What's New in This Edition

The second edition of this book has been revised and expanded for the new features and enhancements in Microsoft SQL Server 6.5. Following are some of the new topics covered in this book:

- Distributed Transaction Coordinator (DTC)
- Replication to ODBC clients
- SQL Enterprise Manager enhancements
- SQL Web Assistant
- Support for Microsoft Exchange
- Enhancements to SQL Distributed Management Objects (SQL-DMO)
- Data warehousing and VLDB enhancements
- SQL language enhancements

This is a summary of the new chapters that we have added to the book:

- Chapter 3, "Introduction to the SQL Enterprise Manager"—A welcome change from the wide array of tools of yesteryear, the SQL-EM package is complete and efficient. If you have been maintaining your SQL Server from the command line, this toolkit will be a refreshing change!

- Chapter 29, "DBCC"—dbcc provides a whole range of capabilities that fall outside the normal range of SQL operations. Its diagnostic and administrative capabilities are a necessary part of regular data maintenance. The other facilities can help you get the best performance out of SQL Server.

- Chapter 39, "Introduction to Client/Server Programming with MS SQL Server"—This chapter introduces you to the concepts of the client/server architecture as it applies to SQL Server.

- Chapter 40, "Client Application Interfaces for SQL Server"—This chapter provides background on the various client interfaces and available APIs.

- Chapter 41, "Planning for SQL Server Applications"—Use the information in this chapter to configure your DB-Library and ODBC client settings to create a successful connection to SQL Server. This chapter also outlines some methods to improve your application's responsiveness by using client-side processing or server-side processing.

- Chapter 44, "Building Dynamic Web Pages with SQL Server"—In this chapter, you learn by example how to build a guest book using the Internet Database Connector: how to build the HTML forms, the IDC definition files, and the HTML template files. You also learn how to use the SQL Server Web Assistant to build Web pages to display data from your database in a semi-static form.

Microsoft® SQL Server™ 6.5

UNLEASHED

Second Edition

David Solomon, Ray Rankins, et al.

SAMS
PUBLISHING

201 West 103rd Street
Indianapolis, IN 46290

This book is dedicated to my wife, Carola, and to my children, Adam and Luke. Goodness knows how much longer they can put up with all of this!

International Standard Book Number: 0-672-30956-4

Library of Congress Catalog Card Number: 96-68299

99 98 97   4   3   2

Interpretation of the printing code: the rightmost double-digit number is the year of the book's printing; the rightmost single-digit, the number of the book's printing. For example, a printing code of 96-1 shows that the first printing of the book occurred in 1996.

Composed in Garamond and MCPdigital by Macmillan Computer Publishing

Printed in the United States of America

Trademarks

Publisher and President	Richard K. Swadley
Publishing Team Leader	Rosemarie Graham
Managing Editor	Cindy Morrow
Director of Marketing	John Pierce
Assistant Marketing Managers	Kristina Perry, Rachel Wolfe

Development Editor
Todd Bumbalough

Software Development Specialist
John Warriner

Production Editor
Robin Drake

Technical Reviewer
Ramesh Chandak

Editorial Coordinator
Bill Whitmer

Technical Edit Coordinator
Lynette Quinn

Resource Coordinator
Deborah Frisby

Formatter
Frank Sinclair

Editorial Assistants
Carol Ackerman
Andi Richter
Rhonda Tinch-Mize

Cover Designer
Tim Amrhein

Book Designer
Gary Adair

Copy Writer
Peter Fuller

Production Team Supervisor
Brad Chinn

Production
Debra Bolhuis
Georgiana Briggs
Kevin Cliburn
Bruce Clingaman
Jason Hand
Daniel Harris
Casey Price
Laura Robbins
Bobbi Satterfield
Ian Smith
Susan Van Ness
Marvin Van Tiem

Indexer
Ginny Bess

Overview

Contents

Part II Transact-SQL Programming

Part III   Performance and Tuning

Part IV System Administration

Part V Introduction to Open Client Programming

Acknowledgments

These *Unleashed* books are never the work of a single individual. This second edition reflects the hard work of many authors of the original edition, and many who also chipped in to make certain that this second edition saw the light of day.

Among the original authors of this material are Ray Rankins, whose contributions throughout the performance and tuning sections made this book much of what it is. Brian Tretter wrote a great deal of the original material about administering SQL Server when we collaborated on a book on Sybase. Some of that material, flavored with Brian's real-life experience, has made its way into this book. Dan Woodbeck contributed to the first Microsoft edition, keeping us Sybase graduates focused on the special characteristics of the MS SQL Server. He helped to develop the structure and focus of this second edition.

On this edition, Kalen Delaney contributed with both expertise and a genuine concern for the quality of the book. Jeff Steinmetz helped enormously both in writing huge chunks of the programming section and in constructing the large version of the pubs database.

Employees at Microsoft joined several of our readers in letting us know about problems with the first edition. Their comments on database design and segments helped us restructure the performance section of the book.

The production people at Sams were characteristically helpful. In particular, Robin Drake's editorial remarks demonstrated a surprising comprehension of some amazingly dense material. Her humor and good spirit helped us all see this project through. Robin and the tech editor caught several errors and dramatically improved the quality of the book. Whatever errors remain are the authors'.

- David Solomon

About the Authors

David Solomon, President of Metis Technologies in Troy, NY, writes, speaks, teaches, and consults on SQL Server design, application, and implementation. With more than five years of experience in SQL Server, he is an expert on query analysis and troubleshooting, logical database design, and application design and implementation. He specializes in advanced SQL techniques and physical database design. You can reach David at CompuServe 75600,615 or at dsolomon@metis.com.

Ray Rankins is currently the director of technical services for Northern Lights Consulting and a Certified Sybase Professional Database Administrator. A computer professional for more than 11 years, Ray has been working with Sybase and Microsoft SQL Server since 1987 as a DBA, application developer, database designer, project manager, consultant, and instructor. He has worked in a variety of industries, including financial, manufacturing, health care, retail, insurance, communications, public utilities, and government. His expertise is in SQL Server performance and tuning, SQL Server application and database design and development, client/server architecture, and Very Large Database design and implementation, and he teaches and speaks on these topics from the local to the international level. He is also coauthor of *Sybase SQL Server 11 Unleashed*, *Microsoft SQL Server 6 Unleashed*, and *The Sybase SQL Server 11 DBA Survival Guide*, all published by Sams Publishing.

Kalen Delaney is an independent SQL Server trainer and consultant based in the Pacific Northwest. She has been working with SQL Server since 1987, when she joined the Sybase Corporation. Kalen spent five years at Sybase doing technical support and customer training. Prior to working for Sybase, she taught for eight years at UC Berkeley in the Computer Science department. As an independent consultant, Kalen has done internal training at both Microsoft and Sybase, and her most recent projects include working with Microsoft to develop advanced SQL Server training materials. Kalen loves to teach; in addition to teaching all the official Microsoft SQL Server courses, she teaches her own custom SQL Server curriculum at client sites around the world.

Tej Dhawan is the president of Advanced Technologies Group, Inc. in West Des Moines, Iowa. Tej started working with Visual Basic and SQL Server in March 1992 and continues development of large-scale systems using the above in conjunction with Microsoft NT, Exchange, and the Internet Information Server. Tej also teaches classes based on the Windows API and is a Microsoft Certified Professional.

Stuart Evered is the principal consultant at Madison Information Sciences, based in Madison, Connecticut. The company provides services and expertise with multiuser database technologies, focusing on client/server architecture across a diverse industry base including banking and consumer products. Madison Information Sciences specializes in design/management of databases using various SQL engines, including SQL Server, Sybase, and Informix OnLine, a sophisticated data modeling background, using Erwin to apply business rules to relational models, as well as advanced interface/reporting design using Borland Delphi, Microsoft Access, PowerBuilder, and Visual Basic.

Ahsan Farooqi is a Microsoft Certified Trainer and a Microsoft Certified System Engineer as well as a CNA-3 and CNE-4. He has been working in the field for about six years and training for three. He led the development of the client/server and networking program for the training division of Chubb Computer Services of Chubb & Sons (a Fortune 100 company). He has authored many student and instructor manuals. He specializes in Novell and NT BackOffice, including NT Server, SQL Server, and SMS Server. He is the president of Farrisons Enterprise USA, Inc., and can be reached at A_Farooqi@msn.com. (Watch for www.Farrisons.com, coming shortly.)

George Ghali began writing software at the age of 15, working for Westwood Studios in Las Vegas. It was there that he acquired the training and skills to which he attributes much of his later success as a programmer. In the process, he created applications for such companies as Disney and SSI. George received his undergraduate degree from the University of Southern California. He also took the opportunity to study abroad in both England and France. His first consulting position was with Andersen Consulting in Los Angeles. He is currently working as a contractor for Redmond Technology Partners in Seattle.

Dwayne Gifford has been a developer/analyst in Access, Excel, SQL Server, and Visual Basic for the past five years. He has also been a professional trainer in Access, Excel, Visual Basic, and Microsoft Project. In addition to organizing and writing *Tricks of the Visual Basic 4 Gurus* and *Access 95 Unleashed*, he has contributed to *Office 95 Unleashed*. He has chosen topics that are important in that the reader can gain a general-to-extensive knowledge of the powers of these Microsoft applications. He is currently a lead systems analyst for Excel Data Corporation on contract to Microsoft, where he supports the operations of their largest internal systems. He can be contacted at a-dwayg@microsoft.com.

Jeffrey R. Garbus is president of Northern Lights Software, Ltd. Since 1989, Jeff has taught thousands of programmers, systems administrators, and database designers about SQL Server administration and tuning, based on his experience as a consultant to some of the most complex SQL Server installations in the world. His current interests are in design, tuning, and maintenance of Very Large Databases (VLDBs).

Arthur Knowles is president and founder of Knowles Consulting, a firm specializing in systems integration, training, and software development. Art is a Microsoft Certified System Engineer. His specialties include Microsoft Windows NT Server, Windows NT Workstation, SQL Server, Systems Management Server, Windows 95, and Windows for Workgroups. Art is the author of *Microsoft BackOffice Survival Guide*, Second Edition and *Internet Information Server 2 Unleashed*, and has served as a contributing author to several books, including *Designing and Implementing Microsoft Internet Information Server 2*, *Windows 3.1 Configuration Secrets*, *Windows NT Unleashed*, and *Mastering Windows 95*. He is the forum manager of the Portable Computers Forum on The Microsoft Network. You can reach Art on the Internet at webmaster@nt-guru.com or on his Web site at http://www.nt-guru.com.

A. Nicklas Malik is the president of Malik Information Services, a Seattle-based consulting and training firm. He is a consultant, designer, author, and instructor specializing in enterprise database management, client/server development, user interface design, and artificial intelligence. He is a recognized expert in Visual Basic and is a recipient of the prestigious Microsoft MVP award for his contribution to Visual Basic on CompuServe. Nick also contributed to the book *Tricks of the Visual Basic Gurus*, also by Sams Publishing. He can be reached at 76055.2722@compuserve.com.

Brian Moran is president of the Washington D.C. SQL Server Users Group and a senior architectural engineer focused on database technology for the New Technology practice of The Spectrum Technology Group. Brian writes a monthly SQL Server column for *Windows NT Magazine*, has spoken about SQL Server across the world, and is triple certified as a Microsoft Certified Systems Engineer (MCSE), Solution Developer (MCSD), and Trainer (MCT). His time is split providing SQL Server and Windows NT training and developing quality SQL Server solutions with a focus on the physical design and performance-tuning needs of complex SQL Server environments. You can reach him at brian@spectrumtech.com.

Orryn Sledge is a client/server consultant in the metropolitan Pittsburgh, PA, area. He specializes in developing high-performance, mission-critical systems using Microsoft SQL Server, Sybase SQL Server, PowerBuilder, Visual Basic, and Access. He has been actively involved with SQL Server consulting since 1992. In addition to SQL Server consulting, he has trained several Fortune 500 companies on SQL Server administration and development. In early 1995, he was one of the first developers in the nation to complete the Microsoft Certified Solution Developer (MCSD) program. He is also certified by Microsoft in SQL Server Administration, SQL Server Database Implementation, Windows NT Server and Workstation, Access, Windows System Architecture I, and Windows System Architecture II. In addition to his Microsoft certifications, he is a Certified PowerBuilder Developer (CPD). Along with Mark Spenik, Orryn wrote the book *Microsoft SQL Server 6.5 DBA Survival Guide*, Second Edition, also by Sams Publishing. Orryn can be reached on CompuServe at 102254,2430 or on the Internet at 102254.2430@compuserve.com.

Mark Spenik is the manager of Client/Server Technologies at Keiter, Stephens Computer Services, Inc. Mark, who is a graduate of George Mason University in Fairfax, VA, entered the computer industry in 1985. He has designed and coded large-scale C/S applications and has consulted with numerous firms in C/S development, implementation, and migration. He has a broad programming background, including assembly language, C, C++, and Visual Basic. Mark has hands-on experience with database implementation and administration, including Oracle RDBMS, Sybase SQL Server, and Microsoft SQL Server. His specialty is Microsoft SQL Server, which he has used extensively since the early OS/2 days. Currently, Mark is involved with clients in Richmond, Virginia, who are using NT, SQL Server, and Visual Basic. Mark is a Microsoft Certified Solution Developer and charter member, and is frequently invited to speak at Microsoft Developer Days. He is also certified in Microsoft SQL Server administration, SQL Server database implementation, and Windows NT. Along with Orryn Sledge, Mark wrote the book *Microsoft SQL Server 6.5 DBA Survival Guide*, Second Edition, also by Sams Publishing. Mark can be reached on CompuServe at 102045,1203 or on the Internet at mspenik@kscsinc.com.

Jeff Steinmetz is a senior consultant with a Microsoft Solution Provider. He is both a Microsoft Certified Solutions Developer and a Microsoft Certified Systems Engineer. Jeff has done development work using virtually every Microsoft product and technology, as well as providing systems integration expertise on SQL Server, Windows NT Server, and the Microsoft Internet Information Server. His first experiences in programming began in the days of the lesser-known Radio Shack Color Computer. Jeff also contributed to *Office 95 Unleashed* from Sams Publishing. He can be reached via e-mail at jeffs@logicontech.com or by Web browser at http://www.logicontech.com/staff/jeffs.

Michael W. Watterud is lead systems architect for Anatec, an international systems integration consulting company based in Indianapolis, IN, specializing in Internet, intranet, and client/server. He specializes in enterprise-wide client/server information systems, both DSS and OLTP. With experience in both business and system design and development, he has worked with Oracle, Sybase, and Microsoft SQL Server databases, and a large variety of front-end tools. He has spent the last several years working with Microsoft SQL Server, PowerBuilder, and Visual Basic. His current projects include integrating corporate information systems with the Internet.

Daniel Woodbeck is an instructor and consultant for ARIS Corporation in Bellevue, WA. Dan started working with SQL Server in 1991, developing client/server applications for Baxter International using Microsoft SQL Server for OS/2 1.0 and PowerBuilder 1.0. Dan has the unique perspective of having worked for both Sybase and Microsoft, doing consulting and training for Sybase as part of Sybase Professional Services, and teaching internal education classes for Microsoft's database and development tool technologies to consultants and developers in the Microsoft Consulting Services division. Dan is a Sybase Certified Professional, as well as a Microsoft Certified Product Specialist on both SQL Server and Visual Basic. He currently teaches the Microsoft curriculum for Windows NT, SQL Server, Visual Basic, and Microsoft Access, and the Sybase curriculum as well.

Introduction

Welcome to Microsoft SQL Server 6.5

With Version 6.5, Microsoft continues to challenge traditional database vendors by providing a product that can perform on a par with many far more advanced (and expensive!) database managers. Microsoft has

- Extended the overall power and performance of SQL Server
- Supplied important new syntactic structures to simplify programming and provide better control to the programmer
- Addressed multi-server transactions in a way that's easy to program and easy to administer, offering a method of scaling SQL Server systems beyond the capabilities of a single physical computer

SQL Server 6.5 is a relational database management system (RDMS or RDBMS, depending on where you grew up) that's capable of handling large amounts of data and many concurrent users while preserving data integrity and providing many advanced administration and data distribution capabilities.

Here are a few of the capabilities of SQL Server 6.5:

- Complete data integrity protection, from complex transaction support and advanced security to objects that support your business rules as an implicit part of your database
- Integration with Windows NT, allowing complete multithreading, symmetric multiprocessing on SMP systems, and integration into distributed administration environments
- Outstanding performance on a low-cost platform
- First-class administration tools (see the later section "What Will I Learn from This Book?" for details)
- Built-in support for multi-server "distributed" transactions

Is This Book for Me?

This *Unleashed* book is meant for anyone who's responsible for designing, building, administering, and tuning SQL Server 6.5. Among other things, this book contains performance information that you may not find anywhere else, including SQL Server internals, tuning methods, and advanced SQL techniques that are undocumented or not well-described:

■ *System administrators* will learn how to install and administer SQL Server. You also learn about important standards and protocols to ensure that SQL Server applications can be maintained and supported for the long haul, and you'll understand how SQL Server integrates into Windows NT to help you understand how to tune server-wide performance and configuration and how to automate server administration.

■ *Database administrators* will learn to make the best use of SQL Server 6.5 objects and datatypes, and how to write effective stored procedures and triggers. The "Performance and Tuning" part of the book will help you understand what's going on under the hood of SQL Server, including a detailed analysis of the query optimizer and the physical storage mechanisms used by SQL Server. You can start to understand what performance you can reasonably expect with SQL Server, so that you can focus on problems that you can really fix and on practical solutions.

■ *Programmers* will learn how to write code that runs well on SQL Server, and will acquire a complete understanding of how SQL Server interprets SQL statements when running. We also provide a solid foundation for your work in C and Visual Basic with DB-Library and ODBC in Part V, "Introduction to Open Client Programming."

What Will I Learn from This Book?

If you have installed Microsoft SQL Server Version 6.5, you probably have seen the program group pictured in Figure I.1.

FIGURE I.1.

SQL Server places a set of administration utilities in a single program group in Program Manager during server installation. These utilities are a good starting place for exploring the capabilities of SQL Server.

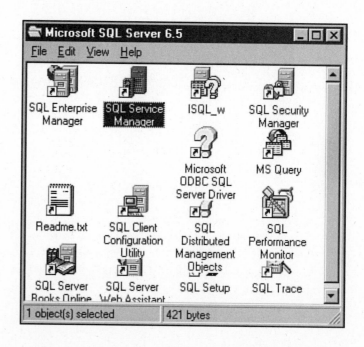

Understanding SQL Server starts with understanding—both functionally and conceptually—the tasks that these utilities represent. In general, this book is *task-oriented*, not tool-oriented. If you need specific instructions on what a particular tool does or how to use a particular button, the online help is a good starting place. In this book, we explain the important tasks, describe when they need to occur, and then show you how to perform them with the appropriate tools.

For your convenience, here's a quick list of the utilities provided with SQL Server, their general uses, and how we refer to each utility in the course of this book:

- SQL Enterprise Manager (SQL-EM) is a utility you will use on a daily basis. The Enterprise Manager is new to SQL Server 6.5, and its capabilities are very broad, though in places a little thin. Throughout this book, we discuss tasks as diverse as creating users, setting up tables, and setting up replication, all of which can be performed using SQL Enterprise Manager. Almost all of the tasks can also be performed by writing Transact-SQL statements. In cases where a Transact-SQL method is available, we show that method first, and then discuss how to perform the task in the SQL Enterprise Manager.

- SQL Service Manager (the stoplight icon) allows you to start and stop SQL Server and related services, including the SQL Executive. Usually, SQL Server starts whenever your NT operating system starts. You can control this setup in the Control Panel, under Services. In production situations, you'll rarely need to bring SQL Server itself down or restart it. We discuss how to use SQL Service Manager in Chapter 24, "SQL Server Installation and Connectivity."

- ISQL/w is another utility you'll use on a daily basis. This tool allows you to open a session (or several sessions) with one or several servers. Then you can submit ad hoc Transact-SQL queries and get results. You can also analyze query behavior with this tool. It's typical for programmers to use ISQL/w to test queries—without the complications introduced by an application program—to make certain that the SQL code is efficient and performing as expected. System and database administrators use the tool to perform routine and emergency maintenance tasks. We provide sample Transact-SQL code examples for ISQL/w throughout this book. You may find yourself always keeping a session or two open to test a query or look at the contents of a table.

- SQL Security Manager provides a graphical method of mapping NT security entities (users and groups) to those in SQL Server for integrated or mixed security. If your organization is using standard security, you set up login IDs using SQL Enterprise Manager or Transact-SQL statements. We look at the different security options in Chapter 27, "Security and User Administration."

- SQL Setup is the installation and configuration management tool. After SQL Server is installed, you only use the setup utility to upgrade a server release; change network, language, or security settings; or to remove SQL Server. You can also use this utility to rebuild your master database in a crisis. This utility is examined most closely in Chapter 24.

- The two help files, Microsoft ODBC SQL Server Driver and SQL Distributed Management Objects, provide detailed information about the two major APIs for addressing SQL Server in application programs. ODBC is used to perform data modifications and queries, while SQL-DMO provides programmatic access to important administrative features. These are covered in detail in the programming part of this edition.

- MS Query is new to Version 6.5. It's a simple visual query interface to provide easy access to SQL Server data.

- The README file contains important up-to-date information about the release of the server.

- SQL Client Configuration Utility, as its name implies, enables you to manage the configuration of SQL Server client software. In particular, it helps you to examine and maintain different versions of the connectivity software on client systems. We look at client configuration management as part of installation, in Chapter 24.

- SQL Performance Monitor is a special invocation of the Windows NT Performance Monitor, designed to provide only SQL Server information instead of the broad range of system information regularly available. We talk about use of the Performance Monitor in Chapter 33, "Measuring SQL Server System Performance."

- SQL Server Books Online is the documentation shipped with SQL Server. Most of the documentation is excellent and quite complete (although from time to time you will wish there were more examples).

- SQL Server Web Assistant (new in Version 6.5) enables you to generate HTML pages based on SQL Server data.

- SQL Trace (also new in Version 6.5) allows you to monitor detailed SQL Server user activity to determine performance tuning requirements.

NOTE

The SQL Transfer Manager no longer appears as a separate program as of Version 6.5. It has been incorporated into the Enterprise Manager.

What's in This Book?

This book consists of seven parts:

- Part I, "The SQL Server Architecture," discusses client/server architecture in general and looks closely at how Microsoft SQL Server implements a client/server database system.

- Part II, "Transact-SQL Programming," discusses the language constructs of Transact-SQL and discusses how objects are created and maintained. You learn about the different datatypes in SQL Server and how their use can affect performance, data maintenance, and capacity. We look closely at programming issues in writing procedures and triggers, examine cursor programming, and explain the ins and outs of transaction programming.

- Part III, "Performance and Tuning," describes in detail how SQL Server stores data, how it decides on optimization strategies, and how locking and multiuser issues impact overall performance. Perhaps the most important point here is that you can start to understand the kinds of expectations you should have for the system: when the query performance is as good as you can expect, and when it can get a lot better. Chapter 22, "Common Performance and Tuning Problems," describes some performance pitfalls that are easy for newcomers to SQL Server to miss, but also easy to avoid once you know they are there.

- Part IV, "System Administration," describes the tasks needed to get SQL Server up the first time and to keep it running all the time. (The performance and tuning section worries about making SQL Server fast; the system administration section worries about making it reliable.) You learn how to make backups, how to restore them, and how to develop a backup and maintenance regimen that ensures that your data is safe. Chapter 38 looks at some of the issues associated with building Very Large Databases (VLDBs).

- Part V, "Introduction to Open Client Programming," provides a first look at the programming issues with SQL Server. Of course, this is a topic for a whole other book, but you learn in these chapters the basics of DB-Library and ODBC programming for both Visual Basic and C++.

- Part VI, "SQL Server and the World Wide Web," looks at approaches to integrate SQL Server databases and Web pages for both Internet and intranet access.

- Part VII, "Appendixes," includes two appendixes: a quick reference on DB-Library functions, and the legal details for the CD-ROM included with this book.

What's Next?

If SQL Server 6.5 isn't yet installed, you might want to start with Chapter 24 to get SQL Server up and running, and then continue to the other sections of this book.

If You Are New to SQL Server...

Start at the beginning and read about how this stuff is built. (You'll never make the time later, and you really need to understand this stuff to make good use of SQL Server.)

As a system administrator, you should read Chapter 3, because you'll need to know some SQL. Then you can jump right to Chapter 23 and work through the administration section.

As a database administrator, you'll need to understand Transact-SQL programming, so work through the book in order from Chapter 3 to about Chapter 14. Before you design a system ready to go into production, you should finish the performance section and try some stuff using a hands-on approach. Then you need to understand thoroughly Chapters 28 (on database logging) and 31 (on server configuration and performance). Read Chapter 22, "Common Performance and Tuning Problems," before you take a production system online. If you're working with large databases, be sure to read Chapter 38.

As a programmer, you should probably read the chapters in order through Chapter 10, and then make the time to look at Chapters 12 through 16 to make sure you understand the kinds of performance issues and problems you might run into. If you'll be writing in Visual Basic or C++, read the section on open client programming. (It may help you to choose the best architecture for your application.) Finally, make the time to read Chapter 19, "Application Design for Performance," and Chapter 20, "Advanced SQL Techniques."

Installing the `bigpubs` Database

In case you are interested in experimenting with SQL Server data that is larger than the standard `pubs` database, we have provided a 60 megabyte database on the CD-ROM enclosed with this book to demonstrate some of the performance issues. The `bigpubs` database has the same structure as the `pubs` database—with a lot more data.

Following are the commands to install the database. Before you can start this process, you will need to have installed the server, started `ISQL/w`, and logged in as the system administrator (`sa`).

You will need:

- The drive letter of your CD-ROM drive (the following text uses drive E: as an example)

- A path where SQL Server can create two files requiring a total of 60 megabytes of space (the example path is `c:\mssql\data`)

- The name of the SQL Server where the database should be created
- The sa password for the server

Although you can execute all of these changes graphically in the SQL Enterprise Manager (and by the time you have finished this book, you will be able to do so easily), it's easier at this stage to just let you know the commands to type to install the database quickly and with a minimum of fuss. (If anything goes wrong along the way, you may consider completing the installation in the Enterprise Manager after you've read about how to use it.)

Here are the steps and the corresponding commands:

1. From the Windows NT command prompt, log into the SQL Server, using ISQL:

   ```
   isql -Usa -Ppassword -Ssqlservername
   ```

2. Create a 35 megabyte device to store the data portion of the database. Here's what my command looked like, using my data directory:

   ```
   disk init
   name = "bigpubs_data",
   physname = "c:\mssql\data\bigpubs.dat",
   vdevno = 5,
   size = 17920
   ```

3. Create a 25 megabyte device to store the transaction log for the database:

   ```
   disk init
   name = "bigpubs_log",
   physname = "c:\mssql\data\bigpubs.log",
   vdevno = 6,
   size = 12800
   ```

   `disk init` statements don't return any output. (In many cases with SQL Server, no news is good news!)

4. Create the database so that you can create the tables and load the data:

   ```
   create database bigpubs
   on bigpubs_data = 35
   log on bigpubs_log = 25
   ```

   When the command is complete, you should get a response like this:

   ```
   CREATE DATABASE: allocating 15360 pages on disk 'bigpubs_data'
   CREATE DATABASE: allocating 12800 pages on disk 'bigpubs_log'
   ```

5. From the Windows NT command prompt, run the `createbigpubs` batch file on the CD:

   ```
   e:
   cd \source\bigpubs
   createbigpubs servername password
   ```

   (If the sa password for the server is still null, just leave it out of the command.)

The last step goes through a set of operations that includes building all the tables, loading the data, creating indexes, and updating statistics on all tables. (You'll get a lot of output back from these operations.) If you want to check quickly whether everything appears to have worked, go back to ISQL (see step 1) and execute these statements:

```
use bigpubs
go
sp_spaceused
```

If everything worked as planned, you should get a report that looks *roughly* like this one, which reports the amount of free space left over after the data was loaded into the 60 megabyte database we created earlier:

```
database_name                   database_size      unallocated space
-----------------------------   --------------     ----------------
bigpubs                         60.00 MB           43.35 MB

reserved           data              index_size         unused
-----------        ----------        ----------         ----------
17046 KB           12856 KB          3416 KB            774 KB
```

The important number to note here is the size of the reserved space (17046KB), the data (12856KB), and the index (3416KB). If these numbers approximately correspond to your system, the database has been loaded correctly. If these numbers are very different (especially if the data number is much lower, or if the value for the index size is 0), something went terribly wrong during the load. Drop the database (drop database bigpubs) and restart the load.

When the fourth step is complete, the database is ready for use. Good luck!

Conventions Used in This Book

We've tried to be consistent in our use of conventions here. When the Microsoft SQL Server version is stated as Version 6, that usage indicates that the topic of discussion applies to *both* Version 6.0 and Version 6.5. In cases where the topic specifically involves one version or the other, the appropriate version number is indicated.

Names of commands and stored procedures are presented in a special monospaced `computer typeface`. Because SQL Server doesn't make a distinction between upper- and lowercase for SQL keywords in SQL code, many code examples show SQL keywords in lowercase, and the text of this book has followed that convention.

We have purposely not capitalized the names of objects, databases, or logins/users where that would be incorrect. That may have left sentences starting like this: "sysdatabases includes..." with an initial lowercase character.

Code and output examples are presented separately from regular paragraphs and also are in a monospaced computer typeface. Here's an example:

```
select id, name, audflags
from sysobjects
where type != "S"

id              name                            audflags
---------       ------------------------------  ----------
144003544       marketing_table                 130
```

> **NOTE**
>
> Perhaps the most controversial convention in the book is to use lowercase to spell dbcc, the database consistency checker.

When we provide *syntax* for a command, we've attempted to follow the conventions in the following table.

Key	Definition
command	Command names, options, and other keywords
variable	Indicates values you provide
{}	Indicates that you must choose at least one of the enclosed options
[]	Means the value/keyword is optional
()	Parentheses are part of the command
¦	Indicates that you can select only one of the options shown
,	Means you can select any of the options shown separated by commas
[...]	Indicates that the previous option can be repeated

Consider the following example:

```
grant {all ¦ permission_list} on object [(column_list)]
     to {public ¦ user_or_group_name [, [...]]}
```

In this case, the `object` value is required, but the `column_list` is optional. Note also that items shown in plain computer type, such as grant, public, or all, should be entered literally as shown. Placeholders are presented in italics, such as `permission_list` and `user_or_group_name`; a placeholder is a generic term for which you must supply a specific value or values. The ellipsis in the square brackets ([...]) following `user_or_group_name` indicates that multiple user or group names can be specified, separated by commas. You can specify either the keyword public or one or more user or group names, but not both.

Our editors were enormously helpful in finding inconsistencies in how we used these conventions. We apologize for any that remain; they are entirely the fault of the authors.

Good Luck!

You are in good shape now. You have chosen a fine platform for building database applications, one that can provide outstanding performance and rock-solid reliability at a reasonable cost. And you now have the information you need to make the best of it.

I wish you all the best with SQL Server.

The SQL Server Architecture

PART

I

Overview of Client/Server

1

Welcome to the first chapter of this book. To give you some background before tackling the rest, this chapter covers the following topics:

- Comparative architectures
- Definition of client/server
- Roles of clients and servers

Roots of Client/Server Computing

Strictly speaking, *client/server* is a style of computing where a client process requests services from a server process. Client/server computing is a broad area within *cooperative processing,* a field that looks at interactive computing between systems. What most distinguishes client/server computing is how processing is distributed between independent applications.

That's all well and good, but in the real world of business computing, the term *client/server* has come to describe the interaction between *fourth-generation language* (4GL) front-end applications, and *relational database-management systems* (RDBMSs). That is certainly how the term will be used in this book.

Client/server computing represents the marriage of two older processing models: mainframe or host-based computing and PC/LAN (local area network)-based computing. Let's look more closely at these two models to understand the purpose of client/server.

For this discussion, let's break down a typical business data-processing application into four components:

- *User interface* elements control keyboard and screen features, including the implementation of function keys, the field-to-field behavior of the cursor, and the display of data.

- *Application program* elements manage screen-to-screen behavior of the system and menuing as well as mapping field information to a logical data model.

- *Logical data processing* is the application of *business rules* to application data. This includes data validation and referential integrity. *Data validation* involves ensuring that a provided value is in a valid format or within a valid range of values. (Is `price` greater than $0.00? Is `social_security_number` in the format `###-##-####`?) Referential integrity involves verifying that the data "referenced" in one table exists in a "related" table. (Does the `pub_id` value in the `titles` table exist in the `publishers` table? Is `item_number` found in the `items` table?) It also includes rules particular to a specific organization or application (for example, promised ship dates are always seven days from the date of order; only managers may fill in an override column; and so forth).

- *Physical data processing* maps logical data to a physical storage structure. It handles locking, data caching, and indexing, as well as the reads and writes from media.

Host-Based Computing

In the *host-based* environment, almost all processing occurs on the central host. What little local processing does occur (for instance, with an advanced terminal) is restricted to cursor handling from field to field and handling of individual keystrokes. After a screen of data is transmitted, the host resumes control.

In this environment, applications and data are centralized and exist solely on the host computer. Communications are almost never a bottleneck, even when the host and the terminal are separated by hundreds of miles and only share a relatively slow asynchronous connection. Application development and maintenance are also centralized, providing an important measure of control and security. Administration of the system (backup, data maintenance) is handled centrally as well.

Host-based computing has been the platform for most business database applications for the past 20 years. Mainframes and traditional minicomputers have provided solid, reliable performance, but at a tremendous cost. Purchase prices are stratospheric compared to PCs, but the intolerable burden of mainframes has been the cost of maintenance. The combined effect of high purchase prices and exorbitant maintenance fees was that processing cycles centralized on the host became far more expensive than the processing cycles on a PC.

PC/LAN-Based Computing

When those central mainframe costs were billed to a department manager's budget, the manager turned to a PC to solve departmental problems. The low cost and high availability of PC computing was extremely attractive to people who were forced to wait in line to pay high prices for mainframe processing.

Of course, the real nightmare of host processing has always been the tremendous backlog of applications waiting to be developed and maintained. PC users found they could build their own applications (they were admittedly amateur, but often more usable than the enterprise applications) faster than they could fill out the forms requesting apps from the central MIS group.

> **NOTE**
>
> Years ago, a colleague of mine switched to a PC to do all his data analysis and number crunching, even though his data sets were typically large and fairly complex. As he explained, "It takes my PC seven minutes to do what the mainframe can do in one-half second, but I have to wait a week to run my job on the mainframe."

Small, private, PC-based databases grew into multiuser, LAN-based databases because it made sense—users found ways to share data and be more efficient. Although file server-based

LANs are well qualified to handle most office-automation (OA) tasks (word-processing document storage, shared printing devices, and central OA application maintenance), performance is problematic when managing databases with large amounts of data and/or increasing numbers of concurrent users. Moreover, much of the data entered in those PC-based databases was redundant with information stored in other systems. The reentry or data conversions required to populate the data often resulted in corrupted, duplicate, or inaccurate data.

The performance problem relates to the breakdown of application processing on the LAN. User-interface processing is performed entirely on the local PC, as is application processing. Logical data processing also occurs on the PC, which can create a data integrity problem (discussed later in this chapter). Physical data processing is split between the local PC and the central file server.

A file server is a lot like a hard drive attached to your computer by a very long cable (the network), and that cable is usually shared by many users. When your application needs to find a particular record in a database, it retrieves a set of physical blocks from the file server file. It is up to the application to find the required record in the data stream that is transmitted.

The efficiency of each request (defined as the ratio of data required to data returned) depends significantly on the capabilities of the application programmer. Using clever indexing strategies, a skilled programmer can write applications in the file server environment that support hundreds of thousands (even millions) of records.

On the other hand, ad hoc query performance can be disastrous. Users without a sophisticated understanding of how to manipulate indexes to improve performance can initiate queries that—while accurate—require that the system return all records for review by the local PC. Not only is this time-consuming, but it also can lock up system resources for the hours it takes to retrieve the results.

The problem is that the file server doesn't know anything about the data itself. All it understands is the physical storage of information on the hard drive. The result is that a simple query could take hours, filling the network with useless traffic and slowing down every other operation at the same time.

> **NOTE**
>
> Here is a useful analogy to help you understand LAN-DBMS computing.
>
> If you call Information to get a telephone number for John Murphy on Cedar Street, the conversation might go like this:
>
> OPERATOR: "Information. What city, please?"
>
> YOU: "Murphysville, please. I would like a number for John Murphy on Cedar Street."
>
> OPERATOR: "Please hold for the number."

[Pause]

RECORDING:

"Abbott, James, 555-1234."

"Abbott, Martin, 555-1299."

"Abby, Philip, 555-9999."

... (Two hours later—are you still waiting?)

...

"Murphy, James, 555-8888."

"Murphy, John, 555-6666."

Of course, by this time, John Murphy has probably moved to another city.

You didn't call to have someone play a recorded telephone book—you called to get a specific number. With LAN-based databases, the server sends your application the telephone book, and it's up to the application program to find the number you need.

The other problem with the PC/LAN-based approach to database applications is as much cultural as technical. There are plenty of outstanding PC programmers and sophisticated power users, but every shop seems to have its share of dBASE programmers whose background in computer systems left them with no understanding of the craft of software development.

This latter group tends to be very productive in the early stages of development, but software maintenance is another issue. Because data-integrity checks are housed in the application software, and application software is distributed, version control and related data-integrity control can often fall victim to deadlines and software enhancements.

The fact of life is that application development, report development, and data analysis are gravitating toward individuals with less experience and less training in the information disciplines. This means that the "system" (to be better defined later) needs to become more intelligent, more protective of data integrity, and more efficient.

The host-versus-LAN dichotomy is summarized in the following table.

Host	*LAN*
High speed	Low cost
Central administration	Local processing
Geographical distribution	High-speed communication
Maturity	Opportunity

The issue of maturity versus opportunity is where a lot of people are stuck right now. Mainframes represent a stable, predictable environment, with dependable utilities, well-developed infrastructures, and large budgets. PCs represent a dynamic, uncontrolled world, short on administrative utilities, long on risk, and with very low cost expectations from management.

Client/Server to the Rescue!

Client/server computing seeks to merge the best of both worlds: the sheer power and central control of mainframes with the lower cost and better processing balance of PCs. How is this achieved?

First, what is client/server computing? For many, *client/server* is another way of saying *cooperative processing*. By that definition, any time two computers are communicating, you are in a client/server world. Broadly speaking, client/server is a subset of cooperative processing, which is a peer-to-peer architecture.

In the real world (that is, when you see the words "client/server" in the classified ads), the term client/server refers to the interaction between user workstations and central database servers. The workstations run application programs that query and update data stored centrally on the database server.

The following are the key points about this client/server model:

- The client process and server process may be (but are not required to be) connected by a LAN or a wide area network (WAN). They both could be running on the same computer.

- The basic language used to communicate between the client and a database server is Structured Query Language (SQL).

> **NOTE**
>
> SQL is a highly abstract language in which the programmer or user describes his or her requirements (add a row of data to a particular table, display rows having the following characteristics, and so forth) without needing to understand or define the physical approach to answering the question. The database server is fully responsible for interpreting an abstract request, finding the fastest method to retrieve the data, and managing the locking and data integrity.
>
> Because SQL is so abstract, the implementation of client and server software tools and client/server applications does not require the close coordination ordinarily required for cooperative processing. In client/server, both sides write to a common API with some confidence that the final result will provide sufficient functionality and good performance.

Client/server provides a new approach to the central/local distribution of work and responsibility. Like a host-based system, client/server is capable of exerting stringent central control over data integrity, administration, and security. Because data is stored centrally, client/server enables the administrator to back up work centrally and to perform periodic maintenance against data stored in a central and secure location.

Because application programs run entirely on the client systems and only database requests are handled centrally, intricate and processor-intensive user interfaces (for example, Windows applications and highly graphical data presentations) are performed using local processors and local memory.

> **NOTE**
>
> The other resource that can become a bottleneck is the network, especially in a multi-user environment with graphical applications. Anyone who has tried to execute intricate X Window applications with multiple X terminals on a busy network will tell you that executing graphical-application processing on a host can cause serious performance degradation on a LAN. (With lots of users, CPU and memory resources on the server can quickly run dry.)
>
> Local application and interface processing (using local CPUs and local memory) make the client/server model work.

Client/server is particularly efficient (when properly implemented) at responding to ad hoc queries. A LAN-DBMS often responds to simple requests by delivering huge amounts of useless data, but client/server systems return an answer. This answer, called a *result set,* is only the rows and columns of data you requested from the server in a SQL statement.

As mentioned before, SQL should not dictate a specific method of answering a query; it defines only the data required. How does the server know how to answer the question?

SQL Server includes a *query optimizer,* the responsibility of which is to analyze the SQL query, consider the data it is to act on, and decide on an *optimization plan.* The SQL Server optimizer is very powerful and a major factor in the success of the product. (The optimizer is also a fascinating part of the system, and understanding how it works can have a major impact on system performance. For more on the optimizer, take a look at Chapter 13, "Understanding the Query Optimizer.")

The other implication of client/server computing (particularly under the SQL Server model) is that application programming can be distributed without creating havoc in the database. SQL Server (and now other competitive products) provides several data-integrity structures to perform server-side validation and processing within the database.

Because the server is able to manage data integrity, this burden can be lifted (in part or in whole) from the application development at the client. Consider each item in this list. Where was this processing taking place before? Data integrity was managed within the application, not the database. Application programmers were fully responsible for data integrity. An error in implementing data integrity in an application would likely result in having "bad" data in the database. The detection, identification, and clean-up of this data could require hundreds (or thousands!) of hours. Database administrators (DBAs) could do no more than provide guidelines, review code, and hope for the best.

The DBA is able to become more active now. The database has extensive capabilities and the DBA can use the data integrity objects to enforce guidelines on the server side. In many cases, this enables the elimination of thousands of lines of redundant code within applications. Applications become simpler, they are faster to develop, and it's less likely to be a disaster when they contain an error.

The Critical Factor: Cost

Of course, the driving force behind the move to client/server is cost. Mainframe hardware and software are expensive to buy and expensive to keep. Annual maintenance costs alone make MIS managers see red (instead of black), and the rightsizing trend is intended to bring systems cost to an acceptable level. For some organizations, this can mean the elimination of a mainframe or not having to perform an expensive mainframe upgrade to handle new application requirements.

> **NOTE**
>
> There is some discussion of using mainframes as giant database servers, and some organizations are already doing this. Because NT systems are now able to provide more storage options in hundreds of gigabytes, they will be more attractive as super servers. As of this writing, mainframe DASD storage costs approximately 30 times what NT drives cost for the same capacity (and that gap is actually widening).
>
> Mainframes as database servers represent an enormous integration problem as well. There is a very limited choice of RDBMS software, and sophisticated connectivity on the mainframe is substantially more difficult than on Windows NT. The proprietary architecture of mainframes imposes a substantial burden on an integrator because of the problems in transferring knowledge and tools from one environment to the other.

Cost issues extend beyond the purchase and maintenance costs of computing equipment. LANs are not cheap and they can become enormously complex. On the other hand, most organizations are building LANs and WANs for other uses, including office automation, telephony, and videoconferencing. Client/server architecture creates substantially less traffic on the network than some of these other systems.

Many businesses have bought into client/server to gain access to advanced development tools, such as PowerBuilder, Visual Basic, Visual C++, and many useful query and analysis products as well. The opportunity to develop products in less time does more than reduce development costs; it also enables an organization to move more rapidly into new markets, to improve customer service, and to be more competitive.

> **WARNING**
>
> It is crucial that you understand the business case for client/server in your organization in order to gauge management's expectations of your new systems. Many MIS shops have succeeded in implementing newer technologies, but have failed in the eyes of management because of a marked difference between what was implemented and what management expected.

This book looks at SQL Server from several perspectives. In this first part you learn about the fundamental architecture of SQL Server. In Part II you learn the basic structures that SQL Server supports and how to address those structures. In Part III you will begin to understand how SQL Server implements those structures in order to implement the system to get the best performance. Part IV looks at SQL Server from an administrative standpoint. This is so you can understand the strengths and weaknesses of the product, along with the background you need to develop an aggressive approach to maintaining and tuning the server. In Part V you look at some programming interfaces for writing client applications. Part VI introduces you to the complexities and features of serving Web pages with SQL Server.

Summary

You and your organization have traded in the maturity and stability you were used to with mainframe systems for the dynamism and opportunity of the client/server environment. Maybe you decided to step up from a LAN DBMS to a database capable of supporting hundreds or thousands of users and hundreds of gigabytes of information.

This book provides you with the information you need to bolster the system and to provide the reliable service your organization expects from its data resources.

Understanding the Microsoft Client/ Server Architecture

2

From the time that client/server became an overused, misinterpreted computer buzzword, different vendors have been attempting to refine their implementations of the concepts discussed in Chapter 1, "Overview of Client/Server." This section compares different database engine architectures—the heart of any client/server DBMS. From that comparison, the history of the Sybase/Microsoft client/server architecture, starting in 1986 with the first release of SQL Server 1.0, will be more understandable. The chapter culminates with a discussion of how Microsoft, through increased investments in time, developers, and support personnel, has created a version of SQL Server that is very much its own, but still recognizable for its Sybase roots.

Comparative Database Architectures

The current client/server world includes two dominant architectures for writing database engines. Understanding these architectures aids in understanding how yours will work, so let's take a look at both.

The first type is the *multiprocess engine*, which is characterized by multiple executables running simultaneously. Typically, these engines consume significantly higher system resources than the other type, but they appear (with limited testing) to scale to dramatically larger platforms more easily than their counterparts.

The second type is the *single-process, multithreaded architecture*, which is used by SQL Server. Instead of running distinct executables or applications for each task, this architecture relies on multithreading work within a single application. The benefit is substantially lower hardware requirements for a given performance level.

Multiprocess Database Engines

Some database engines rely on multiple executable applications to perform user query work. In this architecture, each time a user logs in, he or she is actually starting a separate instance of the database engine itself. Each user, therefore, is running his or her own instance of the database application. To coordinate many users accessing the same sets of data, these executables work with other global-coordinator tasks to schedule operations among these various users. Applications in a database of this type communicate using a proprietary *interprocess communication (IPC)* facility. Although not necessarily efficient, Dynamic Data Exchange under Microsoft Windows is one IPC.

Multiprocess database engines are typically used on mainframe databases, and are popular on the MVS operating system because MVS provides IPC facilities for applications.

The most popular example of a multiprocess database engine isn't typically run on mainframes. Oracle Corporation's Oracle Server is a true multiprocess database engine. Sixteen different types of executables are loaded by the Oracle Server to perform different tasks. User connections start user-database executables, executables that manage multiuser access to data tables, executables that maintain transaction logging and versioning, and other features such as distributed transactions, data replication, and so on.

Each time users connect to an Oracle database, they load a distinct instance of the Oracle database executable. Queries are passed to that executable, which works in concert with the other executables on the server to return result sets, manage locking, and perform other necessary data-access functions. (See Figure 2.1.)

FIGURE 2.1.

With process-per-user architectures, a separate instance of the database engine starts for each user.

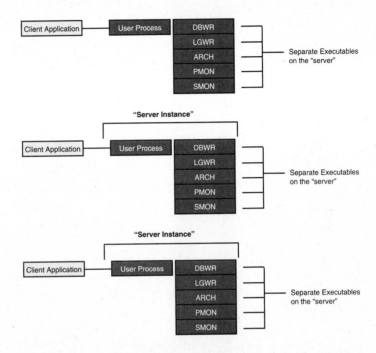

Pros and Cons of Multiprocess Database Engines

Most multiprocess database engines were developed before operating systems supported features such as threads and preemptive scheduling. As a result, "breaking down" a single operation meant writing a distinct executable to handle that operation. This system provided two important benefits for database processing:

- A database could support multiple simultaneous users, providing for data centralization on a network.
- It provided for scalability through the addition of more CPUs in the physical machine.

In a multitasking operating system, the OS divides processing time among multiple applications (tasks) by giving each task a "slice" of the CPUs available work time. In this way, there is still only one task executing at a time. However, the tasks share the processor, because the OS grants a particular percentage of the CPU's time to each task. As a result, multiple applications appear to be running simultaneously on a single CPU. The real advantage, however, comes when multiple CPUs can be used by the operating system.

Applications love operating systems that support multitasking as well as symmetric multiprocessing. The ability to schedule distinct tasks to distinct processors gives applications the true capacity to run simultaneously. As a result, today's multiprocess, database-management systems scale to larger numbers of processors more readily than their counterparts. Most industry polls and publications acknowledge that Oracle Server can scale to large numbers of processors and do so efficiently—that is, as new processors are added, Oracle takes advantage of that processor, producing a net gain in processing power for the database. As the following discussion on multithreaded DBMSs shows, that setup may or may not be what your business really needs.

Single-Process, Multithreaded Database Engines

Multithreaded database engines tackle the thorny issue of multiuser access in a different way, but using similar principles. Instead of relying on a multitasking operating system to schedule applications on a CPU, a multithreaded database engine takes on this responsibility for itself. In theory, the database engine's ability to fend for itself gives it greater portability, because the database manages scheduling individual task execution, memory, and disk access.

Multithreaded systems are more efficient for a given hardware platform. Whereas a multiprocess database uses between 500KB and 1MB of memory for each user connection (remember that memory is protected and dedicated to an executable file), a multithreaded DBMS uses only 50KB to 100KB of RAM.

In addition, because the database executable itself manages these multiple threads, you don't need a costly and inefficient interprocess communication mechanism. Instead, the database engine itself coordinates the multiple operations it must perform, and it sends these instructions to the operating system for final execution. In this way, the database time-slices individual operations by taking individual threads, one at a time, and sending the user instructions on those threads to the operating system. Instead of the OS time-slicing applications, the DBMS time-slices threads. (See Figure 2.2.)

In this way, the database uses a finite element of work (a thread) for a variety of operations (user instructions, locking data pages, disk I/O, cache I/O, and so on) instead of a multiprocess DBMS, which uses specialized applications for each.

This architecture forms the heart of all Sybase SQL Server versions through release 10.x, and, without the multiprocessing features, also for SQL Server on OS/2. In fact, Sybase developers wrote the code that Microsoft distributed for its then-new operating system, OS/2. Microsoft has since assumed more and more responsibility for this code base, but the underlying architecture is identical to the one Sybase developed in its first release of SQL Server.

As shown in the discussion on how Microsoft has altered this idea with SQL Server for Windows NT (later in this chapter), there are different means to implement thread services, memory management, and, most importantly, thread scheduling and SMP services.

FIGURE 2.2.

A single-process, multithreaded database simulates operating-systems threads; as a result, the DBMS is responsible for scheduling user tasks and commands internally.

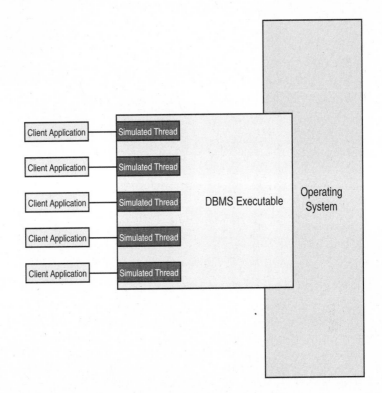

Pros and Cons of Multithreading Database Engines

Sybase was quick to point out the performance it could achieve on relatively small hardware platforms when SQL Server first debuted. In fact, SQL Server was typically one of the fastest DBMSs (if not *the* fastest) for any given database size or hardware platform. That performance is derived in part from the efficiency of a multithreaded DBMS relative to other multiprocess competitors. A single executable running multiple internal threads consumes far fewer system resources, and it uses those it consumes much more effectively than in other architectures.

> **NOTE**
>
> As a developer using SQL Server 1.0 for OS/2 a few years ago, I was able to convince my management to buy what was at the time the hottest PC available—a 486/DX33 with 16MB of RAM, and three SCSI hard disks. With a 16 Mbps Token Ring adapter, we were able to support 50 simultaneous users with almost instantaneous query response, using databases as large as a full gigabyte (remember, this was 1991). We thought that this performance was amazing from a hardware platform that cost only $12,000 (again, this was 1991) but could run "real" applications.

Today, that $12,000 could buy a two-processor Intel machine with 64MB of RAM, a Fast Ethernet (100 Mbps) network card, a stack of 1.0 or 2.0GB SCSI fixed disks, a 10GB database, and it could support literally dozens if not hundreds of users!

A major benefit from this enhanced efficiency is the reduction in RAM requirements for the server, saving precious megabytes for data and procedure caching. Cache is a critical element for any serious database application, and maximizing both the quantity and usage of that cache is an important performance factor. Although the need for such efficiency has been somewhat mitigated by falling RAM prices, memory is still a precious commodity. As shown by Chapter 31, "Configuring and Tuning SQL Server," there's no such thing as too much memory.

The most significant detractor of a multithreaded DBMS is more implementational than architectural, but it still reflects choices the database vendor may make.

Scalability with multithreaded DBMSs can be an issue, if only because the degree to which a multithreaded database is scaleable is a function of the database vendor's ability to take a single operation and break it down so that multiple threads can work on that single operation. Up to now, the availability of symmetric multiprocessing hardware, particularly on Intel-based platforms, has been severely restricted—obviating the need for an SMP database. As these platforms continue to expand and become common items, a database's ability to take advantage of the additional processing power will be an important purchasing and implementational decision factor.

Single-process DBMSs aren't inherently restricted from using SMP hardware. Quite the contrary. Their efficient use of threads makes them better candidates for such platforms, because of their capability to squeeze the most from the least. However, SMP support competes with portability, because different hardware vendors implement SMP support in different ways.

As a result, Sybase has been forced to implement an operating-system-neutral means of accessing operating-system- and hardware-level SMP support. This setup has contributed overhead to SQL Server, limiting its capacity to scale to larger processor counts and hardware platforms. This is more a function of the parallelization of threads than anything else. SQL Server has implemented user connections as individual threads—but only as single-thread operations, not multithread operations. Therefore, when a user executes a query that scans a 4GB table, that user has only one thread of execution to do the scanning. Because threads are the most finite element of work in SQL Server, a single thread can be scheduled to only one CPU at any given time. Therefore, there is no parallelization of work for this user, because single tasks are running on a single CPU at any given time. Any performance benefits resulting from SMP are the result of another processor being made available before the existing processor would be—which is a scheduling benefit, not a true processing benefit.

In fact, it's this very problem that Microsoft sought to address in SQL Server 4.2x for Windows NT and has succeeded in addressing in SQL Server 6.x for Windows NT. The next section defines how Microsoft has achieved this end, and at what cost.

SQL Server for Windows NT and the Symmetric Server Architecture

With Windows NT, Microsoft was making the leap to building a true application server. Although many pundits would argue that they missed the mark with the first release, few would argue that Windows NT (in Versions 3.5 and 3.51) is a true network-enabling, application-server platform. This platform forms the heart of Microsoft's effort to "go it alone."

> **NOTE**
>
> There is substantial confusion about what SQL Server 4.2 for Windows NT was or was not. If you talk to Sybase, it's a relic piece implementing an outdated feature set. If you talk to Microsoft, it's a complete reengineering of database technology. As usual, the truth is somewhere between.

With Windows NT, Microsoft finally had a 32-bit operating system with preemptive scheduling, protected memory, and a kernel-based architecture that supported symmetric multiprocessing. It would be difficult for any application developer to pass up access to those kinds of resources—which has long been the Sybase approach. Instead of treating Windows NT like just another operating system, Microsoft decided to use it to best advantage.

Depending on whom you talk to, anywhere from 70 to 85 percent of the core Sybase database kernel was tossed out and rewritten by Microsoft. The interesting part is that the behavior of the server that application developers saw didn't significantly change! With SQL Server for Windows NT, Microsoft created a database engine that looked like SQL Server, walked like SQL Server, and even quacked like SQL Server—but it was no ordinary SQL Server.

Microsoft rewrote SQL Server to use native operating system services for threads, memory management, disk I/O, symmetric multiprocessing support, and even Windows NT's networking services. This was a complete break with the past. Sybase was used to writing all of these facilities for itself—a necessity of its portability in that Sybase can't count on features like threads, protected memory, or network protocols in all the operating systems that Sybase wants to support.

Microsoft took a different approach, relying on the portability of Windows NT to achieve cross-platform compatibility. Because Windows NT can run on a variety of platforms, Microsoft can count on Windows NT services for connectivity and resource management. As a result, SQL Server from Microsoft runs only on Windows NT, but it runs on all platforms, including SMP platforms, that are supported by Windows NT. So what about this version number thing?

Microsoft wanted to ease customer concerns about migrating to a new database version and a new operating system; complete, guaranteed backward compatibility with existing SQL Server 4.2 for OS/2 databases was a must. So, the decision to use the 4.2 version number was marketing-driven. SQL Server, however, behaved exactly like the 4.2 for OS/2 release. Underneath, there was little that was left untouched.

Thread Services for Microsoft SQL Server

The biggest change came in SQL Server's use of threads. Instead of simulating threads in the database kernel, as Sybase had done, SQL Server used native Win32 operating system threads—meaning that those threads ran in protected memory spaces, preemptively scheduled by the Windows NT OS kernel. This, in marketing-ese, became the Symmetric Server Architecture shown in Figure 2.3.

FIGURE 2.3.

The Symmetric Server Architecture of SQL Server for Windows NT marked Microsoft's first effort to differentiate the Microsoft version of SQL Server from Sybase's versions.

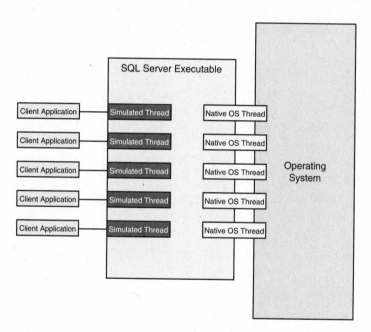

In the Sybase architecture, a user connection is given a distinct thread in the database kernel. This is true for Microsoft SQL Server as well, except that, with Microsoft SQL Server on Windows NT, that thread is a Win32 operating system thread. It's bound by the restrictions of Windows NT's memory protection, thread scheduling, and hardware-access rules, but it also has all the features of a Win32 thread—out-of-the-box support for multithreading, access to striped hardware devices, and memory protection for individual threads. With this architecture, a single corrupt thread no longer crashes the entire executable; instead, SQL Server can trap the offending thread and continue execution.

In Microsoft SQL Server, there is a pool of 1,024 "worker threads" capable of serving user connection requests. That thread pool is distinct from another of 255 threads, one for each disk device that SQL Server supports. (More on this in Chapter 25, "Defining Physical and

Mirror Devices.") Why a pool of threads? An important SQL Server configuration option indicates that SQL Server supports a maximum of 1024 worker threads. Because one connection gets one thread, the maximum number of user connections should be 1,024—but instead, the numeric limit is 32,767. SQL Server will dynamically round-robin user connections to available threads, even if the number of user connections exceeds the threads available. If you're supporting more than 1,000 users on a single SQL Server, you obviously don't sleep much. But the capacity is present in SQL Server to expand beyond even its own resources.

SQL Server 6.5 has different pools of threads for different purposes, including parallel table scanning, backup striping, disk-device management, and user connections.

This architecture continues in SQL Server 6.5, and it has been enhanced to provide multiple threads of operation for single queries—a substantial advantage for using SMP hardware with SQL Server. For more about this, see Chapter 32, "Optimizing SQL Server Configuration Options."

Network Services for Windows NT

SQL Server always supported any network protocol you could want—so long as it was the native protocol of the operating system you used to host SQL Server. For Sybase and UNIX platforms, that meant TCP/IP. For OS/2, Named Pipes using NetBEUI (that lovely little nonroutable rascal), and for NetWare, IPX/SPX. This wasn't necessarily a limitation, because most environments rarely mixed operating systems, and products such as SQL Bridge from Microsoft closed the gap between Named Pipes and TCP/IP.

With Windows NT, Microsoft changed network interoperability by offering an operating system that would work with anybody's protocol. Through the NWLink network subsystem, Microsoft ensured IPX/SPX interoperability with Novell NetWare clients and servers. Windows NT has always had built-in TCP/IP support, which SQL Server has used since being released on Windows NT. Through the two years that Windows NT has been available, Microsoft has added support for DECNet Sockets, Banyan VINES, and the Apple Datastream Protocol (ADSP, or AppleTalk).

Because SQL Server is written as a Win32 application, it too can take advantage of these networking services. As such, SQL Server supports all the protocols that Windows NT supports, allowing a Windows NT machine running SQL Server to support clients of almost any network—NetWare clients, UNIX workstations, Macintoshes, and even ordinary PCs.

With SQL Server 6.0, Microsoft added an extra network library called the *Multiprotocol Network Library* (*MPNL*). MPNL takes two core Windows NT network services—network services and network-enabled operating system remote procedure calls—and integrates them. With MPNL, SQL Server can use Windows NT RPCs as its interprocess communication, and it can take advantage of Windows NT RPC features such as encryption. MPNL appears as just another option in Windows NT's setup routine. However, that network library enabled TCP/IP, IPX, and Named Pipes workstations to communicate with Version 6.0 SQL Servers using encrypted connections. These connections feature two-way encryption, meaning that both queries and result sets are encoded using RSA encryption (the encryption algorithm Microsoft used for RPCs).

> **WARNING**
>
> During the internal testing phases of SQL Server 6.0's development, I spoke with many people on the development team. Using MPNL in these interim beta releases resulted in a 10–15 percent performance decrease in network throughput, caused primarily by the overhead of using OS-level RPCs. In addition, selecting the "encryption" option caused another 10–15 percent performance degradation at the network level. My own informal testing of the released version of SQL Server 6.0 and 6.5 has shown these levels to hover right around 10 percent for each, but my testing methods weren't formal or scientific. The features are unique and very useful for secured environments, but there is a modest cost to using them.

Windows NT and Disk Systems

Sybaser SQL Server and Microsoft SQL Server for OS/2 (essentially the same product, with different distribution channels for most of their lives) supported fault tolerance through internal mirroring of physical disks and files. Sybase and Microsoft guaranteed fault tolerance, but there was no integration with the operating system or the underlying hardware platform. Microsoft changed yet another Sybase standby through its use of Windows NT.

From its first release, Windows NT has supported both RAID 0 (simple data striping across multiple physical disks) and RAID 5 (data striping with parity checks). Windows NT uses NTFS and stripe sets to spread data writes across multiple disks. Although SQL Server maintains full compatibility and support for its own mirroring, using the operating system is recommended unless hardware RAID devices are available.

SQL Server and caching disk controllers have never really been a good combination. SQL Server assumes that when it writes a data page to disk, the page is actually written on disk. However, caching controllers take that data page and write it to a hardware cache that SQL Server doesn't know about. Because of this setup, the page may or may not actually be written to disk. This situation hasn't changed much, although hardware vendors are now developing disk controllers with on-board caches that make themselves aware to the operating system—and on Windows NT, that means SQL Server knows about them as well. In most cases, SQL Server will "write through" the operating system so that neither Windows NT nor the hardware platform will cache data writes SQL Server thinks it has committed.

In sum, Microsoft has changed the direction of its SQL Server permanently by using an operating system that provides network connectivity, hardware scalability, and proper thread and memory protection. Sybase's efforts at portability focused on assuming a generic standard of nonexistence for most of these features, forcing them to be implemented in the database kernel. Microsoft, through its use of Windows NT's portability, has eliminated the duplication of this code and its incumbent overhead.

The Two APIs of Any Client/Server Database

Most computer professionals are familiar with some form of database technology. Business applications are worthless without some central data store. However, accessing that data is the job of programmers, who require two distinctly different languages. There is a host language, which for ages now has been COBOL. However, COBOL isn't a database language—it's a generic programming language with file-access capabilities. To access a database, you need a language to get to that database.

Through most of the 1970s, database access came through embedded languages and precompilers. Statements that accessed the database were inserted using special codes or function calls that marked the source code as a flag for the precompiler. The source code was fed to the precompiler first, and the database-specific code was compiled into separate instructions. The host-language compiler took the standard COBOL code, turned it into a binary object, and linked it so the operating system could understand it as an executable.

Host Language APIs for SQL Server

That same process of using two different native languages to write an application goes into writing SQL Server applications, with an interesting twist—there is no precompiler. Instead, the database-specific calls reside in the source code of the application merely as strings—and they stay that way through the host-languages compilation process. In the resulting executable, all the database queries are still stored as strings. In fact, those queries won't see SQL Server until the source code is properly compiled and runs for the first time!

Most books and documentation written about SQL Server (or any client/server database, for that matter) don't address this issue. They discuss SQL syntax, and they discuss client library API calls—but integrating the two is a topic most people just assume. It's a dangerous assumption. Improperly using DB-Library or ODBC API calls, or similarly, Transact-SQL calls, can contribute to bad applications just as easily as bad design can.

This fundamental difference between interface types defines a *call-level interface*. Both DB-Library and ODBC are call-level interfaces, in that the host application makes native language calls into a library of database functions. The data-manipulation statements are stored as strings, instead of being marked for precompilation like those in embedded languages.

For SQL Server, there are two different APIs that every application will use. The client host-language API that traditionally has been the SQL Server standard is DB-Library. Sybase introduced DB-Library with the original version of SQL Server, and Microsoft used DB-Library for all versions of SQL Server. In fact, Chapter 42, "DB-Library Programming for SQL Server," discusses in detail Version 6.5-specific enhancements in this new release. Marking a change in SQL Server's focus, ODBC is actually now the strategic API for Microsoft—as evidenced by the substantial work being put into ODBC by Microsoft not only in terms of developing database drivers, but also by working with other companies such as Visigenic and InterSolv to move ODBC to non-Windows platforms such as UNIX and Macintosh.

Microsoft introduced support for embedded languages with the E-SQL Developer's Kit for OS/2 SQL Server. This toolkit gave PC-based COBOL and C developers access to an embedded language, if that was their preference. Most developers, however, have chosen DB-Library as their API, and more are switching to ODBC.

SQL is an API?

Transact-SQL (T-SQL) is the second of the two APIs for SQL Server. Why define T-SQL as an API? Most importantly, because it fits the definition! An API is an access point to the resources of an operating system or application that provides a specific set of services. Transact-SQL, through its enhancements to the SQL standard in the form of functions, datatypes, logical operators, and branching logic, is the access point to SQL Server's data-processing resources and services. It's the second of two APIs for SQL Server because DB-Library and ODBC are also access points to a different but still necessary set of resources and services.

SQL Server applications need both in order to function. A standard SELECT statement is useless unless it can be passed to SQL Server. A SQLLOGIN% C-language function is used to open a connection to SQL Server, but that connection is equally useless unless T-SQL statements can be passed over that connection, prompting SQL Server to pass results back to the client.

Sound like fun? It gets better. As already mentioned, Transact-SQL is a dialect of ANSI-standard SQL. ANSI has two primary standards—one codified in 1989, the other in 1992. SQL Server is ANSI 1989 compliant, and SQL Server 6.5 is ANSI 1992 compliant.

How SQL Server Processes Queries

SQL Server doesn't process SQL statements until they're passed to the server over the network. There are some implicit assumption here:

- The client application is capable of formulating queries.
- A network exists for transporting these query instructions to the server.
- The server is capable of using the network to return the results of the query.

These assumptions form the architecture that makes up the SQL Server client/server architecture. With any query you execute, whether interactively through ISQL/w or within an application, all of the following steps take place:

1. DB-Library receives a SQL string from the client application.

2. DB-Library associates that string with a particular user connection opened at the server.

3. DB-Library passes the string along that connection to the network library.

4. SQL Server's Network Library "disassembles" the SQL string into a data packet for the network you're running. The data chunk of the packet conforms to SQL Server's formatting, which is called *Tabular Data Stream.*

5. The network delivers those packets to SQL Server.

6. SQL Server has a Network Library, too, which listens for queries to arrive. The server-side Network Library reassembles the query into a string, and passes that string to the SQL Server query processor.

7. SQL Server processes the query and, if it's a select statement, generates a result set.

8. SQL Server passes the result set to the server-side Network Library, which disassembles the result set into Tabular Data Stream packets.

9. The client-side Network Library receives the packets and reassembles them into a result set, which resides on the client in a connection-specific memory region.

10. DB-Library API calls access the memory region, extracting the data held there and putting it into host-language variables (variables that are local to the client application) for display to the user.

Although this may seem like too many steps, the process has been broken down to a very low level. (For more detail, see Chapter 42, "DB-Library Programming for SQL Server," and Chapter 43, "ODBC Programming for SQL Server," which cover DB-Library and ODBC programming for SQL Server.)

What's most significant about this process is that, regardless of the operating system, these steps are followed every time you send a query to SQL Server.

Summary

With SQL Server for Windows NT, Microsoft has taken a popular, high-performance architecture for client/server databases and made some critical modifications. While some may debate the "openness" of making SQL Server a Windows NT-only application, making the most of Windows NT's security, portability, and scalability means that SQL Server for Windows NT can run on a variety of platforms and scale to support very large applications.

Although all client/server databases make use of two APIs for developing applications, only SQL Server uses DB-Library and Transact-SQL (or ODBC, if you're so inclined) to provide the two necessary means to access SQL Server's powerful features.

Introduction to the SQL Enterprise Manager

The SQL Enterprise Manager (SQL-EM) merges the functions of several system management utilities for SQL Server into a unified application, keeping in sync with the Explorer view of Windows 95 and Windows NT 4.0. It follows the tree metaphor to manage the various SQL Servers available on an enterprise network and can be used by any user with access to SQL Server. Permissions to individual SQL Server objects are controlled by the access rights given to the individual user ID.

SQL-EM provides the tools to manage Version 6.0 and 6.5 servers, a function not available through the Version 6.0 SQL-EM. It can be used to manage devices, databases, tables, logins, replication, security and much more. It provides the functions of starting, pausing, and stopping the SQL Server previously available through the command line, SQL Executive, or the NT Services dialog box. Along with the management of devices and databases, SQL-EM also provides the tools to manage the database objects such as views, tables, and indexes.

This application is a powerful tool and deserves attention, especially for the database administrator (DBA) who previously had to rely on a set of tools from different vendors to manage one or more SQL Servers.

> **NOTE**
>
> SQL-EM uses several icons to denote object types as well as the state of services. To learn more about the icons or to have a lookup table handy, choose File | Toggle Legend from the SQL-EM menu.

Getting Started with SQL-EM

SQL-EM requires a few steps before it can be used. The tree view when SQL-EM is first launched shows a globe listed as Microsoft SQL Servers with a branch off of it labeled SQL 6.5. This is the starting point of SQL-EM and the place where the administrator configures SQL-EM for use. This is where a server is registered with SQL-EM for the availability of management control. Figure 3.1 shows a sample of the default view.

Registration of a SQL Server provides SQL-EM with the necessary login and password information so that it can send the appropriate commands to the SQL Server as they're executed through SQL-EM.

Server Groups

Modular management dictates the placement of servers in well-defined groups. As SQL-EM starts, it automatically provides the SQL 6.5 group. This is where you'd ideally place all Version 6.5 servers, but it can also be used to place groups based on organizational divisions.

FIGURE 3.1.

The default SQL-EM view.

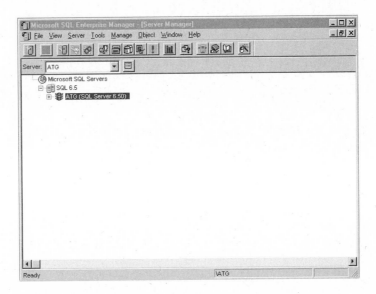

Similar to setting up domains under NT, groups can be set up for organizational or functional divisions. In a manufacturing organization, for example, you might set up the following groups to logically separate the servers for management:

- Production
- Accounting
- Engineering

To create a server group, choose Server | Server Groups from the SQL-EM menu. This action brings up a Manage Server Groups dialog box. For the manufacturing example, you'd need to create a top-level group for the three departments. To accomplish that, you type the names of the new groups and click Add after each one. The groups appear immediately in the SQL-EM window.

If a group was being set up for a department such as Information Systems, you could conceivably have subgroups within the top-level groups. For subgroups, select the parent group in the Manage Server dialog box and choose the Sub-Group Of radio button. Any names added will appear under the parent group, as shown in Figure 3.2.

Registering Servers

After the groups have been created, individual SQL Servers can be placed within them. This placing of a server is called *registering a server* and is done by choosing Server | Register Server from the SQL-EM menu, and then providing the server name, the login specifics, and group membership information.

FIGURE 3.2.

Organizational departments set up as groups with subgroups.

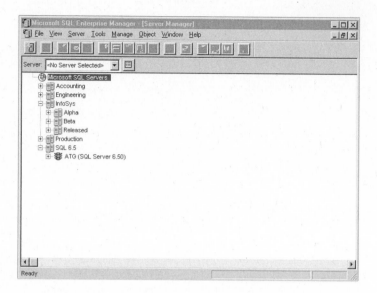

The server name is the name of the server created during installation of the server. Type the name directly into the Server drop down list box. If the server was installed with integrated or mixed security mode, the Trusted Connection option may be used to validate the connection, using Windows NT security. If mixed/integrated security wasn't used, a SQL Server ID and password are required in the appropriate edit boxes. For the DBA, this is usually sa and the appropriate password.

Registration information is now complete. A registered server appears in the SQL-EM window—notice the ATG (SQL Server 6.50) group in Figure 3.2.

Errors after clicking the Register button happen due to one of two reasons:

- **Invalid login.** If the standard security mode is in use, make sure that the password and user ID are correct. If integrated or mixed mode is selected, make sure that the server was installed with that form of security.
- **Server not found.** This problem happens due to network protocol incompatibilities. Make sure that the server and client are set to use the *same* protocol.

SQL-EM gives you the option of registration even if failures like these occur. It's recommended, however, that problems like these be resolved before continuing the registration process, as the problems will occur in almost every SQL Server application if left unresolved.

Security

Data is an asset of almost any organization and should be protected. SQL Server, an enterprise server, provides a large number of security options manageable from SQL-EM. You can define groups of users and specify individual rights for each user at a very micro level.

Groups

A *group* is a set of users who have certain rights within a database. Much like network accounts, all users belong to a global group called `public` but, unlike network accounts, each user can belong to *only* one other SQL Server group.

Groups are used to implement rights across a set of users, by setting the permissions for the group rather than for each individual user. Groups are created for databases, so, from the SQL Server listed under a group, open a database tab and click Groups/Users. The object Groups/Users can now be modified.

In SQL-EM, choose Manage | Groups to reveal a dialog box where one or more user groups can be added, and each new group can be modified to contain one or more database users. (You can also delete a group by "dropping" it from the same dialog box.) Figure 3.3 shows the Manage Groups dialog box.

FIGURE 3.3.

Group management.

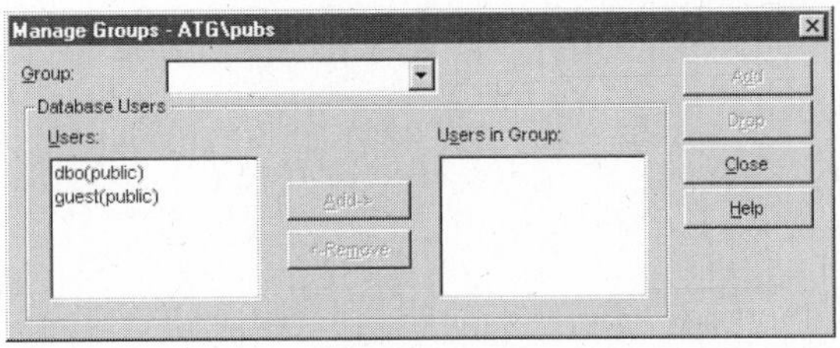

Logins

Database users can also be added from the Manage menu. Choose Logins to show the dialog box in Figure 3.4, where you can add users and assign permissions to databases. Their group memberships can also be set here.

FIGURE 3.4.

The Manage Logins dialog box.

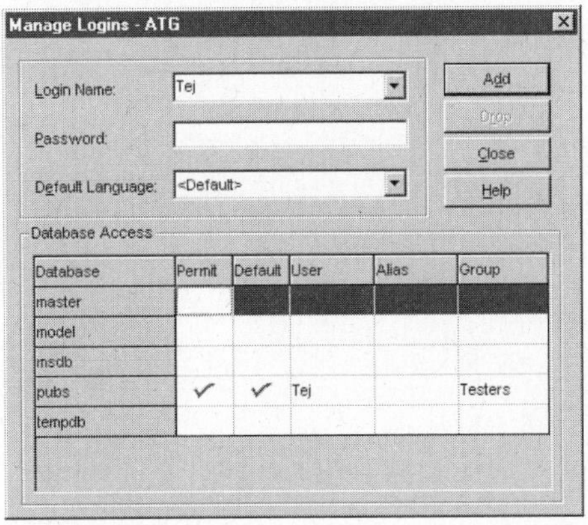

Devices

A *device* is a virtual drive where objects such as tables, indexes, triggers, views, stored procedures, and the like are stored and managed through other databases. They can be used for a few different reasons, as described in the following sections.

Database Devices

A *database device* stores actual data, indexes, and other database objects used by users of the database. To create such a device, choose Manage | Database Devices from the SQL-EM menu, to display the current devices and the space consumed by each device (see Figure 3.5). Devices can be added, modified, or deleted by using the buttons on the toolbar or the options presented under the File menu. The toolbar buttons are self-explanatory and provide Tooltips.

FIGURE 3.5.

Viewing the devices on the current server.

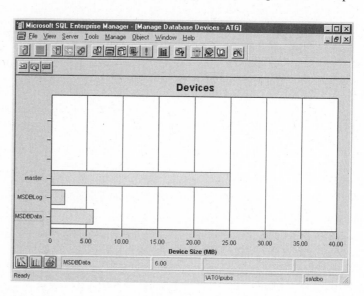

To add a device, click the appropriate button or choose File | New Device to open the New Database Device dialog box (shown in Figure 3.6).

Creating a database device is a crucial step and should be handled carefully. Because a device is a repository of all database objects, its size and properties should be carefully evaluated. The main areas of concern are as follows:

- **Size.** The size of a device should be carefully set to provide enough room for all objects and have room to grow in the near future. The available storage space on the hard disk is shown in a graph. The devices shouldn't be too large because the larger the devices, the more memory SQL Server is going to require to manage them.

Similarly, the smaller the device, the more frequent the management required to expand it to meet the data storage needs.

- **Name.** This is the name that uniquely identifies the device—not necessarily the name that users will see. For easier administration, however, this name should follow some form of standard naming conventions. Appending the word _log to a log device is an example that provides readability during maintenance and administration.

- **Creation time.** The device-creation process is a fairly disk-intensive task and if at all possible shouldn't be performed during production hours. To create the device immediately, choose Create Now in the New Database Device dialog box. To create the device during low usage or routine maintenance, you may want to click the Schedule button and schedule the creation of the device at a certain time and date. This option is highly recommended when creating large devices due to the large I/O load a device creation process can place on the SQL Server, affecting performance of applications using the SQL Server.

- **Mirroring.** This is the process whereby a device can be duplicated onto another hard disk for online backups. You can select a mirror device on another hard drive, but remember that this choice will slow the transactional processes due to interaction with two separate devices.

FIGURE 3.6.

The New Database Device dialog box.

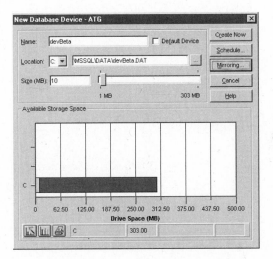

Backup Devices

Devices can be for different kinds of uses and are created accordingly. They can be used to store databases, transaction logs, and backups. Transaction log devices are created in the same way as databases devices (see the preceding section). A backup device is slightly different in that it could be either a file-based device or a tape-drive-based device. To create a backup device, right-click the Backup Devices folder and select New Backup Device from the pop-up menu to display the dialog box shown in Figure 3.7.

FIGURE 3.7.

Creating a backup device.

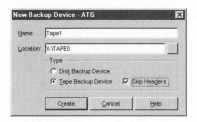

Creating a disk-based device isn't much different from creating a database device or transaction log device, but a tape device has an option concerned with ANSI headers on the tape. If the tape is to be used with SQL Server only, it's safe to ignore the tape headers and go straight for the backup. A tape device is only *virtually* created until used for the first time, when the device information is actually written to tape. The instruction to skip headers during backup overrides any skip header options that may have been set during the creation of the device.

The ANSI headers on a tape contain such vital information as tape expiration (which specifies when a tape should tell the user of the end of its useful life), along with any user restrictions that may be set on the tape. A new tape typically has a blank ANSI header; once used by any application, including SQL Server, the header will contain information about the backup.

SQL Server creates the headers, whether or not the option to skip headers is selected, once it has been told to back up to tape.

Server Activities

SQL-EM lends itself to being an integrated server manager and provides a good set of tools to do just that. The following sections discuss some of the common server management tasks that can help coordinate the DBA's server-management tasks.

Monitoring the Server

At any given time, a SQL Server is working on several tasks. When troubleshooting problems, monitoring for shutdowns, or just keeping tabs on the pulse of the server, it's necessary to see exactly what the server is doing. The menu sequence Server | Current Activity provides the DBA with just a table of tasks by user, as shown in Figure 3.8.

From this monitor window, you can view detailed user activity by clicking the Detail Activity tab. If the DBA notices illegal or inefficient activities, a message can be sent to the client workstation (if messaging is enabled on the client). In more drastic instances, where a user's processes might be interfering with the normal operation of the SQL Server, the DBA can kill the user's process from this window.

FIGURE 3.8.

Current activity on the server.

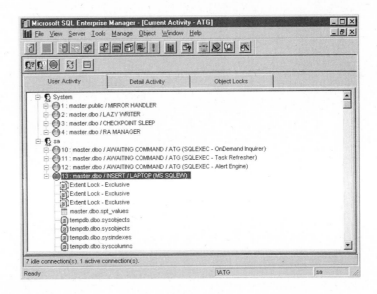

Scheduling Tasks

SQL Server provides a stable and thorough mechanism for scheduling processes to minimize the impact of systems administration on normal operation of the server. Scheduled processes might include creating a device, re-index databases, importing or exporting data—any process that lends itself to a non-immediate need. To manage scheduling, choose Server | Scheduled Tasks (see Figure 3.9).

FIGURE 3.9.

Managing scheduled tasks.

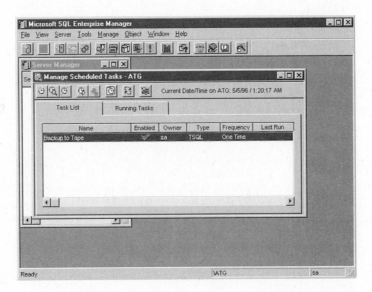

To create a new task, choose File | New Task and specify the name for the task. If the task isn't a Transact-SQL statement, specify the type of task. The database that the task will affect is selected next, followed by the command to be executed. For example, you could use a command like this to back up the pubs database to the tape device Tape1:

```
dump database pubs To Tape1
```

A schedule can be set by using the Change button if the task is to be run at times other than the default time selected by the SQL Server. By clicking the Options button, you can set other options related to the schedule—such as e-mail/pager notification, event logging, and retry intervals. Tasks that are currently running can be viewed by clicking the Running Tasks tab; you can also cancel operations from the same location.

You can optimize your use of schedules with a little advance planning. Experiment with creating and testing schedules for various tasks on a test server before modifying data in a production database.

Alerts

SQL Server's operation and efficiency can be affected by many events. The DBA may want to know of certain events that would affect the operation of the SQL Server significantly; and the way to accomplish that objective is with *alerts*. Alerts are messages sent by SQL Server through e-mail or by pager to a DBA-specified user. (The e-mail operation happens through Microsoft Mail's SQL Server e-mail account.)

The alert processes require both SQL Server and SQL Executive to be running. (Microsoft Mail, also needed for alerts, is included with SQL Server.) To create an alert, choose File | Alert/ Operators to display the dialog box shown in Figure 3.10.

FIGURE 3.10.

Managing alerts and operators.

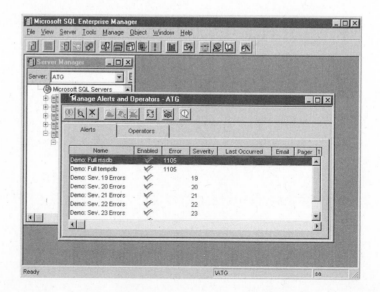

Adding alerts isn't much different from controlling schedules or any other objects. You can select a new alert either by right-clicking or choosing File | New Alert. The Manage Alerts and Operators window is similar to the Manage Scheduled Tasks window, but differs in the event-action relationship, and that deserves attention here. In the Demo: Full msdb example shown in Figure 3.10, for example, the alert fires if error 1105 occurs. This error occurs when additional space for an object can't be allocated in a particular database. The error is severe, as it refers to an "out of space"-like error and should really be sent to an operator or DBA for immediate check.

The operators are defined with the options on the Operators tab. Details such as work start/stop times, e-mail/pager methods, and types of alerts assigned to the operator can be set.

Error Logs

SQL Server starts a new log file at each startup, and keeps tracks of most system events and messages. This log file is a text file in the SQL\Logs directory, and can be viewed with any text editor (such as Windows Notepad). You can also view this log from SQL-EM by choosing Server | Error Log, which displays the current error log in a window (see Figure 3.11). Prior error logs can be selected using the drop-down list box called Error Log.

FIGURE 3.11.

The error log for the current server.

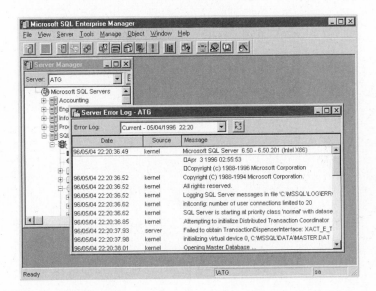

Server Configuration

Server configuration is probably the most useful area of server management, from an administration viewpoint. Here is where you modify parameters such as user connections and memory, security settings, SQL Server boot options, startup parameters, e-mail parameters, and tape drive support. The Server Configuration/Options dialog box (see Figure 3.12) also displays a detailed sheet about server parameters and configuration. To reach the dialog box, choose Server | SQL Server | Configure.

FIGURE 3.12.

Use this dialog box to set server configuration options.

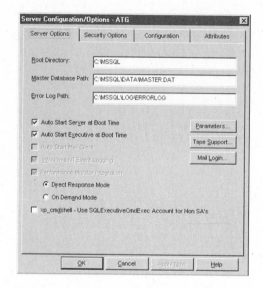

Server Options

The server options determine how SQL Server starts up or boots at system startup time or when manually started. These options are necessary to ensure that the server comes up properly after a system reboot.

SQL Server can be set to auto start when the system reboots. This is similar to setting up the NT Service Manager to start the SQL Server and SQL Executive processes automatically on boot. Additional parameters—typically sent through the command line—can be specified in the Server Configuration/Options dialog box by clicking the Parameters button. For example, if changing options on SQL Server has made it impossible to start the SQL Server properly, the -f parameter starts the SQL Server with a minimal configuration to correct the configuration problems.

Security Options

SQL Server provides three different setups for managing security: Standard, NT Integrated, and Mixed. The Security Options dialog box allows for setting those options and for auditing connection successes and/or failures. For further information about security options, see Chapter 27, "Security and User Administration."

Changing the Configuration

SQL Server configuration changes such as those in memory, database sizes, locks, maximum open databases, or network packet size can be made through Transact-SQL, but the SQL-EM interface makes it easier to make changes.

When adding additional RAM to the system, you need to configure the server to use the additional memory added. To accomplish that objective, scroll down to the Memory tab and change the current value to the new value.

> **NOTE**
>
> The Memory number isn't the actual number of kilobytes, but rather the number of 2KB units of memory. So, if you add 32MB of RAM to the server, you would add 16384 (32MB * 1024 /2) to the value already in the cell.

System Tools

SQL-EM provides several tools to easily administer tasks such as backup-and-restore or database transfers. The SQL Transfer Manager from Version 4.2 has been replaced by a Database/Object Transfer tool, and the dump database command syntax has been made easier with the Database Backup/Restore tool. An external query utility, ISQL/w, is still provided with SQL Server, but its functionality has also been added to SQL-EM. These tools are available under the Tools menu for SQL-EM.

Database Backup/Restore

Unless you have access to a backup tool such as Arcada Backup Exec 6.1 or above, which has tools to back up SQL Server databases during a normal system backup, you'll probably rely on the SQL-EM Database Backup/Restore capability for your daily backups (see Figure 3.13). The options on the Backup tab allow for selection of one or more tables in a database to be backed up to a backup device, such as disk or tape. The scheduling options allow as much flexibility as the task-scheduling features of SQL-EM, discussed earlier in the chapter.

Database Object/Transfer

When manually transferring a subset of data or entire databases from one server to another, you can use the SQL-EM Database Object/Transfer tool to copy the structure, data, dependencies, etc. of SQL Server objects such as databases from one server to another. (See Figure 3.14.) As with most other server-intensive tasks, this can be scheduled for running at low-usage times.

FIGURE 3.13.

The Database Backup/Restore dialog box.

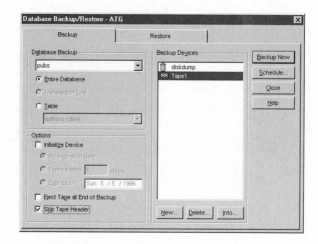

For routine database transfer and copying, you may want to consider replication, discussed in Chapter 36, "Introduction to SQL Server 6.5 Replication."

Query Tool—ISQL/w

SQL-EM integrates the dialog box from ISQL/w to provide a query tool within the SQL-EM environment. The tool can be used to create, save, and execute any valid query on SQL Server, just like ISQL. The tool duplicates the function of ISQL, but is still useful because of its integration into SQL-EM.

FIGURE 3.14.

Use this dialog box to manage database or object transfer from one server to another.

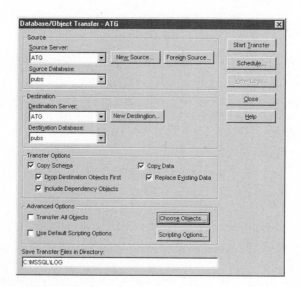

Database Management

Several database management tools have been integrated from the old SQL Object Manager into SQL-EM. These tools provide for the creation of tables, rules, stored procedures, triggers, and indexes. Some of these functions are discussed in the following sections.

Tables

Tables are an integral part of SQL Server and can easily be created using SQL-EM. To create a table, select a database within which the table will be created. If a database needs to be created, you can accomplish that by right-clicking the Databases folder and selecting New Database from the pop-up menu. The New Table command brings up a dialog box like the one in Figure 3.15, where fields can be created for the table.

FIGURE 3.15.

Creating fields for a table.

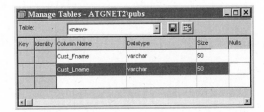

Indexes

A natural successor to the creation of a table is the process of placing indexes on columns in the table. The indexes are created by using the Manage | Indexes menu command, which displays the dialog box shown in Figure 3.16.

FIGURE 3.16.

Creating indexes for the table.

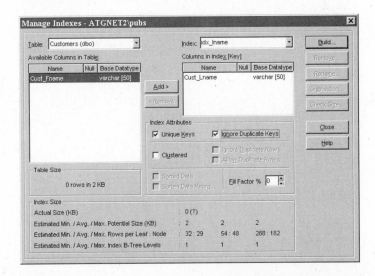

The attributes for the indexes are set here, and an estimate of the index's impact on size of the database is displayed. Name the index with the Index drop-down list box; the Build button starts the process to create the index.

Triggers, Views, and Stored Procedures

These database objects are created using SQL queries through SQL-EM, ISQL, or other database management products. Once a database is selected in the Server Manager window, selecting the menu option Manage allows for selection of triggers, views, and stored procedures. Selecting the menu item Stored Procedures, for example, brings up a window into which a query can be typed or a preexisting stored procedure selected from the Procedure drop-down list. (A shell SQL statement related to the task is placed within the window to start the user on the right track.) An example of a view-creation window is displayed in Figure 3.17.

FIGURE 3.17.

Creating views.

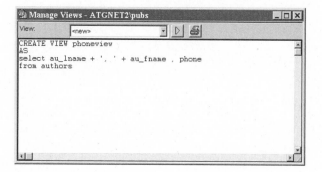

User-Defined Data Types

When default data types such as char or binary don't quite suit the task at hand, it's useful to be able to define a data type for use in the database. In the pubs database, for example, there are three user-defined types. Suppose that you wanted to add another one, for use as an ID for businesses. Similar to the SSN for an individual, the IRS has a federal ID for businesses. The SSN follows this format:

- ## -

The federal ID is formatted a little differently:

-

To add this custom ID, you'd choose Manage | User-Defined Datatypes and type the values shown in Figure 3.18.

FIGURE 3.18.
User-defined data types.

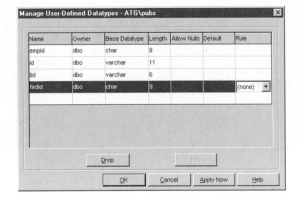

Object Permissions

When each database is created in SQL Server, it's necessary to check the permissions given to users for this database. The permissions can be checked by user or by object, and are set with the Object | Object Permissions menu sequence.

Setting Permissions by User

To set the permissions by user, choose Object | Object Permissions and click the By User tab in the resulting dialog box. The dialog box lists all objects within the current database, and provides a drop-down list box for users and groups. To assign a particular right to a user or group, select the user/group from the drop-down list box and click within the cell(s) containing the desired right(s).

To limit the object list to specific types of objects, such as tables or views, check or uncheck the appropriate boxes in the Object Filters section of the dialog box.

For example, to assign the `select` right to all members of the `public` group for the `customers` table, click within the cell on the `Customers` row under the `Select` column (see Figure 3.19). A green check mark will appear, indicating a right assigned but pending until the Set button is clicked. Clicking the same cell again allows you to change the right to Revoke or Cancel.

Setting Permissions by Object

Permissions can also be assigned by object when most users will have the same right to the object. For example, allowing all users to read data from a table used only for lookups can be easily accomplished by giving the `select` right to the lookup table. To grant the `select` right to `Authors`, click the cell corresponding to `Select` and `public` as displayed in Figure 3.20.

FIGURE 3.19.

Assigning object rights to users.

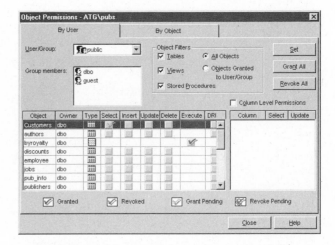

FIGURE 3.20.

Assignment of object rights.

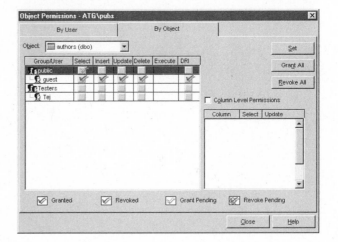

Replication

Replication is the process of duplicating tables and transactions from one database to another, from a local to another local or to a remote server. SQL-EM provides an easy-to-use interface to install replication and set up the publishers and subscribers of data.

Installing Publishers

To install replication, your SQL Server should have at least 16MB of RAM allocated to it. When less than 16MB is allocated to the SQL Server, an attempt to install replication results in an error message asking for more memory.

Choose Server | Replication Configuration | Install Publishing from the SQL-EM menu to open the dialog box in Figure 3.21. If the replicated database is local, select the Local radio button and fill in the names for the new database and device parameters. For a remote database, select the remote distribution server from the drop-down list.

FIGURE 3.21.

Configuring SQL Server for replication.

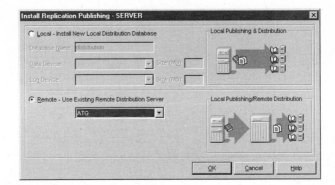

Setting Up Subscribers

To enable subscribing, choose Server | Replication Configuration | Subscribing from the menu; then select the publishing servers to use for subscriptions, followed by the selection of the subscribed databases.

Once set up, the publications and subscriptions can be managed through the Manage menu. This option allows for adding, editing, or deleting of replication objects. See Chapter 36 for further details on subscriptions and publications.

Help

A discussion of SQL-EM would be incomplete without a reference to the plethora of online help available through its Help menus. The SQL-EM Help itself gives ample ideas about the use of the tool and the Transact-SQL help provides guidance through writing SQL scripts for a variety of tasks. For the dedicated administrator, there is also a "Tip of the Day" feature that has crept into SQL-EM, and provides tidbits of information on the use and utility of SQL-EM.

Summary

A welcome change from the wide array of tools of yesteryear, the SQL-EM package is complete and efficient. If you have been maintaining your SQL Server from the command line, this toolkit will be a refreshing change!

PART

II

Transact-SQL Programming

Introduction to Transact-SQL

New in SQL Server 6.5

SQL Server 6.5 introduces some new structures and behaviors for select, insert, and update:

- You can use the keyword AS to designate column headings.
- Multiple instances of null values are treated as equal for distinct operations.
- You can designate an escape character for like clauses.
- group by now includes with cube and rollup to provide *super-aggregate* results.
- SQL Server now supports ANSI-standard join operators.
- The insert statement can insert rows based on a stored procedure result set.

What Is Transact-SQL?

To communicate with the SQL Server and to manipulate objects stored in SQL Server, client programs and stored procedures use a variation of *Structured Query Language* (*SQL*) called *Transact-SQL* or *T-SQL*. T-SQL provides most of the capabilities of *ANSI SQL 89 and 92*—the standard 1989 and 1992 versions of SQL as published by the American National Standards Institute—as well as several extensions to provide greater programmability and flexibility in the language. SQL-92 support has been enhanced dramatically with the 6.5 release of the server, particularly with regard to join operations.

Structured Query Language

SQL provides a language for accessing data objects, using substantially less programming code than required by a third-generation language. A SQL query addresses data in sets rather than requiring you to construct a typical loop. For example, the following pseudocode resembles the code required to modify a set of rows in a table:

```
open file
while not(eof)
begin
   lock record
   read record
   if column-value = value
   write record
   unlock record
end
close file
```

Using SQL, you can accomplish the same task with a single statement like this:

```
update table-name
set column-name = new-value
where column-value = value
```

The individual SQL statement is far more likely to represent a work unit than is the atomic line of code in a third-generation language. This greater level of abstraction means better reliability, easier maintenance, and more readable, more meaningful code.

SQL provides some additional benefits:

- *No need for explicit locking statements*—the server manages all locking.
- *No reference to the physical location of the data*—the server translates a logical name into a linked set of physical locations.
- *No specification of indexing or search strategy*—the server identifies the most efficient method of finding the requested data.

Later chapters explore the mechanics of locking in SQL Server, the method the server uses to manage table storage, and query-optimization strategies. This chapter discusses the basics of T-SQL.

T-SQL and ANSI-SQL

Standard SQL provides mechanisms to manipulate and manage data. Some components of SQL include

- *Data Definition Language* (DDL) to create and drop data structures and to manage object-level security
- *Data Modification Language* (DML) to add, modify, and remove data in tables

Standard SQL was originally conceived as a query-and-execution language, not as a full-fledged programming language. Transact-SQL extends SQL by adding program flow-control constructs (`if` and `while`, for example), local variables, and other capabilities that enable you to write more complex queries and to build code-based objects that reside on the server, including stored procedures and triggers.

> **NOTE**
>
> If you already know SQL, you might want to skim most of this chapter. Look at the notes, which highlight performance characteristics of SQL on SQL Server. Be sure to read about the use of worktables in ordering data and in performing aggregate functions, and look at the new ANSI join syntax.
>
> If you are just learning SQL, plow through this chapter and try executing some of the queries presented to get a feel for the language.

This book is not intended to be a detailed text on SQL syntax; there are several other excellent books that can help you learn the intricate details of SQL programming. Here you'll get some SQL background and then forge into those areas where the Transact-SQL language differs from standard SQL.

Who Uses SQL and Transact-SQL?

Whether you are working from PowerBuilder, writing a C/C++ application in Windows NT or MS-DOS, or using Microsoft Access, Visual Basic, or Visual FoxPro, you will ultimately submit a SQL query to the server. Some tools do the dirty work for you, by providing a visual interface to enable you to identify the components of the ultimate query and then submit the query behind the scenes. You might never see the SQL, but it is still there.

So, if you want to interact with SQL Server data, you need to submit a query in SQL. If you want to write a program to store as a SQL Server stored procedure, you need to write in Transact-SQL.

This chapter discusses the basic SQL data-retrieval and data-modification capabilities. Chapters 5 and 6, "Transact-SQL Datatypes" and "Creating and Altering Database Objects," explore SQL datatypes and the creation of tables and views. Chapters 7 and 8, "Transact-SQL Programming Constructs" and "Transact-SQL Program Structures," show you how to use the programming constructs with T-SQL; Chapter 9, "Transaction Management," reviews how to build objects based on SQL code.

Statements, Batches, and Elements of T-SQL

A Transact-SQL statement almost always includes at least one command: a verb indicating an action. For example, `select` asks the server to retrieve rows of data and `update` tells the server to change the contents of the specified rows. This chapter looks closely at four commands: `select`, `insert`, `update`, and `delete`.

NOTE

The one case where a command is not required is in the execution of a stored procedure. When the name of a stored procedure is the first element of a batch submitted to SQL Server, the `execute` command is optional.

Commands in SQL are one kind of *keyword*—reserved words that have special meaning to the server. Other keywords introduce new elements of a SQL statement. For example, the `from` keyword tells the server that a list of source tables follows. The `where` keyword introduces a list of logically connected conditions specifying the rows affected by a statement.

The application program or user submits T-SQL statements to the server in batches. A *batch* is a set of statements sent to the server at a single time. Every SQL Server application has a mechanism for telling the server to execute a batch of statements. For example, in the following ISQL session, the go directive tells ISQL to submit the three preceding lines as a batch to the server:

```
1> select au_lname, au_fname, phone
2> from authors
3> where state = "CA"
4> go
```

Server Processing Steps

When you submit a SQL batch to the server, the batch is parsed as a whole, optimized and compiled as a whole, and then executed statement-by-statement.

Let's look more closely at each of these steps. The server parses the batch to check the syntax of each command and keyword and to validate table and column names. During optimization, the server determines the most efficient method for resolving a query. (Part III of this book, "Performance and Tuning," contains much more on optimization.) Compilation creates an executable version of the batch. Execution is the step-by-step performance of each statement in the batch.

If parsing or compilation fails for any reason (for example, a syntax error or a type mismatch occurs), the batch fails and no statements are executed. If the batch fails because of an error during execution, some subset of the entire batch might have been executed. Look at the error messages returned by the server to determine what actually happened during execution.

How Do I Test SQL Queries?

If SQL Server is installed on your network, you need a SQL editor that enables you to write SQL statements and submit them to the server. There are three obvious choices:

- Use the Windows-based utility ISQL/w, which is included in the client utilities for SQL Server. After you run Setup to install the utilities on your workstation, start the application. Connect to a server; you are prompted for a login name and password. If you are the system administrator and nobody has ever used the server before, the login is sa and the password should be left blank. If this is not the case, get your login and password from your administrator.

- Use the Query Tool provided as part of SQL Enterprise Manager (SQL-EM). (This turns out to be exactly the same product as ISQL/w, bundled in with SQL-EM.)

- Use the MS-DOS-based utility ISQL, which is one of the utilities provided when you install the server. To run ISQL, you need to set some environment variables (see Chapter 24, "SQL Server Installation and Connectivity," for more on this topic).

We will step quickly through the basics of connecting to SQL Server. The chapters on installation (Chapter 24, "SQL Server Installation and Connectivity) and security (Chapter 27, "Security and User Administration") clarify many of the details we are glossing over in this section.

Logging in to a Server

You need a *connection* to a server to test T-SQL queries. First, find out the three pieces of information you need to log in:

- The name of the server
- Your login name
- Your password

> **NOTE**
>
> If you just installed SQL Server on your own workstation, you can use the default server name for the name of the server. The login name you use (for now) is sa and the password is blank (also for now).

Start up ISQL/w or SQL Enterprise Manager and get to the connect dialog box displayed in Figure 4.1.

FIGURE 4.1.

Use the connect dialog box in ISQL/w *to log in to SQL Server. In this example, the server is named* website, *the login is* sa, *and the password is blank.*

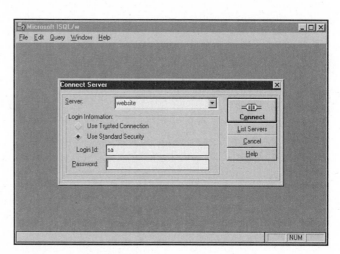

A Quick Tour of the ISQL/w Window

After you have logged in successfully, you get a connection window within the ISQL/w window (see Figure 4.2).

FIGURE 4.2.

The ISQL/w *window after logging in displays information about the server, user, and current database in the title bar. Notice that the query window is maximized.*

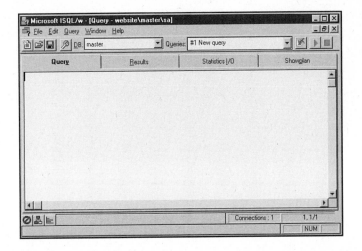

Here's a quick tour of the features of ISQL/w.

The menus are pretty self-explanatory. File menu options control the saving, retrieving, and printing of queries, as well as controlling connections to servers. The Edit menu enables you to cut-and-paste and search for strings. The Query menu executes queries and provides access to some common connection settings. The Window and Help menus behave pretty much like they do in any Windows application.

The toolbar buttons provide one-click access to the same features as the menus, but some of the buttons are pretty handy. The first button on the left (the *New Query button*) creates a new query window *and a new connection* to the same server, using the same login ID and password, and automatically using the same database as your current connection. Multiple connections are handy because they enable you to operate like two separate users, testing locking and multiuser behaviors, or looking up a quick value to help you write a complex query in another window.

WARNING

Many users believe that they are getting an additional query window using the same connection. This is not the case. You are establishing a new connection to the server. If your license limits the number of connections on the server, you will run out quickly if each user has 10 concurrent connections. (This situation isn't a national disaster—some users just need to close some connections to let others in. But it is puzzling the first time it happens.)

The other useful buttons are at the right side of the query window. (Make certain that your window is wide enough to see the three buttons to the right of the Queries drop-down list box.) The leftmost button of the three (a query icon with an X drawn on it) closes the current query and connection. This is how you reverse the effect of the New Query button.

The second button is a right-pointing arrowhead that turns green when you insert any text in the text area of the query window. This is the *execute* (or *do-it!* or *go!*) *button*. Click it when you have written a query, and the text of the query is submitted to the server. The button is gray when no text is in the window or when a query is already being processed.

The third button is a square that turns red when you are executing a query. This is the *query cancel button*. It's handy to use this after you tell the server to sort a 5 billion-row table, and then realize you don't need the answer.

There's lots of other cool stuff to do here, but it will be discussed when appropriate.

Using a Database

For the following examples (and for most examples of SQL you will encounter here and in other reference sources), use the pubs database. (Later you'll learn what actually happens when you "use" a database.) In ISQL/w, pull down the list of databases from the top window and select pubs (see Figure 4.3).

FIGURE 4.3.

To select a database, use the database drop-down list box.

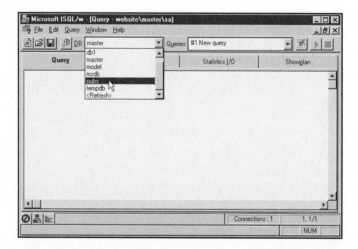

NOTE

The pubs database is a sample database consisting of tables referenced in almost every example you will see in the system documentation and in every book or article you ever read about SQL Server. The database is automatically created and populated when you install SQL Server.

We have also provided a bigpubs database for helping you understand some of the issues in performance and administration as tables get larger. For now, we'll use pubs, but in later chapters you will want to install bigpubs.

If you are not using ISQL/w, you can specify the pubs database by using the following command:

```
use pubs
```

To execute this command, use the mouse to select a button that says "execute" or "go" or has a green arrow (depending on the program you are using) or, if you are using ISQL, type the word go on its own line. Now you are ready to execute the examples in this chapter.

Retrieving Data with select

When people think of SQL, they think first of the select statement. A select statement asks the server to prepare a result and return it to the client. In standard SQL, you use it to retrieve data from tables and views for review in a client application. In T-SQL, select also enables the user to retrieve information from the system and to set the values of local variables for further work on the server.

Tables, Rows, and Columns

Most SQL statements retrieve data from tables. Logically, a *table* is a two-dimensional structure consisting of rows (or *instances*) of data, each having one or many columns (or *attributes*; they used to be called *fields*). In Chapter 5, you learn how to create tables. For now, you'll retrieve data from the tables in the pubs database.

What's in the pubs Database?

The pubs database is a collection of tables containing sample data related to a fictitious book-distribution company. There are *publishers* who publish books, *authors* who write the books, *titles* (the books themselves), and *stores* that sell the books. There are also tables stating the relationships between the tables: the titleauthor table shows which author(s) wrote which title(s), and the sales table lists which store(s) purchased which title(s) and how many title(s).

> **NOTE**
>
> There are other tables with special characteristics to demonstrate additional features of the server, including the pub_info table to demonstrate *binary large objects* (*BLOBs*) consisting of text or images, and discount and royalty to show how to perform more offbeat joins and other kinds of queries.

If the pubs database is not installed on your server, you should install it or ask your administrator to do so. All the examples in the Microsoft documentation, as well as many of the examples in this book, are based on this database.

Selecting Data from a Table

To retrieve data from a table, you submit a `select` statement. The (extremely) simplified syntax for the `select` statement is

```
select column-list
from table-name
```

The following example retrieves the last and first names of all rows in the `authors` table:

```
select au_lname, au_fname
from authors
```

The first and most important point about SQL is that it operates on *sets* of data, not individual rows. This statement returns all rows specified—in this case, all rows in the table. (Shortly, you'll explore how to limit affected rows with a `where` clause.)

SQL Result Sets

Execute this query by clicking the query execute button (or pressing Ctrl+E). The server executes the query and returns the results to the text area of the Results tab. Figure 4.4 shows the results returned from this query.

> **NOTE**
>
> If you get slightly different results, don't despair. In general, your `pubs` database configuration should be no different from mine, but I might have somewhat different indexes or some other variation.

FIGURE 4.4.

Click the Results tab to see the rows returned by the query.

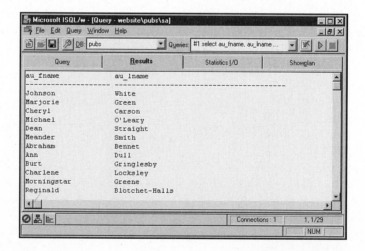

Here are all of the results (listed as text) for you to review. Because you specified two columns in the select list, the result set contains two columns:

```
au_lname                                   au_fname
--------------------------------------     -------------------
White                                      Johnson
Green                                      Marjorie
Carson                                     Cheryl
O'Leary                                    Michael
Straight                                   Dean
Smith                                      Meander
Bennet                                     Abraham
Dull                                       Ann
Gringlesby                                 Burt
Locksley                                   Charlene
Greene                                     Morningstar
Blotchet-Halls                             Reginald
Yokomoto                                   Akiko
del Castillo                               Innes
DeFrance                                   Michel
Stringer                                   Dirk
MacFeather                                 Stearns
Karsen                                     Livia
Panteley                                   Sylvia
Hunter                                     Sheryl
McBadden                                   Heather
Ringer                                     Anne
Ringer                                     Albert
(23 rows affected)
```

> **NOTE**
>
> This is a complete result set, with each of the 23 rows displayed. Most of the result sets that follow are truncated, with ellipses (...) to stand for the missing rows. Complete results sets are included only where it's necessary to see all the data to understand the example.

The results returned by most queries are actually similar to tables themselves, consisting of one or more columns with zero or more rows of data.

> **NOTE**
>
> You can redirect standard result sets into a new table by using the into keyword. Some keywords yield a result set that is not a pure table. For example, the compute keyword produces additional result rows that don't fit the column/row structure. You can't direct a result set into a new table in combination with a compute clause.

Column-Based Expressions

You can manipulate the contents of columns in the select list, as in the following example, where the proposed increase in the price of books is 10 percent of the current price:

```
select title_id, type, price, price * .1
from titles
```

Following is the result set, containing four columns of data. The fourth column is an expression derived from price.

```
title_id type          price
-------- ------------  --------------------  ----------------------
BU1032   business                    19.99                 1.99900
BU1111   business                    11.95                 1.19500
BU2075   business                     2.99                 0.29900
BU7832   business                    19.99                 1.99900
MC2222   mod_cook                    19.99                 1.99900
...
PS7777   psychology                   7.99                 0.79900
TC3218   trad_cook                   20.95                 2.09500
TC4203   trad_cook                   11.95                 1.19500
TC7777   trad_cook                   14.99                 1.49900

(18 rows affected)
```

NOTE

The heading in the price column looks out of alignment in this example because the column heading (price) is short and the column contents have few digits. The last column has no heading because it's an expression, not a column value.

In expressions, the basic arithmetic operators are available (+, -, *, /, %), as well as bitwise logical operators (AND &, OR |, XOR ^, NOT ~) and string concatenation (+).

Here is an example of string concatenation, combining the contents of two columns and a constant string expression:

```
select au_lname +", " + au_fname
from authors
```

```
------------------------------------------------------------
White, Johnson
Green, Marjorie
Carson, Cheryl
O'Leary, Michael
Straight, Dean
Smith, Meander
Bennet, Abraham
Dull, Ann
Gringlesby, Burt
Locksley, Charlene
```

```
Greene, Morningstar
Blotchet-Halls, Reginald
Yokomoto, Akiko
del Castillo, Innes
DeFrance, Michel
Stringer, Dirk
MacFeather, Stearns
Karsen, Livia
Panteley, Sylvia
Hunter, Sheryl
McBadden, Heather
Ringer, Anne
Ringer, Albert

(23 rows affected)
```

Manipulating Column Names in the `select` List

Look closely at the column headings for each of the result sets provided in the preceding section. Wherever a column appears unmodified in the `select` list, the column name is provided as the default column heading. Where any kind of expression or manipulation takes place, the column heading is blank.

To provide a column heading for a blank column, or to replace the default heading, you specify a *column alias*. Here are a couple of examples:

```
select title_id, type, price "original price", price * .1 discount
from titles
title_id type             original price         discount
-------- ------------     ----------------------  ----------------------
BU1032   business                  19.99                 1.99900
BU1111   business                  11.95                 1.19500
BU2075   business                   2.99                 0.29900
BU7832   business                  19.99                 1.99900
MC2222   mod_cook                  19.99                 1.99900
...
TC4203   trad_cook                 11.95                 1.19500
TC7777   trad_cook                 14.99                 1.49900

(18 rows affected)

select "Full Author Name" = au_lname +", " + au_fname
from authors

Full Author Name
-----------------------------------------------------------
White, Johnson
Green, Marjorie
Carson, Cheryl
O'Leary, Michael
Straight, Dean
Smith, Meander
Bennet, Abraham
...
Karsen, Livia
Panteley, Sylvia
```

```
Hunter, Sheryl
McBadden, Heather
Ringer, Anne
Ringer, Albert
```

(23 rows affected)

The two examples do the same thing in different ways. The first, which is the ANSI-SQL standard method, states the alias after the column expression. Note that `"original price"` appears in quotes because the alias itself contains two words. The quotes do not appear in the result heading. In the second example, the alias precedes the column expression with an equal (=) sign. The two aliasing methods have the same effect.

TIP

Newcomers to SQL often forget commas in the `select` list, which is a difficult and subtle problem to catch unless you know it can happen. For example, look at this query and the result:

```
select city state from publishers
state
--------------------
Boston
Washington
Berkeley

(3 rows affected)
```

What happened to the `state` column? Without the comma between `city` and `state`, the word `state` was interpreted as a column heading for the `city` column. Unless you knew to look for this problem, you could spend hours trying to fix your server, your network, and your workstation—without looking at the query.

A simple solution to troubleshooting SQL is to always ask an easy question first: How many columns did I request, and how many came back? If those numbers differ, look at the query and make certain that you really asked for the right number of columns of data.

NOTE

SQL 6.5 allows you to include the keyword AS to specify a column heading, as in this example:

```
select title_id, type, price AS "original price", price * .1 AS discount
from titles
```

Using `distinct`

The `distinct` keyword removes duplicate rows from the result set. Without `distinct`, this query returns one result row per row in the source table:

```
select type
from titles
type
-----------
business
business
business
business
mod_cook
mod_cook
UNDECIDED
popular_comp
popular_comp
popular_comp
psychology
psychology
psychology
psychology
psychology
trad_cook
trad_cook
trad_cook

(18 rows affected)
```

Adding `distinct` instructs the server to remove duplicate rows from the result set:

```
select distinct type
from titles
type
-----------
UNDECIDED
business
mod_cook
popular_comp
psychology
trad_cook
```

The scope of the `distinct` keyword is over the entire `select` list, not over a single column. In the next query, containing two columns, the `distinct` keyword identifies unique *combinations* of city and state in the `authors` table. Here is the complete list of cities and states in the `authors` table:

```
select city, state
from authors
city                  state
--------------------  ----
Menlo Park            CA
Oakland               CA
Berkeley              CA
San Jose              CA
Oakland               CA
```

```
Lawrence        KS
Berkeley        CA
Palo Alto       CA
Covelo          CA
San Francisco   CA
Nashville       TN
Corvallis       OR
Walnut Creek    CA
Ann Arbor       MI
Gary            IN
Oakland         CA
Oakland         CA
Oakland         CA
Rockville       MD
Palo Alto       CA
Vacaville       CA
Salt Lake City  UT
Salt Lake City  UT
```

(23 rows affected)

Here is the same result set with `distinct`:

```
select distinct city, state
from authors
```

```
city                 state
-------------------- ----
Ann Arbor            MI
Berkeley             CA
Corvallis            OR
Covelo               CA
Gary                 IN
Lawrence             KS
Menlo Park           CA
Nashville            TN
Oakland              CA
Palo Alto            CA
Rockville            MD
Salt Lake City       UT
San Francisco        CA
San Jose             CA
Vacaville            CA
Walnut Creek         CA
```

(16 rows affected)

In the result set, note that many rows can contain the same value for a specific city or state; the distinct operator removes only duplicate combinations.

TIP

Don't use distinct if you don't need it. It forces the server to perform extra sorting and processing that will slow down your work when distinct isn't necessary.

select *

You can include an asterisk (*) in the `select` list in place of a column or columns. The asterisk
stands for all columns in a table:

```
select *
from publishers
```

As shown in the following example, this is a convenient shortcut for ad hoc queries because it
displays all columns in logical order (the order in which they were declared when the table was
created), and the user doesn't need to know the names of columns to display information:

```
pub_id  pub_name                             city                 state
------  -----------------------------------  -------------------  ----
0736    New Age Books                        Boston               MA
0877    Binnet & Hardley                     Washington           DC
1389    Algodata Infosystems                 Berkeley             CA

(3 rows affected)
```

Filtering Rows with where

SQL is a set-processing language, so data-modification and data-retrieval statements act on all rows in a table unless a where clause limits the scope of the query. The where clause must follow the from clause:

```
select column-list
from table-name
where condition
```

In the following example, the where clause restricts the result set to authors from California:

```
select au_lname, au_fname
from authors
where state = "CA"
```

This section examines the methods available for limiting the number of rows affected by a query.

Equality and Inequality Operators

In the preceding example, the condition is in the form

```
column name = constant expression
```

The server evaluates each row to determine whether the search expression is true.

> **NOTE**
>
> The server doesn't always need to examine every row in a table to find rows that match a query. It can use indexes to speed searches if it decides that method is more efficient. The various search methods used by the server are described in detail in Chapter 13, "Understanding the Query Optimizer."

The search condition is more generally in the form

```
expression operator expression
```

where either *expression* is any valid combination of constant, variable, and column-based expressions, and where the operator is =, <> or != (equivalent symbols meaning "not equals"), >, <, >=, or <= (or !>, not greater than, or !<, not less than).

For example, the following query compares price, year-to-date sales, and advance sales in the titles table:

```
select type, title_id, price
from titles
where price * ytd_sales < advance
```

Inequalities and Character Data

When you use inequalities to compare character strings, the server determines which string would appear first in the current server *sort order*. Using the default sort order, which is based on the ASCII character set cp-850, the server selects and orders character data based on the standard ASCII character set. For example, the condition

```
type < "mod_cook"
```

would find the value business, but would also find UNDECIDED, because uppercase characters appear before lowercase characters in the ASCII character set.

Logical or and and

You can connect multiple search conditions with the or and and keywords. This example displays authors from California or from Salt Lake City:

```
select au_id, city, state
from authors
where state = "CA" or city = "Salt Lake City"
au_id       city                    state
---------- -------------------- ----
172-32-1176 Menlo Park              CA
213-46-8915 Oakland                 CA
238-95-7766 Berkeley                CA
267-41-2394 San Jose                CA
274-80-9391 Oakland                 CA
409-56-7008 Berkeley                CA
427-17-2319 Palo Alto               CA
472-27-2349 Covelo                  CA
486-29-1786 San Francisco           CA
672-71-3249 Walnut Creek            CA
724-08-9931 Oakland                 CA
724-80-9391 Oakland                 CA
756-30-7391 Oakland                 CA
846-92-7186 Palo Alto               CA
893-72-1158 Vacaville               CA
899-46-2035 Salt Lake City          UT
998-72-3567 Salt Lake City          UT

(17 rows affected)
```

between and Ranges of Data

You can search for data in a range by using a condition in this form:

expression between *expression* and *expression*

In the following query, the search condition compares a column to a specific range. This is the most common use of the between operator:

```
select title_id, price
from titles
where price between $5 and $10
```

Note that between includes the endpoint values; thus between has the same effect as two conditions connected with and:

```
select title_id, price
from titles
where price >= $5 and price <= $10
```

Use not between to identify rows outside the range, as in this example:

```
select title_id, price
from titles
where price not between $5 and $10
```

Note that not between *excludes* endpoint values; not between has the same effect as two conditions connected with or:

```
select title_id, price
from titles
where price < $5 or price > $10
```

Lists of Possible Values with in (...)

Use in to provide a list of possible values for a column or expression:

```
select title_id, price
from titles
where type in ("mod_cook", "trad_cook", "business")
```

The server reviews the value of type in each row; if the value appears in the list, the condition is true for the row. Note that in has the same effect as multiple equality conditions (one per value in the list) connected with or:

```
select title_id, price
from titles
where type = "mod_cook"
    or type = "trad_cook"
    or type = "business"
```

Use not in to provide a list of ineligible values:

```
select title_id, price
from titles
where type not in ("mod_cook", "trad_cook", "business")
```

The value must *not* be found in the list for the condition to be true. Note that not in has the same effect as multiple inequality conditions (one per value in the list) connected with and:

```
select title_id, price
from titles
where type <> "mod_cook"
    and type <> "trad_cook"
    and type <> "business"
```

Wildcards with `like`

SQL also provides a pattern-matching method for string expressions using the `like` keyword and three wildcard mechanisms: % (percent sign), _ (the underscore character) and [ ] (bracketed characters). See Table 4.1 for details.

Table 4.1. Wildcard mechanisms with the `like` operator.

Wildcard	Meaning
%	Any number (0 to many) of any character(s)
_	Any single character
[ ]	Any single character listed in the brackets

You can freely combine wildcards in a single expression.

> **NOTE**
>
> The % and _ methods are supported by ANSI-SQL; the [ ] pattern is recognized only by the Microsoft and Sybase SQL Servers.

Let's look at some uses of the wildcard. In the first example, the `where` clause matches any row where the city starts with the word *Spring* (including Spring Hill, Springdale, Springfield, and even Spring itself):

```
select au_lname, au_fname, city, state
from authors
where city like "Spring%"
```

In the following example, the underscore matches only a single character in an expression, so the query finds only rows with a single character between the *B* and *1342* in the `title_id`.

```
select type, title_id, price
from titles
where title_id like "B_1342"
```

Possible matches for `title_id` include BA1342 to BZ1342, but also include numerics (for example, B71342) and other non-alphanumeric characters (B*1342 or even B%1342). Notice that B1342 and BAB1342 do not match the pattern, because the underscore always stands for a single character.

The bracket notation enables you to define a set of valid values for a position in a string. For instance, the next example more accurately specifies the value for `title_id` from the preceding example (only the specific alphabetic characters U, A, or N should be permitted in that position):

```
select type, title_id, price
from titles
where title_id like "B[UAN]1342"
```

Note that you could also write this query as a set of equality statements, much like an `in` clause:

```
select type, title_id, price
from titles
where title_id = "BU1342"
    or title_id = "BA1342"
    or title_id = "BN1342"
```

As well as listing possible values, you can specify a range of values with a hyphen as in the following example, which permits any alphabetic character (upper- or lowercase) in the same position of the earlier `titles` query:

```
select type, title_id, price
from titles
where title_id like "B[A-Za-z]1342"
```

NOTE

This last example could conceivably be written with lots of equality conditions connected by or …

```
where title_id = "BA1342"
    or title_id = "BB1342"
    or …
    or title_id = "Bz1342"
```

It would require 52 `where` clauses connected by `or` to replace the wildcard capabilities. The pattern-matching strengths of the [ ] become increasingly clear as the number of permutations and combinations increases:

```
where title_id like "[A-Z][A-Z][0-9][0-9][0-9][0-9]"
```

This example would require more than 6 million `where` clauses!

WARNING

Remember that the wildcard characters are meaningful only after the `like` keyword. In all other circumstances, the wildcard characters are treated as actual characters, usually with odd results. In this query, only rows with individuals whose names end in a percent sign (probably very few) would be returned:

```
select au_lname, au_fname
from authors
where au_lname = "G%"
```

Using an Escape Character with `like`

The one problem posed by the `like` operator is how you search for the wildcards themselves. For example, what if you wanted to find a string containing the literal character % (percent)? Within a `like` clause, the percent normally has a special meaning. To release it from that special meaning, you use an *escape character*.

For example, here is a four-row, one-column table containing character strings.

```
ch1
----------
[ABC]
(ABC)
<ABC>
%ABC%
```

To find any string starting with a literal percent sign requires that you be able to specify the literal % character, not its wildcard value. In this example, the first percent was intended as a literal character, the second as a wildcard (starts with % and any characters after), but it is interpreted in both positions as a wildcard, so all rows are found:

```
select *
from like_ex
where ch1 like "%%"
```

```
ch1
----------
[ABC]
(ABC)
<ABC>
%ABC%
```

In this example, the backslash (\) is specified as an escape character. Any time the percent appears directly after the backslash, it is interpreted as a literal character, not a wildcard.

```
select *
from like_ex
where ch1 like "\%%" escape "\"
```

```
ch1
----------
%ABC%
```

Notice that any character can function as the escape character. In this example, the letter T is used as the escape character:

```
select *
from like_ex
where ch1 like "T%%" escape "T"
```

> **NOTE**
>
> Chapter 5 describes the column, variable, and expression datatypes available to the DBA and programmer. Look for information there on the interaction of specific datatypes with the comparison operators.

Ordering Result Sets with `order by`

In most cases, you can't count on SQL Server data being sorted in any particular order. The rows returned in an unsorted result set are ordered according to the most efficient method for resolving the query. To force the output to be sorted by a particular value, you must specify an `order by` clause:

```
select au_lname, au_fname
from authors
order by au_lname
```

You can also sort based on two or more columns, separating the sort keys with commas, as follows:

```
select au_lname, au_fname
from authors
order by au_lname, au_fname
```

> **NOTE**
>
> Sorting result sets introduces a performance cost, because the server adds a sorting step subsequent to preparing the set of rows to be returned. This additional step can be circumvented if the server can make use of an index on the sort columns.

You can specify the sort column by name or by position in the `select` list, as in the following example, where titles are sorted by year-to-date dollar sales, derived from `price` and `ytd_sales` (unit sales):

```
select title_id, price, ytd_sales, price*ytd_sales "ytd dollar sales"
from titles
order by 4
```

If you want to sort by an expression in the `select` list, make certain that the expression in the `order by` clause exactly matches the expression in the `select` list, as follows:

```
select title_id, price, ytd_sales, price*ytd_sales "ytd dollar sales"
from titles
order by price*ytd_sales
```

It's usually a good idea to name the full column or expression in the `order` by clause. Otherwise, when a programmer makes a change to the `select` statement (adding `type` after `title_id`, for example), he or she could inadvertently change the sort column.

Ascending and Descending Ordering

In the preceding example, it might be more common to sort the data by sales in descending order, showing the best-performing items first. To reverse the sort order (highest items displayed first), use the `desc` keyword:

```
select title_id, price, ytd_sales, price*ytd_sales "ytd dollar sales"
from titles
order by price*ytd_sales desc
```

By default, sort order is ascending. The `asc` keyword (for "ascending") is included as part of SQL for completeness, but is very seldom used.

`asc` and `desc` ordering affects only a single column. The following query displays best-selling books by type (ascending) and then by quantity sales (descending):

```
select title_id, type, ytd_sales
from titles
order by type, ytd_sales desc
```

Ordering by Columns Not Appearing in the `select` List

Every example so far in this chapter has demonstrated sorting by a column or columns included in the `select` list. ANSI-SQL requires that sort columns be included in the `select` list, but SQL Server doesn't. Sometimes this leads to confusing results, as in the following query, where the data is sorted by the invisible `city` and `state` columns:

```
select au_lname, au_fname
from authors
order by city, state
au_lname                                    au_fname
----------------------------------------    -------------------
del Castillo                                Innes
Carson                                      Cheryl
Bennet                                      Abraham
Blotchet-Halls                              Reginald
Gringlesby                                  Burt
DeFrance                                    Michel
```

Smith	Meander
White	Johnson
Greene	Morningstar
Karsen	Livia
Straight	Dick
Stringer	Dirk
Green	Marjorie
MacFeather	Stearns
Dull	Ann
Hunter	Sheryl
Panteley	Sylvia
Ringer	Anne
Ringer	Albert
Locksley	Chastity
O'Leary	Michael
McBadden	Heather
Yokomoto	Akiko

```
(23 rows affected)
```

A user trying to determine the sort order of these results would be driven nuts trying to find the pattern.

Ordering by a column not in the `select` list can provide better performance. In the following example, the query displays a discount derived from price, but sorts by the price column itself:

```
select title_id, discount = price * .15
from titles
where price between $10.50 and $15.00
order by price
```

The logical result of the query is the same as if you had ordered by the expression `price * .15`; however, because you create indexes only on columns (not on expressions), it's always better to sort by a column than by an expression derived from that column. If there were an index on the `price` column, this query would probably be generated without the intermediate worktable, providing substantially better performance.

> **NOTE**
>
> By now, you have noticed that the behavior of the server can't always be predicted—that it will "probably" use an index or "in many cases" it will make use of an intermediate worktable. Even given a specific table structure and query, you can't predict universally how the server will answer a question until you also understand the distribution of the data. It is the work of the optimizer to decide, on a query-by-query basis, what is the most effective method for resolving queries.
>
> Experienced programmers often have a difficult time getting used to the idea that the server makes these decisions for them, but this is one of the primary benefits of the SQL Server implementation. Programmers can worry about how to logically define their requirements; database administrators worry about how to efficiently satisfy those requirements.

Retrieving Aggregate Data

SQL provides functions for describing data as a whole rather than as a set of rows. The *aggregate* functions (so named because they "aggregate" many rows of data into a single row) are listed in Table 4.2.

Table 4.2. The aggregate functions.

Function	Description
sum()	Totals numeric expressions
avg()	Averages numeric expressions
min()	Returns the lowest numeric expression, the lowest sorting string expression, or the earliest date
max()	Returns the highest numeric expression, the highest sorting string expression, or the latest date
count()	Returns the number of non-null expressions
count(*)	Returns the number of rows found

Take a look at the following query and result set. The avg() function returns a single average for all title rows in the table:

```
select avg(price)
from titles
```

```
-----------------------
            14.77
```

```
(1 row affected)
```

Notice that the query examined all rows of the titles table but returned only a single row.

> **TIP**
>
> The result column for the aggregate has no default column heading. It is useful to assign headings such as sum and avg to SQL result sets, but you need to assign these headings in quotes because these are reserved words as names of functions:
>
> ```
> select avg(price) "avg" ...
> ```

Combine where clauses with aggregates to specify the rows to be included in the aggregate. In this example, the query asks for the average price of business books:

```
select avg(price) "avg"
from titles
where type = "business"
```

You can include many aggregates in the same `select` list if they relate to the same rows within a table:

```
select avg(price) "avg", sum(price) "sum"
from titles
where type in ("business", "mod_cook")
avg                      sum
------------------------ ------------------------
              12.98                     77.90
```

```
(1 row affected)
```

Counting Rows with `count(*)`

An important aggregate function is `count(*)`, which counts rows matching a set of conditions. The following query determines the number of authors in California:

```
select count(*)
from authors
where state = "CA"
----------
        15
```

```
(1 row affected)
```

Aggregates and Null Values

Aggregate functions don't include null values. Consider a table, `test_table`, containing four rows, with the following values in the `c2` column:

```
c2
----
100
150
200
null
```

The following example provides the values for each of the aggregate functions; this displays the behavior of each of the aggregate functions on a table containing a null value:

```
select sum(c2) "sum", count(c2) "count", avg(c2) "avg",
       min(c2) "min", max(c2) "max", count(*) "count(*)"
from test_table
sum         count       avg         min         max         count(*)
----------- ----------- ----------- ----------- ----------- ----------
        450           3         150         100         200          4
```

```
(1 row affected)
```

Null values do not imply any value (not even zero). Notice that the `count(c2)` is 3, meaning that three rows in the table contain non-null values in the column `c2`. The average disregards the null value and the minimum is 100, not zero or null, because nulls are disregarded.

Note, however, that the `count(*)` column includes all *rows*, regardless of nulls.

Sub-Aggregates with group by

The count(*) query provides the overall average and sum of prices for business and modern cooking books, but how do you determine the average and sum of each of these individual types of books? The answer is to return subaverages and subtotals by type, using group by, like this:

```
select type, avg(price) "avg", sum(price) "sum"
from titles
where type in ("business", "mod_cook")
group by type
type            avg                 sum
----------- ------------------------ ------------------------
business                    13.73                   54.92
mod_cook                    11.49                   22.98

(2 rows affected)
```

The result set includes one row per type value among the selected rows. Aggregates return a single row for each unique value in the column specified in the group by clause.

When two or more columns are included in the group by statement, aggregates are based on unique combinations of those columns. In the following example, the server returns the average and total price for business and modern cooking books for each combination of type and publisher ID:

```
select type, pub_id, avg(price) "avg", sum(price) "sum"
from titles
where type in ("business", "mod_cook")
group by type, pub_id
type        pub_id avg                sum
----------- ------ ------------------------ ------------------------
business    0736                2.99                    2.99
business    1389               17.31                   51.93
mod_cook    0877               11.49                   22.98

(3 rows affected)
```

Filtering Results with having

You can use the having keyword to select rows from the result set. If you wanted to display by type the average price of books costing more than $10, you would use a where clause:

```
select type, avg(price)
from titles
where price > $10
group by type
type
----------- ------------------------
business                    17.31
mod_cook                    19.99
popular_comp                21.48
```

```
psychology                      17.51
trad_cook                       15.96
```

```
(5 rows affected)
```

The where clause selects rows from the table before the averaging takes place.

A having clause enables you to select rows from the result set. This example displays only those types of books with an average price greater than $20:

```
select type, avg(price)
from titles
where price > $10
group by type
having avg(price) > $20
type
------------ -----------------------
popular_comp                    21.48
```

```
(1 row affected)
```

TIP

One useful application of the having keyword is to identify rows in a table that have duplicate keys. (*Keys* are unique identifiers. Duplicate keys are a terrible idea, but they often crop up during a data transfer from older systems.)

To find all rows in the authors table that share the same key, use this query:

```
select au_id, count(*)
from authors
group by au_id
having count(*) > 1
```

Worktables and Aggregate Functions

To resolve a query containing a group by clause, the server uses an intermediate worktable. Figure 4.5 shows the role of the worktable in the resolution of a query. The server resolves where clauses and grouping while building the intermediate worktable. distinct, having, and order by are resolved after the worktable is generated, while preparing the final result set.

The server needs to use an intermediate result set to resolve this query:

```
select type, avg(price)
from titles
where pub_id = "1289"
group by type
having avg(price) > $15
order by avg(price) desc
```

First, rows matching the where clause are averaged into a worktable. Then the server filters and sorts the result set.

FIGURE 4.5.

The worktable helps the server resolve complex queries involving grouping and ordering.

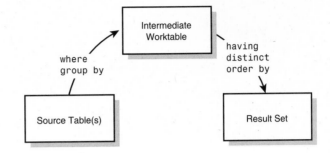

cube **and** rollup

SQL 6.5 introduces two new operators with group by: cube and rollup. These operators add *super-aggregate* values to the result set.

Here is a simple select statement with a group by clause. Each row appears as a part of only one row in the ultimate result:

```
select product_id, item_id, sum(qty) "SUM"
from cubit
group by product_id, item_id
```

```
product_id  item_id SUM

----------  ------  -------------------------------------------------
1           A       0.01
1           B       0.10
1           C       1.00
2           A       10.00
2           B       100.00
2           C       1000.00
3           A       10000.00
3           B       100000.00
```

When the cube operator is added, the result includes rows that aggregate the already-aggregate rows. Those super-aggregates appear in boldface in the result set. Note that, whenever a (null) value appears in the result set, this indicates that the sum includes rows for all values of this column. Thus, the row with 1 for product_id and (null) for item_id provides a sum for all rows where product_id is 1, regardless of the value of item_id:

```
select product_id, item_id, sum(qty) "SUM"
from cubit
group by product_id, item_id
with cube
```

```
product_id  item_id SUM
----------  ------  ------------------------------------------------
1           A       0.01
1           B       0.10
1           C       1.00
```

```
1          (null)  1.11
2          A       10.00
2          B       100.00
2          C       1000.00
2          (null)  1110.00
3          A       10000.00
3          B       100000.00
3          (null)  110000.00
(null)     (null)  111111.11
(null)     A       10010.01
(null)     B       100100.10
(null)     C       1001.00
```

```
(15 row(s) affected)
```

As you can see, a single value can appear as part of several different aggregate values within the final set.

The `rollup` operator acts similarly to the `cube` operator, but it suppresses rows that could be perceived as unnecessary. The last several rows in the `cube` result are super-aggregates for columns not appearing first in the `group by` list. These rows are suppressed in the `rollup` output:

```
select product_id, item_id, sum(qty) "SUM"
from cubit
group by product_id, item_id
with rollup
```

```
product_id  item_id SUM
----------  ------  ------------------------------------------
1           A       0.01
1           B       0.10
1           C       1.00
1           (null)  1.11
2           A       10.00
2           B       100.00
2           C       1000.00
2           (null)  1110.00
3           A       10000.00
3           B       100000.00
3           (null)  110000.00
(null)      (null)  111111.11
```

> **TIP**
>
> The key point here is that the `rollup` operator prioritizes columns based on the `group by` order, and `cube` doesn't. Use `rollup` to aggregate up a hierarchical relationship—for example, from department to division to company. Use `cube` to see the complete interaction between freely varying values, as with products and customers.

Joins

All the queries considered so far have addressed only one table at a time, but most SQL queries need to address multiple tables at one time. For example, to display the titles of books and the names of publishers in a single query, you need to draw information from both the `titles` and `publishers` tables.

> **NOTE**
>
> As we prepare this second edition dealing with SQL Server 6.5, one of the largest syntactic issues relates to the new ANSI-92-compliant join syntax. This syntax will provide access to some new features and will be the best-supported approach to writing joins in future releases. For now, many readers will be making the transition to the new syntax.
>
> All examples in this chapter are presented using both methods, so that you can become equally familiar with both. In later chapters, most of the examples are presented in the older format. Remember that the new ANSI syntax is not supported prior to SQL 6.5.

Let's look more closely at how you would write a query to join the `titles` and `publishers` tables.

When two tables are joined, they must share a *common key* or *join key*, which defines how rows in the tables correspond to each other. For example, in the case of `titles` and `publishers`, the tables share a common key, `pub_id`. In the `publishers` table, `pub_id` uniquely identifies a row in that table. In the `titles` table, `pub_id` uniquely identifies a row in the `publishers` table; titles with this `pub_id` belong to publishers having the same `pub_id`.

> **NOTE**
>
> It's not exactly accurate to say that tables must share a common key to be joined. But to receive reasonable, rational results from a query you must normally provide a common key. See the next section for details.

When you join two or more tables in SQL Server, the server does not implicitly understand the relationship between the tables; you need to tell it about common keys. In the next example, the selection is drawn from two tables (see the `from` clause). The `where` clause of the query defines how those tables relate to each other:

```
select title, pub_name
from titles, publishers
where titles.pub_id = publishers.pub_id
```

Notice that the `from` clause now names two tables. Also notice that the join condition specifies a table name before each column name (`titles.pub_id`). Column names must be *qualified* (that is, you must specify the exact table name) whenever there is possible ambiguity because of duplicate column names in multiple tables.

In this case, because `pub_id` appears in both the `titles` and `publishers` tables, the `pub_id` column needs to be qualified. On the other hand, the `title` and `pub_name` columns are not qualified, because each appears only in a single table among those named in the `from` clause.

Here is the alternative, ANSI-standard syntax to specify the same join result:

```
select title, pub_name
from titles JOIN publishers
ON titles.pub_id = publishers.pub_id
```

What Happens When You Fail to Specify a Common Key?

When you write a join without specifying a common key, the server returns all possible combinations of rows between the tables. Consider this example:

```
select title, pub_name
from titles, publishers
```

When the `where` clause is left out, the server returns a list containing each title many times, once for each publisher. This is a meaningless result, because only a single publisher would have published each book.

A result set based on a query missing a proper join condition is called a *Cartesian product*. Cartesian products can take forever to resolve and—once resolved—are usually utterly useless.

The ANSI standard provides a method of retrieving this result, which it refers to as a *cross-product* or *cross-join*:

```
select title, pub_name
from titles CROSS JOIN publishers
```

Recipe for Writing Queries Containing Joins

Here is a simple recipe for writing joins if you have been assigned to write a specific query or report:

1. Build the `select` list, naming each column or expression.
2. Name the tables where the columns in the `select` list reside, as well as any tables required to connect those tables.
3. Provide the join conditions to connect the tables.

For example, imagine writing a query to determine the average price of all books purchased by a single publisher. In that case, the `select` list might look like this:

```
select pub_name, avg(price)
```

> **NOTE**
>
> This example uses an aggregate expression based on the `price` column. In spite of this added wrinkle, the join method is the same as elsewhere and the recipe described previously is valid.

The next step is to determine the tables where these columns are found, and any tables that must be identified between them, like one of the following:

```
from titles t, publishers p
```

> *or*

```
from titles t JOIN publishers p
```

> **NOTE**
>
> Earlier, you saw how column aliases enable you to specify a substitute column name. The previous example included *table aliases*, which don't affect the final results but do enable you to simplify the SQL syntax. In a later section, you see how self-joins require table aliases; however, in all other circumstances table aliases are completely optional. It is important to understand that once you have specified an alias, any subsequent reference to a table *for this SQL statement* will require the table alias rather than the full name.

The final step is to name the `where` clauses and complete the SQL. Here is the complete query (in two versions):

```
select pub_name, avg(price)
from titles t, publishers p
where t.pub_id = p.pub_id
group by pub_name
```

> *or*

```
select pub_name, avg(price)
from titles t JOIN publishers p
ON t.pub_id = p.pub_id
group by pub_name
```

> **NOTE**
>
> You can combine joins with every other aspect of SQL, including grouping, ordering, `having`, and other complex `where` conditions.

Dealing with More than Two Tables

You can join up to 16 tables at a time. This example joins the `titles` and `authors` tables to determine which author wrote each psychology title. Following the recipe for a join, here is the `select` list:

```
select au_lname, au_fname, title
```

In the `from` clause, you could simply name the tables `authors` and `titles`, but note that the tables do not share a common key. To connect them, you need to include the `titleauthor` table, which shares a common key with both tables:

```
from authors a, titles t, titleauthor ta
```

   or

```
from authors a
     JOIN titleauthor ta
     JOIN titles t
```

Now it's time to name the join conditions. Because there are three joins, there are two required join conditions:

```
where ta.title_id = t.title_id
and a.au_id = ta.au_id
```

   or

```
from authors a
     JOIN titleauthor ta ON a.au_id = ta.au_id
     JOIN titles t ON ta.title_id = t.title_id
```

TIP

When joining two tables, you must specify one join condition in order to avoid a Cartesian product. When joining three tables, you must specify two join conditions. As a general rule, when joining *n* tables, you must specify *n*-1 join conditions.

Now all that is required is to put the whole query together and add the condition to limit the result set to psychology books, and you're done:

```
select au_lname, au_fname, title
from authors a, titles t, titleauthor ta
where ta.title_id = t.title_id
and a.au_id = ta.au_id
and type = "psychology"
```

   or

```
select au_lname, au_fname, title
from authors a
     JOIN titleauthor ta ON a.au_id = ta.au_id
     JOIN titles t ON ta.title_id = t.title_id
     where type = "psychology"
```

> **NOTE**
>
> Does the order in which the tables are named have an effect on the overall behavior of the server or on performance? Using the older join syntax, in a very few cases, and only in cases where more than four tables are named, table order can have an impact on performance. See Chapter 13, "Understanding the Query Optimizer," Chapter 15, "Analyzing Query Plans," and Chapter 17, "Managing the SQL Server Optimizer," for more on performance issues and how they relate to the actual syntax of a select statement.
>
> Using the ANSI join syntax, you need to provide the table names in an order that allows the parser to make sense of your table references. For example, if you were to execute this query, the server would not be able to determine the meaning of the ta reference in the first join condition:
>
> ```
> /* this example will NOT work */
> select au_lname, au_fname, title
> from authors a
>         JOIN titles t ON ta.title_id = t.title_id
>         JOIN titleauthor ta ON a.au_id = ta.au_id
> ```

The Meaning of * in a Multitable Query

In a multitable query, an unqualified asterisk (*) means "all columns from all tables." For example, in the following query, it means "every column from both the titles and publishers tables":

```
select *
from titles t, publishers p
where t.pub_id = p.pub_id
```

If you qualify the * as in the following example, you get only the columns from a single table:

```
select t.*, pub_name
from titles t, publishers p
where t.pub_id = p.pub_id
```

Subqueries

With SQL Server, you can use a *subquery* in place of a constant expression to tell the server to derive a result before processing the remainder of the query. In the following example (shown on next page), you ask the server to show you all books published by a specific publisher. Note that a subquery might return only a single column of data:

```
select title
from titles
where pub_id =
    (select pub_id
     from publishers
     where pub_name = "Algodata Infosystems")
```

The subquery must always appear in parentheses.

When a subquery appears as part of an equality condition (for example, pub_id = (...)), the server expects to resolve the subquery before it starts work on the main query, and *the subquery must return only a single row.*

> **TIP**
>
> To be certain to return only a single row, use a unique key or other unique identifier in the where clause of the subquery, or use an aggregate.

Subqueries with `in`

Although a subquery returns only a single column of data, it can return multiple *rows* of data when used with `in` and `not in`. In the following example, the server displays all publishers of business books:

```
select pub_name
from publishers
where pub_id in
    (select pub_id
     from titles
     where type = "business")
```

The server returns a list of valid publisher IDs to the main query and then determines whether each publisher's pub_id is in that list. Here is the result set from the query:

```
pub_name
----------------------------------------
New Moon Books
Algodata Infosystems

(2 rows affected)
```

Subqueries Versus Joins

The SQL Server treats the subquery in the same way as a join. Here is a query using a join condition to return a similar result:

```
select pub_name
from publishers p, titles t
where p.pub_id = t.pub_id
and type = "business"
```

Here is the result set:

```
pub_name----------------------------------------
New Age Books
Algodata Infosystems
Algodata Infosystems
Algodata Infosystems

(4 rows affected)
```

Subqueries with `exists`

Why does the server return duplicate rows in the result set? Because each query asks for *all matching rows.* There are two ways to solve this problem. The first method is to use the `distinct` keyword to force the server to find only unique results. The problem with `distinct` is that it requires an additional sorting step using a worktable, with an often severe performance penalty on large data sets.

The second method is to use the `exists` keyword to find only rows matching the condition, and to stop looking for results after the first match is found for a particular value. Here's the same query with an `exists` clause. Look at the example; then you'll step through it to understand how it is written and how it is resolved:

```
select pub_name
from publishers p
where exists
    (select *
     from titles t
     where p.pub_id = t.pub_id
     and type = "business")
```

There are a number of syntactic oddities to observe. First, note that `exists` takes neither an equals sign nor an `in`, and applies not to a relationship between columns, but to a relationship between tables. Because of that, you do not specify a column name in the `select` list of the subquery; always write `select *` instead.

Finally, notice that the subquery refers to a table alias, p, in the `where` condition (`p.pub_id`), even though this table alias is not declared in the `from` clause of the subquery itself. The table alias p, of course, relates to the `publishers` table, which is declared in the outer portion of the query.

`exists` (and some other situations we won't look at right now) usually uses a *correlated subquery* in which the subquery will not run on its own. To resolve the correlated subquery, the server must execute the subquery once for each row in the outer query, testing for a match on `pub_id`.

Here is the result set of the query with `exists`:

```
pub_name
----------------------------------------
New Age Books
Algodata Infosystems

(2 rows affected)
```

The duplicates are eliminated without an intermediate worktable.

> **TIP**
>
> Always use `exists` rather than joining tables and using `distinct`. The performance benefits are dramatic.

not exists and not in

Certain results can be defined only with a subquery; for example, non-membership and non-existence can be expressed only in that way. Which publishers *do not* publish business books? This query cannot be expressed with a join, but it can be expressed using `not exists` or `not in`:

```
select pub_name
from publishers p
where not exists
    (select *
     from titles t
     where t.pub_id = p.pub_id
     and type = "business")
select pub_name
from publishers
where pub_id not in
    (select pub_id
     from titles
     where type = "business")
```

> **TIP**
>
> In most cases, `not in` and `not exists` are identical in their behavior. However, using `not exists` enables you to compare tables where the join condition consists of multiple columns. You can't use `not in` to compare tables like that. (If you're not sure about this, try it!)

Subqueries with Aggregates in where Clauses

One specific case where a subquery is required appears when you want to use an aggregate function in a where clause. The next example returns the type and price of all books whose price is below the average price. This condition in a where clause would be illegal:

```
where price < avg(price)
```

The server requires that the average price be derived in a subquery, as follows:

```
select type, price
from titles
where price <
    (select avg(price)
     from titles)
```

> **NOTE**
>
> Don't confuse this use of a subquery with a having clause. Consider this example:
>
> ```
> select type, avg(price)
> from titles
> group by type
> having avg(price)<
>             (select avg(price)
>              from titles)
> ```

union

The SQL union keyword enables you to request a logical union of two or more result sets, listing rows where values are found in either result. This query requests the city and state of each author and each publisher in a single result set:

```
select city, state
from authors
union
select city, state
from publishers
```

The server resolves each element of the union, placing the results in an intermediate worktable. When all the results are available, the server automatically removes duplicate rows from the final result.

> **TIP**
>
> To prevent the server from removing duplicates, use union all to force all result rows to be returned.

Each result set must have the same number of columns as the first result set, and each column must be of the same datatype as one in the corresponding position in the first result set. The name of each column is drawn from the column names in the first result set.

> **NOTE**
>
> Column datatypes do not have to match exactly, but they do have to allow an implicit conversion. For example, the server automatically converts strings of different length, and it will convert numeric values of different types. It will not, however, automatically convert dates to numeric values, or numbers to strings. For more on implicit data conversions, see Chapter 5.

You can sort the result of a `union` operation. The `order by` clause appears after the final `select` statement, but it references the column names or expressions in the first `select` list. In the following sample query, authors' and publishers' cities and states are sorted by state, and then city:

```
select city, state
from authors
union
select city, state
from publishers
order by state, city
```

This operation is most often used to connect active and archive data, or data that has been separated by year, into a single result set. The following example draws data from the fictional `salescurrent` and `saleshistory` tables, where the two tables have the same structure:

```
select 95 "year", month, sum(dollar_sales)
from salescurrent
group by month
union
select 94, month, sum(dollar_sales)
from saleshistory
group by month
order by year, month
```

Notice that the `union` keyword enables you to create result sets using `group by` and `where` clauses, each of which is specific to its own `select` operation. Also note that the `order by` clause might optionally reference the column aliases defined in the first result clause instead of the column expressions.

Using `select` with `into`

You can direct the `select` statement to create a table on-the-fly, consisting of the rows in the result set, rather than returning the output to the user. This is a common mechanism for creating temporary tables that will be used for subsequent reporting. The structure of the table is defined by the select list itself. The columns are created in the order of the select list, with column names and datatypes drawn from the select list as well.

This example instructs the server to create a table with each of the book types included in the titles table:

```
select distinct type
into type_lookup
from titles
```

The resulting type_lookup table has one column named type whose datatype is the same as the datatype stored in the titles table.

When creating a table with select ... into, you can use any of the SQL syntax you have seen so far in this chapter. This query prepares a master list of all California cities for publishers, authors, and stores:

```
select city
into cal_cities
from publishers
where state = "CA"
union
select city
from authors
where state = "CA"
union
select city
from stores
where state = "CA"
```

> **NOTE**
>
> The into must be stated after the first select list when combined with a union statement.

It is often useful to create an empty copy of an existing table. This query creates an empty copy of salesdetail:

```
select *
into new_salesdetail
from salesdetail
where 1 = 2
```

Even though no rows are found, a table with no rows is created.

Adding Rows with insert

So far, you have explored SQL only for retrieving data. The next couple of sections look at queries that modify the data in tables, using the keywords insert, update, and delete.

To add rows to a table, use the `insert` statement. You can either insert specific values that you state in the query or insert based on a selection from another table.

Inserting Specific Values

The following query inserts a row in the `authors` table, providing values for five of the nine columns in the table:

```
insert authors
    (au_id, au_lname, au_fname, phone, contract)
values
    ("123-45-6789", "Jones", "Mary", "415 555-1212", 1)
```

In the `insert` statement, the number of columns in the `values` list must match those in the column list. The datatype of the values must enable an implicit conversion to the datatype of each corresponding column. Columns that are not specified are set to their default value (see Chapter 5 for information on default values), where one is defined; if there is no default value for a column not specified in the column list, a null value is inserted for the column.

> **NOTE**
>
> If a column does not allow null values, has no default value, or is not an *identity* (automatically sequentially numbered) or *timestamp* (automatic version control) column, SQL Server will return an error if no value is provided in the `insert` statement. In those cases, in order to enter a row, a value must be provided for the column.

The `insert` statement in which you provide specific values inserts only one row at a time. Each additional row requires that you specify the `insert` keyword again, providing again the name of the table and related columns.

Inserting Several Rows with `select`

In addition to inserting individual rows with a `values` list, you can also insert one row or many rows, based on the result set from a `select` query embedded in the `insert` statement. In the following example, the query inserts rows in the fictitious `authors_archive` table, based on rows in the `authors` table:

```
insert authors_archive
    (au_id, au_lname, au_fname, phone, city, state, zip)
select au_id, au_lname, au_fname, phone, city, state, zip
from authors
where state = "CA"
```

> **NOTE**
>
> A single `insert` statement can insert zero, one, or many rows. This is an important point to remember about inserting rows when writing insert triggers. For more on this, see Chapter 8.

Omitting the Column List

The column list in an `insert` statement is optional, but when it is left out, you must provide values for each column in the table *in the order in which the columns were defined*. If you fail to provide the correct number of columns, the server returns a syntax error and the insert fails. This query inserts a row in the `publishers` table, but does not specify any column names:

```
insert publishers
values
    ("1235", "New World Books and Prints", "Atlanta", "GA")
```

If you specify values in an incorrect order, the server traps invalid data types where appropriate. Otherwise, the wrong data simply appears in each column. For example, this insert to the `publishers` table has the city and state in the wrong order:

```
insert publishers
values
    ("1235", "New World Books and Prints", "GA", "Atlanta")
```

The server won't catch this error because all of the columns are character or variable-character datatypes, enabling implicit conversions and length adjustments. In this case, the value GA would be inserted as the city and the value At (truncated to two characters to match the `state` column definition) would be inserted for the state.

> **WARNING**
>
> Omitting column names from `insert` statements, particularly when the statements are embedded in application programs, stored procedures, and triggers, can result in ugly code-maintenance problems. What if someone added a column named `zip` to the `publishers` table? An `insert` statement including the column names to be inserted would succeed, although `zip` would be stored as a null value. But an insert without column names would fail, because the statement now requires five values instead of four.
>
> Here is an important coding standard for your organization: All `insert` statements will name the columns to be inserted.

Inserting from a Stored Procedure

SQL Server 6.5 allows you to insert rows in a table based on a result set from a stored procedure. In this example, a stored procedure p1 selects rows from the titles table based on the type value passed as a parameter (in this case, "business"). The results from that stored procedure are directed into the newtitles table in the following statement:

```
insert newtitles
exec p1 "business"
```

> **NOTE**
>
> This capability is particularly useful when performing multi-server work. A remote procedure can return rows from a remote server. Those rows can be inserted into a table on the local server. Without this capability, the client would be responsible for receiving the rows from the remote server, and then transmitting them to the local server. For more on remote servers, see Chapter 34, "Remote Server Management."

Modifying Rows with update

To modify values within tables, use the update statement. update statements consist of three main components:

- The table to be updated
- The columns to be updated, with the new values
- The rows to be updated, in the form of a where clause

This statement changes the name of a publisher to Joe's Press:

```
update publishers
set pub_name = "Joe's Press"
where pub_id = "1234"
```

An unqualified update statement (one without a where clause) modifies every row in the table:

```
update titles
set price = price * 2
```

> **TIP**
>
> By far the hardest element of SQL for experienced database programmers to grasp is the need for a where clause to define the set of rows to be updated. This is particularly true when writing an online update system, where the row to be modified is visible on-screen.

When you pass the update statement, SQL Server has no idea which row or rows you might have on-screen; each statement is taken on its own, without a reference to other processing. Therefore, the statement

```
update publishers
set name = "Joe's Books and Prints"
```

instructs the server to change *every row in the table.*

You can update only one table at a time, but you can set values for many columns at a time, as in the following statement, which updates the entire address record for a contact:

```
update contacts
set address1 = "5 West Main St.",
    address2 = "Apartment 3D",
    city = "Hartford",
    state = "CT",
    zip = "03838"
where contact_id = 17938
```

TIP

Setting many columns in a single statement is always more efficient than issuing many update statements.

Removing Rows with `delete`

To remove rows from a table, issue the delete statement. delete statements include the name of the table and a where clause defining the rows to delete. This example removes all business books from the titles table:

```
delete titles
where type = "business"
```

An unqualified delete statement removes every row from the table:

```
delete titles
```

This is usually unintended; if not, see the next section on truncate table. (Refer to the earlier Warning in the "Omitting the Column List" section of this chapter.)

You can delete rows from only a single table at a time.

Clearing a Table with `truncate table`

There are times when you want to clear all rows from a table but leave the table definition as is. To clear a table, issue the `truncate table` command:

```
truncate table titles
```

`truncate table` simply deallocates all space allocations to a table and its indexes instead of removing each row from the table one by one. This is substantially faster than an unqualified `delete`, especially on large tables.

> **WARNING**
>
> You probably are not ready for this information, but you will be reminded of it later when you are reading about transaction logs and data backup.
>
> `truncate table` is fast because it does not log individual row deletions as it deallocates space. Your ability to recover your database in case of disaster is compromised after `truncate table` until you run a backup, and you will not be able to run an incremental backup (`dump transaction ...`) until you have run a full backup (`dump database ...`) first.

`truncate table` is most commonly used when moving large blocks of test data in and out of the server and when preparing the server for a rollout.

Summary

SQL provides a flexible, English-like method of retrieving and modifying data in tables. The query language is fairly simple, yet powerful. It is the only way to access data in a SQL Server and is supported by every product that supports SQL Server itself.

The following chapters look more at Transact-SQL, the extensions to the standard SQL language that enable SQL Server to store programmatic, SQL-based objects, and to manage data integrity at the server.

Transact-SQL Datatypes

5

This chapter looks at the datatypes supported by SQL Server. *Datatypes* are predefined, named methods for storing, retrieving, and interpreting categories of data values. As in most programming environments, the system defines the datatypes available to you; you are not permitted to improvise your own.

> **NOTE**
>
> SQL Server supports user-defined datatypes, but these enable the user only to subclass an existing datatype, not to define a new type with new storage and retrieval characteristics. For more on user-defined datatypes, see Chapter 6, "Creating and Altering Database Objects."

Datatypes Supported by SQL Server

You must choose a datatype whenever you create a column in a table or when you declare a local variable. In each case, the choice of a datatype determines the following:

- The kind of data that can be stored in the column (numbers, strings, binary strings, bit values, or dates)
- In the case of numeric and date datatypes, the range of values permitted in the column
- In the case of strings and binary data, the maximum length of data you can store in the column

> **WARNING**
>
> Column datatype selection is one of those incredibly important topics that has ramifications in space utilization, performance, reliability, and manageability of your system. Unfortunately, it is also something you need to do very early in the process of implementing SQL Server, long before you will really understand the ramifications of your choices.
>
> Whatever else you don't have the time to understand, be certain to understand this point: *After you have created a column and declared its datatype, you cannot change that datatype without dropping and re-creating the table. The more data in the table, the more time that process will take, and the more disruption it will cause in system availability.*
>
> This chapter doesn't go into detail on physical storage structures (how rows and pages of data are stored, how indexes are physically managed, and so forth). Before you get deeply into production on systems that require optimal performance, you should finish this chapter and also carefully read Chapter 11, "Understanding SQL Server Storage Structures." If you are planning to build very large tables or tables that need to perform extremely well, take the time now to read that chapter before you define your tables and columns.

Nullability and Datatypes

When you define a column, you must also decide whether to allow null values in that column. A column that allows nulls requires more space to store a value and might have other performance or storage implications. In this chapter, be sure to notice any special concerns related to nullability for each datatype.

> **NOTE**
>
> This chapter will probably be more helpful if you understand the context in which you define a datatype. Here is a brief example of a table-creation statement:
>
> ```
> create table my_table
> (id int not null,
> value float not null,
> description varchar(30) null)
> ```
>
> This query creates a three-column table named `my_table`. Each column is assigned a datatype, and the variable-length column description is also assigned a maximum length of 30 characters.
>
> For much more about table definition, see Chapter 6.

Character and Binary Datatypes

Store strings using character datatypes. There are three valid datatypes for storing strings:

- `char`, for storing fixed-length strings
- `varchar`, for variable-length strings
- `text`, for strings of virtually unlimited size (up to two gigabytes of text per row)

Binary datatypes store *binary* strings—strings consisting of binary values instead of characters. The most common uses of binary data are for `timestamp` and `image` datatypes (described later):

- `binary`, for fixed-length binary strings
- `varbinary`, for variable-length binary strings
- `image`, for storing large binary strings (up to two gigabytes of image data per row)

char **and** varchar

The most common string datatypes are fixed-length (`char`) and variable-length (`varchar`) character types. Columns defined as `char` (or `character`) will store trailing blanks to fill out a fixed number of characters. Columns defined as `varchar` (or `character varying`) will truncate trailing blanks to save space.

Column Length

The maximum length of a character column is 255 columns. When you define a char or varchar column, you must also specify a column length to indicate the maximum number of characters the column will store. Here are some column definitions and likely datatypes:

```
name varchar(40)
state char(2)
title varchar(80)
comments varchar(255)
title_id char(6)
```

In the examples, name, title, and comments will vary in length. The server will not reserve space to handle trailing blanks, so a value of George in SQL Server will store only the first six characters in the name column. The columns title_id and state are fixed-length char types because the user is likely to insert (or *might* be restricted to inserting) only strings of the stated length.

TIP

The decision to use char or varchar depends on how frequently the user will provide data of *exactly* the length specified in the column definition. Variable-length structures require additional overhead for their storage (one extra byte per row to store the length of the variable-length data). In addition, SQL Server must store one extra byte per row if there is any variable-length data at all in the table definition. Finally, certain operations are more efficient with character data.

The extra cost in overhead of storing variable-length data is often worth the substantial space savings provided by not storing trailing blanks. If a column is defined as char(20) but averages only 8 bytes of data per row, SQL Server still stores (on average) 12 additional padding spaces per row. That might not seem like much but, over a million rows, that's at least 12 megabytes of additional space.

Until you have a firmer understanding of how SQL Server stores data, you may not make the correct choice between char and varchar. As a rule of thumb, the more the data varies in length, the more important it is to use varchar. Note that there is no reason at all to define a varchar(1) column.

Chapter 11 discusses the details of physical data storage in more detail. (There, for example, you will find the specifics on variable-length column overhead.)

> **NOTE**
>
> Nullable character columns are stored as variable-length columns. For example, the `description` column in this table is stored exactly like a `varchar(50)` column:
>
> ```
> create table null_char_example
> (id int not null,
> description char(50) null)
> ```
>
> The `description` column is not stored with trailing blanks, and the server will use extra overhead in each row to keep track of the actual length of the data.

Character Insert Format

When inserting character data into the server or searching for a value in a `where` clause, pass the value in single or double (matched) quotations. The following `insert` statement provides four character values:

```
insert publishers
      (pub_id, pub_name, city, state)
values
      ("1234", "Stendahl Publishing", "Paris", "France")
```

> **NOTE**
>
> For some reason, when the original `pubs` database was defined, the `publisher`, `title`, `store`, and `author id` columns were all defined as character data. This is not usually as good a choice for a key as an integer or other numeric type, which can be stored far more efficiently. (See the section titled "Numeric Datatypes," later in this chapter.)

Here is an example of an `update` statement with character data:

```
update publishers
      set pub_name = "Press of St. Martins-in-the-Field"
      where pub_id = "1234"
```

Truncation with Character Strings

SQL Server simply truncates character strings that are longer than the column definition, without reporting an error. Let's create a table with four rows to demonstrate the behavior of character strings under a variety of circumstances:

```
create table chars
(id int not null,
c1 char(6) not null)
```

Here are the `insert` statements. Note that the second `insert` includes a character string that is longer than the defined length of the `c1` column. The server truncates the string after six characters, but it returns no error message or warning:

```
insert chars values (1, "abc")
insert chars values (2, "abcdefg")
insert chars values (3, "   ef")
insert chars values (4, "ab ef")
```

Now retrieve the rows to see how the server stored them:

```
select id, c1, ">" + c1 + "<" c1_too
from chars

id            c1      c1too
------------- ------- --------
1             abc     >abc   <
2             abcdef  >abcdef<
3                 ef  >    ef<
4             ab ef   >ab ef<
```

As expected, the server has truncated the g from the end of the second entry. Notice how blanks are treated in a non-null `char()` column: The server stores trailing blanks in the first row.

sysname **Datatypes**

Earlier in the chapter, it was mentioned that user-defined datatypes enable you to subclass an existing system datatype to provide a common structure for many columns sharing a single type and having consistent data-integrity requirements. When you install SQL Server, two user-defined datatypes are already available: `sysname` and `timestamp`. (For more on `timestamp` data, see the section titled "Timestamps," later in this chapter.)

> **NOTE**
>
> SQL Server uses `sysname` to identify `varchar(30)` columns bound by the naming restrictions for objects, columns, and databases, primarily regarding permitted and restricted characters.
>
> The `sysname` type is not typically assigned to columns in user tables. It is mentioned here so that you understand what it means if you happen across it in the `systypes` table.

binary **and** varbinary

SQL Server binary datatypes are similar to character datatypes. When you specify a column as `binary` or `varbinary`, you must also specify a maximum data length for the column. The server truncates binary values that are too long. As with character columns, variable-length columns have some overhead, but fixed-length ones pad shorter values with trailing zeros.

Treatment of binary columns is similar to character types in terms of null or non-null columns (see the earlier note on nullability of character data). Null columns require an additional byte of storage where a value exists, but store less data if no value is available.

To specify a binary column, use the `binary` datatype, as in this example:

```
create table binary_example
      (id int not null,
      bin_column binary(4) not null)
```

Binary Data Insert Format

To insert binary data in a column, specify it without quotation marks, starting with `0x` and providing two hexadecimal characters for each byte of data. This `insert` statement adds a row containing a four-byte value into the example table specified previously:

```
insert binary_example
      (id, bin_column)
values
      (19, 0xa134c2ff)
```

Timestamps

The most common use of binary columns is in the application of another preinstalled, user-defined datatype: the *timestamp*. Timestamp columns enable the user to uniquely identify *versions* of each row in the table.

> **NOTE**
>
> If you didn't understand that statement, you probably are not alone. Keep reading and it will probably make more sense.

There are three important steps involving timestamps:

1. Creation of a table with a timestamp column.
2. Automatic updating of a timestamp column.
3. Optimistic locking, using the timestamp value.

To create a table with a timestamp column, use the timestamp datatype in the table-creation statement. Note that in the following example, the column is named `ts`, but you can use any legal column name:

```
create table timestamp_example
      (id int not null,
      code char(3) not null,
      ts timestamp not null)
```

> **NOTE**
>
> A single table might have only one timestamp column.

To insert a row in a table and update the timestamp value, just insert the row. All updating of the timestamp is automatic, so you don't have to indicate a timestamp value. This `insert` statement is an example in which the server provides a unique timestamp value:

```
insert timestamp_example
    (id, code)
values
    (17, "AAA")
```

When you retrieve the rows from the table, you should see that the timestamp has been assigned a binary value. Look at the output that is received after inserting a row into the `timestamp_example` table:

```
select id, code, ts
    from timestamp_example

id          code ts
----------- ---- -------------------
         17 AAA  0x000000010000198a
```

> **NOTE**
>
> How does the server provide a unique timestamp for each row? Every modification to a row in a SQL Server table is written first to the transaction log. The server uses the unique row identifier in the transaction log as the timestamp value for that row.
>
> You can see the timestamp values steadily escalate if you execute the timestamp `insert` several times. When you retrieve the rows, you should see that the unique log identifier is incrementing by three or four per row. (The increment is not one, because the log has additional work to record during an insert.) For more on log writes, see Chapter 13, "Understanding the Query Optimizer," in the section "Updates and Performance."

In fact, *the server does not allow you to specify a timestamp value.* This command will generate an error message:

```
insert timestamp_example
    (id, code, ts)
values
    (18, "BBB", 0x01)
```

The third step in the use of the `timestamp` column is with *optimistic locking*. Here's a brief description of how you implement optimistic locking, but see Chapter 16, "Locking and Performance," for a more in-depth discussion of this technique.

Optimistic locking uses a new system function, `tsequal()` (pronounced "Tee-Ess-equal," for *timestamp equal*). Most locking techniques warn concurrent users when they attempt to retrieve a record for modification. Optimistic locking warns users when they are performing conflicting modifications.

Consider two users, Mary and Al, each attempting to modify a row in the `timestamp_example` table used earlier. Each retrieves the row with a `select` statement, planning later to update the row:

```
select id, code, ts
from timestamp_example
where id = 17
```

Each user retrieves the current, unchanged value of the `timestamp` column. Mary then modifies the code value of the row with an `update` statement, using the `tsequal()` function to be certain that the row has not changed since she retrieved it:

```
update timestamp_example
set code = "BBB"
where id = 17
and tsequal(ts, 0x000000010000198a)
```

It's important to understand why this where clause is written as it is. In order to use the `tsequal()` function, the rest of the where clause must identify a unique row. The `id` column is a primary key for the table (and has a unique index, as it turns out), so the where clause specifies only one row. (If the value of 17 were not found in the table, the update statement would complete and SQL Server would report that no rows were processed by the query.)

After the rest of the query identifies the row, SQL Server evaluates the `tsequal()` function for that row. It retrieves the value of the `timestamp` column (`ts` in this example) and compares it to the constant expression passed with the function (`0x000000010000198a` in this example). If those values are the same, the update is allowed.

If you retrieve a `timestamp` value from the server and then return that value to the server at the next step, why would the `tsequal()` function ever fail to match? Mary's update works because the `timestamp` failed, but during the update the server automatically updates the `timestamp` value again. Now think about poor Al, about to update the same row in the table:

```
update timestamp_example
set code = "CCC"
where id = 17
and tsequal(ts, 0x000000010000198a)
```

Al's update fails in this example because the `timestamp` value he retrieved when he originally read the record is no longer the current value. When Mary updated the row, the `timestamp` value changed. Al gets error number 532:

```
The timestamp (changed to 0x000000010000387c) shows that the row has been updated
by another user.
```

> ## TIP
>
> If you are writing applications and are planning to use optimistic locking, you should definitely plan to trap this error and document for users how to work around it.

Text and Image Data

The longest variable-length column is only 255 characters. The maximum row length in SQL Server is limited by the size of the data page, which is 2KB.

> ## NOTE
>
> The rows themselves are restricted to a maximum of 1962 bytes because of page and transaction log overhead. Chapter 11 discusses row storage in detail and helps you understand the actual row-length limitations (there are many).

Many applications need to store much larger data than a 255-byte column or a 2KB page will allow. Long comments, detailed descriptions, telephone call log notes, and graphical objects like digitized photos, screen shots, and online images all need much larger capacity than 2KB. SQL Server provides a mechanism for storing binary large objects (BLOBs) as large as two gigabytes per row, using the text and image datatypes.

Defining text and image Columns

The following example table, texts, has three columns, including a text column, textstring:

```
create table texts
    (id int identity,
     item int not null,
     textstring text null)
```

Let's insert four rows in the table and then look at the characteristics of the text columns. You can insert a string into a text column exactly as you do a regular char or varchar column:

```
insert texts (item, textstring) values
    (1, null)
insert texts (item) values
    (2)
insert texts (item, textstring) values
    (3,"the rain in spain falls mainly on the plain")
insert texts (item, textstring) values
    (4,replicate("the rain in spain falls mainly on the plain", 7)
```

The first two text values inserted are null; the following two rows are not. The last row uses the replicate function to write a fairly long value. Notice that the insert statement will not insert a text value longer than about 1200 bytes.

Most of the string functions return only 255 characters because they are limited to the maximum length of a `varchar`. String concatenation of text data is also illegal.

writetext, readtext, and updatetext

SQL Server provides three statements to enable the manipulation of long string and binary data, to improve performance, and to simplify access to `text` and `image` columns. Text and image data is stored in a chain of separate 2KB pages, apart from the rest of the row data. In the row itself, SQL Server stores a pointer to the page where the chain of `text` or `image` data begins. The three text/image statements—`writetext`, `readtext`, and `updatetext`—use that pointer to find the page chain and are able to write directly to that chain without modifying the underlying row. (To do this, you must already have a non-null page pointer stored in the row itself.)

To retrieve the page pointer for a row, use the `textptr()` function. Here are the page pointers for the rows already inserted in the example table, `texts`, along with the length of the `text` data (using the `datalength()` function):

```
select id, textptr(textstring) textptr,
       datalength(textstring) datalength
from texts

id          textptr                               datalength
----------- ------------------------------------- ----------
1           (null)                                0
2           (null)                                0
3           0x69010000000000000010000009a080000   43
4           0x6a0100000000000001000000a1080000    225

(4 row(s) affected)
```

The page pointers for the first two rows are null. Before you could use any of the three text/image statements, you would need to update the column with data or a null value, or insert data into the `text` or `image` column during the original `insert` statement.

Let's write a new `textstring` value to the third row, using the `writetext` statement. Here is the syntax for `writetext`:

```
writetext table_name.column_name text_ptr
[with log] data
```

> **NOTE**
>
> The `writetext` and `updatetext` statements enable *nonlogged* modifications to text columns, which can substantially improve the performance of text operations (see Chapter 21, "Miscellaneous Performance Topics"). If the database option, `select into/bulkcopy`, has not been set, you must include `with log` to allow the modifications to be logged.

`writetext` completely replaces the existing `text` or `image` value with the new value. This `writetext` statement replaces the existing string with the replacement string. Notice that you must first retrieve the page pointer and then pass it to the `writetext` statement in a variable:

```
declare @pageptr varbinary(16)
select @pageptr = textptr(textstring)
      from texts
      where id = 3
writetext texts.textstring @pageptr
"Mary had a little lamp, its fleece was white as snow"
```

> **NOTE**
>
> All text and image operations, whether performed manually with `writetext` or automatically with `insert` or `update` statements, require two physical steps: SQL Server must first find a page pointer in the row itself, and then go to that page and perform the requested operation.

In the `writetext` example, there was an error in the text string; Mary should have had a little *lamb*. To change `lamp` to `lamb`, we can use the `updatetext` command. Here's the syntax:

```
updatetext table_name.dest_column_name dest_text_ptr
{NULL | insert_offset} {NULL | delete_length} [with log]
{inserted_data | table_name.src_column_name src_text_ptr}
```

Let's break this down and look at some examples of this statement. To replace existing text, specify where to start (`insert_offset`) and how many characters to replace (`delete_length`), and then provide the new data. To replace a single character with another single character, `delete_length` should be 1:

```
declare @pageptr varbinary(16)
select @pageptr = textptr(textstring)
      from texts
      where id = 3
updatetext texts.textstring @pageptr 21 1 "b"
```

A null value for the `insert_offset` means that the data will be appended to the end of the existing data, so the rest of the rhyme is added to the existing text:

```
declare @pageptr varbinary(16)
select @pageptr = textptr(textstring)
      from texts
      where id = 3
updatetext texts.textstring @pageptr NULL 0
", and everywhere that Mary went that lamb was sure to go."
```

Instead of retrieving the data from a string constant, you can also use another text column as the source data. This example copies the contents of the third-row text data into the text column of the first row (first, though, you need to update the text column to create a text pointer). This example requires two page pointers for the source and destination pages:

```
update texts
      set textstring = ""
      where id = 1
declare @from_ptr varbinary(16), @to_ptr varbinary(16)
select @from_ptr = textptr(textstring)
      from texts
      where id = 3
select @to_ptr = textptr(textstring)
      from texts
      where id = 1
updatetext texts.textstring @to_ptr 0 NULL
texts.textstring @from_ptr
```

The null value for the `delete_length` instructs SQL Server to delete all characters from the insert point to the end of the existing text data before inserting.

Although this example moves data between rows of the same table, you can also move data between text or image columns of different tables.

WARNING

Before you use text and image datatypes, see Chapter 21 for more information about the drawbacks of BLOBs and alternative implementation methods.

The last thing to do here is use a `while` loop (see Chapter 7, "Transact-SQL Programming Constructs," for details) to append the same string repeatedly and build a very long value for one row in the texts table. This code has comments delimited with `/* */` to help you understand what is going on (continued on the next page):

```
/* declare three variables for from, to, and counter */
declare @from_ptr varbinary(16), @to_ptr varbinary(16), @ctr int
/* set up the pointers and initialize the counter at 1 */
select @from_ptr = textptr(textstring), @ctr = 1
      from texts
      where id = 3
select @to_ptr = textptr(textstring)
      from texts
      where id = 3
/* MAIN LOOP */
while @ctr < 10
```

```
begin
/* increment the counter */
     select @ctr = @ctr + 1
/* repeatedly double the size of the text by appending */
     updatetext texts.textstring @to_ptr NULL NULL
     texts.textstring @from_ptr
end
```

Let's see how long the text string is now:

```
select id, datalength(textstring) "col length"
from texts
where id = 3

id          col length
----------- ----------
3               55808
```

A select statement will return only the first 255 bytes of this value, but you can now use readtext to retrieve any sequence of characters in the column. This readtext statement retrieves the 50 bytes starting in position 40000 into the result set listed here:

```
declare @pageptr varbinary(16)
select @pageptr = textptr(textstring)
     from texts
     where id = 3
readtext texts.textstring @pageptr 40000 50

textstring
--------------------------------------------------
go.Mary had a little lamb, its fleece was white as
```

datetime Datatypes

SQL Server enables you to store date and time values. Columns using datetime or smalldatetime will store both a date and a time value for each row. This create table statement creates a two-column table, consisting of an integer and a datetime column:

```
create table date_example
     (id int not null,
     dateval datetime not null)
```

datetime versus smalldatetime

SQL Server supports two date-storage types: datetime and smalldatetime. Generally speaking, smalldatetime is less precise and covers a smaller range of dates, but it occupies less space. Table 5.1 outlines the details.

Table 5.1. A comparison of `datetime` and `smalldatetime` columns.

	datetime	smalldatetime
minimum value	Jan 1, 1753	Jan 1, 1900
maximum value	Dec 31, 9999	Jun 6, 2079
precision	3 milliseconds	1 minute
storage size	8 bytes	4 bytes

NOTE

Here's a question to stump your friends with while watching "Jeopardy!" Why does SQL Server track `datetime` values starting with Jan 1, 1753? The answer is that the Gregorian and Julian calendars were 13 days apart until they were synchronized in September of 1752. Date accuracy prior to 1753 is meaningless using our calendars.

(I heard recently that there was a lot of anger and resentment when the calendar change took place. Apparently, there were people who thought that they had lost 13 days of their lives, believing that the *date* when they would die was preordained. This brings up an interesting question: What if the day you were to die was one of the days that was skipped? Sounds like the premise for an episode of "The Twilight Zone"!)

`datetime` Inserts

`datetime` values are passed to the server in a character string. SQL Server is responsible for conversion and validation of `datetime` data. This statement inserts a date and time into the sample table created earlier:

```
insert date_example
     (id, dateval)
values
     (19, "September 25, 1996 3:15PM")
```

SQL Server permits the entry of many date formats, and it will provide default values for the date and time if they are omitted. Table 5.2 summarizes the entry value and the return value for several date formats.

Table 5.2. SQL Server accepts many date formats for entry.

Insert Format	datetime *Value*	smalldatetime *Value*
Sep 3, 1996 13:17:35.332	Sep 3 1996 1:17:35:333PM	Sep 3 1996 1:18PM
9/3/96 1pm	Sep 3 1996 1:00:00:000PM	Sep 3 1996 1:00PM

continues

Table 5.2. continued

Insert Format	datetime *Value*	smalldatetime *Value*
9.3.96 13:00	Sep 3 1996 1:00:00:000PM	Sep 3 1996 1:00PM
3 sep 96 13:00	Sep 3 1996 1:00:00:000PM	Sep 3 1996 1:00PM
13:25:19	Jan 1 1900 1:25:19:000PM	Jan 1 1900 1:25PM
3 september 96	Sep 3 1996 12:00:00:000AM	Sep 3 1996 12:00AM
4/15/46	Apr 15 2046 12:00:00:000AM	Apr 15 2046 12:00AM

Let's look at each of these examples. The first example demonstrates the complete date specification, including the month, day, and year, as well as time in hours, minutes, seconds, and milliseconds. Note that the datetime value is rounded to the nearest three milliseconds and the smalldatetime value is rounded to the nearest minute.

Lines 2 through 4 show alternate methods of entering dates, with slashes and periods, and with the name of the month specified as well. Dashes (hyphens,–) are also a legitimate delimiter in this format.

Line 5 demonstrates how the server handles a time without a date value. When you specify a time without a date, the server provides the "zero" date for the system of Jan 1, 1900.

> **NOTE**
>
> In general, it makes no sense to enter a time without a date in SQL Server.

In line 6, the server uses the default value of 12:00 midnight (a.m.) for the time when none is provided. You almost always need to use a range search method (between *x* and *y*) when searching for specific dates (see the section "Search Behavior with Dates," later in this chapter).

Line 7 shows how the server treats two-digit year values less than 50. As you can see, all two-digit years less than fifty are assumed to be in the twenty-first century (20*xx*), whereas two-digit years greater than or equal to 50 are treated as twentieth-century dates (19*xx*).

dateformat Options, Languages, and Date Formatting

By default, the server treats a date in the format *xx/yy/zz* as a month/day/year sequence. Microsoft calls this the *mdy* date format. SQL Server also supports several other date orderings. Using the set dateformat command, you can choose other date orders. Valid choices are *mdy, dmy, ymd, ydm, myd,* and *dym.*

This is a *session-level* option, which means that it must be set when the user logs in to the server. For example, to change your date-ordering from the default setting to *yy/ mm/ dd* format, execute this statement:

```
set dateformat ymd
```

> **NOTE**
>
> When a user's language option is changed, it also changes his default date format. The server supports us_english (this is the default language) as well as french and german. A user's language option can be set at the server level for all users, as a characteristic of an individual's login account, or within a session by executing the set language statement.

Search Behavior with Dates

How do you find rows having a specific date or time value? Consider a table having the values listed in Table 5.2 (shown earlier in the chapter) in a date column. The where clause of the select statement needs to specify a date range, not a single date value. All the select statements that follow might be expected to bring back the same rows, but the first will return rows only where the time is exactly midnight:

```
/* this won't work ... only matches on time = midnight */
select *
from date_table
where date = "9/3/96"
```

The next examples properly state a range of times within a single day, but note how they interact with different data types. This example only works with datetime columns (not smalldatetime):

```
/* this will work for datetime columns, not smalldatetime
   ... it states a range of times for the date */
select *
from date_table
where date between "9/3/96" and "9/3/96 23:59:59.999"
```

If you are working with a smalldatetime column, you should only specify a value up to the minute. Otherwise, the value will round up to the next day at midnight.

```
/* this will work for smalldatetime columns, not datetime
   ... it states a range of times for the date */
select *
from date_table
where date between "9/3/96" and "9/3/96 23:59"
```

The final example works with both data types.

```
/* this will work ... and it might be easier to type */
select *
from date_table
where date >= "9/3/96" and date < "9/4/96"
```

In the last example, notice that the upper bound is *open* (less than) and the lower bound is *closed* (greater than or equals). This is a general formula for returning a range of dates, and is flexible with regard to data type. Here are some other examples of search conditions returning a range of dates:

```
/* month */ where date >= "9/1/96" and date < "10/1/96"
/* year */ where date >= "1/1/96" and date < "1/1/97"
```

NOTE

The good news here is that the server interprets a between condition in exactly the same way that it interprets a range stated as two separate conditions—there's no optimization penalty for stating the range as two conditions.

WARNING

As you work with SQL Server, you will discover other techniques for date manipulation. These include the date-parsing functions, datename() and datepart(), and the convert() function, which are all covered in the "Date Functions" section of Chapter 7. These functions can be used in search conditions to determine whether a date falls in a range. For example, you can use datepart() to determine the month and year of a date as in this select statement, which finds rows with a date in September of 1996:

```
select *
from date_table
where datepart(mm,date) = 9
and datepart(yy,date) = 96
```

The problem with using parsing functions in the search condition of a query is that the server can't use an advanced performance strategy to speed the query. For example, if there were an index on the date column of this table, the range searches ("date between x and y" and "date >= x and date < y") listed in the example might provide a faster access path to the specific rows that match the search condition.

When you ask the server to perform a function on a column in a search condition, the only way the server can resolve the query is to step through each row of the table, convert the date column in each row, and test its value. This method of query resolution is called a *table scan* and usually takes much longer than index access, particularly when tables are large.

In general, to get better performance, avoid using parsing functions in your search conditions. For much more on this and related topics, see Chapter 20, "Advanced SQL Techniques," Chapter 13, "Understanding the Query Optimizer," and Chapter 15, "Analyzing Query Plans."

Logical Datatype: `bit`

SQL Server supports a logical datatype of `bit` for flag columns that store a value of 1 or 0. `bit` columns are used for on/off or true/false columns. The following table includes a `bit` column:

```
create table bit_sample
    (id int not null,
    description varchar(30) null,
    active bit not null)
```

`bit` columns have several unique characteristics:

- They don't permit null values.
- They can't be indexed.
- Several `bit` columns can occupy a single byte (SQL Server collects up to eight `bit` columns into a single byte of physical storage).

NOTE

The many uses for `bit` columns include status flags, active account indicators, and item-availability columns. Advanced data-warehousing systems could use `bit` columns to stand for larger columns, substantially shortening data rows and improving performance.

A `bit` column is inappropriate in many cases. For example, inexperienced database administrators will create a `bit` column to indicate whether an account is active, as well as a date column to store the activation date. The active `bit` column depends on the activation date in this example. This not only violates basic normalization rules, but it also requires additional overhead to keep the two columns in sync.

Numeric Datatypes

SQL Server provides many ways to store numeric values, which provide flexibility in precision, range of values, and data storage size. Numeric types fall into four basic categories:

- Integers, including `int`, `smallint`, and `tinyint`
- Floating-point datatypes, including `float` and `real`

- Exact numeric datatypes, `numeric` and `decimal`
- Money datatypes, `money` and `smallmoney`

Integer Datatypes

Integer columns store exact, scalar values. There are three integer datatypes—`int` (or `integer`), `smallint`, and `tinyint`—for storing varying ranges of values, as Table 5.3 summarizes.

Table 5.3. Integers can store a larger range of values, but are larger than `smallint` and `tinyint`.

	int	smallint	tinyint
minimum value	-2^{31} (-2,147,483,647)	-2^{15} (-32,768)	0
maximum value	2^{31} (2,147,483,647)	2^{15-1} (32,767)	255
storage size	4 bytes	2 bytes	1 byte

Integers make useful keys because they can record a large number of exact values in very few bytes. Where possible, use integers for numeric columns because of the efficient storage mechanism. They are also handled natively and are thus much quicker on every platform. The following is a `create` statement including all three integer types:

```
create table auto_sales
     (id int identity,
     make varchar(25) not null,
     model varchar(25) not null,
     year smallint not null,
     age_at_purchase tinyint not null)
```

Consider how each of the integer type columns is used in this example. The `id` column should be an `int` column in order to allow up to 2 billion unique row keys in this table.

NOTE

The `identity` keyword tells the server to maintain an automatic counter using this column. The server will waste some counter values because of failed insertions, so even if you know exactly how many rows will be contained in a table, you need to make a provision for the counter to grow to a higher value. Using `smallint` for the key in this example could result in the server being unable to insert rows in the table once the next available value is higher than the maximum value for the datatype.

For more on `identity` and other characteristics of tables, see Chapter 6.

In the example, the model year of the car is a good use of smallint because the range of values is likely to be from about 1900 to 20*xx*.

NOTE

By the way, this is a terrible place to use a smalldatetime column. You are not recording the date of the car's manufacture (which would require date and time specificity), but the model year of the car. Aside from inefficient storage (smallint requires only two bytes; smalldatetime requires four), smalldatetime does not permit date entry with only a year. For example, to find all orders in 1990, you would have to parse the order date:

```
select order_id, ...
from orders
where datepart(yy, order_date) = 1990
```

In the case of a model year, where the date specifics are not required, an integer value for the year is much easier to search for:

```
select make, model
from auto_sales
where year = 1990
```

The age_at_purchase column in the auto_sales example is a good example of tinyint (until people start living for 256 years!).

WARNING

Remember that you can't change the datatype of a column. If you discover late in the game that a decode table requires more than 256 unique keys, so a tinyint was a bad choice for a primary key, you have to drop the table and re-create it with the proper datatype. You also have to drop and re-create any table(s) that reference that key.

An integer should be transmitted to the server as a number with no decimal place, as in this insert statement:

```
insert auto_sales
      (make, model, year, age_at_purchase)
values
      ("Ford", "Taurus", 1996, 42)
```

Pass integers in search conditions the same way:

```
select make, model
from auto_sales
where year >= 1993
and age_at_purchase between 18 and 25
```

Floating-Point Datatypes

SQL Server provides two approximate numeric datatypes, `float` (or `double precision`), and `real`, for handling numbers with a very large range of values requiring the same precision, no matter how large or how small the number. In Table 5.4, you can see that `float` and `real` differ only in precision and storage size.

Table 5.4. `float` **columns take up more space per row than** `real` **columns, but they provide greater precision.**

	float	real
smallest value	±2.23E-308	±1.18E-38
largest value	±1.79E308	±3.40E38
precision	up to 15 digits	up to 7 digits
storage size	8 bytes	4 bytes

NOTE

Floats and reals are often written in scientific notation. In Table 5.4, 1.79E308 means 1.79 times 10 raised to the 308th power.

Scientific notation makes it possible to talk about extremely large and extremely small numbers without needing to write out meaninglessly long numbers. To write 1.79E308 without scientific notation, I would have to write something like this:

179,000,000,000,000,000,000,000,000,000,000,000,...,000

(It would actually require 306 zeros. I only wrote 36 zeros, and then I got lazy.) The part of the number where the digits are meaningful (1.79) is called the *mantissa*. The part where the scale of the number is indicated (E308 or 10^{308}) is called the *exponent*.

`float` and `real` columns are useful for scientific and statistical data where absolute accuracy is not required, and where the data in a single column might vary from extremely large to extremely small.

DATATYPE PRECISION

`float` columns use an internal algorithm to store numbers as a mantissa and exponent. The algorithm is not perfectly precise; what you put in is not always *exactly* what you get back. For example, a number with 15 significant digits entered in a `float` column might see some variance in the last digit.

That was why I was surprised to learn from a client at one of the New York City financial-trading companies that they had adopted a standard of using float for all stock and bond share prices. I had assumed that they would use money or smallmoney instead (see the later discussion on money datatypes).

The problem with money and smallmoney was that they were rounding to the fourth decimal place, which was inaccurate when dealing with shares trading at $1/32$ of a dollar ($0.03125) or $1/64$ of a dollar ($0.015125). In spite of the fact that a float is an approximate money type, it was perfectly exact in this case, where the number of significant digits in the value did not approach the precision of the datatype.

What is important to keep in mind about float and real datatypes is this: What we commonly think of as precision is the number of decimal places that are accurately returned. In the case of approximate datatypes, precision is the number of significant digits in the value. The value of $1/32$, 0.03125, requires five decimal places for storage, but a real or float datatype sees only four significant digits in the mantissa, 3.125, as well as an exponent, 10^{-2}. The value of $325 1/32$, 325.03125, also requires only five decimal places, but it requires eight-digit precision in a real or float datatype to record all of the significant digits.

This means that the decimal precision of float and real data decreases as the number to store increases. A real column is sufficient to store $1/32$ exactly, but it will not store $325 1/32$ precisely.

Inserting float and real Data

To insert float or real data, simply supply the number (always include a decimal). If you need to specify both a mantissa and an exponent, use standard scientific notation in the form $\pm m.mmmE \pm ee$, where *m.mmm* is the mantissa (up to 15 digits precision) and *ee* is the base-ten exponent, as in the following example:

```
insert float_example
      (id, float_col)
values
      (1, 1.395E3)
```

Precision of float

float permits the user to specify an optional precision, ranging from 1 to 15. float columns with a precision of 1 to 7 are stored as a real in 4 bytes; those with a precision of 8 to 15 bytes are stored like a float (without a specified precision) in 8 bytes.

Exact Numeric Datatypes

SQL Server supports two exact numeric datatypes: decimal (or dec) and numeric. The two are synonymous and interchangeable, but note that only numeric can be used in combination with identity columns. Use numeric data where the *precision* (number of significant digits) and *scale* (number of decimal positions) are known from the start. This is a useful datatype for handling monetary columns.

To create an exact numeric column, specify in the table-creation statement the datatype, along with the precision (maximum is 28) and scale (less than or equal to the precision) for the column, as in this example:

```
create table numeric_example
    (id int not null,
    num_col numeric(7,2))
```

The column, num_col will store numbers up to ±99,999.99, with two digits following the decimal place.

The storage size for a numeric value depends on the precision. A 28-digit numeric column will occupy 13 bytes per row.

Money Datatypes

The preceding sections showed that float and numeric datatypes are useful options for monetary values. SQL Server also provides two datatypes specifically for this purpose: money and smallmoney. Both money and smallmoney are exact datatypes with four-digit decimal precision. (See Table 5.5.)

Table 5.5. money **columns require twice as much space per row as** smallmoney, **but they accommodate much higher numbers.**

	money	smallmoney
range	±922,337,203,685,477.5808	±214,748.3647
storage size	8 bytes	4 bytes

NOTE

You probably noticed that the maximum smallmoney value is the same as the maximum integer value, but the decimal is shifted four positions to the left. Essentially, money and smallmoney are treated like integers for arithmetic operations; then the decimal shifts to the correct position for output.

> **NOTE**
>
> The correct format for entering money is with a dollar sign ($) and no commas:
>
> ```
> insert dollar_table
> (id, dollars)
> values
> (95, $12345.93)
> ```
>
> IMPORTANT: Your language option does not affect the currency symbol or choice of decimal separator.

See Table 5.6 for a list of column datatypes.

Table 5.6. Column datatypes.

Datatype	Range of values	Size in bytes	Sample Input
Character datatypes			
char[(n)]	1<=n<=255	n (default is 1)	'Fred'
varchar[(n)]	1<=n<=255	data length (default is 1)	'14 Main St.
text	BLOB up to 2, 147, 483, 647 chars	16+multiple of 2k	'Fred'
Binary datatypes			
binary(n)	1<=n<=255	n	0xa1b3
varbinary(n)	see binary,	n+1	0xf1
image	BLOB up to 2, 147, 483, 647 bytes	16+multiple of 2k	0xf1...
timestamp	Used for change management	16	N/A
Data datatypes			
datetime	Jan 1, 1900 to Dec 31, 9999 accuracy 3-millisecond interval	8	'jan 2, 1770 13:15:17.12'
smalldatetime	Jan 1, 1900 to Jun 6, 2079 accuracy minute	4	'jan 2, 1970 15:18'
Logical datatypes			
bit	0 or 1	1 (up to 8 bit columns/byte)	1
Numeric datatypes			
int	±2,147,483,647	4	1234567
smallint	±32767	2	2134
tinyint	0 to 255	1	32
float[(precision)]	machine dependent	4 (precision<16) 8 (precision>=16)	123.1397864
double precision	machine dependent	8	123.1397864
real	machine dependent	4	123.1324
numeric(p,s) decimal(p,s)	±10 to 38th power, p is precision (total digits, 1-38), s is scale (decimal digits, <=p)	2 to 17	12345.55
money	±$922,337,203,685,477.5807	8	$1596980.23
smallmoney	±$214,748.3647	4	$10000.25

System Tables and Datatypes

SQL Server datatypes are not keywords; instead, they are stored as *data values* in a database-level system table, systypes. The systypes table contains both system- and user-defined datatypes.

If you view all the names of the types, you will see all the entries described in this chapter. You will also see entries for nullable versions of many datatypes. For example, systypes includes both money and moneyn—one for non-null and one for nullable versions of the money datatype.

Summary

Datatype selection is one of the truly critical decisions the DBA must make when defining a database. Because a column datatype cannot be easily modified after a table is created, you need to anticipate the changing needs of your system and understand the ramifications of your datatype choices.

The next chapters in this part of the book show how to build SQL Server objects, referring to columns and variables belonging to these datatypes.

Creating and Altering Database Objects

In this chapter, you learn two methods for maintaining SQL Server objects. One method requires writing Transact-SQL (T-SQL) statements to develop and maintain objects; the other allows you to use a graphical interface. Why bother learning the syntactic approach when it is so easy to do the work using a graphical tool? Three reasons:

First, as you become more accomplished with the language, you will find it easier to create a fast example for testing by writing code than by using the tool.

Second, and more important, when you are finished designing your database using the SQL Enterprise Manager, you will need to make a backup version of that design, and you might want to distribute that design (perhaps with minor modifications). The method of backing up and publishing a database *design* (as opposed to a database and its *data*) is to generate SQL scripts that can automatically reproduce the database structure.

Finally, even if you use the Enterprise Manager to do most of your tasks, it's always a good idea to be knowledgeable in the syntactic structures. You can't do *everything* using the Enterprise Manager. You may find yourself in certain situations where you'd need to write (or understand) code instead of using the Enterprise Manager.

New for SQL Server 6.5

- `union` is available in a view definition
- Use of the `default` keyword with `insert` and `update`

Creating Database Objects

All objects created within SQL Server require a frame of reference—a logical way of putting your arms around all the related objects. This logical grouping of objects is called a *database*. We assume that you are working, now, in an existing database. Do *not* begin playing in the `master` or `msdb` databases; instead, create one of your own if you are experimenting or learning.

> **NOTE**
>
> If you don't have a test database and you are working on a server where it's acceptable to make some mistakes, here are some quick instructions on how to create a new test database. If it's not acceptable to make mistakes on your server, you should carefully read Chapter 26, "Defining, Altering, and Maintaining Databases and Logs," before creating a test database. (You will need to be able to log in as `sa` to do this. If you can't log in as `sa`, ask your SQL Server administrator to create a database for you.)
>
> To create a test database, use `ISQL/w` to execute this command:
>
> ```
> sp_helpdb test
> ```

If you get an error message saying that the database "test" does not exist, that's good. (If not, try "test1" and "test2" and so forth until you find an unused name.)

Now execute this statement to create the database:

```
create database test on default = 2
```

This creates a two-megabyte database named test on a device that was set up for default use. If you get an error message saying that there isn't enough space on the default disk, or if no default disk is found, there's more work to do; read Chapter 26.

This chapter demonstrates how to use the database object creation and management features of *SQL Enterprise Manager* (*SQL-EM*). It assumes that you are able to run the SQL Enterprise Manager application and that you have permissions, both over the network and on the SQL Server, to perform the operations discussed. If you do not have proper permissions to perform these functions, contact your SQL Server administrator.

In SQL Enterprise Manager, you can find the databases on your server by opening a connection to the server you are working with and opening the Databases folder. (See Figure 6.1.)

FIGURE 6.1.

SQL Enterprise Manager enables you to browse a variety of resources, including database names.

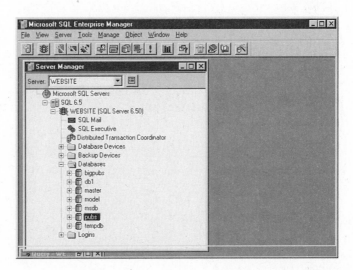

SQL Server supports a variety of database objects that enable you to better utilize, access, and care for your data. In this chapter, you learn about the use and creation of the various SQL Server object types:

- Tables, to store SQL Server data
- Temporary tables, to store temporary result sets
- Views, to provide a logical depiction of data from one or more tables

■ Rules, to validate column data

■ Defaults, to provide a column value when none is provided by the client application

■ Constraints, to validate column data, and to maintain consistency between tables

In this chapter, you also learn about other structures (not properly *objects*, but relevant to this discussion):

■ User-defined datatypes, to maintain consistent rule and default enforcement among related columns

■ Indexes, to maintain uniqueness and improve performance

■ Keys, to document the structure of individual tables and relationships among tables

SQL Server also supports two code-based object types, which are discussed in Chapter 8, "Transact-SQL Program Structures":

■ Stored procedures

■ Triggers

Tables

Tables are logical constructs used for storage and manipulation of data in the databases. Tables contain *columns*, which describe data, and *rows*, which are unique instances of data. Basic relational database design (in conjunction with your shop standards) determines table and column names, as well as distribution of columns within the tables.

Table creation is accomplished by using one of two tools: the SQL Enterprise Manager table editor, or Transact-SQL's `create table` statement. If you are typing a T-SQL statement, here is the fundamental syntax:

```
create table table_name
(column name datatype {identity ¦ null ¦ not null}
[, ...]
)
```

For example, you could create a four-column table called `demographics` by using this statement:

```
create table demographics
(user_id numeric(10,0) identity,
last_name varchar(30) not null,
first_name varchar(30) not null,
comments varchar(255) null)
```

In SQL Enterprise Manager, you can graphically create tables using the Table Editor. To use the Table Editor, you must open a database, and then open the Objects and Tables folders that are nested under Databases. Right-clicking the Tables folder presents the menu illustrated in Figure 6.2.

FIGURE 6.2.

SQL Enterprise Manager uses a hierarchy of objects and collections to manage tables and other database objects.

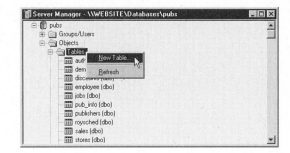

When you select the New Table item, the Table Editor opens. This dialog box can also be activated by using the Manage | Tables menu sequence, but any tables created here will be created in the current database you have open.

Figure 6.3 shows a table named `demographics`, which is composed of four columns: `user_id`, `last_name`, `first_name`, and `comments`. This table at creation time is accessible only to the user who created it. This user may choose to grant permissions to other users (see Chapter 27, "Security and User Administration").

FIGURE 6.3.

SQL Enterprise Manager provides a graphical tool for creating and editing database tables.

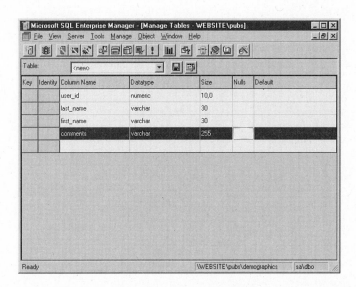

Table names are unique for a user within a database; this means that all users could potentially have their own tables entitled `demographics`. It also means that every user could have only one table called `demographics`.

128

To remove a table and its structure, use the `drop` command. The basic syntax to remove most database objects is `drop object_type object_name`:

```
drop table table_name
```

```
drop table demographics
```

> **WARNING**
>
> There is no `UNDROP`. Once it's gone, it's gone. The only way to get a dropped object back into the database is to have the system's administrator restore it from a dump. If that object did not exist in its entirety at the time of that dump, you are completely out of luck.

Dropping a table can be performed more easily in the Enterprise Manager application. Open the Tables folder for the database you are working with and select the table that you would like to drop. By right-clicking the table name, you can display the menu in Figure 6.4. Select Drop from the menu, and the table, both its structure and data, will be destroyed, as if you had run `drop table table_name`. Unlike the `drop table` command, which requires no confirmation, Enterprise Manager prompts you first, just to make sure you are certain you want to drop the table. After you confirm your wishes, Enterprise Manager executes the `drop table` command, and the table cannot be recovered.

FIGURE 6.4.

Administrators can use Enterprise Manager to edit, create, and destroy database tables.

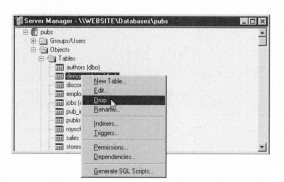

Enterprise Manager enables you to drop tables in groups by using the multi-select feature of its drag-and-drop interface. By holding down the Ctrl key while selecting table names from the Tables folder, you can select multiple tables, all of which will be dropped. If you select a table name, hold down the Shift key, and select another table name in the list, Enterprise Manager highlights the tables between these points and includes them in the drop list. If you are familiar with other Windows applications that use multi-select, you can see that SQL Enterprise Manager behaves consistently with those other applications. In Figure 6.5, Enterprise Manager is prompting the administrator for confirmation of a multi-table drop.

FIGURE 6.5.

SQL Enterprise Manager allows you to execute administrative tasks on multiple objects simulta- neously. Here SQL-EM prompts the user for confirmation before dropping several tables.

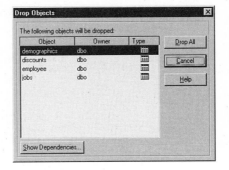

If you're running ISQL/w, you can get information on the table you've created by executing the sp_help system stored procedure.

> **NOTE**
>
> sp_help is the Swiss Army knife of SQL Server. Without any parameters, it provides a list of all objects and user-defined datatypes in a database. If you pass a table name, it shows you the structure of the table (see the next example). If you pass a procedure name, it shows you the parameters.

Here's the syntax for the sp_help stored procedure when asking for detailed information about a table:

```
sp_help table name
```

In this example, the user requests information about the demographics table with sp_help.

```
sp_help demographics

Name          Owner   Type         When_created
—————————     —————   ——————       ——————————
demographics  dbo     user table   Nov 13 1995  8:50PM
( 0 rows affected)


Data_located_on_segment
——————————————————
default
( 0 rows affected)


Column_name   Type     Length Prec  Scale Nullable
—————————     —————    ———    ——    ——    ——————————
user_id       numeric  6      10    0     no
last_name     varchar  30                 no
first_name    varchar  30                 no
comments      varchar  255                yes
( 0 rows affected)
```

```
Identity      Seed      Increment
_ _ _ _ _ _   _ _ _ _   _ _ _ _ _ _ _ _ _ _ _
user_id       1.0       1.0
( 0 rows affected)

Object does not have any indexes.

No constraints have been defined for this object.

No foreign keys reference this table.
```

Alternatively, sp_help without an object name gives you a list of all objects in the database:

```
sp_help

Name              Owner   Object_type
_ _ _ _ _ _ _ _   _ _ _   _ _ _ _ _ _ _ _ _ _ _
demographics      dbo     user table
sysalternates     dbo     system table
sysarticles       dbo     system table
syscolumns        dbo     system table
syscomments       dbo     system table
sysconstraints    dbo     system table
sysdepends        dbo     system table
sysindexes        dbo     system table
syskeys           dbo     system table
syslogs           dbo     system table
sysobjects        dbo     system table
sysprocedures     dbo     system table
sysprotects       dbo     system table
syspublications   dbo     system table
sysreferences     dbo     system table
syssegments       dbo     system table
syssubscriptions  dbo     system table
systypes          dbo     system table
sysusers          dbo     system table
( 0 rows affected)

Sort Order:  Object_type Name


User_type     Storage_type   Length Prec Scale
        Nullable    Default_name   Rule_name
_ _ _ _ _ _   _ _ _ _ _ _ _ _   _ _ _ _  _ _  _ _  _ _ _ _ _  _ _ _ _ _ _ _  _ _ _ _ _
( 0 rows affected)

Sort Order:  User_type
```

This information is particularly useful if you are trying to identify what objects are within a database, if you think you created a database object and don't remember what you called it, or if you are sure you created one and it doesn't appear to be there.

Although the traditional SQL Server methods inherited from Sybase SQL Server provide useful information, that information can be accessed more easily using SQL Enterprise Manager. In SQL-EM, you can view a table's columns, indexes, keys, and so forth in the Table Editor window described earlier. If you want to see the objects in a database, you can open that database's Objects folder for a list of object types, also presented as folders (see Figure 6.6). In each object type folder, the list of objects of that type is listed. By right-clicking an object, you open SQL Enterprise Manager dialog boxes that enable you to create new objects of that type, as well as to modify or remove existing objects.

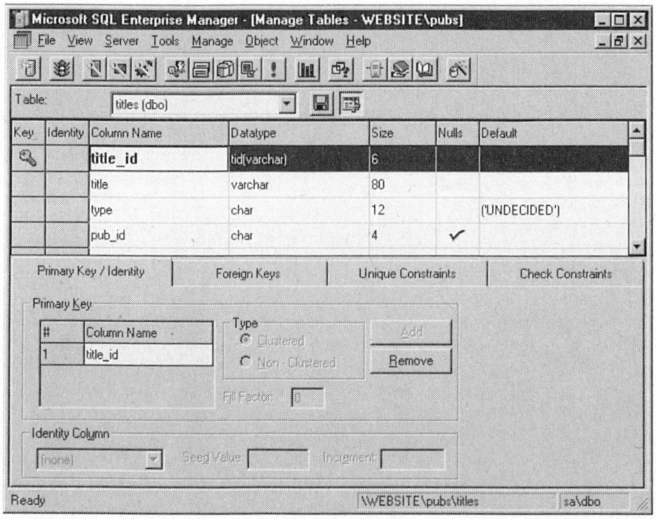

FIGURE 6.6.

SQL Enterprise Manager enhances traditional SQL Server functionality by presenting database object information in a more usable format.

TIP

If you can't find an object you created, run `sp_help` or look for it in the proper folder in SQL-EM. You may need to `refresh` the screen after creating a new object (see the View menu). Look for the table name and remember that *SQL Server object identifiers are case-sensitive*. Additionally, check to see if the object owner changed. If you created an object as `user1` and are now the `dbo` (`dbo` is short for *database owner*), you have to qualify the object name (for example, `user1.demographics`).

Tables are composed of up to 250 user-defined columns, each of which has three characteristics: a name, a datatype, and a property.

SQL Server Object Names

All SQL Server object names are up to 30 characters in length, and are case-sensitive. The character limitation is imposed by the maximum length of the name columns in the `sysobjects` and `syscolumns` system tables. Note that keywords, by definition, are case-insensitive.

The following is the full name of any SQL Server object:

```
database_name.owner_name.object_name
```

Note that *database_name* defaults to the database you are in, and does not need to be explicitly named. *owner_name* defaults to the user name within the database of the person who signed in. If there's no object owned by the person who signed in, the server defaults to the database owner (dbo).

For example, pubs.dbo.authors is a table named authors, owned by the dbo, in the pubs database (included with installation). pubs.user1.authors may coexist in that database and be owned by user1, and user1.authors.au_lname is the name of a column in the table authors owned by user1 in the current database; however, you know this only by looking at the names and making sense of them. If you look at this by convention only, it could as easily be a table called au_lname owned by authors in the database user1.

TIP

In a production database, all objects should be owned by the dbo to simplify ownership, avoid confusion, and ease a permission scheme (see Chapter 27).

SQL Enterprise Manager displays owner names as well. In the list of objects in a particular object folder, the owner name for an object appears in parentheses immediately following the object name. Two objects with a similar name but different owners is sorted in ascending order, using the object name first and then the owner name, rated with the two demographics tables in Figure 6

FIGURE 6.7.
SQL Enterprise Manager tracks objects with common names by sorting on the Object Owner value (david and dbo, respectively, for the titles table).

Column Properties

Columns can have the followi

- Null (a value does not n ... specified for a column)
- Not null (a value must be specified for the column)
- Identity (the server is to maintain a row counter on the table)

A value of null (in the column) means that the column has not been assigned a value. This is *not* equivalent to having a value of zero (for a numeric type) or spaces (for a character type). In fact, from a Boolean standpoint, one null column value isn't equal to any other null column value, because null isn't a value at all; it is the absence of a value.

If a column has a property of not null, a value must be assigned at insert time or the row will not be inserted, and any attempt to update a non-null column with a null value will fail.

Identity columns are used for sequential, unique numbering of rows being inserted into the table. When you include an identity column in a table, you use the keyword identity in place of null or not null:

```
create table table_name
(column_name {int ¦ smallint ¦ tinyint ¦ numeric(p,0)} identity [,...] )
```

Example

```
/* this table has first, last names and an automatic key */
create table names2
 (auto_key int identity,
 first varchar(30) not null,
 last varchar(30) not null
 )
```

You can have a maximum of one identity column per table, which will be (by default) not null. Identity columns may be of any integer or whole-number numeric datatype. In addition, you can set an initial value for the counter field, as well as specify an incremental value for the counter to use. You could set the initial value to 1000 and count by 10, or set the initial value to 100 and count by 50. The syntax for this is to include, in parentheses, the seed value followed by the increment value. The defaults for these are 1 and 1, respectively, meaning that an identity column will start with value 1 and increment values in the field by 1 as new rows are added.

In this example, the identity column will start with the value –10000 and increment by 1:

```
create table foo
(field1 int identity (-10000,1),
 field2 ...)
```

The right choice of datatype for an identity column is very important, because it is impossible to modify the datatype once the table has been created and rows have been added. In addition, identity columns are limited to the range of values for that particular datatype. In simpler terms, a column of type tinyint can store only 256 distinct values, in the range of 0 through 255. By using tinyint as the datatype for an identity column, you have effectively limited your table to holding 256 rows!

If an upper or lower limit is reached for a datatype, inserts can no longer be processed on that table. SQL Server does not automatically reuse values that have been skipped or deleted, nor does the counter "cycle" back to the beginning to hunt for available values. In that way, your identity fields are limited by the datatype you select.

> **TIP**
>
> If your tables require an identity column and you anticipate them growing to be quite large, remember that any whole-number datatype will suffice. A numeric or decimal field allows you up to 38 decimal places for storing numbers. When specifying the datatype for such a column, use decimal (38,0) for the datatype. You'll have 38 decimal places, which should be plenty of row numbers (but if you don't use all those numbers, you may be wasting a lot of empty space).
>
> Also keep in mind that identity counters are not restarted from 1 or 0 if you delete all the rows in the table, and then start inserting again. On the other hand, truncate table *does* reset the identity counter to its seed value.

To insert rows into a table with an identity column, do not specify the identity column in the insert statement. In the first example insert statement, the column names have been omitted, and SQL Server expects values for all the columns in the table except the identity column. In the second example, the column names are specified; SQL Server expects values for only the named columns.

```
insert names values ("John", "Smith")
insert names (first, last) values ("Tom", "Jones")
select * from names
go

auto_key first         last
____ _____ _____
1        John          Smith
2        Tom           Jones
```

The last value applied to an identity column for a session is available in the @@identity global variable (see more on global variables in Chapter 7, " Transact-SQL Programming Constructs"). @@identity retains its value until the session inserts another row into a table with an identity column.

You can use the identitycol keyword in other SQL statements to refer to the identity column (or you can identify it by the column name):

```
select auto_key, first, last
     from names
/* OR */
select identitycol, first, last from names
/* update a row in names2 table */
update names2
     set first = "John"
     where identitycol = 2
```

Notes on Identity Columns

Updates to identity columns are never allowed. You have to delete the old row and insert the new row.

WARNING

Identity column values are not row numbers. SQL Server attempts to use sequential numbers for identity column values, but may not be able to do so based on seed value, increment value, and the failure of transactions to complete. Any of these three issues can contribute to gaps in the identity values SQL Server generates. SQL Server does not support internal row number operations, and identity columns are not a 100-percent-reliable method of implementing such processing!

The table owner, database owner, or sa can explicitly insert identity values if the following set option is enabled:

```
set identity_insert table_name on
```

```
set identity_insert names on
insert names (10, "Jane", "Doe")
set identity_insert names off
go
```

This option enables you to set a seed value for identity columns or to fill in gaps in identity sequences.

WARNING

It is possible, with this option on, to insert duplicate identity values into a table if there is no unique index or unique constraint defined on the identity column. Identity columns do not validate unique values—they merely generate numbers according to a sequence!

Views

Views are a logical way of looking at the physical data located in the tables. In fact, to a select statement, a view looks exactly like a table.

NOTE

A view does not represent any physical data—merely a window into the physical data. Dropping a view has no effect on the underlying table(s).

Creating a view is as simple as writing a select statement. Views (like other objects) require unique names *among all objects in the database*.

```
create view view_name [ (col_name, ...) ]
as select statement
[ with check option ]
```

If you omit the column names in a view, the view columns inherit the column names from the base table(s) at the time the view is created:

```
/* make view with two columns from authors table */
create view author_name as
    select last = au_lname, first = au_fname
    from authors
```

If you use column headings, as in this example, the column headings become the column names in the view.

> **NOTE**
>
> Make sure that your column headings would also be valid column names.

In almost all ways, you can treat a view like a table:

```
/* retrieve all rows and columns from view */
select * from author_name
last                          first
——————————————————————        ——————————
White                         Johnson
Green                         Marjorie
Carson                        Cheryl
O'Leary                       Michael
Straight                      Dean
Smith                         Meander
Bennet                        Abraham
Dull                          Ann
Gringlesby                    Burt
Locksley                      Charlene
Greene                        Morningstar
Blotchet-Halls                Reginald
Yokomoto                      Akiko
del Castillo                  Innes
DeFrance                      Michel
Stringer                      Dirk
MacFeather                    Stearns
Karsen                        Livia
Panteley                      Sylvia
Hunter                        Sheryl
McBadden                      Heather
Ringer                        Anne
Ringer                        Albert
( 23 rows affected)
```

To remove a view, use the drop view statement, which has a syntax similar to that of other drop statements:

```
drop view view_name
```

This example drops the `author_name` view.

```
/* drop the author_name view */
drop view author_name
```

> **TIP**
>
> Remember, dropping the view has absolutely no effect on the data, but it might cause problems for other views that refer to to the one you are dropping. To make sure that you are not leaving a big hole in your database, use SQL-EM or `sp_depends` to search for dependent objects before dropping a view.

Examining Views in SQL Enterprise Manager

SQL Enterprise Manager also offers a Views folder similar to the Tables folder for a particular database. All views in the database are listed here. Double-clicking a view displays a text-editor window where SQL-EM puts the original creation statement for the view. From here, you can edit the creation statement, resubmit it, and effectively re-create your view. (See Figure 6.8.)

FIGURE 6.8.

SQL Enterprise Manager provides a convenient interface for editing creation statements for views.

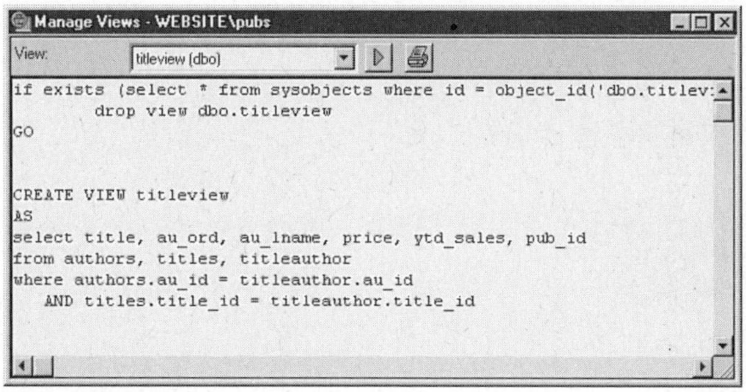

Views as Security—Vertical

You can use a view to limit access to selected *columns* in a base table. (See Figure 6.9.) This is a normal approach to restricting access to a user, while not requiring the user to write a lot of SQL. In this example, the view includes only three of the four columns in the `titleauthor` table:

```
/* create a view to show 3 of 4 titleauthor columns */
create view ta_limited as
     select au_id, title_id, au_ord
     from titleauthor
```

FIGURE 6.9.

The view displays only the named columns. Those columns not named are invisible to users accessing the table through the view.

au_id	title_id	au_ord
172-32-1176	PS3333	1
213-46-8915	BU1032	2
213-46-8915	BU2075	1
...	...	...
998-72-3567	PS2106	1

When you select from the view, you will only see the columns specified in the view. The `royaltyper` column in the `titleauthor` table is not displayed here and is unavailable from this view.

```
select * from ta_limited

au_id       title_id au_ord
_____ _____ ___
172-32-1176 PS3333   1
213-46-8915 BU1032   2
213-46-8915 BU2075   1
238-95-7766 PC1035   1
267-41-2394 BU1111   2
...
899-46-2035 PS2091   2
998-72-3567 PS2091   1
998-72-3567 PS2106   1
( 25 rows affected)
```

When you use a view for security, grant the user permission to select from the view, but not from the base table.

This view can now be used to join `titles` and `authors`:

```
/* select title and author name using ta_limited view */
select au_lname, title
from authors a, titles t, ta_limited ta
where a.au_id = ta.au_id and t.title_id = ta.title_id

au_lname            title
_____ _____
Green               The Busy Executive's Database Guide
Bennet              The Busy Executive's Database Guide
O'Leary             Cooking with Computers: Surreptitious Balance Sheets
MacFeather          Cooking with Computers: Surreptitious Balance Sheets
Green               You Can Combat Computer Stress!
Straight            Straight Talk About Computers
del Castillo        Silicon Valley Gastronomic Treats
DeFrance            The Gourmet Microwave
Ringer              The Gourmet Microwave
Carson              But Is It User Friendly?
Dull                Secrets of Silicon Valley
Hunter              Secrets of Silicon Valley
Locksley            Net Etiquette
MacFeather          Computer Phobic AND Non-Phobic Individuals:Behavior Variat
Karsen              Computer Phobic AND Non-Phobic Individuals: Behavior Varia
Ringer              Is Anger the Enemy?
```

```
Ringer              Is Anger the Enemy?
Ringer              Life Without Fear
White               Prolonged Data Deprivation: Four Case Studies
Locksley            Emotional Security: A New Algorithm
Panteley            Onions, Leeks, and Garlic: Cooking Secrets of the Mediterr
Blotchet-Halls      Fifty Years in Buckingham Palace Kitchens
O'Leary             Sushi, Anyone?
Gringlesby          Sushi, Anyone?
Yokomoto            Sushi, Anyone?
( 25 rows affected)
```

Views as Security—Horizontal

You can use a view to limit access to specific *rows* in a base table by writing a where clause in the view that restricts rows to those a user should see. In this example, the cal_publishers view contains only rows where the state has the value CA:

```
/* create view with only California publishers */
create view cal_publishers as
    select *
    from publishers
    where state = "CA"
```

When you select from the view, only publishers from California are displayed:

```
/* retrieve all rows and columns from the view */
select * from cal_publishers

pub_id pub_name              city          state country
—— —— —————————————— ———————————— —— ————————
1389   Algodata Infosystems  Berkeley      CA    USA
( 1 row affected)
```

Views to Ease SQL

Views can be used to simplify queries. It has been my direct experience that the best programmers are the lazy ones; they find efficient ways of doing things and are therefore more productive. Views are useful for hiding complex joins or denormalized tables from end users and easing the SQL for programmers. In this example, the view joins three tables, allowing users to query a complex data structure as if the data were stored in a single flat table:

```
/* create a view to handle a three-way join */
create view titles_and_authors as
    select title, au_lname, au_fname, type
    from titles t, ta_limited ta, authors a
    where t.title_id = ta.title_id
    and a.au_id = ta.au_id

/* retrieve all rows and columns from the view */
select *
    from titles_and_authors
    where type = "business"
```

```
title                                       au_lname     au_fname    type
_____ _____ _____ _____
The Busy Executive's Database Guide         Green        Marjorie    business
The Busy Executive's Database Guide         Bennet       Abraham     business
Cooking with Computers: Surreptitious Balanc O'Leary     Michael     business
Cooking with Computers: Surreptitious Balanc MacFeather  Stearns     business
You Can Combat Computer Stress!             Green        Marjorie    business
Straight Talk About Computers               Straight     Dean        business
( 6 rows affected)
```

> **NOTE**
>
> This view contains the `ta_limited` view that was created earlier. A view is permitted to refer to other views.

Views can contain the following:

- Aggregate functions and groupings

- Joins

- Other views (up to 16 levels of nesting)

- A `distinct` clause

- `union`

Views cannot include the following:

- `select into`

- A `compute` clause

- An `order by` clause

You can use an `order by` statement when selecting from the view, however.

> **NOTE**
>
> The availability of `union` in a view is new to SQL 6.5 and substantially simplifies design issues with very large tables when you split them horizontally into multiple tables, often in multiple databases.

Data Modifications and Views

SQL Server allows you to insert into, update, and delete from views, with some restrictions.

`insert` adds rows to one base table. `update` and `delete` affect rows in one base table:

```
/* delete rows from a view ...
** corresponding rows in the table are deleted */
delete author_name
     where last = "Smith" and first = "Joseph"

/* change the name of a publisher */
update cal_publishers
 set pub_name = "Joe's Books and Magazines"
 where pub_id = "1389"
```

When a view includes columns from more than one table, you can't do the following:

- Delete rows from the view (this would affect multiple base tables).

- Update columns from more than one table in a single `update` statement:

```
/* this is NOT permitted */
update titles_and_authors
   set type = "mod_cook", au_fname = "Mary"
   where title = "The Gourmet Microwave"

/* INSTEAD, update each table in turn */
update titles_and_authors
   set type = "mod_cook"
   where title = "The Gourmet Microwave"
update titles_and_authors
   set au_fname = "Mary"
   where title = "The Gourmet Microwave"
```

Inserts are not allowed into views unless all underlying columns in the base table not included in the view either are defined to allow `null` values or have a default defined on the columns.

Inserts are allowed on views containing joins as long as all columns being inserted into the view belong to a single base table.

Finally, you can't update, delete, or insert into a view containing the `distinct` clause.

Views with check option

In previous releases of SQL Server, it was possible for users to insert or update a row, creating a row they could not retrieve with `select`:

```
insert into cal_publishers
     (pub_id, pub_name, city, state)
values
     ("1234", "Joe's Books", "Canton", "OH")

/* update creates an "invisible" row */
update cal_publishers
  set state = "OH"
/* would make ALL rows "Invisible" */
```

The `with check option` flag prevents insertion or updating of rows that will subsequently not meet the view criteria. Notice that `with check option` appears as the last element of the query:

```
create view view_name [ ( colname, ... ) ]
     as select_statements
     [with check option]
```

In the following example, the update fails because, after the update, the modified rows would fail to appear in the view:

```
/* create view with only California publishers */
create view cal_publishers_ck as
     select *
     from publishers
     where state = "CA"
with check option

update cal_publishers_ck
  set state = "OH"
```

Here is the actual error message:

```
Msg 550, Level 16, State 2
The attempted insert or update failed because the target view either
specifies WITH CHECK OPTION or spans a view which specifies WITH CHECK
OPTION and one or more rows resulting from the operation did not qualify
under the CHECK OPTION constraint.
Command has been aborted.
```

Views Created with encryption

Microsoft SQL Server enables you to encrypt creation statements. By including the keywords with encryption in the create view statement, you can prevent any user from viewing the original SQL source of a view (the create view statement that was originally executed). Many independent software vendors (ISV's) use this feature to hide views and other objects that their applications create. Typically, views and stored procedures (discussed in Chapter 8) are encrypted according to standard internal security practices for your organization.

Getting View Information

sp_help lists all objects in a database, including views and tables. To get a list of just the views defined in a database, run the following select statement:

```
select name from sysobjects
     where type = "V"

name
_ _ _ _ _ _ _ _ _ _ _ _ _ _
titleview
author_name
ta_limited
cal_publishers
titles_and_authors
cal_publishers_ck
( 6 rows affected)
```

To see a list of columns in a view, use sp_help:

```
sp_help view_name
```

```
Name                    Owner        Type                    When_created
_____     _____        _____     _____
cal_publishers_ck       dbo          view                    Nov 14 1995  6:12PM
( 0 rows affected)


Data_located_on_segment
_____
not applicable
( 0 rows affected)


Column_name             Type                     Length Prec  Scale Nullable
_____     _____      _____  _____
pub_id                  char                     4                  no
pub_name                varchar                  40                 yes
city                    varchar                  20                 yes
state                   char                     2                  yes
country                 varchar                  30                 yes
( 0 rows affected)
...
 ( 0 rows affected)
```

Renaming Objects

You cannot change the owner of an object or its database, but you can change its name. To rename an object (for example, a table or a view), use sp_rename. In the example, the table name is changed from names2 to new_names2.

```
sp_rename old_name, new_name

/* change the table names2 to new_names2 */
sp_rename names2, new_names2
```

> **NOTE**
>
> Even though the name of the table has changed, objects like views and procedures that refer to the table by name are not affected by the change in the name. That's because SQL-based objects such as views and procedures are stored both as text in the syscomments table (so you can output the original text with SQL-EM) and as a pre-parsed *query tree* identifying related objects by ID instead of name. When a table name changes, a dependent view still works—because the object ID of the table (stored in sysobjects) does not change.

After a table has been created, columns cannot be removed, datatypes cannot be changed, and null status cannot be changed. However, columns can be renamed by using sp_rename:

```
sp_rename 'table_name.old_col_name', new_col_name
/* change the au_lname column to "last_name" */
sp_rename 'authors.au_lname', 'last_name'
```

> **NOTE**
>
> Quotation marks are optional when passing character data to stored procedures unless
> the character string includes punctuation or spaces (for example, authors.au_lname).
> Note that old needs a table name, but that new cannot have one.

Adding Columns to a Table

You can add columns to an existing table by using the alter table command. Here is a simplified version of the alter table syntax that shows you how to add a column to a table:

```
alter table table_name add
    col_name datatype { null ¦ identity } [, ...]
```

In this example, the alter table command adds two new columns to the names2 table:

```
/* add middle name and fax columns to names table */
alter table names2 add
middle_name varchar(20) null,
fax varchar(15) null
```

New columns must either be identity columns or allow null values; otherwise, rows existing
in the database would become invalid. The keyword null is required in the command.

A table can have only one identity column. When you add an identity column with alter
table, SQL Server generates identity values for all existing rows.

Adding Columns with
SQL Enterprise Manager

You also can add columns to tables by using the Table Editor in SQL Enterprise Manager.
Double-clicking a table brings up the Manage Tables window. By using the last empty line of
the Table Editor, you can add a new column, and specify its datatype, default value, and null
status. By clicking the floppy-disk icon in the toolbar, you can save these changes. As with using
T-SQL, Enterprise Manager commits the changes without requesting confirmation. Remember, once you add a column, you can't remove it!

Enterprise Manager also automatically flags an added column for null status, which is required
when adding columns to existing tables.

Temporary Tables

Temporary tables are real tables created in the `tempdb` database, usually for the purpose of holding an intermediate result set. Temporary tables are identified by a number sign (#) before the table name. They exist only for the duration of a user session or the stored procedure in which they are created. If the server crashes unexpectedly, these tables are lost, with no recovery possible. All SQL Server users have permission to create temporary tables.

One way to create a temporary table is to use the `create table` statement:

```
/* create temp table in tempdb for use in this session */
create table #temp (a int, b int)
```

More typically, temporary tables are created with `select into`:

```
/* create titles and authors table in tempdb
** for use in this session */
select au_lname, au_fname, title, pub_id
    into #titles_and_authors
    from authors a, titleauthor ta, titles t
    where a.au_id = ta.au_id
    and t.title_id = ta.title_id
```

Now, a two-table join may be made between `publishers` and `#titles_and_authors` to find out what publishers use which authors.

Global and Permanent Temporary Tables

Ordinary temporary tables last only as long as your session, and are only available to your session. To create a *global* temporary table—that is, one available to all users—use two pound signs (##):

```
select *
into ##titles
from titles
```

The `##titles` table is available to all users, but will be dropped when the session that created the table logs out.

You can create a *permanent* temporary table in `tempdb` by fully qualifying the table name with the name of the database:

```
select *
into tempdb..titles
from pubs2..titles
```

Permanent temporary tables exist until explicitly dropped or until the SQL Server is restarted (that is, after a shutdown or a crash). They are useful for nonpermanent data that needs to be shared between multiple users.

Rules

Rules provide a mechanism for enforcing domain constraints for columns or user-defined datatypes. The rules are applied before an `insert` or `update` command, prior to the execution of the command.

Creating Rules

A rule is created in much the same way as any other database object:

```
create rule rule_name as
    @variable operator expression
    [{and¦or} ...]
```

Here are some examples of rules:

```
/* orders must fall into a range */
create rule order_quantity as
    @quantity between 100 and 150000

/* specify a list of valid colors */
create rule color_rule as
    @color in ('black', 'brown', 'red')

/* provide a rule for pub_id */
create rule pub_id_rule as
    @pubid like ('99[0-9][0-9]')
    or @pubid in ('0736', '0877', '1389')

/* date must be >= to current date */
create rule date_rule as
    @date >= getdate()
```

The variable (`@date` in the last example) is a placeholder and has no bearing on the column name. It must be no more than 30 characters in length, including the `@`.

Rules can use any of the comparison operators available in a `where` clause, so long as the comparison operator works for the underlying datatype of the field to which the rule will be bound. In other words, a `like` clause works only with strings, so creating a rule that uses `like` as a comparison operator wouldn't be much use on a column that stores integers. For further information on this, see Chapter 4, "Introduction to Transact-SQL," on using the `where` clause, datatypes, and datatype conversions.

Rules are a Transact-SQL method for implementing *domain integrity*, which is the capability of maintaining a valid list of values for a column. Domain integrity can also be implemented using ANSI standard SQL syntax, which is discussed in the section "Check Constraints," later in this chapter. ANSI SQL syntax enables data object definitions to be portable to other ANSI-supported platforms, but using Transact-SQL statements means the data-definition language can be used only with SQL Server.

If a rule isn't bound to any columns or user-defined datatypes, you can drop it with `drop rule`, whose syntax is (amazingly!) similar to other `drop` statements:

```
drop rule rule_name

/* remove rule from database */
drop rule key_rule
```

Rule Usage

A *rule* is a separate and distinct database object. In order for a rule to take effect, you must bind the rule to a column in a table or tables by using `sp_bindrule`:

```
sp_bindrule rule_name, 'table.column_name'
```

> **TIP**
>
> Remember that the quotation marks are necessary because of the separator, the period (.) in the parameter being passed to the `sp_bindrule` stored procedure.

This example binds the rule, `key_rule`, to the column `user_id` in `demographics`:

```
/* bind key_rule to user_id column in demographics table */
sp_bindrule key_rule, 'demographics.user_id'
```

You can instruct the server to stop applying a rule (*unbind* a rule) by using `sp_unbindrule`. Here's the syntax:

```
sp_unbindrule 'table_name.column_name'

/* unbind rule from user_id in demographics table */
sp_unbindrule 'demographics.user_id'
```

Rule Limitations

A rule can deal only with constants, SQL Server functions, and edit masks. It can't perform a table lookup (use a trigger if this is necessary), nor can it compare a column against other columns in the table.

Only one rule may be bound per column. If you bind a rule to a column and an existing rule is bound to the column, it's replaced by the new rule.

A rule will not be retroactively applied to existing data in a table, but it will be applied when an existing row is updated.

A rule may not be dropped if it is bound to a column or user-defined datatype; you must first unbind it from all columns and datatypes.

> **WARNING**
>
> Rules aren't applied when you bulk copy data into the system.

Creating Rules with SQL Enterprise Manager

SQL Enterprise Manager can do many things, but it can't create syntax for you. As a result, you should study the preceding section carefully, because portions of the syntax described are necessary for creating rules using SQL Enterprise Manager. You'll see examples of this as we take a look at an alternate method for creating and managing rules.

SQL Enterprise Manager provides a Rules folder that holds a list of all rules contained in a particular database. By right-clicking this folder, you can open the Manage Rules dialog box (see Figure 6.10). In this dialog box, you can define the rule name as well as the rule's description, which is how you define the restrictions the rule will implement.

FIGURE 6.10.

SQL Enterprise Manager provides a graphical interface for managing rules, but you still need to know some SQL syntax.

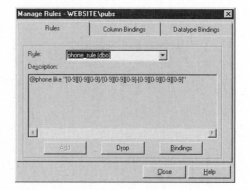

How do you define a description? You do it the same way that you define a rule, with a slight modification. The syntax that is included after the as clause of a rule is the same syntax you should use for the description. Therefore, if you write a rule creation statement as

```
create rule title_id_rule as
@title_id like '[A-Z][A-Z][0-9][0-9][0-9][0-9]'
```

the description field should contain this text:

```
@title_id like '[A-Z][A-Z][0-9][0-9][0-9][0-9]'
```

Remember that the `@title_id` variable name is irrelevant. It could be `@Fred` or `@Barney` and have no effect on the application. (See Figure 6.11.)

FIGURE 6.11.

The syntax for creating rules in SQL Enterprise Manager is identical to that used by Transact-SQL.

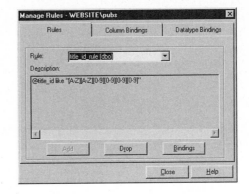

After you create the rule, SQL Enterprise Manager enables you to define the bindings for the rule immediately by selecting the Column Bindings or the Datatype Bindings window tabs. (See Figure 6.12.)

FIGURE 6.12.

SQL Enterprise Manager enables you to define rule and default bindings immediately during rule creation, using both column-wise binding and datatype-wise binding.

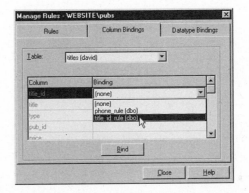

Remember that SQL Enterprise Manager relies on underlying T-SQL syntax to do its work. As such, when you work with establishing and removing bindings of rules and defaults, SQL Enterprise Manager, in the background, is running `sp_bindrule` and `sp_unbindrule` for you!

Defaults

Defaults provide a value for a column when one is not supplied at insert time. Like rules, they exist only as database objects; after creation, they must subsequently be bound to columns.

To create a default, use the `create default` statement:

```
create default default_name
    as constant_expression
```

Examples

```
/* default country value is "USA" */
create default country_default as
    'USA'

/* default age is 16 */
create default age_default as
   16

/* default time is the current system time */
create default time_default as
   getdate()
```

> **NOTE**
>
> There are *no quotation marks* around the 16. It is dangerously easy to make a mistake about the datatype of a default value. The server will not catch datatype mismatches until the first time the value is used in an `insert` statement.

To drop a default, use the `drop default` statement. Here's the syntax:

```
drop default default_name

/* remove default definition from database */
drop default age_default
```

Default Usage

You bind a default to columns in a table or tables by using `sp_bindefault` according to this syntax:

```
sp_bindefault default_name, 'table_name.column_name'

/* apply the default to country in demographics */
sp_bindefault country_default, 'demographics.country'
```

To unbind a default, use `sp_unbindefault` following this syntax:

```
sp_unbindefault 'table.column_name'

/* remove default from country in demographics */
sp_unbindefault 'demographics.country'
```

> **NOTE**
>
> How many *d*s in `sp_unbindefault`? Only one. The standard naming system always removes duplicated letters when they occur between words in the names of system procedures. So, `bind` + `default` becomes `sp_bindefault` and `help` + `protect` becomes `sp_helpprotect`. However, `add` + `dump` + `device` becomes `sp_addumpdevice`. (Only one d is removed.)

Declarative Defaults

SQL Server also permits the declaration of a default value for a column during table creation. Note that the `default` expression falls between the datatype and the nullability:

```
create table table_name
(col_name datatype
     [default expression]
     [{null ¦ not null ¦ identity}]
[, ... ]
)
```

Here the definition of the price column includes a default value of $12.95:

```
create table items
(item_id char(6)_not null,
price money default $12.95 not null)
```

Use the `alter table` statement to add or drop a default clause from a table:

```
/* To remove the default defined on price */
alter table items
     replace price default null

/* To define a default on ssn */
alter table items
     replace item_code default "N/A"
```

Defaults in SQL Enterprise Manager

SQL Enterprise Manager enables you to define two types of defaults for tables. If you use the Manage Tables dialog box illustrated earlier in this chapter, you can assign a default value by using that dialog box either when the table is created or by merely adding it in the interface. Using this method is equivalent to using the `ansi default` clause in a table creation statement, or by using an `alter table` command to add a `default` constraint if the table already exists.

If you are going to create Transact-SQL based constraints, you must use the Defaults folder of the database with which you are working. By right-clicking the Defaults folder, you can create a new default, using the Manage Defaults dialog box.

If it looks strangely familiar, you're catching on. The interface is visually identical to the Manage Rules dialog box. However, instead of typing in the contents of a `where` clause, as you did with rules, here you need only enter the default value itself. Remember that default values for `char` and `varchar` columns require paired quotes to mark the values as strings.

As with binding rules, the Column Bindings and Datatype Bindings window tabs for this dialog box enable you to define to which columns and/or datatypes this particular default will be bound.

Remember, if you plan to use your data definition language to create databases on a different ANSI SQL-compliant database, using Transact-SQL based defaults in this fashion will not work.

You can use ANSI-defined `default` clauses only as described previously. If you want your DDL to be portable, use the Manage Tables dialog box and create your defaults there.

Default Limitations

■ A column can have a default defined by a `default` clause or a default bound to the column, but not both.

■ A default can set only one constant or SQL Server function value; it can't make a decision or perform a table lookup (use a trigger if this is necessary).

■ Only one default may be bound per column. If you attempt to bind a second default to a column, you get an error message from SQL Server—Error 15103 (Severity 16). You can't bind a default to a column that was created with or altered to have a default value.)

■ Make sure that the datatype of the value in the default is compatible with the datatype of the column to which it is bound. Like rules, a default is not retroactively applied to existing data in a table.

■ Make sure that defaults are consistent with any rule on the column; otherwise, rows with defaults will not be inserted (though this may be a way of forcing a nullable column to be made not null).

■ The default is applied before the rule is checked; this enables the rule to be applied to the default rather than to the null value.

■ Defaults are applied during bulk copy.

■ A default may not be dropped if it is bound to a column or user-defined datatype; you must first unbind the default from all columns or datatypes before dropping it.

When a Default Is Applied

Defaults are applied only when no value is specified for a column during insert, or when you provide the `default` keyword. Consider this example:

```
/* define table with two columns */
create table table1
(id int not null,
price smallmoney null)

/* define a default price of $15 */
create default price_default as $15

/* bind the default */
sp_bindefault price_default, "table1.price"
```

To use the default value, the column must be assigned no value in the `insert` statement. An insert that doesn't specify columns must provide all values:

```
/* value is provided for price, default not applied */
insert table1
values (1, $30)
```

The following insert format uses the default:

```
/* default is applied */
insert table1 (id)
values (5)
```

Alternatively, you could apply the default by specifying the keyword `default`.

```
/* default is applied */
insert table1 (id, price)
values (5, DEFAULT)
```

Inserting an explicit `null` overrides the default:

```
/* Explicit null value provided for price, default not applied */
insert table1 (id, price)
values (1, null)
```

Defaults on update

Updates can also use the default value by referencing it in the `set` clause:

```
update table1
set price = DEFAULT
where id = 1
```

Examining Rules and Defaults

To list rules and defaults, along with all other objects in a database, use `sp_help`.

To list all rules or defaults in a database, use the following:

```
select name from sysobjects
    where type in ( "R", "D" )
```

To examine the rules and defaults bound to columns in a table, use this:

```
sp_help table_name
```

In the output of `sp_help`, the names of defaults and rules are displayed in the `Default_name` and `Rule_name` columns:

```
sp_help authors

Name                          Owner                    Type
-----------------------       --------------------     ----------------
authors                       dbo                      user table
Data_located_on_segment                When_created
-----------------------------          --------------------------
default                                Sep 27 1993  3:14PM

Column_name  Type       Length Nulls Default_name Rule_name
-----------  ---------  ------ ----- ------------ ----------
au_id        id            11    0 NULL          NULL
au_lname     varchar       40    0 NULL          NULL
au_fname     varchar       20    0 NULL          NULL
```

```
phone        char        12    0 phonedflt   NULL
address      varchar     40    1 NULL        NULL
city         varchar     20    1 NULL        NULL
state        char         2    1 NULL        NULL
country      varchar     12    1 NULL        NULL
postalcode   char        10    1 NULL        NULL
```

You can get a wealth of information from the system tables if you know how. For example, to list all columns in a database bound to a rule, use this SQL:

```
/* list tables and columns for a rule */
select "table" = o.name, "column" = c.name,
    "user" = user_name(uid), "rule" = object_name(domain)
from syscolumns c, sysobjects o
    where o.id = c.id
    and object_name(domain) = "insert rule_name"
order by 1, 2
```

To list all columns in a database bound to a *default*, use the following:

```
/* list tables and columns for a default */
select "table" = o.name, "column" = c.name,
  "user" = user_name(uid), "default" = object_name(cdefault)
from syscolumns c, sysobjects o
where o.id = c.id
  and object_name(cdefault) = "insert default_name"
order by 1, 2
```

The text used to create a rule or default can be examined by using the `sp_helptext` stored procedure.

```
sp_helptext object_name
```

User-Defined Datatypes

A user-defined datatype (UDDT) is not really a new datatype; it is a way of describing an existing datatype. It provides a mechanism for enforcing data type consistency across and within a database or server. It also can simplify management of frequently used rules and defaults.

> **NOTE**
>
> A user-defined datatype is not a database object and therefore isn't listed in `sysobjects`; it's listed in `systypes`, but follows object naming conventions.

Creating User-Defined Datatypes

Define and remove user-defined datatypes with `sp_addtype` and `sp_droptype`:

```
sp_addtype type_name,
    system_type,
    {null ¦ "not null" ¦ identity}

sp_droptype type_name
```

System types that include *separators* (for example, parentheses in char or commas in numeric) must be enclosed in quotes.

Here's an example of the use of a UDDT:

```
/* add a social security number datatype */
sp_addtype ssn_type, 'char(9)', "not null"

/* add a price datatype */
sp_addtype price_type, money, null

/* drop the datatype */
sp_droptype price_type
```

User-Defined Datatype Notes

You can't drop a user-defined datatype if it is used in the definition of an existing column; you first have to drop all tables using the defined datatype.

You bind rules and defaults directly to the datatypes by using sp_bindrule and sp_bindefault:

```
/* bind price_rule to price datatype */
sp_bindrule price_rule, price_type

/* bind price_default to price datatype */
sp_bindefault price_default, price_type
```

Any column created with the price_type datatype automatically inherits the rule and default through the datatype, unless a rule or default has been explicitly bound to the column itself.

Defining and Using User-Defined Datatypes

The following is a typical sequence of events when using datatypes:

1. Create a user-defined datatype:

   ```
   sp_addtype ssn_type, 'char(9)', 'not null'
   ```

2. Create a rule and default:

   ```
   create rule ssn_rule as
       @ssn between '000001111' and '999999999'
       or @ssn = 'N / A'
   create default ssn_default as
       'N / A'
   ```

3. Bind the rule and default to the datatype:

   ```
   exec sp_bindrule ssn_rule, ssn_type
   exec sp_bindefault ssn_default, ssn_type
   ```

4. Create the tables using the datatype:

```
create table test_table
(ssn ssn_type, name varchar(30) )
```

Typically, user-defined datatypes are defined in the model database and propagated to the user databases as the new databases are created.

Defining User-Defined Data Types in SQL Enterprise Manager

SQL-EM can manage user-defined datatypes as well as rules and defaults. The User Defined Datatypes folder contains a list of all UDDTs defined for the database. From here, you can create, modify, or destroy any user-defined datatypes in a database. Because a UDDT requires a unique name and base datatype, those fields are mandatory in the dialog box shown in Figure 6.13. The Rule and Default fields are optional, but enable you to define the rule and default you want to use with this datatype.

FIGURE 6.13.

SQL Enterprise Manager makes managing user-defined datatypes easier by encapsulating the creation and binding of datatypes into a single interface dialog box.

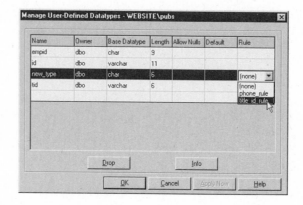

After you fill in the form, SQL-EM executes the proper CREATE statements and BIND procedures to create the UDDT you specified.

Binding Precedence with Rules and Defaults

Rules and defaults are maintained in a "stack of depth one":

```
/* bind a rule to a column */
sp_bindrule "rule_r", "table_t.col_c"
```

```
/* bind another rule to the column */
/* the first rule is replaced */
sp_bindrule "rule_s", "table_t.col_c"
/* unbind the rule - no rule is bound now*/
sp_unbindrule "table_t.col_c"
```

A rule or default bound explicitly to a column overrides a rule or default bound to a datatype. A subsequent bind to the datatype replaces the bind to the column as long as the column and datatype have the same rule or default prior to modification. If you unbind a rule or default from a column, future binds to the datatype apply to the column.

Indexes

The primary purpose of an index is to provide faster access to data pages than scanning every page. Secondarily, it is sometimes used as a mechanism for enforcing uniqueness.

Index Types

SQL Server provides two types of indexes: *clustered* and *nonclustered*. Both are B-Tree indexes. For clustered indexes, data is maintained in clustered index order; as a result, only one clustered index per table can exist (because data can be physically sorted only one way). Alternatively, you can have 249 nonclustered indexes per table, because nonclustered indexes maintain pointers to rows (not data pages).

An index can contain from 1 to 16 columns, but the total index entry width must be no greater than 255 bytes. Indexes are maintained and used internally by the server to improve performance or to enforce uniqueness. Under normal circumstances, the application programmer does not usually refer to indexes.

Clustered Index Mechanism

With a clustered index, there is one entry on the last intermediate index-level page for each data page. This means that the data page is the *leaf*, or bottom, level of the index. (See Figure 6.14.)

In Figure 6.14, which diagrams a clustered index on last name, to find Fred Amundsen you look first in the root page. Because Amundsen is between Albert and Jones, you follow the Albert pointer to the appropriate intermediate page. There, Amundsen is between Albert and Brown, so you again follow the Albert pointer to the data page. Note that the data page must be scanned (which is very quick) to find the actual data row.

FIGURE 6.14.

A clustered index stores pointers matching the physical sort of the data. At the lowest index level, rows in the index point to pages in the table itself.

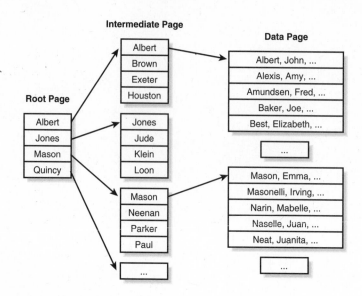

Nonclustered Index Mechanism

The nonclustered index has an extra leaf index level for page/row pointers. Figure 6.15 depicts a nonclustered index on first name (but a clustered index on last name). Let's find all the Amy entries. First, look into the root page. Amy is between Amy and George; therefore you follow the Amy pointer. Proceed until you get to the leaf page, then read the list of row IDs from the leaf page(s) and read each of the Amy entries, retrieving rows as appropriate.

FIGURE 6.15.

The nonclustered index introduces an extra leaf level with one row of index for every row in the table.

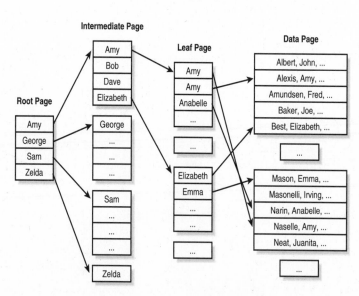

Clustered Versus Nonclustered

A clustered index *tends to be* one I/O faster than a nonclustered index for a single-row lookup, because there tend to be fewer index levels. Clustered indexes are excellent for retrieving ranges of data, because the server can narrow down a range of data, retrieve the first row, and scan the data without returning to the index for more information.

Nonclustered indexes are a bit slower and take up much more disk space, but are the next best alternative to a table scan. Nonclustered indexes can cover the query for maximal retrieval speed. This means that if the data required is in the index, the server does not need to return the data row.

> **WARNING**
>
> When creating a clustered index, you need *free space* in your database approximately equal to 120 percent of the table size. This enables space for the table to coexist in the database while it is being sorted.

Creating Indexes

Create your clustered indexes before creating nonclustered indexes, so that the nonclustered index entries will not need to be resorted or reshuffled during the data sort. (In reality, SQL Server actually drops and re-creates these indexes anyway.) Here is the syntax for creating an index on a table:

```
create [unique] [clustered ¦ nonclustered] index
    index_name on table_name (column [, ...])
```

Here are some index examples:

```
create unique clustered index name_index
    on authors (au_lname, au_fname)

create index fname_index
    on authors (au_fname, au_lname)
```

By default (unless otherwise specified), an index is nonunique and nonclustered.

Notes on Indexes

- Only one index can be defined on an ordered set of columns in a table (this is a new feature).
- When an index is defined as `unique`, no two rows can have the same index value (null counts as one value). The uniqueness check is performed at index creation, on `insert`, and on `update`.

- Often, a clustered index is used for the primary key; this is not always the best performance selection. Having a clustered index on all tables is a good idea; otherwise, space is not reused from deleted rows. If the table doesn't have a clustered index, all new rows (and updated rows) are placed at the end of the table.

- As the number of indexes increases (past five or so) the overhead at update to maintain the indexes gets excessive; in an executive information system (EIS) where there is virtually no real-time update, the only constraint on the number of indexes is disk space.

- An OLTP system usually is configured with as few indexes as possible to speed update, insert, and delete activity.

- Watch out for datatype mismatches in where clauses, especially char and varchar. They can't be optimized effectively because the optimizer may be unable to use the data distribution statistics for the index. This is easy to do unintentionally in stored procedures. Using user-defined datatypes can help avoid this problem.

Managing Indexes with SQL Enterprise Manager

In addition to the syntax provided by Transact-SQL for managing indexes, SQL Enterprise Manager adds many important index management features into its interface. By selecting the Manage | Indexes menu sequence in SQL-EM, you get the rather complex dialog box displayed in Figure 6.16.

FIGURE 6.16.

SQL Enterprise Manager extends the T-SQL index management syntax by providing useful index statistics and maintenance options.

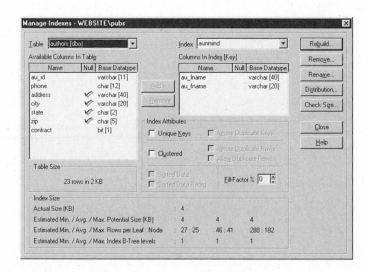

In this dialog box, you can manage all aspects of table indexing, on a table-and-index basis. The left box displays the table structure, including datatypes and null status. The right combo box displays which index you are currently viewing. Selecting the combo box enables you to pick the index on the particular table you want to view. The index attributes, such as whether the index is unique or clustered, are automatically displayed, and any options that were not used are available for selection, should the index be rebuilt.

In addition, at the bottom of the screen, SQL Enterprise Manager calculates valuable index statistic information. By including the keys/page and levels information, you can plan how large an index will be, as well as how efficient that index will be for query resolution. Index usage is discussed further in Chapter 13, "Understanding the Query Optimizer," but the general principle is that an inverse relationship exists between the number of levels in an index and its efficiency for solving queries. Minimizing index levels (by minimizing key size) is a smart optimization technique.

New indexes can be created by selecting the new index entry from the Index combo box. All the options are set to their defaults. You can choose the fields of the index, the index attributes, and so forth, and SQL Server will generate the proper creation statement and estimate the index size for you. You can add columns to the index by highlighting the column in the Available Columns in Table list box and selecting the Add button. (See Figure 6.17.)

FIGURE 6.17.

Creating new indexes by using Enterprise Manager can be more efficient than using SQL syntax, because an administrator can view the size and relative efficiency of that index before it is created.

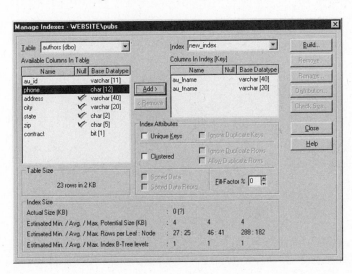

Adding new columns to and removing existing columns from a new index forces SQL Enterprise Manager to recalculate the index size, keys/page ratio, and the number of levels. The initial values are approximated based on current data distribution information or statistics. For the most accurate information, you can update the statistics for an index or table.

The lower portion of this dialog box presents very useful, if advanced, information about indexes. The Index Size panel of the dialog box holds the computed sizes of both leaf and node pages of the index, as well as various other statistics. What are these statistics?

A B-Tree index has three classes of pages: a single *root* page, which is the entry point to the tree; typically multiple *node* pages, which are intermediate pages in the tree; and *leaf* pages, which are the lowest level of the index. Because root and node pages store different information than leaf pages do, they can typically store more information per page.

In the interface, the Actual Size value represents the total size, in kilobytes, of all index pages. To calculate the total number of pages in the index, divide this number by 2048 (2KB per page). The Estimated Min/Avg/Max Potential Size is the largest size this index can be, given the current data distribution (more on that in a minute) and key size. The Estimated Min/Avg/Max Rows per Leaf:Node Page gives you information on the number of index keys a given leaf page can store, as well as the number of rows a given node page can store. Notice that for the aunmind index, the leaf page can store between 27 and 288 rows per leaf page, but the node page can store between 25 and 182 rows per node page. These values are calculated by using an algorithm discussed in Chapter 13, so refer to that chapter for more detail.

The Estimated Min/Avg/Max Index B-Tree Levels value shows you how high your tree is. This value is actually more critical in most cases than actual index size because it acts as a multiplier for page reads. A query that needs to navigate only from the root to the leaf has one level—that is, no node pages. In that way, the height value reported here represents the number of jumps a query must make from the root page to the leaf pages.

> **NOTE**
>
> Minimizing the number of index levels is an important part of optimizing queries. Although there are many methods to accomplish this (they are discussed in Chapters 13 through 16), the easiest method to implement is minimizing the index key size. The smaller your index keys, the more key values can fit on a given page, reducing both the total number of pages and the total number of index levels.

SQL Server depends on statistics it collects about table data to decide on index selection. The process of using these statistics is discussed in more detail in Chapter 13, but understanding what these statistics are and how important it is to maintain them is an appropriate discussion for this chapter.

SQL Enterprise Manager provides an easy way to browse and maintain table data statistics that are stored on the *distribution page*. The distribution page stores the distribution of data in the table as a histogram—that is, how many of value X does the table have, how many of value Y, and so forth. The statistics page is created at the time an index is created. However, the statistics page is never automatically updated unless the index is dropped and re-created. As a result, the statistics page may hold information that represents an inaccurate distribution of table data.

By selecting the Distribution button in the Manage Indexes dialog box, you can view the current data distribution and update that information in the Index Distribution Statistics dialog box shown in Figure 6.18.

FIGURE 6.18.

SQL Enterprise Manager gives administrators a tool for examining and updating table data-distribution statistics, allowing you to see what the optimizer sees when estimating data distribution.

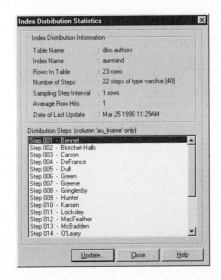

By clicking the Update button, you can update the statistics for this particular index or for all indexes on the table you have selected.

> **WARNING**
>
> Updating distribution page statistics can be a very time- and disk-intensive process. To build the statistics page, SQL Server must scan each row of the table and take a sample of the table data to construct the appropriate values. This causes a heavy drain on I/O and CPU resources and should be performed only during off-hours or normal maintenance cycles.

Constraints

Constraints provide an alternative to rules and defaults. SQL Server enforces three general types of constraints:

- Primary and unique key constraints
- Check constraints
- Referential integrity constraints

A later section of this chapter ("Which One Should You Use?") discusses when rules, constraints, and defaults should be used.

Primary-Key and Unique Constraints

SQL Server permits the declaration of a primary key or a unique constraint at table definition time. Unique constraints require that all non-null values be unique and allow a single null value for the column in the table. At definition, SQL Server automatically creates a unique index, nonclustered by default.

Primary key constraints require that all values in a table be unique, and the column(s) cannot allow null values. They also automatically create a unique index, though clustered by default.

All standard index-creation options are available as part of the syntax for primary key and unique constraints. Here is the syntax for creating the constraints:

```
create table table_name
 ( col datatype [ {identity ¦ null ¦ not null} ]
    [ constraint constraint_name ]
        {unique ¦ primary key}
            [ {clustered ¦ nonclustered} ]
  [ , ... ]
 [ [, constraint constraint_name ]
    {unique ¦ primary key}
        [{clustered ¦ nonclustered}]
            (col [, ...] )
 [, ... ] ] )
```

Primary-key and unique constraints can be defined at the column level or the table level. A table-level constraint can apply to a single column or multiple columns in the table. If you are defining a primary key or unique constraint on multiple columns (a composite key), the constraint must be defined at the table level:

```
/* create names table: primary key on ssn (table level) */
create table names
 (ssn varchar(9) not null,
 name varchar(20) not null,
 constraint names_pk primary key (ssn) )

/* create names2 table: primary key on ssn (column level),
   nonclustered, unique key on name, ssn, clustered (table level) */
create table names
 (ssn varchar(9) not null
    constraint ssn_pk primary key nonclustered,
  name varchar(20) not null,
  constraint name_key unique clustered (name, ssn))
```

Check Constraints

Check constraints specify a domain for columns (similar to rules) and may be slightly faster. They are defined for a table by using the `create table` or `alter table` command. Check constraints can be defined at the column level or the table level. Table-level constraints can perform multicolumn checks.

Multiple constraints can be associated with a single column. Check constraints can't compare against values in other tables (use triggers), although they can look in the current row, and can't contain aggregates. Here's the syntax for the `create table` statement, including declarative defaults and check constraints:

```
create table table_name
 ( col datatype
    [ default constant_expression ]
    [ {identity ¦ null ¦ not null} ]
    [ [ constraint constraint_name ]
        check (search_condition) ]
  [ , ... ]
  [ [, constraint constraint_name ]
    [ [ constraint constraint_name ]
        check (search_condition) ]
    [ , ... ]
 )
```

Here are some examples of check constraints. The first example checks an `item_code` to make certain that inserted values consist of four characters, all numeric:

```
/* two column table with column level check
** constraint on key and default on price */
create table prices
 (item_code char(4) not null
    constraint item_code_constraint
    check (item_code like "[0-9][0-9][0-9][0-9]"),
  price smallmoney default $15 not null
 )
```

The inventory table created here consists of three columns. Note that the high and low columns each have a constraint requiring that the value be above zero; then a table-level constraint requires that the high and low volumes have a specific relationship to each other (high must be greater than low and they must be no more than 1000 apart).

```
/* inventory table with column level check
** constraints and table level constraint comparing
** two columns */
create table inventory
 (item_code char(4) not null
    constraint item_code_constraint
    check (item_code like "[0-9][0-9][0-9][0-9]"),
  high_volume int not null
    check (high_volume > 0),
  low_volume int not null
    check (low_volume > 0),
  constraint check hi_lo_check
    (high_volume >= low_volume
      and high_volume - low_volume < 1000)
 )
```

Referential Integrity Constraints

Referential integrity (RI) in a database is the property of all foreign keys in a referencing table having an associated primary key in referenced tables. For example, if the titles table contains a pub_id, the publishers table should have a corresponding publisher. You can also add constraints to enforce referential integrity at table creation time or later with an alter table statement. Referential integrity constraints prevent data modifications which would leave foreign keys pointing at nonexistent primary keys. (For example, no title is permitted to have a pub_id that does not match an existing pub_id in the publishers table. (See Figure 6.19.)

FIGURE 6.19.

Referential integrity defines the relationship between two tables. The referencing table contains a foreign key, pub_id, that references a primary key in the referenced table.

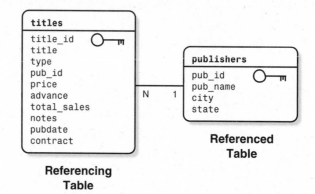

Constraints can enforce both primary and foreign key integrity checks without programming; this is called *declarative referential integrity*. Constraints can support both column level (single-part) keys and table level (multi-part) keys.

Single-part keys can also be defined as table-level constraints.

Declarative constraints roll back an update or insert when the RI constraint is violated. More advanced RI options currently require using triggers or SQL transactions.

Primary-Key Constraints

Primary key constraints require that all values in a table be unique, and require a value in each column identified in the primary key (no nulls) for every row. They automatically create a unique clustered index, and all standard index creation options are available:

```
create table table_name
  ( col datatype [ {identity | null | not null} ]
      [ constraint constraint_name ]
          primary key [ {clustered | nonclustered} ]
  [ , ... ]
[ [, constraint constraint_name ]
              primary key [{clustered | nonclustered}]
          (col [, ...] )
  [, ... ] ] )
```

In each of these examples, ssn is defined as the primary key for the names table. A unique, clustered index will be created on that column automatically:

```
/* primary key on ssn (table level) */
create table names
 (ssn varchar(9) not null,
  name varchar(20) not null,
  constraint names_pk primary key (ssn) )

/* primary key on ssn (column level, nonclustered)*/
create table names
 (ssn varchar(9) not null
     constraint ssn_pk primary key nonclustered,
  name varchar(20) not null)
```

Foreign-Key Constraints

Foreign keys are declared by using the reference constraint in the create table or alter table statement. Reference constraints can be defined at the column level (single-part key) or at the table level (single- or multi-part keys):

```
create table table_name
 (column_name datatype
     [ [ constraint constraint_name ]
       references ref_table [(ref_col)] ]
 [, ... ]
 [, [ constraint constraint_name ]
     foreign key (column_name[, ...])
       references ref_table [(ref_col[, ...])] ]
 )
```

Here a salesdetail table is created that references two tables, titles and sales. Note that the titles reference is a column-level constraint on the title_id column, but the sales reference is a table-level constraint, because the foreign key consists of two columns, stor_id and ord_num:

```
create table salesdetail
 (stor_id char(6),
  ord_num char(10),
  title_id tid
     constraint tid_fk_constraint
     references titles (title_id),
  qty int,
  discount real,
  constraint sales_fk_constraint
     foreign key (stor_id, ord_num)
     references sales (stor_id, ord_num)
 )
```

Constraint Notes

- Reference constraints currently are restrictive only. Tables named in a references statement cannot have rows deleted if existing rows in the referencing table match the primary key. Primary key columns can't be updated if they are referenced by a reference constraint and there are matching foreign key entries in the referencing table.

■ Inserts or updates of foreign key values into a referencing table are allowed if the value of the new foreign key entry does not exist in the primary key column of the referenced table. No reference checks are performed when primary keys are inserted.

■ Tables referenced in reference constraints must have a primary key constraint defined on the referenced columns or a unique index—via a unique constraint or create index statement. If you do not provide the referenced column names in a reference constraint, there must be a primary key constraint on the appropriate columns in the referenced table.

■ The datatypes of the referencing table columns must exactly match the datatypes of the referenced table columns.

■ Constraint names must be unique within the current database. If the constraint name isn't supplied, SQL Server generates a unique system-generated name. (Note that the automatic names aren't guaranteed to be consistent if you create the same table on several different servers.)

■ To reference a table you do not own, you must have references permission on the table. (This was new in SQL Server Version 6.0.)

A table can include a reference constraint on itself. A referenced table cannot be dropped until the referencing table or reference constraint is dropped. Tables referenced in constraints must exist. If tables are to cross-reference one another, use alter table to add a reference after the tables have been created, or use the create schema command.

Modifying Constraints

You can add and drop primary and foreign key constraints by using alter table:

```
alter table table_name add        [constraint constraint_name ]
    { primary_key [ clustered ¦ nonclustered ]
        ( col_name [, ...] ) }
    ¦ foreign key (col [, ...])
        references ref_table [(ref_col [, ...])] }

alter table table_name
    drop constraint constraint_name
```

This example adds a primary key constraint to the publishers table and automatically creates a unique, clustered index on pub_id. Even though the primary key is a single column, this is considered a table-level constraint because it was added at the table level using an alter table statement:

```
alter table publishers
    add constraint pub_pk_constraint
        primary key (pub_id)
```

This `alter table` statement adds a foreign key constraint to the `titles` table, referencing the primary key established in the prior example. No rows can be added to `titles` if a corresponding `pub_id` cannot be found in the `publishers` table:

```
alter table titles
     add constraint pub_fk_constraint
          foreign key (pub_id)
          references publishers (pub_id)
```

The foreign key constraint on the `titles` table has been dropped, and the restrictions on the table are lifted:

```
alter table titles
     drop constraint pub_fk_constraint
```

Adding Constraints

To add a constraint to an existing table, use the `alter table` statement. All new constraints are defined as table-level constraints; column-level constraints can be created only at table or column creation time:

```
alter table table_name add
     [constraint constraint_name ]
     { {unique ¦ primary_key }
          [ clustered ¦ nonclustered ]
          ( col_name [, ...] )
          ¦ check (search_condition) }
```

Here a check constraint is added to the `prices` table, requiring `price` to be greater than zero:

```
/* add a table level check constraint: prices > 0
** note that constraint is table-level,
** but only checks a single column */
alter table prices add
     constraint price_chk
     check (price > $0)
```

As with any object, to modify a constraint, you must drop and re-create it.

Removing Constraints

To remove a constraint from a table, use the `alter table` command:

```
alter table table_name drop
     constraint constraint_name

/* remove the item_code constraint */
alter table prices
     drop constraint price_chk
```

For information on the constraints on a table, use `sp_helpconstraint`:

```
sp_helpconstraint publishers
Object Name
_____
publishers
( 0 rows affected)
```

```
constraint_type              constraint_name              constraint_keys
_____        _____      _____
PRIMARY KEY (clustered)      UPKCL_pubind                 pub_id
CHECK on column pub_id       CK__publisher__pub_i__089551D8  (pub_id = '1756'
                             or (pub_id = '1622' or (pub_id = '0877'
                             or (pub_id = '0736' or (pub_id = '1389'))))
                             or (pub_id like '99[0-9][0-9]'))
DEFAULT on column country    DF__publisher__count__09897611 ('USA')

Table is referenced by
_____
pubs.dbo.titles: FK__titles__pub_id__0E4E2B2E
pubs.dbo.employee: FK__employee__pub_id__2FAF1EF9
pubs.dbo.pub_info: FK__pub_info__pub_id__3567F84F
```

Managing Constraints with SQL Enterprise Manager

SQL Enterprise Manager, through the Manage Tables dialog box, enables you to define, manage, and remove constraint definitions graphically and to view constraint information. By selecting the Advanced Features button in the Manage Tables dialog box, you can extend the dialog box to show four different constraint types: primary keys, foreign keys, checks, and unique constraints (see Figure 6.20).

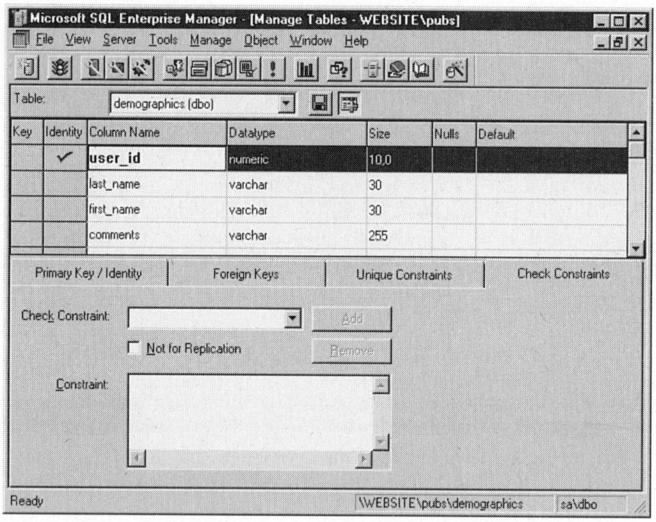

FIGURE 6.20.

SQL Enterprise Manager makes constraint management easier by presenting the domain and reference constraints graphically for a given table in the Manage Tables dialog box.

When you are defining primary-key constraints, remember that the primary key requires a unique index in order to work. Therefore, the primary key represents the unique row identifier for each row in a table. If you are defining primary keys that are to be referenced by other tables, make sure that you are defining foreign keys on those other tables.

When you define foreign-key constraints, remember that you are working from the current table, and that it holds *foreign key records that relate to a different primary key table.* For example, the `titles` table in the `pubs` database serves as a primary-key table for a relationship with the `titleauthor` table. However, the `titles` table is also a foreign-key table in relation to the `publishers` table. As a result, to establish the proper key relationships, you have to create a primary key on the `publishers` table, and then create a foreign key on the `titles` table. You also have to create a primary key on the `titles` table and then a foreign key on the `titleauthor` table that referenced `titles`. Understanding proper key-creation order can prevent many headaches when dealing with large numbers of table relationships!

When defining unique and check constraints, you need worry only about the current table with which you are working. Because these two constraint types enforce domain integrity (the valid values possible for a column or set of columns), you don't need to worry about creation order.

All the information about constraints, including their creation, modification, and configuration, can be seen through this dialog box. Pieces of the information presented in the dialog box are retrieved by using the very same stored procedures described previously, so understanding both can give you a useful toolkit—preventing your dependence on an otherwise very graceful utility.

Guidelines on Constraints

- Rules and check constraints both enforce domains.

- Tables can have both rules and check constraints. The set of allowable values will be the intersection of the rules and check constraints. Constraints enable you to define data integrity requirements as part of a table creation statement. Table-level check constraints can access other columns in the table.

- Using datatypes with rules and defaults, you can manage the data integrity requirements of many columns centrally, through a single mechanism.

- Constraint names must follow SQL Server object naming conventions, if named. If you do not name your constraint, it will be named for you:

  - `tablename_colname_uniquenumber` for column constraint

  - `tablename_uniquenumber` for table-level constraint

- For ease of maintenance, it is recommended that you explicitly name constraints.

Comparing Data Integrity Methods

Rules, defaults, and indexes are T-SQL extensions to the ANSI-89 SQL standard. Rules and defaults are reusable database objects and can be bound to many datatypes or columns. User-defined datatypes can simplify maintenance of rules and defaults for common columns and datatypes. Indexes can be created on columns other than primary key and unique columns to improve query performance.

Constraints

Constraints are ANSI-89 SQL-compliant. They are specific to the table in which they are defined. Check constraints can perform multi-column checks within a table. Because they are stored in the table definition, this documents data integrity checks within the table. Constraints also enable display of custom error messages when the constraint is violated.

Keys

SQL Server enables the definition of logical keys for a database design within the database. The key definitions are for documentation purposes only. The server does not use these for any purpose whatsoever. (As a result, the discussion here will be short.) Their only practical application is that some applications (for example, APT-Forms) use the key information to help define join candidates between tables within the application. These differ from constraints (which enforce referential integrity) and indexes (which enforce uniqueness—for example, of primary keys).

Do not confuse keys with indexes. Keys are logical entities, which have meaning to logical database designers. Indexes are physical database objects, whose purpose is performance:

Key Type	Description
Primary key	Unique row identifier
Foreign key	Primary key from another table, typically used for joins
Common key	Usually an alternate, shorter primary key, used for joins

Use these stored procedures to identify keys in your tables:

```
sp_primarykey table_name, col1 [, col2, ...]

sp_foreignkey table_name, pk_table_name,
    col1 [, col2, ...]

sp_commonkey table1_name, table2_name,
    col1a, col2a [, col1b, col2b , ...]

sp_helpkey table_name
```

Which One Should You Use?

Which one should you use? As with all things that are fairly complex, the simple answer is "it depends." There are some important distinctions. First, constraints have proven to be consistently faster than T-SQL data validation objects such as rules and defaults. The reason for this is that constraint-based validation of data happens as a code path within the SQL Server executable, and data-validation object processes require fetches from disk to read the validation object. For example, if you establish a check constraint and a rule on a column, the check constraint is always faster.

Why? Because the constraint is part of the SQL Server executable, meaning that its instructions are always in working memory. With a rule, the instructions for validating data are out in the disk subsystem, or, at best, reside in cache. Either way, instead of simply jumping to the code path, SQL Server must search for the resolved rule, execute the rule's instructions, and process the results. Because this involves reads to cache or disk, the process is inherently less efficient than using a check constraint. This principle also holds true for default constraints. As a general rule, constraints are always faster than the equivalent T-SQL data validation object.

In the case of referential integrity constraints, there are some other issues to consider. As of Version 6.5, SQL Server is only base-level ANSI 92-compliant. (The CASCADE option was announced with the early releases but did not make it into the final shipped product.) As a result, its referential integrity features support "restrict-only" operations. Therefore, if you have orders that you want deleted from the orders table whenever the corresponding customer is deleted, constraints do not work. Constraints work only where the goal is to *prevent* any multi-table operations. SQL Server will not *cascade* any multi-table operations.

In order to implement cascading multi-table operations, you must still write triggers using Transact-SQL coding. Creating triggers, particularly referential-integrity triggers, is discussed in Chapter 8 on SQL Server Programming Objects. Until SQL Server's ANSI 92 compliance is expanded to support declarative referential integrity with cascade options, triggers are your only choice for implementing cascading RI functions at the database level.

The issue of portability is important for some shops, as well. In areas where multiple relational databases are used, the ability to move from one server platform to another quickly is a basic objective. As a result, some shops insist on ANSI 92 SQL compatibility for data definition language. In such cases, your only choice is to use ANSI constraints, because SQL Server data validation objects are, by definition, proprietary enhancements to the ANSI 89 SQL standard. They do not work on any other server platform.

In the end, the issues boil down to functionality, performance, and portability. Based on the requirements of your applications, deciding on constraints versus T-SQL objects breaks down along these lines. If one doesn't work, the other probably will.

Summary

This chapter explores the creation and use of several database objects, all of which center on the manipulation and control of user data in tables. You could probably start designing a database with what you know right now, but there is a great deal more to learn about how these tables and indexes are physically stored in the server, what kinds of database design choices you need to make to provide the best select versus update performance, how SQL Server really uses indexes, and so forth. Proper database design and implementation is a major factor in the long-term performance and usefulness of a system, and it turns out to be fairly difficult to change the design of a production system. So keep reading!

In Chapter 7, "Transact-SQL Programming Constructs," you learn about the extensions to the basic SQL language that make up Transact-SQL. These extensions are the building blocks for stored procedures and triggers, which you need to understand to begin designing effective databases for SQL Server.

Transact-SQL Programming Constructs

7

What's New in SQL Server 6.5?

With this version of SQL Server, Microsoft continues to enhance and modify the programming structures in SQL Server to provide better integration with Windows NT and more complete adherence to the evolving ANSI SQL standards.

Here is a quick list of the changes to programming structures. Details on each of these changes can be found in place in the text:

- `raiserror` has changed to use different default error numbers based on the severity of the error. Prior to this release, all ad hoc errors used message number 50000. With this release, only ad hoc errors with severity greater than 10 use 50000; others use message number 0.

- Cursor `fetch` statements can use variables with both absolute and relative `fetch` statements.

- Use the `update` statement to store values in local variables at the same time that you are updating rows in a table.

Extensions to ANSI SQL

Many books discuss the relative merits of the ANSI standard SQL language, not the least of which is the one published by ANSI. SQL Server supports 98 to 100 percent of the ANSI standard, but the ANSI standard doesn't really provide the capability of doing anything other than querying the database. From the start, SQL Server has sought to provide a more complete service than a simple query-and-result engine. The developers understood that SQL Server could provide methods of enforcing *business rules* related to the data.

For example, the relational model calls for relational database management systems (RDBMSs) to enforce datatype integrity within a column. If a user tries to insert numeric data in a column defined for character data, the system should prevent it. SQL Server extends the definition of data integrity to include data characteristics specific to the business application. For example, a two-character `state` column can check not only that the value is a character value (not a number or date), but also that the value passed is a legitimate abbreviation for a state.

Earlier chapters describe how SQL Server allows you to define rules, constraints, and defaults to enforce business rules; however, many business rules are more complex than can be enforced through these declarative constructs. SQL Server provides extensions to the ANSI standard for things such as extended functions and programming constructs. These extensions to the standard SQL are called *Transact-SQL* (*T-SQL*).

This section covers the following topics:

- Functions: built-in, mathematical, string, and date manipulation
- Extensions to insert, update, and delete

■ Programming constructs (if, while, and so forth)

■ Cursors

SQL Server Functions

ANSI-89 SQL allows standard arithmetic operators (+, −, *, /, and ^) in both select and data modification statements.

Following are some examples of how these operators work. In this example, the third column is derived from the price column. For each row, SQL Server divides the value of price by 10.

```
/* display 10% of each price */
select title, price, price / 10
    from titles
```

title	price	
The Busy Executive's Database Guide	19.99	2.00
Cooking with Computers: Surreptitious Balance Sheets	11.95	1.20
You Can Combat Computer Stress!	2.99	0.30
Straight Talk About Computers	19.99	2.00
Silicon Valley Gastronomic Treats	19.99	2.00
The Gourmet Microwave	2.99	0.30
The Psychology of Computer Cooking		
But Is It User Friendly?	22.95	2.30
Secrets of Silicon Valley	20.00	2.00
Onions, Leeks, and Garlic: Cooking Secrets of the Mediterranean	20.95	2.10
Fifty Years in Buckingham Palace Kitchens	11.95	1.20
Sushi, Anyone?	14.99	1.50

(18 rows affected)

You can also use an arithmetic operator in the set clause of an update statement. Here SQL Server increases each price by 10 percent by evaluating the expression once per row:

```
/* use an operator in an update statement */
update titles
    set price = price * 1.1
    where type = "business"
```

The concatenation operator enables you to connect multiple string expressions into a single column. Again, the result of the concatenation is calculated once per row:

```
/* perform concatenation with "+" */
select location = city + ', ' + state
    from publishers
```

```
location
____ _____ ____
Boston, MA
Washington, DC
Berkeley, CA
Chicago, IL
Dallas, TX
München,
New York, NY
Paris,
( 8 rows affected)
```

SQL Server data functions provide advanced data manipulation, including the following:

- String functions
- Math functions
- Date functions
- System functions

String Functions

Table 7.1 lists the SQL Server string functions, which can be used as part of any character expression. These functions enable manipulation, parsing, and conversion of character strings.

Table 7.1. SQL Server string functions.

Function	Definition
Length and Parsing	
datalength(*char_expr*)	Returns the integer # of the characters in *char_expr*, ignoring any trailing spaces
substring (*expression, start, length*)	Returns part of the string
right (*char_expr, int_expr*)	Returns *int_expr* characters from the right of *char_expr*
Basic String Manipulation	
upper (*char_expr*)	Converts *char_expr* to uppercase
lower (*char_expr*)	Converts *char_expr* to lowercase
space (*int_expr*)	Generates a string of *int_expr* spaces
replicate (*char_expr, int_expr*)	Repeats *char_expr, int_expr* times
stuff (*char_expr1, start, length, char_expr2*)	Replaces *length* characters from *expr1* at *start* with *expr2*
reverse (*char_expr*)	Reverses text in *char_expr*
ltrim (*char_expr*)	Removes leading spaces
rtrim (*char_expr*)	Removes trailing spaces
Conversions	
ascii (*char_expr*)	Returns the ASCII value of the first character in *char_expr*
char (*int_expr*)	Converts ASCII code to character

Function	Definition
Conversions	
str (*float_expr* [, *length* [, *decimal*]])	Numeric-to-character conversion
soundex (*char_expr*)	Returns the soundex value of *char_expr*
difference (*char_expr1*, *char_expr2*)	Returns the difference between the soundex values of the expressions
In-String Searches	
charindex (*char_expr*, *expression*)	Returns the starting position of the specified *char_expr*, else zero
patindex ("%*pattern*%", *expression*)	Returns the starting position of the specified pattern, else 0

Basic String Manipulation and Parsing

Many of the string manipulation and parsing functions that you may have used in other languages are available in T-SQL. Here are some tips on how to use these functions:

- data_length is useful for determining the length of a variable-length string. With a fixed-length string (char datatype), it always returns the defined length of the column. To determine the actual length of the string (without padding):

```
select datalength(rtrim(column-name))
from table-name
```

- right returns the rightmost *n* characters, but there is no "left" function; to retrieve the leftmost positions, use the substring function and start in position 1.

- upper and lower are case conversions, which are useful for text comparisons.

> **WARNING**
>
> Don't use these conversion functions in a where clause without any other conditions. SQL Server can't use an index to resolve a function and so must scan the table. For more on this topic, see Chapter 19, "Application Design for Performance."

soundex

The `soundex` function is useful in determining whether character strings are likely to sound similar. The function returns a value representing the first letter and each of the significant consonant sounds, as in this example:

```
select soundex('marsupial')

--
M621
( 1 row affected)
```

In this example, the `soundex` value consists of the initial m followed by a number for each of the next three consonants (r, s, and p). Vowels, semivowels, and duplicated letters are ignored, and if the word has fewer than four useful sounds, the value is padded with zeros.

The idea is that if two strings have the same `soundex` value, they are likely to sound similar. For example, look at the results from this query:

```
select name, "soundex" = soundex(name)
from smith_table
```

name	soundex
Smith	S530
Smyth	S530
Smithe	S530
Smythe	S530
Smithson	S532
Smithsonian	S532
Smithers	S536
Smothers	S536

Properly used, the `soundex` function provides the capacity to search for certain values that sound similar but are spelled differently. The problem is that a `where` clause based on a `soundex` function (and the related `difference`) will not be able to make use of an index:

```
select id, name
from smith_table
where soundex(name) = soundex("Smythe")
```

This query must scan the table, *even if there is an index on the* name *column*, because the query processor can't optimize the query. You can actually store `soundex` values in a table and then index those values, if you need to search for them:

```
insert smith_table (name, sdx)
values ("Smythe", soundex("Smythe"))

select id, name
from smith_table
where sdx = soundex("Smythe")
```

In this case, SQL Server can use an index on the sdx table, resolving the one constant `soundex` expression before starting the search.

There are substantial limitations with `soundex` and `difference`, mostly because of the oddities of English spelling. `soundex` will fail to match the names *Klein* and *Cline* and will consider the word *Phone* an exact match with *Pen* but not *Fan*. For these reasons, the `soundex`-based functions should be used cautiously in applications.

Searching Within Strings with `charindex`

Use the `charindex` function to search for matching strings within strings. `charindex` returns the position of the first match. This query determines the position of the first comma in the string:

```
select charindex (",", "red, white, blue") "First Comma Location"

First Comma Location
- - - - - - - - - - -
4
```

> **NOTE**
>
> If you need to look for rows containing matching character strings, don't use `charindex`. Instead, use the `like` operator with a pattern (see the next section, "Wildcards").

Wildcards

SQL Server provides *wildcards* to enable pattern matching in text searches. This is roughly like the matching you use in the Windows Explorer to look for a missing file. Table 7.2 lists the SQL Server wildcards used with the `like` operator.

Table 7.2. SQL Server wildcards.

Wildcard	Description
%	Matches any quantity of characters, or no characters
_	(Underscore) Matches any single character (a place holder)
[ ]	Specifies a range of valid characters, or an "OR" condition (this is a SQL Server extension)

Within the brackets, a couple of operators are available. The caret (^) in the first position means NOT, so the pattern `[YyNn]` means "capital or lowercase Y or N" versus `[^YyNn]`, which means "any character *except* capital or lowercase Y or N."

The hyphen (-) indicates any character within a range, so the pattern [AC] means "capital A or C", but [A-C] means "any capital between A and C."

Here are some samples of the use of the bracket, along with the values it would match. *Remember that the [ ] represents a single character in the string.*

```
[ABG]          /* matches "A" or "B" or "G" */
[A-CE-G]       /* matches "A", "B", "C", "E", "F", "G" */
[^ABG]         /* matches any except "A", "B", "G" */
[^A-C]         /* matches any except "A", "B", "C" */
```

WARNING

It is *very* important to use wildcards with the like operator rather than =.

```
/* this will work */
select * from authors
     where au_lname like "[Ss]mith%"
/* this will not work as expected! */
select * from authors
     where au_lname = "[Ss]mith%"
```

In the first example, the server returns rows with values such as Smith, smith, Smithers, and Smithsonian. In the last example, the server is being instructed to look for an author whose last name is [Ss]mith%. You would not expect any rows to be returned.

The escape Clause

To include wildcard characters as literals in a search string, use an escape character.

SQL Server, by default, uses the square brackets ([ ]) to escape a wildcard, which means that you want to use the wildcard as a literal character. In this example, the brackets enclose the percent sign, which otherwise behaves as a wildcard.

```
/* find a string containing the value 20% */
select * from test_tab
     where description like "%20[%]%"
```

The ANSI-89 SQL Standard defines the escape clause to specify an escape character:

```
like char_expression escape "escape_character"
```

In a pattern, the escape character restores the wildcard to its natural meaning as a character. Here, the number sign allows the following percent sign to match with the percent sign character appearing in the description column:

```
/* find a string containing the value 20% */
select * from test_tab
     where description like "%20#%%" escape "#"
```

An escape character retains its special meaning inside square brackets (unlike wildcard characters). It's valid only within its `like` predicate and doesn't affect other `like` predicates in the same statement. Finally, it affects only the single character following it.

Using Wildcards with `patindex`

The `patindex` function enables you to search for patterns, rather than exact matches within strings. `patindex` uses the same wildcards as the `like` operator. Here's an example of `patindex`, similar to the `charindex` example above:

```
select patindex ("%[,. !]%", "red, white, blue") "First Punctuation"

First Punctuation
— — — — — — —
4
```

Note that the pattern as a whole must match the string, so it's typical to include your search string in percent signs (%). The location of the first matching non-wildcard character is reported by the query.

String Function Examples

In this example, you build a name column from two columns, the last name column and the first name column, using the concatenation operator, +:

```
select au_lname + "," + au_fname
    from authors

— — — — — — — — — — — — — — — — — — — — — — — — — —
White,Johnson
Green,Marjorie
Carson,Cheryl
O'Leary,Michael
Straight,Dean
Smith,Meander
Bennet,Abraham
Dull,Ann
Gringlesby,Burt
Locksley,Charlene
Greene,Morningstar
Blotchet-Halls,Reginald
Yokomoto,Akiko
del Castillo,Innes
DeFrance,Michel
Stringer,Dirk
MacFeather,Stearns
Karsen,Livia
Panteley,Sylvia
Hunter,Sheryl
McBadden,Heather
Ringer,Anne
Ringer,Albert
( 23 rows affected)
```

This example finds all rows where the last name has an identical soundex value to the name Green:

```
select au_id, au_lname
    from authors
    where difference (au_lname, "Green") = 4

au_id       au_lname
_ _ _ _ _   _ _ _ _ _ _ _ _ _ _ _ _ _ _ _ _ _ _
213-46-8915 Green
527-72-3246 Greene
```

Notice that you get the same results from this query:

```
select *
    from authors
    where soundex (au_lname) = soundex ("Green")
```

This update statement uses the stuff function to replace the fourth character in each phone number with a hyphen (–):

```
/* replace characters within a string */
update authors
    set phone = stuff(phone, 4, 1, "-")
```

Functions can be embedded, as in this example, which shows the difference in length between a fixed-length column and one that has been right-trimmed of trailing blanks:

```
select distinct type, datalength(type), datalength(rtrim(type))
    from titles

type
_ _ _ _ _   _ _ _ _   _ _ _ _ _
UNDECIDED    12        9
business     12        8
mod_cook     12        8
popular_comp 12        12
psychology   12        10
trad_cook    12        9
```

This example displays all titles containing the word Computer, using the like operator and wildcards to identify many rows:

```
select title
    from titles
    where title like "%Computer%"

title
_ _ _ _ _ _ _ _ _ _ _ _ _ _ _ _ _ _ _ _ _ _ _ _ _ _ _ _ _ _ _
Computer Phobic AND Non-Phobic Individuals: Behavior Variations
Cooking with Computers: Surreptitious Balance Sheets
Straight Talk About Computers
The Psychology of Computer Cooking
You Can Combat Computer Stress!
```

Mathematical Functions

SQL Server performs standard arithmetic operations using normal precedence:

- Functions and parentheses are evaluated first.
- Next, multiplication, division, and exponents.
- Finally, addition, subtraction, and logical operations.

All operations proceed from left to right.

> **NOTE**
>
> SQL Server doesn't include a built-in arithmetic operator for exponents. Instead, exponents are derived with the `power()` function. For example, to raise 2 to the 12th power, use:
>
> ```
> select power(2, 12)
> ```
>
> Be careful when using the `power()` function for advanced work. The result of the `power()` function is of the same datatype as the first parameter passed. For example, 2 to the [1/2] power should be the square root of 2 or 1.414... If you execute this `select` statement, the datatype of the first parameter is `numeric` with a scale of 0 (no decimal places):
>
> ```
> select power(2., .5)
> ```
>
> SQL Server returns the value 1. As you add additional decimal places to the first parameter, you get increasing accuracy:
>
> ```
> select power(2.000000000, .5)
> ```
>
> The result is 1.414213562. It might be safest to declare a variable and use the variable in the function, like this:
>
> ```
> declare @base numeric (14, 9)
> select @base = 2
> select power(@base, .5)
> ```
>
> This returns the same result, with nine decimal digits.

SQL Server also supports the standard trigonometric functions and a number of other useful ones. Table 7.3 lists the SQL Server mathematical functions.

Table 7.3. SQL Server mathematical functions.

Function	Description
abs (*numeric_expr*)	Absolute value of the specified value
ceiling (*numeric_expr*)	Smallest integer greater than or equal to the specified value
exp (*float_expr*)	Exponential value of the specified value
floor (*numeric_expr*)	Largest integer less than or equal to the specified value
pi ()	Returns the constant value of 3.1415926...
power (*numeric_expr,power*)	Returns the value of *numeric_expr* to the power of *power*
rand ([*int_expr*])	Returns a random float number between 0 and 1, optionally using *int_expr* as a seed
round (*numeric_expr, int_expr*)	Rounds off a numeric expression to the precision specified in *int_expr*
sign (*int_expr*)	Returns the positive (+1), zero (0), or negative (–1)
sqrt (*float_expr*)	Returns the square root of the specified value

WARNING

The randomizer function needs a random seed in order to provide a random value.

Date Functions

SQL Server includes date functions to perform date parsing and date arithmetic (see Table 7.4).

Table 7.4. SQL Server date functions.

Function	Description
getdate ( )	Returns the current system date and time
datename(*datepart, date_expr*)	Returns the specified part of *date_expr* value as a string, converted to a name (for example, June) if appropriate
datepart(*datepart, date_expr*)	Returns the specified part of the *date_expr* value as an integer

Function	Description
`datediff(datepart, date_expr1, date_expr2)`	Returns `date_expr2` minus `date_expr1`, as measured by the specified `datepart`
`dateadd(datepart, number, date_expr)`	Returns the date produced by adding the `number` of the specified `datepart` to `date_expr`

Date Parts

Date parts are used in conjunction with the date functions to specify an element of a date value for parsing or date arithmetic. (See Table 7.5.) Note that the minimum value for `year` is `1753`. For an explanation of why, see Chapter 5, "Transact-SQL Datatypes," in the section titled "`datetime` versus `smalldatetime`."

Table 7.5. SQL Server date parts.

Date Part	Abbreviation	Value Range (in `datepart`)
year	yy	1753-9999
quarter	qq	1-4
month	mm	1-12
dayofyear	dy	1-366
day	dd	1-31
week	wk	1-54
weekday	dw	1-7 (1=Sunday)
hour	hh	0-23
minute	mi	0-59
second	ss	0-59
millisecond	ms	0-999

Here are some examples of how to use the date functions. Use the `getdate()` function to return the current SQL Server date and time:

```
/* what is the current date and time */
select getdate()
```

```
- - - - - - - - - - - - - -
Jul 14 1996 10:39AM
```

> **NOTE**
>
> When you return a datetime value to the client using select, it's automatically converted to a formatted character string in the format Mmm dd yyyy hh:mmAM. This can sometimes prevent you from realizing that the getdate and dateadd functions return datetime or smalldatetime values.

Here's a query that uses the datediff function to determine how old unpaid invoices are:

```
/* how old are unpaid invoices? */
select invoice_no,
    datediff (dd, date_shipped, getdate()) "invoice aging"
    from invoices
    where balance_due > 0
```

To get a positive value from datediff, state the earlier date first (date_shipped is prior to today). Also, notice that we have requested the difference in number of days (dd) in the invoice aging column.

In this query, the datename function returns the *name* of the month (mm) part of the publication date:

```
/* what month were these books published? */
select title, datename ( mm, pubdate )
    from titles

title
_ _ _ _ _ _ _ _ _ _ _ _ _ _ _ _ _ _ _ _ _ _ _ _ _ _ _ _ _ _ _  _ _ _
The Busy Executive's Database Guide                            June
Cooking with Computers: Surreptitious Balance Sheets           June
You Can Combat Computer Stress!                                June
Straight Talk About Computers                                  June
Silicon Valley Gastronomic Treats                              June
The Gourmet Microwave                                          June
...
Emotional Security: A New Algorithm                            June
Onions, Leeks, and Garlic: Cooking Secrets of the Mediterranean October
Fifty Years in Buckingham Palace Kitchens                      June
Sushi, Anyone?                                                 June
```

> **TIP**
>
> Avoid sorting on datename, or you'll discover that the first month of the year is April and the first day of the week is Friday!

convert

The convert function is used to change data from one type to another when SQL Server can't implicitly understand a conversion (for example, float to real to integer are all dynamically converted for comparison purposes). The syntax of the convert function is similar to the casting seen in C and C++:

```
convert (datatype [(length)], expression)
```

In this example, the convert function changes advance (a money column) to a character string so that it can be concatenated to a string:

```
/* return one column of data ...the conversion is
** required to allow concatenation of literal
** string with a numeric */

select "Advance = "
     + convert (char(12), advance)
from titles


_ _ _ _ _ _ _ _ _ _
Advance =      5000.00
Advance =      5000.00
Advance =      10125.00
Advance =      5000.00
...
Advance =      7000.00
Advance =      4000.00
Advance =      8000.00
```

SQL Server makes any reasonable conversion; if you choose an unreasonable conversion, you get an error message, as in this query, which attempts to use a conversion function to get a Julian date:

```
/* convert pubdate to a julian integer value?  Nope! */
select pubdate, convert (int, pubdate) AS "julian date"
from titles

Msg 529, Level 16, State 1
Explicit conversion from datatype 'datetime' to 'int'
is currently unimplemented.
```

Date Conversions

A special version of the convert function enables datetime and smalldatetime values to be converted to character types. The syntax of this version of the convert function includes a third parameter, *format*:

```
convert (datatype [(length)], expression, format)
```

The *format* parameter tells SQL Server which date format to provide in the converted string. Table 7.6 lists the SQL Server date formats.

Table 7.6. SQL Server date formats available with the convert function.

Without Century	With Century	Format of Date in Converted String
	0 or 100	mon dd yyyy hh:miAM (or PM)
1	101	mm/dd/yy
2	102	yy.mm.dd
3	103	dd/mm/yy
4	104	dd.mm.yy
5	105	dd-mm-yy
6	106	dd mon yy
7	107	mon dd, yy
8	108	hh:mi:ss
	9 or 109	mon dd, yyyy hh:mi:ss:mmmAM (or PM)
10	110	mm-dd-yy
11	111	yy/mm/dd
12	112	yymmdd

Using the convert function, you can display dates in almost any format without resorting to explicit string manipulation.

```
/* return pubdate in mon dd, yyyy format*/
select "Pubdate" = convert (char(12), pubdate, 107)
     from titles

Pubdate
– – – – – –
Jun 12, 1991
Jun 09, 1991
Jun 30, 1991
...
Jun 12, 1991
Jun 12, 1991
( 18 rows affected)
```

> **NOTE**
>
> This is probably a good time to make certain that you understand how the convert function is used, and how it varies from the dateformat set option. convert is used to display SQL Server information in a specific format. You typically won't store converted date information, and the convert function certainly won't affect how the data is *stored* or how it is *displayed by default.* The scope of this command is only the current query.

It may be useful to return date information converted into a specific format because your front end lacks useful date parsing capabilities, or can't interact with the encoded `datetime` format used by the server and passed as part of the data stream.

There's also a set option that defines the *default date format* for passing date values to the SQL Server:

```
set dateformat format
```

The `format` used in this statement defines the order in which date information is passed when all date values are numeric. This script demonstrates the use of the `dateformat` option. (Each go statement separates a batch from the previous and next batches to allow the statements to be parsed after the settings have changed. The use of go is explained in more detail a little later in this chapter.)

```
create table dates
(dtfmt char(3), dt datetime)
go
set dateformat mdy
go
insert dates (dtfmt, dt) values ("mdy", "1/2/3")
go
set dateformat dmy
go
insert dates (dtfmt, dt) values ("dmy", "1/2/3")
go
set dateformat ymd
go
insert dates (dtfmt, dt) values ("ymd", "1/2/3")
go
select dtfmt, dt, convert(char(8), dt, 1)
from dates
go
```

The script creates a table, inserts one row using each of three `dateformat` values, and displays how the server interpreted the numeric value of each. Here's the output from the `select` statement:

```
dtfmt dt
__ _____ _____
mdy   Jan 2 2003 12:00AM       01/02/03
dmy   Feb 1 2003 12:00AM       02/01/03
ymd   Feb 3 2001 12:00AM       02/03/01
```

In the `select` statement, the `convert` function is used to display the data in a specific format *for that specific* `select` *operation*. The `dateformat` option is used to provide a method of interpreting date values sent from the client.

(Also note that the `language` server configuration setting and user set option can also affect the default `dateformat`.)

System Functions

System functions are used to display information about the SQL Server, database, or user. These functions tend to be used a lot by programmers and DBAs, but not very often by users. System functions with optional parameters return values for the current user, database, and process if a parameter isn't specified. System functions enable quick conversion of system and object information without writing several join clauses. They are used heavily in system stored procedures. Table 7.7 lists the SQL Server system functions.

Table 7.7. SQL Server system functions.

Function	*Returns*
Access and Security Information	
host_id ( )	Current host process ID number of the client process
host_name ( )	Current host computer name of the client process
suser_id (["*login_name*"])	User's SQL Server ID number
suser_name ([*server_user_id*])	User's SQL Server login name
user_id (["*name_in_db*"])	User's ID number in the database
user_name ([*user_id*])	User's name in the database
user	User's name in the database
show_role()	Current active roles for the user
Database and Object Information	
db_id (["*db_name*"])	Database ID number
db_name ([*db_id*])	Database name
object_id ("*objname*")	Database object ID number
object_name (*obj_id*)	Database object name
col_name (*obj_id*,*col_id*)	Column name of the object
col_length ("*objname*", "*colname*")	Length of the column
index_col ("*objname*", *index_id*, *key #*)	Indexed column name
valid_name (*char_expr*)	Returns 0 if *char_expr* isn't a valid identifier
Data Information	
datalength (*expression*)	Returns the length of *expression* in bytes

In this example, the user retrieves a value for the ID of the current user from the sysusers table within the database. Many system functions return the current value when no parameters are specified:

```
/* return current user ID*/
select user_id ()

- - -
1
```

This query returns the name of the login whose ID is 1 from the master..syslogins table:

```
/* return login name of the login whose ID is 1 */
select suser_name (1)

- - - - - - - - - - - - - -
sa
```

> **NOTE**
>
> The system user ID (suser_id) of the sa is always 1 because sa is the first login added to the syslogins table during installation.
>
> Likewise, the user ID (user_id) dbo is always user 1 (user_name "dbo") in every database because the dbo is the first user added to the sysusers table during database creation.

The object_name and object_id functions convert id values in the sysobjects table to names and vice versa. In this example, the user determines the name of an object whose ID is known:

```
/* Return name of the object specified by the ID */
select object_name (112003430)


- - - - - - - - - - - - - -
publishers
```

Here's another example of a system function used to convert a table name to an ID:

```
/* Return list of all indexes for titles table */
select name from sysindexes
    where id = object_id("titles")

name
- - - - - - - - - - - -
UPKCL_titleidind
titleind
```

> **TIP**
>
> This example could also be written like this:
>
> ```
> select i.name
> from sysindexes i, sysobjects o
> where i.id = o.id
> and o.name = "titles"
> ```
>
> Aside from being more verbose (especially when involved in a more elaborate join), explicit `select` operations from system tables are demonstrably slower than system functions. Use the system functions rather than direct accesses against the system tables to get good performance and keep your SQL simple.

compute and compute ... by

The `compute` and `compute ... by` keywords enable you to prepare both detail and summary information in a single pass of the table.

compute

A `compute` clause reports overall aggregate values for a result set. The `compute` clause in this example requests an overall highest price to be listed after the list of all prices:

```
/*list titles and prices, show overall max price*/
select title, price
    from titles
    compute max(price)
```

```
title                                                           price
_____   _ __
The Busy Executive's Database Guide                             19.99
Cooking with Computers: Surreptitious Balance Sheets            11.95
You Can Combat Computer Stress!                                 2.99
Straight Talk About Computers                                   19.99
Silicon Valley Gastronomic Treats                               19.99
The Gourmet Microwave                                           2.99
The Psychology of Computer Cooking
But Is It User Friendly?                                        22.95
Secrets of Silicon Valley                                       20.00
Net Etiquette
Computer Phobic AND Non-Phobic Individuals: Behavior Variations 21.59
Is Anger the Enemy?                                             10.95
Life Without Fear                                               7.00
Prolonged Data Deprivation: Four Case Studies                   19.99
Emotional Security: A New Algorithm                             7.99
Onions, Leeks, and Garlic: Cooking Secrets of the Mediterranean 20.95
Fifty Years in Buckingham Palace Kitchens                       11.95
Sushi, Anyone?                                                  14.99
                                                                23
```

The price of the most expensive book is 23 (notice the last line). The format of this output varies from one reporting tool to the next. Some tools (including ISQL) produce a header in the line before the output, but this is completely dependent on the application program. The server merely returns rows marked as compute columns, and it's up to the application to determine a format. Here is what the ISQL output might look like:

```
max

          =========================
                             22.95
```

> **NOTE**
>
> Many organizations don't use compute for a variety of reasons. First, because it isn't ANSI-standard SQL, organizations avoid writing important queries that might need to be modified dramatically to be ported to other database environments. Second, any decent reporting tool will provide all the totaling and subtotaling directly within the report definition, with much more flexibility about the actual handling of the computed values. If you plan to use compute, make sure that you've spent the necessary time testing how your application reads and presents computed values.
>
> Also, take a look at cube and rollup operators (see Chapter 4, "Introduction to Transact-SQL"), which can sometimes provide more useful output than the compute statement.

compute by

A compute by clause displays subtotals within a result set, but not totals. In this example, the server returns both detailed result rows and the maximum price (an aggregate function) for each type (output continues on the following page):

```
/* display type, title and price,
** and show the maximum price for each type */
select type, title, price
from titles
where price > $18
order by type
compute max(price) by type

type          title                                             price
------        ---------------------------------------------     ---
business      The Busy Executive's Database Guide                19.99
business      Straight Talk About Computers                      19.99

                                                                max
                                                                ======
                                                                19.99
```

```
type         title                                         price
------      ----------------------------------------      ----
mod_cook     Silicon Valley Gastronomic Treats             19.99

                                                           max
                                                           ======
                                                           19.99


type         title                                         price
------      ----------------------------------------      ----
popular_comp But Is It User Friendly?                      22.95
popular_comp Secrets of Silicon Valley                     20.00

                                                           max
                                                           ======
                                                           22.95


type         title                                         price
------      ----------------------------------------      ----
psychology   Computer Phobic AND Non-Phobic Individuals: Behavio 21.59
psychology   Prolonged Data Deprivation: Four Case Studies 19.99

                                                           max
                                                           ======
                                                           21.59


type         title                                         price
------      ----------------------------------------      ----
trad_cook    Onions, Leeks, and Garlic: Cooking Secrets of the M 20.95

                                                           max
                                                           ======
                                                           20.95

(13 row(s) affected)
```

> **NOTE**
>
> When you execute a select statement with a compute clause, don't be surprised to see a different *layout* of the results. The compute clause causes results to be returned to the client application in a different format from standard results, and client DB-Library applications use different function calls to unpack compute results. After the data is retrieved, it is anyone's guess as to how the application plans to use it.

compute by columns must match, *in order,* columns in the order by clause. You can specify only a subset of the order by columns. Consider a query containing this order by clause:

```
order by a, b, c
```

The only allowed compute by clauses are the following:

■ compute by a, b, c

■ compute by a, b

■ compute by a

If you try to perform a compute by operation without a corresponding order by clause, the server returns this message:

```
A compute-by item was not found in the order-by list.
All expressions in the compute-by list must also be present in the order-by list
```

To show subtotals and totals, combine compute by and compute in one select statement:

```
/*display details with subtotals and grand totals*/
select pub_id, title_id, ytd_sales
from titles
where price > $18
order by pub_id
compute sum(ytd_sales) by pub_id
compute sum(ytd_sales)
pub_id title_id ytd_sales
--- ---- -----
0736   PS3333   4072

              sum
              ===========
              4072

pub_id title_id ytd_sales
--- ---- -----
0877   MC2222   2032
0877   PS1372   375
0877   TC3218   375

              sum
              ===========
              2782

pub_id title_id ytd_sales
--- ---- -----
1389   BU1032   4095
1389   BU7832   4095
1389   PC1035   8780
1389   PC8888   4095

              sum
              ===========
              21065
              sum
              ===========
              27919

(12 row(s) affected)
```

The final compute example displays the results of a grand total, but doesn't include any subtotals because there's no compute by clause. Note that expressions in a compute or compute by clause must match exactly the corresponding expression in the select list.

```
select type, price, price*2 "Twice the price"
from titles
where type = "business"
compute sum(price), sum(price*2)

type          price                    Twice the price
_ _ _ _ _     _ _ _ _ _ _ _ _ _ _ _    _ _ _ _ _ _ _ _ _ _ _ _

business      19.99                    39.98
business      11.95                    23.90
business      2.99                     5.98
business      19.99                    39.98
              54.92                    110
(5 rows affected)
```

isnull

Sometimes, when calculating aggregates or printing reports to end users, you want to have null values treated as if they have a value. To define that value, use the isnull function to substitute a specified value whenever a null value appears in a column or expression.

Consider an invoices table containing four rows and a column, total_order. The four values of total_order are as follows:

```
total_order
_ _ _ _
100
50
25
(null)
```

The avg function, like all aggregate functions, ignores nulls:

```
/* average of orders excluding nulls */
select avg ( total_order ) "avg"
     from invoices

avg
_ _ _ _
58
```

Using the isnull function, you can force the aggregate function to treat a null value as if it had a specific value *for the current query*. The next two examples substitute the values 0 and 10 for any null values, respectively:

```
/* average of orders using 0 for orders
** that have a null  total */
select avg ( isnull ( total_order, 0 ) ) "avg using 0"
     from invoices

avg using 0
_ _ _ _
43
```

```
/* average of orders using 10 for orders
** that have a null total */
select avg ( isnull ( total_order, 10 ) ) "avg using 10"
     from invoices
```

```
avg using 10
- - - - -
46
```

Use `isnull` whenever you need to force specific behavior for unknown or unavailable values, rather than ignoring the values entirely. Remember that the result of most expressions involving null values is a null value. For example, `11 + null` is `null`. The most unexpected `null` result comes from the `sum` function when the aggregate finds no non-null values in a column:

```
/* sum only null values - the result is null */

select sum(price)
from titles
where price is null
```

You may want to use the `isnull` function to return these aggregate results as zeros:

```
select isnull(sum(price), 0)
from titles
where price is null
```

nullif

SQL Server also provides a `nullif` function that sets a value equal to null if two expressions are equivalent. This is especially useful for evaluating aggregates on columns that have values with a special meaning. Consider a `prices` table containing a `price` column that doesn't permit null values:

```
create table prices
(item int not null,
 price money not null)
```

Certain rows may contain a price of -1, indicating that the item is not priced:

```
insert prices values (1, $10)
insert prices values (2, $25)
insert prices values (3, -$1) -- means no price (nulls not permitted in column)
```

Values of -1 shouldn't be included in averages. To determine the average price, use a null value whenever -1 is found:

```
select avg(price) "incorrect average",
       avg(nullif(price, -1)) "correct average"
from prices
```

```
incorrect average          correct average
- - - - - - - - - - -      - - - - - - - - - - -
11.33                      17.50
```

coalesce

The `coalesce` statement allows you to return the first non-null expression in a list:

```
coalesce (expression1, expression2)
coalesce (expression1, expression2, ..., expressionN)
```

In a table with multiple phone number columns (`workphone` and `homephone`), for example, you can list home phone numbers where they are available, work numbers for all others:

```
select name, homephone, workphone,
     coalesce (homephone, workphone) as "phone number"
from telephones

name       homephone    workphone    phone number
————       ————————     ————————     ————————
Al         (null)       555-9999     555-9999
Joe        555-1234     555-8888     555-1234
Martin     (null)       555-6263     555-6263
```

In the results, note that the `workphone` is displayed wherever the `homephone` is `null`.

Programming Constructs

Transact-SQL provides a set of *programming constructs* (syntactic structures used to write procedural code) to help those writing stored procedures and triggers to write structured, modular code that's resident at the database server. Here are the important syntactic features for writing procedural code:

- Batches
- Comments
- Local and global variables
- Message handling
- Error handling
- `while` loops
- `if...then` loops
- `begin...end` loops

Batches

A *batch* is the entire packet that's passed from the client to the server. A batch can consist of only one SQL statement or it may contain several statements. Statements in a batch are parsed as a group, compiled as a group, and executed as a group. This means that none of the statements in the batch is executed if there are any syntax errors in the batch.

NOTE

If a stored procedure isn't the first statement in a batch, it must be preceded by the `exec` keyword. When a stored procedure is the first statement in the batch, `exec` is optional.

Here are some sample batches; each contains two SQL statements:

```
/* this batch performs two selections */
select * from authors
select * from titles
go

/* this batch binds defaults to several columns at once */
sp_bindefault "my_default", "my_table.col_3"
exec sp_bindefault "my_default", "my_table.col_2"
go

/* this batch sets security on a table */
grant select, insert to mary on mytable
revoke select, insert from mary on mytable(col_3)
go
```

> **NOTE**
>
> Because a batch represents a unit of SQL transmitted to the server, if you're going to separate your batches (which you often will—some tasks require their own batch), you need either to send twice or use some sort of separator that instructs the front end to transmit separate batches. In many tools, this is the keyword go. go *is not* T-SQL. It's an instruction to the front end to transmit to the server everything that precedes go.

Certain application errors are caused by a lack of knowledge about batches. For example, this batch fails to execute because the second statement contains a parsing error:

```
/* a parsing error in the second statement
** prevents the entire batch from running */
insert publishers (pub_id, pub_name)
    values ("1234", "Publisher A")
insert publishers (pub_id, pub_name)
    values ("1235", "Publisher B", "Nashville", "TN") -- too many values!
insert publishers (pub_id, pub_name)
    values ("1234", "Publisher C")
go
```

SQL Server fails to parse this code because there are too many values passed for the number of columns named in the insert statement. None of the insert statements is executed because the error occurs at the parsing stage.

Certain errors occur during execution. When a fatal execution error is encountered, the batch stops processing and only the statements that preceded the error are executed. Most execution errors don't stop batch processing. Instead, the offending command fails, but the rest of the batch continues processing.

In the following example, the table tiny has only one column, c1, which is a tinyint (allowing only integer values from 0 to 255). SQL Server detects the datatype mismatch (–1 is out of range) at runtime and the statement fails. The rest of the statements in the batch execute successfully and two rows are inserted in the table (on the next page):

```
create table tiny (c1 tinyint not null)
go
insert tiny (c1) values (1)
insert tiny (c1) values (-1)
insert tiny (c1) values (12)
go
```

> **NOTE**
>
> Sometimes the successful execution of only a part of the batch is disastrous. In that case, you need to use transaction control statements to group a set of statements together as a single logical unit of work and ensure that all the statements execute successfully—or none do. Here's the same set of `insert` statements, executed as a transaction:
>
> ```
> begin transaction
> insert tiny (c1) values (1)
> if @@error != 0 goto error_handler
> insert tiny (c1) values (-1)
> if @@error != 0 goto error_handler
> insert tiny (c1) values (12)
> if @@error != 0 goto error_handler
> commit transaction
> return
> error_handler:
> rollback transaction
> return
> ```
>
> See Chapter 9, "Transaction Management," for more on transactions.

Comments

Comments can be included in batches, and it's a good practice to include descriptive comments in stored procedures. Many of the preceding examples included comments.

There are two forms of comments: multiple-line comments bracketed with /* and */, and single-line comments identified with two hyphens (—). In both cases, the comment is transmitted to the server (and included along with the code in recorded views, stored procedures, and triggers), but the parser and optimizer ignore the text of all comments.

In this example, SQL Server ignores the multi-line comment at the beginning of the batch as well as the single-line comment falling at the end of the `values` clause.

```
/* a parsing error in the second statement
** prevents the entire batch from running */
insert publishers (pub_id, pub_name)
    values ("1234", "Publisher A")
insert publishers (pub_id, pub_name, city, state)
    values ("1235", "Publisher B", "Nashville", "TN") -- corrected!
insert publishers (pub_id, pub_name)
    values ("1234", "Publisher C")
go
```

SQL Server permits nested multi-line comments, as in this example:

```
/* testing a nested comment
/* inside */
   outside */
print "parsed!"
```

Local Variables

Variables for use in a batch or stored procedure are defined with the `declare` statement.

> **TIP**
>
> Local variables exist only for the life of the batch, stored procedure, or trigger where they are declared. When the batch is complete, all information stored in the local variables is lost. (SQL Server supports *global variables*—see the next section for details—but these variables are read-only values that are used by the server to report the status of your session.)
>
> You can transmit the *value* of a variable to the user with a `select` statement or `print` statement. Stored procedures can return a variable as an `output` parameter (see Chapter 8, "Transact-SQL Program Structures").
>
> All structures can use temporary or permanent worktables as a method of retaining the values stored in variables. Note that temporary tables created during a procedure are dropped when the procedure exits, but a global or permanent temporary table can persist. For more on these structures, see the section "Global and Permanent Temporary Tables" in Chapter 6, "Creating and Altering Database Objects."

To declare a local variable with the `declare` statement, provide the name of the variable and its datatype. Variable names must be preceded by a single @ and can be no longer than 30 characters. Variables can use any system or user-defined datatype. The syntax of the `declare` statement looks like this:

```
declare @variable_name datatype [, ...]
```

This example declares a variable to contain an error value:

```
declare @last_error int
```

If you need to declare several variables, use a single `declare` statement for better efficiency. Feel free to format the statement so it's easy to read:

```
/* declare two variables in a single statement */
declare
    @name varchar(30),
    @type int
```

Assigning Values to Local Variables

SQL Server 6.x provides two methods of assigning local variables.

The most common method of assigning values is a select statement, generally referred to as an *assignment* select. The syntax looks similar to the assignment of a column heading:

```
select @variable_name = expression [, ...]
[from ...
[where ...]]
```

Notice that an assignment select doesn't need to include a from clause or refer to a table. In the first example, a scalar constant is assigned to the @int variable:

```
/* set a variable equal to a constant expression */
declare @int_var int
select @int_var = 12
go
```

Until you assign a value to a local variable, the value of the variable is null. You must assign a value first, especially in looping constructs. Here's how to build a loop that will execute 10 times in Transact-SQL:

```
declare @counter int
select @counter = 0
while @counter < 10
begin
      select @counter = @counter + 1
      select @counter
end
```

In the next example, the select statement identifies a single row (identified by a unique ID), and then assigns the column values for that row to the variables. Again, it's more efficient to assign multiple columns in a single statement:

```
/* multiple variables set in a select statement */
declare @single_auth varchar(40),
        @curdate datetime
select @single_auth = au_lname,
        @curdate = getdate()
    from authors
    where au_id = '123-45-6789'
```

A single select statement can retrieve data or assign values to variables, but not both. This batch tries to do both and fails with the error message provided:

```
/* this won't work */

declare @lname varchar(40)

select @lname = au_lname, au_lname

from authors

where au_id = "172-32-1176"

Msg 141, Level 15, State 1
A SELECT statement that assigns a value to a variable must not be combined
with data-retrieval operations.
```

NOTE

An assignment select should return only a single row. If an assignment select that retrieves data returns multiple rows, the local variable is assigned the value for the last row returned. Because SQL Server may use different indexes to arrive at the same result, depending on the circumstances (see Chapters 11 through 14 for more on this topic), you can't predict what the "last row" will be unless you include an order by clause in your select statement. Here's an example of an assignment select that behaves unpredictably because it fails to specify a single row:

```
/* this behaves unpredictably */
declare @lname varchar(40)
select @lname = au_lname
from authors
print @lname
```

There are two methods of guaranteeing that a single specific value is returned to the variable:

- Use a primary or unique key in a where clause (see the example above)
- Use an aggregate function in the select list

Here's an example of an aggregate function used to guarantee that the last alphabetic name is returned to the variable:

```
declare @lname varchar(40)
select @lname = max(au_lname)
from authors
print @lname
```

If an assignment select that retrieves data returns no rows, the local variable retains the value it had prior to the execution of the select statement. In this example, the user sets up a counter variable in the same statement used to find a specific row in a table:

```
/* if no rows are found, both variables are null */
declare @lname varchar(40), @ctr int
select @lname = au_lname, @ctr = 1
from authors
where au_id = "172-32-1178"
```

Because the au_id isn't found, no rows are returned and both variables are unaffected. This is one case where it might be more effective to use two select statements to set two variables:

```
/* if no rows are found, both variables are null */
declare @lname varchar(40), @ctr int
select @ctr = 1
select @lname = au_lname
from authors
where au_id = "172-32-1178"
```

Assigning Local Variables with update

You can use the update statement to define variables. In earlier releases of the server, you couldn't retrieve values and set them in a single statement. To guarantee that the same value was inserted and retrieved to the variable, you would need to execute two separate statements as part of a transaction, and hold locks while you work:

```
/* WARNING - don't use this example verbatim without reading more !!! */
declare @qty smallint
begin transaction
select @qty = qty * 2
   where title_id = "BU1032"
   and stor_id = "6380"
   and ord_num = "6871"
   holdlock              — this guarantees no changes to the row by others
                         — until the transaction is committed
update sales
   set qty = @qty
   where title_id = "BU1032"
   and stor_id = "6380"
   and ord_num = "6871"
commit transaction
select @qty as "New Quantity"
```

While this approach achieves the objective of setting the variable and making the update, the use of holdlock establishes a potentially blocking lock and often leads to deadlocks (see Chapter 9). In the next example, the variable is set in the update statement, simplifying the code and avoiding the problematic holdlock:

```
declare @qty smallint

update sales
   set @qty = qty = qty * 2
   where title_id = "BU1032"
```

```
    and stor_id = "6380"
    and ord_num = "6871"

select @qty as "New Quantity"
```

SQL Server performs many implicit data conversions automatically within an assignment `select`, but will not perform any automatic conversions when assigning with the `update` statement. In the previous example, declaring the variable as an integer (`int`) creates a datatype mismatch reported by the server:

```
Msg 425, Level 16, State 1
Datatype 'int' of receiving variable not equal
to datatype 'smallint' of column 'qty'.
```

The need to exactly match datatypes means that certain uses of the `update` statement to assign variables can't work at all. In this example, the `update` statement fails because the `@ytd_sales` variable is defined as an `int` but the `ytd_sales` column is defined as `int null`:

```
declare @ytd_sales int
update titles
set @ytd_sales = ytd_sales =
    (select sum(qty)
    from sales
    where title_id = "BU1234")
where title_id = "BU1234"
Msg 425, Level 16, State 1
Datatype 'int' of receiving variable not equal to datatype 'int null' of column
'ytd_sales'.
```

Because you can't define a variable as "`int null`", this statement can't succeed. You need to perform this assignment/update in two steps.

Global Variables

Global variables are used by the server to track server-wide and session-specific information. They can't be explicitly set or declared. Global variables can't be defined by users and aren't used to pass information across processors by applicants (as defined in many third- and fourth-generation languages). Although they're called "global" variables, they're not *server-wide* values. Instead, they provide information about your current session. Other users' values will almost certainly vary from your own at any given time. Here's a list of the more commonly used global variables:

Function	Description
@@rowcount	Number of rows processed by the preceding command
@@error	Error number reported for the last SQL statement
@@trancount	Transaction nesting level
@@transtate	Current state of a transaction
@@tranchained	Current transaction mode (chained or unchained)

continues

Function	Description
@@servername	Name of the local SQL Server
@@version	SQL Server and O/S release level
@@spid	Current process ID
@@identity	Last identity value used in an `insert`
@@nestlevel	Number of levels nested in a `stored_procedure/trigger`
@@fetch_status	Status of previous `fetch` statement in a cursor

Most of these variables are described in context elsewhere in this book. There are some things about the most-commonly-used global variables that you should know right now.

@@rowcount

@@rowcount changes after every statement except `declare`. If you need to use the value repeatedly or refer to it after performing some intermediate processing, declare an `int` variable and then store the value of @@rowcount in that variable, like this:

```
declare @rows int
select @rows = @@rowcount
```

This is a particularly useful technique inside of a trigger, where you often need access to @@rowcount to be certain that all the rows in the table are valid.

> **NOTE**
>
> When you write a trigger, you need to be specially aware of how @@rowcount is affected by every statement. Notice, however, that when you exit the trigger and continue processing, @@rowcount is restored to the value originally set by the statement that fired the trigger.

@@error

@@error should be checked after every SQL statement, particularly in stored procedures and triggers. If you want to streamline your code a little more, check @@error only after data-retrieval and data-modification statements. If the value of @@error isn't zero, an error was raised by the execution and you should perform some error checking.

Client application programs rely on callback functions that alert the application or the user when server-originated errors occur. The way you trap those errors depends on your application. You need to use @@error most frequently when writing server-based routines (stored procedures, triggers, and complex batches) where the decision to go ahead and work on the next SQL statement depends on the success of the prior statement.

Notice that @@error presents the same coding challenge as @@rowcount: The value changes with every SQL statement. Look at the output from this batch:

```
raiserror ("miscellaneous error message", 16, 1)
if @@error <> 0
    select @@error as "last error"

Msg 50000, Level 16, State 1
miscellaneous error message
last error
- - - - -
0
```

The actual error raised was number 50,000, as the output indicates. The error trap worked, identifying the fact that @@error wasn't 0 after the previous statement. The if statement was successful, though, so the attempt to display the contents of @@error failed because it had changed by the time it was reported.

If you need to take different action based on the error number, or hope to record errors in an error log table, you need to capture the value of @@error immediately after the statement, and then evaluate it:

```
declare @my_error int
raiserror ("miscellaneous error message", 16, 1)
select @my_error = @@error
if @my_error <> 0
    select @my_error as "last error"

Msg 50000, Level 16, State 1
miscellaneous error message
last error
- - - - -
50000
```

Now the select statement returns the correct error number (50,000).

@@trancount

The value of @@trancount is greater than zero if a transaction is currently uncommitted within the session, and zero if no transaction is pending. See Chapter 9 for an in-depth discussion of @@trancount.

@@version

@@version tells you the current release and hardware platform for the server. This variable is useful for technical support and sometimes helpful to identify an unnamed server in your network. This is the version information for a beta release of the server:

```
Select @@version
- - - - - - - - - - - - - - - - - - - - - - - - - - - - -
Microsoft SQL Server 6.50 - 6.50.187 (Intel X86)
    Feb 23 1996 10:44:46
    Copyright (c) 1988-1996 Microsoft Corporation
```

print

The print statement is used to pass a message to the client program's message handler. Messages can include up to 255 characters of text. You can pass only a literal character string or a single character-type variable to print. (Although you can pass global variables, the only currently-supported, character type global variable is @@version.) Here's the syntax:

```
print {character_string | @local_variable | @@global variable }

/* send a string to the message handler */
print "This is a message"

This is a message
```

You can't perform any concatenation or substitution in the print statement itself. Instead, use a select statement to build the character string in a variable, and then pass the variable to the print statement:

```
/* send a variable to the message handler
** the variable needs to be of a character type */
declare @msg varchar(30)
select @msg = "Hello, " + user_name()
print @msg

Hello, dbo
```

Notice how the second example uses a variable to store the final string to be passed to the print statement. The concatenation performed in the select statement can't be performed by the print statement.

raiserror

SQL Server will handle most error reporting for you automatically, transmitting a message to the user and identifying the problem. The raiserror command is provided to enable you to initiate an error yourself. Returning and identifying an error condition to a calling procedure or batch is useful in stored procedures and complex batches. It's particularly useful when you encounter an error in a trigger and must issue a rollback statement.

Error messages consist of four basic elements:

- Error number
- Severity
- State
- Message

The server and client applications use each of these elements to inform the user or administrator and to make programmatic decisions.

Error *number* is a unique integer value between 50,001 and 2,147,483,647 ($2^{31}-1$). Client programs trap certain errors, but pass others straight through to the user. The server itself also monitors the errors being generated and can take action in response to an error:

- The error handler in a client program identifies errors it needs to trap to handle internally. Deadlocks are a common error handled by the programmer with no user intervention.

- Other general errors are often reported directly to the user. The attempt to enter a duplicate key in a table is often reported directly to the user.

- You can set up alerts so that SQL Server can respond to specific error conditions by number. One common error to trap with an alert is a full database transaction log.

Severity describes the general type of error. Severity values include 0 and all of the integers from 10 to 25:

- Severity levels 0 and 10 are informational; both are returned to the client application as severity 0.

- Severity levels 11 through 16 are errors that the user can typically correct. They include syntax errors, security violations, data-validation violations, and other common database occurrences.

- Severity levels 17 through 19 indicate a software or hardware problem. You usually can continue working, although the statement you executed to generate the error may not work. These errors should be reported to a system administrator immediately.

- Severity levels 20 to 25 indicate system problems. They are fatal and, depending on the error, could result in the user losing his connection—or may result in the whole server shutting down. In any case, something heavy is going down.

State describes the "invocation state" of the error. State is an integer value from 1 to 127. Because the state of the error depends on when it's called, you don't store the message state as part of the error.

> **NOTE**
>
> I'll be brutally honest here. I'm quoting the Microsoft SQL Server Books Online. With over five years of experience in SQL Server, I still haven't heard a convincing explanation of how to use this information.

Message is the text of the error message will be reported to the user if the error occurs. It can't exceed 255 characters.

> **NOTE**
>
> When you raise an error, you provide *either* the message number *or* the message text. If you pass the number, the server looks up the text in the master..sysmessages table (see the following section). If you pass the text (this is called an *ad hoc message*), the server automatically assigns a message number to @@error of 50000 if the severity is greater than 10. @@error is set to 0 for severity 1 through 10.
>
> This is new in SQL Server 6.5. In prior releases, all ad hoc messages used message number 50000 regardless of their severity. If you programmed on the basis of this earlier behavior, you can force all ad hoc messages to return 50000 by using the with seterror option with raiserror.

To generate a SQL Server error programmatically, use the raiserror command, which places the error number you specify in the @@error global variable and transmits the error number, severity, state, and the text of the error message to the client application. It's also possible to transmit error messages to the SQL Server error log and the Windows NT event log.

Managing SQL Server Errors

SQL Server provides a number of internal error messages related to predefined events within the parsing, optimizing and execution subsystems. These errors are stored in a system table, master..sysmessages. You can add your own messages to the master..sysmessages table and then refer to those messages in a raiserror statement. When you raise an error, you can send an ad hoc error message and number created directly in your SQL code, or you can refer to one of your predefined messages.

To provide better system documentation and greater consistency between development and support teams, you should store all error messages in master..sysmessages.

Using SQL-EM to Manage Messages

SQL Enterprise Manager provides a graphical method of managing server-wide error messages. To manage error messages, use the Server | Messages menu option (see Figure 7.1).

The Manage SQL Server Messages dialog box allows you to search for system and user-defined messages by text, severity, or error number (see Figure 7.2). If you have previously defined error messages and need to modify or delete them, search for them in this dialog box.

FIGURE 7.1.

Use the Server | Messages menu option to manage error messages.

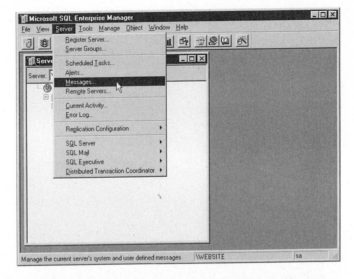

FIGURE 7.2.

Search for system and user-defined messages in this dialog box.

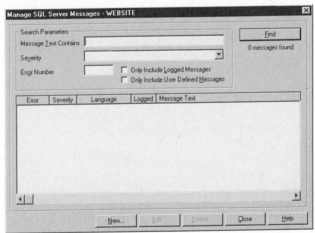

To create new error messages, click the New button (see Figure 7.3). In the resulting dialog box, specify the message number and text, severity, language, and logging behavior of the error message.

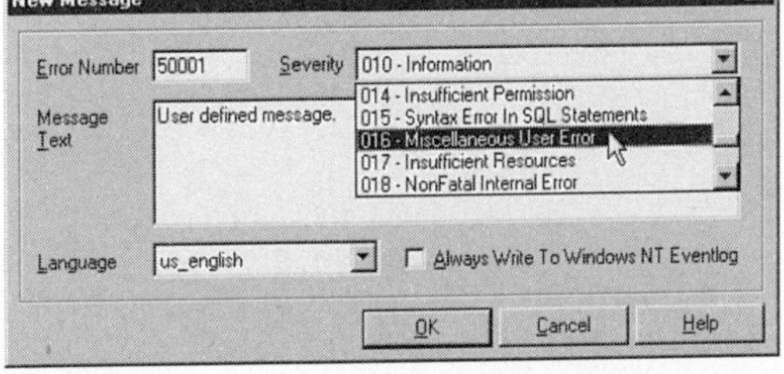

FIGURE 7.3.

The New Message dialog box enables you to create new, user-defined error messages.

The server always provides the next available message number (user-defined messages start at 50,001). You need to specify the text of the message, which is limited to 255 characters. If you plan to support many languages, indicate the language of this message. You can store one message per message number per language.

You can also indicate that the error should be logged to the Windows NT event log. When an error is logged to the event log, you can use SQL Server *alerts* to respond to the error in a number of useful ways. For example, an e-mail message or page can be sent to an *operator*, or a SQL statement can be executed at this server or another server. See Chapter 35, "The MS SQL Server Distributed Management Framework," for more on alerts and operators.

> **NOTE**
>
> Figure 7.3 shows a list of severity levels in the drop-down list box. While you specify a severity level for an error message, it is only the documented, recommended severity for that message. The `raiserror` statement always overrides the value you specify here.

You can include C-like formatting instructions (for example, with the `printf()` function) in the message text to allow substitution of arguments at runtime. For example, this message permits you to pass a string as an argument to be substituted for `%s`:

```
"Insert an argument here %s then continue"
```

If you pass the argument `@my_value`, the output string would be

```
Insert an argument here @my_value then continue
```

In the example in Figure 7.4, the message allows a string argument.

FIGURE 7.4.

Use C formatting strings to allow function arguments in your messages.

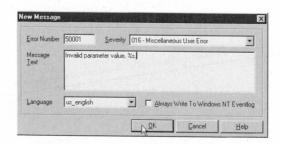

To test your error messages, use the `raiserror` statement and identify the message by number. Use ISQL/w or the Query Analyzer in SQL-EM to execute a `raiserror` statement, as in Figure 7.5.

FIGURE 7.5.

Raise errors in SQL-EM to test errors and argument handling.

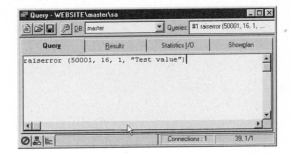

In the example, the fourth argument in the `raiserror` statement (`"Test Value"`) is the substitution value for the string indicated with `%s`. Figure 7.6 shows the output from `raiserror`.

FIGURE 7.6.

The output from `raiserror` shows that the argument has been substituted for the `%s` substitution value.

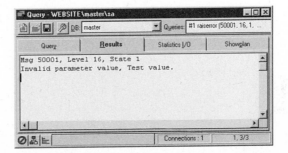

Managing Messages with Stored Procedures

SQL Server also provides three stored procedures to help you maintain your error messages. Use the stored procedures to develop a script to distribute tables of errors to multiple servers.

`sp_addmessage` adds messages to the table:

```
sp_addmessage msg_id, severity, "text of message"
    [, language[, {true¦false} [, REPLACE ]]]
sp_addmessage 52000, 16, "Invalid customer id in order", "us_english", true
```

SQL Server enables you to provide several different language versions of a single error message. When a program generates an error, the version of that error for the user's current language is returned to the user. The default language is `us_english`. The `true¦false` element indicates whether the error should be recorded in the SQL Server error log when raised.

`sp_altermessage` changes the logging behavior of a message:

```
sp_altermessage msg_id, WITH_LOG, {true¦false}
sp_altermessage 52000, WITH_LOG, "false"
```

The words `WITH_LOG` must be literally supplied; then you provide the `true` or `false` value to indicate whether the error should be logged when it occurs. Only the system administrator can run this command. Notice that you can even change the behavior of a system-supplied error message.

`sp_dropmessage` removes an error message from the table:

```
sp_dropmessage msg_id [, language | 'all']
```

```
sp_dropmessage 52000
```

You can drop all language versions of a message, or just a version of a message in one language. If you don't provide a language value, the server drops the message in the currently active language.

The `raiserror` Command

Although many error messages are generated automatically by the SQL Server, at times a SQL batch or a SQL programming object (a trigger or stored procedure) will need to raise an error.

NOTE

Server-side errors are reported to the client application as part of the *Transaction Data Stream* (TDS). Most client applications implement an interrupt-based error handler using a callback function or event handler. How the client application deals with error events or how it displays errors to the user is entirely up to the application developer.

Here's the syntax for `raiserror`:

```
raiserror ({msg_id | msg_str}, severity, state
    [, argument1 [, ...]] )
    [WITH LOG]
```

NOTE

SQL Server supports an alternative syntax for `raiserror` with ad hoc messages:

```
raiserror msg_id msg_str
```

Before version 6.0, this was how errors were raised under all circumstances. Don't use this syntax in new applications unless they also need to run in SQL Server 4.21.

Here are some examples of `raiserror`:

```
/* raise the error and send a message */
raiserror ( 52000, 16, 1 )
```

In this case, SQL Server requires that error message 52000 already exist in the `sysmessages` table. If you raise an error that doesn't exist, SQL Server returns this error:

```
Msg 2758, Level 16, State 1
RAISERROR could not locate entry for error 52000 in Sysmessages.
```

You need to add the message with `sp_addmessage`, and then raise it.

To raise an ad hoc error message (one that isn't already in `sysmessages`), provide the text of the message instead of the error message ID:

```
raiserror ("Invalid customer id in order", 16, 1)

Msg 50000, Level 16, State 1
Invalid customer id in order
```

Ad hoc error messages always use message ID `50000`.

`raiserror` enables you to provide *arguments* that are then substituted into the text of the message, using syntax similar to the C-language `printf` command. This substitution permits your error message to be more specific and useful. In this example, the actual customer ID that caused the error is passed as an argument to the `raiserror` statement:

```
raiserror ("Invalid customer id %s in order", 16, 1, "AB52436")

Msg 50000, Level 16, State 1
Invalid customer id AB52436 in order
```

The value `AB52436` is substituted for `%s` in the message when it's returned. You can also pass arguments to messages stored in `sysmessages`. Here's the message added to `sysmessages`:

```
sp_addmessage 52000, 16, "Invalid customer id %s in order"
```

Now raise the error, referring to the specific message by its ID and passing the argument:

```
raiserror (52000, 16, 1, "AB52436")

Msg 52000, Level 16, State 1
Invalid customer id AB52436 in order
```

You need to specify the datatype of the arguments you intend to pass in the message text. Indicate a string with `%s` and signed integers with `%d` or `%i`. (There are also other, more exotic types, including octals and hexadecimals.)

When you consider `raiserror` in context, the benefits of predefined error messages and user-specified arguments are clearer. Here's a brief example of a stored procedure for deleting rows from a table. The database programmer is able to provide a detailed error message if the row can't be deleted because it belongs to someone else:

```
create proc pr_del_cust
(@cust_id char(4))
as
declare @resp_user varchar(30)
select @resp_user = resp_user
    from cust_table
    where cust_id = @cust_id
if user_name() != @resp_user
begin
    raiserror (58000, 14, 1, @cust_id, @resp_user)
    return 1
end
delete cust_table
where cust_id = @cust_id
return 0
```

Here's error message `58000`:

```
sp_addmessage 58000, 14, "Customer %s belongs to %s. You may not delete it."
```

If the user attempts to delete a row that doesn't belong to him, the server returns a descriptive and specific error:

```
pr_del_cust "AB12"

Msg 58000, Level 14, State 1
Customer AB12 belongs to david. You may not delete it.
```

Conditional Execution: `if...else`

Statements to be executed conditionally are identified with the `if...else` construct. This setup allows a statement or statement block to be executed when a condition is `true` or `false`. Here's the basic syntax for `if...else`:

```
if boolean_expression
    {statement ¦ statement_block}
[else
    {statement ¦ statement_block}]
```

In the following example, the condition depends on the comparison between a subquery and a constant value. If the Boolean expression contains a `select` statement, the statement is treated as a subquery and must be enclosed in parentheses:

```
/* check for average price of business books
** and return a message */
if (select avg(price) from titles
        where type = "business") > $19.95
    print "The average price of business books is greater than $19.95"
else
    print "The average price of business books is less than $19.95"

The average price of business books is less than $19.95
```

`if exists`

The `if exists` test is used to check for the existence of data, without regard to the number of matching rows. The existence test is better than a `count(*) > 0` for an existence check because the server stops processing the `select` as soon as the first matching row is found.

```
if [not] exists (select_statement)
    {statement ¦ statement_block}
[else
    {statement ¦ statement_block}]

/* check for authors named Smith */
declare @lname varchar(40), @msg varchar(255)
```

```
select @lname = "Smith"
if exists (select * from titles
          where au_lname = @lname)
    begin
    select @msg = "There are authors named " + @lname
    print @msg
    end
else
    begin
    select @msg = "There are no authors named " + @lname
    print @msg
    end
go
```

> **WARNING**
>
> `if` statements can be nested up to 150 levels. If you're nesting deeply, make sure that your sa has configured your stack size adequately.

Statement Blocks: `begin...end`

To treat multiple SQL statements as a single block, use the `begin...end` construct:

```
begin
    SQL Statements
end
```

In the following example, the `if exists` executes one statement block if the condition is true or the other statement block if the condition is false:

```
/* check for a smith and do two things */
if exists (select * from authors
          where au_lname = "Smith")
    begin
        print "Smith exists"
        exec found_proc
    end
else
    begin
        print "Smith not found"
        exec not_found_proc
    end
```

Although `begin...end` can be used almost anywhere, it's most commonly used in combination with `while` and `if...else`.

Repeated Execution: `while`

To write programs that require a programming loop, use the `while` construct. Here's the basic syntax (shown on the following page):

```
while boolean_condition
    [{statement ¦ statement_block}]

[break]

[continue]
```

`break` unconditionally exits the `while` loop and continues processing with the first statement after the `end` statement. `continue` reevaluates the Boolean condition and begins processing from the top of the loop if the condition is true.

This is a nasty example of a `while` loop that demonstrates the use of `break` and `continue`:

```
/* loop until average price equals or exceeds $25*/
while (select avg (price) from titles) < $25
    begin
        update titles set price = price * 1.05
        /* if fewer than 10 books are less than
        ** $15, continue processing */
        if (select count(*) from titles) < 10
            continue
        else
        /* If maximum price of single book exceeds
        ** $50, exit loop */
          if (select max(price) from titles) > $50
            break
    end
```

If you want to understand what's going on, read the comments describing each step. Notice that the condition governing the loop is evaluated before any processing begins.

NOTE

Of course, this is a horrible example of a `while` loop. Nobody in his right mind would run the same table scans over and over. So remember that the example is meant to help you understand how the looping structures (`while`, `break`, `continue`) are used and what they do.

The right way to write this code is to consider in advance the conditions regarding the looping and run each statement only once, making heavy use of variables:

```
declare
    @avg_price money,
    @max_price money,
    @count_rows int,
    @times_thru_the_loop int
select
    @avg_price = avg(price),
    @max_price = max(price),
    @count_rows = count(*),
    @times_thru_the_loop = 0
    from titles
```

```
while @avg_price < $25 and (@count_rows < 10 or @max_price < $50)
begin
   select
       @avg_price = @avg_price * 1.05,
       @max_price = @max_price * 1.05,
       @times_thru_the_loop = @times_thru_the_loop + 1
end
/* now update the titles one time based on the no of times through the loop */
if @times_thru_the_loop = 0
   select @times_thru_the_loop = 1
update titles
   set price = price * power(1.05, @times_thru_the_loop)
```

Keep in mind that the traditional reason for looping syntax in a database application using a third-generation language would be to walk record-by-record through a file until you reach the *end of file* (EOF) mark. That makes no sense in SQL Server unless you are using a cursor. Instead, almost all of your interaction with tables using SQL is performed using *set processing*. For example, this query instructs the server to update all rows in the table sharing a certain characteristic:

```
update authors
set city = "Pittsburgh"
where city = "Pittsburg"
```

If you want to see better examples with while, check out the section titled "Cursors," later in the chapter.

Repeated Execution: goto

goto is provided to allow you to continue processing starting at a labeled statement. Here's the basic syntax:

```
goto label
...
```

```
label:
```

Although structured programming avoids using goto statements because of the syntactic problems it can create, here's a simple example (seen in an earlier note) that uses a goto statement to simplify error handling:

```
begin transaction
insert tiny (c1) values (1)
if @@error != 0 goto error_handler
insert tiny (c1) values (-1)
if @@error != 0 goto error_handler
insert tiny (c1) values (12)
if @@error != 0 goto error_handler
commit transaction
return
error_handler:
rollback transaction
return
```

Be careful not to use goto statements in ways that will confuse the parser. This batch fails to parse because the first reference to the table #mytemp attempts to reference an object that hasn't yet been created. Parsing doesn't follow the logical flow of the program. Instead, the single-pass parser identifies each object from top to bottom:

```
goto label2
label1:
    insert into #mytemp values (1)
    return
label2:
    create table #mytemp  (a int)
    goto label1

error 208 invalid object name #mytemp
```

The server can't resolve the backward references.

Event Handling: waitfor

The waitfor statement is used to cause a query to pause for a period of time or until an event occurs. SQL Server puts the process on the sleep queue and awakens it when the event occurs.

Here's the syntax of the waitfor statement:

```
waitfor {delay "time" ¦ time "time" }
```

delay pauses for the specified amount of time. time waits until the specified time of day. The time specified for delay and time is in hh:mm:ss format—you can't specify dates. time can't exceed a 24-hour period, and you can't specify a variable.

> **TIP**
>
> Although you can't use a variable in the waitfor time or waitfor delay statement, you can use the execute statement to formulate a variable execution string like this one, which performs an action once per hour, on the hour, for a day (in this case, reporting who is on line):
>
> ```
> declare @exec_string char(255),
>     @start datetime,
>     @ctr tinyint
> select @start = getdate(),
>     @ctr = datepart(hh, getdate())
> while datediff(hh, @start, getdate()) < 24
>     begin
>     select @exec string = "waitfor time '"
>         + str(@ctr) + ":00:00'"
>     execute (@exec_string)
>     execute sp_who
>     end
> ```

The first example demonstrates how to wait for a particular time:

```
/* Pauses until 10pm */
waitfor time "22:00:00"
```

The second example is an infinite loop that displays a list of current users every 30 seconds:

```
/* display current logins every 30 seconds */
while 1 < 2
begin
     waitfor delay "00:00:30"
     exec sp_who
end
```

return

To exit a batch, stored procedure, or trigger unconditionally, use the return statement. In this example, return is optional and has no real effect:

```
select * from authors
print "finishing now"
return
```

return is often used with if statements to allow the server to end a batch when a condition is identified:

```
/* return can be used with a conditional statement
** to terminate processing */
if not exists (select * from inventory
               where item_num = @item_num)
     begin
          raiserror 51345 "Not found"
          return
     end
print "No error found"
return
```

Chapter 8 discusses how to use the return statement to pass back a *return status value* indicating the reason that a stored procedure completed.

set Options

Options affect the way the server handles specific conditions. Options only exist for the duration of your connection, or for the duration of a stored procedure or trigger if they are set in that context (more examples on the next page):

```
set condition {on ¦ off ¦ value}

/* instruct the server to return only the first 100 rows of data */
set rowcount 100

/* asks the server for the number of logical and physical page requests */
set statistics io on

/* requests execution time */
set statistics time on
```

```
/* tells the server to stop reporting the number of rows returned */
set nocount on

/* asks the server for the final optimization plan for the query */
set showplan on

/* parse and optimize, but don't execute the query (often used in conjunction
** with showplan for looking at a plan without running a query) */
set noexec on

/* checks the batch for syntax, and then stops. */
set parseonly on
```

Cursors

ANSI-SQL provides the capability of addressing a set of rows individually, one row at a time, by a *cursor*. A cursor is a pointer that identifies a specific working row within a set. This section explores the syntactic structures used to define and use cursors.

Before looking at how to use a cursor, you need to understand what cursors can do for your application. Most SQL operations are set operations: A where clause defines the set of rows to address, and the rest of the statement provides definitive instructions on what to do with or to the rows.

Consider a typical reporting requirement in which the sales manager wants to evaluate the probable value of all sales opportunities for the next three months.

> **NOTE**
>
> It's extremely difficult to come up with compelling examples of cursor programming. The problem is that cursors introduce a staggering performance penalty in your applications and nearly always need to be avoided.

A typical table to track sales opportunities contains these columns:

```
create table leads
 (id int identity,
  cust int not null,
  est_sale int not null,
  close_date smalldatetime
     default dateadd(dd, 30, getdate()) not null,
  prob tinyint default 20 not null,
  sales_id char(3) not null,
  descr varchar(30) not null)
```

Here's some sample data that might occur in the leads table:

```
id  cust est_sale close_date          prob sales_id descr
-   --  ----  -------------------  --  -----  -----
 1    1 5000     Jan 17 1996 12:00AM 25   JJJ      software
 2    1 9000     Jan 28 1996 12:00AM 60   DDD      hardware
```

```
3     1 9000    Jan 30 1995 12:00AM 70    RRR    hardware
4     2 2000    Jan 31 1995 12:00AM 60    XXX    hardware
5     3 8000    Jan 20 1995 12:00AM  5    MMM    misc
6    12 2000    Jan 24 1995 12:00AM 95    PPP    software
7     3 8000    Jan 19 1995 12:00AM 70    DDD    software
8     1 2000    Jan 29 1995 12:00AM 50    JJJ    hardware
9    23 4000    Feb  5 1995 12:00AM 55    DDD    hardware
10    1 2000    Jan 30 1995 12:00AM 55    SSS    hardware
11   43 4000    Jan 16 1995 12:00AM 25    RRR    software
12    2 6000    Feb  5 1995 12:00AM 50    AAA    misc
```

A simple sales projection method is to multiply the estimated sale (est_sale) by the probability of a sale occurring (prob), and then total those discounted projections:

```
select est_total = sum(est_sale * prob)
from leads
```

Suppose that you want to write a sales projection that's far more scientific. Here are some facts you need to add to your sales projection:

- Some of the salespeople are way too optimistic, others too conservative. JJJ's probabilities are always 20 percent high, and DDD's are always 50 percent low.

- Customer number 2 is known for asking for bids he never buys. His projections should also be lowered by 80 percent (except JJJ's, which are already sufficiently discounted).

- Anything projected for February should be discounted by an additional 20 percent.

- Salespeople have typically been selling more hardware than they expect, so increase the sale amount in the projection by 15 percent.

Some Approaches

You could certainly write a program using a client-side application program, and many of these programs are written that way. What if there are 5 million lead rows, however? What impact will that fact have on your application?

You could use a set of temporary tables and build a standard query or set of queries to perform this step, but it may be easier to write a query that uses cursors, examining each row individually to see whether it fits any of the rules, and make any necessary adjustments.

> **NOTE**
>
> See the earlier note. I really don't like cursors because they are *substantially* slower than the typical set-processing mechanisms. In this chapter, I come not to praise cursors but to bury them (that is, describe them).

Cursor Example and Some Syntax

Take a look at the following code. This is the actual cursor program to execute the sales projection, given the functional requirements stated previously.

```
declare leads_curs cursor for
select  cust_id, est_sale, close_date, prob, sales_id, descr
from leads
for read only

declare
  @cust_id int,
  @est_sale int,
  @close_date smalldatetime,
  @prob tinyint,
  @sales_id char(3),
  @descr varchar(30),
  @sum_sales int

select @sum_sales = 0

open leads_curs
fetch leads_curs into
  @cust_id, @est_sale, @close_date, @prob, @sales_id, @descr

while (@@fetch_status = 0)
begin
    if @sales_id = "DDD"            /* increase DDD's sales */
      select @prob = @prob * 1.5
    if @sales_id = "JJJ"           /* decrease JJJ's sales */
      select @prob = @prob * .8
    else
      if @cust_id = 2              /* decrease cust 2's sales */
        select @prob = @prob * .8
    if datepart(mm, @close_date) = 2 /* decrease feb sales */
      select @prob = @prob * .8
    if @descr = "hardware"         /* increase hardware sales */
      select @est_sale = @est_sale * 1.15

    select @sum_sales = @sum_sales + @est_sale * @prob / 100
    fetch leads_curs into
      @cust_id, @est_sale, @close_date, @prob, @sales_id, @descr
end

close leads_curs
select @sum_sales "Weighted projected sales"
deallocate leads_curs
go
```

Let's review in detail each element of the example program.

Declaring Cursors

Here's the statement that declares the cursor:

```
declare leads_curs cursor for
select cust_id, est_sale, close_date, prob, sales_id, descr
from leads
for read only
```

The example declares a cursor that selects from a single table. The cursor will be used only to read values, not to update rows (`for read only`).

The cursor is optimized and compiled when it's declared. If the cursor contains a `where` clause and could use an index, it's a good idea to make it a SARG and support it with an index (see Chapters 11 through 15 for more on SARGs and indexes).

Cursor names are restricted by the same rules as object names—30 characters and no reserved characters. The `select` statement is unchanged. (There are some restrictions, which are detailed later.)

Declaring Variables

When fetching rows, you can do one of two things with cursor data:

- Return the row to the user, in which case the data looks just like a one-row result set from a `select` statement.
- Retrieve the data into variables.

This example retrieves the data into variables in order to perform additional processing. Here's the `declare` statement that sets up all of the variables:

```
declare
  @cust_id int,
  @est_sale int,
  @close_date smalldatetime,
  @prob tinyint,
  @sales_id char(3),
  @descr varchar(30),
  @sum_sales int

select @sum_sales = 0
```

To retrieve the data into variables, the variables need to be declared first. The variables must be of the same type and length as the columns specified in the `select` list of the `select` statement (no implicit conversion is allowed).

As a convention, you usually name the variables exactly the same as the column names in the `select` list. In the example, the columns are `cust_id`, `est_sale`, and so forth, and the variables are `@cust_id`, `@est_sale`, and so forth. (This is a compelling reason to limit column names to 29 characters. That way, the variable names still fit in 30 characters with the addition of the `@` symbol.)

Opening Cursors

When you open a cursor, the server executes the `select` statement to fix the membership and ordering of the cursor set. When you open the cursor, the row pointer is above the first row in the cursor; you must fetch a row to move the pointer to the first row:

```
open leads_curs
```

You can repeatedly open and close a cursor. When you do, the cursor select is re-executed to determine a revised ordering and membership for the set, and the row pointer is moved above the first row in the set again.

Fetching Rows

Once a cursor is open, you can fetch rows from the cursor set. In this example, the cursor is retrieving into variables. Notice that one variable is required for every column in the select list. (If you provide too many or too few, you get a runtime error.)

```
fetch leads_curs into
  @cust_id, @est_sale, @close_date, @prob, @sales_id, @descr
```

The `fetch` keyword in this case is forward-going only: each subsequent `fetch` statement moves you one row forward in the keyset. The later section "Scrolling Capabilities" looks at other ways to scroll through a cursor set with `fetch`.

The Main Loop

This is the reason for writing a cursor, right? This is the main loop, where you retrieve all the rows one at a time, perform some conditional processing on each one, and then move on to the next:

```
while (@@fetch_status = 0)
begin
   if @sales_id = "DDD"            /* increase DDD's sales */
     select @prob = @prob * 1.5
   if @sales_id = "JJJ"            /* decrease JJJ's sales */
     select @prob = @prob * .8
```

```
    else
      if @cust_id = 2                  /* decrease cust 2's sales */
        select @prob = @prob * .8
    if datepart(mm, @close_date) = 2 /* decrease feb sales */
      select @prob = @prob * .8
    if @descr = "hardware"           /* increase hardware sales */
      select @est_sale = @est_sale * 1.15
    select @sum_sales = @sum_sales + @est_sale * @prob / 100
    fetch leads_curs into
      @cust_id, @est_sale, @close_date, @prob, @sales_id, @descr
end
```

NOTE

This looks a lot like old-fashioned programming, something you might do in COBOL or Pascal or BASIC. The problem is, SQL Server is rotten at old-fashioned programming.

This program took about 8 seconds to run against 12 rows on my Pentium. (That's a long time for 12 rows!)

The moral of the story is that old-fashioned programming is typically a bad choice in SQL Server. Write set-based programs whenever you can, even (most of the time) if it means making multiple passes of a single table or set of tables.

You should note the global variable, @@FETCH_STATUS, which has three states after you execute a fetch statement:

- 0 means that a row was successfully fetched.
- -1 means that the fetch exceeded the results set (in this case, out of rows).
- -2 means that the row returned is no longer in the table (it was deleted from the table after the cursor was opened but before the row was retrieved). In this case, the row retrieved will consist entirely of NULLs.

TIP

Some additional code is required in the main loop to handle the case when @@FETCH_STATUS is -2, and to do other appropriate error checking, before this cursor code can go into production.

Closing the Cursor

When you finish working with a cursor, close it, and then do your end-of-process programming. Some open cursors hold locks that block others' work, and an open cursor uses other resources as well. You can reopen a closed cursor; the row pointer returns to the top of the set:

```
close leads_curs
select @sum_sales "Weighted projected sales"
```

Deallocating Cursors

When you finish working with a cursor, deallocate it. The cursor optimization plan takes up space in memory, so it should be freed as soon as possible. Once a cursor is deallocated, you need to declare it again before issuing the open statement:

```
deallocate leads_curs
```

Updating with Cursors

The sales projection example demonstrates only how to read data by using a cursor. Cursors can also be used to modify (update or delete) rows in a table. To enable update and delete statements to deal with the current row in a cursor set, SQL Server includes the where current of *cursor_name* condition:

```
update table_name
set column = expression [, column = expression[, ...]]
where current of cursor_name

delete table_name
where current of cursor_name
```

Here are a couple of examples:

```
update leads
set est_sale = est_sale * .8
where current of leads_curs

delete leads
where current of leads_curs
```

Declaring a Cursor for update

In order to update or delete using a cursor, you need to declare the cursor for update. Here's the complete syntax for the declare statement:

```
declare cursor_name [insensitive] [scroll] cursor
   for select_statement
   [for {read only ¦ update [of column_list]}]
```

For now, let's look at the last line of the statement, where you set up the cursor as a read-only cursor or as an updateable cursor. (The next few pages look into insensitive and scroll.) If a cursor is declared as read only, you can fetch rows but you can't use the where current of construction to modify the contents of the set.

In the example of the leads_curs, the updateable version looks like this:

```
declare leads_curs cursor for
select cust_id, est_sale, close_date, prob, sales_id, descr
from leads
```

You can declare a cursor `for update` or `for update of` *column_list*. If you don't specify a list of columns, all columns in all tables are considered updateable. This means that you can update the contents of several tables during the processing of a cursor containing a join.

> **NOTE**
>
> Is it a good idea to update many tables using a single cursor? Possibly, but it seems as if it would be easy to get confused.

If you plan to update only one table in the cursor, but need to access information in another, the cursor should be declared `for update`. You can use the `shared` keyword to indicate which tables you will read from and which will be modified. In this example, you need to access the `publishers` table to increase prices on titles published in Massachusetts, but no modifications will be made to the `publishers` table:

```
declare tp cursor for
select title_id, type, price
from titles t, publishers p shared
where t.pub_id = p.pub_id
and state = "MA"
for update of price
```

In addition to limiting updates to the `price` column of the `titles` table, this cursor also maintains only shared locks on the `publishers` table, improving multiuser operations.

Scrolling Capabilities

If you use the keyword `scroll` in your cursor declaration statement, you can use `fetch` to move forward, backward, and to absolute row locations within the cursor set (the keyset). For example, here's a scrollable version of the `leads_curs` declaration:

```
declare leads_curs scroll cursor for
select cust_id, est_sale, close_date, prob, sales_id, descr
from leads
for read only
```

Once you declare a cursor with the `scroll` keyword, the `fetch` statement is far more flexible. Here's the complete syntax for `fetch`:

```
fetch [[next|prior|first|last|absolute n|relative n] from cursor_name
[into @variable_name1, @variable_name2, ...]
```

Let's look at some examples.

This is the standard `fetch` statement. The keyword `next` is optional. You don't need a scrollable cursor to use `next`:

```
fetch next from leads_curs
     into @cust_id, @est_sale, @close_date, @prob, @sales_id, @descr
```

Here, you retrieve the prior row:

```
fetch prior from leads_curs
    into @cust_id, @est_sale, @close_date, @prob, @sales_id, @descr
```

In this case, the cursor moves back one row. If the cursor is already on the first row of the set, the value of @@fetch_status is set to -1 to indicate that the fetch exceeded the cursor set.

This example retrieves the first row in the set:

```
fetch first from leads_curs
    into @cust_id, @est_sale, @close_date, @prob, @sales_id, @descr
```

Use last to fetch the last row in the set.

You also can retrieve a row in an absolute position in the set. For example, to retrieve the tenth row in the cursor, use this:

```
fetch absolute 10 from leads_curs
    into @cust_id, @est_sale, @close_date, @prob, @sales_id, @descr
```

Again, your program should check the value of @@fetch_status to be certain that the absolute position is valid.

The last fetch operator uses relative row scrolling:

```
fetch relative -5 from leads_curs
    into @cust_id, @est_sale, @close_date, @prob, @sales_id, @descr
```

Relative scrolling can be forward (positive values) or backward (negative values). This example scrolls back five rows in the set. Again, always check @@fetch_status after each relative scroll to make sure that the new row position is still valid.

SQL Server 6.5 allows you to use a variable with absolute and relative fetch statements, as in this example:

```
fetch absolute @ctr from leads_curs
    into @cust_id, @est_sale, @close_date, @prob, @sales_id, @descr
```

insensitive cursors

If you declare a cursor with the insensitive keyword, the server makes a copy of the affected data into a temporary worktable. The contents of the worktable are what you see as you fetch rows in the cursor. The contents of an insensitive cursor don't change as the underlying data in the actual table changes, so you can use this mechanism to take a "snapshot" of data at a particular moment in time, and then use a cursor to process and report on that data.

Obviously, an insensitive cursor isn't updateable.

Avoiding Cursors

In general, you should try to avoid cursors. The example cursor program took 8 seconds to process 12 rows. For the record, here's how you could use a case expression in a select statement to replace the cursor processing:

```
select "Sum of Sales" = sum(
    est_sale * prob * .01
    *
    case descr
    when "hardware" then 1.15
    else 1.
    end
    *
    case datepart(mm, close_date)
    when 2 then .8
    else 1.
    end
    *
    case sales_id
    when "JJJ" then .8
    when "DDD" then 1.5
    else 1.
    end
    *
    case
    when cust_id != 2 then 1.
    else
        case sales_id
        when "JJJ" then 1.
        else .8
        end
    end
    )
from leads
```

This query took less than a second to run. On a large data set, a performance improvement of more than 80 percent is well worth a little hard work.

Summary

This chapter has considered the syntactic extensions and special features of the Transact-SQL. The following chapters look at using these structures to manage transactions and write stored procedures and triggers.

Transact-SQL Program Structures

8

Now that you understand how to code batches, you need to find ways to make these batches permanent. This is done with triggers and stored procedures. *Triggers* are database objects that are bound directly to tables. *Stored procedures* exist independently from tables (although they typically reference tables).

This chapter looks at the creation and maintenance of triggers and stored procedures.

Triggers

A *trigger* is a special type of stored procedure that is executed automatically as part of a SQL data modification statement. A trigger is created on a table and associated with one or more data modification actions (insert, update, or delete). When one of those actions occurs, the trigger fires automatically. In essence, it becomes an integral part of the data modification statement, occurring within the very transaction in which the modification occurs.

Triggers are one of the features that originally drew database engineers to SQL Server. Triggers provide to the DBA the opportunity to permit users to interact freely with SQL tables, making standard SQL-based modifications using insert, update, and delete. The trigger can guarantee data integrity and consistency, promising that every modification operates within the integrity requirements of the organization.

Triggers can do all of the following:

- Compare *before* and *after* versions of data
- Read from other tables and other databases
- Modify other tables and other databases
- Execute local and remote stored procedures
- Roll back invalid work

Of course, anyone responsible for writing triggers should read this section. It contains useful, tested examples of how to accomplish specific tasks by using triggers, and advice about how to write them efficiently and effectively. DBAs and system administrators should read about triggers to understand how they work and to decide where they should be used appropriately. Programmers should learn what effect triggers might have on applications, so they need to understand when a trigger fires and some of the actions that might take place in triggers.

Benefits and Uses of Triggers

Before the introduction of declarative referential integrity (DRI) constraints with SQL Server Version 6.0, triggers were the only mechanism for enforcing server-based RI. DRI constraints now handle ordinary RI enforcement, and check constraints have expanded the capabilities of declarative domain checking originally handled by rules. As a result, triggers are used to handle more complex and difficult problems.

Before SQL Server introduced declarative referential integrity, the main job of triggers was to do that work. Now that DRI handles the brunt of referential integrity checking, these are the most common applications of triggers:

■ Complex defaults—A trigger can refer to the contents of other columns or other tables to determine the default contents of columns in a table. In these cases, you also may want to consider an approach that uses a stored procedure.

■ Complex column constraints—Advanced domain checking (including inter-row and multi-table lookups) is often best done in a trigger.

■ Nonstandard referential integrity—If your application calls for alternative actions in response to RI violations, occasionally permits users to override protections, or requires unusual RI checking, a trigger is often the most efficient method available.

■ Maintenance of duplicate and derived data—Updates to additional tables based on changes to one table can be distributed by using a trigger. If the distribution of these changes can be deferred until a later time (not explicitly run as part of the transaction), you may also want to consider using replication to handle this kind of application problem.

When Not to Use Triggers

Complex or poorly written triggers can create havoc in a system requiring good throughput and update performance:

■ Triggers hold open locks, prevent updates in place, and can create additional transaction log overhead.

■ Triggers should be avoided when an application program or stored procedure can perform the same work with minimal I/O overhead.

■ Triggers should never be used to handle simple data validation or simple DRI.

In any case, triggers must be written to run quickly and return as soon as possible.

Trigger Execution

To write effective triggers, you need to understand trigger execution. Unlike stored procedures, triggers can't be executed by name. Triggers are executed automatically by the SQL Server, after all modifications are complete, within the transaction of the statement that fired the trigger. A trigger is executed only one time per statement, even if the statement modified several rows.

NOTE

This is really the key point in this very critical paragraph. *A trigger is executed only one time per statement.* Remember: A statement can modify multiple rows. So a trigger needs to be ready to deal with changes to zero, one, or many rows in the table. The need to deal with the multi-row case sometimes makes your trigger code more complex. The examples in this chapter demonstrate how this is done efficiently.

Triggers are fired automatically when the appropriate statement is executed. For example, if there were an `update` trigger on the `titles` table, the trigger would fire when a user executed the following query:

```
update titles
set price = price * 2
where type = "business"
```

TIP

When you're working with triggers, and especially triggers that modify other tables, it may help you to start by stating clearly the sample query that will fire the trigger.

Remember three critical points about this `update` statement:

- The statement might have modified zero, one, or many rows, depending on the data.
- The trigger fires one time, even if the original statement modifies one row, many rows, or no rows at all.
- The trigger fires *as an integral part of the transaction* within which the statement operates.

Here's what the SQL Server does when the statement fires (see Figure 8.1):

1. Begins a transaction by recording a `begin tran` marker in the transaction log (in cache) and setting `@@trancount` to 1.

FIGURE 8.1.

A trigger occurs within the transaction of the statement that executes it.

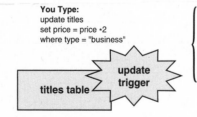

You Type:
update titles
set price = price *2
where type = "business"

titles table   update trigger

What actually happens:
begin transaction
delete titles in log
delete titles in data
insert titles in log
insert titles in data
execute trigger
commit transaction

2. Records the original contents of the affected rows in the log (in cache).

3. Deletes the original rows from the data pages (in cache).

4. Records the revised contents of the affected rows in the log (in cache).

5. Inserts the revised rows into the data pages (in cache).

6. Executes the update trigger.

7. Commits the transaction by recording a commit tran marker in the log (in cache), reduces @@trancount by one, then writes all dirty (modified) log pages to disk.

To maintain triggers, you need to know how to create and remove them and how to examine their contents. The next section of the chapter looks at these mechanical steps. A later section, "Special Trigger Syntax," discusses the special capabilities provided for writing triggers.

Creating Triggers

You use the Manage Triggers window in the SQL Enterprise Manager to maintain triggers on tables. There are two ways to access the Manage Triggers window. The first is to select Manage | Triggers from the main menu after highlighting the correct database in the Server Manager window (see Figure 8.2).

To go directly to the triggers on a specific table, right-click the table in the Objects list (in order, open the server, database icon, Objects folder, and Tables folder to get there). From the pop-up menu that appears (see Figure 8.3), choose Triggers to open the window.

FIGURE 8.2.

Use the Manage | Triggers menu option to access the Manage Triggers dialog box.

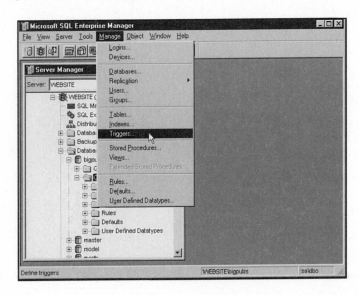

FIGURE 8.3.

Examine triggers for the current table by right-clicking and selecting Triggers from the pop-up menu.

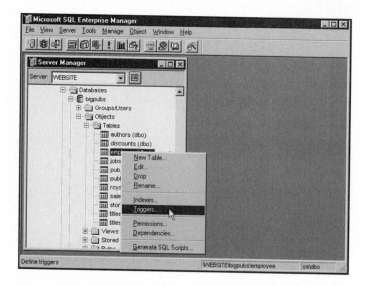

You can manage triggers from any SQL editing session (from ISQL/w or the Query Analyzer, for example). The Manage Triggers window simplifies trigger management by allowing you to see at a glance the triggers on a specific table and to quickly retrieve the existing text of a trigger.

The title bar of the Manage Triggers window includes the name of the server and database you are currently using. Within the toolbar, the drop-down list on the left allows you to view and change the table whose triggers are being managed. The drop-down list on the right displays the name of the current trigger, along with the actions it performs. In Figure 8.4, the <new> trigger includes two icons, for insert (a plus sign) and update (a pencil). This means that no trigger is currently assigned to insert or update actions. A trigger is assigned to the delete action, so the delete icon (an X) isn't visible, and the default create statement includes only insert and update.

FIGURE 8.4.

The Manage Triggers window allows you to see immediately the actions associated with a new or existing trigger.

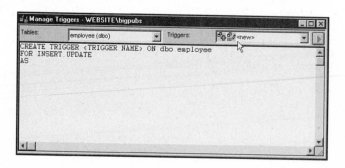

To create a trigger on a table, make sure that the correct table is listed in the Tables list box and then select the <new> option. In this example, we'll create a trigger that reports the number of rows deleted in the employee table in bigpubs.

Because a trigger is a SQL code-based object, you need to know some Transact-SQL syntax to create it. Here's the basic create trigger statement:

```
create trigger trigger-name
on table-name
for { insert ¦ update ¦ delete [, ...]}
as
SQL-statements
[return]
```

These are a few things that you should notice about the statement itself:

- Triggers are objects and must have a unique name in the database. It's useful to use a naming convention to clearly identify triggers, such as starting or ending the name with the letters *tr*.

- A trigger is created on a table for an action or set of actions. A trigger can respond to several actions (insert, update, and/or delete). A trigger *cannot* be placed on more than one table.

- While you can't replace a trigger with another having the same name without dropping the original trigger first, you can replace a trigger with another *performing the same action on the same table.*

- Triggers can optionally include the return statement to indicate successful completion. When the trigger returns (or ends without return), the originating statement that fired the trigger is considered complete and will commit. You can't return a return status code with the return statement, as you can when writing stored procedures.

When you select a <new> trigger in the Manage Triggers window, SQL-EM provides a code template to allow you to start writing the trigger. You need to substitute a name for the trigger according to your conventions, and you should decide which actions the trigger will affect. Although SQL-EM lists only actions that are currently unassigned (in the case of the employee table, insert or update), you can add other actions that the trigger should affect.

Once you execute the create statement, the new trigger will be responsible for any actions indicated in the FOR clause of its create statement.

Here's the create trigger statement that reports the number of rows whenever employees are deleted:

```
create trigger tr_employee_d ON dbo.employee
FOR DELETE
AS
declare @msg varchar(50)
select @msg = str(@@rowcount) + " employees deleted by this statement"
print @msg
return
```

The number of rows affected by the statement firing the trigger is available when executing the trigger in the @@rowcount global variable.

Figure 8.5 shows the Manage Triggers window with the revised trigger. After you create the trigger, the trigger name is added to the Triggers drop-down list and the <new> option is no longer available.

FIGURE 8.5.

The drop-down list of triggers displays the triggers currently on the table and the actions associated with each trigger.

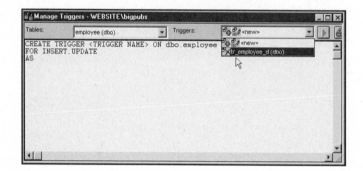

Dropping and Replacing Triggers

When you select the tr_employee_d trigger, you'll notice that SQL-EM has added code to automatically drop and re-create the trigger if you need to modify it. Triggers can't be modified in place. You need to drop an object before creating another with the same name. To drop a trigger, use the drop trigger command:

```
drop trigger trigger-name
```

Triggers are automatically dropped when the referenced table is dropped.

You don't need to drop a trigger to replace it. To replace a trigger for an action on a table, create a new trigger with a different name. The original trigger is replaced. If the original trigger is no longer responsible for any action on the table, the trigger is dropped.

Consider this example, where a trigger is created on a table for insert and update:

```
create trigger tr_titles_iu
on titles for insert, update
as ...
```

The first trigger is still maintained to handle inserts, even after a second trigger, tr_titles_u2, takes over responsibility for the update:

```
create trigger tr_titles_u2
on titles for update
as ...
```

Note, however, that the text of the code of tr_titles_iu stored on SQL Server and displayed in SQL-EM hasn't changed. The original trigger still claims to work on insert and update!

When a new trigger, tr_titles_i2, is assigned to handle inserts, the first trigger is automatically dropped because it isn't responsible for any action:

```
create trigger tr_titles_i2
on titles for insert
as ...
```

WARNING

SQL-EM automatically writes a script to drop and create a trigger in the Manage Triggers window. This strategy seems to allow very straightforward maintenance of triggers; however, you need to be careful if you're running a production system where users are dependent on triggers to maintain database integrity.

When triggers play a vital role in transaction processing, it's critical that *no transactions take place without the protection of a trigger.* The drop/create statements executed automatically by SQL-EM aren't treated as a transaction, meaning that a user could possibly execute a transaction on a table when neither the old nor the new trigger is in place.

There are two solutions. First, you can use SQL-EM, but only manage triggers when no users are working. You should place the database in single-user mode before performing this work. This scheme blocks out any other users while you're maintaining triggers. Turn off single-user mode to make the database available to others.

Your second choice is not to use SQL-EM to manage existing triggers. Instead, use ISQL/w or the Query Analyzer and execute explicit create trigger statements. Don't drop the trigger before creating the new one. Instead, create a new trigger that performs the same action *but has a different name.* SQL Server will replace the old trigger with the new in a single transaction, and no user transactions on the table will proceed without being subject to one trigger or the other.

The example just described isn't the most sophisticated example of a trigger, but it does allow you to start to understand trigger processing. With the trigger in place, let's go ahead and delete some employees from the database.

> **TIP**
>
> If you want to test the `delete` trigger without deleting employees, execute a `begin transaction` statement before starting this work. When you're finished testing the trigger, execute a `rollback transaction` to undo all the deletions and return the rows to the table.

In the Query Analyzer, execute this statement:

```
delete employee
where emp_id = "PMA42628M"
```

Following is the output from the statement. The first line is from the trigger, the second from SQL Server itself (to suppress that output, set `nocount on`):

```
    1 employees deleted by this statement
```

```
(1 row(s) affected)
```

In this preceding example, the query modified one row, and the trigger was executed one time. In the following example, delete all employees:

```
delete employee
```

```
    42 employees deleted by this statement
```

Even though all the employees were deleted, the trigger fired only once. Here's one more test:

```
delete employees
where 1 = 2
```

Even if no rows are affected, the trigger still fires one time:

```
    0 employees deleted by this statement
```

To drop a trigger using SQL-EM, display it in the Manage Triggers window. Then use the Object | Drop menu option to get to the dialog box where you can remove a trigger from a table (see Figure 8.6).

The Drop Objects dialog box should now display the name of the trigger, its owner, and the type of object affected (see Figure 8.7).

FIGURE 8.6.

To drop the currently displayed trigger, use the Object | Drop menu option.

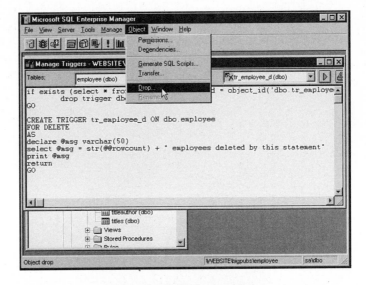

FIGURE 8.7.

The Drop Objects dialog box allows you to drop a trigger.

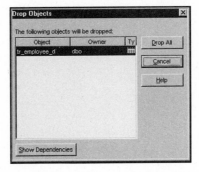

Before dropping the object, click the Show Dependencies command button to see the objects on which the trigger depends (see Figure 8.8). The dialog box displays a chain of objects on which the trigger depends (upper pane) and those objects that depend on the trigger itself (lower pane). Before dropping a trigger, always check this dialog box for dependencies of which you might have been unaware.

FIGURE 8.8.

The Object Dependencies dialog box shows you what objects might be affected when you drop an object. Always check this box carefully before dropping objects.

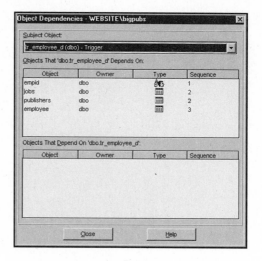

Displaying Triggers

Use SQL-EM to retrieve trigger text and to look at dependent objects. You can also use system stored procedures in the Query Analyzer to learn about triggers.

To display the text of a trigger:

```
sp_helptext trigger-name
```

To display all dependencies for a table (including triggers):

```
sp_depends table-name
```

To display tables (and other objects) referenced in a trigger:

```
sp_depends trigger-name
```

You can also query the database system tables to see all triggers on all user tables in the database. SQL Server stores trigger information in these tables:

- Triggers are objects, with one row per trigger, stored in sysobjects.
- The sysobjects entry for each table includes pointers to its insert, update, and delete triggers.
- A row is created in sysdepends (this is what was reported in the Object Dependencies dialog box).
- The text of the trigger is stored in syscomments.
- A pre-parsed version of the query is stored in sysprocedures.

Here's a query that displays the triggers for every user table in the database:

```
select id, name, "insert" = object_name(instrig),
    "update" = object_name(updtrig), "delete" = object_name(deltrig)
from sysobjects
where type = "U"
```

id	name	insert	update	delete
16003088	authors	(null)	(null)	(null)
112003430	publishers	(null)	(null)	(null)
192003715	titles	(null)	(null)	(null)
288004057	titleauthor	(null)	(null)	(null)
368004342	stores	(null)	(null)	(null)
416004513	sales	(null)	(null)	(null)
496004798	roysched	(null)	(null)	(null)
544004969	discounts	(null)	(null)	(null)
592005440	jobs	(null)	(null)	(null)
688005482	pub_info	(null)	(null)	(null)
752005710	employee	employee_insupd	employee_insupd	(null)

To see the same output for a single table, include a `where` clause to select rows by `name`:

```
select id, name, "insert" = object_name(instrig),
    "update" = object_name(updtrig), "delete" = object_name(deltrig)
from sysobjects
where type = "U"
and name = "table-name"
```

Special Trigger Syntax

Before starting to write triggers, you need to learn their special syntactic capabilities:

- Access to versions of rows before and after modification with the `inserted` and `deleted` tables
- Information about which columns were modified by a statement with the `update()` function

`inserted` and `deleted` Tables

The `inserted` and `deleted` tables are actually views of the transaction log having the same structure as the table on which the trigger was created. Consider this statement:

```
update titles
set price = $15.05
where type like "%cook"
```

When the statement is executed, a copy of the rows to be modified is recorded in the log, along with a copy of the rows after modification. These copies are available to the trigger in the `deleted` and `inserted` tables, respectively.

If you want to see the output displayed in the following examples, create a copy of the titles table, and then create a trigger like this one on your copy:

```
create trigger t1 on titles
for insert, update, delete
as
print "inserted"
select title_id, type, price from inserted
print "deleted"
select title_id, type, price from deleted
rollback transaction
return
```

Using this approach, you can execute a data modification statement and review the contents of inserted and deleted without changing the contents of the table.

The inserted and deleted tables are available after insert, update, and delete. Here are the contents of inserted and deleted, as reported by the trigger:

```
inserted
title_id  type          price
--------  ------------  --------------------------
MC2222    mod_cook                          15.05
MC3021    mod_cook                          15.05
TC3218    trad_cook                         15.05
TC4203    trad_cook                         15.05
TC7777    trad_cook                         15.05
deleted
title_id  type          price
--------  ------------  --------------------------
MC2222    mod_cook                          19.99
MC3021    mod_cook                           2.99
TC3218    trad_cook                         20.95
TC4203    trad_cook                         11.95
TC7777    trad_cook                         44.99
```

A trigger that executes after more than one statement (insert, update, or delete) can identify which statement initiated the trigger by examining the contents of the inserted and deleted tables. The following table summarizes what you'll find in these tables after each statement.

Statement	Contents of inserted	Contents of deleted
insert	Rows added	Empty
update	New rows	Old rows
delete	Empty	Rows deleted

Scope of `inserted` and `deleted` Tables

The `inserted` and `deleted` tables are local to the current trigger. This means that each trigger that's executed will materialize its own versions of these tables from the contents of the log for the current statement in the current context. `inserted` and `deleted` aren't available if the trigger calls a stored procedure, and if the trigger executes an action causing another trigger to fire, that trigger will see only its own `inserted` and `deleted` tables.

In some circumstances, it will be important to pass `inserted` and `deleted` rows to a procedure or other process. Because procedures accept only scalar parameters (and not arrays of values or tables), you may need to find alternate methods of communicating the contents of `inserted` and `deleted` to stored procedures.

You can't create a temporary table within a trigger, but, as Figure 8.9 shows, you can use a predefined local or global temporary table or a permanent worktable.

FIGURE 8.9.

A trigger can pass the contents of `inserted` *and* `deleted` *to stored procedures, using predefined temporary or permanent tables.*

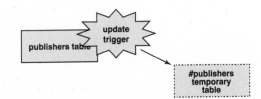

Here's a quick example of how a trigger could use a temporary table. In the first step, an empty temporary table meant to duplicate the structure of the `publishers` table is created within the session. That temporary table is available from any subsequent procedure or trigger call until the connection logs out or the table is explicitly dropped:

```
select *
into #publishers
from publishers
where 1 = 2
```

In this example, the next step is to create a trigger. Notice that the temporary table must exist when the trigger is created, and of course must exist when the trigger executes. In this example, the trigger simply copies the contents of `inserted` into the temporary `#publishers` table:

```
create trigger p
on publishers for update
as
insert #publishers
select * from inserted
return
```

To test the trigger, update the `publishers` table, in this case affecting every row but making no actual change to the data:

```
update publishers
set city = city
```

After the trigger has run, the user has access to the temporary table with the contents of the inserted table. Using this method, further action can be taken on the modified rows, both within the trigger and after execution. Here are the contents of the temporary table after the update statement is complete:

```
select * from #publishers

pub_id pub_name                              city                  state country
------ ------------------------------------- --------------------- ----- --------
0736   New Moon Books                        Boston                MA    USA
0877   Binnet & Hardley                      Washington            DC    USA
1389   Algodata Infosystems                  Berkeley              CA    USA
1622   Five Lakes Publishing                 Chicago               IL    USA
1756   Ramona Publishers                     Dallas                TX    USA
9901   GGG&G                                 München               (null)Germany
9952   Scootney Books                        New York              NY    USA
9999   Lucerne Publishing                    Paris                 (null)France

(8 row(s) affected)
```

WARNING

Referencing local and global temporary tables from within triggers can lead to some problems with reliability. If the temporary table isn't created properly, or for some reason is unavailable when the trigger fires, SQL Server returns a runtime error message like this one:

```
Msg 208, Level 16, State 1
Invalid object name '#publishers'.
```

You may choose instead to use a permanent worktable for all trigger executions for a particular table, and to identify rows within the worktable by server process ID (@@spid).

The update() Function

The update() function is available only inside an insert or update trigger. The function allows a trigger to determine whether a column was affected by the insert or update statement that fired the trigger. By testing whether a column has changed, a trigger can avoid performing unnecessary work.

Here's the basic syntax for the update() function:

```
if update(column-name)
```

In this example, changes to the price column must be recorded in an audit table. The update() function tests for changes to the column:

```
create trigger tr_titles_iu
as
if update(price)
   insert audit_table (dt, descr, usr)
   values (getdate(), "price update",
      user_name())
return
```

When Is update() True?

The update() function doesn't really tell you whether the column was modified—only if it was *referenced* in the insert or update statement that fired the trigger. After an insert statement, the function is true if a value (null or non-null) was specified by the insert statement. Here are some examples, with comments describing whether the update() function is true:

```
/* update(price) is true because a value was specified */
insert titles (title_id, ..., price)
values ("BU1234", ..., $15.95)

/* update(price) is true because an explicit null was specified */
insert titles (title_id, ..., price)
values ("BU1234", ..., null)

/* update(price) is false because no value was specified */
insert titles (title_id, ...)
values ("BU1234", ...)
```

In the last example, update() is false because no value for price was specified. However, if a default exists for the column, the update() test is true.

After an update statement, the update() test returns true if the column was included on the left-hand side of a set statement:

```
/* update(price) is true because the price column
   appears in the set clause */
update titles
set pubdate = "12/4/96",
   price = $15.95
where ...

/* update(price) is false because the price column
   is not included in the set clause */
update titles
set pubdate = "12/4/96"
where ...
```

The next example underscores the point that update() tells you only whether the column was included in the set statement, not whether the column was actually modified. In this example, update() is true, even though the price clearly will not change:

```
update titles
set pubdate = "12/4/96",
   price = price
where ...
```

Trigger Restrictions

Triggers can't create or drop objects or perform work that affects the contents of the transaction log, including any of these commands:

- create or drop objects
- select ... into
- alter table,
- alter database
- truncate table
- grant or revoke
- update statistics
- reconfigure
- load database or load transaction
- Disk commands (disk init, disk mirror, etc.)

Triggers and Transactions

One of the most common applications of triggers is to perform complex row validation. If the trigger determines that the data modification statement that fired it was invalid, it can roll back the transaction. To do so, you execute the rollback transaction within the trigger itself. When a trigger executes rollback transaction:

- All work performed by the trigger is rolled back.
- All work performed by the statement *and its entire transaction* is rolled back.
- The trigger runs to completion.
- When the trigger returns, the batch continues processing.

> **WARNING**
>
> The last three versions of SQL Server have exhibited different behavior when a trigger executes rollback transaction. In Version 4.2 (and all versions of Sybase SQL Server), rollback transaction immediately ended all processing in the trigger itself and in the batch. Thus, no statements following the rollback statement were executed in the trigger, and no statements following the data modification that fired the trigger were executed in the batch.
>
> In Version 6.0, processing continued through completion in the trigger after rollback, but the batch would return immediately after the trigger completed execution.

In Version 6.5, processing continues both in the trigger and in the batch. It's up to the programmer to detect the error and end processing.

This behavior is very easy to test. Build a table with one or two columns for testing trigger behavior:

```
create trigger trigtable
(c1 int, c2 int)
```

Now write an `insert` trigger that prints messages before and after you roll back the transaction:

```
create trigger instrig on trigtable for insert as
print "inside trigger before rollback"
rollback transaction
print "inside trigger after rollback"
return
```

Finally, execute a batch that prints messages before and after the `insert` statement:

```
print "in batch before insert"
insert trigtable values (1,1)
print "in batch after insert"
```

Here's the output from the batch with Version 6.5:

```
in batch before insert
inside trigger before rollback
inside trigger after rollback

(1 row(s) affected)

in batch after insert
```

As you can see, processing continues both inside and outside the trigger, even after a `rollback transaction` statement. Check the behavior of this transaction in every version of SQL Server you're running to ensure that you can predict the behavior of your code and write error handlers to deal with any inconsistencies.

What doesn't `rollback transaction` do? It doesn't send a `print` statement, an error message, or any warning at all to the user. It's critical to raise an error when executing a rollback, because your error message is the only warning the user will receive that the transaction failed.

Here's an example of a trigger that rolls back transactions on Sunday:

```
create trigger tr_publishers_d
on publishers for delete
as
if datepart(dw, getdate()) = 1 /* Sunday */
begin
    raiserror ("Cannot delete publisher on Sunday", 16, 1)
    rollback tran
end
```

> **NOTE**
>
> There's a question about how exactly to code the error handler inside a trigger. For performance reasons, because locks persist until you execute the `rollback` statement, shouldn't you `rollback` before you `raiserror`?
>
> The answer depends on how you plan to use your trigger code. Prior to Version 6.0 (and in all releases of Sybase SQL Server), `rollback transaction` in a trigger automatically and immediately aborts trigger processing. Thus, if you were to write the following trigger error handler for those early versions, no error message would be returned:
>
> ```
> ...
> if error_condition
> begin
>     rollback tran
>     raiserror ...
> end
> ...
> ```
>
> Because the rollback doesn't implicitly cause an error, the user would receive *no error message at all*, and would believe (rationally) that the transaction had successfully completed.
>
> Recommendation: To get absolutely the best performance from SQL Server 6.5, roll back first, and then raise an error. If you are at all concerned about compatibility with earlier releases or with Sybase, raise the error before you roll back.

Trigger Applications

This section shows some examples of triggers that perform data validation or maintain a derived value in another table. These examples are meant to show the basic trigger programming techniques and help you start to conceive of useful applications for triggers in your own systems. These are the applications demonstrated in this section:

- Special RI: Cascade `delete`
- Special RI: Trickle `insert`
- Override trigger validation
- Maintain derived data

In each case, a template of the trigger is presented with an example, followed by a detailed line-by-line review of the trigger code. In the case of the RI examples, it might be useful to look at the section on maintaining declarative referential integrity using constraints in Chapter 6, "Creating and Altering Database Objects."

Special RI: Cascade `delete`

Normally, a `delete` to a referenced table fails if there are related rows in a referencing table (see Figure 8.10). In this example, a deletion to a referenced table (`stores`) results in the deletion of all related rows in referencing tables.

FIGURE 8.10.

Cascading deleted stores
causes deletions of related
rows in sales.

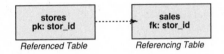

stores	sales
pk: stor_id	fk: stor_id
Referenced Table	Referencing Table

Here's the `delete` statement that should fire the trigger:

```
delete stores
where stor_id like "70%"
```

A cascade `delete` trigger is always placed on the *referenced* table and deletes rows from the *referencing* table. The template code is in Listing 8.1, which you can find on the CD-ROM distributed with this book, in `\source\ch8\list01.sql`.

Listing 8.1. To use this template for a cascade `delete` trigger, provide the names of the referenced and referencing tables and specify the join keys in the where clause of the `delete` statement.

```
create trigger trigger-name
on referenced-table for delete
as
if @@rowcount = 0
   return
delete referencing-table
from deleted d, referencing-table r
where d.join-key = r.join-key
if @@error != 0
begin
   raiserror ("error encountered in trigger processing", 16, 1)
   rollback tran
   return
end
return
```

In this example of a cascade `delete` trigger (see Listing 8.2, `list02.sql` on the CD-ROM), the `stores` table is referenced, meaning that the trigger should cascade deletes from the `stores` table to the `sales` table.

Listing 8.2. This trigger cascades deletes from stores to sales.

```
create trigger tr_stores_d
on stores for delete
```

continues

Listing 8.2. continued

```
as
if @@rowcount = 0
   return
delete sales
from deleted d, sales s
where d.stor_id = s.stor_id
if @@error != 0
begin
   raiserror ("error encountered in trigger processing", 16, 1)
   rollback tran
   return
end
return
```

A Detailed Look

This section provides a detailed line-by-line review of the trigger. The statement from the trigger is presented first, followed by a brief discussion of its purpose and application.

```
if @@rowcount = 0
   return
```

Triggers can hold open locks, even if no rows were affected by the statement firing the trigger. Therefore, every trigger should return immediately if no rows were affected.

> **NOTE**
>
> `@@rowcount` provides the number of rows modified by the statement firing the trigger. The value of `@@rowcount` changes throughout the trigger, after each SQL statement (except `declare`). If you need to refer to the original value of `@@rowcount` later in the trigger, you should store it in a variable.

```
delete sales
from deleted d, sales s
where d.stor_id = s.stor_id
```

At the next step, the trigger cascades the deletion to the `sales` table by deleting rows in `sales` having a `stor_id` in the `deleted` table. To understand this action better, consider what happens when a statement deletes rows from the `stores` table, and then calls the trigger:

```
delete stores
where stor_id like "70%"
```

Tables 8.1 and 8.2 show the contents of the `deleted` and `sales` tables when the trigger fires (the `inserted` table is empty after a `delete` statement).

Table 8.1. Two columns from the `deleted` table.

stor_id	stor_name
7066	Barnum's
7067	News & Brews

Table 8.2. Key columns from the `sales` table before trigger execution.

stor_id	ord_num
5023	AB-123-DEF-425-1Z3
5023	AB-872-DEF-732-2Z1
...	...
6380	356921
7066	BA27618
7066	BA52498
7066	BA71224
7067	NB-1.442
7067	NB-3.442
7131	Asoap132
...	...

For each row in `deleted`, SQL Server finds and deletes corresponding rows from the `sales` table. In this case, the five rows with a `stor_id` of `7066` and `7067` are deleted.

```
if @@error != 0
begin
    raiserror ("error encountered in trigger processing", 16, 1)
    rollback tran
    return
end
```

Good error checking will avoid unpleasant surprises with SQL Server. Check `@@error` after each SQL statement in a trigger, and roll back after reporting an error to the user.

Nested Triggers

When a trigger modifies another table, ordinarily the trigger on the second table is fired. This is called *nested triggers*. By default, the server will execute nested triggers up to 16 levels deep. If the nesting goes more than 16 levels, the trigger will fail with error 217:

```
Maximum stored procedure nesting level exceeded (limit 246).
```

A system configuration setting determines whether SQL Server will execute nested triggers. The sa can execute this statement to turn off nesting (a value of 1 turns it back on):

```
sp_configure 'nested triggers', 0
```

> **NOTE**
>
> This configuration can also be managed through SQL-EM with the Server | Configurations menu choice, using the Configuration tab in the Server Configuration/Options dialog box.

Special RI: Trickle `insert`

An `insert` to a referencing table is normally blocked if the foreign key can't be found in the referenced table. In this example, the user needs to insert a new row on-the-fly into the referenced table. This is sometimes called *trickling* an insert. These statements should fire the trigger:

```
insert sales (stor_id, ...)

insert sales (stor_id, ...)
select stor_id, ...
from #sales
```

A trickled insert trigger is placed on the *referencing* table and inserts rows into the *referenced* table. The template for this trigger is in Listing 8.3 (`list03.sql` on the CD-ROM).

Listing 8.3. To use this template, replace the names of tables and join keys, and provide the names and columns to be substituted.

```
create trigger trigger-name
on referencing-table for insert
as
declare @rows int
select @rows = @@rowcount
if @rows = 0
   return
if @rows <> (select count(*)
   from inserted i, referenced-table r
   where i.join-key = r.join-key)
if @@error <> 0
begin
   raiserror ...
   rollback tran
end
begin
   insert referenced-table (col-list)
   select distinct col-list
   from inserted
```

```
    where join-key not in
       (select join-key
        from referenced-table)
    if @@error <> 0
    begin
       raiserror ...
       rollback tran
    end
end
return
```

One thing you will notice about this trigger is that there may be several column values for the referenced table that are unavailable or will need to use default values. For this reason, the trickle may be appropriate only in extraordinary circumstances. In the example using sales and stores (Listing 8.4, list04.sql on the CD-ROM), only the stor_id is provided for an inserted row in the stores table. Additional non-null columns will require a column default or should be specified in the trigger code.

Listing 8.4. This insert trigger for the sales table checks for missing rows in the stores table and adds corresponding stores where they are not found.

```
create trigger tr_sales_i
on sales for insert
as
declare @rows int
select @rows = @@rowcount
if @rows = 0
    return
if @rows <> (select count(*)
    from inserted i, stores s
    where i.stor_id = s.stor_id)
if @@error <> 0
begin
    raiserror ("error in tr_sales_i", 16, 1)
    rollback tran
end
begin
    insert stores (stor_id)
    select distinct stor_id
    from inserted
    where stor_id not in
       (select stor_id
        from sales)
    if @@error <> 0
    begin
       raiserror ("error in tr_sales_i", 16, 1)
       rollback tran
    end
end
return
```

A Detailed Look

Here's the `@@rowcount` code again:

```
declare @rows int
select @rows = @@rowcount
if @rows = 0
   return
```

Before testing `@@rowcount`, capture it in a variable if you plan to use it later in the trigger. Remember that every statement (except `declare`) changes the value of `@@rowcount`.

```
if @rows <> (select count(*)
   from inserted i, stores s
   where i.stor_id = s.stor_id)
```

This is a basic integrity check, testing whether joins for all rows exist in the referenced tables. To understand it better, consider the statement firing the trigger and the resulting contents of the `inserted` and `stores` tables (see Tables 8.3 and 8.4):

```
insert sales (stor_id, ...)
select stor_id, ...
from #sales
```

Table 8.3. Two columns from the `inserted` table.

stor_id	ord_num
3345	RS-5555535
7066	JK-111123
7066	LM-53-99-A
7067	KK-12341

Table 8.4. Two key columns from the `stores` table.

stor_id	stor_name
7066	Barnum's
7067	News & Brews
7131	Doc-U-Mat: Quality Laundry and Books
8042	Bookbeat
6380	Eric the Read Books
7896	Fricative Bookshop
5023	Thoreau Reading Discount Chain

In this case, one of the inserted `stor_id` values is missing from the `stores` table. The number of rows found when joining the tables is 3 where the value of `@rows` is 4, so if `@rows <> ( ... )` is `true`, the next statement is executed.

> **TIP**
>
> It's generally better to avoid two-pass processing (one to check for missing rows, the second to perform the insert) if you expect to fail to find rows. If most of the time the values entered are available, it's advantageous to avoid the exclusive locking caused by an `insert` statement inside the trigger. In this case, the two-pass processing was determined to be infrequent, so the code includes the test.

```
insert stores
    (stor_id, stor_name)
    select distinct stor_id, null
    from inserted
    where stor_id not in
        (select stor_id
         from sales)
```

In this final step, the trigger inserts `distinct` new rows in the referenced table. The `distinct` keyword prevents duplicate stores in the case where multiple inserted rows share the same missing `stor_id`.

Override Trigger Validation

If an application needs to permit only certain users to make modifications to data, using some sort of override key, you can use a trigger to permit those changes. In this example, a negative `qty` in the `sales` table represents a merchandise credit for a customer, which only selected users may perform.

This trigger allows negative amounts only if a value of `"Y"` is inserted in an `override` column in the same row. The catch is this: Only certain users have been granted permission to update that column.

To set up this example, add the `override` column to the `sales` table, and then grant the proper permissions on the table and column:

```
alter table sales
    add override char(1) default "N" null
revoke update on
    sales(override) from public
grant update on
    sales (override) to supervisors
```

Listing 8.5 (`list05.sql` on the CD-ROM) displays the trigger to handle the override authorization.

Listing 8.5. The update trigger checks the override code and updates the table if necessary.

```
create trigger tr_sales_u
on sales for update
as
if @@rowcount = 0
   return
if update(qty)
begin
   /* check for new rows with negative qty, no override */
   if exists (select * from inserted
      where qty < 0
      and override <> "Y")
   begin
   raiserror ("invalid update", 16, 1)
   rollback tran
   return
   end
update sales
set override = "N"
from sales s, inserted i
where s.stor_id = i.stor_id
and s.title_id = i.title_id
and s.ord_num = i.ord_num
and s.override = "Y"
end
/* if @@error <> 0 ... */
return
```

The important part of this trigger is the update statement to turn off the override value wherever it's turned on. (Otherwise any user could update that row in a subsequent statement, regardless of their access to the override column itself.) A trigger can modify the table on which it is written *without executing the trigger again*, in what would otherwise be an infinite loop.

Maintaining Derived Data

It's often useful to store a data value in more than one place to improve performance when reading the value from SQL Server. (This technique, called *denormalization*, is discussed in detail in Chapter 18, "Database Design and Performance.")

For example, it might be useful to keep a copy of the title of a book right in the sales table to improve select performance on that table (see Figure 8.11). The problem is, how do you manage the derived title column in the sales table after changes in the titles table?

FIGURE 8.11.

A duplicate title *column in the* sales *table could improve* select *performance on the* sales *table.*

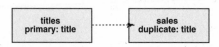

There are several methods of maintaining duplicate and derived data, including the following methods:

- Client-based application code
- A stored procedure
- A trigger

The benefit of using triggers is that they can maintain data integrity automatically after each SQL statement. This means that, regardless of the method used to prepare and issue a data modification statement, the data can't be modified without running the trigger.

> **NOTE**
>
> There are two notable exceptions, which are unlogged data modification statements. `truncate table` removes all rows from a table without checking DRI constraints or executing triggers. `bcp` (the bulk copy program) inserts rows without checking constraints or triggers.

Here's an example of an `update titles` statement that would fire the trigger on the `titles` table. The problem is to write a trigger that copies the revised title to the related rows in the `sales` table:

```
update titles
set title = "Sushi, Really!"
where title = "Sushi, Anyone?"
```

The greatest complication in writing a trigger to handle data maintenance is dealing with the case where more than one row is modified by the initial statement. You need to rely on the set-processing capabilities of SQL to handle the multi-row instances, rather than using a row-wise mechanism (such as cursors).

Here's the trigger code. Notice the Transact-SQL version of an `update` statement to handle the update based on a join:

```
create trigger tr_titles_u
as
if @@rowcount <> 0 return
if update(title)
    update salesdetail
    set title = i.title
    from salesdetail sd, inserted i
    where sd.title_id = i.title_id
if @@error <> 0 ...
return
```

Trigger Summary

Triggers hold exclusive locks and are active in the transaction log. They're slow compared to other, non-SQL-based structures like constraints, rules, and defaults. But they're faster than many other mechanisms used to manage data integrity (particularly client-based tools), and they provide nearly bulletproof resistance to data corruption when written properly.

Triggers must be

- Fast
- Efficient
- Effective on the multi-row case
- Well tested

Triggers should not

- Try to wait for user input
- Select data for the user
- Sort out bad and good data
- Use cursors

Triggers can play a critical part in the implementation of a typical database design. Whether providing access to advanced referential integrity capabilities or performing automatic maintenance of denormalized data, triggers allow you to implement the kinds of complex, real-life business rules that make systems effective and robust.

Stored Procedures

A *stored procedure* is an executable database object that exists independently of a table. It can be called from a client or from another procedure or trigger, parameters can be passed and returned, and error codes can be checked. This section explores the following topics:

- Creating stored procedures
- Passing parameters in and out
- Handling return codes
- Effects on the optimizer

Stored Procedure Advantages

Stored procedures provide many benefits over executing large and complex SQL batches from a client workstation:

- **Faster execution.** Stored procedures, after their first execution, become memory-resident and don't need to be reparsed, reoptimized, and recompiled.

- **Reduced network traffic.** Stored procedures can consist of hundreds of individual SQL statements, but can be executed with a single statement. This allows you to reduce the size of the call from the client to the server.

- **Modular programming.** Procedures provide a method of breaking things into smaller, more manageable pieces.

- **Restricted, function-based access to tables.** You can grant permissions in such a way as to allow a user access to tables *only* through the stored procedure.

- **Reduced operator error.** There's less information to pass.

- **Enforced consistency.** If users are accessing tables only through your stored procedures, problems resulting from ad hoc data modifications are eliminated.

- **Automated complex or sensitive transactions.** By requiring all interaction with certain tables to take place in a stored procedure, you can guarantee data integrity on those tables.

Running Stored Procedures

Stored procedures improve overall system performance because optimization and compilation by the SQL Server enhances procedure performance and storing procedures where they are to be used reduces network traffic. The first time a procedure is executed, the server must optimize and compile it. That compiled optimization plan is stored in procedure cache and may be available when the procedure is run later. If so, the optimization and compilation steps are skipped:

First Execution	Subsequent Executions
Locate stored procedure on disk and load into cache	Locate stored procedure in cache
Substitute parameter values	Substitute parameter values
Develop optimization plan	
Compile optimization plan	
Execute from cache	Execute from cache

Notice that the second time the stored procedure is run, it's in memory and is therefore much faster to locate. You don't need to optimize or create an executable plan.

> **NOTE**
>
> Sometimes skipping the optimization step leads to worse performance. (More on this under create proc ... with recompile and execute proc with recompile.)

Creating Stored Procedures

To write a stored procedure, you need to provide the procedure with a unique name, and then write the sequence of SQL statements to be included in the procedure. It's good programming practice to end the stored procedure with a `return` statement. Here's the simplified syntax for a stored procedure and a quick example:

```
create proc procedure_name
as
SQL statements
[return [status_value]]

create proc pub_titles
as
select t.title, p.pub_name
  from publishers p join titles t on p.pub_id = t.pub_id
return
```

To execute a stored procedure, simply invoke it by name (just like you execute system stored procedures like sp_help). Use the `execute` keyword if the call to the stored procedure isn't the first statement in the batch.

> **NOTE**
>
> Some of these rules seem awfully arbitrary unless you think about how the parser works. If the parser sees an unknown word appearing first in the batch, it tries to find a stored procedure with that name. In most other contexts, it will simply try to fit that unknown name into the syntax of the current statement being executed. For example, the parser might think that the stored procedure call in this next example was an alias for the `titles` table:
>
> ```
> select * from titles
> sp_help
> ```
>
> The server needs to know that this unknown word is really the name of a stored procedure. You indicate this with the `execute` keyword:
>
> ```
> select * from titles
> execute sp_help
> ```
>
> Whenever you're having a problem understanding the parsing and syntax rules, try to be a parser yourself, and see if you can make sense out of the syntax you sent!

Here's the syntax for the execution step:

```
[exec[ute]] proc_name
```

These two examples do the same thing—execute the procedure created above:

```
pub_titles
```

```
exec pub_titles
```

To drop a stored procedure, use the `drop proc` statement:

```
drop proc proc_name
```

SQL Server and Temporary Stored Procedures

Normally, stored procedures are permanent, persistent objects. They're retained in the database catalogs until explicitly dropped. SQL Server allows you to create temporary and global temporary stored procedures. By putting a # as the first character, a *temporary stored procedure* is unique to a user connection and is destroyed either when the user disconnects or when the server is shut down. *Global temporary procedures* begin with ## and are available to *any* user connection. They're dropped when the server is restarted.

Display and Maintenance

Procedures can be renamed by using sp_rename. To modify a stored procedure, drop the procedure and re-create it; a stored procedure must be dropped before it can be re-created with the same name by the same user.

You can't drop and re-create an object in the same batch. The following batch fails because SQL Server parses the whole batch before execution. When it reaches the `create proc` statement with the parser and checks to make sure that no such procedure exists before creating it, the procedure is still there, so the whole batch fails:

```
/* this batch will fail to execute ... why?
Objects cannot be dropped and created in the same batch */
drop proc titles_for_a_pub
create proc titles_for_a_pub
as ...
```

The next example includes a `go` statement, which separates the two executions into separate batches. This example works fine:

```
/* this batch succeeds because drop and create are in separate batches */
drop proc titles_for_a_pub
go
create proc titles_for_a_pub
as ...
```

A better method is the following:

```
/* check if the procedure exists and drop it */
if exists (select * from sysobjects
    where name = "titles_for_a_pub"
    and type = "P" and uid = user_id())
  drop proc titles_for_a_pub
go
create proc titles_for_a_pub
as ...
```

Why even worry about this? It's a standard and very important practice to maintain copies of your stored procedures in scripts, both for documentation and for capability of modifying the procedures (there's no "modify procedure" or "alter procedure" statement).

SQL Enterprise Manager provides the Manage Stored Procedures window for managing stored procedures in a database. Use the Manage | Stored Procedures menu option from SQL-EM (see Figure 8.12).

FIGURE 8.12.

Use the Manage | Stored Procedures menu option to access the window. Make sure that the correct database is currently selected.

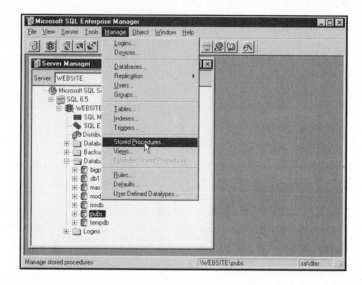

When the Manage Stored Procedures window appears, you're provided with the framework of a new procedure. To retrieve an existing procedure, use the drop-down list box in the toolbar of the window (see Figure 8.13). To retrieve procedures from another database, you must close the Manage Stored Procedures window, select the correct database, and reopen the window.

FIGURE 8.13.

You can retrieve existing stored procedures with the drop-down list box of procedure names for the current database.

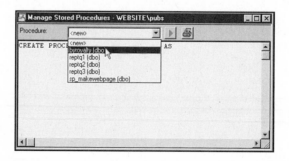

Notice that when you retrieve a procedure, SQL-EM automatically supplies the code to drop and re-create the procedure.

Displaying Procedure Code in ISQL/w

To display the text of a stored procedure in the database in which it was created, use the sp_helptext stored procedure, whose syntax is spelled out here:

```
sp_helptext procedure_name
```

Here's how to retrieve the create proc statement from the titles_for_a_pub procedure:

```
sp_helptext titles_for_a_pub

text
-------------------------------------------------------
create proc titles_for_a_pub
    (@pub_name varchar(40))
as
select t.title from publishers p, titles t
    where p.pub_id = t.pub_id
    and pub_name like @pub_name
return

( 0 rows affected)
```

> **NOTE**
>
> SQL Enterprise Manager and sp_helptext both reverse-engineer this information from the system table syscomments, where the text of stored procedures (and triggers and views) is stored. If objects (including the procedure itself) are renamed, the text of the procedure *will not be maintained automatically.*

sp_help reports parameters' names and datatypes for a stored procedure:

```
sp_help procedure_name
```

The last part of this sample output from sp_help displays information about the parameters of the procedure (continued on the following page):

```
sp_help titles_for_a_pub

Name                 Owner      Type                  When_created
-------------------- ---------- --------------------- --------------------
titles_for_a_pub dbo           stored procedure   Aug 15 1996  3:58PM
( 0 rows affected)


Data_located_on_segment
----------------------
not applicable
( 0 rows affected)
```

```
Parameter_name    Type     Length Prec Scale Param_order
---------------   -------  ------ ---- ----- -----------
@pub_name         varchar   40     40          1
( 0 rows affected)
```

Procedures and Parameters

Stored procedures can accept parameters to improve their usefulness and flexibility. The parameters are declared at the top of the procedure:

```
create proc procedure_name
     (parameter_name datatype [, ...])
as
sql_statements
[return [status_value]]

[exec[ute]] procedure_name [expression] [, ... ]
```

Here's an example of a stored procedure with a single parameter, @pub_name. You need to declare a datatype for parameters, and you can use user-defined datatypes if they exist in the database where the procedure is created:

```
create proc titles_for_a_pub
     (@pub_name varchar(40))
as
select t.title from publishers p, titles t
     where p.pub_id = t.pub_id
     and pub_name like @pub_name
return
```

The procedure accepts a publisher name and looks up publishers based on that name.

Example: Procedure Usage

Here's an example of how a procedure with a parameter might be used. Note that the quotes around the parameter value, Algo%, are required because the string includes a special character, % (quotes are also required around character data that includes spaces, punctuation, or any reserved words):

```
titles_for_a_pub 'Algo%'

title
-------------------------------------------------------
The Busy Executive's Database Guide
Cooking with Computers: Surreptitious Balance Sheets
Straight Talk About Computers
But Is It User Friendly?
Secrets of Silicon Valley
Net Etiquette
( 6 rows affected)
```

```
exec titles_for_a_pub 'New Moon Books'

title
- - - - - - - - - - - - - - - - - - - - - - - - - - - - - - - - - - - - - - - - -
You Can Combat Computer Stress!
Is Anger the Enemy?
Life Without Fear
Prolonged Data Deprivation: Four Case Studies
Emotional Security: A New Algorithm
( 5 rows affected)
```

Parameter names, like local variables, require an "at" sign (@), and can be up to 30 characters long. You are still restricted by all the other SQL Server naming guidelines—no spaces or punctuation, case sensitivity, etc. You can define up to 255 parameters per procedure.

If you use user-defined datatypes, make sure that they're defined in the database—and aren't inadvertently deleted! Rules, defaults, and column properties like nullability and identity don't apply to parameters defined with user-defined datatypes. All parameters are nullable.

Microsoft SQL Server can use text and image datatypes as read-only stored procedure parameters.

Executing with Parameters

At execution time, parameters can be specified by position or by name. If passed by name, parameters can be passed in any order. Following is the basic syntax:

```
[exec[ute]] procedure_name
    [[@parm_name = ]expression] [, ... ]
```

> **TIP**
>
> Because stored procedure parameter names are public, try to use meaningful names to help users and programmers pass the proper values.

Here's an example of a stored procedure that requires three parameters:

```
create proc myproc
    (@val1 int, @val2 int, @val3 int)
as
...
go
```

In this example, the parameters are passed by position. The execute statement doesn't provide any parameter names, so the values are assigned to the parameters in the order they were defined in the create statement (@val1, @val2, @val3):

```
/* parameters passed by position here */
exec myproc 10,20,15
```

In this example, the parameters are passed by name. The execute statement provides specific parameter names for each value, so the values are assigned to the parameters explicitly, according to the specifications of the execute statement:

```
/* parameter passed by name here */
exec myproc @val2 = 20, @val1 = 10, @val3 = 15
```

After you start passing parameters by name, all subsequent parameters must be passed by name.

Passing parameters by name is more flexible and self-documenting than passing parameters by position; however, passing by position is marginally faster.

Default Parameter Values

Stored procedure parameters can be assigned default values if no value is supplied during execution. You can improve your stored procedure code by defining defaults for all parameters:

```
create proc procedure_name
      (@parameter_name datatype = default_value
      [,...])
as
SQL Statements
[return [status_value]]
```

Example: Procedure Creation

```
/* check for a pub_name before executing query */
create proc titles_for_a_pub
      (@pub_name varchar(40) = null)
as
if @pub_name = null
  begin
  print "Pass in the pub_name as a parameter"
  return
  end
select t.title from publishers p, titles t
      where p.pub_id = t.pub_id
      and pub_name like @pub_name + "%"
return
```

Here, you pass in a parameter and verify that the parameter has actually been passed. If you hadn't specified a default, SQL Server would have sent a generic error message (and the procedure wouldn't execute) if no procedure name was passed at execution time. If you specify a default value for a parameter, the stored procedure executes, giving you the chance to check the default and take action within the stored procedure.

If you execute without providing a parameter value, you get the error message you wrote:

```
/* without a parameter, you get the message */
titles_for_a_pub
go

Pass in the pub_name as a parameter
```

If you provide a parameter, you get the typical procedure execution:

```
/* with a parameter, you get the results */
titles_for_a_pub "Algo%"
go

title
-------------------------------------------------
The Busy Executive's Database Guide
Cooking with Computers:Surreptitious Balance Sheets
Straight Talk About Computers
But is it User Friendly
Secrets of Silicon Valley
Net Etiquette
```

Passing Parameters In and Out

Stored procedure parameters can be passed both in and out. The output keyword identifies parameters that can be returned to the calling batch or procedure. Notice in the syntax the use of output in both the create proc and execute statements:

```
create proc procedure_name
  [ (@parm_name datatype = default_value [output]
    [, ... ] )]
as
SQL Statements
[return [status_value]]

[exec[ute]] procedure_name
      [[@parm_name = ] expression [output] [, ... ]
```

In this example, the procedure accepts two parameters, @title and @ytd_sales. The second parameter is keyed for output, meaning that its value at the end of the procedure will be available for return to the calling process. The procedure finds a row in the titles table for the @title value and then stores the value of ytd_sales for that title in the parameter:

```
/* passing a parameter back to calling batch */
create proc ytd_sales
  (@title varchar(80) = null,
   @ytd_sales int output)
as
if @title = null
  begin
  print "Syntax: ytd_sales title, @variable [output]"
  return
  end
select @ytd_sales = ytd_sales
  from titles
  where title = @title
return
```

The execute statement needs to declare a variable to store the returned value (@sales_figure). The datatype of the variable should match the datatype of the output parameter. The execute statement itself needs to include the keyword output to complete the chain and permit the value of the parameter to be returned to the variable. The final `select` statement demonstrates the use of that returned value:

```
/* variable must be set up first to accept output value
** in this example, total sales are returned by position */
declare @sales_figure int
exec ytd_sales 'But Is It User Friendly?', @sales_figure output
select 'ytd sales of But Is It User Friendly?  = ', @sales_figure
go
```

```
-------------------------------------------- -----------
ytd sales of But Is It User Friendly?  =   8780
( 1 row affected)
```

This example shows the same execution as directly above, except that the parameters are passed by name (`@title = ...`) instead of position:

```
/* in this example, total sales are returned by name */
declare @sales_figure int
exec total_sales @title= 'But Is It User Friendly?',
               @ytd_sales = @sales_figure output
print "total sales of But Is It User Friendly?= %1!", @sales_figure
go
```

Returning Procedure Status

Every stored procedure automatically returns an integer status value: `0` is returned on successful completion, `-1` through `-99` are returned for SQL Server-detected errors. Use a `return` statement to specify a return value greater than `0` or less than `-99`. The calling program can set up a local variable to receive and check the return status. Here's the syntax for the creation and the execution:

```
create proc procedure_name
 [ (@parm_name datatype = default_value [output]
   [, ... ] ) ]
as
SQL Statements
return [integer_status_value]

[execute] [@status_var = procedure_name
    [[@parm_name = ] expression [output] [, ... ]
```

When you create the procedure, you need to define any error conditions and associate them with integral error codes. It's best if the error codes are well defined and consistent throughout your application (or, even better, throughout your organization). They must at least be documented and well defined between a stored procedure and a calling batch. In this example, the value `15` means that the user failed to provide a necessary parameter, the value `-101` means that no publisher with the specified name was found, and the value `0` means that the procedure ran without error. In a long stored procedure, it's useful to define error status in a comment in the procedure header:

```
/* procedure sets an error status on error */
create proc titles_for_a_pub
```

```
        (@pub_name varchar(40) = null ) as
if @pub_name = null
    return 15
if not exists (select * from publishers
        where pub_name = @pub_name)
    return -101
select t.title from publishers p, titles t
    where p.pub_id = t.pub_id
    and pub_name = @pub_name
return 0
```

During procedure execution, the execute keyword is followed by a local variable that can accept a return status code. This allows the batch or application to take action if an error occurred during procedure execution:

```
/* check for status and report errors */
declare @status int
exec @status = titles_for_a_pub 'New Age Books'
if @status = 15
    print "Invalid Syntax"
else if @status = -101
    print "No publisher by that name found"
```

SQL Server Status Codes

In addition to your own status codes, SQL Server provides error codes if a stored procedure terminates unexpectedly during execution. The following table lists return status codes currently in use by SQL Server.

Status Code	Meaning
0	Successful return
-1	Missing object referenced
-2	Datatype mismatch error
-3	Process chosen as deadlock victim
-4	Permission error
-5	Syntax error
-6	Miscellaneous user error
-7	Resource error, such as out of space
-8	Nonfatal internal problem (bug)
-9	System limit reached
-10	Fatal internal inconsistency (bug)
-11	Fatal internal inconsistency (bug)
-12	Table or index corrupted
-13	Database corrupted
-14	Hardware error

Stored Procedures and Transactions

SQL Server notes the transaction nesting level before calling a stored procedure. If the transaction nesting level when the procedure returns is different from the level when executed, SQL Server displays the following message:

```
Transaction count after EXECUTE indicates that a COMMIT or ROLLBACK TRAN is missing
```

This message indicates that transaction nesting is out of whack. Because a stored procedure doesn't abort the batch on a `rollback transaction`, a `rollback` inside the procedure could result in loss of data integrity if subsequent statements are executed and committed.

A `rollback transaction` statement rolls back all statements to the outermost transaction, including any work performed inside nested stored procedures that haven't been fully committed (that is, `@@trancount > 0`). A `commit tran` within the stored procedure decrements the `@@trancount` by only one.

> **TIP**
>
> Develop a consistent error-handling strategy for failed transactions or other errors that occur within transactions. Implement this strategy consistently across procedures and applications. Implement transaction control in nested stored procedures. Check whether the procedure is being called from a transaction before issuing a `begin tran`.

Because a `rollback transaction` from a procedure doesn't abort the batch calling the procedure, follow these guidelines:

- Procedures should make no net change to `@@trancount`.
- Issue a `rollback tran` only if the stored procedure issues the `begin tran` statement.

Here's a code template for a stored procedure that can provide transactional integrity whether it's run as part of an ongoing transaction or as its own transaction:

```
/* proc to demonstrate no net change to @@trancount
** but rolls back changes within the proc
** VERY IMPORTANT: return an error code
** to tell the calling procedure rollback occurred */

create proc p1
as
declare @trncnt int

select @trncnt = @@trancount   -- save @@trancount value

if @trncnt = 0   -- transaction has not begun
   begin tran p1  -- begin tran increments nest level to 1
```

```
else               -- already in a transaction
  save tran p1     -- save tran doesn't increment nest level

/* do some processing */

if (@@transtate = 2) -- or other error condition
  begin
  rollback tran p1   -- rollback to savepoint, or begin tran
  return 25          -- return error code indicating rollback
  end

/* more processing if required */

if @trncnt = 0       -- this proc issued begin tran
  commit tran p1     -- commit tran, decrement @@trancount to 0
                     -- commit not required with save tran

return 0 /* successful return */
```

Here's a template for the calling batch that might execute the stored procedure listed here. The main problem you need to solve is how to handle return codes properly and respond with the correct transaction handling:

```
/* Retrieve status code to determine if proc was successful */
...

declare @status_val int, @trncnt int

select @trncnt = @@trancount   -- save @@trancount value

if @trncnt = 0       -- transaction has not begun
  begin tran t1      -- begin tran increments nest level to 1
else                 -- otherwise, already in a transaction
  save tran t1       -- save tran doesn't increment nest level

/* do some processing if required */

if (@@transtate = 2) -- or other error condition
  begin
  rollback tran t1   -- rollback to savepoint,or begin tran
  return             -- and exit batch/procedure
  end

execute @status_val = p1 --exec procedure, begin nesting

if @status_val = 25 -- if proc performed rollback
  begin             -- determine whether to rollback or continue
  rollback tran t1
  return
  end

/* more processing if required */

if @trncnt = 0       -- this proc/batch issued begin tran
  commit tran t1     -- commit tran, decrement @@trancount to 0
  return             -- commit not required with save tran
```

Cursors in Stored Procedures

You can declare cursors in stored procedures (these are called *server cursors*). When the procedure returns, the cursor is automatically deallocated. As Figure 8.14 illustrates, if stored procedures are nested, they can access cursors declared in higher-level stored procedures in the call tree.

FIGURE 8.14.

Nested stored procedures can access cursors declared in higher-level stored procedures in the call tree.

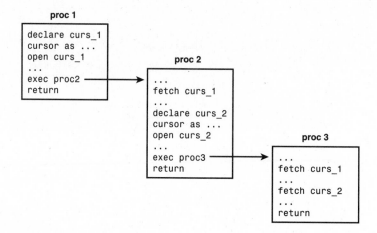

Here's an example of a procedure with a server cursor:

```
create proc title_price_update
as
declare @ytd_sales int, @price money
/*declare cursor*/
declare titles_curs cursor for
  select ytd_sales, price from titles
  for update of price
open titles_curs
fetch titles_curs into @ytd_sales, @price
if (@@fetch_status = 2)
  begin
     print "No books found"
     close titles_curs
     deallocate titles_curs
     return
  end
while (@@fetch_status = 0)
  begin
     if @ytd_sales = null
       begin
       update titles set price = @price * .75
          where current of titles_curs
       end
     else
       if @price > $15
            update titles set price = @price * .9
               where current of titles_curs
```

```
        else
            update titles set price = @price * 1.15
                where current of titles_curs
            fetch titles_curs into @ytd_sales, @price
    end
if (@@fetch_status = 1)
    raiserror 55555 "Fetch of titles_curs failed"
close titles_curs
deallocate titles_curs
return
```

Inserting Data with Procedure Result Sets

SQL Server 6.5 allows you to use the results from a procedure as the basis for an insert into a table. While this adds some flexibility in writing application code, its most important application is the ability to execute a *remote procedure* on another SQL Server and use those results as the basis of an insertion. In prior versions, you would need to retrieve the rows in a client application and retransmit them to the local server. (For more on the use of remote procedures and remote servers, see Chapter 34, "Remote Server Management.")

Here's the syntax of the new insert statement:

```
insert tablename [(columnname [, ...])]
execute [@statusvar =] procedurename [parameter [output][, ...]
```

Here's a simple example of a procedure-based insert. The procedure itself returns a single result set, whose columns will correspond with the column-list of the insert statement in both datatype and logical use:

```
create procedure ins_proc
as
select "1390", pub_name, city, state
from publishers
where pub_id = "1389"
return 0
```

Here's the insert statement:

```
declare @status int
insert publishers (pub_id, pub_name, city, state)
execute @status = ins_proc
```

Procedure Limitations and Notes

A stored procedure can't create views, defaults, rules, triggers, or procedures, nor issue the use statement. (If you want a stored procedure to operate within the context of the database from which it's called, create a system stored procedure.) You can create tables in stored procedures. Typically, you create temporary tables for storing intermediate results or as worktables. Temporary tables used within stored procedures are dropped at procedure termination. A table can't be created, dropped, and re-created with the same name in a single procedure.

Stored procedures are parsed in a single pass and will not resolve forward or backward references. For example, when defining a stored procedure that references a temporary table, either the stored procedure must create the temporary table prior to referencing it, or the temporary table must exist at the time the stored procedure is created.

Procedures are reusable, but not reentrant. Stored procedures can be recursive.

Stored procedures can reference objects in other databases and call other procedures to a nesting level of 16 deep.

Objects Referenced in Procedures

To display a list of objects referenced by stored procedure, use sp_depends:

```
exec sp_depends procedure_name
```

To display a list of stored procedures that reference a specific table or view, use sp_depends this way:

```
exec sp_depends {table_name ¦ view_name}
```

If you rename an object referenced by a stored procedure, the stored procedure still references the original object. If you drop the original object and create a new object with the original object's name, the stored procedure is recompiled to reference the new object. If you create a new object with the original object's name and the original object still exists, you need to drop and re-create the stored procedure to reference the new object.

If you drop any object referenced by the stored procedure, and don't re-create it with the same name, you get a runtime error. If you drop an index used by the query plan of a stored procedure, SQL Server will generate a new query plan the next time it's executed.

Optimizing Stored Procedures

The SQL Server query optimizer generates a query plan for a stored procedure based on the parameters passed in the first time it's executed. This query plan is then run from cache for subsequent executions. To force a new query plan to be generated, use the with recompile option either at creation time or execution time. with recompile specified at procedure creation time causes the optimizer to generate a new query plan for every execution. If it's specified at procedure execution time, it causes the optimizer to generate a new query plan for that execution only and will be used for subsequent executions.

Examples:

```
create proc advance_range
     (@low money, @high money)
     with recompile
```

```
       as
select * from titles
    where advance between @low and @high
return
go
/* if the procedure has not been created with the
** 'with recompile' option, execute as follows to
** recompile */
exec advance_range $1000,$2000 with recompile
```

Here are some cases when you might consider using with recompile:

■ When a stored procedure can generate widely different query plans, depending on the parameters passed in, and there's no way of predicting the best query plan for all executions

■ When statistics have been updated on a table and you want the stored procedure to generate a new query plan based on the updated statistics

■ When an index has been added to a table that you want the optimizer to consider to generate a new query plan for the stored procedure

WARNING

If the procedure contains select * from tablename and alter table has been used to add a column to the table, with recompile won't force all the columns to be displayed. Instead, you have to drop and re-create the stored procedure to display the new column.

Remote Stored Procedures

Remote stored procedures are procedures residing on other servers. Fully qualify the stored procedure name with the server name to execute procedures on other servers:

```
[exec[ute]] server_name.db_name.owner.proc_name
```

Transaction control statements don't affect work performed in remote procedure calls.

Stored Procedure Guidelines

■ Stored procedures should be solid because they're server-resident and called frequently.

■ Check parameters for validity, and return an error if there's a problem.

- Ensure that the parameter datatypes match the column datatypes with which they're compared, to avoid datatype mismatches.
- Check @@error after each SQL statement.
- Comment your code.
- Always use a return statement.
- Develop a method for maintaining versions of stored procedure source code.

Stored Procedure Debugging Techniques

To get the syntax right on a stored procedure, write small parts of it as a batch first; then store the procedure after the whole operation starts working.

Get showplan output with recompile. The output from showplan and dbcc are generated by the query optimizer, which operates only when a procedure is recompiled. To see the effect of different parameters on optimization, create the procedure with recompile; then drop and re-create the procedure without recompile when you go into production.

Summary

When SQL Server was first introduced, stored procedures and triggers helped differentiate the product from competitive database products. Even now, the capabilities of effective stored procedures and triggers make your system operate better, with better integrity and usually better performance.

Understand the capabilities and limitations of stored procedures and triggers before writing lots of code. A well written application runs fast and clean; poorly written code makes the server run sluggishly and inefficiently.

Transaction Management

New in SQL Server 6.5

Most of the transaction behavior in SQL Server 6.5 remains unchanged from version 6.0, except for the items described here:

- New behavior after `rollback transaction` in a trigger
- Bound connections allow multiple connections to share a single transaction space

What Is a Transaction?

A *transaction* is a set of operations to be completed at one time, as though they were a single operation. A transaction must be fully completed or not performed at all. Standard examples of transactions include bank transfers (withdraw $500 from checking, add $500 to savings) and order-entry systems (write an order for five widgets, remove five widgets from inventory).

All SQL statements are inherently transactions, from `grant` and `create` statements to the data-modification statements `insert`, `update`, and `delete`. Consider the following `update` example:

```
update titles
set price = price * 1.02
```

This statement modifies all rows in the `titles` table. SQL Server guarantees that, regardless of the size of the `titles` table, all rows will be processed or no rows will be processed at all. What if half the rows are modified and the server fails? When the server comes back up (but before the database is available for use), it rolls back the incomplete transaction, recording the roll-back in the transaction log. This is all part of an automatic *recovery* process that takes place on each database every time the server is restarted. (For more on recovery and other characteristics of transaction logs, see Chapter 26, "Defining, Altering, and Maintaining Databases and Logs.")

SQL Server also includes transaction-control syntax to group sets of SQL statements together into single logical work units:

- `begin transaction` starts a unit of work
- `commit transaction` completes a unit of work
- `rollback transaction` cancels a unit of work

The following example consists of two separate statements—one that enters an order and another that depletes inventory—in a single transaction:

```
begin transaction
   update inventory
      set in_stock = in_stock - 5
      where item_num = "14141"
   insert orders (cust_num, item_num, qty)
      values ("ABC151", "14141", 5)
commit transaction
```

Because the two data-modification statements are wrapped inside a `begin transaction...commit transaction` structure, SQL Server guarantees that the inventory won't change unless the order is also entered.

Look at the same example, but with the `rollback transaction` statement instead of `commit`:

```
begin transaction
    update inventory
        set in_stock = in_stock - 5
        where item_num = "14141"
    insert orders (cust_num, item_num, qty)
        values ("ABC151", "14141", 5)
rollback transaction
```

When the server encounters the `rollback` statement, it discards all changes in the transaction and returns the data to the state it was in before work began.

Transaction Programming

The programming issues associated with writing transactional SQL are fairly straightforward. After you issue a `begin transaction` statement, the server performs all the subsequent work without formally writing a final record of the work. At any time after issuing a `begin transaction` statement, you can roll back the entire transaction or commit it.

The SQL Server implicitly commits work executed outside of explicit transactional control. For example, this set of statements includes no explicit transactional syntax:

```
insert publishers (pub_id, pub_name, city, state)
    values ("1111", "Joe and Mary's Books", "Northern Plains", "IA")
update titles
    set pub_id = "1111"
    where pub_id = "1234"
delete authors
    where state = "CA"
```

Each of these statements is treated as its own transaction. Thus, the server issues *implicit* instructions on transaction control for each individual SQL statement. The server would treat the preceding batch like this:

```
[implicit BEGIN TRANSACTION]
insert publishers (pub_id, pub_name, city, state)
    values ("1111", "Joe and Mary's Books", "Northern Plains", "IA")
[implicit COMMIT TRANSACTION]

[implicit BEGIN TRANSACTION]
update titles
    set pub_id = "1111"
    where pub_id = "1234"
[implicit COMMIT TRANSACTION]

[implicit BEGIN TRANSACTION]
delete authors
    where state = "CA"
[implicit COMMIT TRANSACTION]
```

Each statement would include implicit begin and commit instructions (indicated by italics).

What does the inclusion of implicit begin and commit instructions mean for the integrity of this batch? Each statement is guaranteed to be carried to completion or rolled back to the beginning. If the server went down unexpectedly after the titles update had started but before it was complete, the server would roll back any work already performed by the update statement. On the other hand, the work associated with the insert to publishers would have already been completed and committed (by the implicit COMMIT operation), so only part of the batch would be complete.

Transactions and Batches

In the preceding example, you may have wanted the whole operation to complete or do nothing at all. The obvious solution is to wrap the entire operation in a single transaction, like this:

```
begin transaction
insert publishers (pub_id, pub_name, city, state)
    values ("1111", "Joe and Mary's Books", "Northern Plains", "IA")
update titles
    set pub_id = "1111"
    where pub_id = "1234"
delete authors
    where state = "CA"
commit transaction
```

Now the server treats all three operations performed in the batch as a single modification.

There is no inherent transactional quality to batches. As you have seen already, unless you provide the syntax to form a transaction out of several statements, each statement in a batch is its own transaction, and each statement is carried to completion or fails individually.

Transactions can also span batches. You could write an application that begins a transaction in one batch and then asks for user verification during a second batch. The SQL might look like this:

First Batch:

```
/* DON'T DO THIS ... EVER!!! */
begin transaction
insert publishers (pub_id, pub_name, city, state)
    values ("1111", "Joe and Mary's Books", "Northern Plains", "IA")
if @@error = 0
    print "publishers insert was successful. Please go on."
else
    print "publisher insert failed. Please roll back"
```

Second Batch:

```
update titles
    set pub_id = "1111"
    where pub_id = "1234"
delete authors
    where state = "CA"
commit transaction
```

In a few pages (in the "Transactions and Locking" section), you'll look at the locking issues associated with transactions. At that time, you'll see that transactions force data modifications (insert, update, delete) to hold locks that persist until a commit transaction or rollback transaction statement is encountered.

Writing transactions that span multiple batches is usually a bad idea. The locking problems can get very complicated, with awful performance implications. (What if this operation waited for a user to say okay before going on, but the user went to Cancun and didn't come back for two weeks? Locks would be held until the user got back and said okay.) In general, you want to enclose each transaction in a single batch, using conditional programming constructs to handle situations like the preceding example. Here's a better way to write that program:

```
/* DO THIS INSTEAD !! */
begin transaction
insert publishers (pub_id, pub_name, city, state)
    values ("1111", "Joe and Mary's Books", "Northern Plains", "IA")
if @@error = 0
begin
    print "publishers insert was successful. Continuing."
    update titles
        set pub_id = "1111"
        where pub_id = "1234"
    delete authors
        where state = "CA"
    commit transaction
end
else
begin
    print "publisher insert failed. rolling back transaction"
    rollback transaction
end
```

The important point in this example is that the transaction now takes place within a single batch.

Savepoints

SQL Server enables you to mark a *savepoint* in a transaction. Savepoints let you do some work inside a transaction and then roll back just that work, based on circumstances. In this example, the program sells several items and then tests inventory (which is automatically updated through a trigger) and rolls back a portion of the work if inventory is insufficient:

```
begin tran

save tran item111     /* mark a savepoint before each insert */
insert order (ord_no, item_no, qty)
    values ("2345", "111", 15)
if (select in_stock from inventory where item_no = '111') < 0
begin
    rollback tran item111    /* roll back just this item if incorrect */
    print "Item 111 would be back-ordered, cancelling order"
end
```

```
save tran item999
insert order (ord_no, item_no, qty)
    values ("2345", "999", 5)
if (select in_stock from inventory where item_no = '999') < 0
begin
    rollback tran item999
    print "Item 999 would be back-ordered, cancelling order"
end

save tran item444
    insert order (ord_no, item_no, qty)
values ("2345", "444", 25)
if (select in_stock from inventory where item_no = '444') < 0
begin
    rollback tran item444
    print "Item 444 would be back-ordered, cancelling order"
end

commit tran
```

By wrapping the inserts in a transaction, the programmer gets two benefits. First, the overall effect of each insert can be observed before the work is committed, which makes it easy to reverse the effects of problem updates. The second benefit is that all the legitimate inserts included in the batch go in; the rest are rejected. (In your business, it may not be appropriate to allow a partial transaction. The proper use of savepoints depends on a good understanding of transaction logic in your application.)

The scope of transaction savepoint names is local, so you don't have to worry about generating unique names for your savepoints. Savepoints and related rollback statements don't affect program flow. Rolling back to a savepoint allows processing to continue forward from that point.

Nested Transactions

It's important to note that SQL Server doesn't implicitly commit work when you log out. For example, what if you issue the following statement and then log out?

```
begin transaction
insert publishers (pub_id, pub_name, city, state)
    values ("1111", "Joe and Mary's Books", "Northern Plains", "IA")
```

Any uncommitted transactions are rolled back automatically when you log out. How does the server know that you have uncommitted transactions? SQL Server retains a *transaction nesting level* for each user connection.

NOTE

SQL Server maintains a list of active connections in master..sysprocesses. The primary key of that table is spid (server process ID). You can retrieve the server process ID for your current connection by using the global variable, @@spid:

```
select @@spid0
```

The transaction nesting level can be retrieved for your connection with the global variable @@trancount. You need to understand how each transactional statement affects @@trancount to write properly nested transactions and to manage transactions through triggers and stored procedures.

Table 9.1 summarizes the effect of transactional statements on @@trancount.

Table 9.1. How transaction control statements affect @@trancount.

Statement	Effect on @@trancount
begin transaction	@@trancount = @@trancount + 1
commit transaction	@@trancount = @@trancount − 1
save transaction	(no effect)
rollback transaction	@@trancount = 0
rollback transaction save_name	(no effect)

Following is a summary of how transactional control relates to @@trancount:

- When you log in to SQL Server, your session @@trancount is zero.
- Each time you execute begin transaction, SQL Server increments @@trancount.
- Each time you execute commit transaction, SQL Server decrements @@trancount.
- Actual work is committed only when @@trancount reaches zero again.
- When you execute rollback transaction, the transaction is canceled and @@trancount returns to 0. Notice that rollback transaction cuts straight through any number of nested transactions, canceling the overall main transaction. This setup means that you need to be careful how you write code that contains a rollback statement.
- Savepoints and rolling back to a savepoint don't affect @@trancount or transaction nesting in any way.
- If a user connection is lost for any reason when @@trancount is greater than zero, any pending work for that connection is automatically rolled back. The server requires that transactions be explicitly committed.

Take a look at how the server handles transaction nesting. In this example, transactions are nested two levels deep:

```
begin tran
    update titles
        set price = price * 1.1
        from titles
        where pub_id = "1234"
    begin tran
        update titles
```

```
            set advance = advance * 1.15
            where pub_id in
              (select pub_id from publishers
                where state = "MA")
    commit tran
    delete titles
        where type = "UNDECIDED"
commit tran
```

Let's track @@trancount through each statement. Assuming that @@trancount starts out at zero, Table 9.2 shows the effect of each statement on @@trancount.

Table 9.2. How statements in the example affect `@@trancount`.

Statement	Effect on `@@trancount`
begin tran	@@trancount = @@trancount + 1 = 1
update titles	@@trancount = 1
begin tran	@@trancount = @@trancount + 1 = 2
update titles	@@trancount = 2
commit tran	@@trancount = @@trancount − 1 = 1
delete titles	@@trancount = 1
commit tran	@@trancount = @@trancount − 1 = 0

Nested transactions are *syntactic only*. The only commit tran statement that has an impact on real data is the last one, the statement returning @@trancount to 0, which forces physical data to be written to disk.

Transactions and Locking

To ensure data integrity, SQL Server places exclusive locks on the pages modified during a transaction. In the previous example, pages in both the titles and publishers tables are involved. As SQL Server progresses through the query, locks are acquired on each table modified by a statement and are then held until SQL Server reaches a commit tran that sets @@trancount to 0 (or a rollback tran). A long-running transaction performing data modifications to many different tables can effectively block the work of all other users in the system (see the section titled "Long-Running Transactions," later in this chapter). Because of this possibility, you need to be aware of the performance and concurrency issues involved with writing transactions. When writing transactional code, keep these things in mind:

- Keep transactions as short as your application allows.
- Avoid returning data with a select in the middle of a transaction.

■ Try to write all transactions within stored procedures.

■ Avoid transactions that span multiple batches.

Transactions and Triggers

Triggers are considered part of the transaction in which a data modification is executed. In this example, an update trigger on the `titles` table fires as part of the transaction:

```
begin tran
    update titles
        set price = $99
        where title_id = "BU1234"
commit tran
```

@@trancount and Implicit Transactions

What is the value of `@@trancount` as SQL Server processes each of the statements in the previous example? If `@@trancount` starts at 0, `begin tran` makes it 1, the `update` statement leaves it at 1, and it returns to 0 with the `commit tran` statement.

What is the value of `@@trancount` inside the `update` trigger? To determine the value, you need a trigger that prints out the contents of `@@trancount` during execution. Here is an example:

```
/* DON'T LEAVE THIS KIND OF TRIGGER LYING AROUND!! */
create trigger tr_stores_upd
on stores
for update
as
declare @tc varchar(80)
select @tc = "Trancount = " + convert(char(1), @@trancount)
print @tc
raiserror 99999 "this update statement will never commit ... test trigger in place"
rollback tran
return
```

Here's a transcript of the `ISQL` session when you update the `stores` table:

```
1> update stores
2> set city = "Pittsburgh"
3> go
Trancount = 1
Msg 99999, Level 16, State 1:
this update statement will never commit ... test trigger in place
```

Inside the trigger, `@@trancount` equals 1. As mentioned earlier, each individual SQL statement is a transaction in and of itself. From this example, you can see that SQL Server uses the same transaction-nesting methods with implicit and explicit transaction control. Also, you can see that any work completed in the trigger is part of the `update` statement itself (see Figure 9.1).

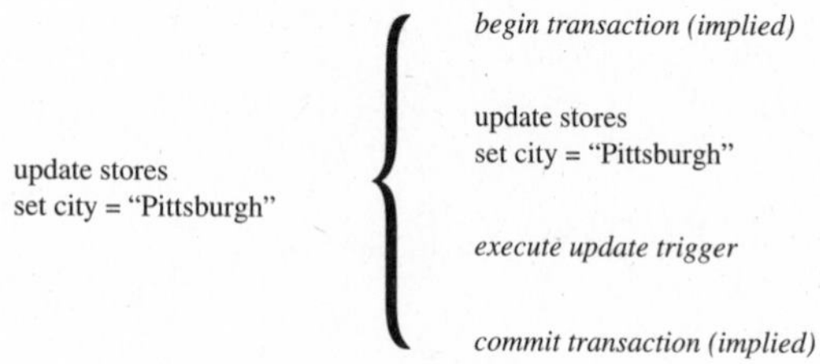

FIGURE 9.1.

*A simple SQL data-
modification statement.*

update stores
set city = "Pittsburgh"

{

begin transaction (implied)

update stores
set city = "Pittsburgh"

execute update trigger

commit transaction (implied)

Watch what happens when the same trigger executes if the update runs as part of an explicit transaction:

```
1> begin tran
2> select "Before Update Trancount " , @@trancount
3> update stores
4> set city = "Pittsburgh"
5> select "After Update Trancount " , @@trancount
6> commit tran
7> go

------------------------- ----------
Before Update Trancount  1

(1 row(s) affected)

Trancount = 2
Msg 99999, Level 16, State 1
this update statement will never commit ... test trigger in place

(6 row(s) affected)


------------------------- ----------
After Update Trancount  0

(1 row(s) affected)

Msg 3902, Level 16, State 1
The commit transaction request has no corresponding BEGIN TRANSACTION.
```

When `begin tran` executes, `@@trancount` is set to 1, as reported by the `select` statement. The update statement executes and the update trigger fires. The update trigger reports that `@@trancount` is 2 (again reflecting the effect on `@@trancount` of implicit transactions).

> **NOTE**
>
> Please don't allow this section to confuse you about transaction control and individual SQL statements. It's crucial to understand that data-modification statements (`insert`, `update`, `delete`) have *no net effect* on `@@trancount`.

rollback transaction in a Trigger

In the preceding example, you should note that the select statement after the update is executed. Rollback-transaction statements, in addition to reversing the effect of the current data-modification statement, *neither return from the trigger nor abort the batch*. (This is new to SQL Server V. 6.5. Earlier versions behaved differently. See Chapter 8, "Transact-SQL Program Structures," for more on rollback transaction in a trigger.)

Transactions and Stored Procedures

Writing all your transactions in stored procedures can provide better performance by avoiding partial transactions, especially because the server provides error messages to help you manage the transaction nesting level within procedures. The biggest concern you have is how to handle rollback transaction statements within stored procedures. Mistakes in using rollback statements in procedures can result in data-integrity problems.

Consider this stored procedure, which inserts a row into a table, tests the table after the insert, and rolls back the insert if more than three rows exist with that value:

```
/* stored procedure example coded improperly (see below) */
create proc p2
(@parm int)
as
begin tran
insert tally_table (c1) values (@parm)
if (select count(*) from tally_table
    where c1 = @parm) > 3
begin
    raiserror 99997 "too many rows with that value - rolling back"
    rollback tran
    return 99997    /* error ... rolled back */
end
else
begin
    commit tran
    return 0        /* no error */
end
```

If you execute the stored procedure when the table contains only two rows with c1 = 1, the procedure runs properly and the insert is entered:

```
1> exec p2 1
2> go
1> select * from tally_table
2> go
 c1
 _____
        1
        1
        1

(3 rows affected)
```

When you run the procedure again, the `rollback` statement executes, and you receive the following error message:

```
1> exec p2 1
2> go
Msg 99997, Level 16, State 1:
too many rows with that value - rolling back
1> select * from tally_table
2> go
 c1
 _ _ _ _ _
          1
          1
          1

(3 rows affected)
```

As expected, the procedure works properly and the table contains only three rows after the `insert` fails.

The problem with this procedure arises only when it's executed from within a transaction. Consider this example:

```
begin tran
    exec p2 1
    exec p2 2
commit tran
```

What you intended by writing this as a transaction was that the inserts with value 2 would not occur unless you could make the related insert with value 1; both inserts should go in as a unit or no inserts should take place. Let's look at the output when the table contains three rows with value 1:

```
1> select * from tally_table
2> go
 c1
 _ _ _ _ _
          1
          1
          1

(3 rows affected)
1> begin tran
2>     exec p2 1
3>     exec p2 2
4> commit tran
5> go
Msg 99997, Level 16, State 1:
too many rows with that value - rolling back
Msg 266, Level 16, State 1:
Transaction count after EXECUTE indicates that a COMMIT or ROLLBACK
TRAN is missing. Previous count = 1, Current count = 0.
Msg 3902, Level 16, State 1:
The commit transaction request has no corresponding BEGIN TRANSACTION.
1> select * from tally_table
2> go
 c1
```

```
 _ _ _ _ _
            1
            1
            1
            2
```

(4 rows affected)

Before the batch, the table contains three rows; afterward, it contains four rows. The new row contains the value 2, so only half of the transaction was executed. The integrity of the transaction has been lost. Let's look at the output from the batch closely to understand what has occurred; then we'll write the stored procedure and batch properly to make certain that this doesn't occur:

```
Msg 99997, Level 16, State 1:
too many rows with that value - rolling back
```

Error 99997 is the error message we wrote, generated because the first `insert` failed. Here's a system-generated message that is also returned because of the way the application was written:

```
Msg 266, Level 16, State 1:
Transaction count after EXECUTE indicates that a COMMIT or ROLLBACK
TRAN is missing. Previous count = 1, Current count = 0.
```

This error occurs because the transaction nesting level (that is, the value of `@@trancount`) when the procedure starts is different from when it ends. Why? `rollback transaction` returns `@@trancount` to 0 regardless of the prior transaction nesting level. Clearly, this is a problem if the calling batch is unaware of the nesting level. Table 9.3 steps through the batch one statement at a time, understanding the impact of each statement on `@@trancount` (and on the transaction).

Table 9.3. Tracking `@@trancount` during procedure execution.

Calling Batch	Procedure	@@trancount
begin tran		1
exec p2 1		1
	begin tran	2
	insert tally_table (c1) values (@parm)	2
	if (select count (*) from tally_table	
	where c1 = @parm) > 3	2
	begin	0 (a)
	raiserror 99997 "too many rows with that value - rolling back"	
	rollback tran	

continues

Table 9.3. continued

Calling Batch	Procedure	@@trancount
	return 99997 /* error ... rolled back */	
	end	
exec p2 2		0
	begin tran	1
	insert tally_table (c1) values (@parm)	1
	if (select count (*) from tally_table	
	where c1 = @parm) > 3	1
	begin	0 (b)
	commit tran	
	return 0 /* no error */	
	end	
commit tran		0 (c)

You should look at three specific events (noted in the table as a, b, and c) to understand the problems in data integrity. Note (a) points out the problems caused by rollback transaction in a procedure. When you write the procedure, you need to make allowances so that a user can execute it whether or not a transaction is currently running. Note (b) shows that the second execution of the procedure, when it reaches the commit statement, forces @@trancount to zero, performing an actual commit of the data modifications since the prior begin tran statement. Finally, the commit statement at note (c) tries to decrement @@trancount, which is already zero. When this happens, the server returns the message seen earlier:

```
Msg 3902, Level 16, State 1:
The commit transaction request has no corresponding BEGIN TRANSACTION.
```

These two messages (3902 and 266) are your warnings that the transaction nesting is not properly managed in the stored procedure.

There are several methods of coding stored procedures with transactions to ensure that the procedure works properly as a stand-alone transaction or as a part of a larger, nested transaction. Here is one example of how to write a stored procedure with transaction control:

```
/* proc to demonstrate no net change to @@trancount
** while still rolling back changes within the proc
** VERY IMPORTANT: return an error code
** to tell the calling procedure rollback occurred */

create proc p1
as
declare @trncnt int
```

```
select @trncnt = @@trancount   -- save @@trancount value

if @trncnt = 0    -- transaction has not begun
  begin tran p1   -- begin tran increments nest level to 1

else              -- already in a transaction
  save tran p1    -- save tran doesn't increment nest level

/* do some processing */

if (@@transtate = 2) -- or other error condition
  begin
  rollback tran p1  -- rollback to savepoint, or begin tran
  return 25         -- return error code indicating rollback
  end

/* more processing if required */

if @trncnt = 0     -- this proc issued begin tran
  commit tran p1   -- commit tran, decrement @@trancount to 0
                   -- commit not required with save tran

return 0 /* successful return */
```

As important as it is to write the stored procedure properly, it's equally important to write the batch calling the procedure to make proper use of the information provided by the stored proc return codes. Here is an example of how to manage nested procedures from the calling batch:

```
/* Retrieve status code to determine if proc was successful */
...

declare @status_val int, @trncnt int

select @trncnt = @@trancount  -- save @@trancount value

if @trncnt = 0    -- transaction has not begun
  begin tran t1   -- begin tran increments nest level to 1
else              -- otherwise, already in a transaction
  save tran t1    -- save tran doesn't increment nest level

/* do some processing if required */

if (@@transtate = 2) -- or other error condition
  begin
  rollback tran t1  -- rollback to savepoint,or begin tran
  return            -- and exit batch/procedure
  end

execute @status_val = p1 --exec procedure, begin nesting

if @status_val = 25 -- if proc performed rollback
  begin             -- determine whether to rollback or continue
  rollback tran t1
  return
  end

/* more processing if required */
```

```
if @trncnt = 0     -- this proc/batch issued begin tran
  commit tran t1   -- commit tran, decrement @@trancount to 0
return             -- commit not required with save tran
```

Whether or not you choose to adhere to these coding standards, the important point is that stored procedures and the batches that call those procedures need to be consistent with each other to provide proper data-integrity control. You must establish coding standards for both that enable transactional control to work whether the transaction commits successfully or is rolled back.

Long-Running Transactions

There is no specific definition of a *long-running transaction*, but as transactions get longer, problems arise. Long-running transactions aren't inherently different from shorter ones, but they do stress elements of the system that otherwise run quite well. In particular, you may encounter performance or concurrency problems because of issues related to the transaction log, the caching system, and locking.

Some of the symptoms of long-running transactions include the following:

- Your transaction log fills up. Some transactions can actually exceed the size of your transaction log. Unlike some other database systems, SQL Server doesn't let you define a temporary, emergency overflow log to handle this situation. Instead, you need to assign—permanently—a transaction log large enough to hold all your largest transactions.

> **NOTE**
>
> Why not just clear half the transaction and continue? The dump tran commands (and other transaction-log-maintenance methods, such as trunc. log on checkpoint) don't allow the server to prune pending, uncommitted transactions.

- You're holding blocking locks that prevent all work by other users from continuing. You may be able to resolve this specific problem by looking at your lock escalation level (see Chapter 16, "Locking and Performance").

- Ordinarily, all transactional work is performed in memory. Only when a commit is executed are the changes to the transaction log flushed to disk; changes to tables and indexes wait until a system-initiated checkpoint. If a transaction gets too long, the caching system may run out of unused memory and initiate a checkpoint to release additional memory. This action could slow down your transaction as well, and a rollback following a checkpoint is far more disk-intensive than one that is executed only in memory.

Reducing the size of your transactions is usually helpful when you start to encounter performance or blocking problems. There are two ways to reduce the log space consumed by long-running transactions. One is to reduce the size of the logical unit of work. For example, you could take a single-transaction task and execute it in two steps, each as its own transaction. This plan may require that you write program code to handle the data integrity in cases where the first half of the transaction works, but the second half fails (you would need to write your own transaction handler to deal with the rollback processing).

On the other hand, before changing the definition of a unit of work, you should look for technical fixes to your code to reduce the amount of log work required for each step. For example, if you can get the server to perform an update in place instead of a deferred update, you could substantially reduce the amount of information recorded in the transaction log to perform the same work (see Chapter 13, "Understanding the Query Optimizer").

> **NOTE**
>
> Reducing the number of indexes on a table also reduces the number of log writes required to handle complex modifications.

Bound Connections and Multi-Connection Transactions

SQL Server 6.5 introduces *bound connections*, which allow multiple connections to work in a single, shared transaction space. The connections are able to share locked data, avoiding concurrency problems typically faced by application programmers writing multi-connection work.

Support for bound connections allows SQL Server to handle long-running transactions more efficiently. It also allows applications requiring parallel tasking to be split up among multiple client processes more efficiently.

There are two types of bound connections. A *local bound connection* allows two connections attached to the same server to interact with the same transaction space. A *distributed bound connection* between two servers allows work across multiple servers to be committed as a single unit of work. (For more on distributed bound connections and multi-server transactions, see Chapter 34, "Remote Server Management," and Chapter 35, "The MS SQL Server Distributed Management Framework.")

There are two aspects to the implementation of bound connections. First, you need to understand how to set up a bound connection. Second, you need to look at some of the application programming considerations in implementing this in real life. The following sections discuss these issues.

How to Bind Connections

Several steps are involved in setting up a bound connection:

1. One connection needs to set up the transaction and retrieve a *connection token.* The connection token is a variable character string that identifies the transaction space.

2. Each additional connection to be bound to the transaction must join that transaction space by passing the token to the SQL Server.

3. The connections perform their work.

4. The connections disengage the bound connection by logging out or by explicitly ending the binding.

Bound Connections: An Example

In this example, we bind two connections, server process IDs 10 and 11. The first step is for connection 10 to set up the shared transaction workspace with `sp_getbindtoken`. The procedure requires an output parameter to retrieve the token:

```
declare @bindtoken varchar(255)
exec sp_getbindtoken @bindtoken output
select @bindtoken "Token"
```

Here is the return value from `sp_getbindtoken`. As you can see, the return value is a meaningless character string:

```
Token
— — — — — — — — — — — — — — — —
PQ5---5--->5iL\L8X<1EeV-//\kHZh
```

SQL Server has set up a shared transaction space for this connection and uses the token to identify that space. Another connection can use that token to share that space with the `sp_bindsession` stored procedure:

```
sp_bindsession "PQ5---5--->5iL\L8X<1EeV-//\kHZh"
```

If the binding token is correct and accepted, the stored procedure returns no results. Otherwise, you get an error, warning you that the token is incorrect or corrupt.

After the two connections are working within the same transaction space, the server can treat their locks as though they were created by a single connection. When connection 10 executes this batch, it obtains an exclusive lock by executing an `update` statement in a transaction:

```
begin transaction
update test_bc
set c2 = c2 * 2
where c1 between 1 and 10
```

The exclusive lock is held until the transaction is committed or rolled back. The current activity dialog in SQL-EM displays the locks held by connection 10 (see Figure 9.2).

FIGURE 9.2.

Current activity shows that connection 10 holds an exclusive lock on the table, test_bc.

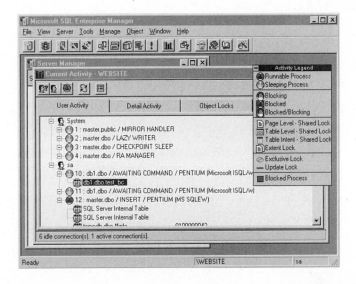

When another process that has not joined the bound connection (in this case, connection 13) attempts to select from the table, its attempt to read is blocked by the exclusive lock. Figure 9.3 shows current activity while connection 13 waits for the lock to clear. Notice that the lock held by connection 10 is now highlighted, indicating a blocking lock, and the icon for connection 13 shows that its process is blocked.

FIGURE 9.3.

Connection 13 (not a part of the bound connection) is blocked by the exclusive lock held by connection 10.

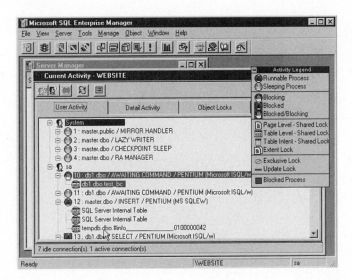

The exclusive lock doesn't block another process involved in the bound connection. The lock space between the two processes is shared, so each connection is able to read through the other's locks. Here is another `update` statement, this time executed by connection 11. The `update` requires its own exclusive lock:

```
begin transaction
update test_bc
set c2 = c2 * 2
where c1 between 1 and 10
```

The statement executes immediately. Now examine the current activity in Figure 9.4 to see what has happened with locks.

FIGURE 9.4.

After connection 11 executes within the distributed transaction space, the exclusive table lock moves to that connection.

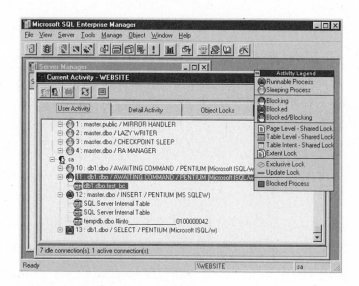

Notice that the blocking lock moved to connection 11, which was the most recent bound connection to work with the object. SQL Server freely moves locks between bound connections, maintaining blocks against other, unenlisted processes.

Programming Issues with Bound Connections

It's tempting to use bound connections heavily to coordinate work between multiple connections within a single client application, and to handle most large batch operations by using this method.

There's a substantial limitation to bound connections. Only one connection at a time can work in the shared transaction workspace. Other processes are blocked until the current process is complete. It's most useful to bind connections between clients when each client process must perform a large proportion of its processing locally, without referring to the server.

From an application programming standpoint, the danger of performing a single update twice, or of making a mistake in coordinating sequential updates on a set of rows, should remind you of the usefulness of the automatic transaction isolation provided by SQL Server.

> **TIP**
>
> The most useful application of this technique is probably with extended stored procedures that need to share a connection workspace with a currently running SQL Server process.

Summary

A transaction is a logical unit of work. SQL Server provides several automatic and programmatic mechanisms, including Transact-SQL transaction control statements, the transaction log, and transaction isolation through locking, to preserve data integrity while transactions are running. Transactions enable you to tie together logically related operations, allowing the server to maintain data integrity. Remember, when writing applications that include transaction control, you need to pay special attention to how you write and work with triggers and stored procedures.

PART

III

IN THIS PART

Performance and Tuning

Defining Performance Expectations

10

This section of the book helps you deal with the problem of tuning and optimizing SQL Server. The first step is to understand how the server stores and retrieves data, and the performance mechanisms already in place in the server. After that, you learn methods to take advantage of those fundamental system characteristics (as well as when to stay out of the server's way and let it run). In time you will discover that performance tuning is more science than art—a combination of sound principles, ingenuity, and determination.

What Can You Expect?

The first problem in tuning a SQL server is to understand what level of performance you can expect. If it ain't broke, don't fix it. You need some effective measures to help you understand whether the performance you're getting makes sense, given the query and the data. When you tune performance, you should apply your time and effort to problems that demand your attention, and to those that you can fix.

Focusing Tuning Efforts Where It Counts

Let's start by understanding basic physical limitations. The weak link in the performance chain is often the physical disk drive. Today's fast-caching RAID arrays can deliver about 2MB of data per second to SQL Server, sometimes more. With multiple I/O channels and read-ahead threads on a multi-processor NT server, you can look for two to three times that volume of data. So a front-to-back scan (a table scan) of a 100MB table could run in less than a minute with a fast drive subsystem. For many users, however, that's simply too long to wait for an answer.

Several techniques can improve that performance. Even faster, larger drives would deliver the data faster to cache; an enormous data cache would improve the chance that some portion of the table would be available to you in memory when you ran the query; the DBCC PINTABLE command could force the table to persist in data cache once it was read (although this is probably a rotten idea with such a large table).

Another method might be to add CPUs and count on read-ahead threads to improve scan times. Depending on your disk configuration and the amount of contention on the system, this strategy may reduce scan time by a factor of 40 percent or more.

Like all hardware-based, brute force techniques, these approaches have fairly limited effectiveness, and their cost may become prohibitive. The solution to this problem may be to deliver the same result while reading less data. That may involve storing derived or duplicate values, or changing the basic design of the table to reduce its size. Adding a nonclustered index may also lead to useful performance improvements.

In any event, what your users perceive as a problem does allow some improvement and may be worth addressing.

On the other hand, users can retrieve a single well-defined row from a well-indexed table in less than a second, regardless of the size of the table. In fact, dozens or even hundreds of users could read single rows from the same table without a noticeable loss of performance. Is there room for improvement? Perhaps. Is it worth your attention? Almost certainly not.

So, when you choose where to focus your tuning efforts, there are two key issues:

- Where are the problems that need to be solved?
- Which problems are the result of physical limitations?

It's crucial to understand the performance capabilities of SQL Server, and to establish an understanding of how your hardware and software configuration relates to the finite limitations of the system. Based on that, you can develop reasonable expectations about what the server can do, and help others (users!) to understand those limitations and capabilities as well.

To help you develop proper performance expectations and focus your tuning activities, this chapter discusses the following topics:

- Defining performance
- Expectations
- Tracking down bottlenecks
- A basic tuning approach

Defining Performance

There are three basic ways to define SQL Server performance:

- **Response time for queries.** How much time elapses when running a specific query? Many organizations demand subsecond response time for simple queries. Of course, more complex queries take longer than a second. Comparing required response time to actual response time is an important measure of performance.

- **Throughput.** This level is typically measured in transactions per second, or TPS. A variety of industry-standard benchmarks (TPC-A, -B, and -C, for example) can help you to compare the performance of database servers running on various platforms, but they won't help you define or predict the actual performance of the system, because they don't reflect your own transactions.

  Carry out your performance benchmarking with your own queries and data to get meaningful throughput measures. You need to make sure that your database and server are up to the challenge of managing the number of queries in the amount of time you need.

- **Concurrency.** This standard can reasonably be considered a subset of throughput. Here's the basic question: Can our system handle 5,000 users? Answering this question is usually a substantial task that requires you to profile predicted query and throughput traffic, and then to answer the response time and throughput questions under load. You need to configure for this (and test for this) differently than for throughput.

- **Combination of throughput and concurrency.** Can this system handle online transaction processing (OLTP), decision support systems (DSS, also called data warehousing or EIS—Executive Information Systems), and batch processing (management and offline report systems) at one time?

  This is the hardest thing to tune for, particularly on single-processor SQL Servers. More on this later.

Tradeoffs

Tuning for a single definition of performance is reasonably simple. For example, to tune for fast response time to queries is usually simple if throughput and concurrency don't matter. Tuning for throughput is less complicated with very few concurrent users.

Approaches that solve single performance include

- Normalization (eliminating duplicate data)—can speed throughput
- Denormalization (storing duplicate data)—can speed retrieval time
- Creating or dropping indexes
- Partitioning tables across databases
- Adding hardware or reconfiguring software

Where solving a single problem is fairly straightforward, finding a way to solve multiple performance needs is usually a delicate balancing act. For example, you may choose to speed throughput by removing indexes used to improve query performance. Modifications to tables are much faster without the additional indexes, so transactions require less work and the system can handle more transactions per second. The tradeoff is that queries previously supported by an index now might need to perform a table scan. A query that used to take three minutes may now take several hours!

Common Tradeoffs

You need to consider some common tradeoffs when you're looking at performance issues. None of these tradeoffs is simple or has a standard response. As you evaluate your performance options, it's vital that you be able to state clearly what you're getting and what you're giving up.

Update Performance versus Read Performance

Most database administrators (DBAs) develop database designs using a two-step approach that starts with a logical design and then moves to a physical design. A *logical database design* is a representation of data intended to remove all duplication and to express clearly the relationship between data elements. The *physical design* is a plan for how to store the data on a particular system.

One of the first hurdles to overcome in physical design is understanding that it has a separate purpose from logical design. Logical design is for understanding and describing data; physical design is for performance.

The first tradeoff is `update` performance versus `select` performance. A normalized database allows updates to run fast, but it also requires more joins to resolve multi-entity queries, and joins are costly. If you denormalize, you reduce joins; thus many queries run faster.

Storage Efficiency versus Cost

This brings up the next tradeoff: storage efficiency versus cost. Denormalizing frequently demands more storage because it requires the storage of duplicate data, and that isn't free; however, it's often cheap compared to the cost of unresolved performance issues.

Fast Execution versus Ad Hoc Access

Balancing OLTP and DSS is a specialized problem. OLTP applications typically support a fixed set of data operations, most of them `update` operations, allowing you to predict the appropriate data design and index selections. Small, lean tables and few indexes provide the best performance in those circumstances.

DSS applications are based on ad hoc queries where users ask questions you can never anticipate. Wide tables and lots of indexes help DSS apps, where retrieval time matters much more than the time to maintain the data.

Before you can address your performance issues, you need to define your requirements and boundaries. You need to provide a physical design to enable the response times that you want to achieve. In the next three chapters, you learn how to set and adjust these parameters.

Expectations

Let's take a look at some specific queries and try to identify the expectations. These queries are based on a table and index defined as follows (the table definition is incomplete, and you should forget for a moment that you don't yet understand how SQL Server uses indexes):

```
create table orders( ...
       item_num int,
       warehouse int,
       ...)

create index ord_index on orders (item_num, warehouse)
```

Here are some potential queries you might run against the table, with their response times:

```
/* QUERY A: response time subsecond */
select sum(qty) from orders
where item_num = 1234 and warehouse = 432

/* QUERY B: response time 600 seconds */
select sum(qty) from orders
where warehouse = 432

/* QUERY C: response time 50 seconds */
select sum(qty) from orders
where item_num in (1234,2345) and warehouse = 432
```

Now let's pose two important, distinct questions:

- Which queries have acceptable response times? (Of course, your answer to this question depends on your users' demands.)
- Which have expected response times?

Look first at Query A. Is the response time acceptable? Clearly, if you have subsecond response time, it's fruitless to waste time trying to decide whether response time is acceptable. Move on to the next problem. Is the response time expected? If you have a reasonable amount of data for the test, again the answer is to look for real problems elsewhere.

Query B has response time that is unacceptable for most real-time operations, so we'll define it as unacceptable. We must then ask ourselves, "Is the response time expected? Should this query take 600 seconds?" This is a more difficult question to answer because it requires an understanding of the data, the physical design, and how the server uses the physical design. Let's handle this in reverse order of the questions just posed. First, how can the server handle the physical design? Can SQL Server use the index to resolve the query? Because the table is indexed on the item_num column, and item_num isn't in the where clause, the server can't use the index. Therefore, the only way to resolve the query is with a table scan, which is the process of reading every page in the table.

Next comes *understanding* the data: How many pages of data do we have to read to resolve the query? It also opens up a hardware question: How many pages of data can SQL Server read in a second? If the data isn't in cache, query performance depends on physical drive performance. Depending on the server hardware, SQL Server can read between 200 and 1,000 pages (400KB to 2MB) per second (typically) from a SCSI disk drive. This is a huge discrepancy, and makes another point clear: You must understand the physical limitations of your system to be able to have reasonable expectations and from there to make physical design decisions.

Back to Query B. How many pages of data must we read? (SQL Server reads one page at a time.) If the amount of data that needs to be read takes several hundred seconds (for example, the table is 800MB), and you're willing to allow a few seconds for overhead, 600 seconds might be an expected result—even though it isn't an acceptable one. During your physical design phase, you need to identify the fact that you have a potential problem query, with expected results that are unacceptable, and you need to figure out a way to improve performance (this can be an additional index, a summary table, or one of many other possible decisions).

Query C gets a bit trickier. It looks like a subset of Query A. Why does this take (at least) 50 times the elapsed time of Query A? Back to basics: Is the response time acceptable? Let's assume that it isn't; that's why we're analyzing the query, after all.

One of the first things to do is break up the query. (If both components of the query are resolved in less than a second, it's time to call Microsoft technical support and report a bug.) If one query takes less than a second (which we know from Query A) and the other takes 49 seconds, what's the problem? The most likely issue is that you have substantially more data for item_num 2345 than for 1234 in the warehouse. To have appropriate expectations, you need a solid understanding of the distribution of your data.

Bottlenecks

A *bottleneck* is a resource that limits system throughput. A typical bottleneck is a physical disk drive. You may need to get data from the disk drive a bit faster and be limited by the speed of data retrieval from the drive. But is this the real problem? Is the problem the disk drive, the controller, or the operating system?

Unfortunately, eliminating a bottleneck has the net effect of shifting the bottleneck to some other limiting resource. With any luck, though, the new bottleneck will be wider.

It's essential to understand where bottlenecks can occur, where they tend to occur, and under what circumstances. Potential bottlenecks are your performance variables—those things that you adjust, tune, and balance to get the best possible results for your application.

Performance Variables

A number of components can be bottlenecks. Some of these are based on configuration options that can be set; others are built in and unchangeable. This section discusses variables that affect performance and helps you understand how to affect them.

> **NOTE**
>
> As you read this section, you'll find some components that you can affect, and some that are fixed and require hardware upgrades to change. The intent of this section isn't to identify how to fix all the problems associated with these variables (you'll be doing that throughout the book), but to identify potential problem areas you need to think about.

Physical Architecture

Physical (hardware) architecture specifically relates to these components:

■ CPU configuration

■ Disk I/O performance

■ Network

■ Concurrency

CPU performance is an important element in performance, but seldom the bottleneck. Can you improve performance by reducing dependence on CPU performance? The best approach is to make your code more efficient by simplifying SQL and reducing cursors.

Can you make better use of multiple CPUs? By tuning configuration options to improve the efficiency of read-ahead caching (RA configuration options), you may be able to improve multi-processing performance for a single query.

You can't change the I/O rate for a physical device, but you can reconfigure the physical design by introducing a RAID device or splitting up data across multiple disks. You can also reduce the amount of requested data. (For example, limit the maximum number of rows to be retrieved from the database. Will a user really need all 4,000,000 rows? Usually not.)

The network is an unreliable component. In many systems, network performance is very fast, but with increasing dependence on intranets, more and more users are running client/server applications across a WAN. For most applications, you should regard the network as a bottleneck: make a point of reducing network traffic whenever and wherever possible. You can do this by reducing the number of packets transmitted or by increasing the TDS packet size. You can also use stored procedures.

Concurrency issues are not tuneable, but can sometimes be contained. For example, if logging overhead is causing problems, you can try committing transactions less frequently or putting the log on a higher-speed device. Additionally, if sequential reads are slower than you would expect, you may be able to redistribute the data on your disks. Overall server architecture also affects concurrency. For example, additional memory often helps the server handle greater numbers of users more efficiently. Along those lines, some dedicated hardware is normal for high-transaction-volume or high-concurrency systems.

Application

Application components relevant to database performance include three critical elements:

■ Query

■ Logical design

■ Physical design

The most important issue from an application-tuning standpoint is to make sure that your user writes queries properly. Substantial user training is critical, particularly where ad hoc queries are involved, because horrid SQL is probably the number one cause of bad performance. Bad queries can have a variety of flavors: unnecessary joins, insufficient joins, lack of search arguments (more on this later), or an inability to take advantage of server features (for example, the update in place).

Logical design issues may involve changing table normalization to reduce joins, or data partitioning to take infrequently referenced data out of the scanned table.

Physical design is often the first place to start working on performance problems. Correct index selection can often fix—that is, improve the performance of—otherwise problematic queries. Adding indexes tends to help queries but hurts update performance. You can also store summary or redundant data.

Cursors are a favorite way programmers can foul up performance, particularly concurrency. A poorly written cursor can lock huge amounts of data. Cursors are also a dramatically slower way than other approaches to retrieving data. Tell your programmers that cursors are a way of treating a set-processing language like a row-processing language, and that it's usually the wrong approach.

Server

Server performance relates to these elements:

- Configuration
- Optimizer
- Lock management
- Concurrency
- Maintenance activity
- Dump/load
- Index creation
- Batch activity
- Concurrency management

The database server is the most tuneable component of your environment. For example, you can configure and reconfigure memory, cache, locks, disk-resource dissemination, connections, and dozens of other things. There are also some components you can't easily tune.

One thing you can't change is the optimizer. The optimizer chooses its own path, join order, and/or other search tactic.

> **NOTE**
>
> You can, for a particular query or session, force a join order or index selection on the optimizer. First you identify what the optimizer is doing, and then you identify ways of saying, "I think that's a bad idea. Do it my way instead." Note that it's very unusual to select a better query plan than the optimizer. (For more details on how the optimizer operates, see Chapter 13, "Understanding the Query Optimizer.")

Most lock management is handled automatically by the server; the maximum number of overall locks is configured by the system administrator. The SQL Server manages the use of the locks. You can improve performance by keeping transactions short and by avoiding manual locking behavior. Also avoid situations where deadlocking becomes likely.

Server overhead can sometimes be handled with hardware, such as using a solid-state device for the log to increase transaction throughput where the log has been positively identified as a bottleneck.

Concurrency

You probably will want to identify a batch window for performing (among other things) maintenance activity such as dbcc and database dumps, index creations and re-creations, or other batch activity (reporting, mailing labels, long-running ad hoc queries). All of these activities tend to hog an entire processor. It's also the type of activity that can lock tables or databases, which reduces OLTP concurrency.

Fitting all your work into a batch window is sometimes a highly specialized art form, particularly in 24x7 shops (shops that require 24-hours-a-day, 7-days-a-week operation).

Tuning Your Approach

Before beginning to tune, gather as much information as possible about the circumstances surrounding the perceived performance problem. Remember that you can't tune for everything. You need to identify and prioritize problems before addressing them. For example, you have a problem query that runs for 40 hours. You can fix the problem by denormalizing your database and adding four indexes to the tables. The cost of this solution is six additional disk drives and three hours added to your batch (dump) window.

Ask yourself whether it's worth the cost. Are you fixing this query for the CEO of the company, who needs this report updated every two hours, or is this query being run every six months by an associate accountant (who has completely fouled up your expense checks for the past four months)? Sometimes the decisions are easy.

Spotlight obvious problems. Over the course of the next several chapters, you get a feel for what the problems are going to be, if you haven't had that type of experience already. If you're tuning an existing system, choose options that are transparent to users (for example, indexes and segments) over those that require changes to programming (like changing table structure).

Estimate your requirements prior to the final rollout. Find or build a tool that simulates user activity, and act on the information you acquire. It's rare for users or application designers to estimate data requirements adequately, but you should make sure that you can handle *at a minimum* the stated system requirements.

When you have specific problems, follow these steps:

1. Identify baseline time for your CPU and controllers so that you can state your expected results.
2. Decide whether the results are expected but unsavory, or unexpected *and* unsavory.
3. Examine the problem query. Is it too complex? Does the query solve the user's actual need? (Frequently, the answer is no.)
4. Are the indexes appropriately selected in the physical design? Is the optimizer using the indexes you think it should? (This issue is covered in Chapter 13.)
5. Is the optimizer selecting the correct approach?
6. When in doubt, break down the query. Do individual components take too long?
7. Finally, prioritize the problem. Does the situation, user, or application warrant physical-design changes or other work on your part?

Summary

Set your expectations appropriately, based on a thorough understanding of your system's strengths and limitations and your data. You'll find that there are physical limitations to your system, which you must understand. Set your expectations and lay your plans accordingly.

Understanding SQL Server Storage Structures

11

To get the best performance from a high-performance vehicle, you occasionally need to tune the engine. However, before you can begin tuning a high-performance vehicle, you need to have a good understanding of the internal structures of the engine and how it works. Likewise, in order to tune SQL Server effectively, you need to have a good understanding of the internal storage structures and how SQL Server stores and manages objects and data within the database.

This chapter explores the basic storage structures in SQL Server and how they are managed and maintained. This information will help you better understand performance issues raised in subsequent chapters.

SQL Server Storage Structures

SQL Server doesn't see data and storage in exactly the same way a DBA or end-user does. A DBA sees initialized devices, device fragments allocated to databases, segments defined within databases, tables defined within segments, and rows stored in tables. SQL Server views storage at a lower level as device fragments allocated to databases, pages allocated to tables and indexes within the database, and information stored on pages (see Figure 11.1).

There are two basic types of storage structures in a database: linked data pages and index trees. All information in SQL Server is stored at the page level. When a database is created, all space allocated to it is divided into a number of pages, each page 2KB in size. There are five types of pages within SQL Server:

- Data and log pages
- Index pages
- Text/image pages
- Allocation pages
- Distribution pages

All pages in SQL Server contain a *page header*. The page header is 32 bytes in size and contains the logical page number, the next and previous logical page numbers in the page linkage, the object_id of the object to which the page belongs, the minimum row size, the next available row number within the page, and the byte location of the start of the free space on the page.

The contents of a page header can be examined by using the dbcc page command. You must be logged in as sa to run the dbcc page command. The syntax for the dbcc page command is as follows:

```
dbcc page (dbid | db_name, page_no [, 0 | 1 | 2 ])
```

The display options (0, 1, 2) determine how the page contents will be displayed. 0 is the default and displays only the page header, without the page contents. 1 displays the page header and a hex dump of the page contents individually by row. 2 displays the same information as 1, but displays the page contents as a single block of data.

FIGURE 11.1.

*Difference between how a
DBA and SQL Server view
data storage.*

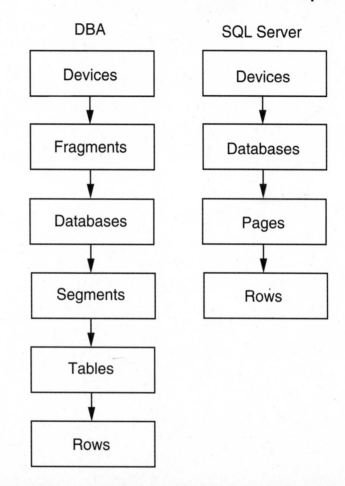

DBA

SQL Server

DBA	SQL Server
Devices	Devices
Fragments	Databases
Databases	Pages
Segments	Rows
Tables	
Rows	

Here is a sample page header:

```
dbcc traceon (3604)
dbcc page (perftune, 424, 0)

PAGE HEADER:
Page header for page 0xac0000
pageno=424 nextpg=0 prevpg=0 objid=288004057 timestamp=0001 00000b46
nextrno=25 level=0 indid=0  freeoff=832 minlen=2
page status bits: 0x1
```

The following is an explanation of the fields visible in the page header:

- `pageno` is the current page number (logical page number assigned when `page` is allocated to `database`).
- `nextpg` is the pointer to the next page in the page linkage.
- `prevpg` is the pointer to the previous page in the page linkage.
- `objid` is the object ID of the object to which this page belongs.
- `indid` is the index ID of the index to which this page belongs.
- `level` is the level within the index in which this page is found.
- `nextrno` is the row number of the next row to be inserted on this page.
- `freeoff` is the location of the free space at the end of the page.
- `minlen` is the minimum allowable length of any row on the page.

If `indid` is `0`, this is a data or nonindex page. If it is an index page (`indid != 0`), `level` indicates the level within the index in which this page is found. (Index levels and index structures are covered in more detail later in this chapter, in the "Indexes and the B-Tree Structure" section.)

You might be wondering, with five different types of pages within a database, how SQL Server keeps track of which object a page belongs to, if any. The allocation of pages within SQL Server is managed through the use of *allocation units* and *allocation pages*.

Allocation Pages

Space is allocated to a SQL Server database by the `create database` and `alter database` commands. The space allocated to a database is divided into a number of 2KB pages. Each page is assigned a logical page number starting at page `0` and increasing sequentially. The pages are then divided into allocation units of 256 contiguous 2KB pages, or 512 bytes (1/2 megabyte) each. The first page of each allocation unit is an allocation page that controls the allocation of all pages within the allocation unit (see Figure 11.2). The first allocation page is logical page number `0`, and subsequent allocation pages are stored at each multiple of 256.

The allocation pages control the allocation of pages to tables and indexes within the database. Pages are allocated in contiguous blocks of eight pages called *extents*. The minimum unit of allocation within a database is an extent. When a table is created, it is initially assigned a single extent, or 16KB of space, even if the table contains no rows. There are 32 extents within an allocation unit (see Figure 11.3).

FIGURE 11.2.

Allocation units within a SQL Server database.

0	1	2	3	4	5	6	7
8	9	10	11	12	13	14	15
16	17	18	19	20	21	22	23
24	25	26	27	28	29	30	31
32	33	34	35	36	37	38	39
40	41	42	43	44	45	46	47
...							
...							
...							
248	249	250	251	252	253	254	255

256	257	258	259	260	261	262	263
264	265	266	267	268	269	270	271
272	273	274	275	276	277	278	279
280	281	282	283	284	285	286	287
288	289	290	291	292	293	294	295
296	297	298	299	300	301	302	303
...							
...							
...							
504	505	506	507	508	509	510	511

512	513	514	515	516	517	518	519
520	521	522	523	524	525	526	527
528	529	530	531	532	533	534	535
536	537	538	539	540	541	542	543
544	545	546	547	548	549	550	551
552	553	554	555	556	557	558	559
...							
...							
...							
760	761	762	763	764	765	766	767

. . .

■ = Allocation Page

FIGURE 11.3.

Extent within an allocation unit.

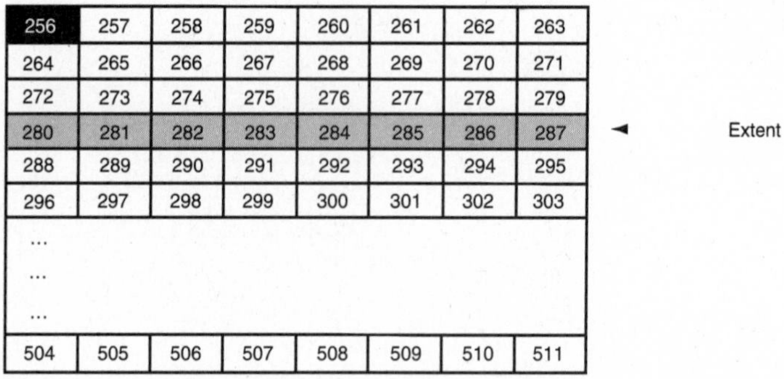

256	257	258	259	260	261	262	263
264	265	266	267	268	269	270	271
272	273	274	275	276	277	278	279
280	281	282	283	284	285	286	287
288	289	290	291	292	293	294	295
296	297	298	299	300	301	302	303
...							
...							
...							
504	505	506	507	508	509	510	511

◄ Extent

An allocation page contains 32 extent structures for each extent within that allocation unit. Each extent structure is 16 bytes and contains the following information:

- Object ID of object to which extent is allocated
- Next extent ID in chain
- Previous extent ID in chain
- Allocation bitmap
- Deallocation bitmap
- Index ID (if any) to which the extent is allocated
- Status

The *allocation bitmap* for each extent structure indicates which pages within the allocated extent are in use by the table (see Figure 11.4).

FIGURE 11.4.

Diagram of the extent structures in allocation page 0, showing the allocation bitmap for extent ID 24.

Allocation Bit Map
for extent id 24

24   31

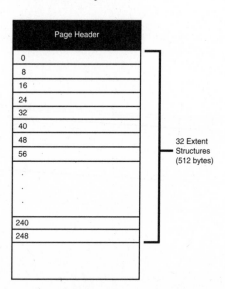

Allocation Page

Page Header

0
8
16
24
32
40
48
56
.
.
.
240
248

32 Extent Structures (512 bytes)

If the allocation bit is on, the page is currently in use by the table or index. If the allocation bit is off, the page is reserved, but not currently in use. The deallocation bit map is used to identify pages that have become empty during a transaction that has not yet been completed. The actual marking of the page as unused does not occur until the transaction is committed, to prevent another transaction from allocating the page before the transaction is complete.

Pages not currently in use are reserved for use by that table or index and cannot be used by any other table or index within the database. This is the information you see reported by the sp_spaceused stored procedure. For example, consider the following output:

```
sp_spaceused titles
name          rows    reserved  data    index_size  unused
------        ----    ----      ----    -----       ------
titles        18      48 KB     6 KB    8 KB        34 KB
```

reserved is the total number of kilobytes allocated to the table and its indexes (should be a factor of 8), data is the total number of kilobytes in use for data, index_size is the total number of kilobytes in use for all indexes on the table, and unused are allocated pages for the table and its indexes that are currently not being used. unused indicates the amount of space that can be used for the table or its indexes before additional extents need to be allocated. The titles table has 24 pages allocated to it—3 used for data, 4 used for its indexes, and 17 allocated pages that currently are not in use. This information is contained in the sysindexes table (see Table 11.1).

Table 11.1. The sysindexes table.

Column	Datatype	Description
name	varchar(30)	If indid >=1 and <= 250, name of index If indid = 0 or 255, name of table
id	int	ID of table related to this sysindexes row
indid	smallint	Index ID: 0 = table, no clustered index 1 = table and clustered index > 1 and <= 250 = nonclustered index 255 = text or image data
dpages	int	If indid = 0 or indid = 1, count of used data-only pages If indid > 1 and <= 250, count of leaf-level index pages

continues

Table 11.1. continued

Column	Datatype	Description
reserved	int	If indid = 0 or indid = 1, total number of pages allocated for all indexes and data If indid = 255, total number of pages allocated for text or image data If indid > 1 and <= 250, total number of pages allocated to nonclustered index
used	int	If indid <= 1, total number of all used index and data pages for the table If indid = 255, total number of pages used for text or image data If indid >1 and <= 250, total number of pages for this index
rows	int	If indid <= 250, number of rows in the table If indid = 255, 0
first	int	If indid <= 1 or = 255, pointer to first data or text/image page If indid > 1 and <= 250, pointer to first leaf index page
root	int	If indid >= 1 and < 250, pointer to root page of index If indid = 0 or 255, pointer to last page in data or text/image chain
distribution	int	If indid >= 1 and < 255, pointer to distribution page for that index
OrigFillFactor	tinyint	The original fillfactor value used when the index was created
segment	smallint	Segment ID for segment from which this object is currently allocating space
status	smallint	Bitmap status for index: 1 - Abort command if attempt to insert duplicate key (IGNORE_DUP_KEY not specified) 2 - Unique index 4 - Abort command if attempt to insert duplicate row in nonunique clustered index (IGNORE_DUP_ROW not specified) 16 - Clustered index 64 - Clustered index allows duplicate rows (ALLOW_DUP_ROW set)

Column	Datatype	Description
		2048 - Index defined by PRIMARY KEY constraint
		4096 - Index defined by UNIQUE constraint
rowpage	smallint	Maximum allowable number of rows per page
minlen	smallint	Minimum row width
maxlen	smallint	Maximum row width
maxirow	smallint	Maximum width of a nonleaf index row
keycnt	smallint	Number of columns in index
keys1	varbinary(255)	If indid >0 and <=250, description of index columns
keys2	varbinary(255)	If indid >0 and <=250, description of index columns
soid	tinyint	ID of sort order the index was created with (= 0 if no character data in the index)
csid	tinyint	ID of character set (= 0 if no character data in the index)
UpdateStamp	varbinary	Used for internal synchronization of updates to the row and page counts

When a table or index requires more space, it checks the sysindexes table and compares the reserved column to the used column. If any reserved pages are not used (reserved - used > 0), it allocates space to the table by using the following method:

```
if space is available on the current page then
    add record to the current page
else if there is a free page in the current extent
    add record to a free page in the current extent
    mark page as used
else if there is a free extent in the current allocation page
    allocate extent from current allocation page
    add record to first page in new extent
    mark page as used
else search all allocation pages for object following extent chain
        to locate a free extent
    allocate first free extent found
    add record to first page in new extent
    mark page as used
else
    allocate new extent from next allocation page in database with free extent
    add record to first page in new extent
    mark page as used
```

Data Pages

A *data page* is the basic unit of storage within SQL Server. All the other types of pages within a database are essentially variations of the data page. Figure 11.5 shows the basic structure of a data page.

FIGURE 11.5.

Structure of a SQL Server data page.

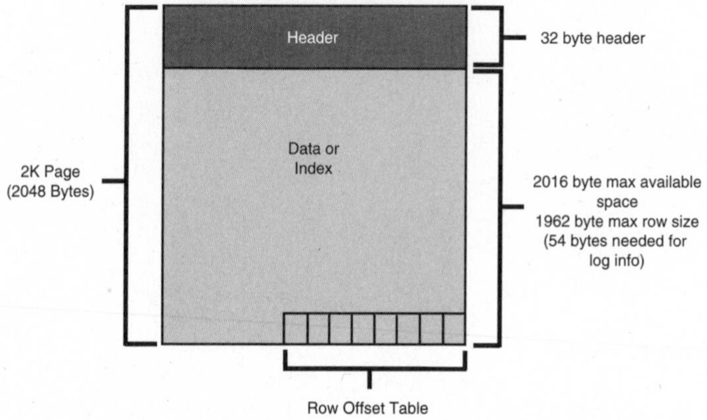

All data pages contain a 32-byte header, as described earlier. With a 2KB page (2048 bytes) this leaves 2016 bytes for storing data within the data page. In SQL Server, data rows cannot cross page boundaries. If not enough space is available at the end of a page to hold the entire row, it is stored on the next page in the page linkage. The maximum size of a single row within SQL Server is 1962 bytes, including row overhead, because pages in the transaction log are 2KB pages as well. For a row with no nullable or variable-length columns, the total amount of data that can be stored in the row is 1960 bytes, because each data row has at least 2 bytes of overhead. If you have variable-length or nullable columns, the amount of overhead per row is greater, so the actual amount of data is less (see the "Data Rows" section in this chapter for a discussion of row structure and row overhead).

When a data row is logged, for example during an `insert`, the entire row is written to a log page along with some logging information. This log information is 54 bytes per log record. Like data rows, log records cannot cross page boundaries. Because there are only 2016 bytes available to store the log record, 2016 bytes minus 54 bytes of overhead leaves 1962 bytes for the data row. Therefore, 1962 bytes is the maximum data row size.

TIP

You can create a table with data rows that could conceivably exceed 1962 bytes if it contains variable-length columns. SQL Server creates the table but gives you the following warning message:

> The total row size, 2575, for table 't3' exceeds the maximum number of bytes per row, 1962.
>
> If you attempt to insert a data row that actually exceeds 1962 bytes of data and row overhead, or update the row so that its updated length exceeds 1962 bytes, the insert or update will fail and you receive the following error message:
>
> ```
> Msg 511, Level 16, State 2
> Updated or inserted row is bigger than maximum size (1962 bytes) allowed for
> this table.
> ```

Data pages are linked to one another by using the *page pointers* (prevpg, nextpg) contained in the page header (see Figure 11.6). This page linkage enables SQL Server to locate all rows in a table by scanning all pages in the link. Data page *linkage* can be thought of as a two-way linked list, because each page contains the previous and next page pointer. This enables SQL Server to easily link new pages into or unlink pages from the page linkage by adjusting the page pointers. If nextpg equals 0, it indicates that the current page is the last page in the page chain. If prevpg equals 0, it indicates that the current page is the first page in the page chain.

FIGURE 11.6.

Linked data pages.

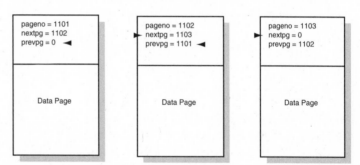

In addition to the page header, each data page also contains data rows and a *row offset table* (see Figure 11.5). The row offset table grows backward from the end of the page and contains the location of each row on the data page. Each entry in the row offset table is 2 bytes wide.

Data Rows

Data is stored on data pages in *data rows*. The size of each data row is a factor of the sum of the size of the columns plus the row overhead. Each record in a data page is assigned a row number. A single byte is used within each row to store the row number. Therefore, SQL Server has a maximum limit of 256 rows per page, because that is the largest value that can be stored in a single byte. Figure 11.7 displays the structure of a data row.

FIGURE 11.7.

Structure of a data row.

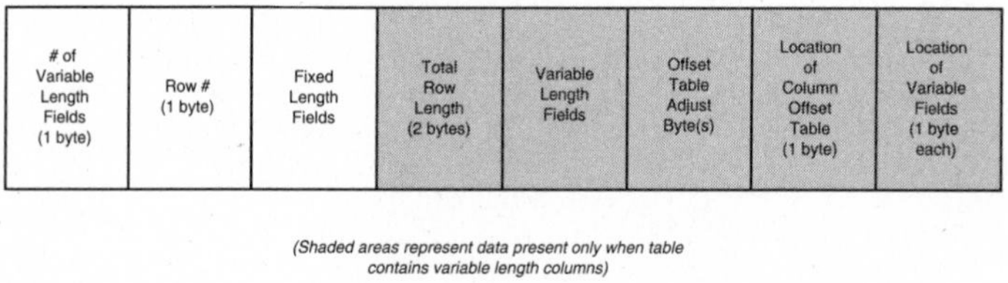

# of Variable Length Fields (1 byte)	Row # (1 byte)	Fixed Length Fields	Total Row Length (2 bytes)	Variable Length Fields	Offset Table Adjust Byte(s)	Location of Column Offset Table (1 byte)	Location of Variable Fields (1 byte each)

(Shaded areas represent data present only when table contains variable length columns)

For a data row containing all fixed-length columns, there are four bytes of overhead per row:

- 1 byte to store the number of variable-length columns (in this case, 0)
- 1 byte to store the row number
- 2 bytes in the row offset table at the end of the page to store the location of the row on the page

If a data row contains variable-length columns, there is additional overhead per row. A data row is variable in size if any column is defined as varchar, varbinary, or allows null values. In addition to the 4 bytes of overhead described previously, the following bytes are required to store the actual row width and location of columns within the data row:

- 2 bytes to store the total row width
- 1 byte per variable-length column to store the starting location of the column within the row
- 1 byte for the column offset table
- 1 additional byte for each 256-byte boundary passed (adjust table)

Within each row containing variable-length columns, SQL Server builds a column offset table backward for the end of the row for each variable-length column in the table. Because only 1 byte is used for each column with a maximum offset of 255, an adjust byte must be created for each 256-byte boundary crossed as an additional offset. Variable-length columns are always stored after all fixed-length columns, regardless of the order of the columns in the table definition.

Figure 11.8 demonstrates the row structure for the following table with all fixed-length fields:

```
create table t1
        (cola char(10),
         colb char(25),
         colc int)
```

Figure 11.9 shows the row structure for the following table:

```
create table t2
        (col_a char(10),
         col_b varchar(25),
         col_c int,
         col_d varchar(10))
```

FIGURE 11.8.

Diagram of a row with all fixed-length fields.

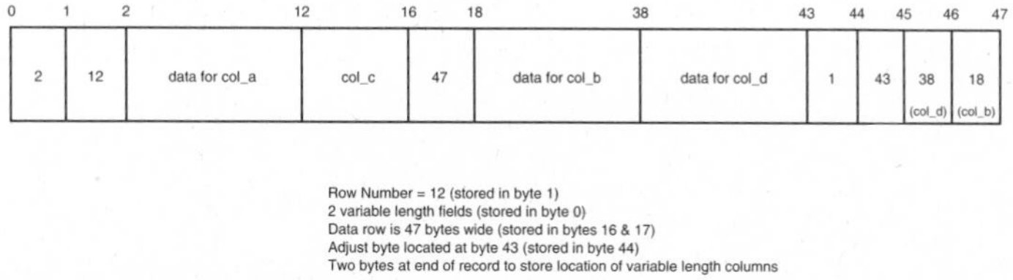

0	1	2		12		37	41
0	10	data for cola		data for colb		colc	

Row Number = 10
No variable length fields (Byte 0 = 0)
No row length stored
Data row is 41 bytes wide

FIGURE 11.9.

Diagram of a row with variable-length fields.

0	1	2	12	16	18	38	43	44	45	46	47
2	12	data for col_a	col_c	47	data for col_b	data for col_d	1	43	38 (col_d)	18 (col_b)	

Row Number = 12 (stored in byte 1)
2 variable length fields (stored in byte 0)
Data row is 47 bytes wide (stored in bytes 16 & 17)
Adjust byte located at byte 43 (stored in byte 44)
Two bytes at end of record to store location of variable length columns

Estimating Row and Table Sizes

Knowing the size of a data row and the corresponding overhead per row helps you determine the number of rows that can be stored per page. (The number of rows per page is important when you explore performance issues in subsequent chapters.) In a nutshell, a greater number of rows per page can help query performance by reducing the number of pages that need to be read to satisfy the query. Conversely, fewer rows per page helps improve performance for concurrent transactions by reducing the chances of two or more users accessing rows on the same page that may be locked.

These topics are explored in greater detail in subsequent chapters, but for now, let's take a look at how you can estimate row and table sizes. If you have only fixed-length fields in your table and none that allow null values, it's easy to estimate the row size:

> Sum of column widths
>
> + 1 byte to store the row number
>
> + 1 byte to store the number of variable-length columns
>
> + 2 bytes per row in the row offset table

Every data row requires at least 4 bytes of overhead. For example, consider table t1, described previously, which contains three fixed-length columns (char(10), char(25), and int). The total row size is the following:

> (10 + 25 + 4) + 4 = 43 bytes per row

If the table contains any variable-length fields or nullable columns, the row width is determined as follows:

Sum of all fixed column widths

+ 1 byte to store the row number

+ 1 byte to store the number of variable-length columns

+ 2 bytes per row in the row offset table

+ sum of average size of variable-length columns

+ number of variable-length columns (1 byte per column)

+ 1 byte (for column offset table within row)

+ 2 bytes (for row length)

= subtotal

+ subtotal/256 rounded up to next integer

= average row size

Each row containing variable-length columns has a minimum 4 bytes of overhead, plus a minimum of 5 bytes of overhead if it contains at least one nullable or variable-length field. Let's examine table t2, which contains two fixed-length columns (char(10) and int) and two variable-length columns (varchar(25) and varchar(10)). Let's assume that the average data size for both col_b and col_d is half the column size—13 and 5 bytes, respectively. The calculation of the average row size is as follows:

14 (10 + 4 for fixed fields)

+ 4 (for overhead)

+ 18 (13 + 5 for sum of average size of variable fields)

+ 2 (number of variable fields)

+ 1 (for columns offset table)

+ 2 (for row length)

= 41 (subtotal)

+ 1 (41/256 rounded up to adjust table bytes)

= 42 bytes (average row size)

> **NOTE**
>
> For a listing of SQL Server datatypes and their corresponding sizes, see Chapter 5, "Transact-SQL Datatypes."

When you know the average data row size, you can determine the number of rows per page by dividing the row size into the available space on the data page, 2016 bytes. For example, if your average row size is 42 bytes, the average number of rows per page is the following:

2016 / 42 = 48 rows per page

Remember to "round down" any fractions, because you can't have only a portion of a row on a data page. If the calculation works out to something like 24.8 rows per page, it actually requires two pages to store 25 rows, because the 25th row won't fit entirely on the first data page. If you are using a fill factor other than the default (covered later in this chapter), you need to multiply the number of rows per page times the fill factor percentage as well. For this example, assume that the default fill factor of 0 is used, which indicates that the data pages are 100 percent full.

When you know the average number of rows per page, you can calculate the number of pages required to store the data by dividing the total number of rows in the table by the number of rows per page. To follow the example, if you have 100,000 rows in the table, you need the following number of pages to store the data :

$$100,000 / 48 = 2083.333...$$

In this case, you "round up" the value to get the actual number of pages (2084) required to store all the data rows. The size of the table in pages is also the cost in number of page I/Os to perform a table scan. A table scan involves reading the first page of the table and following the page pointers until all pages in the table have been read. The table scan, as you will explore in subsequent chapters, is the fallback technique employed by the SQL Server optimizer to satisfy a query when there is no less-expensive alternative, such as a clustered or nonclustered index, to find the matching data rows.

The Row Offset Table

The location of a row within a page is determined by using the row offset table at the end of the page (see Figure 11.10).

FIGURE 11.10.

Row offset table on data page.

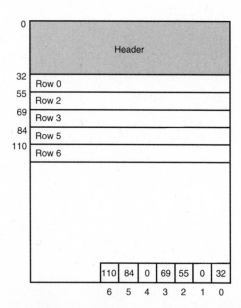

To find a specific row within the data page, SQL Server looks in the row offset table for the starting byte address within the data page for that row ID.

Note that SQL Server keeps all free space at the end of the data page, shifting rows up to fill in where a previous row was deleted and ensuring no space fragmentation within the page. However, the row IDs for the remaining rows don't change. This helps to reduce the amount of overhead involved to maintain row ID pointers in nonclustered indexes (covered later in this chapter, in the "Indexes and the B-Tree Structure" section).

If the offset table contains a zero value for a row ID, that indicates that the row has been deleted. The next row to be inserted into the table reuses the first available row ID, and the row offset is set accordingly. Whether the new row is inserted at the end of the page or between existing rows depends on whether there is a clustered index created on the table that requires the rows to be in sorted order. Let's examine both scenarios, first looking at a table without a clustered index.

A table without a clustered index is stored as a heap structure. All new rows are added at the end of the table on the last data page. No sorting of the data rows is maintained. Assume that the page displayed in Figure 11.11 is the last page in the table.

FIGURE 11.11.

Deletion and insertion of a row without clustered index.

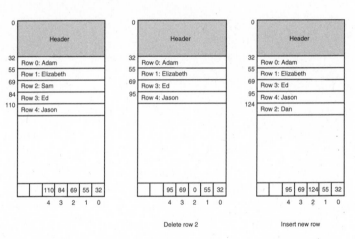

Delete row 2   Insert new row

As row 2 is deleted, all remaining rows on the page are shifted upward, the offsets are adjusted, and the offset for row 2 in the row offset table is set to 0. As a new row is inserted back into the page, it is assigned row ID 2, but is inserted after the last existing row on the page. The offset for row 2 is set to the location of the new row on the page.

If the table has a clustered index defined on it, the rows must be kept in physically sorted order within the data page. Figure 11.12 demonstrates the sequence of events when deleting and inserting rows in a sorted table.

FIGURE 11.12.

Deletion and insertion of a row with clustered index.

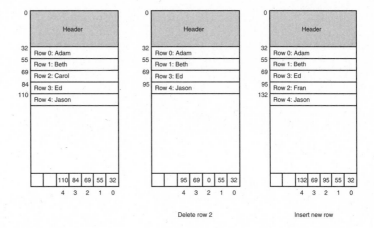

Again, you'll notice that all rows below row 2 are moved up on the page when row 2 is deleted, but the row IDs don't change. The row offsets are adjusted to reflect the new row locations within the page, and the row offset for row 2 is set to 0. When a new row is inserted into the page, it is inserted in the proper sort order between rows 3 and 4, and row 4 is shifted down on the page. The new row, however, is reassigned row ID 2, and the offset table is adjusted accordingly for rows 2 and 4. Although the row IDs may not be in physical order, the actual data values are. Remember, the advantage of this approach is to minimize updates to row pointers in the nonclustered indexes. If the row ID for an existing row does not change, the index row pointing to that data row does not need to be updated.

Text and Image Pages

Occasionally, you need to store large text values or *binary large objects* (*BLOBs*) in a database—data values that could be millions of bytes. However, SQL Server is limited to a maximum row size of 1962 bytes.

To address the need to store large data values, SQL Server provides the text and image datatypes that enable you to store data values up to 2G in size. This is accomplished by storing the text/image data across a number of linked pages separate from the page containing the data row itself.

The data row contains a 16-byte field, defined as a varbinary(16), containing a pointer to the first page containing the text/image data for that column. The text/image data is then spread across as many pages as necessary to store the data, up to 2G (see Figure 11.13). Each text/image page contains an embedded pointer to the next linked text/image page for that column.

A *text/image page* is a standard data page with a 32-byte header, plus an additional 112 bytes of overhead per page. A text page can store up to 1800 bytes of information. Therefore, a data value that is 1801 bytes requires two 2KB pages to store the data.

FIGURE 11.13.

SQL Server text/image pages.

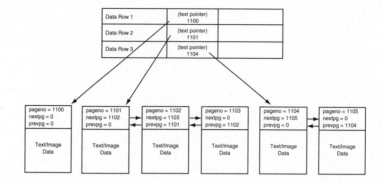

If a row is inserted into a table containing a text/image column that allows null values and the column is initially null, the column is not initialized with a text page pointer, saving 2KB of storage for that row. However, once the text value for that row is updated to something other than null, at least one text/image page is linked to that row, even if the text/image column is subsequently set to null.

Text/image data is retrieved by reading the pointer in the data row, reading the data from the page pointed to by the text/image pointer, and following the embedded page pointers in the text/image pages until nextpg equals 0, signaling the end of the text data for that column.

For any table containing any text/image columns, an additional row is added to the sysindexes table with an indid of 255. The name of the index is system-generated by prepending a t to the name of the table. For example, the name in sysindexes for the titles table would be ttitles. This row is used for allocating and maintaining the text/image pages for that table. Text/image pages are allocated from a different set of extents than the data or index pages.

Indexes and the B-Tree Structure

To this point, you have examined only the table structure. A table with no clustered index is stored as a heap structure. All data is added at the end of the table. You can think of it as a single file where all new records are merely added to the bottom of the file.

This structure is the fastest way of adding data to the table. When there is no clustered index on the table, there is a row in sysindexes with an indid of 0. The root column of this row points to the last page in the table where inserts are to occur (see Figure 11.14). SQL Server adds records to this page until the page is full and then links in a new page to the table.

Needless to say, this is not a very efficient method for retrieving data. To find a specific record, you have to start at the top of the pile and read through each record until you find the requested record. This is referred to as a *table scan*. Because SQL Server doesn't know whether the first found record is the only record to be found, it continues reading all records until it reaches the end of the table. If a table is of sufficient size—for example, 100,000 pages—you probably don't want to have to scan all 100,000 pages to read or modify a single record.

FIGURE 11.14.

SQL Server heap storage.

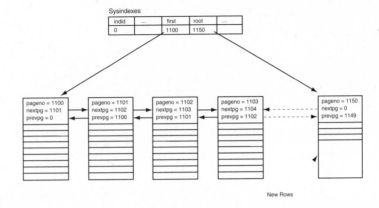

You need to have a mechanism to identify specific records within a table quickly and easily. SQL Server provides this mechanism through two types of indexes: clustered and nonclustered.

Indexes are storage structures separate from the data pages in the table itself. The primary functions of indexes are to provide faster access to the data and provide a means for enforcing uniqueness of your data rows.

All SQL Server indexes are *B-Tree*, or *Balanced-Tree structures* (see Figure 11.15). There is a single root page at the top of the tree, branching out into *N* number of pages at each intermediate level until it reaches the bottom, or leaf level, of the index. The index tree is traversed by following pointers from the upper-level pages down through the lower-level pages. In addition, each index level is a separate page chain.

There may be many intermediate levels in an index. The number of levels is dependent on the index key width, the type of index, and the number of rows and/or pages in the table. The number of levels is important in relation to index performance, as described later in this chapter, in the "Indexes and Performance" section.

FIGURE 11.15.

B-Tree structure.

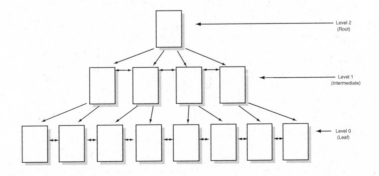

SQL Server 6.5 indexes are limited to a maximum of 16 columns in the index, with a maximum total index key width of 255 bytes for single column indexes, and 900 bytes for multi-column indexes.

Clustered Indexes

When a clustered index is created on a table, the data in the table is physically sorted in clustered index key order. SQL Server allows only one clustered index per table because there is only one way physically to sort the data in the table. A *clustered index* can be thought of as a filing cabinet. The data pages are like the folders in a file drawer in alphabetical order, and the data rows are like the records in the file folder, also in sorted order.

The intermediate index levels can be thought of as the file drawers themselves, also in alphabetical order at a higher level up, assisting you in finding the appropriate file folder. Figure 11.16 shows an example of a clustered index.

FIGURE 11.16.

Clustered index structure.

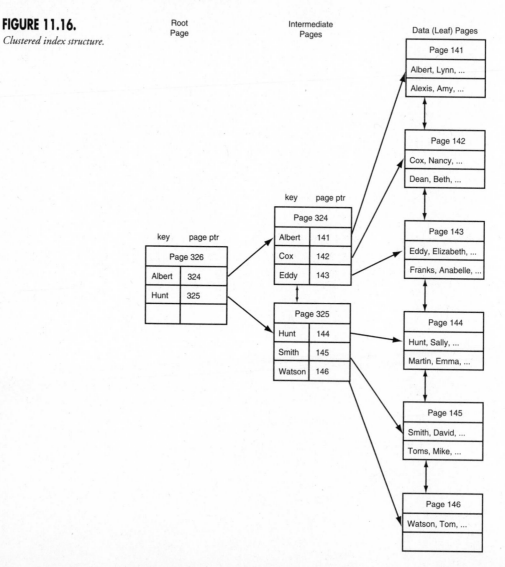

Notice that in Figure 11.16 the data is stored in clustered index order. This feature makes clustered indexes useful for range-retrieval queries, because the rows within the range are physically located in the same or adjacent data pages.

The data pages and clustered index are tightly coupled to each other. The clustered index contains a pointer to every data page in the table. In essence, the data page is the leaf level of the clustered index. To find all instances of a clustered index key value, you must eventually access the data page and scan the rows on that page.

SQL Server performs the following steps when searching for a data row by using the clustered index:

1. Queries sysindexes for the table where indid = 1 and gets the address of the root page.

2. Compares the search value against the key values on the root page.

3. Finds the highest key value on the page where the key value is less than or equal to the search value.

4. Follows the page pointer to the next level down in the index.

5. Continues following page pointers as in steps 3 and 4 until the data page is reached.

6. Searches the rows on the data page to locate a match for the search value. If a matching row is not found on that data page, the table contains no matching rows.

Because clustered indexes contain only page pointers, the size and number of levels in a clustered index is dependent on the width of the index key and the number of pages in the table. The structure of a clustered index row is detailed in Figure 11.17.

FIGURE 11.17.

Clustered index row structure.

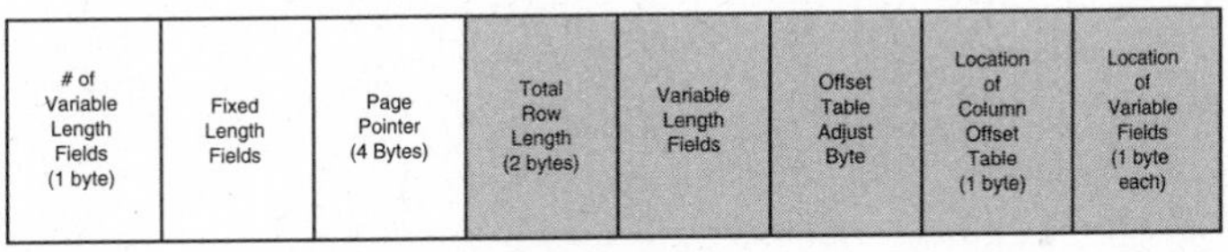

| # of Variable Length Fields (1 byte) | Fixed Length Fields | Page Pointer (4 Bytes) | Total Row Length (2 bytes) | Variable Length Fields | Offset Table Adjust Byte | Location of Column Offset Table (1 byte) | Location of Variable Fields (1 byte each) |

(Shaded areas represent data present only when index contains variable length columns)

Estimating Clustered Index Size

The formula for determining clustered index row width with all fixed-length fields is the following:

> Sum of fixed-length fields
>
> + 1 byte (number of variable columns)
>
> + 4 bytes (page pointer)

The formula for determining clustered index row width with variable-length fields is this (on the next page):

Sum of fixed-length fields

+ 1 byte (number of variable columns)

+ 4 bytes (page pointer)

+ 2 bytes (index row width)

+ sum of average width variable columns

+ 1 byte (adjust table)

+ 1 byte (location of offset table)

+ 1 byte per variable-length column

Assume you have a clustered index on a `char(10)` column that doesn't allow null values. Your index row size would be the following:

10 bytes

+ 4 bytes (page pointer)

+ 1 byte (number of variable columns = 0 in this case)

= 15 bytes per index row

Because the clustered index contains a pointer to each data page in the table, the number of rows at the bottom level of the index is equal to the number of pages in the table.

If your data row size is 42 bytes, you can get 48 data rows per data page. If you have 100,000 rows in the table, it works out to 2084 pages in the table. Therefore, you have 2084 rows in the bottom level of the clustered index. Each index page, like a data page, has 2016 bytes available for storing index row entries. To determine the number of clustered index rows per page, divide the index row size into 2016 bytes and multiply by the fill factor. For this example, assume that the default fill factor is being applied, which fills clustered index pages about 75 percent full:

2016 / 15 = 134.4 rounded down to 134 rows per page $\times$ .75 = 100 rows per page

At 100 rows per page, you need 2084 / 100 = 20.84, rounded up to 21 pages, to store all the rows at the bottom level of the index.

The top level of the index must be a single root page. You need to build levels on top of one another in the index until you reach a single root page. To determine the total number of levels in the index, use the following algorithm:

```
N = 0
divide number of data pages by number of index rows per page
while number of index pages at level N is > 1
begin
    divide number of pages at level N by number of rows per page
    N = N+1
end
```

When the number of pages at level N equals 1, you are at the root page, and N+1 equals the number of levels in the index. The total size of the clustered index in number of pages is the total sum of all pages at each level.

Applying this algorithm to the example gives the following results:

Level 0: 2084 / 100 = 21 pages
Level 1: 21 / 100 = 1 page

Thus, the index contains two levels, for a total size of 22 pages, or 44KB.

The I/O cost of retrieving a single row by using the index is the number of levels in the index plus a single data page. Contrast this with the cost of a table scan for the example:

2 index levels + 1 data page = 3 page I/Os

Table scan = 2084 page I/Os

You can easily see the performance advantage that having an index on the table can provide during a select. An index is also helpful during data modifications to quickly identify the rows that are specified to be updated or deleted.

Nonclustered Indexes

A *nonclustered index* is a separate index structure independent of the physical sort order of the data in the table (see Figure 11.18). SQL Server allows up to 249 nonclustered indexes per table. Without a clustered index, the data is stored in the table as a heap structure, with no specific sort order applied.

You can think of an nonclustered index like a index in the back of a road atlas. The towns are not located in any sort of structured order within a road atlas; rather, they seem to be spread randomly throughout the maps. To find a specific town, you look up the name of the town in the index that contains all towns in alphabetical order. For the town name you are looking for, you find a page number and the coordinates on that page where the town can be found.

A nonclustered index works in a similar fashion. The data rows may be randomly spread throughout the table. The nonclustered index tree contains the index keys in sorted order, with the leaf level of the index containing a pointer to the data page and the row number within the page where the index key value can be found. There is a row in the leaf level for every data row in the table.

The intermediate and root level pages contain the entire leaf level row information plus an additional page pointer to the page at the next level down containing the key value in the first row.

FIGURE 11.18.

*Nonclustered index
structure.*

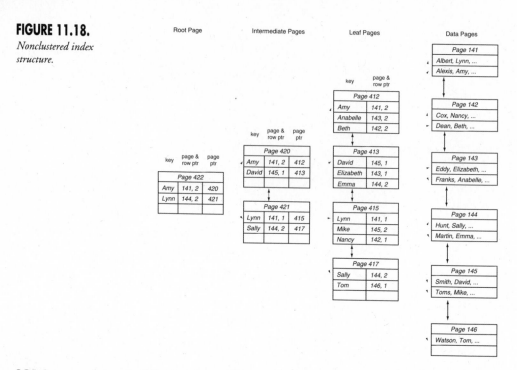

SQL Server performs the following steps when searching for a data row by using the nonclustered index:

1. Queries `sysindexes` for the table where `indid > 1` and `<= 250` and gets the address of the root page for this index.

2. Compares the search value against the key values on the root page.

3. Finds the highest key value on the page where the key value is less than or equal to the search value.

4. Follows the page pointer to the next level down in the index.

5. Continues following page pointers as in steps 3 and 4 until the leaf page is reached.

6. Searches the rows on the leaf page to locate a match for the search value. If a matching row is not found on that leaf page, the table contains no matching rows.

7. If a match is found on the leaf page, follows the pointer to the data page and row ID to retrieve the requested data row.

Because nonclustered indexes contain page and row pointers, the size and number of levels in a nonclustered index is dependent on the width of the index key and the number of rows in the table. The structure of an nonclustered index row is detailed in Figure 11.19.

FIGURE 11.19.

Nonclustered index leaf row structure.

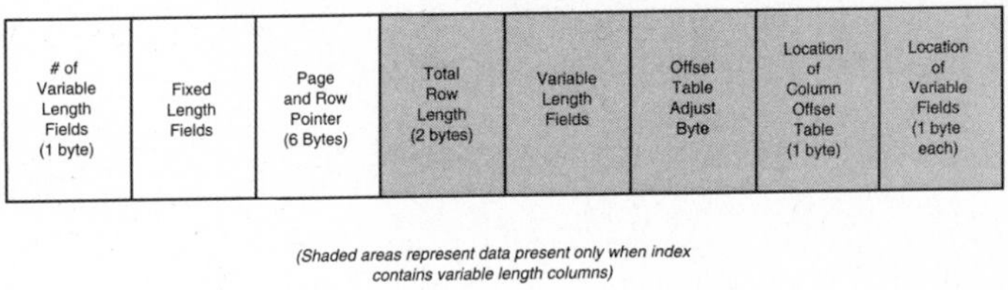

# of Variable Length Fields (1 byte)	Fixed Length Fields	Page and Row Pointer (6 Bytes)	Total Row Length (2 bytes)	Variable Length Fields	Offset Table Adjust Byte	Location of Column Offset Table (1 byte)	Location of Variable Fields (1 byte each)

(Shaded areas represent data present only when index contains variable length columns)

The nonleaf rows of a nonclustered index contain the entire leaf row information—index key plus page and row pointer—and an additional page pointer to point to the pages at the next lower level. The nonleaf rows of a clustered index are constructed similarly to a clustered index (see Figure 11.20).

FIGURE 11.20.

Nonclustered index nonleaf row structure.

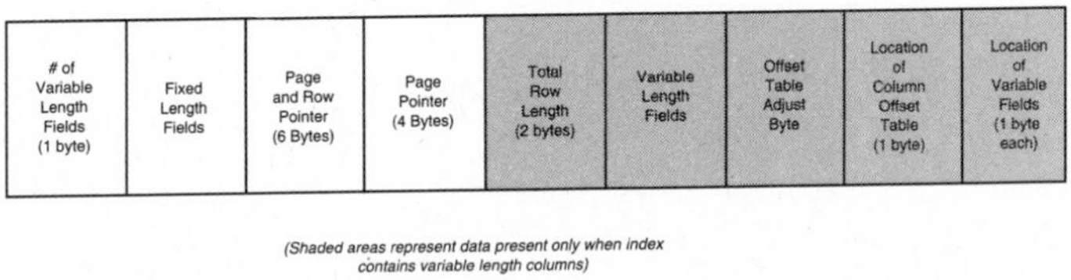

# of Variable Length Fields (1 byte)	Fixed Length Fields	Page and Row Pointer (6 Bytes)	Page Pointer (4 Bytes)	Total Row Length (2 bytes)	Variable Length Fields	Offset Table Adjust Byte	Location of Column Offset Table (1 byte)	Location of Variable Fields (1 byte each)

(Shaded areas represent data present only when index contains variable length columns)

Estimating Nonclustered Index Size

The formula for determining nonclustered leaf index row width with all fixed-length fields is this:

> Sum of fixed-length fields
>
> + 1 byte (number of variable columns)
>
> + 6 bytes (page and row pointer)

Use this formula to determine nonclustered leaf index row width with variable-length fields:

> Sum of fixed-length fields
>
> + 1 byte (number of variable columns)
>
> + 6 bytes (page and row pointer)
>
> + 2 bytes (index row width)
>
> + Sum of average width variable columns
>
> + 1 byte (adjust table)
>
> + 1 byte (location of offset table)
>
> + 1 byte per variable-length column

Let's assume that you have a nonclustered index on a char(10) column that doesn't allow null values. The leaf index row size is the following (on the next page):

> 10 bytes
>
> + 6 bytes (page and row pointer)
>
> + 1 byte (number of variable columns = 0 in this case)
>
> = 17 bytes per leaf index row

Because the leaf level of a nonclustered index contains a pointer to each data row in the table, the number of rows at the leaf level of the index is equal to the number of rows in the table.

If you have 100,000 rows in the table, you'll have 100,000 rows in the nonclustered leaf level. Each nonclustered index page, like a data page, has 2016 bytes available for storing index row entries. To determine the number of nonclustered leaf index rows per page, divide the leaf index row size into 2016 bytes:

> 2016 / 17 = 118.6 rounded down to 118 rows per page × .75 = 88 rows per page

At 88 rows per page, you need 100,000 / 88 = 1136.4, rounded up to 1137 pages, to store all the rows at the leaf level of the index.

The nonleaf rows of a nonclustered index are like clustered index rows in that they contain pointers to all pages at the next level down in the index. Each nonleaf row contains the full index row from the leaf level plus an additional page pointer, 4 bytes in size. Therefore, the size of the nonleaf rows equals this:

> Size of leaf row
>
> + 4 bytes (page pointer)

For the example, the nonleaf rows are the following:

> 17 bytes (leaf index row size)
>
> + 4 bytes (page pointer)
>
> = 21 bytes per nonleaf index row

To determine the number of nonclustered nonleaf index rows per page, divide the nonleaf index row size into 2016 bytes and multiply by the fill factor. For this example, you use a fill factor of 75 percent:

> 2016 / 21 = 96 rows per page × .75 = 72 nonleaf rows per page

Like the clustered index, the top level of the index must be a single root page. You need to build levels on top of one another in the index until you reach a single root page. To determine the total number of levels in the nonclustered index, use the following algorithm:

```
N = 0
divide number of data rows by number of index rows per page
while number of index pages at level N is > 1
begin
    divide number of pages at level N by number of rows per page
    N = N+1
end
```

When the number of pages at level N equals 1, you are at the root page, and N+1 equals the number of levels in the index. The total size of the nonclustered index in number of pages is the total sum of all pages at each level.

If you apply this algorithm to the example, you get the following results:

> Level 0: 100,000 / 88 = 1137 pages
> Level 1: 1137 / 72 = 16 pages
> Level 2: 16 / 72 = 1 page

Thus, the nonclustered index contains three levels, for a total size of 1154 pages, or 2308KB.

The I/O cost of retrieving a single row by using the index is the number of levels in the index plus a single data page. Contrast this with the cost of a table scan for the example:

> 3 index levels + 1 data page = 4 page I/Os
>
> Table scan = 2084 page I/Os

Although a nonclustered index defined on the same column as a clustered index typically consists of one additional level, resulting in one additional I/O, it is still significantly faster than a table scan. You can easily see the performance advantage that having an index on the table can provide during a select. An index is also helpful during data modifications to identify quickly the rows specified to be updated or deleted.

Indexes and Performance

You've seen how indexes, by their nature, can help speed up data retrieval by giving you a direct path to the desired data and avoiding a costly table scan. However, indexes have an adverse impact on update performance because the indexes need to be maintained "on-the-fly" by SQL Server to keep the proper sort order within the index and table.

The disadvantage of clustered indexes is that, during inserts, the rows must be inserted into the appropriate location to maintain the sort order. This is just like a filing system. If you don't put the files away in alphabetical order, your filing system becomes worthless. Similarly, SQL Server maintains the sort order of your data when you update, insert, and delete data rows.

If there is not a clustered index on the table, rows are added at the end of the table as a heap. Any nonclustered indexes have the new row added in the appropriate location within the index leaf page, depending on the index key value.

With or without a clustered index on a table, every time you insert, delete, or update a row, causing the row to move within the table, all nonclustered indexes on the table need to be updated to reflect the new row location. With a large number of indexes on a table, the overhead during data modification may become excessive. For tables involved in Online Transaction Processing (OLTP) types of applications, you should try to keep the number of indexes to fewer than five.

Let's examine what occurs in SQL Server when you modify data with indexes on the table.

SQL Server Index Maintenance

SQL Server indexes are self-maintaining structures. That is, they allocate additional space as needed and deallocate space as rows are deleted, while maintaining the sort order of the index tree. There is typically no need to perform a "reorg" on SQL Server indexes to rebuild and resort the index tree, because SQL Server typically keeps the index tree balanced on-the-fly.

50-50 Page Splits

Normally, when inserting data into a table with a clustered index, the row is inserted into the appropriate position within the appropriate data and/or index page. If the data or index page is full, SQL Server performs a 50-50 page split (see Figure 11.21).

FIGURE 11.21.

50-50 page split.

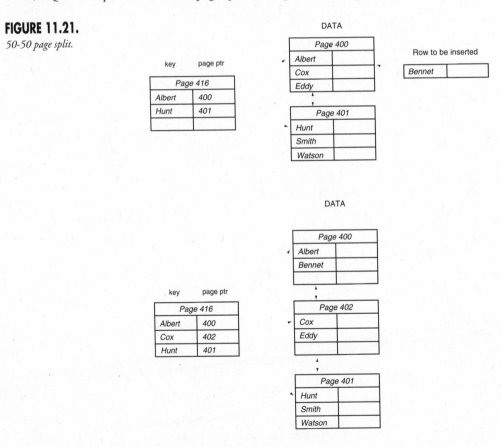

Whenever a page split occurs, the following steps also occur:

1. A new page is linked into the page chain.
2. Half of the rows on the affected page are moved to a new page.

3. The new row is inserted into the appropriate location.

4. The clustered index is updated to reflect the new data page; entries for new index pages are added to the next higher index level.

5. An entry for the new data row is added to all nonclustered indexes on the table.

6. All nonclustered indexes on the table are updated for each row that moved as a result of the page split.

A 50-50 page split obviously incurs index maintenance overhead and slows insert and update performance when it occurs. However, it helps to improve subsequent inserts and updates because the affected pages now are, on average, only about 50 percent full, leaving free space for additional rows before another page split occurs. SQL Server index and table pages typically average out to about 75 percent full for any table that is sufficiently active. This is desirable in an OLTP environment so that 50-50 page splits don't occur excessively.

Be aware that, on occasion, a page split might cascade up multiple levels within the index tree if the index pages are full as well. If the root page splits, a new root page is created and the index tree grows an additional level.

100-0 (Monotonic) Page Splits

If the table has no clustered index, or the clustered index is on a sequential key and data rows are inserted in sequential key order, all new rows are added to the end of the last page in the table. When a data or index page is full and a new row needs to be added to the end of the page, SQL Server performs a *monotonic page split* (see Figure 11.22).

When a monotonic page split occurs, the following steps also occur:

1. A new page is linked into the page chain.

2. The new row is added to the new page.

3. An entry for the new data page is added to the clustered index; entries for new index pages are added to the next higher index level.

4. An entry is added for the new data row to all nonclustered indexes on the table.

As you can see, when you have a monotonic page split, there is less index maintenance and overhead involved. The downside to monotonic page splits or storage in a heap structure is that free space on previous pages isn't reused, because all new rows are added at the end of the page chain. The only way to recover this "lost" space is to rebuild the clustered index and reapply a new fill factor, which you will learn about shortly.

FIGURE 11.22.

Monotonic (100-0) page split.

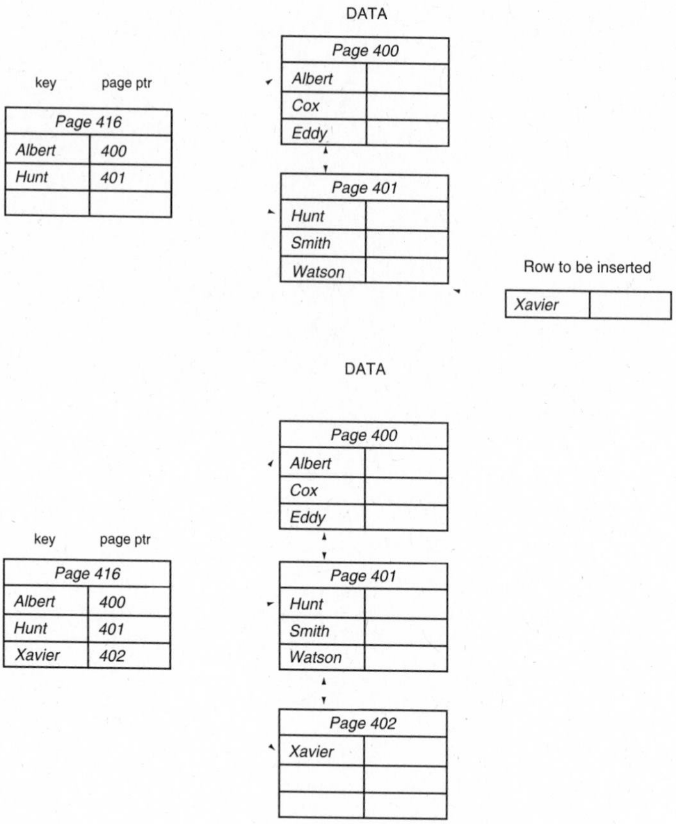

DATA

key	page ptr

Page 416	
Albert	400
Hunt	401

Page 400	
Albert	
Cox	
Eddy	

Page 401	
Hunt	
Smith	
Watson	

Row to be inserted

Xavier	

DATA

key	page ptr

Page 416	
Albert	400
Hunt	401
Xavier	402

Page 400	
Albert	
Cox	
Eddy	

Page 401	
Hunt	
Smith	
Watson	

Page 402	
Xavier	

Overflow Pages

Let's examine what happens if you have a nonunique clustered index that allows duplicate rows and you need to add a duplicate value to the end of the page (see Figure 11.23).

At first, this insert looks similar to a monotonic page split, but it is slightly different in that the new page does not get recorded in the clustered index—because it is in essence an "overflow" of a duplicate value from the previous page. An overflow page is generated only if the duplicate key value matches the last data row on the page and no more room exists to store additional rows on that page. The clustered index still points to the original data page, and the data page points to the overflow page.

Theoretically, this setup violates the normal B-Tree scheme, but gives you a way of handling duplicate key values in a clustered index. If duplicate key values are split across normal data pages, you can miss the rows on a preceding data page if you use the normal method of traversing the index tree. For example, in Figure 11.23, if you had an index pointer to page 402 for the key value Eddy, you would traverse the index tree directly to page 402 and scan for all values of Eddy from that point forward, missing the entry for Eddy on page 400.

FIGURE 11.23.

Overflow page.

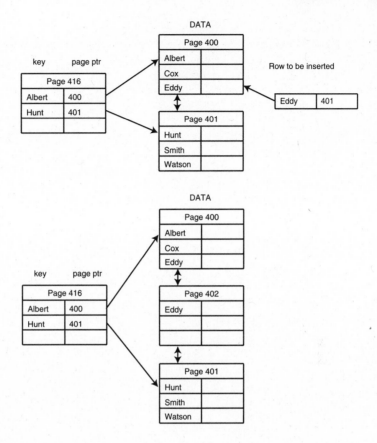

With all the overhead involved in maintaining a sort order, why would you want to use clustered indexes? True, there is an overhead penalty paid when a page split occurs, but clustered indexes also provide a number of advantages:

- Because clustered indexes maintain a sort order and insert data into the appropriate location within the table, clustered indexes make use of free space in pages throughout the table, resulting in less wasted space.
- Clustered indexes can help improve performance for certain types of queries, such as range retrievals and queries with order by, as shown in Chapter 12, "Designing Indexes for Performance."
- Clustered indexes take up much less space than nonclustered indexes defined on the same column(s).
- Clustered indexes typically provide a faster access path to the data than a similarly created nonclustered index, unless the nonclustered index can cover the query (which is also covered in Chapter 12).

■ Clustered indexes are updated less often then nonclustered indexes. Review the previous examples. Every time you performed some form of operation on a data row, you had to update the nonclustered indexes. However, the clustered indexes needed to be updated only if you allocated or deallocated a data page.

I had a customer who was convinced that clustered indexes were a bad thing and got rid of all clustered indexes within his database. When I outlined the previous five points for him, he realized the error of his thinking and redefined his indexing scheme. In general, if you have one and only one index for a table, it is best to define it as a clustered index. If you have multiple candidates for a clustered index and are not sure which column(s) to create the clustered index on, read Chapter 12, which covers index selection and provides guidelines on how to determine what indexes best support your queries and transactions.

Page Merges

As you delete data rows from pages, the remaining rows are shuffled upward on the page to keep all free space at the end of the page. However, if the clustered index key does not cause random inserts into these pages, the free space is not reused. This occurs if the clustered index is defined on a key value that tends to concentrate inserts to a specific portion of the table, such as at the end of the table if defined on a sequential key.

With no clustered index at all, the table is a heap structure and all inserts occur at the end of the page, with no preceding space being reused at all.

When all rows are deleted from a data page, the following occurs:

1. The page is removed from the page linkage.
2. The page is marked as unused in the extent structure bitmap on the allocation page, for the allocation unit within which the page is located.

This page is still reserved for use by the table to which it is allocated. Unused pages are not deallocated from the table until all eight pages within the extent are marked as unused. At that point, the extent is deallocated and may be used by any object within the database that requires additional storage. Until the extent is deallocated, the table or index reuses the unused pages before a new extent is allocated to the table.

Pages within an index are managed similarly to data pages when rows are deleted—with one exception. When only one row is left on an index page, SQL Server merges the index row into an adjacent index page at the same level and removes the now-empty page from the index. This behavior helps to keep the index tree smaller and more efficient.

If the empty space within data and/or index pages is not reused, your table can become fragmented and may take up more space than anticipated. It also can cause your index tree to become unbalanced, with a crowding of data values at the end of the tree and the pages at the beginning of the tree being rather sparse.

This scenario is one of the few times you may have to perform a sort of "reorg" on your indexes to rebalance the index tree and defragment the data. Do this by dropping and re-creating your clustered index, reapplying a fill factor to the data to even out the distribution across the data pages.

The Fill Factor

The *fill factor* is a percentage specifying how full you want your leaf index and/or data pages when the index is created. A lower fill factor has the effect of spreading the data and leaf index rows across more pages by leaving more free space in the pages. This reduces page splitting and dynamic reorganization, which can improve performance in environments where there are a lot of inserts and updates to the data. A higher fill factor has the effect of packing more data and indexes per page, by leaving less free space in the pages. This is useful in environments where the data is relatively static, because it reduces the number of pages required for storing the data and its indexes, and helps improve performance for queries by reducing the number of pages that need to be accessed.

Providing a fill factor when creating a clustered index applies to the rows on the data pages for the table. A fill factor on a nonclustered index affects only the leaf index rows and doesn't affect the data pages. Also, the fill factor is applied only at index creation time and is *not* maintained by the SQL Server. Once you begin updating and inserting data, the fill factor eventually is lost. Therefore, it is only useful to specify a fill factor if the table contains data.

Setting the Fill Factor

The default fill factor is set at the server level, but it is typically provided at index creation time. The typical default fill factor set at the server level is 0. A fill factor of 0 indicates that data and leaf pages are to be completely filled (100 percent) and that sufficient space is left on nonleaf pages for at least one additional index row. This setting minimizes your data storage requirements, but leaves some free space within the index tree to prevent excessive page splits within the nonleaf pages.

If you want to change the server-wide default for the fill factor, use the sp_configure command:

```
sp_configure 'fill factor',N
```

Typically, you specify the fill factor to be used for the index within the index creation statement:

```
create index idx_name on table (column)
    with fillfactor=N
```

In both cases, N is the fill factor percentage to be applied. N can be any valid integer between 0 and 100. 100 is typically used for static tables—all index leaf pages or data pages will be completely filled. For an OLTP environment, you may choose to use a lower fill factor value, such as `50`, leaving your nonclustered leaf index pages or data pages only half full.

In SQL Server 6.5, you can also apply the fill factor to the nonleaf pages in an index, by specifying the `pad index` option along with the `fillfactor` option when creating the index. For example, to apply a 50 precent fill factor to the leaf and nonleaf pages in a clustered index on `title_id` in the `titles` table, execute the following code:

```
create index title_id_index on titles (title_id) with pad_index, fillfactor = 50
```

Because SQL Server indexes are self-maintaining and self-balancing, there is typically no need to reapply a fill factor to the index and/or data. With random activity and normal 50-50 page splits occurring, the data and indexes average out to about 75 percent full.

When might you need to reestablish the fill factor for your indexes or data? Some shops in intensive update situations drop and reload indexes periodically to spread the data and minimize page splits during heavy OLTP activity.

How can you determine whether you are experiencing excessive page splits? One way is to count the number of page splits recorded in your transaction log, by running the following query:

```
select count(*) from syslogs where op = 16
```

By monitoring this value over time, you can determine when your page split count is increasing and also evaluate the effectiveness of various fill factor settings in reducing page splits.

In addition, if a table becomes very large and then very small, rows may become isolated within data pages. This space will not be recovered until the last row on the page is deleted and the page is marked as unused. To reclaim this space, you need to reapply the fill factor to your clustered index.

Reapplying the Fill Factor

To reintroduce the fill factor on a table or index in SQL Server 6.5, you can drop and recreate the index, specifying the new fill factor, or use the `dbcc reindex` command. `dbcc reindex` is useful for reapplying fill factor settings, as it doesn't require that you run the original index creation scripts. You can rebuild a single index on a table or all indexes on a table, and optionally specify a new fillfactor setting or apply the original fill factor used for each index (the original fill factor setting is stored in the `sysindexes` table). The following is the syntax of the `dbcc reindex` command:

```
dbcc reindex (tablename [, indexname [, fillfactor [,{ sorted_data ¦
➥sorted_data_reorg}]]])
```

If the `indexname` parameter is not provided, all indexes on the specified table will be rebuilt. To apply the original fill factor on an index, specify 0 for the `fillfactor` value. The `sorted_data` and `sorted_data_reorg` options apply for clustered indexes. To reapply the fill factor to the data pages, specify the `sorted_data_reorg` option when rebuilding the clustered index.

For example, to reapply the original fill factor to all data and index leaf pages on the `titles` table, execute the following:

```
dbcc reindex (titles, "", 0, sorted_data_reorg)
```

Updates and Performance

All updates within SQL Server are essentially a `delete` followed by an `insert`, unless performed as a direct update in-place. With a clustered index on the table, the row is reinserted to the appropriate location on the appropriate data page relative to its physical sort order. Without a clustered index, the row is inserted into one of three locations:

- The same physical location on the same data page
- The same data page if there is room
- The last page in the heap

SQL Server performs two types of updates:

- Deferred updates
- Direct updates

Direct updates can occur as in-place or not-in-place updates.

Deferred Updates

A *deferred update* is a multi-step process that occurs when the conditions are not met for a direct update to occur. Deferred updates are always required for the following:

- Updates that include a join
- Updates to columns used for referential integrity
- Updates in which the data modification statement can have a cascading effect

For example, consider a table with a unique index on an integer column and sequential data values stored in that column. The following update is executed:

```
update invoices set invoice_num = invoice_num + 1
```

If you start at the first row and update `invoice_num` from 1 to 2, and there is already a row with an `invoice_num` of 2, you violate the uniqueness of the index, and the update fails.

To perform this sort of update, SQL Server uses the deferred update method. With deferred updates, the following steps are executed:

1. All records to be modified are copied to the transaction log to reflect the old and new values for the column(s) to be modified.

2. SQL Server reads the transaction log, deletes the affected rows from the data pages, and deletes any affected index rows.

3. SQL Server rereads the transaction log, inserts the new rows from the log into the table, and inserts any affected index rows.

This method typically has the effect of generating more than the usual number of log records than a direct update. It also incurs the following additional overhead:

- Three data page accesses for each data row
- Four log records generated for each updated row
- Two log records generated for each affected index row
- Two index traversals for each affected index
- Two scans of the log records

SQL Server may also apply the deferred method for inserts and deletes. Consider running the following insert on a table with no clustered index:

```
insert authors select * from authors
```

Because the table is a heap structure, all new rows are added at the end of the table. How does SQL Server know which rows are newly inserted rows and which are existing rows? SQL Server uses a deferred method of inserting the records, by copying the data rows to be inserted into the transaction log. Then it reads the records in the transaction log, inserts the new data rows into the table, and inserts the new index rows into any affected indexes as well.

Due to the additional processing overhead incurred when performing deferred updates, SQL Server attempts to perform direct updates whenever possible.

Direct Updates

Direct updates can be performed either in-place or not-in-place. A direct update not-in-place is still a delete followed by an insert, but the updates can be applied in a single pass. Direct updates not-in-place can occur if the following criteria are met:

- The number of rows affected can be determined at query compile time—that is, the where clause has a search argument (SARG) that can be satisfied by a unique index.
- The index chosen by the optimizer to satisfy the query is not being updated by the query.
- No join clauses are used in the update statement.

For a direct update not-in-place, the row is deleted from the table, modified, and reinserted back into the table. Whether the updated row is inserted back into the table onto the same data page or a different data page depends on two things:

- Whether space is available for the modified row on the current page

■ Whether the update statement caused a change to a clustered index key value, forcing the row to be reinserted into a different data page

Figure 11.24 demonstrates a direct update not-in-place.

FIGURE 11.24.

Direct update not-in-place.

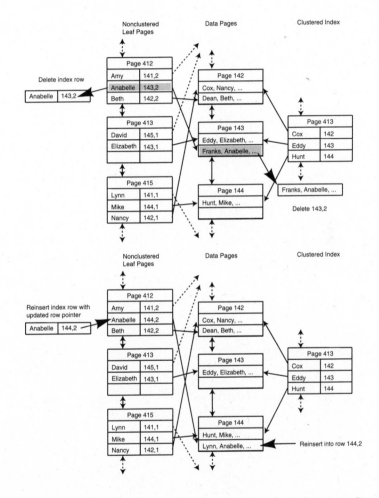

In this example, the update had to be performed not-in-place because the column being modified was the clustered index column, necessitating that the row be moved to a new page.

Even if the data row is reinserted in the same data page, it may be assigned a different row number than previously if there are any unused row numbers (row offset equals 0) less than the previous row ID for the affected row. This behavior necessitates that all index rows pointing to the data row be deleted and reinserted as well, in order to reflect the new page/row pointer information.

A direct update not-in-place produces the following overhead:

- A single data page access for each data row updated
- Two log records (DELETE, INSERT) generated for each updated data row
- Two log records (IDELETE, IINSERT) generated for each affected index row

If the column being modified is not part of an index, and the row is deleted and reinserted in the same page with the same row ID, no index maintenance is required, because no index pointers need to be updated.

Direct updates not-in-place incur less overhead and are faster than deferred updates. Direct updates not-in-place are performed whenever possible.

Direct Updates In-Place

By default, SQL Server treats a direct update as a delete followed by an insert. An update in-place is a method for modifying the record directly, without the necessity for the delete. Because the row is modified in-place and doesn't move, updates in-place are faster than updates not-in-place—they incur fewer log writes and fewer index updates.

In SQL Server 6.5, the following criteria must be met for a direct update in-place of a single row to occur:

- The update statement can't modify a clustered index column because this obviously requires the data row to move.
- An update trigger can't exist on the table because the trigger requires the before and after image of the row.
- The table can't be marked for replication.
- The column(s) being updated can be of variable length if the row will still fit on the same page.
- The column(s) being updated can also be part of a nonunique nonclustered index, if the index key is a fixed-width column.
- The column(s) being updated can be part of a unique nonclustered index, if the index key is fixed-width and the where clause criteria matches only one row.
- The new row size can't differ from the previous row size by more than 50 percent, and the total number of noncontiguous bytes is less than 24.

SQL Server 6.5 also now performs direct updates in-place for multi-row updates if the following criteria are met:

- The column being updated must be of fixed length.
- The column being updated can't be part of a unique nonclustered index.
- The column being updated can be part of a nonunique, nonclustered index, if the column is a fixed-width column.

- The index used to find the rows doesn't contain a column to be updated.
- The table doesn't contain a timestamp column.

A direct update in-place produces the following overhead:

- A single data page access for each data row updated
- A single log record (MODIFY) generated for each updated data row
- Two log records (IDELETE, IINSERT) generated for any affected index row (only if a column being updated is part of a nonclustered index)

Direct updates in-place incur the least amount of overhead of all the update methods. Direct updates in-place result in the fewest number of log records generated and the smallest opportunity for any index rows to need to be updated. SQL Server performs direct updates in-place whenever possible, rather than updates not-in-place.

Confirming Updates In Place

One of the trickier tasks is determining whether a direct update occurs in-place or not-in-place. The SQL Server query optimizer reports only whether an update was direct or deferred, not whether it was in-place or not-in-place.

The only way to determine accurately whether a direct update occurs in-place or not-in-place is to examine the transaction log for the update in question. The easy way to examine the transaction log records is to execute the update statement in question and to execute the following immediately:

```
select * from syslogs
```

As long as no one else has run a logged operation in that database between the time you execute your update statement and the time you run the select against the syslogs table, the last rows retrieved should be the rows related to the update statement in question.

If you are hoping for an update in-place, you want a row where op equals 9 sandwiched between a 0 and a 30. Table 11.2 lists some common op code values and the type of log record to which they relate.

Table 11.2. Common transaction log op codes.

op	Description
0	BEGIN TRANSACTION
4	INSERT
5	DELETE
6	INSIND (indirect insert)

continues

Table 11.2. continued

op	Description
7	IINSERT (index insert)
8	IDELETE (index delete)
9	MODIFY (update in-place)
11	INOOP (deferred insert)
12	DNOOP (deferred delete)
13	ALLOC (page)
15	EXTENT (allocation)
16	PAGE SPLIT
17	CHECKPOINT
30	END TRANSACTION (commit or rollback)

If you have trouble remembering what the different op codes relate to, there is another way to examine the transaction log—use the dbcc log command. You have to log in as sa to run this command.

> **WARNING**
>
> *Do not* run dbcc log in a database if you have the 'trunc. log on chkpt.' option set to true for that database. There apparently is a rare situation where, if you are running dbcc log at the same time that the SQL Server is attempting to truncate the log, you could end up with a corrupted transaction log and your database will be marked as suspect.
>
> If your log ever gets corrupted, you will need a fairly recent backup of your database, because there is no way to fix a bad transaction log—other than to restore your database to a point prior to the log's getting corrupted.

dbcc log displays a translated hex dump of the log contents. One nice thing it does for you is translate the op codes into a textual representation of the type of operation.

To examine the transaction log, follow these steps:

1. Log in as sa.
2. Put the database in single-user mode to avoid having other users adding additional log records (not required, but recommended).
3. Run dbcc traceon (3604) to route dbcc output to your terminal.

5. Truncate the transaction log to make it as small as possible (again, not required, but recommended because dbcc log can generate tons of output if the log hasn't been pruned recently).

6. Execute the update statement in question.

7. Execute dbcc log to print out the contents of the transaction log (this output can be quite large and you may want to redirect it to a file).

8. Examine the last few log records, which should correspond to your update command.

The BEGINXACT and ENDXACT records in the dbcc log output represent the beginning and end of the transaction. If an update in-place occurred, a MODIFY record should be between the BEGINXACT and ENDXACT records. You can match the transaction records to their corresponding BEGINXACT and ENDXACT records via the transaction ID (xactid). The following is sample output for a single row update in-place:

```
BEGINXACT(517 , 25)
attcnt=1 rno=25 op=0 padlen=3 xactid=(517 , 25) len=60 status=0x0000
masterid=(0 , 0) lastrec=(0 , 0)   xstat=XBEG_ENDXACT
spid=11 suid=1 uid=1 masterdbid=0 mastersite=0 endstat=3
name=upd   time=Nov 15 1995 12:37AM


MODIFY(517 , 26)
attcnt=1 rno=26 op=9 padlen=2 xactid=(517 , 25) len=52 status=0x0000
tabid=80003316 pageno=376 offset=296 status=0x0000
old ts=0x0001 0x000020b8   new ts=0x0001 0x000020ba


ENDXACT(517 , 27)
attcnt=1 rno=27 op=30 padlen=4 xactid=(517 , 25) len=40 status=0x0000
endstat=COMMIT time=Nov 15 1995 12:37AM
```

If the update is not in-place, there should be at least two records, a DELETE followed by an INSERT record.

The following output is an example of a single row update not-in-place:

```
BEGINXACT(517 , 21)
attcnt=1 rno=21 op=0 padlen=3 xactid=(517 , 21) len=60 status=0x0000
masterid=(0 , 0) lastrec=(0 , 0)   xstat=XBEG_ENDXACT
spid=11 suid=1 uid=1 masterdbid=0 mastersite=0 endstat=3
name=upd   time=Nov 15 1995 12:35AM


DELETE(517 , 22)
attcnt=1 rno=22 op=5 padlen=1 xactid=(517 , 21) len=72 status=0x0000
tabid=80003316 pageno=376 offset=275 status=0x0000
old ts=0x0001 0x000009d4   new ts=0x0001 0x000020b7


INSERT(517 , 23)
attcnt=1 rno=23 op=4 padlen=0 xactid=(517 , 21) len=76 status=0x0000
tabid=80003316 pageno=376 offset=275 status=0x0000
old ts=0x0001 0x000020b7   new ts=0x0001 0x000020b8


ENDXACT(517 , 24)
attcnt=1 rno=24 op=30 padlen=4 xactid=(517 , 21) len=40 status=0x0000
endstat=COMMIT time=Nov 15 1995 12:35AM
```

If you see any IINSERT and IDELETE records, these represent index row updates. The following output is an example of an update in-place on a nonclustered index column, resulting in the corresponding nonclustered index row update:

```
BEGINXACT(517 , 28)
attcnt=1 rno=28 op=0 padlen=3 xactid=(517 , 28) len=60 status=0x0000
masterid=(0 , 0) lastrec=(0 , 0)   xstat=XBEG_ENDXACT
spid=11 suid=1 uid=1 masterdbid=0 mastersite=0 endstat=3
name=upd   time=Nov 15 1995 12:41AM

IDELETE(517 , 29)
attcnt=1 rno=29 op=8 padlen=2 xactid=(517 , 28) len=56 status=0x0000
tabid=80003316 pageno=392 offset=222 status=0x0000
old ts=0x0001 0x00000cd4   new ts=0x0001 0x000020bc

MODIFY(517 , 30)
attcnt=1 rno=30 op=9 padlen=4 xactid=(517 , 28) len=56 status=0x0000
tabid=80003316 pageno=376 offset=280 status=0x0000
old ts=0x0001 0x000020ba   new ts=0x0001 0x000020bd

IINSERT(517 , 31)
attcnt=1 rno=31 op=7 padlen=2 xactid=(517 , 28) len=56 status=0x0000
tabid=80003316 pageno=392 offset=32 status=0x0000
old ts=0x0001 0x000020bc   new ts=0x0001 0x000020be

ENDXACT(516 , 0)
attcnt=1 rno=0 op=30 padlen=4 xactid=(517 , 28) len=40 status=0x0000
endstat=COMMIT time=Nov 15 1995 12:41AM
```

Summary

By now you should have a reasonable understanding of SQL Server storage structures and how they are maintained and manipulated. Having a reasonable understanding of this information will help you further understand the topics to be discussed in the subsequent performance and tuning chapters.

Now that you have a good understanding of the internal workings of your high-performance vehicle, SQL Server, it's time to starting tuning it to get the best possible performance for your applications.

Designing Indexes
for Performance

12

A number of ways are available to improve SQL Server performance, but the greatest speed improvement results from having indexes that the optimizer can use to avoid table scans and reduce the I/O costs of resolving queries. Proper index design is the most important issue in tuning SQL Server performance. This chapter examines the SQL Server criteria for utilizing indexes and explores the issues and factors that influence index design.

Why Use Indexes?

Two primary reasons exist for creating indexes in SQL Server: to maintain uniqueness of the indexed column(s), and to provide fast access to the data in tables.

If you have primary-key constraints, you need unique indexes to ensure the integrity of the primary key and avoid duplicates. However, you don't have to have indexes in order to access the data. SQL Server can always perform a table scan to retrieve data rows. But table scans aren't an efficient mechanism to retrieve a single row from a million-row table. If the table could store 50 rows per page, it would require 200,000 page reads to access a single row. You need a more direct access path to the data. Indexes can provide this direct access path. The tricky part is deciding which indexes to create, and also which type of index to create: clustered or nonclustered. To make the appropriate decisions, you need to know when SQL Server can use indexes and how they're used. You also need to understand the performance and size implications of indexes.

Index Usage Criteria

To effectively determine the indexes that should be created, you need to know whether they'll be used by the SQL server. If an index isn't being used, it's just wasting space and creating unnecessary overhead during updates. The main criterion to remember is that SQL Server can't use an index defined on a table unless the query contains a column in a valid search argument (SARG) or join clause that matches at least the first column of the index. You need to keep this in mind when choosing the column order for composite indexes. For example, if you had an index on an employee table as follows:

```
create index idx1 on employee (division, dept, empl_type)
```

each of the following queries could make use of the index:

```
select * from employee
   where division = 'accounting'
      and dept = 102
      and empl_type = 'exempt'

select * from employee
   where division = 'accounting'
      and empl_type = 'exempt'
```

```
select * from employee
   where division = 'accounting'
     and dept = 102

select * from employee
   where division = 'accounting'
```

This query couldn't use the index because it doesn't specify the first column of the index:

```
select * from employee
   where empl_type = 'exempt'
```

For the index `idx1` to be used for the last query, you'd have to reorder the columns so that `empl_type` was first—but then the index wouldn't be useful for any queries specifying only `division` and/or `dept`. To satisfy all queries in this case would require defining multiple indexes on the `employee` table.

You may think that the easy solution is to index all columns on a table. While taking up a significant amount of space, this strategy might work in a DSS environment. However, too many indexes can have an adverse impact on performance in an OLTP environment.

Indexes and Performance

Although providing a performance benefit for queries, indexes can be a hindrance to good performance for updates. This situation is due to the overhead incurred to keep indexes up-to-date when data is modified, inserted, or deleted. This problem is common in databases that must support both OLTP and Decision Support-type applications.

In a Decision Support System (DSS), having too many indexes isn't much of a performance issue because the data is relatively static. You typically load the data, create the indexes, and forget about it until the next data load. As long as you have the indexes to support the user queries, and they're getting decent response time, the only penalty of having too many indexes is the space wasted for indexes that won't be used and the additional time required to create the excessive indexes.

In an OLTP environment, too many indexes can lead to significant performance degradation, especially if the number of indexes on a table exceeds four or five. Think about it for a second. Every single row insert is one data page write and one or more index page writes (depending on whether a page split occurs) for every index on the table. With eight nonclustered indexes, that would be a minimum of nine writes to the database. For an update not-in-place of a single row, which is a `delete` followed by an `insert`, you'd be looking at potentially 17 writes to the database. Therefore, for an OLTP environment, you want as few indexes as possible—typically only the indexes required to support the update transactions and enforce your uniqueness constraints.

Meeting the index needs of DSS and OLTP requirements is an obvious balancing act, with no easy solution. It often involves making hard decisions as to which queries have to live with a table scan and which updates have to contend with additional overhead.

One solution is to have two separate databases—one for DSS applications and another for OLTP applications. Obviously, this method would require some mechanism to keep the databases in sync. The mechanism chosen depends on how up-to-date the DSS database has to be. If you can afford some lag time, you could consider using a dump-and-load mechanism. If the DSS system required up-to-the-minute concurrency, you would probably want to consider using replication (see Chapter 36, "Introduction to SQL Server 6.5 Replication").

I wouldn't recommend triggers as a method to keep two databases in sync. I once saw a system in which such a design had been implemented. The performance overhead of the trigger in the OLTP environment was much greater than any overhead caused by having the indexes on the tables. Believe me, replication is a much cleaner, behind-the-scenes approach.

Another possible alternative is to have only the required indexes in place during normal processing to support the OLTP requirements. At the end of the business day, create the indexes necessary to support the DSS queries, which can run as batch jobs after normal processing hours. When the DSS reports are complete, drop the additional indexes, and you're prepared for the next day's processing.

Index Selection

Determining which indexes to define involves performing a detailed query analysis. This involves examining the search clauses to see what columns are referenced, knowing the bias of the data to determine the usefulness of the index, and ranking the queries in order of importance. You have to be careful not to examine individual queries and develop indexes to support one query, without considering the other queries that are executed on the table as well.

Because it's usually not possible to index for everything, index for the queries that are most critical to your applications or those that are run frequently by a large number of users. If you have a query that's run only once a month, is it worth creating an index to support only that query, and having to maintain it throughout the rest of the month? The sum of the additional processing time throughout the month could conceivably exceed the time required to perform a table scan to satisfy that one query.

If, due to processing requirements, you must have the index in place when the query is run, consider creating the index only when you run the query, and then drop the index for the remainder of the month. This is a feasible approach as long as the time needed to create the index and run the query that uses the index doesn't exceed the time needed to run the query without the index in place.

Evaluating Index Usefulness

When the SARGs or join clauses in a query match the indexes on a table, SQL Server evaluates all possible indexes, comparing them to each other and to the cost of a table scan to determine the least expensive method to process the query in terms of page I/Os. SQL Server uses an index only if—depending on the type of query and the data in the table—the index will be more efficient than a table scan.

Also, SQL Server typically uses only one index per table to satisfy a query. The only exception to this rule is when a query contains an or clause and SQL Server can apply the or strategy. (This topic is covered in Chapter 13, "Understanding the Query Optimizer.") If a query has multiple where clauses that can be satisfied by an index, SQL Server evaluates all alternatives, but uses only the index that will result in the most efficient query plan.

How does SQL Server determine the cheapest index to use? For example, how does it know how many rows will be returned by the following query?

```
select * from table
    where key between 1,000,000 and 2,000,000
```

If the table contains 10,000,000 rows with values ranging between 0 and 20,000,000, how does the optimizer know whether to use an index or table scan? There could be 10 rows in the range, or 900,000. How does SQL Server estimate how many rows are between 1,000,000 and 2,000,000? The optimizer gets this information from the index distribution page, as described in the next section.

The Distribution Page

SQL Server keeps distribution information for each index on a separate page in the database, called the *distribution page*. The location of this page is stored in the sysindexes table in the distribution column. The optimizer uses this information to estimate the number of rows that would match the search argument or a join clause for a query.

The optimizer stores two types of information in the distribution page:

■ Sample data values for the first column of the index, in a structure similar to (but not the same as) a histogram

■ The density/selectivity of the index columns

The distribution page is built at index-creation time if the table contains data. If the table is empty, no distribution page is created. In addition, the distribution page isn't maintained by SQL Server as data is inserted/updated/deleted in the table. To update or, if necessary, create the distribution page, the DBA or table owner needs to run the update statistics command. The syntax is as follows:

```
update statistics table_name [index_name]
```

If only the table name is specified, update statistics updates statistics for all indexes on the table. If you want to update statistics for an individual index, specify the index name after the table name.

The general recommendation is that if your data volume changes by more than 10 to 20 percent, or more than 10 to 20 percent of your indexed values have been modified, it's a good time to update statistics. If you want to confirm the last time index statistics were updated, use the stats_date system function. For example, to see the last time statistics were updated on the idx1 index on the pt_sample_lg table, execute this command:

```
select stats_date(pt_sample_lg, idx1)
```

What's Stored on the Distribution Page?

The distribution page is populated by dividing the width of the first column in the index (plus two bytes of overhead) into the space available on the distribution page, to determine the number of slots or "steps" it can store on the distribution page. (See Figure 12.1.) It then reads the leaf rows of the index and stores the appropriate values for the first column of the index in the steps on the distribution page.

The space available on the distribution page is at least 2016 bytes (2048 minus a 32-byte header) minus the additional space required for the index density table. The index density table is stored at the end of the page and requires 2 bytes per each density stored. At least two density values are stored on each distribution page (more on this in a moment), leaving a maximum of 2012 bytes available to store the distribution steps for a single byte key.

The size of each step is dependent on the size of the first column in the index and whether it's a fixed- or variable-length column. For a fixed-width column, the size of each distribution step is the width of the column plus 2 bytes of overhead. For an index with a variable-length column as the first column, the width of each distribution step is the actual data width for the value stored in the step plus 7 bytes of overhead. The additional overhead is extra bytes used to store the row width plus the size of the data value, just like a row with variable-length columns on a data page (see Chapter 11, "Understanding SQL Server Storage Structures," for a discussion of how variable-length data is stored).

The number of distribution steps for a fixed-length column would then be calculated as

(2016 – 2 – (number of key columns * 2)) / (column width + 2)

The number of distribution steps for a variable length column would be determined as follows:

(2016 – 2 – (number of key columns * 2)) / (maximum column width + 2)

Let's consider an example of an index defined on a single integer column that doesn't allow null values. The number of steps that could be stored for this column would be:

(2016 – 2 – (1 * 2)) / (4 + 2)

= 2012 / 6

= 335 steps

FIGURE 12.1.

A graphical representation of a distribution page.

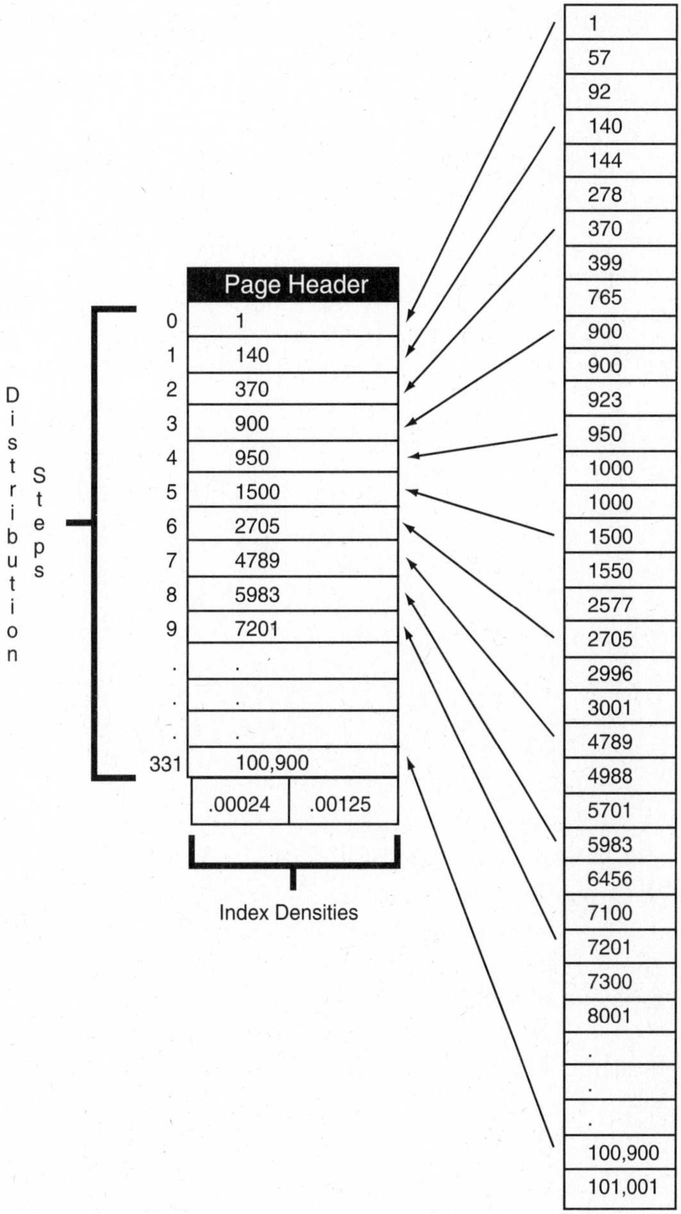

With 10,000,000 rows in the table and up to 335 steps on the page, we can store a sample value for every:

10,000,000 rows / 335 steps = 29,850 rows

SQL Server then populates the distribution table by walking the index and storing the key value in each step for every 29,850 rows, starting with the first row in the table.

How does the optimizer use this information to determine the effectiveness of the index? Consider again the query discussed previously:

```
select * from table
    where key between 1,000,000 and 2,000,000
```

SQL Server estimates the number of rows within the range of values by multiplying the number of steps that the search values are found on or between times the number of rows per step.

In this example, SQL Server compares the search values 1,000,000 and 2,000,000 to the values stored on the distribution page. If it finds 1,000,000 at step 157 and 2,000,000 at step 182, the estimated number of rows would be:

182 − 157 = 25 steps

25 steps × 29,850 rows per step = 746,250 rows

If an index contains a number of duplicate values, the search value could be stored on multiple steps. For an equality search, if a search value matched a number of steps on the distribution page, the estimated number of matching rows would be equal to the number of matching steps × rows per step.

This is why a composite index with many duplicate values in the first column may sometimes result in a higher estimated row count for the index when comparing against the distribution steps. If it's possible, it's often better to put the most unique column as the first column in a composite index. This setup results in more selective distribution steps being stored on the distribution page. However, it also makes the index useless for certain queries where the first column of the index isn't specified in a SARG, so you may have to make a tradeoff here.

Distribution steps are used for equality search clauses (`column = constant`) only when a `constant` expression is compared against an indexed `column` whose value is known at query compile time. In SQL Server Version 6.0 and later, this includes any constant values, arithmetic expressions, system functions, and string concatenation. SQL Server Version 6.0 and later evaluates the `constant` expression and uses the resulting value when compiling the query plan to compare against the distribution steps. Examples of expressions where distribution steps can be used include

- `where col_a = getdate()`
- `where cust_id = 12345`
- `where monthly_sales < 10000 / 12`
- `where l_name like "Smith" + "%"`

> **NOTE**
>
> In versions of SQL Server prior to Version 6.0, the distribution steps could be used only if explicit `constant` values were specified in search arguments.

Some `constant` expressions can't be evaluated until query runtime. For these types of statements, you need some other way of estimating the number of matching rows. These include search arguments containing local variables or subqueries, and also join clauses such as

- `where price = @avg_price`
- `where total_sales > (select sum(qty) from sales)`
- `where titles.pub_id = publishers.pub_id`

Additionally, because distribution steps are kept only on the first column of the index, the optimizer must use a different method for determining the number of rows matching the specified portions of a multicolumn key. If there is an index on one of these other columns, it examines the distribution page on that index to estimate the selectivity of the search clause on that column alone. Otherwise, the optimizer uses the index density values.

Index Densities

When the optimizer doesn't use distribution steps for equality searches (`column = constant`), it uses a value called the *density*. The density is the average proportion of duplicates for the index key(s). Essentially, this number can be calculated as the inverse of the number of unique values in the table. For example, an index on a 10,000-row table with 2,500 unique values would have a density of

$$1/2500 = .0004$$

The index density is applied against the number of rows in the table to estimate the average number of rows that would match any given value. Therefore, any single value compared against the index key on a 10,000-row table with an index density of .0004 would be expected to match

$$10,000 \times .0004 = 4 \text{ rows}$$

The lower the density value, the more selective the index is; the higher the density, the less selective the index. If an index consisted of all duplicates, the density would be 1 or 100 percent.

For multicolumn indexes, SQL Server now stores multiple densities for each sequential combination of columns. For example, if you had an index on columns A, B, and C, SQL Server would store densities for

A alone
A and B combined
A, B, and C combined

Typically, the density value should become smaller (that is, more selective) as you add more columns to the index. For example, if the densities were as follows:

A	.05
A, B	.004
A, B, C	.0001

with 10,000 rows in the table and a search value compared against A alone, you would estimate it to match:

.05 * 10,000 = 500 rows

If the query provided values for both A and B, you would expect it to match:

.004 * 10,000 = 40 rows

If A, B, C are all specified, the query should match only:

.0001 * 10,000 = 1 row

> **NOTE**
>
> Prior to SQL Server Version 6.0, the distribution page contained only a single-density value for all columns in the index.

All density values are stored at the end of the distribution page (refer to Figure 12.1). At least two densities are stored, even for single-column indexes. One is used for determining join selectivity or for search arguments with unknown values and is referred to as the *alldensity value*. This density value is based on all rows in the table, because the join or search value could match a value with a large number of duplicates.

The other density is used for search clauses when the value being searched falls between two distribution steps. If there were a few values in the table with a large number of duplicates, the alldensity value could conceivably refer to a greater number of rows than would exist between the two steps. For example, consider a table with 10,000 rows with an index on a char(8) key:

8 bytes plus 2 = 10 bytes per step
1992 bytes / 10 bytes per step = 199 steps
10,000 rows / 199 steps = 50 rows per step

Let's assume there are 150 unique values in the table. The alldensity would be

1 / 150 = .0067

If a search value was found to be between two steps and the alldensity value was applied, it would estimate

.0067 * 10,000 = 67

that 67 rows would match. However, there are only 50 rows per step, and if the search value falls between two steps, there can't be more than 50 instances of the data value. For this reason, SQL Server stores a regular density value that excludes some values with a high number of duplicates—essentially those values that don't span multiple cells in the distribution. So, when there are a lot of duplicates, the join density is likely to be higher and the regular density value is likely to be lower.

Viewing Distribution Page Values

In an environment where the data is modified, over time your index statistics become out-of-date. You need to run the update statistics command to generate new statistics based on the current data values in the table.

If you want to examine the current contents of the distribution page to determine whether they accurately represent the data values stored in the table, you can use the dbcc page command (see Chapter 11). The contents are displayed in hexadecimal format, however, which is difficult to read and not very useful. Fortunately, SQL Server provides a command that displays the contents of the distribution page in a readable format:

```
dbcc show_statistics (table_name, index_name)
```

Following is a fraction of the output for the clustered index, tx_CIid, on the id column for the pt_tx_CIid table:

```
Updated                Rows          Steps         Density
--------------------   -----------   -----------   ------------------
Nov 19 1995  4:02AM    7282          330           0.000213248

(1 row(s) affected)

All density            Columns
---------------------  ---------------------------
0.000213248            id

(1 row(s) affected)

Steps
-----------
          1
         65
        214
        271
        369
        497
        604
        656
        745
        849
        961
  .
  .
  .
```

```
316606
316996
317462
317913
318409
318866
```

```
(330 row(s) affected)
```

Here you can see the values stored in the distribution steps as well as the stored index densities. Notice that two density values are stored for a single column index: the regular density and the alldensity value. In this example they're the same, because the `id` column is unique and there are no spikes in the data distribution where there would be a large number of duplicates.

If you prefer to see the index statistics in a graphical format, check out the demonstration copy of Aurora Distribution Viewer on the included CD-Rom in the back of this book. In addition to providing multiple ways of graphing the distribution page values, it also can keep a history of distribution page values for tracking the effectiveness of your `update statistics` strategy. The advantage of a graphical display is that it can help you track down spikes in your data distribution.

Index Design Guidelines

Now that you have an understanding of how the optimizer uses indexes and index statistics to optimize queries, let's examine some guidelines to consider when developing your index strategy.

Clustered Index Indications

One thing that I've found in my travels is that too often the database designer (or, as is more often the case, the database design tool) automatically assigns the clustered index to the primary key. This setup may be appropriate if the primary key is the primary access path for that table, but other good candidates for the clustered index to consider are

- Range searches
- Columns containing a number of duplicate values
- Columns frequently referenced in an `order by`
- Columns other than the primary key referenced in join clauses

In most applications, the primary-key column on a table is almost always retrieved in single-row lookups. For single-row lookups, a nonclustered index usually costs you only one I/O more than a similar clustered index. Are you or the users going to notice a difference between three page reads and four page reads? Not at all. However, if you also have a retrieval such as a lookup on last name, will you notice a difference between scanning 10 percent of the table versus a full table scan? Most definitely.

Clustered indexes can improve performance for range retrievals because the clustered index can be used to set the bounds of a search, even if the query involves a large percentage of the rows in the table. Because the data is in sorted order, SQL Server can use the clustered index to find the start and end points within the range, and scan only the data pages within the range. Without a clustered index, the rows could be randomly spread throughout the table and SQL Server would have to perform a table scan to find all rows within the range.

Let's assume that you have 2,000,000 titles in the table, with an estimated 1,000,000 books in the price range between $5 and $10, and you want to run the following query:

```
select title from titles
    where price between $5. and $10.
```

If you had a clustered index on the table, the rows would be grouped together by price; you could start your search at the first row where price is greater than or equal to $5 and scan the rows in order until you find the last row within the range. (See Figure 12.2.)

FIGURE 12.2.

Clustered index range retrieval.

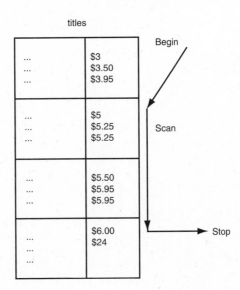

If there are 40 rows per page, with 1,000,000 rows within the range, it would cost you approximately

$$1,000,000 / 40 = 25,000 \text{ data page reads}$$

plus the number of index page reads required to find the first row in the range. This value should be equal to the number of levels in the index.

The same concept holds true for indexes on columns with a large number of duplicates. With a clustered index, the duplicate values are grouped together, minimizing the number of pages that would need to be read to retrieve them.

Another good candidate for a clustered index is a column used frequently in queries for sorting the result set. Most sorts require that the table be copied into a worktable in `tempdb` for sorting purposes. This requirement incurs additional I/O overhead and also increases the potential for I/O and locking contention in `tempdb`. If you have a clustered index on the table and are ordering by the clustered index column(s) on the table, a worktable can be avoided even if the query contains no search arguments. True, the optimizer performs a table scan at this point, but because it knows that the rows are in sorted order (by nature of the clustered index), it can avoid the additional processing to sort the results.

> **NOTE**
>
> If you have a search clause on the table that will be satisfied by a nonclustered index, but are ordering by the clustered index column(s), SQL Server will need to use a worktable to sort the results. This is because the data in this case is being retrieved via nonclustered index order, not clustered index order. Therefore rows aren't sorted in the order specified by the `order by` clause when retrieved.

You also want to try to keep your clustered indexes on relatively static columns to minimize the re-sorting of data rows when an indexed column is updated. Any time a clustered index row moves, all nonclustered indexes pointing to that row also need to be updated.

Clustered indexes can also be more efficient for joins than nonclustered indexes because they're usually much smaller in size, typically at least one level less (see Chapter 11 for a detailed discussion of index structures and sizes). A single page read may not seem like much for a single row retrieval, but add that one additional page to 100,000 join iterations, and you're looking at 100,000 additional page reads.

If you require only a single index on a table, it's typically advantageous to make it a clustered index; the resulting overhead of maintaining clustered indexes during updates, inserts, and deletes can be considerably less than the overhead incurred by nonclustered indexes.

Try to avoid creating clustered indexes on sequential key fields that are inserted monotonically, such as on an `identity` column. This can create a "hot spot" at the end of the table that results in locking contention on the last page of the table and the index. Additionally, the clustered index will not be reusing available space on preceding data pages, because all new rows sort to the end of the table. This situation results in wasted space and your table growing larger than anticipated. I typically recommend that you try to cluster on a data value that's somewhat randomly distributed throughout your table. Some candidates for clustered index keys to randomize your data include the following:

- Date of birth
- Last name, first name

- ZIP code
- A random hash key

Spreading your data throughout the table helps to minimize page contention as well as space utilization. If the sequential key is your primary key, you can still use a unique, nonclustered index to provide an access path via the index and maintain the uniqueness of the primary key.

Because you can physically sort the data in a table in only one way, you can have only one clustered index. Any other columns you want to index have to be defined with nonclustered indexes.

Nonclustered Index Indications

Until tables become extremely large, the actual space taken by a nonclustered index is a minor expense compared to the increased access performance. In an OLTP environment, however, you need to remember the impact on performance of each additional index defined on a table.

Also, when defining nonclustered indexes, you typically want to define indexes on columns with a low number of duplicates (that is, with low density values) so that they can be used effectively by the optimizer. A high number of duplicates on a nonclustered index can often make it more expensive (in terms of I/O) to process the query using the nonclustered index than a table scan. Let's look at an example:

```
select title from titles
   where price between $5. and $10.
```

Again, if you have 1,000,000 rows within the range, those 1,000,000 rows could be randomly scattered throughout the table. Although the index leaf level has all the index rows in sorted order, reading all data rows one at a time would require at least 1,000,000 page reads (see Figure 12.3).

Thus, the I/O estimate for range retrievals using a clustered index is

> number of matching rows
> + number of index levels
> + number of index pages to be scanned to find rows

In the preceding example, if you have 1,000,000 rows in the table, the page cost estimate would be

> 1,000,000 data pages + index pages

Contrast this with the cost of a table scan. At 40 rows per page, and 2,000,000 rows in the table, a full table scan would cost only 50,000 pages. Therefore, a clustered index (25,000 pages) would be most efficient, but if a clustered index is already defined on a better candidate column, a table scan would actually be more efficient than a nonclustered index.

FIGURE 12.3.

Nonclustered index range retrieval.

Index leaf level

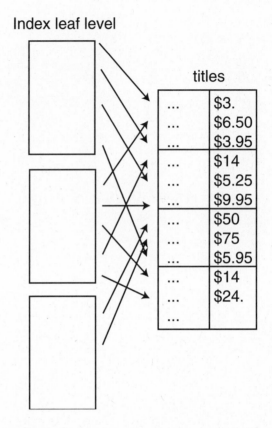

This same principle holds true for nonclustered indexes with a large number of duplicate values (index density is high). As a rule of thumb, nonclustered indexes are more effective if less than 10 to 20 percent of the data is to be accessed via the nonclustered index.

Nonclustered indexes can also help improve performance for certain range retrievals by avoiding the need for a worktable. This occurs when the column(s) in the order by clause match the column(s) in the nonclustered index, and the index is chosen to satisfy the query. For example, if you had a nonclustered index on city, SQL Server could choose to use the nonclustered index to satisfy the following query:

```
select * from authors
    where city in ("Boston", "San Francisco", "Chicago", "New York", "Indianapolis")
    order by city
```

If the index is used, the data rows are retrieved in nonclustered index order, and the additional step of sorting the rows in a worktable can be avoided.

In general, nonclustered indexes are useful for single-row lookups, joins, queries on columns that are highly selective, or queries with small range retrievals. Although they may incur one more page read per row lookup than a clustered index, they are typically preferable to table scans.

Also, when considering your nonclustered index design, don't overlook the benefits of index covering, as described in the following section.

Index Covering

Index covering is a mechanism for using the leaf level of a nonclustered index the way the data page of a clustered index would work. Index covering occurs when all columns referenced in a query are contained in the index itself. Because the nonclustered index contains a leaf row corresponding to every data row in the table, SQL Server can satisfy the query from the leaf rows of the nonclustered index without having to read the data pages.

Because all leaf index pages point to the next page in the leaf page chain, the leaf level of the index can be scanned just like the data pages in a table (see Figure 12.4). Because the leaf index rows are typically much smaller than the data rows, a nonclustered index that covers a query will be faster than a clustered index on the same columns, due to the smaller number of pages that would need to be read.

Adding columns to nonclustered indexes to get index covering to occur is a common method of reducing query time. Consider the following query:

```
select royalty from titles
   where price between $10 and $20
```

If you create an index on only the price column, SQL Server could find the rows in the index where price is between $10 and $20, but it would have to access the data rows to retrieve royalty. With 100 rows in the range, the page cost would be 100 data pages plus the number of index pages, which would have to be scanned. With an index on price, a money field that in this case is assumed to be not null, the index row width would be

> 8 bytes + 7 bytes overhead = 15 bytes per row

With 15 bytes per row, SQL Server could store approximately 100 rows per page with a 75 percent fill factor, costing one additional index page to be scanned plus the number of nonleaf pages necessary to reach the leaf page.

> **NOTE**
>
> If it isn't clear to you how these values are obtained, please read Chapter 11 for a detailed discussion about index structures and size estimation.

However, if you were to create the index on price *and* royalty, the query could be completely satisfied by the index. The number of pages required in this case would be a factor of the number of index leaf pages you would need to scan. An index on price and royalty, both money fields, would be 16 bytes wide:

> 16 + 7 bytes = 23 bytes per row

FIGURE 12.4.
*Scanning the leaf pages of
a nonclustered index to
retrieve data values (index
covering).*

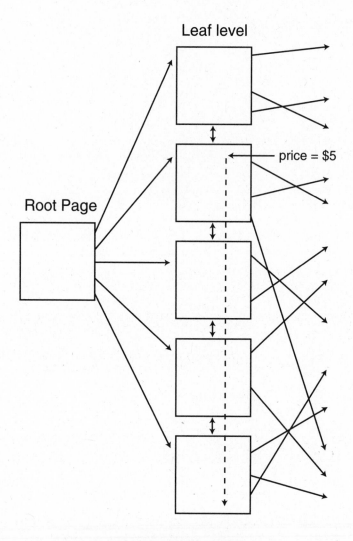

Nonclustered index on price

Leaf level

price = $5

Root Page

Select sum(price) from titles
where price > $5

At 23 bytes per row, SQL Server could store approximately 65 bytes per row with a 75 percent fill factor. Because you can scan all 100 qualifying index rows in order in the leaf pages of the index, the I/O cost for this query would be only two leaf pages plus the number of nonleaf levels in the index.

Index covering also provides a number of performance benefits for queries containing aggregates. Typically, for SQL Server to use an index to satisfy a query, at least the first column of the index must be referenced in the where clause. However, with aggregates, SQL Server can recognize when an aggregate can be satisfied by a nonclustered index without any where clause at all. Consider the following queries:

```
select avg(price) from titles

select count(*) from titles where price > $7.95

select count(*) from titles
```

The first query can use a nonclustered index on price and scan all the index leaf rows to calculate the average price. The second query can again use the nonclustered index on price to find the first leaf row where price is greater than $7.95, and then just scan to the end of the index, counting the number of leaf rows along the way.

The third query is even more interesting. You just want a count of all the rows in the table. You aren't providing any where clauses to cause it to use an index, so it will have to perform a table scan, right? Actually, SQL Server is somewhat clever with this one. Because it knows that any nonclustered index on the table will have as many rows as the table itself, it uses the nonclustered index with the smallest row size, and therefore the fewest number of pages, and simply counts all the rows in the leaf level of that index.

> **WARNING**
>
> When considering padding your indexes to take advantage of index covering, beware of making the index too wide. As index row width approaches data row width, the benefits of covering will be lost as the number of pages in the leaf level increases. As the number of pages approaches the number of pages in the table, the number of index levels increases, and index scan time begins to approach table scan time.
>
> Also, if you add volatile columns to an index, remember that any changes to the columns in the data rows will cascade into indexes as well.

Composite Indexes versus Multiple Indexes

Remember, composite (compound) indexes are selected by SQL Server to satisfy a query only if at least the first column of the index is specified in a where clause. Also, because of the increased width of composite indexes, the index structure will consist of more levels and pages than a narrower index.

At times, it might be more beneficial to have many narrow indexes than one or more larger composite indexes. Having more indexes gives the optimizer more alternatives to look at and possibly derive a more optimal plan. Remember from earlier in this chapter that distribution steps are stored only for the first column in a composite index. If the first column has poor selectivity, SQL Server may choose not to use the composite index.

On the flip side of things, each additional index has a negative impact on update performance.

So how do you determine the optimal index(es) for a table? Let's look at an example:

```
select pub_id, title, notes from titles
   where type = 'Computer'
      and price > $15.
```

The index candidates include

- Clustered or nonclustered index on `type` only
- Clustered or nonclustered index on `price` only
- Clustered index on `type`, nonclustered index on `price`
- Nonclustered index on `type`, clustered index on `price`
- Clustered or nonclustered index on `type`, `price`
- Clustered or nonclustered index on `price`, `type`
- Clustered or nonclustered index on `pub_id`, `title`, `notes`, `type`, `price`

Which are the best options in which circumstances? The answer is entirely dependent on the data distribution and whether the indexes would be unique enough to be worthwhile.

For example, neither `type` nor `price` include very unique values, so would a nonclustered index help in any case for either of them? Probably not, if this is a representative sample of the types of queries going against this table. If you had other queries that could take advantage of index covering (for example, `select avg(price)`), a nonclustered index might help.

What about a clustered index? That's the logical choice if a column contains a large number of duplicate values, or is involved in range retrievals. On which column should you create the clustered index, though? `price` would probably be the better candidate, because there are more distinct prices than there are book types. Actually, there are so few book types—only six—that out of a thousand titles, would an index on `type` be helpful at all? How much I/O would an index on `type` save you in comparison to a table scan? Would the corresponding overhead be worth the minimal time savings?

What if you went the route of creating a composite index on `type` and `price`? That would help if you were searching on `type` alone, and it would help further narrow the result set when you search on `type` and `price`. Unfortunately, that index won't help when you are searching on just `price`. Conversely, an index on `price` and `type` won't help when you search on `type` alone.

The question that needs to be asked at this point is which type of query is most critical. Which query must have good response time?

The last index suggested barely rates consideration. The attempt is to get index covering to take place. However, the index row is so wide that any I/O savings from index covering versus directly accessing the data in the table would be negligible.

As you can see from many of the questions raised in this exercise, you can't examine just one query and devise the best indexing strategy. You need to examine all queries going against the database and design your indexes appropriately to support multiple queries.

Indexing for Multiple Queries

Indexing for multiple queries involves asking many of the questions raised in the preceding section. It really requires that you sit down and perform a detailed query analysis and transaction analysis for all applications going against a database.

After gathering the information, you need to begin ranking the queries/transactions in order of importance. The more critical queries should get a higher priority.

After you've ranked your indexes and decided for which ones you're going to tune the system, you need to examine the where clauses and see what types of indexes you need to support those queries. To evaluate the usefulness of the index, you also need to have a good understanding of the data and the data distribution. Determine which queries actually make effective use of an index on a column. Don't assume that just because a column is referenced in a where clause, it needs an index. Consider also whether other, already-indexed columns are more selective or whether the index, based on the selectivity, would even be used.

> **NOTE**
>
> In some cases, you may find that you need to rewrite a query to have the optimizer make use of an index, depending on how the optimizer treats the search arguments. See Chapter 13 for a more detailed discussion on how the optimizer matches indexes to search arguments.

Start out by devising an indexing strategy for each query independently. Then begin comparing strategies, looking for overlaps between them, to find indexes that satisfy more than one query/transaction. At this point, you may find that a composite index is more useful, or that multiple smaller indexes would be better. Look for a crossover between queries on a significant sort column, or a common range retrieval between queries to identify a good candidate for the clustered index. Look for instances, such as aggregates, where you may be able to take advantage of index covering for a number of queries. Keep in mind the issues of overindexing if you have OLTP activity as well.

After devising your indexing strategy, go ahead and implement and test it, but be prepared to make changes. Few of us predict query performance accurately the first time out. I have actually found trial-and-error to be an acceptable approach to aiding in index design, as well as an excellent learning process.

Let's look at a simple example and apply this strategy. Assume that you have the following customer table:

```
create table customer
   (cust_id   char(6) not null,
    lname     varchar(15) not null,
    fname     varchar(15) not null,
    address   varchar(30) not null,
    city      varchar(30) not null,
    state     char(2) not null,
    zip       char(5) not null,
    zone      char(1) not null)
```

The customer table has 100,000 rows, and six zones with distribution as follows:

> Zone A—70,000 rows
> Zone B—15,000 rows
> Zone C—10,000 rows
> Zone D—3,000 rows
> Zone E—1,500 rows
> Zone F—500 rows

Cust_id is the unique, primary key, and states exist entirely within zones (for example, NY is in Zone A only). The following are samples of the critical queries run against the customer table:

```
select * from customer where zone = 'A'

select * from customer where zone = 'C' and state = 'NY'

select * from customer where cust_id = '345678'

select cust_id from customer where lname like "Smith%"
```

Let's select indexes for each query individually:

■ `select * from customer where zone = 'A'`

Because zone isn't a very unique value for this query, we have the option of either a clustered index on zone or no index at all. For now, choose the clustered index on zone.

■ `select * from customer where zone = 'C' and state = 'NY'`

Again, zone isn't a very unique value, and there's also state. Because states exist within a zone, you can always query state by limiting the result set to zone first. This is a good candidate for a composite index, and again, due to the poor selectivity, you can opt for a clustered index.

■ `select * from customer where cust_id = '345678'`

cust_id is a unique primary key. Let's follow the normal trend and assume a clustered index on the primary key.

■ `select cust_id from customer where lname like "Smith%"`

Again, you have a range type retrieval with more than likely poor selectivity; you can assume clustered index on `lname`.

Let's examine what we've got so far:

- clustered on `zone`
- clustered on `zone, state`
- clustered on `cust_id`
- clustered on `lname`

Obviously, there's some overlap here. Let's make the tradeoffs and decide which one should be the clustered index. Because `cust_id` is a unique key involved in a single row lookup, there's no appreciable benefit to having a clustered index on it when other candidates are available for clustered index.

Next, you have to decide between a clustered index on `zone` or `lname`. If you look closely at the `lname` query, it's only retrieving a list of `cust_ids` from `customer` for a list of last names. You could get away with a nonclustered index on `lname, cust_id`, which would actually be more efficient than a clustered index on `lname`.

Now you're left with a decision on the clustered index on `zone`. Because you have two queries that rely on `zone`, but one that needs to limit the result set to states within a zone, you can make the clustered index on `zone` and `state`. This way, one composite index can effectively satisfy two different queries.

To summarize, the indexes you create initially will be

- Clustered index on `zone, state`
- Nonclustered index on `lname, cust_id`
- Unique nonclustered index on `cust_id`

Remember, you can't tune for everything and everyone. You won't be able to make everyone happy. At some point you'll need to make a tradeoff of some sort:

- OLTP performance needs versus DSS response time
- Critical query versus noncritical query
- Frequently-run query versus rarely-run query
- Online queries versus batch queries

The art is balancing the tradeoffs effectively so that the system is deemed a success.

Summary

The most important aspect to improving SQL Server performance is proper index design. Choosing the appropriate indexes to be used by SQL Server to process queries involves thoroughly understanding the queries and transactions being run against the database, understanding the bias of the data, understanding how SQL Server uses indexes, and staying aware of the performance implications of overindexing tables in an OLTP environment. In general, consider using clustered indexes to support range retrievals or when data needs to be sorted in clustered index order; use nonclustered indexes for single or discrete row retrievals or when you can take advantage of index covering.

I also recommend that you have a good understanding of the SQL Server query optimizer to know how it uses indexes and index statistics to develop query plans. This may be a good time to read Chapter 13.

And always remember—keep your index statistics up to date!

Understanding the Query Optimizer

13

Query optimization is the process of analyzing individual queries and determining the best way to process them. This involves understanding the underlying storage structures and the indexes defined on them to determine whether a way exists to process the query more efficiently. To achieve this end, SQL Server uses a cost-based optimizer. The query optimizer examines parsed SQL queries and, based on information about the objects involved, outputs a *query plan*. The query plan is the set of steps to be carried out to execute the query.

As a cost-based optimizer, the optimizer's purpose is to determine the query plan that will access the data with the least amount of processing time.

To allow the optimizer to do its job properly, you need to understand what types of queries can be optimized, and learn techniques to help the optimizer choose the best query path. Having a good understanding of the optimizer will help you write better queries, choose better indexes, and detect potential performance problems.

> **NOTE**
>
> To better understand the concepts presented in this chapter, you should have a reasonable understanding of how SQL Server manages data objects and indexes, and how indexes affect performance. If you haven't already read Chapter 11 ("Understanding SQL Server Storage Structures") and Chapter 12 ("Designing Indexes for Performance"), I recommend that you review them now.

Optimization Goals

The primary goal of the query optimizer is to find the cheapest access path to minimize the total time to process the query. To achieve this goal, the optimizer analyzes the query and searches for access paths and techniques primarily to do the following:

- Minimize logical page access
- Minimize physical page access

Disk I/O is the most significant factor in query processing costs. Therefore, the fewer physical and logical I/Os performed, the faster the query.

Query Optimization Steps

When SQL Server processes the query, it performs the following steps:

1. Parse and normalize the query validating syntax and object references.
2. Optimize the query and generate the query plan.

3. Compile the query plan.

4. Execute the query plan and return the results to the user.

The optimization step is broken down into multiple phases, as follows:

Phase 1: Query Analysis

1. Find search arguments (SARGs).

2. Find or clauses.

3. Find joins.

Phase 2: Index Selection

4. Choose the best index for SARGs.

5. Choose the best method for ors.

6. Choose the best indexes for any join clauses.

7. Choose the best index to use for each table.

Phase 3: Join Order Processing

8. Evaluate join orders.

9. Compute costs.

10. Evaluate other server options for resolving joins (reformatting strategy).

Phase 4: Plan Selection

If a query is a single table query containing no join clauses, SQL Server skips Phase 3 (Join Order Processing) and jumps directly to Phase 4 (Plan Selection).

The following sections explain these four phases of optimization.

Phase 1: Query Analysis

The first step in query optimization is to analyze each table in the query to identify all search arguments (SARGs), or clauses, and join clauses. The SARGs, or clauses, and join clauses will be used in the next phase to select useful indexes to satisfy a query. For SQL Server to use an index to satisfy a query, at least the first column of the index must match the column in a SARG, or, or join clause. The only exception to this rule is index covering, which is discussed later in this chapter.

Identifying Search Arguments (SARGs)

SARGs exist to enable the optimizer to limit the rows searched to satisfy a query. The general goal is to match a SARG with an index to avoid a table scan. A *search argument* is defined as a where clause comparing a column to a constant. The format of a SARG is as follows:

```
Column operator constant_expression [and...]
```

Valid operators for a SARG are any one of =, >, <, >=, and <=. The inequality operator (!= or <>) isn't a valid operator for a SARG. If you have an inequality operator, the optimizer ignores that statement as a search argument because it can't be used to match a value against an index, unless the query can be solved by index covering (see the later section "Index Covering" for details).

TIP

If you have a search clause containing an inequality operator, try to rewrite it as a SARG so that it can be recognized as a search argument by the query optimizer. For example, consider the following query:

```
select title from titles where price != 0
```

If there is a business rule enforced on the table to prevent any rows where price is less than zero, the query could be rewritten as follows:

```
select title from titles where price > 0
```

and still return the same result set. The difference is that the second version contains a valid SARG that the optimizer will recognize and consider for matching with an index to satisfy the query. True, it still may result in a table scan, but at least it gives the optimizer the option to consider; it wouldn't have done so with the inequality operator.

Multiple SARGs can be combined with the and clause. If an or clause is specified, the SARG is treated differently, as you'll see shortly. Following are examples of valid search arguments:

- `flag = 7`
- `salary > 100000`
- `city = 'Saratoga' and state = 'NY'`

As stated earlier, an inequality operator isn't treated as a search argument. Additionally, if any operation is performed on the column, it's ignored as a search argument as well. Some examples of invalid SARGs follow:

- `gender != 'M'`
- `lname = fname` (comparison against a column, not a constant)
- `upper(city) = 'POULSBO'` (function performed on the column)
- `ytd/12 = 1000` (operation performed on the column)

TIP

The last SARG, `ytd/12 = 1000`, can be rewritten to be treated as a SARG as `ytd = 12000`. When tuning performance of your system, keep an eye out for invalid SARGs. They're a common cause of poor performance because they prevent an index from being used. Many times, invalid SARGs can be rewritten as valid SARGs.

Improvising SARGs

Some SQL statements don't appear to follow the syntax for a valid SARG, but can be improvised as SARGs by the query optimizer. The following are clauses that can be improvised as SARGs:

- `between` becomes `>=` and `<=`

  `price between $10 and $20` becomes `price > = $10 and price <= $20`

  `100 between lo_val and hi_val` becomes `lo_val <= 100 and hi_val >= 100`

- `like` becomes `>=` and `<`

  `au_lname like "Sm%"` becomes `au_lname >= "Sm" and au_lname < "Sn"`

The `like` clause will be improvised as a SARG only if the first character in the string is a constant. The following statement wouldn't be improvised into a SARG:

`au_lname like "%son"`

Also, watch out for the following `between` clause in SQL Server 6.5:

`price between $20 and $10`

This will be improvised into

`price >= $20 and <= $10`

which is an empty result set. SQL Server doesn't generate any error or warning message when this code is encountered.

TIP

In versions of SQL Server prior to 6.0, the optimizer would switch the upper and lower bounds of a `between` if necessary so that the higher value was the upper bound. Unfortunately, this behavior is in violation of the ANSI standard and was changed in Version 6.0 to comply with the ANSI standard.

continues

> *continued*
>
> If you are porting an existing application from SQL Server Version 4.2 to 6.0 or 6.5, you may want to check any queries containing between clauses to verify that the lesser value is always defined as the lower bound.

In some cases, the column in a SARG may be compared with a constant expression rather than a single constant value. The constant expression can be an arithmetic operation, built-in function, string concatenation, local variable, or subquery result. As long as the left side of the SARG contains a column alone, it's still a valid SARG.

Constant Expressions

The issue with a SARG containing a constant expression is whether the optimizer can evaluate the expression prior to query optimization and make use of the distribution steps, rather than having to use the density value to estimate rows. In SQL Server Version 6.0 and later, the optimizer evaluates the constant expression if the value can be determined prior to runtime, and uses the resulting value when evaluating any indexes on the column(s).

The following are examples of expressions that can be evaluated prior to optimization:

```
due_date > getdate()
ytd_sales < 100000/12
lname like "Smith" + "%"%
```

For SARGs containing subqueries or local variables, the value of the constant expression can't be evaluated prior to optimization because the value can't be determined until query execution. The following are examples of constant expressions that can't be evaluated prior to optimization:

```
price < (select avg(price) from titles)
qty < @inventory
```

or Clauses

The next statements the optimizer looks for in the query are or clauses. or clauses are SARGs combined with an or statement rather than an and, and are treated differently than a standard SARG. The format of an or clause is as follows:

```
SARG or SARG [or ...]
```

with all columns involved in the or belonging to the same table.

The in statement:

```
column in (constant1, constant2, ...)
```

is also treated as an or clause, becoming:

```
column = constant1 or column = constant2 or ...
```

Examples of or clauses:

```
where au_lname = 'Smith' or au_fname = 'Fred'
where (type = 'business' and price > $25) or pub_id = "1234"
au_lname in ('Smith', 'Jones', 'N/A')
```

An or clause is a disjunction; all rows matching either of the two criteria appear in the result set. Any row matching both criteria should appear only once.

or Strategy

An or clause can be handled by a table scan or by using the or strategy. Using a table scan, SQL Server reads every row in the table and applies all search criteria to each row. Any row that matches one of the criteria is put into the result set.

If an index exists on both columns in the or clause, however, SQL Server evaluates the possibility of applying the or strategy. The or strategy essentially involves breaking the query into two or more parts; executing each part using the available index and retrieving the matching row IDs; performing a union on the row IDs to sort the rows and remove duplicates; and, finally, using the row IDs as a *dynamic index* to retrieve the final result set from the base table.

If any one of the or clauses requires a table scan to be processed, or if a table scan is cheaper than using the available index, SQL Server simply uses a table scan to resolve the whole query rather than applying the or strategy.

The following steps show how SQL Server would handle the following query if given an index that exists on both au_lname and state:

```
select * from authors
   where au_lname = "Smith"
      or state = "NY"
```

1. Estimate the cost of a table scan.

2. Break the query into multiple parts; for example:

   ```
   select * from authors where au_lname = "Smith"
   select * from authors where state = "NY"
   ```

3. Execute each piece and get the row IDs into a worktable in tempdb as a dynamic index.

4. union the row IDs to sort them and remove any duplicates.

5. Use the dynamic index to retrieve all qualifying rows from the worktable (see Figure 13.1).

The SQL Server query optimizer evaluates the cost of applying the or strategy and compares it to the cost of doing a table scan. SQL Server applies the or strategy only if the sum of the total I/Os to use the or strategy (including the cost of using both indexes and the cost of the sorting) is less than the number of I/Os to process a table scan.

FIGURE 13.1.

Using the dynamic index to resolve the or clause.

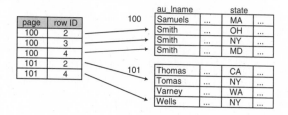

If the or involves only a single column:

```
au_lname = 'Smith' or au_lname = "Varney"
```

and an index exists on the column, the optimizer looks at the alternative of solving it by using a between rather than using the or strategy. Because the data in the index is sorted, the optimizer knows that all values satisfying the or clause in the index are "between" the two values. Therefore, it could find the first matching row for the or clause and simply scan the succeeding root pages of the index until the last matching row was found. In some cases, this approach may result in fewer I/Os than using the dynamic index, as in the following:

```
select * from pt_tx_CIid
   where id in (10000, 15000, 20000, 21000)
```

The or clause would be translated into:

```
id = 10000 or id = 15000 or id = 20000 or id = 21000
```

To process this query using the or strategy would involve using four separate lookups on the pt_tx_CIid table to get the matching rows into a worktable. Using the clustered index, this would have cost two pages per lookup, for a total of eight page I/Os.

By generating an additional SARG as follows,

```
id BETWEEN 10000 and 21000 and (id = 10000 OR id = 15000 OR id = 20000 OR id =
21000)
```

the optimizer now has the option of using the clustered index for scanning all rows in the range and then applying the search criteria to each in a single pass to find all the result rows; it would have cost only five total page I/Os. Because the optimizer always seeks to use the method that results in the lowest I/O cost, SQL Server applies the between strategy and avoids using the dynamic index for this query.

Join Clauses

The last type of statement for which the query optimizer looks during the query analysis phase is the *join clause*. A join clause is a where clause in the following format:

```
Table1.Column Operator Table2.Column
```

A join clause always involves two tables except in the case of a self-join, but even in a self-join you must specify the table twice in the query:

```
select name = e.name, manager = m.name
    from employee e, employee m
    where e.mgr_id = m.id
```

Flattening Queries

SQL Server sometimes attempts to flatten a subquery into a join, to allow the optimizer to select the optimal join order, rather than be forced to process the query inside out.

in, any, or exists Subqueries

In SQL Server Version 6.0 and later, any query containing a subquery introduced with an in, any, or exists predicate is flattened into an existence join unless the outer query also contains an or clause, or unless the subquery is correlated or contains one or more aggregates.

An existence join can be optimized the same way as a regular join, with one exception. With an existence join, as soon as a matching row is found in the inner table, the value TRUE is returned. At this point, SQL Server stops looking for further matches for that row in the outer table and moves on to the next row. For example, the following query would be converted to an existence join:

```
select pub_name from publishers
    where pub_id in (select pub_id from titles where type = 'business')
```

This behavior was modified in SQL Server Version 6.0 from previous versions of SQL Server. Prior to 6.0, the preceding query would have been flattened into a normal join like this:

```
select pub_name from publishers p, titles t
   where p.pub_id = t.pub_id
     and t.type = 'business'
```

The joins would be processed essentially the same way, but the result sets would be different.

If the `titles` table contains four rows where `type = 'business'`, you would get four rows in the result set using a regular join, but only two distinct publisher names. Using an existence join, you would get only the two rows for the publishers who have a match in `titles`.

Materialized Subqueries

If the outer query is comparing a column against the result of a subquery using any of the comparison operators (=, >, <, >=, <=, !=), and the subquery is not correlated, the results of the subquery must be resolved—that is, *materialized*—before comparison against the outer table column. For these types of queries, the optimizer must process them inside out.

An example of this type of query is as follows:

```
select title from titles
   where total_sales = (select max(total_sales) from titles)
```

The subquery must be resolved first to find the value to compare against `total_sales` in the outer query.

Correlated Subqueries

A *correlated subquery* contains a reference to an outer table in a join clause in the subquery. For example, the following is a correlated subquery:

```
select col_a from table_1 t1
   where col_b = (select sum(col_x)
                    from table_2 where col_y = t1.col_c)
```

SQL Server processes correlated subqueries inside out, using an intermediate worktable to hold the subquery results. The worktable is grouped on the correlation columns. For example, the above query becomes

```
select t1.col_c, summ=sum(t2.col_x)
   into #worktable
   from table_1 t1, table_2 t2
   where t2.col_c = t1.col_c

select t1.col_a from table_1 t1, #worktable w
   where t1.col_c = w.col_c
   and t1.col_b = w.summ
```

Phase 2: Index Selection

When the query analysis phase of optimization is complete and all SARGs, or clauses, and join clauses have been identified, the next step is to match them up with any available indexes and to estimate the I/O costs. The index I/O costs are compared with each other and against the cost of a table scan to determine the least expensive access path.

If no useful indexes are found to match a SARG, or clause, or join, a table scan must be performed on the table. A table scan is the fall-back tactic for the optimizer to use if no better way exists of resolving a query.

Evaluating Indexes for SARGs and or clauses

To estimate the I/O costs of using an index for a SARG or an or clause, the optimizer uses the index statistics stored on the distribution page for the index. If no distribution page is available or the table has no index, the query optimizer assumes the following built-in row estimates for the different equality operators:

Operator	Row Estimate
=	10 percent
between, > and <	25 percent
>, <, >=, <=	33 percent

For example, consider a query containing the following search clause:

```
lname = "Smith"
```

With no index statistics, the optimizer assumes that 10 percent of the rows in the table will match the search value of `"Smith"`. If index statistics are available and the value of the constant expression is known during query optimization, the optimizer uses the distribution step information to estimate the number of rows that match the constant expression. If the constant expression can't be resolved until query execution, the optimizer bases its estimates on the index density.

> **NOTE**
>
> In previous versions of SQL Server, certain datatype mismatches would prevent the optimizer from using distribution steps to estimate the number of matching rows in a query. The main culprit was the process of comparing a varchar against a char. This shortcoming seems to have been addressed in SQL Server Version 6.0 and later.
>
> For any datatype mismatch between a column and constant, if a legal implicit conversion can take place, SQL Server performs the datatype conversion to the column datatype and uses the distribution steps.

If a SARG contains the equality (=) operator and there's a unique index matching the SARG, the optimizer estimates that one and only one row will match the SARG.

> **NOTE**
>
> For a more thorough discussion of index selection and index statistics, see Chapter 12.

Evaluating Indexes for Join Clauses

If the query contains a join clause, SQL Server determines whether any usable indexes exist that match the column(s) in the join clause. Because the optimizer has no way of determining what value(s) will join between rows in the table at optimization time, it can't use the distribution steps to estimate the number of matching rows. Instead, it uses the index density, which is an estimate of the number of matching rows in the table for any given value.

If index density isn't available, the estimate for the number of matching rows is determined as follows:

> 1/number of rows in the smaller table

For example, if you have an orders table with 1 million rows joining with a customers table containing 5,000 rows, the join selectivity would be as follows:

> 1/5000 or .0002

Therefore, for every row in the customers table, you would expect to find

> $1,000,000 \times .0002 = 200$

matching rows in the orders table (200 orders/per customer $\times$ 5000 customers = 1,000,000 orders).

If you had a density value available on the join column(s), the density value would be used to estimate the number of rows per join between the two tables. *Density* is based on the percentage of the number of unique values in a table. If you had 1,000 unique values in the orders table, the density would be as follows:

> 1/1000 or .001

Using this density value, for each row in the customers table, you would expect

> $1,000,000 \times .001 = 1,000$

rows to match for any single customer.

A lower density value indicates a more selective index. As the density approaches 1, the index becomes less selective and approaches uselessness.

Ranking Indexes

Unless the or strategy is applied, SQL Server can use only one index per table to satisfy a query. The index chosen is the one that incurs the fewest I/Os to solve the query for that table.

Using the available or built-in statistics, the optimizer estimates the number of page reads necessary to retrieve the estimated number of rows using the candidate index. It then ranks the candidate indexes to determine the index that results in the least I/O.

Keep in mind that there are instances (for example, large range retrievals on nonclustered index columns) in which a table scan may be cheaper than a candidate index in terms of total I/O.

Estimating Page I/O

If no usable index exists, the optimizer performs a table scan. The estimate of the total I/O cost is the number of pages in the table, which is stored in the `sysindexes` table.

If a clustered index is available, the I/O cost estimate is the number of index levels in the clustered index plus the number of pages to scan. The number of pages to scan is based on the estimated number of rows times the number of rows per page.

For a nonclustered index, I/O cost estimate is

> Number of index levels
> + number of leaf pages
> + number of qualifying rows (number of data page reads)

The number of leaf pages is based on the estimated number of rows times the number of leaf index rows per page. Because each leaf index row requires a separate data page lookup to retrieve the data row, the number of data page reads is equal to the number of matching rows in the leaf index level.

For a unique index and an equality join, the I/O cost estimate is one data page plus the number of index levels traversed to access the data page.

Index Covering

When analyzing a query, the optimizer also considers any possibility to take advantage of index covering. *Index covering* is a mechanism for using the leaf level of a nonclustered index to solve a query when all the columns referenced in the query (in both the `select` list and `where` clause, as well as any `group by` columns) are part of the index key. Because at its leaf level a nonclustered index contains the key values for every single row, all the data needed to satisfy the query can be found in the leaf level of the nonclustered index.

This can save a significant amount of I/O if the query doesn't have to access the data page. In most cases, a nonclustered index is faster than a similarly defined clustered index if the nonclustered index covers the query.

Because of the reduced I/O and faster processing, the optimizer attempts to use index covering whenever possible. This is the one exception to the rule that at least the first column of an index must match a SARG in order to be considered by the optimizer. For example, suppose we have a nonclustered index on au_lname and au_fname (in that order) for the authors table. The following query is covered by this index:

```
select au_lname from authors
where au_fname = "Aikiko"
```

Although the first column of the index (au_lname) doesn't match a SARG in the above query, so all columns mentioned in the query are part of the index, the optimizer chooses to satisfy the query by scanning the leaf level of the nonclustered index.

Index covering has particular benefits with aggregates. SQL Server attempts to solve aggregates using index covering whenever possible, even when the query contains no SARGs. For example:

```
select avg (price) from titles
```

can be satisfied by scanning the leaf rows of a nonclustered index on price to determine the average.

NOTE

For a query that simply counts the number of rows in a table without any additional search criteria (such as select count(*) from titles), *any* nonclustered index can be used. Because all nonclustered indexes contain a pointer to every data row in their leaf level, if all you want is the number of rows in the table the optimizer can simply count all the rows in the leaf level of the index. To resolve this type of query, the optimizer chooses to use the nonclustered index with the fewest number of pages in the leaf level, resulting in the fewest total I/Os.

If index covering can take place in a query, the optimizer considers it and estimates the I/O cost of using the nonclustered index to cover the query. The estimated I/O cost of index covering is the number of index levels plus the number of leaf index pages to scan. The number of leaf pages to scan is based on the estimated number of rows divided by the number of leaf index rows per page.

Phase 3: Join Order Processing

If the query contains any join clauses, the next phase in query optimization is to determine the best possible join order.

The optimizer evaluates all possible join orders and, for each join order considered, estimates the cost of the different index alternatives for each table in the join. If no useful indexes are available on one or more of the tables involved in the join, SQL Server also considers applying the reformatting strategy to solve the query efficiently.

The optimal query plan for a join involves choosing the best indexes for each table and the most efficient order in which to process the tables in the join.

Determining Join Order

Joins are performed as a set of nested loops, often called *nested iterations*. Essentially, for each matching row in the outer table, you perform a nested iteration on the inner table to find all matching rows to the outer row. This process is repeated for each row in the outer table.

To process a nested iteration, you need to determine the order in which to process the tables.

Consider the following query:

```
select au_lname, au_fname, title
   from authors a, titleauthor ta, titles t
   where a.au_id = ta.au_id
   and ta.title_id = t.title_id
```

Figure 13.2 shows the possible join orders that could be used to process this query.

FIGURE 13.2.

Possible join order for a query joining titles, titleauthor, *and* authors.

titles ⟶ titleauthor ⟶ authors

authors ⟶ titleauthor ⟶ titles

Because the SQL Server query optimizer is a cost-based optimizer, the order of the tables in the from clause doesn't dictate the order in which the tables are joined. When processing a join, the optimizer evaluates all reasonable join permutations and estimates the total I/O cost in terms of I/O time. The plan resulting in the lowest estimate of I/O time is the plan chosen.

As the number of tables increases, however, the number of permutations that the optimizer must evaluate increases as a factorial of the number of tables in the query, as shown in Table 13.1.

Table 13.1. Number of possible join permutations based on the number of tables in the query.

# of Tables	# of Join Permutations
2	2! = 2
3	3! = 6

continues

Table 13.1. continued

# of Tables	# of Join Permutations
4	4! = 24
5	5! = 120
6	6! = 720
7	7! = 5,040
8	8! = 40,320
9	9! = 362,880
10	10! = 3,628,800
11	11! = 39,916,800
12	12! = 479,001,600
13	13! = 6,227,020,800
14	14! = 87,178,291,200
15	15! = 1,307,674,368,000
16	16! = 20,922,789,888,000

Handling Large, Multi-Table Queries

To minimize the number of permutations that need to be examined, SQL Server breaks up joins of more than four tables into all possible groups of four, to evaluate the join permutations within each group of four. This approach is iterative, repeated until the join order for all tables is determined. The purpose of this approach is to limit the number of permutations that the optimizer has to consider.

The algorithm used by SQL Server to process joins of more than four tables is as follows:

1. Group the tables into all possible groups of four.
2. For each group of four tables, estimate the join cost for each possible permutation.
3. Determine the group of four with the cheapest permutation. The first table of that permutation is marked as the outer table and taken out of the list of tables.
4. Repeat steps 1 through 3 for the remaining tables, until only four tables remain, and determine the best join order for those four as one final step.

The following is an example of this algorithm in practice.

Assume a query that joins six tables: T1, T2, T3, T4, T5, and T6.

Breaking the six tables into all possible groups of four, you would have the following:

> T1T2T3T4, T1T2T3T5, T1T2T3T6, T1T2T4T5, T1T2T4T6, T1T2T5T6,
> T1T3T4T5, T1T3T4T6, T1T3T5T6, T1T4T5T6, T2T3T4T5, T2T3T4T6,
> T2T3T5T6, T2T4T5T6, T3T4T5T6

For each group of four, SQL Server finds the lowest-cost permutation and makes the outermost table for that permutation the outermost table for the entire query. Assume that the best permutation is T3T5T4T2. T3 is set as the outermost table. The remaining tables are regrouped into all possible groups of four, giving you the following:

> T1T2T4T5, T1T2T4T6, T1T2T5T6, T1T4T5T6, T2T4T5T6

Assume that the lowest-cost permutation out of each of these remaining groups of four tables is T4T2T5T6. Table T4 now becomes the second outermost table in the query.

SQL Server is now left with four tables, which the optimizer evaluates as if it were a normal four-table join. Assuming that the best join order for the remaining four tables is T5T2T1T6, this join order is appended to the two previously determined outer tables (T3 and T4). The result is that the final join order for the entire query is as follows:

> T3,T4,T5,T2,T1,T6

This process may seem like a lot of work, but the actual number of permutations examined can be substantially fewer, especially when the number of tables in the query exceeds eight or more tables.

The resulting number of combinations examined with this approach is the sum of $N! / (N-4)!$ for each iteration. For this example, the number of permutations considered would be

> $6!/(6-4)! = 720/2 = 360$
> $5!/(5-4)! = 120/1 = 120$
> $4! = 24$

The total sum of all permutations considered is as follows:

> $360 + 120 + 24 = 504$ permutations

This result represents a savings of 30 percent. As the number of tables increases, the savings become even more significant, as shown in Table 13.2.

Table 13.2. Savings in number of join permutations examined using SQL Server optimizer approach.

# of Tables (N)	N!	Optimizer Method	Savings
6	720	25%	540
7	5040	73.3%	1,344
8	40320	92.5%	3,024
9	362880	98.3%	6,048
10	3628800	99.7%	11,088
16	20922789888000	99.999%	148,512

TIP

Even using the modified approach to identifying join permutations, large multi-table queries are still rather costly to optimize. Sometimes, the time spent optimizing the query can be greater than the time spent processing the query.

In some earlier versions of SQL Server, the optimizer didn't do such a good job of handling queries with more than four tables. The order of the tables in the from clause would sometimes influence the query plan chosen. This behavior sometimes forced developers to write queries in a specific manner, or sometimes to break queries with more than four tables into smaller queries.

The current version of SQL Server, however, seems to handle multi-table queries quite well. In my testing and that of other users, the optimizer consistently tends to arrive at the most optimal plan regardless of the table order. It's typically not necessary to break up large queries anymore.

You may be concerned, however, with the time spent optimizing the query. To reduce the optimization time, consider putting the query into a stored procedure. With the query in a stored procedure, the query plan is determined only for the first execution and then reused for subsequent executions, providing significant time savings if the query is executed repeatedly.

Another alternative is to override the join ordering phase of the query optimizer, using the forceplan option. For details and warnings on using the forceplan option, see Chapter 17, "Managing the SQL Server Optimizer."

Estimating Join Order Costs

For each join permutation considered, the optimizer needs to estimate the cost of that particular join order in terms of total I/O. For comparison purposes, the optimizer estimates the total logical I/Os per table and the total number of physical I/Os per table. It then sums the total physical and logical I/Os for the entire permutation and translates that result into a total elapsed time. The total elapsed time is used only for comparison purposes and doesn't reflect the actual time the query would take to run.

Currently, SQL Server rates a logical read as 2 ms and a physical read as 14 ms, a ratio between logical and physical of 1:7. These are fixed values, regardless of the actual performance of the system on which you're running.

The relative performance of a nested iteration is directly proportional to the number of times that the inner query is done and the number of pages per lookup. The algorithm for determining the total number of I/Os for a nested iteration is as follows:

> \# pages accessed in outer table
> \+ (\# matching rows in outer table
> × \# pages per lookup in inner table)

The total cost of the nested iteration is the total number of logical reads times 2 plus the total number of physical reads times 14.

When determining the total I/O cost, SQL Server makes no assumptions about whether the table currently resides in cache. It always assumes that the first access of the table will be a physical page read and any subsequent accesses or iterations on the table will be logical page reads. For every physical page read, there will also be a corresponding logical page read.

The only time that the data cache is considered is when there is insufficient cache to keep the inner table in memory. When this is the case, the optimizer assumes that, because the table can't stay in cache, all accesses to the inner table will be physical I/Os.

Join Costing Examples

Let's look at a few examples of possible join permutations that the optimizer would consider for the following query:

```
select * from titles t, titleauthor ta
 where t.title_id = ta.title_id and royaltyper < 50
```

For these examples, make the following assumptions:

- 15,000 rows `titles` (15 rows/page), 1,000 pages
- 25,000 rows `titleauthor` (50 rows/page), 500 pages

- Clustered index statistics on `royaltyper` in the `titleauthor` table would indicate that 20 percent have `royaltyper` < 50
- There is sufficient data cache to keep both tables in memory

`titles` to `titleauthor`, No Indexes

The first plan that the optimizer would consider would be joining from the first table in the query to the second table in the query, using no indexes at all. In other words, it would consider doing a table scan on each table for each lookup.

For the outer table, `titles`, this would be a single scan costing 1,000 pages. For each row in `titles`, you would have to look up the matching row(s) in `titleauthor`, using a table scan each time and checking whether `royaltyper` for the joined row is < 50. Because there are 15,000 rows in the `titles` table and no SARG to limit that further, you would perform 15,000 iterations on the `titleauthor` table. Each iterative table scan on `titleauthor` would cost 500 pages.

The total number of I/Os for this query would be estimated as

> 1,000 pages in `titles`
>
> + (15,000 rows in `titles` × 500 pages/lookup in `titleauthor`)
>
> = 7,501,000 I/Os

Next, you need to calculate the relative I/O cost for this permutation. Because SQL Server would perform one scan of `titles`, the first scan would incur 1,000 physical and logical reads. For the `titleauthor` table, because it can fit entirely in cache, only the first iteration would incur physical page reads. All subsequent iterations would be logical I/Os only. Therefore, there would be 500 physical and logical I/Os on the first iteration, and 14,999 × 500, or 7,499,500 logical I/Os, on the subsequent iterations for a total of 7,500,000 logical I/Os. Factoring all this out into the relative I/O cost would result in the following:

`titles`			
1,000 physical reads	14 × 1,000	=	14,000
1,000 logical reads	2 × 1,000	=	2,000
`titleauthor`			
500 physical reads	14 × 500	=	7,000
7,500,000 logical reads	2 × 7,500,000	=	<u>15,000,000</u>
Total		=	15,023,000

The total cost (15,023,000) is the value that the optimizer would use to compare the query plan against the other alternatives.

Next we'll examine some other hypothetical alternatives.

titles to titleauthor, Clustered Index on titleauthor.title_id

For this example, the I/O cost on the `titles` table would remain the same. The difference is the `titleauthor` table. Rather than having to perform a table scan on `titleauthor` for each iteration, you could use the clustered index to find the matching rows. Let's assume that the index density indicates that for any join value, one row would match in the `titleauthor` table. If the clustered index consists of two levels, the I/O cost per lookup on the `titleauthor` table would be three pages (two index levels plus a data page lookup).

The total number of I/Os for this query would be estimated as follows:

1,000 pages in `titles`

+ (15,000 rows in `titles` × 3 pages per lookup on `titleauthor`)

= 46,000 I/Os

Because you still have no way of limiting the query any further at the beginning by `royaltyper`, you still would have to join with every row in the `titleauthor` table during processing of the query to check the value of `royaltyper`. Therefore, at the end of query processing, you still would have examined every page in the `titleauthor` table, for a total of 500 physical page reads. However, each iteration would cost you only three pages, which would be assumed to be logical page reads.

The relative I/O cost would be as follows:

titles			
1,000 physical reads	14 × 1,000	=	14,000
1,000 logical reads	2 × 1,000	=	2,000
titleauthor			
500 physical reads	14 × 500	=	7,000
45,000 logical reads	2 × 45,000	=	90,000
Total		=	113,000

As you can easily see, this plan (113,000) is much cheaper than the previous plan (15,023,000). There still are other plans to consider, however. What if you also had a nonclustered index on `title_id` in the `titleauthor` table?

titles to titleauthor, Nonclustered Index on titleauthor.title_id

Again, the I/O costs on `titles` would remain the same. The only real difference between this query and the last one, which used the clustered index, is that the nonclustered index has one more level than the clustered index and would cost you an extra I/O per lookup.

The total number of I/Os for this query would be estimated as follows:

1,000 pages in `titles`

+ (15,000 rows in `titles` × 4 pages per lookup on `titleauthor`)

= 61,000 I/Os

The relative I/O cost would be as follows:

`titles`			
1,000 physical reads	14 × 1,000	=	14,000
1,000 logical reads	2 × 1,000	=	2,000
`titleauthor`			
500 physical reads	14 × 500	=	7,000
60,000 logical reads	2 × 60,000	=	120,000
Total		=	143,000

This plan (143,000) is more expensive than the plan using the clustered index (113,000) but is still substantially cheaper than the table scan plan (15,023,000). If you had to choose between a table scan and using the nonclustered index, the nonclustered index would still be much cheaper.

This final example pretty much exhausts the alternatives if you join from `titles` to `titleauthor`. Note that even having an index on `titles` wouldn't have aided either of these three plans, because you have no SARG on `titles` to limit the rows that you want to join with `titleauthor`.

You do have a SARG on `titleauthor`, however. The following sections examine some costing examples in which `titleauthor` is the outer table.

`titleauthor` to `titles`, No Indexes

Having no indexes means that for the outer table, `titleauthor`, SQL Server would need to perform a table scan to find the rows where `royaltyper` is < 50. This would be a single scan costing 500 pages. Because you have no index on `titles`, either, you would have to perform a table scan for each lookup on `titles`, costing 1,000 pages each lookup.

The question at this point is how many lookups you would need to perform on the `titles` table. Remember that if no statistics are available to estimate the rows matching a search argument, the built-in statistics are used. For your search argument:

```
royaltyper < 50
```

the built-in estimate is that 33 percent of the rows would match. Therefore, a join would be performed only on the `titles` table for 33 percent, or 8,250 of the rows in the `titleauthor` table. If a row read during the table scan on `titleauthor` didn't have a `royaltyper` < 50, SQL Server would simply skip that row and compare against the next one. Therefore, the optimizer would estimate that you would perform 8,250 iterations on `titles`, rather than 25,000.

The total number of I/Os for this query would be estimated as follows:

500 pages in `titleauthor`

+ (8,250 rows in `titleauthor` × 1,000 pages/lookup in `titles`)

= 8,250,500 I/Os

Because the `titles` table can fit entirely in cache, the relative I/O cost for this plan would be as follows:

titleauthor

500 physical reads	14 × 500	=	7,000
500 logical reads	2 × 500	=	1,000

titles

1,000 physical reads	14 × 1,000	=	14,000
8,250,000 logical reads	2 × 8,250,000	=	16,500,000
Total		=	16,522,000

Next, look at a query plan for when you have a clustered index on `title_id` on the `titles` table.

titleauthor to titles, Unique Clustered Index on titles.title_id

Again, the I/O costs on `titleauthor` would remain the same, but instead of using iterative table scans on `titles`, you would use the clustered index. Because you have a unique clustered index on `title_id`, you know that one and only one row would match a single join value in the `titles` table. Each single row lookup via the clustered index on `titles` would cost you three pages (two index levels plus the data page). You would also use the built-in statistic of 33 percent to estimate the number of rows where `royaltyper` is < 50.

Therefore, the total number of I/Os for this query would be estimated as follows:

500 pages in `titleauthor`

+ (8,250 rows in `titleauthor` × 3 pages per lookup on `titles`)

= 25,250 I/Os

Because you assume that only 33 percent (8,250) of the rows in `titleauthor` match where `royaltyper` is < 50, and only one row in the `titles` table would join with a single value in the `titleauthor` table, you could expect that you would access only 8,250 rows in the `titles` table. At 15 rows per page, that works out to

8,250 / 15 = 550

data pages to be read during processing of this query. This translates into the total physical page estimate for the `titles` table. Based on this information, the relative I/O cost would be as follows:

`titleauthor`

500 physical reads	14×500	=	7,000
500 logical reads	2×500	=	1,000

`titles`

550 physical reads	14×550	=	7,700
24,750 logical reads	$2 \times 24,750$	=	49,500
Total		=	65,200

This is the cheapest plan so far, but you're not done yet! Consider the plan cost if you also have a clustered index on `royaltyper`.

`titleauthor` to `titles`, Clustered Index on `titleauthor.royaltyper`, Unique Clustered Index on `titles.title_id`

Because you have a clustered index on `royaltyper`, you can use the index statistics to estimate the number of rows where `royaltyper` is < 50. In this example, the statistics indicate that 20 percent of the rows have `royaltyper` < 50. Therefore, you could estimate that

$25,000 \times .20 = 5,000$

rows in `titleauthor` have a `royaltyper` < 50. Also, because you can use the clustered index to find the rows, you don't have to scan the entire table. You can start at the beginning of the table and scan the data pages until you find the first row where `royaltyper` >= 50. At 50 rows per page, that would be as follows:

5,000 rows / 50 rows per page = 100 pages

Also, because you still have the unique clustered index on `titles`, one and only one row would match for every matching row in `titleauthor` (3,000 rows). At 15 rows per page, you would have accessed

$5,000/15 = 334$

data pages in `titles` while processing this query. Each single row lookup would still cost you three pages per lookup. Armed with this information, you can estimate the query cost to be as follows:

100 pages in `titleauthor`

+ (5,000 rows in `titleauthor` $\times$ 3 pages per lookup on `titles`)

= 15,100 I/Os

titleauthor

100 physical reads	14×100	=	1,400
100 logical reads	2×100	=	200

titles

334 physical reads	14×334	=	4,676
15,000 logical reads	$2 \times 15,000$	=	30,000
Total		=	36,276

This would be the cheapest plan by far of all the ones considered if the table actually had a clustered index on `royaltyper` in the `titleauthor` table and a unique clustered index on `title_id` in the `titles` table.

TIP

This example also underscores the reason that you need to understand how the query optimizer works. By knowing how the optimizer processes your queries, and examining search arguments, index statistics, and join orders, you can make better-informed decisions about your index design, and write better queries.

For example, having a clustered index on `titleauthor.royaltyper` and a unique clustered index on `titles.title_id` was the cheapest plan (36,276), but wasn't that much cheaper than using no index on `titleauthor` (65,200) relative to the cheapest plan using no indexes at all (15,023,000). This could help you decide whether to index `royaltyper` on `titleauthor` or create the clustered index on a different column, where the cost savings would be more substantial for other critical queries.

Reformatting Strategy

As you saw in the previous set of examples, the worst-case cost scenario for joins is joining a table scan to a table scan. The resulting I/O cost is as follows:

> # pages in the outer table
> + (rows in outer table × # of pages in the inner table)

This can be a significantly large I/O cost, even with tables where the page and row counts number only in the hundreds.

Occasionally, it may be cheaper to build a temporary clustered index on the inner table and use the index to process the query, rather than to repeatedly scan the table. This method is known as the *reformatting strategy*.

When reformatting occurs, SQL Server copies the contents of the inner table into a temporary worktable in `tempdb` and creates a clustered index on the join columns specified in the index. It then uses the clustered index when processing the join to retrieve the qualifying rows from the temporary worktable.

The cost of applying the reformatting strategy is the time and I/O required to create the temporary worktable and build the clustered index on it. The I/O cost of the reformatting strategy alone (that is, copying the table and building the clustered index) is determined as follows:

$$P2 + P2\log_2 \times P2$$

where P2 = the number of pages in the inner table.

The reformatting strategy isn't used unless the estimated cost of processing the query by using the reformatting strategy is less than the cost of joining by using table scans. The total I/O cost for processing the query would be the reformatting cost plus the number of pages in the outer table (P1) plus the number of rows in the outer table (R1) times the number of scans on the outer table (for a normal nested iteration, only a single scan of the outer table). The full equation to estimate total I/O for a query using the reformatting strategy would be the following:

$$(P2 + P2\log2 \times P_2) + P1 + R1$$

If the outer table consists of 300 rows and 200 pages, and the inner table consists of 100 pages, the cost of reformatting would be the following:

$$(100 + 100\log_2 \times 100) + 200 + 300 = 1,300 \text{ I/Os}$$

The cost of processing this query using table scans would be the following:

$$200 + (300 \times 100) = 30,200 \text{ I/Os}$$

In this example, the optimizer would choose to apply the reformatting strategy because it's substantially cheaper than joining with table scans.

TIP

It's nice that the optimizer has the capacity to create a temporary clustered index on-the-fly to process queries on tables without supporting indexes. If you see the reformatting strategy being applied, however, it should set off bells in your head, indicating that you probably don't have the appropriate indexes defined on your tables. True, reformatting is cheaper than joining table scan to table scan, but it's still quite a bit more expensive than if the appropriate index were defined on the table(s) in the first place.

Cross Joins and Outer Joins

SQL Server 6.5 allows an alternate join syntax to conform to the ANSI standard. Using the ANSI-compatible syntax, join criteria are declared in the `from` clause instead of the `where` clause.

The new syntax is as follows:

```
FROM {table_name CROSS JOIN table_name
  ¦ table_name [join_type] JOIN table_name ON search_conditions }
```

`join_type` can be one of the following:

```
        INNER, LEFT [OUTER], RIGHT [OUTER], FULL [OUTER]
```

If you leave out the join clause or use the new CROSS JOIN syntax, this creates a cross product, joining all rows in one table with all possible rows in the other table. The optimizer still will determine which join order is most efficient for processing the cross join.

If the query contains an asterisk (*) on either side of a join operator, or uses the new LEFT OUTER JOIN or RIGHT OUTER JOIN syntax, all rows from the table on the outer side of the join are to be included in the result set—whether or not it joins successfully with the inner table.

For example, to see all publishers whether or not you currently carry any of their titles, the following query could be written as:

```
select pub_name, title from publishers p, titles t
    where p.pub_id *= t.pub_id
```

or

```
select pub_name, title from publishers p LEFT OUTER JOIN titles t
    on p.pub_id = t.pub_id
```

All pub_names will be retrieved from publishers. For any row that doesn't join successfully with titles, the title column contains a NULL for that row in the output.

This syntax is referred to as an *outer join*. The table on the same side of the expression as the asterisk is forced to be treated as the outer table—that is, the first table accessed in a nested iteration.

For this type of query, the optimizer doesn't evaluate the reverse join order.

If you use the FULL OUTER JOIN syntax in SQL Server 6.5, this specifies that all rows from either table be included in the result set, regardless of whether there is a match in the other table. If no match exists, the corresponding columns from the other table are set to NULL. How the optimizer processes a full outer join to determine the optimal join order depends on the other search criteria specified in the where clause. For example, the following query with no where clauses is processed using the reformatting strategy:

```
select pub_name, title from publishers p FULL OUTER JOIN titles t
    on p.pub_id = t.pub_id
```

If you add a where clause specifying search criteria only for the publishers table, SQL Server examines the possible join orders and processes it as a left outer join:

```
select pub_name, title from publishers p FULL OUTER JOIN titles t
    on p.pub_id = t.pub_id
    where p.state = "NY"
```

Optimizing group by, distinct, and order by Clauses

In addition to determining the best indexes and join orders, the optimizer also determines whether worktables are required to further process a query. These are typically queries containing an order by, group by, or distinct clause. Because worktables incur additional processing and I/O, the optimizer determines whether a worktable is required.

group by

For a group by, a worktable must always be created to perform the grouping and hold any aggregate values being generated for each group.

If the group by statement in SQL Server 6.5 also contains the with cube or with rollup clause, a second worktable is created to perform the cube or rollup function on the group by results generated in the first worktable.

distinct

Because the distinct clause applies across the entire row, a worktable is created to sort and remove duplicates. If a unique index exists on the table and all columns in the unique index are included in the result set, a worktable can be avoided, because the unique index guarantees that each row is distinct.

order by

For an order by, the determination of whether a worktable is required is dependent on the indexes on the table and the query containing the order by clause.

For a table with a clustered index, a worktable can be avoided for an order by if the following conditions are met:

- The order by clause specifies at least the first column in the clustered index as the first order by column.
- Only columns that are part of the nonclustered index are listed in the order by clause.
- The query is resolved using either the clustered index or a table scan.

If these conditions are met, the worktable isn't needed to sort the result set, because the rows in the table are already sorted in clustered index order and will be returned in clustered index order.

For example, if the clustered index is defined on `zone` and `state`, a worktable isn't needed for this:

```
select zone, state, customer, zip
    from customers
order by zone, state
```

but a worktable would be required for this:

```
select zone, state, customer, zip
    from customers
order by zone, zip
```

because `zip` isn't part of the clustered index. The data is sorted by `zone`, but a worktable is needed to sort the data by `zip` within a `zone`.

If the table has a nonclustered index, a worktable can be avoided for sorting the results if

- ■ The query is resolved using index covering; and
- ■ The `order by` clause specifies at least the first column of the nonclustered index as the first `order by` column.

For example, if a nonclustered index is defined on `zone` and `state`, a worktable isn't needed for this:

```
select state
    from customers
order by zone
```

because the nonclustered index covers the query and the index rows are already sorted by `zone`. However, a worktable would be required for this:

```
select zone, state
    from customers
order by state
```

because `state` isn't the first column of the nonclustered index. The data is sorted by `zone` and `state` within the index, but a worktable is needed to sort the data by `state` alone.

A worktable also can be avoided for sorting the results if

- ■ The `order by` clause specifies at least the first column of a nonclustered index as the first `order by` column.
- ■ Only columns that are part of the nonclustered index are listed in the `order by` clause.
- ■ The nonclustered index is used to satisfy the query by matching a SARG.

If these conditions are met, no worktable is needed to sort the result set, because the rows will be retrieved from the table in nonclustered index order. For example, if a nonclustered index is defined on `zone` and `state`, a worktable isn't needed for the following example:

```
select zone, state, customer, zip
   from customers
   where zone = "A"
order by zone
```

as long as the nonclustered index is used to satisfy the query. Because the data is retrieved in nonclustered index order already, due to the SARG on zone, no further sorting is necessary. However, a worktable would be required here:

```
select zone, state, customer, zip
   from customers
   where zone = "A"
order by zone, zip
```

because zip isn't part of the nonclustered index. The data is retrieved by zone in zone order, but a worktable is needed to sort the data by zip within a zone.

> **NOTE**
>
> Prior to Microsoft SQL Server 6.0, any order by … DESC always required a worktable because SQL Server only scanned tables and indexes in ascending order. SQL Server Version 6.0 and later now support reverse table and index scans; worktables no longer are required for an order by … DESC if the optimizer can perform a reverse table or index scan to retrieve the results, and the other conditions discussed in this section are also met.
>
> If you mix ASC and DESC clauses in an order by, a worktable will always be needed to resolve the different sort orders.

Phase 4: Plan Selection

At this point in the query optimization process, the optimizer has examined the entire query and estimated the costs of all possible indexes to be used and query processing strategies. Now it needs to choose which plan to pass to the SQL Server for execution.

For a single table query, choosing the best query plan involves choosing the index and query-processing strategy that result in the fewest number of rows and data pages to be scanned to process the query on that table.

For a multi-table query, choosing the best plan involves not only determining the cheapest index and query-processing strategy for each table individually, but also determining the best strategy in conjunction with the optimal join order that results in the lowest estimated I/O time, as discussed in the earlier section on join order processing.

Additionally, if any order by, group by, or distinct clauses are present, the optimizer chooses the most efficient method to process them.

For all of its options, the overriding factor in selecting a plan is total I/O. The optimizer is committed to selecting a query plan that results in the least amount of I/O processing. After the plan is selected, it's passed to the SQL Server for execution.

> **NOTE**
>
> You can examine the query plan chosen by the optimizer by executing the query after running the `set showplan on` command. How to interpret the `showplan` output is covered in Chapter 15, "Analyzing Query Plans," along with a discussion of other tools available for examining the query-plan selection process.
>
> You also have the ability to influence or override the query-plan selection process using the methods discussed in Chapter 17.

Potential Optimizer Problems

So you've written the query and examined the query plan, and the optimizer isn't choosing the plan that you think is best. What's wrong with this query? Before going into a detailed discussion about analyzing and debugging query plans (covered in detail in Chapter 15), let's look at some of the more common problems that may lead the optimizer to choose poor query plans.

Are Statistics Up-to-Date?

One of the more common problems encountered with performance in new production systems is the fact that no index statistics are available, or existing statistics are woefully out-of-date. Before you start tearing queries apart, or tearing your hair out, run `update statistics` on the tables in question and rerun your query.

Are the SARGs Really SARGs?

Look at your `where` clauses very closely. Are what appear to be SARGs actual SARGs in the eye of the optimizer? Watch out for inequality operators, operations on columns, and constant expressions that can't be evaluated at query compile time.

Does the Index Actually Cover the Query?

If you were expecting index covering to take place, double-check the query and index in question to make sure that all columns in the query are contained in the index. It's very easy for a nonindexed column to sneak its way into a query, forcing a data row retrieval.

Was the Stored Procedure Optimized Based on Different Parameters?

Query plans for stored procedures are compiled once and placed into a procedure cache. The query plan created is based on the parameters passed during the first execution. It's possible that the best plan for those parameters may not be the best plan for the current parameters. Chapter 14, "Stored Procedure Optimization," contains a complete discussion on how to deal with this problem.

Is Reformatting Occurring?

If reformatting is taking place, no supporting indexes exist for the query, or the query contains invalid SARGs that can't use any available indexes. At this point, you need to reevaluate your indexing decisions, or rewrite the query to take advantage of an available index.

Summary

The SQL Server optimizer has continuously improved over the years, taking advantage of new techniques and algorithms to improve its capacity to find the cheapest plan. Most of the time, the optimizer makes the correct decision. There are occasions when the optimizer makes the wrong decision, due either to inaccurate or incomplete information in the index statistics. When you suspect that the optimizer is making the wrong decision, SQL Server provides tools to analyze the query plans generated and determine the source of the problem. These tools are described in Chapter 15.

Stored Procedure Optimization

14

Stored procedures are one of the primary features of SQL Server. Almost every application developed on SQL Server makes use of stored procedures at some point. In fact, most administrative tasks in SQL Server are performed with stored procedures. For these reasons, it is important to understand how stored procedures are managed and processed by SQL Server, in order to understand the performance benefits and issues when using stored procedures.

Stored Procedures and Performance Benefits

Stored procedures are parsed and compiled SQL code that reside in the database and can be executed from a client application by name. There are a number of advantages to using stored procedures in SQL Server:

- Faster execution
- Reduced network traffic
- Modular programming
- Restricted, function-based access to tables
- Reduced operator error
- Helping enforce consistency
- Can automate complex or sensitive transactions

Two of the main advantages of using stored procedures are reduced network traffic and faster execution of SQL.

In a client/server environment, the network must always be considered a potential bottleneck, because all communication between clients and servers occurs over the network. Using stored procedures can help to reduce network traffic. A stored procedure can contain large, complex queries or SQL operations that are compiled and stored within a SQL Server database. They are then executed on the SQL Server when the client issues a request to execute the stored procedure. The SQL statements are executed locally within the SQL Server, and typically only the final results are sent back to the client application. With the programming features (if...else, while, goto, local variables, and so on) built into Transact-SQL, the SQL Server itself can evaluate intermediate results and perform any necessary code branching without having to send intermediate results back to the client for processing.

Another performance gain that stored procedures provide over dynamic SQL is that all object references and SQL syntax are checked at the time the stored procedure is created and a parse tree is generated. This parse tree is stored on disk in the sysprocedures table in the database where the stored procedure is created. The parse tree is used by the query optimizer to determine a query plan. When the stored procedure is executed, the parsing and object references do not need to be performed again. With dynamic SQL, the SQL statements must be parsed and all object references checked for every execution, even if the same SQL statements are executed repeatedly. Although the overhead of generating the parse tree is typically minimal, it is additional overhead that can reduce the throughput of a high transaction environment.

In addition to storing the parse tree for a procedure, SQL Server also has the capability of saving the optimized query plan generated by the execution of a stored procedure in procedure cache memory and reusing it for subsequent executions. Avoiding the optimization and compilation phase for subsequent executions can result in significant time-savings on procedure execution, especially for complex queries or transactions. Table 14.1 compares the differences between the first execution of a stored procedure and subsequent executions.

Table 14.1. Comparing the steps performed for first and subsequent stored procedure executions.

First Execution	Subsequent Executions
Locate stored procedure on disk and load into cache	Locate stored procedure in cache
Substitute parameter values	Substitute parameter values
Develop optimization plan	
Compile optimization plan	
Execute from cache	Execute from cache

How Stored Procedures Are Optimized

The SQL Server query optimizer generates a query plan for a stored procedure based on the parameters passed in the first time it is executed. The stored procedure parse tree is read in from disk, and SQL Server generates a query tree for the procedure in procedure cache. The parameters are then substituted and the optimizer generates a query plan in procedure cache. (See Figure 14.1.)

The stored procedure query plan remains in cache after execution for subsequent execution by the same or other SQL Server users, providing there is sufficient cache space available for the query plan to remain in cache.

FIGURE 14.1.

Stored procedure query plans are read in from disk and a query plan is generated in cache for each concurrent user.

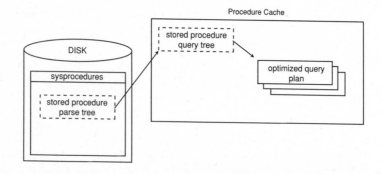

> **NOTE**
>
> If the procedure cache size is not configured large enough by the system administrator, there might not be enough free space in the procedure cache to load another query tree or plan for all users needing them at the same time. Procedure cache space can be freed only if a query tree or plan is not currently in use. If there is insufficient space to load another query tree or plan, error 701, "There is insufficient system memory to run this query," occurs.
>
> Also be aware that there is a maximum number of procedures or other compiled objects allowed in the procedure cache. The number of objects allowed in the procedure cache is a function of the procedure cache size and is displayed in the error log during SQL Server startup as the number of available *proc buffers*. If the number of procedures or objects in use exceeds the maximum, error 701 occurs.
>
> See Chapter 31, "Configuring and Tuning SQL Server," for guidelines on estimating procedure cache space requirements.

It is important to note at this point that stored procedure query plans in SQL Server are reusable, but not reentrant. What this means is that a query plan in cache can be in use by only one user at a time. If multiple users execute the same stored procedure concurrently, SQL Server generates newly optimized copies of the stored procedure query plan in cache for each concurrent user for whom a copy is not available.

The Stored Procedure Dilemma

The advantages of a cost-based optimizer is that it has the capability to generate the optimal query plan for all queries based upon the search criteria. For certain types of queries (for example, range retrievals) the query optimizer might at times generate different query plans based upon the supplied search arguments and the estimated number of matching rows. Consider the following example:

```
select * from orders
  where saledate between @lowdate and @highdate
```

If there were a nonclustered index on `saledate`, the query optimizer would have the option of resolving the query either by using the nonclustered index or by performing a table scan. This decision would be based on the available distribution statistics and the estimated number of rows where `saledate` is between `@lowdate` and `@highdate`. For an execution of the query where there are a small number of rows within the range, the optimizer might choose to process the query using the nonclustered index. For a subsequent execution with a large number of values in the range, the optimizer might choose to process the query using a table scan.

However, the behavior of stored procedures for subsequent executions is to reuse the query plan residing in procedure cache that was generated for the first execution of the stored procedure. This provides a performance gain for queries that consistently use the same query plan, but can cause a performance loss if the wrong query plan is used for subsequent executions.

Consider the previous SQL example and put it into a stored procedure as follows:

```
create proc get_orders (@lowdate datetime, @highdate datetime)
as
select * from orders
  where saledate between @lowdate and @highdate
return
```

Suppose that the first time this procedure gets executed each day, it is passed parameter values to retrieve all order records for the previous day, and is resolved via a table scan. This is the query plan that is placed in procedure cache for subsequent executions. Subsequent executions done on the same day, however, retrieve only order records since the last time the procedure was executed, to provide for real-time monitoring of the orders being received throughout the day. Assuming that the procedure is run every five minutes, the number of records to be retrieved is minimal, which could be sufficiently resolved using the nonclustered index. The query plan from the first execution of this stored procedure still exists in the procedure cache, however, so a new query plan is not generated. The procedure ends up performing a table scan for each execution, thus not providing the expected response-time performance for the query. There needs to be a way to get the SQL Server to recompile a new query plan for the subsequent executions.

Recompiling Stored Procedures

So how do you go about generating a new query plan when a stored procedure is using the wrong one for a particular execution? Fortunately, SQL Server gives you a couple of options. The first is to create the stored procedure with the `with recompile` option:

```
create proc get_orders (@lowdate datetime, @highdate datetime)
with recompile
as
select * from orders
  where saledate between @lowdate and @highdate
return
```

This option forces the SQL Server query optimizer to generate a new query plan for each execution. As you might suspect, this creates a lot of overhead with the optimizer, and you lose the performance gains typically realized with stored procedures by avoiding the query-plan compilation phase for subsequent executions. However, if you are looking at a few milliseconds extra for each execution versus the minutes or possibly hours a stored procedure might run if the wrong query plan is used, it's probably a worthwhile tradeoff, because you can be virtually guaranteed that the proper query plan is being chosen based on the parameters passed on each execution.

The second alternative is to create the procedure normally, but use the `with recompile` option on procedure execution like this:

```
exec get_orders @lowdate = "12/15/94", @highdate = "12/16/94" with recompile
```

Using `with recompile` on stored procedure execution causes the SQL Server optimizer to generate a new query plan based on the supplied parameters only for the current execution. Other existing query plans in cache, except for the one it is replacing, remain unchanged. This method enables you to then explicitly specify when you want the optimizer to examine your parameters and generate a new query plan rather than create a new query plan for each execution, as the `create proc ... with recompile` option does. You typically use this method when you are running a specific instance of a stored procedure with atypical parameters.

> **WARNING**
>
> If multiple copies of a stored procedure query plan are in procedure cache, the stored procedure currently being executed reuses the first available query plan the SQL Server finds in cache. There is no guarantee that a specific user will get the same query plan he generates with the `exec ... with recompile` on subsequent executions. Likewise, another user might unexpectedly get the recompiled query plan, which may not be appropriate for the parameters he is passing in. The SQL Server still returns the appropriate results, but possibly not in the most efficient manner.
>
> Unfortunately, SQL Server provides no mechanism to explicitly flush query plans out of procedure cache. The only way to remove all query plans for a specific stored procedure from procedure cache is to drop and re-create the stored procedure.

Automatic Recompilation

What happens if you drop an index from a table referenced by a stored procedure, and the procedure query plan was using that index to resolve the query? In this instance, SQL Server detects that the index is no longer available and automatically recompiles a new query plan. In Microsoft SQL Server 6.5, the `create index` statement also causes automatic recompilation of stored procedures the next time they are executed. The `update statistics` statement, on the other hand, does not cause recompilation of stored procedures.

Using `sp_recompile`

If you've updated statistics for a table, and want the query optimizer to reexamine the new statistics and generate new query plans for all stored procedures that reference that table, use the `sp_recompile` stored procedure as follows:

```
sp_recompile tablename
```

Using `sp_recompile` causes all query plans in cache that reference the specified table to be recompiled.

When to Use `with recompile`

Consider using the `with recompile` option when a stored procedure can generate widely different query plans, depending on the parameters passed in, and there is no way to predict the best query plan for all executions.

When to Use `sp_recompile`

The `sp_recompile` stored procedure should be applied when

- Statistics have been updated on a table and you want the stored procedure to generate a new query plan based on the updated statistics
- An index has been added to a table and you want the optimizer to consider the new index and generate a new query plan for the stored procedure

When Recompilation Doesn't Work

If a stored procedure contains a `select * from` *tablename*... statement, and `alter table` has been used to add a column to the table, the stored procedure does not pick up the new column(s), even when the stored procedure is executed using the `with recompile` option. This is because the column names and IDs for `select *` are resolved when the stored procedure is created and stored in the parse tree. To pick up the new columns, you need to create a new parse tree. The only way to do this is to drop and re-create the stored procedure. This same situation applies when you rename tables referenced by a stored procedure. Because the stored procedure resolves object references by object ID rather than by name, the stored procedure can still reference the original table. For example, if you rename the `customer` table `old_customer`, your stored procedure continues to work, performing operations on what is now the `old_customer` table. If you subsequently create a new `customer` table, your stored procedures do not recompile to operate on the new `customer` table as long as the `old_customer` table exists. If you drop the `old_customer` table, the stored procedures that reference it are automatically recompiled and a new parse tree is generated to reference the new customer table. If you want to force the stored procedures to reference the new customer table without dropping `old_customer`, you need to drop and re-create all stored procedures that reference the customer table.

Alternatives to Using `with recompile`

Because of the performance issues already identified with using the `with recompile` option, you want to avoid using `with recompile` whenever possible.

Another alternative in SQL Server 6.5 is to use the exec statement to dynamically build the SQL to be executed. Unlike using the `with recompile` option, SQL Server will automatically recompile the query plan for the dynamic SQL statement, but not the other statements in the stored procedure. The following example demonstrates a method for recompiling the range query against the orders table for each execution using the exec statement, while the query against the inventory table is optimized only on the first execution:

```
create proc get_info (@lowdate datetime, @highdate datetime)
as
declare @where varchar(30)

select @where = "'" + convert(char(10), @lowdate, 101) + "' and '"
                + convert(char(10), @highdate, 101) + "'"

exec ("select * from orders where saledate between " + @where)

select * from inventory

return
```

Using the exec statement, however, still incurs additional processing overhead when executing the stored procedure. Instead of creating a procedure with the `with recompile` option or using the exec statement, consider the following solution:

```
create proc get_orders_smallrange (@lowdate datetime, @highdate datetime)
as
select * from orders
  where saledate between @lowdate and @highdate
return
go

create proc get_orders_bigrange (@lowdate datetime, @highdate datetime)
as
select * from orders
  where saledate between @lowdate and @highdate
return
go

create proc range_value (@lowdate datetime, @highdate datetime)
as
if datediff(hh, @highdate, @lowdate) >= 12
    exec get_orders_bigrange @lowdate, @highdate
else
    exec get_orders_smallrange @lowdate, @highdate
```

Using this approach, each subprocedure (get_orders_smallrange and get_orders_bigrange) is optimized on first execution with the appropriate query plan for the different range values specified in the parameters passed to it by the get_orders procedure. Thus, if a user executes get_orders with date values that are greater than 12 hours apart, get_orders executes the get_orders_bigrange procedure, which is optimized for processing large-range retrievals—possibly using a table scan. For a user executing get_orders with date values that are less than 12 hours apart, get_orders executes the get_orders_smallrange procedure, which is optimized for processing smaller range retrievals, possibly using an available nonclustered index. This approach should result in more consistent response times for queries by minimizing the possibility of a user executing a stored procedure with an inappropriate query plan for the parameters specified.

> **NOTE**
>
> To design the stored procedure effectively using this approach requires sufficient knowledge of the bias of your data to know when certain range values result in different query plans.
>
> Also be aware that this technique might increase your procedure cache memory requirements—users now have at least two procedure query plans (get_orders and either get_orders_smallrange or get_orders_bigrange) in cache. However, this approach is typically preferred over having your application check the range values and execute the appropriate stored procedure.
>
> If the range check is hard-coded into your application source code and the bias of your data changes, you have to modify your application source code and recompile it. By performing the range check within the top-level stored procedure, you can easily drop, modify, and re-create the stored procedure to reflect changes in the bias of the data without having to change or recompile the application program.

One other programming consideration with stored procedures that relates to performance and optimal query-plan generation is when stored procedures perform different select statements based on condition branching. Examine the following stored procedure:

```
create proc get_order_data (@flag tinyint, @value int)
as
if @flag = 1
    select * from orders where price = @value
else
    select * from orders where qty = @value
```

At query compile time, the optimizer doesn't know which branch will be followed because the if...else construct isn't evaluated until runtime. On the first execution, the optimizer generates a query plan for all select statements in the stored procedure, regardless of the conditional branching. The query plan for each select statement is based upon the passed-in parameters.

Having distinctly different queries in the stored procedure could result in the wrong query plan being generated for one of the select statements, as its query plan might be based upon inappropriate values for that query.

Again, a better approach would be to break the different select statements into two separate stored procedures and execute the appropriate stored procedure for the type of query to be executed. For example:

```
create proc get_orders_by_price(@price int)
as
    select * from orders where price = @value
return
go

create proc get_orders_by_qty(@qty int)
as
    select * from orders where qty = @qty
return
go

create proc get_order_data (@flag tinyint, @value int)
as
if @flag = 1
    exec get_orders_by_price
else
    exec get_orders_by_qty
return
```

Summary

Stored procedures can provide a number of performance benefits within SQL Server. Having a good understanding of how stored procedures are optimized by SQL Server helps you to develop efficient stored procedures and achieve the maximum performance benefits they can provide.

Analyzing Query Plans

15

The SQL Server's cost-based query optimizer typically does a good job of determining the best plan to process a query. At times, however, you may be a little bit skeptical about the plan that the optimizer is generating. At the least, you'll want to know specifics about the query plan it's using:

- Is the optimizer using the indexes that you have defined, or is it performing table scans?
- Are worktables being used to process the query?
- Is the reformatting strategy being applied?
- What join order is the optimizer using?
- What actual statistics and cost estimates is the optimizer using to make its decisions?
- How do the optimizer's estimates compare to actual I/O costs?

Fortunately, SQL Server provides some tools to answer just these questions, as described in this chapter.

Using and Understanding `showplan`

To determine the query plan that the optimizer has chosen to process a query, SQL Server provides the `set showplan on` option to display the query plan that will be executed. By examining the `showplan` output, you can determine, among other things, which indexes (if any) are being used, what join order was selected, and whether any worktables are required to resolve the query. Interpreting and understanding this output will assist you in writing more efficient queries and choosing the appropriate indexing strategy for your tables.

The `showplan` option is a session-level setting. It won't affect other users, and it's off by default when you first log in to SQL Server. To turn on the `showplan` option, execute the following statement in SQL Server:

```
set showplan on
```

If you're working in ISQL/w, you can turn on `showplan` by typing the command in a query window and executing it, or by turning on the Show Query Plan option in the Query Options dialog box for that query window. (See Figure 15.1.)

Turning on `showplan` by using either of these two methods causes the `showplan` output to be displayed in the query results window along with any data.

When using `showplan` to debug queries, you may also want to use it in conjunction with the `noexec` option. The `noexec` option tells SQL Server to generate a query plan, but not submit it for execution. This option is useful when you're trying to rewrite a long-running query to get it to use a more efficient query plan. You don't want to have to wait hours for the query to run, or wade through thousands of rows of data just to see whether a query would use an index. Setting `noexec` on prevents the query from executing, but SQL Server still generates a query plan and displays it if `showplan` is turned on.

FIGURE 15.1.

Turning on the showplan *option for the* ISQL/w *query window.*

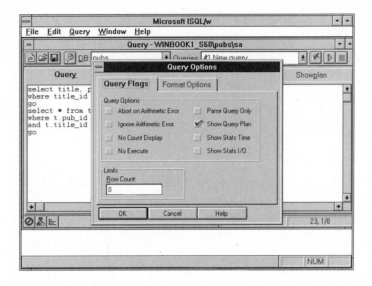

To turn on the noexec option, run the following command:

```
set noexec on
```

Like showplan, noexec is a session-level setting that's turned off by default. It won't affect any other users or sessions that you might have open.

If you're working in ISQL/w, you can set noexec on by typing the command in a query window and executing it, or by turning on the No Execute option in the Query Options dialog box. (Refer to Figure 15.1.) The setting applies only for the current query window.

TIP

When the noexec option is turned on, the only command that SQL Server will execute is set noexec off. Always remember to set all your other session settings, trace flags, and so on before setting noexec on. Otherwise, you'll be pulling your hair out trying to figure out why you're not seeing the showplan output! Also, remember to turn it off when you want to execute the query or another command.

When the showplan option or the statistics io/time options are turned on and you run a system stored procedure, often the showplan/statistics output is rather voluminous, making it difficult to read the stored procedure output. Sometimes, depending on the query tool being used, the amount of output will exceed the tool's results buffer.

Many of the system stored procedures are very large and complex (run sp_helptext on a procedure such as sp_help sometime, and you'll see what I mean). To avoid generating all that output, you'd have to keep switching the showplan/noexec/statistics options off and on. If you're a lazy typist like me, this isn't a viable option. I recommend opening a second session to the SQL Server for running system stored procedures such as sp_help and sp_helpindex, where you don't have any of these options turned on. Use the other session for debugging your SQL code.

The following is an example of the information displayed by showplan:

```
/*QUERY for a simple join with SHOWPLAN ON*/
select sum(ytd_sales) from titles t, publishers p
where t.pub_id = p.pub_id
and p.pub_name = "Macmillan Computer Publishing"

STEP 1
The type of query is SELECT
Scalar Aggregate
FROM TABLE
publishers p
Nested iteration
Table Scan
FROM TABLE
titles t
Nested iteration
Table Scan
STEP 2
The type of query is SELECT


— — — —
28286

(1 row(s) affected)
```

The following sections break down the showplan output and examine the statements displayed.

STEP *stepnum*

Sometimes, SQL Server can't process the entire query in a single step and must break it down into multiple pieces. The STEP *stepnum* statement displays which component of the query the optimizer is processing.

Typical queries that require multiple steps are queries with aggregates, group by or order by clauses, or where a worktable is required to execute the query. The SQL Server must first retrieve the results from the base table(s) into a worktable in tempdb in STEP 1, to calculate the aggregate or group or to sort the result set. In STEP 2, it retrieves the result set from the worktable.

If you examine the sample query, you'll see that there's an aggregate in the query. In the first step, you perform the select from the tables. The value for sum(amount) is stored and calculated in a worktable in tempdb. In the second step, SQL Server retrieves the calculated sum from the worktable.

The type of query is *querytype*

This line simply states what type of command is being executed at each step. If the SQL statement isn't the typical `select`, `insert`, `update`, or `delete`, `showplan` reports what type of statement is being executed. For example:

```
exec proc_1
```

```
STEP 1
The type of query is EXECUTE
```

The type of query is SELECT (into a worktable)

This statement indicates that SQL Server needs to select results into a worktable for processing—for example, when a `group by` clause is used:

```
select sum(ytd_sales), type from titles
group by type
```

```
STEP 1
The type of query is SELECT (into a worktable)
GROUP BY
Vector Aggregate
FROM TABLE
titles
Nested iteration
Table Scan
TO TABLE
Worktable 1
STEP 2
The type of query is SELECT
FROM TABLE
Worktable 1
Nested iteration
Table Scan
```

Notice that this query is a two-step query. The results are first retrieved from the `titles` table into a worktable to do the grouping and calculate the aggregate, and then the final result set is retrieved from the worktable in the second step.

GROUP BY [WITH CUBE ¦ ROLLUP]

This line indicates that the query contains a `group by` clause. Any query with a `group by` will always be a two-step query, because a worktable must be used to calculate the vector or scalar aggregate.

In SQL Server 6.5, showplan now also indicates whether the with cube or with rollup option has been specified for the group by. These queries will still be two-step queries, but a second worktable is created to calculate the cube or rollup values. For example:

```
select pub_id, type, sum(ytd_sales)
    from titles
    group by pub_id, type with cube
```

```
STEP 1
The type of query is INSERT
The update mode is direct
FROM TABLE
titles
Nested iteration
Table Scan
TO TABLE
Worktable 1
STEP 2
The type of query is SELECT
FROM TABLE
Worktable 2
 GROUP BY WITH CUBE
 Vector Aggregate
 FROM TABLE
 Worktable 1
 Using GETSORTED Table Scan
 TO TABLE
 Worktable 2
```

Vector Aggregate or Scalar Aggregate

This line indicates that the query contains one or more aggregate functions without a group by clause. A scalar aggregate contains a single value for the aggregate when the query doesn't contain a group by clause. A scalar aggregate is still a two-step query. The scalar aggregate is essentially a single-column, single-row worktable in tempdb, used to keep a running total for each aggregate as the result rows are processed in the first step. In the second step, SQL Server retrieves the value stored in the scalar aggregate:

```
select sum(ytd_sales), avg(price)
from titles
```

```
The type of query is SELECT
Scalar Aggregate
FROM TABLE
titles
Nested iteration
Table Scan
STEP 2
The type of query is SELECT
```

A *vector aggregate* is created when the query contains one or more aggregates in conjunction with a group by clause. The vector aggregate is essentially a multicolumn table with one column for each column on which you're grouping, and another column to hold the computed aggregate for each distinct group. There will be a row in the worktable for each distinct instance of the column(s) in the group by clause (see Figure 15.2).

FIGURE 15.2.

Worktable for a vector aggregate.

type	avg (price)
UNDECIDED	NULL
business	13.73
mod_cook	11.49
popular_comp	21.48
psychology	13.50
trad_cook	15.96

> **NOTE**
>
> In many of the classes I teach, students have a tendency to misread the showplan output for queries with vector aggregates. They see the Table Scan output in the second step and assume that the optimizer performed a table scan on the base table, when actually it's the query against the worktable that performs the table scan. SQL Server has to do a table scan on the worktable because it isn't indexed.
>
> Be careful not to make this mistake. To determine the access path used by the optimizer, notice the access path listed right after the FROM TABLE statement for the table in question.

FROM TABLE

The FROM TABLE line is typically followed on the next line with the name of the table from which data is being selected. This can be a table in the FROM clause in the query, or a worktable. If aliases were used for tables in the query, the alias will follow the table name. The order of the FROM TABLE information in the showplan information indicates the join order used to process the query. In the following showplan example, the publishers table is the first (outer) table in the join, and the titles table is the second (inner) table:

```
STEP 1
The type of query is SELECT
Scalar Aggregate
FROM TABLE
publishers p
Nested iteration
Table Scan
FROM TABLE
titles t
Nested iteration
Table Scan
STEP 2
The type of query is SELECT
```

Nested iteration

As discussed in Chapter 13, "Understanding the Query Optimizer," all joins are processed as a series of *nested iterations*, looping on the inner table for each row in the outer table. Essentially, all retrievals from a table are one or more sets of loops on the table to retrieve the matching data rows. When you see the Nested iteration statement in the showplan output, it indicates that one or more passes were made on the table.

Table Scan

This line indicates that the access method used to retrieve data was a table scan of the table listed immediately above.

Using Clustered Index

This line indicates that the data was retrieved from the table using the clustered index. The name of the index isn't displayed because there can be only one clustered index on a table. This typically indicates that the query contains a search argument that can be satisfied by using the clustered index.

Index: *index_name*

A nonclustered index was used to retrieve data from the table. The name of the index is displayed to indicate which nonclustered index was used. The nonclustered index may be used if there is a SARG that matches the index or if the query is covered by the nonclustered index.

Using Dynamic Index

If you see this statement in your showplan output, it indicates that the query contains an or statement and the query optimizer applied the OR strategy to solve the query rather than a table scan. Refer to Chapter 13 for a discussion of SQL Server's OR strategy.

Worktable Created for ORDER BY ¦ DISTINCT

This statement indicates that a worktable was needed to process a query containing an order by or distinct clause. When this statement is present, an additional step will be present in the plan, with additional statements to indicate where the sorting and retrieval of data from the worktable occurs:

```
Worktable Created for ORDER BY ¦ DISTINCT
...
    This step involves sorting
...
Using GETSORTED Table Scan
```

If the query contains an order by clause, a worktable needs to be created to sort the final result set if the data can't be retrieved in index sorted order:

```
select * from titles
order by price

STEP 1
The type of query is INSERT
The update mode is direct
Worktable created for ORDER BY
FROM TABLE
titles
Nested iteration
Table Scan
TO TABLE
Worktable 1
STEP 2
The type of query is SELECT
This step involves sorting
FROM TABLE
Worktable 1
Using GETSORTED Table Scan
```

In this example, the rows are retrieved from the titles table into a worktable in tempdb in the first step. In the second step, the rows are retrieved from the worktable in sorted order, using a table scan on the worktable.

If a query contains a distinct clause, the result rows need to be copied into a worktable and sorted so that the duplicate rows can be removed if a unique index isn't part of the retrieved columns to guarantee that each row is distinct:

```
select distinct type from titles

STEP 1
The type of query is INSERT
The update mode is direct
Worktable created for DISTINCT
FROM TABLE
titles
Nested iteration
Table Scan
TO TABLE
Worktable 1
STEP 2
The type of query is SELECT
This step involves sorting
FROM TABLE
Worktable 1
Using GETSORTED Table Scan
```

Worktable Created for REFORMATTING

The reformatting strategy is an alternative used by the query optimizer when no useful indexes are available on either of two tables involved in a join. Joining two tables without an index on either can be very costly. SQL Server compares the cost of joining the tables without an index to the cost of making a copy of one of the tables, creating a clustered index on it, and using the clustered index on the worktable to join it with the other table. The following is an example of the showplan output when the reformatting strategy is used:

```
select * from table1, table2
where table1.number = table2.number

STEP 1
The type of query is INSERT
The update mode is direct
Worktable created for REFORMATTING
FROM TABLE
table2
Nested iteration
Table Scan
TO TABLE
Worktable 1

STEP 2
The type of query is SELECT
FROM TABLE
table1
Nested iteration
Table Scan
FROM TABLE
Worktable 1
Nested iteration
Using Clustered Index
```

In STEP 1, the worktable is being created in tempdb, and the rows from table2 are copied into the worktable. A clustered index is then created on the worktable. In STEP 2, table1 is joined on the worktable, using the clustered index on the worktable to find the matching rows for the join.

Worktable created for SELECT INTO

When you run a select into statement, a new table is created in the specified database with the same structure as the table(s) being selected from. This statement in the showplan output is somewhat misleading in that it's not actually a worktable that gets created, but an actual table in the specified database. Unlike worktables created within other query plans, this table isn't dropped when query execution completes.

The update mode is deferred ¦ direct

When you perform an update operation (update, delete, insert, select INTO), SQL Server can perform the update as a direct update or a deferred update. Refer to Chapter 11, "Understanding SQL Server Storage Structures," for a full discussion of direct and deferred updates. This statement in the showplan output indicates which update method is being used on the specified table.

[NOT] EXISTS: nested iteration

This is a nested iteration that is being performed on a table in a subquery that's part of an existence or nonexistence check in the query. An existence or nonexistence check on the subquery can take many forms, including but not restricted to `exists`, `in`, and `= any`. In SQL Server 6.5, the `showplan` output for existence and nonexistence subqueries has been modified from previous releases. The subquery plan is now indented to differentiate the subquery steps from the outer query steps. For example:

```
select pub_name from publishers
where pub_id in (select pub_id from titles
                 where type = "business")
```

```
STEP 1
The type of query is SELECT
FROM TABLE
publishers
Nested iteration
Table Scan
EXISTS: nested iteration
  FROM TABLE
  titles
  Nested iteration
  Table Scan
```

In earlier releases of SQL Server, this query could have been flattened into a join, but would have resulted in multiple rows for `pub_name`, one for each matching row in the `titles` table. The ANSI standard behavior for such a query is that it should return only distinct instances of `pub_id`. Therefore, the query is processed as an existence join check rather than a standard inner join.

OR ¦ AND EXISTS: nested iteration

In SQL Server 6.5, if multiple existence subqueries are connected using an `and` or an `or` clause, SQL Server will evaluate one of the existence tests to determine whether the second existence test needs to be evaluated. For example, if the first existence check in an `or` evaluates to true, the `or` clause will be true and the second existence check will not need to be evaluated. In the `showplan` output, the `OR EXISTS` step is immediately followed by the plans for the other existence checks, which are indented to differentiate the subquery steps from the outer query steps. For example:

```
select pub_name from publishers
   where pub_id in (select pub_id from titles where type = "business")
      or state in (select state from authors)
```

```
STEP 1
The type of query is SELECT
FROM TABLE
publishers
Nested iteration
Table Scan
```

```
OR EXISTS: nested iteration
  EXISTS: nested iteration
    FROM TABLE
    titles
    Nested iteration
    Table Scan
  EXISTS: nested iteration
    FROM TABLE
    authors
    Nested iteration
    Table Scan
```

SUBQUERY: nested iteration

This clause indicates that the query contains a correlated subquery involving an aggregate. The query plan for the subquery is indented after the SUBQUERY statement to differentiate the subquery steps from the outer query steps. In the subquery plan, a group by clause for a vector aggregate worktable will be displayed, because SQL Server will perform a group by on the correlated columns to evaluate the query. For example:

```
select title_id, ytd_sales from titles t1
   where pubdate = (select max(pubdate) from titles t2
                       where t2.title_id = t1.title_id)

STEP 1
The type of query is SELECT
FROM TABLE
titles t1
Nested iteration
Table Scan
FROM TABLE
Worktable 1
SUBQUERY : nested iteration
GROUP BY
Vector Aggregate
  FROM TABLE
  titles t2
  Nested iteration
  Using Clustered Index
  TO TABLE
  Worktable 1
```

WITH CHECK OPTION

This indicates that data is being inserted or updated in a view containing one or more subqueries that was defined with the with check option.

CONSTRAINT: nested iteration

This clause appears when an insert or update is executed on a table containing a foreign key constraint, and the constraint is enforced. It indicates that a nested iteration join is being applied to enforce the constraint between the current table and the primary key table specified in the constraint. If no matching row is found in the primary key table, the insert or update is aborted.

LEFT ¦ FULL OUTER JOIN: nested iteration

This clause appears when the query contains a left, right, or full outer join. For a left or right outer join, the LEFT OUTER JOIN clause appears after the plan for the left table and is followed by the plan for the right table. The optimizer always converts a right outer join into a left outer join and flip-flops the tables in the query plan:

```
select pub_name, title_id, ytd_sales
   from titles RIGHT OUTER JOIN publishers
      on titles.pub_id = publishers.pub_id

STEP 1
The type of query is SELECT
FROM TABLE
publishers
Nested iteration
Table Scan
LEFT OUTER JOIN : nested iteration
  FROM TABLE
  titles
  Nested iteration
  Table Scan
```

When a full outer join is performed, you should typically also see the reformatting strategy applied and at least two steps to process the full outer join:

```
select title_id, ytd_sales from titles FULL OUTER JOIN publishers
on titles.pub_id = publishers.pub_id

STEP 1
The type of query is INSERT
The update mode is direct
Worktable created for REFORMATTING
FROM TABLE
publishers
Nested iteration
Table Scan
TO TABLE
Worktable 1
STEP 2
The type of query is SELECT
FROM TABLE
titles
Nested iteration
Table Scan
FULL OUTER JOIN : nested iteration
  FROM TABLE
  Worktable 1
  Nested iteration
  Using Clustered Index
```

Using dbcc Trace Flags for Analyzing Query Plans

The showplan option is a very useful tool for determining the query plan that the optimizer has chosen to process the query, but it doesn't give you any indication of why that plan was chosen. Unfortunately, sometimes it may not be clear why a particular plan is being used, or it may appear that the wrong query plan was chosen. So how exactly do you determine whether the optimizer is choosing the appropriate plan?

Well, the hard way would be to force the optimizer to use different query plans, and let it execute the various query plans to see which one actually results in the least amount of I/O and query processing time (see Chapter 17, "Managing the SQL Server Optimizer," for a discussion of how to force specific query plans). This would obviously be very time-consuming, and it would help you to determine whether the optimizer was choosing the correct query plan, but still not necessarily why.

What you really want to know is whether the optimizer is recognizing your search arguments and join clauses, and what information it is using to come up with its row and page I/O estimates.

Fortunately, SQL Server provides some dbcc trace flags, which give you exactly that information. Table 15.1 shows the useful trace flags and the information they provide.

Table 15.1. Useful dbcc traceon commands for interpreting query plans.

Trace Flag	Information Displayed
-1	Sets trace flags for all connections rather than just the current connection, when using dbcc traceon or dbcc traceoff
302	Provides information on the index selection process for each table in the query
310	Provides information on the join order selection process
330	Displays cost estimates for each table in the showplan output
3604	Sends output to the client session
3605	Sends output to the SQL Server error log

You must be logged in as sa to have permissions to run the dbcc traceon command. You can cause some of the options to apply to all user connections by turning on the trace flags in SQL Server startup. If you start SQL Server from a batch file or the command line, you can set trace flag options at SQL Server startup with the -T option:

```
sqlservr -d c:\mssql\data\master.dat -ec:\mssql\log\errorlog -T330
```

If you prefer to start SQL Server by using the SQL Enterprise Manager, you need to set the SQL Server startup parameters in the Server Configuration/Options dialog box. Figure 15.3 shows how to set the 330 trace flag using SQL Enterprise Manager, so that the trace flag will apply when starting SQL Server from the SQL Service Manager.

FIGURE 15.3.

Setting the 330 trace flag as a SQL Server startup parameter. Startup parameters set here will be used when SQL Server is started using the SQL Service Manager.

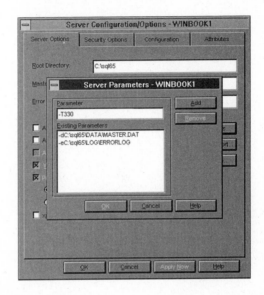

dbcc traceon (-1)

Most dbcc traceon commands, such as the 302 and 310 trace flags, display information only for the current user process in which they were executed. You also must be the sa to have the necessary permission to run the dbcc traceon commands.

If, as the sa, you want to turn on a trace flag globally for all user sessions, you can either specify it as a startup parameter or use the dbcc traceon (-1) command. The dbcc traceon (-1) command causes all dbcc traceon/traceoff commands to apply globally to all currently open user sessions, without having to shut down the SQL Server. For new connections to pick up the trace flags, you'll need to run the dbcc traceon (-1) command periodically.

One advantage of using the -1 trace flags over setting them as command-line options with the -T parameter is that you can turn them on and off without shutting down SQL Server. This capability is useful if you want to prevent generation of trace output during peak processing periods, or turn them on only during periods when particular problems occur.

The 3604 and 3605 Trace Flags

By default, most dbcc traceon flags send their output to the SQL Server error log. To route the output to the client session, run the following command:

```
dbcc traceon (3604)
```

To turn off output to the client session, use the dbcc traceoff command:

```
dbcc traceoff (3604)
```

All users have permission to issue the dbcc traceon (3604) command (unlike the other trace flags). Actually, even though the sa can turn on the dbcc trace flags globally, the user application **will** need to execute dbcc traceon (3604) to have the global trace flag output sent back to the user application.

dbcc traceon (330)

When the 330 trace flag is on, SQL Server reports additional information in the showplan output regarding the row estimates and query cost for each table.

The following is the showplan output with the 330 trace flag turned on:

```
select title, pub_name
   from publishers p, titles t
   where t.pub_id = p.pub_id
   order by type

STEP 1
The type of query is INSERT
The update mode is direct
Worktable created for ORDER BY
FROM TABLE
publishers p
Row estimate:  8
Cost estimate: 16
Nested iteration
Table Scan
FROM TABLE
titles t
JOINS WITH
publishers p
Row estimate:  18
Cost estimate: 60
Nested iteration
Table Scan
TO TABLE
Worktable 1
STEP 2
The type of query is SELECT
This step involves sorting
FROM TABLE
Worktable 1
Row estimate:  18
Cost estimate: 43
Using GETSORTED Table Scan
```

Notice the two additional statements for each table: Row estimate and Cost estimate. Row estimate is the number of rows in the table that the optimizer estimates will satisfy the query.

`Cost estimate` is the I/O cost in milliseconds to retrieve the rows for each table. The total I/O cost for the entire query can be determined by summing the I/O cost displayed for each table. In this example, the total I/O cost for this query would be the following:

```
16 + 60 + 43 = 119 milliseconds
```

Refer to Chapter 13 for a discussion of how the optimizer determines the row and I/O cost estimates.

By displaying this information in the `showplan` output, you can more easily compare the effectiveness of different query plans with one another and see which one results in the lower total I/O cost. This would still require running different versions of a query, however, and forcing particular query plans by invalidating search arguments or using the techniques covered in Chapter 17, "Managing the SQL Server Optimizer." There must be an easier way to examine the different statistics, join orders, and cost estimates that the optimizer uses to find the cheapest query plan. Fortunately, there is.

dbcc traceon (302) and dbcc traceon (310)

The `302` and `310` trace flags give you a look into the cost-analysis process that the query optimizer goes through when determining the best query plan. Additional options are available to view other aspects of the query optimization process, but these two trace flags provide the most useful information regarding optimizer query plan selection. These options are the ones on which this chapter concentrates.

The `302` trace flag displays the index selection phase of the query optimizer. You can examine the search arguments and join clauses identified by the query optimizer and determine whether an index is found on the column(s) that matches the SARG or join clause, whether the statistics page is used, and what the row and page I/O estimates are for each candidate index.

The `310` trace flag is most often used in conjunction with the `302` trace flag, but it's not required. The `310` output displays the join selection phase of the query optimizer, which takes place after the index selection phase. Here you can examine the possible join permutations and costs associated with each one that the optimizer is considering.

As with the other `dbcc` trace flags, you must be `sa` to turn on the `302` and `310` trace flags. These can be turned on for all users, however, by setting the trace flags on as startup parameters or by using the `dbcc traceon (-1)` command. The client application still needs to issue a `dbcc traceon (3604)` command to have the trace output displayed.

As the `sa`, run the following commands to turn on the `302` and `310` trace flags for your current session:

```
dbcc traceon (3604, 302, 310)
```

If you want to turn on the trace flag for all user sessions, run the following command as `sa`:

```
dbcc traceon (-1, 302, 310)
```

The users will then need to run a `dbcc traceon (3604)` to have the `302` and `310` output returned to the client application.

Interpreting the `dbcc traceon (302)` Output

The `302` and `310` trace flags provide a textual representation of the query optimization process. This output, however, obviously was originally intended for the developers of SQL Server to debug the query optimizer code. Over the years, the output has become somewhat more readable, but still can be a bit cryptic. This section examines the output from the `dbcc (302)` trace facility and deciphers each of the statements you may see.

Scoring Search Clauses

The first part of the `302` output is the search clause scoring phase. The process is performed for each valid search argument identified in the query. If no search arguments are identified by the query optimizer for a table, no search clause information is displayed.

For each table on which the optimizer identifies one or more search clauses, you see its information displayed between two strings of asterisks:

```
******************************
Entering q_score_index() for table 'pt_tx_CIid' (varno 1).
The table has 7282 rows and 118 pages.
Scoring the search clause:
AND (!:0xf14da4)  (andstat:0xa)
  GT (L:0xf14d84)  (rsltype:0x3c rsllen:8 rslprec:19 rslscale:4 opstat:0x0)
    VAR (L:0xf14d1e)  (varname:amount right:f14d6a varno:1 colid:2
    coltype:0x3c colen:8 coloff:6 colprec:19 colscale:4 vartypeid:11
    varnext:f14c6a varusecnt:1 varstat:90 varlevel:0 varsubq:0)
    MONEY (R:0xf14d6a)  (len:8 maxlen:4 prec:6 scale:0 value:
    400000.00)

Cheapest index is index 0, costing 118 pages and generating 2403 rows
per scan.
Search argument selectivity is 0.330000.
******************************
```

Pretty straightforward, easily readable output, huh? The following sections break out the important pieces that you need to know to figure out what's going on.

Entering `q_score_index()` for table '*table_name*'

This indicates that you're in a scoring routine for the specified table to find the best index to use for a table, depending on the search arguments or join clauses.

varno *tablenum*

This indicates the location of the table in the FROM clause in the query. 0 is the first table, 1 is the second table, 2 is the third table, and so on.

The table has *N* rows and *n* pages

This is the estimate of the overall table size. These values are taken from the sysindexes table. Essentially, this is the base cost of a table scan against which the cost of using any indexes will be compared to find the cheapest approach. Be sure to double-check these values, because there are instances in which they could be inaccurate or out of date, resulting in the wrong query plan being selected.

Scoring the search clause

This line indicates that the optimizer is scoring a search clause on the specified table. This point is where things get a bit tricky. Breaking out the different variables displayed (in the following sections) should help things make a bit more sense.

Type of Operator

```
AND (!:0xf14da4)  (andstat:0xa)
  GT (L:0xf14d84)  (rsltype:0x3c rsllen:8 rslprec:19 rslscale:4 opstat:0x0)
```

SQL Server always reports one and clause, even for queries with a single search argument. You can pretty much ignore the first one that you see. The next line below it indicates which type of operator is specified in the query:

- EQ: Equal to (=)
- LT: Less than (<)
- GT: Greater than (>)
- LE: Less than or equal to (<=)
- GE: Greater than or equal to (>=)

Remember, not equal (<>, !=) isn't treated as a valid search argument by the optimizer and will not show up in the cost estimates.

NOTE

A between clause is treated by SQL Server as

```
<= upper bound and >= lower bound
```

as seen in the following example:

```
select count(*) from pt_tx_CIamountNCamount
where amount between 100000 and 120000
```

continues

```
continued

*******************************
Entering q_score_index() for table 'pt_tx_CIamountNCamount' (varno 0).
The table has 7282 rows and 88 pages.
Scoring the search clause:
AND (!:0xf14e02)  (andstat:0xa)
  LE (L:0xf14dce)  (rsltype:0x3c rsllen:8 rslprec:19 rslscale:4
  opstat:0x0)
    VAR (L:0xf14e54)  (varname:amount left:f14d66 right:f14d80
    varno:0 colid:2 coltype:0x3c colen:8 coloff:6 colprec:19
    colscale:4 vartypeid:11 varusecnt:2 varstat:8c varlevel:0
    varsubq:0)
    MONEY (R:0xf14d80)  (len:8 maxlen:4 prec:6 scale:0 value:
    120000.00)
  AND (R:0xf14df6)  (andstat:0xa)
    GE (L:0xf14de2)  (rsltype:0x3c rsllen:8 rslprec:19 rslscale:4
    opstat:0x0)
      VAR (L:0xf14e54)  (varname:amount left:f14d66 right:f14d80
      varno:0 colid:2 coltype:0x3c colen:8 coloff:6 colprec:19
      colscale:4 vartypeid:11 varusecnt:2 varstat:8c varlevel:0
      varsubq:0)
      MONEY (R:0xf14d66)  (len:8 maxlen:4 prec:6 scale:0 value:
      100000.00)
```

Be careful dealing with between clauses in SQL Server version 6.0 and later. In previous releases, it didn't matter whether you put the lower bound on the left or right of the search clause. SQL Server would swap the values to ensure that the lower bound was always the smaller value. The ANSI standard doesn't allow this treatment of a between statement. Now in SQL Server, if you state the query as follows:

```
between upper_bound and lower_bound
```

SQL Server will still process the query, but the row estimate will always be 0 because it will return an empty result set.

Also note that for any like clause where the first character of the matching string isn't a wildcard character, it's treated as < upper bound and >= lower bound.

Column Information

```
VAR (L:0xf14d1e)  (varname:amount right:f14d6a varno:1 colid:2
coltype:0x3c colen:8 coloff:6 colprec:19 colscale:4 vartypeid:11
varnext:f14c6a varusecnt:1 varstat:90 varlevel:0 varsubq:0)
```

- ▪ varname indicates the name of the column involved in the search clause. In this example, the column name is amount.

- ▪ varno is the table in the FROM clause to which this column belongs.

- ▪ colid is the ID of the column in the table, as contained in syscolumns.

- ▪ vartypeid is the datatype ID of the column. To find out the actual datatype name for this example:

  ```
  select name from systypes where type = 11
  ```

Datatype and Value of the SARG

```
MONEY (R:0xf14d6a)  (len:8 maxlen:4 prec:6 scale:0 value:
400000.00)
```

This line indicates the datatype and value of the search argument supplied. In this example, the datatype is MONEY and the value is 400000.00. Note that SQL Server converts a constant value to the column's datatype.

Scoring the Indexes That Match the Search Clause

After identifying all the search clauses, the next step is to match the search clauses with any available indexes on the table. For any index that can satisfy the query, a cost estimate in terms of page I/Os will be generated for each index to determine the most efficient index to use. This cost estimate will be based on distribution steps, index density, or built-in percentage estimates if the distribution steps and density information are either unavailable or can't be used.

Unique *type* index found — return rows 1 pages *N*

If the search argument is an equality operation (=), SQL Server knows that only a single row can match a single value. The index *type* can be either clustered or nonclustered. The page cost is estimated to be a single data page read plus a number of index page reads equal to the number of levels in the index. Consider the following example:

```
select company from pt_sample_CIid
where id = 1000


******************************
Entering q_score_index() for table 'pt_sample_CIid' (varno 0).
The table has 5772 rows and 243 pages.
Scoring the search clause:
AND (!:0xf14c6e)  (andstat:0xa)
  EQ (L:0xf14c5a)  (rsltype:0x38 rsllen:4 rslprec:10 rslscale:0
  opstat:0x0)
    VAR (L:0xf14c10)  (varname:id right:f14c40 varno:0 colid:1
    coltype:0x38 colen:4 coloff:2 colprec:10 colscale:0 vartypeid:7
    varnext:f14b4a varusecnt:1 varstat:84 varlevel:0 varsubq:0)
    INT4 (R:0xf14c40)  (len:4 maxlen:4 prec:4 scale:0 value:1000)

Unique clustered index found—return rows 1 pages 2
Cheapest index is index 1, costing 2 pages and generating 1 rows per
scan.
Search argument selectivity is 0.000173.
******************************
```

A unique index was found on the id (varname = id) column for the table pt_sample_CIid, and the search argument is an equality operator. The cost of finding a single row for this table is two pages: one index page read to find the data page, plus one data page read.

If the index isn't a unique index, the optimizer must estimate the number of matching rows by using the index statistics.

Scoring clause for index *index_id*

This line indicates which index (by index ID) matches the search clause and therefore is being evaluated as a potential access path. If the index ID equals 1, it's the clustered index. If the index ID is between 2 and 250, then it's scoring the corresponding nonclustered index:

```
Scoring clause for index 1
Relop bits are: 0x10
Qualifying stat page; pgno: 913 steps: 197
Search value: MONEY value:300000.00
No steps for search value—qualpage for LT search value finds
value between steps 18 and 19—use betweenSC
Estimate: indid 1, selectivity 9.060227e-001, rows 6597 pages 72
```

Scoring SARG interval, upper ¦ lower bound

If the query contains an interval search (that is, between, like, or a pair of greater-than and less-than predicates), SQL Server scores both the upper and lower bound for the interval. It determines the location of the upper bound on the statistics page, determines the location of the lower bound on the statistics page, and estimates the matching number of rows between upper and lower bounds:

```
Scoring clause for index 1
Relop bits are: 0x8,0x4
Scoring SARG interval, upper bound.
Qualifying stat page; pgno: 913 steps: 197
Search value: MONEY value:120000.00
No steps for search value—qualpage for LT search value finds
value between steps 173 and 174—use betweenSC
Scoring SARG interval, lower bound.
Qualifying stat page; pgno: 913 steps: 197
Search value: MONEY value:100000.00
No steps for search value—qualpage for LT search value finds
value between steps 168 and 169—use betweenSC
Net selectivity of interval: 2.551812e-002
Estimate: indid 1, selectivity 2.551812e-002, rows 185 pages 3
```

Relop bits are: ...

You can ignore this line. It simply reiterates the integer bitmap value of the conditional operator.

Index Statistics

The next few lines of output provide information on which index statistics (distribution steps, density, or built-in percentages) are used to estimate row count (see Chapter 13 for a discussion of index statistics and the distribution page). The following sections examine the different alternatives and what the output looks like.

Qualifying stat page; pgno: *pagenum* steps: *numsteps*

A valid statistics page was found for this index at logical page address *pagenum*. The statistics page has *numsteps* steps on it. The optimizer will base its decisions on the information on this statistics page when evaluating that index.

TIP

One of the more common errors made by newcomers to SQL Server is to create a table and all indexes on it before loading the data. If `update statistics` isn't run subsequent to the data load, there will be no statistics page for any of the indexes. SQL Server won't create a statistics page for an index created on any empty table, because there's nothing with which to populate the statistics page.

Also, remember to keep your statistics up to date so that the optimizer can make more valid assumptions about your data distribution when estimating the number of matching rows. The rough rule of thumb is to update statistics when more than 10–20 percent of your data has been modified/inserted/deleted.

If you want to examine the contents of the distribution page, you can use the `dbcc page` command (see Chapter 11), but the contents will be displayed in hexadecimal format and aren't very useful. Fortunately, SQL Server provides a `dbcc` command that displays the contents of the distribution page in a readable format. The command is as follows:

```
dbcc show_statistics (table_name, index_name)
```

Following is a fraction of the output for the clustered index, `tx_CIid`, on the `id` column for the `pt_tx_CIid` table:

```
Updated               Rows      Steps     Density
------------------    -----     -----     ------------
May 19 1996  8:02AM   7282      330       0.000213248

All density           Columns
------------------    ----------------
0.000213248           id

Steps
-----------.
          1
         65
        214
        271
        369
        497
        604
        656
        745
```

```
                849
                961
       .
       .
       .
             316606
             316996
             317462
             317913
             318409
             318866
```

Here you can see the values stored in the distribution steps as well as the stored index densities.

If you prefer to see the index statistics in a graphical format, check out the demonstration copy of Aurora Distribution Viewer on the CD included with this book. In addition to providing multiple ways of graphing the distribution page values, it also can keep a history of distribution page values for tracking the effectiveness of your update statistics strategy.

Search Value: *DATATYPE* value: *N*

This line repeats the datatype and value information from the search clause. This is the value that will be used for comparison against the index statistics.

Match found on statistics page

An exact match of the search value was found on the distribution page. This will be followed by one of the following four messages to indicate where the match was found within the distribution page and the number of steps it matched:

- equal to a single row (1st or last)—use endsingleSC

  The search value matched the first or last step on the distribution page.

- equal to several rows including 1st or last—use endseveralSC

  The search value matched multiple steps near the beginning or end of the distribution page.

- equal to single row in middle of page—use midsingleSC

  The search value matched a single row in the middle of the distribution page.

- equal to several rows in middle of page—use midseveralSC

  The search value matched multiple rows in the middle of the distribution page.

If no exact match is found on the distribution page, SQL Server looks to see which steps the search value would fall between.

No steps for search value – qualpage for LT search value finds

This indicates that no exact match for the search value was found on the distribution page. Based upon where within the distribution steps the search value falls, SQL Server will display one of the following three messages:

- ◼ value between steps *K* and *K+1* — use betweenSC

  The search value falls between the two steps listed.

- ◼ value < first step — use outsideSC

  The search value is less than the first distribution step value.

- ◼ value > last step — use outsideSC

  The search value is greater than the last distribution step value.

If the search value falls less than the first step or greater than the last step, this could indicate that statistics are out of date, especially if the index is created on a sequential key value. This could be a potential problem if a large number of rows are outside the distribution steps, but the optimizer estimates that there are only a few rows. If the estimate of where the search value falls seems inconsistent with your knowledge of the actual data, it's probably time to update statistics for that table or index.

Because SQL Server knows the number of rows between steps, it can make an estimate of the number of rows that match the search value, depending on which of the preceding matches is applied.

The use *XXXXXX*SC statement indicates the algorithm that will be applied to estimate the number of matching rows. The row estimate is determined as a factor of the number of distribution steps matched and the index density. For example, if a search value falls between two step values, SQL Server can't determine exactly how many duplicates there may be for the search value between the two steps. The estimate will be the smaller of the index density times the number of rows in the table, or the number of rows between the steps.

Consider a table with 100,000 rows, 333 steps on the distribution page, and an index density of .00025. The search clause is an equality search (column = constant). If a search value is found between two steps, the number of candidate rows is

  100,000 rows / 333 steps – 2 = 298 rows between 2 steps

  or

  100,000 rows × .00025 = 25 rows based on index density

In this case, SQL Server would use the density estimate that 25 rows would match the search argument rather than 298. This is the typical case for an equality search when the search value falls between two steps.

For search arguments other than equality searches (column = constant), where the search value falls between two steps, the row estimates are determined as follows:

$$\text{column < constant} \quad \text{selectivity} = ((\text{stepnum} + .5 / \text{numsteps}) - (\text{density} /2))$$

$$\text{column <= constant} \quad \text{selectivity} = ((\text{stepnum} + .5 / \text{numsteps}) + (\text{density} /2))$$

$$\text{column > constant} \quad \text{selectivity} = 1 - ((\text{stepnum} + .5 / \text{numsteps}) - (\text{density} /2))$$

$$\text{column >= constant} \quad \text{selectivity} = 1 + ((\text{stepnum} + .5 / \text{numsteps}) - (\text{density} /2))$$

Net selectivity of interval: #.###

This information is displayed if a range search that matches an available index is specified in the query. A between clause will display this information twice, once each for the lower and upper bound. The net selectivity is based on the number of steps in the range.

When Distribution Steps Can't Be Used

A common problem for the optimizer is search arguments that are valid but don't have known values until runtime. This occurs when the constant expression in the search argument contains a local variable or is compared against a subquery. For example:

```
select count(*) from pt_tx_CIamountNCamount
    where amount > (select avg(amount) from pt_tx_CIamountNCamount)
```

or:

```
declare @max_amt money
select @max_amt = max(amount) from pt_tx_CIamountNCamount
select count(*) from pt_tx_CIamountNCamount
    where amount = @max_amt
```

There's no way for the optimizer to know what value the subquery or local variable will have at runtime, because the value can't be determined until the query is executed, and the query can't be executed until a query plan is generated. Sounds like a bit of a Catch-22, doesn't it? Actually, the only limitation on the optimizer in these cases is that it can't use the distribution steps to estimate row counts for equality operations; rather, it has to use the *index density*. Index density is the percentage of unique values in the table. For any other type of operator (for example, >, <), the optimizer has to use built-in, or "magic" percentages. The magic percentages used are dependent on the type of operator:

equality (=)	10 percent
closed interval (>= and <, between)	25 percent
open interval (>, <, <=, >=)	33 percent

> **NOTE**
>
> In releases before SQL Server 6.0, the query optimizer would also be unable to resolve the value for search arguments where the constant expression contained a function, mathematical operation, or string concatenation. This restriction was removed in Version 6.0.
>
> SQL Server now resolves the function, mathematical operation, or string concatenation before invoking the query optimizer. The resulting value can then be compared against the distribution steps, if available, instead of using the index density or "magic" percentages.

When the distribution steps can't be used, the 302 output contains the following:

```
SARG is a subbed VAR or expr result or local variable (constat=number)—use
magicSC or densitySC
```

In most cases, it's preferable for the optimizer to compare values against the distribution steps instead of using the index density, and especially preferable over using the "magic" percentages. Consider the following example:

- 100,000 rows
- .00025 index density (4000 unique values)
- 20,000 rows where id = 100

```
declare @id int
select @id = 100
select count(*) from table_1 where id = @id
```

If the distribution steps were used, SQL Server would estimate that approximately 20,000 rows would match the search argument where id = 100. Because you're using a local variable, however, SQL Server will use the index density to estimate the number of rows, and, in this case, that would be 100,000 × .00025, or 25 rows. Quite a significant difference in row estimates between the two approaches, possibly resulting in a less-than-efficient query plan being chosen.

Another situation where the optimizer is forced to use the "magic" percentages is when the distribution page is unavailable, or no index exists on the column specified in the search argument. With no index on the column, SQL Server will just automatically use the "magic" percentages—no information on index selection is displayed:

```
select count(*) from pt_sample
where id = 1000

********************************
Entering q_score_index() for table 'pt_sample' (varno 0).
The table has 5772 rows and 244 pages.
Scoring the search clause:
AND (!:0xf14d74)  (andstat:0xa)
  EQ (L:0xf14d60)  (rsltype:0x38 rsllen:4 rslprec:10 rslscale:0
```

```
opstat:0x0)
   VAR (L:0xf14db6)  (varname:id right:f14d46 varno:0 colid:1
   coltype:0x38 colen:4 coloff:2 colprec:10 colscale:0 vartypeid:7
   varusecnt:1 varstat:84 varlevel:0 varsubq:0)
   INT4 (R:0xf14d46)  (len:4 maxlen:4 prec:4 scale:0 value:1000)
```

```
Cheapest index is index 0, costing 244 pages and generating 577 rows
per scan.
Search argument selectivity is 0.100000.
*******************************
```

Notice that this query contains an equality operator. The last line states that the selectivity of the search argument is 0.100000, or 10 percent, the "magic" percentage for an equality operator.

If an index exists but no distribution page has been created, the following text is displayed:

```
No statistics page—use magicSC
```

Determining Final Cost Estimates and Selectivity of Indexes

After the row estimates have been determined, using one of the preceding methods, the next step is to determine the I/O cost estimates and overall selectivity of the indexes. Examine the 302 output for the following query:

```
select count(id) from pt_tx_CIamountNCamount
where amount > 300000
```

```
*******************************
Entering q_score_index() for table 'pt_tx_CIamountNCamount' (varno 0).
The table has 7282 rows and 88 pages.
Scoring the search clause:
AND (!:0xf14dac)  (andstat:0xa)
  GT (L:0xf14d98)  (rsltype:0x3c rsllen:8 rslprec:19 rslscale:4
  opstat:0x0)
    VAR (L:0xf14e26)  (varname:amount right:f14d7e varno:0 colid:2
    coltype:0x3c colen:8 coloff:6 colprec:19 colscale:4 vartypeid:11
    varnext:f14df6 varusecnt:1 varstat:90 varlevel:0 varsubq:0)
    MONEY (R:0xf14d7e)  (len:8 maxlen:4 prec:6 scale:0 value:
    300000.00)

Scoring clause for index 1
Relop bits are: 0x10
Qualifying stat page; pgno: 913 steps: 197
Search value: MONEY value:300000.00
No steps for search value—qualpage for LT search value finds
value between steps 0 and 1—use betweenSC
Estimate: indid 1, selectivity 9.973933e-001, rows 7263 pages 80
Scoring clause for index 2
Relop bits are: 0x1000,0x800,0x10
Qualifying stat page; pgno: 945 steps: 197
Search value: MONEY value:300000.00
No steps for search value—qualpage for LT search value finds
```

```
value between steps 0 and 1—use betweenSC
Estimate: indid 2, selectivity 9.973933e-001, rows 7263 pages 7320
Cheapest index is index 1, costing 80 pages and generating 7263 rows
per scan.
Search argument selectivity is 0.997393.
********************************
```

Estimate: indid *I*, selectivity #.###, rows *R* pages *P*

This information is displayed for each index considered, showing the estimated number of matching rows, the page I/O estimate to retrieve the rows, and the overall selectivity of the index, expressed as a floating point value of the percentage of matching rows.

In the preceding example, you see this information twice for the one search argument because you have two indexes on the amount column that can be considered.

For the clustered index, indid 1, you see the estimate of the number of matching rows to be 7263 rows, costing 80 pages to retrieve them. The selectivity is .997393, or approximately 99.7 percent of the rows in the table.

For the nonclustered index, indid 2, the number of matching rows is the same and selectivity is the same, but the I/O cost is 7320 pages.

Both of these alternatives will be compared against the cost of a table scan, which is equal to the total number of pages in the table. The access path resulting in the fewest number of page I/Os is selected as the cheapest approach and is the next bit of information displayed by the optimizer.

Cheapest index is index *I*, costing *P* pages and generating *R* rows per scan

This line merely reiterates the cost estimates for the index determined to be the cheapest access path. Note that if the index ID = 0, a table scan is the cheapest access path.

In the preceding example, the cheapest index is the clustered index (indid 1), resulting in 80 page I/Os. Note that this is only slightly less than a table scan (88 pages), because of the high number of matching rows. If there were no clustered index on the table, a table scan would have been cheaper than the nonclustered index (7320 pages).

Search argument selectivity is #.######

This line displays as a decimal value the selectivity of the chosen index for a search argument.

Scoring Join Clauses

After scoring all search arguments for the query, the next step is to score any join clauses. With joins, a specific value can't be looked up on the distribution page, because the value to be compared is entirely dependent on the row to be joined at runtime.

Therefore, similar to how you deal with search arguments with unknown values, the optimizer uses the index density to estimate the number of rows that match any single row in a join clause. If index density isn't available, the join selectivity is determined as follows:

1 / # of rows in smaller table

The following is an example of a query with join clauses and the resulting dbcc traceon (302) output:

```
select company, amount from pt_sample_CIid s, pt_tx_CIid t
where t.id = s.id


*******************************
Entering q_score_join() for table 'pt_sample_CIid' (varno 0).
The table has 5772 rows and 243 pages.
Scoring the join clause:
AND (!:0xf14d84)  (andstat:0x2)
  EQ (L:0xf14d70)  (rsltype:0x38 rsllen:4 rslprec:10 rslscale:0
  opstat:0x0)
    VAR (L:0xf14d28)  (varname:id right:f14cda varno:0 colid:1
    coltype:0x38 colen:4 coloff:2 colprec:10 colscale:0 vartypeid:7
    varnext:f14b4a varusecnt:1 varstat:84 varlevel:0 varsubq:0)
    VAR (R:0xf14cda)  (varname:id varno:1 colid:1 coltype:0x38
    colen:4 coloff:2 colprec:10 colscale:0 vartypeid:7 varnext:f14bb6
    varusecnt:1 varlevel:0 varsubq:0)

Unique clustered index found—return rows 1 pages 2
Cheapest index is index 1, costing 2 pages and generating 1 rows per
scan.
Join selectivity is 5772.
*******************************


*******************************
Entering q_score_join() for table 'pt_tx_CIid' (varno 1).
The table has 7282 rows and 118 pages.
Scoring the join clause:
AND (!:0xf14d84)  (andstat:0x2)
  EQ (L:0xf14d70)  (rsltype:0x38 rsllen:4 rslprec:10 rslscale:0
  opstat:0x0)
    VAR (L:0xf14cda)  (varname:id right:f14d28 varno:1 colid:1
    coltype:0x38 colen:4 coloff:2 colprec:10 colscale:0 vartypeid:7
    varnext:f14bb6 varusecnt:1 varstat:84 varlevel:0 varsubq:0)
    VAR (R:0xf14d28)  (varname:id right:f14cda varno:0 colid:1
    coltype:0x38 colen:4 coloff:2 colprec:10 colscale:0 vartypeid:7
    varnext:f14b4a varusecnt:1 varstat:884 varlevel:0 varsubq:0)

Scoring clause for index 1
Relop bits are: 0x80,0x4
Estimate: indid 1, selectivity 2.132651e-004, rows 1 pages 2
Cheapest index is index 1, costing 2 pages and generating 1 rows per
```

```
scan.
Join selectivity is 4689.
*******************************
```

Scoring the join clause

This line indicates that the optimizer is now scoring a join clause for this query rather than a search clause. Notice that the output is pretty much identical to the search clause output, except for the fact that you won't see it using distribution steps to estimate the query cost.

Join selectivity is *N*

SQL Server displays the join selectivity as an integer representation of the denominator of the index density. In the example, the clustered index on `pt_sample_CIid` is a unique index. Because the index density is determined as 1/# of unique values in the table, for `pt_sample_CIid`, this would be 1/5772. Therefore, the join selectivity is the denominator of the index density, or 5772.

For the `pt_tx_CIid` table, the index isn't unique, so the density information is used to determine the number of distinct values in the table. In this case, the index density is .0002132651. Multiply that times the number of rows in the table to get the estimate of the number of rows that match any single unknown value:

$$7282 \times .0002132651 = 1.55 \text{ rows}$$

which the server rounds down to approximately 1 matching row per lookup. Therefore, the join selectivity is as follows:

$$1 / .0002132651 = 4689 \text{ unique values in pt\_tx\_CIid}$$

After you have examined the search clause and join clause index selection process, the next step is to examine the join order processing phase.

Cost join selectivity is *N*. Best join selectivity is *N*.

If a table involved in the join also contains a search argument, SQL Server estimates the best join selectivity as the selectivity of the join clause or the search clause, whichever is lower. Look at the previous example with an added search argument:

```
select company, amount from pt_sample_CIid s, pt_tx_CIid t
where t.id = s.id
and t.amount > 400000

*******************************
Entering q_score_index() for table 'pt_tx_CIid' (varno 1).
The table has 7282 rows and 118 pages.
Scoring the search clause:
```

```
AND (!:0xf14e14)  (andstat:0xa)
  GT (L:0xf14df4)  (rsltype:0x3c rsllen:8 rslprec:19 rslscale:4
  opstat:0x0)
    VAR (L:0xf14bb6)  (varname:amount right:f14dda varno:1 colid:2
    coltype:0x3c colen:8 coloff:6 colprec:19 colscale:4 vartypeid:11
    varusecnt:2 varstat:91 varlevel:0 varsubq:0)
    MONEY (R:0xf14dda)  (len:8 maxlen:4 prec:6 scale:0 value:
    400000.00)

Cheapest index is index 0, costing 118 pages and generating 2403 rows
per scan.
Search argument selectivity is 0.330000.
*******************************


*******************************
Entering q_score_join() for table 'pt_sample_CIid' (varno 0).
The table has 5772 rows and 243 pages.
Scoring the join clause:
AND (!:0xf14e08)  (andstat:0x2)
  EQ (L:0xf14d70)  (rsltype:0x38 rsllen:4 rslprec:10 rslscale:0
  opstat:0x0)
    VAR (L:0xf14d28)  (varname:id right:f14cda varno:0 colid:1
    coltype:0x38 colen:4 coloff:2 colprec:10 colscale:0 vartypeid:7
    varnext:f14b4a varusecnt:1 varstat:84 varlevel:0 varsubq:0)
    VAR (R:0xf14cda)  (varname:id varno:1 colid:1 coltype:0x38
    colen:4 coloff:2 colprec:10 colscale:0 vartypeid:7 varnext:f14bb6
    varusecnt:1 varlevel:0 varsubq:0)

Unique clustered index found—return rows 1 pages 2
Cheapest index is index 1, costing 2 pages and generating 1 rows per
scan.
Join selectivity is 5772.
*******************************


*******************************
Entering q_score_join() for table 'pt_tx_CIid' (varno 1).
The table has 7282 rows and 118 pages.
Scoring the join clause:
AND (!:0xf14e08)  (andstat:0x2)
  EQ (L:0xf14d70)  (rsltype:0x38 rsllen:4 rslprec:10 rslscale:0
  opstat:0x0)
    VAR (L:0xf14cda)  (varname:id right:f14d28 varno:1 colid:1
    coltype:0x38 colen:4 coloff:2 colprec:10 colscale:0 vartypeid:7
    varnext:f14bb6 varusecnt:1 varstat:84 varlevel:0 varsubq:0)
    VAR (R:0xf14d28)  (varname:id right:f14cda varno:0 colid:1
    coltype:0x38 colen:4 coloff:2 colprec:10 colscale:0 vartypeid:7
    varnext:f14b4a varusecnt:1 varstat:884 varlevel:0 varsubq:0)

Scoring clause for index 1
Relop bits are: 0x80,0x4
Estimate: indid 1, selectivity 2.132651e-004, rows 1 pages 2
Cheapest index is index 1, costing 2 pages and generating 1 rows per
scan.
Cost join selectivity is 4689.
Best join selectivity is 2403.
*******************************
```

The cost join selectivity on the `pt_tx_CIid` table in this example is the same as the normal join selectivity estimated in the previous example, 4689. You also have a search clause on `pt_tx_CIid`, however, which is even more limiting than the join clause. By using the search argument, you can narrow the number of rows to be joined even further. Therefore, in this case, the best join selectivity is the number of rows matching the search clause.

Interpreting the dbcc traceon (310) Output

The dbcc traceon (310) trace flag displays the cost analysis of the possible join permutations for the query. Here's an example of the 310 output for a simple two-table join:

```
select company, amount from pt_tx_CIid t, pt_sample_CIid s
where t.id = s.id


QUERY IS CONNECTED

J_OPTIMIZE: Remaining vars=[0,1]

permutation: 0 - 1

NEW PLAN (total cost = 3544214):
JPLAN (0x391f594) varno=0 indexid=0 totcost=1760 pathtype=sclause
class=join optype=? method=NESTED ITERATION outerrows=1 rows=7282
joinsel=1 lp=110 pp=110 cpages=110 ctotpages=110 corder=1 cstat=0x20
matcost=25439 matpages=55 crows=7282 cjoinsel=1

JPLAN (0x391f5f0) varno=1 indexid=0 totcost=3542454 pathtype=sclause
class=join optype=? method=NESTED ITERATION outerrows=7282 rows=7282
joinsel=4689 lp=1769526 pp=243 cpages=243 ctotpages=243 corder=1
cstat=0x20 crows=5772 cjoinsel=1 joinmap=[0]


NEW PLAN (total cost = 34290):
JPLAN (0x391f594) varno=0 indexid=0 totcost=1760 pathtype=sclause
class=join optype=? method=NESTED ITERATION outerrows=1 rows=7282
joinsel=1 lp=110 pp=110 cpages=110 ctotpages=110 corder=1 cstat=0x20
matcost=25439 matpages=55 crows=7282 cjoinsel=1

JPLAN (0x391f5f0) varno=1 indexid=1 totcost=32530 pathtype=join
class=join optype=? method=NESTED ITERATION outerrows=7282 rows=7282
joinsel=4689 lp=14564 pp=243 cpages=2 ctotpages=243 corder=1
cstat=0x4 crows=1 cjoinsel=5772 joinmap=[0] jnvar=0 refindid=0
refcost=0 refpages=0 reftotpages=0 ordercol[0]=1 ordercol[1]=1

WORK PLAN (total cost = 35170):

permutation: 1 - 0
WORK PLAN (total cost = 1275268):

NEW PLAN (total cost = 28516):
JPLAN (0x391f594) varno=1 indexid=0 totcost=3888 pathtype=sclause
class=join optype=? method=NESTED ITERATION outerrows=1 rows=5772
joinsel=1 lp=243 pp=243 cpages=243 ctotpages=243 corder=1 cstat=0x20
matcost=24799 matpages=165 crows=5772 cjoinsel=1

JPLAN (0x391f5f0) varno=0 indexid=1 totcost=24628 pathtype=join
class=join optype=? method=NESTED ITERATION outerrows=5772 rows=7282
```

```
joinsel=4689 lp=11544 pp=110 cpages=2 ctotpages=110 corder=1
cstat=0x0 crows=1 cjoinsel=4689 joinmap=[1] jnvar=1 refindid=0
refcost=0 refpages=0 reftotpages=0 ordercol[0]=1 ordercol[1]=1

WORK PLAN (total cost = 31156):

CHOSE PLAN:
JPLAN (0x391e9f4) varno=1 indexid=0 totcost=3888 pathtype=sclause
class=join optype=? method=NESTED ITERATION outerrows=1 rows=5772
joinsel=1 lp=243 pp=243 cpages=243 ctotpages=243 corder=1 cstat=0x20
matcost=24799 matpages=165 crows=5772 cjoinsel=1


CHOSE PLAN:
JPLAN (0x391ea50) varno=0 indexid=1 totcost=24628 pathtype=join
class=join optype=? method=NESTED ITERATION outerrows=5772 rows=7282
joinsel=4689 lp=11544 pp=110 cpages=2 ctotpages=110 corder=1
cstat=0x0 crows=1 cjoinsel=4689 joinmap=[1] jnvar=1 refindid=0
refcost=0 refpages=0 reftotpages=0 ordercol[0]=1 ordercol[1]=1



TOTAL # PERMUTATIONS: 2
TOTAL # PLANS CONSIDERED: 6

FINAL PLAN (total cost = 28516):
JPLAN (0x391e9f4) varno=1 indexid=0 totcost=3888 pathtype=sclause
class=join optype=SUBSTITUTE method=NESTED ITERATION outerrows=1
rows=5772 joinsel=1 lp=243 pp=243 cpages=243 ctotpages=243 corder=1
cstat=0x20 matcost=24799 matpages=165 crows=5772 cjoinsel=1

JPLAN (0x391ea50) varno=0 indexid=1 totcost=24628 pathtype=join
class=join optype=SUBSTITUTE method=NESTED ITERATION outerrows=5772
rows=7282 joinsel=4689 lp=11544 pp=110 cpages=2 ctotpages=110
corder=1 cstat=0x0 crows=1 cjoinsel=4689 joinmap=[1] jnvar=1
refindid=0 refcost=0 refpages=0 reftotpages=0 ordercol[0]=1
ordercol[1]=1
```

Again, this information at first glance appears a bit cryptic, but the following sections give you the keys that you need to wade through this information and fully comprehend what's going in the join processing phase of your query.

QUERY IS [NOT] CONNECTED

This statement indicates whether the proper number of join clauses have been specified to avoid a Cartesian product. You typically hope to see that the query is connected, because Cartesian products can be very expensive in terms of I/O, even on moderate-size tables.

J_OPTIMIZE: Remaining vars = [...]

This line indicates the beginning of the join order processing for the tables in the query. The numbers specified in the brackets correspond to the tables in the order listed in the FROM clause. These numbers are the same numbers assigned during the search clause processing phase (that is, varno).

permutation: 0 - 1 - ...

If this is a multi-table query containing a join, this statement indicates the join order being costed out. This information is repeated for each valid join order that the optimizer considers (for example, 0 - 1 - 2, 2 - 0 - 1, and so on). The numbers correspond to the tables as listed in the query's FROM clause:

> 0 = The first table in the FROM clause (varno = 0)
>
> 1 = The second table in the FROM clause (varno = 1), and so on

NEW PLAN (total cost = ######)

This statement will be printed for each join permutation considered. The total cost indicates the total I/O cost calculated for this plan, in milliseconds.

Following the NEW PLAN line is the JPLAN information, which is repeated for each table in the query. The order in which they appear in the output is the order in which they're joined for this permutation. The first JPLAN listed under NEW PLAN is being considered as the outermost table, the second NEW PLAN is the first inner table, the third JPLAN would be the second inner table, and so on. The output looks similar to the following example:

```
JPLAN (0x391f5f0) varno=1 indexid=1 totcost=32530 pathtype=join
class=join optype=? method=NESTED ITERATION outerrows=7282 rows=7282
joinsel=4689 lp=14564 pp=243 cpages=2 ctotpages=243 corder=1
cstat=0x4 crows=1 cjoinsel=5772 joinmap=[0] jnvar=0 refindid=0
refcost=0 refpages=0 reftotpages=0 ordercol[0]=1 ordercol[1]=1
```

This information is somewhat cryptic, but when you learn to decipher it, you'll see that it contains a bunch of useful information. (Some of the variables are for Microsoft SQL Server engineers to use to debug the query optimizer, and don't provide information useful for monitoring the optimization of query plans.) Table 15.2 shows what some of the more useful variables represent.

Table 15.2. Useful variables displayed by `dbcc traceon (310)` JPLAN output.

Variable	Description
varno	The table number, as listed in the FROM clause (0, 1, …). Matches the varno listed in the 302 output.
indexid	The ID of the index being used on this table for this permutation: 0 = base table 1 = clustered >1 and <= 250 = nonclustered
totcost	The total I/O cost in milliseconds for this table for this permutation. This is the information displayed for the chosen plan as the cost estimate in the showplan output when the dbcc traceon (330) flag is turned on.
pathtype	The access path being used for this table for this permutation: sclause—search clause (using index or table scan to find matching rows) join—join clause orstruct—OR strategy (using dynamic index)
method	The search method used to process this table: NESTED ITERATION—The standard method for reading from the table, making one or more passes (iterations). REFORMATTING—Using the reformatting strategy: building a temporary clustered index on-the-fly. OR OPTIMIZATION—Using the OR strategy: dynamic index.
outerrows	The number of iterations to be performed on this table; corresponds to the number of rows in the outer table. For the outermost table, outerrows is 1.
rows	The estimated number of matching rows in this table. This information comes from the search clause processing phase and is based on the index statistics or built-in statistics. The value here corresponds to the value reported in the 302 output for this table, using the specified index.
joinsel	The best cost join selectivity as reported by the 302 output for this table, using the specified index.
lp	The estimated number of logical page reads. This value is equal to the number of pages per lookup (cpages) times the number of iterations (outerrows).
pp	The estimated total number of physical page reads. For the outer table, this value equals the total number of pages scanned for the single pass of the table. For an inner table, this value equals the total number of pages physically read after all iterations.

Variable	Description
cpages	The estimated number of page I/Os per lookup (index + data pages).
ctotpages	The total number of individual pages to be accessed for this table. If the inner table size is less than the size of the data cache, the total number of physical page reads is the same as the total number of pages to be accessed (ctotpages) for this table. If the table is larger than the data cache size, the total number of physical page reads is equal to the number of pages per lookup (cpages) times the number of iterations (outerrows), or the same as the number of logical page reads.
crows	The estimated number of data rows scanned per lookup.
corder	The ID of the leading column of the index (corresponds to colid in syscolumns for this table).
cjoinsel	The join selectivity for this index for this table, as reported by the 302 output.
matcost	The estimated cost of materializing the left operand of a merge join into a worktable.
matpages	The estimated number of pages in the worktable materialized for a merge join.
	The following values are displayed when the reformatting strategy is considered (they also show up when an index is used on the inner table, but the values are all 0):
refindid	The ID of the temporary clustered index created by the reformatting strategy to be used to satisfy the query.
refcost	The estimated I/O cost, in milliseconds, to apply the reformatting strategy (Chapter 13 explains how this value is determined).
refpages	The number of pages per lookup, using the temporary clustered index.
reftotpages	The total number of pages to be accessed for this table when the reformatting strategy is applied.
ordercol[#]	The column IDs of the joining columns. For the query select * from T1, T2, where T1.a = T2.b, [0] indicates the ID of the first column in the join (T1.a), [1] indicates the ID of the second column in the join (T2.b).

Merge join processing is a new feature of the optimizer in SQL Server 6.5. Merge join processing is similar to the reformatting strategy. Consider the query on the following page:

```
SELECT *
  FROM T1, T2, T3
  WHERE T1.c1 = T2.c1
    AND T2.c2 = T3.c2
```

Suppose that T3 has a clustered index on column c2. When the optimizer picks the merge join, it takes the results of the join between T1 and T2 and puts those rows into a worktable. The worktable is then sorted based on the join column of T3. The worktable is then joined to T3 based on that join column, and because the worktable is already sorted in that order, fewer I/Os are required.

If the optimizer determines that the total I/O cost of creating and sorting the worktable and joining against it is the cheapest way of processing the join, it will choose the merge join strategy.

The I/O cost for each table (totcost) is determined as follows:

> total logical page reads (lp) for each table × 2ms
>
> + (total physical page reads (pp) × 14ms)

The total plan cost is the sum of the total I/O cost (totcost) for each table in the query.

WORK PLAN (total cost = *N*)

This is a plan for which the optimizer began generating the query plan cost, but during processing determined the cost calculated thus far was greater than the cost of a plan already found. The optimizer skipped further processing of this plan.

IGNORING THIS PERMUTATION

At times, the optimizer will determine that some permutations are so unlikely to cost less than any plans examined thus far that it ignores those permutations altogether. This scheme saves processing time for the optimizer, but the optimizer may at times make the wrong assumption and ignore a plan that might be cheaper.

If you want to verify that the optimizer isn't ignoring a plan that may be cheaper, reverse the order of the tables in the FROM clause. This action causes the optimizer to process the table permutations in reverse order and estimate the I/O cost for the previously-ignored permutation. For example, consider the following query:

```
select company, amount from pt_tx t, pt_sample_lg s
where t.id = s.id
```

The 310 output for this query would be as follows:

```
QUERY IS CONNECTED
```

```
J_OPTIMIZE: Remaining vars=[0,1]

permutation: 0 - 1

NEW PLAN (total cost = 56461986):
JPLAN (0x2a3f594) varno=0 indexid=0 totcost=1392 pathtype=sclause
class=join optype=? method=NESTED ITERATION outerrows=1 rows=7282
joinsel=1 lp=87 pp=87 cpages=87 ctotpages=87 corder=0 cstat=0x0
matcost=25439 matpages=55 crows=7282 cjoinsel=1

JPLAN (0x2a3f5f0) varno=1 indexid=0 totcost=56460594 pathtype=sclause
class=join optype=? method=NESTED ITERATION outerrows=7282 rows=92352
joinsel=7282 lp=28203186 pp=3873 cpages=3873 ctotpages=3873 corder=0
cstat=0x0 crows=92352 cjoinsel=1 joinmap=[0]


NEW PLAN (total cost = 197498):
JPLAN (0x2a3f594) varno=0 indexid=0 totcost=1392 pathtype=sclause
class=join optype=? method=NESTED ITERATION outerrows=1 rows=7282
joinsel=1 lp=87 pp=87 cpages=87 ctotpages=87 corder=0 cstat=0x0
matcost=25439 matpages=55 crows=7282 cjoinsel=1

JPLAN (0x2a3f5f0) varno=1 indexid=1 totcost=196106 pathtype=join
class=join optype=? method=REFORMATTING outerrows=7282 rows=92352
joinsel=7282 lp=14564 pp=2431 cpages=2 ctotpages=2431 corder=1
cstat=0x0 joinmap=[0] jnvar=0 refindid=1 refcost=132944 refpages=2
reftotpages=2431


WORK PLAN (total cost = 198378):
JPLAN (0x2a3f594) varno=0 indexid=0 totcost=2272 pathtype=sclause
class=join status=0x10 optype=? method=NESTED ITERATION outerrows=1
rows=7282 joinsel=1 lp=55 pp=55 cpages=87 ctotpages=87 corder=0
cstat=0x0 matcost=25439 matpages=55 crows=7282 cjoinsel=1

JPLAN (0x2a3f5f0) varno=1 indexid=1 totcost=196106 pathtype=join
class=join optype=? method=REFORMATTING outerrows=7282 rows=92352
joinsel=7282 lp=14564 pp=2431 cpages=2 ctotpages=2431 corder=1
cstat=0x0 joinmap=[0] jnvar=0 refindid=1 refcost=132944 refpages=2
reftotpages=2431


permutation: 1 - 0
IGNORING THIS PERMUTATION

CHOSE PLAN:
JPLAN (0x2a3e9f4) varno=0 indexid=0 totcost=1392 pathtype=sclause
class=join optype=? method=NESTED ITERATION outerrows=1 rows=7282
joinsel=1 lp=87 pp=87 cpages=87 ctotpages=87 corder=0 cstat=0x0
matcost=25439 matpages=55 crows=7282 cjoinsel=1


CHOSE PLAN:
JPLAN (0x2a3ea50) varno=1 indexid=1 totcost=196106 pathtype=join
class=join optype=? method=REFORMATTING outerrows=7282 rows=92352
joinsel=7282 lp=14564 pp=2431 cpages=2 ctotpages=2431 corder=1
cstat=0x0 joinmap=[0] jnvar=0 refindid=1 refcost=132944 refpages=2
reftotpages=2431
```

466

```
TOTAL # PERMUTATIONS: 2
TOTAL # PLANS CONSIDERED: 3

FINAL PLAN (total cost = 197498):
JPLAN (0x2a3e9f4) varno=0 indexid=0 totcost=1392 pathtype=sclause
class=join optype=SUBSTITUTE method=NESTED ITERATION outerrows=1
rows=7282 joinsel=1 lp=87 pp=87 cpages=87 ctotpages=87 corder=0
cstat=0x0 matcost=25439 matpages=55 crows=7282 cjoinsel=1

JPLAN (0x2a3ea50) varno=2 indexid=1 totcost=196106 pathtype=join
class=join optype=SUBSTITUTE method=REFORMATTING outerrows=7282
rows=92352 joinsel=7282 lp=14564 pp=2431 cpages=2 ctotpages=2431
corder=1 cstat=0x0 joinmap=[0] jnvar=0 refindid=1 refcost=132944
refpages=2 reftotpages=2431
```

I'll first break out the individual components of this output.

The first join order examined is from pt_tx to pt_sample_lg (0 - 1). The first plan considered for this join order (NEW PLAN (total cost = 56461986) is a table scan on the outer table, pt_tx (varno=0, indexid=0), and a table scan on the inner table, pt_sample_lg (varno=1, indexid=0). The total cost of the first plan considered is 451,252,368 milliseconds.

The processing method used on both tables in the first plan considered is the normal query processing (NESTED ITERATION). Because the outer table, pt_tx, is scanned only once (outerrows=1), the number of logical page reads (lp=87) is the same as the physical reads (pp=87, cpages=87 × outerrows=1). The total I/O cost (totcost=1392) for the pt_tx table is as follows:

> 87 logical page reads × 2ms = 174ms
> + 87 physical page reads × 14ms = 1218ms
> = 1392 ms

Next, the optimizer determines the total I/O cost for the pt_sample_lg table (varno=1).

The total number of pages per iteration on the pt_sample_lg is also 3,873 pages (cpages=3873) because a table scan would be performed for each iteration. The total number of iterations performed is 7,282 (outerrows=7282). This value equals the total number of rows in the outer table, pt_tx (varno=0, rows=7282). Therefore, the total number of logical page reads (and in this example, physical page reads as well) is as follows:

> 7282 iterations
> × 3873 pages per iteration
> = 28,203,186 total logical page reads

Because the table will fit entirely in cache, only the first iteration will incur physical I/Os. Therefore, the total I/O cost for the inner table, pt_sample_lg, is 56,461,986 milliseconds (varno=1, totcost=56461986). This value is determined as follows:

> 28,203,186 logical page reads × 2 ms = 56,406,372ms
>
> 3,873 physical page reads × 14 ms = 54,222ms
>
> = 56,460,594 ms

The total I/O cost for the first plan is estimated to be 56,461,986 milliseconds, or approximately 15.6 hours!

Because neither of these tables has a usable index for this query, the optimizer considered applying the reformatting strategy on the `pt_sample_lg` table (varno=1, method=REFORMATTING). This is the second plan considered (NEW PLAN (total cost = 197498)). The costs for the outer table, `pt_tx` (varno=0) are the same for this plan, but the cost for `pt_sample_lg` are the costs associated with applying the reformatting strategy on `pt_sample_lg`.

The reformatting strategy itself has an I/O cost of 132,944 milliseconds (refcost=132944). The number of pages per lookup using the temporary clustered index (refindid=1, indexid=1) is 2 (refpages=2, cpages=2), and the total number of pages accessed is 2,431 (reftotpages=2431, ctotpages=2431). Because you now have a clustered index on the table and do not have to read the entire table into cache, the number of physical page reads is the same as the number of pages accessed, 2,431 (pp=2431). The total number of logical I/Os is as follows:

2 pages (cpages=2)
× 7282 iterations (outerrows=7282)
= 14,564 logical page reads

The total I/O cost for the `pt_sample_lg`, including the cost of reformatting, is as follows:

14564 × 2ms = 29,128ms
+ 2431 × 14ms = 34,034ms
+ 132,944ms (cost of reformatting)
= 196,106ms (totcost=196106)

The total query plan cost is 197,498ms (NEW PLAN (total cost = 197498)). This is a more reasonable 3.3 minutes. Quite obviously, the cost of using the reformatting strategy is considerably less than the cost of joining via a table scan on the inner table. At this point, however, the optimizer makes the assumption that the reformatting plan is the lowest plan to be found and ignores the alternative permutation of `pt_sample_lg` as the outer table and `pt_tx` as the inner table. Just for fun, and because I am always somewhat skeptical myself, I'll force the optimizer to evaluate this alternative first by switching the order of the tables in the FROM clause:

```
select company, amount from pt_sample_lg s, pt_tx t
where t.id = s.id
```

The 310 output for this example is as follows:

```
QUERY IS CONNECTED

J_OPTIMIZE: Remaining vars=[0,1]

permutation: 0 - 1

NEW PLAN (total cost = 16132434):
JPLAN (0x2a3f594) varno=0 indexid=0 totcost=61968 pathtype=sclause
class=join optype=? method=NESTED ITERATION outerrows=1 rows=92352
joinsel=1 lp=3873 pp=3873 cpages=3873 ctotpages=3873 corder=0
cstat=0x0 matcost=255693 matpages=2639 crows=92352 cjoinsel=1
```

```
JPLAN (0x2a3f5f0) varno=1 indexid=0 totcost=16070466 pathtype=sclause
class=join optype=? method=NESTED ITERATION outerrows=92352
rows=92352 joinsel=7282 lp=8034624 pp=87 cpages=87 ctotpages=87
corder=0 cstat=0x0 crows=7282 cjoinsel=1 joinmap=[0]


NEW PLAN (total cost = 444178):
JPLAN (0x2a3f594) varno=0 indexid=0 totcost=61968 pathtype=sclause
class=join optype=? method=NESTED ITERATION outerrows=1 rows=92352
joinsel=1 lp=3873 pp=3873 cpages=3873 ctotpages=3873 corder=0
cstat=0x0 matcost=255693 matpages=2639 crows=92352 cjoinsel=1

JPLAN (0x2a3f5f0) varno=1 indexid=1 totcost=382210 pathtype=join
class=join optype=? method=REFORMATTING outerrows=92352 rows=92352
joinsel=7282 lp=184704 pp=44 cpages=2 ctotpages=44 corder=1 cstat=0x0
joinmap=[0] jnvar=0 refindid=1 refcost=12186 refpages=2
reftotpages=44

WORK PLAN (total cost = 486402):

permutation: 1 - 0
IGNORING THIS PERMUTATION

CHOSE PLAN:
JPLAN (0x2a3e9f4) varno=0 indexid=0 totcost=61968 pathtype=sclause
class=join optype=? method=NESTED ITERATION outerrows=1 rows=92352
joinsel=1 lp=3873 pp=3873 cpages=3873 ctotpages=3873 corder=0
cstat=0x0 matcost=255693 matpages=2639 crows=92352 cjoinsel=1



CHOSE PLAN:
JPLAN (0x2a3ea50) varno=1 indexid=1 totcost=382210 pathtype=join
class=join optype=? method=REFORMATTING outerrows=92352 rows=92352
joinsel=7282 lp=184704 pp=44 cpages=2 ctotpages=44 corder=1 cstat=0x0
joinmap=[0] jnvar=0 refindid=1 refcost=12186 refpages=2
reftotpages=44




TOTAL # PERMUTATIONS: 2
TOTAL # PLANS CONSIDERED: 3

FINAL PLAN (total cost = 444178):
JPLAN (0x2a3e9f4) varno=0 indexid=0 totcost=61968 pathtype=sclause
class=join optype=SUBSTITUTE method=NESTED ITERATION outerrows=1
rows=92352 joinsel=1 lp=3873 pp=3873 cpages=3873 ctotpages=3873
corder=0 cstat=0x0 matcost=255693 matpages=2639 crows=92352
cjoinsel=1

JPLAN (0x2a3ea50) varno=2 indexid=1 totcost=382210 pathtype=join
class=join optype=SUBSTITUTE method=REFORMATTING outerrows=92352
rows=92352 joinsel=7282 lp=184704 pp=44 cpages=2 ctotpages=44
corder=1 cstat=0x0 joinmap=[0] jnvar=0 refindid=1 refcost=12186
refpages=2 reftotpages=44
```

Notice that, in this example, the total plan I/O cost of applying the reformatting strategy on the pt_tx table with pt_sample_lg as the outer table is 444,178 milliseconds, or approximately 7.4 minutes. This plan is more than twice as long as the cheapest plan estimate in the previous example with pt_tx as the outer table. However, in this example, the optimizer is ignoring that permutation.

This is one of the rare instances when the order of the tables in the from clause does make a difference in whether the cheapest plan is chosen. It's not an overly significant difference in terms of actual query execution time, but it's a good example to show how to use the dbcc trace flags to validate the optimizer's decision.

OR **Strategy Example**

Just for fun, take a look at the dbcc traceon (302,310) output for a query with an or clause:

```
select * from pt_sample_CIid
    where id = 1000
        or id = 100000
```

I'll break out the 302, 310 output into parts and help you understand what's being evaluated/ estimated at each point:

```
********************************
Entering q_score_index() for table 'pt_sample_CIid' (varno 0).
The table has 5772 rows and 243 pages.
Scoring the search clause:

TREE IS NULL

q_new_orsarg built new SARGs:
AND (!:0x15d4be8)  (andstat:0x0)
  LE (L:0x15d4bd4)  (rsltype:0x0 rsllen:0 opstat:0x20)
    VAR (L:0x1276558)  (varname:id left:1276464 right:12764c4 varno:0
    colid:1 coltype(0x38):INT4 colen:4 coloff:2 colprec:10 colscale:0
    vartypeid:7 varusecnt:5 varstat:0xcd varlevel:0 varsubq:0)
    INT4 (R:0x12764c4)  (left:0x12764cc len:4 maxlen:4 prec:6 scale:0
    value:100000)
  AND (R:0x15d4bc8)  (andstat:0x0)
    GE (L:0x15d4bb4)  (rsltype:0x0 rsllen:0 opstat:0x20)
      VAR (L:0x1276558)  (varname:id left:1276464 right:12764c4
      varno:0 colid:1 coltype(0x38):INT4 colen:4 coloff:2 colprec:10
      colscale:0 vartypeid:7 varusecnt:5 varstat:0xcd varlevel:0
      varsubq:0)
      INT4 (R:0x1276464)  (left:0x127646c len:4 maxlen:4 prec:4
      scale:0 value:1000)

Scoring clause for index 1
Relop bits are: 0x80,0x40,0x8,0x4,0x1
Scoring SARG interval, upper bound.
Qualifying stat page; pgno: 2953 steps: 321
Search value: INT4 value:100000
No steps for search value—qualpage for LT search value finds
value between steps 272 and 273—use betweenSC
Scoring SARG interval, lower bound.
Qualifying stat page; pgno: 2953 steps: 321
```

```
Search value: INT4 value:1000
No steps for search value—qualpage for LT search value finds
value between steps 11 and 12—use betweenSC
Net selectivity of interval: 8.132573e-001
Estimate: indid 1, selectivity 8.132573e-001, rows 4694 pages 28
Unique clustered index found—return rows 2 pages 28
Cheapest index is index 1, costing 28 pages and generating 2 rows per
scan.
Search argument selectivity is 0.000347.
*******************************
```

Because the OR clause is on the same column, the optimizer evaluates the cost of using the clustered index on id in a single pass to find all rows where id = 1000 or 100000. Essentially, this is the same as doing a search where id is between 1000 and 100000. The cost of this approach would be 28 pages to yield 2 rows.

The next step is to evaluate the cost of performing two separate lookups on pt_sample_CIid, using the unique clustered index on id:

```
*******************************
Entering q_score_index() for table 'pt_sample_CIid' (varno 0).
The table has 5772 rows and 243 pages.
Scoring the search clause:
AND (!:0x1276516)  (andstat:0x8)
  EQ (L:0x127647e)  (rsltype:0x38 rsllen:4 rslprec:10 rslscale:0
  opstat:0x0)
    VAR (L:0x1276558)  (varname:id left:1276464 right:12764c4 varno:0
    colid:1 coltype(0x38):INT4 colen:4 coloff:2 colprec:10 colscale:0
    vartypeid:7 varusecnt:5 varstat:0x18cd varlevel:0 varsubq:0)
    INT4 (R:0x1276464)  (left:0x127646c len:4 maxlen:4 prec:4 scale:0
    value:1000)

Unique clustered index found—return rows 1 pages 2
Cheapest index is index 1, costing 2 pages and generating 1 rows per
scan.
Search argument selectivity is 0.000173.
*******************************
```

```
*******************************
Entering q_score_index() for table 'pt_sample_CIid' (varno 0).
The table has 5772 rows and 243 pages.
Scoring the search clause:
AND (!:0x1276522)  (andstat:0x8)
  EQ (L:0x12764de)  (rsltype:0x38 rsllen:4 rslprec:10 rslscale:0
  opstat:0x0)
    VAR (L:0x1276558)  (varname:id right:1276464 varno:0 colid:1
    coltype(0x38):INT4 colen:4 coloff:2 colprec:10 colscale:0
    vartypeid:7 varusecnt:5 varstat:0x18c5 varlevel:0 varsubq:0)
    INT4 (R:0x12764c4)  (left:0x12764cc len:4 maxlen:4 prec:6 scale:0
    value:100000)

Unique clustered index found—return rows 1 pages 2
Cheapest index is index 1, costing 2 pages and generating 1 rows per
scan.
Search argument selectivity is 0.000173.
*******************************
```

By using the unique clustered index in two separate lookups, it would cost 2 pages per lookup to find both qualifying rows, for a total of 4 pages.

This is the end of the search clause processing phase. Even though you have no join in the query, there's still a join processing phase to estimate the total I/O cost using the cheapest access method determined during the search clause processing. The 310 output for this query is as follows:

```
QUERY IS CONNECTED

J_OPTIMIZE: Remaining vars=[0]

permutation: 0

NEW PLAN (total cost = 64):
JPLAN (0x2a3f594) varno=0 indexid=0 totcost=64 pathtype=orstruct
class=join optype=? method=OR OPTIMIZATION outerrows=1 rows=2
joinsel=1 lp=4 pp=4 cpages=4 ctotpages=0 corder=0 cstat=0x8 crows=2
cjoinsel=0


CHOSE PLAN:
JPLAN (0x2a3e9f4) varno=0 indexid=0 totcost=64 pathtype=orstruct
class=join optype=? method=OR OPTIMIZATION outerrows=1 rows=2
joinsel=1 lp=4 pp=4 cpages=4 ctotpages=0 corder=0 cstat=0x8 crows=2
cjoinsel=0




TOTAL # PERMUTATIONS: 1
TOTAL # PLANS CONSIDERED: 1

FINAL PLAN (total cost = 64):
JPLAN (0x2a3e9f4) varno=0 indexid=0 totcost=64 pathtype=orstruct
class=join optype=SUBSTITUTE method=OR OPTIMIZATION outerrows=1
rows=2 joinsel=1 lp=4 pp=4 cpages=4 ctotpages=0 corder=0 cstat=0x8
crows=2 cjoinsel=0
```

This shows that the optimizer is using the OR strategy (method=OR OPTIMIZATION) rather than a table scan or normal single-scan index retrieval. Notice that the total physical page reads are 4 (pp=4) and the logical page reads are 4 (lp=4). This is the sum of the I/O cost for the two separate lookups, using the clustered index. Four pages is less than 28 pages, which would have been the I/O cost if a normal single-pass index scan were performed, and significantly less than 243 pages, which would have been the I/O cost of a table scan had the optimizer not been able to apply the OR strategy.

CHOSE PLAN

This section simply reiterates the plan that will be chosen for each table in the final plan.

TOTAL # PERMUTATIONS: *N*

This line represents the total number of possible join orders to be considered. See Chapter 13 for a discussion of how SQL Server evaluates all possible join permutations. For two tables, the number of permutations is 2. For four tables, the number of permutations is 24.

TOTAL # PLANS CONSIDERED: *N*

This value represents the total number of all possible query plans that the optimizer actually evaluated to determine the lowest query cost. This will be the sum of all query plans evaluated for each permutation considered. Any permutations that were ignored won't be figured into this value.

FINAL PLAN (total cost = *N*)

This section of the output simply reiterates the costing information for the permutation with the lowest estimated I/O cost. This is the "final" plan, which will be used to process the query. This is the information that is interpreted and displayed by the showplan output.

Using statistics io and statistics time

To this point, you've seen how the optimizer evaluates your queries, estimates the number of I/Os and the I/O processing time, and picks what it determines to be the cheapest query plan. The decisions that the optimizer makes are based on index statistics and row estimates.

Next you may want to compare the optimizer estimates against the actual number of I/Os and actual query processing time to verify the estimates being generated by the optimizer.

statistics io

SQL Server supplies a set option that causes the actual logical and physical page reads incurred by the query to be displayed. This option is the statistics io option and is turned on by executing the following command:

```
set statistics io on
```

If you're working in ISQL/w, you can set statistics io on by typing the command in a query window and executing it, or by turning on the Show Stats I/O option in the Query Options dialog box for that query window (see Figure 15.4).

FIGURE 15.4.

Turning on the statistics io *option for an* ISQL/w *query window.*

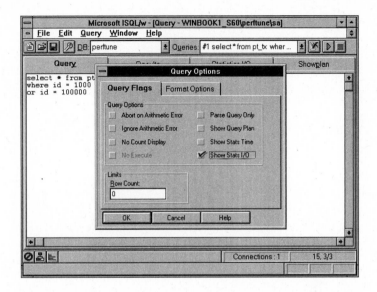

Turning on statistics io in either of these two ways causes the statistics io output to be displayed in the query results window, along with any data. A third way of turning on the statistics io output is by checking it in the Query menu, as shown in Figure 15.5. This option causes the statistics io output for that session to be displayed in a graphical manner on the Statistics I/O tab (see Figure 15.6).

FIGURE 15.5.

Turning on the graphical statistics io *output in* ISQL/w.

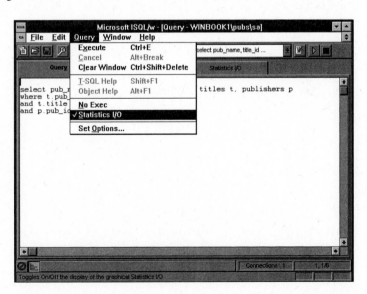

FIGURE 15.6.

ISQL/w's *graphical display of* statistics io.

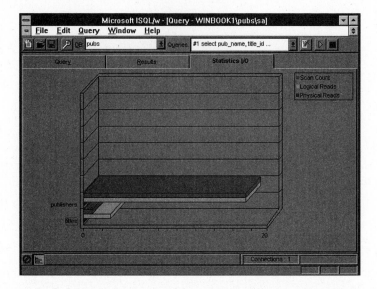

The graphical display makes nice, pretty pictures and gives you a quick glance of what the I/O counts look like, but it's difficult to determine the specific I/O counts from the display. The following examples turn on the showplan option manually to review the textual output.

TIP

If you've been viewing showplans and dbcc trace flag output, make sure that you turn off noexec before running a query with statistics io on. The statistics io values are actual I/O counts generated when the query is executed. If noexec is on, the query won't run and no I/O statistics will be generated.

The statistics io option displays the total logical page reads per table, the total physical page reads per table, the total number of read-ahead reads per table, and the scan count (that is, number of iterations) for each table. Following is a query and a sample of the statistics io output generated for it:

```
select sum(amount) from pt_sample_CIidNCk s, pt_tx_CIid t
where s.id = t.id

Table: pt_sample_CIidNCk  scan count 1,  logical reads: 243,
  physical reads: 9, read ahead reads: 234
Table: pt_tx_CIid  scan count 5772,  logical reads: 11671,
  physical reads: 110, read ahead reads: 0
_ _ _ _ _ _ _ _ _ _ _ _ _
501,590,426.50
```

In this example, pt_sample_CIidNCk is the outer table and is scanned once (scan count 1). pt_tx_CIid is the inner table and is scanned 5,772 times. SQL Server performed 243 logical reads and 9 physical reads on `pt_sample_CIidNCk`, and 110 physical and 11,671 logical reads on `pt_tx_CIid`. Because every physical page read requires a logical page read for SQL Server to process the page, the count of physical page reads never exceeds the number of logical page reads. You could experience a high number of logical page reads, however, and few or zero physical page reads. If physical reads are 0, the table was entirely in cache when the query was executed.

One good use of the `statistics io` output is to evaluate the effectiveness of the size of your data cache. By turning on this option, you can monitor the logical versus physical reads to see how much of your table(s) are staying in cache over time. If the physical page counts are consistently as high as the logical page reads, the table isn't staying in cache, and you may need to modify the SQL Server configuration to increase data cache size (see Chapters 31, "Configuring and Tuning SQL Server," and 32, "Optimizing SQL Server Configuration Options").

Another use for `statistics io` is to evaluate the effectiveness of your `RA pre-fetch` settings. The `read ahead reads` value indicates the number of pages that were found in cache due to the read-ahead pre-fetches. If you're performing a table scan and all pages are sequential, SQL Server is able to recognize this fact and make use of the pre-fetch mechanism to minimize individual physical page reads. For every initial physical page read, SQL Server pre-fetches additional extents into cache as a background process, so subsequent page read requests are satisfied by pages already in cache. In this example, 9 actual physical page reads were performed on the `pt_sample_CIidNCk` table and 234 pages were found in cache due to the pre-fetch. This is an efficient use of the pre-fetch mechanism because the pages in the `pt_sample_CIidNCk` table in this example were completely sequential. As a table becomes fragmented over time, the number of physical reads would be expected to increase and the read-ahead reads would decrease.

> **TIP**
>
> To determine how fragmented a table has become, you can use the `dbcc showcontig` command to display statistics on how contiguous the pages are in the table or leaf level of an index. If the table has become heavily fragmented, you can reduce the fragmentation and improve the read-ahead performance by dropping and re-creating the clustered index on the table, using the `WITH SORTED_DATA_REORG` option. Re-creating the clustered index "repacks" the data, so that the data pages are essentially full and contiguous.

The other common use of `statistics io` is to evaluate the page estimates generated by the query optimizer for a query plan. If the actual numbers differ significantly from the number of pages estimated by the optimizer, it would indicate that the optimizer is making an inaccurate estimate. This could be because of a bug or weakness in the optimizer's costing algorithm, or statistics that are woefully out of date. You should probably try updating statistics first and rerunning the command with `statistics io` on before you call Tech Support with a complaint about the query optimizer.

> **NOTE**
>
> In my experience, the SQL Server optimizer typically does a good job of estimating page I/O. Obviously, the estimates are based on index statistics, so they're not going to match the actual page I/Os exactly. I wouldn't suspect an optimizer problem unless the estimates were substantially different from the actuals—probably any difference greater than 1,000 pages or more than a 10 percent margin of error.
>
> Also, you only want to compare the logical I/O counts against the SQL Server estimates. When the optimizer is making its I/O estimates, it makes no assumptions about any data that may already be in cache. Rather, it takes the more pessimistic view that all initial page reads on a table will be physical page reads.

Take a look at the final plan displayed by the `dbcc traceon (310)` command for the previous query, and compare the page estimates against the actual I/O statistics generated:

```
FINAL PLAN (total cost = 28516):
JPLAN (0x268ea34) varno=0 indexid=0 totcost=3888 pathtype=sclause
class=join optype=SUBSTITUTE method=NESTED ITERATION outerrows=1
rows=5772 joinsel=1 lp=243 pp=243 cpages=243 ctotpages=243 corder=1
cstat=0x20 matcost=21883 matpages=21 crows=5772 cjoinsel=1

JPLAN (0x268ea90) varno=1 indexid=1 totcost=24628 pathtype=join
class=join optype=SUBSTITUTE method=NESTED ITERATION outerrows=5772
rows=7282 joinsel=4689 lp=11544 pp=110 cpages=2 ctotpages=110
corder=1 cstat=0x0 crows=1 cjoinsel=4689 joinmap=[0] jnvar=0
refindid=0 refcost=0 refpages=0 reftotpages=0 ordercol[0]=1
ordercol[1]=1
```

The optimizer estimated that there would be 243 total logical page reads on the outer table `pt_sample_CIidNCk` (varno=0, lp=243). This matches exactly with the actual I/O count generated by `statistics io`. For `pt_tx_CIid` (varno=1), it estimated 11,544 logical page reads and 5,772 iterations. It did perform 5,772 iterations on the `pt_tx_CIid` table, but actually performed 11,671 logical page reads, a difference of 127 pages with an error margin of only 1 percent. At 2 milliseconds per page, this is only about .25 seconds, not a significant amount of time.

And speaking of time, how closely do the time estimates generated by the optimizer correspond to the actual execution times?

statistics time

To display the total CPU and elapsed time to execute a query and the time to parse and compile the query, turn on the `statistics time` option. This option can be turned on with the following command:

```
set statistics time on
```

If you are working in ISQL/w, you can set `statistics time` on by typing the command in a query window and executing it, or by turning on the Show Stats Time option in the Query Options dialog box for that query window (see Figure 15.7).

FIGURE 15.7.

Turning on the statistics time *option for an* ISQL/w *query window.*

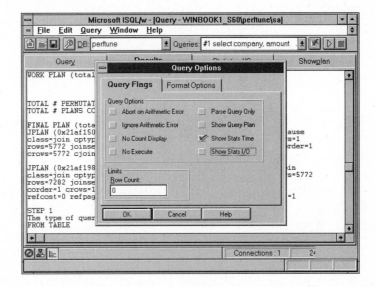

Turning on `statistics time` using either of these two methods causes the `statistics time` output to be displayed in the query results window, along with any data.

TIP

Again, make sure that you turn off `noexec` before running a query with `statistics time` turned on, or the query won't be executed and no time statistics for execution of the query will be generated. The query will still be parsed and compiled; however, no time statistics for those will be generated.

Compare the actual execution time with the estimated I/O times generated by the optimizer for the following query:

```
select count(*) from pt_sample_CIidNCk s, pt_tx_CIid t
where s.id = t.id
```

```
SQL Server Parse and Compile Time:
   cpu time = 10 ms.

— — — — —7282
```

```
(1 row(s) affected)

Table: pt_sample_CIidNCk  scan count 1,  logical reads: 243,
  physical reads: 8,  read ahead reads: 235
Table: pt_tx_CIid  scan count 5772,  logical reads: 11671,
  physical reads: 110,  read ahead reads: 0

SQL Server Execution Times:
   cpu time = 2393 ms.  elapsed time = 3855 ms.
501,590,426.50
```

The times estimated by the SQL Server optimizer can be viewed with the dbcc traceon (310) trace flag:

```
FINAL PLAN (total cost = 28516):
JPLAN (0x268ea34) varno=0 indexid=0 totcost=3888 pathtype=sclause
class=join optype=SUBSTITUTE method=NESTED ITERATION outerrows=1
rows=5772 joinsel=1 lp=243 pp=243 cpages=243 ctotpages=243 corder=1
cstat=0x20 matcost=21883 matpages=21 crows=5772 cjoinsel=1

JPLAN (0x268ea90) varno=1 indexid=1 totcost=24628 pathtype=join
class=join optype=SUBSTITUTE method=NESTED ITERATION outerrows=5772
rows=7282 joinsel=4689 lp=11544 pp=110 cpages=2 ctotpages=110
corder=1 cstat=0x0 crows=1 cjoinsel=4689 joinmap=[0] jnvar=0
refindid=0 refcost=0 refpages=0 reftotpages=0 ordercol[0]=1
ordercol[1]=1
```

In this example, the SQL Server time estimate (28,516 ms) is significantly higher than the actual execution time. But in this case, the SQL Server estimated a greater number of physical reads than actually occurred. Apply the I/O time estimates against the actual logical and physical page counts:

$$(110 + 8) \text{ physical reads} \times 14 \text{ ms} = 1652 \text{ ms}$$
$$+ (11544 + 243) \text{ logical reads} \times 2 \text{ ms} = 23574 \text{ ms}$$
$$= 25226 \text{ ms}$$

This value is still considerably higher than the actual execution time. In addition, the query optimizer's time estimate doesn't factor in network I/O times. If you have a moderately large result set, the time to send the results across the network can exceed the actual query processing time. The elapsed time reported by statistics time is the total time from when the query execution was initiated to when the final DONE packet is sent to the client application. It includes all time spent by the query to send results to the client, any time spent waiting for CPU cycles, and any time spent waiting for a lock request to be granted.

In other words, don't expect the estimated time displayed by the dbcc traceon (310) trace flag to match with the actual execution elapsed time. The optimizer time estimates are primarily for comparison purposes by the optimizer. The time estimates for logical and physical page access times, 2ms and 14ms respectively, are hard-coded values and don't necessarily represent actual I/O rates for the platform on which you're running.

The real useful purpose for the statistics time option is to record the actual CPU and elapsed-time values for queries and transactions, to benchmark and compare execution times for queries. You can also use the output to identify queries with high parse and compile times. Some queries may even have higher parse and compile times than execution times. These would be good candidates to place in stored procedures, to reap the benefits of reusable query plans residing in procedure cache, and avoid the expensive parse and compile steps for each execution.

Before I finish discussing `statistics time`, it's worthwhile to point out a slight difference in how the CPU time is calculated versus how the elapsed time is calculated. This can sometimes result in odd-looking values, such as cases in which CPU time is greater than elapsed time, or when CPU time is 0 and there's substantially more elapsed time.

The elapsed time is based on the system time. It's determined by subtracting the system time when the query initially started execution from the system time when SQL Server sends the final DONE packet to the client application.

The CPU time is factored as the number of CPU ticks tallied for the query, converted to milliseconds. A *CPU tick* is the time interval between clock interrupts on a system. The number of milliseconds per CPU tick is determined by dividing the clock rate by 1,000.

Look at the first scenario in which CPU time exceeds elapsed time (see Figure 15.8).

FIGURE 15.8.

An example of how CPU time can exceed elapsed time.

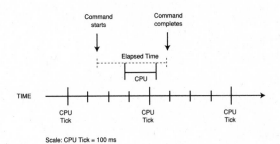

Notice how the process starts just before a clock tick and completes just after. Because it was processing at the time of a clock interrupt, a CPU tick was tallied for that process. If you assume that a CPU tick translates to 100ms, the CPU time for this process would be 100ms. The actual elapsed time from start to finish appears to only be about 75ms, however. Thus, you have a case in which the reported CPU time is more than the elapsed time.

Now look at a second scenario in which you have CPU time of 0 with substantially more elapsed time (see Figure 15.9). In this case, the process starts CPU processing just after a CPU tick and completes before the next CPU tick. Total elapsed time from start to finish in this instance appears to be around 175ms. Here you have a case in which CPU time is is recorded as 0, even though the process did incur CPU processing time.

FIGURE 15.9.

An example of how zero CPU time can be counted.

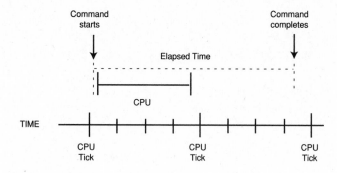

Summary

SQL Server provides a number of tools to view and evaluate the query plans being generated by the query optimizer. You can use the showplan option to view the query plan chosen by the optimizer, and the dbcc traceon (302, 310) trace flags to determine how the optimizer chose that query plan. The statistics io and statistics time options can be used to evaluate the actual performance of queries and validate the cost estimates of the query optimizer.

Through the use of these tools, you may sometimes discover that the optimizer is choosing the wrong plan, or at other times, you may simply want to force the optimizer to process a query differently than it chooses to do. Chapter 17 examines some methods for forcing particular query plans and the conditions for when you may want to do this.

Locking and Performance

16

The Need for Locking

Any multiuser database must have a consistent set of rules for making changes to data. For a true transaction-processing database, the database management system is responsible for resolving potential conflicts between two different processes that attempt to change the same piece of information at the same time. Such a situation can't occur, because the consistency of a transaction can't be guaranteed. For example, if two users were to change the same data at approximately the same time, whose change would be propagated? Theoretically, the results would be unpredictable, because the answer is dependent on whose transaction was completed last. Because most applications try to avoid "unpredictability" with data wherever possible (imagine your payroll systems returning "unpredictable" results, and you'll get the idea), there must be some way to guarantee sequential and consistent data changes.

The responsibility for ensuring conflict resolution between users falls on the SQL Server lock manager. Locks are used to guarantee that the current user of a resource (data page, index page, table, index, database) has a consistent view of that resource from beginning to completion of a particular operation. In other words, what you start with has to be what you work with throughout your operation. Nobody can change what you are working on in mid-state—in effect, intercepting your transaction.

Without locking, consistent transaction processing is impossible. *Transactions*, being defined as complete units of work, rely on a constant state of data, almost a "snapshot in time" of what they're modifying, to guarantee their completion. Transactions and locking therefore are part of the same whole—ensuring the completion of data modifications.

SQL Server Lock Types

SQL Server relies on a variety of lock types and lock granularities in its work. The three basic lock types are as follows:

- *Shared locks*—Used by processes that are *reading* pages. Multiple shared locks can be acquired concurrently on any page; a single shared lock prevents *any* exclusive locks from being acquired. Shared locks are typically held only for the duration of the read on a particular page unless the holdlock keyword is specified (or transaction isolation level 3 is invoked—see the later section "Using Transaction Isolation Levels in SQL Server Version 6.0 and Later" for details).

- *Update Locks*—Used by processes that will update data but haven't yet done so. Update locks are read-compatible with shared locks during the pre-modification phase. Update locks are automatically updated to exclusive locks when the data change occurs.

- *Exclusive Locks*—Used by processes that are currently changing data pages. Exclusive locks prevent both update locks and shared locks from being acquired. Exclusive locks are held on all affected pages until an explicit transaction has completed, or until the command has completed in an implicit transaction (a transaction that has no explicit `begin tran`/`commit tran` pair in its statements).

Table 16.1 summarizes the lock types and levels for SQL statements.

Table 16.1. Lock types and levels for SQL Server commands.

Statement	Index Used		Index Not Used	
	Table Level	Page Level	Table Level	Page Level
`select`	shared intent	shared	shared intent	shared
`select...holdlock`	shared intent	shared	shared	
`update`	exclusive intent	update, then exclusive	exclusive	
`insert`	exclusive intent	exclusive	exclusive intent	exclusive
`delete`	exclusive intent	update, then exclusive	exclusive	

Shared Locks

Shared locks are used by SQL Server for all read operations. A shared lock is by definition not exclusive, meaning that a theoretically unlimited number of shared locks can be on any page at any given time. In addition, shared locks are unique in that the particular page being locked is locked by a process only for the duration of the read on that page. For example, a query such as `select * from authors` would lock the first page in the `authors` table when the query starts. After the first page is read, the lock on that page is released, and a lock on the second page is acquired. After the second page is read, its lock is released and a lock on the third page is acquired, and so on. In this fashion, a `select` query allows other data pages not being read to be modified during the read operation, increasing concurrent access to the data.

To force a table-level lock or force page locks to be held for the duration of a transaction, you can specify the `holdlock` keyword. For example, the query `select * from authors holdlock` acquires a table-level shared lock, holding all pages until either the `select` completes or the transaction containing the `select` is committed or rolled back. In this fashion, a `select ... holdlock` query returns a snapshot of data from the table, and that table data can't be modified during such a read operation. If an index is used to satisfy the query, SQL Server starts out with page-level shared locks and holds them until the `select` or transaction containing the `select` completes. If the page locks are held, SQL Server may escalate to a table-level lock if the lock escalation threshold is exceeded (more on this topic later in this chapter).

Shared locks are *compatible* (in SQL Server terminology) with other shared locks, as well as with update locks. In this way, a shared lock doesn't prevent the acquisition of shared locks and update locks on a given page. User connections requesting shared locks or update locks aren't prevented from doing so if a shared lock already exists on a page. However, shared locks do prevent the acquisition of exclusive locks.

For all versions of SQL Server prior to 6.0, SQL Server mandated the prevention of dirty reads. *Dirty reads* are the ability to read data that has been modified but the changes haven't been committed. The read is considered "dirty" because the actual data value being returned by the read query could subsequently be rolled back by the transaction modifying the data, resulting in the read operation reading invalid data values. Because this result is by definition unpredictable, SQL Server has always prevented such situations from occurring by not allowing shared locks and exclusive locks to be acquired on the same page or table. Version 6.0 of SQL Server introduced the ability to perform dirty reads by not acquiring shared locks for read operations. See the later section "Using Transaction Isolation Levels in SQL Server Version 6.0 and Later" for a discussion of how to allow dirty reads.

> **NOTE**
>
> If a database is used for read-only operations, you may want to turn on the READ ONLY option, using sp_dboption. When this option is set, SQL Server actually disables the lock manager and any locking capabilities for that database. If your database won't receive further updates, using this option yields the easiest database maintenance *and* the best performance improvement available, by eliminating the locking overhead.

Update Locks

Update locks are used to mark pages as those that a user process would like to modify. An update lock is compatible with shared locks, in that both can be acquired on a single data page. Update locks are partially exclusive in that only one update lock can be acquired on any page. In effect, an update lock signifies that a user wants to change a page, keeping out other connections that also want to change that page. As a result, update locks are useful in avoiding deadlock—a situation discussed in detail later in this chapter. When shared locks exist on a page and a user connection acquires an update lock, the update lock waits for all the shared locks to be released. At that point, SQL Server automatically promotes the update lock to an exclusive lock, allowing the data change to proceed.

If the user connection sending the data-change request has done so through an explicit transaction (by including begin tran/commit tran statements in the submitted batch), the exclusive lock is held for the duration of the transaction—that is, until a commit tran is encountered, a rollback tran is encountered, or the server is stopped and restarted (in the case of an aborted transaction).

If the user connection sending the data-change request hasn't defined an explicit transaction, the newly-acquired exclusive lock is released after that particular statement has completed.

Exclusive Locks

Exclusive locks are reserved for those operations that are changing data. Exclusive locks can't be acquired while a data page is being read, and all data reads are prevented on a page or table while an exclusive lock is held. In this way, exclusive locks prevent dirty reads from occurring. Chapter 17, "Managing the SQL Server Optimizer," discusses methods of modifying this default behavior for SQL Server.

Exclusive locks are incompatible with any other lock type. If a page has read locks on it, the exclusive lock request is forced to wait in a queue for the page to become available. If an exclusive lock is on a page, any read requests are similarly queued until the exclusive lock is released.

Exclusive locks are held for the duration of an explicit transaction, or for the duration of a statement in a simple batch.

Transact-SQL Statements and Associated Locks

Different Transact-SQL operations affect locking in different ways, and the combinations of SQL statements can also have an impact.

`select` queries acquire shared locks by default. As described earlier, those shared locks are acquired and released in sequential order as pages are read. The only exception to this rule is when you use the `holdlock` keyword, which is discussed in detail in Chapter 17. `holdlock` forces SQL Server to hold the shared page locks for the duration of the `select` or the transaction containing the `select`. If the `holdlock` keyword is specified and the query must be satisfied by a table scan, SQL Server attempts to acquire a table-level shared lock.

`insert` statements always acquire exclusive page-level locks. `update` and `delete` queries always acquire some type of exclusive lock to perform data modifications. If the query first has to collect the set of rows to be modified before actually updating them, or a `select` statement has shared locks on the pages, a `delete` or `update` statement first acquires an update lock, which subsequently is upgraded to an exclusive lock when the row updates are processed. If the query is an `update` or `delete` of the whole table, or the query requires a table scan to process the `update` or `delete`, SQL Server automatically attempts to acquire a table-level exclusive lock. Once acquired, the lock is held for the duration of the statement or transaction.

SQL Server Lock Granularity

Lock granularity is the minimum amount of data that's locked as part of a query or update. The smaller the lock size, the greater the number of potential concurrent users, but the greater the overhead in maintaining those locks. The greater the lock size, the less overhead required to manage locks, but concurrency is less. (See Figure 16.1.)

FIGURE 16.1.

Tradeoffs between performance and concurrency, depending on lock granularity.

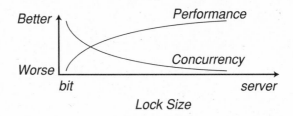

By default, SQL Server balances performance and concurrency by locking at the page level or higher. As you learn later in this chapter, SQL Server 6.5 now allows locking at the row level for insert operations.

The smallest unit of work for any SQL Server operation, including locking, is the data page (for more on data pages, see Chapter 11, "Understanding SQL Server Storage Structures"). In other words, SQL Server typically locks all the rows on a particular page when that page is read or changed. For queries that affect a large percentage of rows in a table, SQL Server may choose to upgrade a collection of page locks to a table lock. In effect, SQL Server trades in a collection of locks of a smaller granularity for one of larger granularity. Any lock, regardless of granularity, consumes the same quantity of resource overhead. Therefore, a single table lock is more efficient than 5,000 individual page locks. A table-level lock introduces a concurrency issue, because other processes can't modify other rows in the table until the table-level lock is released.

Prior to Version 6.0, all SQL Server lock management was internal to SQL Server; there was no application or user level of lock control except for forcing shared locks to be held through the use of the holdlock keyword. SQL Server 6.0 introduced options to control the lock type acquired by SQL commands, and some control over lock granularity (see Chapter 17). However, the lock granularity was limited to table-level or page-level locks. In SQL Server 6.5, you now also have the capability of locking data at the row level for certain types of insert operations.

Table-Level Locks

SQL Server generally tries to lock at the page level to maximize concurrency. While a process has page-level locks on a table, SQL Server also gives the process a corresponding intent lock on the table.

An *intent lock* indicates at the table level the types of locks that are being acquired at the page level. SQL Server applies an intent table lock when a process acquires a page-level shared or exclusive lock. The intent lock is used to prevent another process from acquiring a shared or exclusive table-level lock in case the current process needs to escalate to a table-level lock. Intent locks are held for as long as a process holds a page-level lock on the table.

As the page locks on a table increase, SQL Server may escalate to a table-level lock. Also, if an update or delete command doesn't contain a valid SARG that the optimizer can use to estimate the number of rows to be updated and limit the number of pages scanned, SQL Server automatically grabs a table-level lock. There are two types of table-level locks: shared and exclusive.

A *shared table-level lock* permits other processes to read at the page or table level, but prevents any exclusive locks at the page or table level. A shared table-level lock is acquired under these conditions:

- When a nonclustered index is created on a table
- For certain `dbcc` commands (for example, `dbcc checktable`)
- When a `select` statement specifies the `holdlock` keyword and no valid SARG exists in the query, the SARG doesn't match an available index, or the number of pages locked by the `select` with the `holdlock` statement exceeds the lock escalation threshold.

Consider the following queries:

```
select * from titles holdlock

select * from titles holdlock where price > $10
```

The first query would automatically use a shared table-level lock, because the entire table would be scanned. For the second query, if `price` had no index, SQL Server would automatically acquire a shared table-level lock. If `price` had an index, the query would initially acquire shared page locks and a shared intent lock on the table. Should the number of pages locked exceed the lock escalation threshold, SQL Server would attempt to escalate to a table-level shared lock as long as no conflicting page-level locks (that is, exclusive page locks) existed on other pages in the table.

An exclusive table-level lock prevents any other type of lock from being acquired at the page or table level. SQL Server applies an exclusive table-level lock during creation of a clustered index or for updates and deletes if one of these conditions occurs:

- The query doesn't contain a valid SARG
- The SARG doesn't match an available index
- The number of pages locked by the `update` or `delete` statement exceeds the lock escalation threshold

Consider the following queries:

```
update titles set price = price * 1.10

delete titles where price < $10
```

The first query would automatically use an exclusive table-level lock, because the entire table would be scanned. For the second query, if `price` had no index defined on it, SQL Server would acquire an exclusive table-level lock. If `price` had an index, the query would initially acquire update page locks and an exclusive intent lock on the table. Should the number of pages locked exceed the lock escalation threshold, SQL Server would attempt to escalate to a table-level exclusive lock, as long as no conflicting page-level locks (that is, shared or exclusive page locks) existed on other pages in the table.

Lock Escalation for Large Data Sets

SQL Server attempts to conserve locking resources by upgrading page-level locks to table locks when certain thresholds have been reached. Historically, that threshold has been to upgrade page locks to table locks when 200 page locks have been acquired on any given table. At that point, SQL Server releases the individual page locks and allocates a single table lock for the user process. SQL Server Versions 6.0 and later allow you to modify the lock escalation thresholds within SQL Server. Chapter 32, "Optimizing SQL Server Configuration Options," shows you how to set server-wide configuration values to configure the lock escalation thresholds that SQL Server uses.

Insert Row-Level Locking

By default, the lowest granularity for a lock within SQL Server is the data page. SQL Server 6.5 introduces the option to lock at the row level for insert operations. Insert row-level locking can help to improve performance for insert-intensive applications by minimizing contention and "hot spots" between multiple-user processes. A *hot spot* is a page or group of pages in a table where the majority of insert operations occur. Hot spots are likely to occur on heap tables without a clustered index (because all rows are added at the end of the table), or on tables with a clustered index on a sequential key, where all rows are inserted in sequential-key order.

Historically, the only way to eliminate hot spots and minimize page contention during inserts was to create a clustered index on a key value that would randomly distribute the inserted data rows throughout the table. This plan sometimes forced you to create a clustered index on a column that wasn't necessarily used in queries.

To avoid page contention for inserts in SQL Server 6.5, you can implement row-level locking. By default, insert row-level locking is off. You enable it at either the database or table level, using the sp_tableoption stored procedure. For example, to turn on insert row-level locking for the titles table, execute the following command:

```
sp_tableoption 'titles', 'insert row lock', 'true'
```

To turn on insert row-level locking for all existing tables in the database, execute the following command:

```
sp_tableoption '%.%', 'insert row lock', 'true'
```

The `sp_tableoption` command sets insert row-level locking on or off for the table for all subsequent user transactions. To enable or disable insert row-level locking dynamically within an application, use the `dbcc rowlock` command:

```
dbcc rowlock (dbid, tableid, 0 ¦ 1 )
```

For example, to turn on insert row-level locking for the `titles` table in the `pubs` database, execute the following:

```
declare @dbid int, @tableid int
select @dbid = db_id("pubs"), @tableid = object_id("titles")
dbcc rowlock (@dbid, @tableid, 1)
```

If you want to disable insert row-level locking for the `titles` table in the `pubs` database, execute the following:

```
declare @dbid int, @tableid int
select @dbid = db_id("pubs"), @tableid = object_id("titles")
dbcc rowlock (@dbid, @tableid, 0)
```

Note that enabling or disabling row-level locking with the `dbcc rowlock` command remains in effect for all users until it's disabled or re-enabled with `dbcc rowlock`. For this reason, you should use this command sparingly and always remember to disable/re-enable the row-level locking setting as soon as your transaction completes.

To support insert row-level locking, Microsoft introduced two new lock types for SQL Server:

- *Insert_page locks*—Used by processes that are *inserting* pages into a table configured for row-level locking. Multiple-user processes can obtain insert_page locks on a single page. An insert_page lock is compatible only with other insert_page locks and is held on all affected pages until an explicit transaction has completed, or until the command has completed in an implicit transaction.

- *Link_page locks*—Used by the first process holding an insert_page lock that detects that the current data page is full and a new page needs to be allocated to the table and linked to the current page. The current insert_page lock is escalated to a link_page lock. The link_page lock is compatible only with currently existing insert_page locks. No further insert_page locks are allowed until the transaction acquiring the link_page lock completes.

Using insert row-level locking requires that additional information be logged to the transaction log for recovery purposes, to ensure that the database is brought back to a consistent state in the event of a rollback or SQL Server failure. Enough space has to be

continues

continued

reserved in the transaction log for all concurrent insert row-level locking transactions. Because of the additional logging requirements, you may need to monitor your transaction log more closely and possibly increase your transaction log size or dump the log more frequently.

Simulating Row-Level Locking

Although SQL Server 6.5 allows for row-level locking for inserts, in other instances you may need row-level locking for selects and/or updates and deletes. Additionally, you may have an application that needs to access pre-6.5 SQL Servers that don't support insert row-level locking. To meet these requirements, you need to simulate row-level locking. Two common ways exist to simulate row-level locking. The least efficient is row padding, and the most complex to implement involves optimistic locking.

Row Padding

Row padding is based on a simple concept: If SQL Server locks at the page level, make rows big enough so that only one row fits on a page. Presto! Magnifico! Row-level locking, right? The answer, of course, is a bit more complex. Yes, you have only one row locked at any given time if that data page is locked. However, the storage requirements to support this strategy are substantial; each row, even though it needs to be only 1009 bytes (half of the space available on a page—2016 bytes/2 = 1008 bytes—plus one extra byte), the rows effectively will be 2048 bytes in size. The reason? Only one row can fit on each page. That makes for a very, very big row. In addition, remember that SQL Server optimizes and costs queries based on the number of pages involved. That number has just increased substantially, because the number of pages matches the number of rows.

Depending on the application and the business needs at hand, row padding could very well be a viable alternative to page-level locking. However, carefully consider database size, growth, and application needs before implementing this solution! Row padding can improve performance for OLTP applications by minimizing page contention, but degrade performance for data retrieval by increasing the number of pages that need to be accessed.

Optimistic Locking

A method commonly used to implement a form of row-level locking is to use *optimistic locking*. Optimistic locking allows for user interaction within transactions without holding read locks indefinitely, as locks aren't used to manage the update consistency of retrieved data rows. Optimistic locking is achieved by putting a `timestamp` column on a table. Any applications must then use a "read-then-update" process, driven from the client application, to modify rows using optimistic locking.

To implement optimistic locking, some table structure prerequisites must be met. First, the table must have a primary key or unique index, so that rows can be uniquely identified in a `where` clause. Secondly, the table must have a `timestamp` column. The `timestamp` column is a special column that SQL Server updates automatically to a guaranteed unique value whenever a row is modified.

Instead of simply updating a row directly, an application must first read the row from the database without using the `holdlock` command. The value of the `timestamp` column for each row must be retrieved and stored in the client application.

When the application is ready to update a row, it submits a new query to change the row. However, the `update` statement must include a `where` clause that compares the `timestamp` value held in the client application with the `timestamp` value on disk. If the `timestamp` values match— that is, the value that was read is the same as the value in the database—no changes to that row have occurred since it was read. The change attempted by the application proceeds. If the `timestamp` value in the client application *doesn't* match the value in the data table, that particular row has been changed since the read operation occurred. The row that the application is attempting to modify isn't the same as the row that currently exists. As a result, the change can't occur, because of the "phantom values" problem.

To compare the `timestamp` values, the `update` statement itself must make use of the `tsequal` function in the `where` clause of the `update` statement to compare the `timestamp` value returned by the read (and held in a buffer on the client application), with the `timestamp` value in the data table. If they match, the `update` proceeds. If not, the `update` fails because the `where` clause can't be satisfied.

The following sample illustrates how this process works:

1. The client reads a row:

   ```
   select * from data_table where primary_key_field = <value>
   ```

2. The client prepares an `update` statement with new data values for this row.

3. The client submits the following `update` statement:

   ```
   update data_table set data_field_1 = foo
       where primary_key_field = <value>
           and tsequal (timestamp, 0x13590813570159017)
   ```

In this step, the `update` statement is using the same `where` clause as the `select` statement, identifying the same row by using the same primary key value. This is required to make sure you get the same row, and it explains why a primary key is necessary for this to occur. However, in addition to specifying the primary key, the `where` clause also uses the `tsequal` function. `tsequal` takes two distinct `timestamp` values and compares them for equality. In this case, the `update` statement is comparing the `timestamp` field of `data_table` with an explicit value, `0x13590813570159017`. So how does the application get this value? By reading the row before the `update` statement and fetching it from the result set.

If `tsequal` evaluates to TRUE, the row has been found and will be modified, because both conditions of the `where` clause have been met. If the `tsequal` function is FALSE, the row has been modified since it was retrieved and the update will fail with an error message similar to the following:

```
Msg 532, Level 16, State 1
The timestamp (changed to 0x00000001000013b7) shows that the row has been
 updated by another user.
Command has been aborted.
```

At this point, it's up to the client application to decide what to do. Typically, the new version of the row is retrieved to determine whether the update should still be applied.

> **NOTE**
>
> Take note that the following `where` clause:
>
> ```
> where primary_key_field = <value>
>    and timestamp = 0x13590813570159017
> ```
>
> is not treated the same as this version:
>
> ```
> where primary_key_field = <value>
>    and tsequal (timestamp, 0x13590813570159017)
> ```
>
> With the first `where` clause, if the `timestamp` values don't match, a data row will not be found that matches both search criteria, and the row won't be updated. However, no error message will be issued to indicate why the row wasn't updated.
>
> Use the `tsequal` function to generate the specific error message to indicate that the timestamps don't match. Your client application error handler can then trap the error code 532 and perform specific error handling for a mismatched `timestamp` value.

Although optimistic locking is more efficient in terms of disk resources than row padding, sending multiple query statements back and forth across a busy network simply moves the additional overhead off the disk subsystem and into the network and processor subsystems. As a result, there's no way to simulate row-level locking without incurring additional overhead somewhere in the application.

This last point is an important one to remember, because it defines SQL Server's page-level locking as the most efficient locking system for the greatest variety of applications. Row-level locking needs should be carefully examined for necessity; the overhead cost may outweigh the benefits, and only the architect of the application and the application's business needs can define those parameters.

Locking with Cursors

Because cursors perform row-at-a-time operations on tables, a single row can be associated with many rows on a single page. Hence, attempts to update different rows in different cursors can cause concurrency problems as different user connections fight for the same data page. Understanding how cursors implement locking can prevent application developers from writing queries that use SQL Server's updateable cursors improperly.

For cursors that are declared `for read only`, SQL Server uses a shared lock on the current page being read by the cursor. In other words, a fetch from a cursor result set causes SQL Server to put a shared lock on the page containing the row that was fetched. The shared lock is held for the duration of the fetch operation. All the other pages that the cursor is browsing are unlocked during the execution of the cursor until a row is fetched from the page.

For cursors that are declared `for update`, SQL Server uses an update lock on the page containing the current row being fetched. That update lock is held for the duration of the fetch operation. If the data row being fetched is modified, the update lock is upgraded to an exclusive lock and held as an exclusive lock for the duration of the transaction. If the `update` statement that changed the data page isn't part of a multi-statement transaction or an explicitly defined transaction, the exclusive lock reverts to an update lock after the change has completed. The update lock is then released when fetch operations move to another page. If the `update` statement involved is part of an explicitly-defined or multi-statement transaction, the exclusive lock is held for the duration of the transaction and then released.

Cursors that are declared `for update` can use shared locks instead of update locks if they're declared with the `shared` keyword. Using the `shared` keyword (see the cursor syntax section in Chapter 7, "Transact-SQL Programming Constructs," for syntax examples) allows SQL Server to use shared locks instead of update locks for updateable cursors. The implication of this fact is that, because a cursor is *not* using an update lock, it's possible for a different operation to acquire an update lock. Remember, only one update lock is allowed for any given page. Using `shared` allows multiple connections running multiple cursors to fetch rows that will be updated simultaneously, enhancing concurrency. The shared locks used when the `shared` keyword is specified are automatically upgraded to exclusive locks when a cursor row is updated. This process is identical to the upgrade/downgrade process for update locks and updateable cursors.

This option is particularly useful for multi-table cursors. If you're updating only one of the tables, using the `shared` keyword enables you to avoid putting update locks on all the tables involved in the cursor set, because you can modify only one of the tables at any given time. For example, consider the following multi-table cursor:

```
declare title_pub_cursor cursor
   for select title_id, title, price
        from titles, publishers shared
        where titles.pub_id = publishers.pub_id
           and publishers.state = "NY"
   for update of title, price
```

For the cursor defined, only the `titles` table will be updated, so the `shared` keyword is specified on the `publishers` table. This strategy allows other user processes to acquire update locks on pages in the `publishers` table.

Index Locking

SQL Server locks indexes differently than tables. SQL Server's locking, by default, is internally managed. Ways exist to override this control manually, but only for user-defined queries on user tables. Index locking issues are entirely internal, and actually use a substantially different mechanism.

Because SQL Server uses B-tree indexes, SQL Server indexes have a single root page. As queries use indexes to retrieve rows, that root page receives more than its fair share of attention. As a result, locking this page during index scans and index-based reads creates high levels of contention for the index. Instead of locking all index pages for an index-based read, SQL Server locks and unlocks index pages as they are read through the index tree levels. In this way, a lock is held on an index page only as long as necessary to scan the key values for that page.

With B-tree indexes, there's always the possibility for page-splitting to accommodate index and table growth. (See Chapter 11 and Chapter 12 for more information about B-trees in general and SQL Server's use of them in particular.) When page splits occur, both index pages initially receive exclusive locks, which are then downgraded to update locks after the index row has been modified. The update locks are then held for the duration of the transaction. After the data modification has completed, the update locks are released and the index is re-balanced, if necessary.

The use of update locks on modified pages in indexes allows other transactions to "read through" a lock on an index page if attempting to access data rows contained on data pages that are not exclusively locked by that transaction (see Figure 16.2). This behavior helps to improve query performance by not forcing a `select` to wait for an update on one or more data rows to be committed, before being able to access data rows contained on different data pages.

FIGURE 16.2.

Example of how update locks are used in index pages.

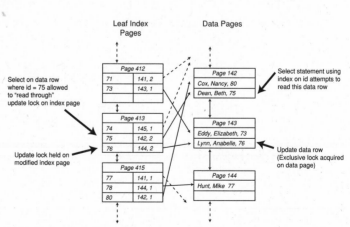

Using Transaction Isolation Levels in SQL Server Version 6.0 and Later

SQL Server is directly responsible for management of individual locking tasks. As noted elsewhere in this chapter, there are some provisions for manually overriding the locking behavior in some circumstances. However, another aspect to locking and lock management is directly tied to transactions; SQL Server also provides for the management of *transaction isolation levels*. Transaction isolation levels are categories of locking behavior within transactions that are defined by ANSI. ANSI has described four different classes of transaction isolation levels, and each implements a different behavior regarding user concurrency versus data consistency:

- Transaction Isolation Level 0, which is named *READ UNCOMMITTED*, allows SQL Server to read pages that are currently being modified—in effect, supporting "dirty reads." This feature was first provided in SQL Server 6.0. In prior versions, no reads of uncommitted changes were ever allowed outside the transaction making the changes. To allow "dirty reads," SQL Server doesn't attempt to acquire read locks on data pages for a select, so the `select` command isn't blocked by any exclusive locks. Because no read locks are acquired, they also don't block any update operations.

> **NOTE**
>
> Even if the transaction isolation level is set to 0, certain utilities like `dbcc` still acquire shared locks for their scans, because these commands must maintain the database integrity by ensuring that the correct data is read before modifying it.

- Transaction Isolation Level 1, *READ COMMITTED*, is the default SQL Server behavior, and has been so historically through all versions of Microsoft SQL Server. With READ COMMITTED as the transaction isolation level, read operations can read only pages where transactions have already been committed—that is, no "dirty reads" are allowed.

- Transaction Isolation Level 2, *REPEATABLE READS*, allows a single page to be read many times within the same transaction and guarantees that the same value will be read each time. This option prevents other users from updating a data row that has been read until the transaction in which it was read is committed or rolled back.

- Transaction Isolation Level 3, *SERIALIZABLE READS*, is designed to prevent "phantom reads," that is, preventing another transaction from updating, deleting, or inserting rows for pages previously read within a transaction. If the first transaction attempts to read the same rows again, using the same search criteria, a different result set would be returned. The SERIALIZABLE option prevents this problem from happening.

All of these options can be configured at the session level, by using the set transaction isolation level command. By default, SQL Server uses READ COMMITTED for all behavior. READ UNCOMMITTED is available as an option for allowing dirty reads and setting Transaction Isolation Level 1. Levels 2 and 3 are synonymous under SQL Server; setting *either* REPEATABLE READ or SERIALIZABLE with this command enables *both* of these options. They can't be set independently because both implement reads on committed transactions.

> **NOTE**
>
> Remember, using the set command to change how SQL Server processes queries remains valid *for the duration of the user connection.* If a user logs out and then reconnects, the new connection reverts to SQL Server's standard behavior, which is READ COMMITTED.

You can determine the current isolation level of a user connection by using the dbcc useroptions command (it doesn't accept any arguments) to determine current configuration option values enabled by set commands.

When running queries in Isolation Level 1, Level 3 can be simulated for a specific query by using the holdlock keyword in a select statement. Likewise, when running queries at Isolation Level 1 or 3, Level 0 for reads can be simulated for a specific query by specifying the nolock keyword in the select statement.

Examining Current Lock Activity

SQL Server locking activity can be monitored by using three different utilities:

- The sp_lock stored procedure
- SQL Enterprise Manager
- Performance Monitor

These three tools are very useful utilities in monitoring and tracking down locking issues that can hamper SQL Server performance.

The following sections describe each option.

Using the sp_lock Stored Procedure

The sp_lock stored procedure supplied by SQL Server returns a "snapshot in time" of all currently allocated locks being managed by SQL Server. This information is obtained from the syslocks table in the master database.

The `sp_lock` stored procedure is useful only for the particular instance in which it runs, because locks are allocated and deallocated dynamically by SQL Server. For example, the following execution of `sp_lock` shows all current locks within SQL Server at the time `sp_lock` is run:

```
sp_lock
```

spid	locktype	table_id	page	dbname
10	Ex_intent	1120007021	0	pubs
10	Ex_page	1120007021	628	pubs
10	Update_page	1120007021	628	pubs
10	Update_page	1120007021	634	pubs
11	Sh_intent	688005482	0	master
11	Ex_extent	0	360	tempdb

Combining this procedure with `sp_who` lets you find out who is locking whom. If `page` `0` is locked, for example, that's a table lock.

The `locktype` column encodes the following information:

- *The type of lock.* Shared locks are assigned a prefix of `Sh_`, whereas exclusive locks receive `Ex_`. Update locks are assigned a type of `Update`.

- *The unit of work to which the lock is assigned.* Units of work can be table, page, or extent. (Extent locks are used only for space allocations, not normal querying operations.)

- *Whether the lock is an intent lock*—that is, will this process want to acquire a shared or exclusive lock on the table at some point?

- *If the locktype value has a suffix of _blk, it's blocking another process.* A user connection can't access the unit of work held by this lock.

If the `page` value is `0`, that fact indicates a table-level lock. A page value other than `0` indicates a lock on a table or index page. To determine whether the page is an index or table page, you use the `dbcc page` command. Use of this command and its syntax is described in Chapter 11.

> **NOTE**
>
> The `sp_lock` stored procedure always displays at least one shared intent lock on the table with ID `688005482` in the `master` database. This is the `spt_values` table. The `sp_lock` procedure acquires the shared intent lock because, to display a `locktype` name in the output, it needs to join the `syslocks` table with the `spt_values` table.
>
> In addition, `sp_lock` also acquires an extent lock in `tempdb` because of the worktable required for sorting the output.

To determine what specific table is being locked, you can use the `object_name()` function to display the name of the table. For the `object_name()` function to return the proper value, you need to be in the appropriate database (in this case, pubs). For example, you can run the following select statement to determine the name of the table whose ID is 1120007021:

```
select object_name(1120007021)
```

```
_ _ _ _ _ _ _ _ _ _ _ _ _ _ _ _ _
```

```
titles
```

Viewing Locking Activity with SQL Enterprise Manager

An alternative to sp_lock is in the SQL Enterprise Manager application. By clicking the Current Activity button in the SQL-EM toolbar (its icon is a bar graph), you can view all the current system logins and their activities. By clicking the Object Locks tab, you can get a prettier version of sp_lock output that's also categorized by database table and login ID (see Figure 16.3). Optionally, you can select the Detail Activity tab and see individual login IDs (see Figure 16.4). Scrolling to the right reveals the Lock Type and Locked Object fields of the grid; these fields show which objects a given user connection has locked and the lock type currently allocated.

FIGURE 16.3.

SQL Server Enterprise Manager provides a facility for viewing current locking activity by object within SQL Server.

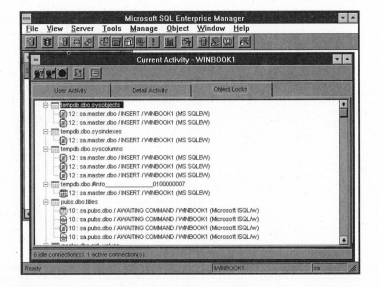

Viewing the Current Quantity of Locks with Performance Monitor

A third option for viewing the current quantity of locks allocated by SQL Server is to use Performance Monitor (using Performance Monitor is discussed more fully in Chapter 33, "Measuring SQL Server System Performance"). An advantage of Performance Monitor over sp_lock is that, in addition to displaying the current lock activity, it also can keep track of the total number of locks allocated by SQL Server, as well as locks allocated on a per-unit basis (that is, total number of shared locks, total number of table locks, and even total number of shared table locks). Chapter 33 discusses how to use the specific counters; the important point here is to understand that SQL Server provides a means for charting its locking activity for use in debugging particular locking and concurrency problems.

FIGURE 16.4.

Viewing current locking activity by user within SQL Server (note that for display purposes, column headings have been truncated to get the information to fit on one screen).

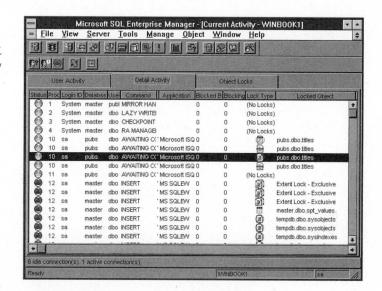

Configuring SQL Server Locking

SQL Server offers a configuration option, the `locks` parameter, for controlling the total number of locks that SQL Server can allocate at any given time. A lock of any type or granularity level consumes the same fixed quantity of overhead, so the lock type or level is unimportant from this perspective.

As a general rule, you should start out configuring SQL Server with a ratio of approximately 20 locks per concurrent user connection. If applications running against SQL Server do large numbers of scanning operations or affect large percentages of tables with individual queries, monitor lock activity closely. Increasing numbers of users, increasing numbers of rows affected by queries, or both, are indicators that the number of locks available to SQL Server may be insufficient.

Using the `sp_configure` stored procedure or SQL Enterprise Manager to configure the `locks` parameter is discussed in Chapter 31, "Configuring and Tuning SQL Server."

Minimizing Locking Contention

To maximize concurrency and performance, minimize locking contention between processes as much as possible. Some general guidelines to minimize locking contention:

- Keep transactions as short and concise as possible—the shorter the period of time locks are held, the less chance for lock contention. Keep commands not essential to the unit of work being managed by the transaction outside the transaction (for example, assignment selects, selects of updated rows, and so on).

- Keep transactions in a single batch to eliminate unnecessary delays between the begin tran and commit tran commands.

- Consider running transactions in stored procedures; stored procedures typically run faster than commands executed from a batch.

- Commit updates in cursors frequently and as soon as possible. Cursor processing is much slower than set-oriented processing and causes locks to be held longer.

> **NOTE**
>
> Cursors can sometimes be used to minimize locking contention for mass updates and deletes by updating a large number of rows, one row at a time, with page-level locks (be sure to commit changes frequently) rather than a potential table-level lock.

- Use the lowest level of locking required by each process. For example, if dirty reads are acceptable, consider using Transaction Isolation Level 0. Use Level 3 or holdlock only if absolutely necessary.

- Consider breaking one large table into multiple tables by using a logical horizontal or vertical partitioning scheme. This strategy minimizes the chances of table-level locks being acquired and increases concurrency by allowing multiple users to go against multiple tables rather than contending for access to a single table. (Table partitioning is covered in more detail in Chapter 38, "Administering Very Large SQL Server Databases").

- Never allow user interaction between a begin tran and a commit tran, because this causes locks to be held for an indefinite period of time. If a process needs to return rows for user interaction and then update one or more rows, consider using optimistic locking in your application.

- Avoid "hot spots" in a table.

- Use insert row-level locking to minimize page locking contention between multiple-insert processes.

- Reduce page locking contention by reducing the number of rows per page.

Decreasing the Number of Rows per Page

If you're trying to minimize locking contention for inserts, consider using a low fill factor when creating the clustered and nonclustered indexes on the table. A low fill factor has a favorable effect on concurrency, by spreading existing data rows across a greater number of pages and leaving extra free space on existing pages for new rows—reducing page splits as well as page contention. (For information on setting the fill factor, see Chapter 11 and Chapter 31.

By reducing page splits, fewer exclusive page locks will be acquired in the index pages. This fact helps to improve overall performance for inserts and updates.

A low fill factor isn't a permanent solution, however. Once you begin inserting or modifying data, the fill factor is lost; it doesn't maintain a consistent number of rows per page. If you want to explicitly limit the number of rows per page, or simulate row-level locking in SQL Server to minimize page contention between processes updating different rows, you need a more permanent solution, as discussed earlier in this chapter.

Deadlocking

Deadlocking is the interesting circumstance of having two different user connections fighting for the same resources. The situation is similar to what happens at major corporations every morning. One person brings in coffee, the other brings in doughnuts. The person with the doughnuts wants the coffee, but *before* having to give up the doughnuts. The person with the coffee wants the doughnuts, but *before* having to give up the coffee. In effect, you have two people trying to keep what they have and grab what the other has at the same time. Welcome to deadlock.

In the case of SQL Server, deadlock uses the same metaphor, with a slightly more technical implementation. One user connection acquires a lock on a particular page. The next step is to acquire a lock on the next page affected by a transaction. However, a different user connection is already locking that page, and requesting a lock on the page that the first user connection has locked. In this situation, neither user connection can continue until the other has finished, and neither can finish until the other has continued—deadlock (see Figure 16.5).

The traditional Sybase architecture for detecting and resolving this problem was replaced in Microsoft SQL Server 4.2 for Windows NT. It was further enhanced in SQL Server 6.0 to improve both deadlock detection and resolution. The details are considered Microsoft proprietary information, but the general process relies on a separate "monitor" that runs internally within SQL Server. This process continually checks for deadlocks, and it automatically aborts one of the conflicting user processes.

FIGURE 16.5.

Diagram of a deadlock.

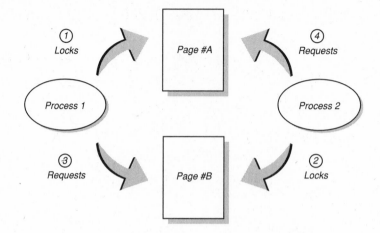

The user process that is aborted has its transaction aborted, but not its batch. The user process that has its transaction aborted is sent error number 1205, indicating that the user process ...has been chosen as the victim of a deadlock process. *Victim* is the right word, because the transaction is aborted and rolled back without any intervention from the user.

All SQL Server applications that use transactions should check for error number 1205, or for return code –3. Both of these error values indicate an aborted transaction as the result of deadlock. If it's detected, typically an application should respond by simply resubmitting the transaction. Because the other user connection involved has been allowed to continue, it probably will have released its locks by the time the transaction is resubmitted.

Unfortunately, the nature of multiuser databases ensures that occurrence of deadlock can only be reduced, not eliminated entirely. As a result, *all* applications should check for error 1205, all stored procedures should check for return code –3 when calling other stored procedures, and application developers should write transactions such that deadlock can be minimized.

NOTE

If you implement insert row-level locking in an application, be aware that a lower locking granularity can result in more frequent deadlocks. For example, consider a transaction that inserts a row on a page and then updates the same row within the same transaction. The insert acquires an insert_page lock. The update command attempts to acquire an exclusive page lock. If another process was running the same transaction simultaneously, it too would have an insert_page lock and attempt to acquire an exclusive page lock. This situation would result in deadlock. If normal page-level locking were employed, this scenario wouldn't occur. Therefore, I recommended that you thoroughly test existing applications and transactions for potential deadlocking problems before arbitrarily implementing insert row-level locking.

How to Minimize the Chance for Deadlock

The steps involved in avoiding deadlock are easy in principle, but they may be difficult to implement, depending on the needs of your application.

The easiest way to avoid deadlock is to put all transaction-based SQL code into stored procedures. The performance advantages of stored procedures becomes most apparent here, because stored procedures allow a transaction to be completed in a dramatically shorter time frame than would be possible by submitting "naked" SQL statements. As a result, the duration that locks are held within transactions is similarly reduced, which reduces the potential for deadlock.

> **WARNING**
>
> If developing a transaction-oriented application, you should try to use development tools that provide access to stored procedures and SQL Server-specific features. This isn't necessarily a consideration for decision-support systems, but for transaction-based systems on SQL Server it can make a substantial difference in performance and concurrency.
>
> Application development tools that don't provide a means to access SQL Server-specific features typically encounter problems with highly transactional systems. These tools often implement their own abstraction layer APIs that shield developers from making database-specific SQL calls directly. As a result, these tools are much more portable, but at a cost. Behind the scenes, each is submitting "dynamic" or "naked" SQL statements to SQL Server that aren't as efficient in transaction-oriented environments as stored procedures.

Another method of speeding transactions is to avoid putting queries that return data in a transaction. The data read allocates additional read locks that extend the time window in which update locks are held, increasing the probability of deadlock. Instead, explicitly defined transactions should be limited to the operation for which they were intended—changing data. If read operations are part of a batch, put them outside the begin tran/commit tran pair. They add locking overhead and extend lock duration needlessly.

Whether using stored procedures or submitting dynamic SQL, using the minimum locking level needed to complete the transaction is always ideal. Although holdlock is a useful option for maintaining shared locks and for implementing repeatable reads, excessive use of these features is a common cause of deadlock. If you have queries that are reading data as a "snapshot in time," consider writing these queries to use the nolock option discussed in Chapter 17.

As other methods to avoid deadlocking, consider using optimistic locking or having the transaction first acquire an exclusive lock. For example, one of the most common deadlock culprits is the sequential number generator. Often they are written as on the following page:

```
begin tran
select new_id from keytab holdlock
update keytab set new_id = new_id + 1
commit tran
```

If two users run this transaction simultaneously, they both acquire the shared lock and hold onto it. When each attempts to acquire an exclusive lock on the keytab table, they deadlock. To avoid this situation, rewrite the transaction as follows:

```
begin tran
update keytab set new_id = new_id + 1
select new_id from keytab
commit tran
```

Written this way, only one transaction can acquire the exclusive lock on keytab. The other process waits until the first one completes, but a deadlock has been avoided.

If read repeatability is necessary within a transaction, consider writing the transaction in such a way as to obtain an initial exclusive lock on the resource, and then reading the data. For example, if a transaction needs to retrieve the average price for all books in the titles table and ensure that that result doesn't change before the update is applied, you can trick the optimizer into giving you an exclusive table lock. Consider the following SQL code:

```
begin tran
update titles set title_id = title_id
    where 1 = 2
if (select avg(price) from titles) > $15
begin
    /* perform some additional processing */

end

update titles set price = price * 1.10
    where price < (select avg(price) from titles)

commit tran
```

In this transaction, it's important that no other process modifies price for any rows in the table, or the value retrieved at the end of the transaction will differ from the value retrieved at the beginning. Notice the update at the beginning of the transaction. The where clause looks kind of funny, doesn't it? Well, believe it or not, it's a perfectly valid where clause as far as the optimizer is concerned, even though it always evaluates to false. When the optimizer processes the query, because it doesn't recognize any valid SARGs, its query plan forces a table scan with an exclusive table lock. When executed, though, the where clause evaluates to false immediately, so no table scan is actually performed, but the process is still granted an exclusive table lock.

Because the process now has an exclusive table lock, you can guarantee that no other transaction modifies any data rows, giving you the read repeatability you need, while avoiding the potential for deadlock that holdlock would cause. Avoiding the deadlock doesn't come without a tradeoff, however. By using the table lock to minimize deadlocks, you increase lock contention on the table. Therefore, before implementing this solution, you need to consider whether deadlock avoidance is more important than allowing concurrent access to the table.

Finally, one of the best methods for minimizing deadlocks is the simple matter of referencing tables in the same order within all transactions. Some possible methods used for ensuring the reference order for tables include sorting them alphabetically by name, by table ID, or some other common sorting order. As a result, if tables are always accessed in similar order, the very issue of two connections requesting conflicting resources is avoided. Locks will be acquired and released in a relatively sequential order, preventing deadlocks by avoiding conflicting re-source requests.

Examining Deadlocks

Because a user transaction is aborted, any locking information that could be returned by sp_lock is no longer available. The user connection with the aborted transaction had all of its locks released by SQL Server when the transaction was aborted. However, you still can debug the situation and find out what went wrong.

Using the dbcc traceon command, you can specify the 3605 and 1204 trace flags to display deadlock output messages in the SQL Server error log file. (See Chapter 26, "Defining, Altering, and Maintaining Databases and Logs," for more information on proper use and maintenance of the error log file.) Because only the sa login can turn on these trace flags, debugging deadlock situations involves testing multiple applications and having a system administrator available to turn on the trace flags and monitor output of deadlock information to the error log file. If you want to have these trace flags on all the time, you can add them as SQL Server command-line parameters, using the -T command-line switch. Command-line parameters are added through SQL Enterprise Manager's Server Configuration/Options dialog box, as shown in Figure 16.6.

FIGURE 16.6.

Adding the deadlock trace flags as SQL Server startup parameters in SQL Enterprise Manager.

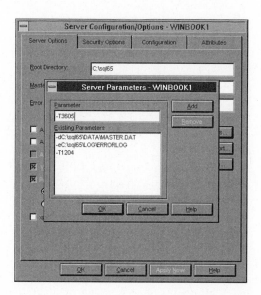

Once these options have been turned on, SQL Server will print information to the error log file similar to that listed below when a deadlock occurs, highlighting the conflicting processes, the pages or tables on which they are deadlocked, and which process was chosen as the victim:

```
95/11/21 23:15:13.39 spid10   *** DEADLOCK DETECTED with spid 11 ***
spid 10 requesting SH_INT (waittype 0x8004), blocked by:
  EX_TAB: spid 11, dbid 5, table 'authors' (0xf43010)
  (blocking at 0x246f9a0)
pcurcmd SELECT(0xc1), pstat 0, input buffer: select * from authors where
au_id = "409-56-7008"
and au_lname = "Bennet"

spid 11 waiting for SH_PAGE (waittype 0x8006), blocked by:
  UP_PAGE: spid 10, dbid 5, page 0x190, table 'titles' (0xb71be83), indid 0
  EX_PAGE: spid 10, dbid 5, page 0x190, table 'titles' (0xb71be83), indid 0
  (blocking at 0x246f9b8)
pcurcmd SELECT(0xc1), pstat 0, input buffer: select * from titles where title_id
= "BU1032"

VICTIM: spid 10, pstat 0x0000 , cputime 40
```

In this example, user process 11 is marked as being involved with a deadlock. Process 10 is requesting a shared lock on the authors table but is being blocked by an exclusive table lock from process 11. Further down the output, you can see that process 11 is waiting for a shared page lock on the titles table, but is being blocked by process 10. As a result, the victim is process 10. Hence, SQL Server aborts process 10's current transaction (similar to process 10 submitting the rollback tran statement, but with SQL Server's "encouragement"), and all the work of that transaction is undone, as well as all locks for that transaction being released.

> **WARNING**
>
> The 1204 trace flag is known to incur additional overhead within SQL Server, and slows performance when turned on. For this reason, I recommended that this option be turned on only in development or test environments, or only temporarily in a production environment when attempting to debug a deadlocking problem.

Summary

Prior to SQL Server Version 6.0, all locking of all resources was controlled solely by SQL Server. SQL Server 6.0 first introduced the ability to manage lock type and granularity at the query level (discussed in the next chapter), or by using specific configuration options to control lock escalation thresholds (discussed in Chapter 32. Prior to SQL Server 6.5, the smallest lock unit of work was the 2KB page, meaning that SQL Server did no row-level locking. Row-level locking had to be simulated, coming at the cost of potentially substantial overhead. SQL Server 6.5 introduced the ability to lock at the row level for insert processes, providing you with a mechanism for reducing lock contention and hot spots within your tables.

Most importantly, remember that locking contention and deadlock can be only minimized, never completely eliminated; understanding how to minimize locking contention and deadlock is an important skill to make the applications you develop on SQL Server both more reliable and faster. Use stored procedures, use the least-restrictive lock type possible (you see how to do this in the next chapter), and make your transactions run as quickly as possible. A well designed application on insufficient hardware is almost always faster and more reliable than a poorly designed application on a killer box!

Managing the SQL Server Optimizer

17

SQL Server uses a cost-based optimizer. The costs with which it works are computed values—computations developed by people. Because people are sometimes fallible, it stands to reason that the computations these people create also might be fallible. This creates the need for discussion of how to tell SQL Server what to do, but only in those instances where it can't figure out the best way to process a query on its own.

This last point is the real issue: How often does SQL Server require manual intervention to execute a query optimally? Considering the overwhelming number of query types and circumstances in which those queries are run, SQL Server does a surprisingly effective job of query optimization.

For all but the most grueling, complex query operations, my own testing has shown that SQL Server's optimizer is quite clever, and very, very good at wringing the best performance out of any hardware platform. For that reason, you should treat this chapter as a collection of techniques to be used only where other methods have already failed.

Overriding the Optimizer

Before indiscriminately applying the topics discussed in this chapter, remember one very important point: Use of these features can effectively hide serious fundamental design flaws in your database or application. In fact, if you're tempted to use these features (with a few more moderate exceptions), it should serve as an indicator that problems may lie elsewhere in your application.

Having determined that no such flaws exist, and that SQL Server really is choosing the wrong plan to optimize your query, you can use the information in this chapter to override the three most important decisions the optimizer makes:

- Choosing which index, if any, to resolve the query
- Choosing the order in which to join tables in a multi-table query
- Choosing the lock type and level to manage multiuser access to tables

WARNING

If you haven't already read Chapters 13 through 16, I'd strongly encourage you to do so now. If you're new to SQL Server, I'd suggest that you go back through them again and make sure that you have a solid grasp of the topics they cover. Understanding how SQL Server behaves normally is essential to making it behave for a particular exception!

SQL Server's optimizer is quite good. SQL Server has a reputation for rather blinding performance, and that reputation is owed in no small measure to the query processor. Remembering this fact as you peruse this chapter will help you keep perspective on how selective you should be in applying these concepts.

Throughout this chapter, one point must remain clear in the reader's mind: These options are considered *exception cases* and are meant to cope with particular problems in particular queries in particular applications. As such, there are no global rules or rules of thumb to speak of, because the application of these features by definition means that normal SQL Server behavior doesn't work.

The practical result of this idea is that you should test every option in *your* environment, with *your* data and *your* queries, and use the techniques discussed in the preceding four chapters to optimize your queries. The fastest-performing query wins, so don't be afraid to experiment with different options—but don't think that these statements and features are globally applicable or fit general categories of problems, either! There are, in fact, only three rules: *test, test,* and *test*!

SQL Server uses indexes to improve query performance, and it locks to guarantee consistency. We'll look at forcing, or, in Microsoft's terms, "hinting" index selection first. Associated with index selection is the ability to force a particular join order for multi-table queries, which is topic number two for this chapter. The section on locking discusses new Microsoft-specific T-SQL keywords that enable you to specify a query-level locking scheme that overrides the one SQL Server might have chosen for you.

Forcing Index Selection

In prior versions of SQL Server, there was an undocumented but commonly known method to force index selection on the optimizer. If you included the index ID number after the table name in a query, SQL Server would use that index. With SQL Server 6, there is a documented method, using index hinting, that allows you to specify the index SQL Server should use for accessing a table.

This `select` statement displays the names of tables and the index names and IDs for those tables. Here's an example of the kind of output you can expect:

```
select "table"=o.name, "index"=i.name, indid
from sysindexes i, sysobjects o
where i.id = o.id
and o.type = "U"      /* user tables only (no system tables) */
order by 1, 2, 3

table                    index             indid
---------------------    ---------------   -----
pt_sample                pt_sample             0
pt_tx                    pt_tx                 0
pt_sample_CIkey2         CIkey2                1
pt_sample_CIcompany      CIcompany             1
pt_sample_CIidNCk        CIid                  1
pt_sample_CIidNCk        NCk                   2
pt_tx_CIamountNCamount   CIamount              1
pt_tx_CIamountNCamount   NCamount              1
pt_tx_NCamount           pt_tx_Ncamount        0
pt_tx_NCamount           NCamount2             2
pt_tx_CIid               tx_CIid               1
```

An index of 0 refers to the base table, an index of 1 is for the clustered index, 2–250 are the nonclustered indexes, and 251–255 are reserved. Remember that every table will have either a 0 or a 1 but not both. After you have the index names and IDs, you can use them to specify the index to be used by the query. Specifying an index ID of 0 can force a scan of the base table.

We'll use showplan to observe the index the server uses to resolve several queries. In this query, the server has three meaningful options for identifying the correct result rows—a table scan, a clustered index search, or a nonclustered index search:

```
set showplan on
go

select *
from pt_sample_CIidNCk
where id between 1 and 500 and
key2 between 30000 and 40000
go
```

Left to its own devices, the optimizer selects the clustered index:

```
STEP 1
The type of query is SELECT
FROM TABLE
pt_sample_CIidNCk
Nested iteration
Using Clustered Index
```

To force selection of a specific index, specify the index name for the index you want SQL Server to use, placing the name in parentheses after the name of the table in the from clause. This example forces the use of the NCk index (see the preceding list of tables and indexes):

```
select *
from pt_sample_CIidNCk (index = NCk)
where id between 1 and 500
and key2 between 30000 and 40000
go
```

As instructed, the optimizer uses the nonclustered index to find rows matching the query:

```
STEP 1
The type of query is SELECT
FROM TABLE
pt_sample_CIidNCk
Nested iteration
Index : NCk
```

> **NOTE**
>
> In versions prior to SQL Server 6, the server let you specify only the index ID, and not the name. The problem with index IDs is that they might change when an index is dropped and re-created. Because you specify the name of the index when you create the index, you're safer specifying an index name.

Using the same method, you can force the optimizer to use the clustered index, by selecting an ID of 1:

```
select *
from pt_sample_CIidNCk (index = 1)
where id between 1 and 500
and key2 between 30000 and 40000
go

STEP 1
The type of query is SELECT
FROM TABLE
pt_sample_CIidNCk
Nested iteration
Using Clustered Index
```

In this example, you've forced the clustered index. Using an index ID of 0, you can even force a table scan:

```
select * from pt_sample_CIidNCk (index = 0)
where id between 1 and 500
and key2 between 30000 and 40000
go

STEP 1
The type of query is SELECT
FROM TABLE
pt_sample_CIidNCk
Nested iteration
Table Scan
```

Let's look at the performance of this query given each of these choices. set statistics io can be used to determine the number of logical I/Os to execute the query, as shown in Table 17.1. (Physical I/Os are problematic because everything is resident in cache by the time you run the query a second time.)

Table 17.1. Summary of logical I/Os to resolve the query by optimization plan.

Index	Logical I/Os
Clustered: CIid (1)	7
Nonclustered: NCk (2)	632
Table Scan (0)	243

Clearly, the server found the most efficient path in this query!

A Case Study

Let's look at a case study where a user might decide that he can outguess the optimizer.

Table 17.2 shows the table structure for a simple transaction table, pt_tx.

Table 17.2. Partial output from `sp_help pt_tx`.

Column	Datatype	Len
id	int	4
amount	money	8
date	datetime	8

There's a non-unique, nonclustered index on the date column.

Consider this query, which looks for the total amount for all Sunday entries:

```
select sum(amount)
from pt_tx
where datename(dw, date) = "Sunday"
```

The output from `showplan` shows that SQL Server has chosen a table scan strategy for this query, at a cost of 88 logical reads:

```
STEP 1
The type of query is SELECT
Scalar Aggregate
FROM TABLE
pt_tx
Nested iteration
Table Scan
STEP 2
The type of query is SELECT
```

Here's the data distribution by the day of the week:

```
select datename(dw, date) "day of week", count(*) "num rows"
from pt_tx
group by datepart(dw, date), datename(dw, date)

day of week     num rows
— — — — — — —   — — — — —
Sunday          25
Monday          1236
Tuesday         1185
Wednesday       1220
Thursday        1248
Friday          1289
Saturday        1079
```

If you run a covered query (see Chapter 15, "Analyzing Query Plans") against this table, using the nonclustered index on `date`, you'll find that a nonclustered index scan costs 55 logical I/Os.

The question is: *Did the optimizer fail to find the best path?* If the server were able to scan the nonclustered index (at a cost of 55 I/Os) and if it were able to convert the date value in the index before deciding whether to read a data page, it would need to read a page from the table itself only 25 times (once for each row where the day of the week is Sunday). The total cost of the query would be:

index scan cost   55

data read cost	+25
total cost	80

This is less than the cost of the table scan by 9 percent (80 versus 88).

Based on this reasoning, let's force the use of the nonclustered index and look at the cost:

```
select sum(amount)
from pt_tx (index = date_ix)
where datename(dw, date) = "Sunday"
```

The cost of this query is 7,337 I/Os, or almost 100 times the cost of a simple table scan. SQL Server didn't evaluate the value of the function before deciding whether to read a page from the table. Instead, for each value in the nonclustered index, SQL Server retrieved the corresponding page from the table, *and then determined whether the row matched the search condition.*

Moral of the Story

If you think you can do a better job of index selection than the optimizer, give it a try. Compare the cost of your choice with the cost of the choice made by the optimizer. In most cases, you'll find that the SQL Server query optimizer made the better choice! From time to time, SQL Server will choose poorly, however, particularly when deciding between several possible nonclustered indexes. For this reason, forcing an index should always be treated as a last resort. Instead of forcing an index, you should usually focus your time on why an incorrect index is being picked. A likely culprit is out-of-date statistics or a condition in the where clause that isn't a SARG.

Forcing Join Order

Forcing join order is another technique to get presumably better performance from SQL Server. You've seen that the order of the joins is as important to performance as index selection. It's tempting to ask, "If I change the join order from the one the server selected, can I pick better?"

> **NOTE**
>
> I have to admit that I haven't been able to outguess the server very effectively, but I've certainly been able to pump up the volume of I/O requests.

You force join order with the forceplan option:

```
set forceplan {on ¦ off}
```

After forceplan is on, the optimizer won't do any evaluation of the costs of different join orders; instead, SQL Server joins the tables in the order listed in the from clause. Once this option is set ON, it will stay on for *every* query until it's set OFF. Note that this is different from forcing an index, which is specified for one particular table, for one query only.

In this query, the optimizer found the most efficient plan by reversing the order of the tables from the order in which they're named:

```
set showplan on
set statistics io on
go

select * from titles, publishers
where titles.pub_id = publishers.pub_id
go

STEP 1
The type of query is SELECT
FROM TABLE
publishers
Nested iteration
Table Scan
FROM TABLE
titles
Nested iteration
Table Scan
Total writes for this command: 0
Table: titles scan count 3, logical reads: 9, physical reads: 0
Table: publishers scan count 1, logical reads: 1, physical reads: 0
Total writes for this command: 0
```

We can see that the join order is publishers outside, titles inside. Current versions of the showplan option list tables outer to inner.

TIP

You can also verify the order by looking at the statistics io output, scan count. In the preceding example, a scan count of 1 says that the table incurred 1 iteration (the outer table), and the scan count of 3 was the inner table (passed through 3 times). Therefore, publishers was the outer table.

Force a join order with the forceplan option (as a matter of tidiness, make sure you set it off when you're done with it):

```
set forceplan on
go

select * from titles, publishers
where titles.pub_id = publishers.pub_id
go

set forceplan off
go

STEP 1
The type of query is SELECT
```

```
FROM TABLE
titles
Nested iteration
Table Scan
FROM TABLE
publishers
Nested iteration
Table Scan
Table: titles scan count 1, logical reads: 3, physical reads: 0
Table: publishers scan count 18, logical reads: 18, physical reads: 0
Total writes for this command: 0
```

The forceplan option instructs the server to execute the query using the join order listed in the from clause and to skip trying to pick a better join order. In this example, titles is being forced to be the outer table in the query, and publishers the inner table. You can see that you're more than doubling the amount of required reads to resolve the query. In large joins, performance can degrade by several orders of magnitude.

One of the things I do when tuning a database for a client who has a performance problem is to go in and add additional indexes, which allows the server to pick different join orders more effectively (allows a join order to use an index instead of a table scan). It isn't unusual to have a change in join order change a query from 30 minutes to 30 seconds *if usable indexes are also present*. In the case just described, all I had to do was take a table that was indexed on (a, b) and index it additionally on (b, a).

> **NOTE**
>
> SQL Server 6.0 introduced reverse index traversal, allowing a middle table in a join to use the index in both directions.

Although forcing a join order can be educational, it can cause problems as the data distribution changes. The optimizer notices when index statistics are updated, but you have to remember to go and change all the code that has been forced to use a particular plan.

Temporary Tables

When joining many tables, join order isn't your only problem. You can also run into built-in limitations regarding the number of joins, or restrictions about inner/outer tables in outer joins. There are many cases where no optimizer could resolve the query in a single pass (although SQL Server will try).

In these cases, you may want to use a temporary table to build one or many intermediate results, and then join those intermediate results together to get a final result. With large, complex queries, queries with many search clauses, and those requiring an intermediate work set that's substantially smaller than the source table(s), consider creating temporary tables. This is by far the most common way to bypass the optimizer.

Query-Level Locking Selection

As a second category of "optimizer hint," SQL Server includes a collection of keywords for defining the particular lock type and lock granularity a query can use for a specific table. Note that this specification is for one query only; SQL Server doesn't allow you to specify a particular lock for all queries of a type on a table. The locking level must be either chosen by the optimizer (the default behavior) or supplied in the form of an optimizer hint, using the keywords discussed in the following paragraphs.

There are nine distinct optimizer hints. The first is index selection, which has already been covered. The remaining eight control locking behavior. All these options except HOLDLOCK were introduced in SQL Server 6.0; HOLDLOCK was available in earlier versions:

- NOLOCK. When this option is used, select statements don't apply read locks, and exclusive locks aren't honored, which means that dirty reads are possible.

- HOLDLOCK. This is the traditional HOLDLOCK that has been part of SQL Server for many versions. It forces SQL Server to hold page or table locks until a statement or transaction has completed, and supports repeatable reads.

- UPDLOCK. This option forces update locks instead of exclusive locks for data page modification. See the section on update locks in Chapter 16, "Locking and Performance," for more details on update locks.

- PAGLOCK. This option forces SQL Server to use individual shared page locks in situations in which it would normally immediately acquire a table lock. PAGLOCK does *not* override the normal escalation to a single shared table lock when the lock escalation threshold is reached.

- PAGLOCKX. This option works like PAGLOCK except that it applies an exclusive page lock where an exclusive table lock would normally be used.

- TABLOCK. This option forces SQL Server to put a single shared lock on the table, rather than attempt to use individual page locks for the table.

- TABLOCKX. This option works like TABLOCK, except that the lock applied is an exclusive table lock.

- FASTFIRSTROW. Because of SQL Server's Parallel Data Scanning features (new as of Version 6.0), SQL Server can execute a table scan-plus-sort operation faster than using a nonclustered index. The table scan-plus-sort can use the Parallel Data Scanning features, while the traversal of the nonclustered index can't. However, rows can't be returned to the workstation until the sort has completed, potentially delaying initial delivery of the result set. FASTFIRSTROW tells the optimizer to use the nonclustered index instead of the scan-plus-sort operation to speed the response time of the first row. Overall query performance might suffer, but the initial results will be returned more quickly.

With each of these options, issues of consistency and concurrency arise, as they did in the previous chapter. These issues are magnified, however, by the application developer's control of these features replacing SQL Server's control of these features. So how can you efficiently and effectively make use of these features?

Note that these locking hints are used primarily for `select` statements. In SQL Server 6.0, only the UPDLOCK hint could be used with an `update` statement. Now, in SQL Server 6.5, PAGLOCK, TABLOCK and TABLOCKX can all be used with an `update` statement, but, in that case, TABLOCK is synonymous with TABLOCKX.

First and foremost, these keywords enable you to overcome performance and locking problems that are created by SQL Server itself. They should be used only to solve a specific, identifiable problem.

For example, many transaction-processing databases must be online 24x7x365. As a result, the question of how to implement reporting has resulted in some curious inventions. Many shops simply do hourly or half-hourly transaction log dumps to disk. The backups are restored to DSS or reporting-only databases on the same server, or even on a different server. From that reporting server, reports can be run on almost-live data.

The critical issues with doing reporting on live transaction data are many. First, reports must run `select` statements, which require shared locks. However, `updates`, `inserts`, and `deletes` require exclusive locks. As a result, the `read` operations for reporting interfere with exclusive lock requests, creating concurrency issues—forcing the use of a separate reporting-only database or server.

The NOLOCK keyword fixes this problem by allowing reports to view live transaction data without interfering by using shared locks or being blocked by the exclusive locks held by the transactions. This setup removes one of the restrictions to using live data for reporting, but the issues of CPU usage and I/O on the data pages involved remain. It isn't a perfect solution, but it's a step in the right direction.

As discussed in the previous chapter, SQL Server's normal behavior is to acquire page locks as needed, until the lock escalation (LE) threshold is reached. However, in the situation where no index is used, and the query also uses the HOLDLOCK optimizer hint, SQL Server will immediately acquire a shared *table* lock. You can override this immediate acquisition of a table lock with the optimizer hints PAGLOCK or PAGLOCKX. Using PAGLOCK or PAGLOCKX can increase the concurrency of your queries by allowing queries to lock only those pages that it needs to reference, rather than locking all table pages for large operations. This is particularly true for PAGLOCKX, which allows other connections to read and write pages that aren't affected by its query's operations. However, these hints won't override the escalation to a table lock when the configured number of page locks have been acquired. For details on configuring the lock escalation thresholds, see Chapter 31, "Configuring and Tuning SQL Server."

The FASTFIRSTROW option highlights the need for testing in *your* environment in order to make these new options work properly. With Parallel Data Scanning features enhancing table- and index-scanning operations, it's actually faster to perform a table scan and then sort the data rows than it is to use a nonclustered index with the keys already sorted in the desired order. As a result, the data rows aren't returned as quickly as they would be if a nonclustered index were used. So, using FASTFIRSTROW enables you to force SQL Server to use the available nonclustered index instead of the scan-plus-sort operation, to return rows more quickly to the client. As a result, the query appears to run faster on the client because results start returning sooner, but in fact it takes longer to prepare the entire result set for the client.

NOTE

The idea of returning the first row of a result set immediately to create the impression of fast query performance isn't new. In fact, Microsoft's own JET database engine (the core engine of both Microsoft Access and Microsoft Visual Basic) uses this technique to make users think that they're getting data back sooner than they are. JET returns rows to the client as they're generated, so that the client gets at least some data right away. The tradeoff is that this scheme increases network performance and client application overhead, because multiple fetches are required to get the entire result set back. As usual, applications have a set of six-of-one-half-dozen-of-the-other compromises from which you, the application developer, get to choose. Testing is the only way to ensure that you're maximizing SQL Server's performance potential.

With all the hinting keywords, it's possible to specify multiple keywords for the same table, if they're separated by spaces. The most restrictive option is the only one that will be used in that query, so the others become redundant and are ignored by the query processor. Following is an example of a query that forces SQL Server to acquire and hold page-level locks on each page of a table:

```
begin tran
select *
from pt_sample (HOLDLOCK PAGLOCK)
commit tran
go
```

Note that Transact-SQL syntax requires that locking hints be inside parentheses. The HOLDLOCK option, which was the only locking option available prior to Version 6.0, can still use the old syntax without parentheses. However, you should use the older syntax only when backward compatibility is required, because the syntax without parentheses isn't guaranteed to be available in future versions.

Summary

SQL Server provides many facilities for forcing optimizer behavior. Indiscriminate use of forcing indexes and forcing join orders often causes more harm than good, but it can be a useful tool for overcoming query-optimization problems. Where necessary, use temporary tables to reduce the cost of large joins.

If you're encountering locking problems, such as substantial quantities of blocked processes or highly contentious queries and tables, the locking hints in this chapter provide an effective means of managing locking granularity for queries.

There's a mandatory testing step that must precede any use of these keywords. If you don't know what's really going wrong with a query, using these options will make life much more painful, not less so. However, with thorough testing, these hints can alleviate locking contention and let client applications work more effectively. Testing! Always think TESTING!

Database Design and Performance

18

Physical and Logical Database Design

A logical database design is a roadmap of all of the data structures in a system (or organization), with the relationships among objects clearly defined. A physical database design is the *implementation* of a database on a specific database engine.

Logical database designers are skilled at understanding how physical and process structures within an organization relate to potential data structures. They draw diagrams that explain the relationship of data within an organization. They develop a set of entities and relationships (which ultimately become tables in the physical database), and assign attributes to each entity and relationship (that is, identifying which columns go into which tables).

Many MIS organizations swear by this design, and require this logical design to be the physical design, simply because it's easy to understand. This isn't a good approach. A logical design doesn't have the same purpose as a physical design. The purpose of the logical design is to understand and represent data and its relationships. *The primary purpose of a physical design is performance.*

Designing databases for performance requires an understanding of the underlying DBMS. Now that you understand the physical structures that SQL Server uses to store and modify data, you are ready to consider how to apply SQL Server to specific performance problems. This chapter explores physical database design techniques for improving SQL Server performance.

Database Design Issues

There are three primary design issues to consider when developing a physical database design:

- Data integrity
- Ease of use
- Performance

When developing a physical database design, you want the design to support your data consistency and *referential integrity* (*RI*) requirements easily. If a data element is represented exactly once within a database, it's easier to track and maintain than if it's represented multiple times. Referential integrity must also be maintained and, if possible, enforced at the server level.

A database administrator (DBA) should consider ease of comprehension in a physical database design. Tables should be browseable so that end users can easily find the data they need and know what data a table contains.

Finally, the DBA typically wants to make database access and modification fast. Speed of data retrieval and update is usually the yardstick used to measure the success of a physical database design. Often, designing a database for access speed or to improve update performance requires modifying the physical design of the database—for example, duplicating or partitioning frequently used data from infrequently used data.

Unfortunately, designing for all three criteria (data integrity, ease of use, and performance) is often impossible because they tend to be mutually exclusive. For example, breaking up a table to improve access speed makes browsing and pulling data together more difficult for the end users. During physical database design, decisions need to be made about balancing these objectives.

What Is Logical Design?

Logical database design is the process of defining end users' data needs and grouping elements into logical units (for example, tables in an RDBMS). This design should be independent of the final physical implementation. The actual physical layout of the tables, access paths, and indexes is provided at physical design time. Database design tradeoffs have ramifications in physical design and performance because an RDBMS can't detect a poorly designed database and compensate accordingly.

One stage of logical design is the reduction (or, if possible, elimination) of redundant data. This usually results in many tables, each with small, compact rows. Sometimes, reducing redundancy in this way ends up increasing the number of joins required to pull related data elements back together for output.

Normalization Conditions

To understand how to change the database in the physical design to suit your performance needs, you first need to understand relational database *normalization*, which is the end result of logical database design. Here's a review of the basic terminology and conditions of normalization:

- An *entity* (table) consists of *attributes* (columns) that define *properties* about each *instance* (row) of the entity.
- Each instance of data refers to a single event.
- Each row is uniquely identified with a *primary key*. The primary key allows you to find the row you want to retrieve.
- The primary key can be a single column or multiple columns (a *compound* or *composite key*).
- Primary keys can't be null (if there's no way of uniquely identifying a row, it doesn't belong in a relational database).

Normal Forms

The relational database model includes a definition of six levels of normalization, or six *normal forms* (first through fifth normal form, and "Bryce-Codd" normal form). Normalization removes redundancy from the data, and requires every data element to be referenced by a primary key. (In this book, third normal form is considered a normalized database because it's pretty much the level that the industry considers a normalized database.)

First Normal Form

For a database to be in *first normal form*, all repeating groups must have been moved into separate tables; one column contains exactly one value.

The following example isn't in first normal form because it has a repeating group of titles; there are many titles for the single `Publisher` row:

Publisher	Title1	Title2	Title3
Smith Publishing	The Tale of...	Cooking with...	Computer and ...

The following example is in first normal form. There are now several rows for `Publisher`, one for each `Title`:

Publisher	Title
Smith Publishing	The Tale of...
Smith Publishing	Cooking with...
Smith Publishing	Computer and...

NOTE

The problem of dealing with repeating groups is not all that simple. There are times when repeating groups really *ought* to be stored in this "horizontal" representation, especially when there is a finite limit to the number of repeating values, and when the data will typically be reported horizontally.

Some databases allow you to store repeating groups within a single column, called a "multi-valued" column. When the relational model was defined, the elimination of multi-valued columns was one of its basic tenets.

Second Normal Form

When *second normal form* is met, non-key fields must depend on the entire primary key. A database without compound primary keys is automatically in second normal form (if first normal form is met).

This example isn't in second normal form because the key is `Publisher` and `Title`, but `Publisher Address` relates to only one part of the key field (`Publisher`) but not to `Title`:

```
Publisher              Title                Publisher Address

Smith Publishing       The Tale of...       New York, NY
Smith Publishing       Cooking with...      New York, NY
Smith Publishing       Computer and...      New York, NY
```

To correct the example, break the table into two parts. Publisher-specific information belongs in the Publisher table:

```
Publisher              Publisher Address

Smith Publishing       New York, NY
```

Title-specific information belongs in the Title table:

```
Publisher              Title

Smith Publishing       The Tale of...
Smith Publishing       Cooking with...
Smith Publishing       Computer and...
```

Third Normal Form

Third normal form dictates that non-key fields must not depend on other non-key fields.

This example table isn't in third normal form because the Location column depends on the department, not the employee, even though Employee is the key field:

```
Employee           Dept               Location

Smith              10                 Bldg C
Jones              .10                Bldg C
Thomas             10                 Bldg C
Alders             8                  Bldg D
```

To bring the table into third normal form, break it into two parts—one for Employee that indicates the department:

```
Employee           Dept

Smith              10
Jones              10
Thomas             10
Alders             8
```

and the other for Dept, indicating the location:

```
Dept               Location

10                 Bldg C
8                  Bldg D
```

Benefits of Normalization

A normalized database reduces redundancy and therefore storage requirements in the database. Data integrity also is easier to maintain in an environment where you have to look in only one place for the data, where each entity is represented only once.

In addition, when the database is normalized, the rows tend to get narrower. This fact enables more rows per data page within SQL Server, which can speed up table scanning and queries that return more than one row, improving query performance for single tables.

Drawbacks of Normalization

The drawbacks to a normalized database design are mostly related to performance:

- Typically, in a normalized database, more joins are required to pull together information from multiple tables (for example, to get employees along with their current location requires a join between the `Employee` table and the `Dept` table).

- Joins require additional I/O to process, and are therefore more expensive from a performance standpoint than single-table lookups.

- Additionally, a normalized database often incurs additional CPU processing. CPU resources are required to perform join logic and to maintain data and referential integrity. A normalized database contains no summary data, because summary data violates normalization in two ways: it's redundant information and it has no independent business meaning. To calculate summary values requires aggregating multiple rows of data, which incurs both greater CPU processing and more I/O.

Normalization and the Database Design Picture

Normalization provides a good place to start a physical database design because data is logically grouped and consistent. Third normal form should always be applied to all database design, at least initially.

Denormalizing the Database

Denormalizing is the process of taking a normalized logical design and intentionally disobeying the rules to increase performance. To denormalize effectively, you must understand both the bias of the data to be loaded into the database and how the data will be accessed.

Advantages of Denormalization

Denormalization can help minimize joins and foreign keys and help resolve aggregates. By storing values that would otherwise need to be retrieved (repeatedly), you may be able to reduce the number of indexes and even tables required to process queries.

Guidelines

Following are some basic guidelines to help you determine whether it's time to denormalize your database design:

■ Balance the frequency of use of the data items in question, the cost of additional storage to duplicate the data, and the acquisition time of the join.

■ Understand how much data is involved in the typical query; the amount of data affects the amount of redundancy and additional storage requirements.

■ Remember that redundant data is a performance benefit at query time, but is a performance liability at update time because each copy of the data needs to be kept up to date. You typically write triggers to maintain the integrity of the duplicated data.

Basic Denormalization Techniques

Be aware that denormalization is a technique for tuning a database for a specific application, and as such tends to be a last resort when tuning performance. Adding indexes to a table is a tuning method that's transparent to your end users and applications (as long as all are writing queries properly!); modifying the database schema isn't transparent. If you change the database design, application code that accesses that database needs to be modified as well.

A variety of denormalization methods can be used to modify the physical database design in an effort to improve performance:

■ Adding redundant data by duplicating columns or defining summary data

■ Changing your column definitions by combining columns or shortening existing columns

■ Redefining your tables by combining tables, duplicating entire tables or portions of a table, and partitioning tables into multiple tables

Redundant Data

Redundant data helps performance by reducing joins or computations, which in turn reduces I/O and CPU processing, respectively. It tends to be either an exact copy of the data or summary data.

Duplicate data should be of exactly the same name, type, and domain, and have the same integrity checking as the original data. Triggers should be used to maintain integrity between the original and the duplicate data. Note that the more volatile the data, the more often you incur overhead to maintain the duplicate data. You need to balance frequency of use and the cost of the acquisition join against the frequency of modification and the cost of the extra update.

Occasionally, duplicating static data to avoid joins is a good idea. In Figure 18.1, moving the title to the Salesdetail table saves you from having to perform a lookup when you need that data for, perhaps, a report on sales by title. Is this a good candidate for duplication? The advantage is that it will improve performance, and the title is a *nonvolatile* data attribute (that is, it won't change much). The disadvantage is that this change might make the `Salesdetail` table a lot larger.

FIGURE 18.1.

Duplicating the title *column from the* Titles *table in the* Salesdetail *table.*

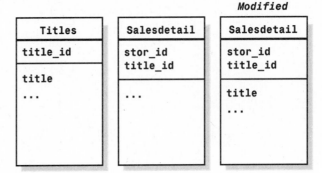

Why is this example denormalized? Because there is redundant data and `title` doesn't depend on the entire key (`stor_id`, `title_id`) of the `Salesdetail` table.

Foreign Key Duplication

Another candidate column for duplication is a foreign key to reduce the number of joins required to retrieve related information.

Figure 18.2 shows a normalized version of a database, requiring a three-table join to retrieve the name of the primary author for a title. If you want to be able to know the primary author for a book 80 percent of the time you retrieve the title, how can you reduce the joins? The easiest way is to add the author ID or author name for the primary author to the `titles` table. (See Figure 18.3.) Author name or author ID is a good candidate for duplication because it's unlikely to change very often.

FIGURE 18.2.

In a normalized version of this database, a three-table join is required to retrieve the name of the primary author.

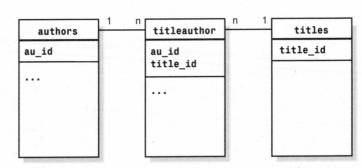

FIGURE 18.3.

Duplicating the primary_auid *value in the* titles *table reduces that three-table join to a two-table join for better performance.*

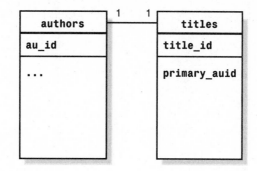

Derived or Summary Columns

Derived columns contain data duplicated for the purpose of avoiding repeated calculations. This is called *summary data.*

In any environment, application designers have recognized that certain summary values need to be maintained and available constantly to speed their retrieval. If you store frequently accessed sums, averages, and running tallies, reports and queries can run substantially faster, but data modification is slowed somewhat.

Figure 18.4 shows the title table with a derived column, total_sales, which contains a sum of the qty column from the salesdetail table for the rows related to that title. The value stored in the derived total_sales column is updated automatically every time a qty is inserted or modified in the salesdetail table. This setup speeds data retrieval, but adds overhead to modifications on salesdetail.

FIGURE 18.4.

Storing a derived value in the title *table,* total_sales, *which is the sum of* qty *for the corresponding rows in the* salesdetail *table.*

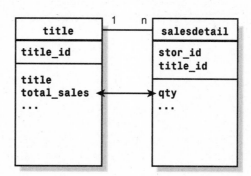

In this example, maintaining a running total_sales column is less expensive than calculating the total sales every time that information is needed. This decision is based on comparing the frequency of the request for the quantity information with the additional cost of the update on salesdetail.

When defining summary data, triggers should be used on the detail tables to maintain the integrity of the summary data, and the summary data needs to be used often enough to justify the update-time overhead created by the triggers.

Changing Column Definitions

You've seen that adding redundant columns and derived columns can enhance performance. You also can see an improvement in performance when you shorten critical columns by using two strategies:

- Contrived columns
- Shortening long columns

When the columns get narrower, a narrower index enables more keys to be searched with fewer I/O operations. The corresponding data rows can also wind up being smaller, enabling more rows per data page, which minimizes the number of I/Os required to scan the data.

Contrived Columns

A *contrived column* is typically a substitute for a long key; it has no business use of its own.

In Figure 18.5, does the Customer table contain enough information to make rows unique? Is name unique enough? City? State? ZIP? Address? Maybe not. George Foreman presumably lives with each of his five sons, all named George, making six George Foremans (Foremen?) at one residence. What about Social Security number? Some people don't have one. Some people lie. Sometimes the Social Security Administration makes a mistake and issues a duplicate number. What do you do? What makes sense for a foreign key in the Order table? Unfortunately, none of the existing columns necessarily makes sense for a foreign key.

FIGURE 18.5.

The Customer *table has no easily identifiable primary key for the* Order *table to reference. A contrived key could have been used as both primary key in* Customer *and foreign key in* Order.

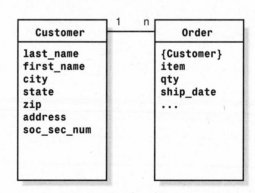

To use a contrived column, add the contrived key to the table and treat it as the primary key for all purposes. Use it as a foreign key in all related tables. In the "George Foreman" example above, a unique integer column (probably an `identity` column) could be added to the `Customer` table. Each row would be uniquely identified by the `identity` value. Each row in the `Orders` table would include a `Customer identity` value that uniquely identifies a row in the `Customer` table.

This strategy is most helpful in long-key or multicolumn-key situations. You save storage in the short *and* long run. Using a contrived column results in a much shorter key than trying to decide how many columns guarantee uniqueness and then using all those columns as the foreign keys.

Access performance also improves because index columns are narrower, speeding individual lookups and joins. In addition, a contrived key is a column that generally doesn't change, so you don't have to worry as much about maintaining the foreign key values. If the customer name is part of the key and is used as a foreign key, any name change has to be cascaded to all foreign key entries as well, increasing the overhead on updates to `Customer`. With a contrived key, you can update customer information without affecting the primary and foreign keys.

Redefining Tables

Creating duplicate tables tends not to be the only solution, and frequently isn't the best solution. It is, however, a viable method of reducing I/O and search speed for specific types of queries.

There are two basic methods of duplicating tables: subsets and partitioning.

Subsets are duplicates of the original data—by row, column, or both. (Note that replication services can do this across SQL Servers automatically!)

Data Partitioning

Data *partitioning* takes on two basic variations:

- Vertically, by separating infrequently used columns
- Horizontally, by separating infrequently used rows

Not all data is appropriate for duplication or partitioning. If the data is fairly stable, duplicating or partitioning a table may be useful; volatile data is less likely to work well. The more volatile the data, the more you have to double your work. Triggers are necessary for maintaining data consistency and integrity of duplicate data, which incurs additional overhead on data modifications. In addition, if both tables of a partition must be checked to satisfy a query, additional code must be written (either a union or a join) to bring the results together into a single result set.

Duplicate data also means that you'll incur an additional storage expense. On the other hand, you may need to scan less data to derive the same results. In addition, your joins will be faster (because the tables are smaller), and you may gain a benefit by archiving some of your historical, infrequently accessed data.

Although the potential benefits of duplication and partitioning may be large, the amount of extra maintenance may be correspondingly large.

Vertical Partitioning

Vertical partitioning is a denormalization technique by which you split a table, by columns, into two or more tables. This technique is typically used to minimize the size of the primary table, or to move infrequently accessed columns to a separate table. Consider the following situation:

> "Our invoicing job won't fit in the overnight batch window. We need to reduce join time between orders and items."

In Figure 18.6, a table with several descriptive columns can be partitioned vertically. The information needed for the active processing is all in the Item_Active table; less-used information is stored in the Item_Inactive table. The Item_Active table is considerably smaller and has a higher row density (rows per page). Given this implementation, order-entry operators can still look at descriptions, take orders, and so forth by performing a simple join between Item_Active and Item_Inactive. Because these are point queries, retrieving one row at a time, the additional cost of the join is negligible. However, the nightly batch process that needs to scan a large number of item numbers and prices at a time speeds up significantly.

FIGURE 18.6.

Vertically partitioning a table creates an active set of data with substantially higher row density.

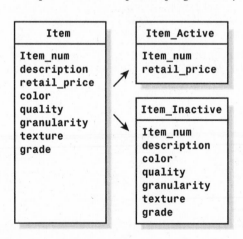

The advantage of partitioning columns is that the number of locks held on tables may be reduced, and table scans may be faster. However, if excessive joining takes place between vertically partitioned tables, and adversely impacts performance, you may need to reevaluate your decision.

Horizontal Partitioning

Table-scan time grows proportionally with table size. When activity is limited to a subset of the entire table, isolating that subset makes sense. This plan is useful not only for production, but also for test tables. Horizontal partitioning is a method of splitting a table at the row level into two or more tables.

The method used to partition the rows horizontally varies, depending on how the data is used. The most common method used is by date, partitioning the most current, active data from the historical, inactive data. Other partitioning options include partitioning by activity, department, business unit, geographical location, or a random hash value.

Consider the following situations:

> "Ninety-eight percent of the time we're using 5 percent of the rows; the rest of the rows are getting in our way."

or

> "The most recent 15 percent of the data is being used 85 percent of the time. Why perform statistics updates on the whole 200,000,000 rows when only a part of the table is volatile?"

Figure 18.7 illustrates an `Orders` table partitioned horizontally, with active rows in one table and inactive rows in another.

FIGURE 18.7.

You can reduce scan time, index size, and index levels by partitioning a table horizontally.

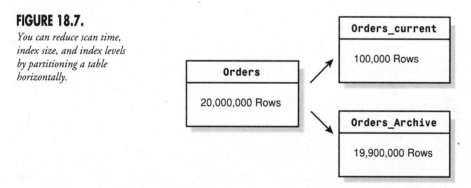

One of the main drawbacks to consider when horizontally partitioning tables is that retrieving data from more than one table as a single result set requires the use of the `union` statement. If you use a random hashing scheme to partition the data, determining where the data resides is more difficult for end users, making the database less browseable.

Views as a Partitioning Tool

One advantage of vertical partitioning over horizontal partitioning is that the vertical partitioning can be hidden from the end user or application developer through the use of views. If you split a table by columns, a view can be created that joins the two table partitions. Users can then select from the view as if it were a single table.

Views can't be used to hide horizontal partitioning from end users or applications because, in the current versions of SQL Server, the union statement isn't permitted in views.

Database Devices and Performance

A database can span many devices. Although some device allocations can be reserved for use by the transaction log, any other devices can be reserved for use by tables and indexes (see Figure 18.8).

FIGURE 18.8.

A single database can span several logical devices. The create database *statement here allocates 100MB on each device for use by the database* perftune.

device_1   device_2   device_3

create database perftune
on device_1 = 100,
on device_2 = 100,
on device_3 = 100

When SQL Server allocates space to a table or index, which device provides a free extent? This section discusses the location of physical data, how to manage its location, and the performance ramifications of choosing from different options for storing and placing databases and objects.

What is at stake here is the ability to improve server performance by spreading out data so that it can be read more quickly, in parallel, from different disk drives using different controllers. In addition, the approaches considered here provide different types of *fault tolerance* in the storage system. (A fault-tolerant system is one that can recover from or run through the failure of a single component, such as a hard disk.) Choices are available:

- ■ SQL Server itself provides one option with *segments*. These are subsets of the space allocated to a database, identified by the logical device of the allocation. Before Windows NT disk functions were integrated into SQL Server, segments made sense. Although we explore segments in this chapter, other options make more sense.

■ The recommended option for SQL Server 6.5 is to use some variation of *RAID* (Redundant Array of Inexpensive Disks).

The following section takes a brief look at the implementation of segments. After that, you learn a way to avoid the administrative overhead of segments and get better performance with RAID technology.

Segments

Figure 18.8 shows a database that is being associated with three devices, perhaps with the following statement:

```
create database perftune on device_1 = 100, on device_2 = 100, on device_3 = 100
```

Now you create a table:

```
create table perf_table (a int, b varchar(255) null)
```

Where will the table reside? Let's break this into two questions:

1. Where will the table structure reside?
2. Where will the table data reside?

The official answer is that allocations are random. (In practice, you'll see that allocation is slightly less than random.) Without segments, you can't control where allocations are made. (See Figure 18.9.)

FIGURE 18.9.

When you don't use segments, allocation of space to a table among several devices is unpredictable.

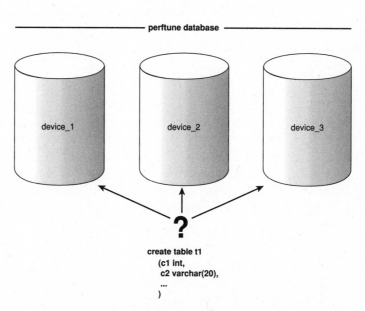

You *can* control the device where your objects reside—by creating named segments. A *segment* is a pointer to a device or set of devices.

> **NOTE**
>
> Try to keep segments and *fragments* straight. A fragment is the unit of space allocated to a database by a single `create database` or `alter database` command (or the corresponding action in SQL-EM). The `master..sysusages` table contains one fragment per entry.
>
> For example, if you create a 100MB database on two devices, and then add another 25MB allocation on the first device, the database would consist of three fragments:
>
> ```
> create database show_frag on dev1 = 50 log on dev2 = 50
>
> alter database show_frag on dev1 = 25
> ```
>
> A segment points to one or many devices containing allocations for a database. In effect, a segment is a way of gathering fragments of a database on those devices. If you created a segment pointing to all allocations of the `show_frag` database on `dev1`, that segment would include the 50MB fragment created by the `create database` statement, as well as the 25MB fragment created by the `alter database` statement. In addition, any new fragments allocated to the database on `dev1` would also be part of the segment.

Before looking at user-defined segments, you need to understand how SQL Server uses system-defined segments to store data. Every database when created consists of three segments:

- The `system` segment, where all the system tables (except `syslogs`) are stored (the `system` segment points to the first device listed in the `create database` statement)
- The `default` segment, where all table and index data is stored
- The `logsegment` segment, where the transaction log (`syslogs`) is stored

When you're using system-defined segments, the `create table` statement inserts rows into several system tables, all stored in the `system` segment:

- A row with a unique identifier for the table is inserted into the `sysobjects` system table (stored in the `system` segment).
- A row is added to the `sysindexes` system table, identified by the key used in `sysobjects`. If the table was created with a primary key (clustered), the row in `sysindexes` has the `indid` value of 1. Otherwise, it has a value of 0. Any nonclustered unique or primary key constraints generate additional rows in `sysindexes` with `indid` values of 2 or greater. (`text` and `image` columns also generate entries in `sysindexes`.)
- One row per column in the table goes into the `syscolumns` system table.
- The table creation is logged in `syslogs` (`logsegment`).

The object itself (your table) is created on the segment named `default`. All tables and indexes are created on the `default` segment unless some other segment is named in the `create` statement. When a database is created, the `default` segment points to all non-log devices.

If you (unwisely) create a database without specifying a separate log device, all three sets of tables (system tables on the `system` segment, user tables and indexes on the `default` segment, and the `syslogs` table on the `logsegment` segment) compete for the same space.

All the system tables are initialized first, and therefore grow on the first device. Tables created on the `default` segment start out on the first available device and continue to grow from the beginning of the database space allocation. The `syslogs` table, however, is actually allocated from the back of the space allocation. In other words, `syslogs` starts from the end and moves forward to the beginning.

In Figure 18.10, you can see that the tables you create will start at the beginning of the database's space allocation and continue to grow toward the end of the space allocation. The `syslogs` table, however, is allocated from back to front. As a result, if a transaction log isn't on its own device, they both compete for the same space and eventually will collide.

FIGURE 18.10.

Unless the log is on its own device, it can grow large enough to fill the entire database.

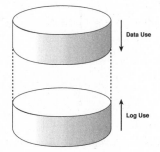

Data Use

Log Use

When the `logsegment` and `default` segments have met, you run out of database space. In this manner, log growth and size can't be controlled because the transaction log is competing with other database objects for the *entire database space allocation.* So how do you control log table growth? By putting the transaction log on its own device.

When you execute the `create database` statement, you have the option of putting the transaction log on its own device. Doing so is highly recommended because the log then uses only the space allocated to it on that device. It can't use any of the other devices allocated for the database.

When a table is created, a single extent (8 2KB pages) is allocated to the table on one of the devices within the `default` segment. The row in `sysindexes` stores the address of that row, as well as a segment ID of 1, which indicates the `default` segment.

NOTE

If the table had been created on a different segment (with `create table ... on` *segmentname*), the allocation would have come from a different device and the `segment` column in `sysindexes` would store the segment ID. Any future allocation of space would come from the segment identified in `sysindexes`.

Why Use Segments?

Why do you want to define and use segments? Although segments are one method of spreading disk activity across many physical disks, they are far from the most efficient to manage or operate.

The only valid reason to use segments is to control space allocation to sets of objects or indexes within a database. Because an object can't grow beyond its segment, you can limit the growth of potentially explosive tables by placing them on a segment that includes only the space that you want to allocate to the table.

The `syslogs` table and volatile tables such as live data feeds are examples of tables whose growth needs to be carefully controlled. (Live data feeds include stock tickers and physical monitoring equipment, such as shop-floor and pollution-control equipment.) Tables that are subject to sudden growth spurts may be less important to your overall system than other, transactional tables with more steady growth. You may want to gather data in these tables, but if you suddenly get a huge number of new rows, you may be willing to have these tables stop accepting data (temporarily) while you deal with a warning about filling a particular segment. In the meantime, you can continue to accept data in other tables that are more critical.

TIP

Better ways exist to control growth of big tables and indexes. You can use the SQL Performance Monitor to watch table and index allocations and perform careful truncations when they grow too large. This is a much more surgical approach to monitoring large table sizes!

You could also isolate large tables in their own database, where they can't hurt any other tables and where they compete only with their own indexes for space. This adds complexity to a backup and recovery system, but resolves the space contention issues fairly simply.

Segment Definition

Now that you know not to do it without cause, here's how to do it. You begin with a `create database` statement like this example:

```
create database perfdb on virtual_device_1 = 100, virtual_device_2 = 100,
➥virtual_device_3 = 100
```

To create named segments, you first must use the database. Segments are *database-specific*: They have meaning only in the database in which they were created.

The next example consists of two batches. The first batch changes the database context. (Remember—segments are managed within the database!) The second batch creates three segments, then extends the third segment so it spans two devices:

```
use perfdb
go

exec sp_addsegment seg1, virtual_device_1
exec sp_addsegment seg2, virtual_device_2
exec sp_addsegment seg3, virtual_device_2
exec sp_extendsegment seg3, virtual_device_3
go
```

Figure 18.11 displays the database and segment allocation at this point. (There will also be segments defined for `default`, `system`, and `logsegment`.)

FIGURE 18.11.

perfdb segment definitions after segments are defined. Notice how a single device can be designated as a part of several segments.

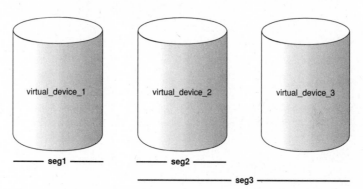

As you can see by looking at the code and the figure, `seg1` refers to all the space allocated to `perfdb` on `virtual_device_1`, `seg2` refers to all the space allocated to `perfdb` on `virtual_device_2`, and `seg3` refers to all the space allocated to both `virtual_device_2` *and* `virtual_device_3`.

Let's dispel some common misconceptions. First, the total space allocated to the database is 300MB. The total space allocated to `seg1` is 100MB; to `seg2`, 100MB; and to `seg3`, 200MB. Note that you can't add up the space allocated to the segments and get the database size. This fact causes some confusion when users receive this error message from the server: `Unable to allocate space for object object_name on segment segment_name`. When you aren't using segments, this message means that you ran out of space in the database or that `syslogs` has filled up. For named segments, it doesn't mean that the database is full; it simply means that no free extents are available on the virtual device(s) assigned to the segment. The object can't grow.

Let's go back to the original questions: If you place an object on seg1, where does that object go? The answer is on `virtual_device_1`. What if the object is placed on seg2? Then data is stored on `virtual_device_2`. What if the object were created on seg3? Then data allocation would be on *either* `virtual_device_2` or `virtual_device_3`. In the seg3 case, it's still unclear whether the object will be allocated an extent on `virtual_device_2` or `virtual_device_3`, but you know for certain that it won't be on `virtual_device_1`.

Next problem: What if more space is available on `virtual_device_1`? For example, assume that `virtual_device_1` is all the space on a 2-gigabyte SCSI device. You are using only a small portion of the disk. You are also using only a small portion of the virtual disk you have defined on it. If you exceed the 100MB, will the object try to grab more space on the device? Again, the answer is no. The segment and space on the segment are limited to space allocated to the database by `create database` or `alter database` statements. (More on `alter database` shortly.) What if space on `virtual_device_1` is allocated to another database? Again, still no difference. The many-to-many relationship of devices to databases doesn't affect segments, as segments are database-specific.

Placing Objects on Segments

At this point, you've provided a mechanism to isolate individual devices defined for databases. Now you need to assign objects to these areas. The common way to place an object on a segment is to specify the segment in the table's creation statement. By using the on *segment name* keyword, you can specify a distinct segment to initialize the table. The `sp_placeobject` stored procedure enables you to move an existing table from one segment onto another segment. The third option uses a unique feature of clustered indexes. By creating a clustered index for a table on a different segment, SQL Server puts both the index and the table data on the new segment:

```
create table volatile_table (a int, b varchar(255) null) on seg1

create index index1 on volatile_table (a) on seg2

create table spread_table table on seg3
```

Note a few things in this example code. First, `volatile_table` will reside on seg1. This isolates the table from the other physical disks. Next, `index1` is a nonclustered index, so it can exist on a device separate from the table. (Clustered indexes are treated as part of the same structure as the underlying table, so if you place a clustered index on a segment, the table itself moves to that segment.) The `spread_table` table can acquire space on either `virtual_device_2` or `virtual_device_3`. Finally, both `index1` and the `spread_table` table will compete for space on `virtual_device_2`. (See Figure 18.12.)

FIGURE 18.12.
Objects are assigned to segments and acquire space according to the definition of those segments.

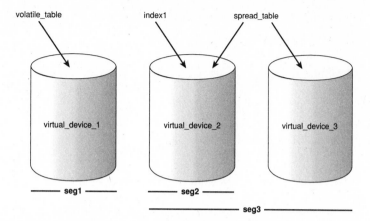

How to Stop Using a Particular Device for a Segment

You can use sp_dropsegment to instruct the server to stop using a particular device for a segment or to completely remove a segment definition (if there isn't already an object for that device). For instance, you might want to instruct the server that you don't want virtual_device_1 to be used for default or system segments any longer:

```
exec sp_addsegment index_segment, virtual_device_1
exec sp_dropsegment "default", virtual_device_1
exec sp_dropsegment "system", virtual_device_1
```

Introduction to RAID Technology

RAID, or Redundant Arrays of Inexpensive Disks, is a relatively new technology, having debuted near the end of the 1980s. The concepts behind RAID aren't new; RAID simply provides a structured framework in which to discuss those concepts. The most basic concept is simple: Instead of using a single, fixed disk to store data, use multiple disks simultaneously and in parallel. When you do this, I/O operations are much faster because the read and write operations happen in parallel across multiple read-write heads on multiple fixed disks, rather than across a single read-write head on a single disk. Simple parallelization of I/O in this way has demonstrated immediate—and drastic—performance improvements. SQL Server has traditionally used segments to achieve this, by breaking up a table across multiple disks.

Currently, six common RAID levels are defined:

- RAID Level 0
- RAID Level 1
- RAID Level 2
- RAID Level 3

- RAID Level 4
- RAID Level 5

RAID Level 0

A RAID Level 0 device provides data striping across multiple disks without providing any mechanism for data redundancy. (See Figure 18.13.) The data is divided into the appropriate number of chunks and striped across all disks in the array. All data reads and writes are handled asynchronously.

The advantages of RAID 0 are the high I/O rate due to small block size and the capacity to read from and write to multiple disks at once. The transfer time for a data request to a RAID 0 device is proportional to the number of devices participating in the array.

FIGURE 18.13.

RAID Level 0 diagram.

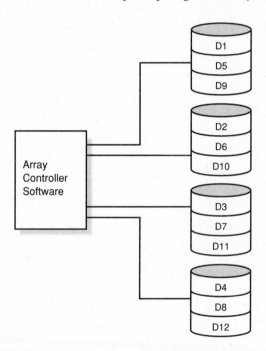

RAID Level 1

RAID Level 1 is your traditional, hardware-level disk mirroring. (See Figure 18.14.) Each disk in the array has one or more exact copies of the disk. There's no data striping. RAID 1 devices provide the highest level of reliability of all the RAID devices, while providing a high I/O rate due to small block sizes. RAID 1 devices support small reads and writes with performance nearly equivalent to that of a single disk, especially if the array performs mirrored writes concurrently. Data access time can also be improved if the controller software allows simultaneous read requests to be spread over both disks.

RAID 1 devices often provide a faster and more efficient mirroring mechanism than SQL Server software-level mirroring.

One disadvantage to RAID 1 is that it has no built-in mechanism for data striping—it's up to the database designer/DBA to spread tables and indexes across devices to evenly spread the I/O. RAID Level 1 also requires the greatest number of disks of any of the RAID technologies (each disk requires an equivalently sized duplicate to provide data redundancy).

As far as performance, large writes to a RAID 1 device generally execute at a speed slower than a single spindle due to the overhead of maintaining a duplicate copy of the data. RAID 1 offers no performance improvement over a single disk when writing data and is definitely slower if a separate controller isn't used for the mirror drive. Read performance, however, is the same as or better than reads from a single spindle. This is because requested data can be read from either side of the mirrored pair and doesn't normally need to read from both disks. With some RAID 1 devices, intelligent controller software can improve read performance by reading from the device closest to the requested data or by splitting concurrent read requests across both devices.

FIGURE 18.14.

RAID Level 1 diagram.

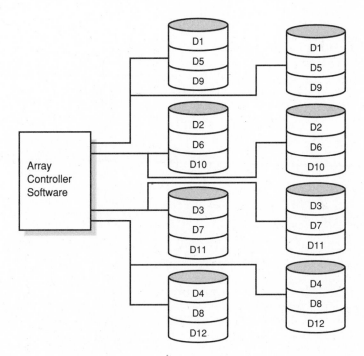

RAID Level 2

A RAID Level 2 device is a parallel-access array. All disks are accessed and written concurrently for every access to a RAID device. RAID 2 uses a bit-level interleaving scheme to spread a data chunk across all data disks in the array. (See Figure 18.15.) Data redundancy is implemented by spreading the corresponding check bits across check disks.

The advantages of using a RAID 2 array are that the array handles error detection and correction rather than individual disks, and that the cost of redundancy in terms of drives is less. Redundancy is maintained by using check bits of the data rather than an exact copy. The disadvantage of RAID 2 is that failure of one disk shuts down the entire array.

FIGURE 18.15.

RAID Level 2 diagram.

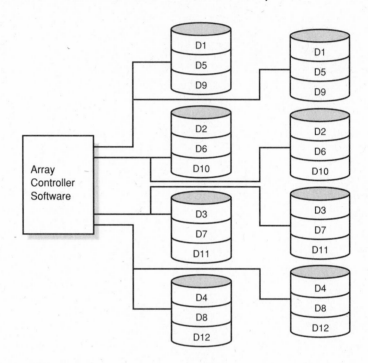

RAID Level 3

RAID 3 also implements a parallel access array. It differs from RAID 2 in that data blocks are spread across devices. A single disk contains parity information (XOR) in order to rebuild a failed device in the array. (See Figure 18.16.)

The advantages of using RAID 3 are that the synchronized parallel access supports fast large-data transfers, and that the cost of maintaining redundancy is lower in terms of the number of devices required compared to RAID 1. RAID 3 also allows hot swapping of a failed data drive (that is, the array doesn't have to be shut down while replacing a failed device). The failed device can be swapped out on-the-fly and the contents will be re-created on the replacement from the contents of the parity disk.

The primary disadvantages of using a RAID 3 device are that the single parity disk is a bottleneck for the entire array, and failure of the parity disk disables the entire array. Also, because of the parallel access architecture, RAID 3 isn't efficient for small block reads.

FIGURE 18.16.

Raid Level 3 diagram.

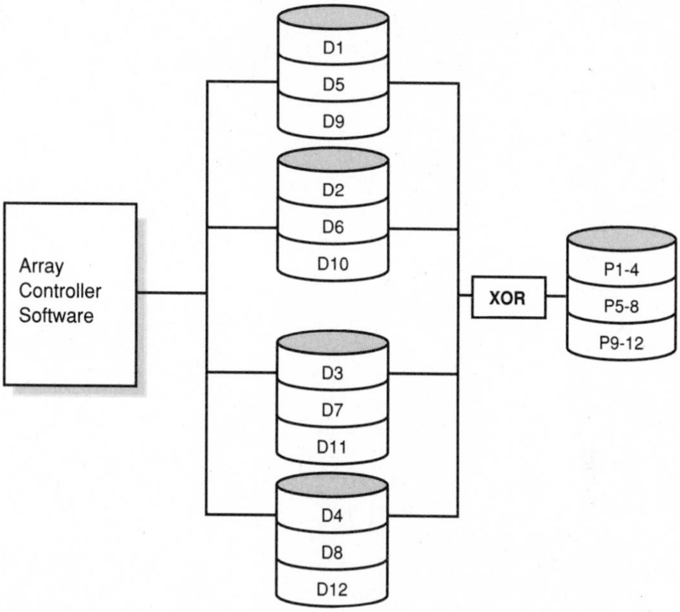

RAID Level 4

A RAID Level 4 device is an independent array. Unlike the parallel access arrays, a single I/O request doesn't require concurrent access to all disks in the array. Data blocks in a RAID 4 device are striped across all data devices in the array. A single disk contains the parity information (XOR) necessary to rebuild a failed device. (See Figure 18.17.)

The primary advantage of RAID 4 over RAID 2 and 3 is that, because it's an independent array, it can process multiple data requests simultaneously. The disadvantage of RAID 4 is that write performance is compromised by the overhead of maintaining the disk parity.

To maintain the parity information, the controller software must read parity information to internal buffers, compute the new parity information, and then write the updated parity information as well as the data to the appropriate devices. This is commonly referred to as the *read/modify/write sequence*. In addition, the single parity disk creates an I/O bottleneck in the array and creates a single point of failure.

FIGURE 18.17.

RAID Level 4 diagram.

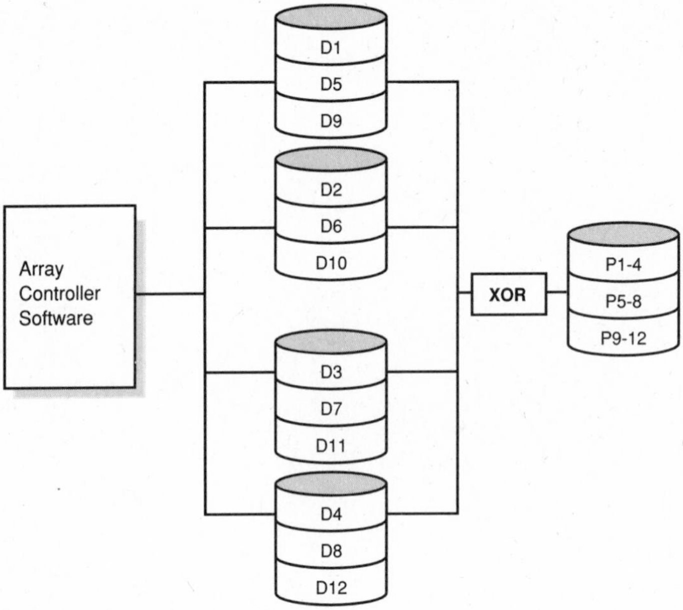

```
                                        D1
                                        D5
                                        D9

                          D2
                          D6
 ┌──────────┐            D10                      ┌─────┐      P1-4
 │  Array   │                                     │ XOR │      P5-8
 │Controller│                                     └─────┘      P9-12
 │ Software │            D3
 └──────────┘            D7
                         D11

                                        D4
                                        D8
                                        D12
```

RAID Level 5

RAID 5 is similar to RAID 4 except that it doesn't maintain a single parity disk. Instead, parity information for the data contained on one disk is spread across the other disks in the array. (See Figure 18.18.)

The additional advantage to this approach is that it eliminates the bottleneck and single-point-of-failure problems of having a single parity disk. The disadvantage of RAID 5 is the slower write performance due to the read/modify/write sequence.

SQL Server and Storage Device Performance

Over time, a table that is used for steady data modifications will become heavily *fragmented.* Fragmentation occurs when the page chain points from extent to extent without consecutive pages in the chain being contiguous in the extent range. Fragmentation is especially damaging to performance with devices that perform large block reads.

SQL Server typically performs small block reads and writes, reading data in 2KB chunks at a time. Consequently, SQL Server is sometimes poorly suited to storage devices that use larger block sizes to achieve performance gains or caching controllers that buffer large block reads.

By reducing fragmentation, you can improve performance with large block devices. To check on fragmentation, use the dbcc show_contig command (see Chapter 29, "DBCC"). To remove fragmentation, drop and re-create the clustered index (without the sorted_data option).

FIGURE 18.18.
RAID Level 5 diagram.

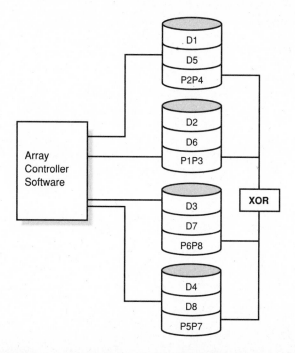

> **NOTE**
>
> You may be able to take better advantage of the performance of devices that perform large block reads if you configure the read-ahead capabilities of SQL Server as described in Chapters 31, "Configuring and Tuning SQL Server," and 32, "Optimizing SQL Server Configuration Options."

DSS and data-warehouse-type applications may benefit from large block devices if they are performing large sequential reads of adjacent data pages. OLTP applications generally perform operations on small blocks of data randomly spread across devices; therefore, they benefit more from devices that perform small block I/O efficiently.

Which RAID Device Should You Use?

Three tradeoffs are involved in choosing a RAID device:

- Cost
- Performance
- Reliability

All three factors tend to be mutually exclusive:

- High performance equals higher cost and lower reliability.
- High reliability equals higher cost and lower performance.

If you're looking into a RAID solution, choose the subsystem that best maps to the desired goal of performance, reliability, and cost, making the tradeoffs where necessary.

DSS and data warehouse implementations require good read performance and high availability. In an OLTP environment, the goal is both high device reliability and maximum write performance. A tempdb device requires high read and write performance, but high reliability typically isn't required.

> **NOTE**
>
> With the capacity to set up stripe sets in Windows NT (see the following section) to support RAID levels 0, 1, and 5, the cost issue of RAID is somewhat mitigated. However, you still need to weigh performance against reliability to determine which RAID implementation to use for different SQL Server environments.

RAID Levels Commonly Used with SQL Server

The three RAID levels most commonly implemented in a SQL Server environment are Levels 0, 1, and 5. RAID Level 0 typically provides the best read/write performance of the RAID devices for the lowest cost, but with the tradeoff of the lowest reliability. A RAID 0 device might be a good device to use for a large tempdb to help minimize tempdb I/O contention.

RAID Level 1 provides the highest reliability of RAID devices, and high performance for small block I/O operations. Typically, RAID 1 provides the best tradeoff between reliability and performance, and is a good candidate for log devices and critical OLTP databases.

RAID 5 provides high reliability and excellent performance for reads, but lower performance for writes. It also requires fewer devices than RAID 1 to maintain redundancy. RAID 5 is typically a good candidate for DSS and data warehouse databases, where OLTP activity is at a minimum and most of the activity is read-oriented.

SQL Server and RAID—Additional Notes

When setting up the log and data devices for a SQL Server database, try to get the log and data onto separate I/O devices, and preferably on completely separate I/O channels so no contention exists between log writes and data reads and writes. This setup gives you the best I/O performance for your database. Because of the striping nature of RAID 0 and RAID 5 devices, if you mix SQL Server data and log on these devices, both log and data will be striped across the same set of disks. Although striping reduces the chances of a log write going to the same disk at the same time as a data read or write, there's no guarantee that log and data I/O will always go to separate physical disks. To eliminate any I/O contention between data and log, and to get the best performance when using RAID, I recommend that you use separate RAID devices for each data and log.

For a transaction log, you may also want to consider using a mix of RAID 0 and 1—essentially, a striped set of mirrored disks. This plan gives you the best of both worlds—the highest level of reliability (RAID 1) with the highest write performance for concurrent writes (RAID 0).

RAID devices provide flexible alternatives for storage devices requiring large volumes, high performance, or high reliability. Choosing the appropriate RAID device requires balancing cost versus performance versus reliability in order to find the proper fit.

Hardware-Based RAID Subsystems

With Microsoft SQL Server, you have two sets of options for using RAID technology: You can use Windows NT to create stripe sets, or you can use a hardware-based RAID disk subsystem.

Hardware-based RAID, although more expensive than using Windows NT, can also be more reliable. For mission-critical, transaction-processing applications, you should be using hardware-based RAID. With hardware-based RAID systems, everything should be duplicated and hot-swappable. Disk drives should be hot-swappable, and most manufacturers of high-quality RAID subsystems have additional disks already plugged into the cabinet, waiting to be turned on in the event of a disk failure. The disks themselves should be hot-swappable, meaning that the physical disk can be removed and replaced without turning off the server or disk subsystem.

Power supplies should also be hot-swappable, and a redundant power supply should already be in the cabinet. Should either of the power supplies fail, the remaining power supply should immediately take over, preventing service interruptions. Most hardware-based RAID systems also use dual controllers—one for managing the disk interface to the computer, the other for managing the striping of data. If possible, both of these controller types should also be duplicated, to prevent controller failure from becoming a single point of failure. Swappable controllers are obviously a more complicated effort, so understand that massive controller failure is still going to keep you up late trying to repair it.

As with all RAID implementations, remember that approximately 25 to 30 percent of the rated disk capacity will be consumed by the parity bit information that's part of RAID 5. You need to remember this when you're planning capacity for databases. Putting a 5GB database on a 5GB RAID array will lead to disappointing results; for 5GB, count on a 7GB or 8GB array being necessary!

Windows NT Stripe Sets

For ultimate disk-level, fault-tolerant protection, hardware-based RAID is the preferred choice. In some situations, however, cost and fault-tolerant expectations need to be lowered, and can be. In these cases, Windows NT can supply both performance improvements and data-integrity enhancements through the use of Windows NT stripe sets. Stripe sets allow the operating system to collect space from various drives, and treat them as a RAID array. Windows NT supports RAID 5, and writes parity bits according to that specification. The advantage here is one of dollar cost. Using existing hard disks in an existing server, you can create a stripe set that provides a majority of the performance offered by hardware RAID, with some of the fault tolerance as well. Windows NT will write parity bits, but drives and power supplies aren't necessarily hot-swappable.

Stripe sets, including step-by-step instructions for their creation and management with the Windows NT disk administrator, are discussed in the Sams title *Windows NT Administrator's Survival Guide*, and are also included in the "Administering Windows NT" multimedia education course available from Microsoft.

RAID versus Segments

Segments provide functionality outside of parallel I/O and fault tolerance. The capability of controlling growth of objects by limiting that growth to a particular device isn't something Windows NT or a hardware-based RAID system can manage. If your database requires this feature, segments are your only option.

However, if you're using segments purely as a performance enhancement, you will be pleased and surprised to learn that not only is RAID faster, it's more reliable *and* cheaper to administer. A RAID volume presents itself as a single logical disk—drive E: or drive F: or whatever you care to label it. By creating a disk device and database on that drive, you have immediately paralleled I/O and fault tolerance.

NOTE

During the development of SQL Server 4.2 for Windows NT, the program manager for performance and tuning issues on the SQL Server development team at Microsoft tested the use of segments versus using Windows NT-based RAID. Despite days of configuration, his best manually configured scenario using named segments was still 10 percent *slower* than using Windows NT stripe sets. Not only do stripe sets eliminate the overhead of administrators manually configuring segments, but you also get a faster database.

Summary

A fully normalized database, although easier to maintain, doesn't necessarily lend itself to optimal performance. To determine whether the database design needs to be modified to improve query performance, identify the problem queries and look at the base tables on which the queries rely. Identify any potential join problems due to column widths and types or due to the large quantity of rows to be accessed. Then consider modifying columns or creating derived, summary, or contrived columns where they might be helpful. Additionally, identify any potential scanning problems in the base tables and consider partitioning tables if no alternatives exist. Due to the impact on end users and application developers, the first choice for query optimization tends to be adding indexes, rather than modifying the physical database design.

SQL Server can use a variety of underlying disk-related technology for improving database performance and reliability. SQL Server for Windows NT has kept features introduced in SQL Server 4.2 (named segments), primarily for the purpose of backward compatibility. Advances in hardware technology have largely rendered these features obsolete.

For small departmental applications, implementing stripe sets with three or four physical disks is a viable option for providing both guaranteed fault tolerance and performance enhancement. Both of these advantages come without the administrative overhead associated with named segments. Even on smaller servers, buying extra hard disks and using stripe sets is cheaper than having an administrator manage segments manually.

For truly mission-critical, high-transaction-volume applications, hardware-based RAID is the best choice for both performance and data fault tolerance. The fault tolerance, hot-swappability of components, and extra performance that hardware-based RAID provides cannot be matched by Windows NT's built in features—but bring your checkbook. The prices are high, but the cost of losing your data through failure or downtime may be even higher.

Application Design for Performance

19

Sometimes it seems like there are a thousand ways to make your application run slowly. This chapter reviews some elements of system design and implementation that affect performance, and then focuses on application-design characteristics that also have an impact on system performance.

At the most general level, system performance is determined by several components:

- Server resources, including fast CPU, sufficient memory, and fast disks
- Network configuration, including sufficient bandwidth for the traffic
- Client configuration, including fast CPU and sufficient memory
- Replication method

More specifically, a bad database or application design can render a good hardware configuration useless. For example, a database design requiring repeated scans of a very large table can bring a powerful server to its knees.

> **NOTE**
>
> A pessimistic theory of systems states that all systems will ultimately fail, but those that gain acceptance obviously fail, because those that gain acceptance always grow in usage and demand until they no longer can handle the load, and fail.
>
> No matter how powerful your hardware and software configuration, it makes sense to build systems to be as lean and efficient as possible in order to delay the time when your configuration no longer is able to handle the demands on the system.

The obvious areas on which to focus in building efficient SQL Server systems include the following:

- Logical database design, to keep data as concise as possible and improve update performance
- Physical database design, to improve query performance
- SQL query syntax, to take advantage of server capabilities
- Proper balance of client and server workload, to ensure that the client and server are each performing optimally

This last item is the focus of this chapter.

Considerations in Balancing Performance

What you're seeking as you build client/server applications is the perfect mix of client processing and server processing. To predict how operations should be distributed, you need to understand the special strengths and weaknesses of servers and clients.

Servers

When properly optimized and configured, a SQL Server is most efficient at finding a needle in a haystack—that is, finding a handful of rows in a huge table or performing hundreds of concurrent modifications on a large table. It's efficient at performing fairly complex data modifications, and its deadlock detection and resolution scheme is acceptable if deadlocks aren't too frequent. The server is acceptably efficient at scanning a medium-sized table and is as good as any relational database at evaluating complex search criteria. The SQL Server can efficiently enforce fairly complex business rules within a database. Overall, the server is best suited to handling set-based data retrieval and modification operations in your system.

A SQL Server is extremely *inefficient* at executing thousands of operations in a loop (as with a cursor). It can be inefficient at scanning an enormous table (though no more inefficient than most other relational database systems, and better than others with read-ahead threads). Large data loads on tables having dozens of indexes will run slowly.

Clients

A properly configured client workstation is most efficient at displaying complex user interfaces, handling data formatting and column- or row-specific data validation. The client can process and display small- and moderate-sized result sets, and is efficient at handling row-wise operations on those sets. For example, client workstations are a good place to prepare detailed reports with summary values based on result sets.

A client workstation is inefficient at consolidating and sorting tens of thousands of rows of data or finding a handful of rows in a large set.

Implications of Server and Client Capabilities

Understanding the fundamental strengths of the components, there are several decisions you need to make regarding application design. Some of those decisions are very straightforward and indisputable; others are more difficult and involve tradeoffs. The following sections examine these topics:

- Network performance issues
- How to handle row processing and data validation
- Complex and multiple-server transactions

The Network as Bottleneck

Don't disregard the importance of the network in client/server systems. In general, you should always treat the network as a primary bottleneck. Even if your system has sufficient *potential* bandwidth to handle a specific operation efficiently, network availability is by far the most unpredictable performance factor. With more and more systems needing to run across the Internet or across a corporate intranet, reducing your dependence on the network is even more important. Moreover, under load, operations that run well for a single user may be unacceptably slow when multiple users run them.

Let's look at ways to reduce network load and make applications more efficient.

Reducing Query Size

SQL (the language) allows complex set operations to be defined in a single statement. Consider the difference between the code required to modify a set of rows having a certain characteristic in a typical third-generation language and SQL. The following pseudocode represents the work of a 3GL to search a set of rows and modify certain ones:

```
open file for update to filehandle
set up rowset
while not (eof)
begin
    lock next row
    read next row into rowbuffer
    if column1 = value
    begin
        update column2 = newvalue
        write rowbuffer
    end
    unlock this row
end
close file
```

Here's a sample SQL statement to perform the same work:

```
update tablename
set column2 = newvalue
where column1 = value
```

In and of itself, the SQL language provides a mechanism for reducing query size; however, complex batches can include dozens or hundreds of SQL queries. For example, the sp_help stored procedure consists of more than 48KB of code. If every time a user needed to know table and column definitions he had to submit a 48KB query, the strain on the network could be substantial.

Thus, one useful way to reduce network traffic is to use stored procedures instead of submitting large SQL queries. A stored procedure with several parameters seldom requires more than a small network packet (512 bytes) to transmit. If your system will have hundreds or thousands of users attached to a single server, using procedures instead of sending large SQL batches will improve network performance.

Reducing Result Sets

The other major drag on the network is large result sets. This is a genuine problem in decision-support systems, which by their nature deal with very large data and often need to return large sets of rows.

On the other hand, I've seen many client systems where programmers fail to take real advantage of the server, instead returning large numbers of rows to the client, and then processing the rows on the client system in order to find the actual rows desired. For example, consider this query:

```
select last_name, first_name, m_init
from names
where upper(last_name) = "GREEN"
```

The query will probably run horribly (the upper function invalidates a SARG and requires a table scan) unless the table is quite small. An experienced SQL programmer will think of several reasonable solutions, including this one:

```
select last_name, first_name, m_init
from names
where upper(last_name) = "GREEN"
and last_name like "G%" or last_name like "g%"
```

The revised query may be able to use an index to identify the rows starting with a capital or lower case *G*. This strategy should speed up the query substantially, allowing use of an index, but a lot depends on exactly what the data looks like.

On the other hand, an inexperienced SQL programmer's reaction to the poor performance of the original query might be to return all rows to his application, and then identify those rows matching his criteria locally, figuring that his local use of an upper() function will be faster than that on the SQL Server. The inexperienced programmer in this case is wrong, and this approach hurts both his query and every other activity on the network, while he monopolizes bandwidth to transmit data.

Certain applications, particularly decision-support applications, legitimately need to bring back enormous quantities of data to the user. It may still be possible to keep that data off the network by submitting the query from a connection established locally on the server. (Use ISQL/w or the command-based ISQL program to do this.) That connection can create a file containing the large result set, which can be transferred to another physical computer across the network at a time when there's less network activity.

Remember that it's almost always more efficient for the server to prepare aggregate results (with group by) than for the raw data to be passed to a workstation and processed there. In addition to the benefit of keeping the result set small, SQL Server also has access to indexes and caching mechanisms that make totaling easier and faster on that device than on a client workstation.

Row Processing

A major application question is how to perform row-by-row processing. Version 6.5 provides improved performance for cursor processing, but the performance of cursor applications remains a serious problem. There are several application problems (most often, batch update processes, complex reports, and logical integrity checks) that seem to call for row-wise processing. It's worth looking for alternative approaches because of the enormous performance penalty introduced by cursor processing. See Chapter 20, "Advanced SQL Techniques," for a discussion of problems and solutions to row-wise, cursor-based processing (and for some alternatives).

Data Validation Methods

An ongoing debate in SQL Server applications is where and how to perform data validation. It was a fairly simple issue in earlier software generations. The application was required to enforce all business rules, from individual column values to interdependencies between columns in a row to complex interdependencies among several tables (including referential integrity). One of the benefits of SQL Server is the capacity to implement rules, constraints and triggers that define the data integrity and consistency requirements for a table or set of tables. At this time, the application designer has several methods of enforcing consistency:

- *Application-based integrity.* This is the traditional place to enforce business rules in a 3GL application, where the database has little or no capability of managing the content or consistency of data. There are correct ways to implement this approach to be certain that you have the desired effect and that locking and transactional problems don't completely lock up the system.

- *Procedure-based integrity.* All data modifications can be performed through stored procedures, allowing all validation to be implemented in those procedures. This is a fairly common choice because it allows a single set of code to manage all data. It's easy to maintain, and it can provide better performance if properly implemented. In this approach, transactions don't typically span procedures (and therefore batches), so fewer locks are held for a long time.

- *Server-based integrity.* This is integrity based on rules, constraints, defaults, and triggers. This is the only approach that allows users to update freely using standard SQL statements, even if they know nothing about the structure or data-integrity requirements of the database. This approach is modular and can be efficient, but it can sometimes be difficult to debug because of the interaction of code in different objects.

- *Mixed-model integrity.* This is integrity enforced at several levels. This is a very common approach, often allowing the best combination of performance, flexibility, and user interface.

Data Validation and Performance

Performance, code maintenance, and interface issues are associated with the method used to enforce business rules on the database. Code running at the client level reduces the load on the server, but the client doesn't have access to other rows in the table or in other tables. Enforcement objects at the server increase the load on the server and can create persistent blocking locks that can damage performance. Server-based enforcement objects apply to all applications and can keep application development simpler and more reliable; server-based objects also permit changes to the rules applied to data shared among several applications with a single modification. Only application-based validation can provide useful, column-level assistance during input and modification steps.

Let's look at each of these approaches and understand its long-term implications. The following sections provide some examples of business rules that might need to be validated before a data modification could be permitted.

> **NOTE**
>
> Understand that there's no "right" way to do this, although there are several wrong ways. Your choice of how to implement data validation depends on your hardware and software configuration, application design and implementation philosophy, and usage and performance requirements.

Rule 1: Items Can Be Deleted Only If the In-Stock Value Is 0

Rule 1 could be implemented in a couple of ways. It would be incorrect to read the row and verify that the in-stock value is 0 locally, and then delete the row with confidence, where you perform the two steps discretely with any time lapse between:

```
select instock
from item
where item_no = 1343
go

/* check instock in a local program */
delete item
where item_no = 1343
go
```

Clearly, the problem is that someone else could jump in and modify the value of `instock` on the item between the time you retrieve the row and when you delete the row. You could solve this with a persistent lock using `holdlock` in a transaction (continued on next page):

```
begin transaction
select instock
from item
```

```
where item_no = 1343
holdlock
go

/* check instock in a local program */
delete item
where item_no = 1343
commit transaction
go
```

This solves the potential hole in data integrity, but it leaves a persistent page-level lock on the item table while you do application-side processing (transactions held open across batches). This scheme can result in "live" locks and deadlocks, both damaging to performance.

> **NOTE**
>
> You could delete the row by simply including the application condition in your SQL code like this:
>
> ```
> delete item
> where item_no = 1343
> and instock = 0
> ```
>
> What if the delete fails to find any rows? Does that mean there's no item, or that the item has a nonzero instock value? Failure to find a row based on either condition will cause the delete to fail.

There is a mechanism that provides sufficient data integrity without creating the locking problem introduced by transactions that cross batches. SQL Server provides an optimistic locking mechanism using timestamp values to guarantee that the version of the row being modified or deleted is the same one that was read:

```
select instock, timestamp
from item
where item_no = 1343
go

/* check instock in a local program */
delete item
where item_no = 1343
and tsequal(timestamp, 0x123456671312)
go
```

In this example, the programmer retrieved the binary timestamp value along with the instock value in the first step, and then used that timestamp value in the tsequal() function to guarantee that the version of the row deleted is the same as the version retrieved. The important point about this function is how different error cases are treated: The server finds the row based on other conditions, and then validates the version with the `timestamp` value. If the row isn't found, the server returns 0 `rows processed`, as you would expect. If the row is found but the `timestamp` value fails to match, the server returns a specific error message (Error 532). For a more thorough discussion of the use of timestamp columns, refer to Chapter 5, "Transact-SQL Datatypes."

The approaches described so far would all work as well or better if performed during a stored procedure. All the locking windows would be narrower, substantially improving performance and reducing the potential impact on other users. Validation of the deletion could also be easily implemented in a trigger:

```
create trigger tr_item_del
on items for delete as
if @@rowcount = 0 return
if exists
    (select * from deleted
    where instock != 0)
begin
    raiserror ("Error: attemp to delete non-zero instock value", 16, 1)
    rollback tran
end
return
```

The trigger simplifies the problem of an application programmer by handling the error case completely. The data is safe from errors made by individual application programmers, who forget to apply the rule or do so improperly. The trigger requires some additional overhead during the deletion, and locks are held during trigger execution. But the overall performance impact of enforcing Rule 1 by using a trigger is probably less than that of the other approaches.

Rule 2: Customer Status Can Only Be ACTIVE, INACTIVE, or PENDING

Rule 2 establishes a list of valid values for an individual column. It's simple enough to enforce this rule in an application program, although there's a chance that a programmer will make an error and allow invalid entries in one program. In addition, users accessing the database using a simple SQL interface like ISQL/w can put any value in the column by using a simple `insert` statement. Nevertheless, validation in the application has two specific benefits. First, the application can prompt the user immediately if an entry is invalid. (This immediate feedback is critical to a good user interface.) A server-based validation technique would prompt the user only when the entire row was submitted to the server. Second, performing column-level validation at the workstation avoids unnecessary network traffic and unnecessary work by the server.

To get efficient use of shared resources (the network and server) and good user interface (field-level prompting) as well as protection against application errors and interactive SQL users, it's common to implement a combination of both client- and server-based validation techniques. In the case of Rule 2, using both application-level tools and a rule or constraint to validate customer status provides the best of both worlds, although it requires additional maintenance if the values change frequently.

Can you perform column-level validation in a stored procedure? Of course, and if all data modifications have been channeled through procedures, that might be appropriate. The benefit of using procedures instead of rules is that all database-consistency requirements are defined in a single unit of code.

Can column-level validation take place in a trigger? It can, but it shouldn't. Remember that triggers execute *after* the modifications are performed on the table. There might be a tremendous amount of disk activity (mostly reads, as most modifications are made in memory until they are committed to disk) to support a data modification. Whenever you can, prevalidate work instead of waiting until the trigger fires, as long as that prevalidation doesn't require additional work (see Rule 1).

Rule 3: Orders Can Be Entered Only for Valid Customer IDs

This is classic referential integrity, in which the referencing table's foreign key (`order.cust_id`) must match a primary key in the referenced table (`customer.cust_id`). You can certainly write code to ensure that the customer exists, either in an application program or in a stored procedure. This will require the same kind of transactional and locking work seen in Rule 1.

SQL Server provides two mechanisms for handling referential integrity more efficiently: constraints and triggers. In general, constraints ought to be more efficient because they're implemented in C code as an implicit part of the SQL Server application rather than in SQL (see Chapter 20 for more on the difference in performance between native C and SQL code performance), so whenever possible we use constraints rather than triggers. (Remember not to rely on constraints when an application must run Version 4.21 as well as Version 6.x.)

Rule 3a: Orders Can Be Entered Only for Customers Having a Status of "ACTIVE"

Here's an example where referential integrity requirements are more complex than a constraint would completely handle. A constraint could catch the first level of data-integrity problems (only valid customers), but a trigger would be required to check the status of the customer:

```
create trigger tr_order_ins_upd
on orders for insert, update as
if @@rowcount = 0 return
if exists
    (select * from inserted i, customers c
```

```
        where i.cust_id = c.cust_id
        and c.status != "ACTIVE")
begin
        raiserror 55556 "Order entered for inactive customer"
        rollback tran
end
return
```

The trigger code is simplified because the constraint has already handled referential integrity. (Note that additional code would be required to allow updates to orders already in the table if the customer status is now "INACTIVE".)

A mixed approach taking advantage of the capabilities of many elements of the system usually provides the best results, but might entail more sophisticated documentation and maintenance than you want to deal with. On the other hand, most single-mode approaches require a compromise on performance or functionality, and sometimes both.

Complex Transactions

Some applications require complex transactions to take place in real time (or as close to real time as possible). Complex transactions could be multirow updates requiring concurrency, or they could involve a dozen tables in a chain of nested triggers. What complex transactions have in common is the following:

- A substantial number of pages must be locked, possibly in many tables
- A large number of log entries are generated

What's substantial? What's a large number? There are no firm numeric guidelines, but if running the transactions is causing serious locking or performance problems, your transactions are complex enough to be worth addressing.

Consider an example of an update to a table that requires a dozen updates to related tables. The best case would be to include those updates as part of a single transaction, but currently the response time is unacceptable to users of the system. What's the best way to perform these complex applications?

The first step is to be absolutely certain that the application is properly coded and that the database design is fully optimized. (You certainly should know by now that too many indexes can slow update performance.) Problems with concurrency or performance can often be sufficiently resolved by using basic optimization techniques, allowing transactions to happen in real time.

The resources that are stressed during execution of a long-running transaction are the locking system, the transaction log, and memory. Locking large numbers of pages will certainly result in blocking—"live" locks as well as some number of deadlocks. If concurrency problems arise, you may be able to reduce them by decreasing the fill factor on small, heavily used tables. Changing the clustered index on a table can sometimes resolve locking problems as well. Using a cursor can reduce locking contention, but at a terrible price in performance.

Another method of reducing locking contention is to change the Lock Escalation configuration values. Page-level locks are escalated to table-level locks during inserts, updates, and deletes when the number of page locks exceeds one of the lock escalation thresholds. By raising the threshold levels, you will probably increase overall system overhead, forcing SQL Server to manage more page-level locks, but you will also reduce the impact of live locks on concurrency.

Transaction log problems are most common with very large transactions (that is, large enough to fill the transaction log between a `begin tran` and a `commit`). But a smaller transaction can cause this kind of problem if sufficient numbers of users are running it at one time. Log capacity isn't the only issue, however. A single transaction could take a long time to commit. If the log is a serious bottleneck, consider moving it onto a nonvolatile RAM drive such as a solid state drive (SSD).

Memory can also cause problems with long-running transactions, and you should allow sufficient space in memory for several users to run a complex transaction concurrently. If SQL Server doesn't have sufficient cache to store all the modified data and log pages in memory, it will need to execute a checkpoint command to write out all the modified pages and obtain some free space in cache. This can lead to repeated reads and writes of the same data pages during a single transaction, known as *thrashing*. By eliminating thrashing, you can typically obtain dramatic performance improvements. Use the Performance Monitor to observe the *cache hit percentage* during a long-running transaction. If the hit percentage is fairly low (below about 70 percent is a decent starting point), consider adding memory.

If long-running transactions continue to present a performance problem, the next step is to consider ways to perform the transaction in a batch mode during off-hours. (Make certain that the operation fits in with the rest of your maintenance schedule.) If you can't wait for a nightly batch, or if you are running a 7x24 system with no maintenance window, you need to devise a different strategy to offload large-scale work. One approach that has worked is to write intermediate values to a permanent worktable, and then to use the SQL Executive Task Manager to run a periodic sweep of worktables, performing these operations in the background.

NOTE

Be careful how you implement background housekeeping operations. If you want to run multiple instances of the operation, you need to build in the code to guarantee data consistency. Remember that background operations introduce additional overhead, but they speed up the perceived performance of the system by users waiting for a response from the system after an update.

Multiple-Server Transactions

With the Distributed Transaction Coordinator (DTC) and the new multi-server transactions provided with SQL Server 6.5, there are more ways to implement transactions that span multiple servers. Before you choose a method, you need to decide whether you require immediate, concurrent data modifications or can tolerate some degree of latency between servers. *Latency* indicates the degree to which an object and its replicated copy are fully synchronized. Zero latency means that every modification to an object is immediately made to its copy *within the same transaction.*

Replication is simpler to implement and more tolerant of problems in network availability than the two-phase commit (2PC) approach used with the DTC. The most significant problem with 2PC occurs when one of the servers is unavailable; at that point, no transactions involving that server can proceed. In a replication approach, transactions involving a server that's unavailable are recorded and subsequently delivered to that server after it becomes available.

In general, avoid designs based on DTC unless you need absolute cross-server data integrity with zero latency. *Do not use DTC simply to reduce latency.* Instead, choose the looser coupling offered with replication, but work on network and configuration characteristics to improve performance and reduce overall latency.

Some General Advice

In order, the things most likely to ruin application performance are

- Bad database design
- Bad application design
- Bad SQL
- Bad server configuration

It may not be a coincidence, but that's also a list of things most difficult to fix in an application. So you need to tend to your database and application design first.

Summary

SQL Server applications perform well when they achieve the right balance of client and server work, and when each of the individual components of the system performs well. Sometimes your design options will be constrained by the functional requirements of the application, especially when it comes to transaction implementation and data validation.

A final point: Never forget that *perceived* performance is as important as actual performance. Users are far more sensitive to operations that are slow to *start* doing work or hang their systems for a long time than they are to operations that take a long time but are unobtrusive.

Advanced SQL Techniques

20

This chapter addresses advanced SQL techniques, particularly for improving individual query performance by understanding the impact of specific syntactic structures on optimization and execution of a query. Specifically, this chapter discusses:

- Identifying problematic statements and queries in application designs before they're created on the server
- Finding problematic or performance-hindering statements in queries and stored procedures, and different methods for fixing these statements and queries

This chapter is likely to be useful for almost anyone responsible for writing efficient SQL. It would be best, however, for you to know some SQL before starting work on this chapter. Following are the general groups of users and developers who can benefit from this chapter:

- Application developers who write queries as part of their applications
- SQL Server developers writing queries and stored procedures for client application developers
- System administrators and DBAs responsible for writing stored procedures for client application developers

System administrators and DBAs who want to optimize SQL Server configuration options and physical database design should look at the appropriate chapters on performance and tuning techniques in this part of the book.

Aggregate Query Resolution

This section covers how SQL Server uses worktables to resolve queries with group by and aggregate functions. In general, aggregate functions automatically require the use of a worktable, which introduces some overhead. Although this overhead can't be avoided, the worktable also has functional implications for certain types of queries. This section looks at the use of having with group by, compares having and where clauses, and considers some advanced issues related to the use of group by.

Combining having Clauses with group by

When used with group by, having restricts the *groups* that are returned by the query after the computation has been completed. When used without group by, having restricts the *rows* that are returned by the query after the computation has been completed (see the following section for details).

having *does not* affect the rows that "go into" a computation; it affects only the rows or groups that come out of a computation. In this example, the server will filter the final results to remove rows containing an average price less than $10:

```
select type, avg(price)
from titles
group by type
having avg(price) >= $10
```

Compare that query to the following, in which the server filters out rows having a price less than $10 before performing the averaging:

```
select type, avg(price)
from titles
where price >= $10
group by type
```

having is always evaluated *after* the computation has completed in the query, but before rows are returned.

where **versus** having

If both where and having clauses restrict rows, why not use having all the time? If a query has no aggregate functions and no group by clause, SQL Server implicitly interprets the having as a where. If a query has aggregate functions or a group by clause, having forces SQL Server to use a worktable to resolve the query.

Query Tracking: having

This example query uses a having clause to retrieve only selected rows from an aggregate result. Look closely at how the server resolves the query in two steps, using a worktable:

```
select title_id, avg(qty)
from sales
where title_id < "C"
group by title_id
having avg(qty) > 500
```

> **NOTE**
>
> This information is accessed using the showplan option, in which SQL Server displays its intended access method for resolving a query. It also includes output from the statistics io option, which provides details about SQL Server physical and logical data access during actual execution. Later in this section, you examine output from dbcc trace flags. If you're unfamiliar with these methods of examining query performance, please see Chapter 12, "Designing Indexes for Performance," for detailed assistance in retrieving and interpreting this information.

In the following showplan output, the server plans to execute the query in two steps. In the first step, SQL Server builds the grouped (*vector*) aggregate; in the second step, it returns only rows in the worktable matching the having criteria:

```
STEP 1
The type of query is SELECT (into a worktable)
GROUP BY
Vector Aggregate
FROM TABLE
sales
Nested iteration
Index : titleidind
TO TABLE
Worktable 1
STEP 2
The type of query is SELECT
FROM TABLE
Worktable 1
Nested iteration
Table Scan
```

The output from statistics io shows that the worktable is scanned several times as the aggregate is prepared:

```
Table: sales  scan count 1,  logical reads: 6905,  physical reads: 4777,
➥read ahead reads: 615
Table: Worktable  scan count 1,  logical reads: 45,  physical reads: 1,
➥read ahead reads: 0
```

Grouping and Worktables

This section looks at advanced issues with group by and worktables, examining the following topics:

- The role of the worktable
- The impact of order by and having on worktables
- having with and without group by

Role of the Worktable

The worktable stores temporary results that can't be evaluated, processed, or returned to the user until after the server has completed the current step. Worktables are used to prepare many kinds of results, including the ones covered in the following list:

- Vector aggregate

  ```
  select type, count(*)
  from titles
  group by type
  ```

- Ordered result set (no useful index)

  ```
  select type, title
  from titles
  order by type, title
  STEP 1
  The type of query is INSERT
  ```

```
The update mode is direct
Worktable created for ORDER BY
FROM TABLE
titles
Nested iteration
Table Scan
TO TABLE
Worktable 1
STEP 2
The type of query is SELECT
This step involves sorting
FROM TABLE
Worktable 1
Using GETSORTED Table Scan
```

How Does SQL Server Process Queries Involving a Worktable?

Figure 20.1 illustrates how the server uses a worktable in resolving a query. `where` and `group by` are resolved as the processor moves rows from the base table(s) to the worktable. `having` and `order by` are resolved as the processor builds a final result set based on the worktable.

FIGURE 20.1.

where *clauses and* group by *take place between the source table(s) and the worktable;* having *and* order by *operate on the worktable in producing a final result set.*

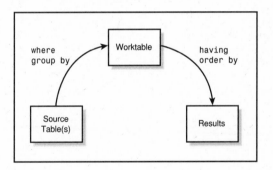

If the server can determine that the column value is dependent on the grouping value, it will perform the grouping properly (and will probably derive the function on-the-fly when displaying results). Here's an example where the `group by` clause refers to the actual column, while the `select` list contains only a function based on that column:

```
select user_name(uid), count(*)
from sysobjects
group by uid
```

Special Topics in Join Processing

This section covers the following special topics in multi-table optimization:

- Joins with or
- Overriding the optimizer
- Breaking up large queries

> **NOTE**
>
> Please review Chapter 12 in detail before reading this section. I assume that you understand the fundamentals of single- and multi-table optimization in this section, and I use this information to lay out areas where you can improve query performance.

Joins with or

FIGURE 20.2.

In this three-way join, results include rows in the titles *table matching rows in the* sales *table, as well as rows in the* titles *table matching rows in the* titleauthor *table.*

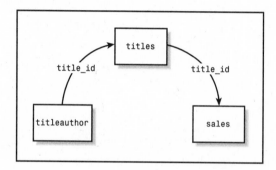

A curious problem arises when you join three tables with two conditions, where a row is included in the result set if either join condition is true. Consider the set of tables shown in Figure 20.2.

Here's an example of a query that joins three tables based on an or condition:

```
select title
from titles t, titleauthor ta, sales sa
where t.title_id = ta.title_id
or t.title_id = sa.title_id
```

On its surface, this query seems to request a list of all titles that either have an author specified or have been sold. I observed a strange behavior with this type of query, however. When either of the optional join tables is empty, the server returns no rows. For example, consider this three-table join:

```
select count(*)
from A, B, C
where A.id = B.id or A.id = C.id
```

Table 20.1 shows the contents of the three tables.

Table 20.1. Contents of Tables A, B, and C.

Table A

id	CA
1	1
2	2

Table B

id	CB
1	1
2	2

Table C (empty table)

id	CC
(no rows)	

Based on the contents of the tables, you would expect that the count would find two rows where table A matched table B. The query appears to work when all the tables contain at least one row, but it fails when any table is empty.

Actually, the query is incorrectly written and fails under all circumstances. The following example adds a couple of rows to table C and then tries the query again:

```
1> insert C values (1, 21)
2> insert C values (2, 22)
3> go
(1 row affected)
(1 row affected)

1> select count(*) from A, B, C
2> where A.id = B.id
3> or A.id = C.id
4> go

    ----------
            6

(1 row affected)
```

With only two rows in A, how did the server find six rows in the join? To understand better, consider this join query:

```
select A.id A, B.id B, C.id C
from A, B, C
where A.id = B.id or A.id = C.id
```

The output of the query shows that the server presented every possible combination of rows:

```
A           B           C
_ _ _ _ _   _ _ _ _ _   _ _ _ _ _
        1           1           1
        1           1           2
        1           2           1
        2           1           2
        2           2           1
        2           2           2
```

When SQL Server doesn't understand your join condition or can find no path to optimize the join, it builds a Cartesian product (the set of all possible combinations), and then tests the validity of each row against the search conditions provided. In this case, you have many duplicate rows, including rows where A is matched to an incorrect B or an incorrect C.

You need to restate the question: Show how many rows in A have a match in B or a match in C. Here's the proper way to write the query:

```
select count(*)
from A
where id in
    (select id from B)
or id in
    (select id from C)
```

This query becomes more problematic if you need to retrieve information from table B or C to be included in the final result set. Your method of resolving that kind of query will depend on your specific requirements, but you probably will need to use a temporary table and prioritize B or C.

In any case, avoid using or to connect join clauses, because it creates duplicate and invalid data.

Overriding the Optimizer

Here's a question. When might the optimizer be wrong?

You've looked at how to override the optimizer in Chapter 15, "Analyzing Query Plans." Now I'll discuss some of the circumstances where that might be an effective approach.

In general, you should override the optimizer if you're absolutely certain that you know something it doesn't. Here are some examples:

- Indexes didn't exist at optimization time
- Statistics are out of date
- Device performance is different from the assumption

The following sections provide a brief look at each of these topics.

If Indexes Didn't Exist at Optimization Time

When you create a temporary table inside a stored procedure, sometimes it's appropriate to index that temporary table so that you can access that index properly during a subsequent join, as in this example:

```
create proc p_temptable as

/* create a temporary table */
select title_id, au_id, title,
    au_fname, au_lname, au_ord, advance / royaltyper, price
into #temp_ta
from titles t, authors a, titleauthor ta
where t.title_id = ta.title_id
and a.au_id = ta.au_id

/* index the table for subsequent joins or other operations */
create unique clustered index on #temp_ta (title_id, au_id)
create nonclustered index on #temp_ta (title)

/* now execute queries ...
** will the procedure use the indexes or identify the best join order? */
select au_id, sum(qty)
from sales s, #temp_ta t
where s.title_id = t.title_id
group by au_id
order by 2 desc

... (other queries)

return
```

Because stored procedure optimization occurs only once, at procedure execution time the temporary table indexes (as well as any index statistics, of course) are unavailable to queries such as the aggregate query in the example. You may want to force a join order or identify a useful index on the temporary table to run the query.

When Statistics Are Out of Date

In most cases, the best cure for badly out-of-date index distribution statistics is to update your statistics. But updating statistics takes time and locks tables. Remember that an index is extremely valuable, even if its statistics are incorrect. Statistics are used only to choose a path, not to execute it. Force the correct index choice and you may get good performance.

Remember, though, that hard-coding a program to use a particular index path might cause trouble later on, when indexes are up to date. Forcing an index is best used with an ad hoc query when you know something about the specific here-and-now situation rather than about a global condition that will change over time. The optimizer is far better at adjusting to changing conditions than your programs are likely to be.

If Device Performance Differs from the Assumption

The optimizer assumes that the ratio of logical to physical read performance is 14:2. What's the effect of this assumption on a typical join? Consider the example in Table 20.2.

Table 20.2. Effects of the ratio on a typical join.

Item	Table A	Table B
Size	10MB (5000 pages)	2MB (1000 pages)
Rows	1MB	250KB
NCI levels/size	4 levels, 500 pages	3 levels, 100 pages

NCI stands for "non-clustered index," CI for "clustered index."

Here's the query you're trying to optimize:

```
select count(*)
from A, B
where A.id = B.id
```

When the server estimates the work required to perform the join, it makes assumptions based on what will fit in cache. If an object will fit entirely in cache, the server assumes that one scan of a table or index will include a physical and a logical cost—number of pages to read × (14 ms + 2 ms), where any subsequent scan of the same object will require only a logical cost (pages to read × 2 ms).

> **NOTE**
>
> Some of the calculations here are a little more crude than what the server is able to do in its algorithm. The server takes into account issues such as percentage of cache to use, and considers index covering and reformatting strategies. I'm considering only alternative join orders in performing a join.

You will now work out the estimated cost of performing the join without assuming any specific values for logical and physical reads. Instead, you will carry two variables, LC (logical cost) and PC (physical cost), and then look at how the ratio of those values affects actual performance.

First, assume that A is the outer table and B the inner (A→B join order), and use a nonclustered index (NCI) on B to correlate tables. Also, assume that table B and the nonclustered index fit in cache:

```
COST(A→B) = 5,000 pgs * PC
              + 1,100 pgs * PC
              + 1,000,000 rows * 4 levels * LC
          = 6,100 * PC + 4,000,000 * LC
```

In layman's terms, the cost equals:

- The number of pages to read all of table A times the physical cost of each read, *plus*
- The number of pages in the nonclustered index times the physical cost to read them, *plus*
- The number of rows in table A times the number of index levels to traverse to find matching rows in B times the logical cost to read them once for each row in A.

Now assume a B→A join order, using a nonclustered index on A to correlate rows. Assume that the nonclustered index of table A (but not the data pages) will fit in cache:

```
COST(B→A) = 1000 pgs * PC
              + 500 pgs * PC
              + 250,000 rows * (4 levels * LC + 4 pages * PC)
          = 1,001,500 * PC + 1,000,000 * LC
```

If you substitute varying values for the ratio of performance between logical and physical reads, you get the graph in Figure 20.3. Some plans are more sensitive to device speed than others. In this example, as the physical device gets faster with respect to memory, the cost of treating B as the outer table in a join is reduced dramatically. SQL Server assumes that the performance ratio of physical to logical reads is 14:2.

FIGURE 20.3.

Expected query performance based on device speed and access path.

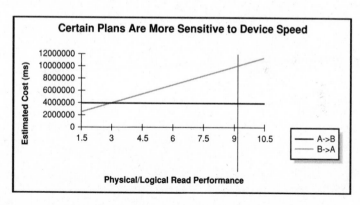

Clearly, the relationship between memory and disk speed relate impacts actual performance. Ordinarily, the ratio is more like 20 to 1 between memory and traditional disk storage, and much higher for nontraditional storage such as WORM and CD-ROM drives, especially without aggressive caching strategies. It's reasonable for the optimizer to discount this benefit because of the effects of multiuser processing consuming available cache, requiring a fall-back to physical memory when memory is insufficient.

Are there times when the actual physical drive performance will be better than 7:1? If you set up tempdb in RAM, or if you are using a solid state device (a nonvolatile, RAM-based hard drive), you may see numbers substantially better than that. Also, new RAID devices include smart read-ahead strategies that could provide substantially better performance than you have experienced in the past. Finally, if you have limited cache space on your server, or if the cache periodically is running over into the NT page file (a really, *really* bad idea, by the way), memory performance could be fairly poor.

The type of device is as important as the access path in some instances; therefore, you may find that drive performance is one area in which you can look to outguess the optimizer and force a specific order.

Breaking Up Large Queries

I've taken and taught dozens of Microsoft and Sybase SQL Server classes, and everywhere I've been, the instructor (including myself!) has said something like this:

> "If you are joining more than four or five tables, you may want to consider breaking up the query into multiple steps, using a temporary table."

This begs the question, "Where, why, when??" If you try it, half of the time the query takes longer. Then, suddenly, it takes half of the time. What's going on??

In this section, I try to demystify the choice of breaking up large queries into multiple steps. We'll examine when it's the right choice, and what strategies to try. After that, you'll still be using a trial-and-error approach, but maybe it'll be a little more focused and fruitful.

Defining Large Queries

A large multi-table query is a query consisting of many tables with sufficient rows in the table to make a join expensive. The critical issue in multi-table queries is *join order*. The server may not be able to find an efficient join order with all the tables in the query. The circumstance may require breaking the query into multiple parts, using one or more temporary tables.

> **NOTE**
>
> This is a strategy that the optimizer will not try.

It isn't surprising that breaking up joins of six or eight tables is useful. What is surprising is that sometimes even a three-table join can benefit from the use of a temporary table. Here's a query to consider breaking into components:

```
select sum(t1.amount)
from A, B, C
where A.id = B.id
and C.id = A.id
and B.id = C.id
and C.key2 between 1000 and 15000
```

The showplan shows that the server chose the join order B→A→C:

```
STEP 1
The type of query is SELECT
Scalar Aggregate
FROM TABLE
B
Nested iteration
Table Scan
FROM TABLE
A
Nested iteration
Using Clustered Index
FROM TABLE
C
Nested iteration
Using Clustered Index
STEP 2
The type of query is SELECT
```

The problem is that table C, the innermost table, has two separate, fairly selective indexes that might be useful for this query: a clustered index to use with a SARG and a nonclustered index that could support the join. Because of the join selectivity estimates, the server has determined (correctly) that using the clustered index at the innermost level is the most efficient approach to this three-table join.

Here are the statistics for each table, retrieved using set statistics io on:

```
Table: A  scan count 7282,  logical reads: 14755,  physical reads: 0
Table: B  scan count 1,  logical reads: 88,  physical reads: 0
Table: C  scan count 11308,  logical reads: 34404,  physical reads: 0
```

How to Break Up a Query

You want to break up queries to allow SQL Server to get the best effect out of all candidate indexes. In the case considered here, only one of the two useful indexes on table C is being used, while table B is being scanned. Here's what you do to make this work:

- Separate the query into components, each of which has an effective strategy.
- Try several approaches to see which gives the lowest total statistics io values.
- Use one or many temporary tables to store and re-join values, especially when you have a highly selective index.

Breaking up a query is most likely to be useful when a SARG in the query is fairly selective (it will significantly reduce the number of relevant rows in a single table), but isn't used in the optimization plan. The best SARGs use a clustered index.

At the first step in breaking up a query, you want to take advantage of that selective index to reduce the overall number of rows in play, partly to reduce the complexity of subsequent steps but also to reduce the size of your temporary table:

```
select C.id, B.amount
into #temp
from B, C
where C.id = B.id
and C.key2 between 1000 and 15000
```

> **NOTE**
>
> This approach to large queries is likely to be less effective if the entire temporary table won't fit in cache.

Here's the `showplan` output for the first step in the plan. The clustered index on the inner table C is used to dramatically reduce the cost of each scan on that table:

```
STEP 1
The type of query is TABCREATE
STEP 2
The type of query is INSERT
The update mode is direct
Worktable created for SELECT INTO
FROM TABLE
B
Nested iteration
Table Scan
FROM TABLE
C
Nested iteration
Using Clustered Index
TO TABLE
#temp
```

In the second step, you join the remaining table(s) with the temporary table to get a result:

```
select sum(t.amount)
from A, #temp t
where t.id = A.id

drop table #temp
```

The server will choose to use the permanent table A as the inner table if the index on `id` is sufficiently selective and if indexes fit in cache. Otherwise, the temporary table, if small enough, will be the inner table. You may want to test this out, examining statistics outputs and optimization plans to make certain that the server finds the most effective plan. You may want to force a join order or use an index if the server isn't making the best choice.

The optimization plan for the second part of the query shows that the server is scanning the new temporary table as the outer table and then using the index on A to build the final result:

```
STEP 1
The type of query is SELECT
Scalar Aggregate
FROM TABLE
#temp t
Nested iteration
Table Scan
FROM TABLE
A
Nested iteration
Using Clustered Index
STEP 2
The type of query is SELECT

STEP 1
The type of query is TABDESTROY
```

FIGURE 20.4.

Breaking up a query into many parts allows more flexibility in identifying an efficient join order.

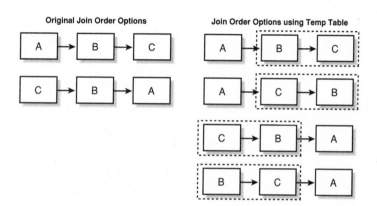

Figure 20.4 shows the original and revised join orders. You can see that the join order presented when the query was broken up allowed the server to make the most efficient use of the indexes available. The more tables involved in the query, the more likely you are to find a better optimization strategy by breaking up the join into more than one step.

Here's the statistics io output from the query. The cost of the original query was about 48,000 logical reads. This query required less than half that many reads to complete:

```
Table: B  scan count 1,  logical reads: 88,  physical reads: 0
Table: C  scan count 7282,  logical reads: 22152,  physical reads: 0
Table: #temp_____000024884F  scan count 0,  logical reads: 554,
          physical reads: 0

Table: A  scan count 550,  logical reads: 1109,  physical reads: 0
Table: #temp_____000024884F  scan count 1,  logical reads: 5,
          physical reads: 0
```

Recommendations

Following are some recommendations for how to break up query tables:

- Understand outer/inner processing with multi-table joins.
- Look for situations in which the optimizer doesn't use all available indexing resources.
- Look for situations in which nested scans of large tables are occurring.
- Break up queries by building temporary result sets.
- Try to encourage the optimizer to make use of many indexes.
- Use the first SQL statement to reduce the number of rows being processed.

Summary

This chapter looked at some ways to manipulate SQL statements to get the best performance out of the SQL Server optimizer. In general, it's important to remember that the optimizer isn't perfect, and that it must make assumptions about the state of the data or its accessibility that aren't necessarily accurate. The optimizer also has specific methods of resolving certain syntactic structures (such as group by or order by). So, the more you understand how the optimizer works, the more likely that you'll find a way to write queries that will run well consistently over a long period of time.

The challenge, of course, is to build powerful, fast, and adaptable systems. Some of the advice people give you about writing queries is appropriate for a specific situation, but problematic over the long term as an application runs under widely-varying conditions. So here are two last pieces of advice:

Miscellaneous Performance Topics

21

There are a number of performance-related issues in SQL Server about which both the programmer and the DBA/system administrator need to be aware. Many of these topics don't fit neatly into previous chapters on understanding and tuning the performance of SQL Server. This chapter presents a selection of these topics, discusses the various performance implications of each, and provides tips and guidelines to alleviate or avoid some of the performance problems.

BCP and Performance

Two Microsoft SQL Server utilities can be used to transfer data. SQL Transfer Manager provides an easy, graphical way to transfer both objects *and* data from one SQL Server database to another. The *bulk copy program* (*BCP*) is a command-line utility that copies SQL Server data into or from an operating system file. The operating system file is defined in a user-specified format.

The BCP program is a very useful utility for transferring data from non-SQL Server data sources into SQL Server (for example, loading a DB2 data extract into a SQL Server database). BCP is the fastest way to insert data into a SQL Server table because, during load, BCP doesn't enforce rules, triggers, or constraints as a normal `insert` statement does. In addition, if the appropriate conditions are met, BCP can also avoid logging of the rows being inserted, greatly reducing the overhead involved and resulting in much faster load times.

When a table has no indexes, BCP performs a "fast" BCP load. The actual data rows being inserted into the table aren't logged as they would be by a normal `insert` statement. Instead, only the new page allocations to that table are logged.

> **NOTE**
>
> In addition to having no indexes on the table, the database must also be configured for `select into/bulkcopy` operations, or else BCP reverts to the slow form of BCP load.
>
> Also, if a table you are inserting into is marked for replication, the individual rows will need to be logged for the replication process in order to be replicated. This requirement also results in a slow, logged BCP to be performed.

> **WARNING**
>
> Selecting the `select into/bulkcopy` option disables transaction log dumps for that database. After completion of a nonlogged activity (`select into`, fast BCP load), a full database dump should be performed.

Minimizing Data Load Time

In addition to performing fast versus slow BCP loads, a number of other methods of tweaking the BCP load performance are available, as described in the following sections.

Configuring Network Packet Size

Network packet size determines the number of bytes (per network packet) sent to and from the SQL Server. Your SQL Server configuration determines the minimum packet size allowed. However, you can override this option on an individual basis with the -a option to BCP.

Increasing packet size can enhance performance on bulk copy operations. The default network packet size used by BCP when copying data into a Microsoft SQL Server is 4096 bytes; 512 bytes is the smallest network packet size. If a larger packet is requested but can't be granted, BCP defaults to 512 (the performance statistics generated at the end of a BCP run show the actual packet size used). Testing has found that packet sizes between 4096 and 8192 bytes provide the fastest performance for BCP operations.

Loading Data with BCP and Indexes

Generally, there are two reasonable sequences of events for initial loading of data into SQL Server. Here's the first sequence:

1. Create the clustered index.
2. Load the data.
3. Create any nonclustered indexes.
4. Update your statistics on the clustered index.

Here's the second sequence:

1. Load the data.
2. Create the clustered index and any nonclustered indexes.

Typically, the second sequence is the most efficient method. Although the cost is high to build all indexes after the data is loaded, the total elapsed time will be substantially less than the time needed to perform a slow BCP into a table with the indexes in place.

Remember, however, that if the data in the source file isn't in clustered-index sort order, you need 120 percent of the size of the table as free space *within that database* for SQL Server to be able to sort the data and build the clustered index. Due to database size constraints, you may need to use the first sequence and load the data with the clustered index in place.

TIP

If the source data file is in clustered-index order, you can load the data into the table without the clustered index. After the data is loaded, create the clustered index with the sorted_data option. This option simply creates the clustered index without re-sorting the data; it doesn't reorganize the table.

However, if this option detects a row out of order during the creation of the clustered index, the index create fails. You then are forced to run a standard clustered-index create and have the necessary free space available.

Also, if you must load the data with the clustered index in place, the load proceeds more quickly with sorted data than with unsorted data.

Dropping nonclustered indexes, loading the data, and re-creating the nonclustered indexes is always faster than loading the data with the indexes in place. The difference is due to the significant amount of overhead incurred to maintain those indexes during the data load. However, whether you are performing a complete refresh of the data or an incremental data load determines whether dropping all indexes prior to running BCP is feasible.

Another advantage to creating indexes after the data load is that the index statistics will be "up to date" because the indexes are created with data in the table. You won't need to run the update statistics command.

Performing Incremental Loads Versus Full Loads

If you are replacing all data for a table, it's faster to drop all nonclustered indexes and truncate the table prior to the data load. After the data is loaded, you re-create the nonclustered indexes. However, be aware that if data volumes are high, index creation time can be substantial. In some cases, if rebuilding the index takes an excessive amount of time (several hours), it may pay to absorb the overhead of leaving the nonclustered indexes in place during the data load. This rule typically applies when performing incremental data loads.

If you're making substantive increases in the amount of data being added to the table (approximately 20 percent or more, as a rule of thumb), the fastest method generally is to drop the nonclustered indexes, load the data, and then rebuild the indexes.

WARNING

Because rules, triggers, and constraints aren't applied during BCP load, integrity controls are bypassed. You need to ensure that the data is completely valid to avoid violating any data or referential integrity conditions (more on this topic later). For this reason, BCP often isn't used for incremental data loads.

If you aren't significantly increasing the amount of the data in the table, a variety of methods are available for performing an incremental BCP load:

- One alternative is to run the BCP load with all indexes on the table. Although this BCP load is the slowest, you won't have to re-create the indexes; however, you will have to update statistics on the table subsequent to the load.

- A second alternative for incremental loads is to drop all nonclustered indexes and load with just the clustered index in place. This approach speeds up the BCP load, but the table still is essentially unusable by applications that depend on the nonclustered indexes for access performance, until the indexes are re-created. Depending on the size of the table, index creation could take hours or even days.

- The third option is to run the incremental BCP load with no indexes on the table. This method allows the fastest load process, but the slowest index creation time. The re-creation of the clustered index acquires an exclusive table lock, which must be completed before the creation of nonclustered indexes can commence. It also prevents any user access to the table until the clustered index creation is complete. Unless you're adding more than 25 percent of the data (that is, adding 500MB to a 2GB table), the time needed to re-create the clustered index and all nonclustered indexes is prohibitive.

Performing Multiple Concurrent BCPs

If you have to load multiple tables, and the tables are on different physical devices, consider running multiple BCP loads concurrently, one into each table. This strategy should help to increase overall BCP throughput over running them in serial. Be aware that there still will be contention for the transaction log between the BCP load processes, unless each table resides in a separate physical database with the transactions logs for each database on separate physical devices as well.

Slow BCP and Logging

When running a slow BCP load, the individual data rows are logged. Remember that for each row being inserted into the table, a corresponding row is being inserted into each existing nonclustered index on the table. This situation can result in a significant number of log records being generated. Large logged BCP loads are notorious for filling up the transaction log. Because the BCP load by default is treated as a single batch transaction, the BCP records in the log can't be truncated until the BCP process completes.

To avoid the log filling up, you can use the -b option to break up the BCP load into multiple batches. At the completion of a batch, SQL Server commits the inserted rows and checkpoints the database. The log records for those inserted rows can now be removed from the log. If you also turn on the trunc. log on chkpt. option for the database, the log is automatically truncated. The size of the BCP batch depends on the size of your transaction log and the amount of other logged activity occurring at the same time.

> **NOTE**
>
> Using the -b option causes BCP to run slower due to the multiple checkpoints that occur during the load. Also, when the log gets truncated, all update/insert activity is suspended until the truncation completes. However, this alternative is much preferred over the log filling up.

One other advantage of using the -b option for large data loads is that if the BCP load process fails at some point you can restart the BCP load from the first row of the batch being loaded at the time the BCP failed. All rows for the previous batches will have been committed and checkpointed. Check the load statistics reported at the end of the failed BCP to determine how many rows were copied. If 40,000 rows were copied into the table, using a batch size of 10,000, you can restart the BCP load at row 40,001, using the -F option as follows:

```
BCP acctg..customers in customer.BCP -Usa -P -c -b10000 -F40001
```

BCP and Data Integrity

BCP doesn't invoke any data integrity checks during load—such as triggers, rules, or constraints—even in "slow" mode. Your data and referential integrity checks are completely bypassed. When bulk copying data into a table with triggers, rules, or constraints, you need to decide how you're going to resolve this issue.

To make sure that new data is valid, you need to run SQL code after the BCP load process completes, in order to check the data validity and decide how invalid rows are to be handled. For example, to check that the loaded data meets your referential integrity constraints, you could run the following code:

```
select cust_id, line_no
   from purchase
   where cust_id not in
      (select cust_id from customers)
```

This query lists all the rows with invalid foreign key values in cust_id.

Because BCP doesn't invoke rules or check constraints, you need to write SQL queries to check that all values in a column match your rules or constraints. Here's an example:

```
select order_id, item_num
   from orders
   where price <= $0.0
```

This query returns all rows that don't meet the rule or constraint that `price` must be greater than zero. You can then make the determination whether to change the rule, remove the rows, or change the invalid data.

Sometimes triggers are also used to keep summary values in sync. For example, consider an item table that has a `total_sales` column containing the sum of the `qty` column in the `orders` table for that item. In this case, your trigger code is structured to handle the incremental adding of data. The overall total value for `total_sales` couldn't be determined by the trigger code. You may have to fully recalculate all summary values for the detail rows in the `orders` table. Determine the SQL necessary to accomplish this task and execute the code, similar to the following example, which uses a correlated subquery:

```
update item
   set total_sales =
       (select sum(qty)
        from orders
        where item.item_num = orders.item_num
        group by orders.item_num)
```

You may wonder, how does all this relate to performance? Well, any corresponding speed gains achieved by running a BCP load are going to be offset by the performance hit the system will take when you have to run these queries. If your tables are large, the processes to validate your data integrity could take hours. These processes will be very I/O- and CPU-intensive; they'll cause other concurrent processes to run more slowly, and may also lock tables from updates or retrievals until they're complete. Some of these processes could essentially bring the SQL Server to its knees.

You may at times find it more beneficial to use a standard `insert` process to add data to your table. This way, all data integrity checks and trigger codes are applied for each individual row inserted. True, this is more overhead on the `insert` process itself, but it allows other processes to continue to run only slightly hindered.

Database Maintenance and Performance

The main issue to address regarding data maintenance and performance is that data maintenance tasks tend to be very resource-intensive and, although you can run many of the SQL Server maintenance tasks online, they may have a significant impact on performance.

One of the main culprits is the `dbcc` command. The database consistency checker validates your table allocation pages and page linkages. In order to do this, `dbcc` performs a huge amount of physical I/O, and locks tables from update activity while running. Although improvements have been made in SQL Server 6.5 to improve `dbcc` performance (for example, parallel threads for `dbcc checktable` to check indexes and parallel read-ahead), it's still very I/O-intensive and can be time-consuming. The locking incurred by certain `dbcc` commands can have a severe impact on online performance. Table 21.1 summarizes the performance impact of the `dbcc` commands.

Table 21.1. Summary of `dbcc` commands and performance implications.

Command Option	Locking and I/O	Performance
`checktable` and `checkdb`	Shared table lock(s); heavy I/O	Slow
`checkalloc` and `newalloc`	No locking; heavy I/O	Slow
`checkcatalog`	Shared page locks on system tables	Fast

In an effort to minimize the total amount of time spent running the `dbcc` commands, you may want to consider running some of them in parallel. `dbcc checkdb` essentially runs `dbcc checktable` on all tables in the database in serial. `dbcc checkdb` can be broken down into multiple `dbcc checktable` commands, which can be executed in parallel. For example, you can try running `dbcc checktable` concurrently for different tables in the database. This strategy can reduce the time needed to run your `dbcc` checks, especially if the different tables are on different physical devices. However, you need to determine the break-even point on your server for running `dbcc` processes in parallel, before the combined CPU and I/O contention between the multiple processes causes them to run more slowly than if they were run sequentially. Additionally, to take full advantage of parallel thread processing and parallel read-ahead for `dbcc checktable`, you need to have a large amount of memory available to SQL Server (approximately more data cache than the largest table in the database) to minimize the impact on other processes and allow the `dbcc checktable` command to run as fast as possible.

Other methods to speed up `dbcc` execution or minimize impact on other processes include the following:

- Using fast disk devices to speed up `dbcc` I/O operations
- Skipping checking nonclustered indexes for `dbcc` commands by specifying the `noindex` option
- Running `dbcc checktable` on individual indexes one at a time rather than on the entire table and all indexes, to avoid holding a table lock for an extended period of time
- Running `dbcc` checks on a copy of the database in a "warm standby" SQL Server

Other data maintenance commands that affect performance adversely are index creation and `update statistics`. Both `update statistics` and nonclustered index creates acquire shared locks on the affected tables. This action prevents updates for the duration of the command. Clustered index creation acquires an exclusive lock on the table until completion, preventing any access by other processes.

> **TIP**
>
> The `update statistics` command updates statistics for all indexes on a table unless you specify an index name:
>
> ```
> update statistics table_name [index_name]
> ```
>
> When run specifying just the table name, the index statistics are updated for each index on the table sequentially. By running it on individual indexes, you can run multiple update statistics processes concurrently, lowering the total time to update the statistics for a table and releasing the shared locks more quickly.
>
> Also, keep in mind that the index statistics are used only for non-unique searches. For unique indexes used only for single-row retrieval (not used for range searches), the distribution page isn't used. Therefore, it wouldn't be critical to update statistics on that index as frequently, if at all.

tempdb and Performance

All users within SQL Server share the same `tempdb` database for worktables and temporary tables, regardless of the database in which they're working. This fact makes `tempdb` a potential bottleneck in any multiuser system. The primary bottleneck in `tempdb` is disk I/O, but there also can be locking contention between processes on the `tempdb` system tables.

There are four basic techniques for eliminating `tempdb` as a bottleneck:

- Add memory to SQL Server
- Put `tempdb` in RAM
- Put `tempdb` on faster devices
- Disseminate disk resources

The following sections discuss each option.

Adding More Memory to SQL Server

Adding more memory to SQL Server can help improve `tempdb` performance by allowing more of the activity in `tempdb` to take place in SQL Server data cache. The main disadvantage to this approach is that it won't help much for `inserts` into temporary tables in `tempdb`, because the modified data pages still have to be written to disk upon `commit`. Therefore, an I/O bottleneck still exists on writes to `tempdb`. Also, there's no guarantee that additional cache will be used exclusively for `tempdb`, because the data cache is shared by all databases in the system.

Putting `tempdb` in RAM

Microsoft SQL Server provides the option of creating `tempdb` in RAM. This scheme allows the `tempdb` to be entirely memory-resident. Using `tempdb` in RAM is safe and won't harm database integrity or recoverability because `tempdb` is used only for intermediate operations and is re-initialized on each SQL Server restart.

Putting `tempdb` in RAM can provide significant performance improvement if it's very write-intensive. However, if `tempdb` isn't used effectively, the RAM allocated to `tempdb` is essentially wasted memory, which could be used more appropriately as SQL Server data cache, and could end up having an adverse impact on overall SQL Server performance.

The use of `tempdb` in RAM can accelerate `tempdb` operations, but depletes memory available for the SQL cache buffer, which reduces the amount of data pages that can fit in cache, resulting in more physical I/O for regular table operations. Therefore, `tempdb` in RAM is a viable solution only if you have excess memory available in your system after meeting your data and procedure cache requirements.

Also, if you have a limited amount of RAM available on your system to be used for `tempdb`, this limitation constrains the maximum size of `tempdb` unless you move it out of RAM. If unforeseen growth requirements for `tempdb` materialize, you'll need to add more memory to the system or move `tempdb` back to regular disk devices.

To determine whether placing `tempdb` in RAM might be beneficial for you, see whether your situation meets the following conditions:

- You have a significant amount of available system RAM (typically >= 128MB).
- Your SQL Server cache hit ratio is poor, even with a lot of available buffer cache.

> **NOTE**
>
> Your cache hit ratio can be determined by using SQL Performance Monitor. For information about using SQL Performance Monitor, see Chapter 33, "Measuring SQL Server System Performance."

- Your applications perform a lot of `tempdb` operations.

> **TIP**
>
> To determine the amount of `tempdb` activity, use `sp_lock` to monitor the locking activity in `tempdb` while queries are running. Or you can monitor the number of objects being created in `tempdb` by running a query against `sysindexes`. Here's an example:
>
> ```
> select sum(id) from tempdb..sysindexes
> ```

- The `tempdb` operations are sized so that they'll fit within the maximum size of `tempdb` made possible by your RAM configuration.

To determine the effectiveness of `tempdb` in RAM, perform the following steps:

1. Identify a set of sample queries that typify your most frequently performed `tempdb`-intensive operations.

2. Run these operations several times, noting the average execution time.

3. Reconfigure your system to put `tempdb` in RAM and run the identical queries. Note the difference in average execution time.

If the amount of improvement isn't significant, it's probably better to take `tempdb` out of RAM and allocate the memory to SQL Server cache.

Faster Devices for `tempdb`

One other way to minimize I/O contention in `tempdb` is to place it on faster devices. These could be high-speed disk devices, disk devices with caching mechanisms, or solid state disk (SSD) devices. SSD devices are essentially nonvolatile RAM devices that appear to the operating system and SQL Server as standard storage devices. SSD devices contain a built-in backup mechanism to maintain contents following a system or power failure. I/O rates to SSD devices are roughly equivalent to reads and writes from system memory.

> **NOTE**
>
> For `tempdb`, the backup mechanism of an SSD is unnecessary, because `tempdb` is reinitialized during SQL Server startup anyway. SSD devices are fairly expensive (approximately $70–100 per megabyte). With the capability to put `tempdb` in RAM, it would be more cost-effective to add memory to the machine and assign it to `tempdb`. However, if you need a larger `tempdb` device than you have available RAM to allocate for `tempdb` in RAM, an SSD device could be used as an alternative solution.

By speeding up I/O operations in `tempdb`, you not only minimize the I/O bottleneck but also minimize the potential for locking contention in `tempdb`. The shorter the amount of time needed to create and insert data into a temporary table, the less time a lock is held on the system tables.

A customer once reported that he was experiencing deadlocking problems in `tempdb`. Further research determined that the deadlocking was occurring on the system tables due to the number of users concurrently creating and dropping temporary tables. When we placed `tempdb` in RAM, I/O operations were speeded up considerably and the deadlocking problem went away. If you don't have sufficient RAM to configure `tempdb` in RAM, a solid state disk device is an alternative solution to this problem.

Disseminating Disk Resources

The goal of disseminating resources is to place the databases and logs within SQL Server across devices in such a way as to spread the I/O and minimize I/O contention. In an ideal world, we would have an unlimited supply of disk drives available so that we could place databases, logs, and objects on their own physical devices when needed. However, very few of us (if any) live in such a world. We frequently have to make do with existing hardware.

The first 2MB of `tempdb` exists by default on the `master` device. If `tempdb` activity is high, you may want to move this 2MB fragment off the `master` so that `tempdb` I/O doesn't conflict with other activity on the `master` device. Unfortunately, SQL Server allows you to expand `tempdb` onto another device, but not to move it off the `master` device. So how do you get rid of the 2MB slice of `tempdb`?

Well, if you're squeamish about directly modifying SQL Server system tables, you can simply drop the `default` and `logsegment` segments from the `master` device for `tempdb` after you've altered it to another device. This setup prevents any temporary tables or worktables and the `tempdb` log from reading or writing on the `master` device. However, the `system` segment is still there, and system table reads and writes still go to the `master` device. To move the `system` segment, you need to define a user-defined segment `tempdb` on the `master` device first, because SQL Server requires at least one segment to be defined on a database device.

With this solution, you can effectively get all of `tempdb` off the `master` device, but you'll have a 2MB slice of the `master` device essentially unused. To move `tempdb` completely off the `master` device, you need to modify the system tables.

> **WARNING**
>
> Modifying the system tables requires that you have sufficient knowledge of the information contained in the system tables. Once you start playing around with system tables, you risk corrupting your system if you modify or delete the wrong information.
>
> It's *strongly* recommended that you perform all system table modifications within a transaction. This way, you can verify your modifications before they are committed. If you really mess up your system tables, you can simply issue a `rollback` statement and you'll be back to square one to try again.

The general steps to move `tempdb` off the `master` device are as follows:

1. Start SQL Server in single-user mode to prevent users from attempting to access `tempdb`. Booting in single-user mode also allows updates to the system tables.
2. Log in as sa.
3. Make a backup of the `master` database in case something goes horribly wrong and you need to restore master.

4. Create a dummy database on the desired device at the size you want `tempdb` to be. (If the device doesn't already exist, you need to create it before taking this step.)

5. Begin a transaction so that you can roll back system table changes if an error is made.

6. Delete all references to the existing `tempdb` database from the `sysusages` and `sysdatabases` tables (that is, where `dbid = 2`).

7. Get the database ID for the dummy database and modify the `sysusages` and `sysdatabases` tables to change the dummy database references to `tempdb` (that is, change `dbid` in `sysusages` and `sysdatabases` to `2` and change the name in `sysdatabases` to `tempdb`).

8. Run `selects` against `sysusages` and `sysdatabases` to verify your changes to the system tables. If everything looks okay, commit the transaction; otherwise, roll back the transaction. Review the steps you performed to determine the cause of the problem and try again.

9. Shut down and restart SQL Server for the changes to take effect.

WARNING

This procedure should be used only on the `tempdb` database—not on any other database. Attempting this procedure on any database other than `tempdb` will corrupt that database. It works only on `tempdb` because `tempdb` is rebuilt each time the SQL Server is rebooted. Also be aware that incorrectly modifying the system tables can cause serious problems within the SQL Server.

The following code example displays a sample session. In this example, the new database that we're going to make `tempdb` will be called `newtemp`. The size of the new database will be 200MB. We'll create it on an existing device called `newdevice`. A dump device called `masterdump` has previously been defined as the dump device for the `master` database. The server has already been booted in single-user mode to allow updates to the system tables, and you are logged in as `sa`.

```
/* backup the master database */
dump database master to masterdump


/* create the database called newtemp on the device called newdevice */
/* This will eventually become the new tempdb */
create database newtemp on newdevice=200


/* remember to begin a transaction before modifying system tables!! */
begin tran
```

```
/* remove tempdb references for tempdb (dbid = 2)
   from sysusages and sysdatabases */
delete sysusages from sysusages u, sysdevices d
where vstart between low and high and dbid = 2


delete sysdatabases where dbid = 2


/* get the database id for the new database */
select name, dbid from sysdatabases
where name = 'newtemp'

name                             dbid
_____          ___
newtemp                           10

/* modify the system table references to the dummy database
   to make it look like tempdb (set dbid = 2 and change name to tempdb) */
update sysusages set dbid=2 where dbid = 10


update sysdatabases set name='tempdb',dbid=2
where name =  'newtemp'


/* verify your modifications by checking sysdatabase and sysusages */

select name, dbid, suid, crdate from sysdatabases
where name = 'tempdb'

name                      dbid  suid  crdate
_____    ___   ___   _____
tempdb                     2     1    Dec  8 1996 10:36AM

select * from sysusages where dbid = 2

dbid   segmap    lstart    size      vstart
___    _____    _____    _____     _____
   2      7         0       51200    16793600
(1 row affected)

/* Everything looks okay, commit the changes */
commit tran


/* shutdown and restart SQL Server for changes to take effect */
shutdown with nowait
```

Other tempdb Performance Tips

When using temp tables for storing intermediate values, select only the columns actually required by the subsequent SQL statements into the temp table. This plan helps to reduce the size of the temp table and speeds access of the data within the temp table because more rows will fit on a data page, reducing the number of data pages that need to be accessed by the query. With a large number of users, this plan can help to minimize the amount of I/O and I/O contention within `tempdb`.

If a table in `tempdb` will be accessed frequently, consider creating indexes on `tempdb` tables where appropriate. The investment in time and space to create the index may be more than offset by the time and I/O savings realized if the table is frequently accessed or used in joins. Also, the index can be used to satisfy the queries rather than table scans.

TIP

SQL Server enables you to create temporary tables and indexes within a stored procedure and subsequently reference them within the same stored procedure. Unfortunately, at the time that the queries are optimized, there's no data in the `temp` table for the query optimizer to estimate the index usefulness. By default, it assumes that the table has 100 rows on 10 pages.

If you want SQL Server to optimize the query based on actual data and index statistics, create the temporary table prior to executing the stored procedure that references it. You can do this easily by creating master procedures and subprocedures as follows:

```
create proc p1 as
select * into #tmp1 from customers
create index idx1 on #tmp1 (cust_id)
exec p2
return


create proc p2 as
select * from #tmp1 where id = 1001
return
```

The only thing to remember when implementing this solution is that the temporary table must exist at the time all stored procedures that reference it are created, so that they can resolve the table's name. To do this, simply add a command in the stored procedure script file that creates the table. Only the table definition must exist, not any data in the table. You can use a `where` clause, which doesn't return any data rows, to create the temporary table template:

```
select * into #tmp1 from customers where 1 = 2
```

Cursors and Performance

SQL was originally designed as a set-oriented processing language. Queries, updates, and deletes operate on sets of data. The set may contain a single row or multiple rows. The `where` clause specified indicates which rows will be included in the set.

What if you want to examine the rows' contents and, based on the values, perform an appropriate action? Within the original SQL language, this would require running multiple update processes, specifying different conditions in the where clause. But what if you had the following situation?

- Increase the price of all items by 10 percent, where price is less than $50
- Decrease the price of all items by 15 percent, where price is greater than or equal to $50

If you tried to run these as two separate update statements, you could potentially update a row twice, no matter in which order you run the queries. If an item was priced at $49.95, the first update would increase its price to $54.95 and it would then be updated again by the second update. Obviously you have a dilemma.

Cursors were designed to give you the ability to handle these types of situations. Cursors give you a way of performing operations on a row-by-row basis. However, this method of row-by-row access incurs significant processing overhead, due to the looping constructs needed to step through the cursor result set one row at a time. The slower processing of cursors can result in increased locking contention between concurrent users.

Be careful to use cursors only when absolutely necessary. Often, cursor processing can be replaced by normal SQL set-oriented processing. Standard SQL set-oriented processing typically runs faster than a cursor performing equivalent operations, even if it requires multiple table scans.

For example, consider the following cursor:

```
declare price_curs cursor for
select price from titles for update of price

declare @price money
open price_curs
fetch next from price_curs into @price
while (@@fetch_status <> -1)
begin
   if (@@fetch_status <> -2)
   begin
      if @price > $50
         update titles set price = price * $1.10
            where current of price_curs
      else if @price > $25
         update titles set price = price * $1.20
            where current of price_curs
      else
         update titles set price = price * $1.30
            where current of price_curs
   end
   fetch next from price_curs into @price
end
```

```
close price_curs
deallocate price_curs
```

The preceding example doesn't need to be performed as a cursor because the result sets don't overlap. It could be replaced with the following code:

```
update titles set price = price * $1.10
   where price > $50
update titles set price = price * $1.20
   where price > $25 and price <= $50
update titles set price = price * $1.30
   where price <= $25
```

In testing against a 5,000-row table, the second example has been observed to run approximately 2.5 times faster than the same processing performed as a cursor.

> **NOTE**
>
> Although cursor processing is slower than set-oriented processing, sometimes row-by-row processing can improve concurrent access to the data.
>
> Consider an update to price for all rows in the items table. With normal set-oriented processing, this would require a table-level lock, locking out all other access to the table until the update completes. With a cursor, locking is performed at the page level, allowing access to other pages in the table by other user processes. If each row is committed as a single transaction, the cursor typically locks only a single page at a time.
>
> However, be aware that committing each row individually could generate significantly more log records.

text **and** image **Columns and Performance**

Inappropriate datatype selection is a common error for database designers new to Microsoft SQL Server. One of the more common mistakes made is the inappropriate use of the text or image datatype.

Chapter 5, "Transact-SQL Datatypes," explains that text and image columns are stored as a 16-byte pointer in the data row, pointing to a separate linked chain of pages to store the text/image data.

What often happens is that the database designer decides, "I need a column for four to five lines of free-format comments. The char or varchar datatypes don't get big enough, so I'll use the text datatype."

The problems with text and image columns should cause you to think twice before using them.

These problems range from potentially enormous space consumption to a serious performance impact. Let's look closely at the drawbacks, and then consider some alternative implementations for storing large text and image data.

text and image columns can demand a substantial amount of storage overhead in your database. Each row in the table itself includes a 16-byte pointer to the first page in the text or image page chain for that data row. (If the data in the text or image column is null, the pointer is null as well.) To store the actual BLOB data, SQL Server allocates space for text data in each row in a linked chain of 2KB pages.

> **NOTE**
>
> This is an extremely important point. The server doesn't pack text data to use space efficiently. If the text column in a row contains the string, "Hello, World!" those 13 characters occupy an entire 2KB data page. One million rows worth of text columns like that take 2GB of storage, where they would take only 13MB if stored in a conventional varchar column.

See Chapter 11, "Understanding SQL Server Storage Structures," for the details on text and image storage.

When you update a row containing a text column, the amount of information logged can create a serious performance problem. text columns can be updated without logging by using the writetext command, but this has an impact on the recoverability of your database, because the text data inserted isn't logged.

> **NOTE**
>
> To allow nonlogged modifications such as a writetext requires that the select into/ bulk copy option be turned on for that database, which disables transaction log dumps.

In addition, any read of text or image data requires a minimum of two page I/Os (one read of the data page to get the text or image pointer, and at least one page read for the text or image data).

Some basic workarounds are available to avoid the problems of text and image datatypes:

- *Store it somewhere else.* This isn't as odd as it seems. Lots of applications store only the path name to an operating-system file containing the text or image data. The path is returned to the application, which in turn executes an operating system file open command to read the data. (Lots of commercial applications are written this way. There are some intricacies in implementing security, but the database application may run more smoothly.)

■ *Use varchar(255) or varbinary(255).* Stringing together a set of varchar or varbinary columns from a sequential set of rows takes a little extra application work, but eliminating the overhead of the BLOBs may provide better performance. (For an example of this, look at how SQL Server stores the text of stored procedures, views, triggers, rules, and defaults in the system table and syscomments.) Another alternative is to break the text or image data across multiple varchar(255) or varbinary(255) columns within a single row. Again, your application program needs to break the data into the appropriate columns on insert and combine them on retrieval.

This approach can help to improve performance by reducing search time for like strings, reducing storage overhead and I/O. The multi-column approach isn't feasible, however, if your data rows exceed the SQL Server maximum allowable row size of 1962 bytes.

■ *Store the text or image information in a related table.* In the pubs database, the pub_info table stores BLOB data separate from the actual publishers table. This setup improves the performance of updates on the publishers table, and the pr_info (text) and logo (image) columns can be placed in a table on a separate database, allowing a nonlogged writetext.

Summary

A number of performance issues must be addressed when working with SQL Server, in addition to server configuration and query tuning. This chapter has looked at only a subset of those issues, but they're the most common issues within standard environments. Mostly, these are issues that you need to be aware of when working in a SQL Server environment, so that you can prevent potential performance problems or address them if they should arise.

Common Performance and Tuning Problems

22

When tuning the performance of SQL Server, a number of esoteric features can be tweaked and tuned to improve overall performance. However, when trying to diagnose existing performance problems, a number of items could be potential culprits. How do you know where to begin to look to track down the performance problem?

Having a good understanding of the preceding chapters will help you to understand how SQL Server processes queries, so you can identify the causes of performance problems and ways to improve them. However, it's one thing to understand the technology, and another to know how to apply it.

In my years as a SQL Server consultant, I've been called in on a number of occasions to track down performance problems. What I've learned is that the majority of performance problems have similar causes—typically the types of mistakes made by developers and DBAs who are new to SQL Server and don't have a full understanding of how SQL Server optimizes queries. Admittedly, I made many of those same mistakes in the past as well.

What I've learned over the years is that it helps to try to identify the common causes of performance problems before delving into areas such as spreading I/O across devices or denormalizing the database.

One thing to remember when tuning the performance of your SQL Server is that there's no one particular strategy to apply that's going to make things faster. It basically depends on your situation and the cause of the performance problem. In addition, every strategy itself has its pros and cons; there often are a number of tradeoffs between tuning options. Making a change to improve performance in one area may hurt performance in another. This chapter serves as a checklist of some of the more common causes of performance problems you may encounter and presents ways to work around or prevent them. No one method is necessarily recommended over another. You need to weigh the pros and cons of the approaches presented and balance the potential performance tradeoffs when tuning your own system.

Out-of-Date or Unavailable Statistics

I was conducting a performance evaluation of an application at a customer site, when the manager of another application-development group in the department asked if I could look at a performance problem they were experiencing. I had some free time later in the afternoon and decided to take a look at it.

The programmer's description of the problem was that initially the queries that populated the screen used to return values with subsecond response time, but over time the application was getting slower as they added data to the tables. This behavior set off a light bulb in my head and prompted me to ask the obvious question, a question so obvious I was almost embarrassed to ask it: "When was the last time you ran update statistics?" His answer was, "What's that?"

The moral of this story is, don't neglect to ask the obvious question. We ran update statistics on the entire database and, like magic, all queries went back to subsecond response time. The problem was solved in a total of about five minutes from diagnosis to solution.

What tipped me off was that the behavior the programmer described was textbook behavior of a database with out-of-date statistics, or no statistics at all (see Chapter 13, "Understanding the Query Optimizer," for a detailed discussion of index statistics and how they're used by the optimizer). This problem often occurs in development environments or newly created production databases. Remember, if indexes are created on empty tables, no index statistics are generated. Without valid statistics to use, the query optimizer must use built-in statistics to estimate index usefulness, which often leads to invalid row and page estimates and might result in the wrong index or a table scan being used to process the query. A table scan may not present a noticeable performance problem when the table is only a few data pages in size, but, as data is added and the table grows, performance begins to degrade more noticeably. When you see this behavior, it's a good indicator that index statistics need to be updated.

> **TIP**
>
> If you've updated the statistics on your tables and/or indexes, don't forget to run `sp_recompile` on those tables. Any existing stored procedures in procedure cache have a query plan associated with them, based on the table statistics the first time they were run. To force them to generate a new query plan based on the updated statistics, run the `sp_recompile` stored procedure on the tables. All stored procedures that reference those table(s) will compile a new query plan on the next execution.

Search Argument Problems

It's the curse of SQL that there are a number of different ways to write a query and get the same result sets—some queries, however, may not be as efficient as others. A good understanding of the query optimizer can help you avoid writing *search arguments* (SARGs) that SQL Server can't optimize effectively. This section highlights some of the common "gotchas" encountered in SQL Server SARGs that can lead to poor or unexpected performance.

No SARGs

Watch out for queries in which the SARG may have been left out inadvertently, like this:

```
select title_id from titles
```

A SQL query with no search argument (that is, no `where` clause) always performs a table scan unless a nonclustered index can be used to cover the query (see Chapter 12, "Designing Indexes for Performance," for a discussion of index covering). If you don't want the query to affect the entire table, be sure to specify a valid SARG that matches an index on the table in order to avoid table scans.

Negative Logic

Any *negative logic* (for example, !=, <>, not in) always results in a table scan being performed, unless index covering can be applied (that is, all columns contained in the query can be found within the leaf level of a nonclustered index). An example of a SQL statement containing negative logic is as follows:

```
select * from orders
where price != $10.95
```

The not in or not equal (!= or <>) statement isn't considered an optimizable SARG by the SQL Server optimizer and isn't evaluated for index matching. This situation typically results in a table scan (unless an index covers the query) to resolve the query. When faced with a !=, consider possible ways to rewrite the query. For example, if you know (based on your data integrity rules) that price can't be less than 0, you can write the following query:

```
select * from orders
where price != 0
```

or

```
select * from orders
where price is not null
```

The query might perform better if written like this:

```
select * from orders
where price > 0
```

This query might perform better than either of the previous two because it avoids the negative logic and is treated as an optimizable SARG. The supplied constant value enables SQL Server to examine the distribution page to estimate the number of rows to be returned, in order to determine whether an index can be used to satisfy the query, rather than a table scan.

Operations on a Column in a where Clause

Any operation on the column side of a where clause causes it not to be treated as a SARG by SQL Server. Therefore, the optimizer can't use an index to match the SARG with an index; a table scan must be performed to satisfy the query. Examples of this type of where statement:

```
select * from orders
where price * 2 < $50.00
```

and

```
select * from customers
where substring(last_name, 1, 1) = "P"
```

These two queries could be rewritten this way:

```
select * from orders
where price < $50.00/2
```

or

```
select * from customers
where last_name like "P%"
```

As rewritten, the queries return the same result set, but the `where` clauses are now treated as SARGs. The optimizer can now consider using an index to satisfy these queries, instead of performing a table scan. The query against the `customers` table uses the distribution steps to estimate the number of rows where `name` begins with `P`. In SQL Server Version 6.0 and later, the optimizer evaluates the arithmetic expression prior to optimization and also uses the distribution steps to estimate the number of matching rows. This is a much better scheme than limiting the optimizer to a table scan because the optimizer can't treat the expression as an optimizable SARG.

Unknown Constant Values in a `where` Clause

The preceding discussion brings up an interesting point regarding how the optimizer treats constant expressions where the value *can't* be known until runtime. These are expressions that contain subqueries or local variables. The SQL Server treats these expressions as SARGs but can't use the distribution steps, because it doesn't have a value to compare against the steps at query compile time. What it does in this situation is use the *index density* information. Index density is stored on the distribution page for the index along with the distribution steps, and is a float value representing the average number of rows that would match against any given value for the index. The index density value is based on the uniqueness of the index. A less unique index has a higher index density—that is, a greater percentage of rows may match any given value. (For an in-depth discussion of index density and distribution steps, read Chapter 12.)

The optimizer generally is able to better estimate the number of rows affected by a query when it can compare a known value against the distribution steps than when it has to use the index density to estimate the average number of rows that match an unknown value. This is especially true if the data in a table isn't distributed evenly. When you can, try to avoid using constant expressions that can't be evaluated until runtime, so that the distribution steps can be used rather than the density value.

To avoid using constant expressions that can't be evaluated until runtime in `where` clauses, consider putting the queries into stored procedures and passing in the constant expression as a parameter. Because the optimizer evaluates the value of a parameter prior to optimization, SQL Server evaluates the expression prior to optimizing the stored procedure. For example, the following query contains a search clause with a local variable. The value of the local variable won't be known until runtime, so the index density would have to be used to estimate the number of affected rows:

```
declare @avg_price money
select @avg_price = avg(price) from orders
select * from orders
   where price < @avg_price
```

To avoid using the subquery or local variable in a `where` clause when comparing the `price` column in the `orders` table against the average price, create the following procedure:

```
create proc proc1 (@var1 money)
as
   select * from orders
      where price < @var1
```

Now, use an assignment `select` statement to retrieve the average price into a local variable and pass it into the stored procedure as a parameter:

```
declare @avg_price money
select @avg_price = avg(price) from orders
exec proc1 @var1
```

In this example, `@var1` is evaluated and a query plan is generated for the stored procedure using a known value, so the distribution steps are used instead of the index density to estimate the number of rows that are less than the specified price contained in the parameter `@var1`. This results in a more accurate estimate of the number of affected rows. More accurate row estimates typically result in more efficient query plans being chosen.

So for best results when writing queries inside stored procedures, use stored procedure parameters rather than local variables in your SARGs whenever possible. This strategy allows the optimizer to optimize the query by using distribution steps, comparing the distribution steps against the parameter value. If you use local variables as SARGs in stored procedures, the optimizer is restricted to using index density, even if the local variable is assigned the value of a parameter.

If you ever need to perform an operation on a parameter inside the stored procedure, do it before using the parameter in a SARG, and store the new value back into the parameter itself—better yet, perform the operation on the parameter within the SARG. For example, the following two procedures return the same results, but are optimized differently:

```
create proc proc1 (@var1 money)
as
   select @var1 = @var1 * 2
   select * from orders
      where price < @var1

create proc proc2 (@var1 money)
as
   select * from orders
      where price < @var1 *2
```

For the first procedure, `proc1`, the `select` against the `orders` table is optimized based on the value passed into `@var1` when the stored procedure is called, not the value `@var1` contains during execution. If the value `10` is passed into `@var1` when the procedure is first executed, the optimizer uses `10` as the value for `@var1` to compare against the distribution steps for an index on price. At optimization time, the previous select statement that assigns a new value to @var1, select @var1 = @var1 * 2, has not yet been executed, so the original value of @var1 (10) is used to optimize the query. Even though this isn't the value @var1 will contain when the query is actually executed, this method still is often preferable to using local variables, because the distribution steps can be used to optimize the query, instead of index density or built-in optimizer statistics.

The second procedure, proc2, *will* evaluate the expression in the SARG, @var1 * 2, and use the value of 20 to optimize the query the first time it's executed, comparing 20 against the distribution steps for an index on price. This is because SQL Server Version 6.0 and later evaluates the expression in the SARG before optimization. By being able to use the distribution steps, the optimizer should be able to determine a more accurate row estimate for proc2 than would be obtained for proc1, and possibly a more efficient query plan to retrieve the same result set.

TIP

If you need to maintain the original value of a parameter for use later in the procedure, save it in a local variable and reassign it back to the parameter when needed, as in the following example:

```
create proc proc3 (@var1 money)
as
declare @initval money

select @initval = @var1

select @var1 = avg(price) * 2 from orders
select * from orders
    where price < @var1

select @var1 = @initval
select * from orders
    where price > @var1
```

When this procedure is optimized, the original value of @var1 will be used to optimize the final select statement in the procedure.

NOTE

For more information on stored procedure optimization, see Chapter 14, "Stored Procedure Optimization."

Datatype Mismatch

Datatype mismatch used to be a problem in earlier releases of SQL Server, but appears to have been eliminated in SQL Server Version 6.0 and later. Previously, if the value being compared against the column was of a different datatype, the index statistics couldn't be used. This was especially easy to do in stored procedures when a char or varchar parameter was being compared in a SARG against a varchar or char column, respectively.

> **NOTE**
>
> Remember that SQL Server stores a char column that permits nulls as a varchar. Therefore, to match a parameter datatype to a column defined as char(10) null, you need to define the parameter as varchar(10) to ensure that the datatypes match.

When examining the index-selection process in SQL Server Version 6.0 and later using the dbcc traceon (302) trace flags (as described in Chapter 15, "Analyzing Query Plans"), observe that SQL Server now converts the value to the datatype of the column prior to checking the index statistics, as long as an implicit conversion between the datatypes can be performed (for example, float converts to int and char converts to varchar, but char doesn't convert to int). To be on the safe side, however, try to match the datatype of the constant expression with the column datatypes.

or Logic in the where Clause

An or clause may cause a worktable to be created if the optimizer chooses to apply the *OR strategy* to create a dynamic index (see Chapter 13 for a discussion of the OR strategy). The dynamic index is created and used instead of a table scan to process the query, if the I/O cost of creating and using the dynamic index is less than the I/O cost of a table scan.

> **NOTE**
>
> Remember, an in clause is treated like an or clause by SQL Server. For example:
>
> ```
> select * from titles
> where title_id in ("BU3075", "BU1025")
> ```
>
> is the same as
>
> ```
> select * from titles
> where title_id = "BU3075" OR title_id = "BU1025"
> ```
>
> In SQL Server 6.5, either of these statements is processed with the option of performing a range retrieval between the highest and lowest values in the where clause to find the matching rows, rather than using a dynamic index.

If any one of the search clauses must be resolved by a table scan, a single table scan is performed to resolve the query. Also, if the resulting cost of using the dynamic index or a range retrieval against the index is estimated to exceed the cost of a table scan, a table scan is performed.

If you're trying to avoid table scans when you have or clauses in your queries, make sure that all clauses involved in the or can be supported by an index and that the index is selective enough to avoid a table scan.

Other Query-Related Issues

The majority of performance-related problems are a result of the way a query is written. The SQL language allows a number of additional clauses and keywords to sort and group the data in different ways. Unfortunately, these additions incur extra work and may cause queries to run more slowly. This section identifies some additional performance issues to be aware of when writing SQL queries, and offers some tips to improve query performance.

The distinct Keyword

The distinct keyword causes a worktable to be created in tempdb for sorting and removing of duplicate rows. This factor can seriously affect performance if the query returns a large result set, because the entire result set is copied into a worktable in tempdb and sorted, and then the duplicates are removed before SQL Server sends the results to the client application. This setup can significantly add to the response time of the query and increase the amount of I/O performed on tempdb.

For single-table queries, if all columns of a unique index are included in the select list, the unique index guarantees that each row is unique and the worktable can be avoided. For multi-table queries, each table must also have a unique index on the join columns.

> **TIP**
>
> Watch out for overuse and misuse of the distinct keyword. I was once at a client site where they were complaining about query response time in their applications. It was several minutes before any rows were being returned to the client application, even for single-table queries. As it turned out, they were using the distinct keyword in every query being issued, even for join queries where no duplicate rows were being returned, because one of the tables had a unique index that was being retrieved. Dropping the distinct keyword from the queries resulted in data results being returned to the client application in seconds rather than minutes.
>
> Be aware of instances when a unique index avoids duplicate rows in your result set, but the optimizer still insists on using a worktable to ensure that no duplicates are returned. Also, you should simply avoid using distinct unless absolutely necessary.

The count() Function

The count(*) function, without a where clause, results in a table scan unless a nonclustered index on the table can be used to cover the query. For the following query, the smallest nonclustered index can be used to satisfy this query because SQL Server can determine how many rows are in the table by counting the number of rows in the smallest nonclustered index:

```
select count(*) from customers
```

However, if the query contains a where clause, a clustered or nonclustered index would need to exist on one of the SARGs to avoid a full table scan.

> **TIP**
>
> If you only want to determine the existence of a row in a table without needing to know the exact count, use the if exists statement rather than select count(*). The if exists statement discontinues processing as soon as a matching row is found, whereas select count(*) continues processing to look for all matching rows.

> **NOTE**
>
> Remember that the count(*colname*) function counts all *non-NULL* values for a column in a table. Unlike count(*), a query with a count(*colname*) function will be covered by an index only if the column being counted is contained in a nonclustered index. If no nonclustered index exists that contains the column, SQL Server needs to scan the entire table to count the non-NULL values, even if the column is defined as NOT NULL.

Whether an index can be used to satisfy a count() function or not, a single-column, single-row worktable still will be created automatically in tempdb for the purpose of calculating and storing the count. This will require a second step in the query plan to retrieve the count from the worktable.

Aggregate Clauses

Without a where clause, aggregates such as avg, min, max and sum generally cause table scans, unless the query can be satisfied by an index. Here's an example:

```
select sum(qty) from orders
    where order_num = "3124"
```

If an index exists on the orders table and contains the order_num column, the query can be satisfied by finding the data rows via the index and calculating the sum of qty. If an index exists on the order_num and qty columns, the query can be satisfied by scanning the index rows without having to access the actual data rows at all.

Also, the following query would be covered by the index and thus avoid a table scan if the index were created on the `qty` column:

```
select sum(qty) from salesdetail
```

If you're expecting an index to cover an aggregate query, but the query optimizer is performing a table scan, make sure that the query truly is covered by the index. All columns in the `select` list, as well as all columns in the `where` clause, must be included in the index definition.

Also, as with the `count()` function, a single-column, single-row worktable is created automatically in `tempdb` for each aggregate function in the query, for the purpose of calculating and storing the aggregate value. Be aware of the increased I/O that occurs from writing to `tempdb`, as well as the performance considerations related to `tempdb` (see Chapter 21, "Miscellaneous Performance Topics," for a detailed discussion of `tempdb` performance issues).

Here's an interesting tip if you want to retrieve the `max` and `min` values for a table on an indexed column. It's actually cheaper in terms of total I/O and processing time to run them as separate `select` statements rather than combine them in a single statement. This is because SQL Server can't walk an index structure in two different directions. For example, to resolve the following query on customers with a nonclustered index on `id`,

```
select min(id), max(id) from customers
```

the query would be covered by the index, but would find the `min(id)` by reading the first row on the first page of the leaf level of the index. Then, to find the `max(id)`, it would have to scan the entire leaf level of the index until it found the last row on the last page (see Figure 22.1 on the next page). Based on the index in Figure 22.1, it would cost five page reads to find the `min` and `max` in a single query.

However, if you ran a query to retrieve just the `min` value, it would cost only one page. SQL Server would simply read the first row on the first page in the leaf level. (As discussed in Chapter 11, "Understanding SQL Server Storage Structures," the location of the leaf page is stored in the `sysindexes` table, so SQL Server doesn't need to traverse the index tree to find the leaf page.)

To retrieve the `max` value, SQL Server would start at the root page and traverse the index tree, following the last row on the last page at each level until it got to the last row on the leaf level. Look at Figure 22.1 again and note that this would cost two page reads (the root page plus the last leaf index page). Therefore, the total number of pages read for two separate queries is only three pages versus five. This example saves only two pages, but in much larger tables and indexes the I/O savings can be substantial.

FIGURE 22.1.

Finding the min *and* max *values in the leaf pages of a nonclustered or clustered index.*

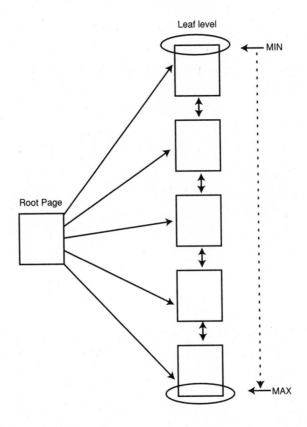

If you need to get the min and max values in a single result row from a single select statement, but want to avoid a scan of the leaf index level, consider coding one of the aggregates as a subquery in the select list like the following:

```
select min(price), (select max(price) from titles)
    from titles
```

This example still performs two separate select statements, but the results are returned in a single result row.

order by and group by

The order by and group by clauses need to use tempdb as a work area for sorting and grouping the result set. When processing a small result set, the response should be subsecond. When a large result set is returned, response time can increase significantly due to the increased I/O in the tempdb database.

With the order by clause, you can avoid a worktable under two circumstances. The first is if there's a clustered index on the table and the result set is being ordered by the clustered index.

Due to nature of the clustered index, SQL Server knows that the data is already sorted by the clustered index.

WARNING

If you're ordering by the clustered index but have a search argument on a column that has a nonclustered index on it, and the nonclustered index is used to resolve the query, a worktable will be generated to sort the result set because the result set is being retrieved in nonclustered index order rather than in clustered index order.

A worktable can also be avoided for an order by if the order by clause matches the SARG and the SARG can be satisfied by a nonclustered index, like the following:

```
select * from customer
    where id between 10 and 20
    order by id
```

Because the result set is being retrieved in nonclustered index order already, additional sorting isn't required.

NOTE

In versions of Microsoft SQL Server prior to Version 6.0, if you had an order by ... DESC clause in your query, a worktable would have been generated in tempdb by the SQL Server to do the sorting, because SQL Server was unable to retrieve the data in descending sort order.

SQL Server Version 6.0 and later can now perform reverse index scans. If an index is used to retrieve the data, and the data is being sorted in descending index order by an order by ... DESC clause, the index can now be scanned in reverse order, and a worktable isn't necessary to re-sort the final result set.

If you have any group by clauses in your queries, a worktable will always be generated by SQL Server to perform the grouping and the calculation of the aggregate(s) for each group.

Join Clauses

When running troublesome queries with the showplan option on, watch out for the following showplan message: Worktable created for REFORMATTING. This message indicates that no useful indexes were available to satisfy the query and that the optimizer has therefore determined that it's more efficient to build a temporary clustered index on the inner table in tempdb on-the-fly than to incur the I/O and processing cost of joining via iterative table scans.

> **WARNING**
>
> This can be a very costly solution in terms of additional I/O and `tempdb` usage. It's better to provide queries with the appropriate indexes than to let the optimizer generate one on-the-fly. If you see the reformatting message in the `showplan` output, perform a query analysis and reexamine your indexing strategy.

You also want to be careful to avoid and watch out for Cartesian products between tables in a join due to a missing join clause. Remember, as a general rule of thumb, if there are *n* tables in a query, there should be at least *n*-1 join clauses.

Providing All Possible Join Clauses

You can improve join performance in joins of three or more tables that share a key by providing all possible join clauses in the query. The key to fast joins is selecting an efficient join order. When the server *joins*, it gets a value from one table and then looks for corresponding values in the next inner table. The order in which the tables are processed determines the amount of work required to answer the query.

The server uses the join clauses you provide in the query to define the universe of possible join orders. For example, if you write the following:

```
select *
   from titles t,salesdetail sd,titleauthor ta
   where t.title_id = sd.title_id
   and sd.title_id = ta.title_id
```

you have the following two possible join orders:

titles	$\rightarrow$	salesdetail	$\rightarrow$	titleauthor
titleauthor	$\rightarrow$	salesdetail	$\rightarrow$	titles

These two join orders are possible because of the two join clauses specified in the query.

Add the third leg of the triangle (`t.title_id = ta.title_id`) to the query to provide more possible join orders (see Figure 22.2):

```
select *
   from titles t,salesdetail sd,titleauthor ta
   where t.title_id = sd.title_id
   and sd.title_id = ta.title_id
   and t.title_id = ta.title_id
```

FIGURE 22.2.

Adding the third join clause completes a triangle of join tables and gives the server complete freedom to choose the most efficient join order.

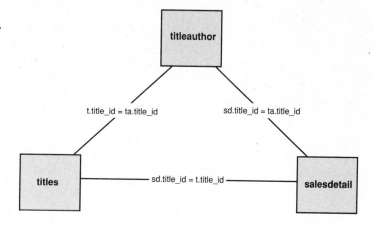

Logically you haven't added anything (you'll get the same result), but you have provided more possible join orders. There are three join conditions specified, so there are now six possible join conditions:

titles	→	salesdetail	→	titleauthor
titleauthor	→	salesdetail	→	titles
titles	→	titleauthor	→	salesdetail
titleauthor	→	titles	→	salesdetail
salesdetail	→	titleauthor	→	titles
salesdetail	→	titles	→	titleauthor

This means that with the additional join clause, you can actually triple your potential number of join orders. You may not always get a faster result, but you do improve your chances of getting that faster result.

SQL Server Configuration

SQL Server configuration has an impact on overall system performance. One of the most important configuration issues to examine when tracking down performance problems is SQL Server memory configuration.

> **NOTE**
>
> For a more detailed discussion about memory configuration, some of the more esoteric SQL Server configuration parameters, and how they affect SQL Server performance, see Chapter 32, "Optimizing SQL Server Configuration Options."

Memory

Memory is probably the most important SQL Server configuration variable in relation to performance. The more data that can be accessed and worked on in data cache, the faster the system performs. You want to make sure that sufficient data cache has been configured for the databases and for the queries being run. Don't assume that memory has been configured properly.

For example, I was at a customer site during a performance and tuning (P&T) engagement and asked them how much memory was on the machine. They reported to me that 48MB was available. Mistakenly, I assumed that was how much they had configured for SQL Server.

One query in question was taking approximately 6 hours to run to retrieve 50,000 records. I tried running it with the showplan and noexec options on, and the query plan generated by showplan indicated that the optimizer was using the expected index to process the query. I then turned off the noexec option and let the query run, and noticed that it was performing a significant amount of physical I/O.

At this point, I decided to take a look at the SQL Server configuration and discovered that the SQL Server was configured at only 8MB of memory. No one had ever reconfigured it after installation!

Anyway, we increased the memory configuration to 32MB, which allowed all data pages required by the query to remain in memory. This also helped to significantly reduce the runtime of the query. Overall, we were able to cut the time required to run the query by about 6 hours—down to approximately 20 seconds!

> **WARNING**
>
> Be careful not to overconfigure memory for SQL Server. If you allocate more memory to SQL Server than is actually available within the Windows NT operating system, SQL Server will end up paging to disk and performance will suffer significantly!

Physical Database Design

The physical design of a database can have an impact on overall database performance. This section identifies some common physical design issues to consider when tracking down performance issues or tuning the performance of a database.

Indexes

Watch out for missing indexes. You should verify that all indexes have been created as defined in design documentation. A common performance problem results from developers writing queries based on expected indexes that might have been created differently—or not created at all. The queries don't use the expected index, thus adversely affecting performance.

Over-Indexing

Avoid over-indexing your tables whenever possible in an On-Line Transaction Processing (OLTP) environment. Perform a thorough transaction-and-query analysis to carefully map out which indexes are really needed. You typically want to identify the most critical, highest-priority transactions that should be supported by indexes.

Index Selection

Poor index selection is another tuning item you should examine. Chapter 12, contains a detailed discussion about index selection and usefulness. The following are a few things to keep in mind:

- For the SQL Server optimizer to consider using a composite index to process a query, at least the first ordered column in the index must be specified in the where clause.

- The first element in the index should be the most unique element (if possible), and index column order in general should be from most to least unique in a compound key. However, remember that selectivity doesn't help if you don't use the first ordered index column in your where clause, so choose the first ordered column that will also be used most in queries.

- Understand that choosing the clustered index for the primary key is correct only some of the time. A more useful alternative is to choose the column(s) that will be accessed by ranges of data ("Give me all the consumers whose ages are between 25 and 45") or for grouping ("Give me sales by customer").

Clustered Indexes

Check to see whether clustered indexes are being used effectively. Any table, if it has only one index, should typically have a clustered index before a nonclustered index, because the overhead involved with maintaining clustered indexes is less than for nonclustered indexes. Also, the space required for a clustered index is significantly less than for a nonclustered index, because the clustered index typically has one less level than a similar nonclustered index. This helps to improve query performance because it results in one less page-read-per-row lookup than does a nonclustered index on the same column.

Examine your clustered-indexing strategy closely. Too often, the clustered index is automatically assigned to the primary key. This setup is fine if it's the exclusive access path to that table and is used frequently in joins. However, in other situations it may be more efficient to create the clustered index on a different column(s) and create a nonclustered unique index to maintain and support the primary key.

Other possible candidates for a clustered index include the column or columns used most frequently to access data in the table, columns frequently specified in order by clauses, and columns frequently used for range retrievals.

> **TIP**
>
> Clustered indexes support range retrievals well because the data within the range is grouped together, minimizing the number of data pages that need to be accessed to retrieve the data rows. For further discussion on selecting clustered versus nonclustered indexes, see Chapter 15.

Avoid Hot Spots

Watch out for potential hot spots when inserting or updating data. Hot spots occur when the most recently inserted rows are clustered together. This situation typically occurs in tables without a clustered index, because SQL Server inserts all new data rows at the end of the table. It can also occur with a clustered index if the clustered index exists on a sequential key and data is inserted in sequential-key order.

If the most recently inserted rows are also the most often accessed, locking contention and potential deadlock problems are possible on those data/index pages between multiple users. Consider implementing a clustered index that will spread the data throughout the table, thus avoiding hot spots. For example, if you have an orders table with a sequential key on order_id, and data is inserted in sequential order, consider creating a nonclustered index on order_id and placing a clustered index on product_id so that new order entries are spread randomly throughout the table by product_id.

DSS versus OLTP

Try to avoid mixing Decision Support System (DSS) activities with high-load On-Line Transaction Processing (OLTP) activity. DSS queries are often long-running and CPU-intensive, causing a slowdown of other transaction activity. In addition, DSS queries and reports typically require a large number of supporting indexes. The greater the number of indexes, the greater the overhead necessary to maintain all those indexes during update processing.

If possible, consider setting up a separate server on a separate machine with duplicate data for performing DSS tasks. This way, you can index the DSS system as heavily as needed and the DSS reports won't affect the OLTP activities.

> **NOTE**
>
> This topic is covered in more detail in Chapter 18, "Database Design and Performance," and Chapter 38, "Administering Very Large SQL Server Databases."

Historical Versus Active Data

You should check to see whether a large amount of historical data that is rarely accessed is being kept online with recent, more active data. If so, consider moving the historical data off into a separate table or database to make the active table smaller. This scheme reduces the amount of data and index pages that need to be searched and also reduces the overhead of index maintenance by making the index trees smaller. This topic is covered in detail in Chapters 18 and 38.

Locking Issues

Watch out for obvious locking-contention problems, which can severely impact system performance. Some of the more likely culprits are:

- Disconnected client processes that have left a session open in the SQL Server that is still holding locks
- Transactions that enable user input, causing locks to be held for indeterminate periods of time
- Use of the `holdlock` keyword in `select` statements
- Long-running transactions
- Nested transactions that don't fully commit properly (thus leaving locks held within a session)

> **TIP**
>
> For a complete discussion of locking issues and solutions, see Chapter 16, "Locking and Performance."

Maintenance Activities

Watch out for maintenance activities such as `dump/load` and `dbcc` that could occur during normal processing periods. They are very I/O- and CPU-intensive and can have considerable impact on the performance of other online activities. Additionally, commands such as `dbcc`, `create index`, and `update statistics` acquire table-level locks until completion, thereby limiting concurrent access to tables.

Summary

A number of potential causes and solutions to performance problems exist within SQL Server. Having a good understanding of the performance issues and SQL Server operations makes you effectively equipped to address and solve performance problems. You should now also have a good feel for the more likely culprits to examine to identify and solve performance problems quickly.

If you've considered and looked into the common problems addressed in this chapter and ruled them out as the cause of your performance problems, it may be time to dig a little deeper into the SQL Server. Just remember, when all else fails, feel free to give Tech Support a call. Who knows? You may have been one of the lucky (?) souls to uncover a bug or "undocumented feature" within SQL Server. Believe me, I've seen my share of those in the years that I've been working with SQL Server.

Remember, too, that every strategy to improve performance has its pros and cons; there are often a number of tradeoffs between tuning options. Making a change to improve performance in one area may hurt performance in another. You need to balance the potential performance tradeoffs when actually tuning your own system. The information presented in this and the preceding chapters will help you make those decisions wisely.

IV

PART

System Administration

Roles and Responsibilities of the System Administrator

23

This chapter looks at the roles and responsibilities of a SQL Server system administrator and how these roles differ from or overlap with those of a database or operating system administrator. The text explains critical terminology and explores the following key concepts:

- System tables
- System stored procedures

Components of SQL Server

As you may recall from Chapter 2, "Understanding the Microsoft Client/Server Architecture," the SQL Server environment consists of clients, servers, and a network that enables them to communicate. Let's review each of these components to understand the broad spectrum of administration required to keep SQL Server operational.

Client components include the following:

- Workstation hardware
- Network interface card (NIC)
- Operating system
- Network software
- Network library software
- Database library software (DB-Library/ODBC)
- Application software

These are the network components:

- Server and client NIC
- Network software
- Hubs, routers, and concentrators
- Cable

The following are server components:

- Server hardware
- NIC
- Windows NT Server
- Network software
- Network library software
- Server library software
- SQL Server software

As the SQL Server system administrator, you probably are only *officially* responsible for the SQL Server software and the various client libraries, but consider a different question: When the server becomes unavailable, which of these components could be the culprit? The answer is any of them. Client/server requires a mastery of several disciplines to maintain solid, reliable performance day in and day out.

As system administrator, you need to muster a team of experts—in client software, server software, and all the networking layers in between. As you work through this chapter, map the examples to your environment; this strategy will enhance your capacity for troubleshooting problems as they arise.

NOTE

People who are worried about job security in the client/server world should think about all the areas of expertise required to make a complex system such as SQL Server really work. Here's a very brief list of specializations:

■ Project manager
■ Analyst
■ Relational database designer
■ SQL Server administrator
■ Network/LAN (for example, Windows NT) administrator
■ Network administrator
■ Help desk staff
■ Database administrator
■ Client OS (for example, Windows 95) specialist
■ Applications programmer

SQL Server Versions

SQL Server has been around for a number of years, and many releases and versions are in production in companies around the world. Microsoft first shipped SQL Server 1.0 for OS/2 in 1988, and it was actually Microsoft's first database product. At this early stage in the relationship, Sybase was responsible for actually porting the 32-bit UNIX version of SQL Server to 16-bit OS/2.

Microsoft followed Version 1.0 with Version 1.1, but both of these were quickly superseded by SQL Server 4.2 for OS/2. Version 4.2 introduced "feature set parity" with the major releases of Sybase SQL Server, which, depending on the platform, had version numbers between 4.0 and 4.2. Sybase continued to introduce new versions, such as 4.8 and 4.9x, and those enhancements weren't folded into the OS/2 version of SQL Server until an update, 4.2a (and then 4.2b), shipped concurrently with the first release of SQL Server for Windows NT.

SQL Server 4.2 for Windows NT was an interesting product. It represented Microsoft's "coming of age" in the development of this application, because approximately 70 percent of the "database kernel" was completely rewritten and optimized for Windows NT. Microsoft's marketing of the product caused some confusion about this point, however. Microsoft kept the 4.2 version number to ease people's concerns about compatibility—Release 4.8 from Sybase required extensive (and expensive) upgrade costs, and Microsoft put backward compatibility with the OS/2 server at the top of its feature list.

However, the database engine actually had features that would debut in Sybase 4.9.2, and even Sybase System 10. In fact, SQL Server 4.2 for Windows NT from Microsoft has the same query optimization enhancements that Sybase originally put in to the System 10 SQL Server.

Microsoft immediately differentiated SQL Server for Windows NT by re-architecting the database kernel—and writing it as a Win32 process so that it could run only on Windows NT. Hardware portability, provided by Sybase through various releases on various versions of UNIX, was accomplished through Windows NT's portability to both Intel-based and RISC-based platforms. Supported platforms for Windows NT now include MIPS, DEC Alpha AXP, and IBM/Apple/Motorola's PowerPC chip. In addition, symmetric multiprocessing support, which Sybase previously shipped in a different version of the software, is also directly supported through SQL Server's use of Windows NT.

Microsoft has gradually weaned its OS/2 customers off that platform and onto Windows NT—and for good reason. SQL Server for Windows NT is dramatically more stable, can address literally hundreds of megabytes of RAM (remember, OS/2 was still a 16-bit OS), and gigabytes of disk space. The combination of Windows NT and SQL Server is a far more stable, far better-performing server application platform than any supported on OS/2, and it now directly competes with a range of UNIX installations.

Microsoft SQL Server 6.0 continued the trend of internal differentiation from the original Sybase product by adapting SQL Server to make use of more native Windows NT services, including the graphical user interface. Whereas SQL Server 4.2 for Windows NT introduced useful graphical tools for administering SQL Server, SQL Server 6.0 introduced a centralized administrative application for managing network-wide SQL Servers. In addition, SQL Server introduced new categories of features, such as parallel query optimization and transaction-based data replication.

SQL Server clients can run on a variety of platforms, including DOS, Windows 3.x, Windows NT, Windows 95, Macintosh, and—by using ODBC—even UNIX. All of these platforms can take full advantage of SQL Server's services and features, allowing developers to write applications for whichever client platform their customers need.

Microsoft SQL Server 6.5 has continued in this trend and introduces several new components on both the server and client side. This has widened responsibilities of the administrator. On the server side, new components include the following:

- MS Query
- SQL Trace
- Microsoft Distributed Transaction Coordinator (MS DTC)
- OLE Automation Stored Procedures
- SQL Server Web Assistant
- Simple Network Management Protocol Management Information Base (SNMP MIB)
- SNMP Agent

New SQL Server 6.5 client components include this list:

- MS Query
- SQL Trace
- MS DTC (Client)
- SQL Server Web Assistant

Together these features enhance the performance, reliability, and scalability of SQL Server by making the processes of replicating data, managing the system, and developing applications easier and more portable. These components are discussed in detail in other chapters.

System and Database Administration

In some organizations, no distinction is drawn between administration of SQL Server and its resident databases. A single individual or group is responsible for all these issues. Certainly, overall system responsiveness and integrity require good coordination between the system and its databases, but there are distinctions between SQL Server and database administration. The system administrator keeps the server available and focuses on the relationship between the server and its operating system. The database administrator focuses on database query performance, transaction throughput, and concurrency. For the most part, this chapter concentrates on server administration issues. Chapter 26, "Defining, Altering, and Maintaining Databases and Logs," examines database administration issues.

The System Administrator (sa) Login

All administrative responsibilities need to be executed by an individual logged in—literally—as sa, for system administrator. Database-level tasks can be assigned to database owners, but administering server-level configuration and optimization parameters requires access to the special sa login.

Responsibilities of the System Administrator

The SQL Server system administrator is responsible for the overall performance and reliability of SQL Server. The following list describes some of the responsibilities of the system administrator (this is probably a pretty good place to start defining the job description of an sa for your organization or workgroup):

- **Server installation and upgrades.** The system administrator installs the software on the server. (When performing an installation, obtaining assistance from a person skilled in the server operating system is always helpful.) A user that exists in the local Windows NT Administrators group must be added to the operating system to perform the SQL Server installation, if no such user exists. This user is also responsible for applying patches and bug fixes to SQL Server and for performing major version upgrades. When installation is complete, the system will contain a login for the sa. The step-by-step installation process is documented in Chapter 24, "SQL Server Installation and Connectivity."

- **Physical device configuration.** SQL Server uses underlying system resources, including disk, memory, and network resources. The system administrator needs to identify physical storage areas and then define logical mappings to those areas.

- **Database creation.** After identifying logical devices, the sa creates databases on those devices, and then often assigns ownership (and administrative responsibility) to another login.

- **System configuration settings.** The system administrator manages system configuration settings, including the amount of server memory and how it's allocated, the number of concurrent user connections and open databases, and the number of locks and system devices. These settings affect system availability and performance.

- **Server monitoring and preventive maintenance.** SQL Server administration requires a well-defined regimen of preventive maintenance. Activities to include along with regular administrative activities are outlined in Chapter 26.

- **Backup and maintenance of the system and user databases.** The master database is a crucial resource where system-wide information is recorded. All stored procedures are maintained in the master database. The model database is the template database for all subsequent database creation. As system administrator, you guarantee the availability and integrity of these databases.

  Unless the sa designates specific owners of databases, the sa is also responsible for backup and restoration of user databases. The sa can transfer database ownership, creating database owners (DBOs) in the process, and these individual DBOs then assume such responsibilities.

  The Database Maintenance Planning Wizard greatly enhances general maintenance of the databases in SQL Server 6.5. The DMP Wizard can also be run from the SQL Enterprise Manager. Further maintenance is facilitated through SNMP.

SNMP applications can also be used to monitor the status of SQL Server installations, view configuration parameters, access databases, and monitor performance information. (This is a new feature in SQL Server 6.5.) SNMP support is discussed in detail in other chapters.

- **Server startup and shutdown.** Only the system administrator is permitted to start and stop the server process. You may require periodic shutdowns to change system parameters or to repair broken equipment. In addition, the system administrator is the backup database administrator (DBO) for all databases.

- **System security.** SQL Server provides several levels of security: server login security, database security, and object security. The sa is responsible for server-level security.

- **Server performance monitoring.** The system administrator provides activity and performance statistics, using the SQL Performance Monitor. The administrator is also responsible for communication enhancement and SQL Server data portability to the Internet server or the Web Server. This is done using the SQL Server Web Assistant (new in SQL Server 6.5).

System Tables

SQL Server stores almost all configuration, security, and object information in its own *system tables*. There are system tables within each individual database, colloquially called the *database catalog*. There are system tables that are unique to the master database as well, and these are colloquially referred to as the *server catalog* or *system catalog*.

NOTE

The system tables that are unique to the master database are sometimes called the *system catalog* or *data dictionary*. It's crucial to remember that system tables are stored within each individual database (including master). All databases, including master, model, tempdb, and so forth, have 18 system tables (such as sysobjects, sysusers, and sysindexes) that make up the database catalog. The master database is unique in that it holds 13 additional system tables that are global to the server (such as syslogins, sysdevices, and sysdatabases) and that also make up the server catalog.

Database Catalog System Tables

These databases are stored in every database, *including* master:

sysalternates	User aliases that allow a database user to be validated using a different server login name.
sysarticles	Stores the definition of a basic replication unit, including base table, publication to which it belongs, and article status. (See syspublications.)
syscolumns	Names and characteristics of every column in every table and view in the database.
syscomments	Contains the creation text of every view, rule, default, trigger, and procedure. This text is accessed through sp_helptext.
sysconstraints	Names and characteristics of table constraints.
sysdepends	Relationships between dependent objects (views to tables, stored procedures to tables, and so forth).
sysindexes	Index and space allocation information for every table.
syskeys	Documented keys for each table.
syslogs	Transaction log, a non-readable record of each logged modification performed within the database. (This is the only system table stored in the log segment—see Chapter 26 for more on segments.)
sysobjects	Object definitions (tables, views, procedures, triggers, rules, defaults, constraints).
sysprocedures	Pre-parsed optimization trees for code-based objects (views, procedures, triggers, rules, defaults, constraints).
sysprotects	Permissions for users on objects (tables, views, procedures).
syspublications	Defines "folders" for individual replication articles, enabling other servers to subscribe to individual tables or groups of tables.
sysreferences	Names and characteristics of each referential integrity constraint declared on a table or column.
syssegments	Database partitions for storing different types or categories of objects and managing object growth below the level of the entire database.
syssubscriptions	Maps individual articles and publications to the servers that will use these objects. New rows are inserted as new subscribers request data from the source server and tables.
systypes	System- and user-defined datatypes available for columns when creating tables.
sysusers	Authorized logins that can access the database.

> **NOTE**
>
> Don't confuse the keys in syskeys with index columns or primary and foreign keys in constraints. Index columns determine the contents of an index, as well as the physical sort order of data (if clustered) and a unique identifier (if unique). Primary and foreign keys constraints define an enforced referential-integrity relationship between tables.
>
> Keys recorded in syskeys (established with sp_primarykey, sp_foreignkey, and sp_commonkey) define the structure of tables *as system documentation only*. Their only real uses come when an application examines these values to suggest a join or to learn about the structure of the tables; however, the keys defined in syskeys are never enforced by SQL Server itself.

Server Catalog System Tables

The following databases are stored in master:

syslogins	Name, password, and configuration information about each serverlogin.
sysconfigures	System configuration values to be used at the next system startup.
syscurconfigs	Current system configuration values.
sysdatabases	Database name, owner, status, and other information.
sysdevices	Physical storage resources available to SQL Server (both active database devices and backup devices).
sysusages	Data allocations and mappings of physical storage areas to individual databases.
sysprocesses	Process IDs, login information, and current status of each logged-in user.
syslocks	Current locks. (This is a memory table only—if the server goes down for any reason, all locks are released).
syslanguages	Installed language sets (in the United States, this is usually only us_english).
syscharsets	Installed character sets.
sysmessages	Server-wide error messages.
sysservers	All servers involved in remote procedure calls.
sysremotelogins	Mappings and login identifiers for users logging in from remote SQL Servers.

System Stored Procedures

SQL Server enables the database developer to store SQL routines within the database; these are *stored procedures.* Stored procedures provide faster performance, reduced network traffic, better control for sensitive updates, and modular programming.

Although stored procedures often support user table processing, SQL Server provides several stored procedures called *system stored procedures* that support system table processing. For example, the sp_helpdb stored procedure returns a complete listing of all system databases. Other system stored procedures (for example, sp_addlogin and sp_bindrule) modify system tables.

Special Characteristics

Names of system stored procedures start with sp_, are stored in the master database, and are created by the instmstr script. Naming a stored procedure with sp_ and storing it in master gives administrators the capability to create new system stored procedures. You can create your own system stored procedures.

> **NOTE**
>
> For shops that use both Sybase System 10 and Microsoft SQL Server 6.5, you'll notice that System 10 has moved the system stored procedures into a new system database called sybsystemprocs. Microsoft continues to store system stored procedures in master. It's one of what will continue to be a growing number of differences in these two products as the manufacturers update them independently.

When you execute a stored procedure whose name starts with sp_, the server first looks in your current database to find the proc. If the proc isn't found in your current database, the server looks for it in master.

Ordinary stored procedures are interpreted in terms of the current database when the procedure is created. For example, if you create a stored procedure in a user database, the stored procedure is immediately bound to the tables within the database. (In the following examples, any characters embedded inside a reversed pair of slashes and asterisks (/* and */) are interpreted as comments and are ignored by SQL Server.) The following example uses the database user1db to create a procedure called show_objects that will select a user from the sysobjects tables. Because we've specified the database as user1db, the procedure can be executed from any database. Let's assume that we're currently in database xyz. If we execute the following code, it will have the same effect as if we executed the code from database user1db:

```
/* create proc in user1db */
use user1db
go
create proc show_objects
```

```
as
select name, user_name(uid)
from sysobjects
go
```

Now assume that we're currently in database xyz, but this time we remove the line use user1db from the code before executing the code. The object is assumed to be in xyz database, which isn't the case. However, if we open database user1db and then execute the code—even after taking the code piece out as just mentioned—we end up with the same result as if we hadn't removed the use user1db line of code.

You can execute this procedure from any database, but you'll always see a listing of objects in user1db, the database in which the procedure was created. To invoke a procedure in one database from a different database, you must qualify the procedure name. The format is *database.owner.procedure*. If the database name isn't provided, the object is assumed to be in the current database. If the owner isn't provided, the procedure will first look for an object owned by you; if you don't own an object of that name, it will then look for an object owned by the user dbo, the database owner. Assuming that the previous procedure was created by dbo, you would execute the procedure in the following manner:

```
/* sample execution of procedure from database user9db */
use user9db
go
user1db..show_objects
go
```

System procedures are always interpreted in terms of the current database *when the procedure is executed.* Create a similar system procedure in master:

```
/* create this proc in master */
use master
go
create proc sp_show_objects
as
select name, user_name(uid)
from sysobjects
go
grant exec on sp_show_objects to public
go
```

When the procedure runs, the system returns the contents of sysobjects in the current database at execution time (remember, you don't need to fully qualify the procedure name with its database and owner if you have prefixed it with sp_):

```
/* sample execution from user9db */
use user9db
go
sp_show_objects
go
```

You'll notice that the last line of code in the preceding example includes a permissions statement. System stored procedures that aren't created by the instmstr script have three requirements. First, they must be created by the sa login. Second, they must be created in the master database. Third, they must have their execution granted to the `public` group in the `master` database. Chapter 27, "Security and User Administration," discusses groups and users. For now, just remember to grant execution to the group `public`.

NOTE

With some practice, you will be creating these stored procedures yourself, without giving it much thought. Don't forget that a stored procedure must be prefaced by execute (or exec) if it isn't the first command in a batch. The following is an example:

```
/* From user9db, execute the */
/* show_objects proc in user1db */
/* AND the sp_show_objects proc */
use user9db
go
user1db..show_objects
exec sp_show_objects
go
```

Useful System Procedures

The following are system procedures you'll find useful:

`sp_who`	Current logins and operations (from `sysprocesses` in the `master` database)
`sp_lock`	Current locks and table identifiers (from `syslocks` in the `master` database)
`sp_help`	Objects in the database or detailed object information (from `sysobjects`, `syscolumns`, `sysindexes`, `syskeys`, and `systypes`)
`sp_helpdb`	Databases on the server (from `sysdatabases` in the `master` database)
`sp_configure`	Current system configuration settings (from `syscurconfigs` and `sysconfigures` in the `master` database)
`sp_helpdevice`	Physical storage and backup devices on the server (from `sysdevices` in the `master` database)

TIP

If you plan to write your own system stored procedures, you probably want to identify your procedures to avoid future versions of SQL Server from overwriting important, working procedures with new standard system procedures. For example, if your company name is *ABC Corp.*, you may want to prefix all your developed, stored procedures with `sp_abc_`.

Summary

As an administrator of a SQL Server, you have several areas of responsibility. System tables record configuration and object information, and system stored procedures enable you to query and modify those system tables. (Although it's possible to update the system tables by hand, Microsoft strongly discourages bypassing the system stored procedures to make changes directly to system tables unless instructed to do so by Microsoft Product Support Services.)

The following chapters examine the many responsibilities of the system administrator, explore the system tables involved in maintenance, and describe the proper usage of most system stored procedures.

SQL Server
Installation and
Connectivity

24

This chapter takes a look at installation and connectivity with SQL Server. You explore some broad guidelines and learn about the traps at this stage. This chapter gives detailed instructions about the process but not about the specific selections, because so many of the choices you need to make relate to your specific environment: your version of SQL Server, your platform, and your choice of client operating system.

SQL Server Hardware and Software Requirements

SQL Server for Windows NT is not shy about consuming hardware. What's amazing isn't its appetite for anything related to hardware, including processors, disk space, disk controllers, RAM, and network access, but that it's able to use these resources so efficiently. Relative to other database servers, a very fast, scaleable SQL Server 6.5 platform can cost half to one-quarter of what a comparable UNIX platform would.

With SQL Server 6.5, Microsoft is acknowledging—in fact, promoting—SQL Server's capability of scaling to even larger hardware platforms. SQL Server 4.2 could handle a 5GB (or even stretch to a 10GB) database; SQL Server 6.5 increases both of these numbers by an order of magnitude. SQL 4.2 could use four processors; SQL 6.5 can use eight. In fact, SQL Server's biggest problem is that only now are hardware vendors catching up to its appetite. Many Intel-based platform vendors, as well as Digital with its Alpha AXP-based systems, are just releasing machines that support a full gigabyte of RAM, multi-gigabyte disk subsystems, and eight or more CPUs. All of this is occurring at price points far below those of such well-known RISC platform vendors as HP, SUN, Data General, and so on.

So what makes a good hardware platform for SQL Server?

Server Hardware Characteristics

SQL Server itself needs to be fast enough to handle the work of several users concurrently, and to manage all the overhead involved in running a complex product. The performance of the hardware platform focuses on the four critical areas of any system:

- CPU power to handle the computing load
- Adequate hard disk throughput for data access
- Sufficient RAM for SQL Server to cache databases effectively
- A network interface that doesn't strangle the other three areas

No one area is any more important than the others. As a SQL Server administrator, part of your job is to analyze the bottlenecks and performance inhibitors of your SQL Server platforms. Each of these components can be a potential problem, and keeping them performing in relatively equal fashion is an important job.

With Windows NT's built-in symmetric multiprocessing support, and SQL Server's use of that support through the Symmetric Server Architecture (discussed in Chapter 2, "Understanding the Microsoft Client/Server Architecture"), sufficient processing power shouldn't be a problem. If a single Intel Pentium 133 MHz processor isn't sufficient, add another. If two aren't sufficient, add two more. If Intel-based systems don't work, any number of RISC vendors are available to make SQL Server run faster.

Physical memory capacity also is critical. After SQL Server has set aside the minimal memory that it needs for users, devices, and databases, the remaining server memory is used for cache. There's a simple rule about SQL Server and memory: More is better. The larger your tables, the more indexes you plan to create; the more users you expect, the greater the memory you should plan to install.

Here are some quick RAM guidelines:

- Development systems can run with only 16MB of actual RAM in the system, provided that replication isn't involved (12MB for Windows NT and 4MB for SQL Server).

- Production systems can have as much as you want to make available. Use the Windows NT Performance Monitor discussed in Chapter 33, "Measuring SQL Server System Performance," to determine your production server's proper memory requirements.

- If you are going to be using SQL 6.5's replication features, the "on the box" minimum memory requirement is 32MB (16MB for Windows NT and 16MB for SQL Server). The practical limit for such systems is 64MB (24MB for Windows NT and 40MB for SQL Server).

- SQL Server's RAM requirements and recommendations are consistent across all of Windows NT's supported platforms, including the RISC platforms and PowerPC. 64MB of RAM on an Intel box is the same to SQL Server as 64MB of RAM on a PowerPC box.

Windows NT also takes advantage of multiple disk controllers and multiple hard disks, as does SQL Server. SQL Server 6.5 builds on this capability to improve parallel of query operations as well, but that only means that it can take better advantage of the underlying hardware.

Networking seems to be the most-forgotten bottleneck for SQL Server systems. I have seen too many shops install SQL Server for Windows NT on multi-CPU Intel or MIPS boxes, with 128MB of RAM and dedicated RAID hardware subsystems. When query response times are dismal, nobody thinks to look at the 4 Mbps token ring network on which they're running. Or the 2 Mbps ArcNET network. These are necessarily deficient networks. In their day, they were sufficient for the needs of simple file and print sharing. But 16 Mbps token ring or 10 Mbps Ethernet are mandatory, and the new 100 Mbps Fast Ethernet and 100 Mbps Asynchronous Transfer Mode (ATM) networks will be the networks of choice for the next five years.

In the end, choosing hardware for SQL Server is a choice in compromises. Bypassing an extra CPU to make sure that the network interface card (NIC) is sufficient is a much better tradeoff than vice versa. More RAM and more disk controllers are a better investment than a fifth processor, but a second processor may be better than the other two. Don't be afraid to test configurations, and don't be afraid to ask questions of other SQL Server users about their optimal hardware platform.

Chapter 33 discusses how to use Windows NT's monitoring utilities to analyze bottlenecks and evaluate whether the cause is software-related, hardware-related, or both.

SQL Server Software Requirements

Windows NT's software requirements are easy. Windows NT Server is all you need. If you haven't upgraded to the most current version, you should. Microsoft also recommends upgrading. Microsoft continues to improve the speed and scalability of Windows NT Server with each new release.

Also, Microsoft makes the interesting (and correct) recommendation that SQL Server *not* be installed on the Primary Domain Controller or Backup Domain Controller. Although the thin veneer of economics would suggest that running one hardware box for both of these is more economical than having dedicated PDC and SQL Server machines, the PDC requires substantial hardware in its own right to maintain domain security and accounts throughout the network. Backup Domain Controllers are also ill-suited to SQL Server work. Backup Domain Controllers are responsible for all logins to the domain, and on busy networks that overhead can be substantial. For performance reasons, a dedicated server is best. If absolutely necessary, putting SQL Server on a BDC will work.

Upgrading to SQL Server 6.5 for Windows NT

This section makes the assumption that you already have installed SQL Server 4.2x or 6.0 for Windows NT. If you aren't upgrading an existing server, you can skip ahead to step-by-step installation; these issues don't apply to you. If you are upgrading, however, consider this section mandatory reading.

SQL Server 6.5 introduces a number of significant changes that affect how you choose to upgrade your server if upgrading from SQL Server 4.2x, and only minimal changes if upgrading from SQL Server 6.0. The actual upgrade process can be very easy and quite painless. The good news is that backward compatibility, including support for existing 6.0 and 4.2x-based applications, has been a top priority. There are, however, some important planning issues to consider when adopting SQL Server 6.5.

Special Considerations When Upgrading from 4.2x to 6.5

Sites that want to run SQL 6.5 in parallel with existing 4.2x-level servers have a number of options. First, the SQL SETUP program can install SQL Server into a different drive and directory, and administrators can switch between SQL 4.2 and SQL 6.5 on the same machine. To accomplish this objective, two criteria must be met, as follows:

- SQL Server 6.5 must be installed in its own subdirectory, not the existing subdirectory where SQL Server 4.2 is installed.

- SQL Server 6.5 must use its own MASTER.DAT file. It can't use the existing MASTER.DAT of the SQL Server 4.2 installation.

SQL SETUP installs SQL 6.5 Registry keys into a different Registry key folder than SQL Server 4.2, so no Registry entry changes are required. After installing, administrators can use DISK REINIT and DISK REFIT to restore the necessary sysdevices, sysusages, and sysdatabases table entries. Because the SQL Server 6.5-level services have been renamed, they appear as different entries in the Control Panel's Service Control Manager. SQL Server 4.2 and SQL Monitor appear as "SQLServer" and "SQLMonitor," while the new SQL Server 6.5 and SQL Executive services appear as "MSSQLServer" and "SQLExecutive," thereby avoiding naming conflicts with the Service Control Manager.

The reason for avoiding naming conflicts? SQL Server 4.2x and SQL Server 6.5 can run side by side, simultaneously, on the same machine. They must be configured to listen on pipes with different default names, but they can run side by side, making any migration path—fast or slow—more practical.

For those who want to install SQL 6.5 on a completely different machine, SQL Server 6.5 can read existing 4.2x-level backup files directly, and SQL Transfer Manager supports both platforms directly as well.

> **NOTE**
>
> The SQL Transfer Manager was a separate application in SQL Server 6.0. In SQL Server 6.5, the Transfer Manager has been integrated into the SQL Enterprise Manager.

This setup provides the capability to gradually move over to the new platform without compromising availability or backward-compatibility of the server or applications that access it. Although more effort is involved in choosing this migration method, a single hardware failure won't destroy both servers.

Special Considerations When Upgrading from 6.0 to 6.5

Before upgrading from SQL Server 6.0 to SQL Server 6.5, note the following list of compatibility issues between the two versions:

- You can't run SQL Server 6.0 and SQL Server 6.5 side by side on the same machine.
- SQL Server 6.5 can read SQL Server 6.0 databases.
- SQL Server 6.0 with Service Pack 3.0 (available from Microsoft) can read a 6.5 database.

General Upgrade Information

For those who choose to upgrade directly from SQL 4.2x or SQL 6.0 to SQL Server 6.5, the process is very simple. Before starting the upgrade process, make sure that the SQL Server Open Databases configuration parameter is equal to or greater than the number of databases on your server (including master, pubs, model, and tempdb). If the parameter is less than the total number of databases on your system, use the SQL Enterprise Manager or the system stored procedure sp_configure to increase the value. Make sure that you have the required amounts of disk space to upgrade your existing SQL Server. If you're upgrading a SQL Server 6.0 installation, you need approximately 20MB; if you're upgrading a SQL Server 4.2x installation, you need approximately 65MB. The free disk space must exist on the same drive where SQL Server is being installed. The SETUP program automatically detects the existence of SQL Server 4.2 or 6.0 and steps through the upgrade process. In almost every case, this process can proceed uninterrupted, and clients will be using SQL Server 6.5 without realizing that the server underneath has changed. In one scenario, however, this statement might not be true; that's the topic of the next section.

Upgrading SQL Server and Potential ANSI Keyword Violations

The enhancements to Transact-SQL in SQL Server 6.5 and 6.0 added many new keywords that weren't part of SQL Server 4.2x. SQL Server 6.5 uses several keywords that were listed in Version 6.0 as future reserved words. As such, existing object definitions in SQL 4.2x and SQL 6.0 databases may cause conflicts with these new keyword definitions. To make the migration process as painless as possible, SQL Server 6.5 includes the CHKUPG65.EXE utility. Located in the \BINN subdirectory of the SQL Server installation directory, CHKUPG65 connects to an existing 6.0 and 4.2x-level SQL Server and scans syscomments, looking for object definitions that may conflict with the keywords defined for Transact-SQL. This fact highlights the constraint with using CHKUPG65: It requires that the syscomments table hold all object definition statements so that CHKUPG65 can scan them in the table. Many third-party applications clear out the text column of syscomments for security purposes. In this case, CHKUPG65 won't work, and the object definitions have to be manually scanned in the SQL Server system tables, both in master and in the other databases. In addition, the SETUP program also relies on syscomments for upgrade information—database and object definitions that aren't present in syscomments cause the upgrade to fail. SETUP notifies the administrator that an upgrade can't be performed during the setup routine to prevent overwriting the existing server and databases. (Note that the CHKUPG65 utility was called CHKUPG in SQL Server 6.0.)

CHKUPG65 uses the standard command-line syntax of all DOS-based SQL utilities, and requires the specification of an output file for the report that it generates on keyword violations. A typical command line would be as follows:

```
CHKUPG65 -Usa -Ppassword -oc:\CHKUPG65.rpt
```

On my own 4.2x test server, I created a device named reference, with a database named primary. In that database I created a table called key, with column names such as constraint, check, and cursor. After the CHKUPG65 utility ran, it generated a report file with the results shown in Listing 24.1.

Listing 24.1. The CHKUPG65 utility generates a report of all ANSI keyword and reserved word violations in 4.2 databases that could cause upgrade problems.

```
=====================================================
Database: master
Status: 8
(No problem)
Missing objects in Syscomments
None
Keyword conflicts
User name: user
Login ID: user
Database: primary
=====================================================
Database: primary
Status: 0
(No problem)
Missing objects in Syscomments
None
Keyword conflicts
Column name: constraint
Column name: cursor
Object name: key
User name: user
=====================================================
Database: pubs
Status: 0
(No problem)
Missing objects in Syscomments
None
Keyword conflicts
None
```

You can see that the report shows which databases, objects, logins, and user definitions will cause the SQL 6.5 SETUP upgrade process to fail. With this information, administrators know where potential problems lie. They now have some choices to make about how these keyword issues can be resolved. The upcoming paragraphs discuss those options. Remember, this is *only* if CHKUPG65 doesn't give your server a clean bill of health. If CHKUPG65 doesn't say it's broken, you don't have to fix anything.

> **WARNING**
>
> Any server that will be upgraded from 4.2x or 6.0 to 6.5 should have CHKUPG65 run against it. If there are keyword violations, SQL Server SETUP will note them as part of the upgrade and *allow you to continue installing SQL Server*! This is problematic because, if the keyword violation is a database name, SQL Server is unable to validate or recover the database. In this case, SQL Server simply stops. You would be forced to reinstall SQL Server and to use existing 4.2x or 6.0 backups to restore your server.
>
> Also, notice that SQL Server checks for missing objects in the syscomments table. Many ISVs who develop applications for SQL Server (PeopleSoft is most notable, among many others) delete the text of their stored procedures from syscomments to prevent the code from being copied. If this is done, SQL Server can't upgrade the server in place, because it can't verify any ANSI keyword violations!

Handling ANSI Keyword Violations

There are two strategies for migrating servers currently using object identifiers that will generate new keyword violations:

- First, you can rename the offending objects, and change references to those objects in stored procedures and SQL statements within client applications that use those objects. This solution isn't trivial, but it's the most thorough way to guarantee that applications can take advantage of SQL Server 6.5 without causing applications to cause otherwise preventable errors. This method is Microsoft-recommended for migrating servers that will encounter this issue.

- If applications take advantage of stored procedure calls instead of passing "naked" Transact-SQL from the client, the work is much easier—simply change the references within the stored procedures, and the client applications will be "automagically" fixed. If changes to the object names are implemented, the identifier-change process must occur before SETUP is run to upgrade the server. SETUP can't "upgrade in place" a 6.0 or 4.2x-level SQL Server that generates ANSI keyword violations under SQL Server 6.5.

If you aren't going to upgrade in place, but instead install SQL Server 6.5 on a different server and rely on BCP, you have another potential option. With the new SET QUOTED_IDENTIFIER command, you have the option of installing SQL Server 6.5 on a separate machine, migrating the databases and objects to the new server using BCP, and using this command to keep the existing object names. Although not necessarily intended as a migration tool, SET QUOTED_IDENTIFIER changes how the query processor interprets double quotation marks. This command allows any T-SQL keyword to be used as an identifier, as long as the string value being used is enclosed in double quotation marks. Through the combination of modifying client applications to add double quotation marks surrounding object references and using SET QUOTED_IDENTIFIER, the object identifiers and definitions at the server can remain as they are. For example, the key table in the code example can be migrated to SQL Server 6.5, using ISQL and BCP. The fully qualified syntax references a database name of primary, an object owner ID of user within the database, the table name key, and the field name constraint. All four of these words are now T-SQL keywords because of SQL Server 6.5's ANSI language support. This statement can become valid if run in the following fashion:

```
SET QUOTED_IDENTIFIER ON
create table "key" ("constraint" int)
SET QUOTED_IDENTIFIER OFF
```

With this example, you can see that existing object definitions may not need to change. At the client application side, the source code for the application must be changed to add two things: double quotation marks to surround object references that would otherwise generate keyword-violation errors, as well as additional DB-LIB commands activating the appropriate SET option for each user connection. Remember, the SET command works at the *user connection* level, not the *global server* level. If your server generates ANSI keyword violations, the client applications must be modified in some form. The effort expended to achieve this is roughly equivalent, so putting the (marginally-minimal) extra effort to rename the offending database objects will be time well spent.

The good news is that an extremely small portion of SQL Server installations have used database or object names that would violate ANSI keyword restrictions, so upgrading should be a simple matter of following the install process.

NOTE

Customers aren't the only ones to have been caught by their refusal to follow sound advice. Microsoft's Systems Management Server, which uses an underlying SQL Server as its data storage area, used a column name of key for any primary key fields. Because key is now an ANSI keyword (primary key and foreign key constraints, and so on), SMS 1.0 would not run on SQL Server 6.0. It would run only on SQL Server 4.2. Microsoft had to write SMS Version 1.1 to use SQL Server 6.0.

Using Existing 4.2x and 6.0 Administration Tools

If you're installing SQL Server 6.5 over an existing SQL Server 6.0 or 4.2 installation, the existing SQL Server administration tools will be upgraded automatically. Before you can administer a SQL Server 6.0 installation with a SQL Server 6.5 SQL Enterprise Manager, you must install the script SQLOLE65.SQL for the SQL Server 6.5 Enterprise Manager to attach to a SQL Server 6.0 installation. To use existing SQL Server 4.2x tools requires installing the scripts ADMIN60.SQL and OBJECT60.SQL. The older tools (the 6.0 SQL Enterprise Manager, 4.2x Object Manager, and 4.2x SQL Administrator) themselves still see the 6.5-level server as a 4.2-level server or 6.0 server, and are limited to the administrative functionality that they already contain. For example, I can't use SQL Administrator to configure server-to-server replication. I need the SQL Enterprise Workbench for that, and other 6.5-specific features. With SQL Administrator, I can create devices or databases and perform all the other operations that both servers have in common.

Choosing a File System for Windows NT and SQL Server

Choosing a file system (FAT or NTFS) can seem a daunting task. Under Windows NT, though, the issue is no longer performance. In fact, when SQL Server 4.2 for Windows NT first shipped, Microsoft made it clear that there were no direct performance differences between the file systems, and a series of tests bore out this claim.

So how do you choose? The answer comes in the form of the features that you need to run SQL Server. The least likely choice will be FAT, because it's quite unusual to insist that a production SQL Server be dual-bootable to DOS and Windows NT. If your server does have this as a requirement, then FAT is your choice. NTFS volumes can't be read by DOS.

If this is a production server, it's a good bet that Windows NT will be the only operating system. As such, NTFS is the choice because of its recoverability within the operating system, its capability to create stripe sets (multiple physical disks seen as a single drive letter), and its capacity to implement RAID 5 fault tolerance on those stripe sets. (See Chapter 18, "Database Design and Performance," for more information on RAID and SQL Server.)

> **NOTE**
>
> NTFS actually uses a transaction-based metaphor for controlling file system recoverability—a concept that the Operating System group at Microsoft copied directly from database technology vendors.

There is a popular but unverified tale of a gentleman performing a file copy operation between two disks in a computer using Windows NT and NTFS on both disks. He opened the case and disconnected the data cable from one of the disks. He sat by the machine for a few moments, and then reconnected the cable. Windows NT continued the file copy until it was complete.

To test his handiwork, this man did a file comparison of the two disks, and found that every byte of data had been copied properly. Ever try that with DOS?

In addition to recoverability features, NTFS also has improved file and disk security features, as well as enhanced protection against computer viruses. Because Windows NT's OS kernel doesn't allow direct access to hardware resources, viruses stored in NTFS partitions are unable to access such critical items as the boot sector or file system allocation tables. It's an extra layer of protection for what will be a storage place for critical information.

Step-by-Step Server Installation

SQL Server 6.5 uses a slightly modified version of the graphical SETUP utility shipped with SQL Server 6.0 for Windows NT. But the most important part of installation is knowing what you need to tell the SETUP utility. SETUP requires the following pieces of information:

- What's the destination drive and directory for the SQL Server system software?
- What's the destination and size for the MASTER.DAT device file?
- What code page and sort order are you going to use?
- What network protocols will you support?
- Do you want SQL Server and SQL Executive to start automatically?
- How is your SQL Server software licensed?

SQL Server Installation Path

Installation copies a number of files to the operating system file system, including the installation program, the server software itself, installation scripts, and utility files. You need to tell the server where this installation path is located in your directory structure.

The SQL Server administrator should have sufficient privileges to run the installation, which means write privileges to the disks on the server. (Later, you may choose to grant users access to the utility programs, the error log, or other parts of the server environment that they might find helpful.)

Master Device Location and Size

The next value required by the server is a location and size for the master device. The *master device* is always a file in the file system, and is typically installed in the default location \MSSQL\data. The default size for the MASTER.DAT file (the physical name of the master device) must be at least 25MB. The discussion on database devices in the next chapter should help you properly size the master device, and also show you how to increase the size of the master device should you make it too small.

Mirror the master device (for more information, see Chapter 25, "Defining Physical and Mirror Devices"). It's an excellent fault-tolerance option for SQL Server, but does require a separate physical disk and controller to be properly implemented. Secure the directory well to prevent other users from stumbling on the master device. Name the file MASTER.DEV or something similar that makes its purpose unmistakable.

Code Page and Sort Order

SQL Server requires a unique *code page* (also called a *character set*) combined with a unique *sort order* to define how data will be organized. SQL Server supports many distinct code pages. A code page corresponds to an alphabet in some ways. The code page defines the character appearance and unique number in the code set. For example, code page 437 (U.S. English) and code page 850 (Multilingual) contain the complete U.S. alphabet. Beyond the standard alphabet, however, the U.S. English code page contains additional graphics characters (blocks and lines in various positions), whereas the Multilingual code page contains accented letters from other alphabets, such as German umlauts and French accent ague and accent grave. The default code page for SQL Server 6.5 is ISO 8859-1. ISO 8859-1 (Latin 1 or ANSI) character set is compatible with the ANSI characters used by Microsoft Windows NT and Microsoft Windows.

SQL Server can also order data in a variety of ways, within the definition of a single code page. SQL Server comes with several predefined sort orders, but other custom sort orders can be added using SETUP. A sort order defines how SQL Server will handle the organization of characters for both data storage and data retrieval operations. In effect, the sort order determines the results of order by and group by queries, because they rely on this underlying layer. Dictionary order, case-insensitive is the default sort order for SQL Server 6.5.

> **TIP**
>
> Microsoft has *informally* tested different sort orders and found that the combination of Code Page 850 with a BINARY sort order (meaning that the letters are sorted in ASCII numeric value) is about 20 percent faster than the next best combination. This may lead to unexpected results. Because the lowercase letters of the English alphabet are assigned larger numbers than uppercase letters, servers installed with this

combination will return data in queries using order by with lowercase letters sorted *after* uppercase letters. The reason? BINARY sort order tells SQL Server that smaller-numbered letters are sorted before larger-numbered letters in the code page, and uppercase letters come first.

Try to balance performance with flexibility: Although SQL Server does provide case-insensitive sort orders, these will affect system performance.

SQL Server Network Support

SQL Server for Windows NT 4.2 introduced a compelling feature: support for heterogeneous clients. NetWare, Named Pipes, TCP/IP, and Macintosh clients could all access a Windows NT-base SQL Server. Coming from the Sybase "any protocol as long as it's TCP/IP" world, this was a welcome relief for administrators wanting to put data in central locations, accessible by different types of clients.

SQL Server 6.5 builds on this feature to provide Integrated Login Security, a special feature of Microsoft SQL Server (see Chapter 27, "Security and User Administration"), over multiple network protocols. In addition, through the use of the new Multi-Protocol Network Library, SQL Server can encrypt connection attempts, queries, and data over network wires.

Selecting a protocol has never been easier. SQL Server supports a myriad, including the following:

- TCP/IP—Fastest in Microsoft's unofficial testing.
- IPX/SPX—Second fastest, according to informal tests.
- Named Pipes—Third fastest, and the only protocol permanently installed with SQL Server.
- DECNet Sockets.
- Banyan VINES—Including support for StreetTalk and the forthcoming ENS for Windows NT.
- ADSP—"AppleTalk" to the rest of us. This is supported using ODBC client software from Visigenic.

SQL Server will install Named Pipes support by default, but it can be removed at installation time.

Depending on your network protocol (TCP/IP, IPX/SPX, or Named Pipes), you need to decide on a listening port within the server. Processes that communicate with SQL Server send a message to the host operating system network address. The message is keyed with the internal address of the SQL Server process. The address that you establish will be used by every client and every server needing to communicate with this SQL Server.

654

In Named Pipes, the internal address of the process is a pipe name, with a default value of

`\\servernameE\pipe\sql\query`

where `servername` is the published name of the host computer. The default pipe name that SQL Server uses can be changed using the SQL Client Configuration Utility on the client workstation.

In IPX/SPX, the server is assigned a standard port address within NetWare. A default value (normally 0x08bd) is included with the server installation. If that value is already assigned, SQL Server provides several other values that you can try. (You are unlikely to encounter any other process with that identifier. Novell has assigned that number to SQL Server processes, and you will rarely find two SQL Servers running on a single Windows NT server.)

In TCP/IP, you identify a single-integer port address within the server. For TCP/IP installations, contact an administrator for a value to use.

When you choose to install SQL Server 6.5 alongside an existing 4.2 installation, you can use different port numbers for the different servers. For IPX/SPX, you should use different IPX/SPX port numbers, selecting them from the provided list. For TCP/IP connections, selecting different IP port addresses for each server guarantees that clients can connect to both servers.

TIP

If you're installing many SQL Servers at your organization, it's helpful to install SQL Server with the same port address everywhere, for the sake of consistency. If you choose not to standardize port addresses, publish port addresses to help those who do workstation setup and administration.

You can use 5000, for example, unless that number is already used. If you're installing several SQL Servers on the same hardware, increment this number by 100 for each new server (check with the administrator to ensure that each value is available).

With the introduction of integrated login security, SQL Server for Windows NT became part of the network security profile. The problem was that only Named Pipes clients could take advantage of this feature. In addition to the client and server network libraries listed previously, Windows 3.x-, Windows 95-, and Windows NT-based clients can also use the new Multi-Protocol Network Library to access SQL Server.

MPNL implements session-level connectivity using Windows NT Network Remote Procedure Calls (or RPCs). Using an underlying transport (NetBEUI, IPX, and TCP are supported currently), a client workstation can open a session-level connection with SQL Server, using these RPCs instead of some other session-level IPC—such as sockets, SPX, and so on.

With MPNL, two new features are available. By selecting the appropriate check boxes in the SQL Server SETUP routine, administrators can take advantage of MPNL's encryption of TDS packets over the network wire. This feature enables encryption of packets sent and received across the network, providing a secure environment. The encryption relies on Windows NT encryption of network RPCs and uses RSA as its encryption method. Because both the server and client network libraries use these RPCs, two-way encryption is supported. Also with MPNL, any Windows-based client can take advantage of integrated login security over Named Pipes, TCP/IP sockets, or IPX/SPX, including Windows 3.x-based clients using Novell SPX over IPXODI.

Integrated security relies on the underlying domain security facility to provide authentication for SQL Server user connections. In SQL Server 4.2, this objective was achieved by querying the Named Pipes API to determine network validation and then allow access to the server through a trusted connection. SQL Server now relies on a prompt for domain connections to servers for which a Named Pipes or RPC domain structure doesn't exist. For example, if a user needs to connect to a Novell network from a Windows NT workstation, and that user attempts to use MPNL to gain a trusted connection to SQL Server, the MPNL connection will prompt the user with a domain login and password dialog box to validate the domain ID. That domain ID is valid for any server on the network that's both listening on the network with the MPNL and also has integrated security enabled. If any of the servers have mixed or standard security enabled, administrators will need to manage logins and permissions for each user on each server independently.

Starting SQL Server and SQL Executive Automatically

SQL Server and SQL Executive run as *services* under Windows NT's Service Control Manager. As such, they can be configured to start automatically by the Service Control Manager. When the server is in production, this is the recommended method of installation, because SQL Server and SQL Executive can start whenever the server is started. During testing, you may want to leave this option off so that you can debug your Windows NT environment without having to worry about SQL Server. If you change your mind about how SQL Server should start, you can set SQL Server's and SQL Executive's startup status by using the Services applet in the Windows NT Control Panel. The service names are MSSQLServer and SQLExecutive.

Server Licensing

In Microsoft's campaign to disseminate disambiguation information (that is, their effort to stop confusing customers), SQL Server can be licensed in one of two modes. The two modes are *per server* and *per seat*. In per server, you license a maximum number of concurrent client connections to SQL Server. Per seat counts the number of licensed client workstations that can access SQL Server and not the maximum number of concurrent connections. Before installing SQL Server, make sure that you choose the proper licensing mode and the correct number of supported workstations. Microsoft has, unfortunately, so confused their customers that most are unsure whether or not they are in compliance with their license agreement. Talk to your Microsoft representative to confirm the licensing plan for SQL Server, just to be safe.

Online Documentation

SQL Server has an online documentation facility that uses Microsoft's MS Developer Network search engine. It's extremely useful, but it takes more than 15MB of disk space. I'd recommend installing it. The search engine is very easy to use, and the complete printed documentation is available online.

Time to Log In!

After all these steps are complete, SQL Server's SETUP utility will now copy all of the necessary files to the source directory and path that you specified earlier, as well as build the master device and install the system databases. On an Intel DX4-100 machine with 32MB of RAM, this process took just over 35 minutes. Because SQL Server adds or changes entries in the Windows NT Registry, installation requires you to reboot the machine. SETUP will prompt you for this action, and you're now ready to go!

You have installed SQL Server. The server is running. It's time to log in, look around, and see what's left to do. You'll use the ISQL/w (Interactive SQL for Windows) application on the server to log in as the sa.

> **NOTE**
>
> The only initial usable login on the server is sa, which has no password upon installation. (See the section titled "Changing Defaults—The Top Ten Items to Address on Installation," later in this chapter.)

If you are successful, you should be able to transmit queries and receive results:

```
Congratulations, you have installed SQL Server!
```

If the Login Didn't Work...

When ISQL/w running on the server fails to work, there are a few simple problems to check, based on the error message you receive.

The easiest message to resolve is Login Incorrect or Login Failed. Both of these messages mean that you found the server but your combination of name and password were entered incorrectly. If you just installed the server, you probably typed something wrong. If you installed the server a while ago, the sa password may have changed, or the sa login may have been disabled. If you really can't get in, make sure that the SQL Server process is running.

Another common message is `Unable to Connect: SQL Server is not available or does not exist`. SQL Server is probably not running. Use the SQL Server Manager applet (commonly known as the SQL Stoplight) to see the status of SQL Server. If necessary, restart the server and try again.

> **NOTE**
>
> This really is a more difficult message to interpret. Troubleshooting the `Unable to connect` message is discussed in detail later in the chapter, but most of the issues there relate to proper addressing and network connectivity. When you execute `ISQL/w` from the physical SQL Server and can't find the server process, the usual problem is that the server process isn't started yet.

If you're still stumped, see the "Troubleshooting" section, later in this chapter. You might find a useful hint on how to resolve the problem.

Shutting Down with `shutdown`

To shut down the server, you execute the SQL statement `shutdown` after connecting to the server.

The `shutdown` command instructs the server to disable all logins except sa, waits for currently executing transactions and procedures to complete, checkpoints all databases, and then exits the server executable process. This is an orderly shutdown, which manages data integrity before downing the server.

The `shutdown with nowait` command shuts everything down immediately, without regard to process status. Transactions aren't allowed to continue to completion and are rolled back upon restart. Databases aren't checkpointed and need to do additional work to recover. This isn't considered an orderly shutdown, but data integrity isn't damaged by a `shutdown with nowait`.

Although the `shutdown` command is available, SQL Server is typically stopped and started using either the SQL Service Manager ("Stoplight" application), shown in Figure 24.1, or the stoplight icon in the SQL Enterprise Manager.

FIGURE 24.1.

The SQL Service Manager.

If you execute the shutdown statement and remain logged in while it proceeds, you lose your connection when the server shuts down and are notified of the dropped connection by your application program. Other users aren't notified until the next time they try to use their connection. To avoid user panic and annoying calls, inform users before executing a shutdown.

Although SQL Server is considered a round-the-clock, 24x7 server, some common administrative tasks require a server shutdown:

- *Changing configuration options.* There are a handful of *dynamic* configuration options that can change while the server is up. Most configuration options require modifications in the allocation of memory or resources that can be made only when the server is restarted.

- *Setting server trace flags.* Server trace flags enable you to access DBCC and monitoring features. They must be set during server startup.

- *Configuring mirroring of the master device.* The mirror parameter must be supplied to the dataserver executable before startup using the -r startup option.

- *Killing certain user connections.* The SQL Server kill statement can kill certain user processes, but other connections (for example, sleeping processes in earlier versions of SQL Server) simply can't be killed without restarting the server.

Client Installation

Getting workstations ready for client/server is a big job, and the more workstations, the more logistical problems overshadow technical ones. If you have existing workstations that require work before they're ready for SQL Server, you have a more complicated problem in making changes to workstation configurations without impacting current capabilities.

This section looks at the SQL Server client software installation to understand how SQL Server provides openness, portability, and modularity to application programmers.

DB-Library Components

The SQL Server workstation software is composed of two components: db-lib and net-lib. db-lib is the set of functions directly accessible to the application, including calls to set up information in the login record (dbsetluser), to log in (dbopen), to store a query in the buffer (dbcmd), to execute the command (dbsqlexec or dbsend), and to process result rows (dbresults, dbnextrow).

db-lib is implemented differently on different platforms. DOS applications use an include file of db-lib function calls; Windows applications use resources in a dynamic link library (W3DBLIB.DLL for Windows version 3.x, NTWDBLIB.DLL for Windows NT).

net-lib provides network transparency. (See Figure 24.2.) Typically several net-libs are available for each supported client operating platform. The net-lib receives the name of a SQL Server from DB-Library and transforms that into a Named Pipe or full address and port identifier for network communication. Applications written for DB-Library name only the server; the rest of the network implementation is managed entirely through `net-lib`.

FIGURE 24.2.

Net-Library provides network transparency to the application developer.

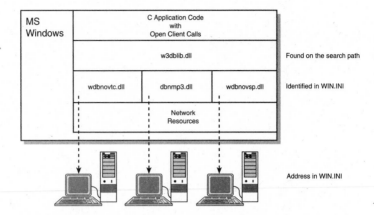

Each `net-lib` applies to a specific protocol and, if appropriate, a version of that protocol. For example, there is a specific `net-lib` for Windows for several different versions of TCP/IP (NetWare, FTP, Microsoft, and so forth), as well as `net-libs` for Named Pipes and IPX.

Windows

Under Windows, you record the names of servers in a text file in the format of a Windows initialization file. With DB-Library, you store server names and addressing schemes in the `WIN.INI` file (in the `Windows` directory) under the heading `[SQLSERVER]`. If you have a `DSQUERY` value listed in the `INI` file, it's used by default if no server is named. Here's the `[SQLSERVER]` section from a sample `WIN.INI` file:

```
[SQLServer]
DSQUERY=DBNMP3
SERVER1=DBMSRPC3
```

Troubleshooting

Client/server works great—when you get it working. Then it works until someone changes something.

Troubleshooting client/server is no different from troubleshooting any other kind of system, except that the vendors are unbelievably non-useful. Why? Because there are simply too many products (and too many combinations of products) for them to be smart about all of them.

You need to be single-minded about *isolating the problem*. Following are some questions to consider (on the next page):

- Is the problem on the server, the client, or the network?
- Is the problem in the workstation application or the operating system?
- Is the problem in the connectivity software or the equipment?

Here's the stated problem: "I can't log in." Or "I can log in, but I can't send a query." Or "I can log in, but periodically my connection hangs." This section presents some of the steps that you can take to isolate this problem.

Step 1: Does SQL Server work?

Start simple. Run the SQL Server Manager (stoplight) application. Select the MSSQLSERVER service from the combo box. If the server isn't started, the light is red. If the server was started but isn't showing up, no lights will be lit, and the message `Server status is indeterminate` appears in the status bar at the bottom of the window. Your first step is to look at the error log and the Windows NT Event Log's Application subsystem to check for SQL Server error messages.

Step 2: Can You Access SQL Server from `ISQL/w`?

The server is working, so now you should find out whether anyone can log in. Remove the network and all the client issues and try to log in from the server. Log in to the hardware where SQL Server resides, and invoke `ISQL/w`. If you can't log in, you may be out of maximum connections (the message for this problem is quite specific).

You also may have a problem in your addressing on the server itself. Remember the port you assigned to the server when you ran the installation? That's also how your client needs to address the server. Look in the Windows NT Registry on the server to make sure that the network and port address listed there is correct. You also may have to set server environmental variables to make this work. In addition, check the client software installation to ensure that the correct port number is specified on the client as well.

At any rate, don't bother trying to get a client process to talk to the server over the network until an `ISQL/w` session can communicate with the server locally.

Step 3: Can You Talk to the Physical Server At All Via the Network?

If a client is having a problem initiating a SQL Server session, first try to initiate a non-SQL Server connection. Try to access a shared drive on the server. If you're running Windows and Named Pipes, see whether an NT server shows up in your workgroup under File Manager's Disk Connect Network Drive option.

If you can't find or ping the server at the operating-system level, you have a network problem. The problem could be a loose or bad cable connection, a bad Ethernet card, out-of-date or incompatible network software, incorrect Ethernet frame types, bad packet sizes... well, you get the idea. This is the part where you call your networking friend and say, "Fix it. It's broken."

Again, don't bother continuing to try to log into SQL Server until this problem is solved.

Step 4: It Worked Yesterday...What Changed?

This is one of the most perplexing problems you'll face. It's especially problematic in Windows. A Windows workstation worked yesterday and doesn't work today, but the user swears that nothing changed:

> "What did you do?"
>
> "Nothing."
>
> "Are you sure??"
>
> "Well, I did install Excel..."
>
> "Aha!"

Microsoft (along with a lot of other vendors) ships DB-Library with many of its products. (Some vendors ship really old, horrible versions.) If the installation program also changes the workstation search path (which, unfortunately, is common), the new DB-Library jumps to the front of the path and sabotages any attempt to find SQL Server.

Step 5: Can You Log into SQL Server?

If you can't log in, first check the capitalization and spelling of your name and password. SQL Server logins and passwords are case-sensitive, and also prevent the use of special characters. As a result, capitalization problems can prevent logins. If the capitalization is correct and your password still doesn't work, your sa should be able to give you a new password, if that appears to be the problem. If you are the sa, you have bigger problems.

Step 6: Does it Happen Only When the Number of Users Increases?

One of the simplest solutions to occasional server lockups or problems with logins is duplicate client TCP/IP addresses. These conflicts cause the server to go completely berserk, so manage those addresses carefully. You can avoid this problem on Windows NT networks that use TCP/IP by using DHCP (Dynamic Host Configuration Protocol). DHCP dynamically "leases" TCP/IP addresses to workstations when they sign on to the network, preventing this problem. Other implementation issues surround the use of DHCP, but it's a viable alternative to hard-coding TCP/IP addresses.

Changing Defaults—The Top Ten Items to Address on Installation

There are some things that you should do as soon as you can log in. Some default settings need to be changed just as soon as you log in as sa.

Securing sa Access

The sa has no password and complete control over the server. You need to fix that problem— *pronto*. (For more on security, see Chapter 27.)

Turning Off the Master Device Default Status

If you don't change this value, you can mistakenly install user databases on the master device. Ultimately, this setup could mean a painful database recovery if you have to reinitialize the master device, and you may have to free up the space later to make room for the master database.

To turn off this value, use the following syntax:

```
sp_diskdefault master, defaultoff
```

For more on default disks, see Chapter 25.

When you back up to diskdump, the backup is amazingly fast and equally fruitless. Nothing is backed up because no physical device is attached. To avoid tragic mistakes, remove the diskdump device:

```
sp_dropdevice diskdump
```

Increasing the Size of tempdb

You probably don't know how large tempdb will need to be yet, but 2MB certainly won't be enough. Use disk init to set up a logical device for tempdb and alter the database to extend tempdb onto the new device (see Chapter 25). For now, 20MB might be a good place to start.

Setting Obvious Configuration Settings

Chapter 31, "Configuring and Tuning SQL Server," reviews the configuration and tuning settings in detail, but here are three values that are always wrong:

■ Open databases

■ Memory

■ User connections

Databases don't consume much server memory, so set this value near the maximum number of databases that you expect to create on the server, with additional room for `master`, `model`, `tempdb`, and `msdb`:

```
sp_configure "open databases", 20
go
reconfigure
go
```

The memory setting probably needs to be changed. The correct value depends on your server. Don't forget that memory is specified in 2KB pages (10240 = 20MB).

Connections should be set as low as reasonable because connections consume memory (about 50KB each):

```
sp_configure "user connections", 25
```

Setting Up the Model Database Objects, Users, and Datatypes

You may want to set up the model database with all the objects (rules, defaults), users (guest, others), and user-defined datatypes that you will want in every database on this server. This is optional.

If this is your first server in your organization, it's really unlikely that you have made any of these decisions yet. If you have other servers, you may already have a set of standards. Make certain that you create everything in model before you create your first user database. Otherwise, you need to copy everything manually into both model and the user database(s) later on.

The pubs Database

The pubs database is installed by default during a SQL Server installation. pubs contains sample tables, views, and data that you can query to observe how the SQL works or how to implement special objects or concepts. All of the examples in the SQL Server documentation—and in most articles you read—use pubs objects.

Summary

If you have already decided on SQL Server, you still need to find all the pieces to make it work. Think of client/server as a scavenger hunt. One medium-sized client eventually bought more than 100 products from more than 40 vendors to build a client/server system.

Your client/server installation will depend on your ability to find high-quality components and knit them together into a seamless system. It's not a one-day job; it's a continual process of building a reliable, functional, simple system.

Use the following checklist to make sure that you have addressed all of the major points covered in this chapter:

- Server hardware vendor and configuration (IBM, MIPS, NEC, HP, Compaq, DEC, and so on)
- Network type (Ethernet, token ring)
- Network protocol (TCP/IP, IPX, Named Pipes)
- Client workstation operating system (DOS, Windows, Macintosh)
- Client workstation configuration (CPU, speed, RAM, and so on)
- Client development and reporting products (PowerBuilder, Visual Basic, Delphi, C++, Forest & Trees, ReportSmith, Clear Access, and so on)
- Server administration tools
- Network administration tools

Defining Physical and Mirror Devices

The server is installed. Now what? For the server to be useful, you need to be able to create and load user databases. With SQL Server, you must first define the physical area that is to be used for the databases; this is done with SQL Enterprise Manager or the `disk init` statement (see Figure 25.1).

FIGURE 25.1.

You must set up devices before setting up databases.

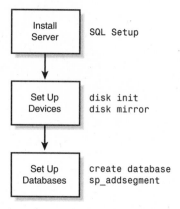

This chapter explores device mirroring at the software level. When you mirror devices, SQL Server keeps an exact copy of each used page from one device on another device that you specify. You set up mirroring with the `disk mirror` statement. This chapter also compares advantages and disadvantages of hardware-level disk mirroring, software-level device mirroring, and RAID (Redundant Array of Inexpensive Disks) striping.

Disk Initialization with `disk init`

Chapter 26, "Defining, Altering, and Maintaining Databases and Logs," discusses database creation and configuration. Before you can set up databases, SQL Server needs to map logical device names to physical disk resources. The logical names that you assign here (*devices*) are used again at database creation (and segment placement) time.

> **NOTE**
>
> Upon server installation, you'll have three devices initialized to house the `master`, `model`, `tempdb`, and `msdb` databases. The `master`, `model` and `tempdb` databases are held on the device with a logical name of `master`. You define the physical location of the `master` device file with the SQL Server Setup utility. The `msdb` database is placed on two disk devices, `MSDBData` and `MSDBLog`. Although you can create user databases on these devices, you should use these devices only for the databases previously mentioned, particularly for production servers.

Several databases can reside on a single physical device, and storage for a single database may span many devices. (Also, a single physical disk can contain several devices.) Figure 25.2 illustrates the many-to-many relationship between devices and databases (discussed at length later in this chapter).

FIGURE 25.2.

A physical device is defined to SQL Server as a logical device, on which zero, one, or many databases may reside. A database can span several physical devices.

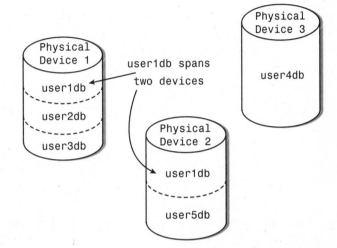

The `disk init` statement provides the server with a method of mapping databases to physical drives. You use databases to contain (provide a context for) data objects such as tables, indexes, and stored procedures.

> **NOTE**
>
> Because `disk init` is used only when defining physical resources to the server, it's easy to forget the syntax. If you're unsure, look it up rather than guess at it.
>
> When working with the parameters, remember that the tricky parts are getting the physical name right, making sure that the vdevno is unique on the server, and stating the size parameter in pages (*not* megabytes).

Parameters

The `disk init` statement requires four mandatory parameters. Every device has both a *logical name* (a reference for SQL Server) and a *physical name* (a reference for the operating system file). In addition, the size of a device is defined at creation time. The following syntax lines show you how to structure the `disk init` code. The parameters are discussed in detail in the following sections:

```
DISK INIT
NAME = 'logical_name',
PHYSNAME = 'physical_name',
VDEVNO = virtual_device_number,
SIZE = number_of_2K_blocks
[, VSTART = virtual_address]
```

Logical Name

The first parameter for `disk init` is the logical name:

```
NAME = 'logical_name'
```

The logical name of the device is the name that you use to refer to the device when creating or altering a database on it, mirroring it (described in detail later in this chapter), or using the `sp_diskdefault` command (also discussed later) to make it a default disk for database creation.

Device names must be unique within a SQL Server. Limitations on device names are the same as with any other SQL Server object: the name must be unique among devices and a maximum of 30 characters in length, with no spaces or punctuation (for example, `data_device`, `log_device`, and `index_device` are all valid names). Don't forget that the server treats device names (like other meaningful identifiers) as case-sensitive.

Physical Name

The second parameter is the physical name:

```
PHYSNAME = 'physical_name'
```

The physical name of the device is its actual location within the operating system. The address is a file system name.

> **NOTE**
>
> Until recently, Microsoft SQL Server used only disk devices. With SQL Server 6.0, Microsoft introduced support for removable-media databases and devices. However, because standard writeable devices have become so cheap (SCSI disks are less than $300 per gigabyte for internal drives), removable media has become undesired in the professional workplace, especially in the corporate environment. A database server may hold important data that must be available 24 hours a day, such as information on airline reservations or IRS or Social Security databases. All these environments must have database servers running around the clock.

Virtual Device Number

The third parameter of `disk init` is the virtual device number:

```
VDEVNO = virtual_device_number
```

The virtual device number is a unique identifier used by SQL Server to identify unique page numbers (it's the high-order byte of an address, hence the 255-device limitation on the servers). These addresses are used to help map the many-to-many relationship between the system tables `sysdevices`, `sysusages`, and `sysdatabases`.

Device numbering begins with 0, and device 0 is set at installation time to be the master device. The first available device number is 3, because `MSDBData` uses `VDEVNO = 1`, and `MSDBLog` uses `VDEVNO = 2`.

> **NOTE**
>
> In previous versions of SQL Server, devices consumed memory for their allocation. As a result, SQL Server needed to be configured to minimize memory allocations for devices without starving the server of database space. With SQL Server 6, that's largely not a problem because of its access to plentiful quantities of RAM. People familiar with running SQL Server for OS/2 or Sybase SQL Server will notice a missing configuration option for defining the maximum number of devices the server allocates when started.

Size

The fourth parameter is the size, which is the size of the device in pages:

```
SIZE = number_of_2K_blocks
```

It has been rumored that the page size will be variable in the future.

> **TIP**
>
> SQL Server generally is excellent at performance, throughput, and a host of other things, but leaves much to be desired in consistency with administration commands. Sometimes, turning flags on means setting them to 1, sometimes it means setting them to `true`, sometimes setting them to `defaulton`, and so forth.
>
> In this case, note that size is in pages. When you create a database, the sizes will be in megabytes, but the confirmation message that database creation returns specifies the number of *pages* allocated. Egad!
>
> *continues*

continued

Moral: If you're unsure about the units of work for a particular command, read the manual. Also, the SQL Enterprise Manager application (discussed shortly) has defaulted all space allocation parameters in dialog boxes to *megabytes*; this is noted in the dialog boxes themselves.

Virtual Address

The sixth line of disk init specifies this parameter:

```
[, VSTART = virtual_address]
```

It's unusual to have to specify this parameter. It defaults to zero; leave it alone unless otherwise directed by Microsoft Product Support Services (PSS).

disk init Examples

The following example of disk init creates a new device in the default SQL Server installation directory:

```
disk init
name = 'data_device_1',
physname = 'c:\MSSQL\data\d_dev_1.dat',
vdevno=3,
size = 512000
```

In this example, the disk init statement creates a device whose logical name is data_device_1. The device is mapped to a physical location:

```
c:\MSSQL\data\d_dev_1.dat
```

The virtual device number is 3, and its size is 1GB (512000 × 2KB).

NOTE

How long does disk init take? That varies with your version of SQL Server. At one point in its evolution, disk init would zero out every page and could take hours. With the Windows NT releases of the server, a disk init of 2GB takes only a couple of minutes.

Physical file creation for disk devices must meet two criteria:

■ The file must not already exist (it will be created by the disk init process).

■ The file must be writeable by the process that's running SQL Server. If you configured the server to start under the Administrator account, the Administrator user must have write permission in the directory and file permission on the file after creation. For this reason, starting SQL Server using the LocalSystem account is recommended, because LocalSystem has access to necessary permissions and privileges.

In the next example, a disk device of 40MB (20,480 pages) is created. A file of 40MB is created during initialization and an entry is made in the sysdevices system table:

```
disk init
name = 'data_device_2',
physname = 'c:\MSSQL\data\data_dev2.dat',
vdevno=4,
size = 20480
```

disk init Error Messages

Errors from disk init statements are normally not very descriptive. Here's an example:

```
Error 5123: DISK INIT encountered an error while attempting to open/create the
physical file. Please consult the SQL Server for more details.
```

When you consult the error log file, you usually find one of three errors:

■ The directory or file name is invalid

■ The file already exists

■ There's not enough space to create the file

Here are some sample error log entries after a disk init error:

```
94/10/29 13:26:30.25 kernel   udcreate: Operating system error 112
(There is not enough space on the disk.) encountered
94/10/29 13:26:38.61 kernel   udcreate: Operating system error 80
(The file exists.) encountered
```

> **NOTE**
>
> For many SQL Server commands (including disk init), no news turns out to be good news. If there's an error with a disk init statement, you'll hear about it. If the command appears to take a few seconds and there's no error, it probably worked. Just run sp_helpdevice to make sure (see an example later in this chapter). After a while, you'll get used to it, but for now, just make a note: If you don't get an error message, it probably worked.

Normally, you can delete a physical file that was created during a failed `disk init`. If you can't delete it, SQL Server failed to release the locks on the file. To delete the file and reclaim the space, you may need to shut down and restart the server and try again. Before doing that, make absolutely certain that the `disk init` actually *didn't* work. You may be trying to delete a valid device!

Using SQL Server Enterprise Manager

The SQL-EM application allows you to define devices, mirror existing devices, and drop devices, all with a point-and-click interface.

To define devices, you must connect to a registered server. As with most SQL-EM operations, you can choose the option from the toolbar, from the menu structure, or by right-clicking the particular component of SQL Server that you want to work with in the Server Manager window. Clicking the Devices button in the toolbar, choosing Manage | Devices from the menu, or right-clicking the Database Devices folder in the Server Manager window pops up the Manage Database Devices - *servername* window, as illustrated in Figure 25.3.

FIGURE 25.3.

The SQL Enterprise Manager displays information about database devices.

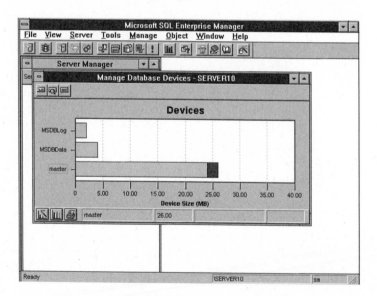

Double-clicking one of the device names in the chart displays detailed information for that particular device—physical location, logical name, and size, as well as the specific databases (and their size allocations) on that device, as shown in Figure 25.4.

NOTE

Directory names on your system may not match those shown in figures here and elsewhere in this book. If you upgrade from SQL Server 6.0 to 6.5, the installation process retains the old directory name (C:\SQL60). For a new installation, the default directory is C:\MSSQL.

FIGURE 25.4.

You can see the allocation of device space by database, as well as other details about the selected device.

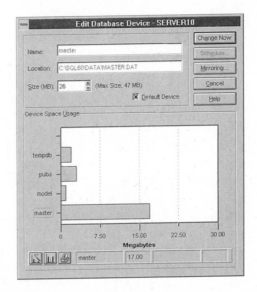

Returning to the Manage Database Devices window, clicking the first button in the toolbar brings up the New Database Device dialog box, where you can define new disk devices for storing databases. (See Figure 25.5.) Notice that the units of measure for these devices are all expressed in megabytes—a welcome change for anyone accustomed to the teeth-gnashing associated with keeping track of SQL Server's inconsistent measurements!

Notice that there's no place in the dialog box to define vdevno for the device. SQL-EM will automatically determine the largest-used device number, increment it by 1, and use the new value for vdevno. Notice also that you can immediately specify mirroring properties for the device, as well as whether it's a default device, directly from this dialog box.

As with all operations in SQL Enterprise Manager, the application is merely executing Transact-SQL commands "behind the curtains" so that, instead of constantly digging up the command reference for disk init, you can point-and-click your way around a server to define devices.

FIGURE 25.5.

You define the name, location, and size of a new database device in this dialog box.

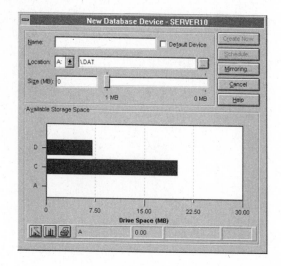

SQL Server Version 6.5 includes enhanced charting capabilities to provide customized charts for the database in study, as shown in Figure 25.6. Additional display options are also available in varieties within the selected graph type. The capacity to show vertical and horizontal graphs greatly emphasizes the capability of SQL Server to graphically represent physical data. This feature is shown in Figure 25.7.

FIGURE 25.6.

This dialog box enables you to control how the Enterprise Manager displays database information graphically.

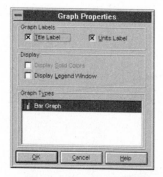

FIGURE 25.7.

Although the graphing features don't compare with those of a spreadsheet or presentation program, you do have some options for controlling the graphs used by SQL-EM.

Effects of `disk init`

The `disk init` command can be performed only by the sa. After the disk initialization is complete, the space described by the physical address is available to SQL Server for storage, and a row is added to the `sysdevices` table in the `master` database.

Figure 25.8 shows the contents of a small `sysdevices` table (use `select * from sysdevices`).

FIGURE 25.8.

The contents of the `sysdevices` *table in an Aurora Desktop window.*

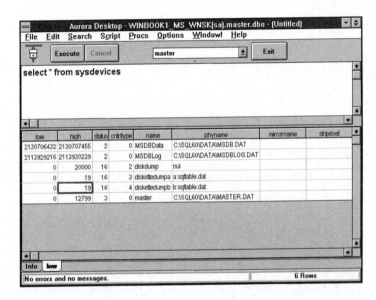

The `sysdevices` table contains one row for each device that the server can access. (Devices include disks for storage of data, and tape and file devices for backups.) Relevant columns in `sysdevices` include the name of the device (and its mirror, if it has one—described later in this chapter), device status, and page range. Can you find the virtual device number? It's actually the high-order byte of the "low" column.

The status is a bitmap describing what the device is used for and what options have been set (if any). Table 25.1 shows the layout of the status byte.

Table 25.1. Bitmap values for the status column of `sysdevices`.

Decimal	Hex	Description
1	0x01	Default disk
2	0x02	Physical disk
4	0x04	Logical disk
8	0x08	Skip header

continues

Table 25.1. continued

Decimal	Hex	Description
16	0x10	Dump device
32	0x20	Serial writes
64	0x40	Device mirrored
128	0x80	Reads mirrored
256	0x100	Secondary mirror side only
512	0x200	Mirror enabled

For instance, the status of the `master` device is 3 (binary 00000011), which corresponds to "database device" and "default disk" (1 + 2 = 3). You can look ahead to Figure 25.10 to see how this looks on-screen.

By far the easiest way of decoding the status bit and virtual device number is to use the system stored procedure `sp_helpdevice`. Here's the syntax:

```
sp_helpdevice [logical_device_name]
```

`sp_helpdevice` can be used without parameters to get a list of defined devices. Figure 25.9 shows all defined devices within a SQL Server. Pass `sp_helpdevice` the name of the disk device to get information on a specific disk. (See Figure 25.10.)

FIGURE 25.9.

A list of all defined devices in an Aurora Desktop window.

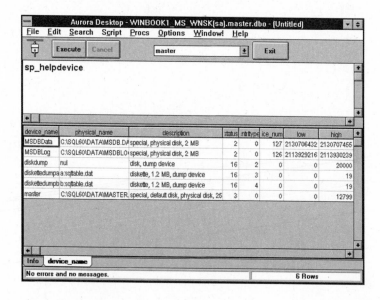

FIGURE 25.10.

Specific disk information in an Aurora Desktop window.

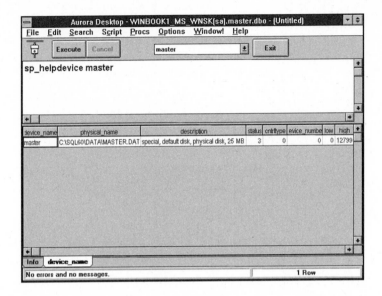

The master device status is 3 (disk device + default device); its controller type is 0 (a device for storage, not backup); its virtual device number (device) is 0; and its low and high values represent the logical page numbers that define the space to be used on the device (12,800 pages = 25MB).

Removing Devices with sp_dropdevice

After a device has been defined, it remains permanently in the data dictionary in the master database until you decide that it has served its purpose and should be removed. A typical reason for removal might be that you are replacing a small, slower, older device with a newer one.

A device is dropped with the sp_dropdevice command. Only the sa can drop a device, in the same manner that only an sa can create a device.

> **NOTE**
>
> Devices can't be removed if databases have been defined on the device; any databases must be dropped first. (The server will check sysusages for any allocated fragments for the device.)

The syntax for sp_dropdevice is illustrated here:

```
sp_dropdevice logical_device_name
```

Here's a typical example:

```
sp_dropdevice data_device_1
```

If your device was created as an operating system file, you must execute the necessary commands to remove the file (dropping the device doesn't automatically delete the file). Also, to be able to use that space, you must shut down and restart the server to release its pointer to the device.

Using Default Disks

The point of defining disks with `disk init` is to store data on them. The data will be stored in databases, which actually allocate space on disks for tables of data, their indexes and related objects, database transaction logs, and so forth. At database creation time, a database must have a disk on which to reside; if no devices are available (no space is left on any defined device), a database can't be created.

When creating databases, you can (and shsp_diskdefaultould) specify the devices where the database will reside. In some cases, you may want the server to determine where the database will reside; to do so, you create a database without specifying a device. The server can use only disks that you have indicated to be default disks, so if a database is created and no device is specified, any default disk can be used as a database device.

The `sp_diskdefault` stored procedure requires a logical device name and the default status of the disk device as mandatory parameters:

```
sp_diskdefault device_name, {defaulton ¦ defaultoff}
```

Here's an example of `sp_diskdefault` usage:

```
exec sp_diskdefault data_device_1, defaulton
```

Here's how you turn off the default status for the `master` database device:

```
exec sp_diskdefault master, defaultoff
```

> **NOTE**
>
> You use execute or exec before any stored procedure that isn't the first statement of the batch. This is a rule for the SQL Server parser.
>
> In the preceding examples, the first use of exec is optional, the second is required.

In the first example, you instruct the server to use `data_device_1` as a default device.

In the second example, you tell the server that you don't want to use database space on the master device unintentionally. This doesn't mean that the master device can't be used; it means that the space can't be used unless it's specifically allocated.

Because the sp_diskdefault command affects server-wide resources, it's limited to system administrators only.

The net effect of the sp_diskdefault command is that the 2^0 bit in the status bit of the sysdevices table for that device is set to 1 (if defaulton) or 0 (if defaultoff).

In most systems, a default is the single option chosen when no selection is made by the user. Because you can set the default bit on or off independently for each device, you can end up with several default disks (or none). It probably seems a little strange to have several default devices. How does the server decide which default disk device to use? Space on default devices is assigned to databases alphabetically, exhausting all space on each default disk device and then proceeding to the next, until all requested space is allocated.

For example, consider the following create database command, which requests that 100MB be assigned to database newdb on a default disk device (or devices):

```
create database newdb on default = 100
```

Assume that you have the default disks and available space on each as outlined in the following table. (Okay, it doesn't follow the Greek alphabet correctly, but then neither does SQL Server.)

Disk Name	Available Space
alpha_device	10MB
beta_device	10MB
delta_device	10MB
gamma_device	1000MB

Where will the server place `newdb`? The obvious answer is that there's room on the `gamma_disk`, so it will go there. But this isn't the way default disks are allocated. Remember that space on default disks is assigned to databases alphabetically. Here's what happens:

- 10MB is allocated on `alpha_device`.
- 10MB is allocated on `beta_device`.
- 10MB is allocated on `delta_device`.
- The remaining 70MB is allocated on `gamma_device`.

The net effect is the same as if you had issued this `create database` command:

```
create database newdb
   on alpha_disk = 10,
      beta_disk = 10,
      delta_disk = 10,
      gamma_disk = 70
```

The effect on the disks is the following:

Disk name	Available space
alpha_disk	0MB
beta_disk	0MB
delta_disk	0MB
gamma_disk	930MB

Note that this isn't necessarily a performance problem. In fact, it's an advantage to spread active tables across disk controllers.

TIP

If you want to find out whether a specific device is a default device, you can check the device status bit in `sysdevices` (if the status is odd, the 2^0 bit is set and it's a default device). Alternatively, use the `sp_helpdevice` command. It specifies whether the device is a default device.

It's normally not a good idea to use default disks. Whatever work it saves you in remembering physical device names is nullified by the enormous pain you'll endure to fix one bad command—for example, any `create database` command that creates a database for use but does so in a place where you don't want to create it. If the defaults aren't all turned off, SQL Server uses the default device unless specifically instructed *not* to do so.

> Moral: Turn off all your `default` statuses and specify device names in your `create database` statements.
>
> In fact, it's unusual to have default disks defined. Systems administrators tend to want to keep a very tight control on physical server resources.

Expanding Disk Devices

For those familiar with previous versions of SQL Server, this section title is sure to induce some head scratching. All previous versions of the Microsoft SQL Server and all versions (including System 10) of the Sybase SQL Server have maintained a fixed allocation for database devices. They couldn't be shrunk or enlarged, only dropped and re-created. Microsoft has added a new command, `disk resize`, to give administrators a way to increase the size allocation for existing devices.

The syntax for `disk resize` is quite simple, as illustrated here:

```
disk resize
name = logical_device_name,
size = final_size
```

The `name` parameter references a unique logical device name, and the `size` parameter is the *final size* for the device. As with `disk init`, the `size` parameter must be specified in 2KB pages. This command isn't generally used (if you're using it too much, you're not properly calculating your space needs in advance), but it's quite useful for expanding the `master` device so that the `master` database can grow. `disk resize` can be used on any valid SQL Server database device.

Disk Mirroring

Occasionally, devices fail. You can ensure against problems caused by device failures by instructing the server to mirror two devices, keeping them in complete sync at all times. You can mirror devices at the hardware, operating system, or SQL Server level. In the last case, SQL Server handles all the disk mirroring work.

WARNING

Disk mirroring at the hardware level may work, and may reduce the load on the CPU, but it's necessary to stress-test the hardware mirroring before counting on it to work with SQL Server in a production environment. Chapter 18, "Database Design and Performance," explains the pros and cons of using different disk storage systems, and their effect on SQL Server.

At a minimum, you should mirror the `master` device and all your log devices. A failed `master` device without backup is agony; a failed `master` device with backup is merely a pain in the backside. (For more about this, see Chapter 30, "SQL Server Database Backup and Restoration.") Failed log devices cook the database; if the log devices don't fail, data device failures can be mitigated at least through log recovery (again, more in Chapter 30).

If you mirror devices across controllers (see Figure 25.11) as well as across physical disks, you can reduce potential single points of failure.

FIGURE 25.11.

Mirroring across devices still leaves you vulnerable to a controller failure. Mirroring across controllers protects against controller failures as well.

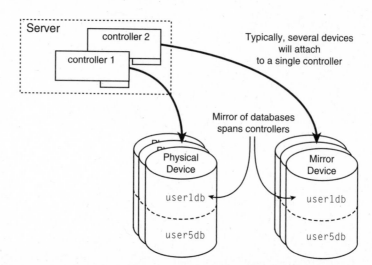

NOTE

SQL Server allows you to specify `noserial` for mirrored disk writes, but in fact it supports only `serial` writes. SQL Server from Microsoft eliminated the `noserial` option starting in Version 6.0, but kept the syntax for compatibility with previous versions of SQL Server.

Although SQL Server currently has a limitation of 255 physical devices, mirroring doesn't take up any of these device connections. (Note the syntax.) Therefore, a mirror device isn't a disk device; it doesn't require a distinct `vdevno`.

Finally, please note that the available space at the physical location of a mirror device must be at least as large as the device it's mirroring.

The disk mirror command syntax is illustrated here:

```
disk mirror
name = 'logical_device_name',
mirror = 'physical_device_name'
[ , writes = {serial ¦ noserial } ]
```

In the `disk mirror` syntax, `logical_device_name` is the name of the device that you initialized (on which you used the `disk init` command). The `physical_device_name` is the device that holds the contents of the mirror. Serial writes—the only option supported on Windows NT versions of SQL Server—ensure that, in case of a power failure, the write will go to at least one of the physical devices if the mirrors are on separate physical devices (they should be). The `noserial` option is kept only for compatibility with prior versions of SQL Server.

Here's an example of the `disk mirror` command:

```
disk mirror
name = 'data_device_1',
mirror = 'r:\MSSQL\mirrors\d_dev_1.mir'
```

In the example, you mirror a device that you initialized and to which you assigned the logical device name `data_device_1`. A copy of all writes to the disk are also written to the physical device at `r:\MSSQL\mirrors\d_dev_1.mir`. Drive R: should be a separate physical disk, and, if possible, connected using a separate controller.

The `disk mirror` Sequence of Events

There are three steps in the `disk mirror` sequence of events:

1. The secondary device (mirror device) is initialized.
2. All used pages on the primary device are copied to the secondary device. Note that, as expected, this isn't a fast process.
3. Bits are set in `sysdevices`—bit 2^6 (device mirrored) and 2^9 (mirror enabled).

> **WARNING**
>
> SQL Server mirrors at the device level, not the database level. If a database is spread across many devices, and any one database isn't mirrored, the database is at risk of a physical failure. For a database to be fully protected, *every device associated with that database must be mirrored.*

Disk Mirroring Information

The easiest way to check on disk mirroring for a device is with the `sp_helpdevice` command.

Alternatively, you can identify all the disk devices (devices with `cntrltype` of 0—the others are backup devices) by using the following SQL statement:

```
select * from sysdevices where cntrltype = 0
```

Deactivating Disk Mirroring

Devices become unmirrored in two ways:

- You, as the sa, issue the `disk unmirror` command.
- SQL Server, in an attempt to write to a primary or secondary device of a mirror pair, is unable to write to one of the devices.

The server maintains the bit flags within the `device status` in `sysdevices` to report on the status of the mirror. When mirrors fail or are disabled for any reason, the server updates the bit flags to indicate which mirror failed. Table 25.2 summarizes the bit flags as they relate to mirror devices. Note that other status flags (`default` or `reads mirrored`) could be set in addition to the flags described in the table.

Table 25.2. Status flags related to mirror devices.

State of Mirror	Status Value		Decoded Status
Not mirrored	2	(2)	Physical disk
Mirrored	578	(2+64+512)	Mirrored, mirror enabled
Secondary failed	66	(2+64)	Mirrored
Primary failed	322	(2+64+256)	Mirrored, half mirrored

Unmirroring a device has the effect of modifying status bits and instructing the server to write to only one specific device of a mirrored pair. If the mirroring is automatic, the server check-points the `master` database so that changes in the `sysdevices` table are permanently reflected on the disk.

The syntax for the `disk unmirror` command is illustrated here:

```
disk unmirror
name = 'logical_name'
[ , side = { "primary" ¦ secondary } ]
[ , mode = { retain ¦ remove } ]
```

The parameter *logical name* is the device that you initialized with the `disk init` command; the `primary` side is the device that you initialized; the `secondary` is the mirror that you specified. You can unmirror either the primary or the secondary device. Defaults are `secondary` and `retain`.

If you specify `retain`, the names of the unmirrored devices are kept in the `sysdevices` table indefinitely, and you can remirror (this is discussed shortly). Automatic unmirroring uses the `retain` option.

An example `disk unmirror` statement is shown here:

```
disk unmirror
name = 'data_device_1',
side = 'primary',
mode = remove
```

This example tells the server that to permanently remove the definition of the primary device from the `data_device_1` device. The effect is that the mirror side becomes the primary (only) device.

Here's another example:

```
disk unmirror name = 'data_device_1'
```

In this example, the server unmirrors the secondary device, and keeps the definition of the device in `sysdevices`. In this case, you can use the `disk remirror` command.

Disk Remirroring

After a device becomes unmirrored automatically, or manually with `mode = retain`, the sa can instruct the server to restart the software mirroring. The `disk remirror` statement will fail unless the device was previously mirrored and the definition still remains in `sysdevices`.

This is the syntax of the `disk remirror` command:

```
disk remirror name = 'logical_name'
```

Here's an example:

```
disk remirror name = 'data_device_1'
```

It isn't necessary to specify anything else. The `logical name` in `sysdevices` already has the necessary information in the row or the command will fail (and you should have used the `disk mirror` command instead).

> **NOTE**
>
> Regardless of the elapsed time of the disk unmirroring process (one second unmirrored, with no updates occurring, for example), an unmirrored disk is considered to be out of synchronization with the primary, and the mirroring process begins anew. This means that the entire device is recopied onto the mirror (or primary, if that was the side unmirrored). Remember that this isn't a fast process.

What happens when you have a device that's being replaced because it's too old, small, or slow? What if you have several databases on the device (or parts of several databases on a device)? One technique is to execute the following steps:

1. Dump all the databases.
2. Drop all the databases. (You can't drop a device if a database is on it.)
3. Drop the "old" device.
4. Cycle the server. (Remember, the device numbers aren't reusable.)
5. Re-create the device.
6. Re-create the databases.
7. Reload the databases.

This is a lot of work. It also needs to be done when your users aren't on the system (and you'd rather be home in bed).

It's possible to use the disk mirroring commands to migrate data from one device to another. This may be extremely useful. Here's the easy way (see Figure 25.12):

1. Mirror the current disk onto the new disk (or an appropriate slice of the new disk).
2. Unmirror the device, `side = primary`, `mode = remove`.

FIGURE 25.12.

It's usually more efficient to migrate data with mirroring than to back it up and restore it.

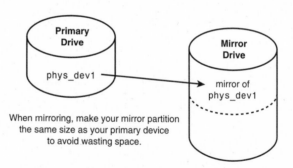

When mirroring, make your mirror partition the same size as your primary device to avoid wasting space.

You should mirror at least the `master` device and all log devices. With the low cost of disk space, there's little excuse not to mirror everything. Think about the cost of having the system down compared to the cost of a 2GB SCSI drive.

Mirroring the master device is *important*. If you lose `master` after a substantive change to your system configuration (but before a backup), you have to piece it back together. If you can't piece it back together, you may lose all contact with your user database(s).

Device SQL

It can be important to determine what devices are available, how much space is initialized on the devices, and how much space is actually utilized. This SQL returns that specific information in a neat report:

```
select 'Database device name' = name,
'In use by databases' = sum (size / 512),
'Space initialized' = (high-low+1)/512
from sysdevices, sysusages
where vstart between low and high
and cntrltype = 0
group by name, low, high
```

Controlling Device Mirroring with SQL Enterprise Manager

SQL-EM allows you to control all of these aspects of mirroring using the Manage Database Devices window that you saw earlier. If you click the Mirror button, SQL-EM displays the dialog box shown in Figure 25.13. With it, you can control all of the options defined previously, using SQL syntax. As with the `disk init` example described previously in the SQL-EM section, SQL-EM is executing the `disk mirror`, `disk unmirror`, and `disk remirror` commands behind the scenes. The difference is that you now know what those commands are and how they should behave!

FIGURE 25.13.

Define mirroring in SQL-EM, using the Mirror Database Device dialog box.

Software Mirroring, Hardware Mirroring, and RAID

SQL Server mirrors data at the software level to ensure that mirroring is possible, regardless of hardware platform or configuration. There are alternatives, however, and most of them are recommended over SQL Server's own mirroring for reasons of cost, performance, or both. Many hardware vendors enable mirroring at the controller level. Alternatively, RAID provides an alternative to mirroring every device, along with a concurrent performance throughput benefit. What kinds of disk-level fault tolerance does SQL Server have available, and what are the tradeoffs of using a particular method?

This section covers three alternate methods of implementing disk fault tolerance for SQL Server, including Windows NT disk mirroring, Windows NT disk striping, and hardware-based RAID.

Software Mirroring

Software mirroring guarantees database stability against hardware failure. It's guaranteed by SQL Server, so if there's a problem, it's handled by Microsoft Product Support Services. In addition, software mirroring enables you to mirror across controllers, minimizing single points of failure.

Software mirroring requires additional writes, however, which require more CPU cycles. Most users of this feature talk about a 10 percent performance hit from software mirroring.

Windows NT also provides operating-system-level mirroring (technically considered RAID level 1) through the Disk Administrator application. Windows NT requires use of NTFS (the native NT File System) for mirrored drives. OS-level RAID 1, or *NTFS mirrored sets*, seems to demonstrate a slight performance increase on reads (the operating system will simply access the drive available first), but writes do encounter a small penalty. Windows NT requires the equivalent of serial writes for all data modifications.

There's no error-checking or parity-bit allocation defined by the generic standard of RAID 1, and Windows NT doesn't do any error checking for mirrored sets. If the machine is capable of dual-booting to DOS, mirrored sets are unavailable (because they use NTFS, not FAT).

Windows NT also provides RAID support for levels 0 and 5. RAID 0 is simple data striping, where a single logical volume (expressed to Windows NT by a drive letter) actually consists of multiple physical devices (called *platters* or *spindles*). This support is available only with NTFS, not HPFS or FAT. With RAID 0, there's only a performance improvement. Both read and write operations can be spread across multiple disks in parallel, improving throughput.

RAID 0 doesn't provide any fault-tolerance options. Instead, RAID 0 hands off fault-tolerance responsibilities to its big brother, RAID 5. Windows NT provides OS-level RAID 5 on NTFS partitions. RAID 5 not only stripes data across multiple disks, it also stripes a parity bit across the disks as well. RAID 5 guarantees the accuracy of data by ensuring that the data bits and associated parity bit are never written to the same physical disk.

RAID 5 is the most reliable of SQL Server's disk fault tolerance options, because RAID 5 provides for "hot fix" support. If a RAID 5 device fails, that device can be removed from the server while the database is processing. When a new device is inserted, the RAID management subsystem of Windows NT will automatically start rebuilding the previously defective disk until all of them are again synchronized. During this time, writes for both data and parity bits are routed to the remaining drives until the new disk is synchronized.

RAID 5 is a viable fault tolerance option, but still leaves a possible bottleneck. Although it can use multiple physical disks (it's recommended that you match this with multiple physical controllers), the power supply actually becomes a point of failure. That's where hardware-based disk mirroring and RAID 5 disk clusters come in.

Hardware Mirroring

Hardware mirroring reduces CPU work. (Hardware mirroring is handled by the controller, or, more important, duplexed controllers.)

Hardware mirroring is guaranteed by the hardware vendor, however. This means that if the mirroring doesn't work out, the hardware vendor will blame the software vendor, and the software vendor will blame the hardware vendor. This isn't a pretty picture when all you want is your data back. (Database restoration is discussed in Chapter 28, "Database Logging and Recovery.")

> **TIP**
>
> If you're going to mirror at the hardware level, be sure to test the mirroring. When the server is under load, pull out one of the drives and see what happens. After mirroring is re-enabled, pull the other drive out and see what happens. (If you smell smoke or ozone, consider software mirroring.)
>
> One point: Network administrators have been pulling the plug on uninterruptible power supplies (UPS) for years, to make sure that the server can run even when the UPS has suffered a lapse in power from the power company. When you pull the power cord on the UPS, however, you can sometimes damage the UPS, and it stops working immediately.

Hardware RAID

With a hardware-based RAID subsystem, there are typically five devices: four contain data and the fifth has redundant hash information. If any device fails, the RAID device notifies the operator and acts as if nothing happened as far as data transmission goes. The operator will replace the bad drive with a "hot" backup. The RAID device will automatically bring the new device up to speed.

Hardware-based RAID systems typically come with duplexed controllers, removing any one disk controller as a point of failure that could bring down the entire system. In addition, better RAID subsystems will also provide duplicate power supplies, so that, should one fail, it can be hot-swapped while the other manages supplying five electricity-hungry disks with the power necessary to keep applications running. (It has the added benefit of keeping the need to update your résumé to a minimum.) The RAID architecture handles all mirroring automatically, and at the hardware level. It's a nifty technology.

RAID is expensive, however. No, that isn't true. It's *breathtakingly* expensive, and not just in purchase price. The parity bit that forms the core of RAID 5 fault tolerance consumes anywhere from 25 to 30 percent of the disk space available, so you'll have to count on needing at least 25 percent more disk than you would if you had bypassed on RAID. You might spend some time looking into advantages at the different RAID levels that you can set. You may decide that performance advantages are outweighed by an inconvenience factor.

Typically, you have to set RAID to level 5 to get the protection you want, and on many platforms you may find that mirrored SCSI disks were faster after all, and don't cost what a good RAID subsystem would. The good news is that RAID subsystem prices are coming down, and quickly.

Summary

In this chapter, you've learned how to implement storage devices using SQL Server, and looked at the use of internal and external mechanisms to provide fault tolerance and to ensure data reliability and availability. The next chapter details how you create databases, using the space created on these devices.

Defining, Altering, and Maintaining Databases and Logs

This chapter addresses how to create and maintain databases and database logs. You learn several approaches to managing disk space on SQL Server, and also about SQL Server segments. If you're familiar with the term *segment* from a different database management system, you need to disregard your preconceived definition when reading this chapter. It's likely that what is defined as a segment for some other database management system is different from how SQL Server defines segments.

With SQL Server 6.5, part of an administrator's job regarding database creation and management is eased through the use of SQL Enterprise Manager. However, many of the fundamental logical and physical concepts on which SQL Server is based are rooted in the original SQL syntax used to define and manage the components discussed in this chapter. Therefore, for the purposes of introducing topics and concepts, the initial references are to the traditional SQL syntax. Where appropriate, and after the discussion of concepts and SQL syntax, additional information and demonstrations on how to implement similar tasks using SQL Enterprise Manager follow. To be a competent administrator, you need to know what an application is doing behind the scenes to your server and databases. Teaching syntax first and GUIs second is a proven method for teaching skills, not just rote tasks.

What Is a Database?

The *database* concept is central to almost all implementation and administration tasks in SQL Server. During the database design phase of a project, you define the tables that are of interest to your organization. From a logical perspective, these related tables are collectively considered a single database. From a physical perspective, however, you can implement these tables in one or many SQL Server databases. The SQL Server database is important because it determines how data is stored physically—how data is mapped to physical devices. Physical space is assigned to a database during database creation, and additional space can be assigned to the database when the need arises.

Several key areas are based at the database level:

■ All SQL Server objects must exist within the database—often referred to as being "in the context of a database." Therefore, how large an object can grow depends on the amount of space allocated to the database. (At a detailed level, limits on object growth truly depend on the amount of space available to a segment in the database, which is described in the section titled "Segments and Object Placement," later in this chapter.)

■ The database is an important element in your security strategy because you must be a user of a database to be able to access objects within it.

■ Some analysis tools, such as DBCC (the Database Consistency Checker), act at the database level.

■ Backups are typically conducted only at the database level, which means that a database is the standard unit of recovery available in SQL Server. (Table-level backups are supported, but only for very special disaster recovery situations. More on that in Chapter 28, "Database Logging and Recovery.")

Databases and Space Management

Logical devices (see Chapter 25, "Defining Physical and Mirror Devices") make space usable to the SQL Server, and databases organize that space, making it available to SQL Server tables and their indexes as well as other objects. Databases can't span physical SQL Servers, nor can tables and their indexes span databases. Therefore, the size of a database will limit the size of any tables and indexes it contains. However, if a table or index grows too large, you can increase the size of the database on-the-fly.

Later, this chapter looks at database segments and how they're used to manage table and index sizes within the database. Although people usually refer to the size of the *database* as determining the maximum size of a table or index, this isn't fully accurate. Each object is created on a segment in a SQL Server database, and objects can't span segments. Therefore, it's the amount of space available to the *segment* that determines the maximum size of an object.

Databases and Security

The owner of a database maps a system login to a database user. Permission to access objects is granted to a database user, either explicitly (to the user) or implicitly (to a user group). (See Chapter 27, "Security and User Administration," for more information.) Therefore, if you don't allow a SQL Server login to be associated with a database user, you have eliminated that user's ability to access the objects within that database.

Databases and Backup

As Chapter 30, "SQL Server Database Backup and Restoration," describes, SQL Server utilities enable you to perform a *full backup* (a copy of the entire database) or an *incremental backup* (a copy of the transactions that have occurred since the last backup). Because transactions are logged in a table within a database, you need to be careful when creating related tables in different databases.

For example, consider a table called customer in the customerdb database and a table called purchase in the purchasedb database. As part of a transaction, you add a new customer to the customer table and that customer's purchases to the purchase table. Each database logs the addition of rows in its own transaction log. If a disaster occurs and you lose the customerdb database, you might be forced to reload this database from backup (assume that the purchasedb database is fine). It's possible that you wouldn't be able to restore the customerdb database to the point at which the disaster occurred, however. Therefore, the purchase table would contain purchases for customers who aren't in the customer table.

When you decide how to distribute related tables in different databases, remember that you may be putting your data integrity at risk.

System Databases

A *system database* is created to support the operation of the server or a SQL Server facility. When SQL Server is installed, it creates at least three system databases (master, model, and tempdb); Version 6.5 also creates a fourth database, msdb:

- The master database records all the server-specific configuration information, including authorized users, devices, databases, system configuration settings, and remote servers.

- The model database is a template database. The contents of model are copied into each new database created after the system is installed.

- tempdb is the temporary database. This database is used as an interim storage area. It's used automatically by the server to resolve large or multi-step queries or to sort data before returning results to the user (if a query contains an order by clause). It can also be used programmatically to provide a worktable to support application processing.

- msdb contains task scheduling, exception handling, and system operator information needed for SQL Executive. This database is discussed in detail in Chapter 34, "Remote Server Management." The msdb database is a critical component of that framework.

> **NOTE**
>
> For shops running both Sybase and Microsoft SQL Server, one change made by Sybase but not copied by Microsoft is the movement of system stored procedures out of the master database and into a new Sybase-specific system database called sybsystemprocs. This database is specific to Sybase System 10. Prior versions of Sybase SQL Server, and all versions of Microsoft SQL Server, put the system stored procedures in the master database.

Database Creation

A primary task of the system administrator is to create databases. This section discusses the syntax of the create database statement, as well as some of the implementation issues involved with database creation.

> **TIP**
>
> As you implement databases, remember that database creation can take a long time. Creation time depends mostly on your physical disk speed—the server initializes every page in a database—and can take between 20 and 60 minutes per gigabyte, depending on your platform. If you are implementing a very large database, this fact could affect your project schedule.

Syntax for `create database`

```
CREATE DATABASE database_name
[ON {DEFAULT ¦ database_device} [= size]
    [, database_device [= size]]...]
[LOG ON database_device [= size]
    [, database_device [= size]]...]
[FOR LOAD]
```

When creating a database, you must provide a database name. Database names must be 30 characters or less, can't include any punctuation or other special characters, and must be unique within the server.

The naming conventions for database names vary widely between organizations. Some shops limit themselves to four or eight characters so that the database can easily map to DOS or MVS filenames. Others use long, descriptive names. Some shops standardize on encoded names, such as `ACTV96TST01` (for "1996 activity test 1").

Database names are case-sensitive; for example, you could create two databases, `customer_db` and `CUSTOMER_DB`. Many organizations standardize on uppercase for database names and object names to enable easier portability to other environments.

I recommend that you keep database names short. After all, people will need to type them. Use names such as `Accounting` or `acctg`, which are easy to remember and easy to type, so your users and programmers won't be cursing you six times a day. And keep the names meaningful and memorable. Names like `AU149305` don't mean much to most mortals. For more on naming standards, see Chapter 37, "Defining Systems Administration and Naming Standards."

A database is created on one or more physical devices. Specifying the device is technically optional, but highly recommended. (Remember, as the system administrator, your first responsibility is to maintain complete control of how SQL Server uses the physical resources of the platform hosting it!) When indicating the device, you use the logical name you specified as part of `disk init`. (See Chapter 25 for more on setting up database devices.)

> **TIP**
>
> If you don't specify the device on which to create the database, a default device will be used (see the "Default Disks" section in Chapter 25). Most DBAs like to know up front where a database is going to be placed. Therefore, always supply the device where you want the database to be created.

You also can specify the size of the database in megabytes. If a size isn't indicated, the server will use the larger of the default size (a configurable value set to 2MB by SQL Server setup) or the size of the `model` database (because the contents of `model` are copied into each new database created). It's a good standard practice to always specify the size when creating a database.

You specify disk size in pages, but you specify database size in megabytes. If you request more megabytes than are available on a device, the server will allocate all remaining space on the device, as long as enough room is available to make a complete copy of the model database. However, there's no guarantee that you'll get all the space you asked for! In a wonderful bout of inconsistency, the confirmation message for the create database statement displays the number of pages allocated on a particular device. Each time you run create database, take the number of pages for each device and add them together. Divide that number by 512, and that number should equal the total space allocation you specified in megabytes in your original create database statement.

> **NOTE**
>
> You can also use the sp_helpdb stored procedure to verify that the created space and allocated space are the same.

Examples of create database

The following are some sample create database statements. In these examples, note how the SQL code has been written to improve readability: Each individual device is listed on its own line. This doesn't affect how the command works, but it certainly makes it easier to read later on. And don't forget to save these create statements in a script, in case you need to execute them later.

The first example sets up a 12MB (8 + 4) database called marketing. In this database, 8MB is allocated for tables, indexes, system tables, and other objects (all of which are broadly classified as *data*), and 4MB is allocated for the transaction log:

```
CREATE DATABASE marketing
ON data_device_1 = 8
LOG ON log_device_4 = 4
```

> **NOTE**
>
> The transaction log is used by SQL Server to log certain activity within a database. Examples of logged activity include creating objects; adding or deleting database users; or adding, deleting, or modifying data in tables.
>
> In general, set up your log segment on a separate drive and, if possible, a separate controller. Performance will be much better. You'll be able to perform incremental backups, and you'll be better able to recover after a disaster. See Chapter 28 for more on transaction logs.

The next example sets up a 30MB (12 + 8 + 10) database called `accounting`. It provides 20MB for data and 10MB for the transaction log:

```
CREATE DATABASE accounting
ON data_device_1 = 12,
data_device_2 = 8
LOG ON log_device_1 = 10
```

This `create database` statement includes several devices and sizes. If you include several devices, SQL Server acquires on each device a fragment of the size you specify. If there isn't enough space on any single device listed, SQL Server allocates as much space as it can on the device. I would suggest that before you create the new database, you check the devices and see how much space is available. Then, after you've created your database, you confirm the size of your new database. A single database can have a maximum of 32 individual fragments.

The next example includes the keywords `FOR LOAD`. You create a database `FOR LOAD` if you're creating the structure for the sole purpose of restoring a database from a backup, where the structure doesn't exist. For example, consider the situation in which you have encountered database corruption and are forced to load from a backup copy. Normally, a corrupt database must be dropped—completely removed from the physical devices. However, you must load the backup copy into an existing database. Because the `LOAD` process replaces the existing structure with the data in the backup, there's no need to go through the time-consuming activity of initializing all the database pages. (See Chapter 30 for more information on restoring databases.)

```
CREATE DATABASE newdb
ON data_device_3 = 12,
data_device_4 = 8
LOG ON log_device_2 = 10
FOR LOAD
```

After a `create database` ... `FOR LOAD`, the only permitted operation on the database is `load database`, the SQL Server method of restoring a database from backup.

What Happens When You Create a Database?

The server performs the following actions when you create a database:

1. Immediately allocate database space.
2. Insert one row in `sysdatabases` (a system table in the `master` database) for the database. You will have a row in `sysdatabases` for every database in a server.
3. Insert one row in `sysusages` (`master` database) for each device fragment.
4. Physically mark each extent. An *extent* is composed of eight data pages. This activity is what takes the bulk of the elapsed time for database creation.
5. Copy the `model` database into the new database.

If the database is created `FOR LOAD`, the server allocates the space from the specified devices but doesn't mark the extents or copy the contents of the `model` database into the structure. The actual marking of extents is an automatic part of the restore process (`load database`).

> **NOTE**
>
> A hospital system using SQL Server experienced a database corruption. Minimizing downtime was critical. By using FOR LOAD, I was able to create the database structure in a few minutes—instead of performing a "normal" database creation, which had originally taken over seven hours. This strategy enabled the system to be up and running almost a full business day sooner than if I hadn't used FOR LOAD.

Here are the steps SQL Server performs when you specify FOR LOAD in a create database statement:

1. Immediately allocate database space.
2. Insert one row in sysdatabases for the database.
3. Insert one row per device fragment in sysusages.
4. Set the database status bit 5 (value = 32), indicating that the database was created FOR LOAD.

Defining Databases with SQL Enterprise Manager

SQL Enterprise Manager enables you to define, expand, and shrink databases the same way create database enables you to do so syntactically. By clicking on the Databases icon in the toolbar, or by selecting Manage | Databases from the menu, you can display the window shown in Figure 26.1.

Double-clicking a particular database name in the window brings up detailed information on that database. (See Figure 26.2.) This is where you set database options (discussed later in this chapter) and assign permissions to database objects for users (discussed in Chapter 27).

FIGURE 26.1.

From SQL-EM, choose Manage | Databases to display a graph of databases, their sizes, and the space available.

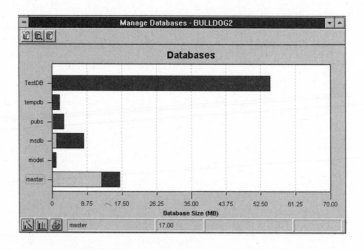

FIGURE 26.2.

Details on a database are available from SQL-EM by double-clicking the database name.

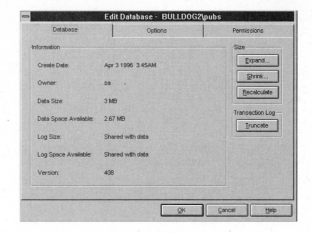

If you're creating a new database, clicking the New Database icon in the toolbar (in Figure 26.1, it's the first button on the left) brings up a dialog box where you can create databases, assign them to data and log devices, and see how creating a new database will affect your total available space on the server.

In Figure 26.3, the administrator is creating a 9MB database, using the `data_1` and `log_1` devices. The graph in the dialog box shows how much space on each device the database will consume and how much, if any, is remaining. The black area shows how much is available.

FIGURE 26.3.

Use the New Database dialog box to create a new database.

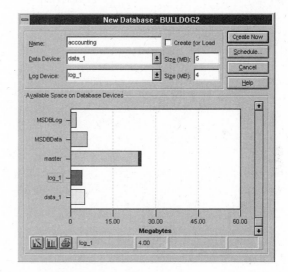

NOTE

With the SQL Enterprise Manager, you're limited to specifying just one data device and, optionally, one log device. If you want to spread the database across other devices, you must expand it by using the Edit Databases dialog box (Figure 26.2), rather than the New Database dialog box (Figure 26.3).

Sizing Databases

By definition, the size of the database is the size of all data fragments plus the size of all log fragments. The data area needs to be large enough to hold all of the system tables and your user tables, as well as any indexes. The log needs to be large enough for the transaction log.

Minimum Size

The minimum database size is the greater of the setting in `sp_configure` (2MB is the default value) or the size of the `model` database (also 2MB by default). If the `model` database won't fit into the allocated space, the database creation will fail.

Default Devices and Sizes

You don't need to specify a device name or a size. If you don't specify the size, the default size is the greater of the size of the `model` database or the value of `database size` in `sysconfigures` (one of the many system tables used by SQL Server 6.5). For example, if `database size` is 2MB but the `model` database is 8MB, the default database size is 8MB.

To change the minimum database size, you can either increase the size of the `model` database with `alter database` (see the section titled "Making Databases Larger," later in this chapter) or change the configured value (which is the recommended approach).

To change the configuration setting to 8MB, use the `sp_configure` stored procedure:

```
sp_configure "database size", 8
reconfigure
```

You need to restart your server before the new setting takes effect.

How Big Should the Database Be?

When you create a database, remember that the data area needs to be large enough to contain the system tables, user tables, and all indexes. You also probably want to leave about 25 percent free space in your database for future growth. To estimate the eventual size requirements of tables, use the stored procedure `sp_estspace`.

> **NOTE**
>
> Use `sp_estspace` whenever you need to estimate how large a table and its indexes will grow. This stored procedure is available on the Microsoft CompuServe forum (`go MSSQL`). You can also find the script on the disk in this book; look for the file named `estspace.sql`.

It's important to remember that databases can easily get larger, but they can only get smaller with great difficulty. Shrinkable databases (discussed later in this chapter) are a new feature for SQL Server 6.5 and are unique to that version. The general approach is to start the database small and let it grow as necessary.

How Big Should the Log Be?

The transaction log records all database modifications. If the log is full, no further modifications are permitted in the database. Under ordinary production circumstances, the only time SQL Server clears the transaction log is after an incremental backup.

The factors influencing log size are database activity level, the frequency of incremental backups, and the volume of simultaneous updates. Because these factors vary dramatically from one system to another, it's impossible to establish firm guidelines on sizing a database log. As a starting point, you might want to consider creating logs that are between 10 and 25 percent of the database size.

Long-running transactions also influence log size. If your system will be updating large amounts of data in a single transaction, the log must be large enough to hold the entire transaction. In that case, you might need the log to be 200 percent or more of the size of the data. If you want your logs to be smaller, you need to break up large updates into smaller transactions (which is usually a good idea anyway), and then dump the transaction log between the transactions to free up space in the log.

> **SETTING UP A SEPARATE AREA FOR THE TRANSACTION LOG**
>
> Most of the examples of database creation in this chapter include a separate allocation for the transaction log. This is accomplished by providing `LOG ON` information to `create database`. Transaction logging and log management are discussed in great detail in Chapter 28, but it's important now to understand some of the characteristics of transaction logs.
>
> A SQL Server transaction log is a record of all modifications made to a database. Every object creation, every security implementation, every row modification (`insert`, `update`, `delete`) is logged in a transaction log. (There are a handful of non-logged
>
> *continues*

continued

activities, which are discussed later; but in a true production environment, all activities are fully logged.)

The transaction log is a *write-ahead log*, which means that logged activity is written to the transaction log before the modifications are made to the tables and indexes themselves. In most cases, the only information that's written to disk at the time of update is the logging information; the data will be brought up to date only at checkpoint time.

There are several crucial benefits to separating your log from your data in your `create database` statement:

■ First, SQL Server incremental backups are actually just copies of the transaction log. If the data and log areas aren't separated, the server can't perform incremental backups; all backups for databases with integrated log and data areas will be full backups.

■ Second, you can get some performance benefits by separating log and data activity, especially if the devices are attached to separate physical disk drives in the server.

■ Third, without separate logs, recovery is more difficult. One implication of writing the log first is that the log is the unit of data integrity in SQL Server. If you lose your data but have your log, up-to-the-transaction recovery is possible (even likely). If you lose your log but still have your data, up-to-the-transaction recovery is impossible, and you can recover only up to the point of your last backup.

The best method of ensuring fault tolerance is to mirror all the devices, or use RAID 5 technology, but sometimes that's not feasible. If you can mirror at least your log devices (which are always smaller than all database devices), you can ensure recoverability. If any log device fails, you still have an alternative device from which you can work. (See Chapter 25 for more information on mirroring.)

How Big Should You Make `tempdb`?

The `tempdb` database is a temporary work area used by the SQL Server to resolve large queries or queries requiring the creation of a worktable. (Queries that might need a worktable include those with `order by` or `distinct` clauses. The `group by` clause always uses a worktable.) Users can also direct SQL Server to create temporary tables with `create table` or `select ... into` statements.

Temporary tables are identified by the number sign (#) in the first character. Remember that when you create a temporary table it can't exceed 20 characters in length—including the # sign. For example, the following statement creates a temporary table, `#authors_and_titles`, in `tempdb`:

```
select au_lname, au_fname, title
into #authors_and_titles
from authors a, titleauthor ta, titles t
where a.au_id = ta.au_id
and ta.title_id = t.title_id
```

The size of the temporary table depends on the size of the tables referenced in the query (authors, titleauthor, and titles).

You can't restrict users from creating temporary tables. The temporary tables persist until the user explicitly drops the table (drop table #titles_and_authors) or until the user creating the temporary table logs out. Temporary tables created by stored procedures are dropped when the procedure ends.

Sizing tempdb depends on a number of factors: how often users create ad hoc temporary tables, whether application programs or stored procedures create temporary tables, how many concurrent users will need to create these tables at one time, and so forth.

TIP

The typical motivation for a programmer to use a temporary table is to avoid a second pass through a large table. By copying a small subset of the data to another location, the user can save many disk operations and improve performance. In general, you want to encourage programmers to think this way because it improves overall system performance.

If you properly select indexes on the primary tables, it might not be necessary to create a worktable to resolve a query. For example, a programmer might want to retrieve data from a table in a particular order. If there was a clustered index created on the columns by which the programmer wants to order the data, the data could be retrieved directly from the primary tables. (The creation of a clustered index on the column or columns of a table physically stores the data in the table in the sort order specified.)

NOTE

If tempdb runs out of space, the transaction aborts and an error is reported in the error log and the Windows NT Event Log.

At first, make tempdb about 25 percent of the size of your largest database, unless you have reason to expect that you'll need substantially more space.

Microsoft introduced a new tempdb option with Version 4.2 for Windows NT: tempdb in RAM. This configuring option enables SQL Server to allocate a block of memory for tempdb. In effect, all operations that require SQL Server to use tempdb are forced into RAM, instead of using a combination of physical disk and cache. The performance improvement is dramatic, but there are some interesting details. First, SQL Server still caches tempdb in the data cache area. In effect, SQL Server can fetch data pages out of the database (which are in RAM) into data cache pages (which are also in RAM). Second, this requires a substantial amount of RAM, because SQL Server might be better able to allocate that RAM as database cache instead.

Microsoft's own recommendations call for tempdb to be loaded into RAM only if the server has more than 64MB of physical memory. Of course, doing so also depends on how heavily your queries make use of tempdb. Chapter 33, "Measuring SQL Server System Performance," discusses using Windows NT's Performance Monitor utility, showing you how to profile your database and queries to determine whether this option will help you.

Database Creation Authority and Database Ownership

Databases are created by the system administrator. The system administrator has the ability to grant create database permissions, but this should be done only with great care.

Whoever creates a database owns it. However, ownership of a database can be transferred (discussed shortly).

Allowing Others to Create Databases

Someone other than the system administrator can create a database if the system administrator grants that person the ability to execute the create database command. (See Chapter 27 for more information.)

Ordinarily, you won't assign the database-creation ability to others, and you shouldn't. Because database creation allocates system resources, manage this task carefully and thoughtfully. Database creation should be a "system administrators only" task.

If you really need to allow others to create databases, do the following:

1. Use the master database:
   ```
   use master
   go
   ```
2. Add a database user in the master database for the particular login:
   ```
   sp_adduser john
   go
   ```
3. Grant the create database privilege to the user:
   ```
   GRANT CREATE DATABASE TO john
   go
   ```

Transferring Database Ownership

Whoever creates a database is designated as its *owner*. It's very common to transfer ownership of a database to another user after the database is created. Database ownership is often transferred to distribute responsibility: A person other than the sa login is responsible for the normal operations of the database (adding users, granting permissions, and so on).

> **NOTE**
>
> The database is the only object that can change ownership. If you try to change the ownership of a table or other object, the system usually marks the entire database "suspect" and you'll need to drop the database and restore from tape. I know, because I tried it.
>
> Database ownership can be changed using the sp_changedbowner stored procedure. The sa login, or the database owner, can change the ownership as needed by using this stored procedure.

Database ownership can't be transferred using the SQL Enterprise Manager. You must run the sp_changedbowner stored procedure if you want to change database ownership. Here's an example:

```
sp_changedbowner john
go
```

In this example, sp_changedbowner takes the parameter john; for this call to work, john must be a valid login.

Making Databases Larger

Use the alter database command to make databases larger. You can enlarge a database while the system is online and the database is in use.

Syntax for alter database

The alter database command is similar to create database:

```
ALTER DATABASE db_name
[ON device_name [= size], [...]]
[LOG ON device_name [= size]]
```

Specify the additional amount of space to be allocated, not the ultimate size of the database. The default increment is 1MB.

Consider the following example of using the create database and the alter database command together:

```
CREATE DATABASE market_db
ON device1 = 50,
device_2 = 100
LOG ON logdev1 = 35
ALTER DATABASE market_db
ON device1 = 50
```

In this example, a 185MB database is created on three devices. The `alter database` command adds an additional 50MB, for a total of 235MB.

Altering a database using SQL Enterprise Manager uses dialog boxes similar to those used in database creation. Using SQL-EM, right-click the database you want to alter; then select Edit from the pop-up menu that appears. This action displays the Manage Databases dialog box. Clicking the Expand button displays the dialog box shown in Figure 26.4.

FIGURE 26.4.

SQL Enterprise Manager makes space allocation easier by presenting a visual image of current space usage and available space for expanding databases.

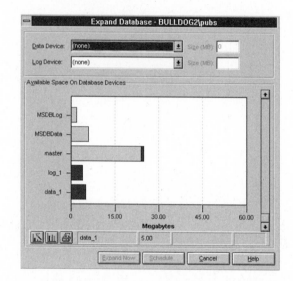

By selecting a device for a specific database portion (data or log), you're instructing SQL Server to expand the space allocation for the current database on that device. However, I can expand the log, or the data area, or both, by selecting devices for them. SQL Server can expand databases online with little performance impact for users, depending on the available hardware platform.

Adding Log Space

Adding log space to a database requires the `LOG ON` keywords (found in Versions 6.0 and 6.5 only) in the `alter database` statement:

```
ALTER DATABASE market_db
LOG ON logdev2 = 35
```

This statement adds 35MB of space to the log of the `market_db` database.

Assigning Space to the Log

Typically, you would assign log space with the `LOG ON` clause in the `create database` or `alter database` statement. It's also possible to assign database space on a specific device to the log retroactively (that is, after a `create` or `alter` statement) with the `sp_logdevice` stored procedure, using this syntax:

```
sp_logdevice databasename, devicename
```

Consider the following examples:

```
CREATE DATABASE test_db
ON device1 = 50,
device2 = 100
LOG ON logdev1 = 35
ALTER DATABASE test_db
ON newdevice = 50
```

After the `alter` statement, the database is 235MB, with 200MB of space for data and system tables (50MB on `device1`, 100MB on `device2`, and 50MB on `newdevice`) and 35MB of space for the transaction log (on `logdevice1`).

The space allocation on additional database devices is assumed to be used for data in SQL Server. In the preceding example, the allocation on `newdevice` is for data because there was no previous allocation of space for the database on the device. If you want to make `newdevice` a log device, use the `sp_logdevice` statement:

```
sp_logdevice test_db, newdevice
```

> **NOTE**
>
> In the previous example, the `create database` statement sets aside 35MB on `logdev1` for the transaction log. All subsequent allocations of space on that device will also be used for the log. The `sp_logdevice` procedure sets aside any space allocations on `newdevice` for the log as well.
>
> This is really the crucial point about space utilization: Space is assigned for data or log by device. This is a special case of the general use of database segments, which is examined in detail a little later in this chapter.

Making Databases Smaller

To make the database smaller in size, click the Shrink button in the Edit Database dialog box. This action opens the dialog box shown in Figure 26.5. Here you are prompted to place the database into single user mode.

Choosing No returns you to the Edit Database dialog box. If you click Yes, the database is placed in single-user mode, and the dialog box shown in Figure 26.6 opens.

Here you indicate to what size you want to shrink the database. The first number shown is the Minimum Size to which the database can be set; Database Size shows the present size. Indicate the desired size of the database in the Database Size box. (Whether or not you make a change in the database size, choosing OK returns you to the Edit Database dialog box.) The shrinking process doesn't change the data segment of your database, only the log segment.

FIGURE 26.5.

SQL Enterprise Manager confirms single-user mode.

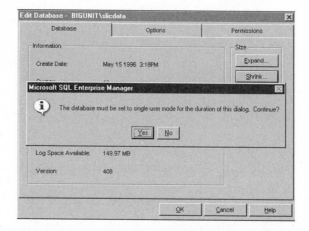

FIGURE 26.6.

Beginning the shrinking process.

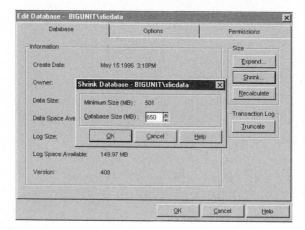

Exploring Databases

It's useful to get under the hood when it comes to databases, particularly if you ever need to do creative work with the system tables to enable a recovery. The following sections explore databases using standard stored procedures and then examine the system tables in more detail.

sp_helpdb

The system stored procedure `sp_helpdb` provides information about databases on the server. If you don't provide a parameter, the system provides a list of all databases on the server:

```
sp_helpdb

name            db_size owner dbid created      status
--------------- ------- ----- ---- ----------- ---------------------------
fred             4.0 MB sa       9 Jan 18, 1996 no options set
master           3.0 MB sa       1 Jan 01, 1996 no options set
model            2.0 MB sa       3 Jan 01, 1996 no options set
perftune         5.5 MB sa       6 Jan 06, 1996 select into/bulkcopy
pubs2            2.0 MB sa       8 Jan 01, 1996 no options set
sybsecurity      8.0 MB sa       7 Jan 01, 1996 trunc log on chkpt
sybsystemprocs  20.0 MB sa       4 Jan 01, 1996 trunc log on chkpt
tempdb           2.0 MB sa       2 Jan 05, 1996 select into/bulkcopy
testdb           4.0 MB sa       5 Jan 01, 1996 no options set
```

If you provide a parameter, you get detailed information about a single database, as in the following example:

```
sp_helpdb pubs2

name            db_size owner dbid created      status
--------------- ------- ----- ---- ----------- ---------------------------
pubs2            2.0 MB sa       8 Jan 01, 1996 no options set

device_fragments size    usage               free kbytes
---------------- ------- ------------------- ----------
master            2.0 MB data and log               480
```

The detailed information from `sp_helpdb` includes a list of database fragments, which are specific allocations of space on each device.

As you have already seen in this chapter, all the information presented by these stored procedures is available in the Manage Database window or one of its accessory dialog boxes.

Database System Tables

When you create and modify databases, three system tables in the master database are involved: `sysdatabases`, `sysusages`, and `sysdevices`. (See Figure 26.7.)

FIGURE 26.7.

The sysusages *table resolves the many-to-many relationship between* sysdatabases *and* sysdevices.

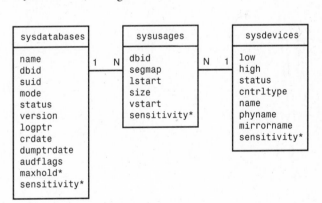

sysdatabases

The server adds a row to sysdatabases for each new database. The user specifies the name, but the server automatically selects the next available integer ID for dbid. There are several important columns in sysdatabases:

name	The name of the database, assigned by the database creator.
dbid	The system-assigned identifier for the database.
suid	The ID of the database owner; at database creation time, this is set to the ID of the login that issued the create database statement. To change the database owner, use the sp_changedbowner stored procedure.
status	An integer consisting of several control bits with information about the database. See the section "The Database Status Flags," later in this chapter.
dumptrdate	The date of the last dump transaction. The server marks this date on the next transaction dump to ensure that all dumps are loaded in order during a restore from backup.

sysdevices

The create database statements don't affect the sysdevices table, but each named device must exist in sysdevices. Information in sysdevices is used to build detailed rows in sysusages, so it's useful to look at sysdevices now. The important columns for this discussion are cntrltype, low, high, and name.

The maximum size of a device on SQL Server is 16 million pages (32GB). A unique range of 16 million pages is allocated to each device upon allocation; these are *virtual page numbers*.

> **NOTE**
>
> The virtual page range is determined by multiplying the virtual device number assigned in the disk init statement by 2^{24}, or approximately 16 million.

The following list describes some of the important columns in sysdevices:

cntrltype	Differentiates between dump devices and database devices. A value of zero is assigned to all database devices.
low	The first virtual page number available on the device.
high	The last virtual page number available on the database device. Although the system reserves the entire range of 16 million pages to the device, the high value reflects the device's actual capacity. To determine the

number of pages on a device, use high – low + 1. To determine the number of megabytes, use (high – low + 1) / 512.

name   The logical name of the device.

Following is a sample listing from the `sysdevices` table for all physical database devices (`cntrltype` = 0):

```
select cntrltype, low, high, name
from sysdevices
where cntrltype = 0
order by low
```

cntrltype	low	high	name
0	0	12799	master
0	16777216	16787455	sysprocsdev
0	33554432	33558527	sybsecurity
0	67108864	67112959	testdevice
0	100663296	100665343	test_dev
0	1342177728	134230015	introdev
0	150994944	151000063	instruct2_data

Values in the low column are even multiples of 16,777,216.

> **TIP**
>
> To determine the virtual device number, divide the low value by 16,777,216; the virtual device number for `testdevice` is 4.
>
> The size of `testdevice` is (67112959 – 67108864 + 1) = 4096 pages = 8M.

sysusages

The `create database` statement automatically adds one row in `sysusages` for each allocation of space on a device. For example, the following `create database` command allocates space on three devices, `DATA_1`, `DATA_2`, and `LOG_1`. Each of these allocations is recorded in a separate row in `sysusages`:

```
CREATE DATABASE market_db
ON DATA_1 = 100, DATA_2 = 100
LOG ON LOG_1 = 50
```

Take a closer look at the useful columns in `sysusages` (more on the following page):

dbid   The database identifier is used to relate information in `sysusages` with `sysdatabases` (`dbid` exists in `sysdatabases` as well).

segmap   Used to map database fragments to segments (see the section "Segments and Object Placement," later in this chapter).

lstart	The first database (logical) page number is the logical page start within the database.
size	The number of contiguous pages.
vstart	The starting virtual page number enables you to map the database fragment to a specific virtual device. The fragment is located on the device if the vstart value falls between the low and high page numbers for the device in sysdevices.

Using SQL to Query the System Tables

The trick to joining sysdevices, sysdatabases, and sysusages is to understand how virtual device numbers in sysdevices are mapped to the vstart column in the sysusages table.

The following output displays the rows in sysusages for a single database. There are three fragments in the database, all on the same virtual device. sysusages includes one row per device fragment per database:

```
select *
from sysusages
where dbid = 9
order by lstart
```

dbid	segmap	lstart	size	vstart	pad	unreservedpgs
9	7	0	1024	67110912		664
9	7	1024	512	67111936		512
9	7	1536	512	67112448		512

The vstart value for each fragment falls between the low and high page numbers (67108864 and 67112959) for testdevice, so each of these fragments is stored on testdevice.

The actual SQL used to join sysusages to sysdevices uses a between test, as in the following fragment:

```
where sysusages.vstart between sysdevices.low and sysdevices.high
  and cntrltype = 0
```

> **NOTE**
>
> Some older SQL Server documentation tells you to join sysusages to sysdevices with the lstart column. This is wrong. Use vstart to make the join to sysdevices.

Following is the SQL used to list allocations of space on devices for each database:

```
select 'Database' = d.name, 'Device' = v.name, u.size
from sysdatabases d, sysusages u, sysdevices v
where d.dbid = u.dbid
  and u.vstart between v.low and v.high
  and cntrltype = 0
order by d.name
compute sum(u.size) by d.name
```

Database Space Usage

Use sp_spaceused to determine space used (and space available) in your database. If the database runs out of space for objects, you can't add data to tables or indexes. You also may not be able to add new views or procedures, depending on where the space shortfall occurred.

The database runs out of space only when it tries to allocate a new extent to an object. For example, the server determines that a page split is required in an index, but the current extent is full. At that time, the server attempts to allocate a new extent (8 pages, which is usually 16KB) to the index. If all extents for the segment are reserved, the update fails and rolls back and the server reports an error (out of space ON segment...).

You usually want about 25 percent free space in your database at all times. This helps you avoid major work stoppages when you're hurrying to add additional space to the database.

The sp_spaceused procedure can report on the space allocated to a table if you pass the table name as a parameter (sp_spaceused *tablename*). However, you should be more concerned with database space usage and availability at this time. No parameters are required to get database space usage for the current database, as in the following example:

```
sp_spaceused

database_name                  database_size
-----------------------------  ------------------
master                         8 MB
(0 rows affected)

reserved      data           index_size     unused
------------  -------------  -------------  -------------
5230 KB       4232 KB        208 KB         790KB
(0 rows affected)
```

> **WARNING**
>
> sp_spaceused can be off by as much as two extents per table.

The output from the procedure can be somewhat misleading, so review it closely. Database size is the total database size, including data and log allocations, but the reserved value is only based on data usage (not logs). If you have allocated data and log separately, you can subtract from the total database size the space allocated to the log to get the total data allocation.

To determine how much space is reserved for objects within the data allocation, take the reserved value in the previous example (5230) and subtract the pages reserved for the log (run sp_spaceused syslogs). That's the space reserved for objects.

To arrive at the space available for allocation to objects, subtract from the total allocation for data the amount reserved for objects.

In the case of the `master` database, where you can't separate the data and log segments, you may have to add the space reserved by `syslogs` to the reserved value to get a total for the space being utilized. Then subtract the total space utilized from the total size of the database to get the amount of space available for allocation.

Database Options

Use `sp_dboption` to enable or disable a database option for a database. Internally, this command sets a status flag for the database. The following list contains several options you can use to define standard processing or to support special requirements.

`columns null by default`	Permits the database owner to decide whether columns that don't specify nullability will permit nulls. For example, the following `create table` statement doesn't specify whether `col_1` permits nulls:

```
create table table_1 (col_1 int)
```

Normally, `col_1` wouldn't permit nulls. If you set `columns null by default` to true before executing the `CREATE TABLE` statement, the column will permit nulls.

`dbo use only`	After setting a database to `dbo use only`, only the database owner (`dbo`) can issue the `use` statement for this database.
`no chkpt ON recovery`	Prevents a checkpoint record from being written to the log after the recovery process is complete.
`offline`	After enabling this option, a removable-media database (mounted on CD-ROM, for example) is no longer accessible by SQL Server or its users.
`published`	This database is a source database for SQL Server 6.5 replication.
`read only`	Enables database users to select from the tables, but prevents all modifications. This option could provide a performance enhancement to decision-support systems.
`select into/bulkcopy`	Enables fast, non-logged actions in a database, including `select ... into`, non-logged `writetext`, and fast `bcp`.
`single user`	Limits database access to one user at a time.
`subscribed`	This database is a destination point for replication processing in SQL Server 6.5.
`trunc log on chkpt`	Automatically truncates the transaction log after every system-generated checkpoint.

WARNING

I've experienced a curious problem with `trunc log on chkpt` on certain systems. A checkpoint clears a portion of the cache to free space or update the data segments of the database. There are three kinds of checkpoints:

- Checkpoints explicitly requested by the database owner
- Checkpoints generated by the server to free space in the cache
- Checkpoints issued by the server checkpoint process, based on the server recovery interval

On some SQL Server platforms, the `trunc log on chkpt` option truncates the log only after the third kind of checkpoint; a manual checkpoint didn't truncate the log.

For more about checkpoints, see Chapter 28. For now, try to understand the potential problem with truncation.

Consider a long-running transaction such as an update of all rows in a large table:

```
update titles
set price = price * 1.02
```

In this transaction, the `titles` table contains several million rows. The transaction is likely to be larger than the total capacity of the transaction log. You have two choices: You can increase the size of the log (ignore that choice), or you can try to run the transaction in smaller pieces, presumably clearing the log after each statement, as in the following:

```
update titles
set price = price * 1.02
where title < "P"
checkpoint
update titles
set price = price * 1.02
where title >= "P"
```

If the checkpoint results in a truncation, all is well. On some servers, the `dbo`-initiated checkpoint doesn't truncate the log, and the log will fill up. What's worse, the explicit checkpoint reduces recovery time, further delaying the server-generated checkpoint that would otherwise have truncated the log.

Default Database Options

On server installation, the following items are true concerning database options:

- All database options are set to false in `model` and in all user databases.
- The `trunc log on chkpt` option for the `master` database is set to false.
- `select into/bulkcopy` is always true in `tempdb`.
- Any option enabled in the `model` database at the time a new database is created will also be enabled for this new database.

Setting Database Options

To set database options, use `sp_dboption`. This is the syntax:

```
sp_dboption databasename, option, {true | false}
```

Here's an example:

```
sp_dboption market_db, "select", true
```

Notes on `sp_dboption`:

- You must be using the `master` database when you execute the `sp_dboption` stored procedure.
- You can abbreviate the name of the database option, as long as the server can distinguish the option from all others. Note that all keywords (such as SELECT) must be placed in quotation marks when they are passed as a parameter to a stored procedure.
- Options can be set `true` or `false`.
- `sp_dboption` without parameters will list all possible parameters.
- Only the `dbo` or `sa` can set database options. `dbo` aliases can't set options.

Typically, changing an option involves the two steps shown in the following code:

```
use master  /* only set options in the master database */
go
sp_dboption market_db, "select into/bulkcopy", true
go
```

Setting Database Options with SQL Enterprise Manager

You can use SQL Enterprise Manager to set database options, using the Options tab of the Edit Databases dialog box, as shown in Figure 26.8. Instead of running `sp_dboption`, you can select the options you want activated or deactivated by using the check boxes provided in the interface.

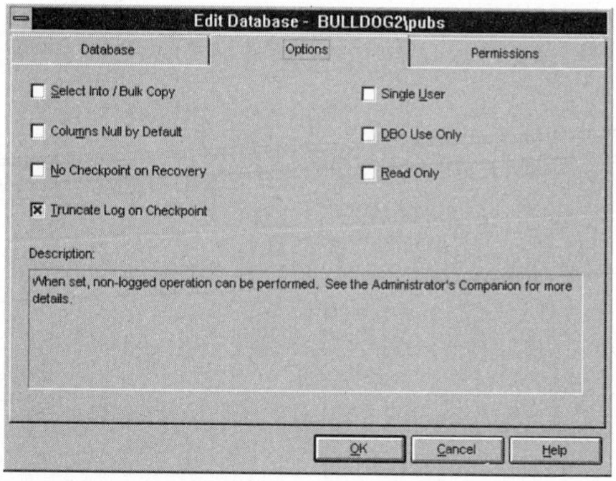

FIGURE 26.8.

SQL Enterprise Manager can be used to configure specific database options.

SQL Enterprise Manager will automatically checkpoint the database, ensuring that changes take effect immediately upon an administrator clicking OK to commit any database option changes.

Examining Database Status

Use sp_helpdb to determine the value of status flags on a database. The status values are decoded to the far right in the output, and you may need to scroll to the end of the report to see the information.

The Database Status Flags

The status column in sysdatabases records information about a database in a bit field. Table 26.1 displays the bit representations of the status column and Table 26.2 displays the bit representations of the status2 column.

Table 26.1. Status column bit representation.

Value	Status
2	Database is in transition
4	select into/bulkcopy
8	trunc log on chkpt
16	no chkpt on recovery
32	Crashed during load
64	Database not recovered yet
128	Database is in recovery
256	Database suspect
1024	read only
2048	dbo use only
4096	single user
8192	Database being checkpointed
16384	ANSI null default
32768	Emergency mode

How to Turn Off the SUSPECT Flag on a Database

If you start the SQL Server before giving external storage devices a chance to warm up, or perhaps if a drive comes unplugged, the server will detect a failure of the device and mark all databases mapped to that device as SUSPECT (status column, bit value 2^8 = 256). Having that value in the status column prevents the server from ever trying to recover that database. To regain access to the database, you need to turn off that bit and restart the SQL Server.

Shortly, you'll learn how to update the sysdatabases table manually and reset the SUSPECT bit. But before you do anything unreasonable, you need to make sure that you correctly understand the problem. If the server is up, run sp_helpdb on your database. Is the SUSPECT flag set? If it isn't, but you still can't access your database, you have a different problem.

If the database is marked SUSPECT, take a look at the error log. You want to see, fairly early in the server startup process, that it failed to start the device where the database is loaded. If you find this message, you're ready to roll. If not, keep reading and try to understand why the database wasn't recovered.

You need to log in as sa to update the sysdatabases table manually. The following example shows the necessary commands to enable you to directly update the status bit in the sysdatabases table:

```
use master
go
sp_configure "allow updates", 1
reconfigure with override
go
update sysdatabases
set status = status - 256
where dbname = "your database name here"
and status & 256 = 256
go
sp_configure "allow updates", 0
reconfigure
go
```

Now shut down and restart the server. If the drives are working, the system should come right up and the databases should be available.

The model Database

Whenever a database is created, the model database is copied to the new database. It's typical to place in the model database any objects that you intend to have in all databases. Typically, model contains rules, defaults, user-defined datatypes, and any logins (for example, guest) that will be created in all databases.

> **TIP**
>
> User-defined datatypes are stored in systypes in each individual database. As new datatypes are created in each database, each datatype is assigned a new integer identifier. For example, if ssn_type was the first user-defined datatype created in one database and age_type was first in another, each would be assigned the same identifier: 100.

> This would create a problem when you move information between databases, especially when you use the `select ... into` command, where the datatype identifier (the numeric value) is copied to the new table structure.
>
> The same problem is more severe in `tempdb`, where the lack of any matching type identifier typically causes `sp_help` to fail.
>
> I recommend that you define user-defined types first in the `model` database before creating any user databases. Then, when the user database is created, the user-defined types will be copied to this new database. I further recommend that as individual databases need to add further datatypes, you should create these datatypes in the `model` database first, and then re-create them in each user database.
>
> Bear in mind that `tempdb` is created every time the server restarts. When `tempdb` is created, it also gets a copy of the `model` database, which means that it gets a complete library of user-defined datatypes.

Consider creating a system stored procedure to handle centralized functions, rather than creating a procedure in `model` to be propagated to all databases. Also consider placing lookup tables in a single central database, rather than propagating lookup tables into every database.

Dropping Databases

To drop a database, simply issue the `drop database` command. Dropping a database removes all the appropriate entries from the various system tables and removes the structure—making that space available to other databases:

```
DROP DATABASE database_name
```

Only the `dbo` (or `sa`) can drop a database, and nobody can be using it at the time it's dropped. When you drop a database, you remove all objects, all data, and all logs associated with the database. The server removes all references to the database in `sysdatabases` and `sysusages`.

Sometimes, you won't be able to drop a database. To remove a corrupt or damaged database, use `dbcc dbrepair`, with the following syntax:

```
DBCC DBREPAIR (db_name, dropdb)
```

Here's an example of how to remove a corrupt database called `corrupt_db`:

```
DBCC DBREPAIR (corrupt_db, dropdb)
```

Segments and Object Placement

If you have a database with space allocated for data on two different physical devices, it's important to understand where the server will place tables, indexes, and other objects as they're created and expanded. For example, suppose that a database was created on devices `DATA_1` and `DATA_2` as follows:

```
CREATE DATABASE market_db
ON DATA_1 = 100, DATA_2 = 100
LOG ON LOG_1 = 50
```

When you create a table in the database, as in the following example, where does the server place the table—on `DATA_1` or `DATA_2`?

```
create table Customer
(name char(30) not null,
 address char(30) not null)
```

The simple answer is that if you haven't set up any segments in your database, it doesn't matter. The server allocates space freely within the data area of the database until all the allocations for data are full.

> **NOTE**
>
> By specifying in the `create database` statement that the 50MB on `LOG_1` was for log use only, you have already set up a *log segment*, a predefined segment for the exclusive use of the `syslogs` table. This section explains how to create your own user-defined segments for storing tables that you want to isolate.

A *segment* is a label that identifies a set of storage allocations within a database. By using segments, you can control where the server places database objects, enabling those objects to expand only within specifically defined areas within the database. Segments can provide two broad benefits: improved performance, and greater control over object placement and growth within the database.

> **NOTE**
>
> Segments aren't widely used in the SQL Server community. An estimate is that less than five percent of all SQL Server sites use any segments beyond those provided as part of SQL Server (see the section titled "Predefined Segments," later in this chapter).
>
> Consider the following discussion and look at the examples before deciding to implement segments. They provide some benefit but require substantial administrative attention, and they can complicate database restoration.

Segments for Performance

Typically, when segments are used to improve performance, the segments point to SQL Server devices that are mapped to different physical disk drives. The performance improvements typically seek to distribute database activity across disks (and controllers). Here are some examples of how activity can be distributed:

- Nonclustered indexes can be stored on one segment, while the table itself is stored on another. This can improve both read and write performance because index I/O can run parallel to table I/O.

  Note that clustered indexes always reside on the same segment as the table indexed. This requirement arises because the leaf level of the clustered index is the table itself.

- A large table can be divided among segments (and disks) to allow different parts of the table to be read at one time.

- Text and image data (Binary Large Objects, or BLOBs) can be placed on a segment, apart from the standard data pages. This can improve read performance when the table is heavily used.

Segments for Control

Segments also enable you to manage the size of objects within the database. Without segments, each object can grow to the full size of the data allocations in the database, contending for space with all other objects. In the previous example, the customer table and its indexes could grow to 200MB, unless other objects were also consuming space in the database.

When you use segments, objects can grow only to the size of the segment. In addition, by implementing segments, you can place thresholds on each segment and define the necessary action when the objects in a segment come near to filling the segment.

Segment Definition

Use the sp_addsegment stored procedure to add a new segment to a database. Use sp_extendsegment to add other device allocations for the database to an existing segment.

Syntax:

```
sp_addsegment segmentname, devicename
sp_extendsegment segmentname, devicename
```

Examples:

```
use market_db
go
sp_addsegment Seg1, DATA_1
sp_extendsegment Seg1, DATA_2
```

Take careful note of the parameters of the sp_addsegment and sp_extendsegment stored procedures: *segmentname* and *devicename*. There are two characteristics you must understand about segments (on the following page):

■ Segments are database-specific. When you create a segment, you establish a mapping to the usage of space on a specific device or set of devices for a database. Fragments of other databases on that device aren't part of that segment.

■ Segments refer to all fragments on a device or set of devices for a database.

Take a look at two examples. In the first example, the acctg database is 240MB, with 200MB for data and 40MB for log. The first segment, Seg1, includes 50MB on DATA_1 and 100MB on DATA_3. The second segment, Seg2, includes 50MB on DATA_2 and 100MB on DATA_3:

```
use master
go
CREATE DATABASE acctg_db
ON DATA_1 = 50, DATA_2 = 50, DATA_3 = 100
LOG ON LOG_1 = 40
go
use acctg_db
go
exec sp_addsegment Seg1, DATA_1
exec sp_addsegment Seg2, DATA_2
exec sp_extendsegment Seg2, DATA_3
exec sp_extendsegment Seg1, DATA_3
go
```

Notes:

■ Segment definitions are database-specific (see Figure 26.9). So Seg1 for acctg_db doesn't conflict with Seg1 for market_db (see the preceding section).

FIGURE 26.9.

A segment is database-specific. Two segments, each with the same name, are created for different databases. They uniquely identify usages on devices for that database.

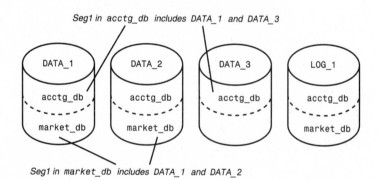

Seg1 in acctg_db includes DATA_1 and DATA_3

Seg1 in market_db includes DATA_1 and DATA_2

The next example adds 50MB to acctg_db on DATA_3. Now Seg1 includes 50MB on DATA_1 and 150MB on DATA_3:

```
ALTER DATABASE acctg_db
ON DATA_3 = 50
```

Segments refer to all fragments on a device or set of devices for a database. When you add 50 megabytes to the database on DATA_3, the additional space is automatically incorporated into every segment that refers to that device for the database (see Figure 26.10).

FIGURE 26.10.

Additional space allocated on a device already mapped to a segment becomes part of that segment.

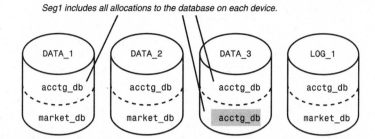

Seg1 includes all allocations to the database on each device.

> **NOTE**
>
> There's a many-to-many relationship between segments and devices. A single segment can include mappings to many devices. A single device can be part of many segments, even within a single database. The section "Segment System Tables," later in this chapter, discusses how this mapping is recorded in the sysusages table.

Predefined Segments

Whenever you create a new database, the server automatically creates three segments in the database:

- default, for tables and indexes
- system, for system tables (including all object definitions)
- logsegment, for storing syslogs

The default and system segments are mapped to all data allocations. logsegment is mapped to any allocations for the log. For example, in the first example you looked at, the allocations on DATA_1 and DATA_2 were mapped to the default and system segments:

```
CREATE DATABASE market_db
ON DATA_1 = 100, DATA_2 = 100
LOG ON LOG_1 = 50
```

Allocations for LOG_1 were mapped to logsegment. (See Figure 26.11.)

FIGURE 26.11.

When a database is created, the default, system, *and* logsegment *segments are defined automatically.*

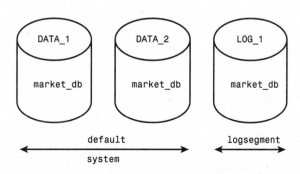

Placing Objects on Segments

Every object is placed on a segment when the object is created. System tables (except `syslogs`) are placed on the `system` segment and the transaction log (`syslogs`) is placed on the `logsegment` segment. Everything else (specifically, tables and indexes) is placed on the `default` segment automatically.

To create an object on a specific segment, add the following to your `create` statement:

```
ON segmentname
```

This example places the `Customer` table (`market_db` database) on `Seg1`. As the table grows, it will use space on `DATA_1` and `DATA_2`, the devices mapped to `Seg1`:

```
CREATE TABLE Customer
(name char(30) not null,
 address char(30) not null)
ON Seg1
```

The next example creates a nonclustered index on `Customer` on a different segment, `Seg2`. A table and its nonclustered indexes can be on separate segments:

```
CREATE INDEX Customer_nci1
ON Customer(name)
ON Seg2
```

The final example explicitly places a table on the `default` segment:

```
CREATE TABLE lookup
(code int not null,
 value varchar(20) not null)
ON "default"
```

The word `default` must be enclosed in quotes, because `default` is a keyword referring to a type of system object.

Changing an Object's Segment

Use `sp_placeobject` to place all of an object's future growth on a specific segment.

> **NOTE**
>
> SQL Server allocates space to objects in 8-page (usually 16KB) extents. `sp_placeobject` instructs the server that all future extent allocations should come from devices mapped to the new segment. It doesn't prevent newly inserted rows from being added to pages that have already been mapped to the earlier segment.

Syntax:

```
sp_placeobject segmentname, objectname
```

Example:

```
sp_placeobject Seg3, Customer
sp_placeobject Seg3, "Customer.Index03"
```

After these statements are issued, all additional space allocations to the `Customer` table and to the `Customer` table `Index03` index will come from `Seg3`.

NOTE

Place the clustered index on a different segment, as in the following:

```
sp_placeobject Seg3, "Customer.ClusteredIndex"
```

This has the same effect as placing the table on the new segment: All future space allocations to the table or clustered index will come from devices mapped to `Seg3`.

One way to use segments is to spread a large table across several devices. To distribute the table evenly, you need to create the table on one segment, load a segment of the data, and then run `sp_placeobject` to point to the next segment, as in the following example:

```
CREATE TABLE spread_table ( ... ) ON Seg1
```

Now load 50 percent of the data:

```
sp_placeobject Seg2, spread_table
```

Now load the rest of the data. At this point, the data is evenly distributed between the two segments:

```
sp_placeobject Seg3, spread_table
```

All future allocations will come from `Seg3`.

The interesting question is this: When should the clustered index be created? If you create the clustered index after the last `sp_placeobject`, the entire table will reside on the `Seg3` segment. So you need to create the clustered index early and enable it to grow across all three segments. To optimize the load, you'll probably choose to create the clustered index after you load the first half of the data but before you place the table on `Seg2`.

Moving an Object to a New Segment

The method you use to move an object to a new segment, including all existing allocations, depends on the object. To move a table without a clustered index to a new segment, create a clustered index on the new segment and then drop the index:

```
create clustered index temp_index on table1(key) on new_seg
drop index table1.temp_index
```

The first statement moves the table to New_Seg and builds a clustered index along the way. The second statement drops the index (if the sole use of creating the index was to enable you to move the table).

NOTE

Whether this is an efficient way to move a table to a new segment depends in part on the size of the table and the resources you have available. It may be faster to create a new table on the desired segment, insert rows from one table to the other, and then drop the old table and rename the new one. It also may be faster to use bcp to copy the data out and then in.

Keep in mind that you can't use the clustered index method to move a table that contains fully duplicated rows. Clustered index creation fails if duplicate rows are discovered in the table.

To move a table that has a clustered index, drop the clustered index first, and then re-create it on the new segment:

```
drop index table1.clustered_index
create clustered index clustered_index on table1(key) on new_seg
```

To move a nonclustered index to a new segment, drop the index and re-create it on the new segment:

```
drop index table1.nc_index
create index nc_index on table1(nckey) on new_seg
```

TIP

Try to remember that sp_placeobject affects only the future growth of an object; it doesn't affect existing allocated space.

Removing a Device from a Segment

Use sp_dropsegment to remove a device from a segment definition or to remove a segment from a database. Remember, every object is created on a segment. If you remove a device from a segment definition, you control which objects can exist on a physical device.

There are some limitations to using `sp_dropsegment`:

- ▪ You can't drop the last segment from a device.
- ▪ You can't use `sp_dropsegment` on a segment if you have previously created or placed objects there.
- ▪ You can't completely drop the predefined segments: `default`, `system`, and `logsegment`.

When you create a database, all data allocations are mapped to the `default` and `system` segments. When you create a new segment for a specific device, you probably want to remove the `default` and `system` segment mappings to that device, to ensure that only objects explicitly placed there use the segment device.

For example, to create a segment to use with indexes in this database, you would create `index_segment` and then drop the `default` and `system` segments from the device:

```
create database market_db
on data_1 = 50, data_2 = 50
log on data_3 = 25

exec sp_addsegment index_segment, DATA_2
exec sp_dropsegment "default", DATA_2
exec sp_dropsegment "system", DATA_2
```

Figure 26.12 illustrates the segment mappings at the end of this process.

FIGURE 26.12.

You can drop the `default` and `system` segments from a data device after you have created a new segment on that device.

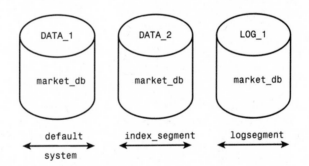

Getting Information on Segments

Use `sp_helpsegment` to get information about segments in your current database. If you don't pass the *segmentname* parameter, `sp_helpsegment` lists all segments in the database. If you pass the name of a segment as a parameter, you get detailed information about the segment, including a detailed list of fragments on devices and the fragment size, as well as a list of all objects stored on the segment. The following example shows you how to get the segment names from pubs and then how to get all the information on the segment log segment:

```
sp_helpsegment

sp_helpsegment system
```

Segment System Tables

Segment changes have an impact on system tables in both the current database where the segments are being defined (syssegments and sysindexes), and the master database (sysusages).

syssegments

When you create a segment, the server makes an entry in the syssegments table in the database. The entry consists of *segment*, *name*, and *status*:

segment	A unique integer value assigned by the system. The maximum value is 31, and there can be no more than 32 segments in a database.
name	A unique name you assign with `sp_addsegment`.
status	A bit column indicating the default segment.

The following example shows the contents of syssegments. There's one row in syssegments per segment in the database; syssegments is a database-level system table:

```
segment name                                    status
------- ------------------------------------    ------
0       system                                  0
1       default                                 1
2       logsegment                              0
3       indexes                                 0
```

sysusages

Creation of a segment also has an impact on sysusages. The segmap column in sysusages is a bitmap of segments mapped to that device fragment.

Segment number	0	1	2	3	4
Bitmap value	$1\ (2^0)$	$2\ (2^1)$	$4\ (2^2)$	$8\ (2^3)$	$16\ (2^4)$
Segment name	system	default	logsegment	Seg1	index_segment
Value	0	0	0	8	16

The value of segmap for the row in sysusages corresponding to the device DATA_2 is 24 (0 + 0 + 0 + 8 + 16).

sysindexes

Object placement is recorded in the segment column of sysindexes. sp_helpsegment displays the segment in which an object is stored.

Querying syssegments

To join syssegments to sysusages, you need to select on dbid and perform a *bit-wise and* (&) between the segmap column in sysusages and the segment values in the database. Your where clause will look like the following:

```
WHERE segmap & power(2, segment) > 0
  AND db_id() = dbid
```

For example, to determine the number of fragments and the total megabytes allocated to each segment, execute the following command:

```
select s.name, count(*) "fragments", sum(size)/512 "allocation"
from master..sysusages u, syssegments s
where segmap & power(2, segment) > 0
  and db_id() = dbid
group by s.name
```

Segments are overlapping. In this database, there's a 3MB allocation to default, logsegment, and system on the same device, as shown in the following output:

```
name                            fragments   allocation
------------------------------- ----------- -----------
default                         1           3
logsegment                      1           3
system                          1           3
```

Summary

Databases are the main storage and allocation structure in SQL Server. Databases provide a way for you to store data logically and physically, to perform backups and recovery with full transactional integrity. They're also a useful security mechanism, as you'll see in the next chapter.

Segments improve database performance and control the growth of objects more carefully than a database alone. Thresholds make segments far more useful because they enable the administrator to monitor the capacity and space availability of each storage unit.

Security and User Administration

27

Implementing a security and user administration plan in a SQL Server database isn't a difficult task, if you first understand SQL Server's security architecture and learn to develop an approach to implementing security. This chapter discusses the basics of implementing an appropriate security regimen, and then recommends some common approaches.

Overview of SQL Server Security Levels

To access server data, a user needs to clear four security levels (see Figure 27.1):

- The client (workstation) operating system
- SQL Server as an application on Windows NT
- The SQL Server database
- The SQL Server object

Each security level can be thought of as a door. If the door is unlocked (unsecured), or you have the key to open it (security access), you can move on to the next door (security level). If you make it past the last door, you'll have access to the data. There's a virtually unlimited number of doors that can be set up to secure data within a database, which can sometimes seem overwhelming. It helps to look at each level independently, as in the following sections.

FIGURE 27.1.

SQL Server security consists of four access levels.

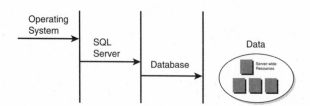

Operating System Security Issues

A user might require some access to several operating systems to run a typical client/server application:

- A client workstation and its file, disk, and presentation resources
- A network operating system for the client/server application (as well as mail, file, and print services)
- The SQL Server host operating system where SQL Server is running

Normally, each of these processes—client, network, and SQL Server—runs on a distinct system; few applications require a client-side SQL Server database engine.

A user doesn't require a login on the host machine where the SQL Server is running unless SQL Server is running locally. Windows NT requires a login to the operating system, so anyone administering SQL Server would need access to that workstation. However, SQL Server can provide access to the server and its databases outside Windows NT's security, because it's directly network-port addressable. (See Chapter 24, "SQL Server Installation and Connectivity," for a detailed discussion of Named Pipes and network port addresses.)

Operating-system security is the responsibility of the OS administrator or, more commonly, of the network administrator. With the growing sophistication of client/server installations, these two distinct jobs are being handled by different employees, so coordinating changes to the underlying OS when administering SQL Server security is even more important. SQL Server's integration with network security makes this coordination even more critical.

SQL Server provides two modes of defining access to the SQL Server itself. *Standard security* is the holdover from Sybase, where a user must supply a distinct login name and password to get access to the server. This login and password are different from any network logins, and can also be different from one SQL Server to the next.

With SQL Server 4.2 for Windows NT, Microsoft introduced *Integrated Login Security*, which allowed SQL Server login names and passwords to be defined based on Windows NT network login names and passwords, thereby enabling users to supply just one network login to get to SQL Server.

The following sections are dedicated to discussing the two methods of security, their proper use, and the benefits of each.

SQL Server Security: Logins

Access to a SQL Server is controlled through a server login and password. Logins can be either standard SQL Server logins or integrated SQL Server logins. Whatever the type, the login ID grants access to the SQL Server process.

After a user makes it past the server door (gains security access to the server), he or she can be faced with a variety of different database doors. The door to the master database is always unlocked, and the user will end up in that room if no default database was specified when the login was set up, or if the user's default database is unavailable. Regardless of the default database, there may be several other doors, including other system databases, along with any user databases that have been created and are available to the user.

SQL Server Database Security: Users

After a user login is created, access to SQL Server databases can be provided in any of the following ways:

- Adding a user to a database (giving the user a key)
- Telling the database to treat a user as some other valid user (an *alias*—giving the user a copy of someone else's key)

- Creating a guest user (unlocking the door and propping it open)
- Making that login the owner of the database (providing the user with a "master" key)

When in a database, a user is able to see definitions for the objects contained in that database. This is because definitions are stored in the system tables, to which any user of a database has `select` access (except for certain sensitive columns). The user still needs permission to access each database object. (Database users are discussed in the "Database Access" section, later in this chapter.)

Object-Level Security: Permissions

When an object (a table, procedure, or view) is created, SQL Server automatically assigns ownership of the object to its creator. Object ownership confers complete control over the object—its access, integrity, and administration. By default, only the object owner can select from a table until access is specifically granted to others.

Object-level security is the last level of security. If a user other than the owner desires access to an object, the owner must grant the intended user *permission* to perform a particular action on the object. For example, a user can select from a table only after the owner has granted the `select` permission to that user. If the user doesn't have the necessary permission, access will be denied.

Although this is the last main level in a security scheme, object security can contain several sublevels. (The "Permission Approaches" section, later in this chapter, shows how the use of dependent objects can tighten the security in your system.) For example, permission can be granted to select from a particular view, but not from its underlying (base) tables. This strategy enables an administrator to deny direct access to tables, but allow access to the data through the view. A similar concept applies to stored procedures and triggers.

SQL Server offers a variety of ways to control access to data. SQL Server login and database user approaches affect the way in which a permissions strategy is implemented.

At the object level, most sites grant broad permissions and then limit or grant specific access as needed to minimize the administrative overhead in implementing a permissions plan. This scheme usually involves granting permissions to `public` or a user-defined group, and then revoking or granting specific permissions to a user-defined group or a specific subset of users.

SQL Server Standard Logins

A SQL Server login provides access to the SQL Server. Logins are usually the first line of defense for the DBA in a security plan. (Remember that OS passwords are usually the responsibility of the OS administrator.) After being granted a login, the user can connect to the server and use the `master` database.

A SQL Server login usually requires a password, although there are exceptions. For example, upon initial installation, the sa login has no password. Passwords aren't required for SQL Server logins, although it's recommended that they be required on all servers. Without the use of passwords, it's difficult to implement any meaningful security in SQL Server.

Logins are added with `sp_addlogin`:

```
sp_addlogin login_name, password [ , defdb [ , deflanguage  ] ]
```

For example:

```
sp_addlogin rbrown, mookie1
```

would create a login name of `rbrown` with a password of `mookie1`. SQL Server responds with this confirmation message:

```
New login created.
```

The next example shows the contents of `syslogins` after running `sp_addlogin` (adding a row to the `syslogins` table in the `master` database):

```
select suid, name from syslogins

suid    name
- - -   - - - - - - - - - - - - - -
1       sa
2       probe
3       mon_user
4       testuser1
5       jeff
6       rbrown
16382   repl_publisher
16383   repl_subscriber
```

In SQL Server 6.5, only the *login_name* parameter is required. *login_name* must be unique for the server and must not be more than 30 characters long. Passwords also must not be more than 30 characters. In SQL Server 6.5, Microsoft has encrypted the `password` field of `syslogins`. In versions prior to 6.0, SQL Server simply revoked permissions on the `password` column.

A default database can be defined for each distinct login. The default database doesn't grant any inherent privilege to use a database; it merely tells SQL Server to *attempt* to use the defined database at login time. If the login doesn't yet have access to the default database, the server issues an error message; the user is logged in and the current database is the `master` database. Any login that doesn't have a default database specified will also default to the `master` database.

TIP

It's important to assign a default database and provide access to that database for each login in your system. In a well-secured system, users can't do any damage to the master database. They can select from the system tables and take up processor time, but real damage shouldn't be possible without the sa password.

To be safe, however, users shouldn't default to the master database. Valid default databases should be set for all users so that they don't end up defaulting to master.

WHY CAN'T I USE THE DATABASE?

There are circumstances when everything has been done correctly, but users still end up pointed to the master database when they log in. Here are a few things to look for, starting with the obvious and moving toward the obscure.

Each of the specific error messages is followed by this general error message:

```
Error 4001: Cannot open default database 'testdb'.
```

The following are common errors, their diagnoses, and the actions which should be taken.

Error received:

```
Message 916: Server user id 6 is not a valid user in database 'testdb'.
```

Diagnosis:

The login has not been added as a user to this database.

Action required:

Add the user to the database with sp_adduser, sp_addalias, or sp_changedbowner; or add the guest user to the database.

Error received:

```
Msg 927, Level 14, State 1:  Database 'test' cannot be opened - it is in
 the middle of a load.
```

Diagnosis:

The database can't be used until a restore from backup is complete.

Action required:

Restore the database from backup. The user must wait until the restore is complete.

Error received:

```
Error 905: Unable to allocate a DBTABLE descriptor to open database 'testdb'.
Another database must be closed or dropped before opening this one.
```

Diagnosis:

The system configuration settings need to enable more concurrently open databases.

Action required:

Increase the open databases setting with sp_configure. In the meantime, another database will need to be closed before this database is available.

The default language option (deflanguage) is used at sites that have loaded other character sets besides us_english (the language that's always available to the server). If this parameter is provided, the user receives all system messages in the language selected.

Note that the optional parameters (defdb and deflanguage) can be updated later, using the sp_defaultdb or sp_defaultlanguage stored procedures.

A user can change his or her own password and default database. The password can be changed using sp_password. Passwords should be changed frequently—at least every month. Users can change their default database with the sp_defaultdb command, assuming that they have security access to the new database.

Special Logins

Two special logins are created as part of the installation of the SQL Server. These two logins are sa and probe.

sa

The sa login is a special login that is created as part of the installation process. The sa login owns the server and the system databases (master, model, tempdb, msdb, and any others installed by the sa). The sa login is the database owner (dbo) within those databases because it's the login that is literally mapped to the dbo user (more on dbo later in this chapter).

> **NOTE**
>
> When a user—that is, a login—creates a database, the server records the suid column from the server's row in syslogins as the database owner in sysdatabases.

Regardless of actual database ownership, the sa is seen as the dbo of any user database.

probe

A probe login is provided as part of installation. This login is used between servers to manage two-phase commit activities.

`repl_publisher` and `repl_subscriber`

The `repl_publisher` and `repl_subscriber` logins are provided as part of installation. They are used to handle replication between servers.

Generic Logins

Some sites add a general login, such as `templogin` or `sybguest`, to be used by temporary users of a server for in-house training or self-study. Often, the logins have no password, or the password is the same as the login name. Of course, many administrators prefer an individual login for each user of a server, as this provides better control and permits auditing of work done by each individual, as opposed to each login.

How Logins Work

When a new login is created, a row is added to the `syslogins` system table in `master`. Each login is assigned a unique system user ID (`suid`), an integer that identifies that user uniquely on the server. During login, the server matches the name passed in the login structure against the `name` column in the `syslogins` table. If a match is found and the password matches, the `suid` is stored in the memory allocated for the new connection.

The login name isn't stored in any table except `syslogins`. The `suid` is the key used in all other tables that refer to a person's login, including those relating server access to database access.

TIP

To retrieve a list of `suid`s and login names, type the following line:

```
select suid, name from syslogins
```

Although you can select the `password` column if you are the sa, the values are encrypted in SQL Server 6.0 and above. Prior to SQL 6.0, the `password` column was plainly readable by the sa:

```
select suid, name, password from syslogins
```

The system functions `suser_name()` and `suser_id()` convert login IDs to names and vice versa. For example, the following line returns the value `probe` (because probe is always the second user inserted in the `syslogins` table):

```
select suser_name(2)
```

Conversely, this line returns the value 2:

```
select suser_id("probe")
```

When the functions are used without arguments, they return the login name or ID for the current user.

These system functions are most useful in accessing data from system tables, where they enable you to decode a name or ID without needing a join against the `syslogins` table, as in the following example. These system functions are also used frequently in the SQL Server–provided system stored procedures:

```
use master
go
select spid, suid, suser_name(suid) "name"
from sysprocesses
order by suser_name(suid)
go

spid   suid   name
___    ___    _____
2      0
3      0
4      0
5      0
6      6      rbrown
1      1      sa
```

Notice that there are rows in `sysprocesses` with a `suid` of `0` (and thus no name). These processes are system processes in charge of mirror, network, and checkpoint handling.

Modifying Login Information

Again, it's not an issue if all of the login information isn't available at the time the login is created. It can be changed at any time using `sp_defaultdb` or `sp_defaultlanguage`:

```
sp_defaultdb login_name, databasename
```

Passwords

A *password* is used to verify the authenticity of a login. There's no minimum password length in Microsoft versions of SQL Server, but there's a maximum length of 30 characters. Passwords can include any printable characters, including A-Z, a-z, 0–9, or any symbols.

As with all passwords, adding symbols or mixing upper- and lowercase makes the password much more difficult to guess.

Changing Passwords

Passwords can be changed by the user or by the sa, using sp_password:

```
sp_password old_password, new_password [ , login_name ]
```

To change a password, a user passes the current password and the new password. If a user who isn't the sa passes a *login_name* to sp_password, the system returns an error message.

An sa changing another user's password passes the sa password, the new user password, and the login name. If the sa omits the login name, the sa password will be changed!

SQL Server Integrated Logins

With SQL Server 4.2 for Windows NT, Microsoft introduced an interesting twist on the traditional Sybase security model: a feature that allowed logins to use their existing network IDs to access SQL Server. Microsoft called the feature *Integrated Login Security* (*ILS*), reflecting the integration of network and SQL Server security—two parts of an overall client/server security architecture that, before this version, were completely exclusive.

There was, however, an important limitation: DOS- and Windows-based client workstations required using Named Pipes as their protocol for connecting to SQL Server. Native IPX/SPX or TCP/IP support wasn't available, but it was still possible to use Named Pipes over either of these protocols. The only problem for network administrators was the potential security gap caused by a resource that they couldn't control existing on their networks.

This restriction, although it appears esoteric, actually defines how ILS works. Windows NT servers can query the Named Pipes API to determine the network login and password information of each user on the network. SQL Server uses this Windows NT feature to validate network packets coming from workstations, bypassing any login or password information supplied for SQL Server. In effect, SQL Server "piggybacks" on Windows NT's network security.

There are actually two different submodes of integrated login security. Pure integrated security means that SQL Server will accept only ILS connections; therefore, all the client workstations are connecting to SQL Server by using Named Pipes. SQL Server will use only the network login and password for the workstation for validation. If an application attempts to use a different SQL Server login and password, SQL Server will ignore the explicit login and use the network login and password instead.

This is obviously very restrictive and requires running dual protocols in non-Windows NT network environments. Therefore, Microsoft also created *Mixed Login Security* (*MLS*), which allows connections on all of SQL Server's supported protocols. If a workstation is using Named Pipes, specifying a SQL Server login and password is optional. If the client supplies an explicit login and password, those explicit values are used for validation. If a Named Pipes client doesn't supply any SQL Server login or password information, an integrated connection is made.

Clients other than Named Pipes are required to supply explicit login and password information. In mixed mode, non-Named Pipes connections are standard connections.

Using the new *Multi-Protocol Network Library* (*MPNL*) described in Chapter 24, true ILS connections can be used over Named Pipes, TCP/IP Sockets, and IPX/SPX connections.

Configuring Integrated Login Security

SQL Server setup for ILS involves a number of steps to configure. However, the most important step is how to plan the security architecture. Because Windows NT networking supports security features that SQL Server doesn't, implementing Integrated Login Security requires careful planning and mapping of SQL Server's security regimen with that of Windows NT. It isn't necessarily rocket science, but it shouldn't be overlooked as trivial either.

Configuring SQL Server ILS involves four basic steps:

1. Run the Server Configuration/Options utility to configure SQL Server to start in Integrated security mode.
2. Define Windows NT network users and passwords, and assign them to one of two groups: `SQLUsers` or `SQLAdmins`.
3. Map the Windows NT network users to SQL Server logins.
4. Test integrated connections, using specific network logins.

Configuring SQL Server

Configuring SQL Server to use ILS can be accomplished using the SQL Enterprise Manager application. When starting SQL Enterprise Manager, use the Server | SQL Server | Configure menu sequence. Selecting the Security Options tab from the resulting window brings up the dialog box shown in Figure 27.2.

The first task is to select a security mode. Standard mode forces all users to use an explicit SQL Server login and password. Integrated mode forces everybody using either Named Pipes or the Multi-Protocol Network Library to use integrated connections. DECNet, Banyan VINES, and ADSP (AppleTalk) customers are out of luck. With Mixed mode, Named Pipes and MPNL connections can use either method, but DECNet, Banyan VINES, and ADSP workstations must use Standard security.

Within all DB-Library applications, the client process is able to identify itself to SQL Server using a *hostname*, which is typically the application name or executable file name. With ILS, SQL Server provides a means of overriding the value of this parameter and substituting the network ID with which the workstation is being validated; thus, you can trace the SQL Server login ID back to its respective network ID. This option should be used with care, however, because it limits DB-Library's capability of tying the login to a specific application or process.

FIGURE 27.2.

Set integrated security using the Server Configuration/ Options dialog box.

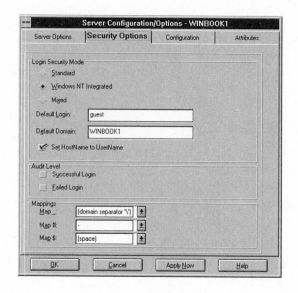

SQL Server is able to audit both successful and failed ILS connections. Auditing these connections tells SQL Server to make entries in the Security subsystem of the Windows NT Event Log each time an event occurs.

Mappings are a crucial element to Integrated or Mixed security. Because Windows NT supports network logins that use special characters—such as spaces, dashes, and (most importantly) the backslash (\) character—to separate domain names from login names, SQL Server must somehow support them as well. However, SQL Server identifiers are restricted from using such symbols. Mappings allow the substitution of SQL Server-approved characters for Windows NT-approved characters. Typically, the default mappings will be sufficient, but the SQL Server administrator should discuss how network logins are defined with the LAN or Windows NT administrator for confirmation.

Choosing OK exits the Configuration/Options window. SQL Server needs to be restarted before these changes can take effect. This is the first step to establishing integrated connections!

Creating SQL Users and Groups with NT User Manager

All Windows NT user and group creation is performed using the Windows NT User Manager. Because this is more of a network administration function than a database administration function, this section isn't going to focus on the ins and outs of defining network users and groups. Instead, it will illustrate why there should be two particular groups for SQL Server logins.

Windows NT's network security structure allows a single network login to participate in many different security groups on the network. Windows NT internally resolves the highest level of permission among these various—and potentially conflicting—groups and permission levels.

A list of network IDs must be supplied for all users who should have access to SQL Server. Also, this list should specify membership in one of two distinct groups: SQLUSers and SQLAdmins. These new network users should be assigned to *only one* of these groups. The network administrator is then responsible for creating the necessary IDs in User Manager.

> **NOTE**
>
> For clarification, the names SQLAdmins and SQLUsers are used only because they're descriptive. They don't represent SQL Server keywords, and they could be replaced with names such as Fred and Ethel, which are equally valid (if somewhat less descriptive) as group identifiers. SQL Server doesn't care which names are used, but they should be descriptive, so that the groups could be easily maintained by others.

SQL Server only supports a single user as part of a single group. Therefore, adding multiple existing network security groups from the Windows NT level could cause conflicts with SQL Server. Windows NT users who need access to SQL Server should be members of SQLUsers or SQLAdmins, but not both. This would cause the very conflict that must necessarily be avoided!

Users assigned to the SQLAdmins group receive sa-level authority, so care should be taken in assigning users to this group. Also, when SQL Server is first started in Integrated or Mixed security mode, SQL Server grants sa privilege to any users in the Administrators group on Windows NT. Users added to the SQLUsers group have unique login and user IDs assigned at the SQL Server level, so their permissions can be assigned individually, if need be.

Also, SQL Server creates database-level groups for each login group created, so the SQLUsers group as defined at the Windows NT level is also defined as the SQLUsers group at the SQL Server level, easing administration and permission assignment tasks.

Mapping NT Users and Groups to SQL Server Logins

SQL Server relies on the Security Manager application to map NT network IDs to SQL Server login IDs. Security Manager reads the Windows NT security database and creates the logins, permissions, and database groups necessary to take full advantage of integrated security.

The first time SQL Security Manager is started, the user is presented with a mostly empty window. This first display shows you who has user-level access to SQL Server. Clicking on the right button in the paired buttons in the toolbar shows the Admin-level users. Figure 27.3 shows a sample server; in this case, all the users are assigned the login of sa.

FIGURE 27.3.

The SQL Security Manager displays mappings between network users and SQL Server logins.

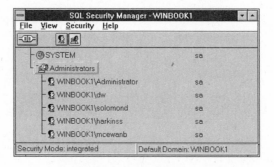

To add new `Admin`-level users, choose Security | Grant New from the menu. This action opens a dialog box listing all the groups defined in Windows NT. Select the `SQLAdmins` group, and the members of that group are automatically added to SQL Server's security domain. (See Figure 27.4.)

FIGURE 27.4.

The SQL Security Manager showing the newly added `SQLAdmins` *group.*

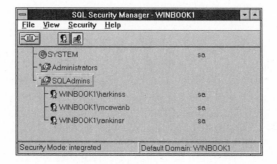

Clicking the left button of the paired buttons displays user-level groups and their associated logins. New user-level IDs are added to SQL Server with the Security | Grant New menu sequence. When adding new user-level IDs, SQL Security Manager checks for any Windows NT user IDs that exist in the group and maps them against any Windows NT user IDs that have `Admin`-level permissions or already exist in `syslogins`. If a user that Security Manager is attempting to add already exists in one of these categories, SQL Server reports it as an error, using the dialog box shown in Figure 27.5.

In this example, there were no errors. SQL Server added not only the login IDs and distinct user names, but also a group within the `master` database for those users (both discussed later in this chapter). Note that unlike the `Admin` users, each of these users has been given his own or her own distinct SQL Server login. All `Admin` users share the `sa` login!

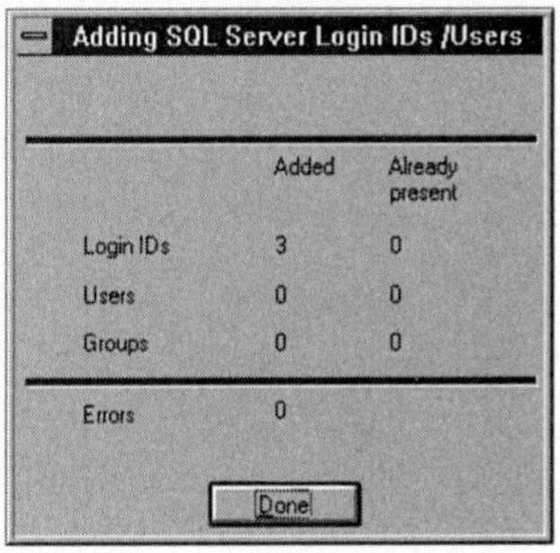

FIGURE 27.5.

This dialog box reports the number of logins, users, and groups added by SQL Security Manager.

	Added	Already present
Login IDs	3	0
Users	0	0
Groups	0	0
Errors	0	

Testing

Testing integrated security is easy. Start any of the SQL Server client applications (ISQL/w is fastest) and simply enter a server name, but no login ID or password, into the Login dialog box. Clicking Connect should result in an integrated security connection.

If the connection doesn't work, there are three areas to check before proceeding:

1. First, check to make sure that the client workstation is using either the Named Pipes or Multi-Protocol Network Library to connect to SQL Server. This can be verified by using the SQL Client Configuration Utility, which is used to define the particular network library that a workstation uses.

2. Next, check that the client workstation actually has access to the network. If a standard login succeeds but an integrated login fails, move on to the next step.

3. Finally, make sure that the network ID is properly defined on the Windows NT machine. This means scanning the ID and group definitions in Windows NT User Manager, as well as running SQL Security Manager to detect conflicts or missing IDs.

SQL Server Logins

To summarize briefly, logins are how users identify themselves to SQL Server. With standard security, the security architecture for SQL Server must be maintained—which is separate from the security architecture for the underlying network. This is the best option for maintaining application portability across different versions of SQL Server. For integrated security, there are additional issues to consider, but there is the benefit of using Windows NT-based security for SQL Server.

Database Access

After server login security, the next level of security is database access. Database access is managed by establishing a link between logins (stored at the server level) and users (stored at the database level). User access to a database is required to use the database (change the current context to the database); it also is required to access any object stored in the database.

NOTE

This information is also added to the memory structure set up for a connection or process, and a review of sysprocesses (built dynamically) shows the uid and database ID (dbid) for a process.

The uid is used to identify ownership of objects within a database. Although the ID assigned to an object is used to identify that object within other tables, there's a unique index on the combination of an object name and a uid (database user ID). This is why more than one user can have an object with the same name. Avoiding the naming confusion that can result is a very important consideration when determining a development approach.

Adding Users

Access to a database is granted by adding a user to the database. Use sp_adduser to add users; it adds an entry in the database-level sysusers table. Here's the syntax of sp_adduser:

```
sp_adduser login_name [ , name_in_db [ , grpname ] ]
```

For example, here's how you add rbrown to the testdb database:

```
use testdb
go
sp_adduser rbrown
go
```

At the completion of the sp_adduser procedure, a row is placed in the sysusers table in the database where the user was added. The following example shows the contents of the database-level table, sysusers, after rbrown has been added to the database testdb:

```
use testdb
go
select suid, uid, name
from sysusers
go

suid   uid   name
---    ---   ----------------
-2     0     public
1      1     dbo
4      3     testuser1
6      4     rbrown
```

The only required parameter is *login_name*, which is checked against the name column in the master..syslogins. (The login name must already exist in the syslogins table.) *login_name* is used to derive the suid to be placed into the sysusers table.

The *name_in_db* parameter is infrequently used in real life, and its purpose is not to be confused with true aliasing (sp_addalias). This parameter is inserted in the name column in the sysusers table.

TIP

Normally, the default value for this parameter is the string specified for the *login_name*, and (unless there's a very good reason) it should always be kept the same. This makes the matching of database users to server users much simpler. In fact, if a value isn't specified or a value of null is provided, it defaults to the *login_name*.

The *grpname* parameter defines the group for the user. By default, a user is placed in the group public, which has a group ID (gid) of 0, although the word public can be specified for this parameter. Groups are discussed later in this section.

Use sp_helpuser to get a list of users in a database or to see specific information about a single user, as in this example:

```
Users_name      ID_in_db Group_name      Login_name      Default_db
_____       ____     _____      _____       _____
dbo             1        public          sa              master
rbrown          4        public          rbrown          testdb2
testuser1       3        public          testuser1       master
```

Special Users

Two special users can exist in a SQL Server database: dbo and guest.

dbo

The dbo is the database owner. dbo is added to the model database as part of installation (and can't be dropped); hence the dbo exists in all databases in a server. The dbo can never be dropped from a database and always has a database user ID (uid) of 1.

NOTE

It's unusual for the user ID (uid in sysusers) and the login ID (suid in master..syslogins) to have the same value. The values are predictably the same only for the sa, who is dbo in all databases.

---

guest

The guest user is provided to grant database access to anyone who logs into the server. The guest user must be explicitly added to a database by using sp_adduser (or added to the model database before a subsequent database creation).

The presence of a guest user means that anyone logged into the server can access the database. This is a catchall to enable access to a database when the login hasn't been explicitly added as a database user (or aliased to another user, as discussed in the next section). The guest user always has a uid of 2. Guest permissions default to the permissions granted to the group public.

> **TIP**
>
> The guest user shouldn't usually be added to the model database, because this means that the guest user will exist in any new database that's created. This could weaken the security strategy.

Adding Aliases (Alternates)

To use a database, a user doesn't necessarily have to be added explicitly as a user of the database. SQL Server provides the capability of relating a login to another login who is already a user of the database.

For example, every database has a user dbo, whose name can be found in the name column in the sysusers table. The sysusers row for dbo includes an suid and a database uid (which is always 1 for dbo). The value specified in the suid column for dbo determines the login ID of the actual database owner—the individual who has all administrative privileges within that database. You can provide database access to additional users as dbo by defining aliases within the database for each such user.

> **TIP**
>
> The most common user privilege to be shared with aliases is dbo, which enables several logins to divide the responsibility for database implementation, evolution, and maintenance. This is most common in a development environment, where several users share responsibility for object creation and maintenance.

sp_addalias adds an entry to the sysalternates table, enabling an additional login to access a database as that user:

```
sp_addalias login_name, name_in_db
```

In the next example, `mwhite` is added as an alias to `rbrown` in the `testdb` database. Now `mwhite` receives all the access and permissions granted to `rbrown` within this database:

```
sp_addalias mwhite, rbrown
```

Both *login_name* and *name_in_db* are required. *login_name* must be a valid entry in `syslogins` with no `suid` entry in `sysusers` or `sysalternates` in the current database. *name_in_db* must be a valid user name within the database.

`sp_addalias` adds a row to the `sysalternates` table. The login ID of *login_name* is stored in the `suid` column. The login ID of the actual login mapped to *name_in_db* is stored in the `altsuid` column.

> **NOTE**
>
> Aliases are added with `sp_addalias` but stored in the `sysalternates` table! Although common sense would dictate the existence of a `sysaliases` table, consistency is never a rule in SQL Server.

Execute `sp_helpuser` with a user name to get detailed information about a user, including aliases, as in this example:

```
sp_helpuser rbrown
Users_name      ID_in_db Group_name      Login_name      Default_db
--------        ----     ----------      ----------      ----------
rbrown          4        public          rbrown          testdb2

Users aliased to user.
Login_name
---------------------
mwhite
```

Examining the contents of the three system tables (`syslogins`, `sysusers`, and `sysalternates`) both before and after executing `sp_addalias` is helpful in understanding the mapping of logins, users, and aliases.

`syslogins` and `sysusers` are joined on `suid`. `syslogins` and `sysalternates` are also joined on `suid`. `sysusers` and `sysalternates` are joined on `suid` and `altsuid`, respectively (see Figure 27.6).

The values from sample versions of `sysusers`, `sysalternates`, and `master..sysobjects` show the correspondence between `suid`, `uid`, and `altsuid` among the tables (continued on the next page):

```
select suid, uid, name
from sysusers
where uid > 0
select *
from sysalternates
select suid, name
```

```
from master..syslogins
sysusers
suid   uid    name
───    ───    ─────────────────
1      1      dbo
4      3      testuser1
6      4      rbrown
( 10 rows affected)

sysalternates
suid   altsuid
───    ───
7      6
( 1 row affected)

master..syslogins
suid   name
───    ───────────────
1      sa
2      probe
3      mon_user
4      testuser1
5      jeff
6      rbrown
7      mwhite
( 7 rows affected)
```

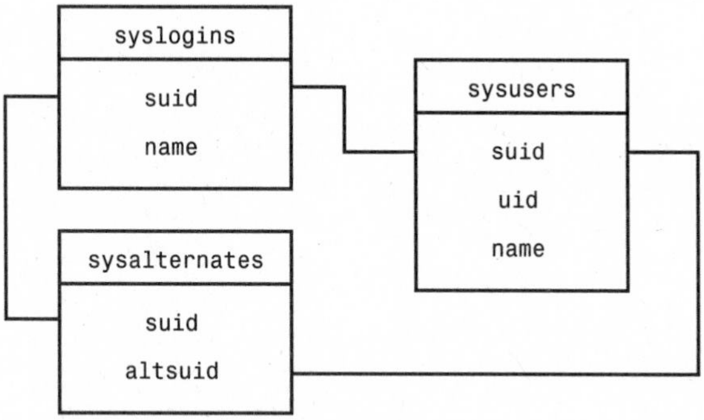

FIGURE 27.6.

*The relationship between the login, user, and alias entities is built on a system user ID (*suid*) column in the* syslogins *tables.*

Here are some features to notice about the contents of these tables:

- The dbo of the database is the sa (suid of the dbo in sysusers equals 1).

- Besides dbo, there are two users of the database—rbrown (suid 6 in syslogins corresponds to suid 6 in sysusers) and testuser1.

- mwhite (suid 7) is aliased to rbrown (suid 6) in this database.

How Database Access Works

So what does the server do when trying to determine access to a database? When a person tries to use a database, the server looks for an entry in sysusers and sysalternates to decide whether to grant access. It first looks in the sysusers table to see whether a match can be made on the suid from syslogins.

A row will be found in sysusers for an suid if the following conditions exist:

- The user has been added through the sp_adduser procedure (normal user addition).
- The user created the database (suid matches with uid of 1, the dbo).
- Ownership of the database has been transferred to the user.

After trying to find a match against the suid in the sysusers table, the server then tries to match the suid column in the sysalternates table.

If a match is found in sysalternates, the server substitutes the value in the altsuid column for the login suid. The altsuid value is then used to match against the suid column in the sysusers table, as was previously illustrated. Then the uid corresponding to the altsuid is what is ultimately used by the user for activities conducted in that database.

If a match isn't found in sysalternates, the server then looks at the sysusers table again to see whether the special user guest has been added. If it has, the person assumes the uid of guest within that database.

If none of these matches can be made, the person is denied access.

The database access validation procedure is outlined in Figure 27.7.

FIGURE 27.7.

SQL Server database permissions depend on user mappings or the presence of a guest *user in the database.*

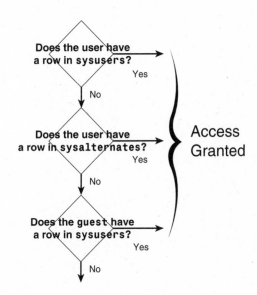

Groups

Groups can be used as part of an effective database security strategy. Object and command permission are granted to users and groups. A user who is a member of a group inherits all the permissions granted to the group.

A user name can be assigned to a group with sp_adduser (discussed earlier) or sp_changegroup. Assigning users to groups is a dbo responsibility. There's a detailed discussion of how to implement groups into your permission strategy in the "Permissions" section, later in this chapter.

> **NOTE**
>
> SQL Server allows a user to belong to only one group. (This isn't *strictly* true, though; a user can belong to one group in addition to public.) It's interesting to see why this limitation exists. It's clear that the structure of the system tables plays a role in that requirement; after all, a user's group membership is recorded in the gid column in sysusers, so there's a many-to-one relationship between users and groups.
>
> Permissions are granted to entries in sysusers. Because groups are stored in sysusers alongside users, all permissions checks require that only two tables be read: sysprotects and sysusers.

The public Group

Every user in a database is a member of the public group.

> **CAUTION**
>
> If a guest user is added to a database, any person who has a valid server login can use that database. The guest user will, of course, be able to perform any functions that have been granted to public.

It's common for an administrator to grant permissions to the public group rather than to each individual user. For example, if a database has 500 users, and all users need to select from the customer table, an administrator could execute a grant statement once for each user (500 statements) or just once for the entire public group.

The public group is found in the sysusers table in each database with a uid of 0, and you can't delete it.

Adding Groups

Although the `public` group is a convenient way to grant universal access to database objects, it's often necessary to grant different permissions to discrete sets of users. Additional groups may need to be created in order to represent different permissions requirements. You add groups with `sp_addgroup`:

```
sp_addgroup groupname
```

For example, to add a `marketing` group to the current database, use the following command:

```
sp_addgroup marketing
```

This procedure adds a row to the `sysusers` table with a `uid` of `16384` or larger.

Reporting, Dropping, and Changing Groups in a Database

To determine the groups that exist in a database, or for more information about an individual group within a database, use `sp_helpgroup`:

```
sp_helpgroup [ groupname ]
```

Without any parameters, `sp_helpgroup` reports all groups in the database:

```
sp_helpgroup
Group_name                     Group_id
– – – – – – – – – – – – – – –   – – – –
marketing_group                16390
public                         0
```

There will always be an entry for the group `public`. Pass the *groupname* as a parameter to list all users in a group:

```
sp_helpgroup marketing_group
Group_name             Group_id Users_in_group        Userid
– – – – – – – – – – –   – – – –  – – – – – – – – – – –  – – –
marketing_group        16390    rbrown                4
marketing_group        16390    testuser1             3
```

Drop groups with `sp_dropgroup`, but only if that group doesn't contain any users:

```
sp_dropgroup groupname
sp_dropgroup marketing_group
```

Use `sp_changegroup` to change a user's group membership (only the `dbo` can execute `sp_changegroup`):

```
sp_changegroup groupname, name_in_database
sp_changegroup marketing_group, rbrown
```

How Groups Work

sp_addgroup adds a row to the sysusers table. The uid and gid (group ID) are assigned the same value (16384 or greater). When users are added to a database without specifying a group name, the group ID of 0 (public) is assigned to them. When a group is specified (either as a parameter in sp_adduser or with sp_changegroup), the gid of that group is placed in the gid column for that user.

> **NOTE**
>
> Once the user has been assigned to a specific group, he or she is no longer explicitly a member of the public group. Nevertheless, any permissions assigned to public will apply to that user. The public group always encompasses *all* users.

Login Approaches

There are several approaches to security in SQL Server systems; following are the major approaches:

- SQL Server login equals the operating system/application (OS/App) login.
- SQL Server login is independent of the OS/App login.
- A single login for all users of an application or user type.

SQL Server Login = OS/App Login

This is a fairly maintainable approach to logins. A user is given a login to the operating system. (The operating system could be the client workstation login, network login, or the user login to the server, if the client application runs on the server.) The operating system sets environment variables for the username (and possibly the password) during its login process. Applications read the environment information when logging into SQL Server.

For example, SQL Server facilities such as ISQL and bcp look for the environment variables USER and PASSWORD when connecting to the server. When the user doesn't need to specify the -U option for ISQL, the application passes the user name from the environment when connecting to the server.

Using the OS login as the SQL Server login simplifies login administration because the procedures (manual or automated) to keep the user (login) names and passwords synchronized are relatively simple.

One drawback to this approach is that users occasionally need to access an application with a different SQL Server login. Applications still must provide a means of supplying a different login name and password from the one stored at the operating-system level.

SQL Server Login Independent of OS/APP Login

To enable separate OS and SQL Server login IDs, applications must include a login function. (Often, when there is some correspondence between SQL Server and OS login IDs, applications automatically populate the login screen with information drawn from the environment.)

This approach is more difficult to administer and maintain than the "SQL Server login equals OS/App login" approach, but it can provide additional security.

Single SQL Server Login

The single SQL Server login approach is often used by sites that want a single point of control for logins to the SQL Server. It's simple, but its simplicity has drawbacks.

Only one login exists for an entire application or for each major application piece. When a person invokes the application, the application connects to the server using hard-coded values for the login name and password. This approach has some benefits:

- Users don't need to log into the server explicitly.
- A password-changing routine doesn't have to be written into the application to accommodate password changes. (Applications that use individual logins with the capability of changing passwords often integrate a password-changing application to shield users from having to connect to the server by using another interface to change their passwords.)
- The administration activity required to manage logins and passwords is extremely low.

However, drawbacks to this approach include the following:

- A database administrator often executes sp_who to see who is logged into the SQL Server. Part of the output from this command is the login name. If all users log into the SQL Server with same name, the output of sp_who will contain numerous processes with the same login name. If a problem is encountered, determining the actual user associated with a process becomes almost impossible. (To overcome this problem, the application can pass the OS login ID as a hostname value when logging in to SQL Server. Hostname values are also included in the sp_who display.)
- Auditing user activity is meaningless. Because every person would be the same application user, only application activities can be tracked. Individual user activities can't be tracked.
- If an outside source is able to determine the application login and password, that source has free rein of the server. As mentioned previously, auditing can't be used to target suspects. The application has to change its password, which could require recompilation of the application—not always a desirable thing to do in production.

Because of these drawbacks, this approach isn't usually recommended. Nonetheless, at times the reduction in administrative overhead justifies the loss of flexibility and security.

SEPARATE LOGIN IDS FOR APPLICATION WORK VERSUS AD HOC QUERY

Users often require access to a system through an ad hoc query generator or other front-end tool, in addition to their regular access through an application. If the user is allowed to use an application login when running an ad hoc tool, the user may be found updating tables or running stored procedures without the protection or validation normally provided by the application.

For example, a user who normally uses the application to delete a row from the ten-billion-row `sales_history` table by retrieving it and pressing a Delete button (complete with `Are you sure?` messages!) might be surprised when the `delete sales_history` statement removes every row from the table.

Unfortunately, most tools can't be restricted from enabling updates to tables or executing stored procedures. Worse, SQL Server never knows whether the user requesting a deletion is running a carefully written application in PowerBuilder or is using `ISQL` after taking a one-day video course on SQL.

What's the solution?

Removing all the different (and interesting) front-end products would work, but one of the most desirable benefits of SQL Server is its accessibility through various front-end querying tools.

Unfortunately, trying to keep the users ignorant of the syntax for `insert`, `update`, and `delete` statements is never a feasible option.

One approach is to create stored procedures for all updates, inserts, and deletes (related objects and permissions are discussed later in this chapter); however, even that solution isn't foolproof. If the procedure can be run from within the application, it can be run from a command-line interface such as `ISQL` as well.

Another approach is to have two sets of logins: one for users running front-end query tools, the other for those using applications that are permitted to perform updates. The first set of logins and passwords is known to the users; the second set is based on the user name but known only to the updating applications.

For example, a user `mdoe` with a password `littlelamb` might have an application user name `mdoe_app` and a password `littlelamb_00946`. The login names for the application are visible from `sp_who`, so the passwords need to be difficult to guess. (The password could be derived from the user password and some hashed version of the `uid`. Keeping the password-derivation method secret is critical here.)

This approach to logins and passwords isn't easy. Making it work depends on preventing the users from running `sp_password`, so password administration becomes the administrator's problem. But perseverance can result in a system that's safe from the errors of a persistent but uneducated user.

Password Approaches

Companies use several standard approaches when identifying a password administration plan. These usually fall into one of three categories:

- Password same as login
- General application login and password
- Password independent of login

Whether or not you use a login approach of "SQL Server login = OS/App login," you still must determine whether the password for that login will be dependent or independent of the login.

Password = Login

At many sites, passwords are identical to logins. Realistically, this is as close to having no password as you can get, because the password for a user is the same as the login name. Therefore, a login for user1 has a password of user1. In this approach, it's very easy for a person to find a way to access the server because only a login name must be determined. Many sites also use a standard for naming logins to a system—for example, market01 through market99, with passwords of market01 through market99, respectively. This is the least secure approach to a user password administration (second only to null). It's also one of the least flexible, because login name and password must remain the same, denying the capability of using password expiration (unless integrated/mixed security is being used).

> **NOTE**
>
> When talking to hackers about methods they use to guess passwords and break into systems, most will invariably say that the first password to try is the login name. (After that come the literal words password or secret.)

General Application Login and Password

Other sites may use a general application login for all users of an application. This means that users access an application, and when the application is connected to the database, it does so as a single general user—regardless of the number of connections it opens. This approach results in a severe reduction in the capability of linking activities to users. When sp_who is executed, for example, all user names are the same. This makes it very difficult to track down who executed a certain command.

Fortunately, this approach often enables changing the general user password, depending on whether the application reads its password information from a configuration file or is hard-coded in the application itself. The latter is generally considered bad practice. Anyone with access to the application can attempt to locate the hard-coded password, and changing the password requires recompiling—and potentially redistributing—the code.

Password Independent of Login

This approach is the most secure. Each user has a distinct password not related to the login name in any way. The user can change the password periodically, and the use of the *password expiration interval* forces the issue. This approach is normally selected at sites that have regulations (federal) regarding their applications, or at sites that are worried about unauthorized access to the database.

Because each user has a password and the capacity to change it, access to sp_password is required. Unfortunately, many sites want to keep users shielded from database operations because they aren't usually accustomed to dealing directly with a database. Because of this fact, a command-line interface (ISQL) isn't an acceptable alternative. This normally results in the creation of a user administration module for users to change passwords. This increases overall application complexity somewhat, but it's done to continue to shield users from the database.

This is naturally the preferred approach by secure sites and is recommended if the environment is structured to handle the administrative complexities.

Permissions

Permissions are used to control access within a database. This is accomplished through the use of the grant and revoke statements. Any permission that can be granted can also be revoked, so when the word *grant* is used within this section, it can be thought of in the broader sense of controlling access (granting *or* revoking).

The granting of permissions results in the addition of rows to the sysprotects system table. Each database contains the sysprotects table, which means that permissions are database-specific. Because permissions are granted to database users, not server logins, there's no way to grant general access to a login.

Users

Permissions are used to control access by users of a database. In this context, a user is essentially any uid that exists in the sysusers table. The sysusers table initially contains rows for the database owner (dbo) and the public group (public). Additional users of a database are added with sp_adduser, and additional groups in a database are added with sp_addgroup. Therefore, the list of users to whom permissions can be granted actually contains both users and groups.

Object Permissions

Granting of permissions on objects is performed using the grant command syntax:

```
grant  {all [ privileges] ¦ permission_list }
  on { table_name [ ( column_list ) ]
  ¦ view_name [ ( column_list ) ]
  ¦ stored_procedure_name }
  to{ group_name ¦ user_name }
[ { , {next_user_or group_} } ...]
  [ with grant option ]
```

Revoking of permissions on objects is performed using the revoke command syntax:

```
revoke [ grant option for ]
  {all [ privileges] ¦ permission_list }
  on { table_name [ ( column_list ) ]
  ¦ view_name [ ( column_list ) ]
  ¦ stored_procedure_name }
  to{ group_name ¦ user_name }
[ { , {next_user_or group_} } ...]
  [cascade ]
```

READING sysprotects

When granting or revoking permissions on a table, SQL Server records that information in a database-level table, sysprotects. Every database includes explicit lines granting permission on system tables to public. (As of this writing, there were 18 rows of default system table permissions in the most recent version.)

The following command adds permissions entries:

```
grant all on marketing_table to public
```

This is the contents of sysprotects after the grant statement:

```
select id, uid, action, grantor
from sysprotects
where id = object_id("marketing_table")
go


id         uid   action grantor
_____ ___   ___ ___
144003544  0     151    1
144003544  0     193    1
144003544  0     195    1
144003544  0     196    1
144003544  0     197    1
```

The id column identifies the table in the database.

The uid column indicates the user (or group) ID to whom permission is granted.

The action column specifies the type of action affected by the permission. The action value can be decoded by referring to the spt_values table in the master database.

continues

continued

Permissions actions are identified with the type T. The output that follows lists all the permission action codes:

```
use master
go
select name, number, type
from spt_values
where type = "T"
and number > 0
order by 2
go

name                    number    type
— — — — — — — — — — — —  — — — —   — —
References              151       T
Select                  193       T
Insert                  195       T
Delete                  196       T
Update                  197       T
Create Table            198       T
Create Database         203       T
Grant                   205       T
Revoke                  206       T
Create View             207       T
Create Procedure        222       T
Execute                 224       T
Dump Database           228       T
Create Default          233       T
Dump Transaction        235       T
Create Rule             236       T
```

grantor records the ID of the user who executed the grant statement.

The object owner grants or revokes permissions on objects to control access to objects within a database. These objects include tables, views, and stored procedures. Permissions default to the object owner, which is why when a user creates an object, he doesn't need to grant himself permissions; however, any other user of the system would have to be granted permission on an object.

NOTE

sa object permissions aren't checked. Object permissions never need to be granted to the sa.

The types of permissions that can be granted/revoked for these objects include select, update, insert, delete, references, and execute. select and update can have a column list specified (to control access at the column level), references applies only to tables (and can contain a column list), and execute applies only to procedures. Table 27.1 summarizes how object permissions can be granted.

Table 27.1. Object permissions.

Permission	Specify Columns?	Can Grant On
select	Yes	Tables, views
update	Yes	Tables, views
insert	No	Tables, views
delete	No	Tables, views
references	Yes	Tables
execute	N/A	Stored procedures

select, insert, update, and delete are pretty straightforward. They indicate whether a user can issue that type of command with a table or view listed in the from clause (a normal select or an insert, delete, or update with a join clause) or as the object of the action (update table or view, insert table or view, or delete table or view).

> **NOTE**
>
> text and image columns enable use of the readtext and writetext commands:
>
> ■ The capability of using the writetext command is transferred through update permission.
>
> ■ The capability of using the readtext command is transferred through select permission.

execute permission is granted on a stored procedure to enable a user to execute the procedure. This can have very powerful implications, because a system can be implemented where users are granted access only to procedures, and not to the underlying tables or views.

The references permission is part of SQL 6.0 and later systems, and it applies to the capability of using declarative referential integrity. When implementing declarative referential integrity, the create table or alter table statement can include a references clause to indicate the relationship between tables. This permission needs to be granted only when objects owned by two different users have referential integrity considerations (a user that owns both objects automatically has references permission). It's unlikely that references permission would have to be granted in a production system, because most production systems have all objects owned by the same user name (dbo).

A permission list can contain a comma-delimited list of permissions or the word all (or all privileges). If all is specified, only the permissions that apply to the type of object on which the permission is being granted are actually granted.

To revoke a user's permissions on an object, the `revoke` command is used:

```
revoke select on table from user1
```

The user can revoke the ability to grant `select` on columns by executing this statement:

```
revoke grant option for select on table(column2) from user1
```

Command Permissions

By default, the `dbo` is the only user who can create objects and perform backups. In some environments, users are granted access to these commands. These are called *command permissions*.

> **NOTE**
>
> It's important to differentiate between command and object permissions. *Command permissions* enable users to create objects themselves. This is rarely granted. *Object permissions* enable users to access objects that already exist. This permission must be granted to enable a system to operate.

Command permissions are granted to users by executing the following `grant` syntax:

```
grant  {all [ privileges] | command_list }
  to{ group_name | user_name }
[ { , {next_user_or group } } ...]
```

Here's the syntax for revoking those command permissions:

```
revoke  {all [ privileges] | command_list }
  on { table_name [ ( column_list ) ]
  | view_name [ ( column_list ) ]
  | stored_procedure_name }
  from{ group_name | user_name }
[ { , {next_user_or group_} } ...]
```

Command permissions are granted and revoked to users to control access to certain commands within a database. These commands include the following:

- `create database` (master database only)
- `create default`
- `create procedure`
- `create rule`
- `create table`
- `create view`

These permissions are most often granted in a development environment to enable developers to create objects in the course of developing a system. In a production environment, these permissions aren't usually needed.

> **WARNING**
>
> The `create database` permission usually shouldn't be granted to users. It should be reserved for the sa login, or those logins with `Administrative` permissions using integrated or mixed security.
>
> The `create database` permission should NEVER be granted to the guest user in the master database!

A command list can contain a comma-delimited list of commands or the word `all` (or `all privileges`). If `all` is specified, only those commands that can be executed in that database are granted. This is only an issue with `create database`; you can grant permission to create databases only within the `master` database. Note the following issues about command permissions:

- The creation of databases usually is performed by the system administrator and normally isn't granted.
- The creation of temporary tables is permitted by any user of the server and doesn't need to be specifically granted.

Permission Approaches

The access requirements of tables, views, and stored procedures should be established during the design phase of a system. As each object is identified, the documentation should contain notes on what types of users need what types of access. It's easier to develop an effective permissions plan if this information is gathered in the early stages.

First, the users of a system should be identified. They should be grouped logically, based on job description, department, or responsibility (for example, managers, clerks, marketing personnel, billing personnel, and so forth). Often when systems are developed, there's only a broad knowledge of user classifications—the actual names of the users will be filled in at a later date. In any case, the first step is to determine which logical groups will be using a database.

The next step is to define what access is needed to which tables, views, and procedures by each group, and by the entire database user community as a whole.

> **NOTE**
>
> Clearly, any approach to permissions is deeply associated with a specific login and user approach. Permissions are granted to either users or groups. Most permission plans focus on controlling access to groups, particularly when large numbers of users are involved.

It's generally easiest to grant broad permissions and then limit access to specified users. The easiest way to implement broad permissions is to grant them to groups. Users assigned to a group automatically have the permissions granted to that group. Recall that a group can be any group that's specifically added to a database or the system group public (which includes all users of a database).

public

The public group is a special group to which all users belong, even when they're specifically added to a user-defined group. It's important to remember that the guest user is, of course, also a member of the public group. Granting permissions to public allows anyone who has access to the database to receive that permission.

If individual users are added to a database (not guest), there's substantial security at the database level. If the database-level security is satisfactory, granting to public allows all the users in the database to perform those functions specified. Using public is a good approach even when there are several user-defined groups in a database.

Often, several groups exist requiring special access to a select number of tables. Most other tables are available to all users of a database.

Take the example of a database with 100 tables and 10 user-defined groups. Granting select permission on all the tables to all users can be accomplished by granting to each user-defined group (10 grant statements) for each table. If all groups need select access to all tables, it's easier to grant select permission to public for each table. This requires only one grant per table. If one group needs insert, update, and delete access as well, additional permission can be granted on that table to that specific group.

public and guest

As indicated previously, the public group contains all users, even the guest user. Combining the addition of a guest user to a database and the use of public as a means for defining permissions should be used only by those sites that are extremely confident with the security enforced at the server level. If a person gains access to the server, that user will then have access to any database that has a guest user defined and consequently can perform any activities granted to public.

Addition of the guest user bypasses control of access at the database level. However, permissions can be granted to public and then revoked from guest to curb the activities the guest user can perform.

> **WARNING**
>
> Permission-related statements combining grant and revoke must be executed in the correct order! SQL Server permissions obey one simple rule:
>
> *Whatever happened last takes effect.*
>
> If a permission is revoked from guest and then granted to public, guest receives the permission because guest is a member of public. There's no hierarchy of permissions. That is, user permissions don't take priority over group permissions, or vice versa.
>
> The safest way to manage permissions is to maintain a script of all the permissions for a particular database. Every time a change must be made, the permission statement should be inserted into the correct part of the script and the entire script should be re-executed. In this way, unexpected consequences from grant and revoke statements can be avoided.
>
> Permissions scripts shouldn't be run when users are online, as this could result in permissions being revoked while users are processing. The only safe way to implement this approach during active hours is to run the script in a transaction or set of transactions, with begin tran and commit tran. However, this method can really slow processing dramatically because of locks placed on the system tables.

Granting to User-Defined Groups

Beyond the use of the public group, granting permissions to user-defined groups is the next easiest way to implement a permission strategy. Of course, this approach is often combined with granting to public or to specific users. The approach is to define logically the access that applies only to a specific group and then grant or revoke permissions to that group.

For example, if only the Marketing group needs to be able to perform select, insert, update, and delete on marketing tables, a marketing group can be added, and the following command executed for each of the marketing tables:

```
grant all on <marketing_table> to marketing
```

If there are billing tables that only Billing personnel need all permissions to, a billing group can be added and the following command executed for each of the billing tables:

```
grant all on <billing_table> to billing
```

What if Billing personnel need to select from marketing tables and Marketing personnel need to select from billing tables? select permission can be granted on each table to the appropriate group, or alternatively to the public group:

```
grant select on billing_table to public
grant select on marketing_table to public
```

Granting to Specific Users

Granting permissions to specific users requires the most administration but offers the greatest control. Normally, it isn't used exclusively in a permission strategy because the addition of each new user requires executing individual grant statements for each object in which access is needed. Granting and revoking to users is most commonly used in combination with granting to public or user-specified groups.

For example, suppose that all marketing users can select, insert, and delete on all marketing tables, but only the user super_market_user can update information in the database. In this case, these commands can be executed:

```
grant select, insert, delete on market_table to marketing
grant update on market_table to super_market_user
```

This assumes that the super_market_user is also a member of the marketing group.

Object Dependencies

Many organizations use dependent objects (views, procedures, and triggers) to implement advanced security structure:

- Views can restrict access to specific rows and columns of data.
- Procedures can restrict and validate all data modifications.
- Triggers can perform related updates or update substantive audit records.

In each of these cases, users need access to the dependent object but shouldn't have direct access to the dependent object.

If object ownership is distributed among several database users, implementing any of these types of advanced security is fruitless. For example, in Figure 27.8, John wants to select from a view owned by Bob, but Mary owns the base table.

The permissions required for this scheme include the following:

```
[Mary:]grant select on basetable to bob
```

```
[Bob:]grant select on viewname to john
```

```
[Mary:]grant select on basetable to john
```

The final grant statement, in which Mary permits John to read the table directly, undermines the effect of a view intended to enforce security.

If both the base object and dependent object are owned by a single user, the owner needs to grant permission to the user only for the dependent object. Because there's no change in ownership between the dependent and base objects, permissions aren't checked.

In Figure 27.9, Mary owns both objects and John wants access to the view.

FIGURE 27.8.

When the owner of an object and a dependent object are different, permissions must be granted explicitly on both objects.

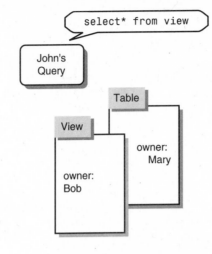

FIGURE 27.9.

When the owner of an object and a dependent object are the same, permissions on the base object aren't checked.

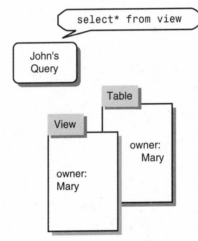

This scheme requires only a single permission statement:

```
[Mary:]grant select on viewname to john
```

Because Mary owns both objects, John's permissions are checked only at the view level and not at the table level. With no change in ownership, permissions aren't checked.

Summary

SQL Server security is implemented in four layers: the operating system, the SQL server, the database layer, and the SQL Server object. Each allows greater or lesser control, depending on your requirements.

SQL Server offers a variety of ways to control access to data. Server login and database user approaches affect the way in which a permissions strategy is implemented.

At the object level, most sites grant broad permissions and grant or revoke specific access as needed to minimize the administrative overhead in implementing a permissions plan. This usually involves granting to `public` or a user-defined group, and then revoking or granting specific permissions to a user-defined group or a specific user.

Database Logging and Recovery

28

SQL Server uses a write-ahead log and automatic forward recovery to maintain up-to-the-transaction data integrity, even in the case of erratic or unexpected server shutdowns. This chapter explores how the SQL Server transaction log works and how it manages recovery. You'll understand commits and checkpoints, and how the server manages data integrity through various server events.

SQL Server's use of terms may differ from your prior experience with other database applications or transaction processing systems. For example, you may think of recovery or disaster recovery as the administrative process of getting back to work after a catastrophe, but it means something quite different in the SQL Server world. You need to nail down the meaning of the crucial SQL Server terms first:

- A *transaction* is a unit of work. Transactions can be long or short, and they can involve changes to millions of rows of data or only one. SQL Server promises that every transaction, no matter how long or complex, will run to completion or will be completely reversed if it can't be completed for any reason. The transaction log is the component of the system responsible for transactional data integrity.

- *Recovery* is the automatic process of reconciling the log and the data. Recovery occurs when the server is started. This chapter examines the recovery process in detail.

- A *backup* is a physical copy of the database or transaction log. The SQL Server term for a backup is a *dump*, and dump is the Transact-SQL command used to initiate backups of either the database or the transaction log.

- *Restoration* is the process of taking a backup of the database from storage and copying it back onto the server.

Backup and restoring are the major topics of Chapter 30, "SQL Server Database Backup and Restoration."

What Is a Transaction?

A *transaction* is a set of operations to be completed at one time, as though they were a single operation. A transaction must be fully completed or not performed at all. Standard examples of transactions include bank transfers (withdraw $500 from checking, add $500 to savings) and order entry systems (write an order for five widgets, remove five widgets from inventory).

All SQL statements are inherently transactions, from grant and create statements to the data modification statements—insert, update, and delete. Consider the following update example:

```
update titles
set price = price * 1.02
```

This statement modifies all rows in the titles table. SQL Server guarantees that, regardless of the size of the titles table, all rows will be processed or no rows will be processed. What if half the rows are modified and the server fails? When the server comes back up (but before the database is available for use), it rolls back the incomplete transaction, removing all evidence that it ever began. That's part of the recovery process, which is discussed later in this chapter.

SQL Server also includes transaction-control syntax to group sets of SQL statements into single logical work units:

- `begin transaction` starts a unit of work.
- `commit transaction` completes a unit of work.
- `rollback transaction` cancels a unit of work.

The following example enters an order and depletes inventory in a single transaction:

```
begin transaction
   update inventory
      set in_stock = in_stock - 5
      where item_num = "14141"
   insert orders (cust_num, item_num, qty)
      values ("ABC151", "14141", 5)
commit transaction
```

SQL Server guarantees that the inventory won't change unless the order is also entered.

Look at the same example, but with the `rollback transaction` statement instead of `commit`:

```
begin transaction
   update inventory
      set in_stock = in_stock - 5
      where item_num = "14141"
   insert orders (cust_num, item_num, qty)
      values ("ABC151", "14141", 5)
rollback transaction
```

When the server encounters the `rollback` statement, it discards all changes in the transaction and returns the data to the state it was in before work began.

This chapter examines the mechanisms used by SQL Server to manage data integrity (both `rollback` and `commit`) in transactions.

What Is the Transaction Log?

The *transaction log* is a database-level system table, called `syslogs`. The `syslogs` table contains a sequential list of all modifications to every object in the database, as well as any information required to maintain data integrity.

The transaction log is

- Shared by all users of a database
- Modified in cache and only flushed to disk at commit time
- Written first (a write-ahead log)

The log is not

- Usefully manipulated or read with SQL
- Readable in any useful format

NOTE

There are now third-party utilities that access the log, allowing some direct interaction with the log and providing some measure of "undo" functions. However, nothing in the standard SQL Server suite allows you to interact directly with the log.

A Write-Ahead Log

Write-ahead means that the log is written first, before the data itself, anytime that a query modifies data.

When modifying data, the server takes the following steps:

1. Write a `begin tran` record in the log (in cache).
2. Record the modification in the log (in cache).
3. Perform the modification to the data (in cache).
4. Write a `commit tran` record to the log (in cache).
5. Flush all "dirty" (modified) log pages to disk.

NOTE

In addition to standard SQL data modification statements (`insert`, `update`, `delete`), all `create` statements, permissions statements (`grant` and `revoke`), and many system stored procedures (such as `sp_adduser` and `sp_bindrule`) change the contents of system tables. The server logs each of these data modifications as well.

Commits

A commit flushes all *dirty* (modified) log pages for that database from cache to disk. Figure 28.1 shows the state of the data after the transaction is complete and the commit has taken place.

The server does all the work in RAM first, before making changes to disk, to improve processing speed. When the process is complete, the only work that is written to disk is any change to the log. However, RAM is volatile. If the server goes down unexpectedly, or if someone pulls the plug out of the wall, the changes to data that are stored only in memory are lost, right? That's where the transaction log earns its keep.

Remember that each modification has been recorded in the log. At recovery time (after the server goes down and is restarted), committed transactions that haven't been written to the data area are rolled forward into the data. This is called *forward recovery*, or *roll forward*. If the commit tran has been executed and the write to the log has been made to disk, the server guarantees that the data can be recovered when the server goes down.

FIGURE 28.1.

The commit process only writes log changes to disk.

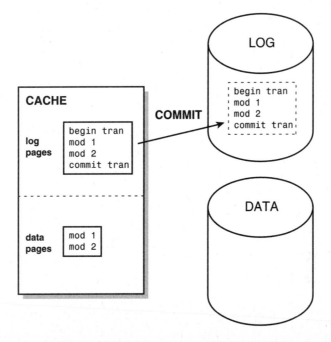

It's interesting to note here that the log is really the part of the database that matters when it comes to recovery and restoring. If the disk on which the data is stored catches fire, you can use the information in the log, in combination with your backups, to restore the system up to the last complete transaction. On the other hand, if the log disk gets wet while you're putting out the fire, you will be able to restore only up to the time of the last backup.

If you have to choose between mirroring logs and mirroring data, mirror the logs.

At recovery time, uncommitted transactions (begin tran markers without a commit tran) are rolled back. All data modifications associated with the transaction are undone. This is *rollback*. But how do uncommitted transactions get into the log in the first place?

Frequently, when transactions overlap, the commit tran flushes any uncommitted—as well as committed—work to disk. In that way, the "dirty" log pages are copied to disk even though the transactions associated with those log pages are incomplete. This action doesn't commit the transactions; it merely writes the pages to disk. The transaction is still uncommitted at this point. Uncommitted work can be identified by a begin tran entry in the log with no

774

corresponding `commit tran`. Figure 28.2 illustrates a `commit` that writes both committed and uncommitted work to the log.

FIGURE 28.2.

The commit process writes all dirty log pages for the database to disk, including those with incomplete transactions.

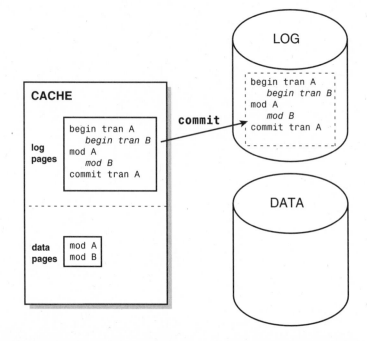

Why write both committed and uncommitted work with every commit? Keep in mind that SQL Server always performs I/O at the page level or higher. Entries in `syslogs` are ordered by a consecutive timestamp value, so transactions that are processing concurrently are intermingled on a single page.

Remember also that the commit process is the crucial bottleneck for an online system. The user is waiting and pages are locked until the commit is complete. By writing out commits at the page level without first weeding out any uncommitted work, the server can streamline commits. If the uncommitted work is subsequently rolled back, the server can record that fact in a later row in `syslogs`.

Checkpoints

The log is the part of the database that keeps track of data integrity, transaction control, and recoverability. For the server to guarantee data integrity, it only needs to make certain that the log is written to disk. However, if enough transactions pile up in the log without being recorded on the data disk as well, after the server goes down it will take weeks for it to recover all the committed transactions. When does the data get updated while the server is running? During a checkpoint.

A *checkpoint* writes all dirty pages for the database from cache to disk, starting with the log (see Figure 28.3). A checkpoint reduces the amount of work the server needs to do at recovery time.

FIGURE 28.3.

The checkpoint process writes all dirty pages for the database, starting with the log.

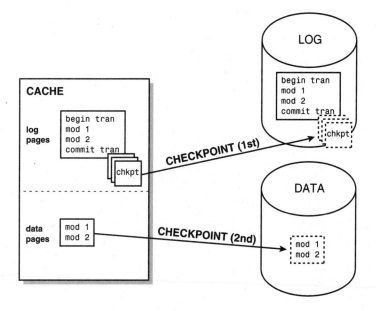

A checkpoint occurs under three different circumstances:

- The dbo issues the checkpoint command.
- The server needs additional cache space.
- The server recovery interval has been exceeded.

Before the checkpoint starts, the server first notes in the log that a checkpoint has been performed in the database. The checkpoint marker enables the server to assume that all committed work recorded in the log prior to the checkpoint marker is reflected in the data.

If long-running transactions are underway when the checkpoint begins, uncommitted work may be written not only to the log but also to the data (see Figure 28.4). The recovery process uses the checkpoint marker in the log to identify work in incomplete transactions that has been written to the data disk by a checkpoint.

FIGURE 28.4.

The checkpoint marker indicates where the last update to the data took place.

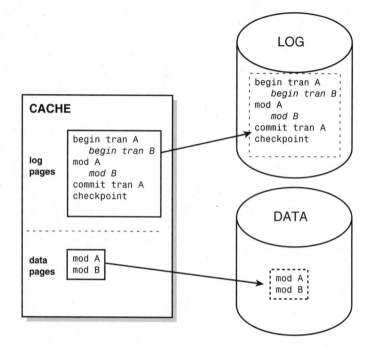

Recovery

Recovery is an automatic process to verify that all completed transactions are in the data and incomplete transactions are removed from the data. Recovery guarantees that any completed transaction is reflected in the data. During the recovery process, the server does the following:

- Checks `syslogs` for each database, backing out incomplete transactions and rolling forward completed transactions not in the data.
- Checkpoints the database.
- Drops and re-creates `tempdb`.

Recovery Interval

With the `recovery interval` configuration option, the sa can set the approximate amount of time per database that he or she will wait for the SQL Server to start up. For example, to set the server recovery interval to 12 minutes per database, use the following:

```
sp_configure "recovery interval", 12
reconfigure
```

`recovery interval` is a dynamic configuration setting, so the new value will take effect as soon as you issue the `reconfigure` statement. Here's how it works. Once a minute, one of the system processes listed in sp_who (which always seems to be stuck on CHECKPOINT SLEEP) wakes up and examines each database in turn. Based on the amount of work recorded in the log for each database, the process determines whether it will take longer than the recovery interval to restore the database. If so, the system process issues an automatic checkpoint. Finally, if the database is set for truncate log on checkpoint, the system process truncates the log.

The length of time it will take your server to recover completely after an unexpected shutdown depends on your recovery interval and the number of databases on the server. The worst-case answer is that it could take the number of minutes attained by multiplying recovery interval times the number of databases. (In other words, 12-minute recovery interval × 20 databases = 4 hours!)

You will seldom encounter the worst case, but even if you do you can access your own database as soon as recovery is complete. (Databases are recovered in order by dbid.)

> **NOTE**
>
> Don't forget that when you shut down the server normally, a checkpoint will be issued automatically for the database. However, if you issue shutdown with nowait (this command is seldom used), the system skips the checkpoint and shuts down immediately. Server recovery is much faster after a normal shutdown than after a shutdown with nowait.

It's tempting to set the recovery interval low to ensure a quick recovery after any shutdown, but the checkpoint process creates overhead when you're running a high volume of transactions through the server. Set the configuration setting to the highest tolerable value.

Recovery Flags

Use the recovery flags setting with sp_configure to display the names of transactions during recovery. If you use transaction names in SQL code, the names will be displayed in the error log if the transaction is rolled back or brought forward during recovery:

```
sp_configure "recovery flags", 1
reconfigure
```

> **NOTE**
>
> Restart the server after this option to have the recovery flags take effect. During the first restart, transaction names won't be listed. Subsequent restarts will display transaction names as they're processed.

Setting recovery flags enables you to determine exactly which work actually made it into the server before a shutdown. To make good use of the error log information, there must be a correlation between SQL Server transaction names and batch-unit or work-unit identifiers in the manual process. For example, if the batch number is 17403, the transaction name might be B_17403. Pass the transaction name to the server with the begin tran statement, as follows:

```
begin tran B_17403
    ...
commit tran
```

When the Transaction Log Fills Up

If the transaction log fills for any reason, all data modifications to the database will fail immediately. Most standard maintenance measures (dump the log, resize the log) will fail as well. The only reliable way to clear the log is to issue the dump tran ... with no_log statement and dump the entire database.

Summary

Transactions ensure consistency of database integrity to manage simultaneous updates and to ensure recovery after a server shutdown. All SQL statements are transactions themselves, and many SQL statements can be combined into a larger transaction.

You need to manage the transaction log, either with thresholds or by regularly monitoring the amount of available space in the log.

DBCC

29

Ask five SQL Server DBAs about how they use the SQL Server database consistency checker (dbcc) and you will probably get five different answers. One might use dbcc to tune performance while another might argue that dbcc is a critical component of backing up a database. Another might use dbcc to assess data fragmentation and index correctness. dbcc is a jack of all trades, allowing DBAs and system administrators to improve the efficiency and reliability of SQL Server databases.

Broadly speaking, dbcc performs the following functions:

- Identifies table and index corruption. As with any database, SQL Server tables occasionally become corrupted. dbcc identifies these tables and indexes.

- Ensures that SQL Server pages are properly allocated. Less dramatic than corruption (but ultimately as destructive), SQL Server page allocation can become inconsistent, normally due to some other system problem.

- Provides access to performance statistics in four major categories: I/O, cache usage, network, and read-ahead. You can use these statistics to develop tuning strategies.

- Shows memory configuration and usage for SQL Server.

- Identifies the oldest open transaction on SQL Server. Databases using extensive transaction logging sometimes encounter problems with the logs failing to clear. Knowing the oldest open transaction on the system can help identify the cause of the problem transaction.

- Shrinks databases to the minimum possible size. Despite an efficient database sizing effort, some SQL Server databases never achieve their estimated size. dbcc promises a tool to shrink the database to its minimum size.

- Shows and corrects log space usage. Incorrect log usage statistics can cause SQL Server to fail. One dbcc command ensures accurate log usage statistics.

- Turns switches ("trace flags") on or off, controlling the behavior of the server.

A General Word of Warning

Although dbcc can be a useful tool, the command should generally be used only by experienced users, typically a dbo or sa. In fact, many dbcc commands can be run only by one or both of these users. Other commands should be run only in single-user mode to avoid unreliable reporting from dbcc.

The reason for this caution is obvious. dbcc makes alterations to the database, including actually dropping the entire database. Running the command in single-user mode ensures that other users won't experience unpredictable application behavior.

Most SQL Server sites will have two notable exceptions to this cautious approach. The first is the use of dbcc checkdb and dbcc checktable. These two commands utilize shared locks in order to validate the structure of SQL Server tables and indexes. For this reason, DBAs should use dbcc to validate database structures before system backups. The second exception to this rule is dbcc DLLName (free). This command frees the memory allocated to a specific DLL. Developers utilizing extended stored procedures, such as e-mail routines, should consider using this dbcc command to return any memory used by the DLL back to SQL Server.

> **NOTE**
>
> A note on capitalization: It's *almost* customary to capitalize many SQL reserved words in books and other reference materials. This is especially true with the dbcc statement.
>
> I wish to resist this custom. Uppercase is loud and unpleasant and—where typography allows—completely unnecessary. Throughout this chapter, dbcc commands are presented in lowercase.

Table 29.1 provides a brief summary of the functions available with dbcc.

Table 29.1. Maintenance tools.

Function	Description
dbcc showcontig(*database-name*)	Returns statistics on disk fragmentation.
dbcc checkdb(*database-name*)	Reports on consistency in a specified database.
dbcc checktable(*table-name*)	Reports on consistency in a specified table.
dbcc checktable(syslogs)	Reports on log usage in a specified database.
dbcc checkcatalog(*database-name*)	Reports on system catalog consistency in a specified database.
dbcc newalloc(*database-name*)	Reports the allocation unit content in a specified database.
dbcc page(*database-name, pagenum, print option,cache, logical*)	Reports the contents of a specified page.
dbcc pglinkage(*database-id, start, number, print option, target, order*)	Shows page linkages for the specified chain.
dbcc fix_al (*database-name*)	Repairs certain errors in a specified database.
dbcc dbrepair(*database-name, dropdb*)	Drops the specified database.
dbcc shrinkdb(*database-name [, size-in-pgs]*)	Shrinks the specified database down to the requested size. Also reports the minimum size of the specified database.

continues

Table 29.1. continued

Function	Description
dbcc opentran (*database-name*)	Reports the oldest open transaction in a specified database.
dbcc updateusage(*database-name*, *table-name*,*index-id*)	Updates inconsistencies in sysindexes for accurate usage statistics from SQL Server.
Performance Tools	
dbcc memusage ()	Reports on three components of SQL Server memory.
dbcc sqlperf (lrustats)	Reports statistics for cache usage.
dbcc sqlperf (iostats)	Reports statistics for I/O performance.
dbcc sqlperf (netstats)	Reports statistics for network usage.
dbcc pintable(*database-id*, *tableid*)	"Pins" a table into cache.

Assessing Data Fragmentation

Many DOS users are familiar with the concept of disk fragmentation and reorganization through the use of tools like Norton Utilities. With a DOS file, pieces (*fragments*) of the file are scattered on the disk drive as a result of creating and updating the file. Similarly, SQL Server pages belonging to tables and indexes become fragmented across many extents and allocation units as users modify data with insert and update commands. On-line transaction processing (OLTP) systems are the most prone to fragmentation, but any system where data is modified is in danger of fragmenting.

Heavily fragmented tables can reduce the efficiency of read-ahead caching and advanced disk caching systems, increasing response time for large table scans. Remember that SQL Server rows are stored in data pages, a physical storage area. Pages, in turn, reside in a 16KB extent, consisting of eight 2KB pages, all allocated to a single table. When a row is added to a full page in a table with a clustered index, SQL Server must split the page and change the linked page chain to include a new page which is out of physical order (see Figure 29.1), except where the split page is the last page in the table. Over time, the table storage becomes less and less contiguous as pages split after many insert and update statements. (For more on the maintenance of physical structures during data maintenance operations, see Chapter 11, "Understanding SQL Server Storage Structures.")

FIGURE 29.1.

The linked list in this diagram becomes fragmented when the value 65 causes an already full page to split into two pages. The location of the new page will be at the next available location, which could be in the same 16KB extent, elsewhere on the same disk, or even on another disk.

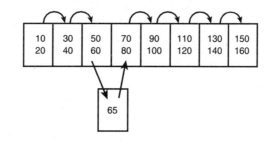

dbcc showcontig

dbcc showcontig analyzes the fragmentation of a table or index. To use the command, provide the id of a table and, optionally, the indid of an index:

```
dbcc showcontig(object_id)

dbcc showcontig(object_id, index_id)
```

You can pass a variable for the object_id and index_id, as in this example from the bigpubs database:

```
declare @id int
select @id = object_id("sales")
dbcc showcontig (@id)
```

By storing the ID in the variable and passing it to the dbcc command, you avoid having to know or type the horrible things. Here's what showcontig reported for the sales table:

```
DBCC SHOWCONTIG scanning 'sales' table...

(1 row(s) affected)

[SHOW_CONTIG - SCAN ANALYSIS]
- - - - - - - - - - - - - - - - - - - - - - - - - - - - - - - - - - - -
Table: 'sales' (432004570)  Indid: 1  dbid:6
TABLE level scan performed.
- Pages Scanned...............................: 8914
- Extent Switches.............................: 1381
- Avg. Pages per Extent.......................: 8.0
- Scan Density [Best Count:Actual Count].......: 80.68% [1114:1382]
- Avg. Bytes free per page....................: 973.1
- Avg. Page density (full)....................: 51.68%
- Overflow Pages..............................: 0
- Disconnected Overflow Pages.................: 0
DBCC execution completed. If DBCC printed error messages, see your System
Administrator.
```

Let's step through the output item by item, understanding what each statistic means, and what it *indicates* regarding fragmentation:

- ▓ `Pages Scanned` is the number of pages in the page chain. In this case, there are 8914 pages in the table.

- ▓ `Extent Switches` indicates how many times the search for a new page required SQL Server to read from a new extent. With eight pages per extent, SQL Server needed to change extents only 1381 times, or about once every 6 pages. Defragmenting a table could reduce the number of extent switches, but the `sales` table isn't very fragmented.

- ▓ `Avg. Pages per Extent` displays how many pages per extent are *in use*. While SQL Server allocates whole extents to an object, the object will use pages only as needed, leaving others reserved but not used. Pages that have been used can empty later as rows are deleted or `update` activities cause them to move. All these factors could contribute to a low number of pages in use per extent. Defragmenting a table could increase the number of average pages per extent to a maximum value of 8. The `sales` table is already using an average of 8 pages per extent, which is optimal.

- ▓ `Scan Density` measures how efficiently the table can be scanned by reading each page with its neighboring pages in the extent. This measures fragmentation on a scale of 0 to 100, where 0 indicates total fragmentation and 100 indicates none at all. At best, the `sales` table could be scanned with 1114 extent switches. Currently, a table scan requires 1382 extent switches. The table has 80.68 percent scan density (1114/1382), which is high enough that the table doesn't warrant additional concern at this time.

  At what level should you consider defragmenting a table? That depends on how the table is used, whether most reads are already from cache, how frequently the table is scanned or accessed with a clustered index, and the availability of read-ahead threads to handle large-block I/O. As a starting point, you might consider reorganizing a table when scan density is below 50 percent.

- ▓ `Avg. Bytes free per page` indicates the average number of free bytes on scanned pages. There are a number of reasons why pages would have a large amount of free space, including the use of a `fillfactor` when creating an index, or a table with fairly long rows (greater than about 750 bytes per row). More common reasons for a table including a lot of space are deletion of rows from those pages, or page splits caused during `insert` or `update` operations. The `sales` table averages 973.1 bytes free per page, meaning that there's a lot of room for growth within the individual pages.

- ▓ `Avg. Page Density` indicates as a percentage how much free space is available per page. This statistic is derived by dividing the available bytes free per page by the maximum bytes stored on a page, 2014 (this is a constant value for all data and index pages), and then subtracting that number from 100 percent. The `sales` table is 51.68 percent full.

  A low value for page density means that the table isn't currently using space efficiently: SQL Server needs to perform more logical and physical work to retrieve a specific number of rows. On the other hand, if the page density is low, as new rows are added there will be fewer page splits and less disruption of the page chain. So, if all the data is already in the table, you want this number to be high. If you're adding a substantial amount of data to the table and the table isn't very fragmented, it's probably good if the number is low.

> **NOTE**
>
> Over time, a table with a clustered index that's receiving a high volume of insert, update, and delete operations will tend to level out at pages that are about 75 percent full.

■ Overflow Pages are created when duplicate rows are added to a table with a clustered index, causing a page to split. Overflow pages can be repaired by re-creating the clustered index. (See Chapter 11 for a complete discussion of overflow pages.) The sales table contains no overflow pages because the clustered index doesn't permit duplicate rows.

■ Disconnected Overflow Pages is a statistic for use only by SQL Server. (I've never seen or heard of disconnected overflow pages anywhere else, but I suspect that their existence might indicate a bug in the SQL Server software.)

Here's what you get if you run dbcc showcontig on the first nonclustered index (indid = 2) on the sales table:

```
declare @id int
select @id = object_id("sales")
dbcc showcontig (@id, 2)

DBCC SHOWCONTIG scanning 'sales' table...
(1 row(s) affected)
[SHOW_CONTIG - SCAN ANALYSIS]
- - - - - - - - - - - - - - - - - - - - - - - - - - - - - -
Table: 'sales' (432004570)  Indid: 2  dbid:6
LEAF level scan performed.
- Pages Scanned...............................: 2181
- Extent Switches.............................: 2180
- Avg. Pages per Extent.......................: 8.0
- Scan Density [Best Count:Actual Count].......: 12.52% [273:2181]
- Avg. Bytes free per page....................: 621.5
- Avg. Page density (full)....................: 69.14%
- Overflow Pages..............................: 0
- Disconnected Overflow Pages.................: 0
```

First, note that the scan occurs at the leaf level of the index. Extent switches are almost one-to-one with pages scanned. The way that the index was built required constant page splitting, resulting in the extremely low scan density (12.5 percent). You probably can't fix the fragmentation in the index, but you shouldn't be surprised if scan performance against the index is slower (page for page) than scan performance against the table itself. (This doesn't mean that an index scan will take longer than a table scan. On the contrary, because the index is only a quarter of the size of the table, it will take much less time to scan the index. But the raw physical retrieval speed for the index—measured in page reads per second—will probably be slower than for the table.)

Resolving Fragmentation

As mentioned in the preceding section, because of the numerous page splits generated as indexes are built, you probably can't reduce the fragmentation of the index leaf level, but you can reduce fragmentation of a table when its scan density is low. Simply rebuilding the clustered index with the `sorted_data` option should result in a table with less fragmentation and more contiguous page chains. You might also experiment with extracting and reloading the contents of a table with `bcp`.

Detecting and Resolving Database Corruption

The most common use of `dbcc` is to detect and resolve database corruption. During the normal course of operations, page allocations can become inaccurate, and tables and indexes can occasionally be corrupted. `dbcc` provides an effective means to ensure the consistency of your data before a small problem balloons into a completely corrupted database.

There are seven `dbcc` commands for detecting database corruption:

- `dbcc checkdb` checks table and index page chains and pointers for every table in the database
- `dbcc checktable` checks table and index page chains and pointers for a single table
- `dbcc checkcatalog` verifies the consistency of system tables
- `dbcc newalloc` checks page allocations for a database
- `dbcc textall` and `dbcc textalloc` check page allocations for text and image data
- `dbcc checkident` makes sure that all identity values are greater than the largest value in the table

Two `dbcc` commands help you resolve database corruption:

- `dbcc fix_al` can resolve some allocation problems
- `dbcc dbrepair` can (when all else fails) drop a suspect database from the SQL Server

Many DBAs use `checkdb` as a regular part of their backup routines to prevent `dump database` from backing up corrupt pages. To ensure that a backup is correct, the system administrator must run `dbcc checkdb` before dumping a database. This section looks at the use of these commands and provides some pointers on how to respond to the information they report.

NOTE

Once you understand how to use these dbcc commands, you should turn to the section on the Database Maintenance Plan Wizard in Chapter 35, "The MS SQL Server Distributed Management Framework." There you learn how dbcc commands fit into an overall database maintenance strategy.

dbcc checkdb

dbcc checkdb checks pointers and data pages on every table and index in a database to ensure proper linkage. checkdb reviews table and index page chains and ensures that index pointers point to the correct pages in each table.

Here's how to execute dbcc checkdb:

```
dbcc checkdb(database_name[, noindex])
```

Here's an example of the output you can expect from dbcc checkdb:

```
dbcc checkdb (bigpubs)

Checking bigpubs
WARNING: NOINDEX option of 'CHECKDB' being used, checks on non-system
indexes will be skipped
Checking 1
The total number of data pages in this table is 4.
Table has 71 data rows.
Checking 2
The total number of data pages in this table is 4.
Table has 53 data rows.
Checking 3
The total number of data pages in this table is 11.
Table has 285 data rows.
Checking 4
The total number of data pages in this table is 1.
Table has 29 data rows.
Checking 5
The total number of data pages in this table is 22.
Table has 142 data rows.
Checking 6
The total number of data pages in this table is 3.
Table has 23 data rows.
Checking 7
The total number of data pages in this table is 1.
Table has 3 data rows.
Checking 8
The total number of data pages in this table is 1.
*** NOTICE:  Space used on the log segment is 0.00 Mbytes, 0.01.
*** NOTICE:  Space free on the log segment is 20.48 Mbytes, 99.99.
Table has 28 data rows.
Checking 9
The total number of data pages in this table is 2.
```

```
Table has 152 data rows.
...
Checking 32003145
The total number of data pages in this table is 8.
Table has 172 data rows.
Checking 128003487
The total number of data pages in this table is 1.
Table has 26 data rows.
Checking 208003772
The total number of data pages in this table is 55.
Table has 537 data rows.
Checking 304004114
The total number of data pages in this table is 8.
Table has 331 data rows.
Checking 384004399
The total number of data pages in this table is 543.
Table has 16067 data rows.
Checking 432004570
The total number of data pages in this table is 8914.
Table has 168725 data rows.
...
Checking 1568008617
The total number of data pages in this table is 1.
Table has 2 data rows.
```

For each table (including system tables), checkdb reports the number of data pages and the number of rows. (This example output has been truncated to save trees.) It also reports any errors found in the page pointers and page chains. (More on these errors in the next section.)

Notice the additional information about the syslogs table (object_id 8). This information is reported only if the log is on its own segment. Also notice the very last message. The output from every dbcc command ends in this message, which you should ignore (and which I will omit from the rest of the examples).

The noindex option skips checking nonclustered indexes, which is by far the process' most time-consuming part. If there are no errors, there's no difference in the output from dbcc checkdb with versus without the no_index option. But the time to run is considerably different. The full version of checkdb took 28 minutes to check the consistency of the bigpubs database on my system (a Pentium with fairly fast disks). With the noindex option, it took only 29 *seconds!*

NOTE

If you're using a server with more than one CPU, this is one place where you should see dramatic performance improvements. SQL Server 6.5 spawns separate threads for each nonclustered index so that it can perform the integrity checks on each index *in parallel.*

Identifying and Repairing Corrupt Databases

checkdb is most often used to detect *potential* problems with a database or its underlying tables. Because checkdb can run for long periods of time (depending on the physical size of the database), problems with specific tables should be addressed with dbcc checktable. At times, of course, an entire database is corrupt. Often, this situation relates to the corruption of system catalogs or a physical problem with the server. dbcc checkdb identifies both database and table corruption problems. Following is a list of database corruption messages (for specific problems relating to tables and their related indexes, refer to dbcc checktable).

Attempt to fetch logical page # in database #. S belongs to object #, not to object #. (Message 605)

This error message implies database corruption, but isn't always accurate. Typically, there's a problem with the second object, such as a damaged page chain. This message may appear without any real corruption. To verify that the page is damaged, run dbcc checkalloc. If no errors are reported, ignore message 605. If errors are reported, load the entire database from a backup.

The next two messages aren't reported exclusively by dbcc, but regular use of dbcc can avoid them.

Database S cannot be opened - it has been marked SUSPECT by recovery. The SA can drop the database with dbcc. (Message 926)

The most feared of all error messages, this one does more than imply database corruption—it flags the database as corrupt and blocks further use. You need to drop the database, and you can't use drop database. Instead, you need to use dbcc dbrepair. For more information on this message, see the section "dbcc dbrepair," later in this chapter.

Database corrupt: The last checkpoint in Sysdatabases is incorrect. Syslogs recorded a different checkpoint.

This error message isn't as dramatic as it sounds, occurring only when the row in sysdatabases hasn't been updated to reflect the latest checkpoint. To resolve this situation, reboot the server and continue its usage normally. This situation doesn't affect SQL Server performance.

Notes:

- dbcc checkdb can be run by only sa or dbo.

- dbcc checkdb(database-name, noindex) runs the same check as checkdb but ignores all indexes. This is useful when you want to perform a quick check on a database with a large number of indexes or very large tables, but you should still check indexes at a later time.

- The time required to run dbcc checkdb varies with the size of the database, because checkdb walks through the database page by page. Establish some benchmarks for your system early on so that you know how long the process should take. Later you can assess whether the command is taking a reasonable amount of time. If checkdb seems to be taking longer than usual, try running `dbcc checktable` to determine whether a specific table is causing a problem.

■ `dbcc checkdb` will often report a page count discrepancy between a table and `syslogs`. This occurs because not all logged operations cause `sysindexes` to be updated. While this condition doesn't cause the database to function incorrectly, it can prevent a DBA from accurately validating the state of a database. To correct this condition, simply run a checkpoint in the specified database:

```
use database-name
go
checkpoint
go
```

■ Beware of databases with transaction logs on the same device as data. Under this circumstance, filling the transaction logs can cause the page count discrepancy to remain even after running a checkpoint.

dbcc checktable

Like `checkdb`, `dbcc checktable` performs logical checks on pages, pointers, and offsets and reports any discrepancies. The difference, of course, is that `dbcc checktable` checks a single table (instead of all the tables in the database), allowing the DBA to break down the work required to perform integrity checks into smaller units.

`dbcc checktable` must be run from the relevant database. You must specify the name of the table, and you can control whether nonclustered indexes will be checked. Here's the syntax for the command:

```
use database-name
go
dbcc checktable(table-name[, noindex ¦ index_id])
go
```

This example checks the integrity of the `stores` table in the `bigpubs` database:

```
use bigpubs
go
dbcc checktable (stores)
go

Checking stores
The total number of data pages in this table is 543.
Table has 16067 data rows.
```

By specifying an `index_id`, you can direct `checktable` to look only at that index of the table (skipping other indexes and the table itself):

```
use bigpubs
go
dbcc checktable (titles, 2)
go
```

Identifying and Repairing Corrupt Tables or Indexes

Various errors are reported by dbcc checktable and checkdb. Following are the most common messages indicating some type of corruption on the server, the likely causes, and some approaches you could consider.

```
Table Corrupt: A page is linked in more than one chain; check this page:page
number=%ld allocation status=%d. (Error 2502)
```

A page in a given table or index is assigned to more than one page chain, potentially resulting in inaccurate result sets. Typically, pages participating in multiple chains result from a previous problem with the database.

You can use dbcc page to determine the actual table where the page was originally allocated (see the section "dbcc page," later in this chapter). If the page is part of a large transactional table, you should probably restore the entire database because this inconsistency may also appear in other tables. If the page is part of a smaller lookup table, you may be able to avoid the full database restore (although that continues to be the best option). If the problem occurs with a system table (identified by an object ID of a number less than 100), restore the database from a backup immediately.

```
Table Corrupt: The index id in alloc page does not match the index id in Sysindexes
(alloc page#=%ld; index id in alloc %ld; index id in Systemindexes=%d) (Error
2504).
```

The mapping of the extent to which the index belongs disagrees with the sysindexes table. Again, this condition can result in incorrect result sets being returned from SQL Server. Run dbcc newalloc in single-user mode. This problem often appears when running dbcc with users on the system, and may in fact be meaningless. If not, determine which object "owns" the problem. Again, if the object ID is less than 100, immediately restore the entire database. If the object is an index, simply dropping and re-creating the index should solve the problem.

Identifying Missing Objects

SQL Server uses system catalogs to maintain information about various entities within the database, including tables and indexes. Occasionally, an application can reference one of these missing objects, returning the following error message:

```
Could not find row in Sysindexes for dbid #, object #, index #. Run dbcc checktable
on Sysindexes. (Error 602)
```

Most likely, the application is using stored procedures to reference a table or view that has since been dropped. This error doesn't imply corruption. To remedy the situation, either re-create the missing table/view or alter the query that references the missing object.

Checking Transaction Log Usage

Most DBAs will remember the problems associated with tracking log usage. Some techniques even reported negative log usage, implying that the log was larger than its physical allocation size. In SQL Server 6.5, this problem is corrected via the use of dbcc checktable, which can be run by only sa or dbo. To check a transaction log's usage, run dbcc checktable on syslogs:

```
use database-name
go
dbcc checktable(syslogs)
go
```

dbcc checktable returns the number of allocated 2KB pages. For kilobytes, multiply the number of pages by two. This method is often more accurate than sp_spaceused, because this procedure utilizes an approximate algorithm for determining log usage statistics.

dbcc checkcatalog

Like user-defined tables and indexes, system catalog tables are subject to page allocation problems and even corruption. Remember, however, that system catalog tables store information on the database structure. Column definitions are stored in syscolumns. Each table has a corresponding row in sysobjects. Each database has a mapping row in sysdatabases in the master database. Without these tables, SQL Server is unable to locate and identify critical pieces of information about a database. Ensuring that these tables are in proper working order is a critical activity for any DBA. To examine these specific tables, use dbcc checkcatalog:

```
dbcc checkcatalog(bigpubs)
go

Checking bigpubs
The following segments have been defined for database 6 (database name bigpubs).
virtual start addr    size      segments
_____            ___       _____
         16777216     5120
                                    0
                                    1
         33554432     5120
                                    2
         50331648     5120
                                    0
                                    1
         67108864     5120
                                    2
         83886080     7680
                                    0
                                    1
```

In addition to reporting errors and corruption in system tables, checkcatalog also reports the segment mappings for the database.

dbcc newalloc

dbcc newalloc provides a vehicle to check page usage and allocation for each extent in a database. Again, to understand the output of this command, we must consider the SQL Server storage structure. Remember that SQL Server databases are built on allocation units of 512KB. In turn, allocation units house 32 extents of eight 2KB pages, of varying page type.

dbcc newalloc output reports the number of extents, used pages, and referenced pages in each allocation unit by extent and page, so that you can determine whether all pages are correctly allocated. In addition, newalloc output indicates whether new objects can be placed on certain extents, which can be useful from a database sizing and maintenance perspective. The used pages and ref(erence) pages should typically be the same, with slight differences attributable to transaction log usage. Note that the extent chain is the information used by SQL Server to determine which pages are owned by a given table.

To execute newalloc, pass the name of a database:

```
dbcc newalloc(database-name)
```

Here's the output from dbcc newalloc on the bigpubs database:

```
Checking bigpubs

Database 'bigpubs' is not in single user mode - may find spurious
allocation problems due to transactions in progress.
*******************************************************************
TABLE: sysobjects        OBJID = 1
INDID=1     FIRST=1      ROOT=8      DPAGES=4     SORT=0
    Data level: 1.  4 Data  Pages in 1 extents.
    Indid     : 1.  1 Index Pages in 1 extents.
INDID=2     FIRST=40     ROOT=41     DPAGES=1     SORT=1
    Indid     : 2.  3 Index Pages in 1 extents.
TOTAL # of extents = 3
*******************************************************************
TABLE: sysindexes        OBJID = 2
INDID=1     FIRST=24     ROOT=32     DPAGES=4     SORT=0
    Data level: 1.  4 Data  Pages in 1 extents.
    Indid     : 1.  1 Index Pages in 1 extents.
TOTAL # of extents = 2
*******************************************************************
TABLE: syscolumns        OBJID = 3
INDID=1     FIRST=48     ROOT=56     DPAGES=11    SORT=0
    Data level: 1.  11 Data  Pages in 3 extents.
    Indid     : 1.  1 Index Pages in 1 extents.
TOTAL # of extents = 4
```

```
****************************************************************
...
****************************************************************
TABLE: titles        OBJID = 208003772
INDID=1    FIRST=408      ROOT=424      DPAGES=55      SORT=0
    Data level: 1.  55 Data  Pages in 7 extents.
    Indid     : 1.  2 Index Pages in 1 extents.
INDID=2    FIRST=672      ROOT=674      DPAGES=1      SORT=1
    Indid     : 2.  15 Index Pages in 2 extents.
TOTAL # of extents = 10
****************************************************************
TABLE: titleauthor       OBJID = 304004114
INDID=1    FIRST=440      ROOT=456      DPAGES=8      SORT=0
    Data level: 1.  8 Data  Pages in 1 extents.
    Indid     : 1.  2 Index Pages in 1 extents.
INDID=2    FIRST=688      ROOT=690      DPAGES=1      SORT=1
    Indid     : 2.  7 Index Pages in 1 extents.
INDID=3    FIRST=696      ROOT=698      DPAGES=1      SORT=1
    Indid     : 3.  8 Index Pages in 1 extents.
TOTAL # of extents = 4
****************************************************************
TABLE: stores        OBJID = 384004399
INDID=1    FIRST=464      ROOT=482      DPAGES=543      SORT=0
    Data level: 1.  543 Data  Pages in 69 extents.
    Indid     : 1.  6 Index Pages in 1 extents.
TOTAL # of extents = 70
****************************************************************
TABLE: sales       OBJID = 432004570
INDID=1    FIRST=496      ROOT=3535      DPAGES=8914      SORT=0
    Data level: 1.  8914 Data  Pages in 1120 extents.
    Indid     : 1.  369 Index Pages in 48 extents.
INDID=2    FIRST=600      ROOT=2436      DPAGES=1      SORT=1
    Indid     : 2.  2215 Index Pages in 279 extents.
TOTAL # of extents = 1447
****************************************************************
...
****************************************************************
TABLE: C       OBJID = 1568008617
INDID=0    FIRST=392      ROOT=392      DPAGES=1      SORT=0
    Data level: 0.  1 Data  Pages in 1 extents.
TOTAL # of extents = 1
****************************************************************
Processed 53 entries in the Sysindexes for dbid 6.
Alloc page 0 (# of extent=31 used pages=43 ref pages=43)
Alloc page 256 (# of extent=27 used pages=77 ref pages=77)
Alloc page 512 (# of extent=22 used pages=104 ref pages=104)
Alloc page 768 (# of extent=10 used pages=35 ref pages=35)
Alloc page 1024 (# of extent=1 used pages=1 ref pages=1)
Alloc page 1280 (# of extent=10 used pages=73 ref pages=73)
Alloc page 1536 (# of extent=32 used pages=256 ref pages=256)
Alloc page 1792 (# of extent=32 used pages=249 ref pages=249)
...
Alloc page 27136 (# of extent=1 used pages=1 ref pages=1)
Alloc page 27392 (# of extent=1 used pages=1 ref pages=1)
Alloc page 27648 (# of extent=1 used pages=1 ref pages=1)
Alloc page 27904 (# of extent=1 used pages=1 ref pages=1)
Total (# of extent=1662 used pages=12384 ref pages=12377) in this database
```

> **NOTE**
>
> This output has been *substantially* abbreviated. The actual output from the command included one section per table and one line per allocation page. (There's one allocation page per 512KB of storage; see Chapter 10, "Defining Performance Expectations," for more on allocation pages and allocation units.) This database is 55 megabytes, or 110 allocation units. An ellipsis (...) shows where something was omitted.

For each object, dbcc newalloc reports some basic information from sysindexes and the number of pages and extents in use for that object, as in this example:

```
TABLE: sales         OBJID = 432004570
INDID=1     FIRST=496      ROOT=3535      DPAGES=8914     SORT=0
    Data level: 1.  8914 Data  Pages in 1120 extents.
    Indid      : 1.   369 Index Pages in 48 extents.
INDID=2   FIRST=600      ROOT=2436      DPAGES=1     SORT=1
    Indid      : 2.  2215 Index Pages in 279 extents.
TOTAL # of extents = 1447
```

newalloc also provides a noindex option, in which the detailed review of index chains is skipped. Here is an extract of the table information reported with the noindex option:

```
TABLE: employee        OBJID = 768005767
INDID=1     FIRST=776      ROOT=840      DPAGES=2      SORT=1
    Data level: 1.  2 Data  Pages in 1 extents.
INDID=2   FIRST=848      ROOT=848      DPAGES=1     SORT=1
TOTAL # of extents = 1
```

Note that a detailed scan of the index pages is skipped for both clustered and nonclustered indexes.

> **TIP**
>
> You'll have to do some testing on your own database to determine whether it's worth using noindex. On my Pentium system, newalloc took 52 seconds; with noindex, the scan took 43 seconds. It's certainly worth 9 extra seconds to me to make certain that index allocations are correct.

Identifying Bad Linkages

Here are some error messages returned by dbcc newalloc, along with some approaches to resolving each problem:

```
Extent chain for object # is not correctly linked. (Message 1117)
```

This message indicates a bad extent chain, clearly requiring you to drop the problem table. If the extent chain is so badly damaged that the server can't drop the table, you'll need to load the database from a backup.

```
Table corrupt: Page linkage is not consistent; check the following pages: (current
page#=#; page# pointing to this page=#; previous page#=indicated on this page=#)
```

This message indicates a page linkage whose maps don't agree. Each page includes pointers to the previous and next page in the chain. If the pointers are inconsistent, SQL Server is unable to traverse this map effectively. To find out which table may have a problem, use dbcc page with the value of the current page number. If the object with the problem is a system or user table, restore the database from a backup. If the problem object is an index, simply drop and re-create the index.

```
Table corrupt: Page# not found. (Message 2529)
```

This message indicates that a page that should contain data appears not to have been initialized. Immediately restore the database from a backup.

```
Allocation Discrepancy: Page is allocated but not linked. (Message 2540)
```

This message simply means that a page is allocated but is not being used. It doesn't imply any data corruption, but does indicate pages that can never be used by a table. To correct this problem, run dbcc fix_al.

```
Table corrupt: Extent id # on allocation pg# had object id # on used bit off.
(Message 2544)
```

Conversely, this message indicates those extents that have been flagged as unused, but actually contain data. To identify the table in question, query sysobjects with the object ID. To correct this problem, restore the database from a clean backup. Note, however, that this error message often appears if the dbcc was run in multiuser mode. To verify this problem, run dbcc with the database in single-user mode.

Notes:

- ■ dbcc newalloc can be run by only sa or dbo.
- ■ For reliable results, dbcc newalloc must be run with minimal database activity on the server. Preferably, issue this command in single-user mode only.
- ■ The noindex option is available with dbcc newalloc.
- ■ dbcc newalloc replaces dbcc checkalloc.
- ■ dbcc newalloc doesn't return extent chain inconsistencies for text and image datatypes. To accurately check these datatypes, use dbcc textall or dbcc textalloc.

dbcc textall and textalloc

Two dbcc commands enable you to verify the allocation of space to text and image (binary large objects, or BLOBs) datatypes. dbcc textall checks all text and image columns in a database. dbcc textalloc checks text and image columns for a specific table. Both commands check the links in the page chains and ensure that all the pages in the chain are actually allocated.

> **NOTE**
>
> Important note: If you have included BLOB columns in your tables, you must run these dbcc commands periodically to check their integrity. Other dbcc commands don't check the integrity of BLOB allocations.
>
> For more on the SQL Server implementation of BLOBs, see Chapter 11 and Chapter 21, "Miscellaneous Performance Topics."

To check allocations for a single table, use textalloc like this:

```
dbcc textalloc("textsample")
```

Here's what dbcc reported for this table:

```
Checking db1
******************************************************************
TABLE: textsample          OBJID = 1692533063
INDID=255      FIRST=552      ROOT=3136      DPAGES=0      SORT=0
    Data level: 1.  8 Data  Pages in 0 extents.
    Indid       : 255.  537 Index Pages in 0 extents.
```

To check allocations for a complete database, pass textall a database name like this:

```
dbcc textall("db1")
```

Both dbcc statements provide a full or fast method. The two methods perform the same integrity check, but the full method returns a more complete report. For example, to request a full check, use:

```
dbcc textall("db1", full)
```

dbcc fix_al

For the most part, dbcc isn't a corrective tool. Instead, the command was designed to diagnose and identify specific problems and inconsistencies within a database. Some problems, however, can be resolved with the use of dbcc. Specifically, dbcc fix_al corrects SQL errors 2540 and 2521. Note, however, that dbcc fix_al presumes that page chains are allocated properly. With this in mind, always run dbcc checkdb before "fixing" the database.

Here's an example that repairs allocations in the `pubs2` database:

```
use master  /*move to a separate database*/
go
dbcc fix_al (pubs2)
go
```

Notes:

- `dbcc fix_al` can be run only in single-user mode.

- Due to its corrective nature, run `dbcc fix_al` from any database other than the one being repaired.

dbcc dbrepair

Perhaps the greatest misnomer in the history of relational technology is `dbcc dbrepair`. This command actually performs no repair operations at all. Instead, the command is used to drop a specified database when the `drop database` command won't work.

For several reasons, databases will eventually be dropped from SQL Server. While this is usually due to normal maintenance and upgrade operations, certain circumstances force the DBA to drop the database. SQL Server automatically marks as suspect any databases that are considered corrupt or unrecoverable, setting the 2^8 (256) bit in the `status` column of the row in `sysdatabases`. Although the DBA can manually change this flag and attempt to recover a database marked as suspect, this type of activity should be approached with extreme caution and cynicism. (Because it usually doesn't work!) SQL Server has marked the database as suspect for a valid reason. Unless you're entirely sure of exactly what occurred on the server, you may be better off following the server's advice and restoring the database from a backup.

> **NOTE**
>
> The one normal exception where resetting the `status` bit can work is when working with removable devices or data devices that were off-line when SQL Server was recovering or attempting to access the database. In this case, you should be able to reset the `status` bit in `sysdatabases` by updating the row:
>
> ```
> /* only do this when you are ABSOLUTELY SURE */
> sp_configure "allow updates", 1
> reconfigure with override
> go
> update master..sysdatabases
> set status = status - 256
> where name = "my_favorite_removable_db"
> go
> sp_configure "allow updates", 0
> reconfigure
> go
> ```

Here's how to drop the suspect database `my_dead_db`:

```
use master
go
dbcc dbrepair(my_dead_db, DROPDB)
go
```

Notes:

- `dbcc dbrepair` will run only on databases with no current users.

- Under certain circumstances, `dbcc dbrepair` will report an error even if the command successfully dropped the database. Having confirmed that the database was deleted, ignore this error message.

- If both `drop database` and `dbcc dbrepair` fail, try the system stored procedure `sp_dbremove`.

Trace Flags and Other Useful Commands

Trace flags can be helpful in interpreting `dbcc` results by enabling and disabling output to the client workstation, and much more.

> **WARNING**
>
> Microsoft emphatically refuses to support the use of these trace flags. Only experienced users should try this. Even then, many of the trace flags should be used only with caution, especially on production databases.

traceon

To enable a trace flag, use `dbcc traceon` with the appropriate numbered flag. This example turns on trace flag `1204` (this trace flag returns the type of locks participating in a deadlock situation, and the current command affected by the deadlock):

```
dbcc traceon(1204)
```

traceoff

To disable a trace flag, use `dbcc traceoff`:

```
dbcc traceoff(1204)
```

tracestatus

To check on the state of a trace flag (on or off), use dbcc tracestatus with the appropriate numbered flag:

```
dbcc tracestatus(1204)
```

Useful Trace Flags

A few of the more common and useful trace flags are described in the following sections.

Optimization Information: 302, 310, 325, 326

Trace flags 302, 310, 325, and 326 provide information about the optimization process. 302 reports how the server evaluates indexes and 310 reports on the selection of an index and join order. 325 and 326 report on sort optimization. See Chapter 13, "Understanding the Query Optimizer," for more on the use of these flags.

Disabling Read-ahead: 652 and 653

Trace flag 652 shuts off read-ahead for the server. Trace flag 653 shuts off read-ahead for the session.

Locking and Deadlock Information: 1200, 1204, 1205

Trace flag 1200 reports locks as they're acquired.

Trace flag 1204 prints information on deadlock chains, enabling system administrators to find out which processes are deadlocked. (Remember that despite SQL Server 6.5's improved deadlock management, deadlocks still happen.) 1205 provides more detailed information about deadlock chains. For more on these trace flags, see Chapter 16, "Locking and Performance."

Temporary Table Information: 1704

Trace flag 1704 reports optimization information when temporary tables are created.

Database Creation: 1802

Trace flag 1802 enables the DBA to build and alter databases without initializing the data pages. The data pages must be initialized at some point before being used by SQL Server; when re-building large databases, however, a DBA can save a significant amount of time by skipping this I/O-intensive activity.

Managing Database Recovery: 3607 and 3608

Trace flags 3607 and 3608 suppress database recovery for all databases. Trace flag 3608 still permits recovery on the master database.

> **WARNING**
>
> *Don't even think* about using this without first working closely with Microsoft technical support, or at the very least backing up everything in sight first.

4030 and 4031

Use trace flag 4030 to see what information is being passed between the client and SQL Server.

Enable trace flag 4031 to determine what information is being passed in the opposite direction, SQL Server to client.

dbcc page

Most SQL Server power users have never used the dbcc page command. Although the command remains largely undocumented, it can be a very effective tool for examining the contents of a specific problem page. At the very least, dbcc page reports the object id for any given page, allowing users to determine the table or index containing inconsistencies.

In the very worst of circumstances, you could also use dbcc page to extract data from a corrupt SQL table. Admittedly, pulling data page by page is a slow and nasty process, but it might be preferable to losing the contents of a critical data page (along with your job). Here's the syntax for the command:

```
dbcc page(database-name, pagenum [, print option[, cache [, logical]]])
```

Here are the values for each of the optional parameters:

print option:

- 0=Print the page header only.
- 1=Print the page header, the data rows, and the table offset.
- 2=Print the page header, the data rows as a single unit, and the table offset.

cache:

- 0=Always retrieve the page from disk.
- 1=Retrieve the page from cache, if available.

logical:

- ◼ 0=Virtual page.
- ◼ 1=Logical page.

Here's an example of a session where dbcc page is used to examine the contents of page 750 in the database bigpubs:

```
dbcc traceon(3604)
go
dbcc page(bigpubs,106,2)
go
dbcc traceoff(3604)
go

PAGE:
Page not found in cache - read from disk.

BUFFER:
Buffer header for buffer 0x2e9f718
    page=0xd90000 bdnew=0x0 bdold=0x0 bhash=0x0 bnew=0x0
    bold=0x0 bvirtpg=16777966 bdbid=6 bpinproc=0 bkeep=0 bspid=0
    bstat=0x0000    bpageno=0

PAGE HEADER:
Page header for page 0xd90000
pageno=750 nextpg=676 prevpg=745 objid=208003772 timestamp=0001
00002f09
nextrno=997 level=0 indid=2  freeoff=1020 minlen=7
page status bits: 0x2

DATA:
00d90020:   019d0100 000b0017 00546865 2042616c   .........The Bal
00d90030:   636f6e79 02140901 9d010000 0d001700   cony...........
00d90040:   54686520 42616c63 6f6e7902 140901c1   The Balcony.....
00d90050:   02000000 001e0054 68652042 61737461   .......The Basta
00d90060:   72642050 72696e63 65021b09 01d90200   rd Prince.......
00d90070:   0009001e 00546865 20426173 74617264   .....The Bastard
00d90080:   20507269 6e636502 1b09012f 03000002    Prince..../....
00d90090:   001f0054 68652042 6567696e 6e696e67   ...The Beginning
00d900a0:   20506c61 6365021c 0901ca02 00000d00    Place.........
00d900b0:   1f005468 65204265 67696e6e 696e6720   ..The Beginning
00d900c0:   506c6163 65021c09 01c10200 0007001a   Place..........
00d900d0:   00546865 2042656e 65666163 746f7202   .The Benefactor.
00d900e0:   170901ce 02000008 001a0054 68652042   ..........The B
00d900f0:   656e6566 6163746f 72021709 01340300   enefactor....4..
00d90100:   0001001e 00546865 20426c61 636b2043   .....The Black C
00d90110:   61756c64 726f6e02 1b0901ca 0200000b   auldron.........
00d90120:   001e0054 68652042 6c61636b 20436175   ...The Black Cau
00d90130:   6c64726f 6e021b09 011f0300 0000001e   ldron...........
00d90140:   00546865 20426c61 636b2053 74616c6c   .The Black Stall
00d90150:   696f6e02 1b09011f 03000004 001e0054   ion............T
00d90160:   68652042 6c61636b 20537461 6c6c696f   he Black Stallio
00d90170:   6e021b09 011c0300 0004002f 00546865   n........../.The
00d90180:   20426f6f 6b206f66 204c6175 67687465    Book of Laughte
00d90190:   7220616e 6420466f 72676574 74696e67   r and Forgetting
00d901a0:   022c0901 2e030000 06002f00 54686520   .,........./.The
```

```
00d901b0:   426f6f6b 206f6620 4c617567 68746572    Book of Laughter
00d901c0:   20616e64 20466f72 67657474 696e6702     and Forgetting.
00d901d0:   2c09011e 03000000 001d0054 68652042    ,..........The B
00d901e0:   6f6f6b20 6f662054 68726565 021a0901    ook of Three....
00d901f0:   2c030000 02001d00 54686520 426f6f6b    ,.......The Book
00d90200:   206f6620 54687265 65021a09 012c0300     of Three....,..
00d90210:   0003001f 00546865 20426f78 63617220    .....The Boxcar
00d90220:   4368696c 6472656e 021c0901 c6020000    Children........
00d90230:   03001600 54686520 42726561 73740213    ....The Breast..
00d90240:   0901dc02 00000100 16005468 65204272    .........The Br
00d90250:   65617374 02130901 9c010000 02002500    east..........%.
00d90260:   54686520 4272656d 656e2054 6f776e20    The Bremen Town
00d90270:   4d757369 6369616e 73022209 01c90200    Musicians."....
00d90280:   000a0025 00546865 20427265 6d656e20    ...%.The Bremen
00d90290:   546f776e 204d7573 69636961 6e730222    Town Musicians."
00d902a0:   0901db02 00000400 22005468 65204272    ........".The Br
00d902b0:   69646765 73206174 20546f6b 6f2d5269    idges at Toko-Ri
00d902c0:   021f0901 1c030000 05001f00 54686520    ............The
00d902d0:   42757264 656e206f 66205072 6f6f6602    Burden of Proof.
00d902e0:   1c0901de 02000004 001f0054 68652042    ...........The B
00d902f0:   75726465 6e206f66 2050726f 6f66021c    urden of Proof..
00d90300:   09019c01 00000100 2f005468 65204275    ......../.The Bu
00d90310:   73792045 78656375 74697665 27732044    sy Executive's D
00d90320:   61746162 61736520 47756964 65022c09    atabase Guide.,.
00d90330:   01c30200 00020027 00546865 20436172    .......'.The Car
00d90340:   64696e61 6c206f66 20746865 204b7265    dinal of the Kre
00d90350:   6d6c696e 02240901 29030000 01001e00    mlin.$..)......
00d90360:   54686520 43617420 696e2074 68652048    The Cat in the H
00d90370:   6174021b 09013403 00000200 1e005468    at....4.......Th
00d90380:   65204361 7420696e 20746865 20486174    e Cat in the Hat
00d90390:   021b0901 2a030000 01002900 54686520    ....*.....).The
00d903a0:   43617420 696e2074 68652048 61742043    Cat in the Hat C
00d903b0:   6f6d6573 20426163 6b022609 012c0300    omes Back.&..,..
00d903c0:   00010029 00546865 20436174 20696e20    ...).The Cat in
00d903d0:   74686520 48617420 436f6d65 73204261    the Hat Comes Ba
00d903e0:   636b0226 0901cd02 00000100 17005468    ck.&..........Th
00d903f0:   65204368 616d6265 72021409           e Chamber...
```

The most useful information is usually in the PAGE HEADER section:

```
PAGE HEADER:
Page header for page 0xd90000
pageno=750 nextpg=676 prevpg=745 objid=208003772 timestamp=0001
00002f09
nextrno=997 level=0 indid=2  freeoff=1020 minlen=7
page status bits: 0x2
```

This page (pageno=750) is between pages 676 and 745 in the page chain. It belongs to object 208003772, and the timestamp tells you the ID of the last transaction to modify the page. The page belongs to a nonclustered index (indid = 2), and is part of the leaf level of that index. The shortest row on the page is 7 bytes, and the next location to write data starts in position 1020.

The report you just examined is in format 2, which is a hex dump of the page with an ASCII representation to the right. The hex dump is very compact, but format 1 presents data in a record-wise manner that may be easier to read. Here's a brief extract from a page output in format 1:

```
Offset 169 -
00d900a9:  01ca0200 000d001f 00546865 20426567  ........The Beg
00d900b9:  696e6e69 6e672050 6c616365 021c09     inning Place...

Offset 200 -
00d900c8:  01c10200 0007001a 00546865 2042656e  .........The Ben
00d900d8:  65666163 746f7202 1709                efactor...
```

Each row is set apart in its own paragraph, with both a hex dump and an ASCII translation. You can see the row boundaries, and determine what row overhead you're using. Some notes:

- To retrieve page information from `dbcc page`, first configure `dbcc` output to the client with `dbcc traceon(3604)`.

- To determine the table name based on the `object_id`, use the `object_name()` function like this:

```
use bigpubs
go
select object_name(208003772)
go
```

Exploring the output from `dbcc page` may teach you more about SQL Server than anything else. You can begin to understand how the server manages data and physically organizes it on a row. While this information is pointless to the typical user, to a database designer or application programmer it may prove priceless.

dbcc pglinkage

`dbcc pglinkage` traces the page chain for a particular object. It could provide a more direct method of evaluating table fragmentation than `scancontig`, but it's far more useful at finding breaks in the page chain, particularly in clustered indexes. Here's the syntax for the command:

```
dbcc pglinkage(dbid, start, number, print option, target, order)
```

Following are the parameters:

`start:`

The decimal start point for the command.

`number:`

The number of pages to be traversed, `0` if the command should follow the chain to the end.

`print option:`

- `0`=Print the total number of pages scanned.
- `1`=Print page numbers for the last 16 pages scanned.
- `2`=Print all scanned page numbers.

```
target:
```

The page at which the command will terminate.

```
order:
```

- `0`=Scan backward.
- `1`=Scan forward.

Here's an example where the page chain is examined for database 2. To find a starting page, retrieve from the `sysobjects` table the `first` page assigned to an object's page chain:

```
select id, first
from sysindexes
where indid = 1
and object_name(id) = "authors"

id          first
_____  _____
32003145    584
```

Now use the `first` page value of 584 as the starting point for `pglinkage`:

```
dbcc traceon(3604)
go
dbcc pglinkage(6,584,0,2,0,1)
go
dbcc traceoff(3604)
go
```

Here's the output. Notice that the pages are in ascending order, with no fragmentation or interruption in the page chain:

```
Object ID for pages in this chain = 32003145.
Page : 584
Page : 585
Page : 586
Page : 587
Page : 588
Page : 589
Page : 590
Page : 591
End of chain reached.
8 pages scanned.  Object ID = 32003145.  Last page in scan = 591.
```

Note that you must pass the database ID as the first argument to `dbcc pglinkage`.

dbcc shrinkdb

`dbcc shrinkdb` enables you to shrink the size of a database. You can specify a size in pages, or you can ask SQL Server to shrink the database to its absolute minimum size. Like many `dbcc` commands, `shrinkdb` requires the database to be in single-user mode.

First, we'll shrink `mydb` from 10 megabytes to 6 megabytes (3072 pages):

```
use master
exec sp_dboption mydb, "single", true
go
use mydb
checkpoint
dbcc shrinkdb(mydb, 3072)
go
use master
exec sp_dboption mydb, "single", false
go
```

In this version of `shrinkdb`, no news is good news: if you get no error message the command completed successfully and the size of the database was changed.

In the next example, SQL Server shrinks the database to its smallest possible size:

```
use master
exec sp_dboption mydb, "single", true
go
use mydb
checkpoint
dbcc shrinkdb(mydb)
go
use master
exec sp_dboption mydb, "single", false
go

Current size of database Size database can be shrunk to
———————————— ————————————————
3072                     1024
```

Notes:

- `dbcc shrinkdb` doesn't require the database to be shrunk to its absolute minimum size. However, it won't allow the database to be shrunk below this value.

- `dbcc shrinkdb` is a logged operation and can be backed out, except on the `master` database.

- *Always* back up a database before shrinking it.

- `dbcc shrinkdb` can reduce both data and log segments.

dbcc opentran

`dbcc opentran` reports information about the oldest open transaction for a database. You can use this feature to avoid problems with truncating the transaction log or getting a database into single-user mode.

Transaction logs are typically truncated by the `dump transaction` command, but `dump tran` can only remove those transactions up to the point of the oldest open transaction. If there are open transactions, a DBA may not be able to clear the log effectively, causing potential system failure if the log fills up. Once you have identified the user holding an open transaction, you can easily identify the problem connection and kill the connection if necessary.

Here's the syntax:

```
dbcc opentran (database-name ¦ database-id)
```

In this example, `dbcc` reports the oldest open transaction in database db1:

```
dbcc opentran(db1)

Transaction Information for database: db1

Oldest active transaction:
        SPID        : 12
        UID         : 1
        SUID        : 1
        Name        : user_transaction
        RID         : (23191 , 18)
        Time Stamp  : 0001 0003E95B
        Start Time  : Oct 16 1996  5:05:46:530PM
```

Use `dbcc opentran (database-name)` with `tableresults` to retrieve data formatted for easy retrieval and processing. Here's a sample of the `tableresults` format:

```
Tag                        Value
————————————————————       ——————————————————————————————
OLDACT_SPID                12
OLDACT_UID                 1
OLDACT_SUID                1
OLDACT_NAME                user_transaction
OLDACT_RID                 (23191 , 18)
OLDACT_TSTAMP              0001 0003E95B
OLDACT_STARTTIME           Oct 16 1996  5:05:46:530PM
```

> **NOTE**
>
> The major difference between the standard and table results is in the way they're returned in the data stream. Most `dbcc` commands (including `opentran`) use print statements to return data through the message handler. When you use `opentran` with `tableresults`, the data returned from `dbcc` looks to your client application like a result set from a `select` statement.

dbcc updateusage

SQL Server avoids constant maintenance of table and index statistics in order to minimize overhead during data modification operations. To eliminate at least some incorrect reporting, use `dbcc updateusage`, which details and repairs most inconsistencies in `sysindexes`. One of the benefits of `updateusage` is more accurate output from `sp_spaceused`, the stored procedure that reports table and index space usage and available space within a database.

Notice that the command can operate on a database, a table, or a single index:

```
dbcc updateusage(database-name[ , table-name[, index-name]])
```

Notes:

- Like other administrative operations requiring a scan, this takes some time. Plan for it, and use dbcc updateusage sparingly.

- Intuitively, DBAs will rush to run this command on the syslogs table in order to get accurate transaction log reporting. Although this will work, the database must be in single-user mode, as dbcc updateusage uses shared locks to make its alterations.

dbcc and Performance

dbcc provides three commands to help manage system performance:

- dbcc memusage reports memory usage.
- dbcc pintable allows you to retain a table in cache after it's loaded.
- dbcc sqlperf lets you analyze system performance.

dbcc memusage

dbcc memusage is perhaps the most useful dbcc command, providing a means to examine SQL Server memory allocation. The memory report from memusage falls into three components: overall memory configuration, 20 largest objects in the data cache, and 12 largest objects in the procedure cache. For more on memusage, see Chapter 32, "Optimizing SQL Server Configuration Options."

dbcc pintable

SQL Server enables database administrators to *pin* tables, flagging the data so that SQL Server doesn't remove it from the cache. Keeping a heavily referenced table in cache should improve performance—as long as the table isn't so large that it dominates the entire cache. To accurately measure the impact of a "pinned" table, use dbcc pintable in conjunction with dbcc memusage.

To allow a pinned table to be paged out of the cache, use dbcc unpintable. Here's the syntax for dbcc pintable:

```
dbcc pintable(database-id, table-id)
```

```
dbcc unpintable(database-id, table-id)
```

After this example is run, SQL Server will maintain table A in database db1 in memory, even after the server is restarted. Notice the warning returned by SQL Server:

```
dbcc pintable(7, 1324531752)
```

```
WARNING: Pinning tables should be carefully considered.
If a pinned table is larger or grows larger than the available
data cache, the server may need to be restarted and the table
unpinned.
```

dbcc sqlperf

sqlperf is another dbcc tool for monitoring and improving performance. Information is available in six categories, including four statistics categories and two status categories:

- I/O statistics provide detailed information about physical reads and writes—that is, interaction with the disk systems.
- Cache statistics enable you to examine how efficiently the server is using data cache.
- Network statistics let you look for network bottlenecks and trouble spots.
- Read-ahead statistics show how efficiently the server uses its read-ahead capabilities.
- sqlperf can list the threads currently spawned by SQL Server.
- A list of free log space lets you track log utilization and avoid transaction log full disasters.

Running sqlperf

sqlperf enables you to choose a category of performance for reporting. sqlperf shows statistics in these categories:

- iostats: disk and log performance
- lrustats: cache utilization
- netstats: network behavior
- rastats: read-ahead effectiveness
- threads: currently active threads
- logspace: current available log space for all databases

sqlperf also enables you to clear certain statistics registers so that you can track statistics for certain queries, operations, sessions, or test conditions.

> **NOTE**
>
> These statistics are also available in the SQL Performance Monitor through a graphical interface.

Here's the syntax:

```
dbcc sqlperf ({iostats ¦ lrustats ¦ netstats ¦ rastats [, clear]} ¦
    {threads} ¦ {logspace})
```

The statistics returned by `sqlperf` are cumulative and are refreshed only when the server is re-started or the system administrator clears them with the `dbcc sqlperf(clear)` option.

I/O Statistics

`dbcc sqlperf` displays a summary of SQL Server I/O activity. The way you might use the information to solve real performance problems varies, depending on your environment. Some cases call for disk striping or some other hardware or software configuration solution.

Data design could also lead to perceived I/O problems. Consider the case of a query performing a join on a 1,000,000 record dataset. If this large table has an attribute in the where clause that has no useful index, I/O measures will almost certainly deteriorate, but not due to any inherent tuning flaw on the server.

Understanding what's causing I/O performance problems requires you to look at your application, the specific problem you're encountering, and what part of the application is too slow. These statistics may help you understand overall how the server is performing, but may not help you isolate a specific problem.

NOTE

You don't need to use `dbcc traceon` to direct `sqlperf` output to your screen.

This example retrieves current I/O system statistics from the server:

```
dbcc sqlperf(IOSTATS)
```

Statistic	Value
Log Flush Requests	604.0
Log Logical Page IO	10820.0
Log Physical IO	1966.0
Log Flush Average	0.307223
Log Logical IO Average	5.50356
Batch Writes	15655.0
Batch Average Size	319.49
Batch Max Size	8.0
Page Reads	210822.0
Single Page Writes	900.0
Reads Outstanding	0.0
Writes Outstanding	0.0
Transactions	492.0
Transactions/Log Write	0.250254

Let's examine each of these measures briefly:

- Log Flush Requests. The number of times log pages were flushed to disk.

- Log Logical Page IO. The number of times requested log pages were read from or written to cache.

- Log Physical IO. The number of times requested log pages were read from or written to disk.

- Log Flush Average. Log flush requests per physical write. If this number is high, the same log page is being written repeatedly as it fills (your transactions are usually small). You may be able to solve a throughput problem by increasing the scope of transactions or placing the log on a faster device. If the number is low, your transactions tend to be larger. If the time to commit is too long, you might consider smaller transaction units (or shorter rows in your tables) with more frequent commits.

- Log Logical IO Average. Logical pages written per physical write. A high number may mean better use of cache to get good log throughput. However, a high number may also mean that the method of updates is inefficient (see the sections on direct and deferred updates in Chapter 11).

- Batch Writes. The number of times SQL Server was able to group multiple writes together into a single set.

- Batch Average Size. The average number of 2KB pages written to disk in a single batch (this tells you how efficiently SQL Server is grouping work).

- Batch Max Size. The maximum number of pending I/O requests (this tells you how far behind the I/O system got, at its worst).

- Page Reads. 2KB page reads from disk.

- Single Page Writes. 2KB page writes to disk (including log writes).

- Reads Outstanding. Pending read requests (not cumulative).

- Writes Outstanding. Pending write requests (not cumulative).

- Transactions. Number of completed transactions.

- Transactions/Log Write. Transactions per physical log write. This number will be higher for shorter transactions, lower for longer ones. (See the earlier bulleted item on Log Flush Average.)

Cache Statistics

By examining how efficiently the server is using cache, you can decide whether to reconfigure memory, add more memory, or pin or unpin a table or set of tables. The next page shows an example of the output from dbcc sqlperf(lrustats):

```
Statistic                Value
_____       _____
Cache Hit Ratio          71.8864
Cache Flushes            13821.0
Free Page Scan (Avg)     0.96416
Free Page Scan (Max)     108.0
Min Free Buffers         409.0
Cache Size               5250.0
Free Buffers             425.0
```

dbcc `sqlperf(lrustats)` returns the following measures:

- `Cache Hit Ratio`. Percentage of read requests satisfied by cache. Low values (less than roughly 80 percent) could mean that the SQL Server is performing many large table scans, or it could mean inefficient use of cache. If the system is performing many large table scans, smaller, frequently used tables could be forced from memory, needing to be repeatedly reread. Consider pinning smaller, heavily read tables in memory.

  Low values could mean that cache is simply too small. Consider reconfiguring to make more room for data cache, or adding more memory to the server or to SQL Server.

- `Cache Flushes`. Number of times a page was flushed from cache. Cache flushes are expensive, especially if the data has changed. If this number increases over time as performance deteriorates, consider increasing available memory.

- `Free Page Scan (Avg)`. Average number of cache pages in the buffer scanned in order to locate a free page. As this number increases, the cost to read a new page increases as well. Adding more memory to data cache will allow more free space (generally) with better read performance.

- `Free Page Scan (Max)`. Maximum number of cache pages in the buffer scanned in order to locate a free page.

- `Min Free Buffers`. Number of pages SQL Server attempts to keep available. When `Free Buffers` drops below `Min Free Buffers`, SQL Server may issue a checkpoint.

- `Cache Size`. Number of 2KB memory pages in data cache (doesn't change during a single SQL Server session).

- `Free Buffers`. Unused buffers (not cumulative).

According to Microsoft, the two critical numbers in this set are `Cache Flushes` and `Free Page Scan (Avg)`. Although the results will accumulate on a daily basis, the number of cache flushes shouldn't exceed 100 over the course of several days of activity. In addition, `Free Page Scan (Avg)` should be around 10. If your numbers are significantly higher, you probably need a larger data cache. If your numbers are in this general range, adding more memory and cache typically won't result in performance increases, as the cache is already large enough to manage the current workload.

Network Statistics

Network performance can dramatically impact client/server systems. Depending on network traffic and activity load, specific applications can see performance drop significantly. SQL Server provides some measures to examine network activity. `dbcc sqlperf(netstats)` maintains cumulative statistics on the relationship between SQL Server and the network. Here's an example of the output from `dbcc sqlperf(netstats)`:

```
dbcc sqlperf(netstats)

Statistic                       Value
_ _ _ _ _ _ _ _ _ _ _ _ _ _     _ _ _ _ _ _ _ _ _ _ _
Network Reads                   0.0
Network Writes                  576.0
Command Queue Length            0.0
Max Command Queue Length        0.0
Worker Threads                  5.0
Max Worker Threads              6.0
Network Threads                 0.0
Max Network Threads             0.0
```

Here's a brief summary of the measurements:

- `Network Reads`. Total network read operations.
- `Network Writes`. Total network write operations.
- `Command Queue Length`. Number of network commands to be processed.
- `Max Command Queue Length`. Largest number of network commands at one time.
- `Worker Threads`. Number of worker threads for network handling.
- `Max Worker Threads`. Highest number of worker threads for network handling at one time.
- `Network Threads`. [undocumented].
- `Max Network Threads`. [undocumented].

Monitor network reads and writes over time to see if there are changes in performance characteristics. Worker thread measures can also be useful. To combat failing values, increase both the worker threads and user connection parameters in SQL Server. Although this may address the `netstats` issues, increasing these parameters also requires additional overhead memory, potentially hurting performance on one of the three memory allocations.

Another solution to poor network performance is to increase the `network packet size` using `sp_configure`. Increase this number if you're sending large result sets to the client or if you're performing large bulk copies.

Read-Ahead Statistics

Read-ahead (RA) statistics enable you to monitor how effectively read-ahead caching is being used by the SQL Server. Here are the RA statistics:

```
dbcc sqlperf(rastats)
```

Statistic	Value
RA Pages Found in Cache	72219.0
RA Pages Placed in Cache	131402.0
RA Physical IO	18422.0
Used Slots	0.0

Here's a detailed look at the RA statistics:

- ■ `RA Pages Found in Cache`. Number of pages already in cache when the read-ahead system was performing a scan. If this number is high, the overhead cost of the read-ahead process may be greater than its benefit.

- ■ `RA Pages Placed in Cache`. Pages read from disk by the read-ahead system. If this number is high and the previous statistic is much lower, the read-ahead system is working too hard and is probably hurting performance more often than it is helping. Read-ahead may need to be turned off or ratcheted down for this server.

- ■ `RA Physical IO`. Number of 16KB I/Os performed by the read-ahead system. These I/Os are roughly eight times more efficient than comparable page reads, if the server makes effective use of them.

- ■ `Used Slots`. Number of current RA slots in use (not cumulative). This isn't a cumulative statistic. It reflects current status at the time you execute the query.

Threads

`dbcc sqlperf` can also list current Windows NT threads used by SQL Server. Threads can support user actions, or can be used to handle log writes, read-aheads, and other system-based activities.

Some thread information isn't cumulative. For instance, the state of each thread reflects its activity at the time the `dbcc` statement is executed. In this sample output, SQL Server shows a modest amount of thread activity:

```
dbcc traceon (3604)
dbcc sqlperf (threads)
dbcc traceoff (3604)
```

Spid	Thread ID	Status	LoginName	IO	CPU	MemUsage
1		sleeping	(null)	0	0	1
2		sleeping	(null)	0	0	0
3		sleeping	(null)	47	0	0
4		sleeping	(null)	6	0	0

```
5                    sleeping    (null)    0          0       0
6                    sleeping    (null)    0          0       0
7                    sleeping    (null)    0          0       0
8                    sleeping    (null)    0          0       0
9                    sleeping    (null)    0          0       0
10    43(0x2b)       sleeping    sa        19         70      1
11    128(0x80)      sleeping    sa        9          120     1
12    158(0x9e)      runnable    sa        7          40      2
13    89(0x59)       runnable    sa        8          7931    8
```

The thread tracks CPU and I/O activity so that you can determine how resources are being consumed by current users. (Once a user logs off, information about his use of the system is cleared.) In the example provided just above, one session (spid 13) is using a large proportion of CPU, but almost no I/O resources. To understand the information more completely, you need to compare it to corresponding output from sp_who:

```
spid   status     loginame   hostname  blk   dbname   cmd
___    _____    _____   _____  ___   _____   _____
1      sleeping   sa                   0     master   MIRROR HANDLER
2      sleeping   sa                   0     master   LAZY WRITER
3      sleeping   sa                   0     master   CHECKPOINT SLEEP
4      sleeping   sa                   0     master   RA MANAGER
10     sleeping   sa         PENTIUM    0     pubs     AWAITING COMMAND
11     sleeping   sa         PENTIUM    0     pubs     AWAITING COMMAND
12     runnable   sa         PENTIUM    0     pubs     SELECT
13     runnable   sa         PENTIUM    0     pubs     CONDITIONAL
```

Use thread information to track down and find processes, applications, and queries that are monopolizing system resources.

> **NOTE**
>
> Notice that the four live sessions (spid 10 to 13) are each assigned an active thread. Threads 1 through 9 in this example are assigned to system resources.
>
> As you configure the server to use additional system threads, the spid assigned to the first user connection will increase to leave sufficient space for system threads.

Log Space

With the logspace option, dbcc sqlperf can display available log space for all databases. Right after installation, the log space report should look similar to this:

```
Database Name        Log Size (MB)    Log Space Used (%)    Status
_____         _____    _____    _____
pubs                 0.0              0.0                    1
msdb                 2.0              0.0976563              0
tempdb               0.0              0.0                    1
model                0.0              0.0                    1
master               0.0              0.0                    1
```

This information is returned formatted like a result set (not like print statements). You can retrieve and track this information over time to watch log utilization.

There are several appropriate responses to logs that are filling up, including performing more common transaction dumps (incremental backups), increasing the size of the transaction log, or reducing the number or complexity of transactions.

This report could be useful *as a testing tool* for tracking log utilization over a period of time to determine the time of day or day of the week when log activity is especially high. This is probably not the tool to use *as an administrative tool* to avoid completely full logs. You are probably better off building an alert based on the capacity of the log, or using the Alert function in the SQL Performance Monitor.

Clearing Statistics Registers

The `clear` option can clear the statistics registers for the four *stats* measures (`iostats`, `lrustats`, `netstats`, and `rastats`). This enables you to measure behavior for a specific period of time. This example clears the `iostats` on the SQL Server:

```
dbcc sqlperf (iostats, clear)

I/O statistics have been cleared.
```

Summary

`dbcc` provides a whole range of capabilities that fall outside the normal range of SQL operations. Its diagnostic and administrative capabilities are a necessary part of regular data maintenance. The other facilities can help you get the best performance out of SQL Server.

SQL Server Database Backup and Restoration

30

Backup is a part of any database environment. A *backup* is a copy of a database (or portion of a database) stored on some type of media (tape, disk, and so on). A *restore* is the process used to return a database to the state it was in at the time a backup was made.

It takes work to define an effective backup-and-recovery plan. This is especially true in very large database (VLDB) environments, because the complexity of administrative activities is magnified. Timing of activities quickly becomes an issue. For large tables and databases, consistency checks (DBCC), updating index statistics, and index creation can take from several hours to days. When making plans for automating backups, you must consider the impact of these activities as well as application activities.

The backup media you choose also can affect your plan. Backing up to tape devices means that the physical tapes have to be managed. You must consider this fact in your plan. Additionally, when a tape is full, a subsequent backup will fail, which can affect your entire backup-and-recovery process. When backing up to file devices, you must consider the organization of the directory structure as well as management of the backup files.

Why Back Up?

Backups are a hassle. Why bother? (Why do you have car insurance?) Backups are the easiest and most foolproof way of ensuring that you can recover a database. Without a backup, all data could be lost and would have to be re-created from the source. This is normally an option only for Decision Support Systems (DSS), because DSS data normally originates in some other system. For On-Line Transaction Processing (OLTP) or On-Line Analytical Processing (OLAP) systems, the majority of data originates on the server. The lost data may not be reproducible.

Backups can guard against table or database corruption, media failure, or user error. They should be performed as frequently as needed for effective data administration. SQL Server backups can be performed while the database is in use, but generally it's more effective to back up during non-peak activity periods.

Roles and Responsibilities

In SQL Server, a backup is done with the dump command and a restore is done with the load command. The capability of executing the dump and load commands defaults to the database dbo. The dbo could be the login who created the database, anyone aliased to the dbo in the database, or the sa login (the sa becomes dbo in any database that the sa uses). Remember that the sa login is the System Administrator, and the dbo is the owner of any particular database. dbo isn't a login; it's a user name, so it resides at SQL Server's database level of security.

You should identify who is responsible for performing backups in your organization. For each of these individuals, create a login and grant the dump database and dump transaction statement permissions. Note that permission for the load database and load transaction statements can't be granted.

As always, the `sa` or `dbo` has the capability of backing up and restoring the database. Any login aliased to the database owner of a database can also back up and restore that database.

Types of Backups

There are two main types of backups: full and incremental. A *full backup* is a copy of all the allocated pages in your database, including all system tables. (See Figure 30.1.) The system tables include `syslogs`, normally referred to as the *transaction log*. The transaction log is backed up with the rest of the system tables to ensure that all transactions have been included.

FIGURE 30.1.

A database backup (`dump database acctg_db`*) copies the entire database, including log and data.*

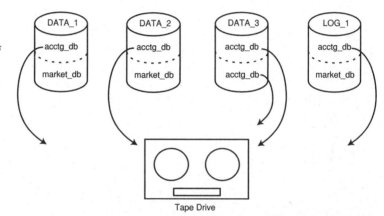

DATA_1 — acctg_db — market_db

DATA_2 — acctg_db — market_db

DATA_3 — acctg_db — acctg_db

LOG_1 — acctg_db — market_db

Tape Drive

WARNING

Full backups don't truncate the transaction log, which often is confusing and sometimes disastrous for new database administrators and backup operators. Even if all your backups are complete backups, you must run the incremental backup process periodically to clear the transaction log. Otherwise, you'll certainly fill up your log, and processing on that database will halt until you clear the log. (See the section titled "Backing Up Transaction Logs," later in this chapter.)

An *incremental backup* is simply a copy of the transaction log (see Figure 30.2). The transaction log contains the transactions that have completed since the last `dump transaction` command. This is similar to incremental backups of file systems, in which only the files that have changed are backed up. Backing up the transaction log truncates the log, unless the `with no_truncate` option is specified.

SQL Server 6.5 allows a third type of backup, a *table backup*. A table backup enables you to backup and restore a single table from a database. A single table can also be restored from a complete database backup. This capability can be useful in a disaster recovery situation, but shouldn't be considered a substitute for regular full database and transaction log backups.

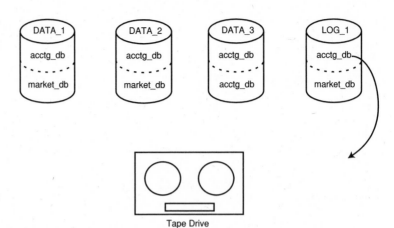

FIGURE 30.2.
An incremental backup
(dump transaction
acctg_db) *copies only the*
transaction log (the
syslogs *table).*

Tape Drive

Backup Devices

A *backup device* is created for the exclusive use of the dump and load commands. When backing up a database or transaction log, you must tell SQL Server where to create the backup. Creating a backup device enables you to associate a logical name with the physical backup media. The two most common types of media are tape devices and disk devices, as described in the following sections.

Tape Devices

A *tape device* records backups to removable tapes. Tape drives can be used alone, or several can be used in parallel for a single backup operation. Purchase as many drives as you can afford, based on the needs of your backup-and-recovery strategy. Tape devices are inherently more secure than disk devices because the media (tape) is removable and portable.

Tape capacity has increased dramatically over the last five years. In 1990, standard [1/4]-inch cartridges held only 150MB of data. Now, smaller cartridges (4mm and 8mm are common sizes) hold over 50 times more data (8GB). The size and compactness of tapes will almost certainly continue to progress.

Tape devices are used by most production sites. Tape devices provide a removable source of backup media that can easily be moved offsite for additional security. Tape devices adapt to changing database size much more gracefully than do disk devices. Dumping a 50MB database to disk can be easily managed by your file system. As the database grows to 50GB, however, backing up to disk will probably prove impossible because most sites don't have that amount of free space in the file system. Additionally, to move the backup offsite, you must back up the files to tape.

Disk Devices

A *disk device* is just a file in a directory, usually stored in the file system of your database server. Backing up to a disk device is faster than backing up to a tape device. When you back up to a disk device, you can actually see the file grow if you check the file size at intervals during the backup operation.

In a break with past behavior, SQL Server 6 for Windows NT doesn't automatically overwrite previous backups. In all versions of SQL Server prior to 6, backing up a database using a pre-existing file resulted in deletion of the original file. Its contents were replaced by the newly created backup. This was called *destructive backup* and was the only behavior SQL Server allowed for both disk backups and tape backups. With SQL Server 6, that default behavior has changed. By default, SQL Server 6 will *append* a backup to an existing file, whether on tape or on disk.

Adding Backup Devices

Use `sp_addumpdevice` to add a new backup device to a SQL Server. Here's the syntax:

```
sp_addumpdevice "tape", logical_name, physical_name, media_capacity
sp_addumpdevice "disk", logical_name, physical_name
```

> **TIP**
>
> Prior to SQL Server 6, adding backup devices using `sp_addumpdevice` was a requirement. With the newest versions of SQL Server, you don't have to add backup devices with `sp_addumpdevice`; you can provide the physical name as part of the `dump` syntax like this:
>
> ```
> dump transaction my_db to disk = "c:\mssql\backups\my_db_t.dmp"
> ```

> **NOTE**
>
> If you upgraded from Version 6.0 to 6.5, the directory name will still be `c:\sql60\backups`.

Logical Name

After executing this command, you can use the logical name for all backups and restores; a good practice is to choose the logical name based on the type of device being added. For tape devices, use a general name for the tape (`Tape1`, `Tape2`, and so forth). For disk devices, use a logical name indicating the database and backup type (`CustomerDB_backup` or `CustomerDB_tran`, for example).

Physical Name

The physical name is normally predefined for tape devices. Tape devices should be specified using the physical name defined by Windows NT. A common example of the physical name is \\.\TAPE0. The following example adds a tape device called Tape1. This device recognizes any ANSI tape labels:

```
sp_addumpdevice "tape", "Tape1", "\\.\tape0", 8000
```

For file devices, it's a good idea to organize a directory structure for all your databases. If using Enterprise Manager to create backup devices, SQL Server will put them in the \mssql\backup directory. For convenience, you may want to use this same directory if you create a backup device using the sp_addumpdevice command. Each database in your server could be a subdirectory. The CustomerDB subdirectory would be \mssql\backup\CustomerDB. The file name created is based on the dump type. Therefore, the two backup devices for the CustomerDB database would be created in the following manner:

```
sp_addumpdevice "disk", "CustomerDB_backup",
    "\mssql\backup\CustomerDB\CustomerDB_backup"
sp_addumpdevice "disk", "CustomerDB_tran",
    "\mssql\backup\CustomerDB\CustomerDB_tran"
```

By standardizing your structure, you can write scripts that accept a database name as a parameter. The entire dump command can be created dynamically. The location of the backup is also known, enabling you to move the file immediately to a different name to avoid having it overwritten.

Don't be stingy with the number of backup devices added. Using a different backup device for each database helps standardize your backup strategy, especially for disk devices.

Media Capacity

The *media_capacity* parameter is used to specify the tape capacity in number of megabytes. Use the maximum size allowable for your tape device. The *media_capacity* parameter is optional with SQL Server 6, because it uses Windows NT to automatically detect the capacity available on the physical backup device. According to Microsoft, this parameter will be removed in future versions of SQL Server, but it's still supported in this release.

SQL Server 6.5 Backup Functions

Backups in SQL Server 6.0 and 6.5 received significant enhancement and now make better use of SQL Server's threading resources. In addition, SQL Server reads and writes 60KB blocks of data for backup, speeding throughput to the backup device. Here are some other new features:

■ Backups can be *striped* (partitioned), enabling you to specify up to 32 separate devices for dumping or loading a database. The backup manager breaks the database into approximately equal portions and backs up those portions in parallel.

■ Backups can be performed remotely, enabling you to back up your database or a portion (stripe) of your database to a device on hardware other than the hardware where your SQL Server resides. This requires a network connection to a remote device, and can support standard Universal Naming Convention network names. (See the Windows NT Server documentation for more information on using UNC names for network resources.) This also requires that the SQL Server service be running under an account that has rights on the remote machine, and not be running under the Local System account.

■ SQL Server uses Windows NT backup tape names and resources, so the CONSOLE program is no longer necessary nor included with SQL Server.

■ Several backups can be recorded on the same tape. A subsequent restore locates only the file it needs to recover.

■ Tape options are expanded.

Creating Backup Devices with SQL Enterprise Manager

You can also use SQL Server's Enterprise Manager to define tape devices, using a GUI interface. In the Server Manager window of Enterprise Manager, right-click the Backup Devices folder and then click the New menu item on the resulting pop-up menu to display the dialog box shown in Figure 30.3.

FIGURE 30.3.

Define new backup devices in the New Backup Device dialog box in SQL Enterprise Manager.

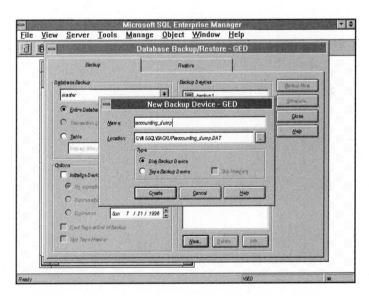

This dialog box enables you to define the logical and physical names, as well as assign the physical location of the device and indicate whether it's a disk or tape device. In the background, Enterprise Manager is simply running sp_addumpdevice, with the parameters containing the values you supply in this dialog box.

Backup and Restore Commands

Now that the basics have been defined, you need to take a close look at the dump and load commands. At this point, you should have the SQL Server up and running and your backup devices identified. Let's look at the options for the dump and load commands for both the entire database and the transaction log. We'll also look at two new features in SQL Server 6.5: single table backup and restore, and restoration to a point in time.

Backing Up the Database

Use dump database to make a full copy of your database. The simplified syntax for the dump database command is as follows:

```
dump database databasename to devicename
```

This command is valid for all versions of SQL Server. In SQL Server 6, however, the dump command needs to handle several other options, including displaying backup statistics, striped backups, and tape handling specifications. Following is the full syntax for the dump database command. Note that the formal syntax uses the term dump_device, whereas the SQL Server 6.5 Enterprise Manager refers to them as *backup devices*.

```
DUMP DATABASE {dbname ¦ @dbname_var}
        TO dump_device [, dump_device2 [..., dump_device32]]
    [WITH options
        [[,] STATS [ = percentage]]]
where
dump_device =
{dump_device_name ¦ @dump_device_namevar}
¦ {DISK ¦ TAPE ¦ FLOPPY ¦ PIPE} =
    {'temp_dump_device' ¦ @temp_dump_device_var}}
[VOLUME = {volid ¦ @volid_var}]
options =
[[,] {UNLOAD ¦ NOUNLOAD}]
[[,] {INIT ¦ NOINIT}]
[[,] {SKIP ¦ NOSKIP}]
[[,] {{EXPIREDATE = {date ¦ @date_var}}
    ¦ {RETAINDAYS = {days ¦ @days_var}}]
```

Table 30.1 presents detailed descriptions of each parameter of dump database.

Table 30.1. The `dump database` parameters.

Parameter	Description
dbname	The name of the database you're attempting to back up.
dump_device	The backup device you defined with `sp_addumpdevice`. Optionally, you can directly specify a disk or tape device, even when you're striping them.
retaindays = *#_of_days*	An option that can be used for any type of backup device. It doesn't allow the backup to be overwritten until the number of days specified has passed. This is an important option for any production backup strategy.
expiredate = *date*	As an alternative to `retaindays`, you can specify the date when the backup expires and can be overwritten.
stats = *percentage*	Returns the percentage of pages backed up (or restored) in increments specified by the value of *percentage*. If *percentage* isn't specified, the statistics will be shown for each 10 percent of the operation.

Several other options focus on how the backup is to be conducted, regardless of the physical device characteristics. You should incorporate several of these options into your backup strategy.

The next four options apply only to tape devices:

- **volume.** The option `volume` labels your backup, which then can be specified during a `load`. For example, specify a value for `volume` as a concatenation of your database name and the date (`CustomerDB_Jan07`). Then, if you have backups for January 7–10 on a single tape, you can easily reload the January 7 backup by specifying `volume` as part of the restore.

- **nounload ¦ unload.** The `nounload ¦ unload` option controls the rewinding of the tape. `nounload` should be used unless this is the last backup you want to have on the tape.

- **noinit ¦ init.** The `noinit ¦ init` option determines whether the backup will be appended to the tape or reinitializes the entire tape volume. Use `init` when backing up to a tape for the first time or to reuse an old tape. You might use `noinit` to allow for multiple backups to a single tape.

- **skip ¦ noskip.** This option indicates whether ANSI tape labels are read (`noskip`) or ignored (`skip`). For example, when `skip` is specified and the ANSI label of a tape warns that it has expired or that you don't have permission to write to it, SQL Server ignores the warning. Or, if the tape to which you're writing is new (and therefore has no ANSI label), SQL Server writes a new label on the first try. The `skip` option prevents unnecessary retries as SQL Server tries to find a label. Specifying `noskip` tells SQL Server to read existing ANSI tape labels on the tape to which you're writing. The default is `noskip`.

The following is an example of striped backups:

```
— Dump the CustomerDB database across 4 backup devices (Tape1-4).
— Name each volume, initialize the tapes, do not rewind,
— prevent other backups from overwriting this dump for 2 weeks,
— and send the messages to the client terminal.
dump database CustomerDB to Tape1 volume = Volume1,
    Tape2 volume = Volume2,
    Tape3 volume = Volume3,
    Tape4 volume = Volume4,
    with init, nounload, retaindays=14
```

Here's an example of multiple backups to a single tape:

```
— Dump the CustomerDB, ProductDB, and SecurityDB to Tape1
— For the first dump, initialize the tape but do not rewind.
— Dump the second database after the first.
— After the third database is dumped, rewind the tape.
dump database CustomerDB to Tape1 volume = CustVol1
    with init
dump database ProductDB to Tape1 volume = ProdVol1
    /* nounload is the default */
dump database SecurityDB to Tape1 volume = SecVol1
    with unload
```

You can back up a database while the server is in use, but doing so can cause a substantial performance degradation. Striping backups across even a small number of devices decreases the total amount of time required to execute the backup, decreasing the negative performance impact. You should benchmark user-response times with and without a backup process running to determine the impact on your system.

Backing Up Databases with SQL Enterprise Manager

So why, exactly, are we talking Transact-SQL syntax when Microsoft is shipping this nifty SQL Enterprise Manager utility? Because SQL Enterprise Manager, behind the scenes, is executing the syntax just described when you use it to back up databases.

When you choose Tools | Database Backup/Restore from the menu, SQL Enterprise Manager displays the Database Backup/Restore dialog box (see Figure 30.4). From this dialog box, you can back up and restore both databases and transaction logs. Enterprise Manager also enables you to create new backup devices, if they're needed.

Selecting the database name from the combo box defines which database you're going to back up. The various syntax options discussed previously are represented as check boxes and other options.

FIGURE 30.4.

SQL Enterprise Manager supplies a graphical interface that hides many of the complexities of backup command syntax.

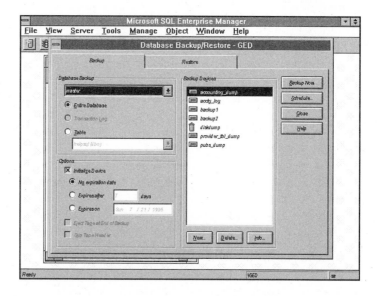

Striped backups are defined by selecting backup devices from the list on the right. Hold down the Ctrl key as you're selecting devices after the first one. SQL Enterprise Manager, when it builds the `dump database` statement it will eventually execute, will use the multiple devices selected to construct the multiple-device clause necessary for striped backup.

Whether used as native SQL syntax in a script, or used through SQL Enterprise Manager, the features of SQL Server backup are identical.

Backing Up Transaction Logs

Use `dump transaction` to make a copy of the transactions that have completed in your database since the last transaction log backup. This is the simplified syntax for the `dump transaction` command:

```
dump transaction databasename to devicename
```

`dump transaction` works similarly to `dump database` and supports the same options. The only difference between the two is in the amount of work they do. This is the full syntax for the `dump transaction` command:

```
DUMP TRANSACTION {dbname ¦ @dbname_var}
      [TO dump_device [, dump_device2 [..., dump_device32]]]
   [WITH {TRUNCATE_ONLY ¦ NO_LOG ¦ NO_TRUNCATE}
      {options}]
where
dump_device =
{dump_device_name ¦ @dump_device_namevar}
¦ {DISK ¦ TAPE ¦ FLOPPY ¦ PIPE} =
   {'temp_dump_device' ¦ @temp_dump_device_var}}
[VOLUME = {volid ¦ @volid_var}]
```

```
options =
[[,] {UNLOAD ¦ NOUNLOAD}]
[[,] {INIT ¦ NOINIT}]
[[,] {SKIP ¦ NOSKIP}]
[[,] {{EXPIREDATE = {date ¦ @date_var}}
    ¦ {RETAINDAYS = {days ¦ @days_var}}]
```

The special-purpose options are in the third line. These options are truncate_only, no_log, and no_truncate, and are described in the following sections.

truncate_only and no_log

The truncate_only and no_log options are used to prune the transaction log without making a copy of it. You normally will either specify one of these two options or indicate a device to which to back up the transaction log. Use truncate_only to truncate the log gracefully. It checkpoints the database before truncating the log. Use no_log when your transaction log is completely full. no_log doesn't checkpoint the database before backing up the log.

Either of these options throws away the log. When the command has been executed, you're exposed. If a disaster occurs before you can back up the database, you won't be able to recover any data that has been added since the last backup. The frequency of backing up transaction logs determines the scope of your exposure.

Any database that doesn't have its transaction log on a separate device can't have incremental backups made. Every system has a database with this characteristic. This usually is discovered when the transaction log for the master database fills up. The database space is shared between data and log, negating the capability of backing up the transaction log.

To avoid this problem, you should periodically prune the master database's transaction log with truncate_only (or no_log, if completely full). Be sure to back up the master database after logged operations (database creation, user addition, and so forth). For databases that don't require up-to-the-minute recovery, and for databases with no separate log segment, set the trunc log on chkpt option on for the database, and back up frequently.

no_truncate

The no_truncate option is exactly the opposite of truncate_only and no_log. no_truncate makes a copy of your transaction log but doesn't prune it. Use this option when you have a media failure of a data device being used by your database. The master database must be available. This option enables the server to back up the transaction log but doesn't try to touch the database in any way. (In a normal dump transaction, a checkpoint is executed. If a database device is unavailable, the checkpoint process can't write the dirty pages. no_truncate simply backs up the transaction log without checkpointing.) Note that the ability to backup the transaction log is disabled after non-logged operations such as non-logged writetext, select into, and fast BCP. You must do a complete database backup after one of these operations.

Transaction Log Backup with SQL Enterprise Manager

As with database backup, SQL Enterprise Manager builds a dump transaction statement that reflects the backup options you select using the Database Backup/Restore dialog box. There's one important distinction. Any database can be backed up using dump database. Only those databases that have a separate transaction log can have incremental backups done using dump transaction. As a result, SQL Enterprise Manager detects whether the database and the log share the same device, and automatically disables the Transaction Log option of the dialog box. Referring to Figure 30.4, the master database is selected for backup, and therefore the Transaction Log option is disabled. For the acctg_db database in Figure 30.5, the Transaction Log option is enabled because acctg_db has its transaction log on a distinct device.

FIGURE 30.5.

SQL Enterprise Manager enables the Transaction Log backup option only when a database has its transaction log on a device separate from the data.

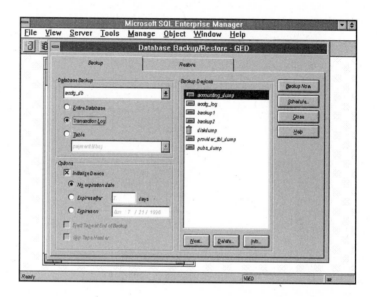

You'll notice that none of the extra transaction log backup options are available from the Database Backup/Restore Dialog Box. In SQL Server 6.5, truncating the log can be done from the Edit Databases dialog box. (You can get to this screen by right-clicking the name of a database in the Server Manager window, and selecting Edit.)The Truncate button will truncate a transaction log even if it's completely full. In order to use the with no_truncate option of dump transaction, you must use the native T-SQL syntax and submit the query from some query-based utility such as ISQL/w or from within the Query Tool window of SQL Enterprise Manager. All other options related to the dump transaction statement are available in the Database Backup/Restore dialog box.

Backing Up a Single Table

In SQL Server 6.5, you can back up and restore individual tables. If you anticipate having to restore individual tables, you can back them up with the dump table command. By backing up specific tables, you can conserve system resources, save time by backing up only tables that have changed, and target high-volume tables for regular backups.

Here's the full syntax for the dump table command:

```
DUMP TABLE [[database.]owner.]table_name
       [TO dump_device [, dump_device2 [..., dump_device32]]]
       [WITH options
           [[,]STATS [= percentage]]]
where
dump_device =
{dump_device_name ¦ @dump_device_namevar}
¦ {DISK ¦ TAPE ¦ FLOPPY ¦ PIPE} =
     {'temp_dump_device' ¦ @temp_dump_device_var}}
[VOLUME = {volid ¦ @volid_var}]
options =
[[,] {UNLOAD ¦ NOUNLOAD}]
[[,] {INIT ¦ NOINIT}]
[[,] {SKIP ¦ NOSKIP}]
[[,] {{EXPIREDATE = {date ¦ @date_var}}
     ¦ {RETAINDAYS = {days ¦ @days_var}}]
```

Restoring the Database

Use load database to restore a backup into an existing database. The database can be the database used to create the backup, but this isn't a requirement. The simplified syntax for the load database command is

```
load database databasename from devicename
```

This command is valid for all versions of SQL Server. Most options available to the dump command can be used in the load. This is the full syntax for the load database command:

```
LOAD DATABASE {dbname ¦ @dbname_var}
       FROM dump_device [, dump_device2 [..., dump_device32]]
     [WITH options
           [[,] STATS [ = percentage]]]
where
dump_device =
{ dump_device_name ¦ @dump_device_namevar}
¦ {DISK ¦ TAPE ¦ FLOPPY ¦ PIPE} =
     {'temp_dump_device' ¦ @temp_dump_device_var}}
[VOLUME = {volid ¦ @volid_var}]
options =
[[,] {UNLOAD ¦ NOUNLOAD}]
[[,] {SKIP ¦ NOSKIP}]
[[,] STOPAT = {date_time ¦ @datetime_var}]
[[,] FILE = fileno]
```

All options listed are identical to the `dump database` command, except for the `stopat` and `file` options. `stopat` is the date and time to stop loading a backup onto the database. This option is discussed later, in the section on restoring to a point in time. The `file` option specifies the file number to be loaded from a tape or disk device that contains multiple database backups. The default is `1`. To determine what's contained in a multiple database device, use the command `load headeronly`:

```
LOAD   HEADERONLY
     FROM dump_device
```

You might consider using this command immediately after a database backup to verify that the restore process can read the backup. It can be used for tape or file devices.

> **NOTE**
>
> No one can use the database while `load` is being executed, including the person executing the `load` command.

Here are some loading examples. The first shows a striped restore:

```
Load database accounting from Tape1, Tape2, Tape3, Tape4
```

The `load database` command restores all used pages from the backup into the target database and runs recovery of the transaction log to ensure consistency. Any unused pages are initialized by the restore process. (This is the primary reason that a restore can take significantly longer than a backup. The time required to back up a database is proportional to the used pages in the database; the time required to restore a database is proportional to the overall number of pages in the database. Therefore, a 50GB database with 20MB of data might take only a few minutes to back up, but the restore could take several hours or days.)

A `load` is executed to restore a database normally after a corruption or user error occurs. If you are restoring for a reason other than a disaster, the current database structure can be used to restore the database backup. This doesn't require any extra work other than ensuring that tapes are loaded (or files are in the correct locations).

Restoring Databases with SQL Enterprise Manager

From within the same Database Backup/Restore dialog box illustrated in Figures 30.4 and 30.5, you can also restore databases by clicking the Restore tab. The new dialog box, shown in Figure 30.6, provides the same syntax options as `load database` and `load transaction` (discussed in the preceding sections).

FIGURE 30.6.

SQL Enterprise Manager supplies the same features and functions that are available in T-SQL for database restoration, but presents them in a more usable format in this dialog box.

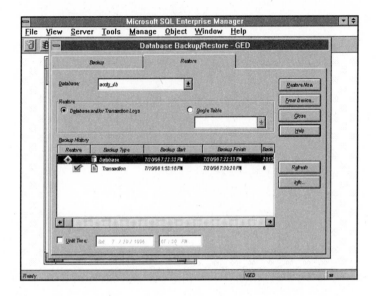

As with the Backup tab, SQL Enterprise Manager automatically detects the database that you want to restore and determines whether you can apply a transaction log backup. If the transaction log is on a separate device, SQL Enterprise Manager enables the Apply Transaction Log option button. Doing so changes the statement that SQL Enterprise Manager constructs from `load database` to `load transaction`. As with dumping databases, loading databases requires a list of source backup devices and a destination database. Having supplied these, and having made sure that the database isn't currently in use, SQL Enterprise Manager sends the appropriate `load` command to SQL Server.

Restoring After a Disaster

If the load is a result of a disaster, the database must first be dropped. The `drop database` might not execute in the case of a corruption. For corrupt databases, use `sp_dbremove`:

```
sp_dbremove database[, dropdev]
```

A new database structure must now be created. If you are creating a database for the exclusive purpose of restoring, use the `for load` option with the `create database` command.

Creating for Load

Creating a database for load allocates the structure but doesn't initialize the pages. Using this option takes significantly less time than a normal `create`. The database will not be usable except for running a `load`. The database must be created in the same fashion as the database that was backed up. For example, if you initially created the `CustomerDB` database with 1GB for data and 100MB for log, and you subsequently altered the database by 500MB for data, execute the following commands:

```
use master
go
create database CustomerDB on DataDevice1 = 1000,
     log on LogDevice1 = 200
     for load
go
alter database CustomerDB on DataDevice2 = 500 for load
go
load database CustomerDB from CustomerDB_dump
go
```

The easiest way to ensure the correct order is to save each `create` or `alter` command in a single create script as the commands are executed. If you haven't saved your scripts, you can retrieve this information from the sysusages table in the `master` database:

```
select segmap, "Size in MB"=size/512
from sysusages
where dbid = db_id ("database_name")
segmap     Size in MB
3          1000
4          200
3          500
```

The `segmap` column refers to the segments defined in your database. Initially, there are three segments in your database: `system`, `default`, and `logsegment`. If you convert the `segmap` number to binary, you can determine how the `segmap` relates to segment names:

2^0 = system segment

2^1 = default segment

2^2 = logsegment

2^3 = first user-defined segment

2^4 = second user-defined segment

The segment mapping for the example database is as follows:

```
            log   data   sys
segmap 2^3   2^2   2^1    2^0   size
3      0     0     1      1     1000
4      0     1     0      0     200
3      0     0     1      1     500
```

Therefore, a `segmap` of 3 indicates a data device (default + system), and a `segmap` of 4 indicates log only.

If you have added user-defined segments (and possibly dropped the default and system segments from a fragment), there are indicators in the 2^3 column and greater. These fragments should be created as data fragments. Because segments are database-specific, the database system tables containing the user-defined segment definitions are loaded in the `load` process, which resolves the segment mapping within the database.

> **NOTE**
>
> If you created your database with the log on a separate device, the log fragments should have a 1 in the log column (2^2) only.

Loading into a Different Database

Occasionally, you'll want to create an exact copy of a database in your system. First, back up the existing database. Then create a new database to load with this backup. The database doesn't have to be the same size as the original. The only requirement is that the destination database must be at least as large as the original database and have the same beginning fragments as the original database. For example, consider loading the backup from the preceding section into a database of 3GB. The command to create this database might be the following:

```
use master
go
create database NewCustomerDB on DataDevice2 = 1000
log on LogDevice2 = 200
     for load
go
alter database NewCustomerDB on DataDevice2 = 500 for load
go
alter database NewCustomerDB on DataDevice3 = 300 for load
go
alter database NewCustomerDB on DataDevice4 = 1000 for load
go
load database NewCustomerDB from CustomerDB_dump
go
```

Restoring a Transaction Log

Use `load transaction` to load a transaction log backup. Transaction logs must be loaded in the order in which they were backed up. If an attempt is made to load a transaction log backup out of sequence, SQL Server will report an error. During a `load database`, the data in the backup is copied over the database. After the `load` is complete, the database contains all the data in the database at the time of the full database backup. Restoring a transaction log is different from restoring a database. The transaction log restore copies the contents of the backup over the current `syslogs` definition. After the log has been restored, a recovery takes place. SQL Server marches through the log, applying changes in the log that aren't reflected in the database (normally, all records in the log are new transactions). The simplified syntax for the `load transaction` command is as follows:

```
load transaction <databasename> from <devicename>
```

Most options available to the `dump` command can be used in the `load`. This is the full syntax for the `load transaction` command:

```
LOAD TRANSACTION {dbname ¦ @dbname_var}
      TO dump_device [, dump_device2 [..., dump_device32]]
   [WITH options]

where
dump_device =
{dump_device_name ¦ @dump_device_namevar}
¦ {DISK ¦ TAPE ¦ FLOPPY ¦ PIPE} =
   {'temp_dump_device' ¦ @temp_dump_device_var}}
[VOLUME = {volid ¦ @volid_var}]
options =
[[,] {UNLOAD ¦ NOUNLOAD}]
[[,] {SKIP ¦ NOSKIP}]
[[,] STOPAT = {date_time ¦ @datetime_var}]
[[,] FILE = fileno]
```

Most of the options listed are explained in the section titled "Backing Up the Database." file is defined in the section titled "Restoring the Database." stopat is discussed in the later section titled "Restoring to a Point in Time."

The load of a transaction log backup usually requires significantly less time than a load database because the size of the log is normally much smaller than the size of the database itself. No modifications should be made to the database between a load database and a load transaction (or between transaction log loads). Once any changes have been made to the database, no further transaction logs can be loaded.

> **NOTE**
>
> There's one situation in which restoring a transaction log could take considerably more time than expected. When an index is created, the only information that's written to the log is the fact that the index has been built, along with the records of the page allocations. If a transaction log is restored that includes the building of an index, SQL Server must rebuild the entire index during the restore process. For a clustered index on a large table, this can take quite a long time.
>
> Because restoration is frequently done as a response to a disaster situation, and you'll want to get the database up and running as fast as possible, you should consider making a complete backup of the entire database whenever a large clustered index has to be (re)built.

Restoring a Single Table

SQL Server 6.5 allows you to restore a single table, either from a table backup or from a complete database backup. Here's the complete syntax for the load table command (continued on the following page):

```
LOAD TABLE [[database.]owner.]table_name
      FROM dump_device [, dump_device2 [..., dump_device32]]
   [WITH options
```

836

```
        [[,] STATS [ = percentage]]]
where
dump_device =
{ dump_device_name ¦ @dump_device_namevar}
¦ {DISK ¦ TAPE ¦ FLOPPY ¦ PIPE} =
    {'temp_dump_device' ¦ @temp_dump_device_var}}
[VOLUME = {volid ¦ @volid_var}]
options =
[[,] {UNLOAD ¦ NOUNLOAD}]
[[,] {SKIP ¦ NOSKIP}]
[[,] FILE = fileno]
[[,] SOURCE = source_name]
[[,] APPEND]
```

All options listed are identical to the load database command, except for the source and append options. source is the name of the source table from which to load the table. This option must be specified if the source and target table names differ. append specifies that all new data will be added to a table that already contains data.

Single tables can also be restored by choosing the Restore tab in the Database Backup/Restore dialog box. Figure 30.7 shows Single Table option selected, and only table backups and database backups are visible in the Backup History list. (No transaction log backups are shown.)

FIGURE 30.7.

When selecting a single table restore, only table backups and database backups are shown in the Backup History list.

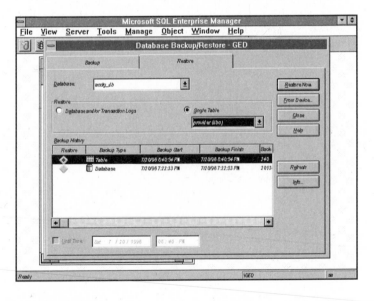

With previous versions of SQL Server, the BCP utility was used to back up and restore the contents of a single table. In SQL Server 6.5, you can use dump table and load table as an alternative. Preliminary testing has shown that load table is significantly faster than using BCP to copy a table into a database.

> **NOTE**
>
> Only a full database and transaction log backups and restores can ensure that all primary key-to-foreign key relationships are consistent. Use table restores only when absolutely necessary.

> **NOTE**
>
> It's recommended that you load a table only from a table backup and not from a full database backup. When backing up a table, an exclusive lock is taken on the table. The table backup is an accurate snapshot of the data at the time the backup was made. A full database backup, however, may have captured transactions in progress. When restoring an individual table from a full database backup, nothing from the transaction log is applied, so you can be left with partial transactions and inconsistent data.

Here are some additional things you should know when doing single-table restores:

- Table restores can't be performed for tables that have text or image columns, or that are published for replication.

- Triggers, rules, defaults, and declarative referential integrity (DRI) aren't enforced for table restores.

- Source and target tables must be identical in their nullability, length, and system datatype.

- Table restores can be performed only when the Select Into/Bulkcopy option is set for the database. A `load table` disables any further `dump transaction` commands until a full database backup is made.

- Table restores can't be done on tables that have indexes; in SQL Enterprise Manager the user will be asked for permission to drop the indexes, which can be rebuilt automatically on completion.

- As with other restore operations, backups from one processor type can't be loaded into a server on another type of processor.

- The target table must be a user table, but the source table can be either a system or a user table.

- Source and target tables can have different names if the `source` option is specified; however, because there's no way to specify a source table name in SQL Enterprise Manager, the `load table` statement must be used.

- There's no way to specify the `append` option in SQL Enterprise Manager; however, if the table already contains data, you'll be asked if you want to append to or overwrite the existing data.

■ The next identity value for any existing identity column is correctly reset after a table restore, even if the table already contains data.

Restoring to a Point in Time

SQL Server 6.5 allows you to restore transaction logs to a specified point in time. The desired date and time are specified with the stopat option of the load transaction command. If you refer to Figure 30.7, you can see the check box to indicate point-in-time recovery, and the text boxes to allow you to enter the desired date and time. Point-in-time recovery is possible only while restoring transaction logs, and isn't possible from a database or table restore.

When restoring a sequence of transaction log backups, if you aren't sure which backup has the date and time needed, you can specify the same date and time for each of the restore operations; this way you can be sure of stopping at the specified date and time.

Point-in-time recovery is possible because SQL Server writes an actual date/time timestamp in the EndTransaction record in the transaction log. When doing point-in-time recovery, SQL Server checks the EndTransaction log records for a timestamp greater than the specified time. Once one is encountered, that transaction and all subsequent transactions will be rolled back. In this case, *subsequent* means EndTransaction records that occur in the log after the one that triggered point-in-time recovery.

If the system time was incorrect when the EndTransaction log record was written, for example, one hour ahead, the log records will have timestamps that are one hour ahead. An EndTransaction record written to the transaction log at 4:30 will have a timestamp of 5:30 and will trigger point-in-time recovery if stopat was set to 5:30. If the system time was subsequently corrected, another EndTransaction record could also have a timestamp of 5:30. Only the first transaction ending at 5:30 would be applied, because once point-in-time recovery is triggered, all subsequent transactions will be rolled back, regardless of their timestamps.

Backup and Restore History

SQL Server 6.5 has four new tables in the msdb database that record the history of backups and restores. These tables are: sysbackuphistory, sysbackupdetail, sysrestorehistory, and sysrestoredetail. These tables are used by SQL Enterprise Manager when displaying the Restore dialog box; the tables allow you to see what backups are available for loading. If you jump back to Figure 30.7, you can see the Backup History list in the middle of the screen. As an administrator, you can also use these tables for generating your own reports of the history of your backups and restores.

Additional Backup Considerations

The pieces of the puzzle are starting to fall into place. You've defined the groundwork necessary to begin development of your backup-and-recovery approach. Now you must consider several issues that can affect your plan.

Frequency of Backups

As mentioned previously, backups should be made as frequently as necessary for effective database administration. This criterion is intentionally vague because the frequency of backups varies based on your requirements. The deciding factor is the amount of time your business can afford for the database to be unavailable after a disaster.

The total time to restore a database is the sum of database restore time plus transaction log restore time. The database restore happens only once during a recovery of a database, and the time can be predicted to some degree. The time to do the transaction log restores, however, is very unpredictable. The time to load transaction logs is based on the amount of activity since the database backup.

Consider the difference between a database backed up yearly versus a database backed up weekly, with transaction logs backed up every day between backups for both. The yearly backup scenario has 364 transaction log backups between database backups; the weekly backup scenario has six transaction log backups. If a disaster occurs on January 4, the time to recover in both cases is identical. Each scenario has a database restore (January 1 database backup) and three transaction log restores (January 2, 3, and 4 transaction log backups). But consider the worst-case scenario. A yearly backup approach could result in having to restore a full year's worth of activity, one day at a time. The weekly backup approach would have a maximum of only a week's worth of activity to restore.

Therefore, back up your database as often as possible. Ideally, database backups should occur with no activity on the system. Although this isn't a requirement, it assures you that the backup contains the state of your database before and after your backup was made. If this isn't possible, make your backups when activity is as light as possible.

Backups can be executed during normal business hours, but they'll have an effect on system performance. Database backups in SQL Server 6 are much less devastating to performance than in earlier versions. This is due to code changes in the implementation of the database backup, increased speed of the process, and the capability of striping backups.

Transaction log backups are often scheduled during normal business hours, but periods of low (or no) activity are obviously preferred. Backing up a transaction log takes significantly less time than a database dump, and the time required is based on the amount of data in the log (which is based on modifications since the last dump transaction). A backup plan for a production system should include transaction log backups to provide up-to-the-minute recovery.

Development environments normally don't dump transaction logs because this type of recovery isn't needed. Fairly frequent database backups usually suffice.

Striped Backups

Backups can be striped across as many as 32 parallel devices in SQL Server 6. This feature can significantly reduce the time required to back up or restore your database or transaction logs.

In spite of the performance improvement, try to avoid striping. Each stripe can be considered a possible point of failure. If one of the stripes can't be read, the load will fail. Consider striping when you decide the time required to back up to a single device is too great to fit the activity in your administration window.

Locking

Although SQL Server enables access to a database during a backup (online backup), there's a particular method to its madness. In the backup process, SQL Server locks extents (8 × 2KB pages) for the entire database. As SQL Server copies out used pages (free space is never backed up), those extent locks are released. SQL Server moves sequentially in extent order through the database, copying pages and releasing extent locks as it proceeds.

User requests, however, can interrupt this process. If a user connection wants to modify a page that hasn't yet been copied out, SQL Server suspends its "in order" copy of pages, jumps to the requested page, and backs up the extent on which that page is found. SQL Server then releases the lock on that extent, enabling the user connection to continue. SQL Server picks up from the last sequentially correct position in the database and continues copying out pages until it has finished, or until a user connection requests another locked page.

In this way, a backup represents a "snapshot" of a database. The changes that the backup process allows don't appear in that particular backup of the database. For that reason, any transactions that are processed after the dump database command is executed by the server must be backed up using a subsequent dump transaction command!

Capturing Statistics

Capture as many statistics as possible about the backup-and-restore processes. This information is invaluable in estimating durations and gives you real statistics about the performance of your system. These are important statistics to gather:

- Total database size (sp_helpdb)
- Total number of used pages (for information about sp_spaceused, see Chapter 26, "Defining, Altering, and Maintaining Databases and Logs")

■ Total execution time (if using the command syntax in T-SQL, you can wrap the `dump` or `load` command with `select getdate()`)

For backups, the time to execute is fairly linear, based on used pages. For loads, the time to execute is based on total database size and used pages.

You need to understand and monitor database size and usage when planning backup regimens for databases that haven't leveled off in size. During the early stages of a system, data volume can be low. Data is added over time. This increase levels off when your purge and archive criteria kick in.

For example, a 15GB database might be created to support your production system. Initially, it may be loaded with only 2GB of base information (used pages). If your application adds 5GB of data each year, and data is purged when it's two years old, the database size levels off at 12GB. Your statistics might show that the 2GB database can be backed up in one hour. If you have a four-hour backup window, you have to start investigating alternative approaches when your database reaches 8GB. By capturing statistics, you would be able to forecast this problem a full year in advance.

Transaction Logging

It's important to prevent the transaction log from running out of space. When the transaction log fills, no other logged operations can be executed until space is available in the log. This is disastrous in production systems. In version 4.x, however, it was a fairly common experience. The DBA was forced to pay close attention to the available space in the log, executing a `dump transaction` before the log ran out of space.

Over time, database activity stabilizes and can be estimated. You should know the amount of time that your system can be active, under normal conditions, before the transaction log completely fills. Based on the amount, schedule transaction log backups often enough to prevent this situation from occurring. (Dump transaction logs when they're about one-half to three-quarters full.)

Even though you have the `dump transaction` activities scheduled, the system might experience peak activities (end of quarter, fiscal year end, and so on) that cause the log to fill at a greatly accelerated rate. The size of the log needs to be monitored so that a full transaction log won't take you by surprise. Version 4.x users are still forced to monitor the log using Windows NT's Performance Monitor application to fix this problem.

Monitoring Available Log Space

SQL Server offers the following two stored procedures to monitor space availability. You can use either to get a report on the `syslogs` table (see the following page):

- sp_spaceused
- dbcc checktable

sp_spaceused checks the reserved column to see how many pages are in use. Relate this to your overall log size to determine availability.

dbcc checktable checks each page in a table and provides an accurate reporting of the number of data pages used. As with sp_spaceused, relate this value to overall log size to determine availability. If your log is on a separate device, the output is easier to analyze. It reports statistics regarding space used and space free in megabytes as well as a percentage of total space:

dbcc checktable (syslogs)

SQL Server can also use Windows NT's Performance Monitor to monitor log space. Performance Monitor's Alert subsystem can monitor total space used in megabytes, as well as the percentage of space used. This latter option is accurate only if the log is on its own device. Performance Monitor enables you to activate ISQL command-line scripts in response to particular events—most notably, setting a percentage threshold over which the log can't grow. Performance Monitor relies on a *polling interval* to determine how large the log is, and there's a performance hit caused by this polling action. For 4.2x-level servers, it's the only option.

SQL Server 6.5 includes two new Performance Monitor counters to help you manage the growth of the log. Max Log Space Used Percentage records the maximum percentage of space in a transaction log that has been used for any selected database during the monitoring session. Max Log Size records the maximum size of the transaction log, in megabytes, that has been allocated for a selected database during the monitoring session. These two counters allow the recording and observing of "high-water markers," so as the log grows and shrinks you can have a record of the largest size reached.

SQL Server 6 users also have the SQL Server Distributed Management Framework, which allows them to set scheduled tasks to perform transaction log backup and pruning, or define exceptions that monitor SQL Server error conditions. That topic is discussed in Chapter 35, "The MS SQL Server Distributed Management Framework."

Developing Your Backup-and-Recovery Plan

Consider all your databases when developing the backup-and-recovery plan. System databases have different requirements than user databases.

System Databases

There are four system databases created as part of server installation: master, model, tempdb, and msdb (three for version 4.2x, which has no msdb). tempdb is temporary (it's actually rebuilt by SQL Server every time it's started); by definition it should be considered exempt from backups. All other system databases should be backed up, however.

Threats

There are two things to watch out for with system databases:

- Database or table corruption
- Damage to the master device

If corruption occurs, follow the steps to rebuild that individual database. If the master device is damaged, it has to be re-initialized. This affects the `master`, `model`, `tempdb`, and possibly the `sybsystemprocs` databases (which can exist on the master device or an alternate device).

The `master` Database

The `master` database isn't a high-activity database. It's fairly small and is created on the `master` device with a default allocation of 17 megabytes. This size is adequate for most small installations, but the requirements of larger installations quickly mandate an increase in size. Because it's on a single device, data and log compete for available space and the transaction log can't be dumped. It can't grow beyond the confines of the `master` device.

The following activities result in the insertion or modification of rows in various system tables:

- Creating, altering, or dropping devices
- Creating, altering, or dropping databases
- Adding or dropping logins or users
- Adding or dropping backup devices
- Reconfiguring SQL Server
- Adding remote servers

Because the `master` database controls SQL Server, a database corruption or the loss of the master device can be devastating. SQL Server is unavailable until the `master` database is repaired. Not having a current backup of the `master` database can be fatal (or at least quite painful). To protect yourself, back up the `master` database whenever commands are executed that insert, update, or delete rows in the system tables. The importance of the backup of this database cannot be stressed enough. Trying to re-create the `master` database from scratch can be extremely difficult, especially if you haven't saved the data from the system tables.

> **NOTE**
>
> The `master` database has no separate log segment, so all backups are full database backups.

Detecting the Problem

If you lose the `master` device, the server goes down, alerting you to the problem. Alert messages appear in the `errorlog` file created by SQL Server, as well as in the Windows NT Event Log application. The normal method of detecting corruption in any database is the suite of `dbcc` commands. If corruption occurs in the `master` database, the system likely will be affected instantaneously. Often, the server goes down and doesn't come up, or major errors appear in `errorlog`.

> **TIP**
>
> If a `dbcc` detects corruption in `master`, log a call to Microsoft Product Support Services. Corruption in `master` or `msdb` could be indicative of a problem with the underlying master device. If you're confident that you can solve the problem yourself, start executing the steps in the recovery process.

You must be proactive to avoid a painful recovery. First of all, avoid striping the `master` database backups, even if it's standard for your user databases. Make sure that all of the `master` dump can fit on a single tape or in an operating-system file. (Based on the normal size of the `master` database, this shouldn't be a problem.) SQL Server must be started in single-user mode to start the recovery process. If the load requires a volume change, you can't open another connection to tell the backup server that the new tape is in place.

Mitigating the Risk

The `master` database should be dumped regularly, probably on the same schedule as your user databases. If you make a change and you don't want to wait for the backup scripts to run, execute it by hand. As always, you should have scripts saved for every activity that modifies `master`. To be extra safe, bulk copy the data from the following tables into separate ASCII files (don't use `dump table` for this, because you'll need to be able to read the files you create):

- `sysdatabases`
- `sysdevices`
- `sysusages`
- `sysconfigures`
- `syslogins`

The SQL Server Setup utility has an option to rebuild the master device.(The check box says that you're rebuilding the `master` database, but what's really happening is that the `master.dat` file is overwritten with the original contents, so you get a whole new `master` device, including a whole new `master` database.) Rebuilding the master device, and allowing the setup process to complete, gives you a `master` device identical to when SQL Server was first installed. At this point, the master database has no knowledge of any user databases in your system. You have to execute one of the following:

- Loading your most recent backup of the master database (preferred)
- Transferring the data, using ISQL or BCP
- Recreating items from DDL scripts

You should have the resources to undertake any of these approaches at any time. It's the only way to ensure that the master database (and SQL Server) will be available when you need it.

model **and** msdb

The model database is copied into any database created with create database. It houses those items you want to be available across all databases (rules, defaults, user-defined datatypes, and users). If you've made any modifications to model, save all DDL files and back up the database after changes are made.

The msdb database holds all the task-scheduling and error-processing instructions that SQL Executive uses for automated task and alert handling. You should back up this database any time you modify it so that you can restore your scheduled and error-based tasks as quickly as possible.

If you detect corruption in either of these databases, you must re-create the entire master database and master device, using the Setup utility described earlier.

User Databases

Your business requirements define whether a database should be backed up. Backups are normally a requirement for production systems. Your approach should define the following:

- *Who?* Identify the person or group responsible for backup and recovery.
- *Name?* Outline your naming standards for database names and backup devices.
- *Which databases?* Identify the databases in your system to be backed up.
- *Types of backups?* Indicate whether you'll back up only the database, or whether you'll also back up the transaction log.
- *How?* Decide whether backups will use disk or file devices and whether the backup is a single process or striped.
- *Frequency?* Identify the schedule for dumping the database and the transaction logs.
- *Execution?* Determine whether backups will be initiated by hand or automated. If automated, detail whether the backup is conducted by an off-the-shelf tool or custom-developed program. Include all code (dump script and scheduler, if applicable) and make sure that it's commented extremely well.

For database recovery, detail the procedures involved in loading each database. If you're using a tool, outline its use.

Considerations for Very Large Databases (VLDBs)

When developing a backup-and-recovery plan for VLDB environments, several items must be considered. The challenge of a VLDB is its sheer size—everything is larger. Tables are measured in gigabytes, and databases are measured in tens or hundreds of gigabytes. The fact that several SQL Server VLDBs exist in industry today gives credence to the product's capability of handling vast amounts of data. VLDBs aren't easy to implement, however, for a variety of reasons. These are the top 10 VLDB issues:

- Impact of corruption
- Time for recovery (how much time)
- Time of backups (when in the day)
- Time to perform initial load of data
- Time to update statistics of indexes
- Time to perform database consistency checks
- Time to create indexes
- Impact of incremental batch data loading routines
- Impact of online activity
- Backup media capacity and backup facilities

Based on these items, you need to make several database architecture choices:

- Physically implementing a single logical database as several smaller physical databases
- Segmenting tables horizontally and/or vertically
- Table or index placement
- Log size and placement
- `tempdb` size and placement

Let's consider the issues in regard to your choices. The time required to perform database backups, loads, updates of statistics, and creation of indexes increases linearly with size. Follow these steps:

1. First, consider the amount of time you're willing to be down while performing a recovery (impact of corruption). If you need a database to be recovered within eight hours, determine the size of a database that can be recovered in that amount of time. Note that the load process is much slower than the dump process. Assume that 4GB is the maximum database size that can be reloaded in the defined window.

2. Taking 4GB as a baseline, analyze table estimates for your database. If you have a 40GB logical database, you might need to implement 10 4GB databases. Are any tables greater than 4GB? How many tables can you fit in a database? Are any tables candidates for segmentation, based on this determination alone?

3. Develop your utopian administration schedule. For every day during a month, determine what periods of time can be dedicated to administrative activities. Weekends might be available, but this isn't always the case. If you determine that you have five hours per night to perform administrative activities, you then need to determine what activities need to be completed and whether they can be distributed over your available administration time.

4. Determine the speed of the backup process. Take into consideration backup media capacity, speed, and the number of databases to be backed up. Benchmark several scenarios. Create a database and load it with about 2GB of data. Perform several database backups with a varying number of backup devices (striped backups). Run several backup processes (for different databases) simultaneously.

5. Determine periodic activity timings for each of your tables. This should be a matrix with table names down one axis and activities (dbcc, update statistics, index creation) across the other axis. After you develop a baseline for these activities, you can easily group tables together to determine the total amount of administration time needed for a certain combination of tables.

6. Determine which activities must take place in a batch window. If you want to perform database consistency checks immediately prior to dumping a database, the time required to perform both activities can be determined from your timings. Assume that a dump takes three hours and a dbcc takes two hours. Although this total fits in your five-hour window, it doesn't consider the fact that you have 10 of these to complete during the course of a week. Perform activities in parallel to determine concurrent processing times. Can you dbcc and dump two databases in a five-hour period?

7. Finalize your schedule and document accordingly.

8. Update your documents periodically based on actual experiences.

Summary

Development of a backup-and-recovery approach isn't a trivial process. You must consider internal and external forces and determine their impact. In the end, you should document your approach so that it's clear how you plan to handle these activities. Be sure to gather statistics on all activities, and use those statistics to predict future performance.

Although building a good backup-and-recovery plan seems like a tremendous amount of work, it's worth the effort in the long run. Project plans must allocate time to create the plan, and it should be in place before you make your production database available.

Configuring and Tuning SQL Server

31

SQL Server contains a number of configuration parameters that control its behavior. This chapter examines the available configuration parameters, describing the aspect of SQL Server each parameter controls, and the defaults and range of values for which each can be configured. Chapter 32, "Optimizing SQL Server Configuration Options," looks in more depth at the configuration parameters that have the greatest impact on performance and provides guidelines for tuning those parameters to optimize SQL Server performance.

Configuration Variables

`sp_configure` is one of the most important weapons in your SQL Server tuning arsenal, giving you control over options ranging from memory utilization, to how CPU's should be utilized on SMP computers, to how many users can be connected at any given time. This section describes all the options available with `sp_configure` and gives advice on tuning the most important ones.

Table 31.1 lists the options for `sp_configure`. Dynamic options are marked with an asterisk (*) and advanced options are shown in bold type.

Table 31.1. Options for `sp_configure`.

name	minimum	maximum	config_value	run_value
affinity mask	0	2147483647	0	0
allow updates*	0	1	0	0
backup buffer size*	1	10	1	1
backup threads	0	32	5	5
cursor threshold*	-1	2147483647	100	100
database size	1	10000	2	2
default language	0	9999	0	0
default sortorder id	0	255	52	52
fill factor	0	100	0	0
free buffers*	20	524288	204	204
hash buckets	4999	265003	7993	7993
language in cache	3	100	3	3
LE threshold maximum*	2	500000	200	200
LE threshold minimum*	2	500000	20	20
LE threshold percent*	1	100	0	0
locks	5000	2147483647	5000	5000
logwrite sleep (ms)*	-1	500	0	0
max async io	1	255	8	8

name	minimum	maximum	config_value	run_value
max lazywrite IO*	1	255	8	8
max text repl size*	0	2147483647	65536	65536
max worker threads*	10	1024	255	255
media retention	0	365	0	0
memory	1000	1048576	4096	4096
nested triggers*	0	1	1	1
network packet size*	512	32767	4096	4096
open databases	5	32767	20	20
open objects	100	2147483647	500	500
priority boost	0	1	0	0
procedure cache	1	99	30	30
RA cache hit limit*	1	255	4	4
RA cache miss limit*	1	255	3	3
RA delay*	0	500	15	15
RA pre-fetches*	1	1000	3	3
RA slots per thread	1	255	5	5
RA worker threads	0	255	3	3
recovery flags	0	1	0	0
recovery interval*	1	32767	5	5
remote access*	0	1	1	1
remote conn timeout*	-1	32767	10	10
remote login timeout*	0	2147483647	5	5
remote proc trans*	0	1	0	0
remote query timeout*	0	2147483647	0	0
resource timeout*	-1	2147483647	100	100
set working set size	0	1	0	0
show advanced options*	0	1	1	1
smp concurrency	-1	64	0	1
sort pages*	64	511	64	64
spin counter*	1	2147483647	10000	10
tempdb in ram (MB)	0	2044	0	0
time slice	50	1000	100	100
user connections	5	32767	20	20
user options*	0	4095	0	0

The descriptions of the five columns in the output are as follows:

- `name` is the description of the variable.

- `minimum` and `maximum` are the valid range of values for the specific variable. Note that these are pulled from the `spt_values` table.

- When the server comes up, the values in the permanent table, `sysconfigures`, are copied into a memory-only table, `syscurconfigs`. *config_value* reflects the value in the `sysconfigures` table, and *run_value* reflects the value in the `syscurconfigs` table. *run_value* and *config_value* may be different for static configuration options.

> **NOTE**
>
> SQL Server 6.5 includes five new `sp_configure` options:
> - affinity mask
> - max text repl size
> - remote conn timeout
> - remote proc trans
> - user options

Configuration options can be dynamic or non-dynamic. *Dynamic values* are those parameters that, when modified, take effect immediately. Some examples are `recovery interval`, `default language`, and `allow updates`. Variables that don't recognize change until the SQL Server is stopped and restarted are considered to be *non-dynamic values*.

> **NOTE**
>
> Don't forget that you need to *cycle* the server to change non-dynamic options (the ones without asterisks). Unfortunately, most important configuration settings require a reboot to take effect.

SQL Server 6.0 was the first to introduce the concept of "advanced" configuration options. The thinking is that some options should be hidden from the casual user, because they're so easy to mess up and should be changed infrequently. To accomplish this, Microsoft added a new setting called `show advanced options`. When this option is turned on (by setting the value to 1), advanced options are shown in `sp_configure` output. If it's turned off (by setting the value to 0), advanced options are hidden from view.

Advanced options can be changed whether or not the `show advanced options` flag is turned on.

Setting options with `sp_configure` is relatively simple. Here's the syntax:

```
sp_configure "option", value
reconfigure [with override]
```

The `with override` option is necessary only to force the server to configure with options it knows to be invalid or force the server to allow direct updates of system tables.

In this example, the recovery interval is being set to seven minutes:

```
sp_configure "recovery interval", 7
reconfigure
```

`sp_configure` can be run in three different modes:

- Executing the procedure with no parameters returns information about all of the configuration options.
- Specifying one option with no parameters returns information about just that setting.
- Specifying one option and one value sets the `config_value` of that option. The `run_value` will be set when the server is rebooted for non-dynamic options, or when the `reconfigure` command is issued for dynamic options.

The `reconfigure` command is always required, even though Books On Line implies that it's not necessary under some circumstances.

You must always run the `reconfigure` command after executing `sp_configure` to change a value; otherwise, the change won't have taken effect when the server restarts! To protect system integrity, system administrators are the only users capable of actually changing a setting with `sp_configure`, but all members of the `users` group can run the procedure to check current configuration settings.

All the examples in this chapter spell out the `configuration` option to avoid confusion. In real life, you only need to include enough of the spelling to make it unique.

However, you should always type the entire name when setting `configuration` options in batch files. If new options are added in a future release, your batch may stop working!

Start SQL Server with the999 `-f` command-line switch if you accidentally configure a value in a way that prevents SQL Server from starting. This allows the server to start with default configuration options so you can fix your mistake. Rebuilding the `master` database using the `SETUP` utility will also reset the configuration parameters to their defaults, but should be avoided because you'll also lose access to your user databases.

SQL Server starts in single-user mode when the `-f` option is used. Single-user literally means one—and only one—connection. You'll need to stop the SQL Executive service or it might grab the only free connection before you have a chance to establish a connection. You should use `ISQL/w` instead of SQL Enterprise Manager (SQL-EM) to reconfigure the bad settings, as SQL-EM will try to grab multiple connections. SQL-EM won't work properly while the server is running in single-user mode!

This is *not* well documented. Forget this tip and you might decide to pull your hair out while trying to recover the server!

Setting Configuration Options with SQL Enterprise Manager

Configuration options can also be modified with SQL Enterprise Manager. Highlight the server you want to configure and choose the Server | SQL Server | Configure... menu sequence to bring up the Server Configuration/Options dialog box. Clicking on the Configuration tab shows the dialog box in Figure 31.1.

You don't need to manually run the `reconfigure` command when changing options through the GUI interface of SQL Enterprise Manager, as one is issued automatically. You can take my word for it, or use the new SQL Trace utility and check it out for yourself!

FIGURE 31.1.

SQL Enterprise Manager provides a dialog box for changing and viewing SQL Server configuration options.

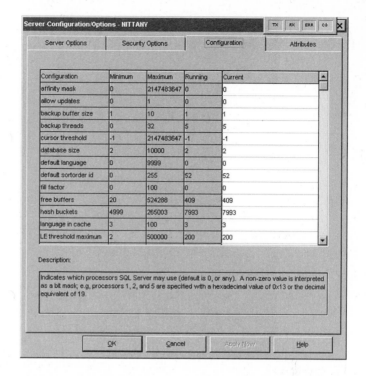

This interface provides access to all the functionality of the command-line version of `sp_configure`. The `reconfigure` command may seem to be missing at first. It's there, but the GUI interface calls it Apply Now. Choosing Apply Now issues `reconfigure` immediately. Clicking OK issues a `reconfigure` command and closes the dialog box.

TIP

Don't forget that configuration options can also be set programmatically by using SQL-DMO.

Configurable Values

The following sections provide a detailed list of configuration settings and how they affect server operations.

affinity mask

Advanced

Units: Decimal bit mask of which processors can be used by SQL Server threads in an SMP environment.

Default: 0 tells SQL Server to use all available processors.

By default, NT schedules threads on whatever processor is available; no guarantee is made to associate a thread with a specific CPU. Threads may move from processor to processor, incurring a certain amount of overhead each time the processor cache is reloaded. Performance can be improved on machines with more than four processors by limiting the processors that NT will use to schedule SQL Server threads. This is called *thread affinity*.

The affinity mask is used to limit which processors SQL Server will use in an SMP environment, and is set at the system level, not the individual connection level. The following table shows how a bit mask can be used to define which processors SQL Server is permitted to use.

Configuration Value	Bit Mask	Processors SQL Server Will Use
1	00000001	0
3	00000011	0 and 1
7	00000111	0, 1, and 2
15	00001111	0, 1, 2, and 3
31	00011111	0, 1, 2, 3, and 4
63	00111111	0, 1, 2, 3, 4, and 5
126	01111110	1, 2, 3, 4, 5, and 6 (isolates SQL Server activity from I/O and DPC processors)
127	01111111	0, 1, 2, 3, 4, 5, and 6 (isolates SQL Server activity from DPC processor only)
254	11111110	1, 2, 3, 4, 5, 6, 7 (isolates SQL Server activity from I/O processor only)

TIP

SQL Server Books On Line (BOL) provides great information on how Windows NT schedules certain low-level system functions like I/O management and NIC handling to specific processors. For example, all I/O handling is always assigned to processor 0, while delayed process call (DPC) activity associated with network cards (NICs) is assigned to the highest numbered processor in the system.

Set the BOL search string to sp_configure (version 6.5) and run a "title only" search to find more information about processor assignment and the best usages for affinity mask.

Excluding processors may improve performance by limiting overutilization of processors that have specific operating-system assignments. This technique can also be useful in evaluating the systems handling of certain NT functions like I/O management, which is always assigned to processor 0.

allow updates

Dynamic

Standard

Units: 0 or 1 (boolean)

Default: 0 (no)

This option determines whether the server allows direct updates to base system tables without using the appropriate system stored procedure.

> **WARNING**
>
> Be very careful with this option! Making direct modifications to system tables can easily destroy your server!

Notes:

■ In order to turn on `allow updates`, you have to issue the `reconfigure` command with override:

```
reconfigure with override
```

■ One of the most reasonable times to enable `allow updates` is after inadvertent device failure. If a device isn't available to the server when the server comes up (the power is down, for example), any databases using that device are recorded in `sysdatabases` as suspect. If you update the `sysdatabases` table (changing the SUSPECT bit), you may be able to bring down the server, power up the offending device, and reconnect to your database. The following example shows the `update` statement you might issue to retry connecting to all suspect databases:

```
update sysdatabases
set status = status - 256
where status & 256 = 256
```

SQL Server uses status bit 256 to mark a database as "suspect." Removing this bit allows SQL Server to attempt to recover the database. Once a database is marked as suspect, SQL Server will not attempt to recover it until the suspect bit is manually removed.

■ After you use the `allow updates` option, be sure to turn it off. A value of 0 says "Don't allow updates"; a value of 1 says "I'm willing to chance it."

> **WARNING**
>
> If you create a stored procedure that modifies system tables while the `allow updates` option is turned on, the procedure will still be able to update system tables after the option is turned back off. Make sure you turn it off ASAP!

backup buffer size

Dynamic

Standard

Units: Integer number of backup buffers

Default: 1

`backup buffer size` specifies the number of 32-page increments that SQL Server will use for backup I/O. The minimum number of buffers is 1, and the maximum is 10. Therefore, if you specified 10 backup buffers for this option, your next database backup would perform I/O in 320×2KB-page increments, or 640KB per I/O.

This option can be very useful for optimizing I/O on very large databases (VLDBs), but setting it is more art than science. Experimentation on your specific platform is the optimal method for using this option.

backup threads

Standard

Units: Integer number of threads

Default: 5

This specifies the maximum number of threads used for a striped database backup operation. Multiple threads allow the backup to occur in parallel, which can have a tremendous impact on performance.

Setting this value to 0 disables all striped backup operations. The maximum is 32, although Microsoft's informal testing has yielded optimal performance of 22GB/hour with just 6 threads.

cursor threshold

Dynamic

Advanced

Units: Integer number of rows returned by a cursor `select` statement

Default: -1 (always create synchronous cursor result sets)

SQL Server uses this option to determine how it should populate cursor keysets. If the result set is larger than this option, SQL Server populates the cursor set asynchronously. If the default of -1 is kept, all cursor result sets are generated synchronously. This option can be useful for cursors that use particularly large result sets. If you are going to use asynchronous cursor population, set this value high; small cursor sets are faster to populate synchronously than asynchronously, and setting the option higher reserves asynchronous population for very larger cursor sets.

database size

Standard

Units: Integer number of megabytes for default database size

Default: 2

This option is the default size for databases, in megabytes, and should match the size of the model database at all times. The minimum value for this option is 1, which allows databases to be created on floppy disks. A create database statement that explicitly defines database size ignores the value for this option.

default language

Standard

Units: Integer value representing a unique language ID

Default: 0 on U.S. English systems

default language tells SQL Server which of the available languages to use for displaying error and print messages back to user workstations. The server always uses the default value (0 for US English), unless the client application login has requested a particular language for that connection. Additional languages receive unique numbers (maximum of 9999) when they're added to SQL Server.

default sortorder id

Advanced

Units: Integer value representing a unique sort order ID

Default: 0 on US English systems

Never change this value using sp_configure! The sort order is actually defined by the BUILDMASTER process in the SQL Server 6.5 SETUP utility. Any changes to the server's sort order should be performed there.

> **NOTE**
>
> The default sort order is the best choice for most situations, but make sure you choose wisely. You'll have to reinstall the server and reload your data if you ever have to change the sort order.

fill factor

Standard

Units: Integer percentage

Default: 0

The `fill factor` is the extent to which index pages should be filled (excluding the root) as indexes are created. This includes the data pages of clustered indexes.

> **NOTE**
>
> The `fill factor` required by `sp_configure` is two words, but the `create index` statement keyword `fillfactor` is a single word.

Low fill factors cause index pages to be partially full, which in turn creates more index levels. The performance benefit comes at insert/update time, when row additions are less likely to cause page splits. (Lots of page splits during updates are bad for performance.)

A fill factor of 0 doesn't mean that pages will be empty. This is a special case. Clustered index data pages and nonclustered index leaf pages are 100 percent full, and some space is left in the intermediate levels (typically 75 percent full). High fill factors fill the pages as much as possible. This reduces index levels and increases query performance.

Fill factors aren't maintained after index creation. To re-create indexes with the fill factors intact, you must drop and re-create the index. Some shops with intensive update applications do this on a nightly basis.

Maintaining fill factors is typically the only reason you might periodically drop and re-create indexes, because SQL Server indexes tend to be self-maintaining and self-balancing.

free buffers

Dynamic

Advanced

Units: Integer quantity of page buffers

Default: 5 percent of `memory` configuration option

Buffers refer to the number of free pages available to SQL Server for managing the data cache. Because SQL Server performs best when the cache hit ratio is high, it's obvious that having an appropriately sized free buffer pool is very important. This setting determines the number of 2KB pages SQL Server will attempt to keep free in the data cache. The `lazywrite` process wakes up and begins flushing pages when the number of free buffers drops about 5–6 percent below the setting of `free buffers`; it stops when the number of available buffers rises about 5–6 percent above the `free buffers` setting.

The minimum value for this setting is 20, and the maximum is one-half the number of buffers available when SQL Server is started. This value can be configured manually but is automatically reset after the `memory` configuration option is changed—to approximately 5 percent of the number of buffers when SQL Server is started. In effect, this default setting guarantees that a minimum of 5 percent of SQL Server's buffer space will be freed, so that free buffers are always available for processing work.

> **TIP**
>
> Execute `sp_configure "memory"`, *xxx* (where *xxx* is the current value of `memory`) when you change a parameter that has a major impact on memory utilization. This may seem silly, but it will force the `free buffers` setting to be reconfigured automatically. Otherwise you run the risk of not having an optimal value in place.

hash buckets

Advanced

Units: Integer prime number of buckets

Default: `7993`

This setting controls the number of buckets for hashing pages to buffers in SQL Server's data cache. SQL Server will hash as close as possible to the referenced page and then traverse the page chain until the correct page is located; performance can suffer if the average chain size is greater than 10 pages. Increasing the number of hash buckets may improve performance by allowing SQL Server to hash closer to the referenced page on its first try.

> **TIP**
>
> `dbcc bufcount`, an undocumented `dbcc` command, allows you to monitor the effectiveness of current hash settings:
>
> ```
> dbcc traceon(3604)
> go
>
> dbcc bufcount
> go
>
> DBCC execution completed. If DBCC printed error messages, see your System
> Administrator.
>
>
> **** THE 10 LONGEST BUFFER CHAINS ****
>
>       bucket number = 7819        chain size = 2
>
>       bucket number = 7835        chain size = 2
>
>       bucket number = 7836        chain size = 2
>
>       bucket number = 7859        chain size = 2
>
>       bucket number = 7864        chain size = 2
>
>       bucket number = 7875        chain size = 2
>
>       bucket number = 7931        chain size = 2
>
>       bucket number = 7945        chain size = 2
>
>       bucket number = 65          chain size = 1
>
>       bucket number = 66          chain size = 1
>
>    The Smallest Chain Size is: 0
>    The Average Chain Size is: 0.035031
>
> DBCC execution completed. If DBCC printed error messages, see your System
> Administrator.
> ```

In general, this option won't need to be changed if you have less than 160MB of physical RAM on your machine, unless you are directed to do so by Microsoft Product Support Services.

language in cache

Standard

Units: Integer number of languages

Default: 3

When using a multilingual character set (code page 850, for example), SQL Server is capable of generating error and confirmation messages in multiple languages. This option specifies the maximum number of languages that SQL Server can use simultaneously.

> **NOTE**
>
> The next section discusses Lock Escalation (LE) thresholds and management. Prior to version 6.0, SQL Server would automatically escalate from individual page locks on a table to a single table lock as soon as the number of locked pages reached 200. This figure was fixed and created problems when working with very large tables. The behavior of current lock escalation parameters hasn't changed since version 6.0. These options are discussed further in Chapter 17, "Managing the SQL Server Optimizer."

LE threshold maximum

Dynamic

Standard

Units: Integer number of pages

Default: 200

This option sets the upper limit on how many single page locks will be acquired before escalating to a single table lock. If the maximum value here has been exceeded, a table lock is applied, regardless of whether the percent value (discussed later) has been exceeded.

LE threshold minimum

Dynamic

Advanced

Units: Integer number of pages

Default: 20

This option is the minimum number of page locks SQL Server must hold on a table before considering escalation to a single table lock. There's a double condition at work: If the minimum value has been exceeded, a table lock will be applied after the maximum or percent values have also been exceeded.

LE threshold percent

Dynamic

Standard

Units: Integer percentage of current table pages

Default: 0 (no threshold percentage in effect)

The percentage of page locks (above the limit specified by LE threshold minimum) that will trigger escalation from multiple page locks to a single table lock for a query. The default value of 0 specifies that this value should be ignored, and table-lock escalation will then occur at the LE threshold maximum configured value.

> **TIP**
>
> It almost always makes sense to change LE threshold percent and LE threshold maximum as soon as the server is installed. Set the threshold equal to 20 percent; this value will handle most of your small and medium-sized tables. Use maximum to prevent your large tables from consuming all the locks configured for your server.

locks

Standard

Units: Integer quantity

Default: 5000

This is the number of concurrent open locks that can be in simultaneous use. If you begin to get error messages saying that locks are unavailable, don't hesitate to bump up the number of available locks by a thousand or two. The memory cost is very low (72 bytes per lock). Note that locks are configured on a server-wide basis, which means that locks are maintained across databases where necessary.

logwrite sleep (ms)

Dynamic

Advanced

Units: Integer number of milliseconds

Default: -1 (no delay, write record immediately)

This option minimizes disk I/O by delaying the log write for *n* milliseconds. This delay allows other processes to fill up the write buffer, so more transactions can be committed with a single write operation. The default value of `-1` specifies that no delay should occur; log writes will occur as `commit tran` statements are processed. The maximum delay is 500 milliseconds.

Setting this value correctly requires a good understanding of your transaction mix. Transactions short in nature that commit very frequently, like those in an OLTP environment, might benefit by using a short delay to pack more transactions into a single log write. Complex transactions that take longer to commit may benefit by forcing a log write as soon as the transaction ends.

max async io

Standard

Units: Integer number of pages

Default: `8`

This option specifies the number of asynchronous write operations that can be requested by commands that force a large number of batch writes to occur. Commands that utilize batch writes include `BCP`, `select into`, `checkpoint`, and `insert using select`.

Raising this value increases the level of asynchronous I/O requests during batch writes. This increased volume will saturate I/O and interfere with read and lazy write requests if the disk subsystem isn't capable of handling the extra load. This situation will cause overall system performance to suffer.

> **TIP**
>
> The easiest way to find an optimal value for your system is trial-and-error. If you have a fast I/O subsystem, bump the value up by increments of 2 or 3 and observe performance. You've found the best value when performance improvements start to level off or actually decrease.

max lazywrite IO

Dynamic

Advanced

Units: Integer quantity

Default: `8`

This value is similar to `max async io`, but controls the number of asynchronous I/O requests generated by the lazy writer instead of common batch write processes like `checkpoint`. It's dynamically configurable up to the *run_value* of `max async io` . Because they control similar functions, consider changing this value for the same reasons and under the same circumstances as changing `max async io`.

max text repl size

Dynamic

Standard

Units: Integer quantity

Default: 65536

Transaction-based replication of text and image data is supported in SQL Server 6.5. This option specifies the maximum size in bytes of text and image data that can be added to a replicated column in a single `insert`, `update`, `writetext` or `updatetext` statement. The limit is imposed to provide support for ODBC drivers and foreign data sources that can't handle large text or image columns. When a published text or image column receives a single `insert`, `update`, `writetext`, or `updatetext` that surpasses this threshold value, the operation fails.

> **TIP**
>
> Change this option to the maximum setting of 2147483647 if all your subscribers are Microsoft SQL Servers. The default setting of 65536 truncates all text and image data columns greater than 64KB during replication.

max worker threads

Dynamic

Standard

Units: Integer quantity

Default: 255

`max worker threads` defines the number of threads reserved for handling SQL Server user connections. If the current number of active user connections is less than or equal to this value, every SQL Server connection is being serviced by its own Windows NT thread. If the current number of connections is greater than this value, SQL Server will automatically "round robin" or "pool" user connections across available worker threads. Systems with low numbers of users usually achieve optimal performance by allowing every SQL connection to be serviced by a private thread, while large numbers of users usually fare better by utilizing a thread pool to handle SQL Server connections. Consider tweaking this value and observing performance as the number of concurrent users rises above 150.

> **TIP**
>
> Compaq published a TPC-C benchmark in October of 1995 running SQL Server 6.5 on Windows NT 3.51 with a ProLiant 4500. They achieved optimal performance servicing 2500 concurrent users, without a TP monitor, with `max worker threads` set to only 100!

media retention

Standard

Units: Integer days

Default: `0`

When you attempt to overwrite a database or transaction log dump, the backup server checks to see how long ago this was dumped. The `media retention` parameter is a safety feature that prevents you from overwriting your dumps prematurely. The operator can override the retention time when he's prompted that there was a violation of the tape retention period. You can also change the tape retention period for a particular dump by using the `retaindays` option on the dump commands.

> **NOTE**
>
> `expiredate` and `retaindays` override the configuration value for `media retention` when specified with the `dump database` or `dump transaction` statements.

memory

Standard

Units: Integer number of 2KB pages

Default: Varies, based on the amount of system RAM at the SQL Server installation

This is probably the single most important parameter you can tune, as it controls the amount of memory Windows NT will provide to SQL Server. A large data cache can reduce the amount of disk I/O that needs to be performed, having a huge impact on performance. In general, if the server is too slow, adding memory is a fairly painless first step to improving performance. But it will help only if memory is your current bottleneck!

> **WARNING**
>
> The server won't start if this value is set too high and Windows NT can't allocate the necessary amount of memory. You can start SQL Server with the `-f` option if this happens, which will temporarily change some settings to their initial settings. The `-f` option starts the server in single-user mode, so you should use `ISQL/w` instead of Enterprise Manager to reconfigure the setting. In some cases, you may even need to stop the SQL Executive service, because it may grab the only connection before you have a chance to get it!

In some environments, 32MB to 64MB is plenty of memory. When tables and indexes get very large, substantially more memory (256MB or more) may be required. Remember that, on Windows NT, the `PAGEFILE.SYS` file must grow proportionally to available physical RAM. Check your Windows NT Server documentation for proper page-file management with increased RAM. Optimizing memory usage is covered in more detail in Chapter 32!

nested triggers

Dynamic

Standard

Units: `0` or `1` (flag)

Default: `1` (yes)

This option determines whether triggers can create a chain reaction—where the first trigger causes a second trigger to fire, and so on. Triggers won't call themselves recursively, and won't fire if nested more than 16 levels deep.

> **WARNING**
>
> Turning off nested triggers can be very dangerous, because applications may be depending on this functionality to enforce cascading referential integrity.

network packet size

Dynamic

Standard

Units: Integer quantity

Default: `4096`

This is the default server packet size for all Tabular Data Stream packets. This value should be evenly divisible by 512. Although it's a server default, individual client applications can override this value on a per-application basis. Microsoft's informal testing has revealed optimal performance to lie between 4096 and 8192 bytes for this parameter. Larger values, up to 8192, should be used for larger data transfers, to make them more efficient on the network.

open databases

Standard

Units: Integer number of open databases

Default: 12

This is the total number of databases for which SQL Server builds internal pointers in its kernel, and for which it can maintain simultaneous connections. This includes master, model, tempdb, msdb, and any user databases that might be used concurrently.

> **TIP**
>
> If the process tries to exceed the configured number, you typically get messages in the error log, describing the incident. Unfortunately, the message reported to the user is fairly confusing. Avoid this problem by configuring the variable to exceed the number of created databases, and then forget about it. The amount of memory taken up is effectively insignificant.

open objects

Standard

Units: Integer quantity

Default: 500

This is the number of concurrent open objects that can be in simultaneous use. If you begin getting error messages saying that object connections are unavailable, increase this number. The memory cost is low (40 bytes).

priority boost

Advanced

Units: Integer 1 or 0

Default: 0

Windows NT groups threads into two generic priority classes. *Variable priority class threads* range from 1–25; *real time threads* range in value from 16–32. Windows NT assigns threads a base priority that can be raised or lowered dynamically by the scheduler, but the current priority can't cross the variable/real time thread boundary.

> **TIP**
>
> Check out these Microsoft Knowledge Base articles for more information on how Windows NT schedules SQL Server threads:
>
> - Q111405 INF: SQL Server and Windows NT Thread Scheduling
> - Q109228SQL Server and Windows NT Thread Scheduling

`priority boost` causes Windows NT to schedule SQL Server threads with a higher base priority than they would ordinarily get, providing performance gains on systems dedicated to SQL Server. This option shouldn't be set on non-dedicated machines, as it will starve other applications competing for processor time.

> **WARNING**
>
> This option can be very dangerous on single-processor machines because the "boosted" SQL threads may starve critical operating-system tasks like disk I/O and network communication. The machine will seem like it's "hung" and may need to be rebooted. In my opinion, the dangers more than outweigh the potential gains, so I never turn on this option unless I have an SMP machine.
>
> If your single-processor machine is too slow, cough up the bucks and buy a faster chip or go to an SMP architecture. The `boost priority` option isn't worth the trouble it can cause.

procedure cache

Standard

Units: Integer percentage

Default: `30`

Compiled stored procedure execution plans are stored in an area of memory called *procedure cache*. Its size is set using `procedure cache`, by specifying a percentage split between the data and procedure caches after memory is first allocated to the SQL Server kernel. Sizing the procedure cache involves tradeoffs with optimizing memory utilization for the data cache.

Obviously, increasing procedure cache means less space for data. Prior to Version 6.5, it was difficult to accurately measure and tune procedure cache utilization. This task is made much easier in SQL Server 6.5 with the introduction of a new Performance Monitor object called Procedure Cache. Using the eight new counters, it's possible to get detailed information about the current procedure cache utilization and track its use over time.

Remember that the procedure cache is measured as a percentage of available memory, not in 2KB pages. This percentage determines how much memory goes to the procedure cache; the leftovers are used by the data cache.

Poor procedure cache management is one of the easiest ways to waste precious memory that could be better used by the data cache. The default value of 30 percent is appropriate for systems without much memory, but can be a waste on systems with large amounts of memory.

Consider this example: The server has 32MB of memory with 16MB allocated to SQL Server, with the procedure cache set to 30 percent. If we assume that the kernel and static options use 4MB, approximately 3.6MB is left for procedures, and the data cache will have 8.4MB. If server memory is raised to 256MB with 192MB allocated to SQL Server, the procedure cache will have about 56MB while the data cache will have about 129MB, the rest being used by the kernel and other configuration needs. That's a lot of space for procedures. Dropping the percentage to a more reasonable value can free up about 40MB or 50MB for the data cache!

> **NOTE**
>
> The numbers don't add to 192 because of memory used by the kernel and configuration options.

Setting procedure cache is more of an art than a science, but it will have a definite performance impact.

> **TIP**
>
> Consider dropping the percentage allocated to procedure cache on systems with large amounts of memory.

The next section discusses Read Ahead (RA) Threading options, which define the operational parameters for Parallel Data Scanning (PDS) operations. Chapter 32 "Optimizing SQL Server Configuration Options," discusses the PDS architecture and implementation in more detail.

RA cache hit limit

Dynamic

Advanced

Units: Integer value of pages

Default: 4

Because read-ahead (RA) asynchronously fetches pages from disk to cache, reads from cache by a read-ahead thread provide no benefit. This number is the limit of cache reads that a read-ahead thread can perform before read-ahead services are suspended. As an RA thread reads pages from disk, it checks to see whether they were already cached. RA will be turned off for this connection if the number of pages already in cache reaches this value. In effect, this option is the "off switch" for read-ahead threading.

> **TIP**
>
> Extensive testing by Microsoft has determined that the default value is optimal and shouldn't need to be changed.

RA cache miss limit

Dynamic

Advanced

Units: Integer value of pages

Default: 3

This option is the "on switch" for parallel read-ahead I/O. With the default of 3, RA is enabled when three consecutive get page requests have to be satisfied with a physical read from disk, and those reads were sequential.

> **TIP**
>
> The default value has been tested extensively by the Microsoft SQL Server lab. The value shouldn't need to be changed.

RA delay

Dynamic

Advanced

Units: Integer value in milliseconds

Default: 15

In a single CPU box, the Windows NT threading model imposes a 10ms delay before preempting an active thread running on the processor. No delay is present in an SMP environment. This option controls how SQL Server handles thread management, by specifying the delay imposed before SQL Server will ask the NT scheduler to preempt an active thread in order to schedule an RA request.

On single-CPU machines this value is set to 15ms; a small delay on top of the standard NT delay is imposed to help reduce overhead associated with context switching. This value should be set to 0 on SMP machines.

RA pre-fetches

Dynamic

Advanced

Units: Integer number of extents

Default: 3

This option sets the number of extents that an RA thread will stay ahead of the original SQL request, to ensure that the original request can always find its data in cache. The query thread issues the individual get page request, while the RA thread will request an extent (an extent is eight 2KB pages, or 16KB). The default setting of 3 instructs SQL Server to stay three extents or 48KB ahead of the query thread. The query must read an entire extent from cache before RA will grab a new one. It's easy for RA to stay ahead of the query because it reads data 16KB at a time compared to 2KB at a time. This allows a single RA thread to handle multiple query requests, which is configured using the RA worker threads and RA slots per thread parameters.

> **TIP**
>
> The default value has been tested by the Microsoft SQL Server lab and should be optimal for most of your needs. There's probably no reason to change it.

> **NOTE**
>
> Reading extents is much more efficient than reading a single 2KB page because most I/O subsystems transfer data in blocks larger than 2KB. In fact, most PC-based hardware transfers data off the disk in blocks of 16KB. This fact means that reading a 2KB page from disk is just as expensive as reading a 16KB extent.

RA slots per thread

Advanced

Units: Integer value of open buckets per read-ahead thread

Default: 5

Because read-ahead threads work at the extent level and typical user threads work at the page level, read-ahead threads are more efficient than the worker threads they're supplying. Therefore, a single read-ahead thread is capable of using its otherwise abundant latency to service other read requests. RA slots per thread defines the number of scanning operations that a single read-ahead thread can satisfy at any one time. The number of slots multiplied by the number of read-ahead threads is the total number of simultaneous read-ahead scanning operations SQL Server can support.

> **NOTE**
>
> The default value is a good starting point. The best number allows all RA threads to keep busy but not run out of worker threads.

RA worker threads

Standard

Units: Integer number of total threads from RA pool

Default: 3

This is the maximum number of threads that can be used to handle RA requests from user queries, not the total number of RA requests that can be handled. We know that each thread has some latency, because it stays ahead of a query by reading data in 16KB rather than 2KB blocks, allowing a single RA thread to handle multiple RA query requests. The number of simultaneous queries that a single thread can handle is configured using the RA slots per thread parameter discussed in the preceding section. Therefore, the total number of RA requests that can be handled is RA worker threads $\times$ RA slots per thread.

RA will never be used for a query if a free slot isn't available when the first RA request is made.

The optimal value for this option is determined by the speed of your I/O subsystem. If you think about it, you'll agree that it doesn't make sense to kink off multiple threads if your data is kept on a single disk. The only thing you'll do is raise contention for the disk and increase the length of the I/O request queue. It becomes appropriate to add worker threads as the number and speed of your disks increase.

TIP

These guidelines will help tune this parameter:

I/O Subsystem	RA Worker Threads
All data on one disk	1
Average I/O setup, 2–6 disks with striping	3
High-end I/O subsystem	5

Of course, these suggestions are simply good starting points. The optimal value for your system can be determined only by monitoring system performance and disk activity. Use as many threads as you can without causing the Avg. Disk Queue Length to become excessive on any one disk. Use the Windows NT Performance Monitor to check disk queue statistics.

---

recovery flags

Standard

Units: 0 or 1 (flag)

Default: 0 (no)

If this option is turned on at startup, the server will list detailed information in the error log for each transaction that's rolled forward or backward. This information includes transaction names that use begin tran and save tran statements. If the option is off, only the database name and quantity of transactions rolled forward or backward are listed.

NOTE

This isn't a dynamic option, so the server needs to be shut down twice for the change to take effect. During your first restart, transactions won't be named.

recovery interval

Dynamic

Standard

Units: Integer number of minutes

Default: 5

recovery interval controls the frequency of checkpoints by setting an upper limit on the number of minutes that the server will take to recover each individual database. The checkpoint process wakes up every 60 seconds and estimates how long it would take to recover the database if it failed at that moment. If estimated database recovery time is greater than the current value for recovery interval, a checkpoint will be issued.

NOTE

It's a common misconception that the recovery interval is the number of minutes between checkpoints. This is not true.

remote access

Dynamic

Standard

Units: 0 or 1 (flag)

Default: 1 (yes)

The remote access variable determines whether this server can communicate with another server. Only the sa login can modify remote access values. This option is dynamic only in SQL Server 6.0 and later versions.

TIP

It's important that this option be turned on when using replication services, because replication requires server-to-server communication.

remote conn timeout

Dynamic

Standard

Units: Integer value from -1 to 32,768 minutes

Default: 10

This option determines how long SQL Server will wait to break an inactive server-to-server connection. This timeout mechanism prevents inactive server-to-server RPCs from staying alive forever.

remote login timeout

Dynamic

Advanced

Units: Integer number of seconds

Default: 5

This option is the amount of time SQL Server waits to make a connection to another server. A value of 0 means that it waits indefinitely.

remote proc trans

Dynamic

Standard

Units: 0 or 1 (flag)

Default: 0 (no)

Support for distributed transactions is one of the most important enhancements included with SQL Server 6.5. This configuration parameter allows existing SQL Server remote procedure calls to take advantage of transaction support across servers, and provides a mechanism for implicitly wrapping a remote procedure call inside a distributed transaction.

The default value of 0 instructs SQL Server not to use the Distributed Transaction Coordinator (DTC) when executing remote procedure calls or queries unless explicitly requested through the use of the begin distributed transaction command.

Turning on this option, by setting the value to 1, allows SQL Server to automatically maintain transaction integrity across server boundaries by using the DTC. This feature is very useful for two reasons. First, it allows remote procedures and queries in existing code to use DTC even though this functionality didn't exist when the code was written. Second, it allows new code to automatically use DTC without having to explicitly use the `begin distributed transaction` command. This fact makes code more transportable and allows older ODBC drivers that may not know about DTC to use its functionality.

> **NOTE**
>
> `remote proc trans` is a server-level option, available through `sp_configure`, controlling the implicit use of DTC for all server connections. `remote_proc_transactions` is a `set` command option that provides similar functionality at the session level.

remote query timeout

Dynamic

Advanced

Units: Integer value in seconds

Default: `0`

This option controls the number of seconds that SQL Server waits to return results from a remote stored procedure call. The default value of `0` indicates that SQL Server waits until the query is finished.

resource timeout

Dynamic

Advanced

Units: Integer value of seconds

Default: `10`

This option needs to be changed only if the SQL Server error log or the Windows NT Event Log's Application subsystem shows many `logwrite` or `bufwait` timeout warnings.

set working set size

Advanced

Units: `0` or `1` (boolean)

Default: `0` (no)

This tells SQL Server to request an initial physical memory range equal to the memory configuration option, or equal to memory and tempdb in RAM if that option is activated. If this value is turned on, Windows NT will preallocate all of SQL Server's memory; if it's turned off, NT will allocate memory on an as-needed basis.

show advanced options

Dynamic

Standard

Units: 0 or 1 (flag)

Default: 0 (no)

SQL Server will hide advanced configuration options by default. Setting this value to 1 enables you to view the other configuration options from Enterprise Manager or from sp_configure output. Advanced options can be set even if they aren't currently visible.

smp concurrency

Advanced

Units: Integer number of active threads

Default: 1

This option controls how many processors SQL Server can use, by limiting the maximum number of threads SQL can activate. For single-processor machines, this value should be 1. If SQL Server is running on a dedicated server machine (strongly recommended), this number should be the number of CPUs on the machine.

This setting allows two special auto-configuration values, 0 and -1. The first causes SQL Server to use the total number of processors detected by SQL Server at startup, minus one. If your server machine has four processors, setting this option to 0 will have SQL Server use three of those processors by default. Setting this value to -1 causes SQL Server to use all available processors.

> **TIP**
>
> Set this option to 0 on SMP machines that are dedicated to SQL Server. Because Windows NT binds some system threads to a particular CPU, you may get better performance by avoiding processors using the affinity mask option, if SQL Server uses anything less than $n-1$ processors on an SMP machine.

sort pages

Dynamic

Advanced

Units: Integer number of pages

Default: 64

`sort pages` defines the maximum number of pages that can be used for query sorting operations. Each individual user connection to SQL Server is given this number of pages for sorting space. The maximum value allowed is 511. Increasing sort pages on SQL Server may require increasing the `memory` configuration option and the size of the `tempdb` database to reflect greater cache and database space usage. Increasing this value may provide performance gains for transaction loads that are sort-intensive.

> **TIP**
>
> Raising this value can have a big impact on sort operations, if you have the memory to spare.

spin counter

Dynamic

Advanced

Units: Integer number of resource acquisition attempts

Default: 10 for single-processor machines; 10000 for SMP machines

This is the number of attempts SQL Server will make to acquire a resource such as a lock, data page, cache page, or worker thread. You need to reconfigure this option manually if a processor is added or deleted after the initial SQL Server installation. SMP machines should be set to 10000, while single-processor machines should be set to 10.

tempdb in RAM

Standard

Units: Integer quantity

Default: 0 (places `tempdb` on disk)

The default of this option places `tempdb` in RAM rather than on the physical disk. Normally, it's best to leave `tempdb` on disk, because NT can manage the cache better than you, but, on systems with large amounts of memory, some application profiles experience significant performance gains by placing `tempdb` in RAM. Don't worry about changing this option if your server has less than 64MB of RAM. Even if your server has that much or more, it's possible that `tempdb` should still stay on disk. Only trial-and-error will tell what's best for your application.

If you do decide to place `tempdb` in RAM, remember that the memory is allocated from the cache managed by Windows NT, not SQL Server. If you make `tempdb` in RAM too big, your server won't start!

> **WARNING**
>
> `tempdb in RAM` is one of the few options that measures space in megabytes rather than 2KB pages. It's easy to set this option too high if you forget this fact! Start SQL Server with the `-f` option if it won't start because the `tempdb` database is too big.

time slice

Advanced

Units: Milliseconds

Default: `100`

`time slice` is theoretically the number of milliseconds that the server allocates to each user process as the server does its own internal multithreading. In practice, the server uses `time slice` as a guideline and may increase or decrease it (transparent to the configuration setting) if processes are taking too long to swap in and out.

> **TIP**
>
> Leave the `time slice` setting alone, unless otherwise directed by Microsoft Product Support Services.

user connections

Standard

Units: Integer quantity

Default: `15`

The `user connections` variable determines the number of users who can log in to the server at any given time. At least one connection is consumed every time a user logs in; some applications actually use several connections. Setting this value too high can waste precious memory, so don't configure the number of users higher than necessary. You need approximately 37KB of memory per user connection. In addition to actual users who are logged into the server, the server consumes user connections for the following:

- One for mirroring SQL Server devices
- One for the checkpoint manager
- One for the checkpoint background I/O manager
- One for the Read-Ahead Threading manager (for parallelizing table scan operations)
- If SQL Executive is started, it will also use two user connections by default (and more if replication is used)
- Additional threads are used by SQL Server for replication processing (which is discussed in Chapter 36, "Introduction to SQL Server 6.5 Replication.")

> **TIP**
>
> The global variable `@@max_connections` is set to the absolute maximum server connections; the actual number of users who can log in equals `@@max_connections` minus the system connections in the preceding list. To determine how many connections are currently in use, execute `sp_who`.

user options

Dynamic

Standard

Units: Integer from 0 to 4095

Default: `0`

This parameter is a bit mask that allows the system administrator to set global user connection defaults for a variety of `set` command options that alter the behavior of query and connection processing. Table 31.2 shows the bit values along with a description.

These bit values match those found in the `@@options` global variable, which is unique for each user connection. You can query `@@options` to determine which settings are active for an individual.

> **TIP**
>
> This code fragment shows you how to determine whether an individual option is turned on at the connection level:

```
DECLARE @UserOptionValue  smallint
SELECT @UserOptionValue = 16 -- this is the option value to test

IF @@OPTIONS & @UserOptionValue  > 0
   print "The option is on"
else
   print "The option is off"
```

Table 31.2. Settings for user options.

Value	Name	Description
1	DISABLE_DEF_CNST_CHK	Controls interim constraint checking.
2	IMPLICIT_TRANSACTIONS	Controls whether a transaction is started implicitly when a statement is executed.
4	CURSOR_CLOSE_ON_COMMIT	Controls behavior of cursors after a commit has been performed.
8	ANSI_WARNINGS	Controls truncation and NULL in aggregate warnings.
16	ANSI_PADDING	Controls padding of variables.
32	ANSI_NULLS	Controls NULL handling by using equality operators.
64	ARITHABORT	Terminates a query when an overflow or divide-by-zero error occurs during query execution.
128	ARITHIGNORE	Returns NULL when an overflow or divide-by-zero error occurs during a query.
256	QUOTED_IDENTIFIER	Differentiates between single and double quotation marks when evaluating an expression.
512	NOCOUNT	Turns off the message returned at the end of each statement that states how many rows were affected by the statement.
1024	ANSI_NULL_DFLT_ON	Alters the session's behavior to use ANSI compatibility for nullability. New columns defined without explicit nullability will be defined to allow NULLs.
2048	ANSI_NULL_DFLT_OFF	Alters the session's behavior not to use ANSI compatibility for nullability. New columns defined without explicit nullability will be defined not to allow NULLS.

Variables That Use Substantial Memory

Several variables use a substantial amount of memory. They're summarized in Table 31.3.

Table 31.3. Variables that use substantial memory.

Parameter	Bytes of Memory per Unit
user connections	37KB
open databases	17KB
open objects	40 bytes
locks	72 bytes
procedure cache	Percentage of cache split between data and procedures
tempdb in RAM	Number specified in megabytes of physical RAM, in addition to memory configuration option

Summary

The options discussed in this chapter have a great impact on how well your server performs, so understanding them is the first step in getting the most out of your hardware. But please, always remember that a well-designed and properly indexed database along with an intelligently designed application is always more important than how tightly you've tuned the server!

Optimizing SQL Server Configuration Options

32

SQL Server 6.5 provides an array of configuration options that directly impact server performance. Used properly, they offer major increases in performance. Used poorly, they quickly turn SQL Server into a performance dog. Chapter 31 discusses all the configuration parameters available through sp_configure and its GUI equivalent. This chapter focuses on a few of the more important options and discusses server tuning strategies in more detail.

Memory Utilization

It's impossible to pinpoint one specific area and claim that this is "the most important tuning issue with SQL Server." Ultimately, speed is increased only by fixing the bottleneck—little is accomplished by tweaking a component that isn't the current bottleneck.

Now that you know that it's impossible to conclusively say which is the most important area bar none, I'm comfortable saying that proper memory utilization is always a major area of concern, and that you can always have a positive impact on performance by managing memory in an intelligent fashion. Memory is so important because it helps alleviate or reduce physical disk I/O, which we all know is the slowest operation a computer knows how to do. Cut down on disk activity and you've improved performance. It's that simple.

This section explores some common tuning mistakes people make in managing their memory resources and helps determine optimum settings for your environment.

In Figure 32.1, the first chunk of physical memory is used by the operating system and any other applications that may be running on the server. Windows NT Server 3.51 requires at least 16MB for its own use, which is the theoretical minimum defined in the OS documentation. The server will boot with that much, but you *won't* be happy with the performance.

> **TIP**
>
> Microsoft documentation claims that the minimum memory requirements for SQL Server and Windows NT Server are 4MB and 16MB, respectively. Use these numbers at your own risk. The server will boot and you'll be able to run queries, but you may not want your job evaluation tied to how fast the server is running. I'd suggest a minimum of 32MB for development environments and much more for some production environments.

The second block of memory is reserved for tempdb, if tempdb in RAM is turned on. The default installation places tempdb on disk, so this block of memory may or may not be used on your system.

Windows NT allocates the remaining blocks of memory to SQL Server based on the current values for memory and procedure cache set using sp_configure. The memory option defines how much memory is allocated to SQL Server as a whole, while the procedure cache option determines how memory is split between the data and procedure caches after SQL Server kernel and user option needs have been satisfied.

FIGURE 32.1.

A representation of physical memory on the server box.

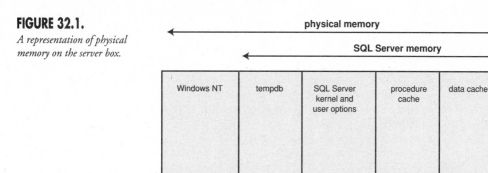

NOTE

SQL Server configuration options normally measure memory in units of 2KB pages. `tempdb in RAM` is one notable exception, as it measures memory usage in megabytes. Be careful setting this option or you may wind up with a number that's very wrong!

The first chunk of memory given to SQL Server is used by the kernel executable and various configuration options set by the user. The kernel uses about 2MB. User options usually require at least 2MB, although this number varies from system to system based on how the system was configured. The remainder of SQL Server's memory is split between the data cache, used for tables and indexes, and the procedure cache, which is used to stored precompiled definitions and execution plans for system- and user-defined stored procedures, based on the current setting of `procedure cache` in `sp_configure`.

If the server doesn't have enough memory to start properly, it doesn't start at all—it's an all-or-nothing proposition. If you manage to configure memory in a way that prevents SQL Server from starting, you can recover by restarting the server using the `-f` command-line switch, which forces default values to be used for many configuration options.

WARNING

Be wary of running SQL Executive or SQL Enterprise Manager (SEM) when the server is started with the `-f` option, because it forces SQL Server to start in single-user mode. SQL Executive and SEM will both try to grab the one and only available connection to the server, locking you out if they succeed. `ISQL/w` is a good replacement for SEM in this scenario. I hope you know your command-line syntax!

WARNING

Never rebuild the master database with the setup option unless you have explored all other possible choices. Rebuilding the master database resets configuration options to their defaults, but it will also render your user databases unusable until you have rebuilt their references in master.

WARNING

If you're running SQL Server on Windows NT 3.1 or 3.5, beware of an unusual memory problem that affects only very-large-scale systems.

Microsoft wrote SQL Server 4.2x to be capable of physically addressing 2GB of RAM (the maximum value for the memory sp_configure option is 1 million 2KB pages). However, until Windows NT 3.51, Windows NT would provide a maximum of 256MB of RAM to any Win32 process—even though all versions of Windows NT are capable of physically addressing 4GB of RAM. Attempting to configure SQL Server to use more than 256MB of memory would result in substantial disk access, as Windows NT paged memory access to virtual memory.

This "undocumented feature" didn't come out until a year after Windows NT 3.1 had shipped. It has since been fixed in Windows NT 3.51 and is part of the reason why NT 3.51 is recommended for SQL Server installations.

Determining the Optimal Memory Configuration for SQL Server 6.5

Because it's a 32-bit operating system, Windows NT provides every application with a virtual address space of 4GB. In reality, the application has access to only half this amount, however, because the upper memory is reserved for Windows NT code. It's important to realize that SQL Server doesn't distinguish between virtual memory and physical memory; it only cares about its private 4GB address space controlled by the Virtual Memory Manager (VMM). It's entirely possible to configure SQL Server to use more memory than is physically available if there is backing storage (that is, available space) in the Windows NT paging file. This is the worst possible thing to do, however, because it fools SQL Server into thinking that it has more memory than is really available. SQL Server will page like crazy and performance will take a nose dive.

TIP

The procedure cache configuration option is often the most overlooked way to improve memory utilization. The default value of 30 is great if your machine doesn't have large amounts of memory, but is often a waste if your server has 64MB or more. Decreasing the percentage of memory allocated for procedures frees up valuable space in the data cache.

When configuring memory on a dedicated server, the basic rule of thumb is to give SQL Server as much memory as possible without causing Windows NT to page on a regular basis. Determining this threshold is easier to do than it may sound. The first step is changing the default SQL Server memory setting to a reasonable value. The following chart, provided by Microsoft, provides a reasonable starting point.

Machine Memory (MB)	SQL Server memory Setting (MB)
16	4
24	6
32	16
48	28
64	40
128	100
256	216
512	464

The next step is to fine-tune this starting point, giving SQL Server as much physical memory as possible, stopping just short of causing Windows NT to begin paging. SQL Server has too much memory if paging happens on a regular basis, which is easy to spot with the Windows NT Performance Monitor.

TIP

Performance statistics vary from server to server, but in general Memory - Pages/sec should be 0 once a dedicated SQL Server has reached a steady state. Paging is degrading your performance if this value shoots above 10 on a regular basis

Start Performance Monitor and choose the Edit | Add to Chart menu sequence to display the dialog box shown in Figure 32.2.

FIGURE 32.2.

Windows NT Performance Monitor allows you to examine finite performance statistics on both Windows NT and SQL Server, making baseline memory configuration easier.

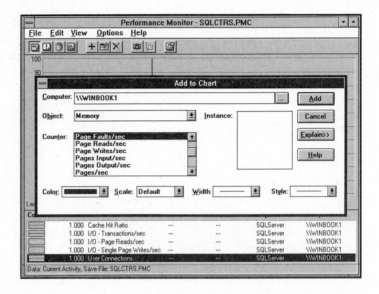

In the Object combo box, select the Memory object. This brings up a fresh list of counters. In the Counter list box, add the Page Faults/sec counter. This monitors Windows NT's inability to satisfy memory requests with RAM, which results in a *page fault*, forcing it to use PAGEFILE.SYS on disk.

Within SQL Server, use sp_configure or SQL Enterprise Manager to change your memory configuration. Shut down and restart SQL Server, and watch the PerfMon counters for page faults to see whether SQL Server is using any paged memory. If not, you can gradually increase SQL Server's memory allocation until it starts to rely on the paging file.

> **TIP**
>
> Memory is probably not a problem if your cache hit ratio is consistently greater than 80 percent. If you're dealing with a huge data warehouse, the cache hit ratio will probably be lower, because it's normally impractical to cache significant portions of the database. Disk utilization becomes the biggest concern in these situations.

Using the tempdb in RAM Option

By default, the tempdb database is created on the master disk device. It can be expanded onto other devices with the alter database command, but it's still on disk. The 4.2 release of SQL Server for Windows NT introduced the option of loading tempdb into RAM, which speeds page-access operations involving temporary tables, worktables, and sorting operations. This sounds like a great idea, but should be used with caution and only on servers with lots of memory, as SQL Server can normally do a better job of managing the cache than you can.

When the `tempdb in RAM` option is set to `0`, the database remains on disk. If the `tempdb` database is extended to other devices, it consumes memory only as its data tables are cached using normal SQL Server caching mechanisms, just as if temporary tables were normal permanent tables. If `tempdb in RAM` is changed to a positive number, the value used represents the number of megabytes of RAM that SQL Server uses to create `tempdb` in main memory. This memory allocation is *in addition to* the memory already provided to SQL Server by Windows NT.

> **TIP**
>
> Microsoft recommends using this option only if your server hardware has more than 64MB of RAM, and only if an application's queries rely heavily on worktables, sorting operations, and temporary tables. Below 64MB of RAM, SQL Server can use the available memory for cache more efficiently than if it were dedicating a portion of system memory for `tempdb`.

Placing `tempdb` in RAM actually causes some of the data to be cached twice, because SQL Server still caches `tempdb` tables in its own data cache as though `tempdb` were still on disk. In other words, SQL Server, for the purposes of cache management and page access, *does not realize that tempdb is in RAM*. A given page might be in RAM twice—once in the `tempdb` allocated memory space, and again in the data cache managed by SQL Server. If your temporary tables grow quite large, you can consume large quantities of memory very quickly as table pages are duplicated in main memory. For this reason, as well as the others already listed, Microsoft recommends using the `tempdb in RAM` option only in specialized cases, and only after benchmarking has determined your specific application benefits from its performance. The safest rule is this: If you want to put `tempdb` in RAM, add enough RAM to contain the entire `tempdb` database. That way, you won't have to sacrifice any of your existing cache space for `tempdb`, and `tempdb` can be accessed in RAM rather than on disk.

> **TIP**
>
> Stop and start the server when `tempdb` is altered if `tempdb in RAM` is turned on. This allows Windows NT to assign a contiguous block of memory to `tempdb`, rather than fragmenting it among multiple blocks. `tempdb` can be altered while in RAM only up to 10 times. After that, you'll be forced to stop and restart the server.

Using dbcc memusage to Validate Memory Configuration

The Database Consistency Checker (dbcc) command can detail your memory allocation, which will help you make the best use of memory resources. Use dbcc memusage to determine whether your tuning guesses were correct. It provides extremely useful information about overall memory size, cache size, and the actual objects stored in the cache. dbcc memusage provides details in three sections:

- Memory usage
- A listing of up to the top 20 buffered data items (tables and indexes) in cache
- A list of up to the 20 largest stored procedures in cache, along with the size and number of compiled plans that are in memory for that procedure

This is the memory usage section of dbcc memusage:

```
Configured Memory: 16.0000            8192      16777216
           Code size:    1.7166       879       1800000
   Static Structures:    0.2559       132       268336
               Locks:    0.2861       147       300000
        Open Objects:    0.1144       59        120000
      Open Databases:    0.0031       2         3220
   User Context Areas:   0.7505       385       787002
          Page Cache:    8.9150       4565      9348032
        Proc Headers:    0.2148       110       225212
      Proc Cache Bufs:   3.6074       1847      3782656
```

> **NOTE**
>
> As the system administrator, you can configure the ratio of data cache to procedure cache. If you have the procedure cache configured to 20 (20 percent), you should have 20 percent procedure cache to 80 percent data cache, for a ratio of 1:4. These numbers are approximate because SQL Server allocates cache pages on 2KB boundaries.

The second part of dbcc memusage is a listing of the top 20 buffered data items (tables and indexes) in cache. The following is a list of the 20 largest contiguous pieces of data in data cache:

```
Buffer Cache, Top 20:
  DB Id  Object Id   Index Id      2K Buffers
  5      240003886   0             118
  5      176003658   0             88
  5      208003772   0             87
  5      176003658   2             57
  5      208003772   2             57
  5      99          0             56
```

1	36	0	6
1	2	0	3
4	1	0	2
4	2	0	2
4	5	0	2
5	176003658	1	2
5	240003886	1	2
1	2	1	1
1	8	0	1
1	30	0	1
1	30	2	1
1	36	1	1
2	2	0	1
2	8	0	1

To understand what each item in this list is, perform the following steps. For this example, we'll determine what the first and fourth items are on the sample output in the list:

1. Use the appropriate database. You need the name of the database first, so use the db_name() function to convert a database ID to a name:

```
select db_name(5)
```

Now use the database:

```
use perftune
```

2. You can use object_name() to convert the object ID to an object name—but note that object_name() works only in the relevant database:

```
select object_name(240003886)
```

3. Using the index ID and the following table, determine what component of a table is cached.

Index ID	Component of Table
0	Table itself
1	Clustered index
2+	Nonclustered index

To determine which nonclustered index is cached when the index ID is greater than 1, try the following select statement from sysindexes:

```
select name, keycnt
from sysindexes
where id = 176003658 /* object id from MEMUSAGE */
and indid = 2 /* index id from MEMUSAGE */
```

To retrieve the column names of the index keys for this index, use the index_col() function:

```
select index_col(object_name(176003658), 2, 1)
```

The last part of dbcc memusage is a list of up to the 20 largest stored procedures in cache, along with the size and number of compiled plans that are in memory for that procedure. An example of the third section is shown in the following output on the next page:

```
Procedure Cache, Top 9:


Procedure Name: sp_MSdbuserprofile
Database Id: 1
Object Id: 1449056198
Version: 1
Uid: 1
Type: stored procedure
Number of trees: 0
Size of trees: 0.000000 Mb, 0.000000 bytes, 0 pages
Number of plans: 2
Size of plans: 0.171600 Mb, 179936.000000 bytes, 90 pages


Procedure Name: sp_helpdistributor
Database Id: 1
Object Id: 1372531923
Version: 1
Uid: 1
Type: stored procedure
Number of trees: 0
Size of trees: 0.000000 Mb, 0.000000 bytes, 0 pages
Number of plans: 2
Size of plans: 0.042969 Mb, 45056.000000 bytes, 24 pages


Procedure Name: sp_server_info
Database Id: 1
Object Id: 361052322
Version: 1
Uid: 1
Type: stored procedure
Number of trees: 0
Size of trees: 0.000000 Mb, 0.000000 bytes, 0 pages
Number of plans: 1
Size of plans: 0.003166 Mb, 3320.000000 bytes, 2 pages


Procedure Name: xp_snmp_getstate
Database Id: 1
Object Id: 921054317
Version: 1
Uid: 1
Type: stored procedure
Number of trees: 0
Size of trees: 0.000000 Mb, 0.000000 bytes, 0 pages
Number of plans: 1
Size of plans: 0.000578 Mb, 606.000000 bytes, 1 pages


Procedure Name: xp_regread
Database Id: 1
Object Id: 585053120
Version: 1
Uid: 1
Type: stored procedure
```

```
Number of trees: 0
Size of trees: 0.000000 Mb, 0.000000 bytes, 0 pages
Number of plans: 1
Size of plans: 0.000578 Mb, 606.000000 bytes, 1 pages


Procedure Name: sp_sqlregister
Database Id: 1
Object Id: 985054545
Version: 1
Uid: 1
Type: stored procedure
Number of trees: 0
Size of trees: 0.000000 Mb, 0.000000 bytes, 0 pages
Number of plans: 1
Size of plans: 0.000822 Mb, 862.000000 bytes, 1 pages


Procedure Name: sp_MSSQLOLE65_version
Database Id: 1
Object Id: 1481056312
Version: 1
Uid: 1
Type: stored procedure
Number of trees: 0
Size of trees: 0.000000 Mb, 0.000000 bytes, 0 pages
Number of plans: 1
Size of plans: 0.001543 Mb, 1618.000000 bytes, 1 pages


Procedure Name: xp_sqlregister
Database Id: 1
Object Id: 953054431
Version: 1
Uid: 1
Type: stored procedure
Number of trees: 0
Size of trees: 0.000000 Mb, 0.000000 bytes, 0 pages
Number of plans: 1
Size of plans: 0.000578 Mb, 606.000000 bytes, 1 pages


Procedure Name: xp_msver
Database Id: 1
Object Id: 1036530726
Version: 1
Uid: 1
Type: stored procedure
Number of trees: 0
Size of trees: 0.000000 Mb, 0.000000 bytes, 0 pages
Number of plans: 1
Size of plans: 0.000578 Mb, 606.000000 bytes, 1 pages
DBCC execution completed. If DBCC printed error messages, see your System
Administrator.
```

NOTE

SQL Server's stored procedures are recursive and reusable, but not reentrant. If many processes want to run a procedure at one time, the server creates a new query plan for each concurrent execution.

It's easy to identify procedures with more than one plan in cache; just check the `Number of Plans` line in the `dbcc memusage` output. If the count is greater than `1`, multiple people have compiled the procedure.

TIP

SQL Server 6.5 includes a new Performance Monitor object called Procedure Cache that allows you to get detailed information on the percentage of procedure cache currently being used.

How to Use dbcc memusage Information

Run `dbcc memusage` regularly to understand how memory is being used in your server. Pay special attention to these issues:

- Look at the overall memory figures to make certain that you have as much data cache as you expected.

- Look at data cache to see whether any particular object is monopolizing the cache at the expense of other objects, because it might be appropriate to take other tuning steps on that object.

- Look at how large stored procedures are, because smaller procedures compile and execute faster.

Configuring Lock Escalation Values

Prior to Version 6.0, SQL Server implemented locking at two different levels for query processing. A single query could lock individual data pages within a table, or it could lock all of the table pages, depending on the number of pages being read. The "magic number" for lock escalation was always 200 pages. In other words, any query was allowed to allocate 200 page locks on a table, but as soon as the query attempted to allocate page lock #201, its locking scheme would be automatically upgraded by SQL Server from 200+ individual page locks to a single table lock. This is done for efficiency purposes in the locking algorithm and to prevent huge amounts of memory from being allocated to satisfy lock resources.

> **NOTE**
>
> Before reading on, you may want to review Chapter 2, "Understanding the Microsoft Client/Server Architecture," for the architectural changes that Microsoft introduced with SQL Server 4.2 for Windows NT. Those changes from the traditional Sybase architecture are responsible for enabling the technological advances discussed in this section.

The capacity to use multiple processors has vastly increased SQL Server's performance potential, but very large databases (exceeding 10 or 20 gigabytes) still pose problems for the server. Although SQL Server's transaction performance is excellent by any measure, some new issues arise with very large databases. Even simple tasks like backups and dbcc become problematic, because scanning large tables with hundreds of megabytes or even gigabytes can be very slow if all I/O is being performed by a single thread (as shown in Figure 32.3).

I/O throughput is the single biggest bottleneck when dealing with VLDBs. If you had a server that could address 4GB of physical memory, you would still be bound by I/O if your database was 200GB!

SQL Server 6.5 uses asynchronous read-ahead (RA) threads to address the limitations of standard table scanning, allowing SQL Server to use multiple threads for I/O operations even though a single thread is processing the actual user query. (See Figure 32.4.) The query threads and RA threads operate independently of one another. The query doesn't know that RA is operating; all it knows is that its data is always in cache so it doesn't need to issue a "get page" request.

Think about what happens when doing a table scan on a 2GB table. Without RA, SQL Server uses a single worker thread for the query, which issues a "get page" request to read a 2KB page from disk when the referenced page isn't already in cache. It's unlikely that many pages will be in cache—because the table is huge—so the query will issue a large number of single "get page" requests.

> **NOTE**
>
> An average disk can perform 50 to 60 I/O operations per second, and high performance disks might handle up to 100 operations per second. Maximum I/O throughput for this query will be limited to 100 to 200 kilobytes per second if SQL Server is using a single thread to read data in 2KB blocks (100 operations per second × 2KB = 200KB per second.) This is extremely inefficient and well below the theoretical 10MB per second transfer rate of SCSI-2 interfaces commonly found in high-end servers.

FIGURE 32.3.

With standard table scanning, table scan performance is bound by both the speed of the disk and the capability of a single worker thread to request pages. RA addresses this problem by allowing multiple threads to read data off disks concurrently.

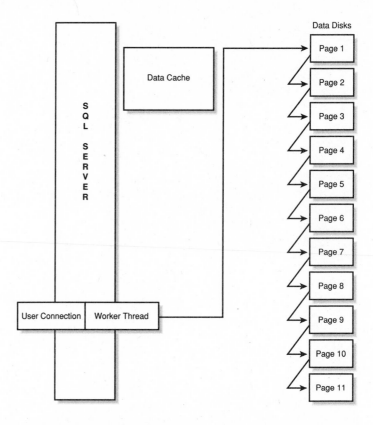

Parallel read-ahead allows SQL Server to use multiple background threads to perform disk I/O *in advance of* a worker thread's request for a particular page. In other words, while a worker thread is "surfing" a page chain for data, an additional thread is reading ahead of the current scanning position, loading pages from disk into cache so that the worker thread is always finding data in cache, not on disk. SQL Server is no longer limited to the 200KB maximum transfer rate possible when using a single thread to perform single 2KB page reads. The process is made even more efficient because the RA thread performs its I/O in 16KB extents rather than 2KB pages.

> **NOTE**
>
> Read-ahead operations are transparent to the query, which still thinks it's doing I/O one 2KB page at a time. The performance gain happens because SQL Server reads the page before the query even requests it. By the time the query needs it, that data is already in cache. This is why the technique works only for sequentially accessed data. Think about it—how would SQL Server know what data to pre-fetch if it wasn't being read in a known order?

# Chapter 32

FIGURE 32.4.

With parallel data scanning, one worker thread can retrieve data pages while another performs the work of a query.

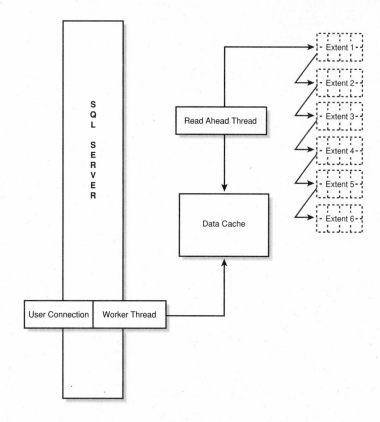

On multiprocessor hardware, the statistical probability of these threads being scheduled to different processors is quite high, so a single query operation can now use multiple processors simultaneously, boosting I/O capacity and increasing query performance even more. The net effect is that read-ahead threads increase the worker thread cache hit ratio by fetching pages from disk into cache before the worker thread actually requests them.

Read-ahead threading is limited to scanning operations, which include both leaf-level index scanning and direct table-page scanning. Therefore, any `select` statements in which the optimizer chooses a table scan, or any execution of `dbcc`, `update statistics`, `create index`, and other such operations that scan tables or leaf index levels, will benefit from read-ahead scanning.

Obviously, there's no benefit to using this feature when the data pages are already in cache. Therefore, a series of new `sp_configure` options define when read-ahead will be used and how it behaves once activated. Activation and deactivation are controlled by two new advanced configuration options: `RA cache miss limit` and `RA cache hit limit`. Because RA provides benefit only when data is on disk and not in cache, the `RA cache miss limit` defines the number of physical get page requests that SQL Server must issue during a sequential read operation before allocating a read-ahead thread to that query. For example, if a query such as `select * from foo` is executed on a 400MB table, SQL Server might find the first 12MB in cache on a large multiprocessor box. As soon as the query encounters three sequential read operations that go to disk (that's the default value), SQL Server acknowledges the read requests and also allocates a read-ahead thread for that query that begins pre-fetching the data.

So how do you turn off read-ahead? That's where the `RA cache hit limit` configuration option comes in (the default is three reads). If the pages that a read-ahead thread is requesting are found in cache, the read-ahead thread contributes little or no meaningful work to the query. `RA cache hit limit` enables SQL Server to turn off the read-ahead thread if it's finding data in cache instead of on disk. SQL Server checks the extent being read in by RA to see if any or all of the pages are already in cache. SQL Server increments a cache hit counter by one if a majority (that is, greater than 50 percent or four 2KB pages) of the 16KB extent is found in cache. Parallel RA I/O is temporarily turned off as soon as this internal counter reaches the current setting of `RA cache hit limit`, which defaults to `4`. RA will be turned back on when the `RA cache hit limit` is exceeded once again.

It's also possible to tune the number of threads used by RA, and how much data each thread will pre-fetch in order to stay ahead of a query. Each RA thread actually services RA requests from multiple user queries, because the RA thread easily stays ahead of a single query's I/O needs by reading data in 16KB extents rather than 2KB pages. The number of RA worker threads and the number of user queries that can be handled by a single thread can also be configured to tune performance under a variety of circumstances.

> **TIP**
>
> RA can sometimes give misleading cache hit ratio readings from the Performance Monitor. The cache hit ratio will be artificially high when RA is running, because user queries will find their data in cache, even though it had been on disk just a few seconds earlier.

How does the read-ahead thread know where to read from? The `RA pre-fetches` configuration option defines the number of extents that a read-ahead thread will keep in cache *ahead of* the current scanning position. With a default value of `3`, a read-ahead thread will keep three extents (24 pages) of data in cache ahead of the worker thread's current read position. Read-ahead threads quickly fetch extra data before the worker thread is ready to process that part of the page chain, because the worker thread reads data in 2KB pages, while the read-ahead thread reads 16KB extents. This leaves the potential for continuous stopping/starting of read-ahead threads, as well as read-ahead thread idle time. SQL Server utilizes this latency and reduces the overhead involved with constant thread creation and destruction by allowing a single read-ahead thread to handle multiple user requests. The number of queries that a single thread will service is tuned with the `RA slots per thread` configuration option, which calls each user query a *slot*.

NOTE

What is an I/O? SQL Server typically thinks of I/O as being a request for a single 2KB page. At the physical disk level, an I/O consists of a request by the disk controller to "connect," "seek," "read," and then "disconnect" from the disk. At this level, data is transferred off the disk in blocks, defined by many I/O subsystems as 16KB. This means that 14KB is thrown away when SQL Server requests a single 2KB page to be read, because 16KB is read off the disk by the controller.

Read-ahead performs I/O at the SQL Server extent level rather than page level, which has a huge impact on performance. As you know, an extent is 8 pages or 16KB. Physically, it takes the disk controller the same amount of time to read a 2KB page as it does a 16KB extent, because it's really working with 16KB I/O blocks anyway. (Of course, this assumes that the underlying hardware implements its blocking scheme in units of 16KB.)

SQL Server allocates user queries, or slots, to RA threads with a very simple algorithm. Each query that requests RA is assigned to the first open slot. A total of 15 concurrent RA requests can be satisfied if RA worker threads is set to 3 and RA slots per thread is left at 5. The queries are assigned sequentially to open slots in the RA threads. The first five RA query requests consume the five slots in the first RA worker thread. A second RA worker thread will be spawned when the sixth concurrent RA request is issued. The third RA worker thread would of course be spawned when the eleventh RA request is made by a user query. The sixteenth RA request is ignored, obviously, because the server is configured to handle only 15 concurrent parallel I/O operations.

TIP

The Windows NT Performance Monitor includes a counter called RA - Slots Used, which can be used to see whether the number of slots is set to an appropriate value. Requests are being ignored if this value consistently reaches the total number of available slots on the server.

Here's an example of might happen:

1. User 1 logs on and executes an update statistics command on a 2GB table.
2. SQL Server allocates a read-ahead thread and assigns the first slot of that thread to User 1.
3. As more users log in, they also begin various large scanning operations. Each of these new users is assigned first to the open slots on the existing read-ahead thread.

4. When five user connections have been serviced and a sixth needs a read-ahead thread, SQL Server allocates a new read-ahead thread and assigns that sixth worker thread to the first slot of the new read-ahead thread.

5. This process continues as read-ahead services are needed.

6. The sixteenth concurrent request is ignored because the server has been configured for only 15 slots. The query will get its data but won't have access to parallel read-ahead I/O. New RA requests can be satisfied when the number of active slots drops below 15.

Multiprocessor hardware is necessary to take full advantage of this technology. The overhead of scheduling a multithread scanning operation on a single CPU is, in theory, sufficient to quash the potential benefit of using multiple threads. Multiple disks are even more important than multiple processors. Spawning multiple RA threads does more harm than good if they simply increase the queue length on an already taxed I/O subsystem.

TIP

You can use the Windows NT Performance Monitor to measure how busy your disks are. `PhysicalDisk: Avg. Disk Queue Length` provides a good indication. Average lengths greater than 2 may indicate that your I/O subsystem is overworked.

SQL Server can achieve substantial performance gains by parallelizing I/O at the thread, processor, and disk levels. Informal Microsoft tests revealed anywhere from 100 to 400 percent faster reads on a two-processor, four-disk, Intel-based hardware platform. Clearly, the right hardware can be an important aspect in making the most of SQL Server.

TIP

You can check performance differences with and without RA by selectively turning it off at the server or connection level using trace flags, as shown in the following table.

Trace Flag	Effect
652	Disables read-ahead for the server.
653	Disables read-ahead for the current connection.

You'll see the performance difference and can empirically measure the increased disk efficiency by checking `PhysicalDisk: Avg. Disk Bytes/Transfer` in the Performance Monitor. This value will drop noticeably if you disable RA on a system that would otherwise benefit from the technology.

The only potential deficiency with asynchronous read-ahead is that the optimizer doesn't yet account for the potential performance benefits. In other words, SQL Server now has three different options for processing a query:

- Using a traditional, single-thread-at-a-time table scan
- Using an index
- Using a table scan that triggers read-ahead threading

The optimizer isn't capable of properly calculating the cost of a query using read-ahead; therefore the optimizer may choose to use an index to process a query when in fact a table scan that takes advantage of parallel data scanning may be quicker.

> **NOTE**
>
> Microsoft is hoping to include true parallel query support with an updated optimizer in SQL Server 7.0. They've publicly committed to releasing a major update to SQL Server every year for the next few years. Of course, that's always subject to change.

Summary

Although SQL Server 6.5 introduces some new areas in which a system administrator can optimize SQL Server's performance, the real performance-tuning work still belongs with those who write queries. Version 6.5 implements more flexible configuration options and enables an administrator to have a potential impact on performance, but those options have the greatest impact on very large systems that rely on multiprocessing, multi-disk-channel hardware platforms.

Measuring SQL Server System Performance

33

Part of the advantage of using Microsoft SQL Server for Windows NT lies in the integration of the database engine with the operating system. That integration allows SQL Server to rely on operating system services and applications that would otherwise be duplicated in the database engine itself, reducing substantial overhead. One area in which this duplication is avoided centers on monitoring system performance. By using the Windows NT Performance Monitor, SQL Server administrators can monitor performance characteristics and hunt for potential bottlenecks, using a graphic interface that presents immediate, real-time data. Before talking about Performance Monitor itself, a short look is necessary to explain what there is to monitor, and why it's helpful to monitor it.

Why Measure Performance?

The capability to measure performance at a system level provides administrators with information they need to configure SQL Server optimally for the environment in which it resides. It's also helpful in tuning particular applications for the specific tasks they execute. Although the activities involved in tuning SQL Server (or any application system) are more witchcraft than pure physics, the ability to observe changes in a standardized format provides genuine information about the cause and effect of changing configuration options. The problem is getting to the information that you need. In the Sybase world, that has usually meant profiling databases and queries, using a stopwatch and some undocumented dbcc commands. Although useful, the lack of support for such things from the vendor makes performance tuning much harder than it needs to be.

Although Microsoft SQL Server typically hasn't supported the size or complexity of applications that Sybase SQL Server can, Microsoft SQL Server, through its integration with Windows NT, has been able to provide administrators with much more information. On the NT platform, a given SQL Server can be monitored and tuned much more effectively than on any other platform.

What Is Performance Monitor?

Windows NT Performance Monitor is an application that ships with Windows NT and is used to monitor a variety of performance counters provided by the operating system. Performance Monitor is a Win32 application that runs only on Windows NT, and relies on Win32 DLLs to interact with the operating system and other applications to provide performance statistics and measurements. Performance Monitor is capable of charting these statistics graphically, as well as taking preventive action based on the scope of those statistics. For example, Performance Monitor can execute a command if a particular measurement crosses a specific threshold. In addition, Performance Monitor can be used to log performance statistics to monitor change over time.

Performance Monitor relies on a defined series of performance *objects*, which are general categories of statistical measures. The performance objects are selected in the Performance option of the Add to Chart dialog box (shown in Figure 33.1).

FIGURE 33.1.

Performance Monitor enables you to monitor objects, counters, and instances to provide very precise information about finite elements of SQL Server and other Windows NT applications.

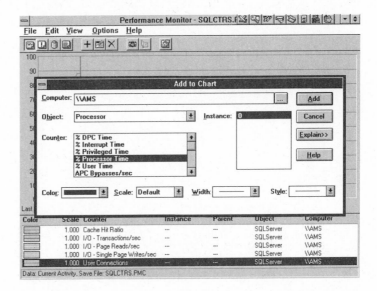

Performance objects include such things as Processor, Physical Disk, Process, and Memory. Each of these has a collection of performance *counters* associated with it—each counter being a particular aspect of that object. For example, the Processor performance object has counters that measure % Processor Time (total percent of available CPU time being used), as well as Interrupts/sec (number of interrupts or requests for services being generated by the system).

Performance objects and counters are defined by DLLs that integrate with Performance Monitor, telling it what to look for. In some cases, a performance object may also have different instances. *Instances* are unique examples of currently active objects. For example, the Processor object on a single-processor machine will have only one instance—the processor itself. If four processors are present, four items will appear in the Instances list box when the Processor object is selected. Depending on the particular object you've selected, the Instances list box may contain different items. For example, if you select the Process object, you'll see a list of the currently active executables and system DLLs under Windows NT. SQL Server will show up in this list as SQLSRVR, because that's the name of the SQL Server executable file.

If you're uncertain about a particular object or counter, the Explain button can show you more information about that particular counter. All the SQL Server performance counters have documentation, albeit a little sparse in places.

The Performance Monitor can be accessed from the Administrative Tools group on the NT desktop, or from the SQL Server 6.5 program group, which displays a SQL Server Performance Monitor Icon (it simply loads the NT Performance Monitor). The default view for Performance Monitor is a standard chart. Depending on how you start Performance Monitor, you'll see different counters and objects already displayed. It also specifies a particular file that contains a predefined list of objects and counters. You can change the statistics that Performance Monitor uses, as well as save your own custom lists of objects and counters.

> **TIP**
>
> The laws of physics are typically unyielding, and both Windows NT and SQL Server are subject to them. Heisenberg's Uncertainty Principle holds true here as elsewhere: You can't measure the direction or velocity of an object without changing either the direction or the velocity. In real English, that means that when you monitor SQL Server's performance you're going to incur performance overhead. Although that overhead can be minimized (or maximized, for the mischievous), it can never be eliminated. Performance Monitor enables you to examine a very precise approximation of SQL Server's performance, not its actual performance.

What to Monitor with SQL Server Performance Counters

Configuring Performance Monitor is discussed in depth in the Windows NT documentation, so instead of repeating step-by-step instructions here, this section discusses what you need to monitor to see how SQL Server is performing.

Any server application requires four basic sets of services: processor, memory, disk, and network. Consequently, you've just defined the four categories of performance objects and counters that you'll want to measure. Although the simplicity of that statement is attractive, you have to remember that not only should you be monitoring the application-level (that is, SQL Server's) performance objects and counters, but you should also be monitoring those same areas at the operating system level. SQL Server provides many areas to create performance bottlenecks, but so does Windows NT. Sharp SQL Server administrators know that not only is SQL Server knowledge required for proper performance monitoring, but also understanding the Windows NT environment as it relates to server applications and networking.

Monitoring the Processor

The first object to monitor is `Processor`. For this object, you'll want to monitor either the `% Processor Time` or the `% User Time` counter. The first counter monitors the total SQL Server processor usage by all applications currently executing on the system. For a dedicated SQL Server, the nominal measure for this should be between 60 and 75 percent. This figure, although approximate, indicates that the processor is capable of handling all normal requests for service, but also has available latency for spikes in usage. If your processor usage exceeds 75 percent on a regular basis, consider installing a faster processor or, if possible, adding a second processor. Windows NT automatically detects new processors and makes them available to SQL Server. (See Chapter 31, "Configuring and Tuning SQL Server," particularly the SMP Concurrency option, for more information on this.)

The counter `% User Time` is an option, because it shows the amount of time being devoted to "non-kernel" functions and applications running on top of the operating system. The counter `% Privileged Time` refers to kernel-level CPU operations, so you want the other two counters to measure SQL Server.

Monitoring Memory

For measuring the `Memory` object, you want to know SQL Server's memory configuration. That value, combined with the database executable, plus the `tempdb` space (if it's in RAM) has a dramatic effect on this counter. For dedicated servers, the `Available Bytes` counter should be set as low as possible without resorting to the use of the paging file. (More on that shortly.)

Monitoring the Disk(s)

The disk drive objects and counters require some special attention before they'll work. Because of the substantial overhead (approximately 5 percent of system performance) that the disk counters exact, they're disabled by default. To enable the disk counters, you must open a Windows NT command window and type `diskperf -y`. The proper Registry entry is now set to allow use of the disk counters. Using this option requires shutting down and restarting Windows NT. Leaving this option on permanently is a good way to needlessly drain operating system resources, so remember to reset it after you have completed your performance-monitoring work.

For both the `PhysicalDisk` and `LogicalDisk` performance objects, Windows NT creates a distinct instance for each *physical volume* that exists in your machine. In other words, if you have a single physical disk partitioned into three logical volumes (hardly wise for a SQL Server installation), Performance Monitor will register a single instance for the `PhysicalDisk` object and three instances of the `LogicalDisk` object. If you have three physical hard disks partitioned as a stripe set, each of those three physical disks will appear as a distinct instance.

You can choose from a variety of counters, including disk reads and writes. What you choose depends on what type of application your SQL Server is supporting. If you're using a decision support system or a data warehouse, disk reads are going to be more important than disk writes—both in percentage and real terms. For servers that do serious amounts of transaction processing, disk writes are obviously more critical.

Monitoring the Network(s)

For the network, monitoring just SQL Server's performance gives you only part of the story, because SQL Server's interface to that network is only part of the equation. The network itself is an entity, but also a component of any client/server architecture. Like the other hardware subsystems, the network is a potential bottleneck. Depending on the cable and topology, it could be a bigger one than you expect. If SQL Server is using only one or two of the available protocols, make sure that you monitor the throughput that those protocols are generating. Performance Monitor allows administrators access to the performance statistics for each protocol stack individually, so comparison testing between protocol stacks for a given application is also possible.

Monitoring the SQL Server Object

With regard to SQL Server-specific counters, the SQL Server object is the most critical and most often used. Here, SQL Server can display transaction performance statistics including transactions/sec and writes/sec, as well as displaying reads/sec for OLAP applications. If you're running SQL Server on a multiprocessing, multidisk channel hardware platform, the SQL Server object also includes a collection of very important counters relating to read-ahead performance statistics. Tuning read-ahead caching involves experimenting with different quantities of threads and slots to maximize the `RA - Pages Fetched Into Cache/sec` and `RA - Pages Found in Cache` statistics. (See Chapter 32, "Optimizing SQL Server Configuration Options," for more information on parallel data scanning.)

Having optimized these two statistics, you then want to make sure that the `RA - Slots Used` counter value and the value of the total number of read-ahead slots (`RA Slots × RA Threads`) are as close as possible; this indicates maximum efficiency from read-ahead operations for a given workload.

Using `dbcc sqlperf`

For SQL Server, most of the performance counters are fetched using undocumented `dbcc` commands. Performance Monitor uses the `SQLCTRS.DLL` file to list the objects and counters that are available. When Performance Monitor polls the `SQLCTRS.DLL` file for performance statistics, `SQLCTRS` goes to SQL Server and runs a series of undocumented `dbcc` commands. The execution of these commands against SQL Server form the majority of the overhead associated with monitoring SQL Server's performance. Certain dbcc options are exposed for general use, however.

The dbcc sqlperf option exposes three different categories of statistics: iostats, lrustats, and netstats. Consequently, these are the three arguments that must be substituted when executing a dbcc sqlperf command:

- iostats generates information about the I/O statistics since SQL Server was last started or since the last time the options were cleared—whichever is most recent. This is equivalent to using Performance Monitor to report on disk reads/sec and disk writes/sec. Remember, though, that instead of charting these statistics over time, dbcc sqlperf generates a "snapshot in time" of the statistics. To monitor performance over time, you would have to run this command at regular intervals and record the results.

- lrustats reports on the caching efficiency of SQL Sever, most notably the cache hit ratio. lru stands for *least recently used*, which is the caching algorithm used by all versions of SQL Server.

- The netstats counter reports on network-related statistics, including bytes sent/sec, bytes received/sec, queue length, and so on.

Why use the dbcc sqlperf counters? Because the performance drain associated with using them is substantially less than that when using Performance Monitor. Performance Monitor queries SQL Server at regular intervals, and retrieves very large numbers of performance statistics so that they can be charted. dbcc sqlperf generates text output using print statements, and returns them as data to a client application. As a result, the responsibility for recording those results, storing them, and charting them becomes a manual process for an administrator. Most often, that's how this command is used. A regularly scheduled command-line ISQL session pipes in a query that runs dbcc sqlperf. That query sends the output to an operating-system text file. An administrator moves or copies that text file to an archive directory. As a result, the complete performance history for a server can be stored in a safe location, with minimal (but still present) performance drains being the result.

Summary

If you're troubleshooting a particular performance problem, use Windows NT Performance Monitor. The quantity and variety of information that's available is worth the additional performance hit that your server will take during performance tuning and optimization time. However, if you simply want to track SQL Server's performance as part of monitoring its operational history, use the SQL task scheduling engine (discussed in Chapter 35, "The MS SQL Server Distributed Management Framework") to configure a regularly scheduled, automatically executed batch file that runs ISQL, gathers the performance statistics, and redirects the output to a text file. Administrators can then examine, log, and archive these files to maintain operational history information.

Remote Server Management

This chapter presents details on the definition and management of remote servers, privileges, and security.

As your systems grow in size, complexity, or geographic distribution, you may find it necessary to enable your servers to communicate with each other directly. Remote server access in a multi-server environment enables applications to share data (in a limited way) and to access data and functions on other SQL Servers and Open Data Services applications. (See Figure 34.1.)

FIGURE 34.1.

Remote servers include SQL Servers and Open Data Services applications. Open Data Services processes require the same remote server administration as SQL Servers.

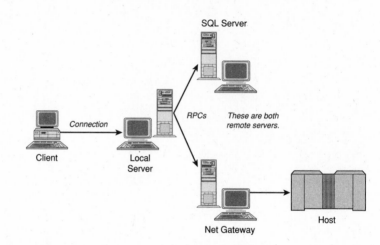

Because the remote server interface can access Open Data Services applications, it also is the mechanism for connecting heterogeneous data sources, including mainframe databases from DB/2 to IMS to VSAM flat files, other non-SQL databases, and nontraditional data sources. The most interesting applications involve the integration of real-time devices (stock tickers, news sources, and data-collection devices).

By definition, a *remote server* is a server that you access as part of a client process without opening a distinct, direct client connection. SQL Server manages communications between servers using *remote procedure calls* (RPC). You call a remote procedure the same way that you call a local procedure; the only difference is that you need to fully qualify the name of the procedure with the name of the server. Here's the syntax:

```
execute remote_server_name.db_name.owner_name.procedure_name
```

You've already used this syntax, with the exception of the `remote_server_name`.

NOTE

With SQL Server and Windows NT, there are actually two different types of remote procedure calls that are available. Windows NT supplies a standards-compliant remote procedure call that enables application-to-application communications both locally and over a network. This RPC is compliant with OSF's DCE (Distributed Computing Environment) RPC specification, so applications that make use of Windows NT RPC services are capable of talking with other DCE-compliant applications, regardless of the hosting platform. For example, a Windows NT application can use RPCs to communicate via TCP/IP to an application running on SunOS or Solaris, and the communication will appear transparent.

SQL Server remote procedure calls are different. Instead of being supplied by the operating system, SQL Server RPCs are supplied by an application, and therefore fall outside normal operating-system services. SQL Server RPCs aren't DCE-compliant, and in fact are a proprietary communication mechanism that works only for Microsoft and Sybase SQL Servers, as well as Microsoft Open Data Services applications and Sybase Open Server applications.

SQL Server RPCs don't interact with the operating system or operating system RPCs. Similarly, Windows NT RPCs neither interact with nor affect SQL Server RPCs. They're mutually exclusive.

No matter what type of external data source you want to access, you need to implement remote servers. Because of the need for remote server features for replication services (discussed in Chapter 36, "Introduction to SQL Server 6.5 Replication"), SQL Server 6 enables remote server access by default.

Definitions

For purposes of this discussion, consider the case in which a client is directly connected to a SQL Server but needs to send and retrieve periodic information to a remote server, using an RPC. (See Figure 34.2.)

FIGURE 34.2.

The remote server is accessed through the local server, and the client maintains only a single connection to the local server.

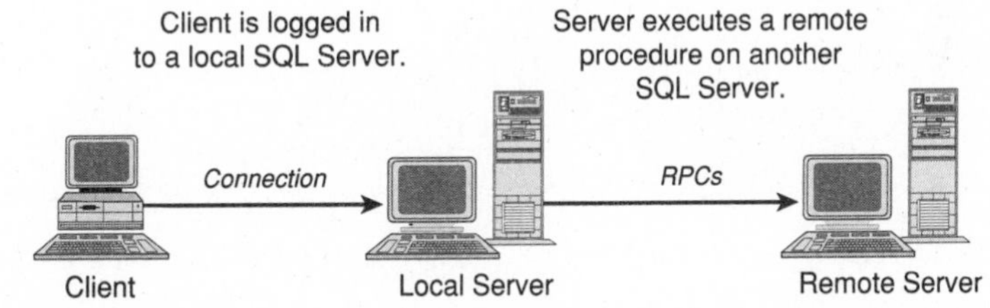

Client is logged in to a local SQL Server.

Server executes a remote procedure on another SQL Server.

Connection

RPCs

Client   Local Server   Remote Server

First, refresh your memory with a few definitions:

- A *local server* is the server you have logged in to.
- A *remote server* is another server to which you would like to connect from the local server.
- *Remote access* means connecting to a remote server.

To illustrate the configuration of remote servers, Figure 34.3 shows an example of two servers: a local server (near_server) and a remote server (far_server).

FIGURE 34.3.

In this example, the name of the local server is near_server. *The remote server is named* far_server.

Client   near_server   far_server

Remote Access Cookbook

Ensuring remote access isn't difficult, but is complex. There are several steps to get remote access working properly:

1. Name the local and remote servers on both servers.
2. Configure each server for remote access.
3. On the remote server, define the method for mapping logins and users to the server's own logins and users.
4. Set the remote option for password-checking.

The following text goes through each step in detail.

Step 1: Name the Servers

Until you start working with remote access, server names seem pretty arbitrary. For example, although you specify a named server when logging in, that server name is transformed into an address and port (or an address and named pipe) long before a packet goes out on the network. The server name that you use on your local workstation doesn't need to correspond to the name in the Registry at the server.

With remote servers, however, the names are relevant to the communication; the names of servers must be defined consistently on each server, or communication won't work properly.

SQL Server 6.5 administrators can manage remote access graphically by using the Enterprise Manager. Version 6.0 administrators must use system procedures to manage remote access.

To manage remote access in Version 6.5, select a server in the Server Manager window of the Enterprise Manager, and choose Server | Remote Servers. This action opens the Manage Remote Servers window (see Figure 34.4). From this window, administrators can manage remote access.

Use sp_addserver to add a server name to the sysservers table in the master database. You need to execute sp_addserver once for the local server name and once for each of the remote servers, as in the following example:

```
sp_addserver local_server_name , local
sp_addserver remote_server_name
```

Note that the local flag distinguishes the name of the local server.

For example, on the local server (near_server), execute the following:

```
exec sp_addserver near_server, local
exec sp_addserver far_server
```

On the remote server (far_server), execute this:

```
exec sp_addserver far_server, local
exec sp_addserver near_server
```

FIGURE 34.4.

*The Manage Remote
Servers window.*

Step 2: Configure Each Server for Remote Access

The syntax is as follows:

```
sp_configure 'remote access', 1
reconfigure
```

For example, on the local server (near_server), execute the following:

```
sp_configure 'remote access', 1
reconfigure
```

On the remote server (far_server), execute this:

```
sp_configure 'remote access', 1
reconfigure
```

Don't forget to shut down and restart each server.

Step 3: Map Remote Logins and Users

This step, on the remote server, maps remote logins and users to the local environment. Here's the syntax:

```
sp_addremotelogin remote_server_name [, local_name [, remote_name]]
```

For example, on the remote server (`far_server`), execute this:

```
sp_addremotelogin near_server
```

Step 4: Set the Remote Option for Password-Checking

This step sets remote options as necessary. Here's the syntax:

```
sp_remoteoption remote_server, login_name, remote_name, option, {true | false}
```

For example, on the remote server (`far_server`), execute this procedure to set up logins without requiring synchronized passwords between servers:

```
sp_remoteoption near_server, near_server_login, null, trusted, true
```

Adding Servers with `sp_addserver`

Use the `sp_addserver` procedure to populate the `sysservers` table. Here's the syntax:

```
sp_addserver server_name [, local]
```

The `local` keyword identifies the name of the server into which you are signed. (There can be only one local server.) You can verify this by selecting the `@@servername` global variable. Note that this doesn't take effect until the server is cycled; until then, RPCs won't work. In this example, you add a local server (`near_server`) and a remote server (`far_server`):

```
exec sp_addserver near_server, local
exec sp_addserver far_server
```

Removing Servers with `sp_dropserver`

To remove a server from the `sysservers` table, use `sp_dropserver`. Here's the syntax:

```
exec sp_dropserver server_name [ ,droplogins ]
```

The `droplogins` keyword also instructs the server to remove all corresponding entries from `sysremotelogins` (discussed next). The following example removes the entry for `server17`, created earlier, and removes all associated logins:

```
sp_dropserver server17, droplogins
```

Adding Remote Logins with `sp_addremotelogin`

Remote logins enable you to map requests to a remote server to that server's local set of privileges and authorizations. *Remote logins are established on the remote server.*

The next three sections explore the three methods for mapping remote logins to local logins on the remote server.

Using the Remote ID as the Local ID

Use this syntax to map the remote ID as the local ID:

```
sp_addremotelogin remote_server_name
```

This is the simplest mapping method. It presumes that the logins are the same on both servers, and maps login to login.

> **TIP**
>
> If users from the remote server need access on your server, don't forget to add them with `sp_addlogin`.

The following example (executed on `far_server`) requires each remote login on `near_server` to have a corresponding entry in `syslogins` on `far_server`:

```
sp_addremotelogin near_server
```

Using a Single Local Login for All Remote Logins

If you want a single local login for all remote logins, use this syntax:

```
sp_addremotelogin remote_server_name, local_name
```

This is another straightforward mapping method. Any legitimate user on a server listed in `sysservers` will be mapped to a single login. In the following example, all logins originating from the server named near_server map to login near_server_user (you need to run `sp_addlogin` near_server_user before running `sp_addremotelogin`):

```
sp_addremotelogin near_server, near_server_user
```

Using a New Local Name for All Remote Users

Here's the syntax for using a new local name for all remote users:

```
sp_addremotelogin remote_server_name, local_name, remote_name
```

The following is an example:

```
sp_addremotelogin near_server, selected_server_user, mdoe
```

In this example, the login named mdoe on near_server can access far_server using the login selected_server_user. (You still need to run sp_addlogin selected_server_user.)

Removing Logins with sp_dropremotelogin

To remove a remote login after adding it, use the sp_dropremotelogin procedure. Here's the syntax:

```
sp_dropremotelogin remote_server [, loginname [, remotename ] ]
```

The following drop statements remove the remote logins added previously:

```
sp_dropremotelogin near_server
sp_dropremotelogin near_server, near_server_user
sp_dropremotelogin near_server, selected_server_user, mdoe
```

Remote Options

Different options can be set for specific servers, logins, and remote names. These options define the way the server deals with the specific logins. Here's the syntax:

```
sp_remoteoption [remote_server [, login_name [, remote_name]],
    option_name, {true ¦ false}]
```

The only option currently available for sp_remoteoption is trusted, which determines whether the local server accepts logins from the remote server without checking passwords. The default is trusted set to false (logins aren't trusted), meaning that passwords require verification.

In the next example (run on far_server), logins from the near_server that map to the near_server_user login on the local server don't need to verify passwords:

```
sp_remoteoption near_server, near_server_user, null, trusted, true
```

If the trusted option isn't turned on, you need to establish and maintain synchronized passwords between servers. Very few applications include the capability to transmit a distinct remote password when necessary. For this reason, the trusted option is typically used when mapping remote logins to different login IDs or a single login ID on the local server, because synchronizing passwords in these situations isn't feasible.

Getting Information on Remote Servers

For information on remote servers defined for your server, you can use the `sp_helpserver` procedure. This procedure reads and decodes information from the `sysservers` table in the `master` database. Here's the syntax:

```
sp_helpserver [server_name]
```

To list all servers defined on your system, use `sp_helpserver` without a server name. By default, only one server will be listed in the `sysservers` table—the name of the local server. Any servers involved with replication will also appear in this list, but only after replication has been configured:

```
sp_helpserver
```

name	network_name	status	id
AMS	AMS	dist	0
KAYDEROSS	KAYDEROSS	rpc,sub	2
NLCWEST1	NLCWEST1	rpc,sub	1

For information on individual logins for a server, use the `sp_helpremotelogin` command:

```
sp_helpremotelogin [remote_server [, remote_name] ]
```

For a list of remote logins, execute `sp_helpremotelogin` without a parameter. In the example that follows, three different remote logins are configured for two different remote servers. The sa logins on both remote servers KAYDEROSS and NLCWEST1 map to the local server login `repl_subscriber`. All other logins from NLCWEST1 map to the `remote_login` login ID on the local server. All remote logins are `trusted`, so passwords aren't verified:

```
sp_helpremotelogin
```

server	local_user_name	remote_user_name	options
KAYDEROSS	repl_subscriber	sa	trusted
NLCWEST1	remote_login	** mapped locally **	trusted
NLCWEST1	repl_subscriber	sa	trusted

Additionally, in Version 6.5 you can retrieve information graphically on remote servers. The following steps explain how to view remote server information:

1. Select a server in the Server Manager window of the Enterprise Manager.

2. Choose Server | Remote Servers to open the Manage Remote servers window (refer to Figure 34.4). From this window, administrators can manage remote access.

Using Extended Stored Procedures and Open Data Services

SQL Server 4.2 for Windows NT introduced an interesting concept: directly accessing operating system resources from within SQL Server. In implementing its desire to more closely tie SQL Server with Windows NT, an interesting benefit arose: SQL Server could directly call Win32 API functions stored in specially written DLLs. This feature was named *Extended Stored Procedures*, and represented the first time that any client/server database could directly access and make use of services available to the operating system on which it was hosted.

In order to accomplish this objective, several requirements must be met. First, for SQL Server to call API functions stored in DLLs, those DLLs must be written as Win32 DLLs using the Windows NT API. The DLLs also must make use of the Open Data Services API, which is an additional application-level, 32-bit programming interface for developing applications that integrate SQL Server clients and other data sources. Finally, the individual API functions' calls must be individually mapped to SQL Server logical names. In effect, creating extended stored procedures is equivalent to writing a header file for a C program or writing an INCLUDE file for a COBOL application.

This level of integration isn't possible on any other platform, because no other version of SQL Server is so closely tied to its underlying operating system. Remember, Microsoft SQL Server for Windows NT runs only on Windows NT. As such, the only limitations on what resources are available are the features of Windows NT itself.

Depending on the application, extended stored procedures may not be the best way to implement certain functionality using Open Data Services. When using extended stored procedures, the DLL that SQL Server calls is loaded into SQL Server's address space, meaning that any corruptions or protection faults that might occur in the DLL will cause SQL Server to protection fault as well. As a result, extended stored procedures introduce an element of potential failure for SQL Server, depending on the quality and robustness of the DLLs being developed for SQL Server access.

As an alternative to using extended stored procedures, you can (and, depending on the application, possibly should) develop a Windows NT application using the Win32 API that also uses the Open Data Services API. By compiling this application as a separate executable, you gain some important benefits:

■ First, because it's an Open Data Services application, you can configure the application to appear to SQL Server as a remote server, using the process described earlier in this chapter. In this way, client applications will connect to the Open Data Services application as though it were another SQL Server. Administration is easier for SQL Server administrators because they can treat the ODS application as if it were "just another" SQL Server, making the task of integrating the administration of this application into normal administration routines much easier. The ODS application isn't considered a special case or exception; it's considered just another SQL Server.

■ Second, because this application is written as a Win32 executable, you have the option of writing it as a Windows NT *Service*. Services in Windows NT are special applications that make use of and conform to the rules of Windows NT's Service Control Manager. Services don't require any desktop interaction; they can run completely in the background. In addition, the Service Control Manager is easily configured, using the Services icon in the Windows NT Control Panel. As a result, the autostarting properties are easily established, making administration of the application much easier.

■ Third and most important, because this application is written and compiled to be a separate executable, it runs within its own address space under Windows NT. If this process should generate a protection fault, *only* the ODS application will be trapped out. SQL Server will continue to run unaffected.

The prospect of SQL Server failing because of an errant DLL is rather intimidating when you consider that, should you use extended stored procedures, not only will the ODS application be closed down, but SQL Server *and all current user connections* will be closed down as well. If, instead, you rely on remote server access to an Open Data Services application, and that application fails, only the ODS application will be closed out. SQL Server and all its current user connections will continue unaffected. The only user connection affected will be the one causing the error in the ODS application. If your application requires high levels of server availability, I recommend that you avoid using extended stored procedures, and use a separate ODS application instead.

Although Microsoft guarantees the integrity of SQL Server in such cases, it can't guarantee SQL Server's integration with other DLLs. As a result, using separate ODS applications accessed via SQL Server remote procedure calls is typically a more reliable solution.

Summary

Making your server accessible to other servers and able to access other servers requires a number of simple steps. Follow the steps presented in this chapter, and remote access should be working. If you think that you followed the cookbook but remote access isn't working, you probably forgot to shut down and subsequently restart the server.

Extended stored procedures represent an interesting and useful technological advance—if properly implemented. More reliable alternatives exist, but the business needs of the applications that you support will dictate which is the best choice for your organization.

The MS SQL Server Distributed Management Framework

35

The SQL Server Distributed Management Framework (DMF) is a collection of administrator applications, Windows NT and SQL Server services, and object programmability libraries aimed at enabling the centralized administration of distributed servers. With the SQL Server Enterprise Manager (SQL-EM), administrators can view and manipulate multiple servers from one central console. To achieve this objective, SQL-EM relies on two other components: the SQL Executive service, and the SQL Distributed Management Objects.

As the rather lengthy discussion in this chapter illustrates, Microsoft has spent considerable effort improving the tools available to administrators of SQL Server databases. With a centralized desktop interface for managing multiple servers, as well as building a programmability interface specifically targeted to server administrators, and making the upgrade/installation process more complete, the SQL Server administrative facilities have come a long way. This framework finally enables administrators to treat Microsoft SQL Server as a legitimate platform for self-administering, high-availability applications. The final question becomes "How do you make SQL Server do all of these things?"—a topic covered in the last section of this chapter.

SQL Server Enterprise Manager (SQL-EM)

With SQL Server 4.2 for Windows NT, Microsoft introduced a suite of very polished administration tools. This was a substantial change for the better. Previous attempts from various vendors—which included such now-historic names as ISQL, SAF, SA Companion, and Desktop DBA—were good efforts, but they didn't integrate into one desktop all the tasks for which a DBA was responsible. Microsoft's SQL Administrator and SQL Object Manager tools, although possessing a complete feature set, were still a collection of independent applications rather than a central desktop for managing multiple servers.

With SQL Server 6, Microsoft introduced a uniform application called the Enterprise Manager. The application begins by collecting the various utilities of the SQL Administrator, SQL Object Manager, SQL Transfer Manager, SQL Server Manager, and SQL Setup. From there, it adds administration capabilities for replication, task scheduling, and a detailed viewer of the current system and activity.

The Enterprise Manager interface can be configured to present any server on the network. Servers can also be grouped into nested hierarchies of folders (or server groups), so that the console can logically organize separate collections and groups of servers—even groups within groups. By relying on a drag-and-drop interface, SQL-EM can easily reorganize the desktop as well.

Configuring the SQL-EM interface doesn't physically change the underlying server in any way. For example, if one administrator creates three server groups named West, Central, and East, and puts servers from cities in those regions into those groups, the servers themselves don't know that any SQL-EM console has grouped them or registered them. Another administrator can configure her groups going vertically across the U.S., such as in North, Central, and South groupings. In both cases, the servers underneath know nothing of the grouping structure on the individual administrator consoles.

In addition, the SQL-EM application doesn't have an interface into the domain structure of the underlying network. If you're running nested domains of Windows NT networks, SQL Server is only aware of servers that are within the local domain, or servers that might be in trusted domains. SQL-EM doesn't group servers according to your domain structure because the server itself doesn't know how it's registered on a particular administrator's console.

> **NOTE**
>
> The Enterprise Manager is capable of managing databases in SQL Server 6.0 and 6.5 fairly easily. However, in order to use the Enterprise Manager with SQL Server 4.2, the system administrator needs to run a script on the 4.2 server. This script installs the stored procedures needed by the Distributed Management Framework to support many of its functions. The script, called SQLOLE42.SQL, can be found in the \SQL\INSTALL directory of any SQL Server 6 installation.

Architecturally, the SQL-EM application is written to Win32 specifications and therefore it runs on Windows NT and Windows 95 workstations. The interfaces of the two versions are functionally identical, providing the same drag-and-drop interface for server management, menus, dialog boxes, and so on, with the Windows 95 version obviously using the new interface components of that operating system. The SQL-EM application has been written to be context-sensitive for right-click operations on both operating systems, so that administrators can choose either desktop—with some important considerations. Because Windows 95 doesn't make use of a Service Control Manager like that in Windows NT, certain API functions for controlling the SCM aren't available in Windows 95. As such, SQL-EM on Windows 95 workstations can't stop, pause, or start the MSSQLSERVER and SQLEXECUTIVE services. For complete control and maximum flexibility of administration for SQL 6 servers, Windows NT is the preferred operating environment for SQL-EM.

SQL Enterprise Manager relies on two other components—the SQL Executive and the SQL Distributed Management Objects—to provide all its administrative functionality. With the SQL Executive, the old SQL Monitor becomes more than a simple task scheduler for SQL Server backup services. Instead, SQL Executive becomes an automated administrator of SQL Server, performing according to schedules and responding to system exceptions.

Instead of diving into a grotesque discussion of menu items and dialog boxes, the demonstration of SQL Enterprise Manager's features and interface in this chapter comes through discussion of configuring automated tasks, exception processing, and configuring alerts and operators.

SQL Executive, Exception Processing, and Task Scheduling

The original SQL Monitor was a useful application for scheduling database backups from within SQL Administrator. With the new SQL Executive service replacing SQL Monitor, the capacity to schedule tasks isn't limited to simple backup routines. Instead, SQL Executive uses a collection of subsystems that invoke different types of tasks according to time-based schedules. SQL Executive relies on these subsystems—as well as a new SQL Server system database, msdb—to provide a complete server-based administrative automation facility to enable timed execution of any SQL Server-related task. Because these various components are all interdependent, discussing them becomes a chicken-and-egg problem.

Let's begin by discussing the SQL Executive service, move into SQL Server's new exception-processing facilities, and then walk through the msdb database that stores the information necessary for all of these features to work. We'll finish with a discussion of the SQL Distributed Management Objects that are used to create and manage these new tasks and open a new world of administrative programmability previously unavailable to administrators strapped by administrative limitations of Structured Query Language.

SQL Executive

SQL Monitor in SQL Server 4.2 enabled administrators to schedule a regular database or transaction log backup. However, what if—before performing that backup—an administrator also wanted to perform a dbcc checkalloc and update statistics in that database? Previously, that plan would have required a third-party client-based application to manage the schedule for executing a script file containing these various commands. That capability has been provided by applications such as SQL Commander or DesktopDBA for some time, but they're always a separate, *client-based* process. As such, they're subject to all the points of failure associated with using such an application; also, multi-server administration becomes a configuration nightmare. Instead, SQL Executive relies on scheduling information stored in msdb tables, in conjunction with its own callable subsystems, to put all the scheduling, activation, and execution history completely within the server itself. The only need for a client process to access this information is for configuration and reporting purposes.

So just what are these subsystems? SQL Server 6 initially ships with five different types of tasks that can be executed. The T-SQL and CmdExec subsystems are for general use. The other three are reserved for data replication, which is discussed in Chapter 36, "Introduction to SQL Server 6.5 Replication." With the T-SQL and CmdExec subsystems, SQL Server can execute Transact-SQL scripts stored within the database or send any command to the Windows NT console command prompt to start off an executable file.

To use the earlier example, an administrator can create a T-SQL script that performs a `dbcc checkalloc` and an `update statistics`, and then performs a complete database backup. This script can either be "naked" Transact-SQL stored in `msdb`, or a stored procedure call that has the necessary T-SQL inside it—allowing you to pass the name of a specific database to process as a parameter, for example. That T-SQL script, whether it's a true script or a stored procedure call, is stored within a table in the `msdb` database and is read as a character value from those tables.

From there, the command string is passed to the T-SQL subsystem, which executes that command against the appropriate server. `CmdExec` enables you to specify the following command string, triggering the subsystem to open a background command-line task and send that string to the `C:\` prompt, executing `ISQL` within that window:

```
isql -Usa -P -ic:\backup.sql -o\backup.out
```

SQL Executive subsystems then become an access point to the outside world for SQL Server.

SQL Executive has been built to use a layered, modular architecture that relies on a different command processor for each type of subsystem command. As subsystems are added, additional command types are available for processing. Figure 35.1 illustrates how these pieces fit together.

FIGURE 35.1.

SQL Executive relies on five additional components for all task scheduling.

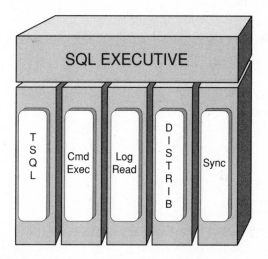

In conjunction with the `msdb` database, SQL Executive executes tasks based on scheduling information held in `msdb`. This scheduling information enables a flexible schedule for task automation, including any combination of time increment or interval measured in months, weeks, days, hours, or minutes. By using the scheduler, for example, administrators can create a backup task that dumps the entire database once each week on Saturday at midnight. A separate task can run on just weekdays at 6 a.m. and perform a transaction log backup instead. Any valid Windows NT command-line syntax or T-SQL command script can be executed in this fashion.

Task-Processing Terminology

With all this new infrastructure, Microsoft has created a bunch of new terminology for you to learn. Understanding these terms at least clarifies the units of work that SQL Server and SQL Executive manage, as well as the areas of work that an administrator must manage. Here are some of the most significant terms:

- **Task.** A series of instructions that are to be processed by one of SQL Executive's five core subsystems. Tasks can be either T-SQL statements (including batches of statements and stored procedures, which includes remote stored procedures) or CmdExec statements, which are executables that are run in background Windows NT CONSOLE sessions (from the command line).

- **Schedule.** The combination of date-and-time interval and increment constructs, which define the execution of a particular task. SQL Executive reads the schedule information associated with each task and executes that task accordingly.

- **msdb.** A new system database, created by SQL Server at installation time, that stores all task scheduling, event handling, and alert notification information, as well as a history of all system- and application-generated events.

- **Operator.** The designated recipient of a particular alert or series of alerts.

- **Event.** A system- or application-generated exception that meets three criteria. First, it's posted to the Windows NT Event Log application. Second, it's posted with a source of SQLServer. Third, the SQL Server error message is registered in the master..sysmessages table.

- **Alert.** Notification that an event has occurred. Alerts are transmitted using, at present, two media: e-mail (via the MAPI interface and a MAPI-compliant e-mail system), or pager (via the TAPI interface and a TAPI-compliant paging system, such as SkyTel or other message-based paging services provider).

Task-Execution Features and Schedules

Task execution isn't just available on a timed, scheduled basis. SQL Executive has also become the heart of the SQL Server 6 exception-processing capability, with which system- and application-generated events can automatically notify scheduled operators and administrators, as well as activate tasks to apply corrective measures automatically.

Before jumping into this topic, some common terms need to be defined. In SQL Server exception processing, *events* are exceptions—generated at the system or application level—that interrupt processing. They're more commonly known as *error messages*, but error messages must meet certain criteria before they can be considered events:

■ First, the error must have a severity level of 19 through 25 (inclusive).

■ Second, the error must be logged into the Windows NT Event Log in the application subsystem.

■ Third, that NT event must have associated with it a source of `MSSQLServer` in the Event Log.

When these three conditions have been met, a true SQL Server event has occurred.

When an event occurs, SQL Server—in conjunction with the SQL Executive—has two processing options: alerts and messages. An *alert*, which is simply notification that an event has occurred, can be sent to an *operator* (or series of operators). An alert can contain alert information, customized messages, and other process-related information. *Operators* are listed and scheduled into the `msdb` database as well, allowing a particular operator on duty at a particular time to be notified of an alert.

In addition to time-based scheduling of operators, messages of a particular type or severity can be assigned directly to particular operators regardless of their schedule. The notification is delivered using any combination of MAPI and/or TAPI, so both e-mail and pagers can be used to send out the alert notification.

Exception Processing

With alert processing, SQL Server now has the capability to deliver a message of an exception within the system or an application to either the current operator on duty or a particular operator, based on the type of message generated. However, simple notification doesn't fix the problem, and automation of those fixes can often be achieved by combining the event detection features of SQL Executive with its capacity to execute T-SQL and `CmdExec` tasks, which is how the term *actions* is defined.

In SQL Server alert processing, an action is a T-SQL script or stored procedure, or a `CmdExec` command-line executable or process, that's executed in conjunction with an event being detected by the SQL Executive. In this way, not only can tasks be scheduled in terms of time-based execution, but SQL Server itself can execute tasks based on exceptions or error conditions that occur at the system or application level. The terms *action* and *task* describe two different ways of invoking a similar command structure. With SQL 6, both *notification* and *execution* of corrective measures can be initiated automatically by the server engine itself, without relying on a separate client application running over the network connected to the specific server.

This feature is available to both the DBMS and any applications running on the DBMS and is achieved through two important changes to the `raiserror` command. Previously, `raiserror` could raise only custom error strings that had an error number outside the range of 0 to 20,000, because SQL Server reserved these error numbers for its own use. Starting with SQL Server 6.0, `raiserror` can be used to call both application-level messages (outside the reserved range) and system-level messages that are in the range. Therefore, an application can now return the dreaded error 1205:

```
Your server command number was deadlocked with another process and has been
    chosen as the deadlock victim...
```

or any other standard error message held in `sysmessages`.

SQL Server 6 has a new system stored procedure, `sp_addmessage`, that enables you to add your own error messages to the `sysmessages` table, allowing `sysmessages` to be a central catalog of error messages both for SQL Server and for any applications using that SQL Server. Any message contained within `sysmessages`—whether created by SQL Server at installation or added later using `sp_addmessage`—can be called using `raiserror`.

In addition, `raiserror` has a new `with log` option that puts the error message into the Windows NT Event Log, with a source of `SQLServer`. This enables the exception-processing capability discussed earlier, by allowing applications to raise both system- and application-level error messages with a severity level greater than 18 (including those added to `sysmessages` by using `sp_addmessage`), logging them into the Event Log (using the `with log` option), and specifying a source of SQL Server (which is handled automatically by `raiserror`). Clearly, this is a powerful exception-handling facility that is providing pleasant relief for database administrators who prefer sleep at 2 a.m. over the insistent cry of a beeper in their ears.

Within the Win32 API, a subset of that API allows applications to register themselves with the Event Log as *callback processes*. In simplest terms, that registration allows an application to define certain actions that the Event Log itself will take if it receives a particular event from a specific source matching particular criteria. When SQL Server 6 starts, part of its initialization routine is to register itself as a callback process with the Event Log, and included in that registration are the requirements that make up a SQL Server 6 event.

Procedurally, the exception-processing architecture of SQL Server 6 is quite elegant as shown in Figure 35.2. In step 1, SQL Server generates an error message that's passed to the NT Event Log. SQL Server, having already instructed the Event Log to notify SQL Executive in case of any errors, sends notification of a potential error to SQL Executive. In step 2, the Windows NT Event Log contacts SQL Executive, which in turn scans the Event Log for the last-generated message. SQL Executive fetches that message and compares it with configuration information held in the `msdb` database, in step 4. Based on the contents of `msdb`, SQL Executive sends e-mail, pages the appropriate operator, or activates the appropriate task, as in step 5.

FIGURE 35.2.

The exception-processing architecture of SQL Server 6.

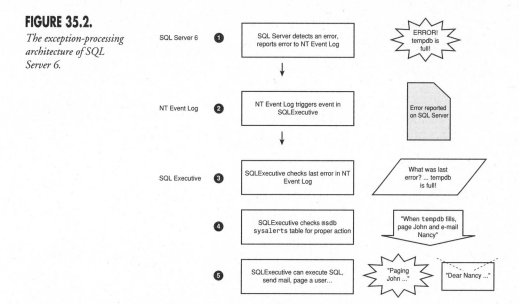

Task Execution and Tracking

There are some important considerations to keep in mind when using exception handling. First, SQL Server records everything it does regarding exception handling. In the sysnotifications table, SQL Server records who was notified and based on which particular event. In the syshistory table, SQL Server records the execution of all tasks, including those activated by the time-based scheduler or those activated in response to an event. This occurs with each instance of a task being executed, and the log is persistent until it's manually cleared. Therefore, on systems where there are large numbers of scheduled and event-based tasks, pruning that history is an important capacity-management consideration.

Second, each exception is processed within its own context. For example, suppose that 12 users are executing a stored procedure at the same time. Each of those processes generates an error condition. Each of those 12 error conditions is received, interpreted, and processed independently of the others—which means that, potentially, 12 e-mail messages, 12 pager beeps, and 12 corresponding tasks can be executed. This situation may or may not be desirable, based on the processing of the application.

In addition, a task called by an exception or event is capable of generating its own events, which starts the process all over again. As you've already seen, this is within a logical and physical context that's independent of any others currently active on the SQL Server. In this way, a lack of forethought, planning, and most importantly *testing* of the exception-handling architecture that you create can lead to a series of closed-loop responses that eventually bring down your server.

The `msdb` Database

The `msdb` database forms the heart of the task-scheduling engine. Within `msdb` are five critical tables that hold all the information necessary for the SQL Executive to function:

- `systasks`
- `sysoperators`
- `sysalerts`
- `sysnotifications`
- `syshistory`

These five tables cooperate with SQL Executive and store all the task, operator, event, alert, and execution information for any task on a particular server. They not only tell SQL Executive what commands to execute, but also on what basis that execution should occur. Finally, a logging feature within SQL Server allows for storage of the complete history of SQL Executive's execution.

systasks

The `systasks` table holds all task information. A *task* is an individual unit of work, which can consist of a command-line batch file name, a Transact-SQL script, or a stored procedure call. Any valid command-line syntax (for the `CmdExec` subsystem) or Transact-SQL statement (for the T-SQL subsystem) is considered a valid task, and that call is stored as a text string in the `systasks` table.

The `systasks` table uniquely identifies each task, using a task ID, and associates the particular subsystem used to execute that task. In addition, the particular database name and all time-based scheduling information are held in this table. Finally, the last column of the table holds the command string that SQL Executive will execute. Therefore, executing `select * from systasks` shows you any command and all scheduling information for that command on the particular server you're querying.

sysoperators

Similar in function to `systasks`, the `sysoperators` table holds information about the operators or administrators who can respond to particular events. With the `sysoperators` table, SQL Server enables you to specify contacting the operator on duty, contacting a particular operator, or contacting a general *fail-safe operator* for each event.

The fail-safe operator is contacted for all events and is a global configuration option for the server. The `sysoperators` table holds information regarding an operator's schedule as well as contact information. For example, an individual operator can be contacted using e-mail or pager, so both of those addresses are held in `sysoperators`, as is the work schedule for that operator.

For example, I might be on duty from 6 p.m. to 6 a.m. every weekday, but I might get weekends off. Or, if I happen to exist farther down the corporate food chain, I might be responsible for Thursday, Friday, Saturday, and Sunday nights. In the event that I can't be contacted when I am on schedule (say, I just happen to jump in my neighbor's Jacuzzi with my beeper still attached to my swim trunks), the fail-safe operator is contacted. All contacts or contact attempts are logged and recorded.

sysalerts

The `sysalerts` table tells SQL Executive which events or exceptions to look for in the Windows NT Event Log and what SQL Executive should do if it ever finds one of those events. The `sysalerts` table enables an administrator to configure an alert to look for particular characteristics of an event, such as the message ID number, the severity level, or (optionally) text included in the error message itself.

In the alert-processing architecture for SQL Executive, the `sysalerts` table is capable of holding a *comparison string* that's used to compare alerts with error messages being generated, so that a single alert could potentially respond to multiple error conditions.

For example, 13 error messages in the `syslogs` table contain the word `syslogs`. However, there's only one `out of space` error for `syslogs`. By using a comparison string of just `syslogs`, I can have a particular alert respond to any of those 13 error messages. However, if I want to trap an `out of space` error, I would use `If you ran out of space in syslogs` as my comparison string, because that string uniquely identifies the error I'm attempting to trap. The `sysalerts` table contains the necessary information about operators and tasks to have either or both directly associated with the error. In `sysalerts`, the `task_id` column is associated with the `systasks.task_id` column, to tell the alert which task it should execute.

sysnotifications

The `sysnotifications` table works with both `sysalerts` and `sysoperators` to join alerts, operators, and the notification method used to contact the particular operator. These are the only three columns in this table.

syshistory

The `syshistory` table is an important one. `syshistory` records the execution history of every task scheduled on a particular SQL Server. With `syshistory`, an individual task's execution data and time are recorded, as is the run duration for the task and its completion status of either success or failure. With this table, SQL Server is capable of maintaining a complete operational history of itself.

There are some important implementational considerations:

- Although `syshistory` can record every task's execution history, it requires data rows in a table to do so. Therefore, the `syshistory` table can grow to be quite large, particularly in "high task count" servers, when much of the exception processing has been automated. Consequently, considerations of space allocated to the database and capacity on the devices must be addressed early on.

- Second, the transaction log for this database can become full quickly because the `syshistory` table will be the destination for many `insert` statements.

- Third, the `syshistory` table and the Windows NT Event Log are duplicating many of the same functions. This may not be desirable, depending on how you want to store the information generated by SQL Executive.

Although the Event Log can hold information, it does run out of space at some point, forcing either a manual save of the file to disk or truncation of the Event Log itself. As such, it doesn't necessarily represent a permanent storage place for event information. In addition, the Event Log provides no querying interface, which makes searching for repeated occurrences of a single event or performing trend analysis on the server very difficult. By keeping that information in `syshistory`, any querying tool can be used to examine the information, and administrators can now keep valid analytical statistics about the server at the server, and start to predict events and trends instead of just responding to them.

SQL Distributed Management Objects (SQL-DMO)

With the creation of System R from IBM in the late 1970s, IBM developers attempted to create a database language that could not only serve as a data-retrieval tool for application support but also have standardized administration syntax for operational support. What has resulted from this effort, in spite of ANSI's best efforts, is a vendor-specific implementation of a variety of commands, procedures, functions, and other inconsistent syntax that have made SQL a kludgy administration facility.

For example, creating a space for database storage in SQL Server requires using the `disk init` command, which specifies a `size` parameter for that space in 2KB page units. However, to remove that space allocation, you must use the `sp_dropdevice` stored procedure. In addition, if you're going to create a database on that device, you must use a number measured in megabytes, not 2KB pages. Such inconsistency has consistently irritated SQL Server administrators. In retrospect, the idea that a data access-and-retrieval language can also function ideally as a server administration language is ill-conceived.

With the SQL Server Distributed Management Objects (SQL-DMO), there's consistency in access to administrative commands, procedures, and configuration parameters for SQL Server. With the SQL-DMO, applications that have an OLE Automation interface can manipulate SQL Server through objects, properties, and methods instead of arcane and inconsistent T-SQL syntax. For example, instead of `disk init` or `sp_dropdevice`, you can use the `CREATE` and `DROP` methods of the `DEVICE` object (in code, this would be `DEVICE.CREATE` and `DEVICE.DROP`) to perform these functions.

OLE Automation applications—in particular, those that have Visual Basic for Applications (VBA) enabled—can use the SQL-DMO libraries to administer any property or configuration option for SQL Server, or even groups of SQL Servers.

The SQL-DMO libraries encompass all facets of server administration, including replication, task scheduling, security, login management, capacity management for disk devices and databases, and object management. The SQL-DMO libraries are called natively by the SQL Enterprise Manager, instead of SQL-EM relying on T-SQL commands and stored procedures.

NOTE

As an implementational note, the SQL-DMO libraries are also Win32-only facilities. Any 32-bit OLE Automation-enabled program can take advantage of the SQL-DMO libraries, such as the 32-bit edition of Visual Basic 4.0 or 5.0, Excel for Windows NT, Excel for Windows 95, and Microsoft Access for Windows 95. However, the resulting application can be used only on a system with Enterprise Manager installed, as there's no legal way to distribute the objects separately from the Enterprise Manager.

Configuring Tasks, Operators, and Alerts

Now that you know what SQL Server can do for you, how do you configure tasks, alerts, and all of the administration-related services? Configuring SQL Server's automated task scheduling begins with the SQL Enterprise Manager application.

Defining Tasks

In SQL Enterprise Manager, you can display the Task Scheduling dialog box by clicking the Task Scheduling button on the toolbar or by choosing the Tools | Task Scheduling menu sequence (see Figure 35.3).

FIGURE 35.3.

SQL Enterprise Manager uses both toolbars and menu sequences to administer servers.

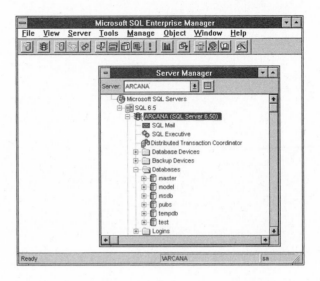

Clicking the first button in the toolbar (the only one that's available, if you have no prior tasks configured) brings up the New Task dialog box in Figure 35.4. In this dialog box, you define the identifying properties of this particular task. We'll get to the task schedule in a moment.

FIGURE 35.4.

SQL Enterprise Manager's New Task dialog box enables you to define task properties graphically, including operator notification and execution schedules.

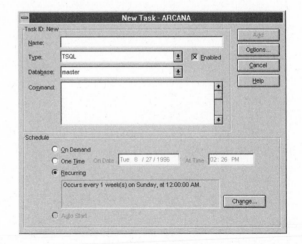

Defining tasks requires defining both the task properties and the task schedule. The properties include the following:

- The task name, which must be unique on the server
- The task type, which for now must be T-SQL or CmdExec because the other task types are reserved for replication

- The database that the task will use (which can be changed in your script, if you choose), particularly if you're calling a stored procedure
- The command string

If you're creating a T-SQL task, the command string must be a valid T-SQL statement or stored procedure call. Fully qualified naming syntax is supported for calling stored procedures that aren't in the current database or the database you define for the task. However, the T-SQL command string will be compiled and executed within the context of the database that you defined in the Database section of the dialog box.

> **NOTE**
>
> Task names must be unique within a server. Because the tasks are stored in the systasks table in msdb, SQL Server has a primary key on the field containing the task name.

There are two other sets of information that you must define for a task. Each task you create has a default schedule, as well as a series of options for the task.

Changing a task's schedule requires you to plan how and when this task should execute. In fact, planning your task-scheduling regimen is far more important than learning how to configure such tasks. However, because planning operational support is a shop-specific task, we'll stick to the technical details.

Suppose that you need a task to dump the pubs database on a regular schedule. Task names conform to the standards for SQL Server identifiers, meaning a maximum of 30 contiguous alphanumeric characters with only the underscore (_) character as punctuation. Let's call this task DumpPubsTx. Because you're executing a dump database command, the command type must be T-SQL. The database is master, because it doesn't need to be changed. The command string for this task is as follows:

```
dump database pubs to disk = "c:\pubs.dmp"
```

> **NOTE**
>
> Notice that T-SQL commands can't return result rows; there's no client application to receive them! However, you can configure a CmdExec task to execute an ISQL script from the command window, using the -i and -o command-line flags to provide input and output files for the session.

Clicking the Change button in the lower half of the New Task dialog box displays the Task Schedule dialog box shown in Figure 35.5.

FIGURE 35.5.

SQL Server Enterprise Manager enables you to define any combination of increment and interval for both date and time information.

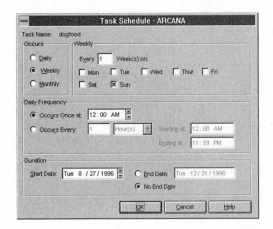

In this dialog box, you first define the increments of days for your task to execute. Execution can be daily, weekly, or monthly, including particular days of the week or days of the month, or particular days during particular weeks during the month.

> **NOTE**
>
> SQL Server 6 lets you shoot yourself in the foot with task scheduling however you choose—one toe at a time, or the whole foot! Using this book and the SQL Server documentation, you should have a clear understanding of how to create tasks. Take the time to plan these tasks carefully.

After you have defined the daily/weekly/monthly section of the schedule, the middle section of the dialog box defines the "time of day" portion of the schedule. Tasks can be recurring during the day, or they can execute only once on each day at a particular time. The bottom section of the dialog box enables you to set start dates and stop dates for the schedule as a whole, suspending the task when the "final day" threshold has been reached.

Task options define how SQL Server will track and execute tasks, as well as what happens if the task fails. Clicking the Options button in the New Task dialog box displays the dialog box shown in Figure 35.6, where you configure task options.

FIGURE 35.6.

SQL Server monitors its own task execution, and it can notify operators if tasks fail or succeed.

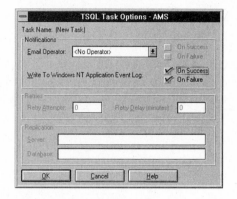

Notice that you can e-mail a particular operator (discussed shortly in the section on alerts), as well as temporarily suspend execution of a task by deselecting the Enabled check box. The task remains defined in the msdb table, but SQL Executive won't execute that task while it is disabled.

Having completed these various options, you can click OK to go back through the maze of dialog boxes, and your completed task is now available for SQL Executive.

Monitoring Task Execution

SQL Server uses the syshistory table to store the execution history of every task, alert, and exception that has occurred on the local server. This information is displayed in the Task History dialog box (see Figure 35.7). All task types, including those used for replication services, are stored here. SQL Server enables you to define a retention period for such log entries, preventing the syshistory table from consuming all the space in msdb. Clicking the Task Engine Options button in the toolbar displays a dialog box that enables you to set the maximum number of rows that syshistory can contain. The syshistory table can also be flushed dynamically by using the Clear Task History Log button.

FIGURE 35.7.

Enterprise Manager's Task History dialog box displays summary information about individual task executions.

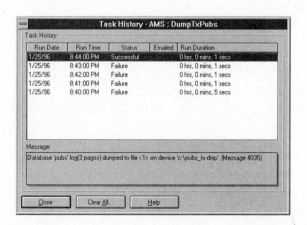

Configuring Operators

Configuring alerts takes place in the SQL Enterprise Manager application. Click the Alerts button in the toolbar (look for the exclamation mark), or use the Server | Alerts menu sequence. Either action opens the Manage Alerts child window, which should list the nine demonstration alerts that SQL Server installs by default. Clicking the Operators tab of the window enables the Operators toolbar, which is highlighted by rather cute firefighter's hats. (Can Microsoft design icons or what?) Clicking the first of the three icons displays the dialog box shown in Figure 35.8, where you can define your operators and their schedules.

FIGURE 35.8.

The New Operator dialog box allows you to define who should be notified in the event of a particular exception or error condition.

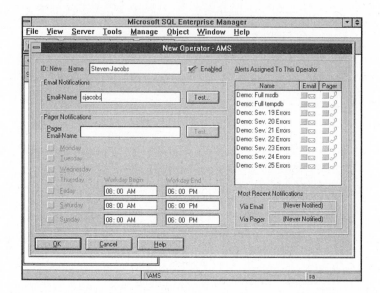

With the New Operator dialog box, you can define operator names, as well as how they are notified. E-mail notification is provided on demand; that is, any time an alert is generated by an error condition, the designated operator will receive e-mail, regardless of day or time. With pager notification, things get a bit more complicated.

Because of the intrusive nature of wearing a beeper, SQL Server enables an administrator to define operator schedules. Operators therefore have a vested interest in being very nice to the administrator, in an effort to avoid carrying a beeper on weekends! The schedules allow for active times during weekdays, as well as distinct active times for Saturdays and Sundays. Notice that these schedules are for the whole week, but they can't be varied by week of the month. So, if you're configured as a SQL Server operator, you're on call every week, but only on particular days of the week. The Enabled check box enables you to suspend an operator's schedule temporarily.

In the grid at the right side of the New Operator dialog box, operators can be assigned particular alerts and tasks to which they respond. They can be notified only by tasks that are in this list, or where they're explicitly configured as an operator (using the Task Options dialog box).

Microsoft requires either the Microsoft Mail 32-bit client or Microsoft Exchange client (which comes with Windows NT Server and Windows NT Workstation) in order to send both e-mail messages and pager messages. If e-mail is your only wish, only Microsoft Exchange is necessary. In fact, setting up a workgroup post office through Windows NT (part of the shipping software) works quite well for small workgroups. Sites that use Microsoft Exchange as their primary messaging service are better served with Microsoft Exchange Server. In particular, Microsoft Exchange Server is required for pager access, because it requires an additional component—the Microsoft Exchange gateway to TAPI (Telephony API) services. SQL Server requires Exchange Server and the TAPI gateway products to send pager alerts to operators.

Remember that configuring operators here means SQL Server is simply adding rows to the `sysalerts` table in the `msdb` database. You can run `select` queries on this table to verify the information you're adding through the SQL-EM interface.

Configuring Alerts

The preceding section mentioned the Manage Alerts child window in SQL Enterprise Manager. Clicking on the Add Alerts toolbar button displays the New Alert dialog box shown in Figure 35.9.

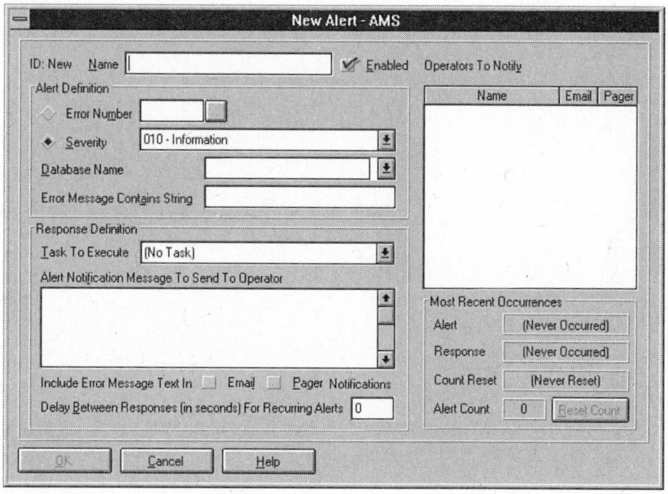

FIGURE 35.9.

SQL Server's New Alert dialog box enables you to define error conditions and specify how SQL Server will automatically respond to those conditions.

Define the error condition in the upper-left corner of the dialog box. Alerts use identifiers, so naming alerts forces you to use SQL Server's naming convention of 30 alphanumeric characters without spaces, but with underscore (_) characters. Errors can be defined using one of three criteria: the error number, the error severity (look at the demonstration errors to see how these are configured), or a passed search string that's compared against the error message itself. For example, you could pass the error string `syslogs`, which is contained in 12 different error messages. Any of the 12 messages could trigger this particular alert.

In the Response Definition section of the dialog box, you specify the *alert response*. This is where SQL Server provides automatic exception processing, by associating a particular task with a particular error condition. In the e-mail or pager message that you send to the operator for this alert, you can include notification that the task was fired, so that the operator is automatically informed that SQL Server has taken corrective action. To prevent repeated paging, the Delay Between Responses interval allows an alert to occur multiple times within a specific period, with no new alert being sent out until that period of time has passed.

SQL Server keeps track of the last date and time a particular operator was notified as well as the last time an alert was generated for a particular exception.

The Alert Engine Options toolbar button displays the particularly powerful dialog box shown in Figure 35.10. The dialog box is important because it allows your server to define a fail-safe operator and pass alerts to another server. The designated server performs the notification operations. The fail-safe operator is notified in the event that no operators are assigned a particular task, or notification attempts for an operator fail the "retry" number of times.

FIGURE 35.10.

The Alert Engine Options dialog box enables you to configure fail-safe operators that are contacted as a last-ditch effort.

The Unhandled SQL Server-Event Forwarding Server section of this dialog allows an error condition to be passed to a different server, and that server's SQL Executive and alert configurations trigger operator notification from that server. It's particularly useful if a server doesn't have access to Microsoft Mail but does have access to the network and another Microsoft SQL Server. Remember, though, that the new server designated as the alert recipient treats that error as a *local* error, so administrators have to ensure that common error-processing routines are specified across all servers.

This feature enables you to centralize all error notification at a single server point. Servers on the network forward their error conditions to the "alert server," which then processes the e-mail and pager notifications. Unfortunately, any task execution must be configured and fired from the local server, so the remote server can't execute tasks configured to fire automatically in the event of an alert. Alerts can be filtered by severity level, allowing only certain levels to be passed to the forwarding server.

Summary

SQL Server's Distributed Management Framework combines a variety of native and foreign technologies to create a new toolkit for SQL Server administrators. Most commonly used will be SQL Server's new exception handling and task automation features, which depend on SQL Executive for their execution. With the delivery of 32-bit development tools for OLE Automation applications, Microsoft now has the additional toolkits necessary to maximize usage of the SQL Distributed Management Objects. By using a standardized object-based API, administrators can circumvent using arcane and inconsistent Transact-SQL statements for server administration.

This chapter represents only the beginning of what you can do with SQL Server's task scheduling features. As is the case with most complex systems, the real difficulties don't lie in the technology or configuring the server. Instead, the real work lies in planning the alert architecture. All of these features require processing power, so careful planning is a must to use those CPU cycles efficiently.

Introduction to
SQL Server 6.5
Replication

36

Introduction to Data Distribution Technologies

One of the most powerful features of host-based applications lies not in the size of databases or the number of users who can access centralized data, but in the availability of data and access to it from all points of the globe. The communications technology supporting the traditional host-based computing structure provided the apparatus necessary for multiple, geographically-distant application sessions to access the one and only centralized data store. There was no need for a data distribution interface or facility, because there was no data distribution. The problem with this system was the inflexible methods of obtaining the data. There was also a problem with manipulating the data to derive information that had relevance to the business.

With relational databases in the client/server environment, the exact opposite was true. The people who could access the data could use tools that allowed a lot of flexibility in how it was accessed, presented, and analyzed. The problem was that the data was often inaccessible to many of the people who needed it. This situation led many MIS professionals to consider client/server and the early versions of SQL Server, Oracle, Informix, and so on as mere wanna-be facsimiles of the "real" mainframe-based databases. Yes, they could work for small applications that the MIS group would otherwise ignore—Marketing, Research, or other isolated departments. But for the real corporate data, give me CICS and the big iron, such as the IBM 3090.

In the last 5 to 10 years, both the database engines themselves and the hardware platforms that host those database engines have now grown sufficiently in size and complexity to host large-scale applications that are crucial to business operations. But unlike the large SNA networks of the past that handled character streams, today's wide area networks connecting remote LANs are too slow and crowded to run the client/server systems of today that deal in characters, numbers, and BLOBs. With work being spread between the client and the server and more information being sent back and forth, WANs become slow and unwieldy for real-time processing of data.

The real data-accessibility question isn't the database server or the application; it's connectivity. Remote users on a mainframe system long ago answered questions that network infrastructure planners are only beginning to grapple with on Windows NT- or UNIX-based networks, and at the forefront of those issues is WAN integration. Until the LAN-to-WAN-to-LAN-to-man (ad nauseam) issues are resolved, corporations need a means of distributing data that's compatible with existing networks and transports, consumes minimal network resources, and is inexpensive. Up to now, the only option has been to choose any two. You could have compatibility, and have it inexpensively, but network consumption was astronomical. You could have compatibility and minimal network drain, but you would have written lots of big zeros in your checkbook. That is, until now.

Asynchronous data distribution has actually been available in SQL Server since Version 1.0, as long as you had a number of well-paid people to manage database backup and restoration. For one project I was involved in early on with SQL Server Version 1.0 on OS/2 (running on Compaq 386/20s with 16MB of RAM, no less!), we took consolidated financial data from Dun & Bradstreet Millenium VSAM files on our mainframe and moved the data through DCA CommServer (another badge of courage in my war chest) to SQL Server. From SQL Server, stored procedures partitioned the data into the 13 divisions of the company. There were 14 databases involved. The primary server held all the consolidated data, and then one database for each of the divisions. The data was partitioned into the divisional databases, and then the databases were backed up to hard disk files. (No, tape wasn't available from Sybase until 4.2, if I recall correctly.) The hard disk files were compressed using a complex data tokening algorithm (commonly referred to as PKZip by its creator, Phil Katz), and the compressed files were then sent to the administrators of the local divisions, who manually restored the files, loaded them into the local SQL Servers, and—voilà!—data replication.

Considering the bronze-age sophistication of the tools available, the biweekly refresh of data proceeded rather smoothly when all parties involved had been properly trained. The problem was that it took 14 well-trained and, at that point, very expensive SQL Server/LAN manager administrators to keep the whole works up and running, not to mention the support staff and processing time on the mainframe side of the equation. Clearly, computing structures that provide distributed data and access to a variety of data sources are going to increase in popularity, and have already done so to the point that Sybase, Oracle, and Microsoft are providing some kind of data replication and distribution technology in their product lines. It's important to remember, though, that whether it's through SQL Server's backup/restore facility or through BCP, data distribution is available and cheap if you don't count "people time."

For those solving problems with technology instead of people, SQL Server has also provided a different, programmatic interface to data distribution, using the 2-Phase Commit (2PC) features of DB-Library. Instead of just distributing data, 2PC actually enables the *physical* distribution of a single *logical* database across multiple servers, for continuously up-to-date copies of the same database on multiple servers. The purpose of this feature is to provide servers and databases that are perfectly synchronized at all times, at the expense of network resource consumption and multiuser throughput. This, in fact, is the key difference between 2PC and data or transaction replication.

2-Phase Commit provides the capability to apply a single transaction to multiple servers at the same time, and with dependent logging. In the specific case of SQL Server, this last part about "dependent logging" is critical because transaction logs that are on different servers operate independently of one another. With 2PC, a client application is able to modify data on the first server, and then modify it on the second server. It validates the change on server 1, and then on server 2. Finally, it commits the transaction on both servers. If the commit on either side fails, *both* sides must have the transaction rolled back. For example, 2PC is an invaluable component to developing applications that rely on fault-tolerant or "hot backup"-capable servers. A single client application applies a single transaction across two servers. If the first server isn't detected, the client application can notify a central administration desk, and then automatically route its transactions over to the backup server. Because both servers have had the same transactions synchronously applied, they are exact replicas of each other during the time they're operational. Although this type of processing is now more commonly implemented with Open Data Services or other gateway applications, 2PC has been a viable alternative for quite some time.

2PC and other distributed transaction types can now be coordinated by using the *Microsoft Distributed Transaction Coordinator* (*MS DTC*). The MS DTC provides three very important features:

- It enables you to update data that resides on two or more SQL Server systems.
- It allows SQL Server to be used by transaction-processing monitoring systems (such as Tuxedo). This in turn allows third-party systems that follow X/Open DTP XA-compliant standards to be used in a three-tier system.
- It provides an easy-to-use graphical user interface for distributed transactions. The GUI interface enables the DBA to monitor all the distributed transactions in progress, look at the log, and actually control the transactions.

The MS DTC is installed and run as a service in NT. When you expand servers in the SQL Enterprise Manager, each server where MS DTC is installed displays an MS DTC icon. You can also access MS DTC via the Server menu.

After you reach the MS DTC, you can perform the following tasks:

- Start and stop MS DTC.
- Open the DTC Transactions window, where you can view all transactions that are running, and the status of each transaction. You can force prepared transactions to resolve as being committed or you can force active transactions to stop. You can also force a coordinating MS DTC server to remove a transaction from its log.
- Open the DTC Trace window, where you can view event log information as well as MS DTC trace information. You can even filter the displayed information by severity level.
- Open the DTC Statistics window, where you can view statistics about MS DTC counters, including the following statistics:
    - Current number of active transactions
    - Peak number of concurrent transactions
    - Number of committed transactions
    - Number of aborted transactions
    - Number of in-doubt transactions
    - Number of administratively resolved transactions
    - Total number of transactions processed
    - Transaction response times
    - The date and time the MS DTC session started

■ Open the DTC Configuration window, where you can set MS DTC update frequency, transaction display retention, log file location, and checkpoint and flush timers.

MS DTC is also added to the control panel at installation.

Obviously, the connection, locking, and network overhead of completing transactions using 2PC between even two servers is substantial, and that, combined with the programming fearlessness necessary to write applications that take advantage of this feature, makes the cost of implementing 2PC applications a very specialized affair. It's also a cost, in terms of overhead and throughput degradation, that's quickly magnified by almost exponential proportions as the number of servers involved increases. Therefore, 2PC isn't ideal for simply copying local tables to remote servers to enable easier access. Although replication is a different answer to the question of distributed *data*, it is *not* in any form an answer to the question of distributed *transactions*, for reasons that you'll see in this chapter.

SQL Server Replication

Replication is the capability to copy one set of data from one source to potentially multiple other sources. But contrary to the term *replicated data*, it isn't the data that's copied, but the transactions that affect the data. Transactions are recorded in the transaction log from one database and marked for replication. These transactions are then copied to the destination database (usually but not necessarily on the same server). The transactions must then be applied to that database in the order in which they were applied to the first database. If the data was the same at the beginning of the process, this will result in identical copies of data on the two machines.

In most cases, replication provides a read-only copy of a specific set of data from a data owner to one or many replicate sites. Yes, sports fans, that's right—the copies of data or transactions that you'll be replicating are read-only, and here's why: Replication is an inherently *asynchronous* process, meaning that the *exact timing* of a data change being applied at the source doesn't affect the exact timing of the change being applied at a replicate site. Therefore, when working in a distributed data environment that uses replication as a model for such data distribution, you usually count on the fact that the *only* truly valid copy of the data is the one at the source, because only that one source can be guaranteed to have applied all data changes up through a specific time. In most instances, if you were guaranteeing that you were applying a change to data at all sites, and validating that change among all sites before continuing, you would be doing 2-Phase Commit processing—and the overhead of that is just what you're trying to avoid here. Replication trades the overhead and development costs of 2PC for restrictions on how data can be distributed and manipulated. There are exceptions to this setup, involving managing the state of ownership. This more complicated scenario is discussed later in the chapter.

In any replication model, each record in a given set of data has only one owner. A single set might consist of multiple records, and each of those records might have a *different* owner, but a single record will always have only *one* owner. The reason for this scheme lies in replication's inability to distribute transactions. In an effort to avoid the network and locking overhead of 2PC, a server must be enabled to process transactions. Because SQL Server works at the database level with transaction logs, "versioning" of record changes can't occur; two servers have no way to figure out which server "owns" the right change. If an application changes record 1 on server 1, and another application changes record 1 on server 2, which change is the "right" change? If you record each change and this information is sent to the other server, you'll set up a Cartesian or repeating change that will never stop changing.

The answer to that situation becomes a *business* question, not a *technological* or *relational* question, because the change itself is tied to the business process, not to any rule or posit of relational theory. The DBMS is responsible only for storing and making available data through means defined by that relational theory. Although deftly written, SQL Server doesn't have the first clue how to resolve the age-old question "Who gets the last donut?" That, unfortunately, is still the domain of the application developer. If you want to have the ability to change data that another server owns, you have to write code to maintain the state of the data and rules (in code, of course) that allow this to happen under controlled circumstances. It's not the easiest thing to accomplish, but it can be done.

Replication provides the capability to distribute read-only copies of a specific set of data to other servers, so that the data is now remotely available to remote users, instead of locally available to remote users. The advantage is data availability that doesn't depend on weak links between LANs and WANs, and significantly more efficient usage of long-distance network links. Instead of 1,200 users accessing a server from all corners of the globe over a WAN, individual groups of local users can access their own *local copies* of read-only data. Or, as you'll soon see, the local data itself might be the writeable data, and sent back to headquarters as part of a read-only roll-up.

Although this might seem like lots of superfluous talk about relational principles and operating constraints, it will make the discussion of SQL Server 6.5's particular implementation of these concepts that much easier to digest. Microsoft has developed an innovative approach to working through some of these constraints, and, in some cases, is still bound by them. Knowing what those constraints are, why they are there, and how to work within them (or choose an alternate technology, such as a transaction processing monitor, customized code, or 2PC-compliant applications), is critical to properly implementing these new features.

SQL Server Replication Terminology

SQL Server 6.5 introduces a slew of new terms aimed at befuddling anybody who has ever worked with SQL Server. (Actually, Microsoft just needed lots of new words to describe the new features.) Some of this terminology focuses on replication and how SQL Server itself functions in a replicated-data environment.

Any single server can function in one, two, or all three distinct roles, based on how you configure SQL Server's operation. These roles are a publication server, a subscription server, and a distribution server:

- The *publication server* is generically defined as a server that is the source of replicated data—data that's published. (I'll describe what data it can provide shortly.) Publication servers use one or more *publication databases* as the source of the information that they are going to make available to other servers for replication. The publication server can have one or more *publications,* the term for a group of tables that will be the source of data for replication. Each table in a publication is called an *article.* Each user database may have one or more publications. This setup allows you to partition data for use by different databases on the same or different servers. More on partitioning data later.

- A *subscription server* has *subscription databases.* A subscription database subscribes to different publications on one or more publication servers, basically becoming the destination for the publications. This database then receives publications consisting of the transactions that hold the data and changes in articles. It applies the transactions that generate that data to the corresponding tables in the subscription database.

- SQL Server uses a "store and forward" metaphor for actual transaction distribution, and this relies on the third of the server roles: *distribution server.* A distribution server contains the *distribution database.* The store-and-forward database has a default name of `distribution`, but any name is considered valid. For the purpose of consistency, the `distribution` database will always be the publisher's store-and-forward database for replication. The distributing server role can be local—that is, a publishing server is also performing its own distribution functions—or a publishing server can rely on the distribution services of another publishing server, thereby using a *remote distribution server.* The distribution server receives all the changes to published data (publications) and stores these publications in the distribution database. Then, depending on schedules and other factors, the distribution server delivers the publications to the subscription servers.

Whether a server is functioning as just a publisher or as both a publisher and a distributor, the server is defined by the location of the distribution database.

Microsoft's architecture for SQL Server replication enables a single server to function in any of these three roles. In other words, the subscribing role that a server performs is distinct from any publishing or distributing services it may provide. A single server can publish data, locally distribute that data to other servers, and yet receive replicated data from different servers as well. You'll see this in more detail in the section "Configuring a Simple One-to-Many Replication Model."

In addition to defining server roles, the individual units of work that SQL Server uses for replication have been defined to enable more flexible options for replicating data than previous applications have provided. SQL Server uses both publications and articles to define what's going to be replicated, and how. An article, which is actually a pointer to a data table, is the smallest unit of work for any SQL 6.5 replication processing. The article is based on a table but isn't a table itself. In fact, an article can be an entire table, a subset of columns from a table, a subset of rows from a table, or a combination of the two. As of yet, only table data can be published. A single table theoretically can have an unlimited number of articles that enable publishing of its data. Articles are defined in the `sysarticles` system table, which is a new addition to the SQL Server database-level dictionary.

By definition, articles must exist within a larger context, which is where publications come in. Any article must be created within a publication. The reason for this setup lies in SQL Server's capacity to subscribe either to individual articles within a publication, or to the publication as a whole—giving you a subscription to all the articles in that publication. By doing this, an administrator can create a publication that contains individual whole-table articles. By subscribing to the publication, another SQL Server database has just subscribed to all the data tables for an entire database!

SQL Server Replication Models

SQL Server 6.5 supports several different "models" of replication. The simplest of these models is the traditional one-to-many data distribution method (see Figure 36.1). In this model, a single SQL Server publishes a database and its tables to a variety of remotely located servers, so that clients at those remote sites have local copies of the data. In this case, the publishing server is also performing its own distribution.

This would fit a scenario where corporate would generate sales and marketing information and replicate it out to the various branches to use for reporting and analysis. One variation on this model would be to replicate only the information for each branch. This variation would require the publication server to publish three publications, one for each branch. Each publication would use horizontal partitioning to make sure that a branch received only information relevant to that branch. Horizontal partitioning is discussed later in the chapter.

In cases in which there might be a dial-up or other slow-link connection, using a remote distribution server (see Figure 36.2) is actually more efficient. By putting the distribution server on the other end of the remote link, the transactions can be distributed using a local LAN connection instead of an expensive and slow WAN connection.

In a complete reversal, SQL Server also supports "corporate roll-ups" of data, although with some additional configuration (see Figure 36.3). Typical examples include sales roll-ups, where individual point-of-sale units or individual warehouses track their own data changes locally, but feed those changes to a corporate data center for reporting and redistribution purposes. In a roll-up scenario, the design of primary keys at each site is of the utmost importance. You must guarantee that there is NO chance of duplication of the primary key of all the data marked for replication.

FIGURE 36.1.

SQL Server supports the typical data-distribution model of a single publisher sending data to multiple subscribers.

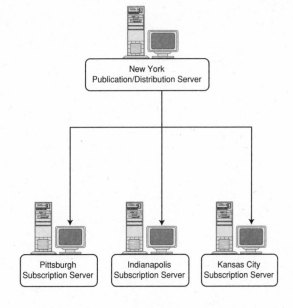

FIGURE 36.2.

SQL Server can also support remote distribution servers, to minimize WAN traffic.

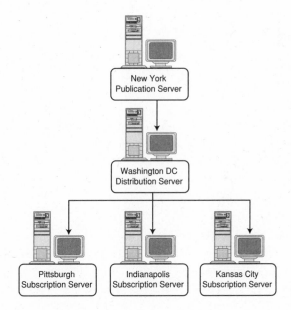

FIGURE 36.3.

SQL Server also supports multiple publishers sending data to a single subscriber, providing "roll-up" capabilities.

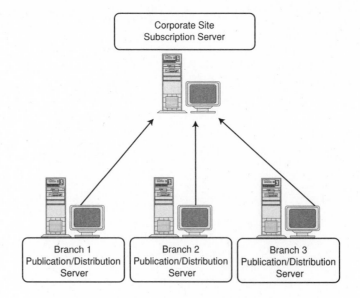

There are several ways to accomplish this objective, but most are variations on the following two:

- The simplest is to use a dual key. The first key would be a sequential number; the second key would be a site code. That combination should be unique for each table.

- The most complex, in terms of both configuration and management, is the many-to-many model. With this scenario, a single server works as a publisher and subscriber, but to different pieces of information. In effect, it's simply a collection of individual one-to-many models, as shown in Figure 36.4. In this example, a publisher provides location-specific data to the other servers. A table would consist of four different logical segments, each identified by the location that owns a particular record. Remember that even in this scenario, all changes to a record must be *local* changes, meaning that only local users on the Seattle server can change records from Seattle, only local users on the Chicago server can change records from Chicago, and so on.

There are scenarios that require the ability to share data at several sites and yet maintain the ability to change that shared data. This is possible but very complicated. You must write the code to do state maintenance (ownership resolution). *State maintenance* is the actual changing of the ownership of the data. By changing the ownership of the data, you can allow multiple sites to be able to change the data. But the changing of state (or ownership) should precede any change. This shouldn't be one of the first replication models that you undertake. It should be done only when there's an overriding business reason for doing it.

One of the more useful features of SQL Server 6.5 replication is that any SQL Server can perform any of the three functions. The biggest benefits to be gained from replication may actually be for highly transactional systems. One of the biggest problems with large corporate databases has been the often mutually exclusive needs of both OLTP (On-Line Transaction Processing) and OLAP (On-Line Analytical Processing) users. Anyone trying to process reports on a high-transaction database knows that both processes kill throughput for everybody. Using replication, the transactional data can be loaded into a different, "reporting only" server, or, if you have the hardware, simply replicate the transactional database to a reporting database on the same server. Replication need not be from server to server; it can actually be from database to database on the *same* server! By replicating the data from a transaction database to a reporting database, you can optimize each one by building an index structure that supports the stated purpose of the server. The table structures are the same, but the indexes are different between the two.

FIGURE 36.4.

SQL Server supports multiple-publisher/ multiple-subscriber replication scenarios, but only with locally updated data.

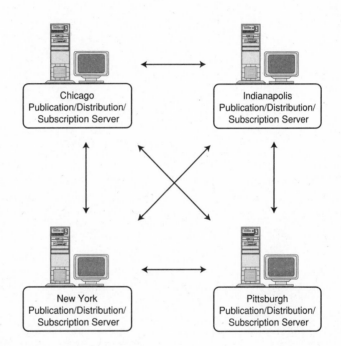

Chicago
Publication/Distribution/
Subscription Server

Indianapolis
Publication/Distribution/
Subscription Server

New York
Publication/Distribution/
Subscription Server

Pittsburgh
Publication/Distribution/
Subscription Server

SQL Server Replication Processing

In the discussion of the SQL Distributed Management Framework in Chapter 35, "The MS SQL Server Distributed Management Framework," SQL Executive was supplied with a total of five subsystems. Two of those subsystems are for generic processing (TSQL and CmdExec), whereas the other three are reserved for replication purposes. The other three are LOGREAD, SYNC, and DISTRIB, and they, in concert with SQL Executive, are the "business end" of SQL Server's replication features.

When a database is marked as "published" (using `sp_dboption`), SQL Server activates the LOGREAD subsystem of SQL Executive. LOGREAD continuously scans the `syslogs` table of the published database, waiting for committed transactions to be flushed to disk. When those transactions are flushed, LOGREAD scans the newly written pages and, based on their contents, reverse-engineers a SQL statement. That SQL statement, now stored as a text string, is added as a row into a table in the `distribution` database. How it does this merits further detail. In the `distribution` database, there are two important tables: `MSjobs` and `MSjob_commands`.

The LOGREAD subsystem's function is dependent not just on what SQL Server logs for transactions, but how those transactions are logged. For example, the query `delete authors` has 23 rows by default, and generates 23 individual `delete` statements, each of which corresponds to a unique index value in the primary key of `authors` (the `au_id` field). As a result, SQL Server logs 23 individual `delete` operations in the `syslogs` table for `pubs`. When the LOGREAD subsystem sees this, it sees 23 individual operations, but they're still part of a single logical operation: the original `delete authors` that the application sent to SQL Server. In effect, there's a 1:23 relationship between the original query and the number of individual operations that SQL Server uses to execute that query. `MSjobs` and `MSjob_commands` provide a way to resolve that 1:N relationship. `MSjobs` gives the whole query a distinct `job_id`, which is used as the common key to `MSjob_commands`. LOGREAD inserts each of the 23 `delete` statements as a separate row in `MSjob_commands`, giving each row a job command ID, and includes the single `job_id` value as well.

After the rows are added to `MSjobs` and `MSjob_commands`, the DISTRIB subsystem is responsible for reading those rows and passing the statements that are held there to the subscribing servers. To do this, DISTRIB uses ODBC and the SQL Server ODBC driver to open the connection. The subscribing SQL Server processes the transaction statement as it would any other. In the event of network failure or other interruptions, SQL Server keeps track of the last successfully executed `job_id` in the `MSlast_job_info` table, which SQL Server automatically creates in the subscribing database.

> **NOTE**
>
> SQL Server 6.5 supports both publishing and subscribing with both SQL Server 6 and 6.5. It supports one-way replication (publish only) to ODBC subscribers that meet certain criteria:
>
> - The ODBC driver must be level-1 compliant.
> - The ODBC driver must be 32-bit, thread-safe, and the processor (Intel, Alpha, etc.) must be the same as the processor on which the distribution server is running.
> - The ODBC driver must not be read-only, must be transaction-capable, and must support DDL. This includes Microsoft Access, Oracle, and any other ODBC program in which the driver meets the above criteria.

Because SQL Server uses transaction statements for replication, rather than simply copying data rows back and forth, replication in SQL 6.5 requires a "baseline" where the publishing table and the subscribing table are synchronized. This is required because each transaction statement represents only a *change* to a value, not a value itself. That's where SYNC comes in. Before distribution of transactions can occur, SQL Server uses the SYNC subsystem to take a "snapshot" of the source data, and copies it to the subscribing database. This involves three important components (`sync`, BCP, `distrib`) in two steps:

- First, SYNC needs to create an object in the destination server, or at least be able to clear an existing object, because SYNC uses BCP to move data. This BCP operation can use either native-format data (if both servers use common code pages and sort orders) or character-format data (if they don't share code pages and sort orders). Obviously, native-format BCP is faster, so establishing common code pages and sort orders is of some benefit for SQL replication. Because BCP only adds new rows (it doesn't clear existing space), the table must be "clean" for synchronization.

- Second, to "clean out" the destination table, SQL Server can auto-generate a *creation script*, which contains the `drop table` and `create table` statements necessary to clear the table. Optionally, SQL Server can use an existing table, and simply `truncate table` any existing rows away. After the table has been cleared, `sync` relies on `distrib` to BCP the source data into the destination table. After the synchronization process has completed, the tables on both the publishing and subscribing servers will be identical—and only then can `distrib` send transaction statements to the subscribing server.

Configuration Prerequisites for SQL Server Replication

SQL Server relies on its own services, as well as others in Windows NT, to provide replication functionality. The most important of these is SQL Executive. Because SQL Executive will be making a standard ODBC connection into the subscribing database, it must have access to network resources. For this reason, SQL Executive must be able to log on to the network. Although it's the default setup option, the importance of creating a distinct Windows NT domain account for SQL Executive is imperative; this is particularly crucial for data replication with SQL Server.

There are two minimum requirements for SQL Server replication. First, you must have adequate disk space for SQL Server, all of its databases, and both the `distribution` database and BCP output files. Second, you must be able to configure SQL Server for 16MB of memory. To install replication, the `memory` option for `sp_configure` must be configured to at least 8192 pages. Both the stored procedures for replication and the SQL Enterprise Manager (SQL-EM) application check this configuration option, and will not allow you to proceed until it has been set properly. Because SQL Executive makes a standard ODBC connection to the subscribing server, increasing the `user connections` option on that server is a good idea as well.

Configuring a Simple One-to-Many Replication Model

Although Windows NT and MS SQL Server supply all the operating system utilities and stored procedures necessary to configure SQL Server replication, using the SQL Enterprise Manager is by far the easiest method to accomplish that goal. What you need to remember is that behind the scenes SQL-EM is simply executing stored procedures and T-SQL commands to configure entries in the `distribution` database, as well as the `syspublications` and `sysarticles` tables of the publishing server.

There are four different configuration steps for using SQL Server replication features:

1. Setting SQL Server's configuration options, using `SETUP` and `sp_configure`.
2. Configuring a server's roles.
3. Creating publications and articles in the published database.
4. Creating subscriptions to the publications and articles.

Setting SQL Server's Configuration Options

Configuring replication begins with changing the necessary `sp_configure` options in SQL Server. Memory must be set to at least 8192 pages, and user connections should be increased by 10—but this number is just my recommendation for testing purposes. The number of publishing and distributing servers, combined with their distribution schedules, will determine how many additional user connections you need to allocate to avoid running out in normal use.

You must also configure SQL Server for INTEGRATED or MIXED login security. SQL Executive, through the SYNC and LOGREAD subsystems, makes an integrated-security connection to SQL Server. Read Chapter 27, "Security and User Administration," for step-by-step instructions for this task using the SQL Server Setup utility or the SQL Enterprise Manager utility. When you have completed these changes, you need to shut down SQL Server and restart it. When you've done that, you're ready to configure SQL Server's publishing features.

Configuring the Server for the Publishing and Distributing Roles

In establishing a replicated-data architecture, SQL Server begins with configuring the data sources to be used. In plain English, that means that you need to configure the publishing and distribution servers before you can configure anything else. In the SQL Enterprise Manager application, choose the Server | Replication Configuration | Install Publishing menu items to open the dialog box shown in Figure 36.5.

FIGURE 36.5.

SQL Enterprise Manager provides the easiest method to configure replication.

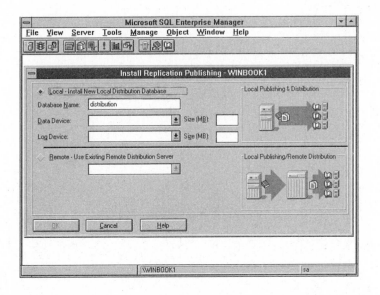

Given that the Install Publishing menu item brought up this dialog box, it might seem odd to define distribution before defining publication. SQL Server needs to know where to place what it's publishing, however, before it can know what to publish. This simple example uses a local publishing server, implementing the first of the replication models described earlier. (Specifying remote distribution enables the second model.) In defining local distribution, SQL Server needs to create the `distribution` database. After having assigned the `distribution` database to a disk device, and optionally a log device, click OK to activate a series of processes:

1. First, SQL-EM edits the Windows NT Registry and sets the name of the store-and-forward database in the following key, supplying the value for this key with the name used for the `distribution` database.:

   `\\HKEY_LOCAL_MACHINE\SOFTWARE\MICROSOFT\MSSQLSERVER\REPLICATION\DistributionDB`

2. Second, SQL-EM runs `create database`, using the name supplied for the `distribution` database.

3. In addition to creating the database, Enterprise Manager's third step is to run the `INSTDIST.SQL` script (supplied in the `\MSSQL\INSTALL` directory by default) in the `distribution` database, which creates the distribution-role-specific tables that SQL Server needs. (The tables `MSjobs` and `MSjob_commands` are among those created by this script.)

4. Finally, the SQL Server must be able to identify itself as both a publishing and distributing server. This is accomplished by altering entries in the `master..syservers` table. Three new status values for a server have been created: `pub`, `dpub`, and `sub`. (Amazing how they correlate, isn't it?) SQL-EM runs the following command to change the `syservers` entry in the master database to `dpub`:

   `sp_addpublisher` *server name*, `'dist'`

If this were only a publishing server, relying on a remote distribution server, it would be set to pub. Because distribution servers must also be publishing servers, dpub handles both options.

After you click OK, SQL-EM asks you whether you'd like to define publishing databases and distribution schedules. Accepting this offer brings up the next major dialog box in replication configuration, illustrated in Figure 36.6.

A single publishing server works with a fixed distribution schedule. That schedule can be time-based or transaction-based. A transaction-based schedule keeps a "batch" of transactions, the size of which you specify. Under certain circumstances, particularly horizontal partitioning, you may want to use a transaction batch size of 1, meaning that each transaction is replicated as it occurs (that is, it's sent to each destination server individually). Because of the impact that this setting can have on network throughput, Microsoft includes recommendations on how to configure this option. Time-based scheduling enables you to send the transactions to replicate every so often—say every three minutes or every hour. Regardless of the number of transactions, the distribution subsystem sends all transactions for that time block to the subscribing servers.

FIGURE 36.6.

SQL Enterprise Manager enables you to define distribution schedules for server-to-server replication, using time-based or transaction-based scheduling.

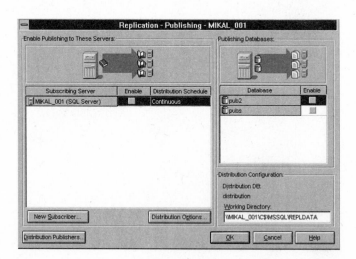

On the right side of this dialog box, you can choose the databases that you want to serve as publishing databases. It is in these database that you create database-specific publications, which will be placeholders for your articles. I'll talk about article and publication restrictions in a moment. Having marked a database as published ("published" and "subscribed" are new sp_dboption parameters), you are now ready to create a publication in your published database.

Configuring a Subscribing Server

For a SQL Server to receive data, it must be configured as a subscribing server. To do the configuring, select Server | Replication Configuration | Subscribing in SQL Enterprise Manager to display the dialog box shown in Figure 36.7.

FIGURE 36.7.

Configuring subscribing servers with SQL-EM.

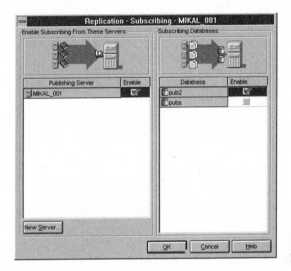

Enterprise Manager puts the name of the server you're configuring as a subscriber in the dialog box's title. The left half of the dialog box lists publishing servers to which you want to subscribe. The list in the right half of the dialog box is the databases that can serve as destination databases for subscriptions.

Select the name of the publishing server, and then select the name of the databases that can serve as destinations for subscriptions. You can select a database as a potential destination; it won't actually become a destination database until you have created a subscription, which will happen shortly.

NOTE

Replication isn't dependent on database names. For example, I can publish data from the pubs database on AMS to the dest database on NLCWEST1. In fact, SQL Server can replicate from one database to another on the same server. As a result, any non-system database can serve as a publishing database, subscribing database, or both.

Creating Publications and Articles

Highlight the database you have published, and choose Manage | Replication | Publications or click the Replication - Publishing icon in the toolbar. Either action opens the Manage Publications dialog box shown in Figure 36.8.

FIGURE 36.8.

Databases that have been marked for publication are listed. This is where you define, change, or remove publications.

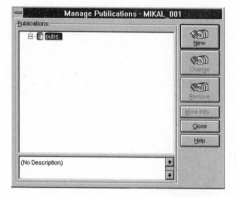

Highlight the database for which you want to create, change, or remove a publication, and click the appropriate command button. This action brings up the Edit Publications dialog box, as shown in Figure 36.9.

FIGURE 36.9.

Defining publications and articles in SQL Enterprise Manager.

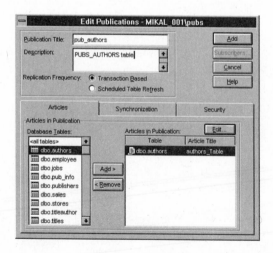

The concept of a publication is one of the more difficult to understand, because it's only an abstraction layer: A publication is nothing more than a logical placeholder for articles. In that way, a publication is similar to a directory in DOS. It doesn't really exist physically, but it can still contain files and other directories. In the same way, a publication is nothing more than table entries that enable a one-to-many relationship: A single publication can hold 0/1/*N* articles, enabling SQL Server to subscribe to individual tables or groups of tables all at once.

Within each publication, theoretically there can be an unlimited number of articles, each of which points to a table. Referring to Figure 36.9, an administrator has created the publication `pub_authors`, and in it is a single article pointing to the `authors` table. You might want to review the definition of an article before reading this next point: A single table can be published many times, because each article is merely a *logical pointer* to a table, not a data table itself. In defining the article, SQL Server is identifying the columns and criteria about those columns in the table. It then monitors those columns and the criteria for any transaction that creates, updates, or deletes data in the columns. If the data also meets any criteria established, then the replication process will *copy the transactions that affect the data*, not the table as an object.

Because of this, a single publication could have 12 different articles, all of which are based on the `titles` table. Each of those 12 tables could be a different view of the data, including combinations of columns, rows, and so on.

Managing Articles

To manage articles, highlight an article in the Edit Publications dialog box, and click the Edit button to open the Manage Article dialog box (see Figure 36.10).

This is where you can tune replication for the many models, some of which were mentioned earlier in this chapter. If I want to roll-up data to a corporate site, I may only replicate certain columns in a table. I would do this by checking the Replicate box in the Manage Article dialog box. This is referred to as *vertical partitioning*. Or maybe I'm replicating copies of sales data out to branch offices. If I have a branch in California, I could use the Restriction Clause box in the Manage Article dialog box to type a `where` clause that would limit the data available in this article. By typing `where state = 'CA'` I could limit the data sent in this article to data for California only. This is *horizontal partitioning*. You can actually use a combination of horizontal and vertical partitioning. The whole purpose is to send only the data that's needed.

FIGURE 36.10.

Articles may be refined to show only certain columns (vertical partitioning) or certain rows (horizontal partitioning) in the Manage Article dialog box. Advanced management can be done with stored procedures that filter the data targeted for replication.

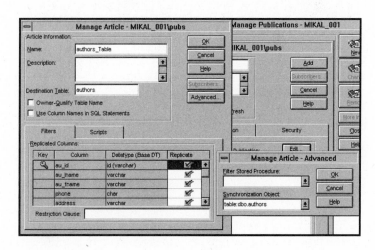

You can get even more elaborate by writing stored procedures that filter what data is replicated. You would define this setting in the Manage Article - Advanced dialog box (shown in the lower-right corner of Figure 36.10). This capability increases the variations and complexity of your replication models.

The Use Column Names in SQL Statements option in the Manage Article dialog box provides a very important enhancement over the replication in SQL Server 6.0. Many times, as copies of databases are established in different locations by different DBAs, certain tables may have columns in different physical order. In SQL Server 6.0, this problem meant that replication would probably fail. The table structures had to be identical, even to physical order; or the insert statements wouldn't use the list of columns. Now you can check the Use Column Names in SQL Statements option; the insert transaction will, after the insert command, list the columns before the values. This feature allows the replication to be successful, even if the columns have a different physical order.

Managing Synchronization and Security

Notice the Synchronization tab in the lower half of the Edit Publications dialog box. This tab section defines how SQL Server will process the initial snapshot that's required to establish a synchronous baseline from which all the transactions will be applied. By default, SQL Server uses a native-format BCP file to copy data across. There's a critical assumption in this default value: Both SQL Servers are using a common code page/sort order combination. If they don't share this, you must manually set synchronization to use a character-format BCP, or perform the synchronization manually. All publications that will have a subscriber that isn't SQL Server 6.5 and are using a common code page/sort order combination must use the character format. This would include ODBC subscribers such as Microsoft Access and Oracle.

The Security tab in the Edit Publications dialog box enables you to adjust your security options down to each publication. This will allow you to deny a server some publications, but still allow that server to subscribe to certain other publications on this server.

If you now click OK in the Edit Publications dialog box, you're doing just fine. You've just created your first publishing/distributing server, and created a publication and article. You're now set to subscribe to this publication and article.

Defining Subscriptions to Publications and Articles

Defining subscriptions can happen on the subscribing server or on the publishing server. If it's defined on the subscribing server, Microsoft calls that a *pull subscription*. If it's defined on the publishing server, Microsoft calls that a *push subscription*. Regardless of the configuration point, the *work source* is still the same. The LOGREAD subsystem still runs on the publishing server; the DISTRIB subsystem still runs on the distributing server.

Defining Pull Subscriptions

A pull subscription in Microsoft terminology is a subscription that's configured from the sub-scribing server. In simpler terms, an administrator uses SQL Enterprise Manager to configure the subscribing server, and in doing so, identifies publications and articles that the subscribing server wishes to consume. To define a subscription using this method, you can use the Manage | Replication | Subscriptions menu options or click the Replication - Manage Subscriptions button in the SQL-EM toolbar. Either option displays the dialog box shown in Figure 36.11.

FIGURE 36.11.

Configuring a pull subscription in SQL Enterprise Manager requires establishing the subscription from the subscribing server.

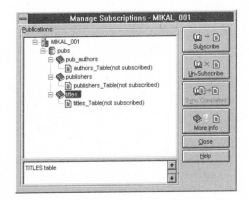

In this dialog box, you can browse the publishing servers to which you have access, as well as the published databases, publications, and articles that are available on those servers. You se-lect the server, database, and publication or article to which you want to subscribe, and then click the Subscribe button. Doing so displays the Subscription Options dialog box shown in Figure 36.12, which enables you to define a number of important subscription properties. Notice that synchronization (the process of making a snapshot copy of the table so that transactions proceed from a common "baseline" of a table image) can be controlled at the individual sub-scription level, and the destination database is assigned from the list of available destination databases that you identified when configuring this server as a subscriber. Only those databases that have check marks in the Enable check box from the Replication - Subscribing dialog box will appear in that list.

FIGURE 36.12.

SQL Enterprise Manager will only allow subscrip-tions to those databases that have the "subscribing" database option enabled.

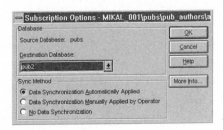

Clicking OK in the Subscription Options dialog box will put a copy of the authors table from the pubs database into the pub2 database. These databases can be on the same or on different servers. You should notice that in the Manage Subscriptions dialog box, the status for the article has changed from "not subscribed" (refer to Figure 36.11) to "subscribed/not sync'ed/ automatic," indicating that automatic synchronization will occur, but hasn't yet occurred.

Defining Push Subscriptions

You can configure a push subscription by using the Manage Article dialog box that you used to define the article (refer to Figure 36.10). By clicking on the Edit button for the article, you display a dialog box that has the all-important Subscribers button in it. In this dialog box, you define which is the subscribing server, and clicking Subscribe enables you to define the destination database for your subscription. After you do this, clicking OK or Close to close out all the dialog boxes runs the stored procedures to configure all of the LOGREAD, DISTRIB, and SYNC tasks necessary to activate the subscription.

This is how you do all the subscriptions to all non SQL Server 6 or later databases. All other subscriptions to all other sources (Microsoft Access, Oracle, etc.), must use the push subscriptions. This makes sense because you need to control the replication from SQL Server. The other program may not have built-in functions to control a pull subscription. But by following the compliance list for ODBC-subscribing data sources (see the earlier section "SQL Server Replication Processing"), the push subscription methods works great.

Defining Subscriptions with the Enterprise Manager Topology Map

By selecting the menu options Server | Replication Configuration | Topology, you can display a graphical representation of the servers on your network, and configure publications and subscriptions using the same dialog boxes that you have used through this process. By right-clicking on a server, you can view the publications and subscriptions of a particular server and perform all the operations that you have already completed to create this new publication.

This map gives you a guide to how replication services are enabled between sets of servers. The current server that you are configuring will always appear in a set of light-gray square brackets; for the example in Figure 36.13, NLCWEST1 is the current server.

What Happens Next?

The answer to this question is easy: You wait. Fortunately, if you configured the SYNC schedule using the defaults, the next five-minute time increment will cause the SYNC process to fire. This creates the native-format BCP file on the local server, and then SYNC calls DISTRIB to copy that file into the destination table. After the SYNC process has completed successfully, the next batch of transactions will cause DISTRIB to be executed, replicating those transactions to the subscribing server and database. You can monitor all of this activity in two different areas of the server. First, you can use the Manage Scheduled Tasks window of SQL-EM to monitor the individual LOGREAD, SYNC, and DISTRIB tasks and make sure that they're running properly. Any error messages they generate will show up here. This window is shown in Figure 36.14.

FIGURE 36.13.

SQL Enterprise Manager enables you to graphically map servers in a replication topology.

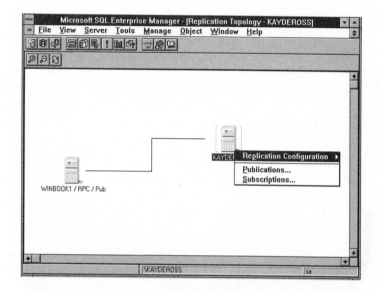

FIGURE 36.14.

SQL Enterprise Manager allows you to schedule tasks (replication is a scheduled task) and follow the tasks through the Manage Scheduled Tasks window.

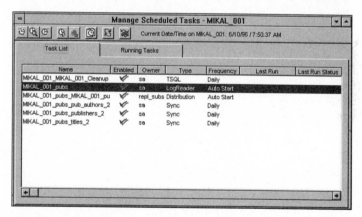

Also, you can use the Manage Subscriptions dialog box on the subscribing server to monitor the status of the subscription itself. Before any subscription has been created, the status will be "not subscribed." After the subscription has been created, but before the SYNC process has run *successfully*, the status will be "subscribed/not sync'ed." Only after the synchronization process has completed will the status change to "subscribed/sync'ed." That's the magic value, because that's the value that DISTRIB needs in order to receive permission to replicate transactions. You'll see DISTRIB's status in the Manage Tasks window, as well. After all this, watch the task history for all the replication-based tasks, to verify their successful completion.

Summary

SQL Server 6.5 replication is clearly a topic that merits its own book. With all the functionality that Microsoft has encased in one small box, from horizontal and vertical partitioning to ODBC-based replication to many other ODBC based systems, SQL Server can now serve as a hub for data distribution through heterogeneous networks. SQL Server 6.5 has one of the most powerful replication tool sets on the market, and it's all yours for just the price of SQL Server. The most important fact to take away from this chapter is that walking through the steps to configure replication is the easy part; knowing how to intelligently configure replication and properly planning an architecture for applications based on distributed data are infinitely more complex. Microsoft has given you the tools to be successful or to hang yourself.

Defining Systems Administration and Naming Standards

37

As the number of applications that you deploy on SQL Server increases, you'll need to develop standards that enable you to administer your servers in a consistent manner. Most companies that successfully implement SQL Server have good standards in place. Standards are created to provide a foundation for administrative tasks, and often result in the establishment of the infrastructure necessary to enable the creation of procedures and scripts to automate activities.

What if you don't have standards in place? The cost of application development without standards is usually very high. The price is paid in effort and delay, as well as credibility. Let's face it: Client/server is really no different from any other application environment. Success comes from the right mix of discipline and creativity. Thoughtful standards provide the discipline within which creativity can thrive.

This chapter focuses on those core standards that are needed to enable you to further develop procedures at your environment. It looks at two core activities:

- Approaches to organizing databases and servers, especially regarding the development environment
- Naming standards, from both a SQL Server and an operating-system level

After you decide on names, directory structure, and how you are going to approach development, you can start building site-specific procedures and scripts to automate activities in your organization.

The SQL Server Environment Approach

You must approach development in a SQL Server environment in a consistent fashion, or each development project is destined to waste time performing certain activities. The approach should focus on providing flexibility for the developer and structure for the database administrator. It also should enable portability of code from the development environment to the potentially many levels of your test environment, and eventually to the production environment.

Understanding Environments

Most people who purchase SQL Server are using it to develop new *production* applications. When developing production software, you should assume there will be a development environment, at least one test environment, and a production environment. You must decide how each environment will be supported by SQL Server.

> **NOTE**
>
> Typical environments include development, system test, volume/stress test, user acceptance test, and production. Because there can be several test environments, this book considers them conceptually as a single environment called *test*.

For each environment, you must determine the following:

- Is the environment supported by a separate (dedicated) SQL Server or does it share the SQL Server with some other function?

- How are the databases organized on the SQL Server? Is there a database per environment rather than a SQL Server per environment?

The most restrictive environment is a single SQL Server with databases for development, test, and production—the needs of one environment conflict with the needs of the others. The development environment might require the SQL Server to be rebooted often, but the production environment is likely to have up-time as an important business requirement. The testing environment often is constructed to be able to gather performance statistics. The activity of the development and production environments, however, might skew these performance statistics, and testing might ruin performance for production. It is *strongly recommended* that development, test, and production activities take place on separate SQL Servers.

The Development Environment

The development environment requires the maximum flexibility for developers while enabling the necessary control structures to provide for consistent promotion of code. In designing this environment, several issues should be considered:

- The SQL Server used for development may or may not be dedicated. A dedicated SQL Server is *strongly preferred* because "bouncing" (shutdown and restart) of the SQL Server is a *very* common activity in development. If the SQL Server is shared by several development groups, frequent reboots of the system may have a significant impact on the productivity of developers.

- The SQL Server may or may not be running on dedicated hardware. Dedicated hardware is preferred, because occasionally the database hardware must be rebooted. Although dedicated hardware provides developers maximum control, it may not be cost-effective. Because this environment is used to unit-test individual modules for *functionality* and not performance, dedicated hardware isn't a requirement.

■ Although flexibility is at a maximum for the developer, so is developer responsibility. A developer has much more responsibility for administrative activities. Developers often create their own objects (tables, indexes, procedures, triggers, and so forth) to satisfy a business problem. Developers often are responsible for managing their own test data. Organized database administration (the DBA group) still has some responsibilities, however. A DBA may create a base set of objects or manage a core set of data. As always, DBAs still get calls about any problems that a developer can't handle (killing processes, adding space, and so forth).

■ Developers must have a set of tables to use when developing. Define how tables will be organized to meet the needs of all developers. (This issue is discussed in detail later in this chapter.)

■ Occasionally, a single logical database is physically implemented as several SQL Server databases in production. The distribution of tables to databases should match the production model. (Remember that relating tables from two different databases requires that at least one of the table names be qualified by the database name. If the development environment doesn't have the same database structure, SQL has to be modified before production implementation, which is likely to introduce new bugs.) Your development environment should look *exactly* like the production environment in the base structure (database, tables, and objects).

If other projects share the development server, create a document to provide information about all groups. It should contain information such as project name, manager, contact name, phone, and specific instructions. Development environments are volatile. You may need to reboot the server to continue development. Because a reboot affects all users on the system, however, you should contact user representatives to prepare them for this situation.

The development environment is the area in which developers first attempt to create new modules of an application. Development is an iterative process. Multiple revisions of code are normally created in the process of satisfying design requirements. Consequently, the code may have unexpected results on tables. During the refinement of a module, database activities such as delete, insert, or update may need several modifications before they're deemed to work correctly. This problem requires the developer to create test conditions to test individual pieces of functionality. Additionally, new requirements may necessitate the addition or deletion of columns from tables to test the new pieces of code. These changes may become permanent modifications to the existing structures, validated by the iterative testing of an application. The development environment needs to be structured to minimize contention between developers.

Due to the nature of development, it's assumed that the development environment will use a SQL Server separate from the test and production environments. Based on that assumption, you can then determine an approach to development at a database and object level.

The development approach is greatly impacted by the number of *actual* SQL Server databases used to represent the single logical database. An initial approach is to put all tables in a single database. If you intend to use the declarative referential integrity features of SQL Server comprehensively, you'll need to leave all your tables in one database. However, under some circumstances, grouping tables into several different databases can have some measurable performance and administrative benefits. As noted earlier, if the production environment is organized using several databases, the development environment should also contain several databases.

There are three main approaches to development in a SQL Server environment:

- Shared database/shared objects and data
- Individual database/individual objects and data
- Shared database/individual objects and data

The differences between the approaches are based on whether the developers share a database and whether they have their own copies of objects and data. The following sections look at these three approaches.

Shared Database/Shared Objects and Data

In the shared database/shared objects and data approach, a single database (or databases) exists for development. All developers use the same objects and data. This approach is sometimes used in small development environments (two or three SQL developers). As the number of developers increases, this approach requires good team management and communication or it will quickly break down.

Advantages:

- One definition of every object means no need for merging different definitions (as in other approaches), a slow and error-prone process.
- This approach simplifies administration. There are fewer objects (tables, indexes, stored procedures, triggers, and so forth) to manage.
- There are reduced storage requirements. There is only one database and one copy of objects and data.

Disadvantages:

- If the database is small, there can be contention for data. James might be testing a delete activity on the same row that Maria is using to test an update activity. Development will be impeded as confusion results from "unexpected" changes to data.

  The best way to avoid this problem is good team communication. If James is known to be working on a set of tables, Maria should either be assigned to work on a different set of tables or should be working closely with James. Similarly, if the tables are grouped into multiple databases, James could be assigned to one database while Maria is assigned to another.

■ In a similar way, there can be contention on the structure of the tables. If James wants to change the schema (drop a column, add a constraint, etc.) to support a hypothesis or test condition, he could affect Maria's work. Because database architectural design is rarely done on-the-fly in professional environments, this risk is fairly minimal. Once again, good communication is the key.

Individual Database/Individual Objects and Data

With the individual database/individual objects and data approach, each developer has a dedicated database for development. Because objects are created in the context of a database, the developer therefore has a personal copy of all objects and data. Normally, developers are responsible for all activities with their databases, including data creation and backups.

Advantages:

■ The developer can change data or structures without affecting other developers.

■ Because object names are created in the context of a single database, all the SQL code can be written to assume the database name, and contains only object names without full database qualification.

Disadvantages:

■ If tables are grouped into several databases, using this development approach is likely to require code changes to promote code to production. In a single database approach, code is consistent from development to production because there's never a need to qualify the name of a table with the database name. In a multiple-database scenario, if a query is executed that refers to tables in different databases, at least one of the tables has to be qualified with the database name. (There's one exception to this rule: when every developer has his or her own SQL Server—a rare situation indeed!)

Consider an example with five developers. The first developer writes code against `customerdb_1` and `purchasedb_1`, the second developer writes code against `customerdb_2` and `purchasedb_2`, and so on. The following is an example of SQL access across databases:

```
select *
from customerdb_1..customer c, purchasedb_1..purchase p
where c.cust_id = p.cust_id
```

Migrating this code into the test or production environments requires changes because these environments likely would contain different database names (`customerdb`, `purchasedb`). You have to modify the code to arrive at the following statement:

```
select *
from customerdb..customer c, purchasedb..purchase p
where c.cust_id = p.cust_id
```

Changing code from one environment to the next isn't recommended. Don't use the private database approach for multiple-database implementations.

■ The amount of space required to support development increases. Each database requires the space necessary to hold a copy of all objects, procedures, and data. In addition, the minimum size of any SQL Server database is the larger of the default database size (normally configured for 2MB) or the size of the model database.

■ On a periodic basis, structural changes made by each developer on his or her own database must merged into a single design, and that design has to be propagated back to everyone's system. This is a time-consuming process that has the risk of bringing the entire team to a standstill for a period of time.

■ During the merge process, it may be discovered that a change made by James in his copy means that Maria has to make extensive changes in her work that James didn't consider. Being proactive about structural changes is the only way to prevent major complications in a team environment.

■ The number of databases in the server increases. This fact complicates administrative tasks. It also can affect the recovery process, because SQL Server recovers databases sequentially in database ID order.

NOTE

I was teaching a class once when the SQL Server crashed and had to be recovered from a backup. Our training databases had database IDs of 70 to 80. It took about an hour for our training environment to become usable.

Shared Database/Individual Objects and Data

In the shared database/individual objects and data approach, a single database (or databases) is used for development. Developers don't share objects or data. Each developer is a true user of the database. Objects are created *and owned* by the developer. The production objects are created by the user dbo. Code written by the developer doesn't refer to user name. The normal SQL Server procedure of looking for an object owned by you before looking for an object owned by dbo is leveraged. The SQL that's written acts against the developer's tables when executed in the development environment, and against the dbo's tables when executed in the test and production environments.

Advantages:

- Each developer has an individual set of data. A developer has complete freedom to update, delete, and insert data without affecting other developers.

- Migration from development environment to the production environment is eased. All developers work with the same database and object names. This setup ensures that any SQL created is identical in all environments. No code changes due to different database or object names is necessary.

- Systems spanning multiple databases don't require modifications to promote to production (unlike the private-database development approach) because the development environment database structure is identical to the production database structure.

Disadvantages:

- The same merging process and structural conflict issues exist in this approach as in the preceding approach, leading to increased requirements on team management and a risk of stalling the development process.

- The number of tables in a single database can be large. A system with 100 tables and 10 developers will have 1,000 tables in the development database.

- Storage requirements are magnified by the number of developers as compared to the shared object approach.

NOTE

Each table and index requires 16KB (one extent) regardless of the amount of data in the table. Therefore, the storage requirements between a private database and a shared database/individual object approach should be equal.

In a private-database approach, however, each developer database has its own free space. On average, the total amount of free space required in the private-database approach is much greater than the shared free space in the shared database/individual object approach.

Recommendations

For small teams or well-organized larger teams, a shared database/shared object approach is the most efficient approach to use. For large or loosely organized teams, especially when using a multiple-database approach, a shared database/individual objects and data approach to development can be beneficial.

> **WARNING**
>
> Your production requirements may not surface until after development has started. The individual database/individual objects approach doesn't work with a multiple-database installation. If the decision to implement with multiple databases occurs after development starts, the shared database/individual objects and data approach is able to readily adapt to the new structure. You may be forced to change your development environment structure completely if you choose the individual database approach. Choose your approach carefully.

The Test Environment

There can be several test environments used in the *software development life cycle* (SDLC). You'll test for function or performance. *Functional testing* is used to confirm that elements of an application or several distinct applications can work together. *Performance testing* is conducted to verify how the database performs under peak numbers of users, data size, or both.

The Functional Testing Environment

Most functional testing can be handled by a single SQL Server. Consider the following issues when planning this environment:

■ A SQL Server used only for testing is *strongly preferred* because SQL Server should be configured for testing, and the configuration for your application may differ from the configuration needed for the testing of some other application.

■ The hardware in which the SQL Server is running may or may not be dedicated. Dedicated hardware is useful in analysis because performance statistics gathered at the hardware level can be related easily to SQL Server, but you're testing functionality and usability across modules here, not performance.

■ Objects are created by database administration. Often the files necessary to build the database structures (DDL scripts) are part of a source-code control system.

■ There's only one copy of each object necessary to support the system. (A development environment may have several copies of each table.)

■ If the tables in the system are physically organized into several databases for performance, recovery, or security reasons, there's only one copy of each database.

■ All objects should be owned by the database owner, dbo. This plan supports the seamless migration of code from the development to the testing environments.

- A core set of data is created that's representative of production data. The amount of data doesn't need to represent production volumes, because it will be used to support feature, integration, and system testing.

- Logins and users of the test system should be representative of production users. This enforces the testing of the system in the same manner as it would be used by the actual production users. By simulating real users, potential problems such as improper permissions can be identified.

Development logins may be added to enable developers to add specific system test data or to assist in the creation of a core set of data. However, developers *should not* have the capability to change the structure of tables or add, drop, or modify any other existing object. Although developers may have access to tables to add or modify data, testing should be conducted using the logins of users representative of production users.

The Performance Testing Environment

Performance testing (or stress testing) should be handled by a SQL Server other than the SQL Server used for your functional testing environment. This environment will have similar features to the functional test environment, except for the following recommendations for servers, hardware, and data:

- The SQL Server used for testing must be configured as it would be in production. Using an identically configured SQL Server is *necessary* because performance data captured is used to estimate production performance.

- The hardware on which SQL Server is running should be configured identically to the production hardware, so that statistics gathered can be considered representative of production performance. This environment is used to validate the system's capacity to handle production loads.

- A core set of data, *representative of production volumes and content*, is created and loaded. The data in this environment is used to test the performance of the system under varying loads. To capture performance and load statistics that are representative of production, production-type data must be used.

- Development logins are normally *not* added to the performance testing server. Logins should be representative of production, and all modifications (data or structure) should be conducted by database administration.

The Production Environment

The production environment is the last and most important environment in the SDLC. The production environment is under maximum control of database administration, and all defined production controls must be implemented and observed. This environment should have the following features:

- The SQL Server and database hardware used for production should be dedicated. A dedicated SQL Server is *preferred* because it greatly simplifies analysis of performance statistics captured at the SQL Server or hardware level. Most production implementations use dedicated hardware for the production SQL Server.

- An initial load of data may be required. Database administration normally is responsible for loading the core supporting data (code tables) as well as any other production data needed to support production use of the application.

- Logins and users are the actual production users. The only other logins added to this server should be for administration reasons. All modifications (data or structure) are conducted by database administration. Security standards and procedures are in place and enforced.

Naming Standards

What's in a name? The answer to this simple question often takes organizations months—or years—to define. Names should be chosen in a consistent manner across all SQL Server systems in your organization; for example, a word shouldn't be abbreviated two different ways in two different places. Consistency with names is one of the building blocks of an infrastructure to which employees and users can become accustomed. Consistent naming enables employees to move from system to system (or software to software) and have basic expectations regarding names. This can help in the transition when learning a new environment.

> **NOTE**
>
> Naming standards are like filing standards. You have to think about the person who's storing the information and the person who will retrieve it. For the person defining the name, the choice should be automatic. For the person retrieving or accessing an object, the name should completely define its content without ambiguity.

Naming standards can be broken into two areas: SQL Server names and operating system names. SQL Server names are the names that you specify in the SQL Server environment (databases, objects, and so forth). Operating system names are the names that you specify for files and directories.

> **NOTE**
>
> A naming convention often debated within many shops is whether to use the under-score (_) character between descriptive words and/or indicators (for example, `sales_detail`) or mixed case (for example, `SalesDetail`). Some programmers prefer using underscores, because that method is considered more readable. Others tend to prefer the latter method because it reduces the need to abbreviate object names. It also saves them from having to search for the underscore key on their keyboards.
>
> The method that you choose to use is entirely up to your or your organization's preference. Throughout the remainder of this chapter, I'll attempt to alternate between both camps in the examples provided to avoid alienating anyone in this ongoing battle, and provide the opportunity for you to see both methods and decide for yourself which you prefer.

Using Indicators

An *indicator* is a string of characters embedded in a name to indicate something about the type of object. In SQL Server, these characters are often used to indicate an object type. For example, `CurrDate_Def` could be used as a name for a default setting a column to the current date and time. There are two schools of thought on the use of indicators:

- An indicator is needed because it simplifies reporting—a DBA can tell the type of object from just a listing of object names. Application designers are cognizant of what type of objects they're accessing (for example, the name tells them whether they're selecting from a table or view). Indicators also enable you to use similar, meaningful names for two objects, once with each indicator (for example, `price_rule` and `price_default`).

- An indicator isn't needed because it can be retrieved from the system tables (the `type` column in the `sysobjects` table) or is indicated by the table from which you're selecting (`sysdatabases`, `sysservers`). Including it in the name is redundant and a waste of valuable characters. Names are limited by SQL Server to 30 characters in length, and naming conventions may often limit them further to be compatible with existing guidelines or other systems (for example, object names within a DB2 environ-ment are limited to 18 characters). An indicator can easily take 4 or 5 characters (`_tbl` or `_view`, for example). This setup limits the number of available characters in an object name. Indicators can propagate (`Customer_Tbl_CIdx`), further reducing the number of available characters. When users need to use a name frequently, indicators also mean extra typing.

> **NOTE**
>
> All object names within a database must be unique for the owner. In other words, the `dbo` may own only one object of any name. If you have a rule named `price_check`, you can't create a constraint named `price_check`. This restriction applies to tables and views as well as rules, defaults, constraints, procedures, and triggers. To avoid being constrained by these names, use indicators, especially for objects with which users don't interact, and whose names they'll never type (rules, defaults, constraints, and triggers).
>
> Entries in `sysindexes` and `syscolumns` must be unique by table (only one index per table named `name_index`, only one column per table named `price`).
>
> User-defined types aren't objects; they're stored in `systypes` instead. Names of types won't clash with objects, but it makes sense to qualify them by type.

If you decide to put an indicator in a name, it's best to make that indicator as short as possible. For object names based on an underlying table (constraints, triggers, indexes), the length of the indicator has an effect on the number of available characters used for the table name. For example, if you decide that insert triggers will be identified by adding the indicator `_InsertTrigger` after the table name, the number of available characters that can be used for the table name can be no greater than 16 (30 characters minus 14 for the indicator). To give as much flexibility to the naming of an object, consider using an abbreviated indicator (such as `_tri`).

Indicators sometimes are placed at the beginning of the name. When this is done, there is rarely an underscore between the indicator and the object name. The insert trigger for the `Customers` table might be `tiCustomer`. The advantage of this method is that a list of all object names groups the objects by type (all tables together, followed by all triggers, etc.). Alternatively, you can do the same thing in SQL:

```
select name, type
   from sysobjects
   order by type
```

Table 37.1 lists the most common indicators used by SQL Server installations throughout the world. Consider that many sites choose no indicators at all. Each of these indicators can be used either before the object name or after the name (separated by an underscore).

Table 37.1. Common SQL Server indicators.

Item	Possible Indicators	Preferred
Server	Server, SERV, serv, SRV	None

continues

Table 37.1. continued

Item	Possible Indicators	Preferred
Database	Database, DATABASE, DB	DB
Table	Table, TABLE, T, TBL, tbl, t	None
Column	col	None
Index	Clustered: ClusIdx, Cidx, clus, C, CI	
	Nonclustered: Idx[#], NCIdx[#], NCI[#], I[#]	CI, Idx[#]
View	V, View, VIEW	None
Rule	Rul, rul, RUL, rule, RULE, R	Rul
Default	Def, def, DEF, default, DEFAULT, D	Def
User-defined datatype	TYPE, Type, TYP, Typ, udt	TYPE
Stored procedure	Proc, PROC, Pr, PR	proc
Trigger	InsertTrigger, InsTrig, ITrg, ITrg, T[iud]	ITrg
Check constraint	Check, constraint, con, CkCon, Chk	Check
Primary key constraint	PK, Pk	PK
Unique constraint	UniqueCons, Unique, Uniq, UN, UQ	Uniq
Foreign key constraint	FK, RI	FK
Data device	DISK[#], Disk[#], DATA[#], Data[#], LOG[#], Log[#], IDX[#], Idx[#]	Data[#], Log[#], Idx[#]

Item	Possible Indicators	Preferred
Publication	PUB, pub, Pub	Pub
Article	ART, art, Art	Art
Subscription table	SUB, sub, Sub	Sub
Replication procedure	RP, rp, PFR, pfr	RP
Dump device	TAPE[#], Dump, Tran, Log, Tape[#], Disk, DUMP, TRAN, LOG, DISK	Dump, Tran, TAPE[#]
Scheduled task	STSK, ST, stsk, st	None
Alert task	ATSK, AT, atsk, at	None

Choosing an Overall Approach

One naming approach is outlined in Table 37.2. You can use these standards at your site or develop your own. *Make sure that you produce a matrix such as this to distribute to application-development projects.*

Table 37.2. Sample SQL Server name standards.

Item	Capitalization	Include Type Name?	Example
Server	ALL CAPS	No	CUST_DEVEL
Database	Mixed case	Yes	CustomerDB
Table	Mixed case	No	CustomerPurchase
Column	Mixed case	No	Age, Name, Address, FaxNumber, HomeNumber
Index	Mixed case	Yes	"TableName[C]Idx[#]": CustomerIdx3 (third nonclustered) CustomerCIdx (clustered)
View	Mixed case	No	CaliforniaCustomer, PartialCustomer
Rule	Mixed case	Yes	ValidSSN_Rul, NonNegative_Rul

continues

Table 37.2. continued

Item	Capitalization	Include Type Name?	Example
Default	Mixed case	Yes	`Zero_Def, CurrDate_Def, CurrUser_Def`

User-defined datatypes	ALL CAPS	Yes	`SSN_TYPE, ADDRESS_TYPE,`
			`NAME_TYPE, PHONE_TYPE,`
			`COMMENT_TYPE, STATE_TYPE, ZIP_TYPE`

Stored procedure	Mixed case	Yes	`Update_Customer Proc, CheckInventory Proc`
Triggers	Mixed case	Yes	`Customer_ITrg, Customer_DTrg,` `Customer_UTrg`
Constraints	Mixed case	Yes	`NonNegative_Check` (check), `Customer_Uniq` (uniqueness) `Customer_PK` (primary key) `CustomerPurchase_RI` (RI)
Publication	Mixed case	Yes	`Pubs2_PUB, Sales_pub`
Article	Mixed case	Yes	`authors_art, sales_art1`
Subscription	Mixed case	Yes	`authors_sub, sales_sub1`

Data devices	Mixed case	Yes	`Customer_DATA1, Customer_LOG1,`
			`Customer_Data1, Customer_Log1,`
			`DISK1, DATADISK1, LOGDISK1`

Dump devices	Mixed case	Yes	`Customer_Dump, CustomerDB_Tran, TAPE1`
Scheduled task	Mixed case	Yes	`DumpAllTxSTSK, UpdAllStats_stsk`
Alert task	Mixed case	Yes	`DumpTxNL_ATSK, AddMoreDBSpace_at`

The standards outlined in this table are used throughout this chapter.

NOTE

It's probably not a good idea to use indicators in the names of tables or views. Many sites use the table name in the name of other objects. The inclusion of _tbl increases the number of redundant characters in the dependent object name (trigger, index, and so forth). In addition, views exist to give users the feeling that their queries are acting against a real table, although they actually are accessing a view. Therefore, the names should be identical in format, and shouldn't contain anything that would distinguish one from the other (_tbl or _view, for example).

Your standards likely will be different, but the important thing is to be consistent in your implementation of names. Knowing the standards up front can save you days or weeks of costly name conversion changes (with SQL code, administration activities, and so forth).

WARNING

If you haven't already read Chapter 24, "SQL Server Installation and Connectivity," do so now. It contains important information on object names and potential ANSI keyword violations.

In previous versions of SQL Server, Microsoft allowed you to use keywords such as primary, reference, user, and key as object identifiers. Because these are now keywords (starting in SQL Server 6.0), they can no longer be used.

In a truth-is-stranger-than-fiction addition to this note, Microsoft itself found this out the hard way. Microsoft's network management application, Systems Management Server, uses an underlying SQL Server as its data storage facility. The SMS team created all the primary key fields with the name of key to make accessing them simpler. Unfortunately, key is now a keyword, meaning that Version 1.0 of SMS doesn't run on SQL Server 6.0 or higher—it runs only on SQL Server 4.2. Microsoft had to endure a costly migration renaming these offending columns, and ship SMS Version 1.1 for use with SQL Server 6. You can avoid such costly mistakes for your applications by reading Chapter 4, "Introduction to Transact-SQL," and avoiding anything resembling an ANSI keyword in naming your objects.

SQL Server Names

In SQL Server, you're responsible for naming the server, each user database, each object in the database (tables and columns, indexes, views), and any integrity constraints (rules, defaults, user datatypes, triggers, declarative constraints). Device names (disk devices and dump devices) have different parameters governing their names because they can be somewhat operating-system-related.

Capitalization standards must be defined for each type of name. (Should names be in all capital letters, all lowercase letters, or mixed case?) This decision can be different for different groups of names (for example, server names could be in all capital letters and object names could be in mixed case).

Consider also whether to use an indicator of the item being named. For example, does the word database or the abbreviation DB get included in a database name? In the end, your standard should identify whether the customer database will be named Customer, CUSTOMER, CustomerDB, or CUSTOMERDB. For most database objects, the structure of names is the personal preference of the person writing the standard.

Naming Servers

Give servers functional names. For example, you probably would much rather have a server named DEVELOPMENT than a server named RSR8_AB100. Several companies name their servers according to cartoons or movies. There are Snow White servers (DOPEY, GRUMPY, DOC, and so forth), Batman servers (BATMAN, ROBIN, JOKER, PENGUIN), and Mickey Mouse servers (MICKEY, MINNIE, GOOFY, DONALD). Although these names are fun, they should be used only for development or general server names, because they don't convey any information as to the purpose of the server. Servers intended to support applications should be named in a consistent manner across *all* applications. The following is a good format:

systemname_environmentname

For the development of a Customer system, you might use CUST_DEVEL, CUST_TEST, and CUST_PROD servers.

> **NOTE**
>
> By default, Microsoft SQL Server for Windows NT takes its name from the NT Server name. This can be changed, but you'd have to edit Registry entries to change it, and it really isn't worth the trouble. Therefore, if an NT Server machine is going to be a

dedicated SQL Server system, name the NT Server as you would want the SQL Server named.

Naming Databases

Databases should be named according to their contents—for example, the type of data (customer or product) or activity (security or administration). A database containing security tables could be named SecurityDB, and a database that contains customer data could be called CustomerDB. The name selected should be intuitive. (If a document is required to relate a database's name to its contents, it probably isn't intuitive.) Some databases are named using a letter followed by three numbers. Would you rather have a database named B123 or ProductDB? *Avoid nondescriptive database names.*

Naming Tables, Views, and Columns

Table and view names should be representative of the underlying data. A customer table should be called Customer; a view of the California customers should be called CaliforniaCustomer. Some organizations like to use nondescriptive table names (TBL0001). *Again, avoid nondescriptive table and view names.* If names aren't intuitive, a decode document may be required to relate the table name to its contents. This setup delays development and makes it harder to write SQL statements.

Column names should indicate the data in the column. Name a column containing the age of a customer Age or CustomerAge.

One useful convention for naming columns is to use words in order from the most general to the most specific. Instead of naming two columns LastName and FirstName, you would name them NameLast and NameFirst. In this way, it's more clearly visible that the data in the columns is related.

Naming Indexes

A table can have one clustered index and up to 249 nonclustered indexes. Index names should contain the table name and an indicator of the type of index. Some DBAs like to include the column as part of the index name, but compound indexes make this naming scheme difficult to implement. The following table shows examples of possible index names for the Customer table.

Index Type	Identifier	Index Name
Clustered (maximum of 1)	_CIdx	Customer_CIdx
Nonclustered (up to 249)	_Idx[#]	Customer_Idx1, Customer_Idx2

TIP

Some application-development tools enable you to perform database administration activities. These tools may already have standard ways to construct names of indexes. Check whether you can modify the format or must change your standards to accommodate this new format.

Naming Rules and Defaults

Rules and defaults are implemented at the database level and can be used across tables. Their names should be based on the function that they provide. A rule that checks for a valid age range could be called ValidAge_Rul, a default placing the current date in a field could be CurrDate_Def.

Naming User-Defined Datatypes

Here's a good format for user-defined types:

CONTENTS_TYPE

Because user-defined datatypes normally are targeted at certain types of columns, the name should contain the type of column for which it is to be used (SSN, PRICE, ADDRESS) followed by the indicator _TYPE.

Naming Stored Procedures

The name of a stored procedure should be meaningful and descriptive enough to indicate what actions are performed by the SQL statements within the stored procedure. For example, a stored procedure that inserts new entries into the Customer table might be called Insert_Customer_Proc.

SQL Server also allows the definition of customized system stored procedures. These procedures must be created in the master database and begin with sp_. Names of user-defined stored procedures should identify the procedures as user-defined procedures and avoid confusion with present or future Microsoft-supplied system stored procedures. It's recommended that an additional prefix be added to the procedure name after the `sp_` to distinguish it from standard system stored procedures. Often, this prefix is an abbreviation of the company name. For example, a custom system stored procedure to display device usage by a database for the XYZ Company could be named `sp_XYZ_disk_usage`. The XYZ indicator identifies this system procedure as one created by the XYZ Company, and prevents it from conflicting with Microsoft-supplied stored procedures.

Naming Triggers

Trigger names should consist of the table name and an indicator of the trigger action (insert, update, delete). A good format is `TableName_[IUD]Trg`. The following table shows some examples.

Object Type	Object Name
Table name	`Customer`
Insert trigger	`Customer_ITrg`
Delete trigger	`Customer_DTrg`
Update trigger	`Customer_UTrg`
Update and delete trigger	`Customer_UDTrg`

NOTE

The indicator consists of seven characters maximum (`_IUDTrg`, for example). To avoid abbreviation problems, no table name should be greater than 23 characters (30 – 7).

Naming Constraints

Constraint names vary based on the scope of the constraint. Constraints can be used to check for valid values, add unique or primary keys, and establish relationships between tables (foreign keys).

A check constraint checks for valid values in a column or number of columns. Its name should indicate the column(s) and type of check.

Unique and primary key constraints are based on a table and should contain the table name and an indicator (`_PK` or `_Uniq`).

A foreign key constraint implements referential integrity between two tables. Its name should contain the tables or columns involved in the relationship and an indicator (`_FK` or `_RI`). Table 37.3 shows a sample list of constraint indicators and names for the `Customer` table.

Table 37.3. Sample constraint indicators and names.

Constraint Type	Indicator	Name Based on	Constraint Name
Check constraint	_Check	Column or columns	ValidAge_Check
Primary key constraint	_PK	Table	Customer_PK
Unique key constraint	_Uniq	Table	Customer_Uniq
Foreign key constraint	_FK	Related tables and/or columns	CustomerPurchase_FK

WARNING

Remember that constraints are objects. For an owner, their names must be unique among all objects within the database. You may want to qualify the constraint name by including the table name as well. (In Table 37.3, different tables might contain columns named ValidAge, and their check constraint names would clash.)

If you decide to include table names in your constraint names, you face a serious limitation in the length of table and column names. For example, if you have a table called Institution and a check constraint on the column Date_of_Enrollment, the constraint might be named with the following:

```
Institution_Date_of_Enrollment_Check
```

which is much longer than the name length limit. The only realistic solution is to abbreviate the name, but that requires having both the person creating the constraint and the person retrieving information about it know the abbreviation rules. You might want to implement standards for abbreviations as described later in this chapter.

Table-level constraints can evaluate many columns. Include in your naming standard the method of naming table-level constraints. For example, the constraint requiring an invoice amount to be greater than zero whenever the type is "SALE" might look like this:

```
constraint Invoice_AmtType_Check
   check ((amt > 0) or (type <> "SALE"))
```

Keep table and column names fairly short, yet descriptive, especially if you plan to use table names in check constraints.

Database Device Naming Standards

A *database device* is physical space that is initialized with the `disk init` command. After a device is initialized, it's available for use by any database (except for `master` and `model`). Selecting the logical name for a device depends on what may exist on that device and on a DBA's confidence factor of the eventual use of that device. Devices can be named generically, by database, or by database contents.

Using a Generic Name

Devices can be named generically according to their number or general contents. For example, you can name a device according to number (`DEVICE1`). This approach is flexible because any part of any database can be placed on the device without confusion. Tracking the databases created on a certain device can't be easily inferred, however. It often is useful in performance analysis if the device can be easily mapped to a database, type of data, or type of activity for a database.

Devices can be generically named to represent the *type* of data that will exist on that device (`DATA1`, `LOG1`, `INDEX1`). This provides a DBA with a guideline as to what portion of a database to place on each device. Indicating in the name the type of data expected on the device can cause confusion, however, if space constraints force you to create the data portion of a database on a device named `LOG1`.

> **NOTE**
>
> After you begin placing database log segments on a device, SQL Server prevents you from mistakenly placing database data segments on that same device. Go ahead and call a device "log-something" if you're planning to put a log on it immediately.

Using the Expected Database Name

Devices can be named to represent the database that will be using the device. The device name can consist of the database name and a device number. For example, the four devices for the `Customer` database might be named `CustomerDB_dev1`, `CustomerDB_dev2`, `CustomerDB_dev3`, and `CustomerDB_dev4`. The name indicates the database intended to be created on the device, but doesn't indicate the type of data. Therefore, log, data, and index data can be created on a device without confusion based on the device name. Indicating the database expected on the device in the name can cause confusion, however, if space constraints force you to create a different database on that device.

Using the Expected Database Contents

Devices can be named to represent the database and the expected contents to be created on that device. The device name can consist of the database name and the type of contents (data, log, index). For example, the four devices for the customer database could be named CustomerDB_Data1, CustomerDB_Data2, CustomerDB_Log1, and CustomerDB_Idx1. The name indicates the database and the type of data expected to exist on the device. This naming scheme requires you to be *very* confident about the placement of databases.

> **NOTE**
>
> Experience has shown that early estimates of index, log, and data requirements are usually way off.

Recommendations

Name devices in the most appropriate manner for your environment, based on the number of databases, whether certain data is placed on separate devices (log, index, data, and so forth), and your confidence that the intended use of the device won't change. (It's probably best if a device named CustDB_Data1 not be used for expansion of the ProductDB database.) Very large database (VLDB) environments are more likely to use the database-contents approach to naming, because databases normally span multiple disks and there's more flexibility for placement.

Dump Device Naming Standards

Chapter 30, "SQL Server Database Backup and Restoration," explains that a dump device is created within the Enterprise Manager or by using the sp_adddumpdevice stored procedure. A dump device is used to back up an entire database or transaction log of a database to some type of media. Normally, this media is a local disk or a local tape device. You're required to provide the logical name and physical name of each dump device. This logical name is linked to the physical name. When dumping a database or transaction log, you can dump the database to the logical name (although the physical name can be supplied). The following are examples of three dump commands for the CustomerDB database:

```
dump database CustomerDB to CustomerDB_Dump
```

```
dump transaction CustomerDB to CustomerDB_Tran
```

```
dump database Customer DB to TAPE1
```

The logical name given to a dump device is normally based on the device type—tape or disk.

Tape Devices

A tape device is usually attached or integrated with your database server hardware. These devices normally take 8mm or 4mm tapes, and the tape capacity can be as great as 8GB. Tape devices have simple names. The string TAPE followed by a number is a common approach to a generic tape device name. For example, if you have three tape devices, they could be named TAPE1, TAPE2, and TAPE3.

Disk Devices

Disk device names should be selected with care. Dumping a database or log to disk creates a file on your file system. Each time a dump is executed to a disk device, a file is created, whether or not a file exists. If you haven't moved the previous dump to a new file name, the file will be overwritten and *lost*. Databases or logs dumped to disk should be copied off to a tape. Disk devices often are used in a development situation, because of the frequency of dumps and the inconvenience of tapes.

It's wise to create two disk dump devices for each database in your system—one for database dumps and one for transaction log dumps. Use the following format for the logical name:

```
DatabaseName_Dump
DatabaseName_Tran
```

The CustomerDB database would have two dump devices created: CustomerDB_Dump and CustomerDB_Tran. Here's an example of the possible commands used to create these devices:

```
/* create a disk dump device for database dumping
** of the CustomerDB database*/
sp_addumpdevice "disk", CustomerDB_Dump,
    "c:\dbdump\CustomerDB\Cust_DB.dmp"
/* create a disk dump device for transaction log dumping
** of the customer database*/
sp_addumpdevice "disk", CustomerDB_Tran,
    "c:\dbdump\CustomerDB\Cust_DB.trn"
```

This approach has a number of benefits. Each database will have separate names for each type of dump. This strategy eliminates the possibility of accidentally dumping the CustomerDB dump over the ProductDB dump. Additionally, a consistent naming standard enables you to automate the backup process more easily. Using uniquely named individual dump files for each database prevents a subsequent database dump from overwriting a dump file for another database, should the SQL Executive Task Scheduler fail to move or rename the file for some reason.

> **NOTE**
>
> Don't name your directories with spaces in the directory names. While SQL Server has no problems using a directory name with spaces in it, some of the dialog boxes in SQL Enterprise Manager don't allow you to enter a space when typing a name or path.

Operating System Names

You need to establish a naming standard for operating system files and directories. This standard normally is needed to organize DDL files. You need a DDL file for *every* important action and object that exists in SQL Server. This includes device creation, configuration changes (sp_configure), adding users and logins, creating and altering databases, creating objects (tables, views, indexes, and so forth), and granting permissions. Place the files in directories organized to enable you to re-create an entire environment from scratch.

When creating directory and file names, you may have to abbreviate the names of databases or database objects in order to meet file naming restrictions. To name your objects consistently and provide for understandable directory/file names, you need to establish some standards for abbreviating names into file names. (See the later section on establishing abbreviation standards.)

WARNING

While Windows NT has full support for Long File Names, not every hardware device (like tape backup drives) can save and restore those names correctly. This can be a problem for SQL Server. For example, suppose that you create a dump device called Datastorage.DAT, the operating system will give it two names: the long name (as you typed it) and the short (8.3) name (DATAST~1.DAT). Some tape drives will save and restore only the short name.

Unfortunately, if you restore your backup file with only the short name, SQL Server won't be able to find it to restore your data unless you manually rename it to the long name. Therefore, before using long file names in SQL Server, make sure that none of your backup and restore procedures will cause you to lose the long file names. If in doubt, use the short names. Short names are assumed throughout this chapter.

Directory Naming Standards

Specifying and organizing directory names should be based on your environment. Here are some important questions to answer:

- How many environments are you supporting (CUSTOMER_DEVEL, CUSTOMER_SYSTEST, CUSTOMER_PERF)?
- How many user databases exist in each server?
- Is there only one database or are multiple databases supported by the server?
- What's the approach to handling Data Definition Language script files (scripts that create the database, tables, indexes, etc., for setup, backup, and documentation purposes)?

- Are all the creation statements in a single file or is there one file per object?
- Are index-creation statements located in the same file as table-creation statements?
- How do you intend to grant permissions?

Assume the greatest complexity and level of detail—a directory structure that can handle multiple SQL Servers and individual creation files for each object.

Base Directory: Server Name

All DDLs for a server/environment should be stored relative to a base directory named according to the server name. For example, if you have three SQL Servers named CUSTOMER_DEVEL, CUSTOMER_TEST, and CUSTOMER_PROD, the base directories would be \CUST_DEV, \CUST_TEST, and \CUST_PROD, respectively.

The base directory should contain every DDL needed to re-create the entire SQL Server. Separating files from different SQL Server environments by directory enables different environments to contain different versions of the same file. This is helpful in regression testing.

First Subdirectory: Database Name

Under the base directory for the server are subdirectories for each of the databases supported by the server. This includes all user databases *and* the system databases (master, model).

User Databases

User databases are created to support applications. The name of the subdirectory should be identical to the database name. For the CustomerDB database in the CUST_DEV server, the directory name is \CUST_DEV\Cust_DB.

For each user database in the server, a number of subdirectories can be created to hold the various DDL files. Table 37.4 lists possible subdirectories under the user database subdirectory.

Table 37.4. Sample subdirectory names.

Object or Activity	Subdirectory Name
Table	..\tbl
Index	..\idx
View	..\view
Rule	..\rul
Default	..\def

continues

Table 37.4. continued

Object or Activity	Subdirectory Name
User-defined datatypes	..\type
Triggers	..\trg
Constraints	..\con
Permissions	..\grant
Stored procedures	..\proc
Remote procedures	..\rproc
Users	..\user
User-defined error messages	..\error

Thus, the directory containing the table-creation statements for the CustomerDB database in the CUST_DEVEL server is the following:

\CUST_DEV\Cust_DB\tbl

The number of subdirectories under the database subdirectory is based on the level of granularity of your DDL files. Some sites like to put all creation statements in a single file. This gives you the least amount of control. To change the creation statement for a particular index, you might have to edit a 70,000-line file. The portion of the file for the index creation is copied into some temporary file or directly into an ISQL session for execution.

The next level of granularity is to put all creation statements of a particular type into a file—all the table-creates in one file, the index-creates in another. You still have the same problems with modification and execution, but you have a greater level of control (object type).

The preferred approach is to have a separate operating-system file for each object in your system. This provides you with the maximum amount of control. Sites that use this approach normally save DDL files in a source-code control system.

master **Database**

The master database subdirectory should contain all files necessary to re-create the base server and all user database structures. After the execution of the scripts in this subdirectory, the server is configured, disk devices are initialized, dump devices are added, logins and users are added, and all user databases are created.

You can use the subdirectories shown in the following table for the master database.

Object or Activity	Subdirectory Name	Extension
Device creation (disk and dump)	`..\device`	`.dsk, .dmp`
Database creation, altering, and setting of options	`..\dbcreate`	`.cre, .alt, .opt`
Addition of logins and users	`..\user`	`.lgn, .usr`

I prefer letting the directory name indicate the type of object or activity with which the script file is associated, and using a generic extension of `.sql` or `.qry`.

Source Code Control

Source-code control software has been used for a number of years in the development of software to manage changes to application code (COBOL, C, and so forth). Source-code control software also can be used to manage changes to DDL. It often acts as a logbook, enabling only one person to check out a file at a time. Checking in a file normally requires text to be provided to indicate why the file was checked out. The version number of the file is incremented each time a file is checked in.

Some sites decide to cross-reference the check-in text with a database change request document. Database changes happen for a reason. These changes usually parallel application changes that can be listed as part of the check-in text.

Capability of "cutting a version" of a group of related files must be provided by the source-code control system. For example, 20 different DDL files (each having its own revision number, based on the number of times it was changed) can be used to create a database structure. Cutting a version relates these 20 files together and logically groups them.

Source-code control gives DBAs a mechanism to manage distinct versions of the database effectively. Through use of this tool, a DBA can identify what versions of DDL files to load to re-create a specific version of a database, object, or stored procedure.

Abbreviation Standards

Because of limitations on the lengths of file names and database object names, it often is necessary to abbreviate descriptive components of file and object names. It's recommended that abbreviation standards be included in your standards definitions so that all users and developers are using a consistent method of abbreviation to avoid confusion.

One method for consistently abbreviating your object names follows:

■ Remove articles (*a, an, the*) and prepositions from the name. `Title_of_Book` becomes `Book_title`.

■ Remove underscores whenever mixed-case names are appropriate. They cease to be useful when abbreviation is necessary. Capitalize the first letter of each word to differentiate the words. `Book_title` becomes `BookTitle`.

■ Place the words so that the most general word is first, followed by increasingly specific modifiers. `LastName` and `FirstName` become `NameLast` and `NameFirst`.

■ Abbreviate common words in identifiers. Create a master list of common words and their abbreviations for your organization, similar to the example provided in Table 37.6.

■ Starting at the right side of the identifier, remove all nonessential vowels and double letters from each non-abbreviated word, until the resulting identifier is short enough. `ControlOfficeSubStationRoutePath` becomes `ControlOfcSbSttnRtePth`.

Table 37.6. Common abbreviations.

Base Word	Abbreviation
NAME	NM
NUMBER	NUM
CODE	CD
COUNT	CNT
AMOUNT	AMT
DATE	DT
TEXT	TXT
ADDRESS	ADDR
FLAG	FL
PERCENT	PCT
TIMESTAMP	TS
IDENTIFIER	ID

Summary

There are a number of SQL Server names to be defined in your environment. Too many SQL Server customers approach development without standards; this is likely to result in costly re-work to bring an existing system up to standard after the standards are defined. Sometimes, customers decide not to change the database because of the cost of conversion. This results in a nonstandard SQL Server implementation in your environment.

Application standards are also important, but are not the focus of this chapter. You need to develop application standards to be able to build high-performing SQL Server applications consistently. The construction of SQL statements can have striking effects on query performance, and the uniform implementation of triggers, procedures, rules, defaults, and constraints is important in providing a consistent approach to developing SQL Server systems. This enables developers to develop more efficiently, because a base structure is provided. It's important that you define standards as early as possible, and monitor adherence to those standards.

It is also important to define naming standards as early as possible and stick with them. Naming standards apply to the operating system as well as to SQL Server. With a consistent approach to naming, you can build on the underlying structure. Scripts can be written to automate activities on the server, decreasing the overall workload.

Administering Very Large SQL Server Databases

When administering a data warehouse or *Very Large Database* (VLDB) environment, a number of items must be considered and re-examined in light of the special issues facing a VLDB. The main challenge of a VLDB is that everything is larger and maintenance tasks take considerably longer. VLDBs provide unique challenges that sometimes require unique solutions to administer them effectively.

What Is a VLDB?

This is the first question most people ask about VLDBs. When does a database become a VLDB?

For some people, it depends on how you define "very large":

- A fixed size (for example, 2G, 20G, 200G, 4000G)?
- When database-restore time exceeds a certain threshold (for example, 4 days)?
- When you're not sure whether to order 25 or 30 more 2G drives?

In general, there's no easy way to quantify the point when a database becomes a VLDB. Possible definitions may include quantifiable parameters, but these tend to be subjective.

Here's the preferred definition:

> *A very large database is any database in which standard administrative procedures or design criteria fail to meet business needs, due to the scale of the data.*

In other words, whenever the size of the database causes you to redesign your maintenance procedures or redesign your database to meet maintenance requirements, you're dealing with a VLDB.

VLDB Maintenance Issues

VLDBs present a number of issues for the database administrator, including these important ones:

- Time required to perform dumps and loads
- Time required to perform necessary database-consistency checks
- Time and effort required to maintain data (that is, update statistics, re-establish fill factors, increment data loads)
- Purging and archiving data
- Managing partitioned databases

This chapter explores these issues and provides guidelines for implementing solutions.

Managing Database Dumps and Loads

Database dumps are necessary to provide recoverability in case of disaster. Although disk mirroring is a viable method to protect you from loss of data and system downtime due to disk failure, it doesn't protect you from other types of failures that can cause data loss. You still need database dumps in addition to disk mirroring to protect you from the following:

- Physical server failure
- SQL Server failure
- Database failure or corruption
- Table or index corruption
- Controller or disk failure
- User error

The main issue with database dumps and VLDBs is the duration of the database dumps. A SQL Server dump makes a physical copy of all the used pages in a database; therefore, dump time is proportional to the amount of data in the database.

If the time to back up a database is excessive, the time to restore it is even more so. During a database restore, SQL Server will replace all data pages in the existing database with the contents of the dump and initialize or "zero out" those pages not loaded. As a result, the load time is proportional to the size of the database.

The typical ratio between dump and load duration is approximately 1:3. That is, if it takes 1 hour to dump the database, it takes approximately 3 hours to restore it.

When developing a backup-and-recovery plan for VLDB environments, several issues must be considered:

- What's the impact of corruption and database loss on the application, end users, and the company?
- What's the allowable and anticipated duration for database recovery?
- What's the allowable and anticipated duration of database dumps?
- What's the allowable and anticipated time to perform database consistency checks?
- How large are the database dumps going to be, and what are your backup media types and capacities?
- Can database dumps be completed within the defined maintenance window?
- Can the database be restored within an acceptable or required time frame?

The most important of these issues is the duration of dumps and loads. If you have an available maintenance window of 4 hours per evening to perform your database dumps, and a full database dump takes 12 hours, what do you do? Conversely, if you have a requirement that the system, in the event of failure, be up and running within 2 hours, and a full database load takes 24 hours, how do you meet the recoverability requirements?

As stated earlier, because you're dealing with a VLDB, you need to take a more creative approach to database dumps and loads in order to meet your requirements.

The first thing to look at is how to speed up database dumps. One method available in SQL Server 6.5 is striping database dumps to multiple dump devices. If you have four dump devices available and a full database dump to a single device takes 8 hours, dumping to four dump devices concurrently should take just over 2 hours.

Another issue to consider is whether dumps are performed locally or across the network. Dumps across the network are inherently slower than dumps to a locally attached database device. For a VLDB, you want to dump locally.

Previous versions of SQL Server allowed only full database dumps and loads. A new feature in SQL Server 6.5 is the ability to back up and load single tables. This can save a significant amount of time if only a single table in a VLDB needs to be restored. However, this approach does have a few drawbacks. Restoring a single table may lead to referential integrity problems between the restored table and other tables in the database. Also, if a data device fails, the entire database is marked suspect and becomes inaccessible—you'll need to restore the entire database to get back online.

To address these concerns, an approach often adopted by organizations working with VLDBs is to physically implement a single logical database as several smaller physical databases, by partitioning the data. There are three advantages to this approach:

- Database dumps for multiple databases can be performed in parallel, minimizing total database dump time.

- Your unit of recovery is smaller in the event of a device failure—a single 2G database loads much faster than a 12G database.

- Tables with referential integrity links can be partitioned into the same database, so referential integrity is maintained when the database is restored.

In order to meet your required dump/load times, you may need to make several database architecture choices. These choices include whether to partition your data horizontally or vertically across databases. This approach essentially breaks a VLDB into a number of "databaselets." There are several advantages to multiple databases:

- If a database failure occurs in one of the databases, database activity may be able to continue in unaffected databases.

- Even if activity can't continue in the event of a single database failure, the entire system can be up and running faster, because the unit of recovery is smaller. Only the smaller single database needs to be restored, because other databases are unaffected.

- Dump load times can be reduced by enabling concurrent dumps of multiple databases.

- Static or archival data that doesn't need to be backed up on a daily basis can be segregated from online, active data.

- It helps to avoid the need to change tapes if database size is less than tape capacity.

The disadvantages to partitioning a VLDB into multiple databases include the following:

- If any relationships exist between tables in different databases, activity may not be able to continue in unaffected databases.

- If any referential integrity constraints exist between tables in separate databases, you may lose referential integrity in event of a database failure.

- Spreading tables across multiple databases may require application changes to fully qualify table references.

- SQL Server security was designed to treat each database as an independent protection domain—setting up users and permissions across multiple databases is more complex and difficult to set up properly.

- Experience has shown that optimizer problems may occur more frequently in cross-database operations than in single database operations.

WARNING

Partitioning a database into multiple databases isn't a decision to be made lightly. Consider the pros and cons carefully before implementing such an approach. You'll probably want to try and stay in one database if you can, partitioning into multiple databases as needed.

Developing a VLDB Backup/Restore Procedure

There are five steps to designing and implementing a backup/restore procedure for a VLDB:

1. Consider the amount of time you're willing to be "down" while performing a recovery (that is, the allowable impact of corruption or database loss). If you need a database to be recovered within eight hours, for example, determine the size of a database that can be recovered in that amount of time.

2. Estimate table sizes for your database, to determine partitioning sizes and options:

   - If you have a 40G logical database, for example, you may need to implement ten 4G databases.
   - Are any single tables greater than 4G?
   - How many tables can you fit in a database?
   - Are any tables candidates for partitioning, based on this determination alone?

3. Develop your utopian administration schedule:

   - For every day during a month, determine what periods of time can be dedicated to administrative activities.

- Are weekends available? This isn't always the case.

- If you determine that you have five hours per night to perform administrative activities, you then need to determine what activities need to be completed and how they can be distributed over your available administrative time.

4. Determine the rate of the dump process:

   - Take into consideration media capacity, backup speed, and backup number.

   - Benchmark several scenarios.

   - Perform several database dumps, varying the number of dump devices (striped dumps) and the number of dump processes that can occur in parallel.

5. Finalize your schedule and document accordingly.

6. Monitor and update the process as needed over time as things change.

Checking Database Consistency

The *database consistency checker* (dbcc) is a systems administration tool that verifies (and, if necessary, repairs) pointers internal to a database and its structures. Remember, dbcc *checks should be run prior to any database dump* to avoid dumping a corrupt database. The worst time to realize you have a bad page pointer is during recovery of a critical database when the load process fails due to inconsistency. (This would probably be a good time to update your résumé!)

The dbcc commands typically lock user tables, indexes, system tables, and/or databases when running. In addition, certain dbcc commands, such as dbcc checkdb and dbcc checktable, are very I/O intensive. The more I/O required, the longer dbcc takes. These are the main issues with running dbcc in VLDBs.

If you want to follow the recommendations and run your dbcc commands prior to a database dump, and you have a daily administrative window of eight hours, but the dbcc commands run for four hours and the database dump runs for six hours, how do you get everything to run within your administrative window?

In addition, although SQL Server allows a dbcc to run while activity is going on in the database, the locking and I/O overhead incurred by dbcc activity may severely impact online performance. If the dbcc commands take several hours to run, this fact will more likely force you to run them online, negatively impacting system performance.

Developing a Consistency Checking Plan

Your database may contain tables with very different processing requirements. Although it's somewhat mysterious how table corruption occurs, a static table is much less likely to encounter allocation problems than is a highly active table with ongoing allocations and deallocations.

To develop a plan for effectively checking your database consistency in a VLDB, you first need to analyze your tables and rank them in order of importance. For example, where would a corruption have the most serious effects on your system?

Next, analyze each nonclustered index on your table and rank it in order of importance to determine which indexes are most important to check.

Plan to check your high-activity tables as close to your dump as possible, because these tables are more likely to encounter allocation problems. Verify the consistency of these tables as close to the dump as possible. Static tables should need to be checked only after data loads. It's unlikely that corruption will occur once the data has been loaded and indexes created. Therefore, it shouldn't be necessary to check the static tables on a daily basis.

You should always run dbcc `checkcatalog` immediately prior to the database dump. This dbcc command is relatively inexpensive to run and runs quickly, even on large databases. However, the duration of your `checkalloc` and `checkdb` commands may not allow them to be run immediately before the dump, due to time constraints.

To estimate execution times for your dbcc commands, run dbcc `checkalloc` and dbcc `checkdb` for each database in your system and note the time for completion, running them serially (one after the other) and in parallel (multiple databases at the same time). It's probable that dbcc `checkalloc` and dbcc `checkdb`, using either of these two methods, can't be completed in a reasonable time for most VLDBs. Thus, you need to develop a plan that breaks activities into smaller pieces.

Gather data into a table or spreadsheet, recording various dbcc times for your tables. This data is needed only for the large tables in your system. All others, such as code tables, can be grouped and considered fairly negligible. The following are commands for which you need to record times:

- ▰ dbcc `checktable` for each large table
- ▰ dbcc `checktable` skipping checking of nonclustered indexes
- ▰ dbcc `checkalloc` skipping checking of nonclustered indexes

Next, categorize each table as either *static* or *active*. Static tables aren't updated (or are rarely updated) by the application (for example, tables containing historical data only). In active tables, rows are inserted, updated, or deleted by the application on a regular basis. Rank the active tables based on importance to the overall success of the system.

In ranking the importance and criticality of a table, consider whether the data exists only in SQL Server (it's created as part of the application) or can be re-created or reloaded from other sources. For example, a purchase table may be updated continuously throughout the day by the application, but a product table may be re-created from a source table on a host machine.

For your static tables, list the frequency with which data is added (weekly, monthly, yearly, and so forth). This figure determines the frequency with which you need to run your dbcc commands on the static tables.

If a nonclustered index is corrupted, it can be dropped and re-created, or you can run the dbcc reindex command, as long as the base table is okay. Therefore, consistency of nonclustered indexes are of secondary priority. However, each index is used differently: One index may be used in 80 percent of the queries, but another index may be used in only 3 percent of the queries. The frequently-used index is much more important to the system and is a higher priority for checking than the infrequently-used index.

Determine the amount of time you have to perform consistency checks in the batch window when you perform database dumps. You'll use this time to determine which tables to check in that window. To be confident that a table is free of corruption, you need to run dbcc checktable on the table. Determine the time to perform dbcc checktable, starting with the highest-ranked activity table and working downward to determine which tables can be checked within your batch window.

If you can execute dbcc checktable on all high-activity tables within the batch window, start adding in the highest-ranked index on each table and continue downward through the indexes until you determine which tables and indexes can be checked in the window before the dump. Consider also the possibility of running dbcc checktable on different tables concurrently, as a way of accomplishing more tasks in a limited time period.

If all active tables can't be checked within a batch window, during the next maintenance window, start with the point where you left off during the last window. This way, over a certain time period (for example, two days or one week) you'll have checked all the critical, active tables in the database. Plan to work in checks on your static tables as needed (weekends are a good time to run full checks on all tables).

When putting together a consistency-checking plan, it's easy to concentrate on your application tables and forget about the system tables. It's possible for corruption to occur in system tables, and it's essential that you periodically run dbcc commands on the system tables as well.

Data Maintenance

In addition to performing database dumps and checking database consistency on a VLDB, there are other data-maintenance commands that need to be performed on a database. These include updating statistics, as well as purging and archiving data.

Updating Statistics

Index statistics are used by SQL Server to choose the correct access path at query optimization time. SQL Server creates statistics pages for every index in the database at index-creation time, but they aren't kept up to date by SQL Server as data values change or data is updated and deleted.

The DBA should update statistics when the data distribution changes, to ensure that valid information is contained on the statistics page.

update statistics Scheduling

Typically, you update statistics on your tables by using the `update statistics` command on a table:

```
update statistics customer
```

However, this command updates the index statistics serially. `update statistics` takes a shared lock on the table for the length of time needed for completion. This action makes the table unavailable for update. On a very large table, this period of time can be significant.

To speed the `update statistics` process, you can update statistics concurrently on multiple indexes by executing `update statistics` commands in parallel.

For example, if you have a `customer` table with a clustered index named `customer_clus` and four nonclustered indexes named `customer_idx1`, `customer_idx2`, `customer_idx3`, and `customer_idx4`, you create five files like the following:

```
/* file 1*/
declare @starttime datetime
select @starttime = getdate()
update statistics customer(customer_clus)
select "The number of minutes to update statistics for customer_clus is:",
    datediff(mi, @starttime, getdate())
go
```

Create a similar file for each of the other four indexes and run the five `update statistics` processes in parallel. This strategy reduces the overall amount of time necessary to update statistics for all indexes on the table, making the table available to users more quickly.

> **CAUTION**
>
> If you aren't using SMP-capable hardware, this plan may cause considerable strain on the system. Be wary of other activities you're trying to complete in the same time period!

Determine possible periods during the week when the statistics can be updated with little to no impact on online users. For OLTP systems, this point will likely be after business hours (during the batch window). For DSS/Data Warehouse systems, the activity is primarily read-only, so `update statistics` can be scheduled during business hours.

In a VLDB database, you may not be able to update the statistics for all indexes on a table in a single batch window. With that fact in mind, consider spreading the updating of statistics across several days as part of your overall maintenance plan. In addition, you may want to put together an index maintenance plan based on the usefulness and purpose of each index.

The distribution page is used by the query optimizer for estimating rows for non-unique searches or range searches. If you have a unique index on a table and a SARG with an equality operator (=), the optimizer knows that one and only one row will match a single value, so the distribution page isn't used to estimate matching rows. For non-unique or range searches, the distribution page is used to estimate the number of matching rows within the range of values.

Indexes used in range retrievals are your highest priority for updating statistics. For a unique index used in single-row lookups, the statistics don't need to be updated as often, if at all.

Consider a `customer` table with the following indexes:

1. `customer_id`

   Unique, nonclustered. Used for enforcement of uniqueness and single row searches by `customer_id`.

2. `state, last_name`

   Non-unique, clustered. Used to spread activity throughout the table to minimize I/O and page contention (activity is by state) and 20 percent searches.

3. `last_name, first_name`

   Non-unique, nonclustered. Used for 65 percent of name searches.

4. `city, state`

   Non-unique, nonclustered. Used primarily for management reporting at the end of the month.

5. `phone, last_name`

   Non-unique, nonclustered. Used for 15 percent of online searches.

The maintenance plan for updating the index statistics might be as follows:

- Every Sunday, update indexes 3, 2, and 5 (or update index 3 on Sunday, index 2 on Tuesday, and index 5 on Friday).
- On the 25th of each month, update index 4 to support the monthly report.

Update of index 1 isn't required.

Purge/Archive Procedures

The data in a VLDB or Data Warehouse may grow to a size approaching or exceeding the maximum available database space. At this point, the decision needs to be made either to expand the database or to purge or archive data to free space. Purging of data is often necessary.

When purging or archiving data, a number of issues need to be addressed:

- Locking implications
- Performance implications
- Storage and retrieval of archived data

There are typically two ways of dealing with historical data: purging or archival. *Purging* is the process of removing data from its current location via a delete process. *Archiving* is the process of moving data from its current location to an archival area via a delete-and-insert process.

To develop a purge/archival strategy, you need to project database growth over the expected life of your system. Is the database 100G, growing by 100M per year, or 500G, growing by 100G per year? Over 10 years, the first system grows to only 101G. The second system, however, grows to 1500G. Based on physical limitations and the cost of performing dumps and `dbccs`, purging/archival of data is absolutely critical for the second system.

If your growth estimates necessitate removing data from your system periodically, you must decide whether to purge or archive. These are the questions you need to answer to make your decision:

- Do current business requirements indicate which data is no longer useful to the company?
- Are there any legal requirements regarding data retention?
- Is it possible that data requirements may change in the future?
- Can the data be re-created from another source?

To be able to purge or archive data from your system, you must be able to identify the rows within a table to be purged or archived. Common data characteristics used to purge or archive data include the following:

- *Time-based.* Data is removed after a certain period of time. Common data elements that can be used are creation date or date of last activity.
- *Non-time-based.* Data is removed based on some element other than time, such as geography (state) or a customer or product list (generated from some source).

Systems are often designed, developed, and put into production with no regard to purge/archive criteria. If the purge/archive process isn't incorporated into the original system design, retrofitting a system to handle purge/archive criteria once it's in production can be extremely difficult and expensive. The time to identify purge/archive criteria is during the requirements analysis of a system, because it's possible that your purge/archive requirements will influence the database design.

To put together your purge/archive requirements and design your purge/archive process, identify the following information:

- How long data should remain in the table
- The frequency with which data will be purged and archived
- The element (column) in the table that will be used to identify the rows to purge and archive

Whether you're purging or archiving data, rows must be deleted from the current table. There are four main areas of concern in purge/archive activities that also need to be factored into the design of the purge/archive process:

- Locking
- Logging
- Referential integrity
- Transactional integrity

Locking and Performance Considerations

When deleting a large amount of data from a table, you must consider the locking implications of the delete and its impact on other online activities. SQL Server escalates page locks to a table lock when the configured lock-escalation (LE) point is reached by a single process during a transaction. Extensive archiving also acts as a batch process (which it is, in effect) and grabs an increasing share of a single processor's resources. Additionally, the I/O utilization for the affected disks can create a bottleneck.

One way to avoid locking problems is to perform archival activities when users aren't using the system. Here are alternatives to avoid table-level locks:

- Use cursors to restrict rows being modified to one at a time
- Use set rowcount to affect a limited number of rows at a time
- Use some other site- or table-specific value to limit the number of pages that are being modified to less than the lock-escalation threshold

If the clustered index is on the element used to identify the rows to purge in a table, the necessary rows are organized in clustered index order on the data pages. The number of rows that can be deleted before a table lock is acquired depends on the lock-escalation threshold settings. The number of pages to be locked should be less than the lock-escalation point to avoid a table-level lock. Assuming the LE threshold percentage is left at the default of 0, the number of rows that can be deleted without a table lock escalation of the pages that are contiguous is the following:

LE Threshold Maximum $\times$ (# of rows per page)

If data isn't clustered on the element you're using to purge, the pages locked are likely not to be contiguous, possibly a different page for each row. Therefore, you should assume that the number of rows that can be deleted at a time before a table lock is acquired must be less than the LE Threshold Maximum.

Logging Considerations

Rows being deleted from a table are logged in the transaction log. You determine whether your transaction log is large enough to handle the deletion of a large number of rows in a single transaction. To minimize I/O contention, your log should be placed on a separate disk to distribute the I/O.

Although your transaction log may be large enough to handle a single deletion of 500,000 rows from a table, those records remain in the log until they're dumped. Your purge/archive process should be designed to dump the transaction log after the completion of the purge process, to clear the log for the next purge or normal system activity.

If your log isn't large enough to handle the deletion as a single transaction, break the deletion into multiple transactions, dumping the logs between each transaction.

Referential Integrity Considerations

Data to purge/archive may be spread across multiple related tables. Your purge/archive process must be designed to consider referential integrity (RI) implications. The following are items to consider when dealing with RI:

- If referential integrity is maintained via triggers, cascading delete triggers may exist on a table where data is to be removed. The deletion of rows from one table thus may cause the deletion of even more rows from a related table. Even though your log may be able to handle the delete from the first table, the cascading effects could fill your log, causing the purge to fail. It could also lead to exclusive table locks throughout your system.

- If declarative RI is used to enforce referential integrity, or a delete trigger is designed to disallow a delete if rows exist in a related table, you have to delete from related tables first. Design the process to delete from the tables furthest removed from the base table, and work inward to the base table.

- If the purge/archive process is a batch job run during administrative periods, you can drop the triggers or RI constraints before running the purge/archive. If the purge/archive is to be conducted during business hours, you probably should leave the triggers on the table.

- If there are cascading delete triggers, you may need to perform deletes in small quantities with regard to the number of rows deleted in each table in the relationship, to avoid table-level locks.

Transactional Integrity Considerations

A *transaction* is a logical unit of work. All activities in the transaction must complete successfully or they all should fail. During an archive process, you'll likely insert data into a table in a different database and remove the data from its current location. If an error occurs that prevents the process from inserting the data into the new database, your archive process mustn't delete the data from its current database. Therefore, the insert/delete activity should be conducted in a transaction.

When archiving data with relationships across multiple tables, the design may require you to write transactions that transfer the data from all the related tables before deleting any of the rows. Make sure that your design considers multi-table relationships.

Storage/Retrieval of Archived Data

To decide how and where you'll archive the data, you need to answer some questions first:

- How available does the archived data need to be? What's the maximum amount of time your business can wait before having access to the data?
- Does the system need near "real-time" access to the data?
- What are any legal requirements for storage and security?

The answers to these questions dictate whether the archived data must be stored online or can be saved into external storage locations, such as BCP files.

Typically, the reason systems are designed with archive mechanisms is to separate infrequently-accessed data from frequently-accessed data. With VLDBs, this is often required to permit backup of the active data in a reasonable time period or to improve performance for the application that accesses the most frequent data.

"Old" data can often be handled on an exception basis, so a delay in accessing the data may be acceptable to the business and the historical data thus need not be stored online.

Possible Archive Solutions

The following options are possible alternatives for archiving data, depending on the required accessibility of the data:

- If the data is accessed periodically (more than several times per day), the data should be stored online. The data can be stored in a separate table in the same database or in a separate database.
- If the data is accessed infrequently (several times per month), the data can be stored externally with a mechanism to make the data available within a certain time period (minutes, hours, or days).
- If the data is rarely or never accessed, but must be maintained for legal purposes, some form of external storage is appropriate. The data can be stored in a database dump or in flat files.

Data Archival and Changes to Database Design

In addition to the problems and issues already discussed with purge/archive processes, another very important concern that's commonly overlooked is structural changes to your database over time. Most databases change over a period of time, even after the system is put into production. It's imprudent to ignore this fact when designing the purge/archive process.

Structural changes have much less impact on purge-only applications. If new columns are added to existing tables, it shouldn't affect your purge application unless the field added is to become part of the key. If new tables are added to the schema, it should be fairly straightforward to accommodate the new table(s).

Structural changes can have a major effect on archive applications. Data that's archived must be accessible at a later time. Your process should be insulated against schema changes as much as possible. If archiving to flat files, create a file with the table schema in place at the time of the archive. If you use version control software, you may be able to associate the version of the script file used to create the table with the archived table.

If you're using a database approach to archive data, design your application so that it detects a difference between the application schema and the archive schema.

Storage Alternatives for Archived Data

There are a number of options for storage of archival data. Any of the following media types can be used for storing archived data:

- Tape
- Disk
- Optical disk

There are advantages and disadvantages for each type of storage media. A possible solution is a combination of more than one device type—for example, storing recently archived data on disk and moving older data to tape or optical disk.

The advantages of archiving to tape include the "unlimited" capacity of tape storage, the reusability and low cost of tape storage, and the security and reliability of data stored on tape. However, databases archived to tape take the longest to restore to an online state and are more difficult to locate than those on disk or optical disk.

The advantage of archiving to disk is that it provides the fastest access to archived data and makes archived files easy to locate. However, disk storage is the most expensive archival solution and the files are less secure. You still need to back up the disk to tape or optical disk to protect against data loss due to disk failure.

Archival to optical disk provides the advantages of high reliability, secure storage, and easier access to archive files than tape. However, unless you use the more expensive rewriteable optical disk, disk platters can be used only once, and access times are slower than disk devices.

Data to be archived can be stored on any of the media types in any of the following formats:

- Database dumps
- BCP files
- Database device files

Database dumps are the simplest method of archiving an entire database. However, to restore the data, the destination database must be the same size as or larger than the original database dumped, and only the entire database can be restored, not individual tables.

BCP files provide an easier method to restore data to individual tables, and the data can be loaded into non-SQL Server databases if necessary.

One approach sometimes used for archiving data is to archive the device file(s) containing the database to be archived. Here's the typical approach to archiving a database by using file system devices:

1. Freeze update activity on the database, set it to read-only, and checkpoint it.
2. Shut down SQL Server.
3. Copy the device file(s) containing the database to the optical disk or another location on the disk.
4. Restart SQL Server.

To restore a version of the database, follow these steps:

1. Shut down SQL Server.
2. Copy the device file(s) from optical disk or magnetic disk to the location of the archive database device(s).
3. Restart SQL Server.

You should now be working with an archived version of the database.

Archiving database device files becomes a more complex procedure if a database spans multiple devices, and it requires a shutdown of SQL Server to copy or replace a device file. This probably isn't a viable approach in a production system. The advantage of this approach is that it's typically the fastest way to bring archived data online.

> **NOTE**
>
> Copying device files isn't a backup method that's generally supported. It's presented here because it has been implemented successfully by a number of SQL Server customers.
>
> Optionally, SQL Server 6.5 allows the creation of a database on removable media, such as optical disk, using the `sp_create_removable` stored procedure to create the archive database and copy data over as you would to any archive database. Once the archive database is populated, use `sp_certify_removable` to move the archive database to the removable media. The archived database can then be brought back online, using the `sp_dbinstall` procedure. This method protects the archived database from modification, because it exists on read-only media. In addition, the database can be installed and brought online without requiring a shutdown of SQL Server. This approach

requires free space on a hard disk equal to the size of the archive database, to create the tables and copy the data into the database before certifying it and copying it to the removable media.

Data-Partitioning Options

When dealing with VLDBs, it may become necessary to partition the database, due to SQL Server size limitations or in order to meet your backup and recovery or data-maintenance requirements. Partitioning a database comes with some disadvantages—consider these when planning database partitioning.

On the administrative side, you'll have more databases for which you'll need to add users, set up permissions, maintain, and back up. If any referential integrity exists between tables in different databases, you need some way to maintain the RI between databases during dump/load, or if a database is unavailable while activity continues on other databases.

There are two primary ways of partitioning databases: vertical partitioning and horizontal partitioning.

Vertical partitioning of data is the process of drawing imaginary lines through a database schema and placing individual tables in different databases (see Figure 38.1). Alternatively, it may also involve partitioning individual tables by columns, to separate the frequently accessed columns from infrequently accessed columns, and then placing the resulting tables in the same or different databases.

FIGURE 38.1.

Vertically partitioning a large database across multiple databases to minimize the size of each individual recovery unit.

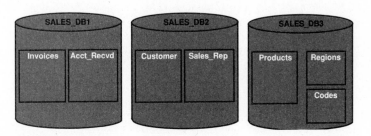

Horizontal partitioning of data involves breaking up tables into logical subsets and placing them into the same or different databases.

Vertical Data Partitioning

The benefits of vertical partitioning over a horizontal partitioning approach is that administration is simplified somewhat, because all data for a given table is in a single table in a single database. Additionally, navigation and data access are simplified for end users, because they don't need to know which portions of a table are in which database.

Another advantage of vertical partitioning is that the vertical partitioning can be hidden from the end user or application developer through the use of views. A single primary database can be defined, containing views of all the tables in other databases. The application developer can write the application against the single database. The views will take care of pointing to the actual table (see Figure 38.2).

FIGURE 38.2.

Using views to hide the location of tables in a vertically partitioned database.

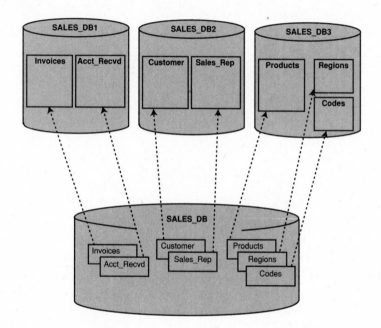

The advantage of this approach is that the tables can be moved without requiring changes to the application code or impacting the end users. The view is typically defined using `select *` against the base table only. Views of this type don't have any detrimental effect on query performance, even if used in joins, because SQL Server merges the view's query tree with the rest of the query before generating a query plan.

If you vertically partition a table by columns, a view can be created that joins the two table partitions together to make it appear to the end user as a single table (see Figure 38.3). Users can then select from the view as if it were a single table.

Joining between tables in more than one databases doesn't require any additional work other than fully qualifying the table names—a standard programming practice in many shops, anyway. Also, no additional programming is needed to handle transactions that span multiple databases within a SQL Server, because SQL Server automatically synchronizes transaction across databases logs (performing an internal two-phase commit), if necessary, in a single-server environment.

FIGURE 38.3.

Using a view to hide the vertical partitioning of a table.

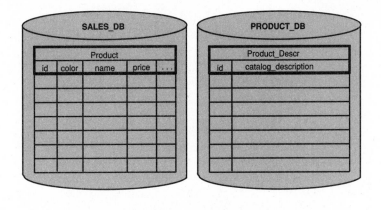

The main drawback to vertical partitioning is that if you break up a database by drawing lines through the schema, and relational integrity must be maintained across those lines, recovering an individual unit may be tricky or impossible while still maintaining the referential integrity between the different units. Backups need to be orchestrated and coordinated between databases to maximize RI and minimize recovery time.

Loss of a single database may also cause navigational problems across the entire database or application, if necessary tables aren't accessible.

When partitioning vertically, you want to identify the components of the database that get accessed most heavily, in order to spread them across databases or devices. This strategy enables you to gain maximum performance by minimizing I/O contention.

TIP

While moving tables around to balance I/O, the shuffling will require the application developers to modify their code to reference the tables.

You might want to consider creating a table that contains a list of tables and the databases in which they reside. Application programmers can use this lookup table in their code to qualify the table names dynamically.

continues

> *continued*
>
> Another alternative is to create views in a single database, as described earlier in this
> section, that hide the actual location of the tables from the end users and developers.

Horizontal Data Partitioning

One of the primary reasons for horizontally partitioning a VLDB is to separate the active data from the historical or inactive data. This plan helps to speed access of the active data by keeping it in a smaller table, so users don't need to wade through a lot of historical data to access the current data they need most frequently.

Another reason to horizontally partition tables is to spread activity across databases or devices, minimizing locking overhead and contention and improving performance for table access. Horizontal partitioning also can serve as a security mechanism by enabling access to specific subcomponents of data through normal database-security mechanisms.

The main drawback to horizontal partitioning is that retrieving data from more than one table as a single result set requires the use of the `union` statement. For example, if an `orders` table is partitioned by year into separate databases, pulling data together for a three-year period requires the following command:

```
select name, state, order_num
    from address a, customer c, sales_1993_db.orders o
    where a.custid = c.custid
    and c.custid = o.custid
union
select name, state, order_num
    from address a, customer c, sales_1994_db.orders o
    where a.custid = c.custid
    and c.custid = o.custid
union
select name, state, order_num
    from address a, customer c, sales_1995_db.orders o
    where a.custid = c.custid
    and c.custid = o.custid
    order by state, name, order_num
```

Unlike vertical partitioning, horizontal partitions can't be hidden from the end user by using views. `union` isn't allowed in a view. Queries requiring data from multiple tables have to include the `union` statement explicitly. If you redefine your partitions and move tables around, your users and application developers need to update their queries or application code to reflect the changes. Horizontal partitioning is usually broken down by using a logical boundary, such as a date-time field, geographical location, department number, or other logical grouping value (see Figure 38.4). The advantage to this approach is that it's easy to determine the location of data. However, logical groupings may not provide an even breakup of your tables, or certain logical groupings may be more active than others. If you want to spread your data evenly, and randomly spread the access, consider using a random hash-partitioning scheme.

In Figure 38.4, horizontal partitioning enables the inactive and static data for previous-year activity to be stored in a database separate from the active, current-year data, which needs to be backed up on a nightly basis. At the end of the fiscal year, the current database is renamed and made a historical database, and a new SALES_CURR_DB database is created.

FIGURE 38.4.

Horizontal partitioning of sales data by year across databases.

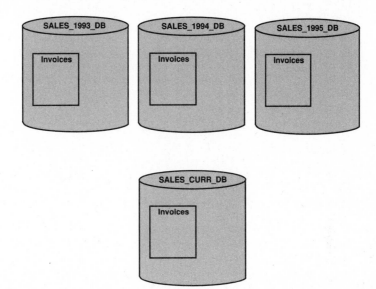

Hash partitioning is horizontal partitioning based on deriving a hash key, rather than along logical boundaries. The hash key is usually generated by using an algorithm to generate some random value. The benefits of a hashing approach are realized if you experience performance problems with hot spots in your data. Hashing the table is a way of randomly spreading the data across resources, balancing the I/O and data access.

The main drawback to a hashing scheme is that it's harder for end users to determine where the data resides. It's also more difficult to determine the logical recovery unit if a single partition is lost. When using a logical boundary for partitioning your data—for instance, by fiscal year—in the event of loss of a single table you can rebuild the table by loading the data for that fiscal year. With a hash partition, it's more difficult to determine which rows were lost, and rebuilding the table may require reloading data from multiple source files.

Summary

Although not originally designed as a data-warehousing system, SQL Server is capable of handling large data volumes. The proof is in the fact that a number of people have successfully implemented VLDBs in SQL Server. This is not to say that there aren't a few bumps in the road to making a VLDB work. It requires some advance planning—and, at times, creative solutions—to deal with the size-related limitations of SQL Server.

V

PART

Introduction to Open Client Programming

Introduction to Client/ Server Programming with MS SQL Server

39

The fundamental components of client/server computing are, as most would guess, the *client* and the *server*. The client is an application that uses the services of the server. The client can be an application that makes requests to a server for display to the user, or simply a process of sharing or distributing work with different computers. The server processes client requests, and returns the results to the client.

How SQL Server Fits Into the Client/Server Model

Client/server, as it applies to developing for SQL Server, provides the following key components: the "front end" component and the "back end" component. The client application (front end) presents and manipulates the data on the workstation. The server (back end) stores, retrieves, and protects the data.

SQL server is the back end component that acts as a gateway between the clients and the physical data. No client applications have direct access to the data (the physical data on the hard drive). All requests must be sent to the server for processing. The server first verifies that the client has the proper privileges to access the requested data; it then processes the request, accesses the data on behalf of the client, and finally returns the results to the client (see Figure 39.1).

FIGURE 39.1.

Interaction between the client and server.

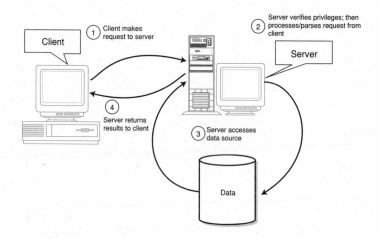

This is a simplified description of SQL Server, but it provides an important distinction between a client/server application and a shared-file application. For example, it's a misconception that Microsoft Access alone can be used to create a client/server application. You may feel that if you place your Access database file on a shared network drive, you have created a client/server database. This would not be a client/server application, but an application that shares a common resource. In this scenario, the file server is not adding any value to the application. The workstation still must perform all the processing when it selects rows, performs updates, or runs any query, for that matter.

In this shared-resource configuration, all users of the database have a physical connection to the data. As the number of users grows, the chances of the network being bogged down increases. There is no server that processes requests and accesses the data on behalf of the client. Access has acceptable performance on tables with a few thousand records, but begins to suffer as the record sizes increase, and when the number of users accessing the tables grows.

> **NOTE**
>
> Chapter 41, "Planning for SQL Server Applications," discusses how Microsoft Access can be used to develop client applications that use SQL Server as a back end.

An Access database can usually be stored on a local PC or a moderately-sized file server without problem. By contrast, imagine a database application with millions of rows of data, such as an order processing system that accepts thousands of transactions per day. The client/server architecture allows such data to be housed on an aptly suited server or mainframe. In the case of Microsoft SQL Server, the server hardware can be configured with multiple Pentium processors, as well as Alpha or MIPS processors, which, at the time of this publication, had clock speeds surpassing 200MHz. Microsoft NT Server can handle up to 4GB of RAM, 408 million terabytes of disk storage, and symmetric multiprocessing (SMP) supports up to 32 simultaneous processors. SQL Server can have databases up to 1 terabyte in size.

> **NOTE**
>
> 1 terabyte (TB) = 1024 gigabytes or about 1,000,000,000,000 bytes.
>
> SQL Server accesses databases on logical devices (the actual physical file on the hard drive). Each logical device can be a maximum of 32GB, and each database can have a maximum of 32 device fragments (32GB * 32 = 1 TB).
>
> SQL Server can also handle up to 32,767 simultaneous user connections.

SQL Server provides to developers more than just a method to fetch data; it also provides powerful functionality that, in most cases, is transparent to the developer. It provides data integrity and data recovery, and acts as a powerful number and data cruncher. As an application developer, you may be asked to investigate the advantages of using the client/server architecture, or may be asked to migrate a monolithic application to client/server. The client/server architecture can add value to your application in the following ways (the list is on the next page):

- Hardware improvements such as memory, processors, and disk drives can be localized to the server. The expense of upgrading the server is localized, yet the benefits of increased processing power are permeated to the clients.

- Security can be enforced at one central location.

- SQL Server optimizes network resources. Only the data requested by the client needs to be sent across the network.

- Business rules can be localized on the server. If something needs to be enforced after an application has been rolled out, the client software in many cases doesn't need to change. The change only needs to occur on the server.

- Because client requests are processed on the server, the workstation doesn't need to wait for results before continuing with other processing. This is known as an *asynchronous transaction*. Usually it's used to provide a 'cancel' function, so that users need not wait on an unintentional request to the server that returns several rows of data or may require a large amount of processing time.

- Several APIs and OLE interfaces to SQL Server are available to the developer. The developer can choose from one of many development tools and still leverage the server's capabilities.

- A variety of clients (MS-DOS, Windows, Macintosh, UNIX) can access the same data sources via one of SQL Server's many supported network protocols.

Methods of Programming SQL Server

When developing an application with SQL server, three roles may be carried out by one or more people: database administration, database implementation, and client development. Many times, all three hats are worn by the same person. Even if you will not be involved in all roles, having a basic understanding of each of these areas will help in your understanding of the client application development process. It is hard to imagine getting away with application development without delving into SQL Server's database implementation features or the Transact-SQL syntax. Chapters 10–38 deal with database implementation issues such as data integrity, query techniques, and retrieving and modifying data. Chapters 4–9 will help in your understanding of the Transact-SQL syntax.

The following chapters concentrate on the client development process.

Transact-SQL

If all users of an application understood the syntax of Transact-SQL and didn't mind text-only interfaces, your job as an applications developer would be in jeopardy. You would simply give each user a copy of the `isql` utility (a utility that ships with Microsoft SQL Server and provides a text-based query interface), and be done with it. Each user could execute stored procedures, run select queries, and perform table inserts and updates by entering Transact-SQL commands right in the query window. Of course, this isn't the case.

The native language of SQL Server is Transact-SQL, but not everybody knows its dialect. As an applications developer, you may have a vast understanding of its syntax, or know only basic commands. Either way, you can use one of the many client application interfaces to create a useful application. Chapter 40, "Client Application Interfaces for SQL Server," provides a background on the interfaces available for your development needs.

DB-Library and Net-Library

The way in which you connect, send requests, and retrieve results from SQL server is through the DB-Library interface. Unless you plan to program with the native DB-Library API, most of the complexities are shielded from you by higher level APIs such as ODBC, DMO, DAO, and RDO. Chapter 40 introduces you to these APIs and gives contrasts and similarities. DB-Library is the common underlying interface for all of these higher-level APIs, and thus key to the client/server architecture.

At the lowest level in the client/server architecture, DB-Library must physically send its requests via the network. Here is where the Net-Library shields the developer from these concerns. Net-Library isn't meant for the application developer to use directly. Your only concern is that the correct library is installed on the client machines, and that SQL Server has been configured to recognize your particular network protocol. Chapter 41, "Planning for SQL Server Applications," discusses the different Net-Library implementations and how they affect the deployment of your application.

By way of DB-Library and Net-Library, clients that can access SQL Server include MS-DOS, Windows 3.1 (and 3.11), Windows 95, and Windows NT. SQL Server also includes AppleTalk, DECnet, and TCP/IP network protocols; with the correct DB-Library, clients such as Apple Macintosh, VMS, and UNIX can access SQL Server as well. A block diagram of the Net-Library architecture is shown in Figure 39.2.

Open Data Services (ODS)

Although the following chapters discuss how to write "client" applications for SQL Server, Open Data Services (ODS) is worth mentioning at this point. Because DB-Library and Net-Library do much of the client/server communication for you, it is possible to take advantage of these libraries and write your own server-side gateways or extended stored procedures with ODS.

ODS is useful in writing "server" side applications, and doesn't necessarily have to communicate with SQL Server. When you write an application with the Open Data Services Library, it runs as a server software process on the network, just as SQL Server does. By leveraging the existing client/server communications established with DB-Library and Net-Library, you can concentrate on the services you want to provide in your ODS application. ODS applications are written in C for the Win32 API, and thus take advantage of the Win32 API features on Window NT, such as security, threads, and memory management.

FIGURE 39.2.

Net-Library architecture.

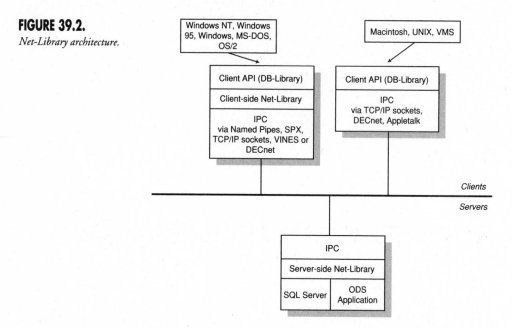

Your ODS application can even be installed as a Windows NT service, once registered with the Service Control Manager (SCM). This service can then respond to commands such as net stop, net start, and net pause.

SQL Server uses the same ODS library as that which can be used for your own application development. This means that your ODS applications benefit from the same features that SQL Server received from the ODS library. Your ODS application can use SMP-capable threading and pooling, and can handle simultaneous network protocols.

What Happens When I Send a Query?

Regardless of which programming interface you use, eventually calls are made at the DB-Library level (or, in the case of ODBC, a SQL Server driver that acts much like DB-Library). When a connection is first established (with dbopen), DB-Library needs to determine which client-side Net-Library should be loaded to communicate with SQL Server.

> **NOTE**
>
> Under the Windows 95, Windows NT, Windows, and OS/2 operating systems, Net-Libraries are implemented as dynamic link libraries (DLLs), and multiple Net-Libraries can be loaded simultaneously. Under the MS-DOS operating system, Net-Libraries are implemented as terminate-and-stay-resident (TSR), and only one can be loaded at any given time.

After the connection is made, SQL Server will use a server-side Net-Library and ODS layer to interface with the client. This architecture and subsequent layers are shown in Figure 39.3. The ODS functions act as the network handler between the server and the client. This interface is using the same ODS library mentioned earlier. ODS manages the network, listens for new connections, cleans up failed connections, acknowledges attentions such as canceling a query, returns result sets, returns messages, and returns status.

> **NOTE**
>
> Curious about what is being sent back and forth between the client and the server? It's known as *Tabular Data Stream (TDS)*. The TDS data stream uses "tokens" that describe column names, datatypes, events, and return status. Only the DB-Library and ODBC interfaces write directly to the TDS. These open interfaces mean that application developers need not worry about the details behind TDS.

FIGURE 39.3.

SQL Server's internal architecture.

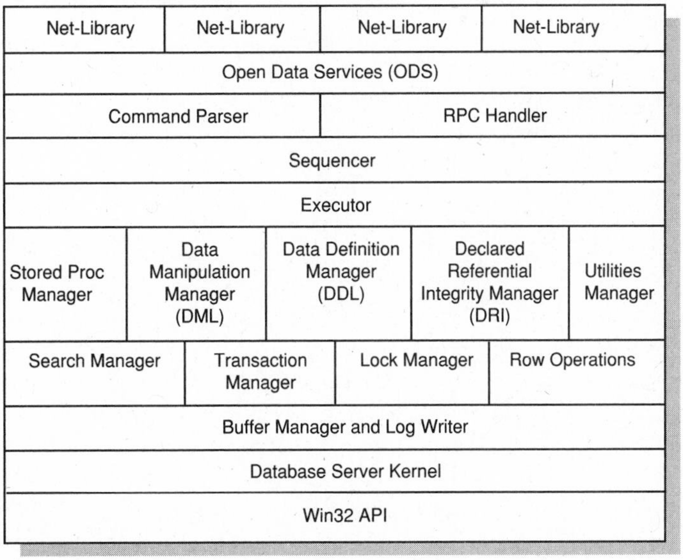

Net-Library	Net-Library	Net-Library	Net-Library
Open Data Services (ODS)			
Command Parser		RPC Handler	
Sequencer			
Executor			
Stored Proc Manager	Data Manipulation Manager (DML)	Data Definition Manager (DDL)	Declared Referential Integrity Manager (DRI)	Utilities Manager
Search Manager	Transaction Manager	Lock Manager	Row Operations
Buffer Manager and Log Writer			
Database Server Kernel			
Win32 API			

After the ODS interface receives the request from the client, it passes the request to the command parser. The command parser checks the syntax of the client request and translates the Transact-SQL commands into a format that is used internally by SQL Server. This internal format, known as a *sequence tree*, is then sent to the sequencer. If the command can be handled directly, the RPC Handler handles the request. These RPC requests are non-language-related requests (those that don't need to be parsed). It also sets up a sequence tree for the sequencer.

The sequencer takes the sequence tree result from either the command parser or the RPC handler and prepares it for execution by compiling the batch, optimizing queries, and checking security.

The executor loops through the batch until it is completed. As it walks through the batch, it hands off tasks to one or more handlers. These handlers are depicted in Figure 39.3 as the two levels below the executor. They are implemented as follows:

- Stored Procedure Manager—Stored procedures are dispatched here. For example, `EXEC sp_helpserver`.

- Data Manipulation Manager (DML)—When a `SELECT`, `UPDATE`, `INSERT`, or `DELETE` is encountered, it will be dispatched here.

- Data Definition Manager (DDL)—Table creations and alterations are handled here. These are calls such as `CREATE TABLE`.

- Declared Referential Integrity Manager (DRI)—Declared Referential Integrity was introduced in SQL 6.0. It maintains constraints for primary key/foreign key relationships. Although it is shown in the diagram at the same level as DML, it actually works in conjunction with DML. Before DRI was introduced, triggers had to be used to enforce referential integrity.

- Utilities Manager—Calls to SQL utility functions are handled here. An example of a utility function would be `dbcc`.

- Search Manager—This performs scans on tables, indexes, and index objects. It handles the retrieval rows in response to a client's "get next row" type of requests. It also tracks the current row being accessed, as in cursor operations.

- Transaction Manager—Any request that includes a `BEGIN TRAN` statement will require that the Transaction Manager become involved with any one of the above managers. These statements can then be followed by `COMMIT TRANSACTION` and `ROLLBACK TRANSACTION` statements.

- Lock Manager—The Lock Manager creates and releases shared locks, intent locks, extent locks, and exclusive locks. It also determines whether locks should be escalated to table locks.

- Row Operations—After the Search Manager, Transaction Manager, and Lock Manager have performed functions in response to a client's request, the row operations can retrieve or update information for a particular row.

Any access to the physical data is handled through the Buffer Manager and Log Writer. If the requested data is not cached in memory, it performs the necessary file I/O functions through the underlying database server kernel and the Win32 API. The Buffer Manager and Log Writer ensure that all transactions are "written ahead" in the log. This provides a data recovery mechanism, as all file I/O must move through the Buffer Manager and the Log Writer.

Finally, results are returned via the ODS interface back to the client. The client can then request more results, or more rows from the result set.

Summary

This chapter has introduced you to the concepts of the client/server architecture as it applies to SQL Server. One key point to remember is that SQL Server provides the back end processing in the client/server model. This means that data manipulation and data access are offloaded to the server. The clients (or workstations) only need to make requests for the data. The server processes the requests and accesses the data on behalf of the client.

Chapter 40 looks at the specific interfaces that allow an application developer to create client/server applications with SQL Server.

Client Application Interfaces for SQL Server

40

When you undertake the task of writing client applications for SQL Server, you will soon realize that you have many development tools from which to choose. This chapter introduces you to the various application interfaces that you can use to create applications for SQL Server, compares the different APIs associated with each interface, and compares the development tools that use these interfaces.

Overview of DB-Library Programming

Chapter 39 discusses SQL Server's client/server model, introducing the native interface used to connect to SQL Server: *DB-Library*. DB-Library handles all the connections to SQL Server and negotiates which network protocol to use. When you write an application using DB-Library, you call SQL Server's native API functions. This approach offers a rich set of functions to the developer, yet introduces complexities that are hidden in some of the other interfaces discussed later in this chapter.

With DB-Library, you can

- Browse available servers
- Open connections
- Format queries
- Send query batches to the server and retrieve the resulting data, including multiple result sets returned from a single query
- Bulk-copy data from files or program variables to and from the server
- Bind columns to your own variables
- Control two-phase commit operations between several participating SQL Servers
- Execute stored procedures on remote servers

The libraries' functions provide developers with fine-grained control of data flow back and forth between the client and the server. DB-Library supports C compilers and Visual Basic.

When developing with a C compiler, you can choose from one of several environments:

- A multithreaded dynamic link library (DLL) for the Windows NT and Windows 95 operating systems
- Medium and large model static-link libraries for MS-DOS, for both Microsoft and Borland compilers
- A DLL for the Windows operating system
- A DLL for the OS/2 operating system

Figure 40.1 shows a high-level diagram that depicts the DB-Library layers under Windows. As described earlier, the type of DLL loaded is dependent on the operating system. In addition, DB-Library will load the appropriate Net-Library, which handles network communications with SQL Server.

# Chapter 40

FIGURE 40.1.

The DB-Library interface automatically loads the appropriate Net-Library. Different operating systems require different DLLs to be loaded.

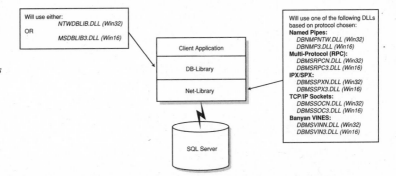

> **WARNING**
>
> Although programming DB-Library with Win32 allows the creation of threads, you need to be aware that DB-Library functions that access the same DBPROCESS are not reentrant.

Visual Basic and DB-Library

With Microsoft Visual Basic, you can create applications with similar functionality to those built with C compilers. The Visual Basic Library for SQL Server (VBSQL) is a version of the DB-Library API specifically tuned for use with Visual Basic, and provides virtually all the functions available in DB-Library.

The VBSQL Library is provided as a custom control. To use VBSQL, you need to include either VBSQL.VBX (Win16) or VBSQL.OCX (Win32) in your Visual Basic application. Note these points when using VBSQL:

■ You can't create multi-threaded applications in Visual Basic, yet C compilers can.

■ You can't bind column names to variables.

■ The VBSQL control must convert Visual Basic Pascal calling convention to the C calling convention (CDECL).

■ The VBSQL control converts data coming back from SQL server to a VB string.

Pros and Cons of Using the DB-Library API

Whether you're programming in Visual Basic or C, DB-Library gives application developers a powerful set of functions to interact with SQL Server. But this wide range of functionality does have a tradeoff: added complexity. Please refer to the following comparisons when determining the feasibility of DB-Library programming for your particular situation.

Advantages

- Access to virtually all SQL Server functions
- A native interface to SQL Server
- Specific API calls to address each SQL Server feature
- API for bulk copy (BCP) functions
- Interrupt driver error and message handling
- Server-side cursor support on SQL 6.0
- Application interfaces for several operating systems: MS-DOS, Win16, Win32, OS/2. Code written for DB-Library can be ported to various operating systems with little or no alteration.

Disadvantages

- Provides access only to Microsoft SQL Server (and some versions of Sybase); not portable to another DBMS
- Larger learning curve than other higher-level APIs
- Direct interaction with the Win32 API and with DB-Library increases the risk of access violations (the error formerly known as GPF)
- All data binding to user interface controls must be programmed manually
- Queries to be sent to SQL Servers must be formatted in its native language: Transact-SQL

Overview of ODBC Programming

Open Database Connectivity (ODBC) is Microsoft's strategy to give application developers a single API to divergent database engines, relational, and non-relational database management systems (DBMS). The ODBC API is intended to give application developers similar functionality, regardless of the type of data they are accessing—whether ISAM database, text data (Excel), or SQL databases. This objective is accomplished by requiring each ODBC driver to adhere to one of the predefined conformance levels. To be considered an ODBC driver, the driver must conform to the core ODBC specifications. This requirement ensures that the application developer can always expect the same functionality, regardless of what data is accessed. If the data format being accessed doesn't directly support the core functionality, the ODBC driver must emulate the functionality.

This API is an abstraction away from the actual data source, as shown in Figure 40.2. These calls provide the developer with a method to work with data sources using the same SQL grammar defined in ODBC. In addition, the method of connecting to data sources, receiving error messages from data sources, and standard login interfaces are common across all drivers. To provide this commonality, the drivers will adhere to the core API requirements described in the following sections.

FIGURE 40.2.

ODBC can access different types of data sources through the same API.

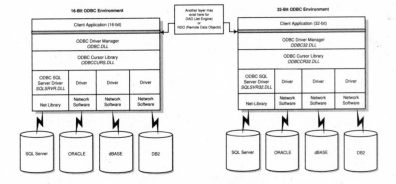

ODBC Core API Conformance Requirements

- Allocate and free environment, connection, and statement handles
- Connect to data sources; use multiple statements on a connection
- Prepare and execute SQL statements; execute SQL statements immediately
- Assign storage for parameters in a SQL statement and result columns
- Retrieve data from a result set; retrieve information about a result set
- Commit or roll back transactions
- Retrieve error information

Most ODBC applications rely on the driver to provide Level 1 conformance. The most common use of the Level 1 extensions is to obtain information on the types of data and functions the driver and data source support.

ODBC Level 1 Conformance

- Core API functionality
- Connect to data sources with driver-specific dialog boxes
- Set and inquire values of statement and connection options
- Send part or all of a parameter value (useful for long data)
- Retrieve part or all of a result column value (useful for long data)
- Retrieve catalog information (columns, special columns, statistics, and tables)
- Retrieve information about driver and data source capabilities, such as supported data types, scalar functions, and ODBC functions

The final ODBC level provides powerful features such as scrollable cursors, catalog information, and parameter arrays.

ODBC Level 2 API Conformance Requirements

- Core and Level 1 API functionality
- Browse connection information and list available data sources
- Send arrays of parameter values; retrieve arrays of result column values
- Retrieve the number of parameters and describe individual parameters
- Use a scrollable cursor
- Retrieve the native form of a SQL statement
- Retrieve catalog information (privileges, keys, and procedures)
- Call a translation DLL

ODBC SQL Conformance Levels

Each database engine uses a slightly different mechanism to access its data, whether a variation of the SQL grammar or a custom/proprietary application. In addition, the data you want to access may not have an engine at all, as in a flat file exported from a spreadsheet. If an ODBC driver exists for the data source, it can be accessed through a common core SQL grammar. ODBC provides a core grammar that roughly corresponds to the X/Open and SQL Access Group SQL CAE specification. If you're familiar with SQL Server's Transact-SQL syntax, the ODBC SQL grammar will not introduce an increase in your learning curve. The degree to which you can use the core SQL grammar depends on the conformance level the ODBC driver supports. Following is a list of the requirements associated with each conformance level:

- The *Minimum SQL Conformance Level* provides familiar Data Definition Language (DDL) and Database Management Language (DML) statements such as `select`, `update`, `delete`, `insert`, `create table`, and `drop table`. The datatypes this level supports are `char` and `varchar`.

- The *Core SQL Conformance Level* adds additional DML grammar such as `alter table`, `create index`, `drop index`, `create view`, `drop view`, `grant`, and `revoke`. This level adds full `select` functionality and additional data types such as `decimal`, `numeric`, `smallint`, `integer`, `real`, `float`, and `double precision`. A driver that supports this conformance level also allows expressions such as `sum` and `min`.

- The *Extended SQL Conformance Level* adds additional DML support for outer joins, positioned `update`, positioned `delete`, `select for update`, and unions. Additional scalar functions included are `substring`, `abs`, `date`, `time`, and `timestamp`. Additional datatypes included are `bit`, `tinyint`, `bigint`, `binary`, `varbinary`, `long varbinary`, `date`, `time`, `timestamp`. A driver that supports this conformance level allows batch SQL statements and procedure calls.

The good news is that the ODBC driver for Microsoft SQL Server supports all API conformance levels and all SQL conformance levels. This fact isn't surprising because all the conformance levels directly correlate to the capabilities of Transact-SQL.

How ODBC Benefits the End User

End users don't use the ODBC API directly, but they may come in contact with an application that uses ODBC. The data sources are implemented as *Data Source Names* (*DSN*). This setup gives the user a common method to select a data source across various applications.

Users of ODBC applications only need to understand the industry standard SQL grammar, regardless of what database they are accessing. In addition, the end user has the capacity to access data on new platforms as they arise, using the functionality with which he or she is already familiar.

How ODBC Benefits an Application Developer

If an application developer writes only to the core ODBC API functions, the same code will work on any ODBC data source. If you need additional functionality to exploit the data source's capabilities, you can use the higher-level ODBC API functions, or extended SQL grammar support.

The applications you write can be coded to a familiar ODBC SQL grammar, regardless of the data source. If the ODBC driver claims conformance for a particular level, you can assume either that the data source provides the functionality, or that the ODBC driver emulates the functionality. This emulation is totally transparent to the application developer.

How ODBC Benefits a Database Developer

Only one driver needs to exist for your DBMS. Once an ODBC driver is in place, users gain immediate access to your DBMS with existing tools already found in the marketplace today.

A Perspective on the Performance of ODBC

As an application developer, you need to weigh the functionality that ODBC provides against the performance that it yields. Don't assume that the performance of ODBC will always be worse than that of native drivers, or that the performance of native drivers will always be better. The truth is that there are good ODBC drivers, and poorly-written ODBC drivers. Some ODBC drivers are actually layers of abstraction from the native DBMS driver.

The good news for a SQL Server application developer is that Microsoft tried to make ODBC more akin to the native driver. If you look back at Figure 40.2, you may notice that DB-Library is nowhere in the picture. The layer above the Net-Library is SQLSVR32.DLL (SQLSRVR.DLL for Win16). This ODBC driver has been optimized for SQL Server. The only thing between you and the native driver is the ODBC driver manager.

> **NOTE**
>
> You may be wondering about the ODBC cursor library, which seems to be floating somewhere between the ODBC driver manager and the ODBC driver. The cursor library doesn't always come into play when you are accessing the driver. This library gives Level 1 drivers the capability of forward and backward scrolling. It also provides the capability of supporting snapshots.

The driver manager handles the connections for you, provides you with common error messages, and passes your queries to the SQL Server ODBC driver. The most noticeable location where you see a performance penalty is during connection time. A few more interactions happen when a connection is made, versus the native API. The ODBC driver DLLs must load, and some requests are made to the server regarding system information and datatype information. After you begin to send queries and retrieve result sets, the performance holds up well to that of the native API.

DAO, RDO, and MFC Database Classes

Two higher-level APIs take advantage of the ODBC API: Data Access Objects (DAO) and Remote Data Objects (RDO). This section covers how development platforms support these interfaces, as well as which APIs are available only on certain versions of Visual Basic or Visual C++.

Database Access Objects (DAO)

The DAO API works in conjunction with the Microsoft Access Jet engine. The Jet engine acts as a layer between all data sources—whether native Microsoft Access databases, data sources (such as other ISAMS) linked to Microsoft Access databases, or ODBC data sources.

As Figure 40.3 shows, Data Access Objects manipulate databases in either the native Jet database engine .MDB format or in other installable ISAM (Indexed Sequential Access Method) database formats, including Fox, dBASE, Excel, Btrieve, Paradox, and delimited text. The Jet engine is well suited for these types of local ISAM databases, as the Microsoft Access database (.MDB) files themselves are a type of ISAM file.

In addition, you can use the Microsoft Jet database engine to access Microsoft SQL Server and any other database that can be accessed via ODBC.

FIGURE 40.3.

The Jet engine acts as a layer between all data sources in the DAO model.

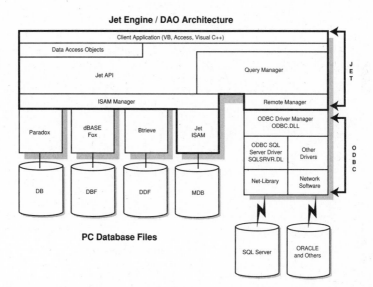

One benefit to this architecture is that the same code works for all formats—whether it's an ISAM or an ODBC data source. Even though ODBC has drivers available for ISAM files, the Jet engine will outperform those drivers. This architecture is suitable if you will be doing a large amount of data access on ISAM databases, and still need a heterogeneous method to connect to SQL Server.

The DAO interface has been around since the introduction of Visual Basic 3.0. This version of Visual Basic introduced the *data bound control*, which provides the capacity to bind a user interface element to a specific column in a table/query, or bind a control to an entire table/query.

In essence, the DAO interface has added an object-oriented programming interface to the Jet 1.1 engine. Visual Basic 4.0 introduced new features in the Jet 3.0 engine, which was then also made available to Visual C++ 4.0 developers. Several other Microsoft products inherited the DAO objects, including the entire Microsoft Office suite (Access, Excel, and Word—PowerPoint is part of the office suite, but it has no programming capabilities that apply to database access). In general, any applications that support VBA (Visual Basic for Applications) also support DAO.

Visual C++ (32-bit) MFC 4.1 introduced classes to wrap the DAO interface. These include CDaoDatabase, CDaoRecordset, and other related classes. The member functions and properties of the MFC classes directly correlate with their Visual Basic counterparts, making the transition from one to the other somewhat painless.

RDO and ODBC MFC Classes

Visual Basic 4.0 (Enterprise Edition only) introduced yet another object-oriented database access method: *Remote Data Objects* (*RDO*). This method provides a more direct route to ODBC data sources, when the Jet engine isn't needed. The performance of this API is similar to straight ODBC API calls. The properties and methods have a similar architecture to the ODBC API. For example, rdoConnection is akin to the ODBC connection, rdoEnvironment is akin to the ODBC environment, and so on. If you are considering programming directly with the ODBC API, RDO may be a less painful solution.

One advantage that RDO has over ODBC is the capacity to easily bind controls to data with the *Remote Data Control* (*RDC*). The RDC connects to an ODBC source in the same manner as RDO, yet provides functionality similar to the data bound controls of DAO.

If you would like to avoid making ODBC API calls during your C++ development, look to the MFC classes CDatabase, CRecordset, and CRecordView. These classes wrap the ODBC functionality with class implementations that provide functionality similar to RDO and RDC. With these class implementations, you can bind dialog controls to database objects, just as in Visual Basic.

DB-Library Versus ODBC and Its Higher-Level APIs

Table 40.1 shows a feature comparison of the interfaces. As a general rule, if your main concern is speed, look to the lower-level interfaces; if your main concern is portability and ease of development, look to the higher-level interfaces. (Chapters 42 and 43 provide specific programming examples that show what's involved in using the various interfaces.)

Table 40.1. Comparison of data access options.

← Easier to Program, More Portable

Faster Performance, Harder to Program →

Feature	DAO	RDO	ODBC API	VBSQL
Types of cursors supported	dynaset, snapshot	keyset, dynamic, static, and forward only	keyset, dynamic, static, and forward only	keyset, dynamic, static, and forward only
Automatic background population of cursors while users work	Yes, using the Jet data	Yes, using the remote data control and asynchronous mode of RDO	No	No
Asynchronous queries	No	Yes	Yes	Yes
Support for Microsoft SQL Server server-side cursors	No	Yes	Yes	Yes
Row access without cursors	Yes	Yes	Yes	Yes
Result set caching	Yes	Yes	Yes	No
Stored procedures (SP)	Yes, with SQLPassThrough	Yes, with singleton execution or in batches	Yes, with singleton execution or in batches	Yes, with singleton execution or in batches
SP results	Yes	Yes	Yes	Yes
SP output parameters	No	Yes	Yes	Yes
SP result codes	No	Yes	Yes	Yes

continues

Table 40.1. continued

← Easier to Program, More Portable
Faster Performance, Harder to Program →

Feature	DAO	RDO	ODBC API	VBSQL
Support for multiple SQL statements in batches	Yes, with SQLPassThrough	Yes	Yes	Yes
Error handler	Populate the errors collection and raise trappable error	Populate rdoErrors collection and raise trappable error	After function returns SQL_ERROR call process SQLError to retrieve error	Use VBX or OCX error and message event; error based on values passed to event
Retry/continue after query timeout	No	Yes (in asynchronous mode)	Yes (in asynchronous mode)	Yes (in asynchronous mode)
Complex data type	Automatic through bound controls and programmable	Automatic through bound controls and programmable	Programmable	Programmable
Access to bound controls	Yes	Yes	No	No
Heterogeneous joins from multiple databases	Yes	Yes	No	No

Programming Tools

Thus far, this chapter has mentioned only two tools that can be used to build SQL Server applications: Microsoft Visual Basic and Microsoft Visual C++. But many other development tools and desktop applications can be used to access SQL Server.

These tools fall into one of three categories:

- Visual programming tools (sometimes called *rapid application development tools*)
- Language (compiler) tools
- Data-aware desktop applications and reporting tools

Visual Programming Tools

The visual programming tools reduce the need to understand hefty SDKs or APIs. With these tools, many operating-system-related issues are hidden from the developer. More time can be focused on writing the application, and less time digging through manuals or other laborious tasks. Here are some examples of visual programming tools and their features:

- Microsoft Visual Basic 3.0/4.0 Professional Edition provides DAO controls; the Enterprise Edition adds the RDO/RDC controls. Based on Visual Basic scripting language. Includes Crystal Reports, a tool used to create custom reports from databases and then integrate them into your application.

- Powersoft's PowerBuilder provides robustness similar to that found in mission-critical mainframe applications. Provides an integrated data dictionary. Price/performance considerations should be noted for the Enterprise version, as its price targets Fortune 1000 companies (thousands of dollars more, compared to Microsoft Visual Basic). Uses the object-oriented programming paradigm.

- Borland's Delphi is based on the Object Pascal programming language. Can create standalone EXEs and DLLs. Also includes a data dictionary similar to that of PowerBuilder.

Language Compiler Tools

Several language compiler tools are available, most of which are C/C++ compilers. They include Microsoft Visual C/C++, Borland C++, Symantec C++, and Watcom C/C++. All of these have MFC library support, although you need Microsoft's MFC Version 4.1 to use the DAO classes. Each has a variation of database support as part of its features. Because C/C++ is for the most part a standard language, each product can best be compared based on its development environment features and other bells and whistles. If you have access to the SDKs and APIs (ODBC, DB-Library), any of these tools can get the job done, with varying degrees of success.

> **TIP**
>
> Many developers are religious about one vendor or one language, so go with what you know.

Data-Aware Desktop Applications and Reporting Tools

The final group includes data-aware desktop applications and report generators. By *desktop applications*, I mean products such as those found in Microsoft Office. Microsoft Access is unique in that it transcends several of the groupings I have outlined. It could fall into the rapid application development group, the report generation group, and the general desktop application group. You can use it for simple data access, creating sophisticated reports, or creating sophisticated applications.

One major milestone in the history of Microsoft Office was the introduction of Visual Basic for Applications. If you have a working knowledge of Visual Basic, it can be applied to any of the applications in the Office suite. Microsoft Excel is database-aware as well; you can populate cells with ODBC and DAO data sources, or write Visual Basic code that creates reports in Excel.

In addition to Microsoft Access, several other reporting tools are worth mentioning:

- Visual Basic ships with Crystal Reports, which enables you to integrate reports right into any Visual Basic (or VBA) application. The standalone version, Crystal Reports Professional, contains a report builder that can be used by developers or end users.

- Microsoft Query ships with several products, including Microsoft Office, and several SDKs. It has a query builder similar to that in Microsoft Access. One feature of this tool is that it is practically free.

- Other available reporting and query tools include Forest and Trees, Monarch, Intersolv's DataDirect Explorer, and many others that I am sure I've missed.

> **NOTE**
>
> Chapter 41 shows an example of an Access database connecting to SQL Server, in the discussion on creating ODBC data sources.
>
> For a more comprehensive description of the report-generation features of Microsoft Access or Microsoft Excel, see *Microsoft Office 95 Unleashed*, SAMS Publishing, ISBN 0-672-30819-3.

Summary

This chapter has provided some background on the various client interfaces and APIs available. After you have decided which path suits your development needs, you may want to look to the following chapters:

- To understand what files are needed for various interfaces, see Chapter 41, "Planning for SQL Server Applications." This chapter discusses how to install and configure the interfaces discussed thus far. It also provides insights on various operating system configuration issues and networking issues.

- Programming examples and development topics are covered in depth in Chapter 42, "DB-Library Programming for SQL Server," and Chapter 43, "ODBC Programming for SQL Server."

- Useful data is a key element to comparing and benchmarking your development options. See Chapter 4, "Introduction to Transact-SQL," for a discussion on the pubs database. The CD for this book includes a larger database example for use in later chapters: the bigpubs database.

Planning for SQL Server Applications

41

1058

Before you embark on writing applications for SQL Server, the client machine must have the SQL Server interfaces properly installed, and must meet some minimum requirements. In addition, some issues should be considered on how your clients will connect to SQL Server via your network. These considerations include what type of processing should be done on the client as opposed to being done on the server. This chapter delves into these issues.

Installing Client Interfaces

There are no minimum requirements for the client's hardware, other than those outlined by the operating system and the requirements your software will impose. Several operating systems can connect to SQL Server, including MS-DOS, Windows 3.1, Windows 95 and Windows NT.

You can run a DB-Library application on any of the operating systems just mentioned. This portability between operating systems is considered one of the strong points of this library.

> **NOTE**
>
> To try the examples in Chapters 42 and 43 ("DB-Library Programming for SQL Server" and "ODBC Programming for SQL Server," respectively), you need Windows 95 or Windows NT, as well as Visual Basic 4.0. If you want to try the RDO examples in Chapter 43, you need Visual Basic 4.0 Enterprise Edition.

You have two methods available to install the SQL Server client components:

- Run the Setup program appropriate for your operating system
- Distribute the required components with your application and register them properly

If you run \I386\SETUP.EXE from your SQL Server distribution CD-ROM, you have the option to set up SQL Server or the client utilities.

> **NOTE**
>
> When you run SETUP.EXE from the SQL Server CD-ROM on Windows NT, it will give you the option to install SQL Server and/or the client utilities. If you run SETUP.EXE on a Windows 95 client, you have only the option to install/uninstall the client utilities. This is an appropriate behavior, because SQL Server itself runs only on Windows NT.

Running SETUP.EXE from the SQL server CD-ROM is probably the approach you'll take for the workstation on which you intend to develop, because it also installs other utilities such as BCP, ISQL/w, Enterprise Manager, Security Manager, Microsoft Query, and SQL Trace. One component that's always installed is the SQL Client Configuration Utility, which is discussed later in this chapter.

When you use this approach to set up the SQL Server client components, it installs DB-Library components, Net-Library components, and ODBC components.

If you want to install the client components for MS-DOS or Win16, look in the CLIENTS directory on the SQL Server distribution CD. When you run \CLIENTS\WIN16\setup.exe, you can install the Win16 version of ISQL/w and all the 16-bit DB-Library and Net-Library components. You also will find an ODBC setup application in \CLIENTS\WIN16\ODBC.

MS-DOS implements the DB-Library as a TSR (terminate-and-stay-resident program). The DB-Library components are found in \CLIENTS\MSDOS\. To use these interfaces, you need to load them during startup (in the AUTOEXEC.BAT file), or just before you start your DB-Library application.

> **WARNING**
>
> Only one TSR can be loaded at a time. You need to know which Net-Library protocols are supported by your SQL Server, and choose from only one of these on your MS-DOS clients.

Configuring DB-Library and ODBC

After the client interfaces are installed, a few steps are required to configure your client in order to connect successfully to SQL Server. The following sections describe the steps involved.

Using the Client Configuration Utility

The most straightforward method of configuring your client is to use the Client Configuration Utility, which was installed when you ran the SQL Server client setup. Although this method isn't suitable for configuring all the workstations that will be using your client applications, it's a good starting point for this discussion.

The DBLibrary tab in the Client Configuration Utility window displays the DB-Library version and allows you to select default behavior configurations. For example, the Automatic ANSI to OEM option converts characters from OEM to ANSI when communicating to SQL Server, and from ANSI to OEM when the server returns results to the client. The Use International Settings option is available on Win32 clients only. Enabling this option allows DB-Library to retrieve date, time, and currency formats from the client system, as opposed to relying on hard-coded formatting.

The Net Library tab (shown in Figure 41.1) lets you specify the default Net-Library protocol (Named Pipes, Multi-Protocol, NWLink IPX/SPX, TCP/IP Sockets, Banyan VINES). When selecting one of the libraries, you also can get information on its version and the DLL path.

FIGURE 41.1.

The Client Configuration Utility enables you to set up the default behavior for DB-Library and Net-Library, as well as the behavior for specific connections.

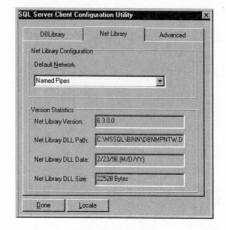

The configuration settings determine the default settings used when any connection is made to SQL Server. If you need to connect to various servers using different libraries, click the Advanced tab (see Figure 41.2). These options let you assign connection information to server names that you provide.

FIGURE 41.2.

The advanced options in the Client Configuration Utility allow you to specify specific connection information for various servers.

The example in Figure 41.2 shows that two servers have been configured with specific connection information. SERVER2 has been configured to use the Multi-Protocol (RPC) Net-Library. The connection string is an alternative pipe to connect to this server. WAN_SERVER has been configured to use TCP/IP Sockets, and connects to the server with an IP address of 191.50.90.50 on port 1433. Port 1433 is the default port that SQL Server listens to for connections over

TCP/IP. The "Networking Considerations" section of this chapter shows how these settings are applied to real-world scenarios.

> **TIP**
>
> For Windows-based clients, ODBC uses the settings you provide with the Client Configuration Utility. Any server names you supply in the Advanced section of the utility also are available when you configure ODBC data sources.

Configuring Clients Automatically

The SQL Server utilities provide a graphical method to configure the needs of a client workstation. Chances are that you need to distribute your application on a larger scale; you shouldn't be expected to configure each workstation manually, as shown with the Client Configuration Utility.

To configure your application automatically, either with a batch file for a DOS client or a setup script for a Windows client, you need to know where the configuration settings are. Many setup tools (for example, Install Shield, WISE Installation, and the Visual Basic Setup Wizard) are capable of creating the appropriate Registry entries under Win32, altering .INI files under Win16, and altering AUTOEXEC.BAT files under DOS. Look to these types of tools to aid in deploying your application.

Each operating system requires the settings to be found in a specific location, as described in the following sections.

Windows 95 and Windows NT Clients

These operating systems use the Registry database. You need to use the Win32 Registry API or an installation tool to ensure that the proper keys are installed into the Registry:

HKEY_LOCAL_MACHINE\SOFTWARE\Microsoft\MSSQLServer\Client\ConnectTo

HKEY_LOCAL_MACHINE\SOFTWARE\Microsoft\MSSQLServer\Client\DB-Lib

HKEY_LOCAL_MACHINE\SOFTWARE\Microsoft\MSSQLServer\Client\PrefServers

As you can see, there are three keys under Client: ConnectTo, DB-Lib, and PrefServers. Figure 41.3 shows an example of the ConnectTo key. The entries reflect the configurations made earlier in this chapter with the Client Configuration Utility:

- The DSQUERY entry is used for default connections.
- The DB-Lib key holds the AutoToAnsiOem and the UseIntlSettings options.
- The PrefServers key holds the name of the server to which connection dialog boxes default.

FIGURE 41.3.

The Registry entries shown here are the result of using the Client Configuration Utility.

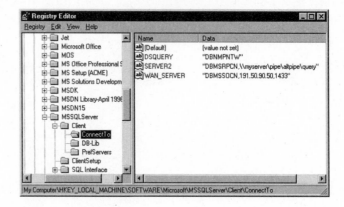

16-Bit Windows Clients

Windows 3.1 and 3.11 use .INI text files for configuration information. The entries for SQL Server are found in WIN.INI. The entries in the [SQLSERVER] section of WIN.INI have the following format:

```
logical_name = Net-Library_Name[,network_specific_ parameters]
```

MS-DOS Clients

The Net-Library TSR must be loaded before running your DB-Library application. MS-DOS environment variables are used to set network connection information. The format looks like this:

```
set logical_name = network_specific_parameters
```

For example:

```
set SERVER1 = \\myserver\pipe\altpipe\query
```

Configuring Clients for ODBC

As with the DB-Library installation, there are two ways to set up ODBC:

- Run the ODBC setup application that comes with SQL Server.
- Install the appropriate DLLs and create the configuration entries in the Win32 Registry, or in .INI files for 16-bit Windows.

Regardless of which method you choose, you still need to create a Data Source Name (DSN) that maps to your SQL Server box. These DSNs enable ODBC applications to connect to data sources with a single connection string. In the case of SQL Server, the DSN maps the ODBC connection to the appropriate server, uses the required Net-Library, and uses any alternate

Net-Library connection strings that have been set up. Figure 41.4 shows the DSN `SQLBigPubs` being created.

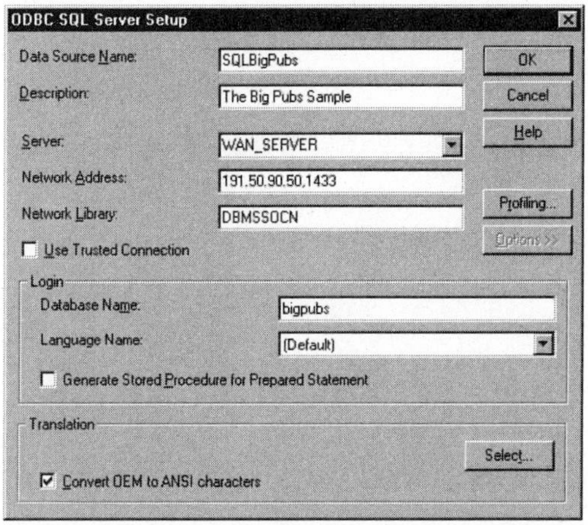

FIGURE 41.4.

The ODBC Control Panel applet enables you to create Data Source Names that map to SQL Server connections.

NOTE

The `SQLBigPubs` DSN is used later in this chapter, as well as in Chapter 43. It's important that you understand how to configure this ODBC data source before attempting the related examples. Before you can point an ODBC DSN to the `bigpubs` database, you should install and run the scripts that build the `bigpubs` database on your server. Look to the inside back cover of this book for CD-ROM installation, as well as to any `readme` files on the CD-ROM.

If you don't want to install this database on your server, possibly due to space considerations, you can point the ODBC DSN to the `pubs` database. The `pubs` database is installed by default when SQL Server is installed. The only drawback is that the `bigpubs` database has a larger set of data than `pubs`, and provides better benchmarking comparisons for the chapters to follow.

To manually configure an ODBC DSN, use the ODBC Administrator found in the Windows Control Panel. (The example in Figure 41.4 is using the `WAN_SERVER` created earlier in this chapter for the DB-Library configuration. Your server name should be used in place of this example server name.) This example shows how the DB-Library configuration is carried over to the ODBC environment.

If you don't need to specify a network address or network library, leave these settings set to `(default)` to use the default Net-Library settings. The default settings imply that ODBC will use the settings enforced earlier in the DB-Library configuration. It also implies that the server name can be enumerated over the network without an alternate connection string. Later in this chapter, we discuss how network name resolution occurs.

To configure your ODBC data sources automatically, without the ODBC Control Panel applet, configure either the Registry or .INI file, based on your target operating system. The following sections outline the necessary settings required for this process. (These sections include Windows clients only, as DOS clients don't support ODBC. For DOS-only clients, look to DB-Library programming, as described in Chapter 42.)

Windows 95 and Windows NT Clients

As with the DB-Library configurations, the ODBC settings just created can be found in the following keys:

```
HKEY_CURRENT_USER\Software\ODBC\ODBC.INI\ODBC Data Sources
```

```
HKEY_CURRENT_USER\Software\ODBC\ODBC.INI\SQLBigPubs
```

The ODBC Data Sources key lists all the DSNs that you have created. Each DSN that you create has its own Registry key, as in the SQLBigPubs key. The SQLBigPubs key holds information such as the server name, the ODBC driver DLL to use, and the default SQL Server database to use after the connection is established. In our example, we want the SQLBigPubs DSN to log onto the bigpubs database by default.

The ODBC installation also creates entries under the following key:

```
HKEY_LOCAL_MACHINE\SOFTWARE\ODBC\ODBCINST.INI
```

This Registry entry lists which ODBC drivers have been installed and the directory path required to find each driver.

Windows 3.1 and 3.11

The same types of entries found in the Win32 Registry are located in matching .INI files under 16-bit Windows. Here's a sample of the ODBC.INI file with the SQLBigPubs DSN already configured:

```
[ODBC Data Sources]
MS Access Databases=Access Data (*.mdb)
SQLBigPubs=SQL Server

[MS Access Databases]
Driver=C:\WINDOWS\SYSTEM\SIMBA.DLL
FileType=RedISAM
SingleUser=False
UseSystemDB=False

[SQLBigPubs]
Driver=C:\WINDOWS\SYSTEM\sqlsrvr.dll
Description=The Big Pubs Sample
Server=SERVER1
UseProcForPrepare=Yes
Database=bigpubs
```

```
OEMTOANSI=No
Trusted_Connection=
(c)LastUser=
```

The `ODBCINST.INI` has the following entries:

```
[ODBC Drivers]
SQL Server=Installed

[SQL Server]
Driver=C:\WINDOWS\SYSTEM\sqlsrvr.dll
Setup=C:\WINDOWS\SYSTEM\sqlsrvr.dll
APILevel=2
ConnectFunctions=YYY
DriverODBCVer=02.50
FileUsage=0
SQLLevel=1
```

Networking Considerations

The network is the link between your client application and the server. You must put some thought into your SQL Server application development strategy if the application will run on a large corporate LAN (local area network), and even more so if it will run across a WAN (wide area network).

As the size of the network increases, more emphasis needs to be put on reducing the amount of network traffic that your application creates. When a WAN is involved, you may be faced with slow network connections, and you may need to weigh the advantages of client-side versus server-side processing.

Protocols such as NetBEUI and IPX/SPX implement a browsing scheme to find computers on the network. Named Pipes, Multi-Protocol, and NWLink are the Net-Libraries that use these network protocols, and thus don't necessarily require additional network connection string information to find the correct server. In the real world, however, you may not always be able to get away with using NetBEUI and IPX/SPX protocols on your network. Large networks and WANS usually involve a routable protocol.

When you don't use a routable protocol, network broadcasts are made across your entire network when a computer name needs to be found. NetBEUI is the "chattiest" of all the protocols. IPX/SPX is routable, yet still tends to be more "chatty" than TCP/IP.

A brief description of routable protocols is in order here. With a routable protocol, each computer on the network has a unique identifier. Let's take TCP/IP as an example. In the sample DB-Library configuration created earlier in the chapter, we set up a server named WAN_SERVER, with an IP address of 191.50.90.50. SQL Server is running on an NT machine that has its network address set to this value. When SQL was installed on this server, TCP/IP Sockets was enabled to be one of the available protocols. When you use an alternate connect string (also called the Network Address in the ODBC configuration dialog boxes), you are bypassing the need to browse the network in order to find the computer name. A routable network moves packets around, shipping them in the right direction as it progresses toward its final destination.

Figure 41.5 shows how the packets intended for the Chicago office get routed directly to the correct location, while no network traffic is created across the telecommunications link when the packets are intended for the Minneapolis segment.

FIGURE 41.5.

A routable protocol reduces the network traffic by moving packets to the desired location, and eliminates the need for broadcasts to be made to other portions of the network.

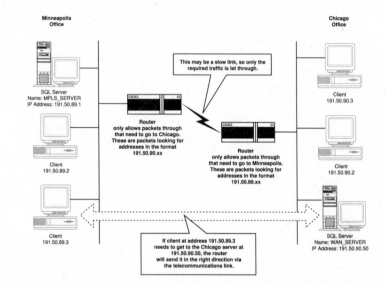

Our DB-Library and ODBC configuration examples use a network address rather than a server name to connect to the Chicago office's SQL server at 191.50.90.50. Connecting with a specific address eliminates the need to look up a server and fulfills the desire to reduce network traffic. Another benefit gained from this method is a decrease in the time required for the client application to connect to the server. The decrease occurs because you eliminate the name-resolving step.

You can use server names in a routable protocol, and thus not need network addresses in your DB-Library and ODBC configurations. For a TCP/IP network, this strategy usually involves setting up the Windows Internet Name Service (WINS) on one of your NT Servers. After it's installed, you can browse a TCP/IP network just as you can a NetBEUI network.

This overview of a routable network architecture is by no means complete. You should work closely with your network administrator to determine how to apply the client configuration options explored thus far. Because of the complexities of routable networks, they should be considered a solution only for large networks. Gaining performance for your SQL Server application isn't reason enough to switch, because of the maintenance required for such a network. Other approaches are available to optimize your network resources.

In addition to optimizing your network architecture as described here, you may want to look at where some of your processing is done, either on the client or the server. The following section presents some ideas on how to improve performance through various programming techniques.

Client-Based Processing versus Server-Based Processing

During your client application development process, you should be aware of opportunities where performing client-based processing could increase the performance of your application.

Determining which components of your application benefit from either client- or server-based processing is a case-by-case situation. Sometimes server-based processing reduces network traffic, and sometimes client-based processing reduces network traffic.

Server-based processing should be considered in cases where large amounts of data would otherwise need to be moved across the network—for example, when using a report writer on the client that performs sums on groups of data. If the client needs to group the data and perform the aggregate functions, it requires that all of the data be sent up to the client. In this case, you may want to create a stored procedure that the report can call. With a stored procedure, the server can perform the grouping and aggregate functions, and then return only the data required to complete the report.

Reducing network traffic with client-based processing is also possible. Consider a table on the server that remains fairly static, such as state or country codes. Rather than accessing these tables every time the data needs to be cross-referenced, you may want to retrieve it only once, at application startup. You could use a local client lookup table or an array, if the size of the data is within reason. A client-based approach may also make your application more responsive. Consider how sluggish an application might become if every list box on the screen was populated from a server-side table. Every time the form or dialog box was loaded, the user would be required to wait for the server to respond to the client's request. In the case of the state or country codes mentioned earlier, you could retrieve the data for the list boxes once by storing them in an array. This approach would make the application more responsive.

Network traffic isn't the only issue involved. Server-side processing eliminates redundant code and provides a central location to enforce business rules. Take for instance a report that totals the sales of each bookstore in the `bigpubs` sample database. These sales are then totaled by region. The Central District might comprise Wisconsin, Minnesota, and Illinois. Using these states as a basis for the Central District, you then distribute this report to all the users of your application. What would happen if your company suddenly decided that the Central District was now also going to include Iowa? Using a client-side approach would mean re-creating the report code and redistributing it to your users.

Had this report been based on a stored procedure, you could change it in just one central location—the server. With the new criteria in place, every user would see the new report being generated with the inclusion of Iowa, and it would have required a change to only one line of code in your stored procedure.

To demonstrate the Central District sales report scenario just described, a Microsoft Access database has been included on the CD-ROM that accompanies this publication. The database contains two reports: one that demonstrates client-side processing, and one that demonstrates server-side processing. This database also gives you a chance to test the ODBC Data Source Name configured earlier (SQLBigPubs). Make sure that you have this ODBC source configured with the name of your SQL server, and that you have run the scripts necessary to build the bigpubs sample database.

This Microsoft Access database was created by linking to the SQL Server tables via ODBC. Each of the tables from the bigpubs database is linked as a remote table. The database contains two query objects: Central District Net Sales, and SP Central Sales. Central District Net Sales is a query built locally with Access. It performs the following query:

```
SELECT DISTINCTROW dbo_stores.stor_name AS ["Store Name"],
[dbo_sales].[qty]*[dbo_titles].[price] AS ["Title Sales"], dbo_stores.state
FROM (dbo_titles INNER JOIN dbo_sales ON dbo_titles.title_id =
dbo_sales.title_id) INNER JOIN dbo_stores ON dbo_sales.stor_id =
dbo_stores.stor_id
WHERE (((dbo_stores.state) In ("MN","WI","IL")))
GROUP BY dbo_stores.stor_name, [dbo_sales].[qty]*[dbo_titles].[price],
dbo_stores.state
ORDER BY dbo_stores.state;
```

The SP Central Sales query is a SQL Passthrough query defined as follows:

```
execute CentralSales
```

This calls a stored procedure defined in the bigpubs database on SQL Server. To create this stored procedure, you must run the following SQL script with either Enterprise Manager or ISQL/w:

```
USE bigpubs
go
CREATE PROCEDURE CentralSales AS
SELECT stores.stor_name AS Store_Name,
Sum(sales.qty*titles.price) AS Net_Sales,
stores.state
FROM sales, stores, titles
WHERE sales.stor_id = stores.stor_id
AND stores.state In ("MN", "WI", "IL")
AND titles.title_id = sales.title_id
GROUP BY stores.stor_name, stores.state
ORDER BY stores.state
GO
```

Two Access report objects are already created as well: Client Based Central District Report, and Server Based Central District Report. The client-based Central District report is based on the Access query, and performs all the summary calculations on the client (in this case, your Microsoft Access application). The server-based Central District report calls the SQL Passthrough query. In this case, the server performs the calculations, and returns only the summary values to the client. Run both of these reports, and then compare the results. Unless you're running SQL Server on hardware that is better suited as a paperweight, the server-based report should be created much more quickly than the client-based report.

To demonstrate how business rules can be centralized on the server, you can carry out the scenario presented earlier, in which the publishing company decided to add Iowa to the Central District. In this case, you need to change only one line of your stored procedure:

```
AND stores.state In ("MN", "WI", "IL")
```

would become:

```
AND stores.state In ("MN", "WI", "IL", "IA")
```

Now everybody who runs the Central District report from the server sees Iowa as part of the results. Another report, Server Based Central District Report with Graph, is included in the Access database, so that you can easily see states as they are added and removed. The graph at the top of the report shows a pie chart, giving a summary of the total net sales for each state.

Summary

To create a successful connection to SQL Server, you need to configure your DB-Library and/or ODBC client settings as outlined in this chapter. When considering Net-Library options, be sure to take into account the size of your network and the amount of network traffic that your SQL Server application might impose on it.

This chapter also outlined some methods to improve your application's responsiveness by using client-side processing when appropriate, or server-side processing when appropriate.

At this point, you should have a working ODBC connection to the bigpubs database. Chapter 43 uses this connection extensively.

DB-Library
Programming for
SQL Server

42

This chapter creates a simple query application with DB-Library. Specifically, we'll use the Visual Basic VBSQL control. Many of the concepts presented are applicable to C programming as well; the only difference is the syntax used for each DB-Library function call, and a few functions that aren't supported in Visual Basic.

Getting Started

To run the samples listed in this chapter, you need Visual Basic 4.0, the DB-Library control VBSQL.OCX, and a connection to SQL Server, with the bigpubs database installed. The bigpubs database is located on the CD-ROM that accompanies this book. Please refer to the CD-ROM installation information on the inside back cover of the book.

> **NOTE**
>
> Test your connection to SQL Server before trying the sample code. With one of the client utilities that ships with SQL Server, verify that you have a working connection, and that the Net-Library components are working.

DB-Library Documentation and Resources

The SQL Server Books Online contain the most up-to-date information on DB-Library programming. In addition, you may want to subscribe to the Microsoft Developers Library Level 2, which provides in-depth coverage of every Windows API and SDK available, including DB-Library. In addition, the BackOffice SDK gives you access to online references related to all of the BackOffice components.

Comparing VBSQL to DB-Library Programming in C

Most of the Visual Basic DB-Library functions directly map to a similar C DB-Library function. The only difference is the prefix for the functions. The VBSQL functions all start with SQL and the C functions start with db. For example, the VBSQL function SQLLogin maps to dblogin in C. The concepts you learn in this chapter can easily be applied to C programming.

The DB-Library in C provides a few functions not available in Visual Basic. dbaltbind, dbbind, dbconvert and dbwillconvert are available only as C functions. These functions allow your program variables to be bound to a result column. Every time a new row is fetched, program variables will be updated with the data in the bound column. Chapter 43, "ODBC Programming for SQL Server," looks at alternatives in Visual Basic that allow data bound controls. The two-phase commit functions aren't available in VBSQL.

Portability of Your DB-Library Code

Both VBSQL and C applications can be ported easily between 16-bit and 32-bit if a few guidelines are followed.

In Visual Basic, the 16-bit DB-Library functions might use type-declaration characters in their declarations. The majority of the functions either return a string or an integer. For example, SQLOpenConnection% returns an integer (thus the % type-declaration character). In 32-bit VBSQL, all the parameters and return values that were previously integers are now of type *long*—a long integer is a variable stored as a signed 32-bit (4-byte) number. If you're starting out with 16-bit VBSQL, you may want to avoid using type-declaration characters throughout your code. You'll be able to change your code in one location, the function declarations, when it comes time to port between 16-bit and 32-bit.

TIP

Visual Basic 4.0 allows conditional compilation. You can wrap your 16-bit and 32-bit declarations in an #If...Then...#Else statement as follows:

```
#If Win32 Then
Declare Function SqlOpenConnection Lib "VBSQL.OCX" (Server As String,_
➥LoginID As String, Pwd As String, WorkStation As String,_
➥Application As String) As Long

#Else
Declare Function SqlOpenConnection Lib "VBSQL.VBX" (Server As String,_
➥LoginID As String, Pwd As String, WorkStation As String,_
➥Application As String) As Integer

#End If
```

Before creating the executable file, choose Tools | Options, click the Advanced tab in the Options dialog box, and enter an argument, such as Win32=-1, in the Conditional Compilation Arguments field. This action will cause the Win32 directive to return True.

Two C DB-Library functions, dbprhead and dbprrow, aren't supported in 16-bit Windows because they send output to STDIO, but are supported in the Win32 API and can be used when developing applications for the console subsystem. These functions provide a convenient way to send results to the default output device. If these functions aren't used, you should be able to link in either the 16-bit or 32-bit library.

Sample Application

With VBSQL, you can build a simple, yet powerful query utility. This sample application will provide functionality similar to that of the ISQL/w utility that ships with SQL Server. All VBSQL applications that send queries and retrieve results perform a common sequence of functions:

1. Initialize VBSQL with SqlInit.
2. Allocate a login structure with SqlLogin.
3. Connect to SQL Server with the login structure, using SqlOpen.
4. Send a query, using SqlCmd.
5. Execute the query, using SqlExec or a combination of SqlSend and SQLOk.
6. Process the results with SqlResults, and retrieve the rows for each result with SqlNextRow.
7. Close the connection with SqlClose or close all SQL Server connections with SqlExit; then release the memory referenced by VBSQL with SqlWinExit.

With our VBSQL test application, the following sections examine each of these functions, discussing the enhancements and error handlers that have been implemented.

Initializing VBSQL and the Error Handlers

A call to SqlInit is used to prepare Visual Basic to use DB-Library. It also initializes the error handlers that you've provided in your code. The VBSQL control has only two events—Error and Message. These events allow you to capture errors from DB-Library and messages returned from SQL Server. These may include informational messages that shouldn't be treated as severe errors, or syntax error messages returned from SQL Server.

There are two informational messages that we'll always ignore in our sample application: 5701 and 5703. Message 5701 simply informs you that the query caused the database context to change, as in USE pubs. SQL Server supports multiple languages; message 5703 indicates that the language setting has changed, and isn't a severe error.

In addition to SQL Server-generated messages, you can generate your own informative messages to be returned to the user. For example, if you use the print command in a query, it will generate a message that's captured in the VBSQL message handler.

Listing 42.1 shows the VBSQL initialization code and the error handlers.

Listing 42.1. The VBSQL initialization code and error handlers.

```
Sub Main()
    'Initialize VBSQL.
    Dim strReturn As String
```

```
    strReturn = SqlInit()
    If strReturn = "" Then
       MsgBox "VBSQL could not be initialized."
       End
    End If

    frmLogin.Show
End Sub

Private Sub Vbsql1_Error(ByVal SqlConn As Long, ByVal Severity As Long,
ByVal ErrorNum As Long, _
➡    ByVal ErrorStr As String, ByVal OSErrorNum As Long, ByVal OSErrorStr As
String,_
➡    RetCode As Long)

    MsgBox ("DB-Library Error: " + Str$(ErrorNum) + " " + OSErrorStr)
End Sub

Private Sub VBSQL1_Message(ByVal SqlConn As Long, ByVal Message As Long,
ByVal State As Long, _
➡    ByVal Severity As Long, ByVal MsgStr As String, ByVal ServerNameStr
As String, _
➡    ByVal ProcNameStr As String, ByVal Line As Long)
    ' It is common practice to ignore the following messages
    ' Message 5701, Changed database context to '%.*s'.
    ' Message 5703, Changed language setting to '%.*s'.
    ' They are informative, and should not be dealt with as fatal errors

    If Message <> 5701 And Message <> 5703 Then
        MsgBox ("SQL Server Message: " + IIF(Message = 0, "", Str$(Message))
+ " " + MsgStr)
    End If
End Sub
```

Opening a Connection to SQL Server

When a connection is established with SQL Server, you need to pass a login structure, along with the name of the server to which you're connecting. To create a login structure, you use the SqlLogin function. This will return a pointer to a structure that can be passed to several other functions, which can supply values to the structure. These functions include all of the following:

- SqlSetLUser. Supplies the login (user) ID.
- SqlSetLPwd. Supplies the user's password. The password is required only if the user has a password on SQL Server.
- SqlSetLHost. Supplies the workstation name. The workstation name is useful when viewing a server's current activity. The activity monitor (in Enterprise Manager) shows the user name, computer name, and application name.
- SqlSetLApp. Supplies the application name. Like SqlSetLHost, this information is useful when monitoring current server activity. It also may be useful when tracing events logged by SQL Server.

■ SqlSetLNatLang. Supplies the national language preferred.

■ SqlSetLPacket. Supplies the TDS packet size. For large data transfers, such as bulk copies, increasing the packet size may improve network efficiency because fewer reads and writes need to be performed. If you want to increase the packet size, stick with a range between 4092 and 8192.

■ SqlSetLSecure. Requests a secure connection.

■ SqlSetLVersion. Sets DB-Library 6 behavior. If this function isn't called, DB-Library will default to Version 4.2 behavior.

■ SqlBCPSetL. Enables bulk copy operations. By default, SQL Server connections aren't enabled for bulk copy operations.

After the login structure has been allocated with SqlLogin, it's passed to SqlOpen with the name of the server to which you're attempting to connect. The sample application adds an enhancement to this process by enumerating the available servers and presenting them in a combo box. The function SqlServerEnum enumerates the available servers on the network, or those configured locally. This function returns a string that contains all the servers found, and separates them with NULL. A special Visual Basic function needed to be written to parse out the server names, and you'll see this done in FindNullInString.

Once the connection is established, the value returned from SqlOpen is stored in the global variable SqlConn. This connection value is passed to all subsequent DB-Library functions. Listing 42.2 shows this login and connection sequence in Visual Basic.

Listing 42.2. This code shows how to log in to SQL Server and create a connection.

```
Private Sub cmdLogin_Click()
    'Get a Login record and set login attributes.
    Dim Login As Long
    Dim strLoginID As String, strPwd As String, strServer As String

    Login = SqlLogin()
    strLoginID = txtLoginID.Text
    strPwd = txtPassword.Text

    Result = SqlSetLUser(Login, strLoginID)
    Result = SqlSetLPwd(Login, strPwd)
    Result = SqlSetLApp(Login, "VBSL Sample")

    'Get a connection for communicating with SQL Server.
    strServer = cbServerName.Text
    SqlConn = SqlOpen(Login, strServer)
    If (SqlConn <> 0) Then
     Unload Me
     frmQuery.Show
    End If
End Sub
```

Sending a Query

The command `SqlCmd` fills the command buffer with the query that needs to be sent to SQL Server. Once the buffer holds the query text, one of two methods can be used to execute the query: synchronous or asynchronous.

The synchronous method is the easiest to code, as it uses only the one command `SqlExec`. The downside to this method is that control isn't returned to your application until SQL Server has completed the query. The function `SqlSetTime` is used to set the number of seconds DB-Library will wait for SQL Server responses.

> **WARNING**
>
> `SqlSetTime` by default is set to an infinite timeout. If the timeout value isn't changed, `SqlExec` has the potential of hanging forever. It may be wise to reduce the timeout period with `SqlSetTime`, or use the asynchronous method.

The asynchronous method pairs up the functions `SqlSend` and `SqlOk`. `SqlSend` starts the query and immediately returns control to your application. You then need to call `SqlDataReady` to determine that SQL Server has finished processing your request. At this time, you need to call `SqlOk`, which checks the correctness of the batch, and allows further processing of the results. Listing 42.3 shows how to use the `SqlDataReady` function in a loop, which gives the user feedback as the query executes, and allows him to cancel the query at any time. If the query is canceled, a call to `SqlCancel` must be made to free the connection and stop the current batch. If this isn't done, you receive the DB-Library error `10038 Results Pending` whenever you attempt to call another DB-Library function.

Listing 42.3 shows the portion of the code executed when the user sends a query. Notice that the code is using the asynchronous method, and is periodically checking for data readiness. The asynchronous method shown here uses a global variable `bStop` (Boolean) that is set to TRUE when the user selects the Stop button.

Listing 42.3. Executed when the user sends a query.

```
'Put the command into the command buffer.
   sSql = txtSQL.Text
   Result = SqlCmd(SqlConn, sSql)

   'Send the command to SQL Server and start execution.
#If 0 Then ' this waits until SQL Server returns results
   Result = SqlExec(SqlConn)
#Else    ' this will allow user input as it waits for SQL Server results
   nWait = 0
   txtWait = ""
```

continues

Listing 42.3. continued

```
    Result = SqlSend(SqlConn)
    While SqlDataReady(SqlConn) = 0
        DoEvents    ' Allow user to stop query
        If bStop Then
            SqlCancel (SqlConn)
            GoTo Exit_Query
        End If
        txtWait = "Waiting ." + String(nWait, ".")
        nWait = nWait + 1
        If nWait > 5 Then nWait = 0
    Wend
    Result = SqlOk(SqlConn)
    If Result <> SUCCEED Then GoTo Exit_Query
#End If
```

You'll have to run a query that takes a measurable amount of time to execute in order to see the asynchronous method in action. Try calling the CentralSales stored procedure created in Chapter 41, "Planning for SQL Server Applications." In the query window, type the following and then click the Execute button:

```
USE bigpubs
execute CentralSales
```

As the stored procedure runs, the animated Waiting text gives you feedback that the query is executing. At any time, selecting the Stop button cancels the query.

Retrieving the Results

Once the query has executed, DB-Library will have pending results to return to your application. You must either retrieve all results, or call SqlCancel. The procedure for retrieving results, and the rows of each result, are common to most DB-Library applications. The flow chart in Figure 42.1 shows how the sample application processes results returned to DB-Library. This order of operations can be applied to other DB-Library applications as well.

When looking at the flow chart in Figure 42.1, you see that the outer loop is making calls to SqlResults until it returns NOMORERESULTS. This is necessary because a query batch may return several sets of results. The various result sets shouldn't be confused with the multiple rows you receive from each result set. The following is an example of a query that may return several results:

```
select * from jobs
select * from authors
```

This may look like two queries that could have been sent separately, but keep in mind that SQL Server allows query batches. Several requests can be put into a single batch. In addition, stored procedures may return several result sets.

After SqlResults determines that results are available, SqlNumCols can be used to begin retrieving column information. The sample application checks this against 0 to see whether the query returned any data. If valid column information exists, the application calls the functions SqlColLen, SqlColName, and SqlColType to retrieve column information, to format the width of text columns that are subsequently displayed in the query results window.

The innermost loop calls SqlNextRow continually until it returns NOMOREROWS. When no more rows are available, the outer loop again uses SqlResults to determine whether the results from the entire batch have been retrieved.

For each column from which you want to retrieve data, you need to pass the column number to SqlData. The return value from SqlData is a string containing the data in a result column. For the SQL Server datatypes binary, varbinary, and image, SqlData returns a string of binary data, with one character in the string per byte of data in the result column. For all other datatypes, SqlData returns a string of readable characters. When there's no such column, or when the data is NULL, an empty string is returned. To make sure that the data really is NULL, always check for a return of 0 by using SqlDatLen.

FIGURE 42.1.

This flow chart shows how results are retrieved in most DB-Library applications.

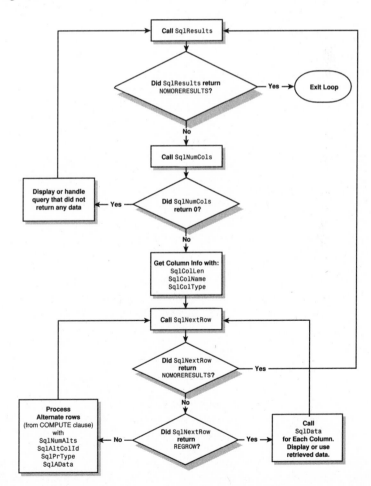

This distinction between an empty string and NULL is important. An empty string still has a length of 1 byte, the NULL character—in other words, a string that contains the character CHR$(0). A truly NULL value has a length of zero, as indicated by SqlDatLen returning 0.

Retrieving Alternate Columns from compute Clauses

There are special cases when the row returned doesn't have data that maps directly to all the columns. SqlNextRow returns the constant REGROW (-1), 0 for failure, NOMOREROWS (-2) when it has reached the end of the result set, or the identification number of the compute clause. These alternate rows are a result of a query that contains compute clauses, as in the following query:

```
SELECT title, type, price, advance
FROM titles
WHERE ytd_sales IS NOT NULL
AND type IN ('trad_cook', 'psychology')
ORDER BY type DESC
COMPUTE AVG(price), SUM(advance) BY type
COMPUTE SUM(price), SUM(advance)
```

To handle these compute clauses, we call our own procedure, ProcessAltRows. This procedure in turn uses the DB-Library functions SqlNumAlts, SqlAltColId, SqlPrType, SqlAltOp, and SqlAData. The function SqlAltColId tells us to which column the compute clause (resulting from MIN, MAX, AVG, SUM, or COUNT) applies. In the example, AVG(price) will return a column ID of 3 because price is the third column in the select clause. SqlAltOp is then used to determine the type of aggregate function in a compute column. This type can be converted to a readable string, using SqlPrType.

The following is the portion of the ProcessAltRows procedure that checks each alternate column and extracts the type and data:

```
numalts = SqlNumAlts(SqlConn, Result)
    For x = 1 To numalts
        AltCol = SqlAltColId(SqlConn, Result, x)
        AltType = SqlPrType(SqlAltOp(SqlConn, Result, x))
        AltValue = SqlAData(SqlConn, Result, x)

        nLen = 0
        For y = 1 To AltCol - 1
            nLen = nLen + colpositions(y).colLen + 1
        Next y
        nLen = nLen + 1
        Mid$(AltStr1, nLen, Len(AltType)) = AltType
        Mid$(AltStr2, nLen, Len(AltType)) = String(Len(AltType), "-")
        Mid$(AltStr3, nLen, Len(AltValue)) = AltValue

    Next x
```

Selecting, Changing, and Retrieving the Current Database

For this to be a truly useful query tool, it should present to the user a list of databases available for the current SQL Server connection. This functionality is part of the sample application, and demonstrates the use of the DB-Library functions SqlName and SqlUse.

In the Form_Load event for frmQuery, we perform a query on the master database's sysdatabases table. This table holds the names of all databases available in SQL Server. This list is then presented to the user in a combo box. When the user makes a selection from the combo box, a call to SqlUse actually performs the database context change.

The sample application uses a helper subroutine named CheckDatabaseName to determine whether the database context has changed, and if so, it updates the current combo box selection to reflect this change. Note that the CheckDatabaseName subroutine is called after any query has been executed, in case the query itself changed the database context, as in the query USE pubs.

Listing 42.4 shows the code for the Form_Load event and the CheckDatabaseName subroutine.

Listing 42.4. The Form_Load event **and the** CheckDatabaseName **subroutine demonstrate database context-change capabilities of DB-Library.**

```
Sub Form_Load()

    Dim sSql As String, sDatabase As String

    CenterForm Me

    ' Get the names of all the databases on the SQL Server.
    sSql = "Select name from master..sysdatabases"
    Result = SqlCmd(SqlConn, sSql)
    'Send the command to SQL Server and start execution.
    Result = SqlExec(SqlConn)
    Result = SqlResults(SqlConn)

    'Process the command.
    If Result = FAIL Then
        MsgBox "Error, Could not retrieve database names."
        Exit Sub
    Else
        While SqlNextRow(SqlConn) <> NOMOREROWS
            cbDatabases.AddItem SqlData(SqlConn, 1)
        Wend
    End If

    ' Place current database name in combo box
    CheckDatabaseName

    ' Select text in query edit box
    txtSQL.SelStart = 0
    txtSQL.SelLength = Len(txtSQL)
End Sub
```

continues

Listing 42.4. continued

```
Sub CheckDatabaseName()
    Dim sDatabase As String
    ' Place the current database name in combobox text
    sDatabase = SqlName(SqlConn)
    cbDatabases.Text = sDatabase
End Sub
```

Timing, Benchmarking, and Limitations

The Windows API call `GetTickCount` is used to determine the time needed to execute the query, as well as the time needed to retrieve the results. Due to the nature of the Visual Basic edit box, the retrieval of the results is somewhat sluggish. Every time a new row is received, it must be appended to the end of the edit box text. The call to `DoEvents` also introduces some overhead.

The Visual Basic edit box has a 64KB limit under Windows 95, and under Windows NT it's limited by available memory. If you retrieve a large number of results under Windows 95, the text box displays only the first 64KB worth of text.

The time needed to execute the query isn't affected by the method you chose to retrieve the results, and is a good way to benchmark how efficiently you've written a query or a stored procedure. In the sample application, the value after `Execution Time (sec):` indicates how long the query took to execute.

In the sample application, the amount of time needed to actually retrieve the rows is listed after the `Rows Retrieved` label.

There are some methods with which you may want to experiment that increase the speed at which this sample query application retrieves the rows. You may want to call `DoEvents` less often. Right now it's called every 10 rows, although the frequency with which you check for events directly correlates with how responsive the Stop button is.

Another improvement is to use a control other than the edit box to display the query results. The sample application has an option called Use Grid. If you select this check box, the Visual Basic grid control is used to display query results (although the grid control isn't well suited for queries that return multiple results or include `compute` clauses). When you use the sample application with the grid control enabled, you see only the first set of results in a query with multiple batches. The remaining results are discarded with `SqlCancel`. For large result sets, retrieving rows into the grid can be twice as fast as the edit box method.

Summary

In this chapter, we created a simple query tool that demonstrates the core functionality required of most DB-Library applications.

The VBSQL concepts presented in this chapter can be applied to any C DB-Library development that you undertake. In addition, all the sample code can be converted to the 16-bit Visual Basic equivalent by replacing the 32-bit definitions with the 16-bit definitions, and using the VBSQL.VBX control in place of the 32-bit OCX control.

For a comparison of VBSQL function calls to C function calls, see Appendix A, "DB-Library Quick Reference."

ODBC Programming for SQL Server

43

In Chapter 42, "DB-Library Programming for SQL Server," we created a simple query application using DB-Library. In this chapter, we'll create a similar sample application using ODBC. The query application is built in such a way that it will allow you to compare DB-Library programming to ODBC programming. In addition, this chapter demonstrates some of the features available to ODBC, such as binding variables, and higher-level interfaces such as *Data Access Objects* (DAO) and *Remote Data Objects* (RDO).

Getting Started

To run the samples listed in this chapter, you need Visual Basic 4.0 Enterprise Edition and a connection to SQL Server, with the `bigpubs` database installed. If you don't have the ODBC Data Source Name (DSN) `SQLBigPubs` configured at this point, please refer to Chapter 41, "Planning for SQL Server Applications." You'll need to properly configure the `SQLBigPubs` DSN before the examples in this chapter will work.

If you don't want to install the `bigpubs` database on SQL Server, you can still create an ODBC data source that points to the `pubs` database, which is created by default when SQL Server is installed. However, you still need to call this ODBC data source `SQLBigPubs` for the sample application to work. The `pubs` database allows you to grasp the concepts of ODBC, but doesn't provide a large enough set of data for performance comparisons.

ODBC Documentation and Resources

The SQL Server books online contain the most up-to-date information on ODBC programming. In addition, you may want to subscribe to the Microsoft Developers Library Level 2, which provides in-depth coverage of every Windows API and SDK available, including the ODBC SDK. You can also find the ODBC SDK on the SQL Workstation distribution CD.

Comparing Visual Basic to C

Because all the calls made in the Visual Basic examples are the same calls made to the ODBC API in C, any concepts learned can be directly applied to C programming. The calls we'll be making in Visual Basic are made possible by DLL function declarations. These function declarations call ODBC via `ODBC32.DLL` (or `ODBC.DLL` in Win16). The following is an example of two function declarations found in the Visual Basic examples:

```
Declare Function SQLAllocConnect Lib "odbc32.dll" (ByVal henv&, phdbc&) As Integer
Declare Function SQLAllocEnv Lib "odbc32.dll" (phenv&) As Integer
```

These same functions defined in C look like this:

```
RETCODE SQL_API SQLAllocConnect(HENV henv, HDBC FAR *phdbc)
RETCODE SQL_API SQLAllocEnv(HENV FAR *phenv)
```

Portability of Your ODBC Code

Both Visual Basic and C applications can be easily ported between 16-bit and 32-bit if a few guidelines are followed.

In Visual Basic, all the function declarations need to reference either `ODBC.DLL` or `ODBC32.DLL`, based on your target operating system (either 16-bit or 32-bit). The call to `SQLDriverConnect` needs to pass a handle to a window, which is also known as an `HWND`. Under Win32, this `HWND` should be declared as a `Long` or 32-bit variable, as opposed to an `Integer` under Win16.

One of the most notable portability features of ODBC is that it allows your application to continue to work, even if the back end database changes. For example, if you write an ODBC application that accesses a Btrieve data source and then the data format changes to dBASE or SQL Server, your application continues to work without modification. The only change that needs to be made is to select the correct driver through the ODBC Driver Manager, as described in Chapter 41.

As long as an ODBC driver exists for your database, your application can use it. The only exceptions are when you use database-specific passthrough queries. In addition, if you've used ODBC functions beyond the core conformance level, the application may not work if the new ODBC driver doesn't support the calls you're making outside of the core level.

Sample Application

The ODBC sample application is broken up into three sections: a query tool, an example of binding columns to variables, and an example of DAO and RDO. The first dialog box presented in the sample application allows you to click a button that brings up one of these three sections.

The Visual Basic code includes all the ODBC API function declarations, and the ODBC constants declarations. These declarations are broken up into four parts:

- ▪ `Odbc32 Core API.bas`—The function declarations required to call ODBC core API conformance functions.
- ▪ `Odbc32 Core Consts.bas`—All the ODBC constants and return codes needed for the core API functions. These also include the constants for the minimum and core SQL grammar data types such as `SQL_CHAR`, `SQL_FLOAT`, `SQL_DOUBLE`, and others.
- ▪ `Odbc32 Ext API.bas`—The Level 1 and Level 2 ODBC function prototypes.
- ▪ `Odbc32 Ext Consts.bas`—The constants used by the Level 1 and Level 2 ODBC functions, as well as the SQL Extended grammar data types, such as `SQL_DATE`, `SQL_TIME`, `SQL_BINARY`, and others.

The ODBC Query Sample Code

The ODBC query tool has the same look and feel as the DB-Library query tool created in Chapter 42. There are some differences between the DB-Library version and the ODBC version worth mentioning.

This ODBC sample application uses connections to ODBC data sources, as opposed to specific SQL Servers. When you select a data source to perform queries against, you're connecting to an ODBC data source that may be configured to connect to SQL Server, an Access database, or a local ISAM database. The query tool doesn't care what the database back end is. In Figure 43.1, notice that the interface presents selections for ODBC data source names, instead of specific databases as in the DB-Library sample.

FIGURE 43.1.

The dialog box for the ODBC query sample allows you to connect to a data source and send ODBC queries to that source.

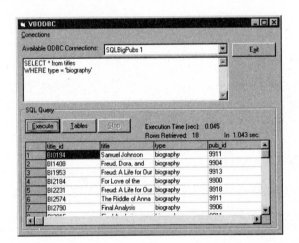

Another point to keep in mind is that you'll be sending queries using ODBC SQL grammar and not the database's SQL grammar (such as Transact-SQL for SQL Server). This is a plus for both the developer and the end user. No matter what data source you have connected to, you can be assured that it will respond to the Minimum SQL Conformance Level, as described in the "ODBC SQL Conformance Levels" section of Chapter 40, "Client Application Interfaces for SQL Server." If needed, ODBC will convert the query text into the syntax required by the database engine. This makes the query tool usable with any ODBC data source, not just SQL Server, as in the DB-Library sample.

Initializing the ODBC Environment

The typical sequence used to perform a query under ODBC includes the following steps:

1. Allocate an ODBC environment handle.
2. Allocate memory for a connection handle within this new environment.

3. Connect to an ODBC driver with this connection handle.

4. Allocate a statement handle.

5. Send a query with the statement handle.

6. Retrieve the results.

7. Free the statement handle.

8. Disconnect from the driver.

9. Free the memory allocated for the connection handle.

10. Finally, free the environment handle.

The same environment handle can be used throughout the application; for our example, it's declared as a global variable, as follows:

```
Global henv As Long
```

To allocate an environment handle, this global variable is passed to SQLAllocEnv.

In our sample application, a global array of a user structure ConnectionInfo is created, called Connection. This setup enables you to have several connections open at one time. Each connection tracks its connection handle, its statement handle, its active/inactive status, and the name of the ODBC DSN to which the connection refers. It's defined as follows:

```
Type ConnectionInfo
    hdbc As Long            ' Connection handle
    hstmt As Long           ' Statement handle
    Status As Integer       ' Active or Inactive
    Tag As String           ' A string of the form "DataSource <number>"
                            ' uniquely identifying a connection
End Type

Global Connection(1 To MaxConnections) As ConnectionInfo
```

When you select the menu sequence Connections | Add New Connection, you'll be presented with the available ODBC data source names. This is done by passing an empty string to SQLDriverConnect. Based on what you select, it returns a string with all the driver information filled in, in this format:

```
DSN=DSN;UID=UID;PWD=PWD;APP=AppName;DATABASE=DatabaseName
```

After the connection is established, this string is parsed and the data source name is added to the list of available connections on which you can perform queries.

If instead you'd like to send the data source name, user identifier, and password as separate strings, the SQLConnect function can accommodate this plan. The syntax for this function looks like this:

```
SQLConnect ( szDSN, szUID, szPassword )
```

For our example, we'll use SQLDriverConnect instead. The code that creates the connection using SQLDriverConnect is as follows:

```
' Allocate a connection handle
  Attempt SQLAllocConnect(henv, Connection(i).hdbc), "Cannot allocate
➥connection handle"

  ' Make the connection
  rc = SQLDriverConnect(Connection(i).hdbc, frmQuery.hwnd, S, Len(S$), Server,
➥Len(Server), cbOut, SQL_DRIVER_COMPLETE)
  If (rc = SQL_ERROR) Or (rc = SQL_INVALID_HANDLE) Then
     DescribeError Connection(i).hdbc, 0
     Screen.MousePointer = vbDefault
     Exit Function
  ElseIf rc = SQL_NO_DATA_FOUND Then
     Screen.MousePointer = vbDefault
     Exit Function
  End If

  ' Allocate a statement handle
  Attempt SQLAllocStmt(Connection(i).hdbc, Connection(i).hstmt), "Cannot allocate
➥statement handle"
```

The Attempt function is simply a helper function to check the return value of all ODBC function calls. It displays the message passed to it if the result code doesn't equal SQL_SUCCESS.

Sending a Query and Returning Results

Once the connection is established, a query can be sent. The text entered in the query window is passed to the ODBC driver via SQLExecDirect.

If all goes well, SQLNumResultCols is called to obtain the number of columns that the query returned. The function SQLNumResultCols is used to obtain the names of each column, so that we can label each of the columns in the grid control.

To retrieve all the rows returned from the query, SQLFetch is called repeatedly until it doesn't return SQL_SUCCESS. The SQLFetch function positions the cursor on the next row of the result set. At this point, the data for each column can be read and placed into the grid control for display. The data is retrieved by a call to SQLGetData for each column in the result set. To retrieve data with SQLGetData, you need to pass it the following information:

- Which column you want to retrieve
- The type of data to which you want the data to be converted
- A reference to the variable where you want the converted data to be placed

The data types you have available are based on the conformance level of the ODBC driver. Since we'll simply display the data in a grid, the SQL_C_CHAR data type conversion is sufficient.

For benchmarking and timing comparisons, the form will display the time it took to return from SQLExecDirect, as well as how long it took to fetch each row with SQLFetch.

The catalog functions that are available in ODBC return result sets in the same manner as SQLExecDirect. One such function is used to retrieve all the available tables in a data source. The query window allows the retrieval of the available tables by clicking on the Tables button. This calls SQLTables in place of SQLExecDirect. Other functions that can be used to obtain catalog information include SQLTablePrivileges, SQLPrimaryKeys, SQLForeignKeys, and SQLProcedures.

Closing Connections and Cleaning Up

When the connection is closed via the menu, or if the query window is closed, all the open connections are closed. The statement handle is closed with SQLFreeStmt, followed by the driver disconnecting with SQLDisconnect. Finally, the connection handle is released with SQLFreeConnect.

When the query window closes, the ODBC environment is no longer needed. The call to SQLFreeEnv releases all memory associated with the environment handle.

> **WARNING**
>
> The use of SQLFreeEnv shouldn't be overlooked. This function releases all memory associated with the environment handle.

Error Handling

The sample application calls SQLError when a previous call to an ODBC function returns SQL_ERROR. Because any ODBC function can post zero or more errors each time it's called, an application may want to call a helper function that describes all of the returned ODBC errors. The DescribeError function in our example does just this. It in turn calls SQLError repeatedly until it doesn't return SQL_SUCCESS. For each error, a message box is displayed, showing the native error code specific to the data source.

All ODBC errors are stored in relation to its statement handle, or HSTMT. The errors are cleared when a call is made to SQLError, or when a related function is called with the same handle. You'll want to check all available errors, as an ODBC environment can store up to 64 errors and will discard subsequent errors once this limit is reached. To create bulletproof code, you should invest a good amount of time creating error-handling routines.

ODBC Bound Column Sample Code

The ODBC API enables you to bind columns from result sets to your own program variables. DB-Library allows similar functionality with C programming, but this functionality isn't available in VBSQL (the Visual Basic DB-Library interface). The bound column sample in this section shows how Visual Basic can use this functionality.

Coding a Predetermined ODBC Connection

In most circumstances, you'll want to connect to an ODBC driver without displaying a user prompt. To do this, a valid connection string is passed to SQLDriverConnect. This string should contain (at the very least) a data source name, a user identifier, and the user's password. The connection code that performs this is as follows:

```
' Make the connection
   S = "DSN=SQLBigPubs;UID=sa;PWD=;APP=Visual Basic 4.0;DATABASE=bigpubs"
   '
   ' We will use Connection(1) throughout the Bound Column example
   '
   rc = SQLDriverConnect(Connection(1).hdbc, Me.hwnd, S, Len(S), Server,
➡Len(Server), cbOut, SQL_DRIVER_COMPLETE)
   If (rc = SQL_ERROR) Or (rc = SQL_INVALID_HANDLE) Then
     DescribeError Connection(1).hdbc, 0
     Screen.MousePointer = vbDefault
     Exit Sub
   ElseIf rc = SQL_NO_DATA_FOUND Then
     Screen.MousePointer = vbDefault
     Exit Sub
   End If
   Connection(1).Tag = "SQLBigPubs"

   ' Allocate a statement handle
   Attempt SQLAllocStmt(Connection(1).hdbc, Connection(1).hstmt), "Cannot allocate
➡statment handle"
   MsgBox "Connection to SQLBigPubs Established", vbInformation
```

Scrollable/Updateable Cursors

This example introduces scrollable cursors. This will allow records to be scanned forward or backward, using ODBC's SQLExtendedFetch function. By passing either SQL_FETCH_NEXT or SQL_FETCH_PRIOR to SQLExtendedFetch, we can navigate freely through the result set.

The query we'll use displays the title and price for each record in the titles table. This query is passed to SQLExecDirect. Before executing the query, we need to set up a scrollable cursor. This is done with SQLSetScrollOptions. In this case, we want to allow updating of the price for each book, so the SQL_CONCUR_LOCK option is used. If this were to be a read-only result set, we could have used SQL_CONCUR_READ_ONLY.

Because we need a scrollable cursor, we set the keyset type to SQL_SCROLL_DYNAMIC. SQLSetScrollOptions lets you define how the ODBC driver will buffer the rows.

The last parameter of SQLSetScrollOptions defines how many rows are retrieved every time SQLExtendedFetch is called. When the keyset type is set to SQL_SCROLL_DYNAMIC, the keys buffered equals the number of keys fetched. By doing so, you're ensured that the application is displaying the latest data to the user. This may be an issue for multiuser databases. If concurrency isn't an issue, you can use SQL_SCROLL_STATIC as an alternative to SQL_SCROLL_DYNAMIC.

Binding Variables to Columns

Binding variables to columns avoids the need to call SQLGetData every time a new record is fetched. Once a variable is bound to a column, it's automatically updated when a new record is fetched. Figure 43.2 shows the interface used to demonstrate ODBC bound variables.

FIGURE 43.2.

The Bound Column Test dialog box allows you to scroll through the titles *table. The variables are automatically updated every time a new row is retrieved.*

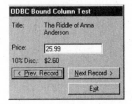

To bind a variable to a column, you pass the following information to SQLBindCol:

- A reference to your variable
- The column to which you want it bound
- The data type to which you want it converted

You must ensure that the variable that will hold the converted data is of the right type and size. For this example, we'll obtain a string and a floating-point value. The second column of our result set is bound to the global variable Price, which is defined as a Double. Listing 43.1 shows how the ODBC data binding was done for our example.

Listing 43.1. This is the code that sets up the scrollable cursor, fetches the first record, and binds the program variables to columns one and two.

```
' Global Declarations
Dim nTitle(80) As Byte
Dim sdDataLen As Long
Dim Price As Double

Sub TitleQuery(ByVal hdbc As Long, ByVal hstmt As Long)

    Dim sQuery As String
    Dim x As Integer

    sQuery = "SELECT title, price FROM titles"
    ' Allow scrollable cursor
    rc = SQLSetScrollOptions(hstmt, SQL_CONCUR_LOCK, SQL_SCROLL_DYNAMIC, 1)
    rc = SQLExecDirect(hstmt, sQuery, Len(sQuery))

    If rc = SQL_SUCCESS Then

        ' Bind columns 1, 2, and 3
        SQLBindCol hstmt, 1, SQL_C_CHAR, nTitle(0), 79, sdDataLen
        SQLBindCol hstmt, 2, SQL_C_DOUBLE, Price, 8, SQL_NULL_DATA
```

continues

Listing 43.1. continued

```
       ' Fetch first row of data.
       rc = SQLExtendedFetch(hstmt, SQL_FETCH_NEXT, 1, _
                              SQL_NULL_DATA, SQL_NULL_DATA)
       If rc = SQL_ERROR Or rc = SQL_SUCCESS_WITH_INFO Then
           DescribeError hdbc, hstmt
       End If
       If rc = SQL_SUCCESS Or rc = SQL_SUCCESS_WITH_INFO Then
           UpdateLabels
       End If
    End If
End Sub
```

> **WARNING**
>
> You may have noticed that a `Byte` array was used to bind column one, where you might think a `String` variable would work. Visual Basic stores its strings as a `BSTR`, which is different from a string in C. A `BSTR` contains a header that stores a pointer to the first character of the string. To pass a reference to the ODBC `SQLBindCol` function, we would actually need to pass the string by value rather than by reference. This would effectively pass the string to the pointer as desired, but this pointer is unstable. Visual Basic will occasionally do housekeeping and move string variables around. This will cause a bound variable to bomb, and produces other undesirable effects.

Once the variables are bound and the first record is fetched, you can navigate through the record set with the two buttons Prev. Record and Next Record. These buttons simply call `SQLExtendedFetch` with `SQL_FETCH_PRIOR` or `SQL_FETCH_NEXT`. Every time a new record is fetched, the display is updated with the new contents of the variables. To show how a bound variable might be used in a real-world application, a 10 percent discount is calculated from the price, and it too is displayed for each new record. In addition, the price can be updated as you move through the records.

Before a new record is fetched, the text entered in the Price edit box is converted to a `double`, and placed into the `Price` variable. Then a call is made to `SQLSetPos`. `SQLSetPos` sets the cursor position in a rowset and allows an application to refresh, update, delete, or add data to the rowset. Because we're fetching only one record at a time into our rowset, we pass 1 as the position. Then we inform ODBC that we'll be doing an update by passing `SQL_UPDATE` to `SQLSetPos`:

```
Sub UpdateData()
    ' Update price data
    Price = CDbl(txtPrice)
    rc = SQLSetPos(Connection(1).hstmt, 1, SQL_UPDATE, SQL_LOCK_NO_CHANGE)
    If rc <> SQL_SUCCESS Then
        DescribeError Connection(1).hdbc, Connection(1).hstmt
    End If

End Sub
```

The ODBC API is powerful and portable, yet it can be a bit awkward to program. The need to use Visual Basic's ByVal argument-passing scheme can also get confusing. To add to these complexities, the ODBC API provides no easy way to link your user interface to underlying data, as is done with DAO and RDO.

RDO/DAO Sample Code

This sample is presented to show how higher-level development tools such as Visual Basic enable you to connect to data sources, bind controls to data, and update data—all without writing a single line of code. The Data Access Objects (DAO) and Remote Data Objects (RDO) leverage ODBC to connect to SQL Server. These object interfaces shield the developer from the complexities of calling the ODBC API functions directly.

The interface in Figure 43.3 was created without any coding, other than that needed to refresh the data grids with the currently entered query found at the bottom of the screen.

FIGURE 43.3.

The grid controls are bound to a result set using either RDO or DAO. This dialog box was created with virtually no code. The grid control also allows updates to the data, as shown for store A041, which is being updated to a quantity of 1.

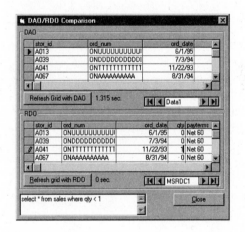

If you look at the properties and methods of the RDO Object Model, you'll see that it closely resembles the functions used by the ODBC API. In fact, RDO is basically a "wrapper" around ODBC.

For instance, if you place a Remote Data Control on a Visual Basic form, it will take care of creating an environment handle, creating connection handles, connecting to drivers, and passing queries to the driver, and will provide a method of navigation through the result set.

To perform data binding, as with SQLBindCol, you simply place a control on your visual basic form and tell it to which Remote Data Control it should bind, as well as from which column it is to retrieve its display data.

All the parameters passed to the ODBC functions SQLDriverConnect, SQLSetScrollOptions, and SQLExecDirect are provided as properties in the Remote Data Control.

Data Access Objects work in much the same way, except by passing through the Jet engine before hitting an ODBC data source. This will introduce a slight penalty in performance, but provides very efficient connections to PC databases such as Microsoft Access and other ISAMS.

> **NOTE**
>
> As this publication was going to press, Microsoft released DAO Version 3.1. It lets you continue to use the Jet engine, or bypass it with ODBCDirect. Now, if you don't need the Jet engine, DAO doesn't even load it. This may bring DAO performance on remote databases into the same realm as RDO.

Timing and Benchmarking

As in the DB-Library samples, we use the Windows API call GetTickCount to determine the time needed to execute the query, as well as how long it takes to retrieve the results.

Both the query sample and the RDO/DAO samples display timing results. Keep in mind that SQL Server caches pages into memory when the same page is accessed several times. The first time a query is run takes longer than when the same query is run subsequent times. This is due to the SQL page caching. You'll notice that the DAO results can take two to three times longer to return than the RDO results. If you continually run the same query over and over with either RDO or DAO, the performance will improve. This should be taken into account when comparing RDO to DAO.

To test this, select the Refresh Grid with DAO button a few times. Then select the Refresh Grid with RDO button a few times as well. This will ensure that SQL Server has cached the pages for both connections. At this point, you'll have a better reference point to do DAO versus RDO timing comparisons.

Summary

In this chapter, we created a simple query tool that demonstrates both core and extended ODBC API functions. We also created a simple user interface that allows updates to be made to SQL Server via ODBC. These examples should help you understand the effort involved in ODBC programming. If the idea of direct ODBC programming doesn't look appealing, you can look to alternatives such as DAO and RDO. Both DAO and RDO provide Visual Basic a simple, yet powerful way to connect your application to SQL Server.

If you'll be developing an ODBC application in C, ODBC provides an excellent method for connecting to SQL Server. Some of the complexities that Visual Basic poses may not be an issue when developing in C.

For a detailed description of the ODBC, DAO, and RDO architectures, see Chapter 40.

VI

PART

SQL Server and the World Wide Web

Building Dynamic
Web Pages with
SQL Server

44

IN THIS CHAPTER

There are several ways to build dynamic Web pages using the Microsoft Internet Information Server. A *dynamic* Web page is one that interacts with the user, or changes periodically. Most people think of ActiveX technologies and Internet Explorer 3.0 when the word *interactive* is mentioned, but this chapter focuses on interacting with ODBC-compliant databases. In this chapter, you explore some of the other options that are provided with the Internet Information Server base product and with Microsoft SQL Server 6.5 for making dynamic Web pages.

Another tool to build interactive Web pages is Microsoft dbWeb. Microsoft dbWeb is an ISAPI application, similar to the IDC, but which uses a Visual Basic application—the dbWeb Administrator—to build Web pages for you. You can download Version 1.1 of dbWeb from the Microsoft Web page at `http://www.microsoft.com/msdownload`. You can also find out more about using dbWeb by picking up a copy of *Internet Information Server 2 Unleashed* by Sams Publishing. Some reasons to use the Internet Database Connector instead of dbWeb:

- **Query control.** If you're an experienced database developer with knowledge of your database's query language, the IDC offers finer levels of control. The IDC requires you to specify a query rather than supplying one for you. This requirement should be considered a blessing rather than a burden, because it provides you fine-tuned control of what will be returned by your query.

- **Layout control.** If you're an experienced HTML developer, the IDC offers finer control over how the user will interact with your Web page. Because you create the input forms used to obtain the query and the Web pages to display the query result, you also get to determine exactly how the Web page will look.

- **Reusability.** You can copy the basic components of an IDC skeleton (the source code, consisting of the Web pages, `.HTX`, and `.IDC` files) to quickly build a variant input form or query result page. Microsoft dbWeb requires that you build an entirely new data source and schema. There's no code reusability.

Using the Internet Database Connector

The Internet Information Server has the built-in capacity to interface with any ODBC-compliant database for which you have a 32-bit ODBC driver. There's more work involved in developing an interactive Web page using the Internet Database Connector (IDC) than in using Microsoft dbWeb, but the IDC provides more fine-tuned control. Another good thing about the IDC is that, unlike dbWeb, the IDC doesn't require form names to start with a number. This means that you can use Microsoft Front Page to develop your forms from start to finish.

In this section, you learn how to use the IDC to create an interactive guest book. There are three steps for the creation of this or any other interactive IDC Web page:

1. Create the Web page form.
2. Create an IDC interface file.

3. Create another HTML file to use as a template for the resulting output created by your query.

These steps are covered in detail in the following sections.

> **NOTE**
>
> You also need to create the ODBC database and the system data source name (DSN) to create an interactive Web page using the Internet Database Connector.

You can use any text editor to create your forms, but I prefer a what-you-see-is-what-you-get (WYSIWYG) editor such as Microsoft Front Page (see Figure 44.1). Microsoft Front Page makes it easy to build your form using the familiar Windows GUI. It isn't imperative that you know how to write HTML documents, although knowing syntax for HTML helps considerably if you have to edit a document manually, or if a problem crops up during the development stage.

FIGURE 44.1.

Creating your form with Microsoft Front Page.

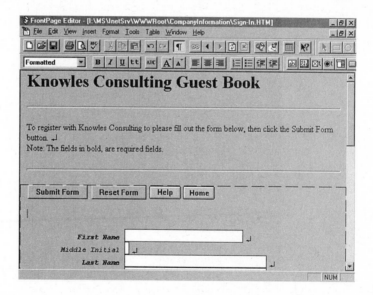

There are two forms you create to build a working guest book:

- First, you need a form to insert information into your ODBC database.
- Second, you need a form to query your database. This form is optional, because you may not want to allow your Internet clients to browse your database. However, I'm including it here because it illustrates the basic techniques required to query your database and display the resulting data on a Web page. The ability to query and to display the data is what really makes a form interactive.

TIP

If you look closely at the HTML source code in the next few sections, you'll see a reference to a database column called Hide. This variable prevents the display of a client's information on the WWW. While you still can view the data by using another ODBC front end, such as Access, the queries used to find and display the guest book specifically exclude any information whose Hide column is set to Y. The user sets this variable by checking the check box Do not post this information on the web for others to see, at the end of the form.

Creating the Input Form

The basic form I created—called Sign-In.HTM—is used to enter information into my guest book. The form was built using the following HTML code:

```
1.    <html>
2.    <head>
3.    <title>Knowles Consulting Guest Book</title>
4.    </head>
5.    <body>
6.    <h1>Knowles Consulting Guest Book</h1>
7.    <hr>
8.    <p>To register with Knowles Consulting to please fill out the form
below, then click the Submit Form button.</p>
9.    <p>Note: The fields in bold, are required fields. </p>
10.    <hr>
11.    <form action="/Scripts/Sign-In-IDC.IDC" method="get">
12.    <p><input type=submit value="Submit Form">
<input type=reset value="Reset Form">
<a href="/CompanyInformation/GuestBookPageHelp.HTM">
<img src="/Graphics/Buttons/help.gif" align=absmiddle border=0></a>
<a href="http://www.nt-guru.com">
<img src="/Graphics/Buttons/home.gif" align=absmiddle border=0></a></p>
13.    <blockquote>
14.    <pre><em>         </em><em><b>First Name</b></em><em> </em>
<input type=text size=25 maxlength=25 name="FirstName">
15.       <em>Middle</em> <em>Initial</em>
<input type=text size=1 maxlength=1 name="MiddleInitial">
16.          <em><b>Last Name</b></em>
<input type=text size=30 maxlength=30 name="LastName">
17.    <em>          Title </em>
<input type=text size=30 maxlength=30 name="Title">
18.    <em>     Company Name </em>
<input type=text size=35 maxlength=50 name="CompanyName">
19.    <em>   Street address </em>
<input type=text size=35 maxlength=35 name="Address">
20.    <em> Address (cont.) </em>
<input type=text size=35 maxlength=35 name="Address_2">
21.    <em>              City </em>
<input type=text size=35 maxlength=35 name="City">
```

```
22.     <em>  State/Province  </em>
<input type=text size=25 maxlength=25 name="StateOrProvince">
23.     <em> Zip/Postal code </em>
<input type=text size=25 maxlength=25 name="PostalCode">
24.     <em>            Country </em>
<input type=text size=25 maxlength=25 name="Country" value="US">
25.     <em>       Work Phone </em>
<input type=text size=14 maxlength=14 name="WorkPhoneNumber">
26.     <em>        Home Phone </em>
<input type=text size=14 maxlength=14 name="HomePhoneNumber">
27.     <em>              FAX </em>
<input type=text size=14 maxlength=14 name="FaxNumber">
28.     <em>             E-mail </em>
<input type=text size=25 maxlength=255 name="E_Mail">
29.     <em>   Home Page URL </em>
<input type=text size=25 maxlength=255 name="URL">
30.               <em>Note</em>
<textarea name="Note" rows=2 cols=44></textarea></pre>
31.<pre><input type=checkbox name="Contact" value="Y">
Please contact me as soon as possible regarding this matter.
32.     </pre>
33.     <pre><input type=checkbox name="Hide" value="Y">
Do not post this information on the web for others to see.</pre>
34.     </blockquote>
35.     <p><input type=submit value="Submit Form">
<input type=reset value="Reset Form">
<a href="/CompanyInformation/GuestBookPageHelp.HTM">
<img src="/Graphics/Buttons/help.gif" align=absmiddle border=0></a>
<a href="http://www.nt-guru.com">
<img src="/Graphics/Buttons/home.gif" align=absmiddle border=0></a></p>
36.     </form>
37.     <table width=100%>
38.<tr><td width=50%><address><font size=2>
<em>Copyright &#169; 1996 Knowles Consulting. All rights reserved</em>
</font> </address>
39.</td><td align=right width=50%><div align=right><address>
<font size=2><em>Last Updated: June 21, 1996</em></font>
</address></div></td></tr>
40.     </table>
41. </body>
42.     </html>
```

NOTE

The preceding HTML code shouldn't include the line numbers. These numbers are included in the text to make the discussion easier to follow.

The first and last two lines of code are required for any HTML document. Line 3 specifies the document title, which will be displayed on the Web browser caption bar. Line 5 specifies the beginning of the document body. Line 6 is the document header. Lines 7 and 10 insert a horizontal rule (line break) into the document to divide the instructions on how to use the form from the header and the form. Line 11 is the beginning of the form, and includes the Internet Database Connector definition, as well as the action type (a get rather than the more commonly used post).

This definition (`/Scripts/Sign-In-IDC.IDC`) file is associated with the Internet Database Connector ISAPI dynamic link library `HTTPODBC.DLL`, which can be found in your `InetSrv\Server` subdirectory. The next section describes the IDC definition files in more detail. For now, just mark this spot in your HTML file as the executable file to which your form's output will be passed.

Moving on, lines 12 and 35 insert the form's Submit Form, Reset Form, Help, and Home buttons. These buttons are used to submit the information entered into the form by the user, to clear the form, to display a help file, and to return to the home page, respectively. Notice that both the Help button and the Home button are image files. When the user selects one of these buttons, the page associated with the hypertext link will be displayed. This is a different action than that performed by the Submit Form and Reset Form buttons, which are really form controls. This is because there are only two basic form buttons supported in the HTML definition: One button submits the form, and one button clears the form.

Line 13 (the `<blockquote>` tag) is used to indent the form's input fields (lines 14 through 33). Line 36 is the end of the form. Lines 37 through 40 include a table definition, the copyright information, and a form last-update notification.

That's about all it takes to create the form that sends an entry to your database. To create a form that allows a user to query your guest book and view the resulting data, use the following code and save it as `SearchGuestBook.HTM`:

```
1: <html>
2: <title>Search the Knowles Consulting Guest Book</title>
3: <BODY>
4: <hr>
5: <h1>Search the Knowles Consulting Guest Book</h1>
6: To search for matching records, enter your search criteria in the fields
below and press the 'Submit Query' button
when completed.
7: <p>Type in any of these boxes to match against people in the guest book.
Use the '%' symbol as a wildcard. A blank
field here will match any entry.<br>
8: <form action="/Scripts/SearchGuestBook.IDC" method=get>
9: <p><input type=submit value="Submit Form">
<input type=reset value="Reset Form"> <a
href="/CompanyInformation/GuestBookPageHelp.HTM">
<img src="/Graphics/Buttons/help.gif" align=absmiddle border=0></a>
<a href="http://www.nt-guru.com">
<img src="/Graphics/Buttons/home.gif" align=absmiddle border=0></a></p>
10: <blockquote>
11: <pre><em>        First Name </em>
<input type=text size=25 maxlength=25 name="FirstName">
12:     <em>Middle</em> <em>Initial</em>
<input type=text size=1 maxlength=1 name="MiddleInitial">
13:         <em>Last</em> <em>Name</em>
<input type=text size=30 maxlength=30 name="LastName">
14: <em>            Title </em>
<input type=text size=30 maxlength=30 name="Title">
15: <em>    Company Name </em>
<input type=text size=35 maxlength=50 name="CompanyName">
```

```
16: <em>  Street address </em>
<input type=text size=35 maxlength=35 name="Address">
17: <em> Address (cont.) </em>
<input type=text size=35 maxlength=35 name="Address_2">
18: <em>             City </em><input type=text size=35 maxlength=35 name="City">
19: <em>  State/Province </em>
<input type=text size=25 maxlength=25 name="StateOrProvince">
20: <em> Zip/Postal code </em>
<input type=text size=25 maxlength=25 name="PostalCode">
21: <em>          Country </em>
<input type=text size=25 maxlength=25 name="Country">
22: <em>       Work Phone </em>
<input type=text size=14 maxlength=14 name="WorkPhoneNumber">
23: <em>       Home Phone </em>
<input type=text size=14 maxlength=14 name="HomePhoneNumber">
24: <em>              FAX </em>
<input type=text size=14 maxlength=14 name="FaxNumber">
25: <em>           E-mail </em>
<input type=text size=25 maxlength=255 name="E_Mail">
26: <em>   Home Page URL </em><input type=text size=25 maxlength=255 name="URL">
27:            <em>Note</em> <textarea name="Note" rows=2 cols=44></textarea>
</pre>
28: <p><input type=submit value="Submit Form">
<input type=reset value="Reset Form"> <a
href="/CompanyInformation/GuestBookPageHelp.HTM">
<img src="/Graphics/Buttons/help.gif" align=absmiddle border=0></a>
<a href="http://www.nt-guru.com">
<img src="/Graphics/Buttons/home.gif" align=absmiddle border=0></a></p>
29: </form>
30: <hr>
31: <table width=100%>
32: <tr><td width=50%><address><font size=2>
<em>Copyright &#169; 1996 Knowles Consulting. All rights reserved</em>
</font> </address>
33: </td><td align=right width=50%><div align=right><address><font size=2>
<em>Last Updated: June 21, 1996</em></font>
</address>
34: </div></td></tr>
35: </table>
36: </body>
37: </html>
```

Although this form looks similar to the form used to enter information into the ODBC database, there are a few differences:

- First, the form title (Line 2), header (Line 5), and instructions (Line 7) are different. This isn't too surprising, as this Web page's purpose is to provide a mechanism for the user to query or search your guest book. The previous HTML document's purpose is to request the user to fill out a form so that he or she can enter the information into your guest book.

- Second, the form calls the /Scripts/SearchGuestBook.IDC IDC interface file (Line 8) rather than the Scripts/Sign-In-IDC.IDC IDC interface file used with the input form. This is because I also wanted to perform a different action—a database query instead of a database insert. Lines 10–29 define the actual form that will be displayed on the Web browser.

■ The rest looks almost the same except for the Contact and Hide database columns, which aren't included on the query form, because a user has no need to search your guest book using these fields as search criteria. After all, while you may want to provide a listing of people who have visited your Web site as a service, you don't want users to know whom you may have contacted or who doesn't want their information made public.

As you can see, creating the forms to insert data into your database or to query and display the results seems quite easy. Unfortunately, there's more to it than this. You also need to create the IDC interface and HTML template files before you can use the forms to enter information into your database or to query and display the result set on the Web.

Creating the Internet Database Connector Interface File

The next step in building your guest book using the Internet Database Connector is to build the IDC definition files. These files contain information about the ODBC data source, the template file used to display the result set, and most importantly, the database query to execute. You will need to create three IDC files:

■ Sign-In-IDC.IDC

■ SearchGuestBook.IDC

■ GuestBookDetails.IDC

Creating the Sign-In-IDC.IDC File

The first file will be called Sign-In-IDC.IDC. It's used by the Sign-In.HTM form you created earlier. The source code follows:

```
1.    Datasource: IISLogs
2.    Username: sa
3.    Template: Sign-In-IDC.HTX
4.    RequiredParameters: FirstName, LastName
5.    SQLStatement:
6.    + if exists (
7.    +    select * from GuestBook
8.    +    where FirstName='%FirstName%' and MiddleInitial = '%MiddleInitial%'
 and
9.    +    LastName='%LastName%' and Address = '%Address%' and
Address_2 = '%Address_2%' and
10.   +    City = '%City%' and StateOrProvince = '%StateOrProvince%' and
11.   +    PostalCode = '%PostalCode%' and Hide = '%Hide%'
12.   +    )
13.   +       select result='duplicate'
14.   +else
15.   +  INSERT INTO GuestBook
16.   +  (FirstName, MiddleInitial, LastName, Title, CompanyName, Address,
17.   +  Address_2, City, StateOrProvince, PostalCode, Country,
WorkPhoneNumber, HomePhoneNumber,
18.   +  FaxNumber, E_Mail, URL, Note, Contact, Hide)
```

```
19.  +  VALUES('%FirstName%', '%MiddleInitial%', '%LastName%', '%Title%',
20.  +  '%CompanyName%', '%Address%', '%Address_2%', '%City%',
'%StateOrProvince%',
21.  +  '%PostalCode%', '%Country%', '%WorkPhoneNumber%', '%HomePhoneNumber%',
22.  +  '%FaxNumber%', '%E_Mail%', '%URL%', '%Note%', '%Contact%', '%Hide%');
```

Line 1 specifies the ODBC system DSN used to access the ODBC database. Line 2 specifies the user name. If you are using SQL Server with the mixed (or integrated) security model, as I am, this option is ignored. Instead, the user account is validated using the IUSR_*ServerName* account (where *ServerName* is the name of the server on which IIS is installed), which is created by the IIS setup program. However, depending on your ODBC database, you may need to supply the Password option and specify a valid password to access your ODBC database. Line 3 specifies the HTML template file, which either informs the user that the data was entered into the database successfully or that a duplicate entry has been found. Line 4 specifies that the First Name (FName) and Last Name (LName) fields must be entered on the form; otherwise, the record won't be entered into the database. The FName and LName variables are used in the query in the GuestBookDetails.IDC file to search for matching records that contain the same values as the First Name and Last Name fields you enter on the form here.

> **NOTE**
>
> There are other defined parameters that you can use in an IDC file. These are summarized later in this section, in Table 44.1.

Lines 5 through 12 are a series of SQL select statements that, when executed, will return a result set containing the first name, middle initial, last name, address lines, city, state, postal code and Hide flag. If all of these fields match the data entered by the user, line 13 is executed and the result is determined to be a duplicate entry. A duplicate entry won't be accepted, and the user will be informed of this fact via the message defined in the HTML template (more on this in the next section). If the record isn't a duplicate, the insert statement after line 14 (the else clause) is executed and the record is inserted into the database. The user will see a success message, as defined by the HTML template.

Creating the SearchGuestBook.IDC File

The query for the guest book requires two IDC definition files. The first one, called SearchGuestBook.IDC, is used to define the search parameters. The source code is as follows:

```
Datasource: IISLogs
Username: sa
Template: SearchGuestBook.HTX
SQLStatement:
+SELECT FirstName, LastName,
+FROM GuestBook
+WHERE FirstName like '%FirstName%'
```

```
+and LastName like '%LastName%'
+and Hide <> 'Y'
DefaultParameters:FirstName=%,LastName=%
```

This source code looks very similar to the `Sign-In-IDC.IDC` file. Indeed, the only real difference is that `SearchGuestBook.IDC` doesn't search for duplicate records. Instead, it executes a query to find records based only on the first and last names specified by the user. If the user doesn't specify one or both of these fields, a wildcard character (%) will be substituted in the empty field (as specified by the `DefaultParameters` entry). The `DefaultParameters` entry is used to create a substitution mechanism to supply default values for a field in the query if the user doesn't explicitly enter a value. When this query is executed, the template file `SearchGuestBook.HTX` will be used to display the result set, which consists of first and last names. At this point, the user can click one of these entries to expand it and display more detail. This will execute the final IDC file, which is described in the next section.

Creating the `GuestBookDetails.IDC` File

Here's the source code for the `GuestBookDetails.IDC` file:

```
Datasource: IISLogs
Username: sa
Template: GuestBookDetails.HTX
SQLStatement:
+SELECT FirstName, MiddleInitial, LastName, Title, CompanyName, Address,
Address_2,
+City, StateOrProvince, PostalCode, Country, WorkPhoneNumber, HomePhoneNumber,
 FaxNumber,
+E_Mail, URL, Note
+FROM GuestBook
+WHERE FirstName = '%FName%' and LastName = '%LName%' and Hide <> 'Y'
```

NOTE

In both of these queries, notice that the `Hide` column is used to make sure that only records containing a `Y` will be displayed. This is to prevent you from displaying information that a user requests remain confidential on the Web.

This IDC definition file uses the `GuestBookDetails.HTX` template file to display the result set on the Web browser. The IDC definition file will display the matching records using the detail form in the template file. The query that's executed will select all the fields that match the user-specified `FName` and `LName` fields. These fields are actually specified in the `SearchGuestBook.HTX` template file, which is examined in the next section.

Table 44.1. The IDC parameters.

Parameter	Description	Note
Datasource	Specifies the data source name (DSN) used to connect to the ODBC-compliant database.	This is a required field.
DefaultParameters	Specifies a default value to be used in the query if the user doesn't explicitly supply a value for a field.	
Expires	Specifies a time, in seconds, to wait before refreshing a cached page.	By default, an output page isn't cached by HTTPODBC.DLL. It will be cached only if the Expires parameter is used.
MaxFieldSize	Specifies the maximum buffer size to be allocated per field by HTTPODBC.DLL.	
MaxRecords	Specifies the maximum number of records to be returned by HTTPODBC.DLL.	
Password	Specifies a password to be used with the associated user name to access an ODBC database.	
RequiredParameters	Specifies the parameters that must be supplied by the user.	
SQLStatement	Specifies the SQL select statement (or query) to be executed.	This is a required field.
Template	Specifies the HTML template file that will be used to display the result set.	This is a required field.
UserName	Specifies a user name that will be used to access the ODBC database.	
Content-Type	Specifies a valid MIME type describing the returned result set.	

Creating the Internet Database Connector HTML Template

Well, you made it to the last step of the process—the creation of the HTML template files, which are described in the following sections:

- `Sign-In-IDC.HTX`
- `SearchGuestBook.HTX`
- `GuestBookDetails.HTX`

Before you go on to the description of the files, it's important to understand how these files work, because the files determine just what the user will see on his Web browser. Before you look at the files, however, it may pay off to learn a bit about what an HTML template (or `.HTX`) file contains. Basically, an `.HTX` file contains extensions to the HTML language. These extensions are enclosed in a `<%' '%>` tag pair. The returned result set is merged with the HTML document between the `<%begindetail%>` and `<%enddetail&>` tag pairs. There are also several HTX variables, summarized in Table 44.2, which, when combined with the `if-else-endif` flow control statement, determine how your output will appear.

Table 44.2. The HTX extensions.

Extension	Description	Note
ALL_HTTP	All HTTP headers that aren't parsed into one of the other listed variables in this table.	
AUTH_TYPE	Specifies the authorization type in use.	If the server has authenticated the user, the return value will be `Basic`. Otherwise, the entry won't be present.
BeginDetail	Specifies the beginning of a detail record block.	
CONTAINS	String includes the specified character.	Can be used only in an `if-else-endif` statement.
CONTENT_LENGTH	The number of bytes the script can expect from the client.	
CONTENT_TYPE	The content type of the information supplied in the post request.	
CurrentRecord	Specifies the current record number.	Can be used only in an `if-else-endif` statement.

Extension	Description	Note
else	else	The else clause of an if-else-endif statement block.
endif	endif	The end of if-else-endif statement block.
<%EndDetail%>	Specifies the end of the detail record block.	
EQ	Equal to.	Can be used only in an if-else-endif statement.
LT	Less than.	Can be used only in an if-else-endif statement.
GATEWAY_INTERFACE	Specifies the revision level of the CGI specification.	
GT	Greater than.	Can be used only in an if-else-endif statement.
HTTP_ACCEPT	Returns special case HTTP header information.	
if	if	The if clause of an if-else-endif statement block.
MaxRecords	The maximum number of records that can be returned.	Can be used only in an if-else-endif statement.
PATH_INFO	Additional path information as given by the client.	This value contains the trailing part of the URL, after the script name but before the query string (if any).
PATH_TRANSLATED	Same as PATH_INFO, but without virtual path name translation.	
QUERY_STRING	Specifies the information after the ? in a script query.	
REMOTE_ADDR	Specifies the IP address of the client.	
REMOTE_HOST	Specifies the host name of the client.	
REMOTE_USER	Specifies the user name supplied by the client and authorized by the server.	

continues

Table 44.2. continued

Extension	Description	Note
REQUEST_METHOD	Specifies the HTTP request method.	
SCRIPT_NAME	Specifies the name of the script being executed.	
SERVER_NAME	Specifies the name of the server (or IP address) as it should appear in self-referencing URLs.	
SERVER_PORT	Specifies the TCP/IP port on which the request was received.	
SERVER_PORT_SECURE	Specifies a 0 or 1, where 1 is an encrypted port (such as a secure port).	
SERVER_PROTOCOL	Specifies the name and version of the request.	Usually HTTP/1.0.
SERVER_SOFTWARE	Specifies the name and version number of the Web server under which the IIS extension is executing.	
UNMAPPED_REMOTE USER	Specifies what the user name was before an authentication filter mapped the user name to a Windows NT user name.	
URL	Specifies the URL of the request.	

Creating the `Sign-In-IDC.HTX` File

The first file is called `Sign-In-IDC.HTX`, and contains the following code:

```
1.    <html>
2.    <title>Knowles Consulting Guest Book</title>
3.    <BODY>
```

```
4.      <hr>
5.      <h1>Knowles Consulting Guest Book</h1>
6.      <hr>
7.      <%begindetail%>
8.      <%enddetail%>
9.      <%if CurrentRecord EQ 0 %>
10.     <h2>Information registered. Thanks!</h2>
11.     <p>
12.     <table border="1" width="100%">
13.     <caption align="top">Details for <%idc.FirstName%> <%idc.LastName%>
</caption>
14      <tr>
15.     <td><%if idc.FirstName EQ ""%>
16.     <%else%>
17.     First Name:</td><td><%idc.FirstName%><td><tr>
18.     <%endif%>
19.     <tr>
20.     <td><%if idc.MiddleInitial EQ ""%>
21.     <%else%>
22.     Middle Initial:</td><td><%idc.MiddleInitial%><td><tr>
23.     <%endif%>
24.     <tr>
25.     <td><%if idc.LastName EQ ""%>
26.     <%else%>
27.     Last Name:</td><td><%idc.LastName%><td><tr>
28.     <%endif%>
29.     <tr>
30.     <td><%if idc.Title EQ ""%>
31.     <%else%>
32.     Title:</td><td><%idc.Title%><td><tr>
33.     <%endif%>
34.     <tr>
35.     <td><%if idc.CompanyName EQ ""%>
36.     <%else%>
37.     Company Name:</td><td><%idc.CompanyName%><td><tr>
38.     <%endif%>
39.     <tr>
40.     <td><%if idc.Address EQ ""%>
41.     <%else%>
42.     Street Address:</td><td><%idc.Address%><td><tr>
43.     <%endif%>
44.     <tr>
45.     <td><%if idc.Address_2 EQ ""%>
46.     <%else%>
47.     Address (cont):</td><td><%idc.Address_2%><td><tr>
48.     <%endif%>
49.     <tr>
50.     <td><%if idc.City EQ ""%>
51.     <%else%>
52.     City:</td><td><%idc.City%><td><tr>
53.     <%endif%>
54.     <tr>
55.     <td><%if idc.StateOrProvince EQ ""%>
56.     <%else%>
57.     State/Province:</td><td><%idc.StateOrProvince%><td><tr>
```

```
58.    <%endif%>
59.    <tr>
60.    <td><%if idc.PostalCode EQ ""%>
61.    <%else%>
62.    Postal Code:</td><td><%idc.PostalCode%><td><tr>
63.    dif%>
64.    <tr>
65.    <td><%if idc.Country EQ ""%>
66.    <%else%>
67.    Country:</td><td><%idc.Country%><td><tr>
68.    <%endif%>
69.    <tr>
70.    <td><%if idc.WorkPhoneNumber EQ ""%>
71.    <%else%>
72.    Work Phone Number:</td><td><%idc.WorkPhoneNumber%><td><tr>
73.    <%endif%>
74.    <tr>
75.    <td><%if idc.HomePhoneNumber EQ ""%>
76.    <%else%>
77.    Home Phone Number:</td><td><%idc.HomePhoneNumber%><td><tr>
78.    <%endif%>
79.    <tr>
80.    <td><%if idc.FaxNumber EQ ""%>
81.    <%else%>
82.    Fax Phone Number:</td><td><%idc.FaxNumber%><td><tr>
83.    <%endif%>
84.    <tr>
85.    <td><%if idc.E_Mail EQ ""%>
86.    <%else%>
87.     E-Mail Address:</td><td><%idc.E_Mail%><td><tr>
88.    <%endif%>
89.    <tr>
90.    <td><%if idc.URL EQ ""%>
91.    <%else%>
92.    Home Page URL:</td><td><%idc.URL%><td><tr>
93.    <%endif%>
94.    <tr>
95.    <td><%if idc.Note EQ ""%>
96.    <%else%>
97.    Note:</td><td><%Note%><td><tr>
98.    <%endif%>
99.    </table>
100.    <p>
101.    <%else%>
102.    <h2><I><%idc.FirstName%> <%idc.LastName%></I> is already registered.</h2>
103.    <%endif%>
104.    <hr>
105.    <table width=100%>
106.    <tr><td width=50%><address><font size=2>
<em>Copyright &#169; 1996 Knowles Consulting. All rights reserved</em>
</font> </address>
107.    </td><td align=right width=50%><div align=right>
108.    <address><font size=2><em>Last Updated: June 21, 1996</em></font>
</address>
109.    </div>
110.    </td></tr>
111.    </table
112.    </body>
113.    </html>
```

Although this code is longer than you might expect, it isn't really as complex at it seems. When the page displays the confirmation message that the client data was accepted, it also creates a table containing the submitted data. If the data wasn't accepted, an error message is displayed, stating that the user is already registered.

The important parts of this record are contained between lines 9 and 101. Line 9 is the start of the major `if-else-endif` statement block. If the `CurrentRecord` parameter is equal to `0`, which will be true if the IDC returns a record in the result set, then the record was accepted. If a result set consists of multiple rows, the `CurrentRecord` parameter will be `0` the first time the `<%begindetail%>` `<%enddetail%>` block is executed. Each subsequent time the `<%begindetail%>` `<%enddetail%>` block is executed, the `CurrentRecord` counter will be incremented by one. Each row statement includes an `if-else-endif` statement block to check whether the column is a non-null value. If it is, the `else` statement is executed, which builds the row. Each row contains a tag and the value of the column. The rest of the document just includes the standard copyright and update information you've already seen.

Creating the `SearchGuestBook.HTX` File

The next HTX file is the `SearchGuestBook.HTX` file. The source code follows:

```
<html>
<title>Guest Book Query Results</title>
<BODY>
<h1>Selected Guest Book Contents</h1>
<%begindetail%>
<%if CurrentRecord EQ 0 %>
<h2>Here are the selected contents of the guest book.
Click a name to get details:</h2>
<p>
<%endif%>
Name: <a href="/Scripts/GuestBookDetails.IDC?FName=<%FirstName%>&
LName=<%LastName%>"><b><%FirstName%>
<%LastName%></b></a>
<p>
<%enddetail%>
<%if CurrentRecord EQ 0 %>
<h2>Sorry, no entries in the guest book match those criteria.</h2>
<%endif%>
<p>
<hr>
<table width=100%>
<tr><td width=50%><address><font size=2>
<em>Copyright &#169; 1996 Knowles Consulting. All rights reserved</em></font>
</address>
</td><td align=right width=50%><div align=right>
<address><font size=2><em>Last Updated: June 21, 1996</em></font> </address>
</div>
</td></tr>
</table>
</body>
</html>
```

This is a very simple .HTX file. Between the `<%begindetail%>` and `<%enddetail%>` tags, you'll find this statement:

```
Name: <a href="/Scripts/GuestBookDetails.IDC?FName=<%FirstName%>&
LName=<%LastName%>"><b><%FirstName%>
<%LastName%></b></a>
```

This is how the hypertext link is created between the search results page and the `GuestBookDetail.HTX` file. I mentioned earlier that the `GuestBookDetails.IDC` file uses the parameters passed to it in the `FName` and `LName` parameters to search the database for matching records to display. Well, this is where they're set and converted to a hypertext link all in one step. What's interesting about this line of code is that a form isn't used; instead, the `GuestBookDetails.IDC` script is executed by the IDC directly, which then passes the `FName` and `LName` parameters to the `GuestBookDetails.IDC` script. Kind of nifty, isn't it?

Creating the `GuestBookDetails.HTX` File

The final file is the detail form used by the `GuestBookDetails.IDC` file to display the result set. It's called `GuestBookDetails.HTX`, and is quite similar to the `Sign-In-IDC.HTX` file. In fact, they share the same table definition code:

```
<html>
<title>Guest Book Entry Details</title>
<BODY>
<h1>Guest Book Entry Details</h1>
<hr>
<%begindetail%>
<p>
<table border="1" width="100%">
<caption align="top">Details for <%FirstName%> <%LastName%></caption>
<tr>
<td><%if FirstName EQ ""%>
<%else%>
First Name:</td><td><%FirstName%><td><tr>
<%endif%>
<tr>
<td><%if MiddleInitial EQ ""%>
<%else%>
Middle Initial:</td><td><%MiddleInitial%><td><tr>
<%endif%>
<tr>
<td><%if LastName EQ ""%>
<%else%>
Last Name:</td><td><%LastName%><td><tr>
<%endif%>
<tr>
<td><%if Title EQ ""%>
<%else%>
Title:</td><td><%Title%><td><tr>
<%endif%>
<tr>
<td><%if CompanyName EQ ""%>
<%else%>
```

```
Company Name:</td><td><%CompanyName%><td><tr>
<%endif%>
<tr>
<td><%if Address EQ ""%>
<%else%>
Street Address:</td><td><%Address%><td><tr>
<%endif%>
<tr>
<td><%if Address_2 EQ ""%>
<%else%>
Address (cont):</td><td><%Address_2%><td><tr>
<%endif%>
<tr>
<td><%if City EQ ""%>
<%else%>
City:</td><td><%City%><td><tr>
<%endif%>
<tr>
<td><%if StateOrProvince EQ ""%>
<%else%>
State/Province:</td><td><%StateOrProvince%><td><tr>
<%endif%>
<tr>
<td><%if PostalCode EQ ""%>
<%else%>
Postal Code:</td><td><%PostalCode%><td><tr>
<%endif%>
<tr>
<td><%if Country EQ ""%>
<%else%>
Country:</td><td><%Country%><td><tr>
<%endif%>
<tr>
<td><%if WorkPhoneNumber EQ ""%>
<%else%>
Work Phone Number:</td><td><%WorkPhoneNumber%><td><tr>
<%endif%>
<tr>
<td><%if HomePhoneNumber EQ ""%>
<%else%>
Home Phone Number:</td><td><%HomePhoneNumber%><td><tr>
<%endif%>
<tr>
<td><%if FaxNumber EQ ""%>
<%else%>
Fax Phone Number:</td><td><%FaxNumber%><td><tr>
<%endif%>
<tr>
<td><%if E_Mail EQ ""%>
<%else%>
E-Mail Address:</td><td><%E_Mail%><td><tr>
<%endif%>
<tr>
<td><%if URL EQ ""%>
<%else%>
Home Page URL:</td><td><%URL%><td><tr>
<%endif%>
<tr>
```

```
<td><%if Note EQ ""%>
<%else%>
Note:</td><td><%Note%><td><tr>
<%endif%>
</table>
<p>
<%enddetail%>
<p>
<hr>
<table width=100%>
<tr><td width=50%><address><font size=2>
<em>Copyright &#169; 1996 Knowles Consulting. All
rights reserved</em></font> </address>
</td><td align=right width=50%><div align=right>
<address><font size=2><em>Last Updated: June 21, 1996</em></font> </address>
</div>
</td></tr>
</table>
</body>
</html>
```

Notice the table definition between the `<%begindetail%>` and `<%enddetail%>` tags. This will display one or more records on the page, depending on the number of records returned in the result set. The only real difference between this page and the others examined earlier in this chapter is that no check occurs to verify that at least one record was found. However, this check isn't needed. After all, to get to this page in the first place, you must have clicked on a hypertext link created in the previous page (`SearchGuestBook.HTX`), which would have been created only if a record was found. There are other tags, like the `<%begindetail%>` and `<%enddetail%>` tags, which you can use in your `.HTX` files. These additional tags are summarized in Table 44.2 (in the preceding section).

Using the SQL Server Web Assistant

While you can use the Internet Database Connector to build dynamic Web pages that interact with the user, you can also use the Web Assistant. The main difference between the IDC and the Web Assistant is that the Web Assistant isn't designed to interact with the user. Instead, it's designed to publish a database online. It does this by creating static Web pages, but perhaps *static* is the wrong word. Most people consider a static page to be a Web page that doesn't change its contents. However, with the Web Assistant, these Web pages can be automatically refreshed when a new record is inserted into the database, or when a specific time interval is reached. This means that the Web page contents could change. In essence, once more you have the ability to create a dynamic Web page. If you combine the IDC with the Web Administrator, you can build a fully-interactive online order system, for example.

Creating an interactive online order system would require an event-driven processing methodology, where you would respond to actions that occur, rather than a hierarchical methodology, where you would control the data flow in a step-by-step process. Let me show you how this could work. First, let's lay the groundwork:

- You have an ODBC database containing your product inventory. This inventory database contains the quantity, price, and a description of the items.
- You want to publish an online catalog using this information.
- You want to accept client orders from the online catalog.

To bring together these three basic ideas and build an interactive order-entry database, you'd have to build the following constructs:

- **Online catalog.** You could use the Web Administrator to build this Web page, using a query designed to select all items from your product inventory database whenever the item quantity is greater than one. Any time the database changes, you could have the Web Administrator rebuild the page. The Web page could include a hypertext link to another Web page containing the order form.

- **Order form.** The order form will use the Internet Database Connector to insert an order record into the Order database.

- **Order database.** This database would contain information about the client and product ordered. It might contain fields for order number, date, name, address, payment, product, and so on. For optimum results, this would be a client/server database (such as SQL Server) rather than an application database (such as Access) so that you could benefit from the capability to execute code automatically (like triggers or scheduled procedures). In this fashion, whenever an order record was entered into the database, your code could automatically decrement the quantity for the item contained in your product inventory database. This same code could automatically notify a sales or shipping representative. This code could update other databases; these databases could be used by applications within your company to automate the shipping and billing processes.

The basic workflow to obtain an order would follow these basic steps:

1. The user connects to your Web site.
2. The user selects your catalog to browse through it.

TIP

You could create a custom query form using the IDC to search for specific items in your catalog. The description field could be used as a searchable text field, for example, so that the user could specify the type of items of interest. The returned result set, based on her query, could be displayed on another custom IDC HTML page. The user could then follow the same order process, once she selects the item to order.

3. The user selects an item and clicks a link to order the item.

4. An order form appears. The user fills out the relevant data fields and submits the form. This submission inserts a record into the Order database.

5. The Order database insert trigger is activated. This could send an e-mail message requesting manual intervention to continue the order and shipping process. Or the trigger could cause a cascade of events to occur in which one or more databases is updated (like the quantity field for the item in the product inventory database), applications are executed, and finally the product is shipped to the user.

6. When the product inventory database is updated to reflect that there is one fewer of the ordered item, the Web Administrator could update the online catalog page so that the next user will see an accurate count for the item. If the current user purchases the item, and then attempts to reorder the item based on her cached online version of the catalog (still showing the purchased item in inventory), your IDC order form would report an error, because the query executed by the IDC would return real-time results (the query would return no records, as the quantity field in the product inventory database would now be 0).

To use the Web Assistant to build your Web pages, follow these steps:

1. Launch the SQL Server Web Assistant, located in the SQL Server 6.5 program group, to display the SQL Server Web Assistant - Login dialog box (see Figure 44.2).

FIGURE 44.2.

Specifying the SQL Server parameters for the Web Assistant.

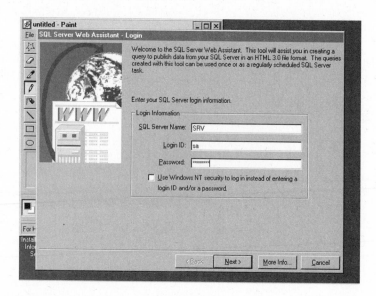

2. Enter the name of your SQL Server installation in the SQL Server Name field.

3. Enter a user name in the Login ID field.

4. Enter a password for the user name in the Password field.

> **NOTE**
>
> If you're using the mixed or integrated security models, you can enable the check box at the bottom of the dialog box (Use Windows NT Security to Log In). This way, your current credentials will be used.

5. Click the Next button to display the dialog box shown in Figure 44.3.

FIGURE 44.3.

Specifying the SQL Server database you want to use.

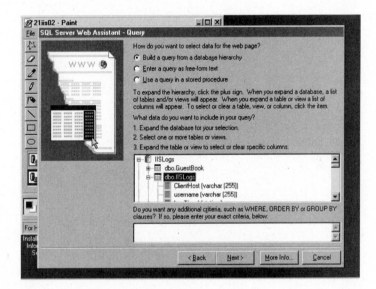

6. In the dialog box, specify one of the following options:

   - Build a Query from the Database Hierarchy. This option specifies that the database table you select will be posted on the Web in its entirety, unless you specify additional restrictions in the query window at the bottom of the dialog box. You can publish multiple tables simply by selecting the tables in the list box shown in Figure 44.3. If you want to publish only part of a table, you can expand the table item and select the specific fields you want to publish.

   - Enter a Query as Free-Form Text. When this option is selected, the dialog box changes to let you choose a database and enter a free-form query. This free-form query is used to return a result set, which will be displayed on the Web page created by the Web Assistant.

   - Use a Query in a Stored Procedure. When this option is selected, the dialog box changes to enable you to choose a database, choose a stored procedure in the database, and enter any command-line arguments for the stored procedure.

For this discussion, I'll assume that you've chosen the Build a Query from the Database Hierarchy option and selected a single table.

7. When you've made your selection, click the Next button.

8. The SQL Server Web Assistant–Scheduling dialog box appears. Choose one of the following options from the Scheduling Options drop-down list box:

   ■ Now. The Web page will be created immediately.

   ■ Later. The Web page will be created once, at a user-specified date and time.

   ■ When Data Changes. The Web page will be re-created automatically whenever the database changes.

   ■ On Certain Days of the Week. The Web page will be re-created on specific days at specific times.

   ■ On a Regular Basis. The Web page will be re-created at scheduled time intervals.

TIP

For high-traffic sites, the last two options could be particularly useful. While the data wouldn't be updated in real-time, it could be updated frequently enough to promote a sense of continuity for the user (for example, new products would constantly be added to the database). This could benefit you by lowering the system resource demands on your server during peak activity periods. This lowering of resource requirements means that your server could support more simultaneous user connections.

---

9. Click the Next button to display the SQL Server Web Assistant–File Options dialog box (see Figure 44.4).

10. Specify a path and file name for the Web page in the first field.

11. Click the A Template File Called radio button and enter the name of the HTML template file to be used to format your output. Or click the other radio button and specify the Web page title and subtitle in the appropriate fields.

12. If you want to add an HTML hypertext link, click one of the Yes radio buttons and supply a single URL and description, or the table name containing this information, depending on which option you selected.

13. Click the Next button to open the SQL Server Web Assistant–Formatting dialog box, as shown in Figure 44.5.

14. Using the options in the middle section of the dialog box, specify how you want the result columns to be formatted.

15. Choose the desired additional options: inserting a time/date timestamp at the beginning of the page, including column name headers on the output, and/or limiting the number of rows on a single Web page.

16. Click the Finish button to build your Web page.

FIGURE 44.4.

Specifying the Web Assistant parameters for the resulting Web page output.

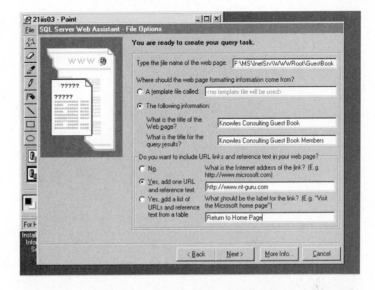

FIGURE 44.5.

Specifying the Web Assistant page formatting parameters.

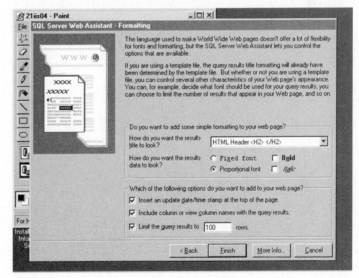

Summary

In this chapter you have learned by example how to build a guest book using the Internet Database Connector. You've learned how to build the HTML forms, how to build the IDC definition files, and how to build the HTML template files. You've also learned how to use the SQL Server Web Assistant to build Web pages to display data from your database in a semi-static form. While not interactive, this method does provide the capacity to publish extremely large amounts of data on the Web. If combined with the interactive capabilities provided by the IDC, an interactive online system can be built.

The primary reason to use the Internet Database Connector over a corresponding Microsoft dbWeb implementation is for enhanced control over the behavior (including the look and feel) of the Web page and the query used to return the resulting data. Because the IDC is a pre-defined interface that uses HTML documents, .HTX, and .IDC files to interface with a database, it's easier than developing a custom CGI application, which requires development with a compiler. Because the IDC is an ISAPI application, it runs in the context of the Internet Information Server. This is a more efficient method than a corresponding custom CGI application, which runs in a separate process address space, meaning that you have less overhead and improved user response time.

IN THIS PART

Appendixes

VII

PART

DB-Library
Quick Reference

A

Core Functions

VBSQL	C/C++	Description
SqlAData	dbadata	Returns the data for a compute column.
SqlADLen	dbadlen	Returns the length of the data in a compute column.
n/a	dbaltbind	Binds a compute column (column of results from a compute clause) to a program variable.
SqlAltColID	dbaltcolid	Returns the column ID for a compute column.
SqlAltLen	dbaltlen	Returns the maximum length of the data for a compute column.
SqlAltOp	dbaltop	Returns the type of aggregate function for a compute column.
SqlAltType	dbalttype	Returns the datatype for a compute column.
SqlAltUType	dbaltutype	Returns the user-defined datatype for a compute column.
n/a	dbanullbind	Associates an indicator variable with a compute-row column.
n/a	dbbind	Binds a regular result column (a column of results from a select statement's select list) to a program variable.
SqlByList	dbbylist	Returns the bylist for a compute row.
SqlCancel	dbcancel	Cancels the current command batch and flushes any pending results.
SqlCanQuery	dbcanquery	Cancels any rows pending from the most recently executed query.
SqlChange	dbchange	Determines whether a command batch has changed the current database to another database.
SqlClose	dbclose	Closes and frees a SQL Server connection.
SqlClrBuf	dbclrbuf	Clears rows from the row buffer.
SqlClrOpt	dbclropt	Clears an option set by dbsetopt (C), or SqlSetOpt (VB).
SqlCmd	dbcmd	Adds Transact-SQL text to the command buffer.

VBSQL	*C/C++*	*Description*
SqlCmdRow	dbcmdrow	Determines whether the current command can return rows.
SqlColInfo	dbcolinfo	Returns information about a regular column or a compute column in a result set, or a column in a cursor.
SqlColLen	dbcollen	Returns the maximum length of the data for a column, in bytes.
SqlColName	dbcolname	Returns the name of a particular result column.
SqlColType	dbcoltype	Returns the datatype for a regular result column.
SqlColUType	dbcolutype	Returns the user-defined datatype for a regular result column.
n/a	dbconvert	Converts data from one datatype to another.
SqlCount	dbcount	Returns the number of rows affected by a Transact-SQL statement.
SqlCurCmd	dbcurcmd	Returns the number of the current command within a command batch.
SqlCurRow	dbcurrow	Returns the number of the row currently being read.
SqlData	dbdata	Returns a pointer to the data (C) or a string containing the data (VB) for a result column.
SqlDataReady	dbdataready	Indicates whether SQL Server has completed processing a command.
SqlDateCrack	dbdatecrack	Converts a machine-readable date-and-time value into user-accessible format.
SqlDatLen	dbdatlen	Returns the actual length of the data for a column, in bytes.
SqlDead	dbdead	Indicates whether a SQL Server connection is inactive.
Use VBSQL Error Event Handler	dberrhandle	Supplies a user function to handle DB-Library errors.
SqlExit	dbexit	Closes and frees all SQL Server connections created as a result of your application.

continues

Core Functions, continued

VBSQL	C/C++	Description
n/a	dbfcmd	Adds text to the DBPROCESS command buffer, using C runtime library sprintf-type formatting.
SqlFirstRow	dbfirstrow	Returns the number of the first row in the row buffer.
SqlFreeBuf	dbfreebuf	Clears the command buffer.
SqlFreeLogin	dbfreelogin	Frees a login record.
n/a	dbfreeequal	Frees memory allocated by the dbqual function.
SqlGetChar	dbgetchar	Returns a character in the command buffer.
SqlGetMaxProcs	dbgetmaxprocs	Determines the current maximum number of simultaneously open connections.
SqlGetOff	dbgetoff	Checks for the existence of Transact-SQL statements in the command buffer.
SqlGetPacket	dbgetpacket	Returns the tabular data stream (TDS) packet size currently in use.
SqlGetRow	dbgetrow	Reads the specified row in the row buffer.
SqlGetTime	dbgettime	Returns the number of seconds that DB-Library waits for SQL Server to respond to a Transact-SQL statement.
n/a	dbgetuserdata	Returns a pointer to user-allocated data from a DBPROCESS structure.
SqlInit	dbinit	Initializes DB-Library.
SqlIsAvail	dbisavail	Determines whether a connection is available for general use.
SqlIsCount	dbiscount	Indicates whether the count returned by dbcount (C) or SqlCount (VB) is real.
SqlIsOpt	dbisopt	Checks the status of a SQL Server or DB-Library option.
SqlLastRow	dblastrow	Returns the number of the last row in the row buffer.
SqlLogin	dblogin	Allocates a LOGINREC structure for use in dbopen (C) or SqlOpen (VB).
SqlMoreCmds	dbmorecmds	Indicates whether there are more commands to be processed.

VBSQL	C/C++	Description
Use VBSQL Message Event Handler	`dbmsghandle`	Installs a user function to handle SQL Server messages.
`SqlName`	`dbname`	Returns the name of the current database.
`SqlNextRow`	`dbnextrow`	Reads in the next row.
n/a	`dbnullbind`	Associates an indicator variable with a regular result-row column.
`SqlNumAlts`	`dbnumalts`	Returns the number of columns in a compute row.
`SqlNumCols`	`dbnumcols`	Determines the number of columns for the current result set.
`SqlNumCompute`	`dbnumcompute`	Returns the number of `compute` clauses in the current set of results.
`SqlNumOrders`	`dbnumorders`	Returns the number of columns specified in a Transact-SQL `select` statement's `order by` clause.
`SqlOpen`	`dbopen`	Allocates and initializes a SQL Server connection.
`SqlOrderCol`	`dbordercol`	Returns the ID of a column appearing in the most-recently-executed query's `order by` clause.
n/a	`dbprhead`	Prints the column headings for rows returned from SQL Server.
Use VBSQL Error Event Handler	`dbprocerrhandle`	Supplies a user function to handle DB-Library errors for a specific `DBPROCESS` connection.
`SqlProcInfo`	`dbprocinfo`	Returns information about a SQL Server connection.
Use VBSQL Message Event Handler	`dbprocmsghandle`	Supplies a user function to handle SQL Server messages for a specific `DBPROCESS` connection.
n/a	`dbprrow`	Prints all rows returned from SQL Server.
`SqlPrType`	`dbprtype`	Converts a SQL Server token value to a readable string.
`SqlResults`	`dbresults`	Sets up the results of the next query.
`SqlRows`	`dbrows`	Indicates whether the current statement returned rows.

continues

Core Functions, continued

VBSQL	C/C++	Description
SqlRowType	dbrowtype	Returns the type of the current row.
SqlServerEnum	dbserverenum	Searches for the names of SQL Servers locally, over the network, or both.
SqlSetAvail	dbsetavail	Marks a SQL Server connection as being available for general use.
SqlSetLApp	DBSETLAPP	Sets the application name in the LOGINREC structure.
SqlSetLHost	DBSETLHOST	Sets the workstation name in the LOGINREC structure.
SqlSetLNatLang	DBSETLNATLANG	Sets the name of the national language in the LOGINREC structure.
SqlSetLoginTime	dbsetlongintime	Sets the number of seconds that DB-Library waits for SQL Server to respond to a connection request.
SqlSetLPacket	DBSETLPACKET	Sets the tabular data stream (TDS) packet size in an application's LOGINREC structure.
SqlSetLPwd	DBSETLPWD	Sets the user's SQL Server password in the LOGINREC structure.
SqlSetLSecure	DBSETLSECURE	Sets the secure connection flag in a LOGINREC structure.
n/a	DBSETLTIME	Sets the connection-specific connection timeout in a LOGINREC structure.
SqlSetLUser	DBSETLUSER	Sets the user name in the LOGINREC structure.
SqlSetLVersion	DBSETLVERSION	Sets the DB-Library client behavior to Version 4.2 or Version 6.0 behavior in a LOGINREC structure.
SqlSetMaxProcx	dbsetmaxprocs	Sets the maximum number of simultaneously-open connections.
n/a	dbsetnull	Defines substitution values for use when binding null values.
SqlSetOpt	dbsetopt	Sets a SQL Server or DB-Library option.
SqlSetTime	dbsettime	Sets the number of seconds that DB-Library waits for SQL Server to respond to a submitted query.

VBSQL	C/C++	Description
n/a	dbsetuserdata	In a DBPROCESS structure, saves a pointer to user-allocated data.
SqlExec	dbsqlexec	Sends a command batch to SQL Server.
SqlOk	dbsqlok	Verifies the correctness of a command batch.
SqlSend	dbsqlsend	Sends a command batch to SQL Server and doesn't wait for a response.
SqlStrCpy	dbstrcpy	Copies a portion of the command buffer to a program variable.
SqlStrLen	dbstrlen	Returns the length, in characters, of the command buffer.
SqlUse	dbuse	Uses a particular database.
n/a	dbvarylen	Determines whether the specified data in a regular result column can vary in length.
n/a	dbwillconvert	Determines whether a specific datatype conversion is available within DB-Library.
SqlWinExit	dbwinexit	Informs DB-Library that the Windows application is about to exit.

Cursor Functions

VBSQL	C/C++	Description
SqlCursor	dbcursor	Inserts, updates, deletes, locks, or refreshes a particular row in the fetch buffer of a client cursor, a transparent server cursor, or an explicit server cursor.
n/a	dbcursorbind	Binds a column of a client cursor, transparent server cursor, or explicit server cursor to an array of program variables. This array of program variables is filled with result data after every fetch or refresh.

continues

Cursor Functions, continued

VBSQL	C/C++	Description
SqlCursorClose	dbcursorclose	Closes the client cursor, transparent server cursor, or explicit server cursor, and releases the memory associated with a cursor handle or connection.
SqlCursorColInfo	dbcursorcolinfo	Returns information about the specified column of a client cursor, transparent server cursor, or explicit server cursor.
SqlCursorData	n/a	Returns the value of the data in a specified row and column of the current fetch buffer for a client cursor, a transparent server cursor, or an explicit server cursor.
SqlCursorFetch	dbcursorfetch	Fetches a block of rows (called the *fetch buffer*) from a client cursor or transparent server cursor, and makes the rows available to either SqlCursorData (VB) or dbcursorbind (C). If you're connected to SQL Server 6.0, you should use the cursorfetchex functions.
SqlCursorFetchEx	dbcursorfetchex	Fetches a block of rows (called the *fetch buffer*) from an explicit server cursor, and makes the rows available to either SqlCursorData (VB) or dbcursorbind (C).
SqlCursorInfo	dbcursorinfo	Returns the number of columns and the number of rows in the keyset for a client cursor, a transparent server cursor, or an explicit server cursor.
SqlCursorInfoEx	dbcursorinfoex	Returns information about a client cursor, a transparent server cursor, or an explicit server cursor.
SqlCursorOpen	dbcursoropen	Opens a cursor.

Stored Procedure Functions

VBSQL	C/C++	Description
SqlHasRetStat	dbhasretstat	Determines whether a stored procedure or a remote stored procedure generated a return status number.
SqlNumRets	dbnumrets	Calculates the number of returned parameter values generated by a stored procedure or a remote stored procedure.
SqlRetData	dbretdata	Returns a return-parameter value generated by a stored procedure or a remote stored procedure.
SqlRetLen	dbretlen	Determines the length of a return-parameter value generated by a stored procedure or a remote stored procedure.
SqlRetName	dbretname	Returns the name of a return parameter of a stored procedure or a remote stored procedure.
SqlRetStatus	dbretstatus	Returns the status number returned by a stored procedure or a remote stored procedure.
SqlRetType	dbrettype	Determines the datatype of a return-parameter value generated by a stored procedure or a remote stored procedure.
SqlRpcExec	dbrpcexec	Executes a single stored procedure, a single remote stored procedure, or a batch of stored procedures and/or remote stored procedures on SQL Server.
SqlRpcInit	dbrpcinit	Initializes a stored procedure or a remote stored procedure.
SqlRpcParam	dbrpcparam	Adds a parameter to a stored procedure or a remote stored procedure.
SqlRpcSend	dbrpcsend	Sends a single stored procedure, a single remote stored procedure, or a batch of stored procedures and/or remote stored procedures to SQL Server to be executed.

Text and Image Functions

VBSQL	*C/C++*	*Description*
SqlMoreText	dbmoretext	Sends part of a large text or image value to SQL Server.
n/a	dbreadtext	Reads part of a text or image value from SQL Server.
SqlTxPtr	dbtxptr	Returns the identifier for a text or image column in the current row.
SqlTxTimeStamp	dbtxtimestamp	Returns the identifier for the text timestamp for a column in the current row.
SqlTxTsNewVal	dbtxtsnewval	Returns the identifier for the new value for a text timestamp.
SqlTxTsPut	dbtxtsput	Places the identifier for the new value for a text timestamp into a column of the current row in the row buffer.
SqlUpdateText	dbupdatetext	Updates an existing text or image value. This function also can change a portion of a text or image value in place.
SqlWriteText	dbwritetext	Sends a text or image value to SQL Server.
SqlTextUpdate1Row	n/a	Updates one row of results in a text column. Subsequent rows, if any, are removed from the results buffer.
SqlTextUpdateManyRows	n/a	Updates all rows of results in a text or image column, starting from the current row.

Browse Functions

VBSQL	C/C++	Description
SqlColBrowse	dbcolbrowse	Indicates whether the source of a result column can be updated with the DB-Library browse mode facilities.
SqlColSource	dbcolsource	Returns the name of the database column from which a result column derives.
SqlQual	dbqual	Returns a string containing the where clause for the current row in a specified table. In a browseable table, this string can be used to update the current row.
SqlTabBrowse	dbtabbrowse	Indicates whether a specified table can be updated with the DB-Library browse mode procedures.
SqlTabCount	dbtabcount	Returns the number of tables included in the current select statement.
SqlTabName	dbtabname	Returns the name of a table based on its number.
SqlTabSource	dbtabsource	Returns the name and number of the table from which a result column is derived.
SqlTsNewLen	dbtsnewlen	Returns the length of the new value of a timestamp column after a browse mode update.
SqlTsNewVal	dbtsnewval	Returns the identifier of the new value of a timestamp column after a browse mode update.
SqlTxPut	dbtxput	Puts the new value of a timestamp column into a specified table's current row in the row buffer.
SqlTsUpdate	n/a	Updates the value of a timestamp column in a specified table.

Bulk Copy Functions

VBSQL	C/C++	Description
n/a	bcp_batch	Saves any rows previously bulk copied from program variables and sent to SQL Server by bcp_sendrow.
n/a	bcp_bind	Binds data from a program variable to a table column for bulk copy into SQL Server.
SqlBCPColfmt	bcp_colfmt	Specifies the format of an operating-system file in a bulk copy into or out of SQL Server.
n/a	bcp_collen	Sets the program variable data length for the current bulk copy into SQL Server.
n/a	bcp_colptr	Sets the program variable data address for the current copy into SQL Server.
SqlBCPColumns	bcp_columns	Sets the total number of columns in the operating-system file for a bulk copy into or out of SQL Server.
SqlBCPControl	bcp_control	Changes the default settings for various control parameters for a bulk copy between a file and SQL Server.
n/a	bcp_done	Ends a bulk copy from program variables into SQL Server performed with bcp_bind and bcp_sendrow.
SqlBCPExec	bcp_exec	Executes a bulk-copy of data between a database table and an operating-system file.
SqlBCPInit	bcp_init	Initializes a bulk-copy operation.
n/a	bcp_moretext	Sends part of a text or image value to SQL Server.
n/a	bcp_readfmt	Reads a data-file format definition from a user file for a bulk copy between a file and SQL Server.
n/a	bcp_sendrow	Sends a row of data from program variables to SQL Server.
SqlBCPSetL	BCP_SETL	Sets the login structure to enable bulk copy operations.

VBSQL	C/C++	Description
n/a	bcp_writefmt	Writes a data-file format definition to a user file for a bulk copy between a file and SQL Server.
SqlBCPColumnFormat	n/a	Sets up the column format for the input file in a bulk copy operation. This is a utility function that combines SqlBCPColumns and SqlBCPColfmt in one step.

Two-Phase Commit Functions (C/C++ Development Only)

C/C++	Description
abort_xact	Marks a distributed transaction as canceled.
build_xact_string	Builds a name for a distributed transaction.
close_commit	Ends a connection with the commit service by calling dbclose.
commit_xact	Marks a distributed transaction as committed.
open_commit	Establishes a connection with the commit service.
remove_xact	Decrements the count of sites still active in the distributed transaction.
scan_xact	Prints the commit service record for distributed transactions.
start_xact	Starts a distributed transaction using the commit service.
stat_xact	Returns the status of the specified distributed transaction.

Legal Agreements Pertaining to the CD-ROM

B

By opening this package, you are agreeing to be bound by the following agreement:

Some of the software included with this product is copyrighted, in which case all rights are reserved by the respective copyright holder. You are licensed to use software copyrighted by the Publisher and its licensors on a single computer. You may copy and/or modify the software as needed to facilitate your use of it on a single computer. Making copies of the software for any other purpose is a violation of the United States copyright laws.

This software is sold as is without warranty of any kind, either expressed or implied, including but not limited to the implied warranties of merchantability and fitness for a particular purpose. Neither the publisher nor its dealers or distributors assumes any liability for any alleged or actual damages arising from the use of this program. (Some states do not allow for the exclusion of implied warranties, so the exclusion may not apply to you.)

By opening this package, you are agreeing to be bound by the following agreement, which applies to products supplied by Northern Lights Software:

Aurora is a copyrighted product of Northern Lights Software, Ltd., and is protected by United States copyright laws and international treaty provisions. Copyright 1994, 1995, 1996. All Rights Reserved. Aurora Utilities for Sybase, Aurora Desktop, Aurora Script Manager, Aurora Distribution Viewer, and Aurora Cost Retrieval DLL are service marks of Northern Lights Software. Sybase is a trademark of Sybase, Inc.

Period of evaluation. By installing the software, it is understood that the provided software is for the purposes of evaluation only, and cannot be used beyond a period of thirty (30) days unless the software is registered. The software can be registered only by Northern Lights Software, Ltd., or its empowered agents.

Limited Warranty. Northern Lights warrants that the SOFTWARE will perform substantially in accordance with the written description delivered with the software, usually in the form of a readme.txt, for a period of ninety (90) days. Any implied warranties are limited to the same period of ninety (90) days.

Remedies. Northern Lights and its suppliers' entire liability and your exclusive remedy shall be, at Northern Lights' option, a refund of the price paid or repair or replacement of the software. This Limited Warranty is void if the failure has resulted from accident, abuse, or misapplication. These warranties are limited to the United States unless you can provide proof of purchase from an authorized non-U.S. source.

No Other Warranties. To the maximum extent permitted by applicable law, Northern Lights disclaims all other warranties, either express or implied, including but not limited to implied warranties of merchantability and fitness for a particular purpose. This limited warranty gives you certain rights. You may have other rights which vary by state and jurisdiction.

No Liability for Consequential Damages. To the maximum extent permitted by applicable law, in no event shall Northern Lights be liable for any damages whatsoever (including, without limitation, damages for loss of business profits, business interruption, loss of business information, or any other pecuniary loss) arising out of the use of or inability to use this product, even if Northern Lights has been advised of the possibility of such damages. Because some states do not allow the limit or exclusion of liability for consequential or incidental damage, the above limitation may not apply to you.

INDEX

UNLEASHED

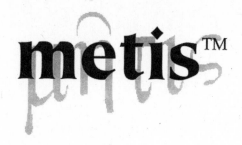

metis™

metis technologies, llc
5 westover road
troy, ny 12180

(800) 638-4711
(800-METIS-11)
fax (518) 273-4256

compuserve 75600,615
info@metis.com
http://www.metis.com

Innovators in technical education and support and

leaders in **using** technology to deliver **knowledge**

Whether you are looking for

WWW-based technical support

or

on-site **mentoring**

whether you need

quality assurance reviews

or

application **performance** assessments

or

formal classroom **training**

look to

metis technologies

Microsoft, Sybase SQL Server

WWW Database Integration

WWW Commerce, Java

Interactive HTML, CGI

Lotus Notes

For more information, call us at 1-800-METIS-11 (1-800-638-4711)

μητις (máy-tis) n.: wisdom, artifice, strategem. **metis**: innovative technologies for a postmodern world

Visible Analyst Workbench

Integrated Enterprise CASE

Planning - Analysis - Design - Construction - Re-Engineering/BPR

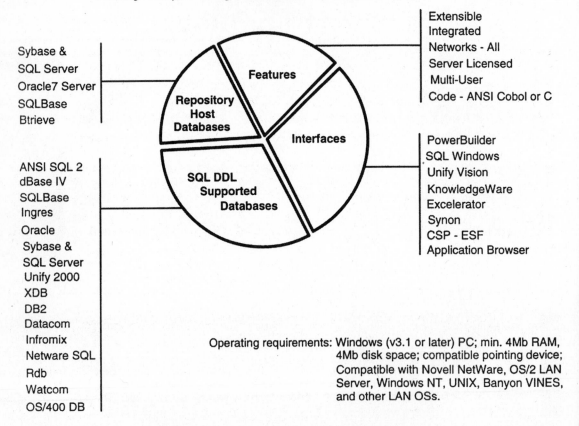

Sybase & SQL Server
Oracle7 Server
SQLBase
Btrieve

Repository Host Databases

Features

Extensible Integrated Networks - All Server Licensed Multi-User Code - ANSI Cobol or C

Interfaces

ANSI SQL 2
dBase IV
SQLBase
Ingres
Oracle
Sybase &
SQL Server
Unify 2000
XDB
DB2
Datacom
Infromix
Netware SQL
Rdb
Watcom
OS/400 DB

SQL DDL Supported Databases

PowerBuilder
SQL Windows
Unify Vision
KnowledgeWare
Excelerator
Synon
CSP - ESF
Application Browser

Operating requirements: Windows (v3.1 or later) PC; min. 4Mb RAM, 4Mb disk space; compatible pointing device; Compatible with Novell NetWare, OS/2 LAN Server, Windows NT, UNIX, Banyon VINES, and other LAN OSs.

The Visible Analyst Workbench® is an object based corporate workgroup CASE tool that combines data, process and objects in an integrated open repository. Powerful modeling support includes Business Modeling, Class Modeling, Entity Relationship Modeling, Data Flow Modeling, State Transition Modeling, and Program Modeling, which is synchronized and cross-balanced, allowing for all development in one singular OO environment. Migration of legacy systems, IEW/ADW and Excelerator data and designs to an OO world make for fast generation of new client/server applications.

Visible Systems Corporation
300 Bear Hill Road
Waltham, MA 02154
Phone: (617) 890-CASE (2273) Fax: (617) 890-8909
Web Page/http://www.visible.com Email: info.visible.com

Free trial copy available on CD-ROM

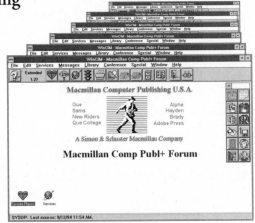

Designing and Implementing Microsoft Internet Information Server 2

Arthur Knowles & Sanjaya Hettihewa

This book details the specific tasks to setting up and running Microsoft Internet Information Server. Readers learn troubleshooting, network design, security, and cross-platform integration procedures. Teaches security issues and how to maintain an efficient, secure network. Readers learn everything from planning to implementation. Covers Microsoft Internet Information Server 2.

Price: $39.99 USA/$56.95 CDN   User Level: Casual—Expert

ISBN: 1-57521-168-8   336 pp.   Internet—Communications/Online

Peter Norton's Complete Guide to Windows NT 4 Workstation

Peter Norton

Readers explore everything from interface issues to advanced topics, such as client/server networking, building their own Internet servers, and OLE. Readers master complex memory-management techniques. Teaches how to build an Internet server. Explores peer-to-peer networking.

Price: $39.99 USA/$56.95 CDN   User Level: Casual—Accomplished

ISBN: 0-672-30901-7   936 pp.   Operating Systems

Windows NT 4 Server Unleashed

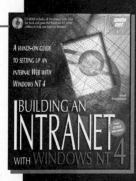

Jason Garms

Windows NT Server has been gaining tremendous market share over Novell, and the new upgrade—which includes a Windows 95 interface—is sure to add momentum to its market drive. *Windows NT 4 Server Unleashed* provides information on disk and file management, integrated networking, BackOffice integration, and TCP/IP protocols. CD-ROM includes source code from the book and valuable utilities. Focuses on using Windows NT as an Internet server. Covers security issues and Macintosh support.

Price: $59.99 USA/$84.95 CDN   User Level: Accomplished—Expert

ISBN: 0-672-30933-5   1,100 pp.   Networking

Building an Intranet with Windows NT 4

Scott Zimmerman & Tim Evans

This hands-on guide teaches readers how to set up and maintain an efficient Intranet with Windows NT. It comes complete with a selection of the best software for setting up a server, creating content, and developing Intranet applications. CD-ROM includes a complete Windows NT Intranet toolkit with a full-featured Web server, Web content development tools, and ready-to-use Intranet applications. Includes complete specifications for several of the most popular Intranet applications—group scheduling, discussions, database access, and more.

Price: $49.99 USA/$70.95 CDN   User Level: Casual—Accomplished

ISBN: 1-57521-137-8   600 pp.   Internet—Intranets

Microsoft Exchange Server Survival Guide

Greg Todd

Readers learn the difference between Exchange and other groupware (such as Lotus Notes), and everything about the Exchange server, including troubleshooting, development, and how to interact with other BackOffice components. Includes everything operators need to run an Exchange server. Teaches how to prepare, plan, and install the Exchange server. Explores ways to migrate from other mail applications, such as Microsoft Mail and cc:Mail.

Price: $49.99 USA/$70.95 CDN   *User Level: New—Advanced*

ISBN: 0-672-30890-8   700 pp.   *Groupware*

Microsoft SQL Server 6.5 DBA Survival Guide, Second Edition

Mark Spenik & Orryn Sledge

This book will turn an inexperienced administrator into a skilled leader in charge of a well-tuned RDBMS. Time-saving techniques show how to maximize Microsoft SQL Server. CD-ROM contains scripts and the time-saving programs from the book. Teaches how to implement day-to-day preventive maintenance tasks. Updated to cover new features—including the new Transaction Wizard.

Price: $49.99 USA/$67.99 CDN   *User Level: Accomplished—Expert*

ISBN: 0-672-30959-9   912 pp.   *Client/Server*

Windows NT 4 Web Development

Sanjaya Hettihewa

Windows NT and Microsoft's newly developed Internet Information Server are making it easier and more cost-effective to set up, manage, and administer a good Web site. *Windows NT 4 Web Development* provides information on all key aspects of server setup, maintenance, design, and implementation. CD-ROM contains valuable source code and powerful utilities. Teaches how to incorporate new technologies into your Web site. Covers Java, JavaScript, Internet Studio, and VBScript.

Price: $59.99 USA/$84.95 CDN   *User Level: Accomplished—Expert*

ISBN: 1-57521-089-4   800 pp.   *Internet—Programming*

Microsoft BackOffice Administrator's Survival Guide

Arthur Knowles

This all-in-one reference focuses on what Microsoft BackOffice is and how it is used in the real world. It includes all the fundamental concepts required for daily maintenance and troubleshooting, and explains the more arcane aspects of managing BackOffice. CD-ROM includes product demos, commercial and shareware utilities, and technical notes. Uses step-by-step written procedures interspersed with figures captured from the tools. Introduces Microsoft's new System Management Server.

Price: $59.99 USA/$81.95 CDN   *User Level: Accomplished—Expert*

ISBN: 0-672-30849-5   1,008 pp.   *Networking*

Add to Your Sams Library Today with the Best Books for Programming, Operating Systems, and New Technologies

The easiest way to order is to pick up the phone and call

1-800-428-5331

between 9:00 a.m. and 5:00 p.m. EST.
For faster service please have your credit card available.

ISBN	Quantity	Description of Item	Unit Cost	Total Cost
1-57521-168-8		Designing and Implementing Microsoft Internet Information Server 2	$39.99	
0-672-30901-7		Peter Norton's Complete Guide to Windows NT 4 Workstation	$39.99	
0-672-30933-5		Windows NT 4 Server Unleashed (Book/CD-ROM)	$59.99	
1-57521-137-8		Building an Intranet with Windows NT 4 (Book/CD-ROM)	$49.99	
0-672-30890-8		Microsoft Exchange Server Survival Guide (Book/CD-ROM)	$49.99	
0-672-30959-9		Microsoft SQL Server 6.5 DBA Survival Guide, Second Edition (Book/CD-ROM)	$49.99	
1-57521-089-4		Windows NT 4 Web Development (Book/CD-ROM)	$59.99	
0-672-30849-5		Microsoft BackOffice Administrator's Survival Guide (Book/CD-ROM)	$59.99	
		Shipping and Handling: See information below.		
		TOTAL		

Shipping and Handling: $4.00 for the first book, and $1.75 for each additional book. If you need to have it NOW, we can ship product to you in 24 hours for an additional charge of approximately $18.00, and you will receive your item overnight or in two days. Overseas shipping and handling adds $2.00 per book. Prices subject to change. Call for availability and pricing information on latest editions.

201 W. 103rd Street, Indianapolis, Indiana 46290

1-800-428-5331 — Orders   1-800-835-3202 — FAX   1-800-858-7674 — Customer Service

Book ISBN 0-672-30956-4

What's on the CD-ROM?

The companion CD-ROM contains the authors' source code and samples from the book and many third-party software products.

Windows 95/NT 4.0 Installation Instructions

1. Insert the CD-ROM disc into your CD-ROM drive.
2. From the Windows 95 desktop, double-click the My Computer icon.
3. Double-click the icon representing your CD-ROM drive.
4. Double-click the icon titled CDSETUP.EXE to run the installation program.

   Installation creates a program group named PN Guide to Programming with MFC. This group contains icons to browse the CD-ROM.

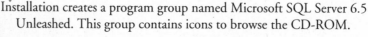

NOTE

If Windows 95 is installed on your computer and you have the AutoPlay feature enabled, the CDSETUP.EXE program starts automatically whenever you insert the disc into your CD-ROM drive.

Windows NT 3.51 Installation Instructions

1. Insert the CD-ROM disc into your CD-ROM drive.
2. From File Manager or Program Manager, choose File | Run.
3. Type *drive*\CDSETUP.EXE and press Enter, where *drive* corresponds to the drive letter of your CD-ROM. For example, if your CD-ROM is drive D:, type D:\CDSETUP.EXE and press Enter.

   Installation creates a program group named Microsoft SQL Server 6.5 Unleashed. This group contains icons to browse the CD-ROM.

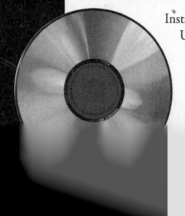